oncooking

a textbook of culinary fundamentals

fourth custom edition

Taken From:

On Cooking: A Textbook of Culinary Fundamentals, Fourth Edition
by Sarah R. Labensky and Alan M. Hause, Steven Labensky and Pricilla Martel

Food Safety Fundamentals
by David McSwane, Nancy R. Rue, Richard Linton, and Anna Graf Williams

Food Safe Kitchens
by Ann Marchiony

Cover photo courtesy of Getty Images.

Taken from:

On Cooking: A Textbook of Culinary Fundamentals, Fourth Edition
by Sarah R. Labensky and Alan M. Hause, Steven Labensky and Pricilla Martel
Copyright © 2007, 2002, 1999, 1996 by Pearson Education, Inc.
Published by Prentice Hall
Upper Saddle River, New Jersey 07458

Food Safety Fundamentals
by David McSwane, Nancy R. Rue, Richard Linton, and Anna Graf Williams
Copyright © 2003 by Pearson Education, Inc.
Published by Prentice Hall

Food Safe Kitchens
by Ann Marchiony
Copyright © 2003 by Pearson Education, Inc.
Published by Prentice Hall

This special edition published in cooperation with Pearson Custom Publishing.

Printed in the United States of America

10 9 8 7 6 5 4 3

ISBN 0-536-43393-3

2007520025

SB

Please visit our web site at *www.pearsoncustom.com*

PEARSON CUSTOM PUBLISHING
501 Boylston Street, Suite 900, Boston, MA 02116
A Pearson Education Company

CONTENTS

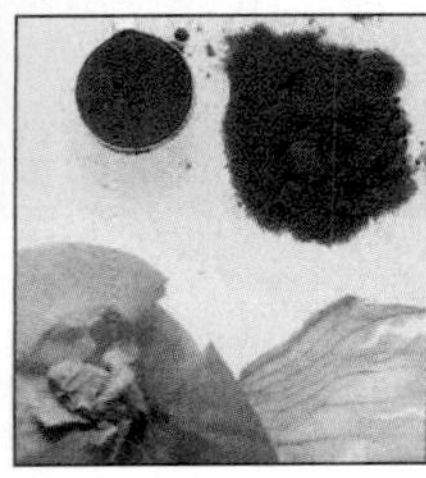

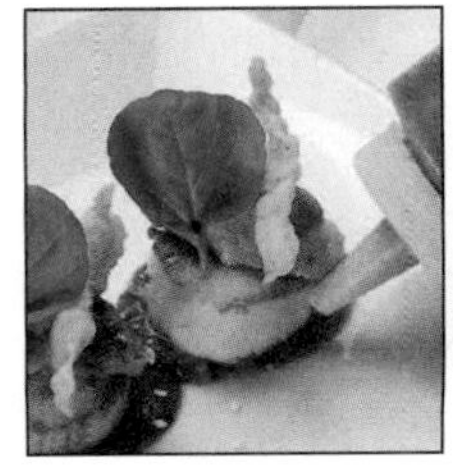

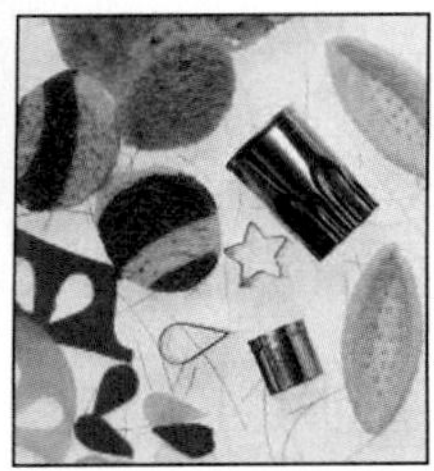

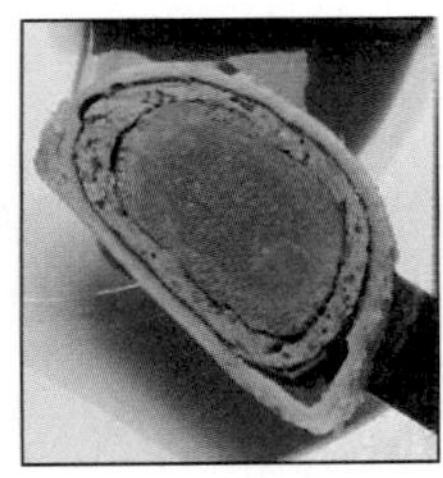

PREFACE

Learning to cook is much more than simply learning to follow a recipe. Consequently, *On Cooking*, fourth edition, is not a cookbook or a collection of recipes. It is a carefully designed text intended to teach you the fundamentals of the culinary arts and to prepare you for a rewarding career in the food service industry.

Many chapters contain extensive illustrated sections identifying foods and equipment. Throughout the book we emphasize culinary principles, not recipes (although we include more than 775 of them). Whenever possible, we focus on the general procedure highlighting fundamental principles and skills, whether it be for preparing a yeast bread or grilling a piece of fish. We discuss both the how and why of cooking. Only then are specific applications and sample recipes given.

Numerous hotel and restaurant chefs throughout the country contributed recipes to this book, usually accompanied by photographs of the dishes as prepared in their kitchens. These recipes and illustrations allow you to explore different techniques and presentation styles. Teaching professionals from culinary schools across the country also share some of their most successful recipes in this book.

In order to provide you with a sense of the rich traditions of cookery, informative sidebars on food history, chef biographies and other topics are scattered throughout the book. Also included are several short essays written by prominent culinarians on topics ranging from tempering chocolate to tasting spicy foods.

We wish you much success in your culinary career and hope that this text will continue to inform and inspire you long after graduation

▸ A Note on Recipes

Recipes are important and useful as a means of standardizing food preparation and recording information. We include recipes that are designed primarily to reinforce and explain techniques and procedures presented in the text. Many recipe yields are intentionally low in order to be less intimidating to beginning cooks and more useful in small schools and kitchens.

All ingredients are listed in both U.S. and metric measurements. The metric equivalents are rounded off to even, easily measured amounts. So, you should consider these ingredient lists as separate recipes or formulas; do not measure some ingredients according to the metric amounts and other ingredients according to the U.S. amount or the proportions will not be accurate and the intended result will not be achieved. Throughout this book, unless otherwise noted:

- *mirepoix* refers to a preparation of 2 parts onion, 1 part celery and 1 part carrot by weight
- *pepper* refers to ground black pepper, preferably freshly ground

- *butter* refers to whole, unsalted butter
- *milk* refers to whole or reduced fat (not nonfat) milk, and
- *TT* means "to taste"

Detailed procedures for standard techniques are presented in the text and generally are not repeated in each recipe (for example, "deglaze the pan" or "monté au beurre"). Variations appear at the end of selected recipes. These variations give you the opportunity to see how one set of techniques or procedures can be used to prepare different dishes with only minor modifications.

A mise en place feature has been added to recipes that appear in the front section of recipe chapters. Ingredients that require preparation before beginning to prepare a recipe are listed in the margin. You should consult this brief checklist after you read the recipe but before you begin to cook. Headnotes that describe the cultural or historical background of a dish or the unique techniques used in its preparation appear with many recipes. This short text should help enhance your understanding of a cuisine or cooking technique.

No matter how detailed the written recipe, however, we must assume that you have certain knowledge, skills and judgment. You should also rely upon the knowledge and skills of your instructor for guidance. Although some skills and an understanding of theory can be acquired through reading and study, no book can substitute for repeated hands-on preparation and observation.

A registered dietician analyzed all the recipes in this book using nutritional analysis software that incorporates data from the U.S. Department of Agriculture, research laboratories and food manufacturers. The nutrient information provided here should be used only as a reference, however. A margin of error of approximately 20 percent can be expected because of natural variations in ingredients.

Preparation techniques and serving sizes may also significantly alter the values of many nutrients. For the nutritional analysis, if a recipe offers a choice of ingredients, the first-mentioned ingredient is the one used. Ingredients listed as "to taste" (TT) and "as needed" are omitted from the analysis. Corn oil and whole milk are used throughout for "vegetable oil" and "milk," respectively. In cases of a range of ingredient quantities or numbers of servings, the average is used.

Throughout this book various recipes are marked with the pyramid symbol.

This symbol identifies dishes that are particularly low in calories, fat, saturated fat or sodium; if appropriate, they may also be a good source of vitamins, protein, fiber or calcium.

Vegetarian dishes are indicated with a vegetable symbol. These recipes do not contain meat, fish, shellfish or poultry, but may contain dairy products and/or eggs. (We do not use this symbol for the baked goods recipes in Chapters 31 through 35, however, because none of them contain meat, fish, shellfish or poultry.) Vegetarian dishes are not necessarily low in calories, fat or sodium; nor are they automatically good sources of vitamins, protein, fiber or calcium.

The World Wide Web icon appears next to end-of-chapter discussion questions whose answers may be researched on the web.

▶ Acknowledgments

This book would not have been possible without the assistance and support of many people. Special thanks to our photographer, Richard Embery, for his talent, professionalism and commitment to quality; and to Sharon Salomon, MS, RD, for preparation of the Nutrition chapter. The nutritional analysis for this edition was prepared by Mindy Hermann, MS, RD, whose thoroughness and prompt replies were greatly appreciated. Thanks also to Stacey Winters Quattrone and

Bill Ingram for their artistry. We are also grateful to the many chefs restaurateurs, writers and culinary professionals who provided recipes and essays for this book.

Alan would like to first of all thank his wife Chantal. This project would not have been possible without her constant and continuing support, guidance criticism and, most importantly, her patience. He would also like to thank his many coworkers and friends who contributed to the success of the text, including: Charles Blonkenfeld, Reynalda Montes, Gregory Reynolds, Steve Ramirez, Rosalino Morales, Estella Morales, Gregorio Alviso, Martin van de Brug, Jim Curry, Christopher Torres, Gayleen Cooley, April Kilgore, Alex Hill and Margarita Nava.

Sarah offers her sincere thanks and appreciation to Priscilla Martel for adding her expertise and insight to this edition of the text. She would also like to thank the many students she has worked with over the years. They are the real reason that books such as this are written.

Priscilla would like to acknowledge the contributions of Carole Pierce and J. Patrick Truhn, two fine writers and editors, and the support of Barbara Kleutsch.

The authors wish to thank the following companies for their generous donations of equipment and supplies: J.A. Henckels Zwillingswerk, Inc., All-Clad Metalcrafters, Inc. and Parrish's Cake Decorating Supplies, Inc. We also wish to thank Shamrock Foods Company, East Coast Seafood of Phoenix Inc., KitchenAid Home Appliances, Taylor Environmental Instruments, Hobart Corporation, Jeff and Sue Reising of Arizona Ostrich Fillet and Randy Dougherty of ISF International.

Finally, we wish to thank everyone involved in this project at Prentice Hall, including Vernon Anthony, Director of Development; Eileen McClay, Executive Editor; Linda Zuk, Production Editor; Marion Gottlieb, Development Editor; Cheryl Asherman, Creative Director; Mary Carnis, Managing Editor; Janice Stangel, Senior Production Editor; and Ryan DeGrote, Executive Marketing Manager. We also remain indebted to Robin Baliszewski, Acquisitions Editor of the first edition and current President of Prentice Hall's Career, Health, Education & Technology Division, for her support and friendship.

The authors would also like to acknowledge the following reviewers for their comments and assistance with this fourth edition. The reviewers of *On Cooking* provided many excellent suggestions and ideas for improving the text. The quality of the reviews was outstanding and played a major role in the preparation of this revision. Their assistance and expertise is greatly appreciated.

Mary Bartholomew, FMP, CCE, Ph.D., Delgado Community College, New Orleans

Jon Bullard, CEC, CCE, Gulf Coast Community College, Panama City, FL

Philip J. Cragg, CEC, CCE, AAC, Atlantic Cape Community College

Kelli M. Dever, AOS, CIA, Boise State University, Boise, ID

Frederick Ferrara, CEC, CCE, CHE, Joliet Junior College, Joliet, IL

Deborah Foster, Ball State University, Muncie, IN

Sally K. Frey, Art Institute of Pittsburgh

Kimberly S. Lukhard, MS, RD, LDN, East Carolina University, Greenville, NC

Lori Marchino, FSE, Vincennes University, Vincennes, IN

Adrienne O'Brien, Luna Community College, Las Vegas, NM

Daniel Rowlson, RD, CCE, Oakland Community College, Orchard Ridge, MI

Jennifer L. Solloway-Malvitz, CEPC, BS, CTET, AS, Fox Valley Technical College, Appleton, WI

▶ Additional Credits

The authors wish to thank the instructors who participated in our focus group and helped us refine the contents of this revision.

Mike Artlip, CEC, CCE, Kendall College; Mary Bartholomew, FMP, CCE, Ph.D., Delgado Community College; Michael Bologna, CEC, Chattahoochee Technical College; Patti Gilbert Curfman, CEC, PattyCakes; Marvis Hinson, CCE, CCWA, Savannah Tech; Mimi Reed, CEC, Renton Technical College; Odette Smith Ransome, MEd, Art Institute of Pittsburgh.

We would like to extend our thanks to the many chefs and instructors who took the time to complete our general survey regarding introductory cooking textbooks. Their feedback has contributed greatly to the production of our text.

Philip J. Cragg, CEC, CCE, AAC, Atlantic Cape Community College; Sally K. Frey, Art Institute of Pittsburgh; Gene Fritz, Ed. M., CCE, Washington State University; Margaret (Meg) Galvin, BBA, Cincinnati State Technical College and Midwest Culinary Institute; Marie Kamp, MBA, RD, LDN, The Pennsylvania State University; Linda Rosner, CEC, CHE, Lexington College, KY; Michele Stalnaker, CEC, Mountain State University; Joseph Zoellin, CEC, Institute of Technology, Culinary Division.

Grateful acknowledgment is extended to the following schools for testing various recipes from this text for accuracy, level of difficulty and appropriateness. Their feedback helped the authors refine recipes so that the concerns of the classroom appear on the printed page.

Sally K. Frey, a culinary instructor at The Art Institute of Pittsburgh, Pennsylvania, and the following students from her department: Emily L. Fielitz, Timothy J. McLaughlin, Brandon K. Snow, Eva M. Wehry; Debbie Foster, Department of Family and Consumer Sciences, Ball State University, Muncie, IN; Katie L. Thomas, CEPC, and Joseph Wollinger, CEC, CCE, Blackhawk Technical College, Janesville, WI; Kelli Dever, Boise State University, Boise, ID; Abby Nash, Cornell University, School of Hotel Administration, Ithaca, NY; Nick DeMarfio, Instructor and Director of Training, and Brett McKinney, Instructor and Director of Purchasing, The Culinary Academy of Long Island, Syosset, NY; Chef Vance C. Roux, CCC, CCE, Delgado Community College, New Orleans, LA; Introductory Foods Lab in the Department of Nutrition and Hospitality Management, East Carolina University, Geenville, NC; Chef Jenn Malvitz and the students at Fox Valley Technical College, Appleton, WI; the instructors and students of Gulf Coast Community College, Panama City, FL; Director Joe Zoellin, CEC, CCE, FMP, the faculty and students of The Institute of Technology, Culinary Division, Clovis, CA; Iowa Western Community College; Mike Artlip, CEC, CCE, and Walter Freund, CEC, Kendall College, Chicago, IL; Linda K. Rosner, CEC, CHE, Lexington College, Chicago, IL; The Luna Community College Culinary Arts Club, Las Vegas, NM; Ozarks Technical Community College, Springfield, MO; Renton Technical College students, Renton, WA, under the guidance of Chef Mimi Reed and Chef John Fisher: Jo Aranowski, Shekinah Brensdal, Cathy Cerda, Denise Hadley, Jesse Savage, Jacqueline R. Thompson, and Adam Willenburg; Marvis Hinson, Culinary Arts Department, Savannah Technical College, Savannah, GA; Stratford University, School of Hospitality and Culinary Arts, Baking and Pastry Arts, Falls Church, VA; Texas Tech University, Lubbock, TX; University of Central Oklahoma food science students, Instructor Marilyn B. Waters, PhD, RD/LD; Connie Holt, RD, MS, Widener University, Chester PA; the class of Professor Lori Ann Marchino at Vincennes University, Vincennes, IN.

We would like to acknowledge the following individuals from the Pearson Imaging Centers:

Rob Handago, Director of Digital Imaging
Joe Conti, Site Supervisor
Ron Walko, Technician
Corin Skidds, Color Tech Support
Greg Harrison, Technician
Rob Uibelhoer, Technician
Shayle Keating, Technician
Luke Landolfi, Technician
Mark Linder, Technician
Tony Barone, Technician
Dennis Sheehan, Technician
Mark Kregger, Site Supervisor
Russell Lip, Technician
John Morgan, Technician
Jane Rees, Technician
JoAnn Shirataki, Technician

We would also like to acknowledge the following individuals from the Image Resource Center at Pearson Education:

Melinda Reo, Director, Image Resource Center
Zina Arabia, Manager, Rights and Permissions
Beth Brenzel, Manager, Visual Research
Karen Sanatar, Manager, Cover Visual Research & Permissions
Fran Toepfer, Image Permission Coordinator

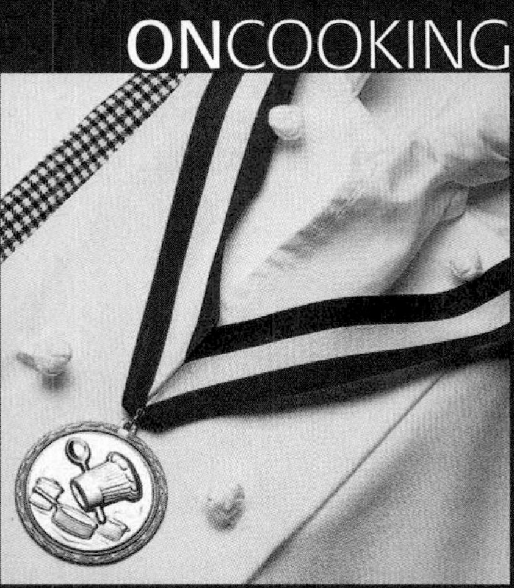
ONCOOKING

CHAPTER**ONE**

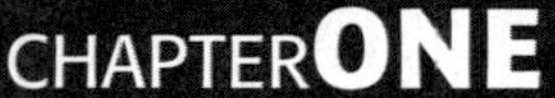

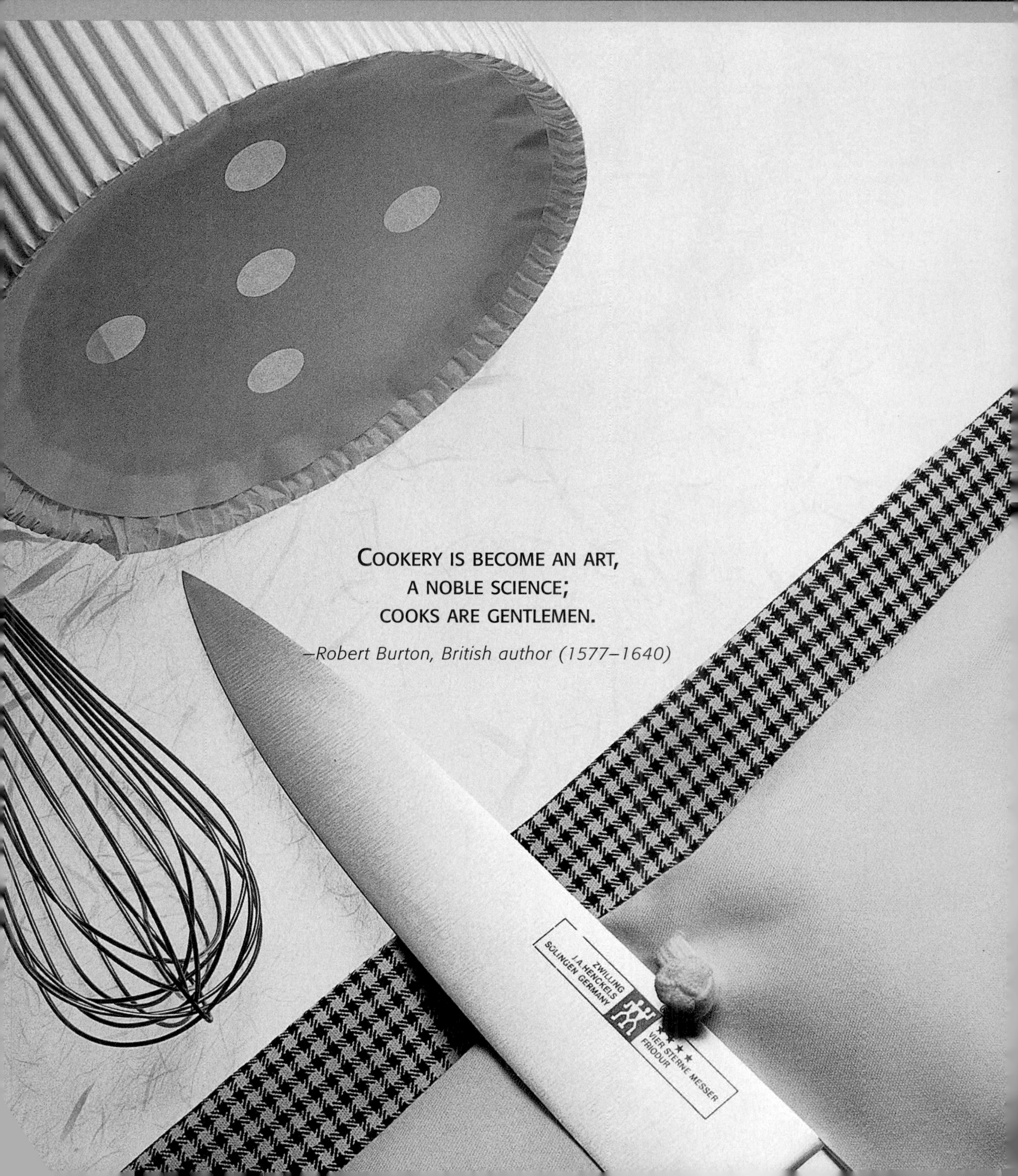

COOKERY IS BECOME AN ART,
A NOBLE SCIENCE;
COOKS ARE GENTLEMEN.

—Robert Burton, British author (1577–1640)

PROFESSIONALISM

AFTER STUDYING THIS CHAPTER, YOU WILL BE ABLE TO:

- discuss the development of the modern food service industry
- name key historical figures responsible for developing food service professionalism
- explain the organization of classic and modern kitchen brigades
- appreciate the role of the professional chef in modern food service operations
- understand the attributes a student chef needs to become a professional chef

Like any fine art, great cookery requires taste and creativity, an appreciation of beauty and a mastery of technique. Like the sciences, successful cookery demands knowledge and an understanding of basic principles. And like any successful leader, today's professional chefs must exercise sound judgment and be committed to achieving excellence in their endeavors.

This book describes foods and cooking equipment, explains culinary principles and cooking techniques and provides recipes using these principles and techniques. No book, however, can provide taste, creativity, commitment and judgment. For these, chefs must rely on themselves.

▶ **cooking** (1) the transfer of energy from a heat source to a food; this energy alters the food's molecular structure, changing its texture, flavor, aroma and appearance; (2) the preparation of food for consumption

▶ **cookery** the art, practice or work of cooking

▶ **professional cooking** a system of cooking based on a knowledge of and appreciation for ingredients and procedures

▶ CHEFS AND RESTAURANTS

Cooks have produced food in quantity for as long as people have eaten together. For millennia, chefs have catered to the often elaborate dining needs of the wealthy and powerful, whether they be Asian, Native American, European or African. And for centuries, vendors in China, Europe and elsewhere have sold to the public foods that they prepared themselves or bought from others.

But the history of the professional chef is of relatively recent origin. Its cast is mostly French, and it is intertwined with the history of restaurants—for only with the development of restaurants during the late 18th and early 19th centuries were chefs expected to produce, efficiently and economically, different dishes at different times for different diners.

THE 18TH CENTURY—BOULANGER'S RESTAURANT

The word *restaurant* is derived from the French word *restaurer* ("to restore"). Since the 16th century, the word *restorative* had been used to describe rich and highly flavored soups or stews capable of restoring lost strength. Restoratives, like all other cooked foods offered and purchased outside the home, were made by guild members. Each guild had a monopoly on preparing certain food items. For example, during the reign of Henri IV of France (1553–1610), there were separate guilds for *rôtisseurs* (who cooked *la grosse viande*, the main cuts of meat), *pâtissiers* (who cooked poultry, pies and tarts), *tamisiers* (who baked breads), *vinaigriers* (who made sauces and some stews, including some restoratives), *traiteurs* (who made ragouts) and *porte-chapes* (caterers who organized feasts and celebrations).

The French claim that the first modern restaurant opened one day in 1765 when a Parisian tavernkeeper, a Monsieur Boulanger, hung a sign advertising the sale of his special restorative, a dish of sheep feet in white sauce. His establishment closed shortly thereafter as the result of a lawsuit brought by a guild whose members claimed that Boulanger was infringing on their exclusive right to sell prepared dishes. Boulanger triumphed in court and later reopened.

Boulanger's establishment differed from the inns and taverns that had existed throughout Europe for centuries. These inns and taverns served foods prepared (usually off premises) by the appropriate guild. The food—of which there was little choice—was offered by the keeper as incidental to the establishment's primary function: providing sleeping accommodations or drink. Customers were served family style and ate at communal tables. Boulanger's contribution to the food service industry was to serve a variety of foods prepared on premises to customers whose primary interest was dining.

Several other restaurants opened in Paris during the succeeding decades, including the Grande Taverne de Londres in 1782. Its owner, Antoine Beauvilliers (1754–1817), was the former steward to the Comte de Provence, later King Louis XVIII of France. He advanced the development of the modern restaurant by offering his wealthy patrons a menu listing available dishes during fixed hours. Beauvilliers's impeccably trained wait staff served patrons at small, individual tables in an elegant setting.

The French Revolution (1789–1799) had a significant effect on the budding restaurant industry. Along with the aristocracy, guilds and their monopolies were generally abolished. The revolution also allowed the public access to the skills and creativity of the well-trained, sophisticated chefs who had worked in the aristocracy's private kitchens. Although many of the aristocracy's chefs either left the country or lost their jobs (and some their heads), a few opened restaurants catering to the growing urbanized middle class.

THE EARLY 19TH CENTURY—CARÊME AND *GRANDE CUISINE*

As the 19th century progressed, more restaurants opened, serving a greater selection of items and catering to a wider clientele. By midcentury, several large, grand restaurants in Paris were serving elaborate meals, decidedly reminiscent of the *grande cuisine* (also known as *haute cuisine*) of the aristocracy. **Grande cuisine,** which arguably reached its peak of perfection in the hands of Antonin Carême, was characterized by meals consisting of dozens of courses of elaborately and intricately prepared, presented, garnished and sauced foods. Other **restaurateurs** blended the techniques and styles of *grande cuisine* with the simpler foods and tastes of the middle class (*cuisine bourgeoisie*) to create a new cuisine simpler than *grande cuisine* but more than mere home cooking.

▶ **grande cuisine** the rich, intricate and elaborate cuisine of the 18th- and 19th-century French aristocracy and upper classes. It is based on the rational identification, development and adoption of strict culinary principles. By emphasizing the how and why of cooking, *grande cuisine* was the first to distinguish itself from regional cuisines, which tend to emphasize the tradition of cooking.

▶ **restaurateur** a person who owns or operates an establishment serving food, such as a restaurant

THE LATE 19TH CENTURY—ESCOFFIER AND *CUISINE CLASSIQUE*

Following the lead set by the French in both culinary style and the restaurant business, restaurants opened in the United States and throughout Europe during the 19th century. Charles Ranhofer (1836–1899) was the first internationally renowned chef of an American restaurant, Delmonico's in New York City. In 1893, Ranhofer published his "franco-american" encyclopedia of cooking, *The Epicurean,* containing more than 3500 recipes.

One of the finest restaurants outside France was the dining room at London's Savoy Hotel, opened in 1898 under the directions of Cesar Ritz (1850–1918) and Auguste Escoffier. Escoffier is generally credited with refining the *grande cuisine* of Carême to create *cuisine classique* or **classic cuisine.** By doing so, he brought French cuisine into the 20th century.

▶ **classic cuisine** a late 19th- and early 20th-century refinement and simplification of French *grande cuisine.* Classic (or classical) cuisine relies on the thorough exploration of culinary principles and techniques, and emphasizes the refined preparation and presentation of superb ingredients.

THE MID-20TH CENTURY—POINT AND *NOUVELLE CUISINE*

The mid-20th century witnessed a trend toward lighter, more naturally flavored and more simply prepared foods. Fernand Point was a master practitioner of this movement. But this master's goal of simplicity and refinement was carried to even greater heights by a generation of chefs Point trained: principally, Paul Bocuse, Jean and Pierre Troisgros, Alain Chapel, Francois Bise and Louis Outhier. They, along with Michel Guérard and Roger Vergé, were the pioneers

MARIE-ANTOIN (ANTONIN) CARÊME (1783–1833)

Carême, known as the "cook of kings and the king of cooks," was an acknowledged master of French *grande cuisine.* Abandoned on the streets of Paris as a child, he worked his way from cook's helper in a working-class restaurant to become one of the most prestigious chefs of his (or, arguably, any other) time. During his career, he was chef to the famous French diplomat and gourmand Prince de Talleyrand, the Prince Regent of England (who became King George IV), Tsar Alexander I of Russia and Baron de Rothschild, among others.

His stated goal was to achieve "lightness," "grace," "order" and "perspicuity" in the preparation and presentation of food. As a pâtissier, he designed and prepared elaborate and elegant pastry and confectionery creations, many of which were based on architectural designs. (He wrote that "the fine arts are five in number, namely: painting, sculpture, poetry, music, architecture—the main branch of which is confectionery.") As a showman, he garnished his dishes with ornamental *hâtelets* (skewers) threaded with colorful ingredients such as crayfish and intricately carved vegetables, and presented his creations on elaborate *socles* (bases). As a *saucier,* he standardized the use of roux as a thickening agent, perfected recipes and devised a system for classifying sauces. As a *garde-manger,* Carême popularized cold cuisine, emphasizing molds and aspic dishes. As a culinary professional, he designed kitchen tools, equipment and uniforms.

Courtesy of Barbara Wheaton

As an author, he wrote and illustrated important texts on the culinary arts, including *Le Maitre d'hotel francais* (1822), describing the hundreds of dishes he personally created and cooked in the capitals of Europe; *Le Pâtissier royal parisian* (1825), containing fanciful designs for *les pieces montées,* the great decorative centerpieces that were the crowning glory of grand dinners; and his five-volume masterpiece on the state of his profession, *L'Art de la cuisine au XIXe siecle* (1833), the last two volumes of which were completed after his death by his associate Plumerey. Carême's writings almost single-handedly refined and summarized five hundred years of culinary evolution. But his treatises were not mere cookbooks. Rather, he analyzed cooking, old and new, emphasizing procedure and order and covering every aspect of the art known as *grande cuisine.*

Carême died before age 50, burnt out, according to Laurent Tailhade, "by the flame of his genius and the coal of the spits." But this may have been the glory he sought, for he once wrote:

> Imagine yourself in a large kitchen at the moment of a great dinner. . . . [S]ee twenty chefs coming, going, moving with speed in this cauldron of heat, look at the great mass of charcoal, a cubic meter for the cooking of entrées, and another mass on the ovens for the cooking of soups, sauces, ragouts, for frying and the water baths. Add to that a heap of burning wood in front of which four spits are turning, one which bears a sirloin weighing 45–50 pounds, the other fowl or game. In this furnace everyone moves with speed; not a sound is heard, only the chef has a right to speak, and at the sound of his voice, everyone obeys. Finally, the last straw; for about half an hour, all windows are closed so that the air does not cool the dishes as they are being served. This is the way we spend the best years of our lives. We must obey even when physical strength fails, but it is the burning charcoal that kills us. . . . [C]harcoal kills us but what does it matter? The shorter the life, the greater the glory.

▶ **nouvelle cuisine** French for "new cooking"; a mid-20th-century movement away from many classic cuisine principles and toward a lighter cuisine based on natural flavors, shortened cooking times and innovative combinations

of **nouvelle cuisine** in the early 1970s. At the same time, Gaston Lenôtre modernized the classic pastries of *grande cuisine,* infusing them with the bright, fresh flavors of *nouvelle cuisine.*

Their culinary philosophy was principled on the rejection of overly rich, needlessly complicated dishes. These chefs emphasized healthful eating. The ingredients must be absolutely fresh and of the highest possible quality; the cooking methods should be simple and direct whenever possible. The accompaniments and garnishes must be light and contribute to an overall harmony; the completed plates must be elegantly designed and decorated. Following these guidelines, some traditional cooking methods have been applied to nontraditional ingredients, and ingredients have been combined in new and previously unorthodox fashions. For chefs with knowledge, skill, taste and judgment, this works.

AUGUSTE ESCOFFIER (1846–1935)

Escoffier's brilliant culinary career began at age 13 in his uncle's restaurant and continued until his death at age 89. Called the "emperor of the world's kitchens," he is perhaps best known for defining French cuisine and dining during La Belle Époque (the "Gay Nineties").

Unlike Carême, Escoffier never worked in an aristocratic household. Rather, he exhibited his culinary skills in the dining rooms of the finest hotels in Europe, including the Place Vendôme in Paris and the Savoy and Carlton Hotels in London.

Escoffier did much to enhance the *grande cuisine* that arguably reached its perfection under Carême. Crediting Carême with providing the foundation for great—that is, French—cooking, Escoffier simplified the profusion of flavors, dishes and garnishes typifying Carême's work. He also streamlined some of Carême's overly elaborate and fussy procedures and classifications. For example, he reduced Carême's elaborate system of classifying sauces into the five families of sauces still recognized today. Escoffier sought simplicity and aimed for the perfect balance of a few superb ingredients. Some consider his refinement of *grande cuisine* to have been so radical as to credit him with the development of a new cuisine referred to as *cuisine classique* (classic or classical cuisine).

His many writings include *Le Livre des menus* (1912), in which, discussing the principles of a well-planned meal, he analogizes a great dinner to a symphony with contrasting movements that should be appropriate to the occasion, the guests and the season, and *Ma cuisine* (1934), surveying *cuisine bourgeoisie.* But his most important contribution is a culinary treatise intended for the professional chef entitled *Le Guide culinaire* (1903). Still in use today, it is an astounding collection of more than 5000 classic cuisine recipes and garnishes. In it, Escoffier emphasizes the mastery of techniques, the thorough understanding of cooking principles and the appreciation of ingredients—attributes he considered to be the building blocks professional chefs should use to create great dishes.

Escoffier was honored as a Chevalier of the French Legion of Honour in 1920 for his work in enhancing the reputation of French cuisine.

THE LATE 20TH CENTURY—AN AMERICAN CULINARY REVOLUTION

During the last 30 years or so, two distinct culinary trends have emerged in the United States: "the hotter, the better" and "fresh food, simply prepared."

The first trend is due, in large part, to an unlikely source: the Immigration Act of 1965. Under its provisions, a large number of Asians immigrated to this country. They brought with them their rich culinary traditions and they ignited America's love affair with fiery hot cuisines. By the late 1970s, many Americans were no longer content with bland or overly salty pseudo-Chinese dishes such as chop suey and chow mein. They demanded authenticity and developed cravings for spicy dishes from Szechuan and Hunan provinces, Vietnam and Thailand. At the same time, Mexican food left the barrio and became mainstream. Burritos and tacos became routine menu items, while authentic regional Mexican dishes were sought out by middle America. Indeed, by the 1990s, people used more salsa than ketchup as a condiment.

During this same time period, restaurateurs and chefs began Americanizing the principles of French *nouvelle cuisine.* When Alice Waters opened Chez Panisse in Berkeley, California, in 1971, her goal was to serve fresh food, simply prepared. Rejecting the growing popularity of processed and packaged foods, Waters wanted to use fresh, seasonal and locally grown produce in simple preparations that preserved and emphasized the foods' natural flavors. Chez Panisse and the many chefs who passed through its kitchen launched a new style of cuisine that became known as **New American cuisine.** As Waters's culinary philosophy spread across the United States, farmers and chefs began working together to make fresh, locally grown foods available, and producers and suppliers began developing domestic sources for some of the high-quality ingredients that were once available only from overseas. Excellent foie gras from Long Island, New York, and goat cheese from Sonoma County, California, are just two examples.

▶ **New American cuisine** a late-20th-century movement that began in California but has spread across the United States; it stresses the use of fresh, locally grown, seasonal produce and high-quality ingredients simply prepared in a fashion that preserves and emphasizes natural flavors

By the mid-1980s, American chefs began to combine aspects of these two trends. Their work resulted in **fusion cuisine.** With fusion cuisine, ingredients or preparation methods associated with one ethnic or regional cuisine are combined with those of another. A fillet of Norwegian salmon might be grilled over hickory wood, then served on a bed of Japanese soba noodles with pesto cream sauce, for example, while duck confit prepared by the traditional French method is seasoned with lemongrass, ginger and chiles.

Along with this new interest in and appreciation for American ingredients and American tastes has come a new respect for American chefs. Many European and American food writers and pundits now consider American chefs to be among the best in the world, a fact they often triumph, while at the same time expressing their concern about the general decline of French cuisine and the exodus of European chefs to America. In addition, the American public has taken food to heart.

Many chefs have been elevated to celebrity status; an entire cable television network is devoted to cooking. Bookstore and library shelves are jammed with cookbooks, and newspapers and magazines regularly review restaurants and report on culinary trends. With gourmet shops and cookware stores in most malls, cooking has become both a hobby and a spectator sport. All this has helped inspire a generation of American teenagers to pursue careers behind the stove—and in front of the camera.

FERNAND POINT (1897–1955)

A massive man with a monumental personality, Point refined and modernized the classic cuisine of Escoffier. By doing so, he laid the foundations for *nouvelle cuisine.*

Point received his early training in some of the finest hotel-restaurant kitchens in Paris. In 1922, he and his family moved to Vienne, a city in southwest France near Lyon, and opened a restaurant. Two years later his father left the restaurant to Fernand, who renamed it La Pyramide. During the succeeding years, it became one of the culinary wonders of the world.

Point disdained dominating sauces and distracting accompaniments and garnishes. He believed that each dish should have a single dominant ingredient, flavor or theme; garnishes must be simple and match "like a tie to a suit." Procedure was of great importance. He devoted equal efforts to frying an egg and creating the marjolaine (a light almond and hazelnut spongecake filled with chocolate and praline buttercreams). His goal was to use the finest raw ingredients to produce perfect food that looked elegant and simple. But simplicity was not easy to achieve. As he once said, "a bearnaise sauce is simply an egg yolk, a shallot, a little tarragon vinegar, and butter, but it takes years of practice for the result to be perfect."

▶ **fusion cuisine** the blending or use of ingredients and/or preparation methods from various ethnic, regional or national cuisines in the same dish; also known as transnational cuisine

▶ INFLUENCES ON MODERN FOOD SERVICE OPERATIONS

From Monsieur Boulanger's humble establishment, a great industry has grown. Today, more than 900,000 public dining facilities operate in the United States alone. The dramatic growth and diversification of the food service industry is due in part to the Industrial Revolution and the social and economic changes it wrought, including the introduction of new technologies, foods, concerns and consumers.

NEW TECHNOLOGIES

Technology has always had a profound effect on cooking. For example, the development of clay and, later, metal vessels that could contain liquids and withstand as well as conduct heat offered prehistoric cooks the opportunity to stew, make soups and porridge, pickle and brine foods and control fermentation. But it was not until the rapid technological advances fostered by the Industrial Revolution that anything approaching the modern kitchen was possible.

One of the most important advancements was the introduction of the cast-iron stove. Prior to the 19th century, most cooking was done on spits or grills or in cauldrons or pots set on or in a wood- or coal-burning hearth. Hearthside cooking did not lend itself well to the simultaneous preparation of many items or to items requiring constant and delicate attention. With the introduction of cast-iron stoves during the 1800s (first wood- and coal-burning; by midcentury, gas; and by the early 20th century, electric), cooks could more comfortably and safely approach the heat source and control its temperatures. They were also able to efficiently prepare and hold for later use or service a multitude of smaller amounts of items requiring different cooking methods or ingredients, a necessity at a restaurant simultaneously catering to different diners' demands.

Also of great importance were developments in food preservation and storage techniques. For thousands of years, food had been preserved by sun-drying, salting, smoking, pickling, sugar-curing or fermenting. Although useful, these procedures destroy or distort the appearance and flavor of most foods. By the

GASTON LENÔTRE (1920–)

Gaston Lenôtre started in the baking trade in the heart of Normandy in the 1930s. By age 15, he had passed his professional exams and set off to work in his hometown. In 1947, he bought the boulangerie/pâtisserie of his boss in Pont Audermer. His bakery became a destination for sophisticated Parisians on their way to their country estates. In 1957 he was enticed to open a shop in Paris at 44 rue d'Auteuil, in the stylish 16th arrondisement. It was the first of more than a baker's dozen of locations, plus a vast catering business, which literally catered to "*le tout Paris*."

Lenôtre chose the village of Plaisir outside Paris for his third location—a vast production kitchen that became the heart of his expanding empire. He saw that to realize his expansion plans, he needed to train workers in his methods. In 1971, he began an in-house school, L'École Lenôtre. But here is where Gaston Lenôtre has shown himself to be much more than a talented baker and inspired businessman. There was a crisis in the trade at the time due to a lack of qualified bakers so Lenôtre opened the school, a few years later, to the entire professional community. For a fee, even his competitors could come learn from his *Meilleurs Ouvriers de France*—chefs recognized by the French government as the best artisans in the trade.

As befitting a native of Normandy, the heart of France's dairy industry, Lenôtre's innovations came in the area of Bavarians, charlottes and fruit mousses. Many of his cakes and tortes became modern classics, copied by pastry chefs worldwide. La Feuille d'Automne, Le Concorde, L'Opéra and the Charlotte Cécile seemed to be in all the Parisian bakeries in the early 1980s. Lenôtre mastered the technique of freezing, using it with respect to protect the quality of his products without adulterating them. He used the latest technology and had a staff of laboratory experts working full-time to maintain the integrity of his products. Proper freezing preserves the product, extending its shelf life without having to use chemicals and preservatives common in industrial food production. Many professionals believe that Lenôtre singlehandedly saved the pastry profession when it was threatened by mass production.

Many consider Lenôtre the father of modern French pastry, and his impact is worldwide. By the early 1980s he had 18 stores in Japan as well as outposts in Germany, Switzerland and England. Today, whether you go to Rio de Janeiro, Disney World in Florida, Lebanon or Las Vegas, you will find Lenôtre's name on the marquee.

ALEX MILES is a pastry chef and culinary educator in Dijon, France.

early 19th century, preserving techniques that had minimal effect on appearance and flavor began to emerge. For example, by 1800, the Frenchman François Appert successfully "canned" foods by subjecting foods stored in sterilized glass jars to very high heat. An early mechanical refrigerator was developed by the mid-1800s; soon reliable iceboxes, refrigerators and, later, freezers were available. During the 20th century, freeze-drying, vacuum-packing and irradiation became common preservation techniques.

While advancements were being made in preservation and storage techniques, developments in transportation technology were also underway. During the 19th century, steam-powered ships and railroads were able to bring foods quickly to market from distant suppliers. Indeed, by the 1870s, Chicago meatpackers were routinely supplying Europe with beef from the western Great Plains. During the 20th century, temperature-controlled cargo ships, trains, trucks and airplanes all were used as part of an integrated worldwide food transportation network. Combined with dependable food preservation and storage techniques, improved transportation networks have freed chefs from seasonal and geographic limitations in their choice of foods and have expanded consumers' culinary horizons.

Engineering advancements also have facilitated or even eliminated much routine kitchen work. Since the start of the Industrial Revolution, chefs have come to rely increasingly on mechanical and motorized food processors, mixers and cutters as well as a wealth of sophisticated kitchen equipment such as high-carbon stainless steel knife blades, infrared thermometers and induction cooktops. More recently, new computer technologies have made managing restaurant kitchens more efficient. And with easy access to the Internet, chefs can now source ingredients from a world of suppliers.

A VERY BIG BUSINESS INDEED

The National Restaurant Association, which closely monitors the economic impact of the U.S. food service industry, issued the following statistics for 2005:

- Daily food service industry sales averaged $1.3 billion; annual sales were approximately $476 billion.
- More than 60 billion meals were eaten in restaurants and school and work cafeterias.
- The average American adult buys a meal or a snack from a restaurant 5.3 times per week
- The food service industry claimed approximately 46.7 percent of the U.S. food dollar.
- More than 12.2 million people were employed in the industry, making it the second-largest employer after the government.
- One-third of all American adults have worked in the food service industry at some time during their lives.

NEW FOODS

Modern food preservation, storage and transportation techniques have made both fresh and exotic foods regularly available to chefs and consumers.

Advancements in agriculture such as the switch from organic to chemical fertilizers and the introduction of pesticides and drought- or pest-resistant strains have resulted in increased yields of healthy crops. Traditional hybridization techniques and, more recently, genetic engineering have produced new or improved grains and, for better or for worse, fruits and vegetables that have a longer shelf life and are more amenable to mass-production handling, storage and transportation methods.

Likewise, advancements in animal husbandry and aquaculture have led to a more reliable supply of leaner meat, poultry and fish. Moreover, foods found traditionally only in the wild (for example, game, wild rice and many mushrooms) are now being raised commercially and are routinely available.

Food preservation and processing techniques have also led to the development of prepackaged, prepared convenience foods, some of which are actually quite good. After careful thought and testing, today's chef can rely on some of these products. Doing so allows greater flexibility and more time to devote to other preparations.

NEW CONCERNS

Consumer concerns about nutrition and diet have fueled changes in the food service industry. Obviously, what we eat affects our health. Adequate amounts of certain nutrients promote good health by preventing deficiencies; good nutrition also helps prevent chronic diseases and increases longevity. Chefs should provide their customers with nutritious foods.

The public has long been concerned about food safety. Federal, state and local governments have helped promote food safety by inspecting and grading meats and poultry, regulating label contents for packaged foods and setting sanitation standards. All these standards, especially sanitation standards, affect the way foods are prepared, stored and served.

Concerns about nutrition and food safety have also resulted in renewed interest in organically grown fruits and vegetables and free-range-raised animals.

NEW CONSUMERS

Demographic and social changes have contributed to the diversification of the food service industry by creating or identifying new consumer groups with their own desires or needs. By tailoring their menu, prices and décor accordingly, food service operations can cater to consumers defined by age (baby boomers and seniors, in particular), type of household (singles, couples and families), income, education and geography.

Since World War II, there has also been a rapid increase in the number and types of institutions providing food services. These include hospitals, schools, retirement centers, sports facilities, private clubs, hotels and resorts (which may in turn have fine dining, coffee shop, quick service, banquet and room service facilities), factories and office complexes. Each of these institutions presents the professional chef with unique challenges, whether they be culinary, dietary or budgetary.

Through travel or exposure to the many books and magazines about food, consumers are becoming better educated and more sophisticated. Educated consumers provide a market for new foods and cuisines as well as an appreciation for a job well done.

Although some consumers may frequent a particular restaurant because its chef or owner is a celebrity or the restaurant is riding high on a crest of fad or fashion, most consumers choose a restaurant—whether it be a fast-food burger

▶ **global cuisine** foods (often commercially produced items) or preparation methods that have become ubiquitous throughout the world; for example, curries and French-fried potatoes

▶ **national cuisine** the characteristic cuisine of a nation

▶ **regional cuisine** a set of recipes based on local ingredients, traditions and practices; within a larger geographical, political, cultural or social unit, regional cuisines are often variations of one another that blend together to create a national cuisine

▶ **ethnic cuisine** the cuisine of a group of people having a common cultural heritage, as opposed to the cuisine of a group of people bound together by geography or political factors

place or an elegant French restaurant—because it provides quality food at a cost they are willing to pay. To remain successful, then, the restaurant must carefully balance its commitment to quality with marketplace realities.

▶ THE FOOD SERVICE OPERATION

To function efficiently, a food service operation must be well organized and staffed with appropriate personnel. This staff is sometimes called a **brigade.** Although a chef will be most familiar with the back-of-the-house or kitchen brigade, he or she should also understand how the dining room or front of the house operates.

▶ **brigade** a system of staffing a kitchen so that each worker is assigned a set of specific tasks; these tasks are often related by cooking method, equipment or the types of foods being produced

THE CLASSIC KITCHEN BRIGADE

Escoffier is credited with developing the kitchen brigade system used in large restaurant kitchens. From the chaos and redundancy found in the private kitchens of the aristocracy, he created a distinct hierarchy of responsibilities and functions for commercial food service operations.

At the top is the *chef de cuisine* or *chef*, who is responsible for all kitchen operations, developing menu items and setting the kitchen's tone and tempo.

His or her principal assistant is the *sous-chef* (the under chef or second chef), who is responsible for scheduling personnel and replacing the chef and station chefs as necessary. The *sous-chef* also often functions as the *aboyeur* (expediter or announcer), who accepts the orders from the dining room, relays them to the various station chefs and then reviews the dishes before service.

The *chefs de partie* (station chefs) produce the menu items and are under the direct supervision of the chef or *sous-chef*. Previously, whenever a cook needed an item, he or his assistants produced it; thus several cooks could be making the same sauce or basic preparation. Under Escoffier's system, each station chef is assigned a specific task based on either the cooking method and equipment or the category of items to be produced. They include the following:

- The *saucier* (sauté station chef), who holds one of the most demanding jobs in the kitchen, is responsible for all sautéed items and most sauces.
- The *poissonier* (fish station chef) is responsible for fish and shellfish items and their sauces. This position is occasionally combined with the sauce station.
- The *grillardin* (grill station chef) is responsible for all grilled items.
- The *friturier* (fry station chef) is responsible for all fried items.
- The *rôtisseur* (roast station chef) is responsible for all roasted items and jus or other related sauces. The grill and fry stations are sometimes subsumed into the roast station.
- The *potager* (soup station chef) is responsible for soups and stocks.
- The *légumier* (vegetable station chef) is responsible for all vegetable and starch items.
- The *potager* and *légumier* functions are often combined into a single vegetable station whose chef is known as the *entremetier*. *Entremets* were the courses served after the roast and usually comprised vegetables, fruits, fritters or sweet items (the sorbet served before the main course in some contemporary restaurants is a vestigial *entremet*).
- The *garde-manger* (pantry chef) is responsible for cold food preparations, including salads and salad dressings, cold appetizers, charcuterie items, pâtés, terrines and similar dishes. The *garde-manger* supervises the *boucher* (butcher), who is responsible for butchering meats and poultry (fish and shellfish are usually fabricated by the fish station chef), as well as the chefs responsible for hors d'oeuvre and breakfast items.

THE DINING ROOM

Like the back-of-the-house (that is, kitchen) staff, the front-of-the-house (that is, dining room) staff is also organized into a brigade. A traditional dining room brigade is led by the **dining room manager** (French *maître d'hotel* or *maître d'*), who generally trains all service personnel, oversees wine selections and works with the chef to develop the menu. He or she organizes the seating chart and may also seat the guests. Working subordinate to him or her are:

- The **wine steward** (French *chef de vin* or *sommelier*), who is responsible for the wine service, including purchasing wines, assisting guests in selecting wines and serving the wines.
- The **headwaiter** (French *chef de salle*), who is responsible for service throughout the dining room or a section of it. In smaller operations, his or her role may be assumed by the *maître d'* or a captain.
- The **captains** (French *chefs d'étage*), who are responsible for explaining the menu to guests and taking their orders. They are also responsible for any tableside preparations.
- The **front waiters** (French *chefs de rang*), who are responsible for assuring that the tables are set properly for each course, foods are delivered properly to the proper tables and the needs of the guests are met.
- The **back waiters** (French *demi-chefs de rang* or *commis de rang*, also known as dining room attendants or buspersons), who are responsible for clearing plates, refilling water glasses and other general tasks appropriate for new dining room workers.

Whether a restaurant uses this entire array of staff depends on the nature and size of the restaurant and the type of service provided. With **American service**, there is one waiter (also called a server) who takes the order and brings the food to the table. The table is then cleaned by a dining room attendant. With **French service**, there are two waiters: a captain and a waiter. The captain takes the order, does the tableside cooking and brings the drinks, appetizers, entrées and desserts to the table. The waiter serves bread and water, clears each course, crumbs the table and serves the coffee. With **Russian service**, the entrée, vegetables and potatoes are served from a platter onto a plate by the waiter. With **buffet service**, usually found in specialty restaurants and some institutional settings such as schools and correctional facilities, diners generally serve themselves or are served by workers assigned to specific areas of the buffet. Restaurants offering buffet service generally charge by the meal; if they charge by the dish, they are known as cafeterias.

- The *tournant*, also known as the roundsman or swing cook, works where needed.
- The *pâtissier* (pastry chef) is responsible for all baked items, including breads, pastries and desserts. Unlike the several station chefs, the *pâtissier* is not necessarily under the sous-chef's direct supervision. The *pâtissier* supervises the *boulanger* (bread baker), who makes the breads, rolls and baked dough containers used for other menu items (for example, bouchées and feuilletés); the *confiseur*, who makes candies and petits fours; the glacier, who makes all chilled and frozen desserts; and the *décorateur*, who makes showpieces and special cakes.
- Depending on the size and needs of any station or area, there are one or more *demi-chefs* (assistants) and *commis* (apprentices) who work with the station chef or pastry chef to learn the area.

THE MODERN KITCHEN BRIGADE

Today, most food service operations use a simplified version of Escoffier's kitchen brigade.

The **executive chef** coordinates kitchen activities and directs the kitchen staff's training and work efforts. The executive chef plans menus and creates recipes. He or she sets and enforces nutrition, safety and sanitation standards and participates in (or at least observes) the preparation and presentation of menu items to ensure that quality standards are rigorously and consistently maintained. He or she is also responsible for purchasing food items and, often, equipment. In some food service operations, the executive chef may assist in designing the menu, dining room and kitchen. He or she trains the dining room staff so that they can correctly answer questions about the menu. He or she may also work with food purveyors to learn about new food items and products, as well as with catering directors, equipment vendors, food stylists, restaurant consultants, public relations specialists, sanitation engineers, nutritionists and dietitians.

The executive chef is assisted by a **sous-chef** or **executive sous-chef,** who participates in, supervises and coordinates the preparation of menu items. His or her primary responsibility is to make sure that the food is prepared, portioned, garnished and presented according to the executive chef's standards. The sous-chef may be the cook principally responsible for producing menu items and supervising the kitchen.

Large hotels and conference centers with multiple dining facilities may have one or more **area chefs,** each responsible for a specific facility or function. There could be, for instance, a restaurant chef and a banquet chef. Area chefs usually report to the executive chef. Each area chef, in turn, has a brigade working under him or her.

Like Escoffier's station chefs, **line cooks** (or section cooks) are responsible for preparing menu items according to recipe specifications. Making the most of time, talent, space and equipment, the chef assigns responsibilities to each of the line cooks.

The **pastry chef** is responsible for developing recipes for and preparing desserts, pastries, frozen desserts and breads. He or she is usually responsible for purchasing the food items used in the bakeshop.

And, as in Escoffier's days, **assistants** and **apprentices** are assigned where needed in today's kitchens.

New styles of dining have created new positions since Escoffier's days. The most notable is the **short-order cook,** who is responsible for quickly preparing foods to order in smaller operations. He or she will work the broiler, deep-fat fryer and griddle as well as make sandwiches and even some sautéed items. Another is the **institutional cook,** who generally works with large quantities of prepackaged or prepared foods for a captive market such as a school, hospital or prison.

A restaurant may employ a **master chef** (Fr. *maître cuisinier*), **master pastry chef** (Fr. *maître pâtissier*) or a **master baker** (Fr. *maître boulanger*, Gr. *bäckermeister*). These titles recognize the highest level of achievement; only highly skilled and experienced professionals who have demonstrated their expertise and knowledge in written and practical exams are entitled to use them. These titles recall the European guild tradition still alive in many countries today. In France and Germany, for example, a chef, pastry chef or baker must pursue many years of classroom and job training, work as an apprentice and pass numerous examinations before acquiring the right to call himself or herself a "master." In the United States, several professional organizations administer programs that certify the professional experience of chefs, pastry chefs and bakers among others in the culinary field. (See Appendix I.)

▸ THE PROFESSIONAL CHEF

Although there is no one recipe for producing a good professional chef, we believe that with knowledge, skill, taste, judgment, dedication and pride a student chef will mature into a professional chef.

KNOWLEDGE

Chefs must be able to identify, purchase, utilize and prepare a wide variety of foods. They should be able to train and supervise a safe, skilled and efficient staff. To do all this successfully, chefs must possess a body of knowledge and understand and apply certain scientific and business principles. Schooling helps. A professional culinary program should, at a minimum, provide the student chef with a basic knowledge of foods, food styles and the methods used to prepare foods. Student chefs should also understand sanitation, nutrition and business procedures such as food costing.

ON EXPERIENCE

Sight, feel, hearing, and smell taught me about food. By touching a piece of meat, I learned to determine its degree of doneness. Raw meat was spongy, well-done meat hard. I learned precisely how to determine all the stages in between by pushing a finger against the surface of the meat. Hearing was significant, too. The snap of an asparagus spear, the crunch of an apple, the pop of a grape are all indicators of freshness and quality. I learned to listen to the sizzling sound of a chicken roasting in the oven. When *le poulet chant* (the chicken sings), I knew that the layers of fat had clarified, signifying that the chicken was nearly done. Smell was of importance in recognizing quality. A fresh fish smells of the sea, seaweed, and salt. Fresh meat has a sweet smell, fresh poultry practically no smell at all. Melon, pears, tomatoes, raspberries, oranges and the like each have their own distinctive fragrance when perfectly ripe.

Excerpt from *The Apprentice: My Life in the Kitchen* by Jacques Pépin.

This book is designed to help students learn these basics. Many chapters have extensive sections identifying foods and equipment. Throughout this book, we emphasize culinary principles, not recipes. Whenever possible, whether it be preparing puff pastry or grilling a steak, we focus on the general procedure, highlighting fundamental principles and skills; we discuss both the how and why of cooking. Only then are specific applications and sample recipes given. We also want students to have a sense of the rich tradition of cookery, so informative sidebars on food history, chef biographies and other topics are scattered throughout the book. The CD-ROM that accompanies this book is designed to enhance the learning experience while exposing students to the usefulness of computer technology in the contemporary kitchen.

In this way, we follow the trail blazed by Escoffier, who wrote in the introduction to *Le Guide culinaire* that his book is not intended to be a compendium of recipes slavishly followed, but rather a tool that leaves his colleagues "free to develop their own methods and follow their own inspiration; . . . the art of cooking . . . will evolve as a society evolves, . . . only basic rules remain unalterable."

As with any profession, an education does not stop at graduation. The acquisition of knowledge continues after the student chef joins the ranks of the employed. He or she should take additional classes on unique or ethnic cuisines, nutrition, business management or specialized skills. He or she should regularly review some of the many periodicals and books devoted to cooking, should travel and should try new dishes to broaden his or her culinary horizons. The professional chef should also become involved in professional organizations (see Appendix I) in order to meet his or her peers and exchange ideas.

SKILL

Culinary schooling alone does not make a student a chef. Nothing but practical, hands-on experience will provide even the most academically gifted student with the skills needed to produce, consistently and efficiently, quality foods or to organize, train, motivate and supervise a staff.

Many food service operations recognize that new workers, even those who have graduated from culinary programs, need time and experience to develop and hone their skills. Therefore, many graduates start in entry-level positions. Do not be discouraged; advancement will come, and the training pays off in the long run. Today, culinary styles and fashions change frequently. What does not go out of fashion are well-trained, skilled and knowledgeable chefs. They can adapt.

TASTE

No matter how knowledgeable or skilled the chef, he or she must be able to produce foods that taste great, or the consumer will not return. A chef can do so only if he or she is confident about his or her own sense of taste.

Our total perception of taste is a complex combination of smell, taste, sight, sound and texture. All senses are involved in the enjoyment of eating; all must be considered in creating or preparing a dish. The chef should develop a taste memory by sampling foods, both familiar and unfamiliar. The chef should also think about what he or she tastes, making notes and experimenting with flavor combinations and cooking methods. But a chef should not be inventive simply for the sake of invention. Rather, he or she must consider how the flavors, appearances, textures and aromas of various foods will interact to create a total taste experience.

▶ **gastronomy** the art and science of eating well

▶ **gourmet** a connoisseur of fine food and drink

▶ **gourmand** a connoisseur of fine food and drink, often to excess

▶ **gourmet foods** foods of the highest quality, perfectly prepared and beautifully presented

JUDGMENT

Selecting menu items, determining how much of what item to order, deciding whether and how to combine ingredients and approving finished items for service are all matters of judgment. Although knowledge and skill play a role in developing judgment, sound judgment comes only with experience. And real experience is often accompanied by failure. Do not be upset or surprised when a dish does not turn out as you expected. Learn from your mistakes as well as from your successes; only then will you develop sound judgment.

DEDICATION

Becoming a chef is hard work; so is being one. The work is often physically taxing, the hours are usually long and the pace is frequently hectic. Despite these pressures, the chef is expected to efficiently produce consistently fine foods that are properly prepared, seasoned, garnished and presented. To do so, the chef must be dedicated to the job.

The dedicated chef should never falter. The food service industry is competitive and depends on the continuing goodwill of an often fickle public. One bad dish or one off night can result in a disgruntled diner and lost business. The chef should always be mindful of the food prepared and the customer served.

The chef must also be dedicated to his or her staff. Virtually all food service operations rely on teamwork to get the job done well. Good teamwork requires a positive attitude and dedication to a shared goal, which is as impressive to a prospective employer as well-honed technical skills.

PRIDE

Not only is it important that the job be well done, but the professional chef should have a sense of pride in doing it well. Pride should also extend to personal appearance and behavior in and around the kitchen. The professional chef should be well-groomed and in a clean, well-maintained uniform when working.

The professional chef's uniform consists of comfortable shoes, trousers (either solid white, solid black, black-and-white checked or black-and-white striped), a white double-breasted jacket, an apron and a neckerchief usually knotted or tied cravat style. The uniform has certain utilitarian aspects: Checked trousers disguise stains; the double-breasted white jacket can be rebuttoned to hide dirt, and the double layer of fabric protects from scalds and burns; the neckerchief absorbs facial perspiration; and the apron protects the uniform and insulates the body. This uniform should be worn with pride. Shoes should be polished; trousers and jacket should be pressed.

The crowning element of the uniform is the toque. A toque is the tall white hat worn by chefs almost everywhere. Although the toque traces its origin to the monasteries of the 6th century, the style worn today was introduced at the end of the 19th century. Most chefs now wear a standard 6- or 9-inch-high toque, but historically, a cook's rank in the kitchen dictated the type of hat worn. Beginners wore flat-topped calottes; cooks with more advanced skills wore low toques and the master chefs wore high toques called *dodin-bouffants*. Culinary lore holds that the toque's pleats—101 in all—represent the 101 ways its wearer can successfully prepare eggs.

CONCLUSION

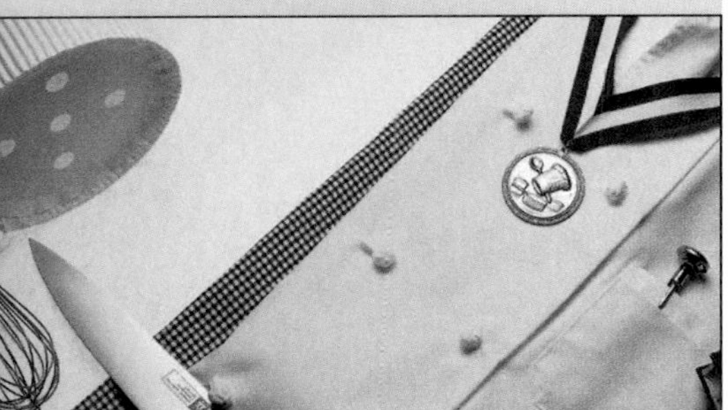

The art and science of cookery form a noble profession with a rich history and long traditions. With knowledge, skill, taste, judgment, dedication and pride, the student chef can become part of this profession. In this book, we provide the basic knowledge and describe the techniques in which students must become skilled. Dedicate yourself to learning this information and mastering your skills. Once you have done so, take pride in your accomplishments. Good luck.

QUESTIONS FOR DISCUSSION

1 Describe the kitchen brigade system. What is its significance in today's professional kitchens?
2 What are the roles of a chef, sous-chef and line cook in a modern kitchen?
3 Describe the differences in a meal prepared by Carême and one prepared by Point.
4 List and explain three technological advances affecting food preparation.
5 Discuss the societal changes that have contributed to diversification in the modern food service industry.

6 The newspapers in most large cities publish restaurant reviews. Use the Internet to find restaurant reviews from a city other than the one in which you live. Select one or two restaurants where you would like to dine the next time you visit that city. Why did you select these particular establishments?

7 The James Beard Foundation recognizes and honors outstanding American chefs each year. Who was James Beard? Which chefs are currently considered some of the most outstanding in the United States? Why?

CHAPTER TWO

OUR LIVES ARE NOT IN THE LAP OF THE GODS, BUT IN THE LAP OF OUR COOKS.

—Lin Yutang, Chinese-American writer,
in The Importance of Living, *1937*

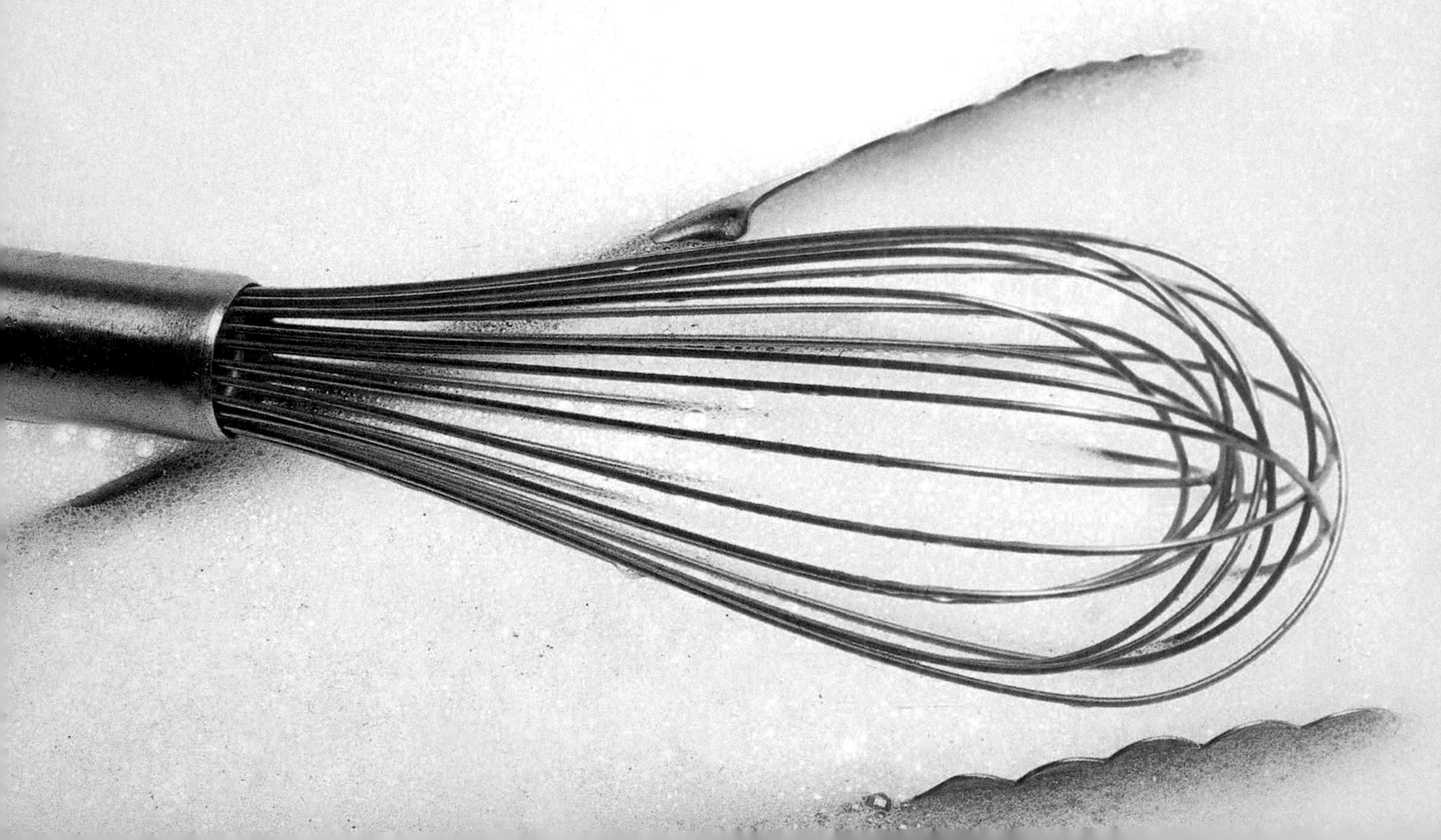

FOOD SAFETY AND SANITATION

AFTER STUDYING THIS CHAPTER, YOU WILL BE ABLE TO:

- identify the causes of food-borne illnesses
- handle foods in a safe manner
- explain and follow a HACCP system
- take appropriate actions to create and maintain a safe and sanitary working environment

The U.S. Public Health Service identifies more than 40 diseases that can be transmitted through food. Many can cause serious illness; some are even deadly. Therefore, providing consumers with safe food is the food handler's most important responsibility. Unfortunately, food handlers are also the primary cause of food-related illnesses.

Understanding what causes food-borne illnesses and what can be done to prevent them will help students be better able to protect their customers. This chapter should alert students to practices that can result in food-borne illnesses.

Federal, state, county, and municipal health, building and other codes are designed in part to ensure that food is handled in a safe and proper manner. Chefs should always consult the local health department for information and guidance, and always be conscious of what they can do to create and maintain a safe product as well as a safe environment for their customers, their fellow employees and themselves.

▶ **biological hazard** is a danger to the safety of food caused by disease-causing microorganisms such as bacteria, molds, yeasts, viruses or fungi.

▶ **chemical hazard** is a danger to the safety of food caused by chemical substances, especially cleaning agents, pesticides, and toxic metals.

▶ **physical hazard** is a danger to the safety of food caused by particles such as glass chips, metal shavings, bits of wood or other foreign matter.

▶ **microorganisms** are singled-celled organisms as well as tiny plants and animals that can be seen only through a microscope.

Sanitation refers to the creation and maintenance of conditions that will prevent food contamination of food-borne illness. **Contamination** refers to the presence, generally unintended, of harmful organisms or substances. Contamination can be (1) biological, (2) chemical or (3) physical. When consumed in sufficient quantities, food-borne contaminants can cause illness or injury, long-lasting disease or even death.

Contamination occurs in two ways: direct contamination and cross-contamination. **Direct contamination** is the contamination of raw foods or the plants and animals from which they come, in their natural settings or habitats. Chemical and biological contaminants such as bacteria and fungi are present in the air, soil and water. So, foods can be easily contaminated by their general exposure to the environment: Grains can become contaminated by soil fumigants in the field, and shellfish can become contaminated by ingesting toxic marine algae.

Chemicals and microorganisms generally cannot move on their own, however. They need to be transported, an event known as **cross-contamination**. The major cause of cross-contamination is people. Food handlers can transfer biological, chemical, and physical contaminants to food while processing, preparing, cooking or serving it. It is therefore necessary to view sanitation as the correction of problems caused by direct contamination and the prevention of problems caused by cross-contamination during processing and service.

Several **microorganisms**, primarily bacteria, parasites, viruses and fungi, can cause biologically based food-borne illnesses. By understanding under what conditions these microorganisms flourish, you'll be better prepared to combat them. Like humans, they need food, a comfortable temperature, the proper pH, and proper atmosphere, and time.

▶ DIRECT CONTAMINATION

FOOD-BORNE ILLNESS

Many people have had food-borne illness and have not even known it. The symptoms of food-borne illness are very similar to those associated with the flu.

THE FOOD-BORNE ILLNESS CRISIS IN AMERICA

America is confronted with a food-related health crisis of unprecedented proportions. The latest official estimate from the Centers for Disease Control and Prevention (CDC) is that there are some 76 million incidents of food-related illness in the United States annually. Of these, an estimated 325,000 Americans are hospitalized and 5,000 die each year. Some recent evidence indicates that these incidents have slightly decreased, and a new study is currently underway. Yet this remains a major crisis, and many Americans who suffer from food poisoning are not even aware of the cause. Symptoms may take a week or longer to appear, and victims frequently incorrectly attribute the distress and discomfort to stomach flu. It is not until the victims' afflictions become acute that tests are taken to determine the real cause. For those at risk—children, the elderly and anyone with a compromised immune system—this is frequently too late and the consequences can be deadly.

In his best-selling book *Fast Food Nation*, Eric Schlosser points out that one cause for this increase in food-borne illnesses is the vast expansion of the meat-packing industry due to increased demand from the fast-food industry. Indeed, recent *E. coli* outbreaks have been traced to meat processors' operations, just as *Salmonella* has increasingly been traced to poultry operations.

While the health problems that Schlosser raises are important and should not be glossed over, they should not be exaggerated either. The Food Safety and Inspection Service (FSIS), a branch of the U.S. Department of Agriculture (USDA), has tested more than 25,000 samples of ground beef since 1996. Of these, only 25 tested positive for *E. coli* and none of these samples were associated with any outbreak of illness. Recently FSIS inspections of meat-processing plants have increased, but incidences of *E. coli* have decreased. Even if health problems in the meat-packing industry were somehow solved tomorrow, food-borne illnesses would likely still be on the rise. The Government Accounting Office has estimated that 85 percent of food-borne illnesses comes from fruits, vegetables, seafood and cheeses—not meat or poultry. Fortunately, poisoning from *E. coli* is among the more uncommon food-borne diseases, with an estimated 73,000 cases each year from all sources.

Schlosser also raises legitimate concerns about the fat and nutritional content of the food served in fast-food establishments. Obesity and high cholesterol can cause health problems, and consuming vast quantities of fast food can contribute to potential illness. However, for most Americans an occasional trip to McDonald's is not hazardous to their health. It just depends on the rest of their diet. And popular images to the contrary, fast-food establishments have a good record of cleanliness when compared with other restaurants—and particularly when compared with home kitchens.

In fact, food safety experts have concluded that the home is the number one place where food-borne illnesses originate. Indeed, most home kitchens would not pass food inspections that public facilities regularly pass with flying colors. And most cases of illnesses caused by *E. coli* and *Salmonella,* even those originating at meat and poultry packers, could have been averted if home cooks had followed basic health procedures: properly storing meat and poultry, frequently washing their hands, promptly disinfecting all areas touched by raw meat or poultry and correctly cooking foods at the appropriate high temperatures for the appropriate period of time.

Of course, food inspections need to be increased and conditions improved at some meat- and poultry-packing plants. However, while blaming particular elements in the food system may bring visibility to serious problems, contamination can occur at many points along the way in the food system. If this food-related health crisis is to be controlled, it must be approached systemically from the farm to the fork.

ANDREW F. SMITH teaches culinary history at the New School University and is the author of eight books on culinary topics. He is editor in chief of the *Oxford Encyclopedia of Food and Drink in America.*

The type of microbe, how much contamination is in the food, and the general condition of the affected person determines the severity of the symptoms. (See Table 2.1.)

Food-borne illness is generally classified as a food-borne infection, intoxication, or toxin-mediated infection. Your awareness of how different microbes cause food-borne illness will help you understand how they contaminate food. (See Table 2.2.)

Table 2.1 GENERAL SYMPTOMS OF FOOD-BORNE ILLNESS

SYMPTOMS USUALLY INCLUDE ONE OR MORE OF THE FOLLOWING:

Headache	Abdominal pain
Nausea	Diarrhea
Vomiting	Fatigue
Dehydration	Fever

THE TEMPERATURE DANGER ZONE

The temperature danger zone is a broad range of temperatures in which most of the bacteria that cause food-borne illnesses multiply rapidly. The *2001 Model Food Code* of the Food and Drug Administration (FDA), August 2003 revision, indicates that the temperature danger zone begins at 41°F (5°C) and ends at 135°F (57°C). Regulations in some localities and with some organizations may vary, however. This text uses the range recommended by the FDA.

Table 2.2 **CLASSISFICATIONS OF FOOD-BORNE ILLNESS**

Infection	Caused by eating food that contains living, disease-causing microorganisms.
Intoxication	Caused by eating food that contains a harmful chemical or toxin produced by bacteria or other source.
Toxin-Mediated Infection	Caused by eating a food that contains harmful microorganisms that produce a toxin once inside the human intestinal tract.

Safety Alert

Onset times vary depending on factors such as the victim's...

- Age
- Health status
- Body weight
- Amount of contaminant ingested with the food.

Food-borne illnesses have different onset times. The **onset time** is the period between the time a person eats contaminated food and when they show the first symptoms of the disease.

FOOD-BORNE HAZARDS

A **food-borne hazard** is a biological, chemical, or physical hazard that can cause illness or injury when consumed along with food.

Biological hazards include bacteria, viruses, parasites, and fungi, and are

- Very small and can only be seen with the aid of a microscope.
- Commonly associated with live animals, humans, and with raw products.
- The most common cause of food-borne illness.
- The primary target of a food safety program.

Chemical hazards are toxic substances that may occur naturally or may be added during the processing of food. Examples of chemical contaminants include agricultural chemical (e.g., pesticides, fertilizers, antibiotics), cleaning compounds, heavy metal (lead and mercury), food additives, and food allergens for allergen-sensitive people. Harmful chemicals have been associated with severe poisonings and allergic reactions. Chemicals and other non-food items should be labeled clearly and never placed near food items.

Physical hazards are hard or soft foreign objects in food that can cause illness and injury. They include items such as fragments of glass, metal shavings, unfrilled toothpicks, jewelry, adhesive bandages, and human hair. These hazards result from accidental contamination and poor food-handling practices that can occur at many points in the food chain from the farm to the customer.

LETTUCE CAUSES ILLNESS...

Seventy-three people became ill with Norwalk virus after a county fair. An investigation was immediately started to determine the cause. The only common food the victims had eaten was chopped lettuce on tacos from a community service club's booth. All the workers in that booth were interviewed and procedures for handling the ingredients were reviewed. The chopped lettuce had been prepared by a food establishment and then placed in plastic bags for use at the venue. All the food workers at the establishment and the booth were tested and one person was positive for Norwalk virus—the employee who had chopped the lettuce. He wore plastic gloves while doing the task and used the same pair even after making several trips to the bathroom.

What do you think went wrong in this situation?

FOOD-BORNE ILLNESS CAUSED BY BACTERIA

Bacteria are single-celled microorganisms that require food, moisture, and specific temperatures to multiply. Bacteria can cause food-borne infections, intoxications, and toxin-mediated infections. In food establishments, most bacteria are destroyed or controlled by

- Monitoring time and temperature
- Good personal hygiene practices
- An effective cleaning and sanitation program
- Measures that minimize cross-contamination

All bacteria exist in a "vegetative state." Vegetative cells grow, reproduce, and produce wastes just like other living organisms. Some bacteria have the ability to form structures called "spores." Spores help bacteria survive when their environment is too hot, cold, dry, acidic, or when there is not enough food. Spores are not able to grow or reproduce. More information about bacteria spores is discussed in greater detail later in this chapter.

However, when conditions become suitable for growth, a spore can germinate much like a seed. The bacterial spore can then return to the vegetative state and begin to grow again. Bacteria can survive for many months as spores, and it is much harder to destroy bacteria when they are in a spore form.

Safety Alert

Keep spores from changing into the dangerous vegetative state where they can grow and cause illness.

Spoilage and Disease-Causing Bacteria

Bacteria are classified as either spoilage or pathogenic (disease-causing) microorganisms.

Spoilage bacteria break down foods so they look, taste, and smell bad. They reduce the quality of food to unacceptable levels. **Pathogenic bacteria** are disease-causing microorganisms that can make people ill if the vegetative bacterial cells or their toxins are consumed with food. Both spoilage and pathogenic bacteria much be controlled in food establishments.

▶ **pathogen** is any organism that causes disease; usually refers to bacteria; undetectable by smell, sight, or taste, pathogens are responsible for as many as 95% of all food-borne illnesses.

Bacterial Growth

Bacteria reproduce when one bacterial cell divides to form two new cells. This process is called binary fission. The reproduction of bacteria and an increase in the number of organisms is referred to as **bacterial growth**. Bacterial growth follows a regular pattern that consists of four phases:

1. **Lag phase**—Bacteria exhibit little or no growth as they adjust to their environment. This phase lasts only a few hours at room temperature but can be increased by keeping foods out of the temperature danger zone.
2. **Log phase**—Bacteria double in number every 15 to 30 minutes.
3. **Stationary phase**—The number of bacteria is steady as the number of new organisms being produced is equal to the number of organisms that are dying.
4. **Death (or decline) phase**—Bacteria die off rapidly because they lack nutrients and are poisoned by their own wastes.

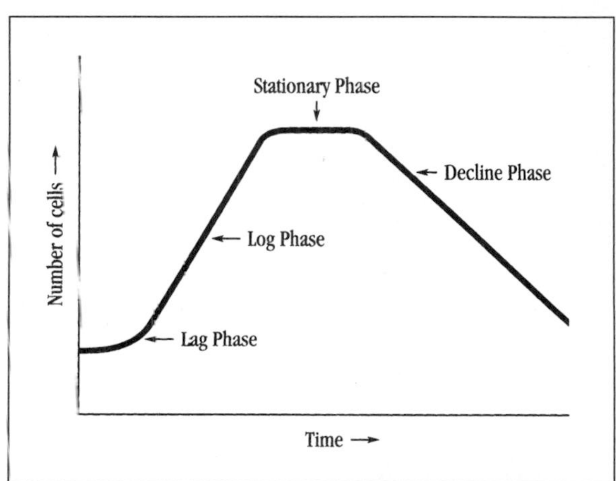

FIGURE 2.1 ▶ Bacterial growth curve.

What Disease-Causing Bacteria Need in Order to Multiply

Disease-causing bacteria need six conditions in order to multiply:

- Food
- Acid
- Temperature
- Time
- Oxygen
- Moisture

An easy way to remember the requirements for bacterial growth is by using the acronym F-A-T-T-O-M. (See Table 2.3.)

Safety Alert

Since many foods naturally contain microorganisms, it is necessary to control one or more of these 6 conditions to prevent bacteria from multiplying.

▶ **Temperature abuse** is the term applied to foods that have not been heated to a safe temperature or kept at the proper temperature to control growth.

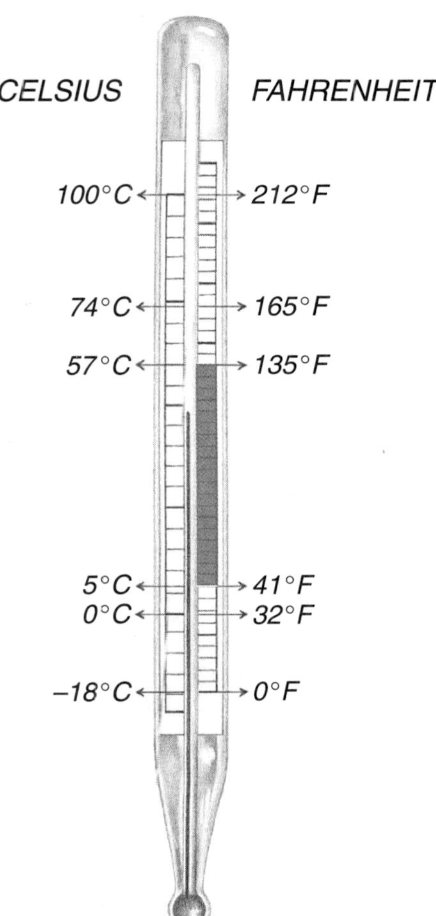

FIGURE 2.2 ▶ Temperature danger zone.

Bacterial cells can double in number every 15 to 30 minutes.

Safety Alert

Careful monitoring of time and temperature is the most effective way to control the growth of pathogenic and spoilage organisms.

Table 2.3 F-A-T-T-O-M

FOOD	High in protein or carbohydrates
ACID	pH from 4.6 to 7.0
TEMPERATURE	From 41°F to 135°F
TIME	Four (4) hours
OXYGEN	Depends on the type of bacteria, some can survive only with oxygen; some only without oxygen; some with or without oxygen; and some with oxygen in very limited amounts
MOISTURE	Water activity greater than 0.85

FOOD A suitable food supply is the most important condition needed for bacterial growth. Most bacteria prefer foods high in protein or carbohydrates like meats, poultry, seafood, dairy products, and cooked rice, beans, and potatoes.

ACIDITY The pH symbol is used to designate the level of acidity or alkalinity of a food. You measure pH on a scale that ranges from 0 to 14.

Most foods are acidic and have a pH less than 7.0. Foods highly **acidic** (pH below 4.6), like lemons, limes, and tomatoes, will not normally support the growth of disease-causing bacteria. Pickling fruit and vegetables preserves the food by adding acids such as vinegar. This lowers the pH of the food in order to slow down the rate of bacterial growth.

A pH above 7.0 indicates the food is **alkaline**. Only a few foods are alkaline. Examples of alkaline foods are olives, egg whites, and soda crackers.

Most bacteria that can cause food borne illness prefer a neutral environment (pH of 7.0) but are capable of growing in foods that have a pH in the range of 4.6 to 9.0. Since most foods have a pH of less than 7.0, we have identified the range where harmful bacteria grow as 4.6 to 7.0. Many foods offered for sale in food establishments have a pH in this range.

TEMPERATURE Most disease-causing bacteria can grow within a temperature range of 41F (5C) TO 135F (37C). This is commonly referred to as the food "temperature danger zone." A few disease-causing bacteria, such as Listeria monocytogenes, can grow at temperatures below 41F (5C), but the rate of growth is very slow.

TIME For most bacteria, a single cell can generate over one million new cells in just a few hours. Because bacteria have the ability to multiply rapidly, it does not take long before many cells are produced. Bacteria need about 4 hours to grow to high enough numbers to cause illness. Table 2.4 includes the total time a food is between 41F (5C) and 135F (57C):

Table 2.4

Time	0	15 min.	30min.	60min.	3hrs.	5hrs.
# cells	1	2	4	16	>1000	> 1 million

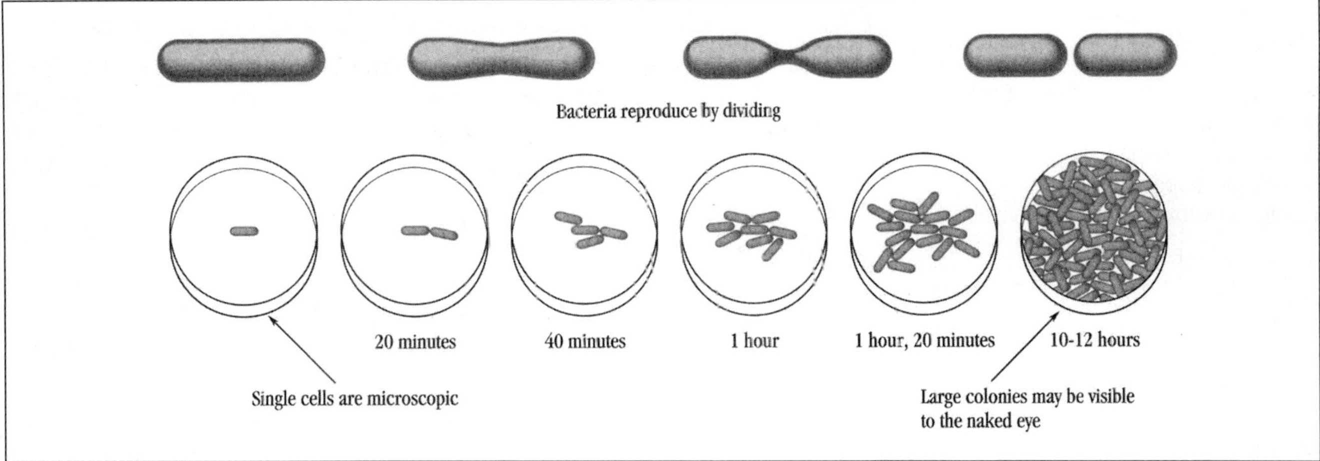

FIGURE 2.3 ▶ One bacterium divides into two; the two bacteria each divide, creating four; the four become 16 and so on. It takes only a very short time for one bacterium to produce millions more.

OXYGEN Bacteria also differ in their requirements for oxygen. **Aerobic bacteria** must have oxygen in order to grow. **Anaerobic bacteria** cannot survive when oxygen is present because it is toxic to them. These bacteria grow well in vacuum-packaged goods or canned goods where oxygen is not available. Anaerobic conditions also exist in the middle of cooked food masses such as in large stockpots, backed potatoes, or in the middle of a roast or ham.

Facultative anaerobic forms of bacteria can grow with or without oxygen.

Safety Alert

Controlling oxygen conditions is not an effective way to prevent food-borne illness. Regardless of available oxygen, some disease-causing bacteria will be able to adapt to the conditions and grow.

MOISTURE Moisture is an important factor in bacterial growth. The amount of water in a food available to support bacterial growth is called water activity. It is designated with the symbol A_w. Water activity is measured on a scale from 0.0 to 1.0. **Water activity** is a measure of the amount of water not bound to the food and is, therefore, available to support bacterial growth.

For example, fresh chicken has 60% water by volume, and its A_w is approximately 0.98. The same chicken, when frozen, still has 60% water by volume but its A_w is nearly zero. Lowering the water activity of foods to 0.85 or below preserves many foods. Drying foods or adding salt or sugar reduces the amount of available water. For example, jams and jellies that contain a lot of sugar have an A_w much less than 0.85. This alone prevents the growth of disease-causing microorganisms.

Preventing Bacterial Intoxications and Infections

All bacteria, like other living things, need certain conditions in order to complete their life cycles. Like humans, they need food, a comfortable temperature, moisture, the proper pH, the proper atmosphere and time. The best way to prevent bacterial intoxications and infections is to attack the factors bacteria need to survive and multiply.

▶ **Disease-causing bacteria** can only grow in foods that have a water activity higher than 0.85.

POTENTIALLY HAZARDOUS FOODS (PHF)

▶ **potentially hazardous foods (PHF)** are food items that require temperature control because they are capable of supporting the rapid growth of infectious or toxin-producing microbes.

Bacteria need food for energy and growth. The foods on which bacteria thrive are referred to as **potentially dangerous foods (PFH)**. They are generally high in protein and include animal-based products, cooked grains and some cooked vegetables. These foods and items containing these foods must be handled with great care.

The *FDA Food Code* classifies the following natural and man-made items as potentially hazardous foods:

- Foods of animal origin that are raw or heat-treated
- Foods of plant origin that are heat-treated or consist of raw seed sprouts
- Cut melons
- Garlic-in-oil mixtures that are not modified in a way to inhibit the growth of disease-causing microorganisms.

If potentially hazardous foods are held in the temperature danger zone [between 41°F (5°C) and 135°F (57°C)] for 4 hours or more, infectious and toxin-producing microbes can grow to dangerous levels. Potentially hazardous foods have been associated with most food-borne disease outbreaks. It is critical to control the handling and storage of potentially hazardous fees to prevent bacterial growth.

▶ **ready to eat foods** are food items that are edible without washing, cooking, or additional preparation by the customer or by the food establishment.

READY-TO-EAT FOODS

Ready-to-eat foods can become contaminated if not handled properly. The *FDA Food Code* identifies the following types of foods as ready-to-eat:

- Raw animal foods that are cooked (e.g., rotisserie chicken) or frozen (e.g., sushi).
- Raw fruits and vegetables that are washed.
- Fruits and vegetables that are cooked for hot-holding.
- All potentially hazardous foods that are cooked and then cooled.
- Bakery items such as breads, cakes, pies, fillings, or icing for which further cooking is not required for food safety.
- Substances derived from plants such as spices, seasonings, and sugar.
- Plant foods for which further washing, cooking, or other processing is not required for food safety, and from which rinds, peels, husks, or shells, if naturally present, are removed.
- Dry, fermented sausages (e.g., dry salami or pepperoni), salt-cured meat and poultry products (e.g., prosciutto ham, country cured ham, and Parma ham), and dried meat and poultry products (e.g., jerky or beef sticks) produced in accordance with USDA guidelines and have been treated to destroy pathogens.
- Thermally processed low-acid foods (e.g., smoked fish or meat) packaged in hermetically sealed containers.

POTENTIALLY HAZARDOUS FOODS

Potentially hazardous foods include the following::

- Food from an animal source (for example, meat, fish, shellfish, poultry, milk and eggs)
- Food from a plant that has been heat-treated (for example, cooked rice, beans, potatoes, soy products and pasta)
- Raw seed sprouts
- Cut melons
- Garlic in oil mixtures that are not acidified or otherwise appropriately modified at a processing plant
- Foods containing any of the preceding items (for example, custards, sauces and casseroles)

FOOD-BORNE ILLNESS CAUSED BY BACTERIA

Biological hazards are important for the food establishment manager to control because they lead to the majority of food-borne illness. Biological hazards are the most common agents that lead to food-borne illness. (See Table 2.5.)

Table 2.5 COMMON BIOLOGICAL HAZARDS IN FOOD ESTABLISHMENTS

BACTERIA	VIRUSES	PARASITES
Bacillus cereus	Hepatitis A	Anisakis spp.
Campylobacter jejuni	Norwalk virus group	Cryptosporidium parvum
Clostridium perfringens	Rotavirus	Cyclospora cayetanensis
Clostridium botulinum		Giardia Lamblia
Listeria monocytogenes		Toxoplasma gondii
Salmonella spp.		Trichinella spiralis
Shiga toxin-producing Escherichia coli		
Shigella spp.		
Staphyloccpccis aureus		
Vibrio spp.		

Food-borne Illness Caused by Sporeforming Bacteria

A spore structure enables a cell to survive environmental stress such as cooking, freezing, high-salt conditions, drying, and high-acid conditions.

Spores are not harmful if ingested, except in a baby's digestive system where Clostridium botulinum spores can cause a disease called infant botulism. It is often recommended parents avoid serving honey to babies due to the possible presence of Clostridium botulinum spores. If conditions in the food are suitable for bacterial growth and the spore turns into a vegetative cell, the vegetative cell can grow in the food and cause illness if eaten.

Sporeforming bacteria are generally found in foods grown in soil, like vegetables and spices. They may also be found in animal products. They can be particularly troublesome in food establishments when foods are not cooled properly.

For example, a 10-gallon pot of chili was prepared for the next day's salad bar display. All the ingredients (beans, meat, spices, tomato base) were mixed together and cooked to a rapid boil. Vegetative cells should die, but spores may survive.

The chili was then stored in the 10-gallon pot and allowed to cool overnight in a walk-in refrigerator. It can take the core temperature of the chili 2 to 3 days to cool from 135°F (57°C) to 41°F (5°C)! If given enough time at the right temperature during the cooling process, sporeforming bacteria that survived the cooking process may change into vegetative cells and begin to grow.

Spores are most likely to run into the dangerous vegetative state when

- They are "heat-shocked" during cooking which can allow the spores to become vegetative cells.
- Optimum conditions exist for growth (high protein or carbohydrates, high moisture, pH greater than 4.6).
- Temperatures are in the food temperature danger zone between 41°F (5°C) to 135°F (57°C) for 4 or more hours.

In the following sections, each type of biological hazard is described, the common foods and route of transmission are identified, and preventive strategies are discussed.

Safety Alert

It is critical hot food temperatures be maintained at 135°F (57°C) or above and cold foods should be held at 41°F (5°C) or below.

Safety Alert

Always cook and cool foods as rapidly as possible (within 4 hours) to limit bacterial growth.

Table 2.6 BACILLUS CEREUS

Causative Agent	*Bacillus cereus*
Type of Illness	Bacterial intoxication or toxin-mediated infection
Symptoms	Diarrhea type: abdominal Vomiting type: vomiting, diarrhea, abdominal cramps
Onset	Diarrhea type: 8 to 16 hours; usually lasts 12 to 14 hours Vomiting type: 30 minutes to 6 hours; usually lasts 30 minutes to 6 hours
Common Foods	Diarrhea type: meats, milk, vegetables, fish Vomiting type: rice, starchy foods, grains, cereals
Prevention	Properly cook and hold at 135°F (57°C), cool rapidly to below 41°F (5°C), and reheat foods.

Safety Alert

Properly cook and hold foods at 135°F and cool rapidly to prevent *Bacillus cereus* illness.

Food-borne Illness Caused by Non-Sporeforming Bacteria

Compared to bacterial spores, vegetative cells are easily destroyed by proper cooking. There are numerous examples of non-sporeforming food-borne bacteria that are important in the food industry.

SPOREFORMING BACTERIA

Bacillus cereus is a sporeforming bacterium that can survive with or without oxygen. It has been associated with two very different types of illnesses: one vomiting, the other diarrhea. Illness due to *Bacillus cereus* is most often attributed to foods improperly stored (cooled, hot-held), permitting the conversion of spores to vegetative cells. Vegetative cells then produce toxin in the food that leads to illness. (See Table 2.6.)

Clostridium perfringens is a nearly anaerobic (must have very little oxygen), sporeforming bactgerium that causes food-borne illness. Potentially hazardous foods that have been temperature abused [not kept hot—above 135°F (57°C); or cold—below 41°F (5°C)] are frequently associated with this problem. *Clostridium perfringens* causes illness due to a toxin-mediated infection where the ingested cells colonize and then produce a toxin in the human intestinal tract. Illness due to *Clostridium perfringens* is most often attributed to foods that are temperature abused, especially those that have been improperly cooled and reheated. Foods must be cooked to 145°F (63°C) or above. Cooked foods must be cooled from 135°F (57°C) to 70°F (21°C) within 2 hours and from 135°F (57°C) to 41°F (5°C) within 6 hours. Foods must also be reheated to 165°F (74°C) within 2 hours and held at 135°F (57°C) until served. For quality and safety reasons, foods should be reheated only once. (See Table 2.7.)

Safety Alert

Cool foods properly to prevent *Clostridium perfringens.*

Table 2.7 CLOSTRIDIUM PERFRINGENS

Causative Agent	*Clostridium perfringens*
Type of Illness	Bacterial toxin-mediated infection
Symptoms	Intense abdominal pains and severe diarrhea
Onset	8 to 22 hours
Common Foods	Spices, gravy, improperly cooled foods (especially meats and gravy dishes)
Pervention	Properly cook, cool, and reheat foods

Table 2.8 CLOSTRIDIUM BOTULINUM

Causative Agent	*Clostridium botulinum*
Type of Illness	Bacterial intoxication
Symptoms	Dizziness, double vision, difficulty in breathing and swallowing, headache
Onset	12 to 36 hours; usually last several days to a year
Common Foods	Low-acid foods (pH above 4.6), which are inadequately heat-processed and then packaged anaerobically (metal can or vacuum pouch), and held in the food temperature danger zone. Examples: home-canned green beans, meats, fish, and garlic or onions stored in oil and butter respectively.
Prevention	Properly heat-process and cook vacuum-packaged and other reduced-oxygen packaged foods. DO NOT use home-canned foods.

Clostridium botulinum is an **anaerobic** (must not have oxygen), sporeforming bacterium that causes food-borne intoxication due to improperly heat-processed foods, especially home-canning. Do not can foods in a food establishment. The organism produces a neurotoxin that is one of the deadliest biological toxins known to man. This toxin is not heat stable and can be destroyed if the food is boiled for about 20 minutes. However, botulism still occurs because people do not want to boil food that has already been cooked. Illness due to *Clostridium botulinum* is almost always attributed to ingestion of foods that were not heat-processed correctly and packaged anaerobically. (See Table 2.8.)

Safety Alert

Properly heat-process and cool vacuum-packaged foods.

NON-SPOREFORMING BACTERIA

Campylobacter jejuni has been reported as the No. 1 cause of bacterial food-borne infection in the United States. This organism tolerates only 3 to 6% oxygen to grow. *Campylobacter jejuni* is often transferred from raw meats to other foods by cross contamination, typically from a food-contact surface (such as a cutting board or knife) or a food employee's hands. (See Table 2.9.)

Safety Alert

Campylobacter jejuni is commonly found in raw chicken.

The *Escherichia coli* (or *E. coli*) group of bacteria includes four food-borne pathogens: enterotoxigenic *E. coli*, enteropathegenic *E coli*, enterohemorrhagic *E. coli*, and enteroinvasive *E. coli*. Of particular importance is a type of enterohemorrhagic *E. coli* called Shiga toxin-producing *E. coli*. This facultative anaerobic bacteria can be found in the intestines of warm-blooded animals, especially cows. The illness caused by Shiga toxin-producing *E. coli* can be an infection or a toxin-mediated infection. Only a small amount of bacteria is required to produce an illness. A potentially hazardous food is not needed for bacterial survival. That's why

Raw chicken

Table 2.9 CAMPYLOBACTER JEJUNI

Causative Agent	*Campylobacter jejuni*
Type of Illness	Bacterial infection
Symptoms	Watery, bloody diarrhea
Onset	2 to 5 days; usually lasts 2 to 7 days
Common Foods	Raw poultry, raw milk, raw meat
Prevention	Properly handle and cook raw meats and poultry, properly clean and sanitize food contact surfaces and properly wash hands.

Table 2.10	ESCHERICHIA COLI
Causative Agent	Shiga toxin-producing *Escherichia coli*
Type of Illness	Bacterial infection or toxin-mediated infection; at special risk are children up to 16 years old and the elderly
Symptoms	Bloody diarrhea followed by kidney failure and hemolytic uremic syndrome (HUS) in severe cases
Onset	12 to 72 hours; usually lasts from 1 to 3 days
Common Foods	Raw and undercooked beef and other red meats, raw finfish, improperly pasteurized milk, unpasteurized apple cider, lettuce
Prevention	Practice good food sanitation, and hand washing; properly handle and cook ground meats to an internal temperature of at least 155°F (68°C) for 15 seconds; prevent cross contamination and keep hot foods above 135°F (57°C) and cold foods below 41°F (5°C). Wash lettuce in sinks used only for food preparation. Use only pasteurized apple cider or fruit juice and milk products.

▶ **rotate stock** to use products in the order in which they were received; all perishable and semi-perishable goods, whether fresh, frozen, canned or dry, should be used according to the "first in, first out (FIFO)" principle.

Safety Alert

Listeria monocytogenes can grow at refrigerated temperatures.

apple cider, which has a pH lower than 4.6 has been implicated in cases of food-borne illness. Shiga toxin-producing *E. coli* is usually transferred to foods such as beef through contact with the intestines of slaughtered animals. Apples used for juice from orchards where cattle grazed are also suspected. Transmission can occur if employees who are carriers do not wash their soiled hands properly after going to the toilet. Cross contamination by soiled equipment and utensils may also spread Shiga toxin-producing *E. coli*. (See Table 2.10.)

Listeria monocytogenes is a facultative anaerobic (can grow with or without oxygen) bacterium that causes food-borne infection. This microbe is important to food establishment operations because it has the ability to survive under many environmentally stressful conditions such as in high-salt foods and, unlike most other food-borne pathogens, can grow at refrigerated temperatures below 41°F (5°C). Transmission to foods can occur by cross contamination by people or equipment or if foods are not cooked properly. (See Table 2.11.)

Table 2.11	LISTERIA MONOCYTOGENES
Causative Agent	*Listeria monocytogenes*
Type of Illness	Bacterial infection
Symptoms	1) Healthy adult: flu-like symptoms 2) Highly susceptible: septicemia, meningitis, encephalitis, birth defects 3) Stillbirth
Onset	1 day to 3 weeks; indefinite duration depending on when treatment is administered
Common Foods	Raw meats, raw poultry, dairy products, cooked luncheon meats and hot dogs, raw vegetables, and seafood
Prevention	Properly store and cook foods, avoid cross contamination, rotate processed refrigerated foods using FIFO to ensure timely use.

Table 2.12 SALMONELLA SPP.

Causative Agent	*Salmonella spp.*
Type of Illness	Bacterial infection
Symptoms	Nausea, fever, vomiting, abdominal crams, diarrhea
Onset	6 to 48 hours; usually lasts 2 to 3 days
Common Foods	Raw meats, raw poultry, eggs, milk, dairy products, pork
Prevention	Properly cook foods; example: *Salmonella* bacteria will be destroyed when poultry is cooked to an internal temperature of 165°F (74°C) for 15 seconds and when eggs are cooked to 145°F (63°C) for 15 seconds. Clean and sanitize raw food-contact surfaces after use; make sure food employees wash their hands adequately before working with food, avoid cross contamination.

Salmonella are facultative anaerobic (grow with or without oxygen) bacteria frequently implicated as a food-borne infection. *Salmonella* are found in the intestinal tract of humans and warm-blooded animals. It frequently gets into foods as a result of fecal contamination or cross contamination. Transmission to foods is commonly through cross-contamination where fecal material is transferred to food through contact with raw foods (especially poultry), contaminated food-contact surfaces (e.g., cutting boards), or infected food employees. (See Table 2.12.)

Shigella spp. is facultative anaerobic bacteria that account for about 10% of food-borne illnesses in the United States. These organisms are commonly found in the intestines and feces of humans and warm-blooded animals. They cause shigellosis, a food-borne infection. The bacterium produces a toxin that causes watery diarrhea. Water contaminated by fecal material and food and utensils handled by employees who are carriers of the bacteria can cause this problem. Illness from *Shigella spp.* is most often attributed to contaminated ready-to-eat foods handled by an infected food handler. (See Table 2.13.)

Safety Alert

Shigella spp. is most often attributed to foods prepared with human contact.

Staphylococcus aureus is a facultative anaerobic bacterium that produces a heat-stable toxin as it grows on foods. This bacterium can also grow on cooked,

Table 2.13 SHIGELLA SPP.

Causative Agent	*Shigella spp.*
Type of Illness	Bacterial infection
Symptoms	Bacillary dysentery, diarrhea, fever, abdominal cramps, dehydration
Onset	1 to 7 days; duration depends on when treatment is administered
Common Foods	Foods prepared with human contact: ready-to-eat salads (e.g., potato, chicken), raw vegetables, milk, dairy products, raw poultry, non-potable water, ready-to-eat meat.
Prevention	Wash hands and practice good personal hygiene, properly cook foods, avoid cross contamination, wash produce and other foods with potable water (water that is safe to drink). Do not allow individuals who have been diagnosed with shigellosis to handle food.

Table 2.14	STAPHYLOCOCCUS AUREUS
Causative Agent	*Staphylococcus aureus*
Type of Illness	Bacterial intoxication
Symptoms	Nausea, vomiting, abdominal cramps, headaches
Onset	1 to 6 hours, usually 2 to 4 hours; usually lasts 1 to 2 days
Common Foods	Foods prepared with human contact; cooked ready-to-eat foods such as luncheon meats, ready-to-eat meat, deli salads (such as taco, potato, egg, and tuna salads), meat, poultry, custards, high-salt foods such as ham, and milk and dairy products, processed foods
Prevention	Wash hands and practice good personal hygiene, avoid coughing and sneezing near food, do not reuse tasting spoons and ladles, properly clean and bandage cuts, burns or wounds on hands and wear plastic gloves. Cooking WILL NOT inactivate the toxin.

and otherwise safe, foods recontaminated by food employees who mishandle the food. *Staphylococcus auerus* bacteria do not compete well when alone and without competition from other microbes. These bacteria are commonly found on human skin, hands, hair, and in the nose and throat. They may also be found in burns, infected cuts and wounds, pimples, and boils. These organisms can be transferred to foods easily, and they can grow in foods that contain high salt or high sugar, and have a lower water activity. They grow well in a high-salt concentration environment such as on hams and luncheon meats. Foods requiring considerable food preparation and handling are especially susceptible. The bacteria are also spread by droplets of saliva from talking, coughing, and sneezing near food. Food employees who improperly use tasting spoons and ladles can transfer bacteria from their mouth to food. Contaminated human hands combined with temperature abuse usually cause most problems associated with *Staphylococcus aureus*. (See Table 2.14.)

There are three organisms within the *Vibrio* group of bacteria connected with food-borne infections. They include *Vibrio cholera*, *Vibrio parahaemolyticus*, and *Vibrio vulnificus*. All are important since they are resistant to salt and are common in seafood.

Since the organism is inherent in many raw seafoods, transmission to other foods by cross contamination is a concern. Most illnesses are caused by the consumption of raw or undercooked seafood. (See Table 2.15.)

Table 2.15	VIBRO SPP.
Causative Agent	*Vibrio spp.*
Type of Illness	Bacterial intoxication
Symptoms	Headache, fever, chills, diarrhea, vomiting, severe electrolyte loss, gastroenteritis
Onset	2 to 48 hours
Common Foods	Raw or improperly cooked fish and shellfish
Prevention	Practice good sanitation, properly cool foods, implement procedures to separate raw and ready-to-eat seafood display cases, buy seafood from approved sources only.

Table 2.16 HEPATITIS A VIRUS

Causative Agent	Hepatitis A virus
Type of Illness	Viral infection
Symptoms	Fever, nausea, vomiting, abdominal pain, fatigue, swelling of the liver, jaundice
Onset	10 to 50 days; a mild case usually lasts several weeks, more severe cases can last several months
Common Foods	Raw and lightly cooked oysters and clams harvested from polluted waters; raw vegetables that have been irrigated or washed with polluted water; foods prepared with contact by infected employee, including salads, sliced luncheon meats, salad bar items, sandwiches, bakery products; contaminated water
Prevention	Buy clams, oysters, and molluscan shellfish from approved sources; keep raw and ready-to-eat foods separate during storage and display; handle foods properly and cook them to recommended temperatures; wash hands and practice good personal hygiene

Food-borne Illness Caused by Viruses

Viruses are now thought to be the Number 1 cause of food-borne and water-borne diseases in the United States. The viruses that cause food-borne disease differ from food-borne bacteria in several ways. Viruses are much smaller than bacteria, and they require a living host (human, animal) to replicate. Viruses do not multiply in foods. However, a susceptible person needs to consume only a few viral particles in order to experience an infection.

Viruses are usually transferred from one food source to another, from a food employee to a food, or from a contaminated water supply to a food. A potentially hazardous food is not needed to support survival of viruses. The viruses of primary importance to food establishments are Hepatitis A and Norwalk virus. Proper hand washing and separation of raw and ready-to-eat foods are important keys to controlling the spread of food-borne viruses.

Hepatitis A virus is a food-borne virus associated with many food-borne infections. Hepatitis A virus causes a liver disease called infectious hepatitis. The Hepatitis A virus is a particularly important hazard to food establishments because employees can harbor the virus for up to six weeks and not show symptoms of illness. Food employees are contagious for one week before onset of symptoms and two weeks after the symptoms of the disease appear. During that time, infected employees can contaminate foods and other employees by spreading fecal material from unwashed hands and nails. Hepatitis A virus is very hardy and can live for several hours in a suitable environment. The virus is transmitted by ingestion of food and water that contain the Hepatitis A virus. Raw seafood and foods handled by infected human hands are the largest threat of transmission and disease from Hepatitis A. (See Table 2.16).

The Norwalk virus is another common food-borne virus associated with many food-borne infections. The virus is primarily transmitted by ingestion of food and water contaminated with feces that contain the Norwalk virus. (See Table 2.17.)

Safety Alert

Raw seafood and foods handled by infected human hands are the largest threat of transmission and disease from Hepatitis A.

Food-borne Illness Caused by Parasites

Food-borne parasites are another important food-borne biological hazard. Parasites are small or microscopic creatures that need to live on or inside a living host

Table 2.17 NORWALK VIRUS

Causative Agent	Norwalk virus
Type of Illness	Viral infection
Symptoms	Vomiting, diarrhea, abdominal pain, headache, low-grade fever
Onset	24 to 48 hours, usually lasts 1 to 3 days
Common Foods	Sewage-contaminated water; contaminated salad ingredients; raw clams, oysters; foods contaminated by infected food employees
Prevention	Use potable water; cook all shellfish; handle food properly; meet time, temperature guidelines for PHFs; practice good personal hygiene and wash hands and fingernails thoroughly; keep raw and ready-to-eat seafood products separate.

Safety Alert

Bottom-feeding fish such as salmon are a common source of *Anisakis spp*.

to survive. Many parasites can enter the food system and cause food-borne illness. In this chapter, we list a few of the most troublesome ones that may appear in food establishments. Parasitic infection is far less common than bacterial or viral food-borne illnesses.

Anisakis spp. are nematodes (roundworms) associated with food-borne infection from fish. The worms are about 1 to 1-1/2 inches long and the diameter of a human hair. They are beige, ivory, white, gray, brown, or pink. Other names for this parasite are "cod worm" (not to be confused with common roundworms found in cod) and "herring worm." The natural hosts of the parasite are walruses, and perhaps, sea lions and otters. The worms are transferred to fish, their immediate host, in the water in which the walruses live. Humans become the accidental host upon eating fish infected with the parasites. Humans do not make good hosts for the parasites. The worms will not complete their life cycles in humans, and eventually die. (See Table 2.18.)

Safety Alert

Wash berries to remove contaminants

Cyclospora cayetanensis is a parasite that has been reported much more frequently beginning in the 1990s. *Cyclospora* frequently finds its way into water and then can be transferred to foods. It can also be transferred to foods during handling. The most recent outbreaks of *cyclosporiasis* have been associated with fresh fruits and vegetables that were contaminated at the farm. *Cyclospora* is passed from person to person by fecal-oral transmission. Foods usually become contaminated after coming in contact with fecal material from polluted water or a contaminated food employee. The *Cyclospora* parasite may take days or weeks after a person eats a contaminated food to become infectious. (See Table 2.19.)

Table 2.18 ANISAKIS SPP.

Causative Agent	*Anisakis spp.*
Type of Illness	Parasitic infection
Symptoms	Coughing if worms attach in throat, vomiting and abdominal pain if worms attach in stomach, sharp pain and fever if worms attach in large intestine
Onset	1 hour to 2 weeks
Common Foods	Raw or undercooked seafood; especially bottom-feeding fish
Prevention	Cook fish to the proper temperature throughout, freeze to meet *FDA Food Code* specifications, inspect seafood and handle carefully, purchase seafood from approved supplier

Table 2.19 CYCLOSPORA CAYETANENSIS

Causative Agent	*Cyclospora cayetanensis*
Type of Illness	Parasitic infection
Symptoms	Watery and explosive diarrhea, loss of appetite, bloating
Onset	Usually within 1 week; symptoms persist for weeks or months if untreated
Common Foods	Contaminated water, strawberries, raspberries, and fresh produce
Prevention	Good sanitation and personal hygiene, purchase foods from reputable supplier

Trichinella spiralis is a food-borne roundworm that causes a parasitic infection. It must be eaten with the infected fleshy muscle of certain meat-eating animals to be transmitted to a new host. Meat-eating, scavenger animals frequently carry this parasite. These animals are exposed to the parasite when they eat infected tissues from other animals and garbage that contains contaminated raw-meat scraps. (See Table 2.20.)

Safety Alert

Cook pork so there is no pink color inside.

Cryptosporidium parvum is a parasite found in water that has been contaminated with cow feces. The parasite causes food-borne infection and is considered an important source of nonbacterial diarrhea in the United States. The parasite could occur, theoretically, on any food touched by a contaminated food handler. It is primarily transmitted by a water supply contaminated with feces and by fecal contamination of food and food-contact surfaces. Parasite prevention starts with providing a potable water supply in the food establishment and handling foods carefully to prevent contamination and cross contamination. Food employees must practice good personal hygiene and wash hands thoroughly before working with food and after going to the toilet. (See Table 2.21.)

Safety Alert

Wash berries to remove contaminants

Problems Caused by Fungi

Yeast and molds make up the group called **fungi**. Yeasts and molds mainly contribute to food spoilage. When yeast grows in a food, it leads to undesirable characteristics of a food, including production of gases, acids, and alcohol. The food may taste or smell "sour" or the package may swell. Yeasts do not lead to food-borne illness. In fact, yeasts are often used to produce fermented foods such as beer, wine, and cheeses. Molds usually grow in foods low in moisture (such as bread or cheese), acidic (fruit juices), or high in sugar (jams and jellies). They often appear very colorful or "cotton-like" or "powdery" in appearance. Like yeasts, molds themselves do not cause food-borne illness. However, if they grow long enough on foods, they can produce a substance called a "mycotoxin." Mycotoxins can cause food-borne illness and some cancers. Mycotoxins are usually considered chemical hazards.

Strawberries

Raspberries

Table 2.20 TRICHINELLA SPIRALIS

Causative Agent	*Trichinella spiralis*
Type of Illness	Parasitic infection from a nematode worm
Symptoms	Early symptoms: nausea, vomiting, diarrhea, sweating, abdominal pain; in later stages: fever, swelling of tissues around eyes, muscle stiffness
Onset	2 to 28 days; death may occur in severe cases
Common Foods	Primarily undercooked pork products and wild game meats (bear, walrus)
Prevention	Cook foods to the proper temperature throughout, i.e., no pink color in cooked pork products

Table 2.21	CRYPTOSPORIDIUM PARVUM
Causative Agent	*Cryptosporidium parvem*
Type of Illness	Parasitic infection
Symptoms	Severe watery diarrhea
Onset	Within 1 week of ingestion
Common Foods	Contaminated water, food contaminated by infected food employees
Prevention	Use potable water supply; practice good personal hygiene and handwashing.

FOOD-BORNE ILLNESS CAUSED BY CHEMICALS

Chemical hazards are usually classified as either naturally occurring or man-made chemicals. Naturally occurring chemicals include toxins produced by a biological organism. Man-made chemicals include substances added, intentionally or accidentally, to a food during processing. A summary of some of the more common naturally occurring and man-made chemicals is provided in Table 2.22.

▶ **naturally occurring chemicals** include toxins produced by a biological organism.

▶ **man-made chemicals** include substances added, intentionally or accidentally, to a food during processing.

Naturally Occurring Chemicals—Food Allergens

Between 5 and 8% of children and 1 to 2% of adults are allergic to certain chemicals in foods and food ingredients. These chemicals are commonly referred to as food allergens. A food allergen causes a person's immune system to overreact. Some common symptoms of food allergies are hives; swelling of the lips, tongue, and mouth; difficulty breathing or wheezing; and vomiting, diarrhea, and cramps. These symptoms can occur in as little as five minutes. In severe situations, a life-threatening allergic reaction called anaphylaxis can occur. Anaphylaxis is a condition that occurs when many parts of the body become involved in the allergic reaction. Symptoms of anaphylaxis include itching and hives; swelling of the throat and difficulty breathing; lowered blood pressure and unconsciousness.

The FDA has identified the "Big Eight" from the 170 different foods known to cause allergic reactions. About 90% of ingredients include the "Big Eight" and are considered to be "major serious allergens." The only way for a person who is allergic to one of these foods to keep from having an allergic reaction is to avoid the food containing the allergen. In many cases, it doesn't take much of the food to produce a severe reaction. As little as half a peanut can cause a severe reaction in highly sensitive people. (See Table 2.23.)

Safety Alert

Foods containing potential contaminants must be properly labeled.

Table 2.22 TYPES OF CHEMICAL HAZARDS IN A FOOD ESTABLISHMENT

NATURALLY OCCURRING...	MAN-MADE CHEMICALS...
Allergens	Cleaning solutions
Ciguatoxin	Food additives
Mycotoxins	Pesticides
Scombrotoxin	Heavy metals
Shellfish toxins	

Source: FDA Food Code

Allergies can be very serious. You need to know which foods in your establishment contain these ingredients. The FDA requires ingredients to be listed on the label of packaged foods. Always read label information to determine if food allergens may be present.

The responsibility of retailers in the case of prepackaged foods is to assure appropriate label warnings are given to potential purchasers. Retailers have special responsibilities in regard to foods sold from open containers (e.g., on delicatessen counters). When such foods contain a major food allergen, the warning should be clearly displayed by the foods in question. Moreover, staff must be trained to take great care to avoid cross contamination such as might occur when using the same ladle or other handling equipment for a food containing a major food allergen and one that does not contain it.

Ciguatoxin poisoning is an example of an intoxication caused by eating contaminated tropical reef fish. The toxin is found in tiny, free-swimming sea creatures called algae that live among certain coral reefs. When small reef fish eat the toxic algae, it is stored in the flesh, skin, and organs. When bigger fish such as barracuda eat the small reef fish such as mackerel, mahi mahi, bonito, jackfish, and snapper, the toxin accumulates in the flesh and skin of the consuming fish. The toxin does not affect the contaminated fish. The toxin is heat stable and not destroyed by cooking. At the present time, there is no commercially known method to determine if ciguatoxin is present in a particular fish. The toxin is transferred to finfish when they eat toxin-containing algae or other fish that contain the toxin. (See Table 2.24.)

Eating foods high in a chemical compound called histamine causes scombrotoxin, also called histamine poisoning. Histamine is usually produced by certain bacteria when they decompose foods containing the protein histidine. Dark meat of fish has more histidine than other fish meat. Histamine is not inactivated by cooking. Over time, bacteria inherent to a particular food can break down histidine and cause the production of histamine. Leaving fish out at room temperature usually results in histamine production. (See Table 2.25.)

Added Man-Made Chemicals

There is an extensive list of chemicals added to foods that may pose a potential health risk. Intentionally added chemicals may include food additives, food preservatives, and pesticides. Pesticides leave residues on fruits and vegetables and can usually be removed by a vigorous washing procedure. Non-intentionally added chemicals may include contamination by chemicals such as cleaning and sanitary supplies. Also, chemicals from containers or food-contact surfaces of inferior metal that are misused may lead to heavy-metal or inferior-metal poisoning (cadmium, copper, lead, galvanized metals, etc.).

Table 2.23 COMMON FOOD ALLERGENS—THE "BIG EIGHT"

Milk	Soy
Eggs	Tree nuts
Wheat proteins	Fish
Peanuts	Shellfish

Safety Alert

Ciguatoxin can be found in marine finfish such as red snapper.

Red Snapper

Table 2.24 CIGUATOXIN

Causative Agent	Ciguatoxin
Type of Illness	Fish toxin originating from toxic algae of tropical waters
Symptoms	Vertigo, nausea, hot/cold flashes, diarrhea, vomiting, shortness of breath
Common Foods	Marine finfish including grouper, barracuda, snapper, jack, mackerel, triggerfish, reef fish
Prevention	Purchase fish from a reputable supplier; cooking WILL NOT inactivate the toxin

Table 2.25 SCOMBROTOXIN

Causative Agent	Scombrotoxin
Type of Illness	Seafood toxin originating from histamine-producing bacteria
Symptoms	Dizziness; burning feeling in the mouth; facial rash or hives; shortness of breath; peppery taste in mouth; headache; itching; teary eyes; runny nose
Onset	Few minutes to half-hour; recovery usually occurs in 8 to 12 hours
Common Foods	Tuna, mahi mahi, bluefish, sardines, mackerel, anchovies, amberjack, abalone, Swiss cheese
Prevention	Purchase fish from a reputable supplier; store fish between 32°F (0°C) and 39°F (4°C) to prevent growth of histamine-producing bacteria; toxin IS NOT inactivated by cooking.

FOOD-BORNE ILLNESS CAUSED BY PHYSICAL HAZARDS

Physical hazards are foreign objects in food that can cause illness and injury. They include items such as fragments of glass, metal shavings from dull can openers, unfrilled toothpicks that may contaminate sandwiches, human hair and jewelry, or bandages that may accidentally be lost by a food handler and enter food. Stones, rocks, or wood particles may contaminate raw fruits and vegetables, rice, beans, and other grain products. (See Table 2.26.)

Physical hazards commonly result from accidental contamination and poor food-handling practices that can occur at various points in the food chain from harvest to consumer.

To prevent physical hazards you should wash raw fruits and vegetables thoroughly; and visually inspect foods that cannot be washed (such as ground beef).

Food employees must be taught to handle food safely to prevent contamination by unwanted foreign objects such as glass fragments and metal shavings. Finally, food employees should not wear jewelry when involved in the production of food, except for a plain wedding band.

Table 2.26 COMMON PHYSICAL HAZARDS IN A FOOD ESTABLISHMENT

Hair	Wood
Fingernails	Stone
Bandages	Metal
Toothpicks	Glass
Staples	

BACK TO THE STORY...

Biological hazards such as bacteria, viruses, and parasites continue to cause problems. An increase in food-borne illness associated with fresh produce was described at the beginning of this chapter. This change is due to several factors. People eat more fruits and vegetables because of the known health benefits. An increase in the number of people in highly susceptible populations exposes more individuals to food-borne illness. The number and types of hazards also seem to be on the increase. Shiga toxin-producing *E. coli* and *Listeria Monocytogenes* were not significant problems until the last decade. Now, these organisms seem to be in the headlines nearly every day. Food establishment managers need to be aware of the change in eating habits, marketing patterns, and emerging pathogens in our food supply.

PROBLEMS IN OTHER COUNTRIES RELATED TO FOOD

Mad Cow Disease or bovine spongiform encephalopathy (BSE) is a fatal brain disorder that occurs in cattle and is caused by some unknown agent. There seems to be a connection between animal feed made from the parts of sheep that carry the organisms called scrapie. Use of animal feed made from such ingredients has been banned in the United States.

The connection between BSE and humans was uncovered in Great Britain in the 1990s when several young people died of a brain disorder, a new variation of a rare problem, Cretzfeldt-Jakob disease (CJD) that typically strikes the elderly.

Efforts of the U.S. Food and Drug Administration (FDA), U.S. Department of Agriculture (USDA), the Centers for Disease Control and Prevention (CDC), and other federal organizations, including state regulatory and health agencies, have kept the diseases from occurring in this country. Advisories are regularly issued to those traveling to Great Britain and Europe about the safety of eating beef and beef products.

Foot- (hoof-) and-mouth disease is not a food safety concern, but is a concern for animal health and economics. The disease is a highly contagious viral infection of cattle, sheep, goats, deer, and other cloven-hoofed animals. It causes blisters on the mouth, teats, and soft tissues of the animal's feet and mouth. The animals rarely recover.

This disease is not a significant health concern for humans and was last found in the United States in 1929. In 2001, an outbreak of foot-and-mouth disease occurred in the United Kingdom (England, Scotland, Wales, Northern Ireland) and Europe. A large number of animals were destroyed to contain the infection. Affected areas were placed under quarantine. The danger from this disease is to animals, not humans; therefore, foot-and-mouth disease is not classified as a food-borne illness.

There are many food-borne hazards a food establishment may encounter. They are classified as biological, chemical, or physical hazards. These hazards differ depending on the type of food and method of preparation involved. Food establishments are typically toward the end of the food production chain. This is where foods are prepared or sold for consumer preparation. Therefore, it is very important to control and prevent food-borne hazards as much as possible to reduce the risk of food-borne illness associated with your establishment. Control and prevention of food-borne hazards in a food establishment starts with understanding the different types of food-borne hazards. The next step is to understand how to control food-borne hazards with time/temperature control, and good personal hygiene.

FACTORS THAT CONTRIBUTE TO FOOD-BORNE ILLNESS

The Centers for Disease Control and Prevention (CDC) is an agency of the federal government. One of the CDC's primary responsibilities is to collect statistics about diseases that affect people in the United States, including food-borne illness. CDC statistics show most outbreaks of food-borne disease occur because food is mishandled. Some of the major contributors to food-borne illness are presented in Table 2.27.

WHAT IS TIME AND TEMPERATURE ABUSE

Controlling temperature is perhaps the most critical way to assure food safety. Most cases of food-borne illness can in some way be linked to temperature abuse. The term **temperature abuse** is used to describe situations when foods are:

- Exposed to temperatures in the temperature danger zone for enough time to allow growth of harmful microorganisms.
- Not cooked or reheated sufficiently to destroy harmful microorganisms.

You've already learned that harmful microbes can grow in potentially hazardous foods when temperatures are between 41°F (5°C) and 135°F (57°C), the temperature danger zone, Keep the internal temperatures, inside the core of a

MAD COW DISEASE

During the past several years, medical authorities have found links between a disease in cattle called bovine spongiform encephalopathy (BSE, popularly known as "mad cow disease") and an extremely rare disease in humans called new variant Creutzfeldt-Jakob disease (nvCJD). Both BSE and nvCJD are slowly degenerative and invariably fatal diseases affecting the central nervous system. Researchers know that these diseases have unusually long incubation periods, but do not know exactly what causes them. They believe that BSE is spread in cattle through feed that has been made, in part, with processed ingredients from slaughtered animals that carried the unknown infectious agent. They also believe that nvCJD is probably contracted by eating meat or other products processed from infected animals. So far, the worst of the known BSE outbreaks has been confined to Europe, principally Great Britain, and even there only a few people have been diagnosed with nvCJD.

There have been very few reported cases of BSE or nvCJD in the United States. For more than a decade, federal authorities have restricted the importation of certain species of live animals and products derived from them originating in countries suffering or suspected of suffering from outbreaks of BSE. They also actively monitor American meat-packing facilities for any signs of BSE in cattle waiting to be slaughtered, and long ago banned the sale of the type of feed associated with BSE in Europe.

Responsible government and nongovernmental authorities continue to assure the American public that it is safe to eat American beef.

Table 2.27 MAJOR CONTRIBUTORS TO FOOD-BORNE ILLNESSES

Contributor	Percent
Improper holding temperature	37%
Poor personal hygiene and improper hand washing	19%
Contaminated equipment	16%
Inadequate cooking	11%
Other	11%
Food from unsafe sources	6%

Source: CDC-MMWR 2000.

Safety Alert

Controlling temperature is the best way to ensure food safety.

Safety Alert

Cooking and reheating are two very important processes for safe food management.

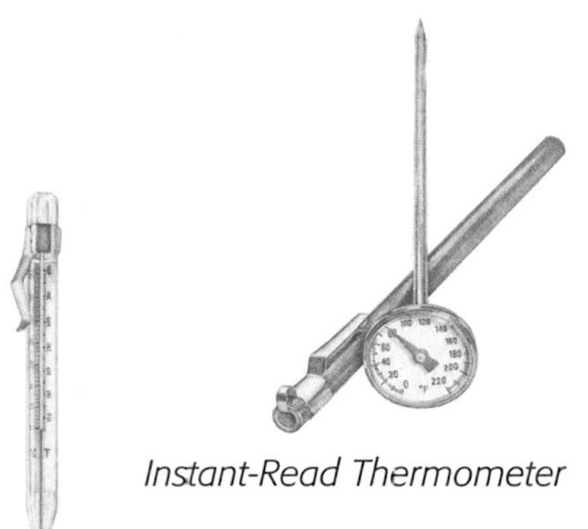

Instant-Read Thermometer

Candy Thermometer

food item, out of the temperature danger zone [41°F (5°C) to 135°F (57°C)] to prevent harmful microbes from growing. Higher temperatures destroy microbes; however, toxins produced by microbes may or may not be affected by normal cooking temperatures.

Keep cold food temperatures below 41°F (5°C) and out of the temperature danger zone to prevent most microbes from growing. Bacteria that can grow at lower temperatures do so very slowly.

There are unavoidable situations during food production when foods must pass through the temperature danger zone such as while cooking, cooling, reheating, and handling (slicing, mixing, and sandwich assembly).

During these activities, you must minimize the amount of time foods are in the temperature danger zone to control microbial growth. When it is necessary for a food to pass through the temperature danger zone, do it as quickly as possible. In addition, foods should pass through the danger zone as few times as possible.

Heating foods improves texture and flavor and also destroys harmful microorganisms. Remember many raw foods naturally contain harmful microbes or can become contaminated during handling. When you cook and reheat foods properly, microbes are reduced to safe level or are destroyed.

HOW TO MEASURE FOOD TEMPERATURES

Maintaining safe food temperature is an essential and effective part of food safety management. You must know how to measure food temperatures correctly to prevent temperature abuse. Thermometers, thermocouples, and other devices are used to measure the temperature of stored, cooked, hot-held, cold-held, and reheated foods. Table 2.28 lists the different types of thermometers and their features.

Table 2.28 TYPES OF THERMOMETERS

THERMOMETER TYPE	FEATURES/USES
Dial-face, metal stem type (bi-metallic)	Most common type of thermometer used Used to measure internal food temperature at every stage in the flow of food Measures temperatures ranging from 0°F (-18°C) to 220°F (104°C) with 2°F increments Stem of bi-metallic thermometer must be inserted at least 2 inches into the food item being measured.
Digital	Displays the temperature numerically Measures a wider range of temperatures than a dial-face thermometer.
Thermocouple	Provides a digital readout of the temperature Has a wide variety of interchangeable probes Sensing portion is often at the tip of the probe.
Infrared	Measures the surface temperature of food without actually touching the food (reduces the chance of cross-contamination) Requires about 20 minutes to adjust after use for hot and cold temperatures ("thermal shock") before use Accuracy must be checked frequently.
T-Sticks (melt devices)	Measure only one temperature Change color when indicated temperature is reached Used to monitor food temperatures and sanitizing temperature in dishwashing machines.
Built-in	Used to monitor air temperature in refrigerated and frozen cases.
Maximum Registering (holding)	Used to measure the temperature of hot water used to sanitize items in mechanical dishwashing machines Becoming less popular in food establishments because it contains mercury (an environmental contaminant).

A temperature-measuring device with a small diameter probe must be available to measure the temperature of thin foods such as meat patties and fish filets.

Guidelines for thermometer include the following:

- Temperature measuring devices typically measure food temperatures in degrees Fahrenheit (denoted a °F), degrees Celsius (denoted as °C), or both.
- Food temperature measuring devices scaled only Celsius or dually scaled in Celsius and Fahrenheit must be accurate to +1.8°F (+1°C). Food temperature-measuring devices scaled in Fahrenheit only must be accurate to +2°F.
- Mercury filled and glass thermometers should not be used in food establishments.
- Clean and sanitize thermometers properly to avoid contaminating food that is being tested. This is very important when testing raw and then ready-to-eat items. To clean and sanitize a food thermometer, wipe off any food particles, place the stem or probe in sanitizing solution for at least 5 seconds, then air-dry.

WHEN AND HOW TO CALIBRATE A THERMOMETER

Before you use a thermometer you need to calibrate it, or make sure it is working correctly. Dial-face metal stem type (bi-metal) thermometers should be calibrated

- Before their first use
- At regular intervals
- If dropped or otherwise damaged
- If used to measure extreme temperatures
- Whenever accuracy is in question.

Calibrate dial-face thermometers by the boiling point or ice point method. Use pliers or an open-ended wrench to adjust the indicator needle.

Boiling Point Method

Immerse at least the first 2 inches of the stem from the tip (the sensing part of the probe) into boiling water and adjust the needle to 212°F (100°C). At higher altitudes, the temperature of the boiling point will vary. Consult your local health department if you have any questions about the boiling point temperature in your area.

Ice Point Method

Insert the probe into a cup of crushed ice. Add enough cold water to remove any air pockets that might remain. Wait until the temperature stabilizes and adjust the needle to 32°F (0°C).

MEASURING FOOD TEMPERATURE

The sensing portion of a food thermometer is at the end of the stem or probe. On the bi-metal thermometer, the sensing portion extends from the tip to the "dimple" mark that is typically 1 inch up the stem. An average of the temperature is measured over this distance. The sensing portion for digital and thermocouple thermometers is closer to the tip of the probe.

The approximate temperature of packaged foods can be measured accurately without opening the package. Place the stem or probe of the thermometer between two packages of food or fold the package around the stem or probe or make good contact with the packaging. (See Table 2.29.)

Table 2.29 HOW TO ACCURATELY AND SAFELY MEASURE FOOD TEMPERATURES

- Use an approved temperature-measuring device that measures temperatures from 0°F (-18°C) to 220°F (104°C).
- Locate the sensing portion of the measuring device.
- Calibrate the measuring device using the ice or boiling point method.
- Clean and sanitize the probe of the temperature-measuring device according to procedure.
- Measure the internal temperature of the food by inserting the probe into the center or thickest part of the item, at least 2 inches for a dial thermometer and 1 inch for digital thermometers.
- Always wait for the temperature reading to stabilize.

Safety Alert

Remember, there has never been a case of food-borne illness that couldn't have been prevented!

PREVENTING TEMPERATURE ABUSE

Controlling temperature of potentially hazardous food is important in almost all stages of food handling. Measuring temperatures of potentially hazardous food is an important responsibility for all food handlers. The following chart lists safe temperature guidelines for working with food throughout the flow of food. (See Table 2.30.)

Keep Cold Foods Cold and Hot Foods Hot!

Frozen foods should be kept solidly frozen until they are ready to be used. Freezing helps to retain product quality. Proper frozen food temperatures do not permit disease-causing and spoilage microorganisms to grow. Cold temperatures also help to preserve the color and flavor characteristics. Frozen foods can be stored for long periods of time without losing their wholesomeness and quality.

Table 2.30 TIME & TEMPERATURE

Receiving and Storing...

Frozen and refrigerated receiving/storage practices prevent or slow the growth of harmful microorganisms

FOOD PRODUCT	INTERNAL TEMPERATURE	TIMES
Frozen Foods	Solidly frozen 0°F (-18°C) recommended	Weeks & months
Refrigerated Foods	41°F (5°C) or lower	As food quality allows
Raw Shell Eggs	45°F (7°C) or below ambient temperature	Until sell-by date has expired

Thawing...

Take food from frozen to non-frozen to minimize the product's time in the temperature danger zone. Keep ready-to-eat foods below 41°F (5°C) at all times.

METHOD	INTERNAL TEMPERATURE	TIMES
In the Refrigerator	41°F (5°C) or lower	Typically take 2-3 days
Submerged under cool running water 70°F (21°C)	41°F (5°C) or lower	4 hours or less (counts toward time in the food temperature danger zone).

Table 2.30 TIME & TEMPERATURE (CONTINUED)

Cooking...

Safely getting a food product from raw to ready-to-eat with minimum time held at internal temperature before serving

FOOD PRODUCT	MINIMUM INTERNAL TEMPERATURE	TIMES
Beef Roast (rare)	130°F (54°C) 140°F (60°C)	112 minutes 12 minutes
Beef (other than roasts), Pork (other than roasts), Fish	145°F (63°C)	15 seconds
Ground Beef, Ground Pork, Ground Game Animals	155°F (68°C)	15 seconds
Beef Roast (medium, Pork Roast, Ham	145°F (63°C)	4 minutes
Poultry, Stuffed Meats, Stuffed Food Products	165°F (74°C)	15 seconds

Hot-Holding...

Keep hot food out of the temperature danger zone.

FOOD PRODUCT	INTERNAL TEMPERATURE	TIMES
Hot-holding of all foods	135°F (57°C) or above	Until product quality is unacceptable

Cold-Food Holding...

Keeping cold food out of the temperature danger zone

FOOD PRODUCT	INTERNAL TEMPERATURE	TIMES
Cold-holding of all foods	41°F (5°C)	Until product quality is unacceptable or sell-by date has expired

Cooking Hot Foods...

Rapid reduction of temperature through and out of the temperature danger zone

PART	INTERNAL TEMPERATURE	TIMES
Hot Food Cooling, part 1	From 135° to 70°F (57° to 21°C)	2 hours or less
Hot Food Cooling, part 2	From 135° to 70°F (57° to 21°C) or below	Within 6 hours or less

Frozen Food Holding...

Keeping food solidly frozen

FOOD PRODUCT	INTERNAL TEMPERATURE	TIMES
Frozen Food	Solidly frozen 0°F (-18°C) recommended	Until product quality is unacceptable

Reheating...

Bringing food back up to serving temperature

METHOD	INTERNAL TEMPERATURE	TIMES
Reheating	165°F (74°C) or above	Within 2 hours

Source: 2001 FDA Food Code

Refrigerated foods are held cold, not frozen. Cold foods should be maintained at 41°F (5°C) or below. Do not forget that some harmful bacteria and many spoilage bacteria can grow at temperatures below 41°F (5°C), although their growth is very slow. By keeping cold foods at 41°F (5°C) or below, you can reduce the growth of most harmful microorganisms and extend the shelf life of the product. For maximum quality and freshness, hold cold foods for the shortest amount of time possible.

Applying heat is another method used to preserve food. Heat food to proper temperatures to destroy harmful bacteria. Established safe cooking temperatures are based on the type of food and the method used to heat the product. Cooked foods, as well as those foods that have been cooled and then reheated, must be maintained at 135°F (57°C) or above until used. You must keep foods hot to stop growth of harmful bacteria.

There are times during food production when foods must be in the temperature danger zone. Recognize the time spent in the temperature danger zone should be minimal for potentially hazardous items.

Improper holding temperatures is the Number 1 contributing factor that leads to food-borne illness. Spores of certain bacteria like *Clostridium botulinum*, *Clostridium perfringens*, and *Bacillus cereus* can survive cooking temperatures. Remember, if spores survive and are exposed to ideal conditions, they can again become vegetative cells and begin to grow in foods.

The *FDA Food Code* contains cooling guidelines that permit foods to be in the temperature danger zone for a total of 6 hours. The *FDA Food Code* specifically states foods must be cooled from 135°F (57°C) to 70°F (21°C) in 2 hours, and from 135°F (57°C) to 41°F (5°C) or less within 6 hours.

To destroy many of the bacteria that may have grown during the cooling process, reheat foods to 165°F (74°C) within 2 hours to prevent the number of organisms from reaching levels that can cause food-borne illness.

Safety Alert

Improper holding temperatures is the Number 1 factor leading to food-borne illness.

Ways to Thaw Food

The preferred method for thawing foods is in the refrigerator at 41°F (5°C) or below. This prevents the food from entering the food temperature danger zone. Other acceptable methods for thawing include using a microwave oven, as part of the cooking process, or submerging under cool running water [70°F (21°C)] for a controlled amount of time. Proper thawing reduces the chance for bacterial growth, especially on the outer surfaces of food.

▶ CROSS-CONTAMINATION

Generally, microorganisms and other contaminants cannot move by themselves. Rather, they are carried to foods and food-contact surfaces by humans, rodents, or insects. This transfer of germs is referred to as **cross-contamination**.

Cross-contamination is the process by which one item, such as your finger or cutting board, becomes contaminated and then contaminates another food or tool. For example, suppose a chef's knife and cutting board are used in butchering a potentially hazardous food such as a chicken, and the chicken was directly contaminated with salmonella at the hatchery. If the knife and board are not cleaned and sanitized properly, anything that touches them can also become contaminated. So even though cooking the chicken to an appropriate internal temperature may destroy the salmonella in the chicken, the uncooked salad greens cut on the same cutting board or with the same knife can contain live bacteria. For example, bacteria from raw chicken can be transferred to a ready-to-eat food such as lettuce or tomato when the same cutting board is used without being washed and sanitized between foods.

Cross-contamination also happens when raw foods are stored above ready-to-eat foods. Juices from the raw product can drop or splash onto a ready-to-eat food. This poses a serious health risk because ready-to-eat items will not be cooked to destroy microorganisms prior to being eaten.

In a food establishment, germs can be transferred by a food employee, equipment and utensils, or another food. The following preventative measures can be used to eliminate the possibility of cross-contamination between products:

- Always store cooked and ready-to-eat foods over raw products
- Keep raw and ready-to-eat foods separate during storage
- Use good personal hygiene and hand washing
- Keep all food-contact surfaces clean and sanitary
- Avoid bare hand contact with ready-to-eat food
- Keep species of meat and poultry separate
- Use separate equipment, such as cutting boards, for raw foods and ready-to-eat foods (color-coded cutting boards may be helpful for this task)
- Use clean, sanitized equipment and utensils for food production
- Prepare ready-to-eat foods first—then raw foods
- Prepare raw and ready-to-eat foods in separate areas of the establishment.

Always keep raw foods separate from ready-to-eat foods. In the refrigerator, ready-to-eat foods must be stored above raw foods. Display cases, such as those used to display seafood items, should be designed to keep raw and cooked food items separate. In addition, separate buckets for in-place sanitizing solutions and wiping cloths should be used for cleaning food-contact surfaces in raw and ready-to-eat food production areas.

OTHER SOURCES OF CONTAMINATION

Raw fruits and vegetables should be treated like ready-to-eat foods. Always wash these foods before use. Washing removes soil and other contaminants. Chemicals may be used to wash raw whole fruits and vegetables. These chemicals must be nontoxic and meet the requirements set forth in the Code of Federal Regulations under Title 21 CFR 173.315.

Safety Alert

Wash hands or change gloves after touching live animals, such as live lobsters.

Utensils used to dispense and serve foods can also be a source of food contamination. Utensils should be properly labeled to identify the type of food they are used to dispense. During hot- or cold-holding of foods, the utensil should be stored in the food. This helps to prevent contamination from employees or customers in self-service areas. It also keeps the utensil that contains food, out of the temperature danger zone. The dispensing utensils (scoops) for ice and dry bulk foods should be clean and kept in an area protected from contamination. Scoops or tongs used in customer service areas also need to be labeled and kept clean.

Animals are not allowed in food establishments unless they are being used for support or special service (i.e., guide dogs for the blind). It is very important food handlers do not touch animals during food preparation and service. If employees should touch an animal for any reason, they must wash their hands before returning to work.

Germs from an employee's mouth can be transferred to food when the employee uses improper tasting techniques. A food employee may not use a utensil more than once to taste food that is to be sold or served.

Safety Alert

Don't touch the parts of utensils that come in contact with food.

Animals, rodents, and pests are common sources for food contamination. Rodents and pests usually enter food establishments during delivery or when garbage facilities are not properly maintained. A good integrated pest management (IPM) program should be established and maintained in every food establishment.

Anything that comes in contact with food must be clean and sanitary. This includes human hands, equipment, utensils, storage and holding area, and self-service areas for customers. In order to protect food from contamination, effective cleaning and sanitizing procedures must be implemented and monitored. The goal of cleaning is to remove visible soil. The goal of sanitizing is to reduce the number of harmful microbes that may be present on a clean surface.

Cross-contamination can occur with bacteria or other microorganisms, chemicals, dirt and debris. Side towels are an especially common source of cross-contamination. If a cook uses a side towel to wipe a spill off the floor, then uses that same towel to dry his hands after visiting the restroom, he has recontaminated his hands with whatever bacteria or dirt was on the floor. Cross-contamination also occurs when raw foods come in contact with cooked foods. Never store cooked food below raw food in a refrigerator, and never return cooked food to the container that held the raw food. Cross-contamination can also occur easily from smoking, drinking or eating, unless hands are properly washed after each of these activities.

Even with proper hand washing, food service workers should strive to minimize direct contact with prepared food by using single-use gloves, clean tongs, tasting spoons, bakery tissue paper and other appropriate tools whenever possible. To avoid food contamination, a two-spoon tasting method should be used when sampling in the professional kitchen. To safely taste food, use a clean spoon to remove some of the food from the pan in which it was made or is being stored. Pour that food into a second clean spoon before tasting it. This prevents the soiled spoon from going back into the food being prepared. Keep a supply of clean spoons for this purpose near all cooking and preparation stations.

REDUCING CROSS-CONTAMINATION

Cross-contamination can be reduced or even prevented by (1) personal cleanliness, (2) dish and equipment cleanliness, and (3) pest management.

THE IMPORTANCE OF HAND WASHING AND GOOD PERSONAL HYGIENCE

To produce clean, sanitary food, all food handlers must maintain high standards of personal cleanliness and hygiene. This begins with good grooming.

Humans provide the ideal environment for the growth of microorganisms. Everyone harbors bacteria in the nose and mouth. These bacteria are easily spread by sneezing or coughing, by not disposing of tissues properly and by not washing hands frequently and properly. Touching your body and then touching food or utensils transfers bacteria. Hands should be washed before and after handling raw food; after smoking, drinking or eating; after coughing or sneezing; after removing the garbage; and after touching dirty clothes, side towels or anything that may contaminate the hands. Human waste carries many dangerous microorganisms, so it is especially important to wash your hands thoroughly after visiting the restroom. An employee who is ill should not be allowed in the kitchen. If during work, an employee develops symptoms such as fever, diarrhea, vomiting, sore throat with fever or jaundice, he or she should report to a manager and request to be dismissed until recovered.

According to the *FDA Food Code*, hands shall be washed in a separate sink specified as a handwashing sink. An automatic handwashing facility may be used by food employees to clean their hands. However, the system must be capable of removing the types of soils encountered in the food operation. Food employees may not clean their hands in a sink used for preparation of dishwashing, or in a service sink used for the disposal of mop water and liquid waste. Hand sanitizing lotions and chemical hand sanitizing solutions may be used by food employees in addition to hand washing. Proper washing helps to remove

STEPS TO PREVENT CROSS-CONTAMINATION

- Wash hands frequently–before and after touching raw food; after touching anything that may contaminate the hands (after removing the garbage, using the restroom, coughing, eating, smoking or touching dirty clothes or side towels).
- Properly sanitize all knives, cutting boards, and equipment.
- Use color-coded cutting boards for poultry, meats, and produce.
- Discard soiled side towels. (Don't use side towels to wipe the floor, then your hands.)
- Use single-use gloves and change them frequently.
- Use clean tongs and bakery tissue paper when handling foods for immediate service.
- Use the two-spoon method when tasting foods.

▶ PROCEDURE FOR PROPER HAND WASHING

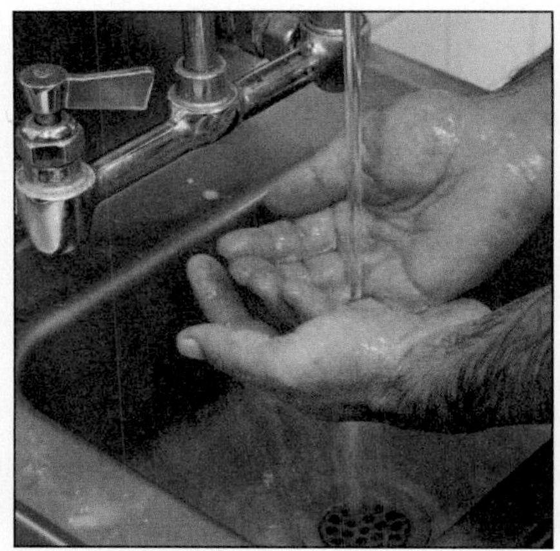

1 Using hot water (100°F/38°C), wet hands and forearms.

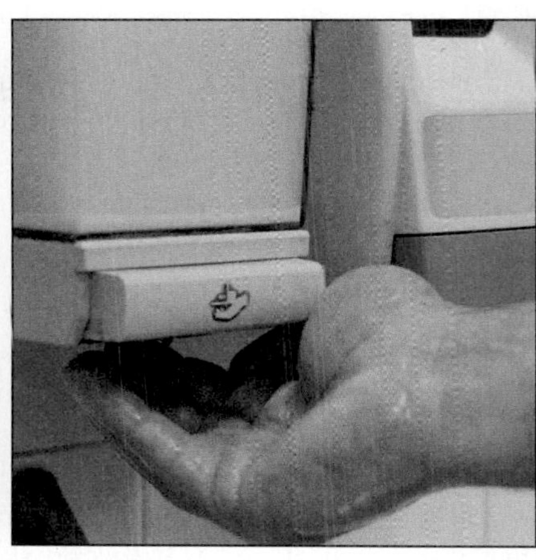

2 Apply an antibacterial soap.

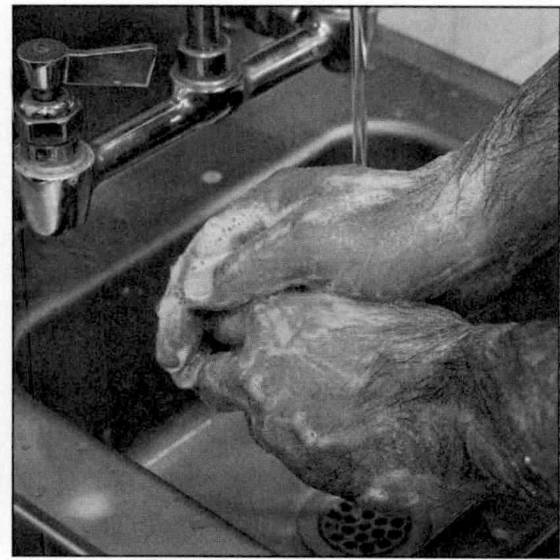

3 Rub hands and arms briskly with soapy lather for at least 20 seconds.

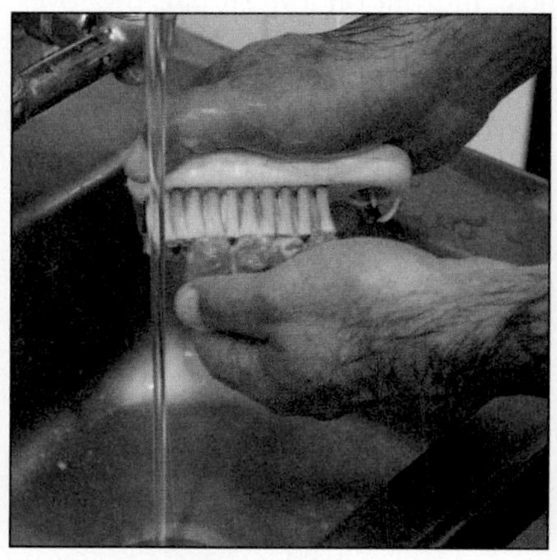

4 Scrub between fingers and clean nails with a clean nail brush.

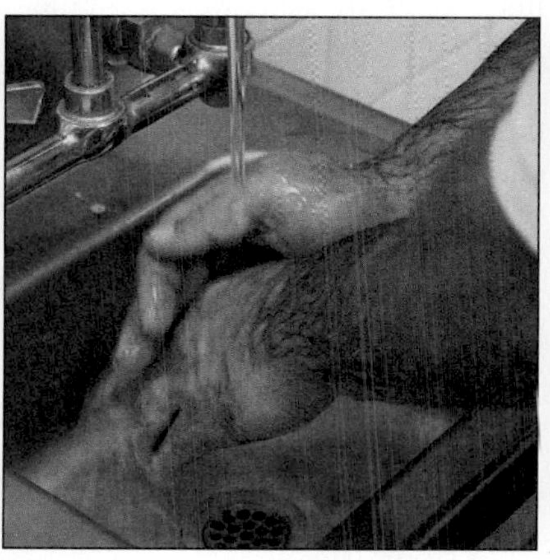

5 Rinse thoroughly under hot running water. Reapply soap and scrub hands and forearms for another 5 to 10 seconds. Rinse again.

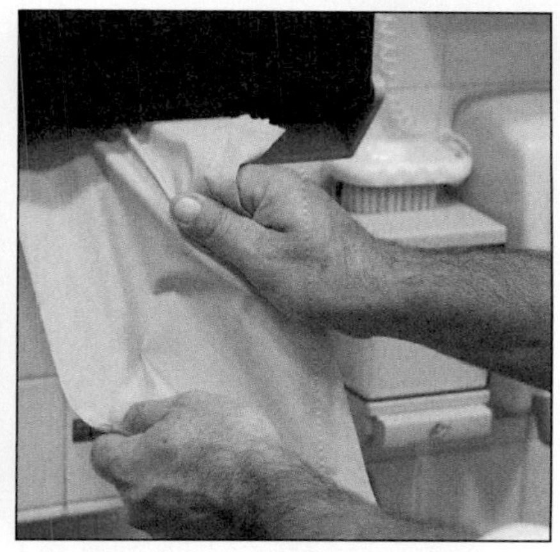

6 Dry hands and arms with a single-use towel, using the towel to turn off the water. Discard the towel in a trash receptacle.

visible hand dirt and the microorganisms it contains. Hand sanitizing lotions must never be used as a replacement for hand washing. It also is critical that hand sanitizers be formulated with safe and approved ingredients because it is likely a food employee's hands will touch food, food-contact surfaces, or equipment and utensils after using the product.

You can do several things to decrease the risk of an illness being spread by poor personal hygiene:

- Wash your hands frequently and thoroughly. Gloves are not a substitute for proper hand washing.
- Keep your fingernails short, clean, and neat. Do not bite your nails or wear nail polish.
- Keep any cut or wound antiseptically bandaged. An injured hand should also be covered with a disposable glove.
- Bathe daily, or more often if required.
- Keep your hair clean and restrained.

- Wear work clothes that are clean and neat. Avoid wearing jewelry or watches.
- Do not eat, drink, smoke, or chew gum in food preparation areas.

Current research shows that the human immunodeficiency virus (HIV), the causative agent of AIDs, is not spread by food. According to the Centers for Disease Control and Prevention (CDC), food service workers infected with HIV should not be restricted from work unless there is another infection or illness.

Using Disposable Gloves

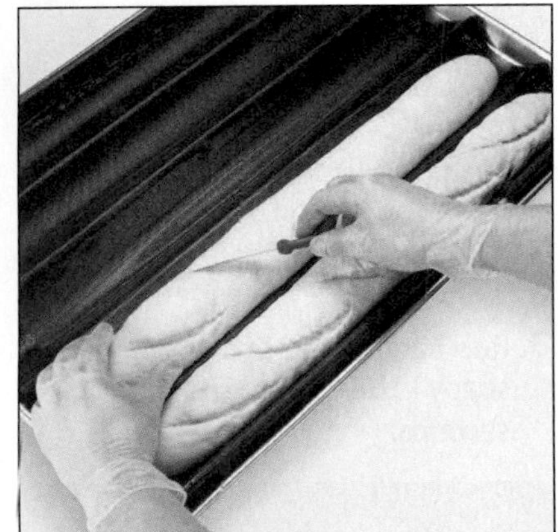

Food establishments sometimes allow their food handlers to use disposable gloves as an extra barrier to help prevent contamination of foods. Gloves can protect food from direct contact by human hands. Gloves must be impermeable, meaning they do not allow anything to penetrate the porous texture of the glove. Use of gloves is often a good idea for food handled extensively by hands such as deli sandwiches, tacos, or when conducting food demonstrations. You must treat disposable gloves as a second skin. Whatever can contaminate a human hand can also contaminate a disposable glove. Therefore, whenever hands should be washed, a new pair of disposable gloves should be worn. For example, if food handlers are wearing disposable gloves and handling raw food, they must discard those gloves, wash their hands, and put on a fresh pair of gloves before they handle ready-to-eat foods.

Food handlers must not handle money with gloved hands unless they immediately remove and discard the gloves. Because money is handled and exchanged by human hands, it is often contaminated with bacteria. Employees must also put on a clean pair of gloves after they complete cleaning, mopping, and similar activities within their work area.

If an employee removes gloves by rolling them inside out, the inner surface of the glove is very contaminated from his or her skin. Again, if you take disposable gloves off, throw them away. Never reuse or wash disposable gloves—always throw them away after each use.

> **Safety Alert**
>
> Whatever can contaminate a human hand can also contaminate a disposable glove.

Personal Habits

Personal hygiene means good health habits including bathing, washing hair, wearing clean clothing, and frequent hand washing. A food employee's fingers may be contaminated with saliva during eating and smoking. Saliva, sweat, and other body fluids can be harmful sources of contamination if they get into food.

Supervisors should enforce rules against eating, chewing gum, and smoking in food preparation, service, and dishwashing areas. The *FDA Food Code* permits food employees to drink beverages to prevent dehydration. The beverage must be in a covered container. The container must be handled in a way that prevents contamination of the employee's hands, the container, exposed food, equipment, and single-use articles.

Jewelry, including medical information jewelry on hands or arms, has no place in food production and dishwashing areas. Rings, bracelets, necklaces, earrings, watches, and other body part ornaments can harbor germs that can cause food-borne illness. Jewelry can also fall into food causing a physical hazard. A plain wedding band that does not contain a stone is the only piece of jewelry that may be worn in food production and dishwashing areas.

Outer Clothing and Apparel

Work clothes and other apparel should always be clean. The appearance of a clean uniform is more appealing to your customers.

Things you can do to prevent food contamination:

- Wear clean clothing.
- If your clothing is contaminated, change into a new set of work clothes.

- Change your apron between working with raw foods and ready-to-eat foods. Aprons should be left in the work area when going on break or to the restroom.
- Don't dry or wipe your hands on your apron.
- Wear a hat, hair coverings or nets, and beard restraints to discourage you from touching your hair or beard. These restraints also prevent hair from falling into food or onto food-contact surfaces.

Personal Health

In an attempt to reduce the risk caused by sick employees, the *FDA Food Code* requires employees to report to the person in charge when they have been diagnosed with any of the following:

- *Salmonella Typhi*
- *Shigella spp.*
- Shiga toxin-producing *Escherichia coli*
- Hepatitis A virus
- Symptoms of intestinal illness or flu-like symptoms (such as vomiting, diarrhea, fever, sore throat, or jaundice) or a wound containing pus such as a boil or infected cut that is open or draining.

If a food employee is directly or indirectly exposed to *Salmonella Typhi, Shigella spp.*, Shig Toxin-producing *Escherichia coli*, or Hepatitis A virus, it must be reported to the supervisor. All these agents are easily transferred to foods and are considered severe health hazards. The person in charge will notify the regulatory authority that a food employee is diagnosed with an illness due to *Salmonella Typhi, Shigella spp.*, Shiga-toxin producing *Escherichia coli*, or Hepatitis A virus.

DISH AND EQUIPMENT CLEANLINESS

One of the requirements for any food service facility is cleanability. But there is an important difference between clean and sanitary. **Clean** means that the item has no visible soil on it. **Sanitary** means that harmful substances are reduced to safe levels. Thus, something may be clean without being sanitary; the visible dirt can be removed, but disease-causing microorganisms can remain.

▶ **Clean** to remove visible dirt and soil.

▶ **Sanitize** to reduce pathogenic organisms to safe levels.

▶ **Sterilize** to destroy all living microorganisms.

The cleaning of all dishes, pots, pans, and utensils in a food service operation involves both removing soil and sanitizing. Soil can be removed manually or by machine. Sanitizing can be accomplished with heat or chemical disinfectants.

Procedures for manually washing, rinsing, and sanitizing dishes and equipment generally follow the three-compartment sink setup shown. The dishwasher must do the following:

1. Scrape and spray the item to remove soil
2. Wash the item in the first sink compartment using 110°F (43°C) water and an approved detergent. A brush or cloth may be used to remove any remaining soil.
3. Rinse the item in the second sink compartment using clear, 110°F (43°C) water.
4. Sanitize the item in the third sink compartment by either
   - **a.** Immersing it in 171°F (77°C) water for at least 30 second, or
   - **b.** Immersing it in an approved chemical sanitizing solution used according to the manufacturer's directions
5. Empty, clean and refill each sink compartment as necessary, and check the water temperature regularly.

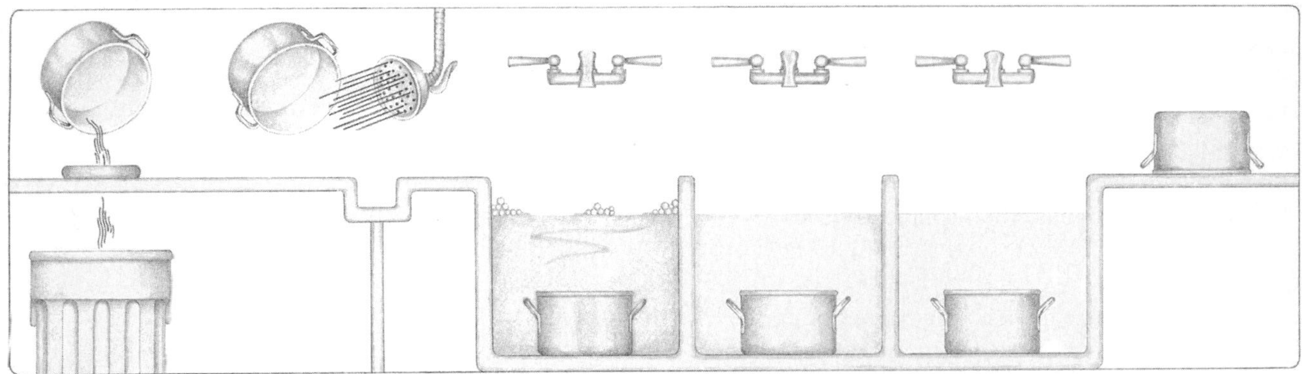

FIGURE 2.4 ▶ The three-compartment sink procedure—scrape, spray, wash, rinse, sanitize and air-dry each item.

Food service items, dishes, silverware, and utensils should always be allowed to air-dry, as towel drying might recontaminate them. And any cracked or chipped china should be discarded as it can harbor bacteria posing a food safety hazard.

Machine-washing dishes or utensils follow a similar procedure. The dishwasher should first scrape and rinse items as needed, then load the items into dishwasher racks so that the spray of water will reach all surfaces. The machine cleans the items with a detergent, then sanitizes them with either a hot-water rinse (at least 180°F/82°C) or a chemical disinfectant. When the machine cycle is complete, items should be inspected for residual soil, allowed to air-dry and stored in a clean area.

Worktables and stationary equipment also must be cleaned and sanitized properly. Equipment and surfaces, including floors, walls, and worktables should be easily exposed for inspection and cleaning and should be constructed so that soil can be removed effectively and efficiently with normal cleaning procedures. A thorough cleaning schedule should be implemented and closely monitored to prevent problems from developing.

The following points are important to the safety and cleanliness of any food service facility:

- Equipment should be disassembled for cleaning; any immersible pieces should be cleaned with detergent, then sanitized with a clean cloth dipped in a sanitizing solution. Combining 1 gallon of (4 liters) lukewarm water with 1 tablespoon (15 milliliters) of chlorine bleach makes an acceptable sanitizing solution. This solution should be replaced every 2 hours. Other chemical sanitizers should be prepared and used according to health department and manufacturer's directions.
- Surfaces, especially work surfaces with which food may come in contact, should be smooth and free of cracks, crevices or seams in which soil and microorganisms can hide.
- Floors should be nonabsorbent and should not become slippery when wet.
- Walls and ceilings should be smooth and light-colored so that soil is easier to see.
- Light should be ample and well located throughout food preparation and storage area. All light bulbs should be covered with a sleeve or globe to protect surrounding from shattered glass.

A kitchen's design can also affect food safety and sanitation. Food preparation equipment should be arranged in such a way as to decrease the chances of

BACK TO THE STORY...

The case study presented earlier raises several areas of concern about food-handling activities employed in areas where ready-to-eat foods are prepared. The handling error that contributed to the food-borne illness was the use of the same knife and cutting board when working with the raw chicken and peaches and watermelon. The cutting board was turned over, but not washed and sanitized. Though sanitizing solutions were available in the bakery and deli, it was not clear that employees cleaned and sanitized food-contact surfaces between raw and ready-to-eat foods.

cross-contamination. The workflow should eliminate crisscrossing and backtracking. Employees should be able to reach storage, refrigeration and cleanup areas easily. Dish- and pot-washing areas and garbage facilities should be kept as far from food preparation and storage areas as possible. Cleaning supplies and other chemicals should be stored away from foods.

Control contamination with proper cleaning and sanitizing. Avoid cross-contamination from one food to another. Keep foods separate and store raw foods below cooked and ready-to-eat foods. Always use proper food-handling techniques.

Keep foods at proper temperature, use good personal hygiene, and control contamination and cross-contamination. These are the essentials of safe food management.

PEST CONTROL

Every food establishment should have a pest control program. The targets of this program are insects and rodents that can spread disease and damage food. These pests carry disease-causing microorganisms in and on their bodies and can transfer them to food and food-contact surfaces. Pests also destroy millions of dollars of food each year by eating it or by contaminating it with urine and feces.

The key element of a successful pest control program is prevention. However, no single measure will effectively prevent or control insects and rodents in food establishments. It takes a combination of three separate activities to keep pests in check. You must

- Prevent entry of insects and rodents into the establishment.
- Eliminate food, water, and places where insects and rodents can hide.
- Implement an integrated pest management (IPM) program to control insect and rodent pests that enter the establishment.

ANOTHER STORY...

Maryland health officials have given conditional approval for a local high school to reopen its lunchrooms, one week after they were shut down because of mice and roach infestations.

Health officials closed two kitchens and a cafeteria at the school after rodent droppings were discovered in the food storage and preparation areas. Breakfast and lunch were prepared at two nearby elementary schools and shipped to the high school during the time the school cafeteria was closed.

In an effort to eliminate the pest infestation problem, school officials took a number of corrective actions. These included sanitizing affected areas, sealing holes in walls and floors, installing screens on windows and discarding old food.

Health officials reinspected the school cafeteria and said the school could reopen the two lunchrooms provide they installed door sweeps, repaired a sink, and cleaned the storage room. These projects were completed and the cafeteria was allowed to reopen.

Insects

What insects lack in size, they more than make up for in numbers. Insects may spread diseases, contaminate food, destroy property, or be nuisances in food establishments (see Table 2.31). Insects need water, food, and a breeding place in order to survive. The best method of insect control is keeping them out of the establishment coupled with good sanitation and integrated pest management (IPM) when needed.

Rodents

Rodents are known to carry microorganisms that can cause a number of human diseases including salmonellosis, plague, and murine typhus. Rodents also consume and damage large quantities of foods each year. Rats typically carry their food back to their nest rather than eat where it is found.

Domestic rodents in the United States include the Norway rat, the roof rat, and the house mouse. The Norway rat is also known as the brown rat, sewer rat, and wharf rat, and is the one most commonly found in the United States.

The Norway rat hides in burrows in the ground and around buildings and in sewers. Norway rats will eat almost any food but prefer garbage, meat, fish, and cereal. They stay close to food and water, and their range of travel is usually no more than 100 to 150 feet.

The roof rat generally harbors in the upper floors of buildings but is sometimes found in sewers. Roof rats prefer vegetables, fruits, cereal, and grain for food. The range of travel for the roof rat is also about 100 to 150 feet.

The house mouse is the smallest of the domestic rodents. It is found primarily in and around buildings, nesting in walls, cabinets, and stored good. The house mouse is a nibbler, and it prefers cereal and grain. Its range of travel is 10 to 30 feet.

Safety Alert

One gallon of lukewarm water combined with 1 Tablespoon of chlorine bleach makes an acceptable sanitizing solution.

Table 2.31 **INSECTS COMMON TO FOOD ESTABLISHMENTS**

Flies	
Common Types:	Houseflies Blowflies Fruit flies.
Common Problems:	When a fly walks over filth, material sticks to its body and leg hairs, which contaminates food when a fly walks over it; the fly vomits on solid food to soften it before eating, spreading bacteria to food and food-contact surfaces.
Control Methods:	Eliminate the insect's food supply; store food, garbage, and other wastes in fly-tight containers; regularly clean kitchen, dining, toilet, and waste storage facilities. Equip windows, doors, and loading and unloading areas with tight-fitting screens or air curtains. Insect electrocuting devices must be installed so dead insects and insect parts cannot fall of food and food-contact surfaces. Non-electrocuting systems, using glue traps and pheromone attractants, are allowed in areas of the establishment where electrocuting devices are not. Chemical insecticides may be applied by a professional pest control operator as a supplement to proper food-handling practices and a clean establishment.
Cockroaches	
Common Type:	German cockroach
Common Problems:	Carry bacteria on their hairy legs and body as well as in their intestinal tract. Commonly hide in cracks and crevices under and behind equipment and facilities.
Control Methods:	Maintain good housekeeping indoors and outside; eliminate hiding places by picking up unwanted materials; fill cracks and crevices in floors and walls and around equipment; doors and windows should be tight-fitting and protected by screening, air curtains, or other effective means. Check incoming food and supplies for signs of infestation such as egg cases and live roaches; store food in containers that are insect proof and have tight fitting lids. Keep floors, tables, walls, and equipment clean and free of food wastes. Residual insecticides and baits can be used when a serious infestation exists.
Moths and beetles	
Common Types:	Indian meal moth Saw-toothed grain beetle Flour weevil Rice weevil
Common Problems:	These insects feed on corn, rice, wheat, flour, beans, sugar, meal, and cereals. These insects create problems of wasted food and nuisance rather than disease.
Control Methods:	Inspect incoming products for signs of infestation Use FIFO system of stock rotation; store opened packages or bags of good in covered containers Clean shelves and floors frequently Keep dry food storage areas cool Residual insecticides and pheromone traps are available to control these pests.

RODENT INFESTATION

It is unusual to see rats or mice during the daytime, since they are nocturnal. Therefore it is necessary to look for signs of their activity. From rodent signs you can determine the type of rodent, whether it is a new or old problem, and whether there is a light or heavy infestation.

DROPPINGS The presence of rat or mouse feces is one of the best indications of an infestation. Fresh droppings are usually moist, soft and shiny, whereas old droppings become dry and hard. Norway rat droppings are the largest and have rounded ends. They look a lot like black jelly beans. Roof rat droppings are smaller and more regular in form. The droppings of the house mouse are very small and pointed at the end. They look something like dark grains of rice.

RUNWAYS AND BURROWS Rats are very cautious and repeatedly use the same paths and trails. Outdoors in grass and weeds, you may see 2- to 3-inch wide paths worn down from repeated activity.

The Norway rat prefers to burrow for nesting and harborage. Burrows are found in earth banks, along walls, and under rubbish. Rat holes are about 3 inches in diameter whereas mouse holes are only about 1 inch in diameter. If a burrow is active, it will be free of cobwebs and dust. The presence of fresh food or freshly dug earth at the entrance of the burrow also indicates an active burrow.

RUB MARKS Rats prefer to stay close to walls where they can keep their highly sensitive whiskers in contact with the wall. As a rat runs along a wall, its body rubs against the wall or baseboard. The oil and filth from the rat's body are deposited on the wall and create a black mark called a "rub mark." Mice do not leave rub marks that are detectable, except when the infestation is especially heavy.

GNAWINGS The incisor teeth of rats grow 4 to 6 inches a year. As a result, rats have to keep these teeth filed down in order to keep them short enough to use. Gnawings in wood are fresh if they are light colored and show well-defined teeth marks.

TRACKS Tracks may be observed along rat or mouse runs both indoors and outdoors. Look for tracks in dust in little-used rooms and in mud around puddles. Rat tracks may be 1 inch long.

MISCELLANEOUS SIGNS Rodent urine stains can be seen with ultraviolet light (black light). Rats leave a different pattern than mice. Rat and mouse hairs may be found along walls, etc. When examined under a microscope, they can be distinguished from other animal hairs.

RODENT CONTROL

The grounds around the food establishment should be free of litter, waste, refuse, uncut weeds, and grass. Unused equipment, boxes, crates, pallets, and other materials should be neatly stored to eliminate places where pests might hide.

> Rodent control begins with a building and grounds that will not provide a source of food, shelter, and breeding areas.

All entrances and loading and unloading areas should be equipped with self-closings doors and door flashing to prevent rodent entry into the establishment. Metal screens with holes no larger than 1/4 inch should be installed over all floor drains to prevent entry.

Traps are useful around food establishments where rodenticides are not permitted or are hazardous. Live traps can be used for collecting live rats. Check traps at least once every 24 hours. Killer or snap traps can also be used as part of a rodent-control program. When using these types of traps, place them at right angles to the wall along rodent runways with the trigger side closest to the wall.

Glueboards are shallow trays that have a very sticky surface. The mouse's feet stick to the board when it walks on it, and it is caught. Glueboards should be placed next to and running parallel with the wall.

Rodenticides are hazardous chemicals that can contaminate food and food-contact surfaces if not handled properly. Baits should be used outdoors to stop rodents at the outer boundaries of your property. Baits should be placed in a tamper proof, locked bat box that will prevent children and pets from being exposed to the toxic chemicals inside. Always make certain pesticides are stored in properly labeled containers, away from food in a secure place. Dispose of containers safely and know emergency measures for treating accidental poisoning.

The use of tracking powder pesticides is prohibited in food establishments. These types of pesticides can be dispersed throughout the establishment and directly or indirectly contaminate food, equipment, utensils, linens, and single-service/single-use articles. This contamination could adversely affect both the safety of the food and the general environment.

▶ **Integrated Pest Management (IPM)** is a system that uses a combination of sanitation, mechanical, and chemical procedures to control pests.

INTEGRATED PEST MANAGEMENT (IPM)

Modern pest control operators use integrated pest management as the primary method to control pests in food establishments. Chemical pesticides are used only as a last result and only in the amount needed to support the other control measures in the IPM program. If chemical pesticides are used, they must be approved for use as specified in the Code of Federal Regulations (40 CFR 152).

The National Pest Management Association (NPMA) recommends a 5-step program for IPM:

- Inspection
- Identification
- Sanitation
- Application of two or more pest managements procedures
- Evaluation of effectiveness through follow-up inspections.

There are many benefits produced by using an integrated pest management program. An IPM program is more efficient and cost effective than programs that rely exclusively on chemicals to control pests. IPM is also longer lasting and safer for you, your employees, and your customers.

BACK TO THE STORY...

The case presented earlier illustrates how pests can pose a very serious problem for food establishments. Pests contaminate food and food-contact surfaces, and they carry disease agents that are harmful to humans. Pests are attracted to food establishments by the food, water, and food odors they find there. In order to keep pests under control, food establishments must prevent them from entering the facility; eliminate sources of food, water, and shelter; and implement an Integrated Pest Management (IPM) program.

ENVIRONMENTAL SANITATION OF MAINTENANCE

Surveys of customers show cleanliness is a top consideration when choosing a place to eat or shop for food. Customer satisfaction is highest in food establishments that are clean and bright and where quality food products are safely handled and displayed.

CONDITION OF THE ESTABLISHMENT

The exterior of the food establishment must be free of litter and debris that could attract and harbor pests and ruin the appearance of the facility. Grass and weeds should be regularly mowed to eliminate harborage areas for insects, rodents, and other pests. Walking and driving surfaces should be constructed of concrete, asphalt, gravel, or similar materials to facilitate maintenance and control dust. These surfaces should also be properly graded to prevent rainwater from pooling and standing on parking lots and sidewalks. To attract customers, the exterior of the building should be clean, attractive, and make a good impression.

Proper Water Supply and Sewage Disposal System

An adequate water supply and proper sewage disposal are vital to the sanitation of food establishments. The water source and ability to meet hot water generation needs should be sufficient to meet demands of the food establishment. Drinking water for food establishments must be obtained from an approved source. Most establishments will be connected to a public water system. However, when a private well or other nonpublic water system is used, it must be constructed, maintained, and operated according to the water quality requirements of the jurisdiction. Wells must be located and constructed in a manner that will protect them from sewage and other sources of contamination. Periodic sampling is required to monitor the safety of the water and to detect any change in water quality.

To render the water safe, a drinking water system must be flushed and disinfected before being placed into service. The *FDA Food Code* dictates that a drinking water system be flushed after construction, repair, or modification and after an emergency situation, such as flood, that may introduce contaminants to the system.

A reservoir used to supply water to devices such as a fountain beverage dispenser, drinking water, vending machine, or produce fogger must be maintained in accordance with the manufacturer's specifications, or according to the following procedures, whichever is more stringent:

1. Drain and completely disassemble the water and aerosol contact parts.
2. Brush-clean the reservoir, aerosol tubing, and discharge nozzles with a suitable detergent solution.
3. Flush the complete system with water to remove the detergent solution and particle accumulation.
4. Rinse by immersing, spraying, or swabbing the reservoir, aerosol tubing, and discharge nozzles with at least 50 ppm hypochlorite solution.

Proper disposal of sewage greatly reduces the risk of fecal contamination of food and water. The *FDA Food Code* requires sewage from food establishments to be disposed through an approved facility that is

- A public sewage treatment plant, or
- An individualized sewage disposal system that is sized, constructed, maintained, and operated according to rules and regulations of the jurisdiction.

Safety Alert

According to the *FDA Food Code*, water from a nonpublic water system must be sampled and tested at least annually and as required by state water quality regulations.

The use of non-potable water sources in food establishments must be approved by the regulatory authority in the jurisdiction and may only be used for non-culinary purposes such as air-handling systems, cooling systems, and fire protection.

CONDITION OF THE BUILDING

The cleanliness and attractiveness customers view upon entering the building influence their overall dining or shopping experience. Entrance doors should be self-closing to discourage flying insects.

Floors, Walls, and Ceilings

Proper construction, repair, and cleaning of floors, walls, and ceilings are important parts of an effective sanitation program. Sanitation, safety, durability, comfort, and cost are the main criteria you will use when selecting materials for floors and walls. Surfaces of floors and walls should be resistant to damage and deterioration from the water, detergents, and repeated scrubbings used to keep them clean. Walls and ceilings should be light colored to show soil and enhance the artificial lighting used in food preparation, handling and display areas.

Consider the specific needs of the different food areas when selecting materials for floors, walls, and ceilings. Some criteria that should be used for all departments are

- Sanitation
- Safety
- Durability
- Comfort
- Cost.

Proper construction, repair, and cleaning of floors, walls, and ceilings are important elements of an effective sanitation program.

Materials used for floors, walls, and ceilings in food preparation areas, store rooms (including dry storage areas and walk-in refrigerators), dishwashing areas, and restrooms must be

- Smooth
- Nonabsorbent
- Easy to clean
- Resistant to damage and deterioration.

▶ **Coving** is a curved sealed edge between the floor and wall that eliminates sharp corners or gaps that would make cleaning difficult and ineffective.

FLOOR The *FDA Food Code* prohibits the use of carpeting in food preparation areas, walk-in refrigerators, dishwashing areas, toilet areas where handwashing lavatories, toilets, and urinals are located, and refuse storage rooms or other areas subject to moisture.

Floors graded to drains are needed in food establishments where water-flush methods are used for cleaning. In addition, the floor and wall must be coved and sealed. Coving is a curved sealed edge between the floor and the wall that eliminates sharp corners or gaps that would make cleaning difficult and ineffective. When cleaning methods other than water flushing are used for cleaning floors, the floor and wall juncture must be covered with a gap of no more than 1/32 inch (1 mm) between the floor and wall.

Use mats and other forms of anti-slip floor coverings where necessary to protect employees from slips and falls. These devices should also be impervious, nonabsorbent, and easy to clean.

Light fixtures, ventilation system components, and other attachments to walls and ceilings must be easy to clean and maintained in good repair.

WALLS AND CEILINGS Walls and ceilings in food production and dishwashing areas must be made of a light colored material to enhance the artificial lighting in these areas. This will make soil and dirt easier to see and will help employees know when they have done an effective job cleaning a surface. Walls and wall coverings should be constructed of materials such as ceramic tile, stainless steel, or fiberglass when used in areas cleaned frequently.

Restroom Sanitation

Toilet facilities near work areas promote good personal hygiene, reduce lost productivity, and permit closer supervision of employees. Toilet rooms in food establishments must be completely enclosed and provided with tight-fighting and self-closing doors. Clean and suitably equipped toilet facilities must be provided for employees. These facilities must be kept clean and in good repair to prevent the spread of disease and promote good personal hygiene.

Materials used in the construction of toilet rooms and toilet fixtures must be durable and easily cleanable. The floors, walls, fixtures in toilet areas must be clean and well maintained. Supply toilet rooms and toilet fixtures must be durable and easily cleanable. The floors, walls, and fixtures in toilet areas must be clean and well maintained. Supply toilet tissue at each toilet. Provide easy-to-clean containers for waste materials and have at least one covered container in toilet rooms used by women.

Handwashing Facilities

Handwashing stations must be properly equipped and conveniently located to enable food handlers to wash their hands as necessary throughout the workday.

Food employees must know when and how to wash their hands. Conveniently located and properly equipped handwashing facilities are key factors in getting employees to wash their hands. Handwashing stations should be located in or near areas where food is prepared or handled and in dishwashing areas. Handwashing stations must also be located in or adjacent to restrooms. The number of handwashing stations required and their installation are usually set by local health departments or plumbing code.

Safety Alert

Poor sanitation in toilet areas can spread disease.

A handwashing station must be equipped with

- Hot and cold running water under pressure
- A supply of soap
- A way to dry hands without contaminating them.

A handwashing lavatory must be able to provide water at a temperature of at least 100°F (38°C) through a mixing valve or combination faucet. If a self-closing, slow-closing, or metering faucet is used, it must provide a flow of water for at least 15 seconds without the need to be reactivated.

Each handwashing station must be equipped with a dispenser containing liquid or powdered soap. The use of bar soap is frequently discouraged by regulatory agencies because bar soap can become contaminated with germs and soil.

Individual disposable towels and mechanical hot-air dryers are the preferred hand-drying devices. Most local health departments do not allow retractable cloth towel dispenser systems because there are too many possibilities for contamination. Common cloth towels, used multiple times by employees to dry their hands are also prohibited.

Safety Alert

Never store food or items associated with food handling in restroom areas.

Safety Alert

Handwashing stations should be clean and well maintained and never be used for purposes other than hand washing. Sinks used for preparing produce and dishwashing must not be used for hand washing.

PLUMBING HAZARDS IN FOOD ESTABLISHMENTS

A properly designed, constructed, and installed plumbing system is very important to food sanitation. Air gaps and mechanical vacuum breakers are used to protect the municipal water supply. Consult a professional plumber or your local plumbing code for details about the plumbing requirements in your jurisdiction.

A properly designed and installed plumbing system is very important to food sanitation. The *FDA Food Code* includes many different components within the definition of plumbing system. In particular, it identifies the

- Water supply and distribution pipes
- Plumbing fixtures and traps
- Soil, waster, and vent pipes
- Sanitary and storm sewers
- Building drains, including their respective connections and devices within the building and at the site.

Numerous outbreaks of gastroenteritis, dysentery, typhoid fever, and chemical poisonings have been traced to cross connections and other types of plumbing hazards in food establishments. The plumbing system in a food establishment must be maintained in good repair. When repairs to the plumbing system are required, they must be completed in accordance with applicable local ordinances and state regulations.

Cross Connections

A cross connection may be either direct or indirect. A direct cross connection occurs when a potable water system is directly connected to a drain, sewer, nonpotable water supply, or source of contamination (sewage, chemicals, etc.) may be blown across, sucked into, or diverted into a safe water supply.

Backflow

► **Backflow** is the backward flow of contaminated water into a potable water supply.

Backflow occurs most frequently under two conditions:

- Backpressure where contamination is forced into a potable water system through a connection that has a higher pressure than the water system.
- Backsiphonage when there is reduced pressure or a vacuum formed in the water system. This might be caused by a water main break, the shutdown of a portion of the system for repairs, or heavy water use during a fire.

In the event of water pressure drop… back-siphonage occurs.

PREVENTING BACKFLOW The plumbing system in a food establishment must be designed, constructed, and installed according to the plumbing code in the local jurisdiction. A properly designed and installed plumbing system will keep food, equipment, and utensils from becoming contaminated with disease-causing microorganisms found in sewage and other pollutants.

PREVENTION DEVICES ON CARBONATORS Carbonators on soft drink dispensers form carbonic acid by mixing carbon dioxide with water. The carbonic acid is then mixed with the syrups to produce the soft drinks. If the carbon dioxide backs up into a copper water line, the carbonic acid will dissolve some of the copper. The water containing the dissolved copper will then be used in dispensing soft drinks, and the first few customers receiving the drinks are likely to suffer the symptoms of copper poisoning. An air gap or a vented backflow prevention device meeting American Society of Sanitary Engineering (ASSE) Standard No. 1022 must be installed upstream from a carbonating device and downstream from any copper in the water supply line to reduce incidences of copper poisoning.

Safety Alert

Failure to properly clean and maintain grease traps can result in the harborage of pests and/or failure of the facility's sewage system.

Grease Traps

Food establishments that do a lot of frying or charbroiling should be equipped with a grease trap. These devices remove liquid grease and fats after they have hardened and become separated from the wastewater. Grease traps are especially important when the food establishment is connected to a septic system or other type of on-site wastewater treatment and disposal system. A grease trap must be located for easily accessible cleaning.

GARBAGE AND REFUSE SANITATION

Proper storage and disposal of garbage and refuse are necessary to prevent contamination of food and equipment and avoid attracting insects, rodents, and other pests to a food establishment. Proper facilities and receptacles must be provided inside and outside the establishment to hold refuse, recyclables, and returnables that may accumulate. Refuse and garbage should be removed from food establishments frequently enough to minimize the development of objectionable odors and other conditions that attract or harbor insects, rodents, and other pests. Insects, rodents, and other pests are also less likely to be attracted to these establishments when garbage and refuse are properly managed. Effective waste management requires:

- Proper handling and short-term storage of the materials inside the operation
- Proper storage of the waste outside the building until it is picked up by a commercial refuse disposal company.

Inside Storage

Waste containers must be provided in all areas in a food establishment where refuse is produced or discarded. Containers used to collect garbage and refuse must be

- Durable
- Cleanable
- Insect and rodent-proof
- Leak-proof
- Nonabsorbent
- Covered with tight-fitting lids when not in use.

Plastic bags and wet-strength paper bags are frequently used to line waste containers. Do not place waste containers in locations where they might create a public health nuisance.

Refuse storage rooms and containers must be cleaned as part of the establishment's routine cleaning program. Keeping the area clean is your best defense against pests. When cleaning this equipment, be careful not to contaminate food, equipment, utensils, linens, or single-service and single-use articles. Wastewater produced while cleaning the equipment and receptacles is considered to be sewage. It must be disposed of through an approved sanitary sewage system or other system constructed, maintained, and operated according to law.

▶ **Garbage** is the term applied to food wastes that cannot be recycled.

▶ **Refuse** is trash, rubbish, and other types of solid waste not disposed of through the sewage system.

Outside Storage

A food establishment should also have an outside storage area and enclosure to hold refuse, recyclables, and returnables awaiting pickup. An outdoor storage surface should be durable, cleanable, and maintained in good repair. Dumpsters and storage areas must be covered with tight-fitting lids, doors, or covers to discourage insects, rodents, and other types of pest.

Dirty equipment, containers, and waste facilities attract insects and rodents.

Refuse and garbage should be removed from the site as often as necessary to prevent objectionable odors and avoid conditions that tract or harbor insects and rodents. Outdoor storage areas must be kept clean and free of litter. Suitable cleaning equipment and supplies must be available to clean the equipment and receptacles. Refuse storage equipment and receptacles must have drains and drain plugs must be in place.

Compactors and other equipment for refuse, recyclables, and returnables must be installed to minimize the accumulation of debris. Always make sure you clean under and around these units to prevent insect and rodent harborage.

Some food establishments may provide redeeming machines for recyclables or returnables. According to *FDA Food Code*, a redeeming machine may be located in the packaged food storage area or consumer area of a food establishment if food, equipment, utensils and linens, and single-service and single-use articles are not subject to contamination from the machine and a public health nuisance is not created.

MANY EMPLOYEES ARE NOT THANKFUL FOR THANKSGIVING LUNCHEON...

A Thanksgiving dinner, catered by a nearly food establishment, left 40 employees with symptoms of food-borne illness. All suffered from nausea, diarrhea, body aches, chills, and fever within several hours after eating the turkey dinner.

Investigators from the local regulatory agency interviewed the supervisors and food workers to determine how the food was prepared. According to the report, four 18- to 20-pound frozen turkeys were placed in the walk-in cooler to thaw on November 17. The turkeys were cooked on November 20. No product temperatures were taken, but the turkeys had pop-up thermometers that indicated when the birds were done. Immediately following cooking, the turkeys were covered with foil and placed in the walk-in cooler. On the day of the company's luncheon, the turkeys were reheated, sliced, and placed into hot holding units for transport to the luncheon. The food workers indicated product temperatures were not routinely monitored during cooling and reheating.

▶HACCP SYSTEMS

The food industry and food regulatory agencies are confronted with a number of new food safety challenges, including

- Emerging pathogens or substances that cause food-borne illness
- A global food supply
- New techniques for processing and serving food
- A growing number of people who are classified as highly susceptible to food-borne illness.

Every year there is an increase in the variety and amount of food products imported into the United States. Also, methods used to process and prepare foods domestically continue to change. In addition, governmental agencies at all levels have reduced staff and services due to increased costs and fewer local, state, and federal funds. Increased responsibility for food safety has shifted to food establishment managers and employees during the recent past.

WHAT IS THE HAZARD ANALYSIS CRITICAL CONTROL POINT SYSTEM (HACCP)

What is the HACCP system and how can it make a difference in food safety management. The HACCP system was developed by the Pillsbury Company and NASA to make the food used by astronauts in space as safe as possible. So why not use it for all food production?

First, food managers identify the biological, chemical, or physical hazards (risk factors) that may be associated with the production of potentially hazardous foods. Then they identify what might go wrong during food production that could result in food-borne illness and when it could happen. Finally they determine how these errors can be prevented or controlled. If these tasks are undertaken in a systematic way, the safety of foods can be assured.

In addition to the HACCP system, there are many other programs and practices that need to be done correctly to protect the safety of foods. These include

- Use of approved products
- Facility design that meets code requirements
- Employees educated and supervised in good personal hygiene practices
- Standard Operation Procedures (SOPs) that ensure uniform food safety compliance
- An effective cleaning and sanitation program
- Proper equipment and maintenance programs
- A commitment from management to facilitate the HACCP system.

In an HACCP food safety system, the focus is on food and how it is handled during storage, preparation and service. A sanitary environment is important for safe food production. however, food can still be contaminated by employees, if

- Proper food-handling techniques are not used
- Good personal hygiene is not practiced
- Food temperatures are not controlled.

The HACCP system helps food managers identify and control potential problems before they happen. It is most effective when tailored to the specific needs of the food establishment. HACCP should not be viewed as a "one size fits all" program. Whether used in restaurants, food establishments, institutions, health care facilities, or other food service operations, the primary goal is always the same—production of safe and wholesome food.

THE HACCP SYSTEM APPROACH TO FOOD SAFETY

▶ **HACCP systems** control factors that contribute to food-borne diseases.

HACCP is the preferred approach to food safety because it provides the most effective and efficient way to ensure food products are safe. By using the HACCP system, food managers can identify the foods and processes that are most likely to cause food-borne illnesses. When a potential problem is identified, the food establishment can initiate procedures to reduce or eliminate the risk of food-borne illness and monitor actions to make sure the procedures are being followed.

The HACCP system uses control of time, temperature, and specific factors that are known to contribute to food-borne disease outbreaks. Records produced in conjunction with the HACCP system provide a comprehensive source of information about the events that occurred during all stages of food production.

The first priority of the HACCP system is to ensure the safety of the potentially hazardous foods on the menu. You will begin by developing HACCP flow charts for recipes that allow you to follow the flow of food from start to finish. In the course of developing HACCP flow charts, you will identify "high risk" activities that occur during food production, which might contribute to a food-borne illness.

You then ask, "What can be done to control these high-risk activities to reduce the risk of food-borne illness?" HACCP recipes are guides for food workers during production. Food managers and supervisors can use the flow charts and production logs to double check for production safety. HACCP records also assist health department personnel as they perform routine inspections of your establishment.

Food managers and supervisors must learn how to effectively develop, implement, and maintain the HACCP system. There are several publications available, including an excellent guide in the *FDA Food Code* that can help you learn more about the HAACP system.

THE SEVEN PRINCPLES IN AN HACCP SYSTEM

The basic structure of an HACCP system consists of seven principles as listed below (see Table 2.32). While each principle is unique, they all work together to form the basic structure of an effective food safety system.

Principle 1—Hazard Analysis

The first principle in an HACCP system is hazard analysis. Hazard analysis starts with a thorough review of your menu or product list to identify all the potentially hazardous foods you serve. As you learned previously, potentially hazardous foods have properties that support the rapid growth of infectious and toxin-producing microbes that can cause the foods to become unsafe. Potentially hazardous foods including the following:

- Foods of animal origin that are raw or heat-treated
- Foods of plant origin that are heat-treated or consist of raw seed sprouts
- Cut melons
- Garlic and oil mixtures that are not modified in a way to inhibit the growth of microorganisms.

All of these foods are commonly found in food establishments.

Table 2.32 SEVEN PRINCIPLES IN A HAZARD ANALYSIS (CRITICAL CONTROL POINT SYSTEM)

1. Hazard Analysis
2. Identify the Critical Control Points (CCPs) in food preparation.
3. Establish a Critical Limit that must be met at each identified Critical Control Point.
4. Establish procedures to monitor each CCP.
5. Establish the corrective action to be taken when monitoring indicates a Critical Limit has been exceeded.
6. Establish procedures to verify the HACCP system is working.
7. Establish effective record keeping that will document the HACCP system.

Source: FDA Food Code.

BIOLOGICAL HAZARDS During hazard analysis, look for steps in food production where foods may become contaminated by bacteria and other biological hazards and where these microorganisms might survive and multiply.

CHEMICAL HAZARDS Chemical hazards are substances that are either naturally present or are added to food during production. Reduce the chance of chemical contamination by purchasing foods from approved sources and by proper handling and storage of chemicals used in the food establishment. When constructing an HACCP flow chart, consider the possibility of chemical contamination.

PHYSICAL HAZARDS Physical contaminations in food can cause injury to the consumer. Glass, metal shavings, a food worker's personal property (jewelry, false fingernails, and hair pins), toothpicks, and pieces of worn equipment are examples of physical agents that may accidentally enter food during production and service.

▶ **Risk** is the probability that a condition or conditions will lead to a hazard.

During hazard analysis, it is important to estimate risk. Risk is the probability that a condition or conditions will lead to a hazard. Some of the factors that influence risk include the following:

- Type of customers served
- Types of foods on the menu
- Nature of the organism
- Past outbreaks
- Size and type of food production operations
- Extent of employee training

Each type of operation and each food establishment pose different levels of risk to the consumers. Focus on your menu's most hazardous foods first. Once your HACCP system has been developed, implemented, and evaluated for these foods, move on to the next most hazardous foods. Within several months, you should be able to include all of the potentially hazardous foods on your menu under the HACCP system.

Table 2.33 SAMPLE MENU

Breakfast			
Orange Juice	Apple Juice	Grapefruit Half	Strawberries
Oatmeal	Cream of Wheat	Shredded Wheat	Raisin Bran
Scrambled Eggs	Bacon	Sausage Links	Hash Browns
French Toast	Sausage Gravy	Cheese Omelet	Pancakes
Belgian Waffle	Breakfast Burrito	White/Wheat Toast	Egg Beaters™
Lunch			
Apple Sauce	Pasta Salad	Potato Salad	Spinach Salad
Chili	Navy Bean Soup	Clam Chowder	Vegetable Soup
French Fries	Hamburgers	Pork Tenderloin	Fish Filet
Chicken Filet	Ham & Cheese	Chicken Wings	Corned Beef & Swiss
Dinner			
Tossed Salad	Cobb Salad	Cottage Cheese	Tuna Salad in Tomato
Baked Potato	Broccoli & Cheese	Wild Rice	Melon Balls
Country Fried Steak	Turkey/Dressing	Liver & Onions	Meat Loaf
Frozen Yogurt	Chocolate Brownie	Cherry Pie	Angel Food Cake
Coffee	Iced Tea	Milk	Soft Drinks

Hazard identification and risk estimation provide a logical basis for determining which hazards are significant and must be addressed in the HACCP plan. The severity of a hazard is defined by the degree of seriousness of the consequences should it become a reality. Hazards that involve low risk do not need to be addressed in the HACCP plan.

Personal experience, facts generated by food-borne illness investigations, and information from scientific articles can be useful when estimating the approximate risk of a hazard. When estimating risk, it is important to separate food safety concerns from food quality issues. For instance, the fact that perishable foods spoil quickly when stored in the food temperature danger zone is a quality issue. However, food-borne disease investigations show that allowing potentially hazardous foods to remain in the temperature danger zone too long is a common contributor to food-borne illness and is a significant food safety issue.

The last phase of the hazard analysis step involves establishing preventive measures. After the hazards have been identified, you must consider what preventative measures, if any, can be employed for each hazard.

Preventive measures commonly used in food establishments include the following:

- Controlling the temperature of the food
- Cross-contamination control
- Good personal hygiene practices
- Other procedures that prevent, minimize, or eliminate an identified health hazard (i.e., limiting the amount of time a potentially hazardous food spends in the temperature danger zone).

Your HACCP system should employ preventative measures that can be easily monitored. Since food temperature and time can be easily monitored, they are the preventive measures used most often in an HACCP system.

Table 2.34 SAMPLE MENU WITH POTENTIALLY HAZARDOUS FOODS CIRCLED

Breakfast			
Orange Juice	Apple Juice	Grapefruit Half	Strawberries
Oatmeal	Cream of Wheat	Shredded Wheat	Raisin Bran
Scrambled Eggs	Bacon	Sausage Links	Hash Browns
French Toast	Sausage Gravy	Cheese Omelet	Pancakes
Belgian Waffle	Breakfast Burrito	White/Wheat Toast	Egg Beaters™
Lunch			
Apple Sauce	Pasta Salad	Potato Salad	Spinach Salad
Chili	Navy Bean Soup	Clam Chowder	Vegetable Soup
French Fries	Hamburgers	Pork Tenderloin	Fish Filet
Chicken Filet	Ham & Cheese	Chicken Wings	Corned Beef & Swiss
Dinner			
Tossed Salad	Cobb Salad	Cottage Cheese	Tuna Salad in Tomato
Baked Potato	Broccoli & Cheese	Wild Rice	Melon Balls
Country Fried Steak	Turkey/Dressing	Liver & Onions	Meat Loaf
Frozen Yogurt	Chocolate Brownie	Cherry Pie	Angel Food Cake
Coffee	Iced Tea	Milk	Soft Drinks

▶ **Critical Control Point (CCP)** is an operation in the flow of food that will prevent, eliminate, or reduce hazards to acceptable levels.

Principle 2—Identify Critical Control Points (CCPs)

The second principle in creating an HACCP system is to identify the critical control points (CCPs) in food production. A critical control point is an operation (practice, preparation step, or procedure) in the flow of food that will prevent, eliminate, or reduce hazards to acceptable levels. A critical control point provides a kill step that will destroy bacteria or a control step that prevents or slows down the rate of bacterial growth.

Examples of CCPs include

- Cooking, reheating, and hot-holdings
- Chilling, chilled storage, and chilled display
- Receiving, thawing, mixing ingredients, and other food-handling stages
- Product formulation (i.e., reducing the pH of a food to below 4.6 or the A_w to .85 below)
- Purchasing seafood, MAP foods, and ready-to-eat foods (where further processing would not prevent a hazard) from approved sources.

The *FDA Food Code* also recognizes specific food handling and sanitation practices including proper thawing methods, prevention of cross-contamination, and employee and environmental hygiene.

The most commonly used CCPs are cooking, cooling, reheating, and hot-/cold-holding. Cooking and reheating to proper temperatures will destroy bacteria, whereas proper cooling, hot-holding, and cold-holding will prevent or slow down the rate of bacterial growth.

These practices are more difficult to measure, monitor, and document. Therefore, many food establishment operators prefer to think of them as "standard operating procedures" (SOPs) or "house policies" rather than CCPs.

For the purpose of this book, CCPs are considered to be operations that involve the following:

- Time
- Temperature
- Acidity
- Purchasing and receiving procedures related to
  - Seafood
  - Modified atmosphere packaged (MAP) foods
  - Ready-to-eat foods where a later step in the food flow would not prevent a hazard
- Thawing of ready-to-eat foods where a later processing step in the food flow would not prevent a hazard.

SOPs include the following:

- Good employee hygiene practice (e.g., hand washing)
- Cross-contamination control (e.g., keeping raw products separate from cooked and ready-to-eat foods)
- Environmental hygiene practices (e.g., effective cleaning and sanitizing of equipment and utensils).

Identification of critical control points begins with a review of the recipe for the potentially hazardous ingredients and the development of a flow chart for the recipe. The flow chart tracks the steps in the food flow from receiving to serving. The specific path food follows will be slightly different for each product. However, some of the more common elements in the flow of food include the following:

There must be at least one critical control point in the production process to qualify it as an HACCP food safety system, and the critical control point must be monitored and controlled to ensure the safety of the food.

- Purchase of products and ingredients from sources inspected and approved by regulatory agencies
- Receiving products and ingredients

- Storage of products and ingredients
- Preparation steps that may involve thawing, cooking, and other processing activities
- Holding or display of food
- Service of food
- Cooling food
- Storing cooled food
- Reheating food for service.

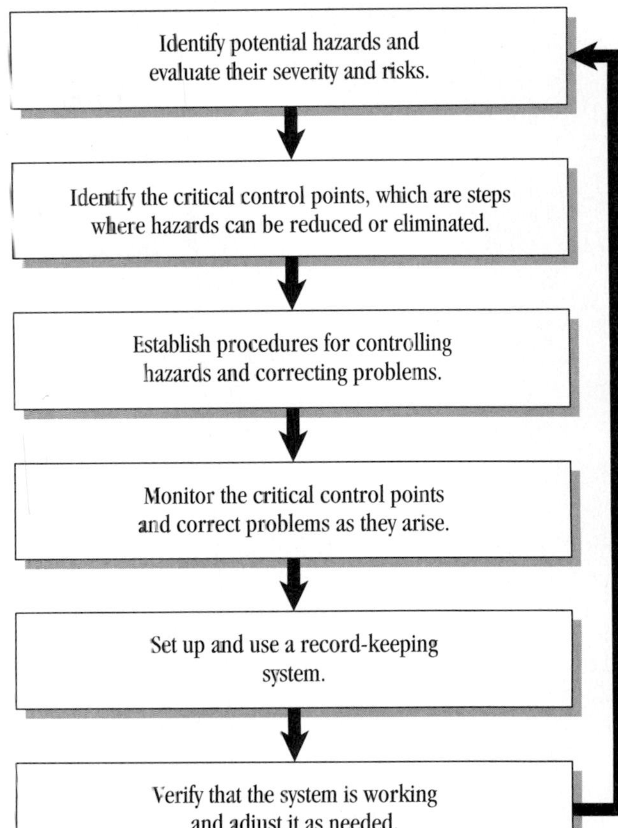

Controlling the temperature of food products throughout the flow of food is the most commonly used technique for ensuring food safety. However, time can also be used as a public health control measures. As you learned earlier, it commonly takes 4 hours or more in the temperature danger zone for bacteria to multiply to levels where they will cause food-borne illness.

There are situations during food preparation and service where foods will be allowed to enter the temperature danger zone. For example, some foods that are cooled and held hot cannot be held at 135°F (57°C) or above without lowering the culinary quality of the food. When fried chicken is held at 135°F (57°C) or above, it can dry out and lose its quality. To prevent this, a food establishment can hold the cooked chicken at less then 135°F (57°C). Rather than controlling the temperature of the food, the emphasis is placed on controlling the amount of time the food is in the temperature danger zone. When time is used as a CCP, do not allow more than 4 hours from preparation to consumption. The food must be properly marked or otherwise identified to indicate the time that is 4 hours past the point in time when the food is removed from temperature control. All foods that exceed the 4-hour limit must be discarded.

Principle 3—Establish the Critical Limits Which Must Be Met at Each Critical Control Point

This principle involves setting critical limits to make sure each critical control point effectively stops a biological, chemical, or physical hazard. Critical limits should be thought of as the upper and lower boundaries of food safety. The critical limit should be as specific as possible, such as "heat ground beef or pork to an internal temperature of 155°F (68°C) or more for at least 15 seconds." A well-defined critical limit makes it easier to determine when the limit has not been met.

Each CCP has one or more critical limits to monitor to assure hazards are

- Prevented
- Eliminated
- Reduced to acceptable levels

Each limit relates to a process that will keep food in a range of safety by controlling

- Temperature
- Time
- The ability of food to support the growth of infectious or toxin-producing microorganisms.

Table 2.35 CRITERIA MOST FREQUENTLY USED FOR CRITICAL LIMITS

CRITICAL LIMIT	BOUNDARIES OF FOOD SAFETY
Time	Limit the amount of time foods are in the temperature danger zone during preparation and service processes to 4 hours or less.
Temperature	Keep potentially hazardous foods at or below 41°F (5°C) or at or above 135°F (57°C). Maintain specific cooking, cooling, reheating, and hot-holding temperatures.
Water Activity	Foods with a water activity (A_w) of .85 or less do not support growth of disease-causing bacteria.
pH (acidity level)	Disease-causing bacteria do not grow in foods that have a pH of 4.6 or below.

One way that a food service operation can make workers aware of potential hazards and the critical actions that are necessary to avoid those hazards is by including detailed safety information in every recipe. The recipe for Beef Stroganoff shows all the critical control points (CCPs) (see Figure 2.5). Writing this much detail into every one of the operation's standardized recipes serves as a constant reminder to employees of both the specific actions necessary and the importance of food safety to the operation.

Principle 4—Establish Procedures to Monitor CCPs

Staff members must be given the responsibility for monitoring critical control points. This involves making observations and measurements to determine whether a critical control point is under control. Monitoring will show when a critical control point has exceeded its critical limit.

Time, temperature, pH, and water activity are the critical limits most commonly monitored to ensure a critical limit is under control. If a product or process does not meet critical limits, immediate corrective action is required before a problem occurs.

Monitoring is a critical part of an HACCP system.

Monitoring must be "doable." Frequent monitoring catches problems early and provides more options for correction (i.e., reheat instead of discard food). If a critical limit cannot be monitored continuously, set up specific monitoring intervals that can accurately indicate hazard control. If early monitoring indicates the process is very consistent, do not monitor as often.

Observations of cross-contamination control, employee hygiene compliance, and product formulation control may also be incorporated into the monitoring system. A record of actions, times, temperatures, and any departure from critical limits provides a history for that item. Once the flow is established, measurements can be recorded on a flow chart. Have employees place their initials by the information they record.

Teach food workers responsible for monitoring CCPs how to accurately measure critical control points and record the information in data records. Explain to employees about the harm that can occur if data is faked or not collected as required.

Monitoring is a critical part of an HACCP system. It provides written documentation that can be used to verify the HACCP system is working properly. An operation that identifies critical control points and establishes critical limits without having a monitoring system in place has not actually implemented an HACCP system. Critical limits without proper monitoring are meaningless.

BEEF STROGANOFF

Yield: 8 Servings, 8 oz. (250 g) each **Method:** Sautéing

Tenderloin tips, émincé	2 lb.	1 kg
Clarified butter	3 Tbsp.	45 ml
Onion, medium dice	4 oz.	120 g
Mushrooms, halved	1 lb.	450 g
Demi-glace	10 fl. oz.	300 ml
Heavy cream	10 fl. oz.	300 ml
Sour cream	8 oz.	250 g
Dijon mustard	1 Tbsp.	15 ml
Fresh dill, chopped	1 Tbsp.	15 ml
Fresh parsley, chopped	1 Tbsp.	15 ml
Salt and pepper	TT	TT
Egg noodles, cooked	24 oz.	700 g

PRE-PREPARATION

A. Wash hands before handling food, after handling raw foods and after any interruptions in work.

B. Cut the beef tenderloin using a clean, sanitized knife and cutting board. Place the émincé into a clean container, cover and refrigerate until ready to use. If work is interrupted, return the beef to refrigerated storage during the interruption.

C. Measure the demi-glace, cream and sour cream, cover and keep refrigerated until ready to use.

D. Chop the onions and herbs using a clean, sanitized knife and cutting board.

PREPARATION

CCP 1. Sauté the tenderloin tips in the butter, searing on all sides. Remove the meat **to a clean container and hold at 135° F (57°C) or higher for no more than 2 hours.**

2. Add the onions to the pan and sauté lightly. Add the mushrooms and sauté until dry.

3. Add the demi-glace. Bring to a boil, reduce to a simmer and cook for 10 minutes.

CCP 4. Add the cream, sour cream, mustard and any meat juices that accumulated while holding the meat. **Cook until an internal temperature of 145°F (63°C) is maintained for at least 15 seconds.**

CCP 5. Return the meat to the sauce. **Cook until the meat reaches an internal temperature of 145°F (63°C).** Stir in the dill and parsley. Adjust the seasonings and serve over hot egg noodles.

HOLDING

CCP Transfer the sauce to a clean steam table pan and cover. Hold for service in a preheated steam table at **135°F (57°C) or higher. Use within 4 hours.**

LEFTOVERS

CCP Place in shallow metal pans with a product depth of no more than 2 inches. **Cool from 135°F (57°C) to 70°F (21°C) within 2 hours and from 70°F (21°C) to 41°F (5°C) or lower within 4 additional hours**, for a total cooling time of not more than 6 hours. Cover and store in a refrigerator so that the internal product temperature is 41°F (5°C) or less. Use leftovers within 4 days.

REHEATING

CCP Reheat Stroganoff to an internal temperature of **165°F (74°C) or higher for 15 seconds within 2 hours**; discard any product that is not consumed within 4 hours.

NOTES:
Measure all internal temperatures with a clean, sanitized thermocouple or thermometer.
Once cooked, egg noodles are a potentially hazardous food and should be held and stored accordingly.

FIGURE 2.5 ▶ A recipe showing critical control points (CCP).

Principle 5—Establish the Corrective Action to Be Taken When Monitoring Shows a Critical Limit Has Been Exceeded

If you detect a critical limit was exceeded during the production of an HACCP monitored food, correct the problem immediately. The flow of foods should not continue until all CCPs have been met.

First determine what went wrong. Next choose and apply the appropriate corrective action. For example, if the temperature of the barbecue pork on your steam table is not at 135°F (57°C) or higher, check the steam table to make sure it is working properly and will keep food hot. At the same time, put the pot on the stove and reheat it rapidly to 165°F (75°C). The pork should be discarded if you suspect it has been in the temperature danger zone for more than 4 hours.

Taking immediate corrective action is vital to the effectiveness of your food safety system.

Principle 6—Establish Procedures to Verify the HACCP System is Working

The sixth principle in the HACCP system is to verify your system is working. First, verify the critical limits you have established for your CCPs will prevent, eliminate, or reduce hazards to acceptable levels. Second, verify the overall HACCP plan is functioning effectively. The HACCP system should be reviewed and, if necessary, modified to accommodate changes in the following:

- Clientele (e.g., more highly susceptible populations)
- The items on the menu or product list (addition of potentially hazardous foods or substitution of low-risk foods for high-risk foods)
- The process used to prepare HACCP productions.

The management team should review and evaluate the establishment's HACCP program at least once a year, or more often if necessary.

Principle 7—Establish an Effective Record-Keeping System That Documents the HACCP System

An effective HACCP system requires the development and maintenance of a written HACCP plan. The plan should provide information about the hazards associated with individual food items or group of food items covered by the system. Clearly identify each CCP and the critical limits that have been set for each CCP. The procedures for monitoring critical control points and record maintenance must also be contained in the establishment's HACCP plan.

The amount of record keeping required in an HACCP plan will vary depending on the type of food processing used from one food establishment to another. The details of your HACCP plan will be determined by the complexity of your food production operation. Keep sufficient records to prove your system is working effectively, but keep it as simple as possible.

Changing a procedure at a CCP but not recording the change on your flow chart almost guarantees similar problems will be repeated. Record keeping is vital to the overall effectiveness of your HACCP system.

A clipboard, work sheet, thermometer, watch or clock, and any other equipment needed to monitor and record these limits must be readily available to the food production staff.

The method you use to record the information is not especially important, as long as it is easy for the staff to use and provides quick access to the information contained in the log.

EDUCATION AND TRAINING

Education and training are keys to a successful HACCP program. Integrate your HACCP system into each food worker's duties, performance plans, and goals.

Table 2.36 EXAMPLES OF DOCUMENTS THAT CAN BE INCLUDED IN THE TOTAL HACCP SYSTEM

- List of HACCP team members and their assigned responsibilities.
- Description of the food product and its intended use.
- Flow diagram of the food preparation steps with CCPs noted.
- Hazards associated with each CCP and preventive measure.
- Critical limits
- Monitoring systems.
- Corrective plans for deviations from critical limits.
- Record-keeping procedures.
- Procedures for verification of the HACCP system.

The content of the training program should provide employees with an overview of the HACCP system and how it works to ensure food safety. The primary goal of your HACCP training program is to provide workers the skills they will need when performing specific tasks (monitoring and recording) which are required by the HACCP plan. Motivate workers by stressing the importance of their roles and their responsibility to the success of the HACCP program.

HACCP training must be an ongoing activity due to the high employee turnover most establishments experience. Keep records of employee HACCP training along with the other documents generated by your HACCP system.

Effective training and supervision will help you achieve the benefits of an HACCP-based operation in a much shorter period of time. This will save you money and, more important, enhance the safety of the products you are serving your clients.

Table 2.37 INFORMATION COMMONLY INCLUDED IN A HACCP PLAN

CONTROL POINT	QUICK CHILL	REHEATING
1 Hazard analysis	Bacteria (especially sporeformers)	Bacteria
2 Identify CCP	Yes	Yes
3 Identify Critical Limit	135°F (57°C) to 70°F (21°C) in 2 hours or less. 135°F (57°C) to 41°F (5°C) in 6 hours or less	Reheat to an internal temperature of 165°F (74°C) or above within 2 hours
4 Monitoring [Procedure Frequency person(s) Responsible]	Cook monitors product temperature every 60 minutes	Cook monitors product temperature every 30 minutes
5 Corrective Action(s)/Person(s) Responsible	Discard product if CCP limit is not met	Continue heating until CCP limit is achieved
6 Verification Procedure(s)/ Person(s) Responsible	Food Manager	Food Manager
7 HACCP Records	Record data on a time/temperature chart and initial	Record data on a time/temperature chart and initial

ROLES AND RESPONSIBILITIES UNDER HACCP

The role of health department personnel and other regulators is to promote the use of HACCP by the food industry. Regulatory personnel will review your HACCP documents periodically to ensure critical control points are properly identified, critical limits are properly set, required monitoring is being performed, and the HACCP plan is being revised when necessary.

The job of the food establishment managers and supervisors is to develop, implement, and maintain the HACCP system. Continuously use and improve your HACCP system to achieve safe food management.

Safety Alert

Be sure to warn people when you must walk behind them, especially when carrying a hot item.

THE SAFE WORKER

Kitchens are filled with objects that can cut, burn, break, crush or sprain the human body. The best ways to prevent work-related injuries are proper training, good work habits, and careful supervision.

The federal government enacted legislation designed to reduce hazards in the work area, thereby reducing accidents. The Occupational Safety and Health Act (OSHA) covers a broad range of safety matters. Employers who fail to follow its rules can be severely fined. Unfortunately, human error is the leading cause of accidents, and no amount of legislation can protect someone who doesn't work in a safe manner.

Safe behavior on the job reflects pride, professionalism, and consideration for fellow workers. The following list should alert you to conditions and activities aimed at preventing accidents and injuries:

- Clean up spills as soon as they occur.
- Learn to operate equipment properly; always use guards and safety devices.
- Wear clothing that fits properly; avoid wearing jewelry, which may get caught in equipment.
- Use knives and other equipment for their intended purposes only. When walking in the kitchen, carry knives close to your side with the point down.
- Keep exits, aisles and stairs clear and unobstructed.
- Always assume pots and pans are hot; handle them with dry towels.
- Position pot and pan handles out of the aisles so that they do not get bumped.
- Get help or use a cart when lifting or moving heavy objects.
- Avoid back injury by lifting with your leg muscles; stoop, don't bend, when lifting.
- Use an appropriately placed ladder or stool for climbing; do not use a chair, box, drawer, or shelf.
- Keep breakable items away from food storage or production areas.
- Never leave a pan of oil unattended; hot fat can ignite when overheated.
- Warn people when you must walk behind them, especially when carrying a hot pan.

BACK TO THE STORY...

When you create an HACCP food safety system, you can avoid situations like the one described earlier. An HACCP recipe and flow chart alerts food workers to potential hazards and critical control points to prevent, minimize, or eliminate them.

Poultry and poultry products have frequently been involved as the source of foodborne salmonellosis. If Salmonella bacteria are present after the cooking process, the bacteria can multiply to high levels that may not be destroyed later by reheating the food. Poultry products should be cooked to an internal temperature of 165°F (74°C) (CCP-1) to kill the germs that may be present in and on the raw birds. The cooked turkey must be held at 135°F (57°C) or above (CCP-2). If not served immediately, the cooked turkey should be divided into smaller portions to ensure it is cooled from 135°F (57°C) to 70°F (21 °C).

FIRE SAFETY

From grease flare-ups on cook tops to major fires cause by dirty ventilation hoods, fires can develop into serious threats in busy professional kitchens. Understanding the danger posed by fires and having a proper fire safety program in place is of utmost importance in a professional kitchen. Fire extinguishers contain different types of chemicals effective on various types of fires. Learn which types of fire extinguishers to use for specific combustible materials. Regulations require that commercial kitchens be outfitted with ventilation hoods and professional sprinkler systems. Grease fires in ventilation hoods are the primary cause of restaurant fires; thorough and regular cleaning prevent hazardous grease buildup. All fire suppression systems should be inspected regularly. When faced with a serious fire, do not waste time. Immediately call for help. Shut off exhaust fans and turn off kitchen equipment if time permits. Close the kitchen doors and evacuate the premises.

Deep-fat fryers pose a serious threat and employee training should include instruction on the proper operation and cleaning of such equipment. In addition, large quantities of hot fat can cause severe burns if not properly handled. When liquids come into contact with the heated fat, hot steam is released. Take care when adding foods to all deep-fat fryers to prevent getting burned. The threat is more extreme when a large quantity of liquid hits the hot grease. Keep containers of water or other liquids away from deep-fat fryers to avoid accidentally spilling liquid into the hot fat and causing a hazardous steam explosion.

IMPORTED CANTALOUPE LINKED TO SALMONELLA POONA OUTBREAK...

An uncommon form of Salmonella bacteria has been identified as the source of a food-borne disease outbreak involving cantaloupes imported from Mexico. The outbreak has caused 47 cases of illness and two deaths in 14 states. The most common symptoms of salmonellosis are headache, stomachache, diarrhea, fever, nausea, and sometimes vomiting. Dehydration, especially among infants and the elderly may be severe. The two people who died from the infection were 78 and 91 years old.

The Food and Drug Administration detained all cantaloupes imported by two Mexican companies, and state and local health agencies instructed food establishments to remove these cantaloupes from their shelves and menus.

FIRST AID

Some accidents will inevitably occur, and it is important to act appropriately in the event of an injury or emergency. This may mean calling for help or providing first aid. Every food service operation should be equipped with a complete first-aid kit. Municipal regulations may specify the exact contents of the kit. Be sure that the kit is conveniently located and well stocked at all times.

The American Red Cross and local public health departments offer training in first aid, cardiopulmonary resuscitation (CPR) and the Heimlich maneuver used for choking victims. All employees should be trained in basic emergency procedures. A list of emergency telephone numbers should be posted by each telephone.

All food service workers are responsible for supplying food that is safe to eat. Microorganisms that cause food-borne illnesses can be destroyed or their growth severely limited by proper food-handling procedures. By learning about food contaminants, how they are spread, and how they can be prevented or controlled, workers can help ensure customer safety. They are also responsible for their own physical safety as well as that of their customers and fellow workers. Maintaining sanitary and safe facilities as well as high standards of personal hygiene are necessary parts of this responsibility.

▸ THE FOOD PRODUCT FLOW

The flow of food at a food establishment begins with receiving and storage. As foods are delivered they are inspected by receiving personnel and then placed quickly into storage. From storage, foods and ingredients are moved or "flow" into the preparation and handling stages of production. Not all food establishment managers will actually purchase food products. However, knowledge of the rules, regulations, and procedures for receiving and storing food is a must for everyone responsible for food safety.

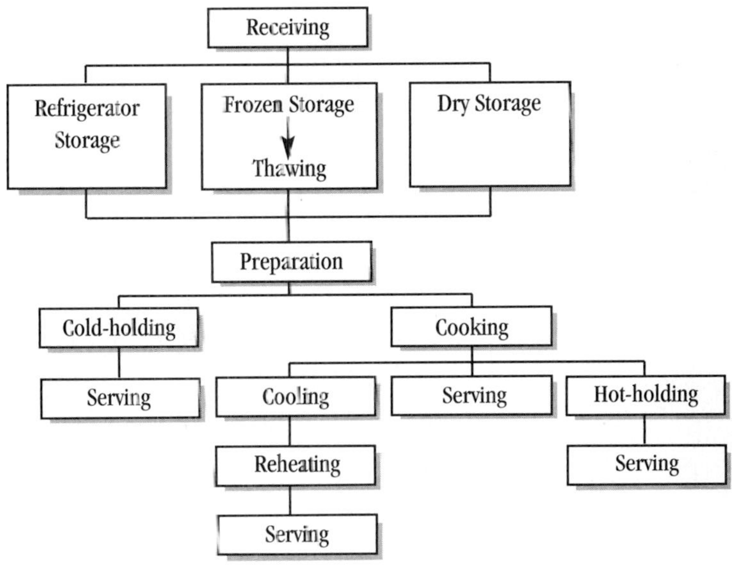

RECEIVING

Inspect all incoming food supplies to make sure they are at the proper temperature, in sound condition, and free from filth or spoilage. Always check product containers for tears, punctures, dents, or other signs of damage. Poor receiving procedures increase the chance of theft, acceptance of underweight merchandise, contamination, waste, or acceptance of products that do not meet specifications.

Schedule deliveries for off-peak times and have enough staff and space on hand to receive products quickly and correctly. Move incoming shipments to storage as soon as they arrive. Merchandise that is damaged, spoiled, or otherwise unfit for sale or use must be properly disposed of, held by the establishment for credit, or returned to the distributor. Distressed merchandise must be put aside to prevent contamination of other foods, equipment, utensils, linens, or single-service or single-use articles.

> **Safety Alert**
>
> Merchandise that is spoiled, or otherwise unfit for sale should be rejected by receiving personnel. Store rejected foods away from good food.

Whatever the size of the establishment, receiving requires prompt handling, quality control procedures, training staff who know product specifications, coding, proper checking of product temperatures, and proper handling of rejected merchandise.

BUYING FROM APPROVED SOURCES

Food quality and safety begin with foods and ingredients from approved sources—processors and suppliers that comply with federal, state, and local food safety laws and regulations. These sources are routinely inspected to make sure they follow good manufacturing practices. Foods prepared in a private home are not from an approved source and must not be used or sold in food establishments. Use of "home-canned" food is prohibited because of the high risk of food-borne illness, especially botulism.

INSPECTING DELIVERY VEHICLES

Suppliers must deliver food products to your food establishments in vehicles that are clean and in good repair. Delivery trucks must

- Maintain perishable and potentially hazardous foods at safe temperatures during transport.
- Be loaded in a manner that separates food items from non-food items (detergents, household cleaners, and pesticides) to prevent contamination and cross-contamination.
- Protect food packages from becoming damaged and torn during transit.

When delivery vehicles arrive at your establishment, receiving personnel should inspect them. Specific items to look for during these inspections are

- Cleanliness of the cargo area
- Temperature of refrigerated and frozen storage areas (if applicable)
- Proper separation of food and non-food items
- Signs of insect, rodent, or bird infestations

PACKAGING OF FOODS

Foods come in many different types of packages, including cans, bottles, jars, pouches, tubs, trays, bags, and boxes. The common purpose of the package is to

- Protect the contents from contamination.
- Provide a source of information about its nutritional contents.
- Provide advertising material.
- Make the product more convenient for customers to transport, prepare, and serve.

Dry foods such as flour, sugar, rice, and beans are commonly packaged in bags. These are not potentially hazardous foods and can be safely stored at room temperature. Check for contamination from chemicals or other substances that could cause food-borne illness.

REDUCED OXYGEN PACKAGING (ROP)

For many foods, oxygen in the air can increase chemical breakdown and microbial spoilage. Many food processors use reduced oxygen packaging to help overcome the effects of oxygen and preserved foods. Some examples of reduced oxygen packaging include vacuum packaging, modified atmosphere packaging, and sous vide foods.

Vacuum packaging removes air from a package and hermetically seals the package so a near-perfect vacuum remains inside. The term hermetic refers to a container completely heat-sealed to prevent the entry and loss of gases and vapors. The most commonly used hermetic packages are metal cans and glass jars. These containers will also stop the entry of bacteria, yeasts, molds, and other types of contamination as long as they remain undamaged.

▶ **hermetic** refers to a container completely heat-sealed to prevent the entry and loss of gases and vapors.

Upon receiving, metal cans must be checked for defects (see Table 2.38).

MODIFIED ATMOSPHERE PACKAGING (MAP)

Modified atmosphere packaging (MAP) helps preserve foods by replacing some or all of the oxygen inside the package with other gases such as carbon dioxide or nitrogen. MAP is used with a wide range of products including meat, fish, precut lettuce, baked products, cheese, coffee, nuts, and dried fruit. The MAP process has been successful in extending the shelf life of many products, and it reduces the amount of additives and preservatives required to prevent deterioration of the food. However, since low oxygen environments can create conditions conducive to the growth of anaerobic bacteria like *Clostridium botulinum*, proper handling of MAP foods is essential. MAP technology requires adequate refrigeration to be maintained during the entire shelf life of potentially hazardous foods. During the receiving process, employees must inspect potentially hazardous foods in modified atmosphere packages to make sure the package is in sound condition and the food is at 41°F (5°C) or below when it arrives at the establishment.

Table 2.38 **DEFECTIVE CANS**

Leaking or bulging	• Do not accept cans if they leak or bulge at either end • Swollen ends on a can indicate gas is being produced inside • Gas may be caused by a chemical reaction between the food and the metal in the container or by the bacteria and other microbes inside the can.
Dented	• Dents in cans do not harm the contents unless they have actually penetrated the can or the seam • Dents found in the side seams or end seams of a can are the most important • Do not accept cans if damage to these areas can affect the physical integrity of the can and may allow microorganisms to enter through tiny pinhole leaks • Shipments with many dented cans or torn labels indicate poor handling and storage procedures by the supplier.
Rusty	• Rust does not harm contents unless it has penetrated the can or seam • Rusty cans indicate exposure to excess moisture.

SOUS VIDE

Sous vide is a French term for "without air." It is a special packaging process where fresh raw foods are sealed in plastic pouches and the air is removed by vacuum. The pouches are then cooked at a low temperature and rapidly cooled to 38°F (3 °C) or below or frozen. The low cooking temperature of the sous vide process kills spoilage microorganisms. However, it does not destroy *C. botulinum* bacteria and their spores. Therefore, potentially hazardous foods processed using sous vide technology must be kept out of the food temperature danger zone during transport, storage, and display. Receiving personnel must inspect sous vide products to make sure the package is in sound condition and the food is at 41°F (5°C) or below as it arrives at the establishment. Some sous vide foods may require even colder temperatures during receipt and cold storage. Check with the manufacturer about cold-holding temperatures for any sous vide foods you purchase. If extended shelf life is desired, a temperature of 38°F (2°C) or lower must be maintained at all times. After receiving, the products should be moved quickly into refrigerated storage until ready for use.

BENEFITS OF ROP PACKAGING

The benefits to ROP packaging are numerous: it creates a largely oxygen-free environment that prevents the growth of aerobic bacteria, yeast, and molds largely responsible for the off odors, slime, texture changes, and other forms of spoilage; it prevents chemical reactions that can produce off odors and color changes in foods; and it reduces product shrinkage by preventing water loss.

Some products cannot be packed by ROP unless the food establishment is approved for the activity and inspected by the appropriate regulatory authority. These products include raw and smoked fish, soft cheeses (ricotta, cottage cheese, and cheese spreads), and combinations of cheese and other ingredients such as vegetables, meat, or fish. Contact your local regulatory authority to obtain a complete set of guidelines for ROP foods and to seek a variance for all food manufacturing/processing operations based on the prior approval of an HACCP plan.

Table 2.39 COMMON ROP PACKAGING CHOICES

Cook-Chill	A process that uses a plastic bag filled with hot cooked food from which air has been forced out and which is closed with a plastic or metal crimp.
Controlled Atmosphere Packaging (CAP)	A system that maintains the desired atmosphere within a package throughout the shelf life of a product by the use of agents to bind or scavenge oxygen or a small packet containing compounds to emit gas.
Modified Atmosphere Packaging (MAP)	A process that employs a gas flashing and sealing process or reduction of oxygen through respiration of vegetables or microbial action.
Sous Vide	A process where fresh raw foods are sealed in a plastic pouch and the air is removed by vacuum. The pouch is cooked at a low temperature and rapidly cooled to 38°F (3°C) or below or frozen.
Vacuum Packaging	Reduces the amount of air from a package and hermetically seals the package so a near-perfect vacuum remains inside.

Table 2.40 THE *FDA FOOD CODE* REQUIREMENTS FOR FOOD ESTABLISHMENTS THAT USE ROP TECHNOLOGY

Have a HACCP Plan	The food establishment must have an HACCP plan in place for the ROP operation that details how the seven principles are incorporated into the operation's food safety management system.
Use Two Microbial Growth Barriers	Because *Clostridium botulinum* is a significant health hazard, the establishment is required to have two microbial growth barriers. Time/temperature are commonly used as one barrier, but they need to be coupled with the use of pH, A_W, or product formulation to assure *Clostridium botulinum* will not grow inside the package.
Maintain foods at proper temperature	All potentially hazardous foods in ROP that rely on refrigeration as a barrier to microbial growth must be maintained at 41°F (3°C) or below.
Set Shelf Life	The refrigerated shelf life is to be no more than 14 days from packaging to consumption or the original manufacturer's "sell-by" or "use-by" date, whichever comes first.
Proper Label Warnings	Packages must be prominently and conspicuously labeled on the principal display panel with the instructions to maintain the food at 41°F (5°C) or below and to discard refrigerated food if within 14 days of its packaging it is not served for on-premises consumption or consumed if served or sold for off-premises consumption.
Use-by or Sell-by dates	Each container must bear a use-by or sell-by date. This date cannot exceed 14 days from packaging or repackaging without a variance granted by the regulatory authority.
Employee Training	Employees responsible for the ROP process must receive training that will enable them to understand the key components of the process, the equipment used, and the specific procedures that must be followed to ensure critical limits identified in the HACCP plan have been met. The training program must also outline the employee's responsibilities for monitoring and documenting the process and describe what corrective actions they must take when critical limits are not met.

FOOD IRRADIATION

Food irradiation is a preservation technique used by some food processing industries. This process involves exposing food to certain forms of radiation in order to destroy disease-causing microorganisms and delay spoilage.

The acceptance of irradiated foods has been limited due to customers' concerns about the safety of foods preserved in this manner. Contrary to many myths, irradiated food is not radioactive and does not pose a risk to the health and safety of people who eat it. Foods processed with irradiation are just as nutritious and flavorful as other foods that have been cooked, canned, or frozen.

Federal law required irradiated food to be labeled with the international symbol for irradiation called a "radura." This symbol must be accompanied by the words "Treated with Irradiation" or "Treated with Radiation."

Irradiation of food can effectively reduce or eliminate pathogens and spoilage microbes while maintaining the quality of most foods. This is a technology proven to be safe and should be welcomed by customers as an effective food preservation technique.

The FDA has approved food irradiation for a variety of foods including fruits, vegetables, grains, spices, poultry, pork, lamb, and, more recently, ground beef.

RED MEAT PRODUCTS

Most red meat and meat products sold in the United States come from cattle (beef), calves (veal), hogs (ham, pork, and bacon), sheep (mutton), and young sheep (lamb). These products are inspected for wholesomeness by officials of the U.S. Department of Agriculture (USDA) or state agencies. Animals must be inspected for wholesomeness to make certain they are free of disease and unacceptable defects. The USDA also offers voluntary meat grading services. Grades for meat represent the culinary quality or palatability of the meat and are not measures of product safety. (You'll find more information about USDA grading in Chapter 11, "Principles of Meat Cookery.")

Meat and meat products are available in several forms such as fresh, frozen, cured, smoked, dried, and canned. Since raw meats are potentially hazardous foods, never accept them if there is any sign of contamination, temperature abuse, or spoilage.

Safety Alert

Reject fresh meat if the product temperature exceeds 41°F (5°C) at delivery.

- Reject fresh meat if the product temperature exceeds 41°F (5°C) at delivery. Fresh meat should be firm and elastic to the touch and have characteristic aromas. Off odors are frequently indicators of spoilage. Sliminess is another characteristic of spoilage and is caused by bacterial growth on the surface of the meat. Control of factors that cause spoilage and sliminess also extends the shelf life of meat products and reduces shrink loss.
- Frozen meats should be solidly frozen when they arrive at the food establishment. Look for signs of freezing and thawing and refreezing such as frozen blood juices in the bottom of the container or the presence of large ice crystals on the surface of the product. Frozen meats should be packaged to prevent freezer burn.

Move fresh meat into refrigerated storage as quickly as possible. Frozen products should be moved from the delivery truck to the freezer while they are still solidly frozen.

Poultry

Some common examples of poultry are chicken, turkey, duck, and geese. USDA or state inspectors must inspect all poultry products to make certain they are wholesome and not adulterated. Adulterated food contains filth or is otherwise decomposed and unfit for human consumption. Inspected poultry products carry a USDA seal on the individual package or on bulk cartons.

Usually poultry is graded also for quality. Grade A poultry must have good overall shape and appearance, be meaty, be practically free from defects, and have a well-developed layer of fat in the skin.

Poultry products support the growth of disease-causing and spoilage microorganisms. The intestinal tract and skin of poultry may contain a variety of food-borne disease bacteria, including *Salmonella spp.* and *Campylobacter jejuni.* The near neutral pH, high moisture, and high protein content of poultry make it an ideal material for bacteria to grow in and on.

USDA inspection stamp for poultry.

Poultry products are also vulnerable to spoilage caused by enzymes and spoilage bacteria. Spoilage is indicated by meat tissue that is soft and slimy; has an objectionable odor, stickiness under the wings, and has discolored or darkened wing tips.

Poultry should be packaged on a bed of ice that drains away from the meat as it melts and held at or below 41°F (5°C).

Game Animals

Game animals are not permitted for sale in food establishments unless they meet federal code regulations. This ban does not apply to commercially raised game animals approved by regulatory agencies, field-dressed game allowed by state codes, or exotic species of animals that must meet the same standards as those of other game animals.

Game animals commercially bred for food must be raised, slaughtered, and processed according to standards used for meat and poultry. Common examples of animals raised away from the wild and used for food are farm-raised buffalo, ostrich, and alligator. The USDA inspects the slaughter and processing of this meat in the usual manner.

Grade stamps for USDA Grade A poultry.

Eggs

Most food establishments sell and use eggs in one form or another. Eggs are usually purchased by federal grades, the most common being AA, A, and B. Grades for eggs are based on exterior and interior conditions of the egg.

The USDA reports approximately 50 billion eggs are sold in the United States each year. *Salmonella enteritidis* bacteria are present in about 1% (approximately 500 million or one in 20,000) of the eggs sold. The bacteria enter the yolk of the egg as it is formed inside the hen. The eggshell surface may contain *Salmonella spp.* bacteria, especially if the shell is soiled with chicken droppings. Even if the shell is not cracked, bacteria can enter through the pores in the egg's shell.

Raw shell eggs should be clean, fresh, free of cracks, and refrigerated at an ambient air temperature of 45°F (7°C) or below when delivered. Shell eggs that have not been treated to destroy all viable Salmonella shall be stored and displayed in refrigerated equipment that maintains an ambient temperature of 45°F (7°C) or less. These eggs must be labeled to include safe handling instructions. The egg, when opened, should have no noticeable odor, a firm yolk, and the white should cling to the yolk. Reject eggs that are dirty or cracked, and remember washing eggs only increases the possibility of contamination.

An egg product is an egg without its shell. As a safeguard against *Salmonella spp*., the FDA requires all egg products, such as liquid, frozen, and dry eggs, be pasteurized to render them Salmonella-free. Pasteurized egg products should be in a sealed container and kept at 41°F (5°C). Egg containers should carry labels that verify the contents have been pasteurized. These products are well suited for facilities that offer food to people in highly susceptible populations.

FLUID MILK AND MILK PRODUCTS

This food group includes milk, cheese, ice cream, and other types of milk products. When receiving milk and milk products, make certain they have been pasteurized. Pasteurization destroys all disease-causing microorganisms in the milk and reduces the total number of bacteria, thus increasing shelf life. All market milk must be Grade A quality. Pasteurization also destroys natural milk enzymes that might shorten the shelf life of the products.

Milk that is marked "UHT" pasteurized has been heated to ultra-high temperatures and placed in aseptic packaging. UHT products can be stored safely for several weeks if kept under refrigeration. These products can be stored without refrigeration for short periods of time. Individual creamers are sometimes processed in this manner.

FLUID MILK

Under the Pasteurized Milk Ordinance, fluid milk can be received at 45°F (7°C) or less. It should be refrigerated immediately upon delivery and held at 41°F (5°C) or below. Individual containers of milk should be clearly marked with an expiration date and the number of the dairy plant that produced it. Check the expiration date of all dairy products before using them.

CHEESE

Cheese should be received at 41°F (5°C) and checked for the proper color, flavor, and characteristics. Reject the product if it contains mold that is not a normal part of the cheese or if the rind or package is damaged.

Emmenthaler (Swiss cheese)

BUTTER

Butter is made from pasteurized cream. Since disease-causing and spoilage bacteria and mold may grow in butter, handle the item as a perishable item. The most common type of deterioration in butter is the development of a strong rancid odor and flavor. Ensure butter has a firm texture, even color, and is free of mold. Packaged butter should be received at 41°F (5°C), intact, and provide protection for the contents.

FISH

Fish includes finfish harvested from saltwater and freshwater, and seafood that comes mainly from saltwater. Seafood consists of molluscan shellfish and crustaceans. Molluscan shellfish include oysters, clams, mussels, and scallops. Crustaceans include shrimp, lobster, and crab. Oysters, shrimp, catfish, salmon, and a few other types of finfish and seafood are being raised on fish farms using a technique called aquaculture.

Fish should be received at 41°F (5°C) or below and shellfish may be received at 45°F (7°C) or below. For better quality and shelf life, the optimum fish and shellfish receiving temperature often ranges from 30°F (-1°C) to 34°F (1.1°C). These products are generally more perishable than red meats even when stored in a refrigerator or freezer. They are commonly packed in self-draining ice to prevent drying and to maximize the shelf life of the food. Slime covering the outside of the fish contains a variety of bacteria that makes them highly susceptible to contamination and microbial spoilage. Fish are rich in unsaturated fatty acids that are susceptible to oxidation and the development of off flavors and rancidity.

Chinook or King Salmon

The quality of fish and seafood is measured by smell and appearance. Fresh finfish should have a mild, pleasant odor and bright, shiny skin with the scales tightly attached. If the fish head is intact, it should have clear, bulging eyes and bright red, moist gills. The flesh of fresh fish should be firm and elastic to the touch.

Mini Coho Salmon

Fish must be commercially and legally caught or harvested—except when caught recreationally—and approved for sale by the regulatory authority. All fish suppliers and warehouse operations must comply with the seafood HACCP program as required in 21 CRS 123. Ready-to-eat raw, marinated, or partially cooked fish other than molluscan shellfish must be frozen to time and temperature guidelines that meet *FDA Food Code* specifications in order to kill parasites. Records must be retained to show how the product was handled.

Shellfish must be purchased from sources approved by the Food and Drug Administration and the health departments of states located along the coastline where the shellfish is harvested. Shellfish transported from one state to another must come from sources listed in the Interstate Certified Shellfish Shippers List. The reason for requiring tight control over molluscan shellfish is to reduce the risk of infectious Hepatitis and other food-borne illnesses that may result from eating raw or insufficiently cooked forms of their product. Molluscan shellfish caught recreationally may not be used or sold in food establishments.

Black Sea Bream

When received at a food establishment, molluscan shellfish should be reasonably free of mud, dead shellfish, and shellfish with broken shells. Damaged shellfish must be discarded.

Molluscan shellfish must be purchased in containers that bear legible sources-identification tags or labels fastened to the container by the harvester and each dealer that shucks, ships, or reships the shellstock. Molluscan shellfish tags must contain the harvester's identification number; the date of harvesting; an identification of the harvest location or aquaculture site including an abbreviation of the state or country in which the shellfish are harvested; the shellfish type and quantity; and a statement in bold, capitalized type that says "THIS TAG IS REQUIRED TO BE ATTACHED UNTIL CONTAINER IS EMPTY AND THEREAFTER KEPT ON FILE FOR 90 DAYS."

Tilapia

If seafood is suspected of being the source of food-borne illness, the investigating team can use the tags to determine where and when the produce was harvested and processed.

For display purposes, shellstock may be removed from the tagged or labeled container in which they are received. The shellstock must be placed on drained ice or held in a display container. Care must be taken to protect shellstock from contamination during display.

Shellstock containers must be kept until every piece of product from that batch is gone.

The identity of the source of shellstock that has been removed from a tagged or labeled container for display must be preserved. This can be accomplished by using an approved record-keeping system that keeps shellstock tags or labels in sequence based upon the date when, or dates during which the shellstock are sold or served. Shellstock from one tagged or labeled container must not be commingled with shellstock from another container before being ordered by the customer. Commingling is combining shellfish harvested on different days or from different growing areas as identified on the tag or label, or combining shellfish from containers with different codes or different shucking dates.

FRUITS AND VEGETABLES

Whole raw fruits and vegetables that will be washed by customers before they are eaten do not need to be washed at the establishment before they are sold.

Most fruits and vegetables have a short shelf life. They continue to ripen even after they are picked. Therefore, they may become too ripe if not properly handled. Microorganisms found in water and soil can also cause fruits and vegetables to spoil. Fruits and vegetables hold their top quality for only a few days.

Purchase raw fruits and vegetables from approved sources and wash them thoroughly to remove soil and other contaminants before they are cut, combined with other ingredients, cooked, served, or offered for human consumption in a ready-to-eat form.

Limes

Most fresh fruits and vegetables are usually not considered potentially hazardous foods (PHFs). Often the acidity and/or outer skin will prevent the entry and growth of harmful bacteria. However, sprouts and cut melons are now considered PHFs and should be handled in the same manner as other PHFs. Even so, the number of cases of food-borne illnesses linked to these kinds of products has increased in recent years. This is largely due to increased consumption of fresh fruits and vegetables and the emergence of microbes that can cause disease with a low number of organisms. Shiga toxin-producing *Escherichia coli*, *Shigella spp*., Hepatitis A virus, and *Cyclospora spp*. can be infective with only a few cells. Therefore, they do not require a potentially hazardous food to multiply. Though not required, whole raw fruits and vegetables may be washed using cleaners. In some cases, an additional anti-microbial rinse (water or bath) is used to reduce the number microorganisms present on the surface. When these types of chemicals are used, they must meet the requirements in the *Code of Federal Regulations* (21 CFR 173.315). The fruits and vegetables should also be rinsed to remove as much of the residues of these chemicals as possible.

Valencia Oranges

Some products, like wild mushrooms, may only be used if they have been inspected and approved by a mushroom-identification expert who is approved by the regulatory authority. Beware of fresh mushrooms packed in Styrofoam trays and covered with plastic shrink-wrap. Mushrooms use up the oxygen inside the package quickly. Unless holes are poked in the plastic wrap that covers the package to permit oxygen inside, oxygen-free conditions may occur that are favorable for the growth of *C. botulinum* bacteria.

JUICE

Juice includes the liquid extract from one or more fruits or vegetables, purees of the edible portions of one or more fruits or vegetables, or any concentrates of such liquid or puree. According to the *FDA Food Code*, this group of foods includes juice as a whole beverage, an ingredient of a beverage, and a puree as an ingredient of a beverage.

Scallions

Most of the juices sold in food establishments are obtained from processors in a prepacked form. These juice processors must have an HACCP system in place. In most instances, the processor will pasteurize or otherwise treat the juice to attain 99.999% reduction of the most resistant disease-causing microorganisms. Juice packed in a food establishment must

- Be treated under an HACCP plan as specified in the 2001 *FDA Food Code* to attain a 99.999% reduction of the most resistant microorganisms of public health significance, or if the juice is not treated to destroy pathogens.
- Bear a warning label that informs customers "This has not been pasteurized and, therefore, may contain harmful bacteria that can cause serious illness in children, the elderly, and persons with weakened immune systems."

White Onions

FROZEN FOODS

Frozen products must be solidly frozen when delivered. Check the temperature of frozen foods by placing the sensing portion of a thermometer between two packages. Receiving personnel should also look for signs the product has been thawed and refrozen.

Common signs of thawing and refreezing are

- Large ice crystals or frost on the surface of the food
- Frozen liquid or juice at the bottom on the package
- Mushy soft products.

Reject frozen foods not solidly frozen or that show signs of temperature abuse.

STORAGE OF FOOD

Employees must check incoming shipments carefully and quickly move received items to proper storage. Stock rotation is a very important part of effective food storage. A first-in, first-out method of stock rotation helps ensure older foods are used first. Product containers should be marked with a date or other readily identifiable code to help employees know which product has been in storage longest. When expecting food shipments, always make certain the older stock is moved to the front of the storage area to make room for the newly arriving products.

TYPES OF STORAGE

The three most common types of food storage areas in food establishments are the refrigerator, freezer, and dry storage.

Refrigeration

Refrigerated storage is used to hold potentially hazardous and perishable foods. It slows down microbial growth and controls quality by holding foods at 41°F (5°C) or below. Some common types of refrigerated storage equipment found in food establishments are walk-in, reach-in, under-the-counter refrigerators, and cold display units, among others.

In order to maintain the temperature of potentially hazardous foods at 41°F (5°C) or below, equipment should maintain the air temperature in the storage compartment at about 38°F (3°C). Fish and shellfish are especially vulnerable to spoilage and should be stored at colder temperatures ranging from 30°F (-1°C) to 34°F (1.1°C). Some fruits and vegetables, such as bananas and potatoes, undergo undesirable chemical changes when they are refrigerated. Therefore, although fruits and vegetables are perishable products, not all types should be refrigerated. For perishability, fresh fruits and vegetables requiring refrigeration should be stored at temperatures between 33°F (1°C) and 41°F (5°C). Unpasteurized juices and potentially hazardous fruits and vegetables, like cut melons and sprouts, must be refrigerated at 41°F (5°C) or below.

The unit should maintain air temperature of 38°F (3°C). Check temperatures daily in the warmest part of the unit to ensure accuracy using an indicating or recording thermometer. Keep the unit door closed to maintain temperature.

Freezing

Freezer storage is designed to keep foods solidly frozen. Freezer equipment must also be equipped with indicating or recording thermometers to monitor the temperature of the ambient air inside the unit. If your freezer is not frost free, defrost it regularly to ensure proper operation. Wrap frozen foods and transfer them to the refrigerator storage area until the defrosting process is complete.

Although bacteria are generally not destroyed by freezing, parasites can be killed if foods are frozen at the proper temperature for the proper length of time. Guidelines have been established for destroying parasites in raw-marinated and marinated, partially cooked fish.

Yellowfin, bigeye, bluefin-northern, bluefin-southern, and certain other species of tuna may be served or sold in a raw, raw-marinated, or partially cooked ready-to-eat form without freezing.

Safety Alert

Food should be frozen throughout to -4°F (-20°C) and held for 7 days in a freezer; or, food should be frozen throughout to -31°F (-35°C) using a blast chiller, and held at that temperature for 15 hours.

Source: 2001 Food Code.

Table 2.41 IMPORTANT PROCEDURES FOR COLD STORAGE

- Keep refrigerated foods at 41°F (5°C) or below and frozen foods solidly frozen during storage.
- Rotate refrigerated and frozen foods on a first-in, first-out (FIFO) basis and store foods in covered containers that are properly labeled and dated.
- Store foods in refrigerated and freezer storage areas at least 6 inches off the floor and space products to allow the cold air to circulate around them.
- Store raw products under cooked or ready-to-eat foods to prevent cross-contamination.
- Keep different species of raw animal foods separate during storage. If limited storage space makes it necessary to store different species in the same area of the refrigerator, store poultry on the bottom shelf, ground beef and pork on the middle shelf, and fish, eggs, and other cuts of red meat on the top shelf.

Dry Storage

Products in dry storage areas are usually packed in labeled cans, bottles, jars, and bags. The area should have a room temperature of 50°F (10°C) to 70°F (21°C) with a relative humidity of 50 to 60% to maximize shelf life of stored products. Windows should be blocked or shaded. When considering dry storage, keep the following in mind:

- Use slatted shelves that allow circulation of air, are at least 6 inches off the floor, and are away from the wall. This allows for cleaning under the shelving and discourages pest harborage.
- When bulk items are moved into bulk food grade containers with tight-fitting lids, include code, labels, and dates.
- Scoops and other utensils should be food grade and have long handles that keep hands from touching food.
- Do not use toilet rooms, locker areas, mechanical rooms, and similar spaces for storage of food, single-service items, paper goods, or equipment and utensils.
- Do not expose products to overhead water and server lines unless the lines are shielded to interfere with potential drips.

Chemical Storage

Toxic chemicals, such as cleaners, sanitizers, and pesticides, are commonly used and sold in food establishments. Most of these products can be poisonous if consumed accidentally.

Many chemicals used in food establishments are poisonous if consumed. Others can cause irritation to skin and respiratory system:

- All products must be labeled and kept separate from food products. If an adequate storage area is not available, use a locked cabinet to store the chemicals.
- Identify the chemical and include directions on proper use.
- Train employees on how to use these products safely.
- It is good practice to post lists of instructions so users can easily see when and how to use the products.

Safety Alert

A good label identifies the chemical, provides directions on how to use it safely, and instructs people on what first-aid measures to use in case of accidents.

Table 2.42 STORAGE CONDITIONS FOR FOOD

PRODUCT	STORAGE CONDITIONS
Meat and meat products	• Store for up to three weeks at temperatures between 28°F (-2°C) and 32°F (0°C) and a relative humidity between 85 and 90%. • Cold temperatures extend the shelf life of red meats by slowing down the growth of bacteria that cause spoilage and reduce shrink loss. • Store for several months when held at 0°F (-18°C) or below. • Frozen meats must be wrapped in moisture-proof paper to prevent them from drying out. • Packaging for frozen foods should also be strong, flexible, and protect against light. • Use by manufacturer's shelf-life criteria.
Poultry	• Store at temperatures between 28°F (-2°C) and 32°F (0°C) for short periods of time. • A relative humidity of 75 to 85% is recommended, as excessive humidity causes sliminess due to excessive bacterial growth. • Poultry should be wrapped carefully to prevent dehydration, contamination, and loss of quality. • Frozen poultry and poultry products can be stored for four to six months when held at 0°F (-18°C) or below. • Use by manufacturer's shelf-life criteria.
Whole shell eggs	• Keep fresh for up to two weeks when stored at 41°F (5°C) or below. • It is recommended to store eggs at 34°F (1°C) to 38°F (3°C) to maintain optimum quality. • Keep eggs covered and store them away from onions and other foods that have a strong odor. • Discard eggs that are dirty or cracked. • Always make sure to wash your hands after handling whole shell eggs. • Egg products (such as whole eggs, egg whites, and yolks) are pasteurized to destroy Salmonella bacteria. • Store products at 41°F (5°C) or below. • Store frozen eggs at 0°F (-18°C) or below and keep them frozen until time for defrosting. • Once dried eggs have been reconstituted, they are considered potentially hazardous and must be stored at 41°F (5°C) or below. • Use by manufacturer's shelf-life criteria.
Milk	• Pasteurized milk may be held at 41°F (5°C) or less for up to ten days or longer. • The optimal storage temperature for fluid milk is 34°F (1°C) to 38°F (3°C), and the shelf life of milk is shortened significantly at higher storage temperatures. • Milk also picks up odors from other foods. Store milk in an area away from onions and other foods that give off odors. • Use by manufacturer's shelf-life criteria.
Fish and Shellfish	• More perishable than red meats even when refrigerated or frozen. • Fish and shellfish should be stored at temperatures ranging from 30°F to 34°F (-1 to 1°C). • Fish should be kept on crushed ice drained away from the product or solidly frozen. Recommend using fresh fish within 24 hours or less. • Shellfish shells should close when tapped. Dead shellfish must be discarded. Lobsters and clams should be kept alive until cooked or frozen. Keep shellfish tags for 90 days after purchase. If a food-borne outbreak occurs, the tags help identify the source.
Fresh fruits and vegetables	• Require temperatures between 41°F (5°C) and 45°F (7°C) in a relative humidity of 85 to 90%. • If fruits and vegetables arrive packed in airtight film, notify your supplier to correct this issue to allow the produce to respire. • Produce should not be washed before storage—wash before using. • Proper circulation is necessary to maintain freshness and firmness. Discard fruits that begin to spoil. • Whole citrus fruits and bananas should not be refrigerated.
Modified atmosphere packaging (MAP) and sous vide products	• MAP products are perishable foods and must be kept at temperatures recommended by the processor. • Most will need refrigeration at 41°F (5°C) or below. If frozen, keep solidly frozen until thawed and used. • Check expiration dates before using. Discard out-of-date products. • Do not use packages that have signs of microbial growth (slime, bubbles, molds, etc.)

PREPARATION OF SERVICE

The preparation and service of foods can involve one or more steps. Small food establishments, such as convenience stores, buy foods in ready-to-eat forms that are stored until sold. Large operations, such as restaurants, supermarkets, and institutional kitchens, prepare large quantities of food. Preparation and service are complex operations in these larger establishments. They can involve many steps and span several hours or days.

Regardless of how many steps are involved in food production and service, food-borne illness prevention requires effective food safety measures that assure good personal hygiene and avoid cross-contamination and temperature abuse.

During preparation, an important technique to follow is "small batch" preparation. Food preparation is usually done at room temperature. This is several degrees into the temperature danger zone. Therefore, you must limit the amount of time the food is in the temperature danger zone by working with small and manageable amounts of potentially hazardous foods and ingredients.

INGREDIENT SUBSTITUTION

For meal solutions and home meal replacements, there is normally a recipe for the products prepared in the food establishment. The receipt usually includes a list of ingredients and instructions for how to prepare, store, and label the food item.

- When one or more of the original ingredients is not available for a recipe, other ingredients may be substituted so the food items can still be prepared and sold.
- All ingredient substitutions should be identified in the recipes before preparation.
- Ingredient substitutions must never compromise the safety of the food and should not be allowed unless they are identified and allowed in the recipe.

AVOIDING TEMPERATURE ABUSE

Temperature and time abuse is when food is kept in the temperature danger zone, 41°F (5°C) to 135°F (57°C), long enough for harmful organisms to grow.

- Monitoring and controlling food temperatures are extremely effective ways to minimize the risks of food-borne illnesses.
- Thermometers are used for stored, cooked, hot-held, cold-held, and reheated foods. Before using a thermometer, make sure it is clean, sanitary, and properly calibrated. Always insert the "sensor" portion or probe stem of the thermometer into the thickest part of the food. In most instances, this will be at the center of the food product or container.

THAWING

The *FDA Food Code* requires raw animal foods to be thawed in less than 4 hours including the time it takes for preparation for cooking or to lower the food temperature to 41°F (5°C) under refrigeration. Thawed portions of ready-to-eat foods should not be allowed to rise above 41°F (5°C) when using the cool water thawing process.

Food establishments will sometimes use a slacking (defrosting) process to moderate the temperature of foods prior to cooking or reheating. During the slacking process, foods can be defrosted under refrigeration that maintains the foods at 41°F (5°C) or less or at any temperature if the food remains frozen. The slacking process is typically used with previously block-frozen food such as spinach.

Under no circumstances should foods be thawed or slacked at room temperature. Room temperature thawing puts foods in the temperature danger zone—the very thing you don't want to have happen. When foods are thawed at room temperature, the outer surface of the food thaws first and will soon reach room temperature. Microbial growth occurs very quickly at room temperature.

Table 2.43 GUIDELINES FOR THAWING FOOD

Refrigeration

- Use refrigeration that maintains the food temperature at 41°F (5°C) or below.

Submerge under Running Water

Completely submerge under running water

- At a temperature of 70°F (21°C) or below
- With enough water force to remove contaminants from the surface of the food
- For a period of time that does not allow thawed portions of ready-to-eat foods to rise above 41°F (5°C)
- For a period of time that does not allow thawed portions of a raw animal food requiring cooking to be in the temperature danger zone for more than a total time of 4 hours.

As Part of the Cooking Process

Thawing for Immediate Service

- Use any procedure (e.g., microwave oven) that thaws a portion of frozen ready-to-eat food prepared for immediate service in response to an individual customer's order.

COLD STORAGE

Most harmful microorganisms start to grow at temperatures above 41°F (5°C). Some bacteria, such as *Listeria moncytogenes*, can grow slowly at temperatures below 41°F (5°C).

FROZEN, READY-TO-EAT FOODS

When large amounts of food are removed from the freezer, they should be marked to indicate the date by which the food must be sold. Ready-to-eat potentially hazardous food must be used within seven calendar days or less after the food is removed from the freezer, minus the time before freezing. Subtract any time if the food is maintained at 41°F (5°C) or less before freezing.

When displaying ready-to-eat potentially hazardous foods like prepared salads and luncheon meats, be sure the refrigerator unit can maintain a safe cold-holding temperature. This may be more difficult in open top and open front refrigerated display cases that do not have doors. Refrigerated display cases have a "safe load line." This line indicates the level below which foods must be stored to ensure the food is held at the proper temperature. It is also important to store foods so the discharge or return air vents are not blocked.

PREPACKAGED FOODS

A refrigerated, ready-to-eat, potentially hazardous food prepared and held in a food establishment for more than 24 hours, or originating from an original contained prepared and packaged by a food processing plant and opened at the food establishment must be discard if it

- Exceeds the prescribed time and temperature requirements,
- Is in a container or package that does not bear a date and time, or
- Is marked with a date or day that exceeds the time and temperature combinations described above.

Table 2.44 COLD HOLDING AT A GLANCE: REFRIGERATORS, DISPLAY CASE AND COLD SERVICE BARS

Cold raw potentially hazardous (like meat)
Temperature: Below 41°F (5°C)

- Physical barriers should be in place to separate different species (meat, poultry, seafood) and to separate raw from ready-to-eat foods.

Fish and seafood
Temperature: Below 41°F (5°C)

- Use ice from potable water
- Transport ice in "approved food-contact" containers
- Liquid must be drained from ice to prevent contamination
- Ice in contact with fish and shellfish is considered contaminated—DO NOT REUSE
- Cooked and raw product should be kept separate.

Cold ready-to-eat potentially hazardous foods
Temperature: Below 41°F (5°C) up to 7 calendar days

- If held more than 24 hours, *FDA Food Code* recommends prepared and held products be marked with "sell-by" or "use-by" dates.

Ready-to-eat salads
Temperature: As cold as possible above 32°F (0°C) and below 41°F (5°C)

- Pre-chill ingredients before using
- Prepare small batches to assure food is not in the temperature danger zone too long.

COOKING

Meat, poultry, fish, seafood, eggs, and unprepared milk should not be prepared and served raw or rare. Establishments that choose to serve raw foods increase the risk of causing a food-borne illness. Raw animal foods need to be cooked to the proper temperatures to be safe. Many states and jurisdictions require an advisory be posted to warn consumers of the risk.

Most foods are cooked using stoves, conventional ovens, and microwave ovens. Because heat transfer can be different depending on the heating source, final temperature requirements have been set for conventional oven cooking and microwave cooking.

Casseroles and other foods that contain a combination of raw ingredients such as meat and poultry must be cooked to a final temperature that coincides with the highest risk food. In this case, 165°F (74°C) is required to destroy pathogens that may be found in the poultry. Food mixtures, such as chili and beef stew, must be cooked to 165°F (74°C) to assure proper destruction of disease-causing agents.

When cooking foods in the microwave oven, the distribution of heat is often uneven. Stirring and rotating the food during the cooking process will enable heat to be distributed more evenly. The *FDA Food Code* requires raw animal foods cooked in a microwave oven to be heated to 165°F (74°C) in all parts of the food. As a common practice, foods cooked in a microwave oven should be allowed to stand covered for two minutes before serving to allow the heat inside the product to disperse more evenly.

The internal temperature of raw animal foods cooked in the microwave oven must reach 165°F (74°C) or above.

Table 2.45 COOKING GUIDELINES FOR POTENTIALLY HAZARDOUS FOODS

FOOD TYPE	MINIMUM INTERNAL TEMPERATURE	MINIMUM TIME HELD AT INTERNAL TEMPERATURE BEFORE SERVING
Beef Roast (rare)	130°F (54°C) 140°F (60°C)	112 minutes 12 minutes
Eggs, Beef and Pork (other than Roasts), Fish	145°F (63°C)	15 seconds
Ground Beef, Ground Pork, and Ground Game Animals	155°F (68°C)	15 seconds
Beef Roast (medium), Pork Roast, and Ham	145°F (63°C)	4 minutes
All Poultry, Stuffed meats	165°F (74°C)	15 seconds

Note: When microwave cooking, heat raw animal foods to a temperature of 165°F (74°C) in all parts of the food.

Source: *FDA Food Code.*

For most foods, the internal temperature will be measured by inserting the probe of the thermometer or thermocouple into the center or thickest part of the food mass. This will give you an accurate reading of the internal temperature of the product.

COOLING

Safety Alert

Improper cooling is one of the leading contributors to food-borne illness in food establishments.

Foods are in the temperature danger zone during cooling and there is no way to avoid it. After proper cooking, potentially hazardous foods need to be cooled from 135°F (57°C) to 41°F (5°C) as rapidly as possible. The *FDA Food Code* recommends hot foods, not used for immediate service or hot display, be cooled from 135°F (57°C) to 70°F (21°C) within 2 hours, and from 135°F (57°C) to 41°F (5°C) or less within 6 hours.

Table 2.46 COMMON METHODS FOR REDUCING COOLING TIME

- Blast chillers
- Walk-in coolers, loosely covered
- Use containers that facilitate heat transfer (stainless steel)
- Transfer food into shallow pans that will allow for a product depth of 3 inches or less
- Transfer food into smaller containers
- Place container of hot food in an ice water bath
- Stir food while cooling
- Use cooling paddles to stir the food
- Add ice as ingredient directly to a condensed food.

Potentially hazardous foods prepared from ingredients, such as reconstituted foods and canned tuna, which have been held at room temperature, must be cooled to 41°F (5°C) or less within 4 hours.

Foods must pass through the temperature danger zone as quickly as possible.

Never assume any one method is working without checking the temperature and time foods take to cool. Always depend on the thermometer reading with any of the methods you use to cool food.

Safety Alert

Always use a thermometer to verify foods are cooling properly.

HOT-HOLDING AND REHEATING

All potentially hazardous foods that have been cooked and are intended to be held hot (not cooled, stored, and reheated) must be maintained at 135°F (57°C) or above.

- Hot-holding is also required when hot potentially hazardous foods are delivered to sites away from the food establishment.
- During hot-holding, never add fresh product to existing product and always work in small batches.
- Reheat to at least 165°F (74°C) within 2 hours.

Ready-to-eat foods commercially prepared and packaged and from a food processing plant under regulatory inspection should be free of harmful microorganisms. Therefore, these foods may be reheated to a temperature of at least 135°F (57°C) for hot-holding [rather than a minimum of 165°F (74°C)]. Commercially prepared and cooked soups would be a good example of a food that would only need to be reheated to 135°F (57°C) or above followed by hot-holding.

While temperature is usually the most important factor in controlling microbes, there are some situations where controlling time can also be used. That is why there is an allowance of four hours in the temperature danger zone for ready-to-eat potentially hazardous food held for food service or immediate consumption. Sliced pizza and fried chicken are good examples. If these potentially hazardous foods were hot-held at 135°F (57°C) or above, the food may dry out and the quality may deteriorate very quickly.

Avoid holding potentially hazardous foods in the temperature danger zone. Most establishments will limit this amount of time to 20 to 30 minutes. In these instances, it is critical to achieve the required cooking temperature and the amount of time foods are held in the temperature danger zone must be carefully monitored and recorded. The procedures and monitoring required when using time as a method of control varies. Consult your local regulatory authority for requirements in your jurisdiction.

SERVING SAFE FOOD

Employees must practice good personal hygiene when serving food. This starts with a clean uniform and an effective hair treatment.

- Food handlers should avoid touching food with their bare hands.
- They can use tongs, serving spoons, disposable gloves, or deli tissue when handling meats, cheeses, prepared salads, or when making sandwiches.
- Employees must hold serving utensils by the handle only, and they must never touch the part of the utensil that comes into contact with food.
- A single utensil should be use for each food item, and the utensil should be stored in the food between uses.
- Always store serving utensils in a way that permits the employee to grab the handle without touching the food.

Food that has been served or sold to and is in the possession of a customer may not be returned and offered for service or sale to another customer. Two acceptable exceptions to this rule are

- A container of non-potentially hazardous food (e.g., a narrow-neck bottle of catsup or steak sauce) that is dispensed in a way that protects the food from contamination and the container is closed between uses; or
- Non-potentially hazardous foods such as crackers, salt, or pepper in an unopened, original package and that is maintained in a sound condition.

Employees must remember to wash their hands after touching soiled equipment, utensils, and cloths. If disposable gloves are used, a fresh pair of gloves should be put on immediately prior to handling any food products.

DISCARDING OR RECONDITIONING FOOD

A food that is unsafe, adulterated, or not honestly presented shall be reworked or reconditioned using a procedure approved by the regulatory authority in the jurisdiction, or it must be discarded.

Food must be discarded if it is not from an approved source or has been contaminated by food employees, consumers, or other persons via soiled hands, bodily discharges (e.g., coughs and sneezes), or other means.

Ready-to-eat foods must be discarded if they have been contaminated by an employee who has been restricted or excluded (e.g., an employee who is ill, or who has been exposed to a contaminant, such as hepatitis).

REFILLING RETURNABLE CONTAINERS

A take-home food container returned to a food establishment may not be refilled with a potentially hazardous food at the establishment. A food-specific container for beverages may be refilled at a food establishment if

- Only a beverage that is not a potentially hazardous food is dispensed into the container.
- The design of the container and of the rinsing equipment and the nature of the beverage, when considered together, allow effective cleaning of the container at home or in the food establishment.
- Facilities for rinsing before refilling returned containers with fresh, hot water that is under pressure and not recirculated are provided as part of the dispensing system.
- The consumer-owned container returned to the food establishment for refilling is refilled for sale or service only to the same consumer.
- The container is refilled by an employee of the food establishment or the owner of the container if the beverage system includes a contamination-free transfer process that cannot be bypassed by the container owner.

Personal take-out beverage containers, such as thermally insulated bottles, nonspill coffee cups, and promotional beverage glasses, may be refilled by employees or the consumer if the refilling process will protect the food and food-contact surface of the container from contamination.

SELF-SERVICE BAR

Self-service salad and hot food buffet bars are very popular in food establishments. They offer convenience and a wide range of selections for customers. The most important food safety goals for this type of operation are to

- Protect foods from contamination by customers.
- Keep foods out of the temperature danger zone.

Keep the following in mind when dealing with a self-service bar in your establishment:

- A properly installed sneeze guard protects the food from contamination by your customers.
- Never place raw animal foods on self-service bars, except for ready-to-eat foods like sushi and shellfish or meats that will be cooked on the premises. Keep hot-held potentially hazardous food at 135°F (57°C) or above and cold foods at 41°F (5°C) or below.
- Use clean and sanitized utensils in a self-service bar and replace any utensils that become contaminated or soiled.
- Use only one utensil for each food items and store it in the food between uses.

If customers are allowed to visit the self-service bar more than once, they must be given a clean plate or bowl for each trip. This will reduce the risk of contaminating food on display at the bar. Beverage cups and glasses may be reused to get refills.

TEMPORARY FACILITIES AND MOBILE FOOD FACILITIES

A temporary food establishment (TFE) is defined by *FDA Food Code* as a food establishment that operates for a period of no more than 14 consecutive days in conjunction with a single event or celebration. TFEs may operate either indoors or outdoors and often have limited physical and sanitary facilities available.

▶ **temporary food establishment** is a food establishment that operates for a period of no more than 14 consecutive days in conjunction with a single event or celebration.

Some food establishments are offering food by way of temporary and mobile facilities. A variety of foods can be prepared and served from temporary stands and trailers. Some examples include sandwiches, pizza, barbecue ribs, gyros, corn on the cob, confections (e.g., cotton candy, funnel cakes, or elephant ears), and beverages.

Mobile facilities are trucks and trailers used to cater events located away from the establishment. The extent of food items offered through catering operations is practically unlimited.

The same food safety practices employed in other areas of the establishment must also be applied at temporary, mobile facilities, and in-store product demonstrations. In particular, food must be protected from

- Temperature abuse
- Infected employees who practice poor personal hygiene and use improper food-handling practices
- Contamination and cross-contamination.

Employees shall use tongs, utensils, and deli tissue to avoid bare hand contact with food. Disposable gloves can provide an additional barrier against contamination. However, gloves must not be viewed as a substitute for proper hand washing.

Safety Alert

Employees must not eat or smoke around food, and they must wash their hands whenever they are contaminated.

Food must be protected from contamination and cross-contamination. Food on display must be protected from contamination by customers and employees. Food equipment must be designed and constructed to make it smooth, easily cleanable, nontoxic, and nonabsorbent.

Use disposable utensils whenever possible. When it is necessary to use multiple-use utensils, they must be washed and sanitized using a four-step process:

1. Wash in hot, soapy water.
2. Rinse in clean water.
3. Use chemical sanitizing rinse.
4. Air-dry.

Garbage and paper wastes should be placed in containers lined with plastic bags and equipped with tight-fitting lids. Food and wastes must be kept covered to avoid attracting insects, rodents, and other pests.

VENDING MACHINES

Safety Alert

It is a good idea to establish sell-by or best-if-used-by dates and codes for these ready-to-eat foods.

A vending machine is a self-service device which dispenses individually sized services of food and beverages after a customer inserts a coin, paper currency, token, card, key, or makes a payment by another means. Some vending machines dispense food and beverages in bulk while others dispense products in individually wrapped packages. Vending machines are available that will dispense potentially hazardous, ready-to-eat foods (e.g., sandwiches, French fries, dairy products, and soup) and non-potentially hazardous foods (e.g., candy, snack chips, pastries, coffee, and soft drinks).

Vending machines that store and dispense potentially hazardous foods must have adequate refrigeration and/or heating units, insulation, and controls to keep cold foods cold and hot foods hot. These machines must also be equipped with an automatic control that prevents the machine from vending food if there is a power failure, mechanical failure or other condition that prevents cold food from being maintained at 41°F (5°C) or below and hot food maintained at 135°F (57°C) or above.

The temperature cutoff requirement does not apply

- In a cold food machine during a period not to exceed 30 minutes immediately after the machine is filled, serviced, or restocked;
- In a hot food machine during a period not to exceed 120 minutes immediately after the machine is filled, serviced, or restocked.

Refrigerated, ready-to-eat, potentially hazardous foods prepared in a food establishment and dispensed through a vending machine (with an automatic shutoff control) shall be discarded if it exceeds the time and temperature combinations prescribed by the *FDA Food Code*, or is not correctly date labeled.

HOME MEAL REPLACEMENT

▶ **Home meal replacements** come in "ready-to-cook," "ready-to-heat," and "ready-to-eat."

Home meal replacements and meal solutions are the terms most often used to refer to high-quality meals prepared away from home but eaten at home. These types of products are now a multi-billion dollar business for food establishments throughout the country. The move toward prepared food has supermarkets selling complete meals instead of just ingredients. Supermarkets and restaurants are now competing head-to-head for the "heat-and-eat" business that has become very popular with today's customers.

Home meal replacements come in "ready-to-cook," "ready-to-heat," and "ready-to-eat."

All three varieties are designed to save time and effort for families that are too tired to cook at the end of the day. Ready-to-eat foods are a common variety of home meal replacements.

Home meal replacements should be labeled so customers understand how to keep the product safe when they take it home. Warn them against keeping the food in the car of keeping it at room temperature when they get home. Pamphlets and brochures stuffed into bags or stapled to the front of bags can help educate customers about safe handling of home meal replacements. Operators must be able to show they've done everything in their power, including written documentation and following industry standards, to make the food safe.

BACK TO THE STORY...

It is most likely the Salmonella Poona organisms were carried from the outside rind of the cantaloupe onto the fruit by knives used to slice and cut the melon. Washing the outer rind of the melon with clean running water and a soft bristle brush can reduce the risk of contamination. Cut melon, including cantaloupe, is classified as a potentially hazardous food and must be held at 41°F (5°C) or below during storage and display.

CONCLUSION

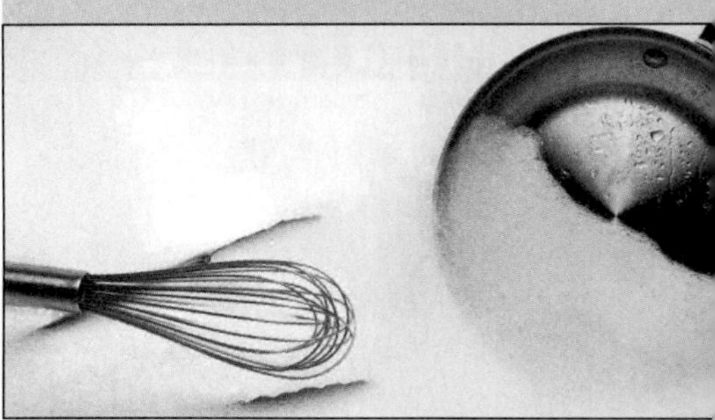

Foods should only be allowed in the temperature danger zone for a short time during thawing, heating, and cooling activities. The three main contributors to food-borne illness in food establishments are

- Time and temperature abuse
- Cross-contamination
- Poor personal health and hygiene practices by food handlers.

These factors must be controlled throughout the flow of food to assure food safety. Preparation and service are critical processes in your establishment because they are the last steps you take before your customer eats the food.

QUESTIONS FOR DISCUSSION

1. Foods can be contaminated in several ways. Explain the differences between biological, chemical and physical contamination. Give an example of each.
2. Under what conditions will bacteria thrive? Explain what you can do to alter these conditions.
3. What is the temperature danger zone? What is its significance in food preparation?
4. Explain how improper or inadequate pest management can lead to food-borne illnesses.
5. Define HACCP. How is this system used in a typical food service facility?

CHAPTER THREE

AND, INDEED, IS THERE NOT SOMETHING HOLY
ABOUT A GREAT KITCHEN?
THE SCOURED GLEAM OF ROW UPON ROW OF METAL VESSELS
DANGLING FROM HOOKS
OR REPOSING ON THEIR SHELVES TILL NEEDED
WITH THE AIR OF SO MANY CHALICES WAITING
FOR THE CELEBRATION OF THE SACRAMENT OF FOOD.

—Angela Carter, British novelist (1940–1992)

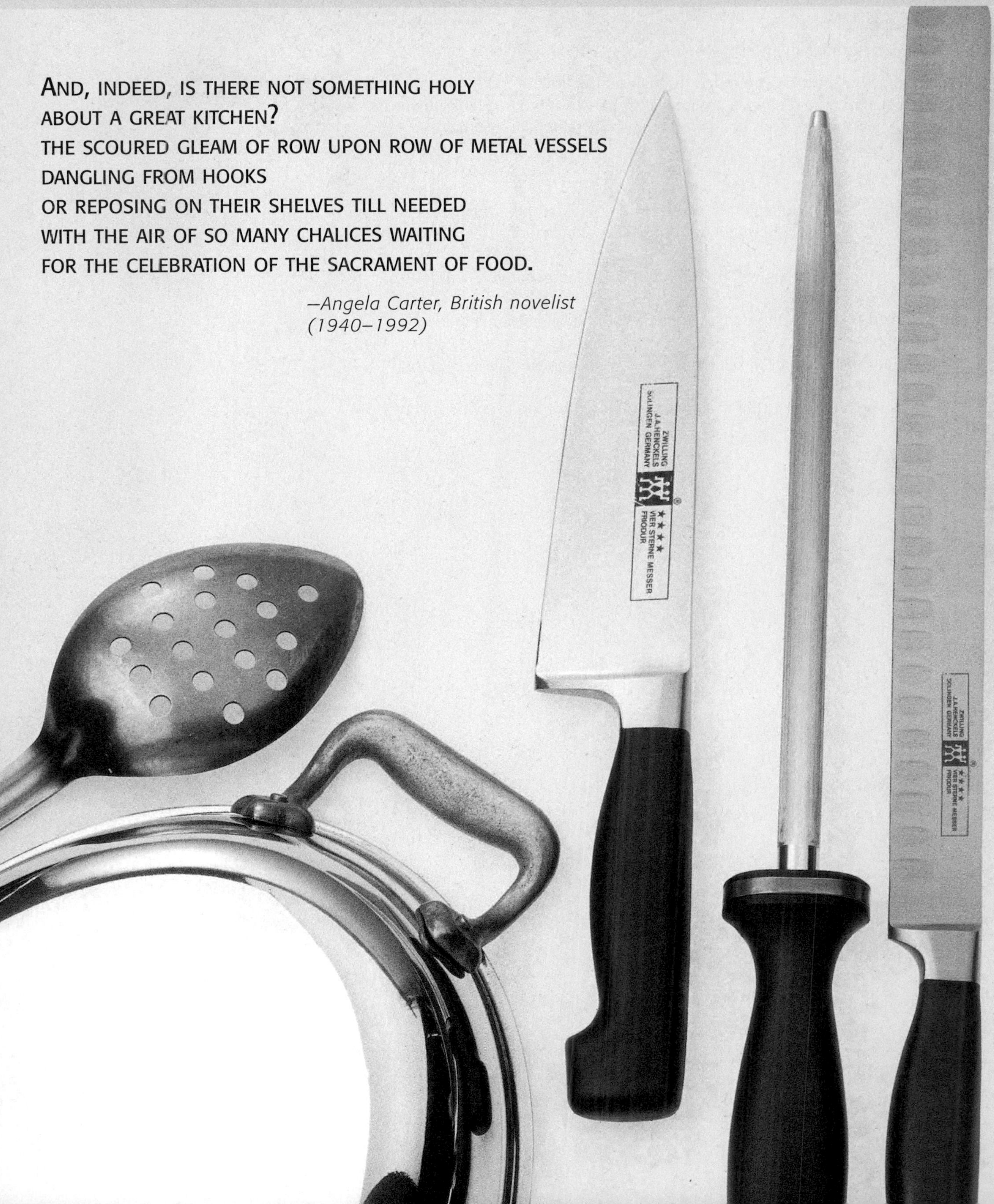

TOOLS AND EQUIPMENT

AFTER STUDYING THIS CHAPTER, YOU WILL BE ABLE TO:

- recognize a variety of professional kitchen tools and equipment
- select and care for knives
- understand how a professional kitchen is organized

Having the proper tools and equipment for a particular task may mean the difference between a job well done and one done carelessly, incorrectly or even dangerously. This chapter introduces most of the tools and equipment typically used in a professional kitchen. Items are divided into categories according to their function: hand tools, knives, measuring and portioning devices, cookware, strainers and sieves, processing equipment, storage containers, heavy equipment, buffet equipment and safety equipment.

A wide variety of specialized tools and equipment is available to today's chef. Breading machines, croissant shapers and doughnut glazers are designed to speed production by reducing handwork. Other devices—for instance, a duck press or a couscousière—are used only for unique tasks in preparing a few menu items. Much of this specialized equipment is quite expensive and found only in food manufacturing operations or specialized kitchens; a discussion of it is beyond the scope of this chapter. Brief descriptions of some of these specialized devices are, however, found in the Glossary.

Before using any equipment, personnel should study the operator's manual or have someone experienced with the particular item instruct them on proper procedures for its use and cleaning. And remember, always think safety first.

▸ STANDARDS FOR TOOLS AND EQUIPMENT

NSF International (NSF), previously known as the National Sanitation Foundation, promulgates consensus standards for the design, construction and installation of kitchen tools, cookware and equipment. Many states and municipalities require that food service operations use only NSF-certified equipment. Although NSF certification is voluntary, most manufacturers submit their designs to NSF for certification to show that they are suitable for use in professional food service operations. Certified equipment bears the NSF mark shown in Figure 3.1.

NSF standards reflect the following requirements:

1. Equipment must be easily cleaned.
2. All food contact surfaces must be nontoxic (under intended end-use conditions), nonabsorbent, corrosion resistant and nonreactive.
3. All food contact surfaces must be smooth—that is, free of pits, cracks, crevices, ledges, rivet heads and bolts.
4. Internal corners and edges must be rounded and smooth; external corners and angles must be smooth and sealed.
5. Coating materials must be nontoxic and easily cleaned; coatings must resist chipping and cracking.
6. Waste and waste liquids must be easily removed.

FIGURE 3.1 ▸ The NSF mark.

▸ Selecting Tools and Equipment

In general, only commercial food service tools and equipment should be used in a professional kitchen. Household tools and appliances that are not NSF-certified may not withstand the rigors of a professional kitchen Look for tools that are well constructed. For example, joints should be welded, not bonded with solder; handles should be comfortable, with rounded borders; plastic and rubber parts should be seamless.

Before purchasing or leasing any equipment, you should evaluate several factors:

1. Is this equipment necessary for producing menu items?
2. Will this equipment perform the job required in the space available?
3. Is this equipment the most economical for the operation's specific needs?
4. Is this equipment easy to clean, maintain and repair?

Table-Mounted Can Opener

▸ Hand Tools

Hand tools are designed to aid in cutting, shaping, moving or combining foods. They have few, if any, moving parts. Knives, discussed separately later, are the most important hand tools. Others are metal or rubber spatulas, spoons, whisks, tongs and specialized cutters. In addition to the items shown here, many hand tools designed for specific tasks, such as pressing tortillas or pitting cherries, are available. Sturdiness, durability and safety are the watchwords when selecting hand tools. Choose tools that can withstand the heavy use of a professional kitchen and those that are easily cleaned.

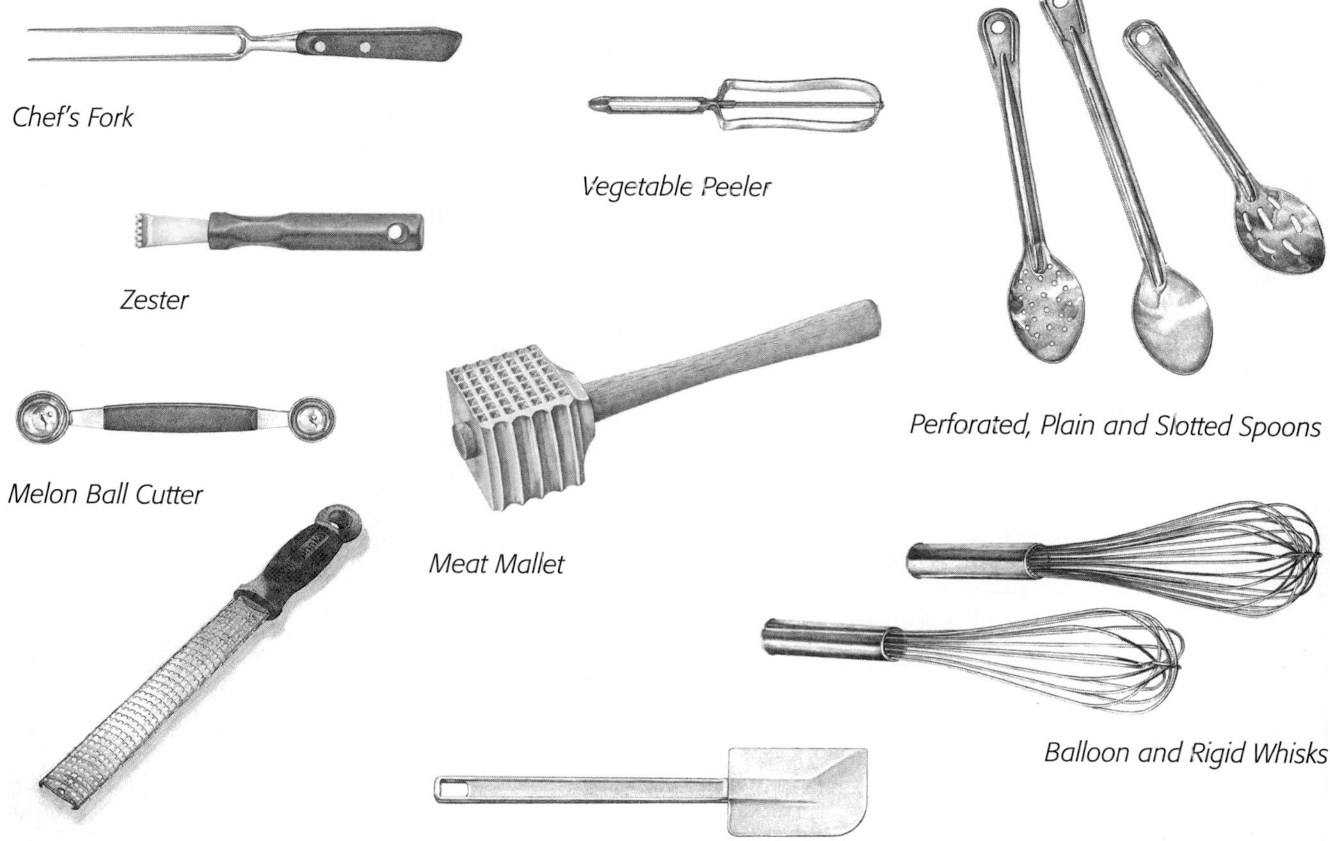

Chef's Fork

Vegetable Peeler

Zester

Perforated, Plain and Slotted Spoons

Melon Ball Cutter

Meat Mallet

Balloon and Rigid Whisks

Rasp-Style Grater

Rubber Spatula

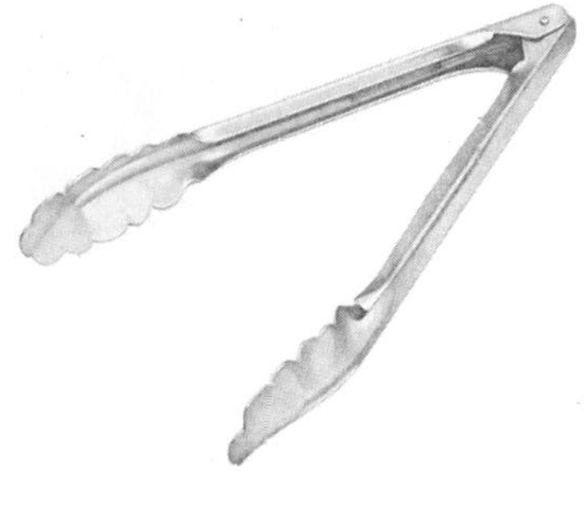

Straight Tongs

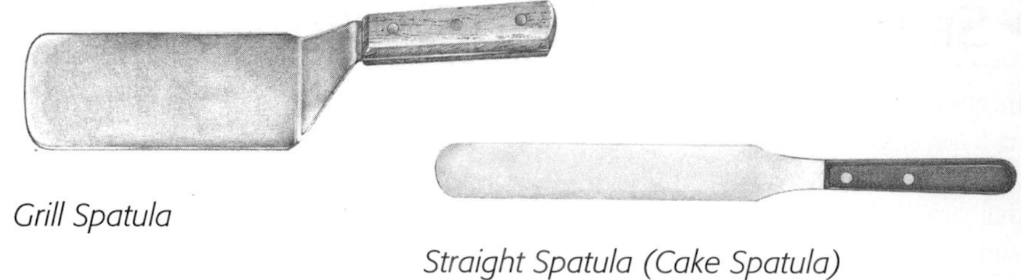

Grill Spatula

Straight Spatula (Cake Spatula)

▶ KNIVES

Knives are the most important items in the chef's tool kit. With a sharp knife, the skilled chef can accomplish a number of tasks more quickly and efficiently than any machine. Good-quality knives are expensive but will last for many years with proper care. Select easily sharpened, well-constructed knives that are comfortable and balanced in your hand. Knife construction and commonly used knives are discussed here; knife safety and care as well as cutting techniques are discussed in Chapter 4, Knife Skills.

KNIFE CONSTRUCTION

A good knife begins with a single piece of metal, stamped, cut or—best of all—forged and tempered into a blade of the desired shape. The following metals are generally used for knife blades:

1 **Carbon steel**—An alloy of carbon and iron, carbon steel is traditionally used for blades because it is soft enough to be sharpened easily. It corrodes and discolors easily, however, especially when used with acidic foods.

2 **Stainless steel**—Stainless steel will not rust, corrode or discolor and is extremely durable. A stainless steel blade is much more difficult to sharpen than a carbon steel one, although once an edge is established, it lasts longer than the edge on a carbon steel blade.

3 **High-carbon stainless steel**—An alloy combining the best features of carbon steel and stainless steel, high-carbon stainless steel neither corrodes nor discolors and can be sharpened almost as easily as carbon steel. It is now the most frequently used metal for blades.

4 **Ceramic**—A ceramic called zirconium oxide is now used to make knife blades that are extremely sharp, very easy to clean, rustproof and nonreactive. With proper care, ceramic blades will remain sharp for years, but when sharpening is needed, it must be done professionally on special diamond wheels. Material costs and tariffs make ceramic-bladed knives very expensive. Although this ceramic is highly durable, it does not have the flexibility of metal, so never use a ceramic knife to pry anything, to strike a hard surface (for example, when crushing garlic or chopping through bones) or to cut against a china or ceramic surface.

A portion of the blade, known as the tang, fits inside the handle, as shown in Figure 3.2. The best knives are constructed with a full tang running the length of the handle; they also have a bolster where the blade meets the handle (the bolster is part of the blade, not a separate collar). Less ex-

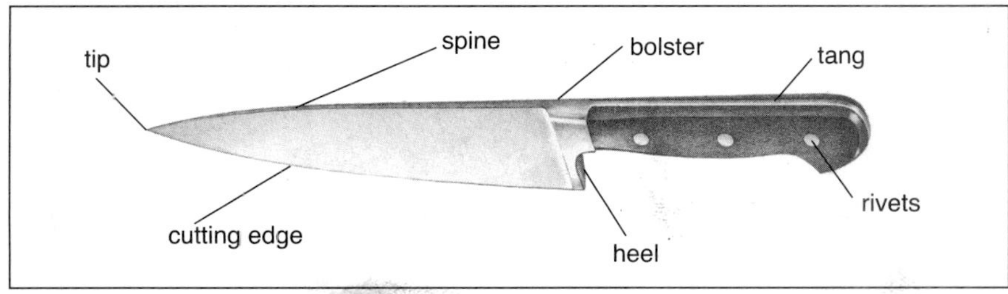

FIGURE 3.2 ▶ The parts of a chef's knife.

pensive knives may have a ¾-length tang or a thin "rattail" tang. Neither provides as much support, durability or balance as a full tang.

Knife handles are often made of hard woods infused with plastic and riveted to the tang. Molded polypropylene handles are permanently bonded to a tang without seams or rivets. Stainless steel handles welded directly to the blade are durable but very lightweight. Any handle should be shaped for comfort and ground smooth to eliminate crevices where bacteria can grow.

KNIFE SHAPES AND SHARPENING EQUIPMENT

A chef will collect many knives during his or her career, many with specialized functions not described here. This list includes only the most basic knives and sharpening equipment.

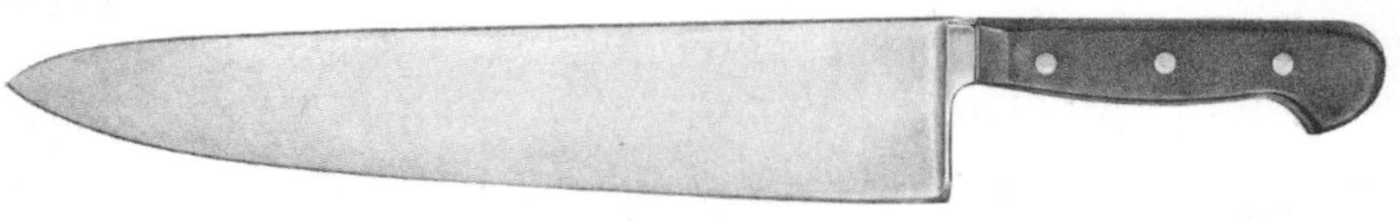

French or Chef's Knife

FRENCH OR CHEF'S KNIFE

An all-purpose knife used for chopping, slicing and mincing. Its rigid 8- to 14-inch-long blade is wide at the heel and tapers to a point at the tip.

Utility Knife

UTILITY KNIFE

An all-purpose knife used for cutting fruits and vegetables and carving poultry. Its rigid 6- to 8-inch-long blade is shaped like a chef's knife but narrower.

Rigid Boning Knife

BONING KNIFE

A smaller knife with a thin blade used to separate meat from bone. The blade is usually 5 to 7 inches long and may be flexible or rigid.

Paring Knife

PARING KNIFE

A short knife used for detail work or cutting fruits and vegetables. The rigid blade is from 2 to 4 inches long. A tournée or **bird's-beak knife** is similar to a paring knife but with a curved blade; it is used to cut curved surfaces or tournée vegetables.

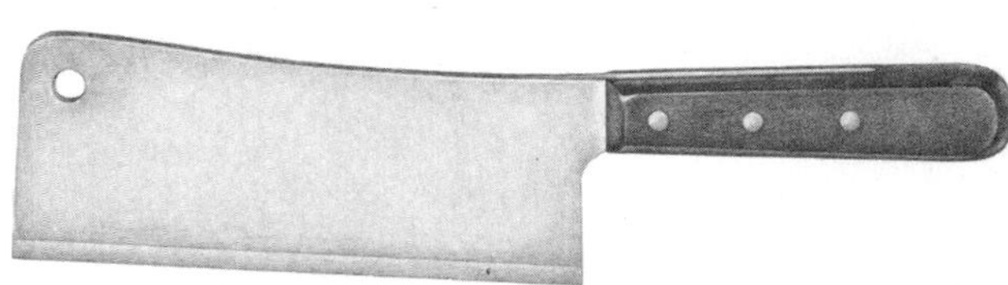

Cleaver

CLEAVER

A knife with a large, heavy rectangular blade used for chopping or cutting through bones.

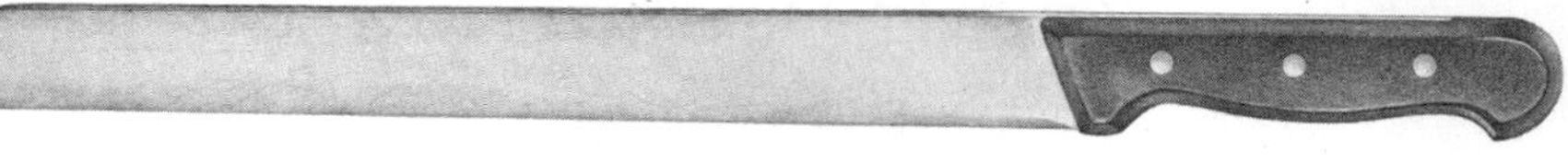

Flexible Slicer

SLICER

A knife with a long, thin blade used primarily for slicing cooked meat. The tip may be round or pointed, and the blade may be flexible or rigid. A similar knife with a serrated edge is used for slicing bread or pastry items.

BUTCHER KNIFE

Sometimes known as a **scimitar** because the rigid blade curves up in a 25-degree angle at the tip, it is used for fabricating raw meat and is available with 6- to 14-inch blades.

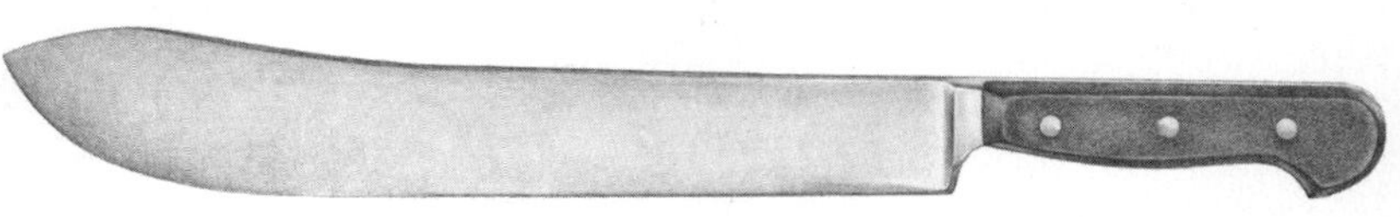

Butcher Knife or Scimitar

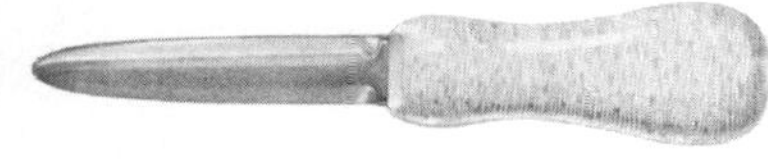

Oyster Knife

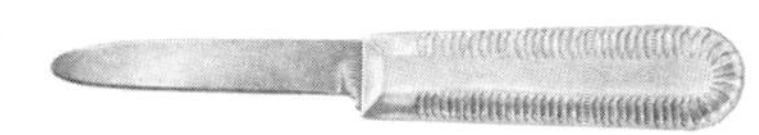

Clam Knife

OYSTER AND CLAM KNIVES

The short, rigid blades of these knives are used to open oyster and clam shells. The tips are blunt; only the clam knife has a sharp edge.

SHARPENING STONE

Also known as a **whetstone,** a flat brick of synthetic abrasives that is used to put an edge on a dull blade. Various grit sizes are available. The most practical sets include both coarse- and fine-grit stones.

STEEL

A scored, slightly abrasive steel rod used to hone or straighten a blade immediately after and between sharpenings.

Three-Sided Sharpening Stone or Whetstone

Steel

▶ MEASURING AND PORTIONING DEVICES

Recipe ingredients must be measured precisely, especially in the bakeshop, and foods should be measured when served to control portion size and cost. The devices used to measure and portion foods are, for the most part, hand tools designed to make food preparation and service easier and more precise. The accuracy they afford prevents the cost of mistakes made when accurate measurements are ignored.

Measurements may be based on weight (for example, grams, ounces, pounds) or volume (for example, teaspoons, cups, gallons). Therefore, it is necessary to have available several measuring devices, including liquid and dry measuring cups and a variety of scales. Thermometers and timers are also measuring devices and are discussed here. When purchasing measuring devices, look for quality construction and accurate markings.

SCALES

Scales are necessary to determine the weight of an ingredient or a portion of food (for example, the sliced meat for a sandwich). Portion scales use a spring mechanism, round dial and single flat tray. They are available calibrated in grams, ounces or pounds. Electronic scales also use a spring mechanism but pro-

Portion Scale

Balance or Baker's Scale

vide digital readouts. They are often required where foods are priced for sale by weight. Balance scales (also known as baker's scales) use a two-tray, free-weight counterbalance system. A balance scale allows more weight to be measured at one time because it is not limited by spring capacity.

Any scale must be properly used and maintained to provide an accurate reading. Never pick up a scale by its platform as this can damage the balancing mechanism.

VOLUME MEASURES

Ingredients may be measured by volume using measuring spoons and measuring cups. Measuring spoons sold as a set usually include ¼-teaspoon, ½-teaspoon, 1-teaspoon and 1-tablespoon units (or the metric equivalent). Liquid measuring cups are available in capacities from 1 cup to 1 gallon. They have a lip or pour spout above the top line of measurement to prevent spills. Measuring cups for dry ingredients are usually sold in sets of ¼-, ⅓-, ½-, and 1-cup units. They do not have pour spouts, so the top of the cup is level with the top measurement specified. Glass measuring cups are not recommended because they can break. Avoid using bent or dented measuring cups as the damage may distort the measurement capacity.

Measuring Spoons

Liquid Measuring Cup

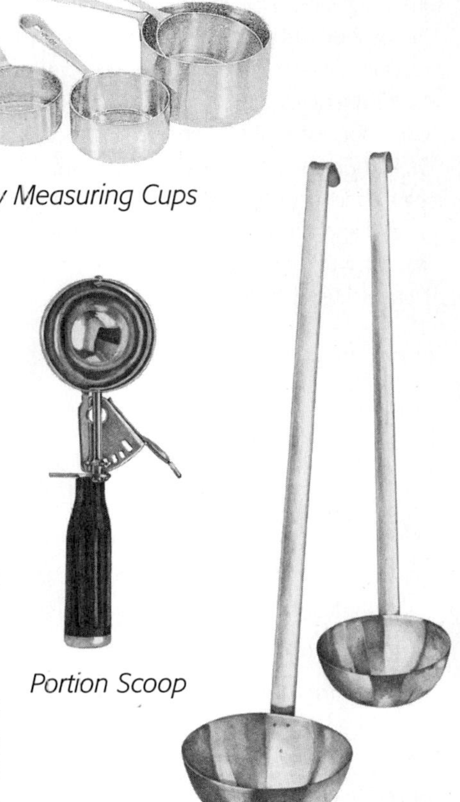

Dry Measuring Cups

Portion Scoop

Ladles

LADLES

Long-handled ladles are useful for portioning liquids such as stocks, sauces and soups. The capacity, in ounces or milliliters, is stamped on the handle.

PORTION SCOOPS

Portion scoops (also known as dishers) resemble ice cream scoops They come in a range of standardized sizes and have a lever-operated blade for releasing their contents. Scoops are useful for portioning salads, vegetables, muffin batters or other soft foods. A number, stamped on either the handle or the release mechanism, indicates the number of level scoopfuls per quart. The higher the scoop number, the smaller the scoop's capacity. See Table 3.1.

Table 3.1 PORTION SCOOP CAPACITIES

	VOLUME		APPROXIMATE WEIGHT*	
SCOOP NUMBER	**U.S.**	**METRIC**	**U.S.**	**METRIC**
6	⅔ c.	160 ml	5 oz.	160 g
8	½ c.	120 ml	4 oz.	120 g
10	3 fl. oz.	90 ml	3–3½ oz.	85–100 g
12	⅓ c.	80 ml	2½–3 oz.	75–85 g
16	¼ c.	60 ml	2 oz.	60 g
20	1½ fl. oz.	45 ml	1¾ oz.	50 g
24	1⅓ fl. oz.	40 ml	1⅓ oz.	40 g
30	1 fl. oz.	30 ml	1 oz.	30 g
40	0.8 fl. oz.	24 ml	0.8 oz.	23 g
60	½ fl. oz.	15 ml	½ oz.	15 g

*Weights are approximate because they vary by food.

HOW TO CALIBRATE A STEM-TYPE THERMOMETER

All stem-type thermometers should be calibrated at least weekly as well as whenever they are dropped. To calibrate a stem-type thermometer, fill a glass with shaved ice, then add water. Place the thermometer in the ice slush and wait until the temperature reading stabilizes. Following the manufacturer's directions, adjust the thermometer's calibration nut until the temperature reads 32°F (0°C). Check the calibration by returning the thermometer to the slush. Then repeat the procedure, substituting boiling water for the ice slush, and calibrate the thermometer at 212°F (100°C).

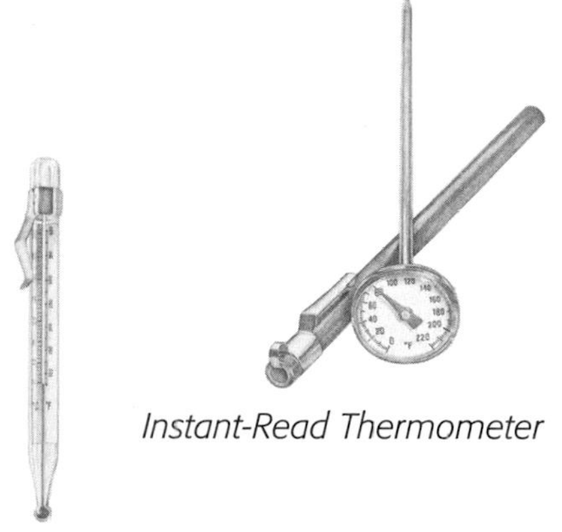

Instant-Read Thermometer

Candy Thermometer

THERMOMETERS

Various types of thermometers are used in the kitchen.

Stem-type thermometers, including instant-read models, are inserted into foods to obtain temperature readings. Temperatures are shown on either a dial noted by an arrow or a digital readout. An instant-read thermometer is a small stem-type model, designed to be carried in a pocket and used to provide quick temperature readings. An instant-read thermometer should not be left in foods that are cooking because doing so damages the thermometer. Sanitize the stem of any thermometer before use in order to avoid cross-contamination.

Candy and fat thermometers measure temperatures up to 400°F (204°C) using mercury in a column of glass. A back clip attaches the thermometer to the pan, keeping the chef's hands free. Be careful not to subject glass thermometers to quick temperature changes as the glass may shatter.

Electronic probe thermometers are now reasonably priced and commonly used in food service facilities. These thermometers provide immediate, clear, digital readouts from a handheld unit attached to a metal probe (some are conveniently designed so that the probe is embedded in the tines of a long-handled fork or the bowl of a ladle). A detachable probe is especially useful inside an oven and for deep-frying and grilling.

The latest advancement in thermometers relies on infrared sensors with laser sightings. Infrared thermometers can instantly monitor the surface temperature of foods during cooking or holding and the temperature of goods at receiving and in storage. Units can respond to a wide range of temperatures in less than a second without actually touching the food, thus avoiding any risk of cross-contamination.

Because proper temperatures must be maintained for holding and storing foods, oven and refrigerator thermometers are also useful. Select thermometers with easy-to-read dials or column divisions.

TIMERS

Portable kitchen timers are useful for any busy chef. Small digital timers can be carried in a pocket; some even time three functions at once. Select a timer with a loud alarm signal and long timing capability.

▶ COOKWARE

Cookware includes the sauté pans and stockpots used on the stove top as well as the roasting pans, hotel pans and specialty molds used inside the oven. Cookware should be selected for its size, shape, ability to conduct heat evenly and overall quality of construction.

METALS AND HEAT CONDUCTION

Cookware that fails to distribute heat evenly may cause hot spots that burn foods. Because different metals conduct heat at different rates, and thicker layers of metal conduct heat more evenly than thinner ones, the most important considerations when choosing cookware are the type and thickness (known as the gauge) of the material used. No one cookware or material suits every process or need, however; always select the most appropriate material for the task at hand.

COPPER

Copper is an excellent conductor: It heats rapidly and evenly and cools quickly. Indeed, unlined copper pots are unsurpassed for cooking sugar and fruit mixtures. But copper cookware is extremely expensive. It also requires a great deal of care and is often quite heavy. Moreover, because copper may react with some foods, copper cookware usually has a tin lining, which is soft and easily scratched. Because of these problems, copper is now often sandwiched between layers of stainless steel or aluminum in the bottom of pots and pans.

ALUMINUM

Aluminum is the metal used most commonly in commercial utensils. It is lightweight and, after copper, conducts heat best. Aluminum is a soft metal, though, so it should be treated with care to avoid dents. Do not use aluminum containers for storage or for cooking acidic foods because the metal reacts chemically with many foods. Light-colored foods, such as soups or sauces, may be discolored when cooked in aluminum, especially if stirred with a metal whisk or spoon.

Anodized aluminum has a hard, dark, corrosion-resistant surface that helps prevent sticking and discoloration.

STAINLESS STEEL

Although stainless steel conducts and retains heat poorly, it is a hard, durable metal particularly useful for holding foods and for low-temperature cooking in which hot spots and scorching are not problems. Stainless steel pots and pans are available with aluminum or copper bonded to the bottom or with an aluminum-layered core. Although expensive, such cookware combines the rapid, uniform heat conductivity of copper and aluminum with the strength, durability and nonreactivity of stainless steel. Stainless steel is also ideal for storage containers because it does not react with foods.

CAST IRON

Cast-iron cookware distributes heat evenly and holds high temperatures well. It is often used in griddles and large skillets. Although relatively inexpensive, cast iron is extremely heavy and brittle. It must be kept properly conditioned and dry to prevent rust and pitting.

OTHER MATERIALS

GLASS

Glass retains heat well but conducts it poorly. It does not react with foods. Tempered glass is suitable for microwave cooking provided it does not have any metal band or decoration. Commercial operations rarely use glass cookware because of the danger of breakage.

CERAMICS

Ceramics, including earthenware, porcelain and stoneware, are used primarily for baking dishes, casseroles and baking stones because they conduct heat uniformly and retain temperatures well. Ceramics are nonreactive, inexpensive and generally suitable for use in a microwave oven (provided there is no metal in the glaze). Ceramics are easily chipped or cracked, however, and should not be used over a direct flame. Also, quick temperature changes may cause the cookware to crack or shatter.

PLASTIC

Plastic containers are frequently used in commercial kitchens for food storage or service, but they cannot be used for heating or cooking except in a microwave oven. Plastic microwave cookware is made of phenolic resin. It is easy to clean, relatively inexpensive and rigidly shaped, but its glasslike structure is brittle, and it can crack or shatter.

SILICONE BAKEWARE

In the 1980s, flexible silicone baking materials became available for use in the professional kitchen. Made from pure silicone or fiberglass impregnated with food-grade silicone, this light material resists sticking and can withstand temperatures from freezing to 485°F (251°C). Baking pan liners made from silicone materials rarely require greasing and are useful for baking as well as candy and chocolate work. Heat-resistant spatulas and pot holders made from silicone are effective and popular. Sheets of baking molds made from these materials are used to form individual cakes, petit fours and desserts, as well as ice cream and frozen desserts. Often these pans are called by the brand names used by their manufacturers, among them Silpats, Flexipan, Gastroflex, Silform and Elastomolds.

ENAMELWARE

Pans lined with enamel should not be used for cooking; in many areas, their use in commercial kitchens is prohibited by law. The enamel can chip or crack easily, providing good places for bacteria to grow. Also, the chemicals used to bond the enamel to the cookware can cause food poisoning if ingested.

NONSTICK COATINGS

Without affecting a metal's ability to conduct heat, a polymer (plastic) known as polytetrafluoroethylene (PTFE) and marketed under the trade names Teflon and Silverstone may be applied to many types of cookware. It provides a slippery, nonreactive finish that prevents food from sticking and allows the use of less fat in cooking. Cookware with nonstick coatings requires a great deal of care, however, because the coatings can scratch, chip and blister. Do not use metal spoons or spatulas in cookware with nonstick coatings.

COMMON COOKWARE

POTS

Pots are large round vessels with straight sides and two loop handles. Available in a range of sizes based on volume, they are used on the stove top for making stocks or soups, or for boiling or simmering foods, particularly where rapid evaporation is not desired. Flat or fitted lids are available.

PANS

Pans are round vessels with one long handle and straight or sloped sides. They are usually smaller and shallower than pots. Pans are available in a range of diameters and are used for general stove top cooking, especially sautéing, frying or reducing liquids rapidly.

Stockpot with Spigot

Sautoir (Straight Sides)

Saucepan

Saucepot

Rondeau/Brazier

Cast-Iron Skillet (Griswold)

Sauteuse (Sloped Sides)

WOKS

Originally used to prepare Asian foods, woks are now found in many professional kitchens. Their round bottoms and curved sides diffuse heat and make it easy to toss or stir contents. Their large domed lids retain heat for steaming vegetables. Woks are useful for quickly sautéing strips of meat, simmering a whole fish or deep-frying appetizers. Stove top woks range in diameter from 12 to 30 inches; larger built-in gas or electric models are also available.

Wok

HOTEL PANS

Hotel pans (also known as steam table pans) are rectangular stainless steel pans designed to hold food for service in steam tables. Hotel pans are also used for baking, roasting or poaching inside an oven. Perforated pans useful for draining, steaming or icing down foods are also available. The standard full-size pan is 12 × 20 inches, with pans one-half, one-third, one-sixth and other fractions of this size available. Hotel pan depth is standardized at 2 inches (referred to as a "200 pan"), 4, 6 and 8 inches.

Hotel Pans

MOLDS

Pâté molds are available in several shapes and sizes, and are usually made from tinned steel. Those with hinged sides, whether smooth or patterned, are more properly referred to as pâté en croûte molds. The hinged sides make it easier to remove the baked pâté. Terrine molds are traditionally lidded earthenware or enameled cast-iron containers used for baking ground meat mixtures. They may be round, oval or rectangular. Timbale molds are small (about 4 ounces) metal or ceramic containers used for molding aspic or baking individual portions of mousse, custard or vegetables. Their slightly flared sides allow the contents to release cleanly when inverted.

Timbales

Pâté en Croûte Mold

ROMAN POTS, SOUTHERN STILLS AND CRAFT FAIRS

Lead is poisonous. Ingesting it can cause severe gastrointestinal pains, anemia and central nervous system disorders, including intelligence and memory deficits and behavioral changes.

The unwitting and dangerous consumption of lead is not limited to children eating peeling paint chips. Some historians suggest that the use of lead cookware and lead-lined storage vessels and water pipes may have caused pervasive lead poisoning among the elite of the Roman empire and thus contributed to the empire's decline. There is also ample evidence that from ancient times until just a few hundred years ago, wine was heated in lead vessels to sweeten it. This had a disastrous effect on the drinker and, for several centuries in countries throughout Europe, on the wine purveyor as well. The former could be poisoned, and the latter could be punished by death for selling adulterated wine. More recently, it was found that much of the moonshine whiskey produced in the American South contained lead in potentially toxic ranges. The source was determined to be the lead solder used in homemade stills, some of which even included old lead-containing car radiators as condensers.

Although commercially available cookware does not contain lead, be careful of imported pottery and those lovely handthrown pots found at craft fairs—there could be lead in the glaze.

▶ STRAINERS AND SIEVES

Strainers and sieves are used primarily to aerate and remove impurities from dry ingredients and drain or purée cooked foods. Strainers, colanders, drum sieves, china caps and chinois are nonmechanical devices with a stainless steel mesh or screen through which food passes. The size of the mesh or screen varies from extremely fine to several millimeters wide; select the fineness best suited for the task at hand.

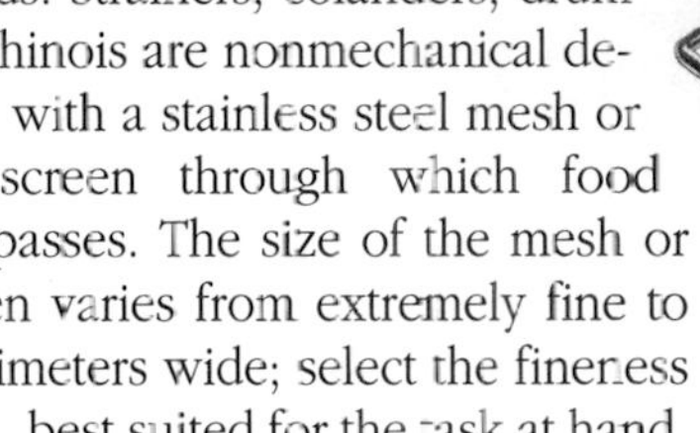

Round Mesh Strainer

Colander

Drum Sieve (Tamis)

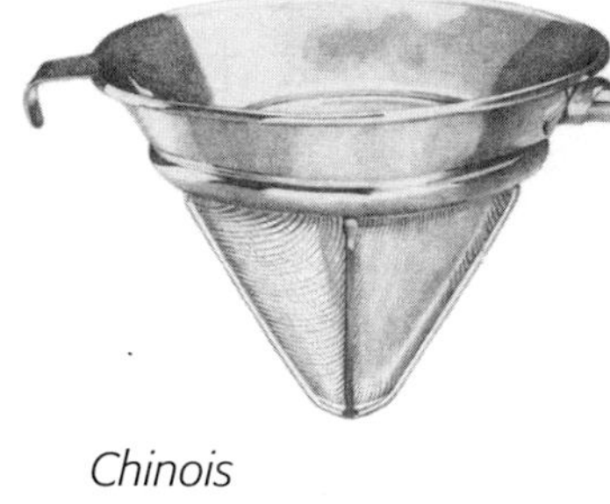
Chinois

China Cap

CHINOIS AND CHINA CAP

Both the chinois and china cap are cone-shaped metal strainers. The conical shape allows liquids to filter through small openings. The body of a chinois is made from a very fine mesh screen, while a china cap has a perforated metal body. Both are used for straining stocks and sauces, with the chinois being particularly useful for consommé. A china cap can also be used with a pestle to purée soft foods.

SKIMMER AND SPIDER

Both the skimmer and spider are long-handled tools used to remove foods or impurities from liquids. The flat, perforated disk of a skimmer is used for skimming stocks or removing foods from soups or stocks. The spider has a finer mesh disk, which makes it better for retrieving items from hot fat. Wooden-handled spiders are available but are less sturdy and harder to clean than all-metal designs.

Skimmer

Spider

CHEESECLOTH

Cheesecloth is a loosely woven cotton gauze used for straining stocks and sauces and wrapping poultry or fish for poaching. Cheesecloth is also indispensable for making sachets. Always rinse cheesecloth thoroughly before use; this removes lint and prevents the cheesecloth from absorbing other liquids.

FOOD MILL

A food mill purées and strains food at the same time. Food is placed in the hopper and a hand-crank mechanism turns a blade in the hopper against a perforated disk, forcing the food through the disk. Most models have interchangeable disks with various-sized holes. Choose a mill that can be taken apart easily for cleaning.

FLOUR SIFTER

A sifter is used for aerating, blending and removing impurities from dry ingredients such as flour, cocoa and leavening agents. The 8-cup hand-crank sifter shown here uses four curved rods to brush the contents through a curved mesh screen. The sifter should have a medium-fine screen and a comfortable handle. The French tamis is a drum-shaped sieve useful for sifting ingredients as well as for straining thick purées to remove lumps and seeds.

Food Mill

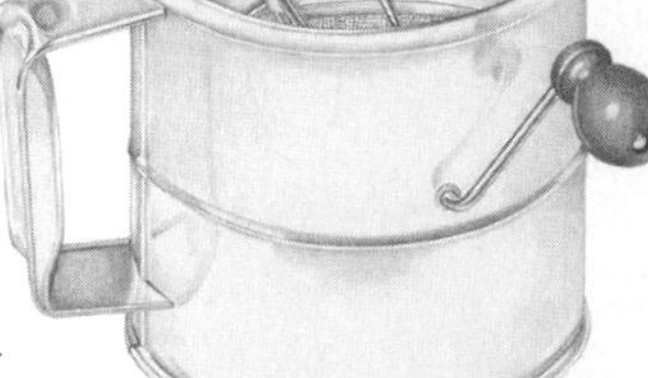
Flour Sifter

▶ Processing Equipment

Processing equipment includes both electrical and nonelectrical mechanical devices used to chop, purée, slice, grind or mix foods. Before using any such equipment, be sure to review its operating procedures and ask for assistance if necessary. Always turn the equipment off and disconnect the power before disassembling, cleaning or moving the appliance. Report any problems or malfunctions immediately. *Never place your hand into any machinery when the power is on. Processing equipment is powerful and can cause serious injury.*

SLICER

An electric slicer is used to cut meat, bread, cheese or raw vegetables into uniform slices. It has a circular blade that rotates at high speed. Food is placed in a carrier, then passed (manually or by an electric motor) against the blade. Slice thickness is determined by the distance between the blade and the carrier. Because of the speed with which the blade rotates, foods can be cut into extremely thin slices very quickly. An electric slicer is convenient for preparing moderate to large quantities of food, but the time required to disassemble and clean the equipment makes it impractical when slicing only a few items.

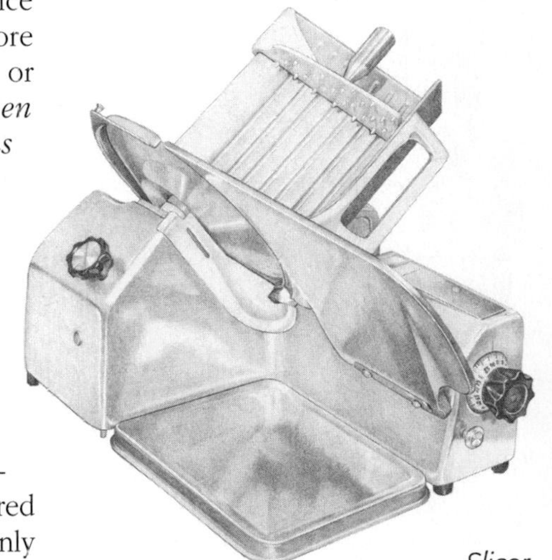

Slicer

MANDOLINE

A mandoline is a manually operated slicer made of stainless steel with adjustable slicing blades. It is also used to make julienne and waffle-cut slices. Its narrow, rectangular body sits on the work counter at a 45-degree angle. Foods are passed against a blade to obtain uniform slices. It is useful for slicing small quantities of fruits or vegetables when using a large electric slicer would be unwarranted. To avoid injury, always use a hand guard or steel glove when using a mandoline.

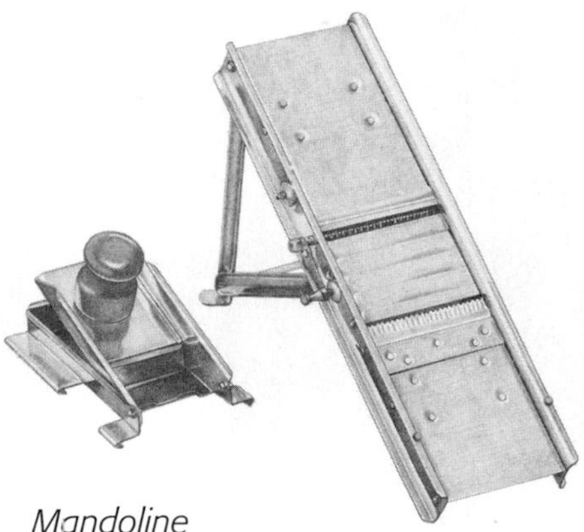

Mandoline

FOOD CHOPPER OR BUFFALO CHOPPER

This chopper is used to process moderate to large quantities of food to a uniform size, such as chopping onions or grinding bread for crumbs. The food is placed in a large bowl rotating beneath a hood where curved blades chop it. The size of the cut depends on how long the food is left in the machine. Buffalo choppers are available in floor or tabletop models. The motor can usually be fitted with a variety of other tools such as a meat grinder or a slicer/shredder, making it even more useful.

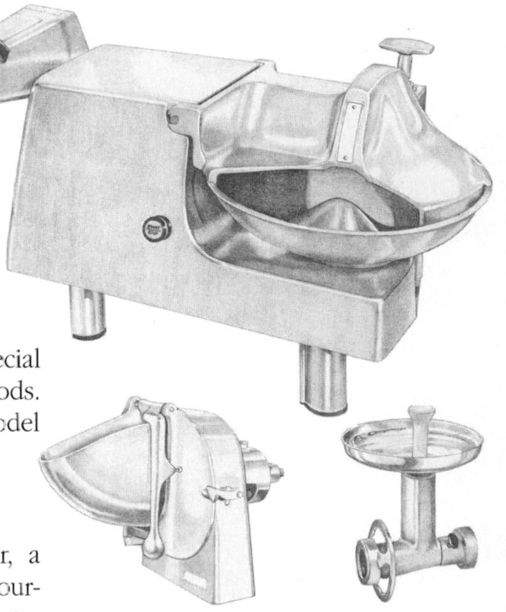

Buffalo Chopper with Slicer and Meat Grinder Attachments

Food Processor

FOOD PROCESSOR

A food processor has a motor housing with a removable bowl and S-shaped blade. It is used, for example, to purée cooked foods, chop nuts, prepare compound butters and emulsify sauces. Special disks can be added that slice, shred or julienne foods. Bowl capacity and motor power vary; select a model large enough for your most common tasks.

BLENDER

Though similar in principle to a food processor, a blender has a tall, narrow food container and a four-pronged blade. Its design and whirlpool action is better for processing liquids or liquefying foods quickly. A blender is used to prepare smooth drinks, purée soups

Heavy-Duty Blender

and sauces, blend batters and chop ice. A **vertical cutter/mixer** (VCM) operates like a very large, powerful blender. A VCM is usually floor-mounted and has a capacity of 15 to 80 quarts.

IMMERSION BLENDER

An immersion blender—as well as its household counterpart called a hand blender or wand—is a long shaft fitted with a rotating four-pronged blade at the bottom. Operated by pressing a button in the handle, an immersion blender is used to purée a soft food, soup or sauce directly in the container in which it was prepared, eliminating the need to transfer the food from one container to another. This is especially useful when working with hot foods. Small cordless, rechargeable models are convenient for puréeing or mixing small quantities or beverages, but larger heavy-duty electric models are more practical in commercial kitchens.

Immersion Blender

20-Quart Mixer and Attachments

MIXER

A vertical mixer is indispensable in the bakeshop and most kitchens. The U-shaped arms hold a metal mixing bowl in place; the selected mixing attachment fits onto the rotating head. The three common mixing attachments are the whip (used for whipping eggs or cream), the paddle (used for general mixing) and the dough hook (used for kneading bread). Most mixers have several operating speeds. Bench models range in capacity from 4.5 to 20 quarts, while floor mixers can hold as much as 140 quarts. Some mixers can be fitted with shredder/slicers, meat grinders, juicers or power strainers, making the equipment more versatile.

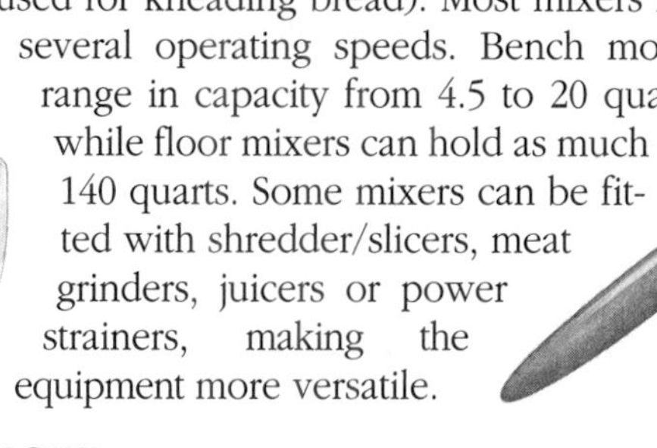

Flat Paddle

Whip

Dough Hook

JUICER

Two types of juicers are available: reamers and extractors. Reamers, also known as citrus juicers, remove juice from citrus fruits. They can be manual or electric. Manual models use a lever arm to squeeze the fruit with increased pressure. They are most often used to prepare small to moderate amounts of juice for cooking or beverages. Juice extractors are electrical devices that create juice by liquefying raw fruits, vegetables and herbs. They use centrifugal force to filter out fiber and pulp.

Citrus Juicer

▶ STORAGE CONTAINERS

Proper storage containers are necessary for keeping leftovers and opened packages of food safe for consumption. Proper storage can also reduce the costs incurred by waste or spoilage.

Although stainless steel pans such as hotel pans are suitable and useful for some items, the expense of stainless steel and the lack of airtight lids makes these pans impractical for general storage purposes. Aluminum containers are not recommended because the metal can react with even mildly acidic items. Glass containers are generally not allowed in commercial kitchens because of the hazards of broken glass. The most useful storage containers are those made of high-density plastic such as polyethylene and polypropylene.

Storage containers must have well-fitting lids and should be available in a variety of sizes, including some that are small enough to hold even minimal quantities of food without allowing too much exposure to oxygen. Round and square plastic containers are widely available. Flat, snap-on lids allow containers to be stacked for more efficient storage. Containers may be clear or opaque white, which helps protect light-sensitive foods. Larger containers may be fitted with handles and spigots, making them especially suited for storing stock. Some storage containers are marked with graduated measurements so that content quantity can be determined at a glance.

Large quantities of dry ingredients, such as flour, sugar and rice, can be stored in rolling bins. The bins should be seamless with rounded corners for easy cleaning. They should have well-fitting but easy-to-open lids and should move easily on well-balanced casters.

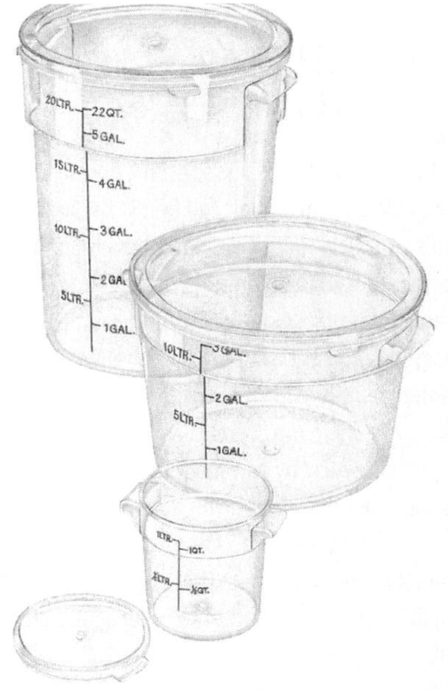

Storage Containers

▶ HEAVY EQUIPMENT

Heavy equipment includes the gas-, electric- or steam-operated appliances used for cooking, reheating or holding foods. It also includes dishwashers and refrigeration units. These items are usually installed in a fixed location determined by the kitchen's traffic flow and space limitations.

Heavy equipment may be purchased or leased new or used. Used equipment is most often purchased in an effort to save money. Although the initial cost is generally less for used equipment, the buyer should also consider the lack of a manufacturer's warranty or dealership guarantee and how the equipment was maintained by the prior owner. Functional used equipment is satisfactory for back-of-the-house areas, but it is usually better to purchase new equipment if it will be visible to the customer. Leasing equipment may be appropriate for some operations. The cost of leasing is less than purchasing and, if something goes wrong with the equipment, the operator is generally not responsible for repairs or service charges.

STOVE TOPS

Stove tops or ranges are often the most important cooking equipment in the kitchen. They have one or more burners powered by gas or electricity. The burners may be open or covered with a cast-iron or steel plate. Open burners supply quick, direct heat that is easy to regulate. A steel plate, known as a **flat top,** supplies even but less intense heat. Although it takes longer to heat than a burner, the flat top supports heavier weights and makes a larger area available for cooking. Many stoves include both flat tops and open burner arrangements.

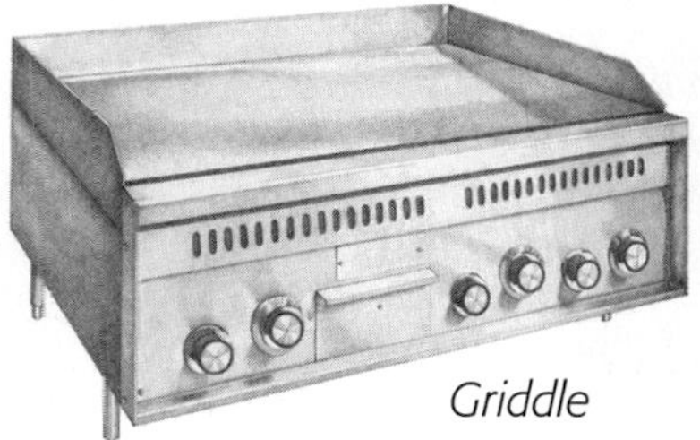
Griddle

Griddles are similar to flat tops except they are made of a thinner metal plate. Foods are usually cooked directly on the griddle's surface, not in pots or pans, which can nick or scratch the surface. The surface should be properly cleaned and conditioned after each use. Griddles are popular for short-order and fast-food-type operations.

OVENS

An oven is an enclosed space where food is cooked by being surrounded with hot, dry air. Conventional ovens are often located beneath the stove top. They have a heating element located at the unit's bottom or floor, and pans are placed on adjustable wire racks inside the oven's cavity. See Figure 3.3. Conventional ovens may also be separate, freestanding units or decks stacked one on top of the other. In stack ovens, pans are placed directly on the deck or floor and not on wire racks.

Convection Oven

INDUCTION—A NEW HEAT WAVE

Induction cooking uses special conductive coils called inductors placed below the stove top's surface in combination with flat-bottomed cookware made of cast iron or magnetic stainless steel. The coil generates a magnetic current so that the cookware is heated rapidly with magnetic friction. Heat energy is then transferred from the cookware to the food by conduction. The cooking surface, which is made of a solid ceramic material, remains cool. Only the cookware and its contents get hot. This means that induction systems are extremely efficient with instant response time because power is directed into the cooking utensil, not the surrounding air.

Induction cooking is gaining acceptance in professional kitchens because of the speed with which foods can be heated and the ease of cleanup. Induction burners are useful in the bakeshop where there may be only a limited need for direct-heat cooking; they are portable and maintain a safer, cooler cooking environment.

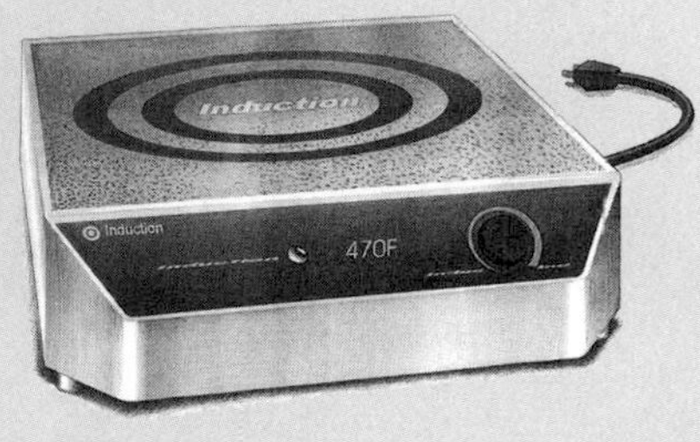

Induction Cooktop

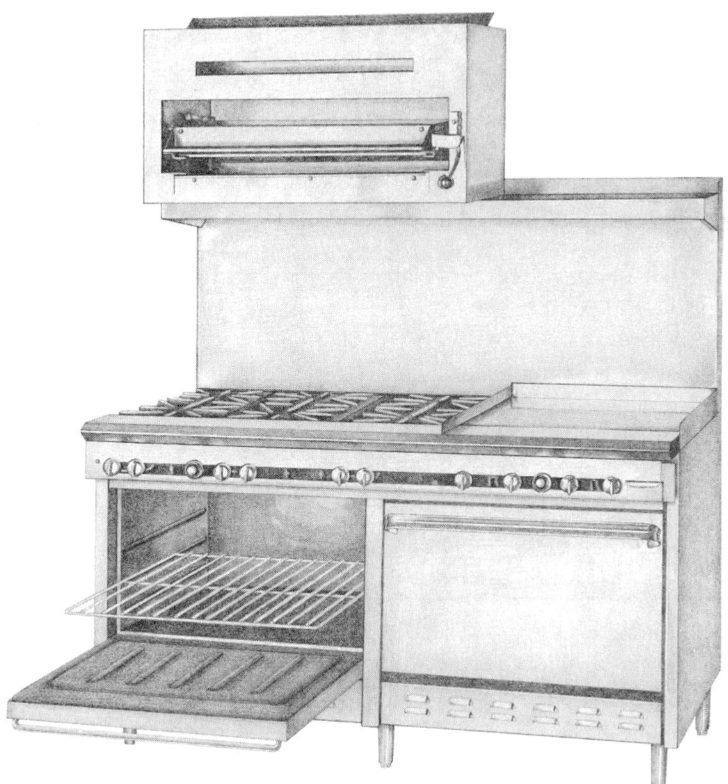

FIGURE 3.3 ▶ Gas burner and flat-top range with dual ovens and an overhead broiler (salamander).

Convection ovens use internal fans to circulate the hot air. This tends to cook foods more quickly and evenly. Convection ovens are almost always freestanding units, powered by either gas or electricity. Because convection ovens cook foods more quickly, temperatures may need to be reduced by 25°F to 50°F (10°C to 20°C) from those recommended for conventional ovens.

WOOD-BURNING OVENS

The ancient practice of baking in a retained-heat masonry oven has been revived in recent years, with many upscale restaurants and artesian bakeries installing brick or adobe ovens for baking pizzas and breads as well as for roasting fish, poultry and vegetables. These ovens have a curved interior chamber that is usually recessed into a wall. Although gas-fired models are available, wood-firing is more traditional and provides the aromas and flavors associated with brick ovens. A wood fire is built inside the oven to heat the brick chamber. The ashes are then swept out and the food is placed on the flat oven floor. Breads and pizzas baked in direct contact with the hot masonry rise better than in a conventional oven and develop a unique crisp crust. The combination of high heat and wood smoke adds distinctive flavors to foods.

Stack Oven

Wood-Burning Oven

MICROWAVE OVENS

Microwave ovens are electrically powered ovens used to cook or reheat foods. They are available in a range of sizes and power settings. Microwave ovens will not brown foods unless fitted with special browning elements. Microwave cooking is discussed in more detail in Chapter 8, Principles of Cooking.

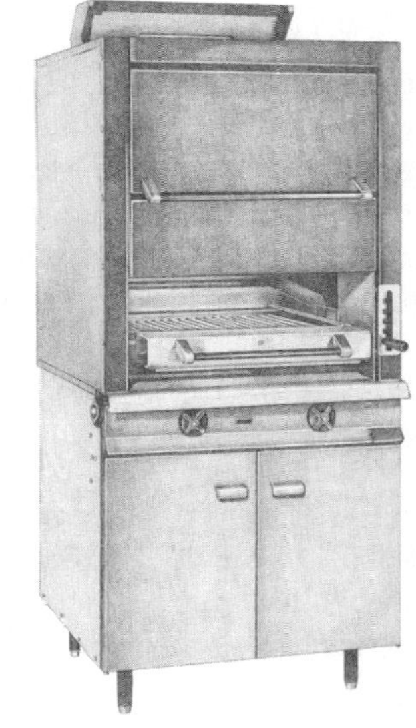

Overhead Broiler

BROILERS AND GRILLS

Broilers and grills are generally used to prepare meats, fish and poultry. For a grill, the heat source is beneath the rack on which the food is placed. For a broiler, the heat source is above the food. Most broilers are gas powered; grills may be gas or electric or may burn wood or charcoal. A **salamander** is a small overhead broiler primarily used to finish or top-brown foods. See Figure 3.3. A **rotisserie** is similar to a broiler except that the food is placed on a revolving spit in front of the heat source. The unit may be open or enclosed like an oven; it is most often used for cooking poultry or meats.

Rotisserie

Gas Grill

TILTING SKILLETS

Tilting skillets are large, freestanding, flat-bottomed pans about 6 inches deep with an internal heating element below the pan's bottom. They are usually made of stainless steel with a cover, and have a hand-crank mechanism that turns or tilts the pan to pour out the contents. Tilting skillets can be used as stockpots, braziers, fry pans, griddles or steam tables, making them one of the most versatile of commercial appliances.

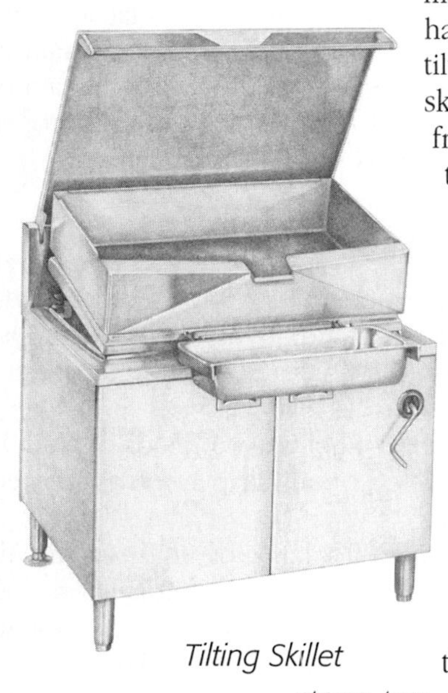

Tilting Skillet

STEAM KETTLES

Steam kettles (also known as steam-jacketed kettles) are similar to stockpots except they are heated from the bottom and sides by steam circulating between layers of stainless steel. The steam may be generated internally or from an outside source. Because steam heats the kettle's sides, foods cook more quickly and evenly than they would in a pot sitting on the stove top. Steam kettles are most often used for making sauces, soups, custards and stocks. Steam kettles are available in a range of sizes, from a 2-gallon tabletop model to a 100-gallon floor model. Some models have a tilting mechanism that allows the contents to be poured out; others have a spigot near the bottom through which liquids can be drained.

Steam Kettle

STEAMERS

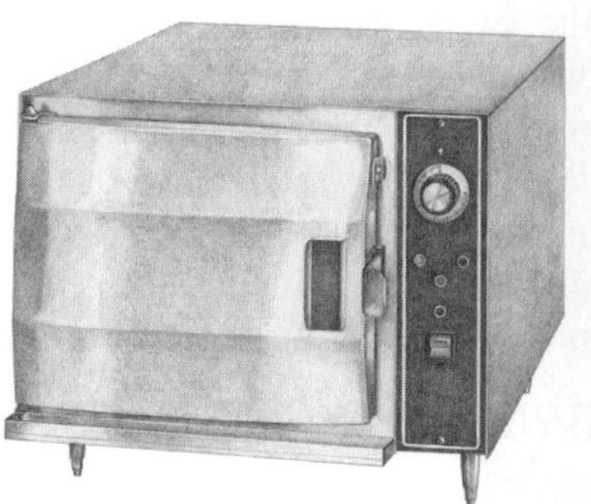
Convection Steamer

Pressure and convection steamers are used to cook foods rapidly and evenly, using direct contact with steam. Pressure steamers heat water above the boiling point in sealed compartments; the high temperature and sealed compartment increase the internal pressure in a range of 4 to 15 pounds per square inch. The increased pressure and temperature cook the foods rapidly. Convection steamers generate steam in an internal boiler, then release it over the foods in a cooking chamber. Both types of steamer are ideal for cooking vegetables with minimal loss of flavor or nutrients.

DEEP-FAT FRYERS

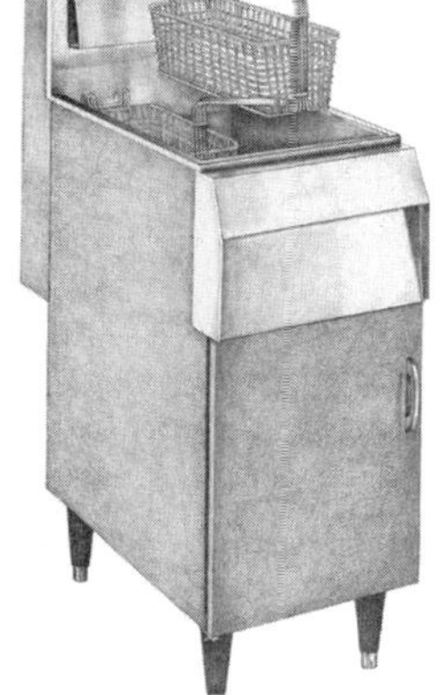
Deep-Fat Fryer

Deep-fat fryers are used to cook foods in a large amount of hot fat. Fryers are sized by the amount of fat they hold. Most commercial fryers range between 15 and 82 pounds. Fryers can be either gas or electric and are thermostatically controlled for temperatures between 200°F and 400°F (90°C and 200°C).

When choosing a fryer, look for a fry tank with curved, easy-to-clean sloping sides. Some fryers have a cold zone (an area of reduced temperature) at the bottom of the fry tank to trap particles. This prevents them from burning, creating off-flavors and shortening the life of the fryer fat.

Deep-fryers usually come with steel wire baskets to hold the food during cooking. Fryer baskets are usually lowered into the fat and raised manually, although some models have automatic basket mechanisms. The most important factor when choosing a deep-fryer is **recovery time.** Recovery time is the length of time it takes the fat to return to the desired cooking temperature after food is submerged in it. When food is submerged, heat is immediately transferred to the food from the fat. This heat transfer lowers the fat's temperature. The more food added at one time, the greater the drop in the fat's temperature. If the temperature drops too much or does not return quickly to the proper cooking temperature, the food may absorb excess fat and become greasy.

REFRIGERATORS

Proper refrigeration space is an essential component of any kitchen. Many foods must be stored at low temperatures to maintain quality and safety. Most commercial refrigeration is of two types: walk-in units and reach-in or upright units.

A walk-in is a large, room-sized box capable of holding hundreds of pounds of food on adjustable shelves. A separate freezer walk-in may be positioned nearby or even inside a refrigerated walk-in.

Reach-ins may be individual units or parts of a bank of units, each with shelves approximately the size of a full sheet pan. Reach-in refrigerators and freezers are usually located throughout the kitchen to provide quick access to foods. Small units may also be placed beneath the work counters. Freezers and refrigerators are available in a wide range of sizes and door designs to suit any operation.

Other forms of commercial refrigeration include chilled drawers located beneath a work area that are just large enough to accommodate a hotel pan, and display cases used to show foods to the customer.

DISHWASHERS

Mechanical dishwashers are available to wash, rinse and sanitize dishware, glassware, cookware and utensils. Small models clean one rack of items at a time, while larger models can handle several racks simultaneously on a conveyor belt system. Sanitation is accomplished either with extremely hot water (180°F/82°C) or with chemicals automatically dispensed during the final rinse cycle. Any dishwashing area should be carefully organized for efficient use of equipment and employees and to prevent recontamination of clean items.

Insulated Carrier

► BUFFET EQUIPMENT

Food service operations that prepare buffets or cater off-premise events need a variety of specialized equipment to ensure that food is handled safely and efficiently and displayed appropriately. Proper temperatures must be maintained during transportation, display and service.

Insulated carriers hold food at its current temperature for a time. They are designed to hold hotel pans or sheet pans, and are available with wheels for easy movement. Some are available with a spigot for serving hot or cold beverages. Any carrier should be easy to clean and of a convenient size for the space available and the type of operation.

Chafing Dish

Temperature remains a concern when arranging food on a buffet table. **Chafing dishes** are commonly used for keeping hot foods hot during service. Chafing dishes are designed so that cans of solid fuel can be placed under a deep hotel pan of hot water. Like a double boiler or bain marie, the hot water then helps maintain the temperature of food placed in a second hotel pan suspended over the first. Chafing dishes, however, should never be used to heat food. Chafing dishes are available in several sizes and shapes, but the most convenient are those based on the size of a standard hotel pan. Round, deep chafing dishes are useful for serving soups or sauces. Exteriors can be plain or ornate, and made of silver, copper or stainless steel.

Roast beef, turkey, ham or other large cuts of meat are sometimes carved on a buffet in front of guests. **Heat lamps** can be used to keep these foods warm. Heat lamps are also useful for maintaining the temperature of pizza or fried foods, which might become soggy if held in a chafing dish.

Pastries, breads and cold foods can be arranged on a variety of platters, trays, baskets and serving pieces, depending on the size and style of the buffet. Some of the most elegant and traditional serving pieces are flat display mirrors. These may be plastic or glass and are available in a wide variety of shapes and sizes. The edges should be sealed in easy-to-clean plastic to prevent chipping.

Although many of these items can be rented, operations that regularly serve buffets may prefer to invest in their own transportation and serving equipment.

Heat Lamp

► SAFETY EQUIPMENT

Safety devices, many of which are required by federal, state or local law, are critical to the well-being of a food service operation although they are not used in food preparation. Failing to include safety equipment in a kitchen or failing to maintain it properly endangers workers and customers.

FIRE EXTINGUISHERS

Fire extinguishers are canisters of foam, dry chemicals (such as sodium bicarbonate or potassium bicarbonate) or pressurized water used to extinguish small fires. They must be placed within sight of and easily reached from the work areas in which fires are likely to occur. Different classes of extinguishers

Table 3.2 FIRE EXTINGUISHERS

CLASS	SYMBOL	USE
Class A		Fires involving ordinary combustibles such as wood, paper, cloth or plastic
Class B		Fires involving grease or flammable liquids such as gasoline, paint or alcohol
Class C		Fires involving electrical equipment or wiring
Class K		Fires involving cooking oils or fat and fats in commercial cooking equipment

Combination extinguishers—AB, BC and ABC—are also available.

Remember the acronym **P.A.S.S.** for the four steps to follow when using any fire extinguisher:

- **Pull**—Pull the safety pin on the extinguisher.
- **Aim**—Aim the extinguisher hose at the base of the fire.
- **Squeeze**—Squeeze the handle to discharge the material.
- **Sweep**—Sweep the hose from side to side across the base of the fire.

use different chemicals to fight different types of fires. The appropriate class must be used for the specific fire. See Table 3.2. Fire extinguishers must be recharged and checked from time to time. Be sure they have not been discharged, tampered with or otherwise damaged.

VENTILATION SYSTEMS

Ventilation systems (also called ventilation hoods) are commonly installed over cooking equipment to remove vapors, heat and smoke. Some systems include fire extinguishing agents or sprinklers. A properly operating hood makes the kitchen more comfortable for the staff and reduces the danger of fire. The system should be designed, installed and inspected by professionals, then cleaned and maintained regularly.

FIRST-AID KITS

First-aid supplies should be stored in a clearly marked box, conspicuously located near food preparation areas. State and local laws may specify the kit's exact contents. Generally, they should include a first-aid manual, bandages, gauze dressings, adhesive tape, antiseptics, scissors, cold packs and other supplies. The kit should be checked regularly and items replaced as needed. In addition, cards with emergency telephone numbers should be placed inside the first-aid kit and near a telephone.

SAFETY ALERT

Storage

- Never store cleaning supplies or other chemicals with or near foods.
- Never store chemicals in a container that originally held food; never store food in a container that once held a chemical.
- Keep chemicals and cleaners in properly labeled containers.

PROTECTIVE GEAR

All kitchens should be equipped with high quality heat-resistant gloves or pot holders to be used when handling hot pans and other equipment. In kitchens where a large quantity of shellfish is opened or a meat slicer is used, steel-mesh safety gloves may be required. Made from stainless steel woven into a fine fiber, these gloves recall medieval armor and are effective at preventing puncture or slicing wounds.

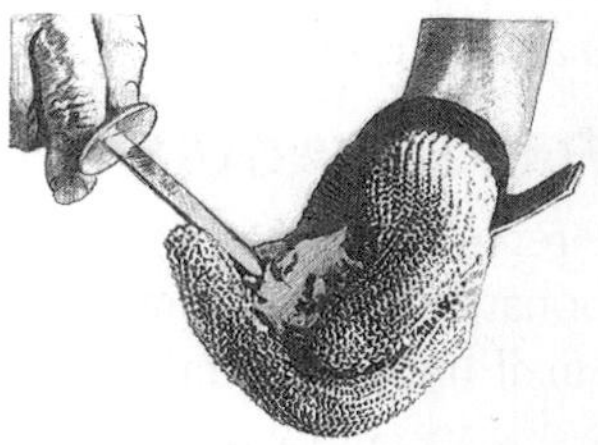

Steel-Mesh Safety Gloves

▶ The Professional Kitchen

The kitchen is the heart of the food service operation. There, food and other items are received, stored, prepared and plated for service; dining room staff places orders, retrieves foods that are ready for service and returns dirty service items; dishes and other wares are cleaned and stored; and the chef conducts business. But commercial space is expensive, and most food service operators recognize that the greater number of customers served, the greater the revenues. Often this translates into a large dining area and small kitchen and storage facilities. Therefore, when designing a kitchen, it is important to use the space wisely so that each of its functions can be accomplished efficiently.

Kitchen design begins with a consideration of the tasks to be performed. Analyzing the menu identifies these tasks. A restaurant featuring steaks and chops, for example, will need areas to fabricate and grill meats. If it relies on commercially prepared desserts and breads, it will not need a bakeshop but will still need space to store and plate baked goods.

Once all food preparation tasks are identified, a work area for each particular task is designated. These work areas are called **work stations.** At a steak restaurant, an important work station is the broiler. If the restaurant serves fried foods, it will also need a fry station. The size and design of each work station is determined by the volume of food the operation intends to produce.

Usually work stations using the same or similar equipment for related tasks are grouped into **work sections.** See Table 3.3. (Note that work stations correspond to the kitchen brigade system discussed in Chapter 1, Professionalism.) For example, in a typical full-service restaurant, there will be a hot-foods section that includes broiler, fry, griddle, sauté and sauce stations. The principal cooking equipment (a range, broiler, deep-fat fryer, oven, griddle and so on) will be arranged in a line under a ventilation hood. During service each work station within the hot-foods section may be staffed by a different line cook, but the proximity of the stations allows one line cook to cover more than one station if the kitchen is shorthanded or when business is slow.

When designing the work area, one must also consider what equipment and storage facilities can be placed beneath or on top of other equipment. For example, in a bakeshop, rolling storage bins for flour and sugar may be located beneath the work surface, while mixing bowls and dry ingredients are stored on shelves above. Ideally, each station should be designed so that the cook takes no more than three steps in any direction to perform all of his or her assigned station tasks.

In addition to the work sections where the menu items are produced, a typical restaurant kitchen includes areas dedicated to the following functions:

1 **Receiving and storing foods and other items.** Most kitchens will need freezer, refrigerator and dry-goods storage facilities. Each should have proper temperature, humidity and light controls in order to properly and safely maintain the stored items. Typically there is a combination of central and section storage. For example, up to 100 pounds of flour and sugar can be stored in rolling bins under a worktable in the bakeshop, while several hundreds of pounds more remain in a central dry-goods area. Similarly, one box of salt can be stored near the hot line for immediate use, while the remainder of the case is stored in a central dry-goods area. Additional storage space will be needed for cleaning and paper supplies, dishes and other service ware.

2 **Washing dishes and other equipment.** These dish- and equipment-washing facilities should have their own sinks. Food preparation and hand-washing sinks must be separate.

3 **Employee use.** Restrooms, locker facilities and an office are also found in most food service facilities.

Table 3.3 **WORK SECTIONS AND THEIR STATIONS**

SECTIONS	STATIONS
Hot-foods section	Broiler station Fry station Griddle station Sauté/sauce station Holding
Garde-manger section	Salad greens cleaning Salad preparation Cold foods preparation Sandwich station Showpiece preparation
Bakery section	Mixing station Dough holding and proofing Dough rolling and forming Baking and cooling Dessert preparation* Frozen dessert preparation* Plating desserts*
Banquet section	Steam cooking Dry-heat cooking (roasting, broiling)
Short-order section	Holding and plating Griddle station Fry station Broiler station
Beverage section	Hot beverage station Cold beverage station Alcoholic beverage station

*These stations are sometimes found in the garde-manger section.

The guiding principle behind a good kitchen design is to maximize the flow of goods and staff from one area to the next and within each area itself. Maximizing flow creates an efficient work environment and helps reduce preparation and service time.

Figure 3.4 shows the several sections of a professional kitchen. It includes an area for front-of-the-house staff to circulate, drop off orders, retrieve finished dishes and return dirty dishes. The design accounts for the flow of foods from receiving, to storage, to food preparation areas, to holding and service areas and then to the dining room as well as the flow of dirty dishes from the dining room back into the kitchen. The work sections are arranged to take advantage of shared equipment. For instance, when the bakeshop is placed next to the hot-foods section, they can share ovens. The garde-manger and dessert sections, both of which rely on refrigerated foods, are conveniently located near the walk-in refrigerator and freezer area. The beverage station is located near the dining room entrance so that food servers do not have to walk through food preparation areas to fill beverage orders. The office is next to receiving so that the chef can easily check and receive orders. The central storage areas are easily accessible to the receiving areas as well as to the food production areas, while the cleaning-supply storage is near the dishwashing area. In general, the design eliminates the need for staff from one work station or section to cross through another station or section.

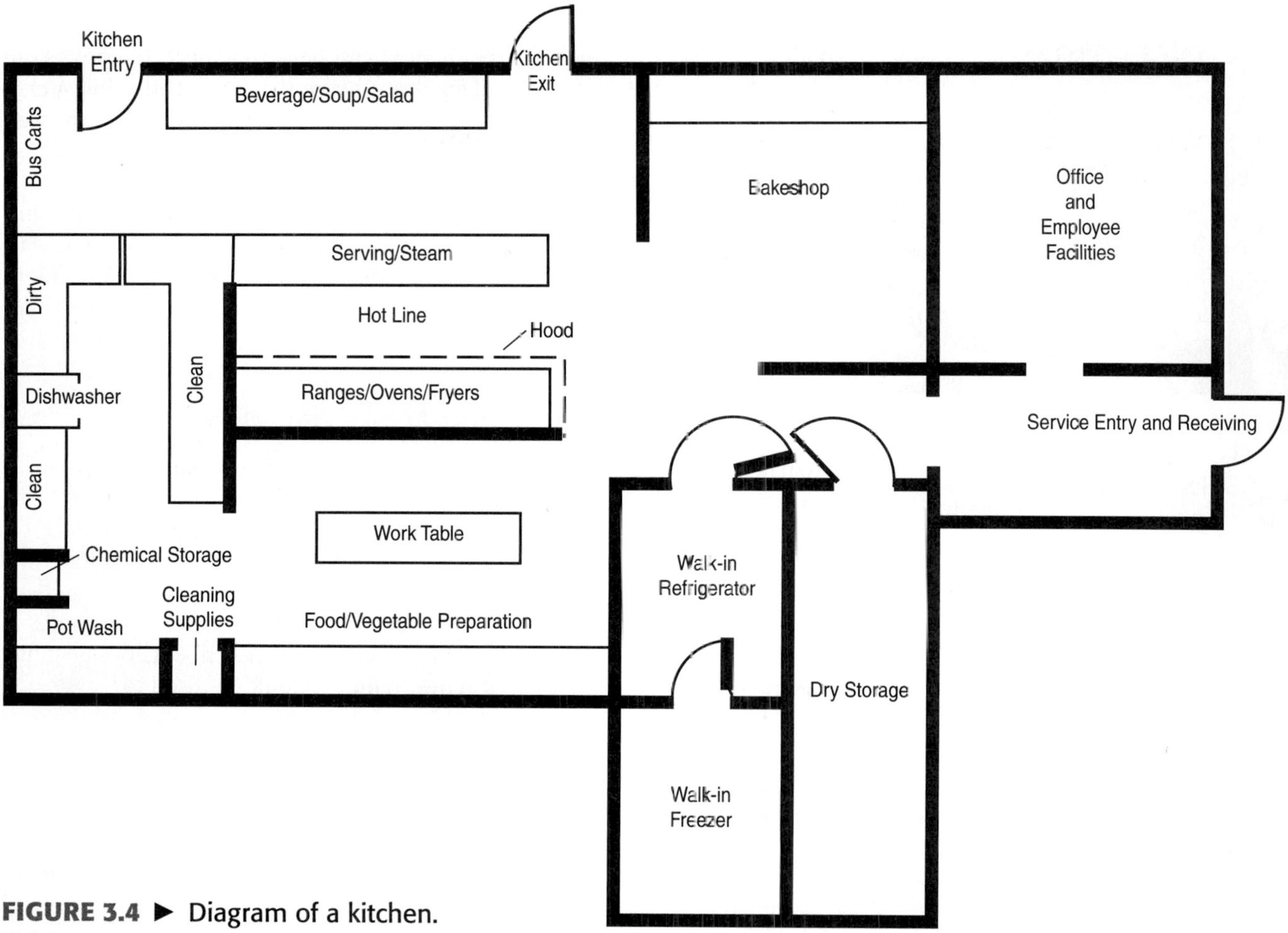

Kitchen Entry
Kitchen Exit
Beverage/Soup/Salad
Bus Carts
Bakeshop
Office and Employee Facilities
Serving/Steam
Dirty
Hot Line
Hood
Clean
Dishwasher
Ranges/Ovens/Fryers
Service Entry and Receiving
Clean
Work Table
Chemical Storage
Walk-in Refrigerator
Cleaning Supplies
Pot Wash
Food/Vegetable Preparation
Dry Storage
Walk-in Freezer

FIGURE 3.4 ▶ Diagram of a kitchen.

ALEXIS SOYER (1809–1858)

The father of the contemporary celebrity chef was Alexis Soyer, a Frenchman whose tragically short working life was spent mostly in London. He was a flamboyant, talented and egocentric showman. He was also a renowned chef, restaurateur, social activist, author, purveyor of prepared foods and inventor.

In 1831, Soyer left his thriving catering business and restaurant in Paris for London. (A scandal was rumored to be behind his sudden departure.) There he quickly established a reputation as a talented chef in the latest French fashion. By 1838, he was employed at a gentlemen's club called the Reform. Able to assist in planning the club's new kitchen facility, Soyer installed the most modern equipment: gas ovens with temperature controls, a steam-driven mechanical spit and a storage locker cooled by running water. From this modern kitchen he produced his signature dish: lamb chops Reform.

The Reform was founded by members of the Liberal party, a political party interested in social reform. Their chef soon joined the party ranks. He developed recipes for inexpensive, nutritious soups for the working class and in 1847 went to Ireland and opened soup kitchens to feed those who were starving as a result of the potato famine.

His most important writings reflect his interests in good food for the masses. The intended audience for *The Modern Housewife* (1849) was the middle class; the growing urban working class was the intended audience for his second book, *A Schilling Cookery for the People* (1855).

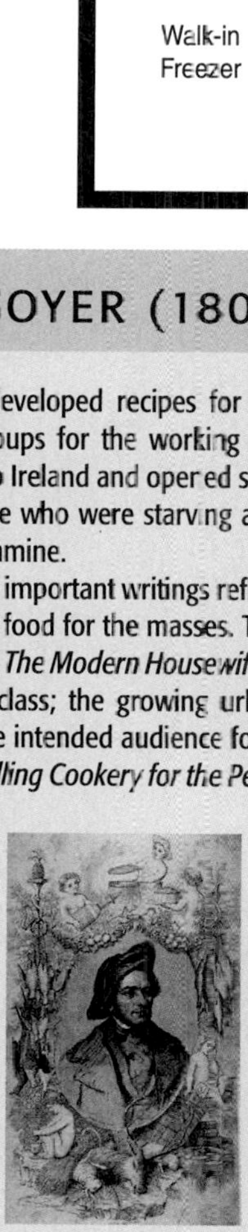

Courtesy of Barbara Wheaton

In 1851, Soyer opened his own lavishly decorated and expensively equipped restaurant called the Gastronomic Symposium of All Nations. It closed shortly thereafter, in part because of Soyer's debts, in part because he lost his operating license as a result of the rowdiness in the restaurant's American-style bar, at which customers were publicly served cocktails for the first time in London.

In addition to cooking and writing, Soyer created and marketed several prepared food items: Soyer's Sauce, Soyer's Nectar and Soyer's Relish. He was also fascinated with kitchen gadgets and invented several, including a sink stopper, jelly mold, egg cooker and coffeepot. The most notable, however, was a portable "Magic Stove" weighing less than 4 pounds, similar to a modern chafing dish. Soyer's final triumph was in the Crimean War (1854–1857). He developed army rations, reorganized field and hospital kitchens and introduced one of his last inventions, the campaign stove. Portable, efficient and requiring little fuel, it was used by the British army for the next 90 years.

CONCLUSION

Hundreds of tools and pieces of equipment can help you prepare, cook, store and present food. Every year, manufacturers offer new or improved items. A chef will use many of them throughout his or her career. Select those that are well constructed, durable and best suited for the task at hand. Then use them in a safe and efficient manner.

The way in which equipment is arranged and stored in a kitchen is also important. Good kitchen design emphasizes the efficient flow of goods and staff from one work section to another as well as within each work section or station.

QUESTION FOR DISCUSSION

1. What is NSF International? What is its significance with regard to commercial kitchen equipment?
2. List the parts of a chef's knife and describe the knife's construction.
3. List six materials used to make commercial cookware and describe the advantages and disadvantages of each.
4. Describe six pieces of equipment that can be used to slice or chop foods.
5. List four classes of fire extinguishers. For each one, describe its designating symbol and identify the type or types of fire it should be used to extinguish.
6. Explain the relationship between work sections and work stations and the kitchen brigade system discussed in Chapter 1, Professionalism.

7. Use the Internet to locate vendors, obtain specifications and compare warranties and prices for a piece of commercial kitchen equipment.
8. Research information on selecting and installing a wood-burning oven in a commercial kitchen.

CHAPTER **FOUR**

EVERY MORNING ONE MUST START FROM SCRATCH,
WITH NOTHING ON THE STOVES.
THAT IS CUISINE.

—Fernand Point,
French restaurateur
(1897–1955)

KNIFE SKILLS

AFTER STUDYING THIS CHAPTER, YOU WILL BE ABLE TO:

- care for knives properly
- use knives properly
- cut foods into a variety of classic shapes

Every professional must become skilled in the use of certain tools. The professional chef is no exception. One of the most important tools the student chef must master is the knife. Good knife skills are critical to a chef's success because the knife is the most commonly used tool in the kitchen. Every chef spends countless hours slicing, dicing, mincing and chopping. Learning to perform these tasks safely and efficiently is an essential part of a student's training.

At first, professional knives may feel large and awkward and the techniques discussed in this chapter may not seem all that efficient. But as students become familiar with knives and practice their knife skills, using knives correctly will become second nature.

Knives are identified in Chapter 3, Tools and Equipment. Here we show how they are used to cut vegetables. The techniques presented, however, can be used for almost any food that holds its shape when cut. Knife skills for butchering and fabricating meat, poultry, fish and shellfish are discussed in Chapter 11, Principles of Meat Cookery, through Chapter 18, Fish and Shellfish.

A note about language: Many of the classic cuts are known by their French names: *julienne,* for example. Although these words are nouns and entered the English language as nouns (for example, a julienne of carrot), they are also used as verbs (to julienne a carrot) and adjectives (julienned carrots).

▸ Using Your Knife Safely

The first rule of knife safety is to think about what you are doing. Other basic rules of knife safety are as follows:

1. Use the correct knife for the task at hand.
2. Always cut away from yourself.
3. Always cut on a cutting board. Do not cut on glass, marble or metal.
4. Place a damp towel underneath the cutting board to keep it from sliding as you cut.
5. Keep knives sharp; a dull knife is more dangerous than a sharp one.
6. When carrying a knife, hold it point down, parallel and close to your leg as you walk.
7. A falling knife has no handle. Do not attempt to catch a falling knife; step back and allow it to fall.
8. Never leave a knife in a sink of water; anyone reaching into the sink could be injured or the knife could be dented by pots or other utensils.

▶ CARING FOR YOUR KNIFE

KNIFE SHARPENING

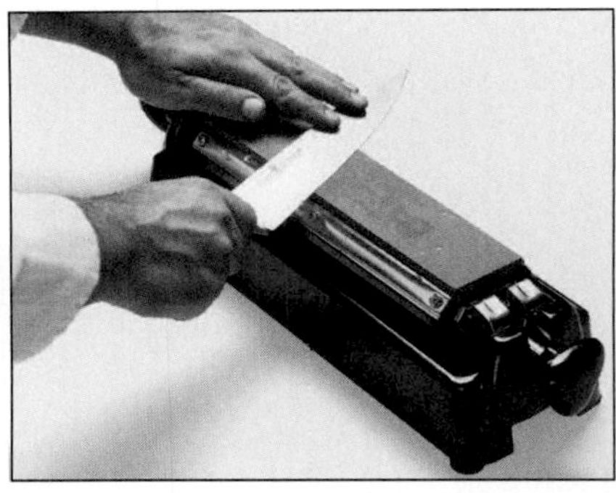

When sharpening a knife against a three-sided whetstone, go from the coarsest to the finest surface.

A sharpening stone called a **whetstone** is used to put an edge on a dull knife blade. To use a whetstone, place the heel of the blade against the whetstone at a 20-degree angle. Keeping that angle, press down on the blade while pushing it away from you in one long arc, as if to slice off a thin piece of the stone. The entire length of the blade should come in contact with the stone during each sweep. Repeat the procedure on both sides of the blade until sufficiently sharp. With a triple-faced stone, such as that shown here, you progress from the coarsest to the finest surface. Any whetstone can be moistened with either water or mineral oil, but not both. Do not use vegetable oil on a whetstone because it will soon become rancid and gummy.

A **steel** does not sharpen a knife. Rather, it is used to hone or straighten the blade immediately after and between sharpenings. To use a steel, place the blade against the steel at a 20-degree angle. Then draw the blade along the entire length of the steel. Repeat the technique several times on each side of the blade.

Honing a knife against a steel straightens the blade between sharpenings.

WASHING AND STORING KNIVES

Proper sanitation of knives is essential to prevent cross-contamination. Always sanitize, rinse and dry knives by hand immediately after each use. Do not wash knives in commercial dishwashers. The heat and harsh chemicals can damage the edge and the handle. In addition, the knife could injure an unsuspecting worker if left in a sink full of water.

To prevent dulling their blades, store knives so that their blades never touch other knives or tools. Slotted knife holders or magnetized strips can be wall-mounted near work stations. The portable knife kit, made from flexible washable material, is designed to hold each knife in an individual protective sleeve.

▶ GRIPPING YOUR KNIFE

There are several different ways to grip a knife. Use the grip that is most comfortable for you or the one dictated by the job at hand. Whichever grip you use should be firm but not so tight that your hand becomes tired. Gripping styles are shown here.

The most common grip: Hold the handle with three fingers while gripping the blade between the thumb and index finger.

A variation on the most common grip: Grip the handle with four fingers and place the thumb on the front of the handle.

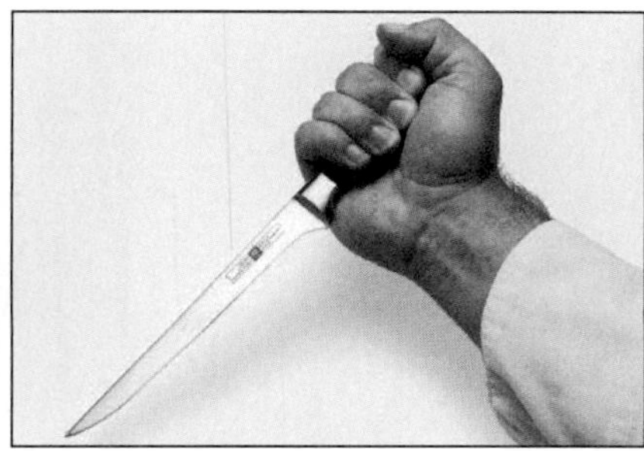

The underhand grip for a rigid boning knife: Grip the handle in a fist with four fingers and thumb. This grip allows you to use the knife tip to cut around joints and separate flesh from bone when boning meat and poultry.

▶ Controlling Your Knife

To safely produce even cuts, you must control (or guide) your knife with one hand and hold the item being cut with the other. Always allow the blade's sharp edge to do the cutting. Never force the blade through the item being cut. Use smooth, even strokes. Using a dull knife or excessive force with any knife produces, at best, poor results and, at worst, a significant safety risk. Cutting without using your hand as a guide may also be dangerous. Two safe cutting methods that produce good results are shown here.

Method A

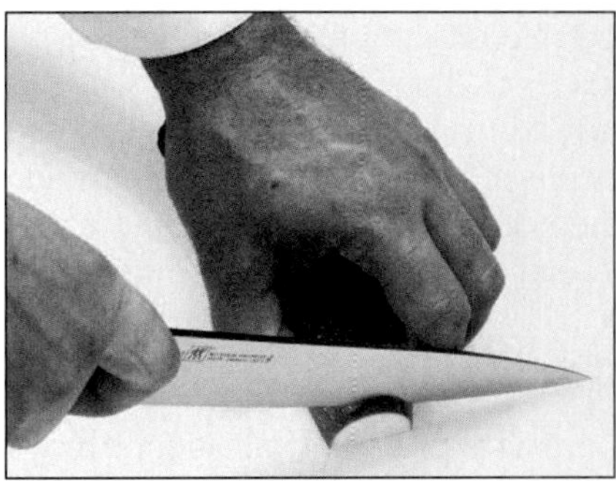

1 Keeping your fingertips curled back, grip the item being cut with three fingertips and your thumb. Hold the knife in the other hand. While keeping the knife's tip on the cutting board, lift the heel of the knife.

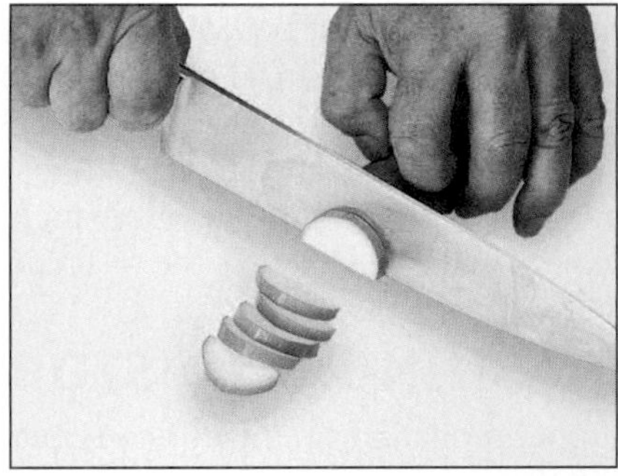

2 Using the second joint of your index finger as a guide, cut a slice using a smooth, even, downward stroke. Adjust the position of the guiding finger after each slice to produce slices of equal size. After a few cuts, slide your fingertips and thumb down the length of the item and continue slicing. For this slicing technique, the knife's tip acts as the fulcrum.

Method B

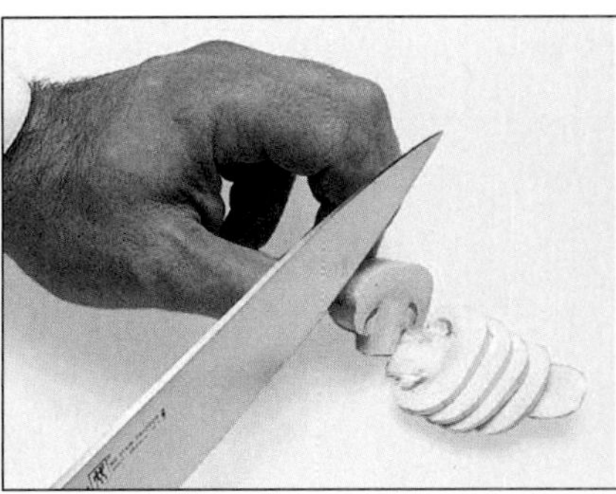

1 Grip the item as described above. Using the second joint of your index finger as a guide, lift the knife's tip and slice by drawing the knife slightly back toward you and down through the item, cutting the item to the desired thickness.

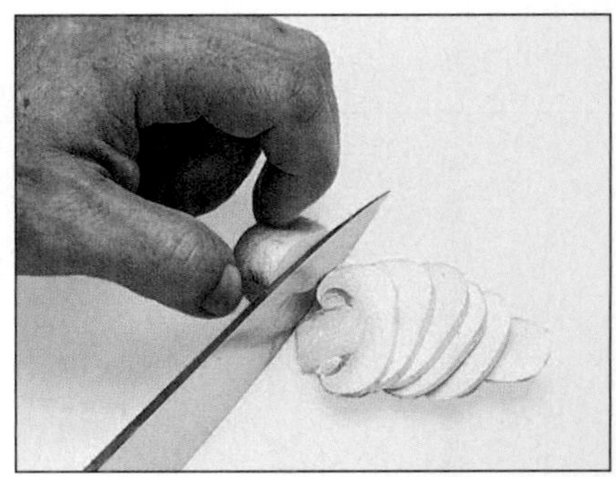

2 The motion of the knife should come almost entirely from the wrist, not the elbow. Allow the weight of the knife to do most of the work; very little downward pressure needs to be applied to the knife. For this slicing technique, your wrist should act as the fulcrum.

► Cutting with Your Knife

A knife is used to shape an item and reduce its size. Uniformity of size and shape ensures even cooking and enhances the appearance of the finished product. Items are shaped by slicing, chopping, dicing, mincing and other special cutting techniques.

SLICING

To slice is to cut an item into relatively broad, thin pieces. Slices may be either the finished cut or the first step in producing other cuts. Slicing is typically used to create three specialty cuts: chiffonade, rondelle and diagonal. Slicing skills are also used to produce oblique or roll cuts and lozenges.

A **chiffonade** is a preparation of finely sliced or shredded leafy vegetables used as a garnish or a base under cold presentations. As shown here, slicing spinach en chiffonade is a relatively simple process.

► **chiffonade** (chef-fon-nahd) to finely slice or shred leafy vegetables or herbs

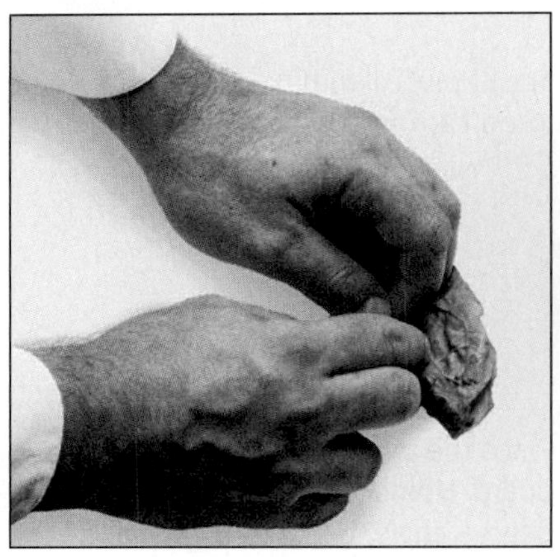

1 Wash and destem the leaves as necessary. Stack several leaves on top of each other and roll them tightly like a cigar.

2 Make fine slices across the leaves while holding the leaf roll tightly.

As seen here, **rondelles** or **rounds** are easily made disk-shaped slices of cylindrical vegetables or fruits.

► **rondelles** (ron-dellz) disk-shaped slices

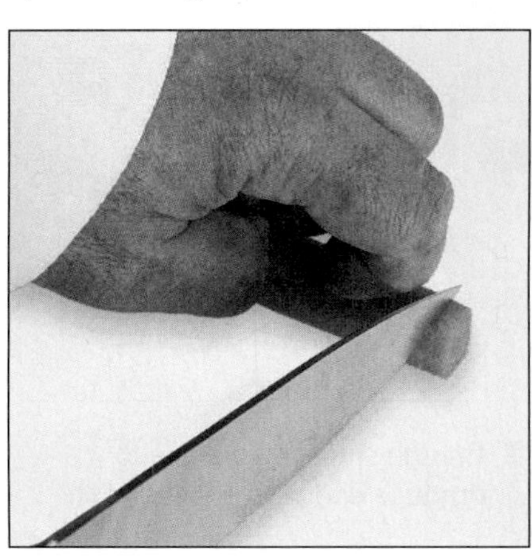

Peel the item (if desired) and place it on a cutting board. Make even slices perpendicular to the item being cut.

▶ **diagonals** oval-shaped slices

Diagonals or bias cuts are elongated or oval-shaped slices of cylindrical vegetables or fruits. They are produced with a cut similar to that used to cut rondelles except that the knife is held at an angle to the item being cut.

Peel the item (if desired) and place it on a cutting board. Position the knife at the desired angle to the item being cut and slice it evenly.

▶ **oblique cuts** (oh-BLEEK) small pieces with two angle-cut sides

Oblique-cut or **roll-cut** items are small pieces with two angle-cut sides. It is a relatively simple cut most often used on carrots and parsnips.

Place the peeled item on a cutting board. Holding the knife at a 45-degree angle, make the first cut. Roll the item a half turn, keeping the knife at the same angle, and make another cut. The result is a wedge-shaped piece with two angled sides.

▶ **lozenges** diamond-shaped pieces, usually of firm vegetables

Lozenges are diamond-shaped cuts prepared from firm vegetables such as carrots, turnips, rutabagas and potatoes.

1 Slice the item into long slices of the desired thickness. Then cut the slices into strips of the desired width.

2 Cut the strips at an angle to produce diamond shapes.

HORIZONTAL SLICING

To horizontal slice is to **butterfly** or cut a pocket into meats, poultry or fish. It is also a method of cutting used to thinly slice soft vegetables.

▶ **butterfly** to slice boneless meat, poultry or fish nearly in half lengthwise so that it spreads open like a book

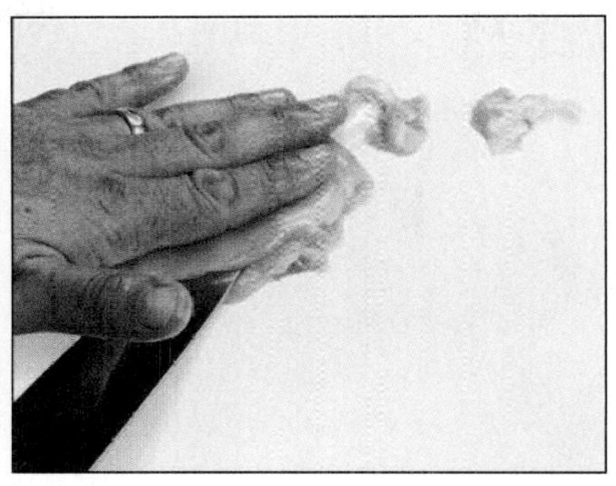

1 With your hand opened and your fingers arched upward, hold the item to be cut firmly in the center of your palm.

2 Holding the knife parallel to the table, slice a pocket to the desired depth, or cut through the item completely.

CHOPPING

To **chop** is to cut an item into small pieces when uniformity of size and shape is neither necessary (for example, coarsely chopped onions for a mirepoix that will be removed from the stock before service) nor feasible (for example, parsley).

▶ **chop** to cut into pieces when uniformity of size and shape is not important

COARSE CHOPPING

Coarse chopping does not mean carelessly hacking up food. Rather, the procedure is identical to that used for slicing but without the emphasis on uniformity. Coarsely chopped pieces should measure approximately ¾ inch × ¾ inch × ¾ inch (2 cm × 2 cm × 2 cm).

Grip the knife as for slicing. Hold the item being chopped with your other hand. It may not be necessary to use your finger as a guide because uniformity is not crucial.

CHOPPING PARSLEY AND SIMILAR FOODS

Parsley can be cut very coarsely or very finely. As shown here, it is easy to chop parsley and similar foods properly regardless of the desired fineness.

1 Wash the parsley in cold water; drain well. Remove the parsley sprigs from the stems.

2 Grip the knife in one hand. With the other hand spread flat, hold the knife's tip on the cutting board. Keeping the knife's tip on the board, chop the parsley sprigs by rocking the curved blade of the knife up and down while moving the knife back and forth over the parsley.

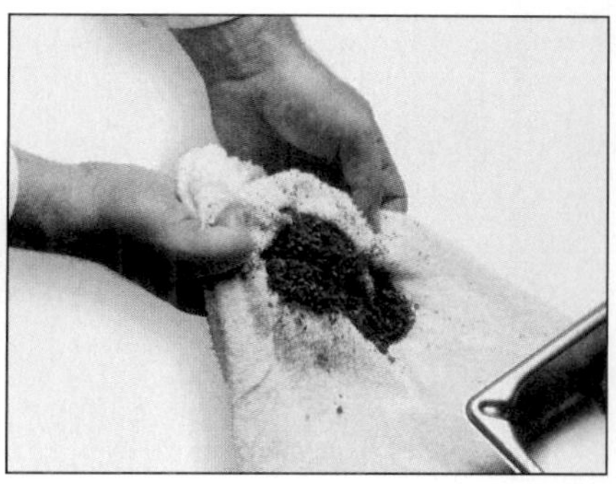

3 Place the chopped parsley in a clean kitchen towel or a double layer of cheesecloth. Rinse it under cold water and squeeze out as much water as possible. The chopped parsley should be dry and fluffy.

CHOPPING GARLIC

A daily chore in many food service facilities, peeling and chopping garlic is a simple job made easy with the procedure shown here.

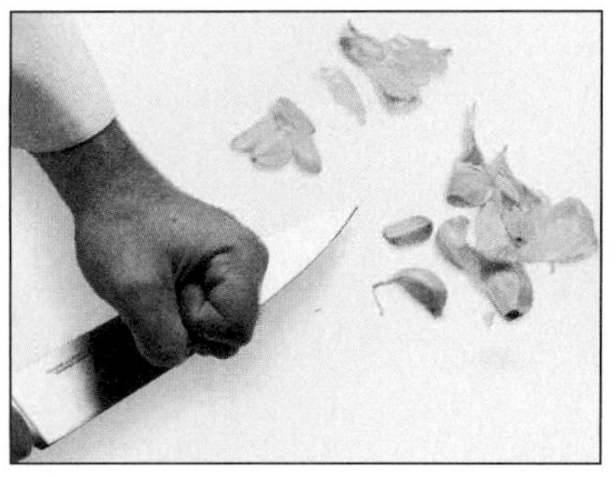

1 Break the head of garlic into individual cloves with your hands. Lightly crush the cloves using the flat edge of a chef's knife or a mallet. They will break open and the peel can be separated easily from the garlic flesh.

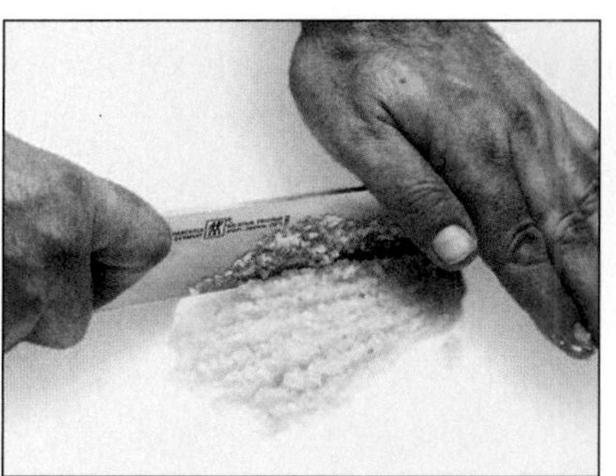

2 With a flat hand, hold the knife's tip on the cutting board. Using a rocking motion, chop the garlic cloves to the desired size. Garlic is usually chopped very finely.

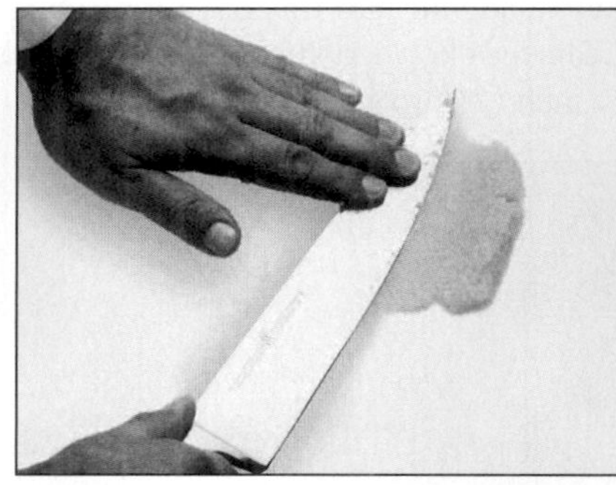

3 Garlic paste can be made by first finely chopping the garlic and then turning the knife on an angle and repeatedly dragging the edge of the knife along the cutting board, mashing the garlic.

CUTTING STICKS AND DICING

To **dice** is to cut an item into cubes. The techniques described here are most often used when uniformity of size and shape is important (for example, julienned carrots for a salad or brunoised vegetables for a garnish).

▶ **dice** to cut into cubes with six equal-sized sides

Before an item can be diced, it must be cut into sticks such as juliennes and bâtonnets. These sticks are then reduced through dicing into the classic cuts known as brunoise, small dice, medium dice, large dice and paysanne. Although most cooks have some notion of what size and shape "small diced" potatoes or julienne carrots may be, there are specific sizes and shapes for these cuts. They are:

Julienne—*(ju-lee-en) a stick-shaped item with dimensions of 1/8 inch × 1/8 inch × 2 inches (3 mm × 3 mm × 5 cm). When used with potatoes, this cut is sometimes referred to as an allumette (al-yoo-MEHT). A fine julienne has dimensions of 1/16 inch × 1/16 inch × 2 inches (1.5 mm × 1.5 mm × 5 cm).*

Bâtonnet—*(BAH-toh-nay) a stick-shaped item with dimensions of 1/4 inch × 1/4 inch × 2 inches (6 mm × 6 mm × 5 cm).*

Brunoise—*(broo-nwaz) a cube-shaped item with dimensions of 1/8 inch × 1/8 inch × 1/8 inch (3 mm × 3 mm × 3 mm). A 1/16-inch (1.5-mm) cube is referred to as a fine brunoise.*

Small dice—*a cube-shaped item with dimensions of 1/4 inch × 1/4 inch × 1/4 inch (6 mm × 6 mm × 6 mm).*

***Medium dice**—a cube-shaped item with dimensions of ½ inch × ½ inch × ½ inch (1.2 cm × 1.2 cm × 1.2 cm).*

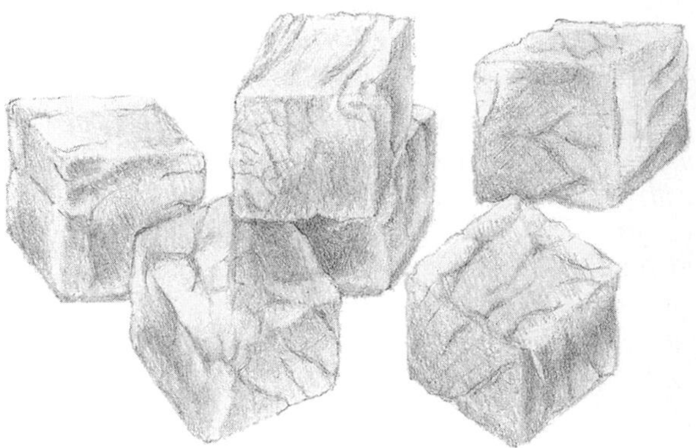

***Large dice**—a cube-shaped item with dimensions of ¾ inch × ¾ inch × ¾ inch (2 cm × 2 cm × 2 cm).*

***Paysanne**—(pahy-sahn) a flat, square, round or triangular item with dimensions of ½ inch × ½ inch × ⅛ inch (1.2 cm × 1.2 cm × 3 mm).*

CUTTING JULIENNE AND BÂTONNET

Julienne and bâtonnet are matchstick-shaped cuts prepared using the same procedure as cutting sticks for dicing.

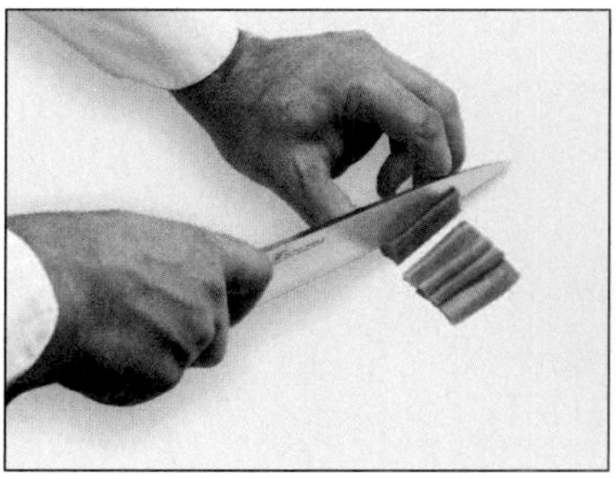

1 Peel the item (if desired) and square off the sides. Trim the item so that the slices cut from it will be the proper length. Cut even slices of the desired thickness, ⅛ inch (3 mm) for julienne or ¼ inch (6 mm) for bâtonnet.

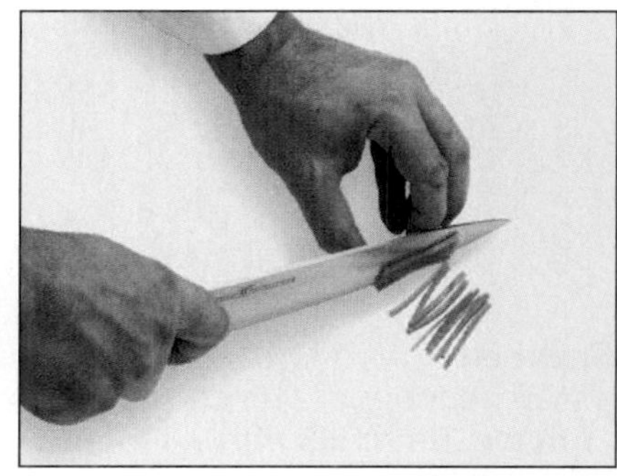

2 Stack the slices and cut them evenly into sticks (also referred to as "planks") that are the same thickness as the slices.

CUTTING BRUNOISE AND SMALL, MEDIUM AND LARGE DICE

Brunoise as well as small, medium and large dice are made by first cutting the item into sticks following the procedure for cutting julienne or bâtonnet, then making cuts perpendicular to the length of the sticks to produce small cubes. Making a ⅛-inch (3-mm) cut perpendicular to the length of a julienne produces a brunoise. Similarly, a fine julienne (1⁄16 inch × 1⁄16 inch × 2 inches) is used to produce a fine brunoise. Making a ¼-inch (6-mm) cut perpendicular to the length of a bâtonnet produces a small dice. A ½-inch (1.2-cm) cut from a ½-inch (1.2-cm) stick produces a medium dice, and a ¾-inch (1.8-cm) cut from a ¾-inch (1.8-cm) stick produces a large dice.

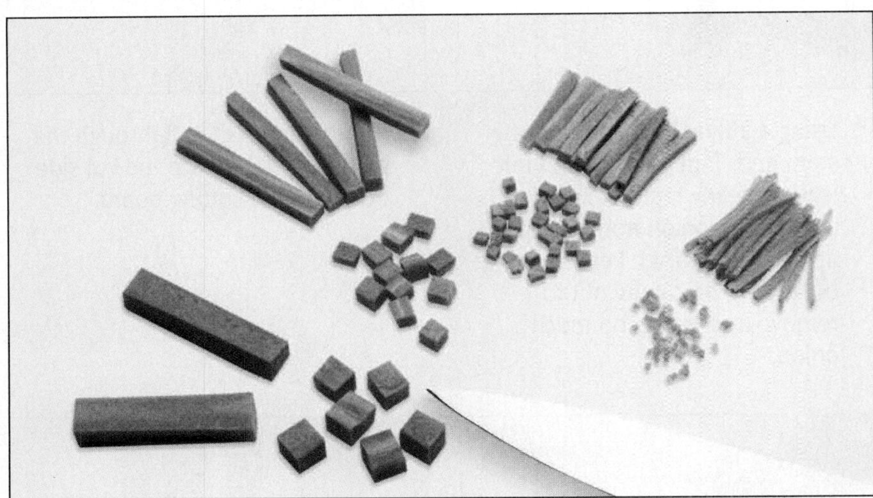

Bâtonnet and julienne sticks and the large, medium, small and brunoise dices cut from them.

CUTTING PAYSANNE

Paysanne is a classic vegetable cut for garnishing soups and other dishes. It could be described as a very thin ½-inch cube. It is produced by following the procedures for dicing, but in the final step the ½-inch × ½-inch (1.2-cm × 1.2-cm) sticks are cut into slices ⅛ inch (3 mm) thick. The term *paysanne* is also used to refer to similarly sized round or triangular pieces.

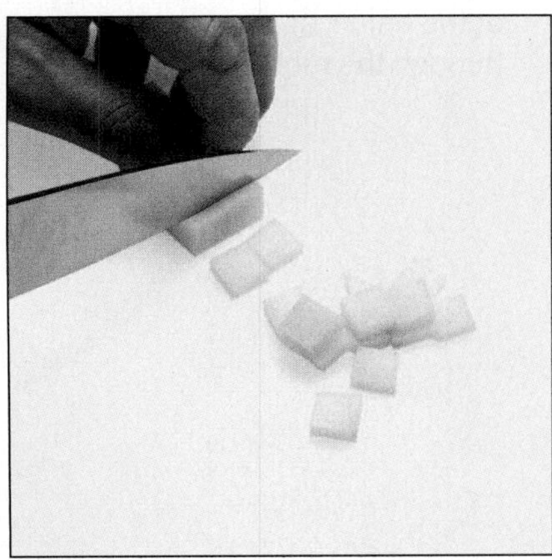

Cutting paysanne from a ½-inch × ½-inch (6-mm × 6-mm) stick.

DICING AN ONION

Onions are easily peeled and diced to any size desired using the procedure shown here.

1 Using a paring knife, remove the stem end. Trim the root end but leave it nearly intact (this helps prevent the onion from falling apart while dicing). Peel away the outer skin; be careful not to remove and waste too much onion.

2 Cut the onion in half through the stem and root. Place the cut side down on the cutting board.

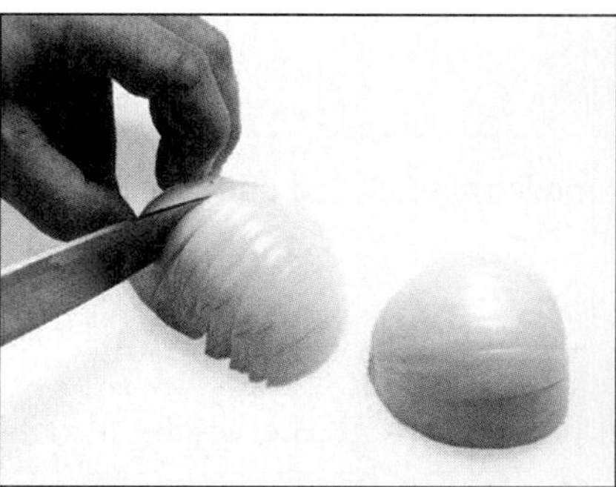

3 Cut parallel slices of the desired thickness vertically through the onion from the root toward the stem end without cutting completely through the root end.

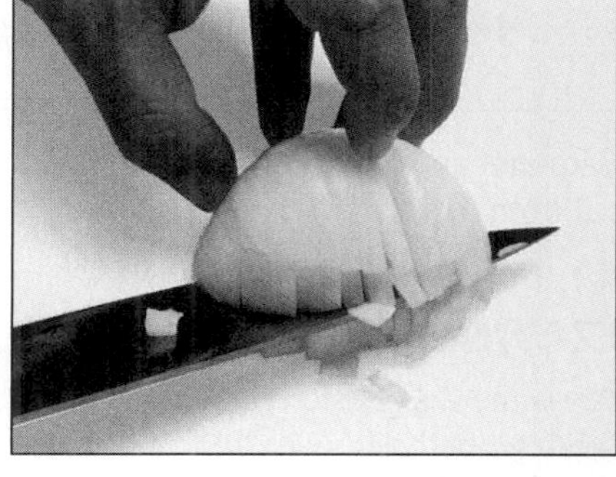

4 Make a single horizontal cut on a small onion or two horizontal cuts on a large onion through the width of the onion, again without cutting through the root end.

5 Turn the onion and cut slices perpendicular to the other slices to produce diced onion.

MINCING

To **mince** is to cut an item into very small pieces. The terms *finely chopped* and *minced* are often used interchangeably and are most often used when referring to garlic, shallots, herbs and other foods that do not have to be uniform in shape.

► **mince** to cut into very small pieces when uniformity of shape is not important

MINCING SHALLOTS

The procedure for mincing shallots is shown here.

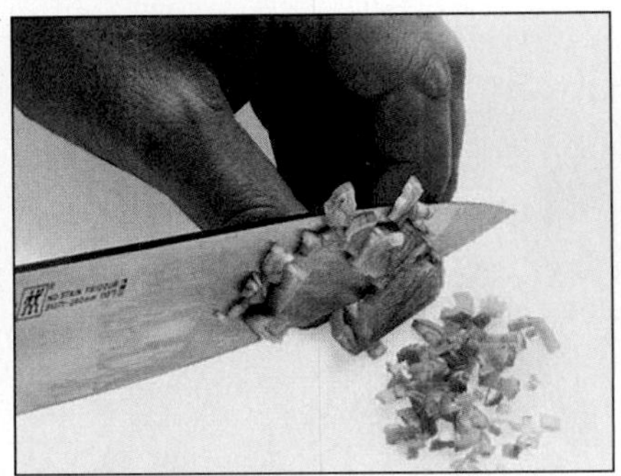

1 Peel and dice the shallots, following the procedure for peeling and dicing an onion.

2 With a flat hand, hold the knife's tip on the cutting board. Using a rocking motion, mince the shallots with the heel of the knife.

TOURNER

Tourner (toor-nay; "to turn" in French) is a cutting technique that results in a football-shaped finished product with seven equal sides and flat ends. The size of the finished product may vary, the most common being 2 inches (5 cm) long and 1 to 1½ inches in diameter. This is a more complicated procedure than other cuts and it takes considerable practice to produce good, consistent results.

► **tourner** (toor-nay) to cut into football-shaped pieces with seven equal sides and blunt ends

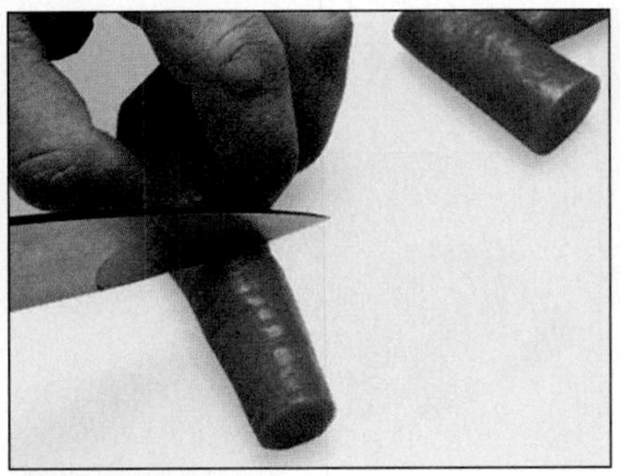

1 Cut the item being "turned" into pieces 2 inches (5 cm) × ¾ to 1 inch (2 to 2.5 cm). Each piece should have flat ends. (Potatoes, turnips and beets may be cut into as many as six or eight pieces; carrots can simply be cut into 2-inch lengths.) Peeling is optional because in most cases the item's entire surface area is trimmed away.

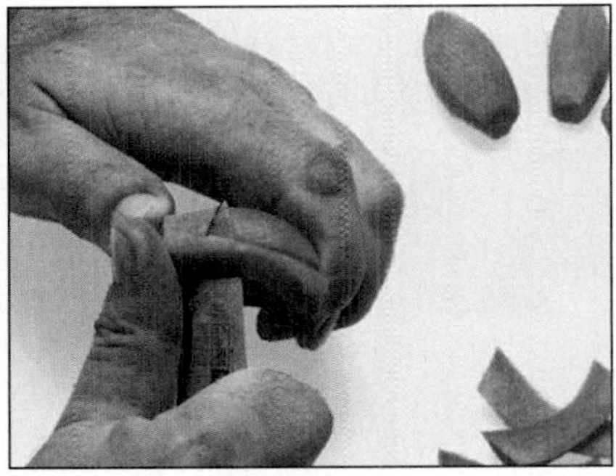

2 Holding the item between the thumb and forefinger, use a tourné knife or a paring knife to cut seven curved sides on the item, creating a flat-ended, football-shaped product.

PARISIENNES

▶ **parisienne** (pah-ree-zee-en) spheres of fruits or vegetables cut with a small melon ball cutter

A melon ball cutter or Parisienne scoop can be used to cut fruits and vegetables into uniform spheres, or **Parisiennes.** Small balls or spheres of fresh melon can be used in fruit salad, while tiny spheres of carrot, turnip, squash and so on can be used as a side dish or to garnish soup or an entrée. Melon ball cutters are available in a range of sizes, the smallest of which has an approximately ⅜-inch (9-mm) diameter and is known as a Parisienne (or Parisian) scoop.

1 Cut each scoop with a pressing and twisting motion.

2 Make the cuts as close together as possible in order to minimize trim loss.

USING A MANDOLINE

▶ **gaufrette** (goh-FREHT) a thin lattice or waffle-textured slice of vegetable cut on a mandoline

The mandoline is a nonmechanical cutting tool. It does jobs that can be done with a chef's knife, such as very thinly sliced apples or large quantities of julienned vegetables, quickly, easily, and very accurately. It can also produce cuts such as a ridged slice or **gaufrette** that cannot be done with a conventional chef's knife.

When using the mandoline, always use the guard or a steel-mesh glove to protect your hand.

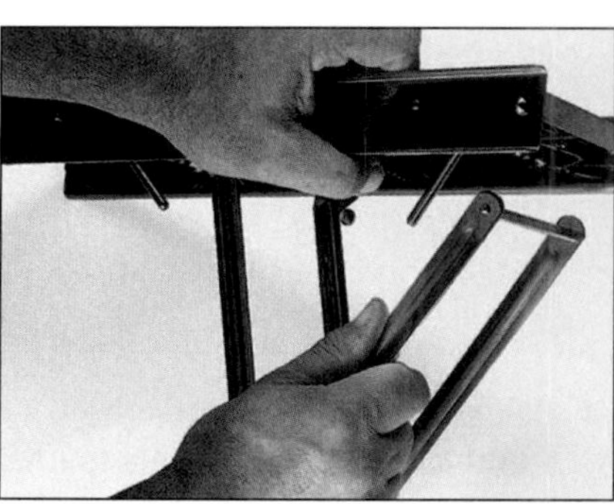

1 To use a mandoline, position the legs and set the blade to the desired shape and thickness.

2 Slide the guard into place.

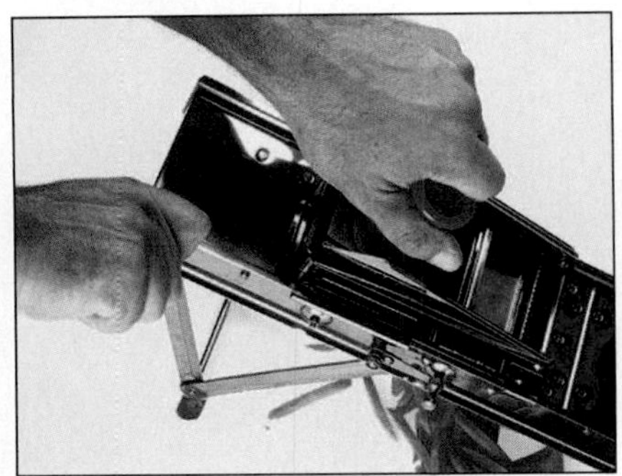

3 To slice, slide the item against the blade with a single, smooth stroke.

4 To cut gaufrette, select the ridged blade and set it to the desired thickness. Make the first slice, turn the item 60 to 90 degrees and make a second slice. Turn the item back to the original position and make another slice, and so on.

CONCLUSION

Although many slicing and dicing machines are available, none can ever completely replace a skilled chef with a sharp knife. Make becoming efficient with knives a high priority. Possessing good knife skills allows more attractive products to be produced in a safe and efficient manner. Chefs will use the classic cuts and techniques outlined in this chapter throughout their careers. Memorize the procedures and practice them often. And remember, a dull or carelessly handled knife is always dangerous.

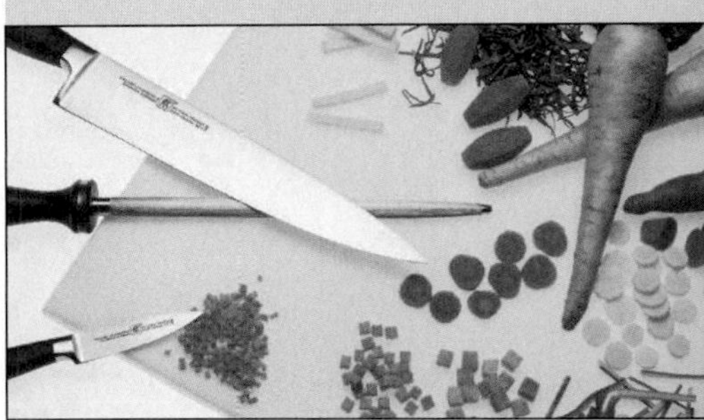

QUESTIONS FOR DISCUSSION

1 Explain the step-by-step procedures for sharpening a knife using a three-sided whetstone.
2 What is the purpose of a steel? How is it used?
3 Why is it necessary to cut vegetables into uniform shapes and sizes?
4 Describe the following cutting procedures: slicing, chopping and dicing.
5 Identify the dimensions of the following cuts: julienne, bâtonnet, brunoise, small dice, medium dice, large dice and paysanne.
6 Describe the procedure for making tournéed vegetables.
7 Describe three preparations for which a mandoline would be useful.
8 A large number of vendors sell professional-quality knives through their Web sites. What are the advantages and disadvantages of buying knives from an online source?

CHAPTER FIVE

FLAVORS AND FLAVORINGS

THE NUMBER OF FLAVORS IS INFINITE, FOR EVERY SOLUBLE BODY HAS A PECULIAR FLAVOR, LIKE NO OTHER.

—*Jean-Anthelme Brillat-Savarin, The Physiology of Taste*

AFTER STUDYING THIS CHAPTER, YOU WILL BE ABLE TO:

- understand the basic principles of the physiology of the sense of taste and smell
- recognize a variety of herbs, spices, oils, vinegars, wines and other flavorings
- understand how to use flavoring ingredients to create, enhance or alter the natural flavors of a dish.

It is the chef's role to consistently present well-flavored foods—to excite the consumer's brain and palate. This can be accomplished by an act as simple as sprinkling a bit of salt over a ripe watermelon to enhance the melon's natural sweetness or as complicated as using a long-simmering stock made from wild mushrooms to enrich a sauce flavored with herbs and wine. In either case, the chef must understand how to flavor foods and be able to recognize flavoring ingredients and know how to use them. This chapter looks at the sense of taste and smell and the flavoring ingredients used in the professional kitchen to enhance foods. Flavorings—the herbs, spices, salt, oils, vinegars, condiments, wines and other alcoholic beverages typically used to create, enhance or alter the natural flavors of a dish—are featured. Flavorings used primarily for baked goods and desserts are discussed in Chapter 28, Principles of the Bakeshop.

▸ FLAVORS

From the simplest grunt of pleasure upon biting into a chunk of meat fresh from the fire to the most sophisticated discourse on the fruity top notes of a full-bodied Cabernet Sauvignon, people have long attempted to describe the flavors of food. This is done by describing physical perceptions ("it tastes tart or sugary" or "it feels greasy") or the recognition of the flavor ("I can sense the rosemary" or "there is a hint of strawberries"). In either case, the terms *flavor* and *taste* are often confused. Although often used interchangeably, they are not synonymous.

A **flavor** is a combination of the tastes, aromas and other sensations caused by the presence of a foreign substance in the mouth. **Tastes** are the sensations we detect when a substance comes in contact with the taste buds on the tongue (sweet, sour, salt, bitter and umami.) Some substances irritate other nerves on the tongue or embedded in the fleshy areas of the mouth. These nerves respond to sensations of pain, heat or cold, or sensations our brain interprets as spiciness, pungency, or astringency. **Mouthfeel** refers to the sensation created in the mouth by a combination of a food's taste, smell, texture and temperature. **Aromas** are the odors that enter the nose or float up through the back of the mouth to activate smell receptors in the nose. Whenever a particular taste, sensation and/or aroma is detected, a set of neurons in the brain is excited and, with experience, we learn to recognize these patterns as the flavor of bananas, chocolate, grilled lamb or sour milk. Each person has a unique ability to recognize and appreciate thousands of these patterns. This compendium of flavors and the ability to recognize them is sometimes referred to as the **palate.**

▸ **flavor** an identifiable or distinctive quality of a food, drink or other substance perceived with the combined senses of taste, touch and smell

▸ **taste** the sensations, as interpreted by the brain, of what we detect when food, drink or other substances come in contact with our taste buds

▸ **aroma** the sensations, as interpreted by the brain, of what we detect when a substance comes in contact with sense receptors in the nose

▸ **mouthfeel** the sensation created in the mouth by a combination of a food's taste, smell, texture and temperature

▸ **palate** (1) the complex of smell, taste and touch receptors that contribute to a person's ability to recognize and appreciate flavors; (2) the range of an individual's recognition and appreciation of flavors

TASTES: SWEET, SOUR, SALTY, BITTER AND NOW UMAMI

Over the centuries, various cultures have developed complex philosophies based, in part, on the basic tastes they found in the foods they ate. For example, as early as 1000 B.C.E., the Chinese were describing the five-taste scheme that they still adhere to today. For them, each of the basic tastes—sweet, sour, salty, bitter and pungent/hot/spicy—is associated with a vital organ of the body, a certain season, a specific element of nature, or an astrological sign. Maintaining the proper balance of tastes in a dish or during a meal assists in the maintenance of good health and good fortune.

About the same time, in what is now India, the practice of ayurvedic medicine was developing. Indians recognized six tastes (and still do): sweet, sour, salty, spicy/pungent, bitter and astringent. Based on the tastes of various herbs and spices, practitioners of ayurvedic medicine associate them with specific vital organs or bodily systems. Indian cooks attempt to create dishes with a balance of all six tastes, in part to encourage good health.

A continent away and several hundred years later, the Greek philosopher Aristotle identified seven tastes in his epic work, *De Anima* (*On the Soul,* ca. 350 B.C.E.). He arranged the various tastes on a sort of continuum with the two primary and contrasting tastes, sweet and bitter, at either end. He placed a secondary taste next to each primary taste: succulent to the right of sweet and salty to the left of bitter. Between these secondary tastes he placed—from left to right—pungent, harsh and astringent. Each taste gave way to the next, creating, along with the other senses, the perception of flavors.

As the understanding of the human body evolved, the definition of taste came to be based more on science than on a balancing of elements. Today, taste is defined as the sensations detected when substances come in contact with the taste buds on the tongue, a process described more fully in the sidebar on page 138. For many years, western cultures have identified four tastes:

Sweet—For most people, sweetness is the most pleasurable and often sought-after taste, although, ironically, the fewer sweet-tasting foods we consume, the more enhanced our ability to recognize sweetness becomes. A food's sweetness comes from the naturally occurring sugars it contains (for example, sucrose and fructose) or sweeteners added to it. This sweetness can sometimes be enhanced by adding a small amount of a sour, bitter or salty taste. Adding too much sourness, bitterness or saltiness, however, will lessen our perception of the food's sweetness.

Sour—Considered the opposite of sweet, a sour taste is found in acidic foods and, like sweetness, can vary greatly in intensity. Many foods with a dominant sour taste, such as red currants or sour cream, will also contain a secondary or slight sweetness. Often a sour taste can be improved by adding a little sweetness or negated by adding a large amount of a sweet ingredient.

Salty—With the notable exception of oysters and other shellfish and seaweed, the presence of a salty taste in a food is the result of the cook's decision to add the mineral sodium chloride, known as salt, or to use a previously salted ingredient such as salt-cured fish or soy sauce. Salt helps finish a dish, heightening or enhancing its other flavors. Dishes that lack salt often taste flat. Like the taste of sweetness, the less salt consumed on a regular basis, the more saltiness we can detect in foods.

Bitter—Although the bitterness associated with tasting alkaloids and other organic substances may occasionally be appreciated, such as when tasting chocolate or coffee, a bitter-flavored ingredient unbalanced by something sour or salty is generally disliked and, as a survival mechanism, is believed to serve as a warning of inedibility or unhealthfulness.

In the past several years, many western researchers have begun to recognize a fifth taste, akin to the **savory** taste long recognized as the fifth taste in Japanese cuisine. Called **umami** (from the Japanese word *umai,* meaning "delicious"), this fifth taste does not have a simple English translation. Rather, for some people it refers to a food's savory characteristic; for others to the richness or fullness of a dish's overall taste, and still others, the meatiness or meaty taste of a dish.

▶ **savory** a food that is not sweet

Taste buds sense umami in the presence of several substances, including the naturally occurring amino acid glutamate and its commercially produced counterpart known as monosodium glutamate (MSG). Cheeses, meats, rich stocks,

HOW WE EXPERIENCE TASTE AND SMELL

The smallest functional unit of taste is the taste bud. These specialized sensory organs can be found on the tongue within three different kinds of **papillae** (Figure 1), as well as the back of the throat and the roof of the mouth. Each taste bud contains several **taste receptor cells,** and **taste compounds** interact with the tops of these specialized cells, which then transmit taste information through a nerve to the brain. The process of tasting begins when a substance is placed in the mouth and taste compounds begin to dissolve in saliva. Mastication, or chewing, further breaks down the substance and increases the concentration of taste compounds dissolved in the saliva. Once dissolved in saliva, the taste compounds have the potential to stimulate taste receptors and ultimately elicit taste sensations. Because compounds must dissolve in the saliva in order to reach the taste receptors, taste compounds must be water-soluble.

The process of smelling begins when odor compounds reach the olfactory neurons, the specialized sensing organs of smell. Olfactory neurons are located at the top of the nasal cavity and are clustered together in the **olfactory bulb** (Figure 2). A separate olfactory bulb rests at the bottom of each hemisphere of the brain and at the top of each nasal cavity. Odor compounds can reach these receptors through two different pathways: orthonasally via the external nares (or **nostrils**) or retronasally via the internal nares. When we sniff or experience odors that are external to our bodies, we are smelling orthonasally. Once we place a substance in our mouths, the aromas we are experiencing are being delivered through the **retronasal path.** Regardless of route, in order for odor compounds to reach the olfactory receptors they must be able to volatilize, or dissolve in air. Since air is hydrophobic, this means most odor compounds do not dissolve well in water, dissolving better in oils.

A pervasive myth (based upon misinterpretation of an article written in German in the 1800s) is that you experience certain taste qualities on only certain areas of the tongue (sweet on the tip, bitter in the back, salt on the front sides and sour on the back sides). In fact, you can taste all taste compounds everywhere on your tongue, and it is easy to prove this to yourself by placing various items representative of sweet, sour, salty, bitter, and even umami on the tip of your tongue. You will be able to immediately perceive any taste at the tongue tip (or anywhere else you have taste buds) and will not need to wait for bitter compounds to diffuse to the back, sour to the back sides, or salt to the sides.

JEANNINE DELWICHE, PH.D., is the head of the Ohio State University Sensory Science Group. She teaches courses on sensory science (which covers the proper way to conduct taste tests) and on wine and beer. Her research focuses on taste, smell and flavor perception, as well as on some of the underlying principles that influence sensory evaluation methodologies. She has also conducted a variety of studies that examine factors that impact product differences and consumer assessments.

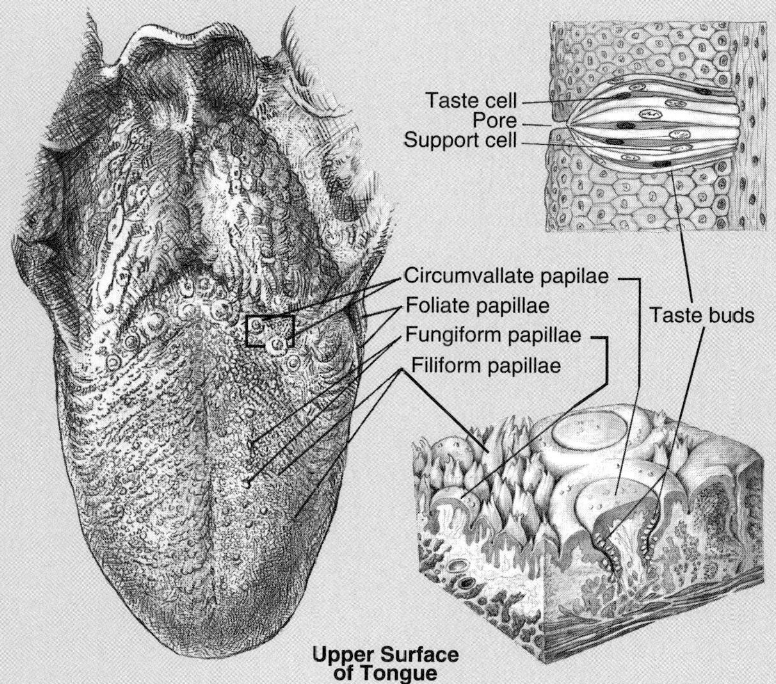

FIGURE 1 ▶ The human tongue and taste buds.

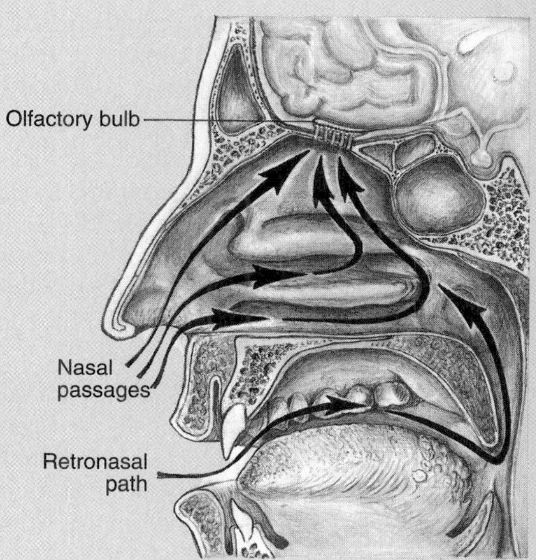

FIGURE 2 ▶ The human olfactory system.

soy sauce, shellfish, fatty fish, mushrooms, tomatoes and wine are all high in glutamate and produce the taste sensation of umami. Aged or fermented foods also provide umami.

Often food professionals and others refer to tastes in addition to sweet, sour, salty, bitter and umami. Typically, they describe something as pungent, hot, spicy or piquant or something that is astringent, sharp or dry. None of these terms, however, fit the definition of a taste, as none are detected solely by taste buds. Rather, these sensations are detected by nerve endings embedded in the fleshy part of the mouth. These nerves, when "irritated" by the presence of compounds such as piperine (the active ingredient in black peppercorns) or capsaicin (the active ingredient in chiles), register a burning sensation that the brain translates as the hot and spicy "taste" of Szechuan or Mexican cuisines, for example.

FACTORS AFFECTING PERCEPTION OF FLAVORS

Obviously, the most important factors affecting the flavor of a dish are the quantity, quality and concentration of the flavoring ingredients. (With practice, a chef gains a feel for the proper proportions.) Other factors that affect one's perception of flavors include the following:

Temperature—Foods at warm temperatures offer the strongest tastes. Heating foods releases volatile flavor compounds, which intensifies one's perceptions of odors. This is why fine cheese is served at room temperature to improve its eating quality and flavor. Foods tend to lose their sour or sweet tastes both the colder and the hotter they become. Saltiness, however, is perceived differently at extreme cold temperatures; the same quantity of salt in a solution is perceived more strongly when very cold than when merely cool or warm. Therefore, it is best to adjust a dish's final flavors at its serving temperature. That is, *season hot foods when they are hot and cold foods when they are cold.*

Consistency—A food's consistency affects its flavor. Two items with the same amount of taste and smell compounds that differ in texture will differ in their perceived intensity and onset time; the thicker item will take longer to reach its peak intensity and will have a less intense flavor. For example, two batches of sweetened heavy cream made from the same ingredients in the same proportions can taste different if one is whipped and the other is unwhipped; the whipped cream has more volume and therefore a milder flavor.

Presence of contrasting tastes—Sweet and sour are considered opposites, and often the addition of one to a food dominated by the other will enhance the food's overall flavor. For example, adding a little sugar to vinaigrette reduces the dressing's sourness, or adding a squeeze of lemon to a broiled lobster reduces the shellfish's sweetness. But add too much, and the dominant taste will be negated. Likewise, adding something sweet, sour or salty to a dish with a predominantly bitter flavor will cut the bitterness.

Presence of fats—Many of the chemical compounds that create tastes and aromas are dissolved in the fats naturally occurring in foods or added to foods during cooking. As these compounds are slowly released by evaporation or saliva, they provide a sustained taste sensation. If, however, there is too little fat, the flavor compounds may not be released efficiently, resulting in a dish with little sustained flavor. Too much fat poses another problem; it can coat the tongue and interfere with the ability of taste receptors to perceive flavor compounds.

Color—A food's color affects how the consumer will perceive the food's flavor before it is even tasted. When foods or beverages lack their customary color, they are less readily identified correctly than when appropriately colored. As color level changes to match normal expectations, our perception of taste and flavor intensity increases. A miscue created by the perceived flavor (the flavor associated with the color) can have an adverse impact on the

SUPERTASTERS, MEDIUM TASTERS AND NONTASTERS

Recent research into the physiology of taste has shown that some people detect a greater degree of a taste in foods than others. Called **supertasters** by Professor Linda Bartoshuk at Yale University, these people may have more taste buds than average, possibly twice as many as **nontasters** or **medium tasters.** In addition to detecting strongly bitter flavors where many people do not (for example, in coffee, broccoli, Brussels sprouts, grapefruit juice and green tea), supertasters also tend to perceive artificial sweeteners as sweeter than do the rest of the population and with a bitter aftertaste that most people miss. Similarly, supertasters find the spicy heat generated by capsaicin to be more pronounced, sometimes unbearably so, than does the average person.

A person's responsiveness to tastes appears to influence food choices. Supertasters tend to avoid strong-tasting foods such as coffee, rich or very sweet desserts, greasy or spicy meats, green leafy vegetables and so on. They also tend not to crave fats or sugars. Cooks who are nontasters may not realize when a food would be too sweet or too bitter to medium- or supertasters. And supertaster cooks may unconsciously avoid using foods that would be perfectly delicious to everyone else. It is easy to determine one's taste level with special chemically treated test papers.

consumer's appreciation of the actual flavor. For example, if the predominant flavor of a dessert is lemon, the dessert or some component of the dessert should be yellow; a green color will trigger an expectation of lime and the possible disappointment of the consumer. Similarly, the dark ruby-red flesh of a blood orange looks different from the bright orange flesh of a Valencia orange. This tonal difference can create the expectation of a different, non-orangey flavor, even though the blood orange's flavor is similar to that of other sweet orange varieties. Likewise, a sliced apple that has turned brown may suggest an off-flavor, although there is none.

COMPROMISES TO THE PRECEPTION OF TASTE

The sense of taste can be challenged by factors both within and beyond one's control. Age and general health can diminish one's perception of flavor, as can fatigue and stress. Chefs need to be aware of the age and health of their clientele, adjusting the seasoning of foods served according to their needs. Here are some factors, described by Jeannine Delwiche, Ph.D., that can affect one's taste perceptions.

Age. "The bad news is that taste and smell sensitivity does decline as we age. The good news is that it declines at a slower rate than our vision and hearing. The sense of smell tends to decline earlier than the sense of taste. There is a great deal of variance across individuals, with some showing declines earlier than others."

Health. "An acute condition, such as a cold, can result in a temporary loss of smell. The presence of mucus can prevent airflow, preventing the odor compounds from reaching the olfactory receptors. In contrast, the sense of taste would remain largely unaffected. Medications can also alter the perception of taste and smell. Some medications suppress the perceptions of saltiness, while others result in chronic perception of bitterness. Still other medications alter salivary flow, making it difficult to swallow dry foods. A further complication is the underlying conditions for taking medication. If an individual is taking high blood pressure medications, not only may the medication have a direct impact on perceived taste, but the same individual is likely to be on a sodium-restricted diet."

Smoking. "Anecdotal reports from those who quit smoking strongly indicate that smoking diminishes odor sensitivity. This is further supported by evidence indicating that people who smoke generally are less sensitive to odors than those who do not. In contrast, evidence indicates that if one waits two hours after smoking, the sense of taste is unaltered. Immediately after smoking, however, taste sensitivity is lowered."

DESCRIBING AROMAS AND FLAVORS IN FOOD

Food scientists and professional tasters make their living describing the smell and taste of foods. Many have attempted to standardize the language used to describe positive and negative aromas and flavors in foods such as beer, cheese, chocolate, coffee and fish. Frequently they employ flavor wheels or other charts to identify types of flavors and tastes found in foods.

One useful list employed by chemists to describe sixteen broad categories of tastes and smells that correspond to the major chemicals found in aromas and tastes is shown in Table 5.1. Such a list is helpful when trying to analyze and describe the flavors in a dish.

DESCRIBING FOOD USING FLAVOR PROFILES

A food's **flavor profile** describes its flavor from the moment the consumer gets the first whiff of its aroma until he or she swallows that last morsel. It is a con-

Table 5.1 COMMON FLAVOR DESCRIPTIONS

TYPE OF AROMA OR FLAVOR	FOODS WITH SUCH CHARACTERISTICS
Green, grassy	Green bell peppers, raw apple skins
Fruity, esterlike	Bananas, apples
Citrus, terpenic	Lemons, limes
Minty, camphoraceous	Fresh mint, rosemary
Floral, sweet	Roses, violets, honey
Spicy, herbaceous	Allspice, cinnamon, nutmeg
Woody, smoky	Smoked foods
Roasty, burnt	Coffee, toasted bread
Caramel, nutty	Burnt sugar, molasses
Bouillon, high vegetable protein	Meat stock
Meaty, animalic	Roasted meat
Fatty, rancid	Fishy smell
Sulfurous, alliaceous	Onions, garlic, rotten egg
Mushroom, earthy	Cooked mushrooms, damp soil, yeasty bread
Celery, soupy	Celery, parsnip
Dairy, buttery	Cheese

venient way to articulate and evaluate a dish's sensory characteristics as well as identify contrasting or complementing items that could be served with it.

A food's flavor profile consists of one or more of the following elements:

Top notes or high notes—the sharp, first flavors or aromas that come from citrus, herbs, spices and many condiments. These top notes provide instant impact and dissipate quickly.

Middle notes—the second wave of flavors and aromas. More subtle and more lingering than top notes, middle notes come from dairy products, poultry, some vegetables, fish and some meats.

Low notes or bass notes—the most dominant, lingering flavors. These flavors consist of the basic tastes (especially sweetness, sourness, saltiness and umami) and come from foods such as anchovies, beans, chocolate, dried mushrooms, fish sauce, tomatoes, most meats (especially beef and game) and garlic. Or they can be created by smoking or caramelizing the food's sugars during grilling, broiling and other dry-heat cooking processes.

Aftertaste or finish—the final flavor that remains in the mouth after swallowing; for example, the lingering bitterness of coffee or chocolate or the pungency of black pepper or a strong mustard.

Roundness—the unity of the dish's various flavors achieved through the judicious use of butter, cream, coconut milk, reduced stocks, salt, sugar and the like; these ingredients cause the other flavorings to linger without necessarily adding their own dominant taste or flavor.

Depth of flavor—whether the dish has a broad range of flavor notes.

These expressions can be applied to any dish to describe its sensory characteristics. For example, Roman-Style Free-Range Chicken has a flavor profile with a top note of rosemary. Its middle notes are contributed by the chicken, and the low notes from the anchovies and garlic. There is an aftertaste of garlic and vinegar. The sauce adds roundness to the chicken, thus creating a dish with a fine

FROM THE LABORATORY TO THE DINING TABLE: HOW FLAVORINGS ARE MADE

Flavor creation, like the culinary art, is a blend of science and creativity. The role of science is to identify the minute trace components of food that define its characteristic odor. This is done using a combination of techniques–gas chromatography, liquid chromatography, mass spectrometry and nuclear magnetic resonance to produce an analysis of the volatile organic compounds in the food. The analysis of sautéed chicken, for example, would contain hundreds of ingredients at levels ranging from parts per million down to fractions of a part per billion.

A purely scientific approach to formulation would involve such complex interactions that it would take a lifetime to make one flavor. At this stage creativity has to take over. The creative process is similar to that used by a chef. The flavorist attempts to form a mental picture of the possible combinations of the key parts of the composition that trigger the recognition of "chicken." Depending on the flavor type, this may be anywhere from two or three components to as many as fifteen. Typically fruits, herbs, and spices are relatively simple; heated or processed foods such as cooked chicken, beer or roasted coffee are more complex.

Once the basic chicken profile has been established, the secondary notes can be built up. In this case we would reproduce the sautéed character. We would also push the character of the flavor in the best direction for the target audience. Whether a skin note should be included would be a typical question.

So far we have considered only odor. It is very easy to confuse flavor, taste and odor, but in reality odor is the key differentiating characteristic that separates great food from simply good food. Although odor is far more important than taste, a flavor lacking any taste components will not taste very authentic. The next step is to build in subtle taste characteristics; perhaps a hint of bitterness would add realism to this flavor?

At this stage our flavor might contain as many as 60 ingredients, which could be chemicals derived from nature or natural extracts, so it is a fairly complex mixture. It will have omitted many of the components found in the analysis and concentrated on the attractive elements of the flavor. The object is not to duplicate nature, but rather to learn from nature and beat her at her own game.

Finally the flavor is tailored to the end use. Many factors in finished food can alter the consumer's perception of flavor; processing temperature, fat content and storage conditions are the most important. High processing temperature will cause a differential loss of the more volatile components, the top notes, and this must be rectified by either modifying the formulation or protecting the flavor from the heat process.

JOHN WRIGHT is Vice President of Global Technical Business Development for International Flavors & Fragrances Inc.

▶ **seasoning** an item added to enhance the natural flavors of a food without dramatically changing its taste; salt is the most common seasoning

▶ **flavoring** an item that adds a new taste to a food and alters its natural flavors; flavorings include herbs, spices, vinegars and condiments; the terms *seasoning* and *flavoring* are often used interchangeably.

▶ **herb** any of a large group of aromatic plants whose leaves, stems or flowers are used as a flavoring; used either dried or fresh

▶ **aromatic** a food added to enhance the natural aromas of another food; aromatics include most flavorings, such as herbs and spices, as well as some vegetables

▶ **spice** any of a large group of aromatic plants whose bark, roots, seeds, buds or berries are used as a flavoring; usually used in dried form, either whole or ground

▶ **condiment** traditionally, any item added to a dish for flavor, including herbs, spices and vinegars; now also refers to cooked or prepared flavorings such as prepared mustards, relishes, bottled sauces and pickles

depth of flavor. An experienced chef is able to taste and evaluate a version of this dish, adjusting flavorings, ingredients and cooking technique as needed to maintain the balance of flavors in the original recipe.

▶ FLAVORINGS: HERBS AND SPICES

Herbs and spices are used as **flavorings. Herbs** refer to the large group of **aromatic** plants whose leaves, stems or flowers are used to add flavors to other foods. Most herbs are available fresh or dried. Because drying alters their flavors and aromas, fresh herbs are generally preferred and should be used if possible. **Spices** are strongly flavored or aromatic portions of plants used as flavorings, **condiments** or aromatics. Spices are the bark, roots, seeds, buds or berries of plants, most of which grow naturally only in tropical climates. Spices are almost always used in their dried form, rarely fresh, and can usually be purchased whole or ground. Some plants—dill, for example—can be used as both an herb (its leaves) and a spice (its seeds).

HERBS

Basil (Fr. *basilic*) is considered one of the great culinary herbs. It is available in a variety of "flavors"—cinnamon, garlic, lemon, even chocolate—but the most common is sweet basil. Sweet basil has light green, tender leaves and small white flowers. Its flavor is strong, warm and slightly peppery, with a hint of cloves. Basil is used in Mediterranean and some Southeast Asian cuisines and has a special affinity for garlic and tomatoes. When purchasing fresh basil, look for bright green leaves;

Basil

avoid flower buds and wilted or rust-colored leaves. Dried sweet basil is readily available but has a decidedly weaker flavor.

Opal basil is named for its vivid purple color. It has a tougher, crinkled leaf and a medium-strong flavor. Opal basil may be substituted for sweet basil in cooking, and its appearance makes it a distinctive garnish.

Opal Basil

Bay (Fr. *laurier*), also known as sweet laurel, is a small tree from Asia that produces tough, glossy leaves with a sweet balsamic aroma and peppery flavor. Bay symbolized wisdom and glory in ancient Rome; the leaves were used to form crowns or "laurels" worn by emperors and victorious athletes. In cooking, dried bay leaves are often preferred over the more bitter fresh leaves. Essential in French cuisine, bay leaves are part of the traditional bouquet garni and court bouillon. Whole dried leaves are usually added to a dish at the start of cooking, then removed when sufficient flavor has been extracted.

Bay Leaves

Chervil

Chervil (Fr. *cerfeuil*), also known as sweet cicely, is native to Russia and the Middle East. Its lacy, fernlike leaves are similar to parsley and can be used as a garnish. Chervil's flavor is delicate, similar to parsley but with the distinctive aroma of anise. It should not be heated for long periods. Chervil is commonly used in French cuisine and is one of the traditional *fines herbes*.

Chives

Chives (Fr. *ciboulettes*) are perhaps the most delicate and sophisticated members of the onion family. Their hollow, thin grass-green stems grow in clumps and produce round, pale purple flowers, which are used as a garnish. Chives may be purchased dried, quick-frozen or fresh. They have a mild onion flavor and bright green color. Chives complement eggs, poultry, potatoes, fish and shellfish. They should not be cooked for long periods or at high temperatures. Chives make an excellent garnish when snipped with scissors or carefully chopped and sprinkled over finished soups or sauces.

Garlic Chives

Garlic chives, also known as Chinese chives, actually belong to another plant species. They have flat, solid (not hollow) stems and a mild garlic flavor. They may be used in place of regular chives if their garlic flavor is desired.

Cilantro (Fr. *coriandre*) is the green leafy portion of the plant that yields seeds known as coriander. The flavors of the two portions of this plant are very different and cannot be substituted for each other. Cilantro, also known as Chinese parsley, is sharp and tangy with a strong aroma and an almost citrus flavor. It is widely used in Asian, Mexican and South American cuisines, especially in salads and sauces. It should not be subjected to heat, and cilantro's flavor is completely destroyed by drying. Do not use yellow or discolored leaves or the tough stems. When used in excess, cilantro can impart a soapy taste to foods.

Cilantro

Curry leaves (Hindi *karipatta; kitha neem*) are the distinctively flavored leaves of a small tree that grows wild in the Himalayan foothills, southern India and Sri Lanka. They look like small shiny bay leaves and have a strong currylike fragrance and a citrus-curry flavor. Often added to a preparation whole, then removed before serving, they can also be minced or finely chopped for marinades and sauces. Choose fresh bright green leaves, if possible, or frozen leaves; dried leaves have virtually no flavor. Although used in making southern Indian and Thai dishes, curry leaves (also known as neem leaves) must not be confused with curry powder, which is discussed later.

Curry Leaves

Dill

Dill (Fr. *aneth*), a member of the parsley family, has tiny, aromatic, yellow flowers and feathery, delicate blue-green leaves. The leaves taste like parsley,

Epazote

but sharper, with a touch of anise. Dill seeds are flat, oval and brown, with a bitter flavor similar to caraway. Both the seeds and the leaves of the dill plant are used in cooking. Dill is commonly used in Scandinavian and central European cuisines, particularly with fish and potatoes. Both leaves and seeds are used in pickling and sour dishes. Dill leaves are available fresh or dried but lose their aroma and flavor during cooking, so add them only after the dish is removed from the heat. Dill seeds are available whole or ground and are used in fish dishes, pickles and breads.

Epazote, also known as wormseed or stinkweed, grows wild throughout the Americas. It has a strong aroma similar to kerosene and a wild flavor. Fresh epazote is used in salads and as a flavoring in Mexican and Southwestern cuisines. It is often cooked with beans to reduce their gaseousness. Dried epazote is brewed to make a beverage.

Lavender is an evergreen with thin leaves and tall stems bearing spikes of tiny purple flowers. Although lavender is known primarily for its aroma, which is widely used in perfumes, soaps and cosmetics, the flowers are also used as a flavoring, particularly in Middle Eastern and Provençal cuisines. These flowers have a sweet, lemony flavor and can be crystallized and used as a garnish. Lavender is also used in jams and preserves and to flavor teas and tisanes.

Lavender

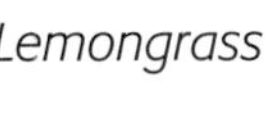

Lemongrass

Lemongrass (Fr. *herbe de citron*), also known as citronella grass, is a tropical grass with the strong aroma and flavor of a lemon. It is similar to scallions in appearance but with a woody texture. Only the lower base and white leaf stalks are used. Available fresh or quick-frozen, lemongrass is widely used in Southeast Asian cuisines.

Lime leaves from a species of thorny lime trees (citrus hystrix) are used much like bay leaves to flavor soups and stews in Thai and other Asian cuisines. These small, dark green leaves have a bright citrus floral aroma. Fragrant lime leaves are available fresh in the United States now that these trees are cultivated domestically.

Fragrant Lime Leaves

Lovage (Fr. *céleri bâtard,* "false celery") has tall stalks and large dark green celery-like leaves. The leaves, stalks and seeds (which are commonly known as **celery seeds**) have a strong celery flavor. Also known as sea parsley and smallage, the leaves and stalks are used in salads and stews and the seeds are used for flavoring.

Marjoram

Marjoram (Fr. *marjolaine*), also known as sweet marjoram, is a flowering herb native to the Mediterranean and used since ancient times. Its flavor is similar to thyme but sweeter; it also has a stronger aroma. Marjoram is now used in many European cuisines. Although it is available fresh, marjoram is one of the few herbs whose flavor increases when dried. Wild marjoram is more commonly known as oregano.

Mint (Fr. *menthe*), a large family of herbs, includes many species and flavors (even chocolate). Spearmint is the most common garden and commercial variety. It has soft, bright green leaves and a tart aroma and flavor. Mint does not blend well with other herbs, so its use is confined to specific dishes, usually fruits or fatty meats such as lamb. Mint has an affinity for chocolate. It can also be brewed into a beverage or used as a garnish.

Spearmint

Peppermint

Peppermint has thin, stiff, pointed leaves and a sharper menthol flavor and aroma. Fresh peppermint is used less often in cooking or as a garnish than spearmint, but peppermint oil is a common flavoring in sweets and candies.

Oregano

Oregano (Fr. *origan*), also known as wild marjoram, is a pungent, peppery herb used in Mediterranean cuisines, particularly Greek and Italian, as well as in Mexican cuisine. It is a classic complement to tomatoes. Oregano's thin, woody stalks bear clumps of tiny, dark green leaves, which are available dried and crushed.

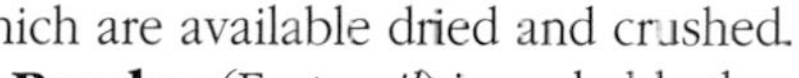

Parsley (Fr. *persil*) is probably the best known and most widely used herb in the world. It grows in almost all climates and is available in many varieties, all of which are rich in vitamins and minerals. The most common type in the United States and Northern Europe is **curly parsley.** It has small curly leaves and a bright green color. Its flavor is tangy and clean. Other cuisines use a variety sometimes known as **Italian parsley,** which has flat leaves, a darker color and coarser flavor. Curly parsley is a ubiquitous garnish; both types can be used in virtually any food except sweets. Parsley stalks have a stronger flavor than the leaves and are part of the standard bouquet garni. Chopped parsley forms the basis of any fine herb blend.

Parsley

Italian Parsley

Rosemary

Rosemary (Fr. *romarin*) is an evergreen bush that grows wild in warm, dry climates worldwide. It has stiff, needlelike leaves; some varieties bear pale blue flowers. It is highly aromatic, with a slight odor of camphor or pine. Rosemary is best used fresh. When dried, it loses flavor, and its leaves become very hard and unpleasant to chew. Whole rosemary stems may be added to a dish such as a stew and then removed when enough flavor has been imparted. They may also be added to a bouquet garni. Rosemary has a great affinity for roasted and grilled meats, especially lamb.

Sage (Fr. *sauge*) was used as a medicine for centuries before it entered the kitchen as a culinary herb. Culinary sage has narrow, fuzzy, gray-green leaves and blue flowers. Its flavor is strong and balsamic, with notes of camphor. Sage is used in poultry dishes, with fatty meats or brewed as a beverage. Sage's strong flavor does not blend well with other herbs. It dries well and is available in whole or chopped leaves or rubbed (coarsely ground).

Sage

Savory

Savory (Fr. *sariette*) has been used since ancient times. Its leaves are small and narrow, and it has a sharp, bitter flavor, vaguely like thyme. It dries well and is used in bean dishes, sausages and fine herb blends. While the variety called *summer savory* is most common and popular, a variety called *winter savory* is also available.

Tarragon

Tarragon (Fr. *estragon*), another of the great culinary herbs, is native to Siberia. It is a bushy plant with long, narrow, dark green leaves and tiny gray flowers. Tarragon goes well with fish and tomatoes and is essential in many French dishes such as béarnaise sauce and fine herb blends. Its flavor is strong

Thyme

and diffuses quickly through foods. It is available dried, but drying may cause haylike flavors to develop.

Thyme (Fr.*thym*) has been popular since 3500 B.C.E., when Egyptians used it as a medicine and for embalming. Thyme is a small, bushy plant with woody stems, tiny green-gray leaves and purple flowers. Its flavor is strong but refined, with notes of sage. Thyme dries well and complements virtually all types of meat, poultry, fish, shellfish and vegetables. It is often included in a bouquet garni or added to stocks.

SPICES

Aleppo Pepper

Aleppo pepper (ah-LEHP-oh) is made from bright red chiles grown in Turkey and northern Syria. The sun-dried Aleppo chiles are seeded and crushed, then used as a condiment. It has a sharp, but sweet, fruity flavor, with only mild heat (15,000 Scoville units, discussed in Chapter 20, Vegetables). Although a member of the *capsicum* family, Aleppo pepper is used more like ground peppercorns (*piper nigrum*) than a chile. Also known as Halaby pepper, it adds an authentic Mediterranean flavor and fragrance to foods.

Allspice

Allspice (Fr. *quatre-épices*), also known as Jamaican pepper, is the dried berry of a tree that flourishes in Jamaica, and one of the few spices still grown exclusively in the New World. Allspice is available whole; in berries that look like large, rough, brown peppercorns; or ground. Ground allspice is not a mixture of spices, although it does taste like a blend of cinnamon, cloves and nutmeg. Allspice is now used throughout the world, in everything from cakes to curries, and is often included in peppercorn blends.

Anise (Fr. *anis*) is native to the eastern Mediterranean, where it was widely used by ancient civilizations. Today it is grown commercially in warm climates throughout India, North Africa and southern Europe. The tiny, gray-green egg-shaped seeds have a distinctively strong, sweet flavor, similar to licorice and fennel. When anise seeds turn brown, they are stale and should be discarded. Anise is used in pastries as well as fish, shellfish and vegetable dishes, and is commonly used in alcoholic beverages (for example, Pernod and ouzo). The green leaves of the anise plant are occasionally used fresh as an herb or in salads.

Anise Seeds

Star Anise

Star anise, also known as Chinese anise, is the dried, star-shaped fruit of a Chinese magnolia tree. Although it is botanically unrelated, its flavor is similar to anise seeds but more bitter and pungent. It is an essential flavor in many Chinese dishes and one of the components of five-spice powder.

Annatto seeds (Fr. *roucou*) are the small, brick-red triangular seeds of a shrub from South America and the Caribbean. Annatto seeds add a mild, peppery flavor to rice, fish and shellfish dishes and are crushed to make Mexican achiote paste. Because they impart a bright yellow-orange color to foods, annatto seeds are commonly used as a natural food coloring, especially in cheeses and margarine.

Annatto Seeds

Asafetida (ah-sah-FEH-teh-dah; also spelled asafoetida) is a pale brown resin made from the sap of a giant fennel-like plant native to India and Iran. Also known as devil's dung, it has a garlicky flavor and a strong unpleasant fetid aroma (the aroma is not transferred to food being flavored). Available powdered or in lump form, it is used—very sparingly—as a flavoring in Indian and Middle Eastern cuisines.

Capers

Capers (Fr. *capres*) come from a small bush that grows wild throughout the Mediterranean basin. Its unopened flower buds have been pickled and used as a condiment for thousands of years. Fresh capers are not used, as the sharp, salty-

A PINCH OF HISTORY

Spices have been used for many purposes for thousands of years. Egyptian papyri dating back to 2800 B.C.E. identify several spices native to the Middle and Far East that were used by the ruling and priestly classes for therapeutic, cosmetic, medicinal, ritualistic and culinary purposes. By A.D. 300, the Romans were regularly importing spices for use as perfumes, medicines, preservatives and ingredients from China and India via long, difficult caravan journeys over sea and land. Spices were extremely expensive and unavailable to all but the wealthiest citizens.

After Rome fell in the second half of the fifth century A.D., much of the overland route through southern Europe became prey to bandits; after Constantinople fell in 1453, the Ottoman Turks controlled the spice routes through the Middle East. Spice costs soared and economies based on the spice trade, such as that of Venice, were at risk.

By then highly spiced food had become common, especially in wealthier households. So, in part to maintain their culinary norm, the Europeans set out to break the Ottoman Turk monopoly. These efforts led to Columbus's exploration of the Americas and Vasco da Gama's discovery of a sea route to India. Although the New World contained none of the spices for which Columbus was searching, it provided many previously unknown foods and flavorings that subsequently changed European tables forever, including chiles, vanilla, tomatoes, potatoes and chocolate.

Formation of the Dutch East India Company in 1602 marked the start of the Dutch colonial empire and made spices from what is now Indonesia, whose Molucca Islands were once referred to as the "Spice Islands," widely available to the growing European middle classes. The transplantation and cultivation of spice plants eventually weakened the once-powerful trading empires until, by the 19th century, no European country could monopolize trade. Prices fell dramatically.

sour flavor develops only after curing in strongly salted white vinegar. The finest capers are the smallest, known as nonpareils, which are produced in France's Provence region. Capers are used in a variety of sauces (tartare, rémoulade) and are excellent with fish and game. Capers will keep for long periods if moistened by their original liquid. Do not add or substitute vinegar, however, as this causes the capers to spoil.

Caraway (Fr. *carvi*) is perhaps the world's oldest spice. Its use has been traced to the Stone Age, and seeds have been found in ancient Egyptian tombs. The caraway plant grows wild in Europe and temperate regions of Asia. It produces a small, crescent-shaped brown seed with the peppery flavor of rye. Seeds may be purchased whole or ground. (The leaves have a mild, bland flavor and are rarely used in cooking.) Caraway is a very European flavor, used extensively in German and Austrian dishes, particularly breads, meats and cabbage. It is also used in alcoholic beverages and cheeses.

Caraway Seeds

Cardamom Seeds

Cardamom (Fr. *cardamome*) is one of the most expensive spices, second only to saffron in cost. Its seeds are encased in ¼-inch- (6-millimeter-) long light green or brown pods. Cardamom is highly aromatic. Its flavor, lemony with notes of camphor, is quite strong and is used in both sweet and savory dishes. Cardamom is widely used in Indian and Middle Eastern cuisines, where it is also used to flavor coffee. Scandinavians use cardamom to flavor breads and pastries. Ground cardamom loses its flavor rapidly and is easily adulterated, so it is best to purchase whole seeds and grind your own as needed.

► For our purposes, *chile* refers to the plant, *chili* refers to the stewlike dish containing chiles and *chilli* refers to the commercial spice powder

Chiles, including paprika, chile peppers, bell peppers and cayenne, are members of the capsicum plant family. Although cultivated for thousands of years in the West Indies and Americas, capsicum peppers were unknown in the Old World prior to Spanish explorations during the 15th century. Capsicum peppers come in all shapes and sizes, with a wide range of flavors, from sweet to extremely hot. Some capsicums are used as a vegetable, while others are dried, ground and used as a spice. Fresh chiles and bell peppers are discussed in Chapter 20, Vegetables. Capsicums are botanically unrelated to *piper nigrum,* the black peppercorns discussed later.

Cayenne, sometimes simply labeled "red pepper," is ground from a blend of several particularly hot types of dried red chile peppers. Its flavor is extremely hot and pungent; it has a bright orange-red color and fine texture.

Cayenne Pepper

Paprika

Paprika, also known as Hungarian pepper, is a bright red powder ground from specific varieties of red-ripened and dried chiles. Paprika's flavor ranges from sweet to pungent; its aroma is distinctive and strong. It is essential to many

Chilli Powder

Spanish and eastern European dishes. Mild paprika is meant to be used in generous quantities and may be sprinkled on prepared foods as a garnish.

Chile powders are made from a wide variety of dried chile peppers, ranging from sweet and mild to extremely hot and pungent. The finest pure chile powders come from dried chiles that are simply roasted, ground and sieved. Commercial chilli powder, an American invention, is actually a combination of spices—oregano, cumin, garlic and other flavorings—intended for use in Mexican dishes. Each brand is different and should be sampled before using.

Crushed Chiles

Crushed chiles, also known as chile flakes, are blended from dried, coarsely crushed chiles. They are quite hot and are used in sauces and meat dishes.

Cinnamon (Fr. *cannelle*) and its cousin cassia are among the oldest known spices: Cinnamon's use is recorded in China as early as 2500 B.C.E., and the Far East still produces most of these products. Both cinnamon and cassia come from the bark of small evergreen trees, peeled from branches in thin layers and dried in the sun. High-quality cinnamon should be pale brown and thin, rolled up like paper into sticks known as quills. Cassia is coarser and has a stronger, less subtle flavor than cinnamon. Consequently, it is cheaper than true cinnamon. Cinnamon is usually purchased ground because it is difficult to grind. Cinnamon sticks are used when long cooking times allow for sufficient flavor to be extracted (for example, in stews or curries). Cinnamon's flavor is most often associated with pastries and sweets, but it has a great affinity for lamb and spicy dishes. Labeling laws do not require that packages distinguish between cassia and cinnamon, so most of what is sold as cinnamon in the United States is actually cassia, blended for consistent flavor and aroma.

Ground Cinnamon and Cinnamon Sticks

Cloves

Cloves (Fr. *clous de girofle*) are the unopened buds of evergreen trees that flourish in muggy tropical regions. When dried, whole cloves have hard, sharp prongs that can be used to push them into other foods, such as onions or fruit, in order to provide flavor. Cloves are extremely pungent, with a sweet, astringent aroma. A small amount provides a great deal of flavor. Cloves are used in desserts and meat dishes, preserves and liquors. They may be purchased whole or ground.

Coriander (Fr. *coriandre*) seeds come from the cilantro plant. They are round and beige, with a distinctive sweet, spicy flavor and strong aroma. Unlike other plants in which the seeds and the leaves carry the same flavor and aroma, coriander and cilantro are very different. Coriander seeds are available whole or ground and are frequently used in Indian cuisine and pickling mixtures.

Coriander Seeds

Cumin

Cumin is the seed of a small delicate plant of the parsley family that grows in North Africa and the Middle East. The small seeds are available whole or ground and look (but do not taste) like caraway seeds. Cumin has a strong earthy flavor and tends to dominate any dish in which it is included. It is used in Indian, Middle Eastern and Mexican cuisines, in sausages and a few cheeses.

Fennel

Fennel (Fr. *fenouil*) is a perennial plant with feathery leaves and tiny flowers long cultivated in India and China as a medicine and cure for witchcraft. Its seeds are greenish brown with prominent ridges and short, hairlike fibers. Their taste and aroma are similar to anise, though not as sweet. Whole seeds are widely used in Italian stews and sausages; central European cuisines use fennel with fish, pork, pickles and vegetables. Ground seeds can also be used in breads, cakes and cookies. The same plant produces a bulbous stalk used as a vegetable.

Fenugreek (Fr. *fenugrec*), grown in Mediterranean countries since ancient times, is a small, beanlike plant with a tiny flower. The seeds, available whole or ground, are pebble shaped and transfer their pale orange color to the foods with which they are cooked. Their flavor is bittersweet, like burnt sugar with a bitter aftertaste. Fenugreek is a staple in Indian cuisines, especially curries and chutneys.

Filé powder (fee-LAY) is the dried, ground leaf of the sassafras plant. Long used by Choctaw Indians, it is now most commonly used as a thickener and flavoring in Cajun and Creole cuisines. Filé is also used as a table condiment to add a spicy note to stews, gumbo and the like. The powder forms strings if allowed to boil, so it should be added during the last minutes of cooking.

Galangal (guh-LANG-guhl) is the rhizome of a plant native to India and Southeast Asia. The rhizome has a reddish skin, an orange or whitish flesh and a peppery, gingerlike flavor and piny aroma. Also known as galanga root, Thai ginger and Laos ginger, it is peeled and crushed for use in Thai and Indonesian cuisines. Fresh ginger is an appropriate substitute.

Ginger (Fr. *gingembre*) is a well-known spice obtained from the rhizome of a tall, flowering tropical plant. Fresh ginger is known as a "hand" because it looks vaguely like a group of knobby fingers. It has grayish-tan skin and a pale yellow, fibrous interior. Fresh ginger should be plump and firm with smooth skin. It should keep for about a month under refrigeration. Its flavor is fiery but sweet, with notes of lemon and rosemary. Fresh ginger is widely available and is used in Indian and Asian cuisines. It has a special affinity for chicken, beef and curries. Ginger is also available peeled and pickled in vinegar, candied in sugar or preserved in alcohol or syrup. Dried, ground ginger is a fine yellow powder widely used in pastries. Its flavor is spicier and not as sweet as fresh ginger.

Grains of paradise are the seeds of a perennial reedlike plant indigenous to the West African coast. Related to cardamom, grains of paradise have a spicy, warm and slightly bitter flavor, similar to peppercorns. In fact, grains of paradise were traditionally used in place of black pepper and are also known as Guinea pepper or Melegueta pepper. Now enjoying a resurgence in popularity and increased availability, they are ground and used primarily in West African and Magreb dishes, and in the spice blend known as ras el hanout.

Horseradish (Fr. *raifort*) is the large off-white taproot of a hardy perennial (unrelated to radishes) that flourishes in cool climates. Fresh roots should be firm and plump; they will not have the distinctive horseradish aroma unless cut or bruised. The outer skin and inner core of a fresh horseradish root can have an unpleasant flavor and should be discarded. Typically used in Russian and Central European cuisines, especially as an accompaniment to roasted meats and fish and shellfish dishes, horseradish is usually served grated, creamed into a sauce or as part of a compound butter or mustard preparation. If horseradish is cooked, heat can destroy its flavor and pungency, so any horseradish should be added near the end of cooking.

Juniper (Fr. *genièvre*) is an evergreen bush grown throughout the Northern Hemisphere. It produces round purple berries with a sweet flavor similar to pine. Juniper berries are used for flavoring gin and other alcoholic beverages, and are crushed and incorporated in game dishes, particularly venison and wild boar.

Mustard seeds (Fr. *moutarde*), available in black, brown and yellow, come from three different plants in the cabbage family. Mustard seeds are small, hard spheres with a bitter flavor. The seeds have no aroma, but their flavor is sharp and fiery hot. Yellow seeds have the mildest and black seeds the strongest flavor. All are sold whole and can be crushed for cooking. Mustard seeds are a standard component of pickling spices and are processed and blended for prepared mustards, which we discuss later. Ground or dry mustard is a bright yellow powder made from a blend of ground seeds, wheat flour and turmeric.

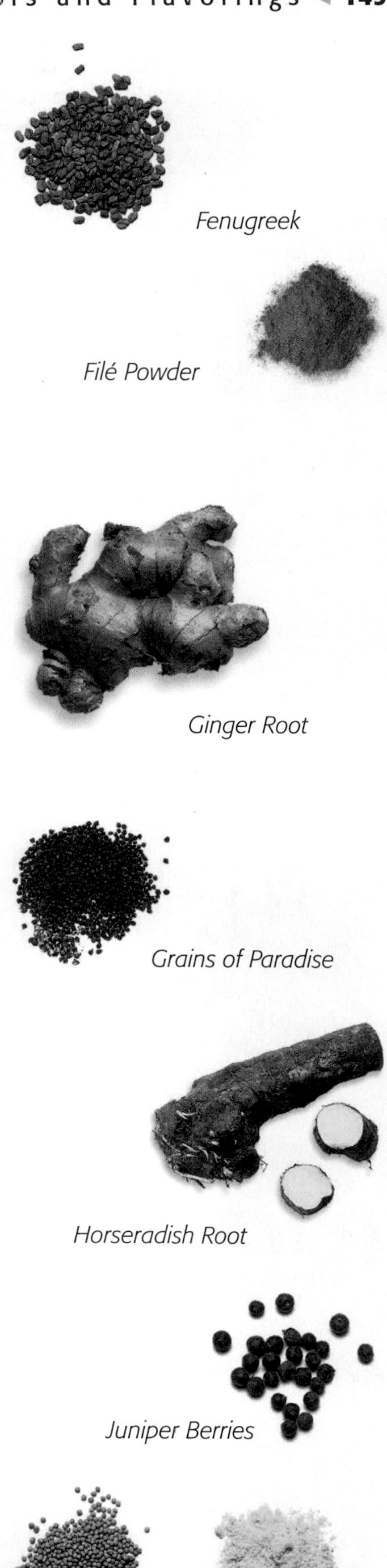

Fenugreek

Filé Powder

Ginger Root

Grains of Paradise

Horseradish Root

Juniper Berries

Mustard Seeds

Ground Mustard

Whole Nutmegs with Ground Mace (left) and Ground Nutmeg (right)

Nutmeg (Fr. *muscade*) and **mace** come from the yellow plumlike fruit of a large tropical evergreen. These fruits are dried and opened to reveal the seed known as nutmeg. A bright red lacy coating or *aril* surrounds the seed; the aril is the spice mace. Whole nutmegs are oval and look rather like a piece of smooth wood. The flavor and aroma of nutmeg are strong and sweet, and a small quantity provides a great deal of flavor. Nutmeg should be grated directly into a dish as needed; once grated, flavor loss is rapid. Nutmeg is used in many European cuisines, mainly in pastries and sweets, but is also important in meat and savory dishes.

Mace

Mace is an expensive spice, with a flavor similar to nutmeg but more refined. It is almost always purchased ground and retains its flavor longer than other ground spices. Mace is used primarily in pastry items.

Peppercorns (Fr. *poivre*) are the berries of a vine plant (*piper nigrum*) native to tropical Asia. Peppercorns should not be confused with the chile (*capsicum*) peppers discussed earlier. Peppercorns vary in size, color, pungency and flavor. Many of these differences are the result of variations in climate and growing conditions. Good-quality pepper is expensive and should be purchased whole and ground fresh in a peppermill as needed. Whole peppercorns will last indefinitely if kept dry. They should be stored well covered in a cool, dark place.

Black Pepper (left) and White Pepper (right)

Black and **white peppercorns** are produced from the same plant, but are picked and processed differently. For black peppercorns, the berries are picked when green and simply dried whole in the sun. Black pepper has a warm, pungent flavor and aroma. Tellicherry peppercorns from the southwest coast of India are generally considered the finest black peppercorns in the world and are priced accordingly. For white peppercorns, the berries are allowed to ripen until they turn red. The ripened berries are allowed to ferment, then the outer layer of skin is washed off. Nowadays, white pepper may be produced by mechanically removing the outer skin from black peppercorns. This is not true white pepper, and the resulting product should be labeled "decorticated." White pepper has fewer aromas than black pepper but is useful in white sauces or when the appearance of black speckles is undesirable.

Green Peppercorns

Green peppercorns are unripened berries that are either freeze-dried or pickled in brine or vinegar. Pickled green peppercorns are soft, with a fresh, sour flavor similar to capers. They are excellent in spiced butters and sauces or with fish.

Pink Peppercorns

Pink peppercorns (Fr. *baies roses*) are actually the berries of a South American tree, not a vine pepper plant. Pink peppercorns are available dried or pickled in vinegar. Although they are attractive, their flavor is bitter and pinelike, with less spiciness than true pepper.

Szechuan pepper (also spelled *Szechwan* and *Sichuan*) is the dried red berries of the prickly ash tree native to China. Also known as anise pepper and Chinese pepper, the berries have an extremely hot, peppery, spicy flavor with citrus overtones and are used in Chinese cuisines and as part of Chinese five-spice powder.

Poppy seeds (Fr. *pavot*) are the ripened seeds of the opium poppy, which flourishes in the Middle East and India. (When ripe, the seeds do not contain any of the medicinal alkaloids found elsewhere in the plant.)

Szechuan Pepper

Poppy Seeds

The tiny blue-gray seeds are round and hard with a sweet, nutty flavor. Poppy seeds are used in pastries and breads.

Saffron (Fr. *safran*) comes from the dried stigmas of the saffron crocus. Each flower bears only three threadlike stigmas, and each must be picked by hand. It takes about 250,000 flowers to produce one pound of saffron, making it the most expensive spice in the world. Beware of bargains; there is no such thing as cheap saffron. Luckily, a tiny pinch is enough to color and flavor a large quantity of food. Good saffron should be a brilliant orange color, not yellow, with a strong aroma and a bitter, honeylike taste. Saffron produces a yellow dye that diffuses through any warm liquid. Valencia or Spanish saffron is considered the finest. It is commonly used with fish and shellfish (a necessity for bouillabaisse) and rice dishes such as paella and risotto. When using saffron threads, first crush them gently, then soak them in some hot liquid from the recipe. Powdered saffron is less expensive but more easily adulterated. It may be added directly to the other ingredients when cooking.

Saffron

Sesame seeds, also known as benne seeds, are native to India. They are small, flat ovals, with a creamy white color. Their taste is nutty and earthy, with a pronounced aroma when roasted or ground into a paste (known as tahini). Sesame seeds are the source of sesame oil, which has a mild, nutty flavor and does not go rancid easily. Sesame seeds are roasted and used in or as a garnish for breads and meat dishes. They are popular in Indian and Asian cuisines, with a black variety of seeds most popular as a Japanese condiment.

Sesame Seeds

Tamarind (Fr. *tamarin;* Sp. and It. *tamarindo*), also known as an Indian date, is the brown, bean-shaped pod of the tamarind tree, which is native to Africa. Although naturally sweet, tamarind also contains 12% tartaric acid, which makes it extremely tart. It is commonly used in Indian curries and Mediterranean cooking as a souring agent and in the West Indies in fruit drinks. Tamarind is sold as a concentrate or in sticky blocks of crushed pods, pulp and seeds, which should be soaked in warm water for about five minutes, then squeezed through a sieve. Tamarind's high pectin content is useful in chutneys and jams, and it is often included in barbeque sauces and marinades. It is a key ingredient in Worcestershire sauce.

Tamarind Pods

Tamarind Paste

Turmeric (Fr. *curcuma*), also known as Indian saffron, is produced from the rhizome of a flowering tropical plant related to ginger. It has a mild, woodsy aroma. It is most often available dried and usually ground although fresh turmeric appears in ethnic markets. Turmeric is renowned for its vibrant yellow color and is used as a food coloring and dye. Turmeric's flavor is distinctive and strong; it should not be substituted for saffron. Turmeric is a traditional ingredient in Indian curries, to which it imparts color as well as flavor.

Turmeric

Wasabi is a pale green root similar, but unrelated, to horseradish. It has a strong aroma and a sharp, cleansing flavor with herbal overtones that is a bit hotter than that of horseradish. Fresh wasabi is rarely found outside Japan, but tins of powder and tubes of paste are readily available. It is commonly served with sushi and sashimi and can be used to add a spicy Asian note to other dishes, such as mashed potatoes or a compound butter.

Wasabi

HERB AND SPICE BLENDS

Many cuisines have created recognizable combinations of flavors that are found in a variety of dishes. Although many of these blends are available ready-prepared for convenience, most can be mixed by the chef as needed. (And commercial blends can contain large amounts of salt.) A few of the more common herb and spice blends are described here.

Chinese five-spice powder is a combination of equal parts finely ground Szechuan pepper, star anise, cloves, cinnamon and fennel seeds. This blend is

Five-Spice Powder

widely used in Chinese and some Vietnamese foods and is excellent with pork and in pâtés.

Curry Powder

Curry powder is a European invention that probably took its name from the Tamil word *kari,* meaning "sauce." Created by 19th-century Britons returning from colonial India, it was meant to be the complete spicing for a "curry" dish. There are as many different formulas for curry powder as there are manufacturers, some mild and sweet (Bombay or Chinese style), others hot and pungent (Madras style). Typical ingredients in curry powder are black pepper, cinnamon, cloves, coriander, cumin, ginger, mace and turmeric.

Fine herbs (Fr. *fines herbes*) are a combination of parsley, tarragon, chervil and chives widely used in French cuisine. The mixture is available dried, or it can be created from fresh ingredients.

Jamaican jerk seasoning is a powdered or wet mixture used on the Caribbean island of the same name made from a combination of spices that typically includes thyme, ground spices such as allspice, cinnamon, cloves, and ginger as well as onions and garlic. Chicken and pork are typically rubbed or marinated in the blend, then grilled

Herbes de Provence

Herbes de Provence (airb duh pro-VAWNS) is a blend of dried herbs commonly grown and used in southern France. Commercial blends usually include thyme, rosemary, bay leaf, basil, fennel seeds, savory and lavender. The herb blend is used with grilled or roasted meat, fish or chicken; in vegetable dishes; on pizza; and even in steamed rice and yeast breads.

Italian seasoning blend is a commercially prepared mixture of dried basil, oregano, sage, marjoram, rosemary, thyme, savory and other herbs associated with Italian cuisine.

Masala (mah-SAH-lah) is a flavorful, aromatic blend of roasted and ground spices used in Indian cuisines. A **garam masala** (gah-RAHM) is a masala made with hot spices (*garam* means warm or hot). A dry garam masala usually contains peppercorns, cardamom, cinnamon, cloves, coriander, nutmeg, turmeric, bay leaves and fennel seeds and is added toward the end of cooking or sprinkled on the food just before service. Adding coconut milk, oil or sometimes tamarind water to a dry garam masala makes a wet garam masala. A wet garam masala is typically added at the start of cooking.

Pickling Spice

Pickling spice, as with other blends, varies by manufacturer. Most pickling spice blends are based on black peppercorns and red chiles, with some or all of the following added: allspice, cloves, ginger, mustard seeds, coriander seeds, bay leaves and dill. These blends are useful in making cucumber or vegetable pickles as well as in stews and soups.

Quatre-épices (kah-tray-PEES), literally "four spices" in French and also the French word for allspice, is a peppery mixture of black peppercorns with lesser amounts of nutmeg, cloves and dried ginger. Sometimes cinnamon or allspice is included. Quatre-épices is used in charcuterie and long-simmered stews.

Ras el hanout (rass al ha-noot) is a common Moroccan spice blend varying greatly from supplier to supplier. It typically contains 20 or more spices, such as turmeric, cinnamon, cloves, grains of paradise, coriander, cumin, cardamom, peppercorns, dried chiles, dried flower petals and, allegedly, an aphrodisiac or two. It is sold whole and ground by the cook as necessary to flavor stews, rice, couscous and game dishes.

Seasoned salts are commercially blended products containing salt and one or more natural flavoring ingredients such as garlic, spices or celery seeds and, often, monosodium glutamate.

STORING HERBS AND SPICES

Fresh herbs should be kept refrigerated at 34°F–40°F (2°C–4°C). Large bouquets can be stored upright, their leaves loosely covered with plastic wrap and their stems submerged in water. Smaller bunches should be stored loosely covered with a damp towel. Excess fresh herbs can be dried for later use in an electric dehydrator or spread out on baking sheets in a 100°F (38°C) oven.

Dried herbs and spices should be stored in airtight, opaque containers in a cool, dry place. Avoid light and heat, both of which destroy delicate flavors. If stored properly, dried herbs should last for two to three months.

USING HERBS AND SPICES

Herbs and spices are a simple, inexpensive way to bring individuality and variety to foods. They add neither fat nor sodium and virtually no calories to foods; most contain only 3 to 10 calories per teaspoon. Tables 5.2 and 5.3 list just a few uses for some of the more common herbs and spices.

Although the flavors and aromas of fresh herbs are generally preferred, dried herbs are widely used because they are readily available and convenient. Use less dried herb than you would fresh herb. The loss of moisture strengthens and concentrates the flavor in dried herbs. In general, use only one-half to one-third as much dried herb as fresh in any given recipe. For example, if a recipe calls for 1 tablespoon of fresh basil, substitute only 1 teaspoon of dried basil. More can usually be added later if necessary. The delicate aroma and flavors of fresh herbs is volatile. Most fresh herbs such as chives, parsley, cilantro, basil and tarragon are best when added at the end of cooking.

Table 5.2 USES FOR SOME COMMON HERBS AND SPICES IN SAVORY FOODS

FLAVORING	FORM	SUGGESTED USES
Allspice	Whole or ground	Fruits, relishes, braised meats
Anise	Whole or ground	Asian cuisines, pastries, breads, cheeses
Basil	Fresh or dried	Tomatoes, salads, eggs, fish, chicken, lamb, cheeses
Caraway	Whole or ground	Rye bread, cabbage, beans, pork, beef, veal
Chervil	Fresh	Chicken, fish, eggs, salads, soups, vegetables
Chives	Fresh or dried	Eggs, fish, chicken, soups, potatoes, cheeses
Cilantro	Fresh leaves	Salsa, salads, Mexican cuisine, fish, shellfish, chicken
Cloves	Whole or ground	Marinades, baked goods, braised meats, pickles, fruits, beverages, stocks
Cumin	Whole or ground	Chili, sausages, stews, eggs
Dill	Fresh or dried leaves; whole seeds	Leaves or seeds in soups, salads, fish, shellfish, vegetables, breads; seeds in pickles, potatoes, vegetables
Fennel	Whole seeds	Sausages, stews, sauces, pickling, lamb, eggs
Ginger	Fresh or powder	Asian, Caribbean and Indian cuisines, pastries, curries, stews, meats
Marjoram	Fresh or dried	Sausages, pâtés, meats, poultry, stews, green vegetables, tomatoes, game
Nutmeg	Ground	Curries, relishes, rice, eggs, beverages
Rosemary	Fresh or dried	Lamb, veal, beef, poultry, game, marinades, stews
Saffron	Threads or ground	Rice, breads, potatoes, soups, stews, chicken, fish, shellfish
Sage	Fresh or dried	Poultry, charcuterie, pork, stuffings, pasta, beans, tomatoes
Tarragon	Fresh or dried	Chicken, fish, eggs, salad dressings, sauces, tomatoes
Thyme	Fresh or dried	Fish, chicken, meats, stews, charcuterie, soups, tomatoes
Turmeric	Fresh or powder	Curries, relishes, rice, eggs, breads

Table 5.3 USES FOR SOME COMMON HERBS AND SPICES IN THE BAKESHOP

FLAVORING	FORM	SUGGESTED USES
Allspice	Ground	Fruits, quick breads and spice cookies
Anise	Dry, whole or ground	Pastries and breads
Basil	Fresh or dried	Savory breads, pizzas and bagels
Caraway	Whole or ground	Rye breads, bagel topping
Cardamom	Ground	Sweet dough, cookies and pastries
Cinnamon	Whole	Infused in syrups and poaching liquid
	Ground	Pies, pastries, breads and ice cream
Cloves	Whole or ground	Poaching liquids for fruit, spice breads and muffins
Dill	Whole seeds or fresh	Breads, bread toppings
Ginger	Fresh	Infused in syrups, ice cream and custards
	Ground	Cakes, cookies, muffins and gingerbread
Mace	Ground	Spice breads and cookies
Mint	Fresh	Infused in sauces and syrups; garnish
Nutmeg	Ground	Custards, spice breads and cookies
Pepper	Whole	Infused in wine for poaching fruit
	Ground	Spice blends for cakes and gingerbread

Spices are often available whole or ground. Once ground, they lose their flavors rapidly, however. Whole spices should keep their flavors for at least six to nine months if stored properly. Stale spices lose their spicy aroma and develop a bitter or musty aftertaste. Discard them.

Most dried spices need to be added early in order for their flavor to develop during the cooking. Whole spices take the longest; ground spices release their flavor more quickly. In some preparations, Indian curries for example, ground spices are first cooked in oil to release their aromas before being added to a dish. Some dried spices such as black pepper may become bitter when cooked for an extended period of time, however. In uncooked dishes that call for ground spices (for example, salad dressings), the mixture should be allowed to stand for several hours to develop good flavor.

Creating dishes with appealing and complex flavors comes with practice and a solid understanding and appreciation of flavoring ingredients. Although some flavoring combinations are timeless—rosemary with lamb, dill with salmon, nutmeg with spinach, caraway with rye bread—less common pairings can be equally delicious and far more exciting. Chef's must be willing and able to experiment with new flavors. But first they must become familiar with the distinctive flavors and aromas of an herb, spice, condiment, vinegar or the like. Then chefs can experiment, always bearing in mind the following guidelines:

- Flavorings should not hide the taste or aroma of the primary ingredient.
- Flavorings should be combined in balance, so as not to overwhelm the palate.
- Flavorings should not be used to disguise poor quality or poorly prepared products.
- Flavorings should be added sparingly when foods are to be cooked over an extended period of time. When reduced during cooking, flavorings can intensify and overpower the dish.
- Taste and season foods frequently during cooking.

Even in a well-tested recipe, the quantity of flavorings may need to be adjusted because of a change in brands or the condition of the ingredients. A chef should strive to develop his or her palate to recognize and correct subtle variances as necessary.

▶ SALT

Salt (Fr. *sel*) is the most basic seasoning, and its use is universal. It preserves foods, heightens their flavors and provides the distinctive taste of saltiness. The presence of salt can be tasted easily but not smelled. Salt suppresses bitter flavors, making the sweet and sour ones more prominent. The flavor of salt will not evaporate or dissipate during cooking so it should be added to foods carefully, according to taste. Remember, more salt can always be added to a dish but too much salt cannot be removed nor can its flavor be masked if too much salt has been added.

Culinary or **table salt** is sodium chloride (NaCl), one of the minerals essential to human life. Salt contains no calories, proteins, fats or carbohydrates. It is available from several sources, each with its own flavor and degree of saltiness.

Rock salt, mined from underground deposits, is available in both edible and nonedible forms. It is used in ice cream churns, for thawing frozen sidewalks and, in edible form, in salt mills.

Rock Salt

Kosher Salt

Fleur de Sel (Sea Salt)

Common **kitchen** or **table salt** is produced by pumping water through underground salt deposits, then bringing the brine to the surface to evaporate, leaving behind crystals. Chemicals are usually added to prevent table salt from absorbing moisture and thus keep it free-flowing. Iodized salt is commonly used in the United States. The iodine has no effect on the salt's flavor or use; it is simply added to provide an easily available source of iodine, an important nutrient, to a large number of people.

Kosher salt has large, irregular crystals and is used in the "koshering" or curing of meats. It is purified rock salt that contains no iodine or additives. It can be substituted for common kitchen salt. Some chefs prefer it to table salt because they prefer its flavor and it dissolves more easily than other salts.

Sea salt is obtained, not surprisingly, by evaporating seawater. The evaporation can be done naturally by drying the salt in the sun (unrefined sea salt) or by boiling the salty liquid (refined sea salt). Unlike other table salts, unrefined sea salt contains additional mineral salts such as magnesium, calcium and potassium, which give it a stronger, more complex flavor and a grayish-brown color. The region where it is produced can also affect its flavor and color. For example, salt from the Mediterranean Sea will taste different from salt obtained from the Indian Ocean or the English Channel.

Sel gris is a sea salt harvested off the coast of Normandy, France. It is slightly wet and takes its gray color from minerals in the clay from which it is collected. **Fleur de sel,** which means "flower of salt," is salt that collects on rocks in the sel gris marshes. It forms delicate crystals and has little color because it has not come into contact with the clay.

Some **specialty salts** are actually mined from the earth, such as that from the foothills of the Himalayan Mountains. The presence of iron and copper along with other minerals gives Himalayan salt a pink hue and distinct flavor. Black salt, common in traditional Indian recipes, is mined rock salt; minerals and other components in the salt give it a dark color and sulfurous taste. **Smoked salt** is a type of flavored salt made by smoking the salt over a smoldering fire. It can also be made by adding liquid smoke to a salt solution before it is evaporated.

Sea salt is considerably more expensive than other table salts and is often reserved for finishing a dish or used as a condiment.

Because it is nonorganic, salt keeps indefinitely. It will, however, absorb moisture from the atmosphere, which prevents it from flowing properly. Salt is

ABOUT FLAVORS

Flavor is to food what hue is to color. It is what timbre is to music. (*Flavor* is adjective; *food* is noun.) Each ingredient has its own particular character, which is altered by every other ingredient it encounters. A secret ingredient is one that mysteriously improves the flavor of a dish without calling attention to itself. It is either undetectable or extremely subtle, but its presence is crucial because the dish would not be nearly as good without it.

Primary flavors are those that are obvious, such as the flavors of chicken and tarragon in a chicken tarragon, shrimp and garlic in a shrimp scampi, or beef and red wine in a beef à la Bourguignonne. Secret ingredients belong to the realm of secondary flavors. However obvious it is that you need tarragon to prepare a chicken tarragon, you would not achieve the most interesting result using only tarragon. Tarragon, in this case, needs secondary ingredients–a hint of celery seed and anise–to make it taste more like quintessential tarragon and at the same time more than tarragon. In this way, primary flavors often depend on secret ingredients to make them more interesting and complex. Using only one herb or spice to achieve a certain taste usually results in a lackluster dish–each mouthful tastes the same. Whether they function in a primary or secondary way, flavors combine in only three different ways: They marry, oppose, or juxtapose.

When flavors marry, they combine to form one taste. Some secondary flavors marry with primary ones to create a new flavor greater than the sum of its parts, and often two flavors can do the job better than one. It may sound like an eccentric combination, but vanilla marries with the flavor of lobster, making it taste more like the essence of lobster than lobster does on its own. And when ginger and molasses marry, they create a flavor superior to either alone.

Opposite flavors can highlight or cancel each other; they can cut or balance each other. Sweet/sour, sweet/salty, sweet/hot, salty/sour, and salty/tart are all opposites. Salt and sugar are so opposed, in fact, that when used in equal amounts they cancel each other entirely. Sweet relish helps cancel the salty flavor of hot dogs. Chinese sauces usually contain some sugar to help balance the saltiness of soy sauce.

Knowing how to combine many flavors and aromas to achieve a simple and pure result (and knowing when not to combine flavors) will make you a better, more confident cook. Good cooks over the centuries have known these things intuitively–but they've had neither the huge variety of ingredients nor the knowledge of world cuisines that we have today.

CHEF MICHAEL ROBERTS is the author of *Secret Ingredients.*

a powerful preservative; its presence stops or greatly slows down the growth of many undesirable organisms. Salt is used to preserve meats, vegetables and fish. It is also used to develop desirable flavors in bacon, ham, cheeses and fish products as well as pickled vegetables.

▶ OILS

Oils (Fr. *huiles*) are a type of fat that remains liquid at room temperature. Cooking oils are refined from various seeds, plants and vegetables. (Other fats, such as butter and margarine, are discussed in Chapter 6, Dairy Products; fats for deep-frying are discussed in Chapter 8, Principles of Cooking.) They are included here as flavorings because each oil, along with its cooking properties, has specific flavor and aroma characteristics that should be considered when choosing an oil as a cooking medium or as a medium to carry other flavors.

▶ **smoke point** the temperature at which a fat begins to break down and smoke

▶ **flash point** the temperature at which a fat ignites and small flames appear on the surface of the fat

▶ **shortening** (1) a white, flavorless, solid fat formulated for baking or deep-frying; (2) any fat used in baking to tenderize the product by shortening gluten strands

When purchasing oils, consider their use, **smoke point,** flavor and cost. Fats, including oils and **shortenings,** are manufactured for specific purposes such as deep-frying, cake baking, salad dressings and sautéing. Most food service operations purchase different ones for each of these needs. Fats break down at different temperatures. When fats break down, their chemical structure is altered; the triglyceride molecules that make up fat are converted into individual fatty acids. These acids add undesirable flavors to the fat and can ruin the flavor of the food being cooked. The temperature at which a given fat begins to break down and smoke is known as its smoke point. Choose fats with higher smoke points for high-temperature cooking such as deep-frying and sautéing.

The flavor and cost of each oil must also be considered. For example, both corn oil and walnut oil can be used in a salad dressing. Their selection may depend on balancing cost (corn oil is less expensive) against flavor (walnut oil has a stronger, more distinctive flavor).

When fats spoil, they are said to go **rancid.** Rancidity is a chemical change caused by exposure to air, light or heat. It results in objectionable flavors and odors. Different fats turn rancid at different rates, but all fats benefit from refrigerated storage away from moisture, light and air. (Some oils are packaged in colored glass containers because certain tints of green and yellow block the damaging light rays that can cause an oil to go rancid.) Although oils may become thick and cloudy under refrigeration, this is not a cause for concern. The oils will return to their clear, liquid states at room temperature. Stored fats should also be covered to prevent them from absorbing odors.

Vegetable oils are extracted from a variety of plants, including corn, cottonseed, peanuts, grape seeds, sesame seeds and soybeans, by pressure or chemical solvents. The oil is then refined and cleaned to remove unwanted colors, odors or flavors. Vegetable oils are virtually odorless and have a neutral flavor. Because they contain no animal products, they are cholesterol-free. If a commercial product contains only one type of oil, it is labeled "pure" (as in "pure corn oil"). Products labeled "vegetable oil" are blended from several sources. Products labeled "salad oil" are highly refined blends of vegetable oil.

Canola oil is processed from rapeseeds. Its popularity is growing rapidly because it contains no cholesterol and has a high percentage of monounsaturated fat. Canola oil is useful for frying and general cooking because it has no flavor and a high smoke point.

Canola Oil

Nut oils are extracted from a variety of nuts and are almost always packaged as a "pure" product, never blended. A nut oil should have the strong flavor and aroma of the nut from which it was processed. Popular examples are walnut and hazelnut oils. These oils are used to give flavor to salad dressings, marinades and other dishes. But heat diminishes their flavor, so nut oils are not recommended for frying or baking. Nut oils tend to go rancid quickly and therefore are usually packaged in small containers.

Hazelnut Oil

Olive oil (Fr. *huile d'olive*) is the only oil that is extracted from a fruit rather than a seed, nut or grain. Olive oil is produced primarily in Spain, Italy, France, Greece and North Africa; California produces a relatively minor amount of olive oil. Like wine, olive oils vary in color and flavor according to the variety of tree, the ripeness of the olives, the type of soil, the climate and the producer's preferences. Colors range from dark green to almost clear, depending on the ripeness of the olives at the time of pressing and the amount of subsequent refining. Color is not a good indication of flavor, however. Flavor is ultimately a matter of personal preference. A stronger-flavored oil may be desired for some foods, while a milder oil is better for others. Good olive oil should be thicker than refined vegetable oils, but not so thick that it has a fatty texture.

Extra Virgin Olive Oil

The label designations—extra virgin, virgin and pure—refer to the acidity of the oil (a low acid content is preferable) and the extent of processing used to extract the oil. The first cold-pressing of the olives results in virgin oil. (The designation "virgin" is used only when the oil is 100% unadulterated olive oil, unheated and without any chemical processing.) Virgin oil may still vary in quality depending on the level of free acidity, expressed as oleic acid. Extra virgin oil is virgin oil with not more than 1% free acidity (oleic acid); virgin oil may have up to 3%. Pure olive oil is processed from the pulp left after the first pressing using heat and chemicals. Pure oil is lighter in flavor and less expensive than virgin oil.

Flavored oils, also known as **infused oils,** are an interesting and increasingly popular condiment. These oils may be used as a dip for breads, a cooking medium or a flavoring accent in marinades, dressings, sauces or other dishes. Flavors include basil and other herbs, garlic, citrus and spice. Flavored oils are generally prepared with olive oil for additional flavor or canola oil, both considered more healthful than other fats.

Top-quality commercially flavored oils are prepared by extracting aromatic oils from the flavoring ingredients and then emulsifying them with a high-grade oil; any impurities are then removed by placing the oil in a centrifuge. Using the aromatic oils of the flavoring ingredients yields a more intense flavor than merely steeping the same ingredients in the oil. Flavored oils should be stored as you would any other high-quality oil.

▶ CONDIMENTS

Strictly speaking, a condiment is any food added to a dish for flavor, including herbs, spices and vinegars. Today, however, condiments more often refer to cooked or prepared flavorings, such as prepared mustards, **relishes,** bottled sauces and **pickles** served to accompany foods. We discuss several frequently used condiments here. These staples may be used to alter or enhance the flavor of a dish during cooking or added to a completed dish at the table by the consumer.

▶ **relish** a cooked or pickled sauce usually made with vegetables or fruits and often used as a condiment; can be smooth or chunky, sweet or savory and hot or mild

▶ **pickle** (1) to preserve food in a brine or vinegar solution; (2) food that has been preserved in a seasoned brine or vinegar, especially cucumbers. Pickled cucumbers are available whole, sliced, in wedges, or chopped as a relish, and may be sweet, sour, dill-flavored or hot and spicy.

Chutney (from the Hindi word for *catnip*) is a pungent relish made from fruits, spices and herbs and is frequently used in Indian cooking.

Fermented black bean sauce is a Chinese condiment and flavoring ingredient made from black soybeans that have been heavily salted, then fermented and either slightly mashed (whole bean sauce) or puréed (paste). Both versions are usually mixed with hoisin, chile sauce or minced garlic to produce a sauce that has an intense, pungent, salty flavor. Yellow bean sauces are similar, but milder and sweeter.

Fermented Black Bean Sauce

Fish sauce (Viet. *nuoc mam;* Thai *nam pla*) is the liquid drained from fermenting salted anchovy-like fish. It is a thin, golden to light brown liquid with a very pungent odor and salty flavor. There is no substitute for the savory richness that it adds to food and it is considered an essential flavoring and condiment throughout Southeast Asia, where it is used in and served with most every sort of dish.

Fish Sauce

Ketchup (also known as catsup or catchup) originally referred to any salty extract from fish, fruits or vegetables. Prepared tomato ketchup is really a sauce, created in America and used worldwide as a flavoring ingredient or condiment. It is bright red and thick, with a tangy, sweet-sour flavor. Ketchup can be stored either in the refrigerator or at room temperature; it should keep well for up to four months after opening. Ketchup does not turn rancid or develop mold, but it will darken and lose flavor as it ages.

Prepared mustard is a mixture of crushed mustard seeds, vinegar or wine and salt or spices. It can be flavored in many ways—with herbs, onions, peppers and even citrus zest. It can be a smooth paste or coarse and chunky, depending on how finely the seeds are ground and whether the skins are strained out. Prepared mustard gets its tangy flavor from an essential oil that forms only when the seeds are crushed and mixed with water. Prepared mustard can be used as a condiment, particularly with meat and charcuterie items, or as a flavoring ingredient in sauces, stews and marinades.

Yellow Mustard

Dijon Mustard

Dijon mustard takes its name from a town and the surrounding region in France that produces about half of the world's mustard. French mustard labeled "Dijon" must, by law, be produced only in that region. Dijon and Dijon-style mustards are smooth with a rich, complex flavor.

English and Chinese mustards are made from mustard flour and cool water. They are extremely hot and powerful. American or "ballpark" mustard is mild and vinegary with a bright yellow color. Unless it contains a high percentage of oil, mustard never really spoils; its flavor just fades away. Because of its high

FROM YOUR GROCER'S SHELF

Even the most sophisticated food service operation occasionally uses prepared condiments or flavorings. The products described here are widely used and available from grocery stores or wholesale purveyors. Some are brand-name items that have become almost synonymous with the product itself; others are available from several manufacturers.

Barbecue sauce—Commercial barbecue sauce is a mixture of tomatoes, vinegar and spices used primarily for marinating or basting meat, poultry or fish. A tremendous variety of barbecue sauces are available, with various flavors, textures and aromas. Sample several before selecting the most appropriate for your specific needs.

Chile sauce—Asian chile sauce, also known as *sambol* or *oelek* or hot sauce, varies somewhat depending on the country of origin or style, but all are thick, reddish-orange and extremely pungent and spicy. They usually contain pieces of chiles and/or garlic and less vinegar than Louisiana-style hot sauce. Asian cuisines incorporate these bottled sauces in curries and other dishes and use them as table condiments. One of the most popular and readily available brands is the Vietnamese-style chili garlic sauce with a rooster logo, made in California. Imported Sauce Sriracha, named after a port town in southern Thailand, is also widely available.

Hoisin sauce—Hoisin sauce is a dark, thick, salty-sweet sauce made from fermented soybeans, vinegar, garlic and caramel. It is used in Chinese dishes or served as a dipping sauce.

Old Bay brand seasoning—Old Bay is a dry spice blend containing celery salt, dry mustard, paprika and other flavorings. It is widely used in shellfish preparations, especially boiled shrimp and crab.

Oyster sauce—Oyster sauce is a thick, dark sauce made from oyster extract. It has a salty-sweet flavor and a rich aroma. Oyster sauce is often used with stir-fried meats and poultry.

Pickapeppa brand sauce—Pickapeppa sauce is a dark, thick, sweet-hot blend of tomatoes, onions, sugar, vinegar, mango, raisins, tamarinds and spices. Produced in Jamaica, it is used as a condiment for meat, game or fish and as a seasoning in sauces, soups and dressings.

Tabasco brand sauce—Tabasco sauce is a thin, bright-red liquid blended from vinegar, chiles and salt. Its fiery flavor is widely used in sauces, soups and prepared dishes; it is a popular condiment for Mexican, southern and southwestern cuisines. Tabasco sauce has been produced in Louisiana since 1868. Other "Louisiana-style" hot sauces (those containing only peppers, vinegar and salt) may be substituted.

Worcestershire sauce—Worcestershire sauce is a thin, dark-brown liquid made from malt vinegar, tamarind, molasses and spices. It is used as a condiment for beef and as a seasoning in sauces, soups, stews and prepared dishes. Its flavor should be rich and full, but not salty.

Whole-Grain Mustard

acid content, mustard is not prone to rancidity, but it will oxidize and develop a dark surface crust. Once opened, mustard should be kept well-covered and refrigerated.

Brown Mustard

Soy sauce is a thin, dark brown liquid fermented from cooked soy beans, wheat and salt. Available in several flavors and strengths, it is ubiquitous in most Asian cuisines. Light soy sauce is thin, with a light brown color and a very salty flavor. Dark soy sauce is thicker and dark brown, with a sweet, less salty flavor. **Tamari** is a Japanese-style soy sauce made without wheat, although its name may be applied to a variety of Japanese-style soy sauces. Necessary for preparing many Asian dishes, soy sauce is also used in marinades and sauces and as an all-purpose condiment. Other common soy-based sauces and condiments include teriyaki sauce and fermented bean paste (miso), made by fermenting soybeans with a grain such as rice or barley.

Soy Sauce

Tahini is a thick, oily paste made of ground toasted sesame seeds. It is thick and slightly grainy, with an ivory to grayish-tan color. Tahini can be bland or salty, depending on the manufacturer. Its toasted, nutty flavor is widely used in Middle Eastern and Mediterranean cuisine, especially in sauces and spreads such as hummus. Tahini is also useful in vegetarian dishes and is relatively high in protein and vitamins.

▶ WINES, BEERS, BRANDIES, LIQUORS AND LIQUEURS

▶ **wine** an alcoholic beverage made from the fermented juice of grapes; may be sparkling (effervescent) or still (non-effervescent) or fortified with additional alcohol

▶ **beer** an alcoholic beverage made from water, hops and malted barley, fermented by yeast

▶ **brandy** an alcoholic beverage made by distilling wine or the fermented mash of grapes or other fruits.

▶ **liquor** an alcoholic beverage made by distilling grains, fruits, vegetables or other foods; includes rum, whiskey and vodka

▶ **liqueur** a strong, sweet, syrupy alcoholic beverage made by mixing or redistilling neutral spirits with fruits, flowers, herbs, spices or other flavorings; also known as a cordial

Wines, beers, brandies, liquors and **liqueurs** are frequently used in the kitchen, most often as flavorings, but also as primary ingredients in marinades and sauces or even as a cooking medium (pears poached in red wine, for instance). Wines are used to flavor and frequently to tenderize foods in marinades, to add flavor during or at the end of cooking, and to deglaze a pan to add flavor to a sauce. Brandy, especially the classic orange-flavored Grand Marnier, is a common bakeshop flavoring. Brandy complements fruits and rounds off the flavors of custards and creams. Liqueurs are selected for their specific flavors: amaretto for almond, Kahlúa for coffee, crème de cassis for black currant. They are used either to add flavors or to enhance other flavors in a dish. Liquors such as rum, bourbon and whiskey can be used for their own distinctive flavors or to blend with other flavors such as chocolate and coffee.

Because alcoholic beverages are used as flavorings, basic information about them is included here. This information is not intended to be a mini-course on wine tasting or Scotch tasting. Rather, it is to familiarize the student chef with the basics of wine, beer and spirits. Brief guidelines for choosing appropriate wines or other alcoholic beverages as flavorings as well as guidelines on how to use them as flavorings are also included. As with other flavoring ingredients, patience, research, experimentation and practice will help develop a chef's feel for what alcoholic beverage—and how much—is the best flavoring for a specific dish.

WINE

THE WINE-MAKING PROCESS

The process of transforming grapes into a still wine is called **vinification.** Freshly harvested grapes are gently crushed in order to release their juices. While in the crusher, stems and other undesirable matter are separated from the juice and grape skins.

▶ **vintner** a winemaker

▶ **viniculture** the art and science of making wine from grapes

▶ **viticulture** the art and science of growing grapes used to make wines; factors considered include soil, topography (particularly, sunlight and drainage) and microclimate (temperature and rainfall)

If the **vintner** is making a **red wine,** both the crushed grapes (typically black-skinned grapes) and the juice (collectively called a **must**) are then transferred to a fermentation tank and allowed to ferment. Stainless steel fermentation tanks are used to create crisper red wines; oak casks are used for a more mellow product. As the red wine ferments, the grape skins release **tannins,** which give many red wines their distinctive astringent characteristic and slightly bitter taste. In order to increase a wine's tannin content, some vintners allow grape stems to remain in the must.

If the vintner is making a **white wine,** the grape skins (typically from white-skinned grapes, although occasionally black-skinned grapes are used) and juice pass through a wine press, where the juice is separated from the skins. For white wines, only the juice is allowed to ferment. If the vintner is making a **rosé wine** (ro-zay) or a blush wine, the grape skins (typcially black) are left in contact with the fermenting juice just long enough to add the desired amount of color.

▶ **fermentation** the process by which yeast converts sugar into alcohol and carbon dioxide

After the must or juice is transferred to a fermentation tank, the vintner adds yeast and sugar to start the **fermentation** process. The type of yeast and amount of sugar depends on the type of grape used and the style of wine the vintner wants to create. During fermentation, the yeast converts the sugars (both those naturally occuring in the grapes and those added by the vintner) to alcohol and carbon dioxide. Fermentation generally lasts for two to four weeks and creates many of the resulting wine's flavors and aromas.

Once fermentation is complete, red wines are pressed to remove the skins from the wine and then filtered to remove the yeast. White wines are allowed to settle and the yeast filtered out. The wines are then stored in either stainless steel

A GOBLET OF WINE HISTORY

People have been consuming wine for thousands of years. Wine making probably began 5000 or 6000 years ago somewhere in the Fertile Crescent in the ancient kingdom of Mesopotamia (today's Iraq) and probably as a happy accident—airborne yeasts came into contact with stored grapes or grape juice and over time the mixture fermented, producing a sweet alcoholic beverage.

From Mesopotamia, grape cultivation and wine making spread throughout the Middle East, from the northern Persian Gulf to the Mediterranean basin. Stone tablets recording grape harvests, paintings of grapes and even vessels with traces of the wine that once filled them have been found in the tombs of Egyptian Pharaohs dating back to 3000 B.C.E. The many images and hieroglyphic records pertaining to grapes and wine suggest that the upper classes of ancient Egypt valued their wine—mostly, a sweet sort of white wine, sometimes flavored with herbs or seawater—as both a social drink and as a component of funerary and other religious rituals.

Wine was also equally prized by the upper classes of ancient Greece. Their poetry, writings and art sing the praises of grapes, wine and wine making. They believed that wine was a gift from a god—Dionysus—and celebrated his gift at a feast held in late December, when the new (and unaged) wines made that year were ready to be consumed. The Greeks stored their wines in clay vessels lined with pine pitch, giving the wines a resinous flavor probably similar to modern Retsina.

As the Romans came to dominate the Mediterranean basin (and ultimately much of Europe) in the centuries following the end of the Golden Era of Greece, upper-class Romans absorbed or emulated many Greek traits, including the appreciation of wine. The Roman god of wine—Bacchus—is the Romanized version of Dionysus. The popularity of Bacchus helped democratize wines and the proliferation of vineyards brought the price of wines down remarkably, thus allowing the lower classes of Rome to enjoy what had once been available to only the upper classes of Egypt and Greece. In fact, it was during the Roman era that bars offering patrons a place to drink wine and sometimes consume food first appeared. The wines they drank were generally red, fruity and sweet (although drier white wines were being produced), sometimes flavored with ingredients such as fermented fish sauce, garlic or onions.

During the centuries following the fall of Rome (mid-fifth century A.D.), much of Europe's grape-growing and wine-making activities shifted to the large Christian monasteries scattered throughout what is now northern Italy, France and Germany. The famous Frankish ruler Charlemagne (ca. 742–814) established vineyards throughout the kingdom, some of which are still in use today, especially in Burgundy. It was during this period—the Middle Ages—that the white wine/red wine divide became more standardized and the ancient practice of adding flavorings fell out of taste. By the 14th century, what are now the famous wine-producing regions of France, especially Bordeaux, were already becoming known for the excellence of their products.

As England became a naval power under the rule of Queen Elizabeth I (1533–1603), many English merchants became wine importers, especially of sherries from Spain, ports from Portugal and Madeira from the island of the same name. Eventually, they also became involved with a complex trading network involving molasses from the West Indies, distilled rum from New England, finished goods from England and slaves from Africa.

By the 1700s, France was recognized as the greatest of the European wine-making nations, especially for the fine wines of Bordeaux. Champagne also appeared during this period, though its discovery was not, as is often attributed, the work of Dom Pérignon, a Benedictine monk who contributed extensively to improving the still wines of the Champagne region. The French widow Nicole-Barbe Clicquot-Ponsardin is credited with improving production techniques and creating the cachet that Champagne still enjoys today.

Ancient Greek urn for storing wine.

In this country, Thomas Jefferson was quite the French wine enthusiast. He was also convinced that the lack of fine American wines was driving his fellow citizens to drink too much hard liquor. So, in an attempt to resolve this perceived social problem, he encouraged Americans to plant European wine grapes (from the botanical family of *Vitis vinifera*). These early attempts to plant European grapes, first in the Ohio River Valley and later in California, were generally unsuccessful and ultimately—for Europe—catastrophic. As *Vitis vinifera* grape vine cuttings were brought back and forth between Europe and America, a very destructive vine louse from America called phylloxera took hold in Europe.

By the 1860s, many of the *Vitis vinifera* vineyards in France and elsewhere were destroyed. European vintners eventually resolved this crisis by grafting the *Vitis vinifera* vines onto a hardy New World grape stock naturally resistant to phylloxera. During this era of turmoil, many French vintners—now unemployed as a result of the phylloxera invasion—relocated throughout Europe, Australia, North America and elsewhere, bringing their talents with them and the foundations for those regions' wine industries.

The European wine industry has, of course, long since recovered. But it is no longer the dominant market leader that it once was. Wines from the United States, Australia, South Africa, New Zealand, Chile and Argentina, among other countries, now command respect throughout the world. Their development is, in part, a reflection of the great glories of Europe, as well as the harnessing of modern technologies that give the vintner near total control over virtually every aspect of the grape-growing and wine-making process, from instruments that measure an individual grape's sugar content to determine the optimum time for harvest, to refrigeration coils that maintain a fermentation tank's temperature, despite fluctuations in the outside temperature, thus allowing the production of high-quality wines in hot climates.

Wooden Cork Pull

Waiter's Corkscrew

Lever-Type Corkscrew

tanks or oak barrels for aging. Aging wines in oak barrels or casks adds a mellow, oaky flavor. (Vintners often subject many red wines and, occasionally, some white wines, to a second, brief, fermentation during aging; called a *malolactic fermentation,* it generally reduces the wine's acidic qualities.) White wines are normally aged for less time than red wines, usually no more than a year. When the vintner has determined that the wine has aged sufficiently, the wine is removed from the tank or barrel and bottled, corked and labeled.

Sparkling Wines

Sparkling wines are still wines that undergo a complete second fermentation. The carbon dioxide generated during this second fermentation gives a sparkling wine its effervescence. The process for making sparkling wines is similar to that used for making still white or rosé wines from the planting of the grapes through the still wine's fermentation stage. From there, the processes diverge. After the initial fermentation, a sparkling wine is allowed to age for approximately five months. The vintner then adds extra yeast and sugar to the wine and allows it to undergo a second fermentation that lasts for a year or so. (This second fermentation should not be confused with the malolactic fermentation noted previously.)

For Champagne (shahm-PAHN-ya) and sparkling wines made like champagne (only a sparkling wine from the Champagne region of France can be called champagne), the second fermentation takes place in the bottle. Called **méthode champenoise,** the process requires that the wine be aged for one to two years after its second fermentation. After aging, the yeast is removed from the bottles through a two-step process. First, the bottle is placed neck down in a rack at a 45-degree angle and rotated one-eighth of a turn every day (this is called **riddling**); during riddling, the dead yeast cells settle into the neck of the bottle. They are then removed through a process called **disgorging:** the neck of the bottle is frozen in an ice-and-salt-water bath and the bottle cap is removed. The internal pressure forces the frozen plug of dead yeast cells out of the bottle. Alternatively, the vintner can use the **charmat process.** With this process, the second fermentation takes place in a tank, eliminating riddling and disgorging.

Regardless of whether the second fermentation takes place in the bottle or tank, once it is completed, the vintner adds a mixture of white wine brandy and sugar called a **dosage.** The sparkling wine is then bottled, corked and secured with a wire, ready for distribution. Champagne and other sparkling wines are classified by their degree of sweetness. From driest to sweetest, they are Natural or Au Sauvage, Brut, Extra Dry, Dry or Sec, Demi-Sec and Doux.

Grape Varietals

With the notable exception of some European, particularly French, wines, most wines sold in the United States are varietal wines. That is, they are labeled and sold according to the grape variety from which they are made. (The U.S. government requires that 75 percent of the wine come from a particular grape before that varietal can be named on the label.)

Most of the world's wine is made from one or more of the many red, black or green grape varieties of the *Vitis vinifera* family of grapes. Several of these varietals are called *noble,* as they are considered to give rise to the world's most regal wines. The red wine grapes generally recognized as noble are Cabernet Sauvignon, Merlot, Nebbiolo, Pinot Noir, Syrah and Sangiovese. Noble white wines sources are Chardonnay, Riesling and Sauvignon Blanc.

Wines not sold as varietal wines may be classified by their place of origin. Thus, for example, Chablis, a popular white wine from the district of Chablis in France's northern Burgundy region, is made from Chardonnay grapes and would be called Chardonnay if made in the United States. A number of countries, led by France and Italy, have implemented systems to ensure that wines bottled and sold under such district names are exclusively from grapes produced in that geographic area. French labels will state "*appelation controlée*" and Italian labels "DOC" (for "*denominazione di origine controllata*") to designate such wines.

In recent years, particularly in the United States, some wines have been given proprietary names in lieu of varietal or geographic designations. Current examples include "Conundrum" by Caymus and "Opus One" by Mondavi-Rothschild, but the practice began in the 1950s with products imported to the United States, such as Lancers and Blue Nun. These made-up trademarked names can be used for blended wines when use of a specific varietal would not be possible because no one grape makes up 75% or more of the blend. They are also popular with winemakers, who wish to create something unique in the marketplace.

Fortified Wines

Wines usually have an alcohol content of 10 to 15%. Fortified wines are wines whose alcohol content has been increased to 18 to 22% by the addition of neutral grape spirits or grape brandy made from the same grapes used to make the wine. If the brandy is added before fermentation is complete, the fortified wine will be quite sweet, as the extra alcohol stops the fermentation process. If the brandy is added after fermentation is complete, the fortified wine will be drier. The best-known fortified wines—and the ones most often used as flavorings—are listed next.

Port is the only significant fortified wine made from red wine. Traditionally, port wine is produced in the Duoro valley of Portugal from a blend of five red wine grape varieties. Ports are generally divided into three categories. **Tawny ports** have a pale brown hue and a mellower, subtle, less fruity flavor than other ports. They are aged in wooden casks, sometimes for 20 or 30 years, and then typically blended with other ports, bottled and consumed. **Vintage ports** have a darker, more brick or burgundy hue and a richer, sweeter flavor than tawny ports. Vintage ports are aged in their bottles, sometimes as long as several decades, before being consumed. They are among the finest of ports, as the vintage designation is given only to ports considered of exceptional quality. **Ruby ports** are blends of younger ports of lesser quality than those designated as vintage ports. They tend to have a bright, almost crimson color and a smooth, sweet, fruity flavor.

Sherry is a fortified white wine from the Jerez region of southern Spain. It is made by an extremely complicated process called *solera* that relies on strict temperature controls and the blending and reblending of wines from different years as they age in wooden casks. During this process, the developing sherry is often exposed to oxygen and, to one degree or another, to a yeast called *flor*. Flor both protects the sherry from too much oxidation and contributes a distinct, somewhat nutty flavor to it. Depending on alcohol content, degree of exposure to flor and other factors, a sherry will be classified as one of six types: **manzanilla,** the driest sherry, which has a very pale golden-yellow color; **fino,** a very dry sherry with a pale golden-brown color; **amontillado,** which has a rich, slightly dry, nutty flavor and a light brown, amber color; **oloroso,** which has a somewhat dry, rich flavor, a full-body and a medium-brown color; **amoroso,** which has a sweet flavor and a medium-brown color that is sometimes artificially darkened; or **cream sherry,** the sweetest sherry, with a dark brown color.

Madeira, a fortified wine from the island of Madeira, is made from white wine grapes. Its characteristic light brown color and toffee-caramel flavor are produced when the developing wine is heated, a process called *estufagem*. This can occur naturally when the Madeira is left in barrels in warm attics for up to 20 years, or artificially when the wine is placed in containers and heated to a temperature of 105°F (40°C) for three to six months. The four principal types of Madeiras differ depending on the grape used. They are, from the driest to sweetest, **Sercial, Verdelho, Bual** and **Malmsey.**

Marsala, a fortified wine from western Sicily that is named for the town associated with its production, is made from grapes that are dried prior to fermentation. This increases the resulting wine's sugar content. After fermentation and fortification, Marsala is often darkened and sweetened with grape juice syrup and then allowed to age in wooden barrels, which mellows its flavors. Marsalas are brown-colored and available in two styles, dry and sweet; the latter has a richer flavor.

Vermouth is a flavored wine, sometimes fortified with brandy. Depending on the producer, vermouths are usually made by steeping various flavoring ingredients such as rose petals, citrus peels, hyssop, elderberries, chamomile, juniper berries, cloves, quinine, nutmeg and coriander in white wine. After a month or so, the flavorings are removed and brandy is added, then the vermouth is aged for two to four years in oak casks. There are two styles of vermouth. One, which is a brick- or ruby-red color, is variously called red (*rosso*), sweet or Italian vermouth. The other, which is clear, is variously called white (*bianco*), dry or French vermouth.

Evaluating Wines

Each grape varietal used to make a wine displays certain hallmark aroma and flavor characteristics in the finished product. This does not mean, however, that all wines made from the same grape varietal will have exactly the same aromas and flavors. Take, for example, a Merlot from Australia and one from California. They may share a certain smooth, juicy, mellow flavor with strong plum, black currant, black cherry and herbal or minty notes. But they will not be identical beverages. Rather, differences in the conditions under which the grapes were grown or the techniques the vintners used to make the wines will create noticeable differences between them. That said, the hallmark flavor and aroma characteristics of several of the world's most popular wine grapes are set forth in Tables 5.4 and 5.5. Often vintners blend two or more grape varietals in order to create a wine with the best attributes of a number of grapes. The infinite combinations account for the wide number of wines available and the vast differences between them.

As with any other flavoring, a chef should evaluate wines before using them. Although this text is not intended as a mini-wine-tasting course, a chef should consider some basics when evaluating a wine: aroma, flavor and body.

- **Aromas**—Most wines present a collection of different aromas. Called a bouquet or nose, individual aromas can often be distinguished (especially with practice) from a complex bouquet; these aromas are usually described by analogy. That is, the aroma reminds the person of some other aroma, usually that of a fruit, flower, herb, spice or other easily distinguished item. For example, when evaluating the bouquet of a Cabernet Sauvignon, many people recognize the aromas of black currants, green bell peppers, chocolate, mint and/or leather as well as fruit jams if the wine is young (new) and cedar and tobacco when it is aged. Likewise, the hallmark aromas of a Sauvignon Blanc are cut grass, fresh green herbs, asparagus and other vegetables. The quickly dissipating first aromas discerned while evaluating a wine's bouquet are often called top notes; the longer-lasting aromas are its medium or base notes.
- **Flavors**—The alcohol in wine contributes very little to its flavor. Rather, vintners try to create flavors by adjusting the balances between the sugars and acids in the wine. These sugars and acids interact, exciting the taste buds to recognize the wine as sweet, dry or somewhere between the two. The resulting flavor attributes are usually described with words based on a sweet/sour continuum (syrupy, sweet, crisp, tart or dry, for example), a general theme (for instance, fruity, herbaceous or spicy) or a reference to an attribute more akin to mouthfeel than flavor: smooth, velvety, silky and so on. **Initial taste** is the first impression of a wine's flavors; when

Table 5.4 **PRINCIPAL RED WINE GRAPES**

GRAPE VARIETALS	HALLMARK FLAVOR AND AROMA CHARACTERISTICS	ACIDITY	TANNINS	BODY	COMMON FOOD PAIRINGS
Cabernet Sauvignon (KA-bair-nay so-veen-yawn)	Assertive, rich, full flavor with fruity, black currant, chocolate, green bell pepper, mint or spice notes; jams when young, cedar and tobacco when older	Moderate	Moderate to prominent	Medium to full	Lamb and beef, especially if grilled; game, especially venison; strong cheeses
Grenache (gruh-NAHSH)	As a red wine, has a hearty flavor with black pepper notes; as a rosé, has a sturdy flavor with raspberry and cherry notes	Moderate	Moderate to low	Medium to full	Highly seasoned, cold-weather dishes such as meaty soups and stews
Merlot (mare-low)	Soft, smooth, juicy, mellow flavor with strong plum, black currant, black cherry and herbal or minty notes	Low	Low to moderate	Medium	Highly spiced dishes; savory foods with a hint of sweetness; grilled meats; fish and shellfish; strong cheeses; chocolate
Nebbiolo (nay-BYOH-low)	Very robust flavor with raspberry, plum, violet and earthy notes	High	Prominent, especially in younger wines	Medium	Game, especially venison; beef; dishes with rich sauces; mushrooms
Pinot Noir (pee-noe nwahr)	Rich, complex, flavor with cherry, raspberry and smoky or earthy notes and a velvety, silky texture	Moderate to high	Low to moderate	Light to medium	Game birds; rich, fatty fish or shellfish; roast beef; strong cheeses
Red Zinfandel (zin-fahn-DELL)	Robust, ripe, fruity, spicy flavors with blackberry or raspberry jam and black pepper notes	Low to moderate	Moderate to substantial	Medium to full	Roasted lamb; dishes flavored with garlic, black pepper and other strong flavorings; chili con carne and other hearty, spicy dishes; vegetable dishes; strong cheeses
Sangiovese (sahn-joe-VAY-zeh)	Earthy, hearty flavor with black cherry, raisin or floral (especially violet) notes	Moderate to high	Moderate	Light to medium	Veal; beef; lamb; hearty chicken dishes; tomato-based dishes
Syrah (see-rah) or Shiraz (shih-rhaz)	Rich flavor with sweet fruity, spice, floral or black pepper notes	Low to moderate	Moderate to prominent	Medium	Peppery, tangy, spicy foods; grilled meats; game

constructing a wine's flavor profile, these would be the top notes. **Finish** is how long the flavor lasts after the wine is swallowed.

Tannins are complex organic compounds concentrated in the grape's skin, pits and stems. Tannins give red wines their characteristic astringent sensation and slightly bitter taste. Because grape parts are separated from the juice early in the white-wine-making process, for the most part, tannins present in a white wine are usually the result of the wine being aged in oak casks.

Because the skins are present during fermentation in red wines, red wines tend to have more dominant and complex fruity flavors than white wines. These

Table 5.5 **PRINCIPAL WHITE WINE GRAPES**

GRAPE VARIETALS	HALLMARK FLAVOR AND AROMA CHARACTERISTICS	ACIDITY	BODY	COMMON FOOD PAIRINGS
Chardonnay (shar-doe-nay)	Full, rich flavor with a buttery texture and apple, green apple or tropical fruit notes; if aged in oak, may have vanilla or spicy notes	Moderate to high	Light to medium	Fish; shellfish, especially lobster; veal; chicken; foods flavored with herbs; foods served with rich or creamy sauces
Chenin Blanc (sheh-nan blahn)	Somewhat muted, tart acidic flavor with pine, melon or citrus notes; also used for a slightly sweet wine with similar notes	Very high	Light to medium	Light, summer foods; sweet or delicately flavored shellfish or fish; chicken; most cheeses; Asian foods
Pinot Blanc (pee-noe blahn)	Dry, full flavor with apple, melon or almond notes	Moderate to high	Medium to full	Duck or goose
Pinot Grigio (pee-noe gree-joe) or Pinot Gris (pee-noe gree)	Crisp, dry, somewhat muted flavor with pine, orange rind and earthy or metallic notes	Moderate	Medium	Vegetables; fish; shellfish; pasta dishes; chicken
Riesling (REESE-ling)	Usually sweet but balanced by a strong steely acidity; apricot, citrus, peach or floral notes	Moderate to high	Light; medium to heavy as a dessert wine	Spicy foods; Asian foods; highly seasoned chicken dishes; shellfish; most cheeses
Sauvignon Blanc (so-veen-yawn blahn)	Bright, crisp, green, tangy flavor with grassy, herb or citrus notes	High	Medium	Spicy foods; tomato-based dishes; rich or fatty fish, especially salmon; most cheeses

fruity flavors tend to mask the acidity more commonly associated with white wines. White wines are generally served chilled because acidic flavors (the tart or sour taste) are less pronounced at colder temperatures.

Body is the weight of the wine in the mouth and is generally related to the amount of alcohol and/or glycerin it contains. A wine's body is usually described as light, medium or full.

MATCHING WINE AND FOOD

The only rule about matching wine and food is that there are no rules. With this in mind, consider the following guidelines.

MATCH COLORS. Traditionally, red wines were served only with beef, veal, pork and lamb; white wines with only fish, shellfish and poultry. Although this rule may still be true for many pairings, do not be afraid to ignore it once in a while. Try, for example, a strong, oaky Chardonnay with grilled beef or a highly acidic, low-tannin red such as Sangiovese (Chianti), Pinot Noir or Beaujolais with fish or shellfish.

MATCH TASTES

▶ **dessert wines** sweet wines made from grapes left on the vine until they are overly ripe, such as Sauternes or wines labeled "Late Harvest"; during fermentation, some of the sugar is not converted to alcohol, but remains in the wine, giving it its characteristic intense sweet taste

- *Sweet.* Dishes with an element of sweetness often pair well with sweet or slightly sweet wines—the sweetness of one complements the sweetness of the other. If the same dish were served with a dry wine, the sweetness in the dish could make the wine taste a bit sour. Because **dessert wines** are so sweet, they are often difficult to pair with any food. A sweet dessert wine such as Sauternes does, however, compliment the fatty richness in foie gras or lobster with a rich cream sauce.

- *Sour.* If a dish has a citrus, especially lemony, top note, usually an acidic wine goes well with it. Wines with a high acid content frequently taste less acidic when paired with salty or sweet foods.
- *Salty.* Salty foods will mute the sweetness and enhance the fruitiness of a wine.
- *Bitter.* Be careful of pairing a wine high in tannins such as a Syrah or Cabernet Sauvignon with a food equally rich in tannins, such as walnuts. The combination will render the wine almost unbearably bitter, dry and astringent.
- *Umami.* The richer the food, often the more robust the wine needed to complement it.

MATCH STRENGTHS. A delicate dish often goes best with a light, gentle wine, usually a white wine. A richly sauced or meaty dish might be best served with a strong, assertive wine, generally a red wine.

MATCH OPPOSITES. Sometimes the perfect wine for pungent, spicy foods is a sweet or slightly sweet wine. Similarly, an acidic wine sometimes goes well with rich creamy or buttery sauces. Along the same vein, pair complex wines with simple dishes and simple wines with complex dishes.

MATCH ORIGINS. Wines often developed alongside regional cuisines and thus they often have an affinity for each other. For example, cheeses or other foods from the Loire Valley of France pair exceptionally well with wines from that region, such as Sancerre (Sauvignon Blanc) or Chenin Blanc.

SELECTING WINES TO USE AS FLAVORINGS

The concepts just described for matching wines with foods have some bearing on what wines a chef should choose as flavoring ingredients. If a chef is wedded to a particular food-and-wine pairing and the dish calls for wine as an ingredient, it is often best to use the same or a similar wine (that is, a less expensive wine made from the same grape varietal) as the flavoring.

Otherwise, the only rules for choosing wines as flavorings are:

- Avoid using anything called cooking wine. These are usually inferior products with added salt and other flavorings.
- Do not cook with a wine that you would not drink.

A chef should choose good-quality wines at cost-effective prices. Finding such wines may take time, but they are available. Often recipes will specify only a general type of wine. Here are some suggestions on what to use if a recipe calls for specific wines:

White wine or dry white wine—Consider a simple, fruity Chardonnay or a dry, herby Sauvignon Blanc; even a dry Vermouth might be used. Avoid wines with a sharp, acidic flavor, and those with an excessive oaky or woody flavor. When a dessert calls for white wine, such as for poached pears, a sweet wine might be appropriate.

Sweet or slightly sweet white wine—Consider a Riesling or Chenin Blanc or even a white Zinfandel.

Red wine or dry red wine—Consider a simple, fruity red wine with a low to moderately low tannin content. A Pinot Noir or a medium-bodied Merlot or red Zinfandel is usually a good choice.

Sweet red wine—Consider the rich flavor of a ruby port or possibly a red Zinfandel.

Sparkling wine—Consider using a sweet, fruity one (sparkling wines lose their effervescence once exposed to air and heat).

Dessert wine—Consider using the classic dessert wine Sauternes, or one labeled “Late Harvest.”

Port—Consider using a ruby port with its rich, sweet, deeply winy flavor; because they are blends, ruby ports offer a greater degree of flavor consistency.

Sherry—Consider using an Amontillo with its roasted, nutty flavor. Generic cream sherry will be sweeter and fruity.

Madeira—Consider a medium-bodied Bual with its toffee-caramel flavor or a more full-bodied, sweet Malmsey.

Marsala—Consider using sweet Marsala with its richer, light caramel-like fruity flavor.

Vermouth—Consider using a dry white Vermouth, a good complement to many savory foods.

BEER

THE BEER-MAKING PROCESS

Beer is made from water, hops and malted barley, fermented by yeast. In Germany, by law only these four ingredients may be used, but in the United States and elsewhere another unmalted, less-expensive grain such as rice or corn is often added to lighten the product.

Barley is converted into malt by steeping the dry grain in cool water for five to nine days, allowing it to germinate and produce the sugar-producing enzymes required for the fermentation process. Once the barley has reached the desired sugar and enzyme levels, the grain is dried with warm air (kilned) to establish color and flavor. The longer the malting period, the darker the resulting malt. A slow, gentle dry produces pale malts and a corresponding light-colored and -bodied brew, while more intense heat develops dark malts that may be characterized as "caramelized" or "toasted." To brew beer, the ground barley malt is "mashed" or soaked in hot water, producing a brown liquid called the wort. **Hops,** the cone-shaped female flowers of the vine *Humulus lupulus,* provide bitterness from their resins and aroma from their oil. They are added to the wort, which is then boiled for 1 to 2 hours, allowing the hops to flavor the brew.

Hops Flowers

Fermentation yeasts, selected according to the type of beer produced, are then added to the cooled wort. The fermentation process, which produces alcohol, can last from a few days in the case of ales to several weeks for lagers. Once fermentation is complete, the beer is transferred to storage vats for conditioning, a process that removes unwanted flavors and develops natural carbonation. This stage can also vary widely, from a few days to a few months. During this stage some brewers subject the beer to such procedures as lagering, *kräusening,* dry hopping, or the addition of other additives to adjust the flavor.

Unlike wine, beer does not improve with age, and is best consumed as soon as possible after production. Light and heat both adversely alter beer's flavor. Brown bottles are generally used to filter damaging rays. Beer is best stored between 50°F and 55°F (10°C and 13°C). Although Americans have a tendency to serve beer ice-cold, this practice limits the appreciation of its full flavor. Lagers are ideally served at approximately 50°F (10°C), while ales should be served at about 60°F (15°C).

EVALUATING BEERS

Many characteristics influence the final outcome of the brewing process: the quality of the water, the type of malt, the hops used, the species of yeast selected for fermentation, the length of the fermentation and conditioning stages, as well as any additives. The combined effects of these elements determine the color, body, astringency, taste, alcohol content, and aroma of the finished product. Beers may be divided into two broad groups: **ales** and **lagers.** Ales are made with yeast that rise to the top during the fermentation process, producing an aromatic, cloudy brew; porter and stout are the darkest and most potent ales. Lagers are made with yeast that falls to the bottom during fermentation and are characteristically light, clear, and crisp. Pilsner is a popular style of pale, light lager associated with the ancient brewing center in Plzen in the Western Czech Re-

Table 5.6 **CHARACTERISTICS OF BEER**

TYPE OF BEER	COLOR	ALCOHOL CONTENT	BODY	FLAVOR	COMMON FOOD PAIRINGS
American pilsner	Light	Very low	Light	Little aroma or bitterness	Spicy foods
Belgian lambic	Light	Moderate	Light	Sour	Sharp cheese; fruit desserts; dark chocolate
Brown ale	Red to brown	Low	Full-bodied	Sweet, nutty	Sausages; smoked fish; game; salad
European lager	Light	Moderate	Moderate	Bitter, floral finish	Most meat and fish dishes; German sausage; pretzels
Pale ale	Light	Low	Moderate	Bitter, fruity, floral	Spicy foods; smoked or fried seafood; beef; lamb; game
Porter	Dark	Moderate	Full-bodied	Bitter	Barbecue; hearty meat dishes; oysters; shellfish; smoked salmon; strong cheeses
Stout; bock	Very dark	High	Full-bodied	Sweet; malty	Chocolate, nut or fruit desserts; heavy meat dishes; goulash; spicy desserts

public. Most of the beer produced and consumed today is lager, with Britain and Belgium the only two markets preferring ale.

The alcohol content of beer ranges from 3% to 12% by volume. The United States has historically preferred lighter beers than Europe or Australia, and in recent decades, in response to calorie consciousness and a desire for lower alcohol content, so-called "light" beers have been developed. These, however, frequently sacrifice taste for the other desired characteristics. Nonalcoholic beers, made by removing the alcohol or adjusting the fermentation process to lower the alcohol content, are produced for consumers who enjoy beer's taste but do not consume alcohol for medical, religious, or other reasons.

Although all ales and lagers share certain general characteristics, within each group there are immense variations, as demonstrated in Table 5.6.

MATCHING BEER AND FOOD

Beer can be served with far more than pizza or barbecue; simply consider the following guidelines.

MATCH TASTES. Fruit beers, such as Belgian *kriek,* are often paired with meat or dessert dishes based on fruits.

MATCH STRENGTHS. Strong beers, such as porter and stout ales or bock lager, are frequently paired with strong tastes, such as sharp cheeses, game and spicy desserts.

MATCH OPPOSITES. Beer, particularly lighter brew, is often preferable as a pairing with particularly spicy foods of East and Southeast Asia, Africa, the southwestern United States or Latin America, which might overpower wine. In Italy, beer is often drunk with pizza, which frequently contains such acidic ingredients as anchovies or artichokes, or multiple ingredients, which would challenge a single wine.

MATCH ORIGINS. Beers of a given country are often paired with foods of that country—for example, German bratwurst or pretzels with German lager, or fiery Thai food with Thai pilsners.

SELECTING BEERS TO USE AS FLAVORINGS

Beer is frequently used as a flavoring in the cuisines of northern France and Belgium, where it appears in such dishes as *carbonnade,* a stew flavored with beer. Because of beer's slight bitterness, sugar or brown sugar is often added to balance the flavor. Beer can also be used in marinades and to deglaze and prepare sauces in the same manner as wine. In the United States, beer is frequently used in batters for foods being deep-fat fried, such as fish, and vegetables, for example Beer-Battered Onion Rings.

BRANDY

Brandy is an alcoholic beverage made by distilling fermented fruit juice or fruit pulp and skin. Brandies typically fall into one of three categories:

- **Grape brandy** is a brandy distilled from white wine or fermented grape pulp and skins. It is aged in wooden casks (usually oak), which contributes to its rich, amber-brown colors and imparts additional mellowing flavors and aromas.

  Cognac, one of the best-known brandies, is made in France's Cognac region (and only brandy made there can be called Cognac). Cognac is twice distilled from blends of various wines that tend to be thin, tart and low in alcohol—bad for drinking but great for brandy making. After distillation, the brandy is aged in oak casks. Virtually all Cognacs sold are blends of brandies from different vintners and different years. Traditionally Cognacs are labeled according to their age. Some common grades are V.S. (Very Special, at least 2½ years old), V.S.O.P. (Very Superior Old Pale, at least 4½ years old) and XO, Napoleon or Extra, at least 6 years old.

  Armagnac is another well-known French brandy from the Armagnac region of southwestern France; it is slightly drier and heavier than Cognac or Cognac-style brandies. **Metaxa** is a Greek brandy with a strong resin flavor. **Brandy de Jerez** is a Spanish brandy aged in a solera system similar to that used for sherry; it is generally heavier and sweeter than Cognac and Cognac-style brandies.
- **Pomace brandy** is a brandy made from pomace, the pressed grape pulp, skins and stems that remain after the grapes are crushed and pressed to extract the juices used to make wine. They are minimally aged, and usually not in wooden casks. They tend to have a harsh flavor. Examples include Italian Grappa and French Marc.
- **Fruit brandy** is any brandy made from fermenting fruits other than grapes. This term should not be confused with **fruit-flavored brandy,** which is a grape brandy that has been flavored with the extract of another fruit. Well-known fruit brandies include **Calvados,** an apple brandy from Normandy, France; **Kirschwasser,** a cherry brandy from Bavaria, Germany; **Framboise,** a raspberry brandy from Alsace, France; **Poire,** a pear brandy from Alsace, France; and **Slivovitz,** a plum brandy from eastern Europe and the Balkans.

As with wines, when choosing a brandy as a flavoring, it does not necessarily pay to skimp on costs. The brandy does not have to be the most expensive brand, but it should have a rich, full, mellow flavor. Try, for example, an inexpensive but genuine Cognac (one that is graded V.S.). If the recipe calls for a fruit brandy, make sure to use one. Do not use a fruit brandy with added artificial flavors, a fruit-flavored brandy or a fruit-flavored liqueur. These products have different flavors, bodies, degrees of sweetness and alcohol contents than fruit brandies.

LIQUORS

Liquors are distilled alcoholic beverages such as gin, rum, tequila, vodka and whiskey. To create these beverages, a liquid made from grains, vegetables or the like is fermented, then the water component is cooked off and the alcohol is concentrated through **distillation.** The resulting clear liquid can be colored or flavored during aging, or bottled for immediate sale. From time to time, a chef may decide to add a distinctive liquor flavor to foods, especially sauces and desserts.

▶ **distillation** the separation of alcohol from a liquid (or, during the production of alcoholic beverages, from a fermented mash); it is accomplished by heating the liquid or mash to a gas that contains alcohol vapors; this steam is then condensed into the desired alcoholic liquid (beverage)

Gin is a clear spirit distilled from grains and flavored with juniper berries as well as herbs, peels and spices. There are various styles of gin; London dry gin, which is a generally recognized style, not a brand, is considered heavier and drier than American gin; Dutch gin is the sweetest.

Rum is distilled from sugar cane and most of it comes from the cane-producing Caribbean countries. Its character varies according to its color: **White rums,** which are clear and colorless, are relatively dry and light; **amber** or **gold rums** are similar to white rums but with a slightly stronger flavor and a pale golden color; **dark rums** have a strong molasses flavor, a dark brown color and a heavy body.

Tequila is a clear to amber-colored spirit made in Mexico from the fermented sap of the agave. Mezcal, which is made from sap extracted from fire-roasted blue agave, is similar to tequila but with a harsher flavor.

Vodka is, traditionally, a flavorless and colorless liquor distilled from potatoes, fruits, grains and/or other plant products. Most of the world's vodka is actually made from wheat. Many newer types of vodka are flavored, either by including the flavorings in the mash during distillation or by adding flavors afterward.

Whiskey (the English, Scots and Canadians spell it without the *e*) is a spirit distilled from various grains that have been pounded and cooked into a mash and allowed to ferment before distillation. After distillation, it is aged in oak barrels until the flavors are mellow and smooth. There are many types of whiskies. **Blended whiskey** is a mixture of straight whiskies and neutral spirits; it is usually aged after blending. **Bourbon** or **bourbon whiskey** is produced in Kentucky and is distilled from a mash containing at least 51% corn, then aged in charred new oak barrels. **Canadian whisky** is usually a blended product with a light body. **Irish whiskey** resembles Scotch, but without the smoky flavor. **Rye whiskey** is an American whiskey made from rye. **Scotch whisky** has a very distinctive, smoky flavor. A single-malt Scotch whisky tends to have a stronger, more complex flavor than a blended Scotch whisky, which is a mixture of malt whiskies and grain whiskies.

LIQUEURS

Liqueurs are traditionally made from herbs, fruits, nuts, spices, flowers or other flavorings infused into an alcohol base. The base can be **neutral spirits,** brandy, rum or whiskey. All liqueurs have varying degrees of added sugar. Many newer liqueurs, especially generic off-brand products, are made with flavoring extracts, essential oils and even artificial flavors. **Cream liqueurs** are liqueurs blended with cream. They are thick, with mild, comforting flavors. They do not keep long once opened, so they need to be stored in the refrigerator. **Crème liqueurs,** such as crème de cacao, crème de menthe and crème de cassis, contain no cream. Rather, additional sugar gives them a thick, syrupy, creamy texture and a very sweet flavor.

▶ **neutral spirits or grain spirits** pure alcohol (ethanol or ethyl alcohol); they are odorless, tasteless and a very potent 190 proof (95% alcohol)

When using a liqueur as a flavoring, look for products with rich, true, natural flavors. In addition, bear in mind that a liqueur and a crème liqueur flavored with the same ingredients are not the same products and should not be used interchangeably. So if a recipe calls for the coffee-flavored liqueur Kahlúa, use it and not a crème de café product; the latter will have a more syrupy texture and a sweeter flavor. Similarly, if a recipe calls for a proprietary blend such as Drambuie or Chambord, do not skimp on some lesser-quality generic product; customers may know the difference. Many of the liqueurs commonly used as flavorings are listed in Table 5.7.

Table 5.7 LIQUEURS COMMONLY USED AS FLAVORINGS

LIQUEUR	ALCOHOL BASE	FLAVORINGS
Amaretto	Grape brandy	Almonds and apricots
B&B	Grape brandy	Benédictine and brandy
Bénédictine	Grape brandy	Herbs, spices and citrus peels
Campari	Neutral spirits	130 different herbs, plants, peels and aromatics
Cassis	Neutral spirits	Black currants, herbs, roots, plants and peels
Chambord	Grape brandy	Black raspberries
Chartreuse	Grape brandy	More than 125 herbs and other flavorings
Cointreau	Grape brandy	Bitter orange peel
Crème de cacao	Neutral spirits	Chocolate
Crème de café	Neutral spirits	Coffee
Crème de cassis	Rum	Black currants
Crème de menthe	Neutral spirits	Peppermint
Curaçao	Grape brandy	Honey
Drambuie	Scotch whisky	Hazelnuts
Frangelico	Neutral spirits	Hazelnuts
Galliano	Neutral spirits	Anise, licorice and vanilla
Grand Marnier	Neutral spirits	Bitter oranges
Irish Crème	Irish whiskey	Cream and sugar
Kahlúa	Neutral spirits	Coffee
Kirsch	Neutral spirits	Cherries
Limoncello	Neutral spirits, vodka	Lemons
Malibu	White rum	Coconut
Midori	Neutral spirits	Melons
Ouzo	Rum	Anise seed and herbs
Pernod	Neutral spirits	Anise seed and licorice
Pimm's No. 1 Cup	Gin	Herbs, botanicals and fruit extracts
Sambuca	Neutral spirits	Anise seed and elderberries
Sloe Gin	Gin	Sloe berries
Southern Comfort	American whiskey	Peaches and oranges
Tia Maria	Cask-aged rum	Coffee beans and spices
Triple Sec	Grape brandy	Bitter orange peel

GUIDELINES FOR COOKING WITH WINES, BEERS, BRANDIES, LIQUORS AND LIQUEURS

- *Use quality products.* Heating a mediocre wine, brandy, liqueur or liquor tends to bring out the worst characteristics of the product, especially its acidic properties.
- *Pay attention to cooking time once wine or other alcoholic beverages have been added.* The longer a dish cooks, the more alcohol evaporates, thus concentrating its flavors, especially acidic flavors. Because alcohol evaporates at a lower temperature than water (172°F/86°C), the flavorings suspended in the alcohol are reduced and concentrated faster than flavorings suspended in water.

- *Brown foods before adding wine or other alcoholic beverages to a dish such as a sauce or stew.* This allows the surface of the foods to caramelize before liquid is added. As the wine is reduced, all of the flavors will blend together.
- *Alcohol and acids in wine may interact with aluminum or cast-iron cookware.* Some chefs therefore prefer to use nonreactive cookware when cooking with wine or other alcoholic beverages.

For many, the consumption of alcohol is a concern. The amount of alcohol left after a wine or other alcoholic beverage has been added as a flavoring depends on how and for how long the dish is cooked. A dish flambéd tableside with Cognac that is allowed to burn out before being served, for example, may retain very little of its original alcohol content. But a chicken breast that has been marinated in white wine and then quickly sautéed could retain as much as 75 percent of the alcohol from the marinade. If, however, the same chicken breast is cooked over medium heat for 15 minutes, as much as 60 percent of the alcohol will evaporate out. Simmering the same chicken breast over low heat for approximately two hours or more will reduce the alcohol content to 10 percent or even less.

▶ VINEGARS

Vinegar (Fr. *vinaigre*) is a thin, sour liquid used for thousands of years as a preservative, cooking ingredient, condiment and cleaning solution. Vinegar is obtained through the fermentation of wine or other alcoholic liquid. Bacteria attack the alcohol in the solution, turning it into acetic acid. No alcohol remains when the transformation is complete. The quality of vinegar depends on the quality of the wine or other liquid on which it is based. Vinegar flavors are as varied as the liquids from which they are made.

Vinegars should be clear and clean-looking, never cloudy or muddy. Commercial vinegars are pasteurized, so an unopened bottle should last indefinitely in a cool, dark place. Once opened, vinegars should last about three months if tightly capped. Any sediment that develops can be strained out; if mold develops, discard the vinegar.

Wine vinegars are as old as wine itself. They may be made from white or red wine, sherry or even Champagne, and should bear the color and flavor hallmarks of the wine used. Wine vinegars are preferred in French and Mediterranean cuisines.

Malt vinegar is produced from malted barley. Its slightly sweet, mild flavor is used as a condiment, especially with fried foods.

Distilled vinegar, made from grain alcohol, is completely clear with a stronger vinegary flavor and higher acid content than other vinegars. It is preferred for pickling and preserving.

Cider vinegar is produced from unpasteurized apple juice or cider. It is pale brown in color with a mild acidity and fruity aroma. Cider vinegar is particularly popular in the United States.

Rice vinegar is a clear, slightly sweet product brewed from rice wine. Its flavor is clean and elegant, making it useful in a variety of dishes, especially those of Japanese or Asian origin.

Flavored vinegars are simply traditional vinegars in which herbs, spices, fruits or other foods are steeped to infuse their flavors. They are easily produced from commercial wine or distilled vinegars, using any herb, spice or fruit desired. Inferior flavored vinegars are made by adding the desired flavoring to low-grade vinegar. The use of flavored vinegars is extremely popular but definitely not new. Clove, raspberry and fennel vinegars were sold on the streets of Paris during the 13th century. Making fruit-flavored vinegars was also one of the responsibilities of American housewives during the 18th and 19th centuries.

FLAMBÉING: COOKING WITH ALCOHOL

Often a dish will require flaming or flambéing, which means igniting brandy, rum or other liquor so that the alcohol burns off and the flavor of the liquor is retained. When alcohol comes into contact with a flame, it can ignite. So, in order to avoid singed eyebrows and kitchen fires, be careful when adding wine, brandy, liqueurs or liquor to a dish on or near the stove.

When a dish calls for flambéing, stand away from the pan being flamed. Never pour alcohol directly from a bottle into a hot pan because the flames can travel up into the bottle, causing it to explode. Heat the liquor until warm. This can be done in the pan in which the food is cooking, such as for Pepper Steaks, or in a separate pan, such as for Strawberry Crêpes Fitzgerald. Tilt the pan away from you before igniting the liquor to avoid having the flames leap from the pan. The flame from a gas burner or match will ignite the alcohol. Allow the flame to subside before finishing the preparation.

Balsamic Vinegar, Raspberry Vinegar and Cider Vinegar

Balsamic vinegar (It. *aceto balsamico*) is newly popular in the United States, though it has been produced in Italy for more than 800 years. To produce traditional balsamic vinegar, red or white wine made from specially cultivated grapes (white Trebbiano and red Lambrusco grapes among others), is reduced, then aged in a succession of wooden barrels made from a variety of woods—oak, cherry, locust, ash, mulberry and juniper—for at least 4, but sometimes up to 50, years. The resulting liquid is dark reddish-brown and sweet. Balsamic vinegar has a high acid level, but the sweetness covers the tart flavor, making it very mellow. True balsamic is extremely expensive because of the long aging process and the small quantities available. Most of the commercial products imported from Italy are now made by a quick carmelization and flavoring process. Balsamic is excellent as a condiment or seasoning and has a remarkable affinity for tomatoes and strawberries.

CONCLUSION

Much of the pleasure of eating comes from savoring the tastes and smells of well-flavored, thoughtfully prepared foods. An understanding of how the human senses of taste and smell work helps a chef develop his or her own palate. With practice a chef will learn how to identify flavorings and learn to balance flavors when preparing recipes or creating new dishes.

Common flavorings include fresh and dried herbs, spices, salt, oils, condiments, wines, brandies, liqueurs, liquors and vinegars. Chefs must be able to recognize, purchase, store and use many of these flavorings. The only way to determine which brands or types of flavorings are best for your particular needs is to taste, smell, sample and use a variety of those available. Cost, convenience and storage factors must also be considered. By maintaining a supply of flavorings, chefs will be able to create new dishes or enhance standard ones at a moment's notice.

QUESTIONS FOR DISCUSSION

1. What are some factors that can affect flavors? Discuss how this relates to cooking certain foods.
2. What is a flavoring? Does every kitchen keep the same flavorings on hand? Explain your answer.
3. What are the differences between an herb and a spice? Give an example of a plant that is used as both an herb and a spice.
4. If a recipe calls for a fresh herb and you only have the herb dried, what do you do? Explain your answer.
5. How are condiments used by chefs and by customers?
6. Describe ways in which wines and other alcoholic beverages are used to flavor foods.

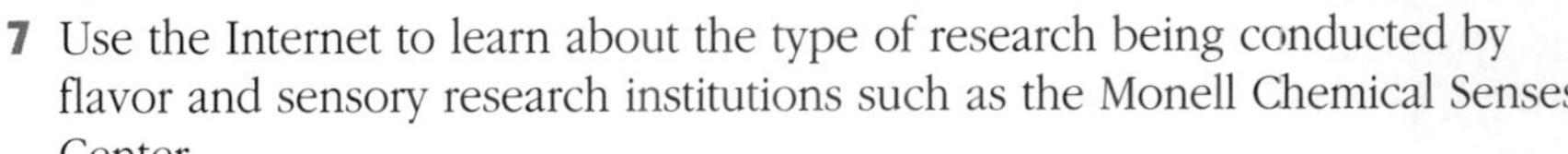

7. Use the Internet to learn about the type of research being conducted by flavor and sensory research institutions such as the Monell Chemical Senses Center.

CHAPTER SIX

FOOD HISTORY IS AS IMPORTANT AS A BAROQUE CHURCH. GOVERNMENTS SHOULD RECOGNIZE CULTURAL HERITAGE AND PROTECT TRADITIONAL FOODS. A CHEESE IS AS WORTHY OF PRESERVING AS A SIXTEENTH-CENTURY BUILDING.

—Carlo Petrini, Italian journalist (1950–)

DAIRY PRODUCTS

AFTER STUDYING THIS CHAPTER, YOU WILL BE ABLE TO:

- identify, store and use a variety of milk-based products
- identify, store and serve a variety of fine cheeses

Dairy products include cow's milk and foods produced from cow's milk such as butter, yogurt, sour cream and cheese. The milk of other mammals, namely, goats, sheep (ewe) and buffalo, is also made into cheeses that are used in commercial food service operations. Dairy products are extremely versatile and are used throughout the kitchen, served either as is or as ingredients in everything from soups and salads to breads and desserts.

▸ MILK

▸ **ewe's milk** milk produced by a female sheep; it has approximately 7.9% milkfat, 11.4% milk solids and 80.7% water

▸ **goat's milk** milk produced by a female goat; it has approximately 4.1% milkfat, 8.9% milk solids and 87% water

▸ **water buffalo's milk** milk produced by a female water buffalo; it has approximately 7.5% milkfat, 10.3% milk solids and 82.2% water

Milk is not only a popular beverage, it is also an ingredient in many dishes. It provides texture, flavor, color and nutritional value for cooked or baked items. Indeed, milk is one of the most nutritious foods available, providing proteins, vitamins and minerals (particularly calcium). But milk is also highly perishable and an excellent bacterial breeding ground. Care must be exercised when handling and storing milk and other dairy products.

Whole milk—that is, milk as it comes from the cow—consists of water primarily (about 88%). It contains approximately 3.5% milkfat and 8.5% other milk solids (proteins, milk sugar [lactose] and minerals).

Whole milk is graded A, B or C according to standards recommended by the U.S. Public Health Service. Grades are assigned based on bacterial count, with Grade A products having the lowest count. Grades B and C, though still safe and wholesome, are rarely available for retail or commercial use. Fresh whole milk is not available raw, but must be processed as we describe shortly.

PROCESSING TECHNIQUES

PASTEURIZATION

By law, all Grade A milk must be pasteurized prior to retail sale. Pasteurization is the process of heating milk to a sufficiently high temperature for a sufficient length of time to destroy pathogenic bacteria. This typically requires holding milk at a temperature of 161°F (72°C) for 15 seconds. Pasteurization also destroys enzymes that cause spoilage, thus increasing shelf life. Milk's nutritional value is not significantly affected by pasteurization.

ULTRA-PASTEURIZATION

Ultra-pasteurization is a process in which milk is heated to a very high temperature (275°F/135°C) for a very short time (2 to 4 seconds) in order to destroy virtually all bacteria. Ultra-pasteurization is most often used with whipping cream and individual creamers. Although the process may reduce cream's whipping properties, it extends its shelf life dramatically.

ULTRA-HIGH-TEMPERATURE PROCESSING

Ultra-high-temperature (UHT) processing is a form of ultra-pasteurization in which milk is held at a temperature of 280°F–300°F (138°C–150°C) for 2 to 6 seconds. It is then packed in sterile containers under sterile conditions and aseptically sealed to prevent bacteria from entering the container. Unopened UHT milk can be stored without refrigeration for at least three months. Although UHT milk can be stored unrefrigerated, it should be chilled before serving and stored like fresh milk once opened. UHT processing may give milk a slightly cooked taste, but it has no significant effect on milk's nutritional value. Long available in Europe, it is now gaining popularity in the United States.

HOMOGENIZATION

Homogenization is a process in which the fat globules in whole milk are reduced in size and permanently dispersed throughout the liquid. This prevents the fat from clumping together and rising to the surface as a layer of cream. Although homogenization is not required, milk sold commercially is generally homogenized because it ensures a uniform consistency, a whiter color and a richer taste.

MILKFAT REMOVAL

Whole milk can also be processed in a centrifuge to remove all or a portion of the milkfat, resulting in reduced-fat, low-fat and nonfat milks. All reduced-fat milks must still be nutritionally equivalent to full-fat milk and must provide at least the same amounts of the fat-soluble vitamins A and D as full-fat milk.

Reduced-fat or less-fat milk is whole milk from which sufficient milkfat has been removed to produce a liquid with 2% milkfat. **Low-fat** or little-fat milk contains 1% milkfat. **Nonfat** milk, also referred to as fat-free, no-fat or skim milk, has had as much milkfat removed as possible. The fat content must be less than 0.5%.

STORAGE

Fluid milk is a potentially hazardous food and should be kept refrigerated at or below 41°F (5°C). Its shelf life is reduced by half for every five-degree rise in temperature above 41°F (5°C). Keep milk containers closed to prevent absorption of odors and flavors. Freezing is not recommended.

CONCENTRATED MILKS

Concentrated or condensed milk products are produced by using a vacuum to remove all or part of the water from whole milk. The resulting products have a high concentration of milkfat and milk solids and an extended shelf life.

Evaporated milk is produced by removing approximately 60 percent of the water from whole, homogenized milk. The concentrated liquid is canned and heat-sterilized. This results in a cooked flavor and darker color. Evaporated skim milk, with a milkfat content of 0.5%, is also available. A can of evaporated milk requires no refrigeration until opened, although the can should be stored in a cool place. Evaporated milk can be reconstituted with an equal amount of water and used like whole milk for cooking or drinking.

Sweetened condensed milk is similar to evaporated milk in that 60 percent of the water has been removed. But unlike evaporated milk, sweetened condensed milk contains large amounts of sugar (40 to 45 percent). Sweetened condensed milk is also canned; the canning process darkens the color and adds a caramel flavor. Sweetened condensed milk cannot be substituted for whole milk or evaporated milk because of its sugar content. Its distinctive flavor is most often found in desserts and confections.

Dry milk powder is made by removing virtually all the moisture from pasteurized milk. Dry whole milk, nonfat milk and buttermilk are available. The lack of moisture prevents the growth of microorganisms and allows dry milk powders to be stored for extended periods without refrigeration. Powdered milks can be reconstituted with water and used like fresh milk. Milk powder may also be added to foods directly, with additional liquid included in the recipe. This procedure is typical in bread making and does not alter the function of the milk or the flavor in the finished product.

CREAM

Cream is a rich, liquid milk product containing at least 18% fat. It must be pasteurized or ultra-pasteurized and may be homogenized. Cream has a slight

IMITATION AND ARTIFICIAL DAIRY PRODUCTS

Coffee whiteners, imitation sour cream, whipped-topping mixes and some whipped toppings in pressurized cans are made from nondairy products. These products usually consist of corn syrup, emulsifiers, vegetable fats, coloring agents and artificial flavors. These products are generally less expensive and have a longer shelf life than the real dairy products they replace, but their flavors are no match. Imitation and artificial products may be useful, however, for people who have allergies or are on a restricted diet. If you choose to use these products, you cannot claim to be using real dairy products on menus or labels.

SAFETY ALERT

Milk Storage

Canned milks, aseptically packaged milks and dry milk powders are shelf-stable products needing no refrigeration. After the can or box is opened or the powder is reconstituted with water, however, these become potentially hazardous foods and must be handled just as carefully as fresh milk. Do not store an open can of milk in its original container, and keep all milk products refrigerated at or below 41°F (5

yellow or ivory color and is more viscous than milk. It is used throughout the kitchen to give flavor and body to sauces, soups and desserts. Whipping cream, containing not less than 30% milkfat, can be whipped into a stiff foam and used in pastries and desserts. Cream is marketed in several forms with different fat contents, as described here.

Half-and-half is a mixture of whole milk and cream containing between 10% and 18% milkfat. It is often served with cereal or coffee, but does not contain enough fat to whip into a foam.

Light cream, coffee cream and **table cream** are all products with more than 18% but less than 30% milkfat. These products are often used in baked goods or soups as well as with coffee, fruit and cereal.

Light whipping cream or, simply, **whipping cream,** contains between 30% and 36% milkfat. It is generally used for thickening and enriching sauces and making ice cream. It can be whipped into a foam and used as a dessert topping or folded into custards or mousses to add flavor and lightness.

Heavy whipping cream or, simply, **heavy cream,** contains not less than 36% milkfat. It whips easily and holds its whipped texture longer than other creams. It must be pasteurized, but is rarely homogenized. Heavy cream is used throughout the kitchen in the same ways as light whipping cream.

STORAGE

Ultra-pasteurized cream will keep for six to eight weeks if refrigerated at or below 41°F (5°C). Unwhipped cream should not be frozen. Keep cream away from strong odors and bright lights, as they can adversely affect its flavor.

CULTURED DAIRY PRODUCTS

Cultured dairy products such as yogurt, buttermilk and sour cream are produced by adding specific bacterial cultures to fluid dairy products. The bacteria convert the milk sugar **lactose** into lactic acid, giving these products their body and tangy, unique flavors. The acid content also retards the growth of undesirable microorganisms; thus cultured products have been used for centuries to preserve milk.

▶ **lactose** a disaccharide that occurs naturally in mammalian milk; milk sugar

Buttermilk originally referred to the liquid remaining after cream was churned into butter. Today, buttermilk is produced by adding a culture (*Streptococcus lactis*) to fresh, pasteurized skim or low-fat milk. This results in tart milk with a thick texture. Buttermilk is most often used as a beverage or in baked goods.

Sour cream is produced by adding the same culture to pasteurized, homogenized light cream. The resulting product is a white, tangy gel used as a condiment or to give baked goods a distinctive flavor. Sour cream must have a milkfat content of not less than 18%.

Crème fraîche is a cultured cream popular in French cuisine. Although thinner and richer than sour cream, it has a similar tart, tangy flavor. It is used extensively in soups and sauces, especially with poultry, rabbit and lamb dishes. It is easily prepared from the following recipe.

Yogurt is a thick, tart, custardlike product made from milk (either whole, low-fat or nonfat) cultured with *Lactobacillus bulgaricus* and *Streptococcus thermophilus.* Though touted as a health or diet food, yogurt contains the same amount of milkfat as the milk from which it is made. Yogurt may also contain a variety of sweeteners, flavorings and fruits. Yogurt is generally eaten as is, but may be used in baked products, salad dressings and frozen desserts. It is used in many Middle Eastern cuisines.

BUTTERMILK IN A PINCH

To make a buttermilk substitute when none is available, combine 8 fluid ounces (240 milliliters) whole milk with ½ fluid ounce (15 milliliters) white vinegar or lemon juice. The mixture should begin to curdle in 15 minutes. Stir well before using. Combining 2 fluid ounces (60 milliliters) whole milk with 6 fluid ounces (180 milliliters) plain yogurt will also work as a buttermilk substitute.

CRÈME FRAÎCHE

RECIPE 6.1

Yield: 16 fluid ounces (500 ml)

Heavy cream, not ultrapasteurized	16 fl. oz.	500 ml
Buttermilk, with active cultures	1 fl. oz.	30 ml

1. Heat the cream to approximately 100°F (43°C).
2. Remove the cream from the heat and stir in the buttermilk.
3. Allow the mixture to stand in a warm place, loosely covered, until it thickens, approximately 12 to 36 hours.
4. Chill thoroughly before using. Crème fraîche will keep for up to 10 days in the refrigerator.

Approximate values per 1-fl.-oz. (30-ml) serving: **Calories** 90, **Total fat** 10 g, **Saturated fat** 6 g, **Cholesterol** 35 mg, **Sodium** 10 mg, **Total carbohydrates** 1 g, **Protein** 1 g, **Vitamin A** 10%, Claims—very low sodium

STORAGE

Cultured products are potentially hazardous foods and should be kept refrigerated at or below 41°F (5°C). Under proper conditions, sour cream will last up to four weeks, yogurt up to three weeks and buttermilk up to two weeks. Freezing is not recommended for these products, but dishes prepared with cultured products generally can be frozen.

BUTTER

Butter is a fatty substance produced by agitating or churning cream. Its flavor is unequaled in sauces, breads and pastries. Butter contains at least 80% milkfat, not more than 16% water and 2–4% milk solids. It may or may not contain added salt. Butter is firm when chilled and soft at room temperature. It melts into a liquid at approximately 93°F (33°C) and reaches the smoke point at 260°F (127°C).

Salted butter is butter with up to 2.5% salt added. This not only changes the butter's flavor, it also extends its keeping qualities. When using salted butter in cooking or baking, the salt content must be considered in the total recipe.

European-style butter contains more milkfat than regular butter, usually from 82 to 86%, and very little or no added salt. It is often churned from cultured cream, giving it a more intense, buttery flavor. It may be used in lieu of any regular butter in cooking or baking.

Whipped butter is made by incorporating air into the butter. This increases its volume and spreadability, but also increases the speed with which the butter will become rancid. Because of the change in density, whipped butter should not be substituted in recipes calling for regular butter.

Clarified butter is butter that has had its water and milk solids removed by a process called clarification. Although **whole butter** can be used for cooking or sauce making, sometimes a more stable and consistent product will be achieved by using clarified butter. The clarification process is described in Chapter 7, Mise en Place.

GRADING BUTTER

Government grading is not mandatory, but most processors submit their butters for testing. The USDA label on the package assures the buyer that the butter meets federal standards for the grade indicated:

- USDA Grade AA—butter of superior quality, with a fresh, sweet flavor and aroma, a smooth, creamy texture and good spreadability.
- USDA Grade A—butter of very good quality, with a pleasing flavor and fairly smooth texture.
- USDA Grade B—butter of standard quality, made from sour cream; has an acceptable flavor but lacks the flavor, texture and body of Grades AA and A. Grade B is most often used in the manufacture of foods.

▶ **whole butter** butter that is not clarified, whipped or reduced-fat

STORAGE

With its high fat content, butter is extremely prone to **rancidity.** Butter that is rancid will develop a harsh bitter taste and deep yellow to brown color. To preserve its freshness, butter should be well wrapped and stored at temperatures between 32°F and 35°F (0°C and 2°C). Unsalted butter is best kept frozen until needed. If well wrapped, frozen butter will keep for up to nine months at a temperature of 0°F (−18°C).

▶ **rancidity** the decomposition of fats by exposure to oxygen, resulting in off-flavors and destruction of nutritive components

MARGARINE: FROM LABORATORY BENCH TO DINNER TABLE

Margarine was invented by a French chemist in 1869 after Napoleon III offered a prize for the development of a synthetic edible fat. Originally produced from animal fat and milk, margarine is now made almost exclusively from vegetable fats.

In *On Food and Cooking: The Science and Lore of the Kitchen,* Harold McGee recounts the history of margarine. He explains that margarine caught on quickly in Europe and America, with large-scale production underway by 1880. But the American dairy industry and the U.S. government put up fierce resistance. First, margarine was defined as a harmful drug and its sale restricted. Then it was heavily taxed; stores had to be licensed to sell it and, like alcohol and tobacco, it was bootlegged. The U.S. government refused to purchase it for use by the armed forces. And, in an attempt to hold it to its true colors, some states did not allow margarine to be dyed yellow (animal fats and vegetable oils are much paler than butter); the dye was sold separately and mixed in by the consumer. World War II, which brought butter rationing, probably did the most to establish margarine's respectability. But it was not until 1967 that yellow margarine could be sold in Wisconsin.

MARGARINE

Margarine is not a dairy product but is included in this section because it is so frequently substituted for butter in cooking, baking and table service. Margarine is manufactured from animal or vegetable fats or a combination of such fats. Flavorings, colorings, emulsifiers, preservatives and vitamins are added, and the mixture is firmed or solidified by exposure to hydrogen gas at very high temperatures, a process known as hydrogenation. Generally, the firmer the margarine, the greater the degree of hydrogenation and the longer its shelf life. Like butter, margarine is approximately 80% fat and 16% water. But even the finest margarine cannot match the flavor of butter.

Margarine packaged in tubs is softer and more spreadable than solid products and generally contains more water and air. Indeed, diet margarine is approximately 50% water. Because of their decreased density, these soft products should not be substituted for regular butter or margarine in cooking or baking.

Specially formulated and blended margarine is available for commercial use in making puff pastry, croissant doughs, frostings and the like.

▶ NUTRITION

Dairy products are naturally high in vitamins, minerals and protein. Often liquid products such as milk are fortified with additional vitamins and minerals, especially vitamins A and D. Because milk and butter are animal products, they do contain cholesterol. Their overall fat content varies depending on the amount of milkfat left after processing.

▶ NATURAL CHEESES

Cheese (Fr. *fromage;* It. *formaggio*) is one of the oldest and most widely used foods known to man. It is served alone or as a principal ingredient in or an accompaniment to countless dishes. Cheese is commonly used in commercial kitchens, appearing in everything from breakfast to snacks to desserts.

Hundreds of natural cheeses are produced worldwide. Although their shapes, ages and flavors vary according to local preferences and traditions, all natural cheeses are produced in the same basic fashion as has been used for centuries. Each starts with a mammal's milk; cows, goats and sheep are the most commonly used. The milk proteins (known as *casein*) are coagulated with the addition of an enzyme, usually rennet, which is found in calves' stomachs. As the milk coagulates, it separates into solid curds and liquid whey. After draining off the whey, either the curds are made into fresh cheese, such as ricotta or cottage cheese, or the curds are further processed by cutting, kneading and cooking. The resulting substance, known as "green cheese," is packed into molds to drain. Salt or special bacteria may be added to the molded cheeses, which are then allowed to age or ripen under controlled conditions to develop the desired texture, color and flavor.

Cheeses are a product of their environment, which is why most fine cheeses cannot be reproduced outside their native locale. The breed and feed of the milk animal, the wild spores and molds in the air and even the wind currents in a storage area can affect the manner in which a cheese develops. (Roquefort, for example, develops its distinctive flavor from aging in particular caves filled with crosscurrents of cool, moist air.)

Some cheeses develop a natural rind or surface because of the application of bacteria (bloomy rind) or by repeated washing with brine (washed rind). Most natural rinds may be eaten if desired. Other cheeses are coated with an inedible wax rind to prevent moisture loss. (Cheeses that are smoked are frequently coated with a brown wax rind.) Fresh cheeses have no rind whatsoever.

Moisture and fat contents are good indicators of a cheese's texture and shelf life. The higher the moisture content, the softer the product and the more perishable it will be. Low-moisture cheeses may be used for grating and will keep for several weeks if properly stored. (Reduced water activity levels prohibit bacterial growth.) Fat content ranges from low fat (less than 20% fat) to double cream (at least 60% fat) and triple cream (at least 72% fat). Cheeses with a high fat content will be creamier and have a richer flavor and texture than low-fat products.

Most cheeses contain high percentages of fat and protein. Cheese is also rich in calcium, phosphorus and vitamin A. As animal products, natural cheeses contain cholesterol. Today, many low-fat and even nonfat processed cheeses are available. Sodium has also been reduced or eliminated from some modern products.

The FDA allows the manufacture and distribution of raw-milk cheeses provided that they are aged more than 60 days at a temperature not less than 35°F (2°C).

CHEESE VARITIES

Cheeses can be classified by country of origin, ripening method, fat content or texture. Here we classify fine cheeses by texture and have adopted five categories: fresh or unripened, soft, semisoft, firm and hard. A separate section on goat's-milk cheeses is also included.

FRESH OR UNRIPENED CHEESES

Fresh cheeses are uncooked and unripened. Referred to as *fromage blanc* or *fromage frais* in French, they are generally mild and creamy with a tart tanginess. They should not taste acidic or bitter. Fresh cheeses have a moisture content of 40 to 80% and are highly perishable.

Cream cheese is a soft cow's-milk cheese from the United States containing approximately 35% fat. It is available in various-sized solid white blocks or whipped and flavored. It is used throughout the kitchen in baking, dips, dressings and confections and is popular as a spread for bagels and toast. **Feta** is a semisoft Greek or Italian product made from sheep's and/or goat's milk. It is a white, flaky cheese that is pickled (but not ripened) and stored in brine water, giving it a shelf life of four to six weeks. Its flavor becomes sharper and saltier with age. Feta is good for snacks and salads and melts easily for sauces and fillings.

Feta

Mascarpone (mas-cahr-POHN-ay) is a soft cow's-milk cheese originally from Italy's Lombard region. It contains 70 to 75% fat and is extremely smooth and creamy. Mascarpone is highly perishable and is available in bulk or in 8- or 16-ounce tubs. With its pale ivory color and rich, sweet flavor, it is useful in both sweet and savory sauces as well as desserts. It is also eaten plain, with fresh fruit or spread on bread and sprinkled with cocoa or sugar.

Mascarpone

Mozzarella (maht-suh-REHL-lah) is a firm Italian cheese traditionally made with water buffalo's milk (today, cow's milk is more common) and containing 40 to 45% fat. Mozzarella becomes elastic when melted and is well known as "pizza cheese." Fresh mozzarella is excellent in salads or topped simply with olive oil and herbs. It is a very mild white cheese

Mozzarella

MAKING MOZZARELLA

In Italy, mozzarella is made every day; it is meant to be consumed just as often. Before there was refrigeration, the balls of mozzarella were stored in well water to keep them cool, which is where the tradition originated of storing fresh mozzarella in liquid.

Once the milk is coagulated and the curds are cut, the mass is slowly stirred to enhance the whey's expulsion. A few hours later, when the curds are mature, they are removed from the whey, chopped or shredded and then mixed with hot water.

To test the exact amount of maturity, a handful of curds is dipped into a bucket of hot water for 10 seconds. When the curds are removed, they should be kneaded briefly and then, holding the mass with two hands, it should be pulled and stretched out to determine its maturity. When it can be stretched as thin and opaque as tissue paper, it is exactly ready to be strung. At this point, small amounts of curd are dumped into a small vat and stirred with hot water using a paddle. This is known as "stringing" the cheese because as the curds are mixed with the water they begin to melt somewhat and become stringy. The more the cheese is stirred, the longer the strings are stretched. Eventually, all the strings come together to make a large mass of satiny-smooth cheese. In Italian, the word *filare* means "to string"; therefore, all cheeses that are strung are members of the *pasta filata* family.

When stringing is complete, the cheese is ready to be shaped and hand-formed into balls. The balls are tossed immediately into vats of cool water so they will maintain the desired shapes. When cool, the balls are immersed in brine solution and then wrapped in parchment paper.

PAULA LAMBERT owns the Mozzarella Company in Dallas, Texas.

Queso Oaxaca

best eaten within hours of production. Commercial mozzarella is rather bland and rubbery and is best reserved for cooking, for which it may be purchased already shredded.

Queso Oaxaca (KEH-soh wah-HA-kaa), also known as Quesillo or Asadero, is one of the most popular cheeses of Mexico. It is a cow's-milk *pasta filata* or stretched-curd cheese that is kneaded and wound into balls, then soaked in brine for several minutes. It is pulled apart into thin strings before being used to fill tortillas or melted over cooked dishes. Queso Oaxaca is a good melting cheese with a smooth semisoft texture, white color and 45% fat content. It is invaluable in preparing Mexican and Mexican-American dishes such as quesadillas, nachos and tacos, and is also available blended with herbs, spices or chiles.

Ricotta (rih-COH-tah) is a soft Italian cheese, similar to American cottage cheese, made from the whey left when other cow's-milk cheeses are produced. It contains only 4 to 10% fat. It is white or ivory in color and fluffy, with a small grain and sweet flavor. Ricotta is an important ingredient in many pasta dishes and desserts. It can be made easily with the following recipe.

Ricotta

RECIPE 6.2

RICOTTA CHEESE

THE ART INSTITUTE OF WASHINGTON, ARLINGTON, VA

Former Chef Instructor John Harrison

Yield: 8 oz. (225 g)

Milk	1 qt.	950 ml
Fresh lime juice	3 fl. oz.	85 ml

1. Allow the milk to reach room temperature in a covered container.
2. In a stainless steel saucepan slowly heat the milk to 180°F (82°C), stirring often. Hold the heated milk at 180°F (82°C) for 5 minutes.
3. Remove the milk from the heat and gently stir it while adding the lime juice. Continue to stir until curds form.
4. Gently pour the curds into a strainer or china cap lined with new, rinsed cheesecloth. Allow the whey (liquid) to separate and drain away from the curds (solids). Discard the whey.
5. Allow the cheese to rest undisturbed for 1 hour. For a firm, dry ricotta, lift the corners of the cheesecloth and tie them together with twine. Suspend the bag in a tall, covered container, place it in the refrigerator and allow the cheese to drain for 4 hours or overnight.
6. Unwrap the cheese. Season it with salt if desired. Use the cheese as you would use commercially produced ricotta.

Approximate values per 1-oz. (30-g) serving: **Calories** 80, **Total fat** 4 g, **Saturated fat** 2.5 g, **Cholesterol** 15 mg, **Sodium** 60 mg, **Total carbohydrates** 7 g, **Protein** 4 g, **Calcium** 15%

1 Heat the milk to 180°F (82°C).

2 Gently stir in the lime juice.

3 Strain the mixture through cheesecloth.

4 The finished ricotta.

SOFT CHEESES

Soft cheeses are characterized by their thin skins and creamy centers. They are among the most delicious and popular of cheeses. They ripen quickly and are at their peak for only a few days, sometimes less. Moisture content ranges from 50 to 75%.

Bel Paese (bell pah-AYZ-eh) is a 20th-century Italian creation made from cow's milk and containing approximately 50% fat. It is mild and creamy with a fruity flavor. The inside is yellowish, and the outside is brown or gray. Bel Paese is excellent for snacking and melts easily.

Brie (bree) is a rind-ripened French cheese made with cow's milk and containing about 60% fat. Brie is made in round, flat disks weighing 2 or 4 pounds (1 or 2 kilogram); it is coated with a bloomy white rind. At the peak of ripeness, it is creamy and rich, with a texture that oozes. Selecting a properly ripened Brie is a matter of judgment and experience. Select a cheese that is bulging a bit inside its rind; there should be just the beginning of a brown coloring on the rind. If underripe, Brie will be bland with a hard, chalky core. Once the cheese is cut, it will not ripen any further. If overripe, Brie will have a brownish rind that may be gummy or sagging and will smell strongly of ammonia. The rind is edible, but

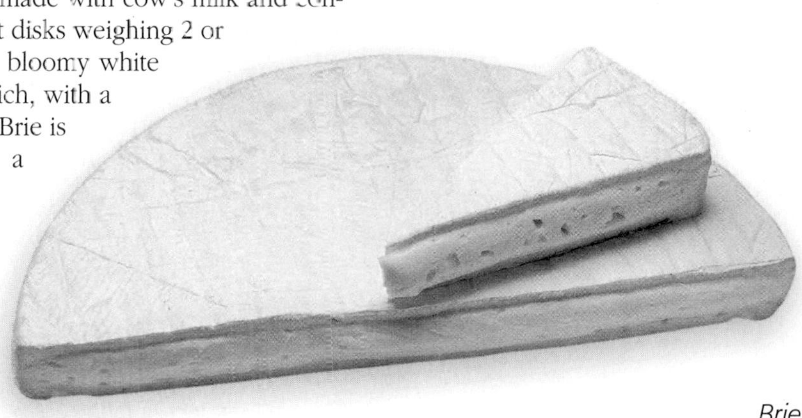

Brie

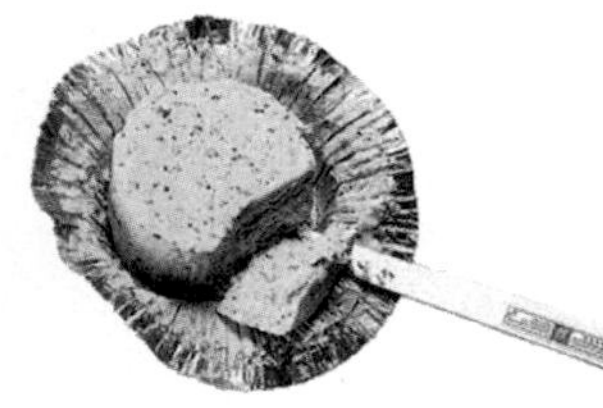

Boursin

trim it off if preferred. The classic after-dinner cheese, Brie is also used in soups, sauces and hors d'oeuvres.

Boursin (boor-SAHN) is a triple-cream cow's-milk cheese from France containing approximately 75% fat. Boursin is usually flavored with peppers, herbs or garlic. It is rindless, with a smooth, creamy texture, and is packed in small, foil-wrapped cylinders. Boursin is a good breakfast cheese and a welcome addition to any cheese board. It is also a popular filling for baked chicken.

Camembert (kam-uhm-BAIR) is a rind-ripened cheese from France containing approximately 45% fat. Bavaria also produces a Camembert, though of a somewhat lesser quality. Camembert is creamy, like Brie, but milder. It is shaped in small round or oval disks and is coated with a white bloomy rind. Selecting a properly ripened Camembert is similar to selecting a Brie, but Camembert will become overripe and ammoniated even more quickly than Brie. Camembert is an excellent dessert or after-dinner cheese and goes particularly well with fruit.

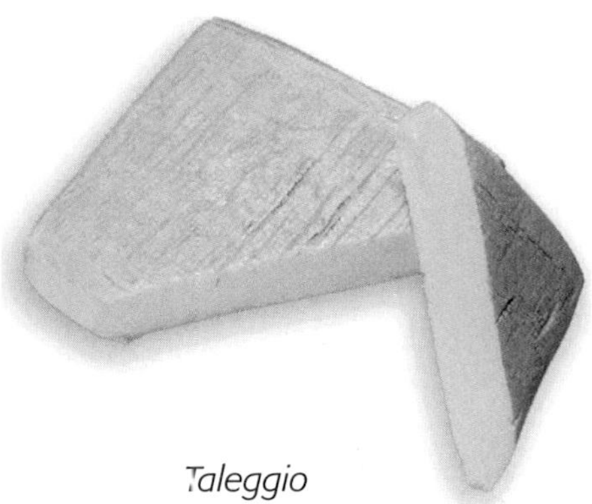

Taleggio

Taleggio (tahl-EH-gee-oh) is a semisoft cheese that has been produced since the 10th century in a small town near Bergamo in the Lombardy region of Italy. Made with pasteurized or unpasteurized cow's milk, it contains 48% fat and is aged for one to two months. Taleggio has an orange-colored washed rind that is edible but pungent. It is molded in a distinctive 8-inch square, approximately 2 inches thick. Its nutty, salty flavor and strong aroma become softer, creamier and more piquant with age. Serve as a dessert cheese with a strong red wine, crusty bread and fruit, or with a salad at the end of a meal.

SEMISOFT CHEESES

Semisoft cheeses include many mild, buttery cheeses with smooth, sliceable textures. Some semisoft cheeses are also known as monastery or Trappist cheeses because their development is traced to monasteries, some recipes having originated during the Middle Ages. The moisture content of semisoft cheeses ranges from 40 to 50%.

Cabrales

Cabrales (kah-BRAH-layss) is a blue-veined Spanish cheese made primarily from a blend of raw goat's, ewe's and cow's milks and containing 45 to 48% fat. Its wrapper made from large maple, oak or sycamore leaves is easily recognized. The outer foil wrapper is marked with the *Denominación de Origen* (D.O.) logo, and each 5- to 9-pound (2.5- to 4.5-kg) wheel is stamped with a unique number. It is aged for three to six months under the cold, humid and breezy conditions in natural caves found in the Asturias region. Cabrales has a moist, crumbly interior with purple-blue veins and a rough, salt-cured rind. It has a thick, creamy texture, a strong aroma and a complex sour, piquant flavor. Cabrales is especially good with salami and a full-bodied red wine or for dessert with a sweet sherry such as Pedro Ximenex.

Doux de Montagne (doo duh mahn-TAHN-yuh) is a cow's-milk cheese from France containing approximately 45% fat. Produced in the foothills of the Pyrenees, it is also referred to as **pain de Pyrenees.** Doux de Montagne is pale yellow with irregular holes and a mellow, sweet, nutty flavor. It is sometimes studded with green peppercorns, which provide a tangy flavor contrast. It is usually shaped in large, slightly squashed spheres and coated with brown wax. Doux de Montagne is good before dinner and for snacking.

Doux de Montagne

Fontina (fon-TEE-nah) is a cow's-milk cheese from Italy's Piedmont region containing approximately 45% fat. The original, known as **Fontina Val D'Aosta,** has a dark gold, crusty rind; the pale gold, dense interior has a few small holes. It is nutty and rich. The original must have a purple trademark stamped on the rind. Imitation Fontinas (properly known as **Fontal** or **Fontinella**) are produced in Denmark, France, Sweden, the United States and other regions of Italy. They tend to be softer, with less depth of flavor, and may have a rubbery texture. Real Fontina is a good after-dinner cheese; the imitations are often added to sauces, soups or sandwiches.

Gorgonzola (gohr-guhn-ZOH-lah) is a blue-veined cow's-milk cheese from Italy containing 48% fat. Gorgonzola has a white or ivory interior with bluish-green veins. It is creamier than other blues such as Stilton or Roquefort, with a somewhat more pungent, spicy, earthy flavor. White Gorgonzola has no veins but a similar flavor, while aged Gorgonzola is drier and crumbly with a very strong, sharp flavor. The milder Gorgonzolas are excellent with fresh peaches or pears or crumbled in a salad. Gorgonzola is also used in sauces and in *torta con basilico,* a cakelike cheese loaf composed of layers of cheese, fresh basil and pine nuts.

Gorgonzola

Gouda (GOO-dah) is a Dutch cheese containing approximately 48% fat. Gouda is sold in various-sized wheels covered with red or yellow wax. The cheese is yellow with a few small holes and a mild, buttery flavor. Gouda may be sold soon after production, or it may be aged for several months, resulting in a firmer, more flavorful cheese. Gouda is widely popular for snacking and in **fondue.**

Havarti (hah-VAHR-tee) is a cow's-milk monastery-style cheese from Denmark containing 45 to 60% fat. Havarti is also known as **Danish Tilsit** or by the brand name **Dofino.** Pale yellow with many small, irregular holes, it is sold in small rounds, rectangular blocks or loaves. Havarti has a mild flavor and creamy texture. It is often flavored with dill, caraway seeds or peppers. Havarti is very popular for snacking and in sandwiches.

Havarti

Port du Salut (por doo suh-LOO) is a monastery cow's-milk product from France containing approximately 50% fat. Port du Salut (also known as Port Salut) is smooth, rich and savory. It is shaped in thick wheels with a dense, pale yellow interior and an edible, bright orange rind. The Danish version is known as Esrom. One of the best and most authentic Port du Saluts has the initials S.A.F.R. stamped on the rind. Lesser-quality brands may be bland and rubbery. It is popular for breakfast and snacking, especially with fruit.

Roquefort (ROHK-fohr) is a blue-veined sheep's-milk cheese from France containing approximately 45% fat. It was first mentioned in a text dated to 79 A.D. and Roquefort producers have held a legal

Roquefort

LEFTOVER CHEESE

Never discard those little leftover bits and pieces of cheese lurking in your refrigerator. The tag ends of Brie, cheddar, farmer cheese, chèvre, Roquefort, mozzarella and scores of other cheese can be quickly transformed into a tasty mixture that the thrifty French call *fromage fort* ("strong cheese"). Seasoned with fresh garlic and a few splashes of wine, it makes an assertively flavored topping for toast or thick slices of bread and tastes best when briefly melted under the broiler.

To make *fromage fort,* gather 1 pound [450 grams] leftover cheese (three kinds is enough, six or seven will be even better). Trim off any mold or very dried-out parts from the surface. Toss three or four peeled cloves of garlic into a food processor and process for several seconds until coarsely chopped. Add the cheese to the garlic along with ½ cup [120 milliliters] dry white wine and at least 1 teaspoon [5 milliliters] freshly ground black pepper. Process until the mixture becomes soft and creamy, about 30 seconds. Remove the mixture from the processor and transfer it to a crock or bowl. Cover tightly with plastic wrap and refrigerate.

STEVE JENKINS is the author of *Cheese Primer.*

► **fondue** a Swiss specialty made with melted cheese, wine and flavorings; eaten by dipping pieces of bread into the hot mixture with long forks

▶ **blue cheese** (1) a generic term for any cheese containing visible blue-green molds that contribute a characteristic tart, sharp flavor and aroma; also known as a blue-veined cheese or bleu; (2) a group of Roquefort-style cheeses made in the United States and Canada from cow's or goat's milk rather than ewe's milk and injected with molds that form blue-green veins; also known as blue mold cheese or blue-veined cheese

monopoly over making this cheese since 1411. Roquefort is intensely pungent with a rich, salty flavor and strong aroma. It is a white paste with veins of blue mold and a thin natural rind shaped into thick, foil-wrapped cylinders. Roquefort is always aged for at least three months in the limestone caves of Mount Combalou. Since 1926, no producer outside this region can legally use the name Roquefort or even "Roquefort-style." Roquefort is an excellent choice for serving before or after dinner and is, of course, essential for Roquefort dressing.

Stilton is a blue-veined cow's-milk cheese from Great Britain containing 45% fat. Stilton is one of the oldest and grandest cheeses in the world. It has a white or pale yellow interior with evenly spaced blue veins. Stilton's distinctive flavor is pungent, rich and tangy, combining the best of blues and cheddars. It is aged in cool ripening rooms for four to six months to develop the blue veining; it is then sold in tall cylinders with a crusty, edible rind. Stilton should be wrapped in a cloth dampened with salt water and stored at cool temperatures, but not refrigerated. It is best served alone, with plain crackers, dried fruit or vintage port.

Stilton

FIRM CHESSES

Firm cheeses are not hard or brittle. Some are close-textured and flaky, like Cheddar; others are dense, holey cheeses like Emmenthaler. Most firm cheeses are actually imitators of these two classics. Their moisture content ranges from 30 to 40%.

Cheddars are produced in both North America and Great Britain. **American Cheddar** is a cow's-milk cheese made primarily in New York, Wisconsin, Vermont and Oregon, containing from 45 to 50% fat. The best cheddars are made from raw milk and aged for several months. (Raw milk may be used in the United States provided the cheese is then aged at least 60 days.) They have a dense, crumbly texture. Cheddars may be white or colored orange with vegetable dyes, depending on local preference. Flavors range from mild to very sharp, depending on the age of the cheese. **Colby** and **Longhorn** are two well-known mild, soft-textured Wisconsin Cheddars. Cheddars are sold in a variety of shapes and sizes, often coated with wax. Good-quality Cheddars are welcome additions to any cheese board, while those of lesser quality are better reserved for cooking and sandwiches. **English Cheddar** is a variety of cow's-milk cheese produced in Great Britain containing approximately 45% fat. Perhaps the most imitated cheese in the world, true English Cheddar is rarely seen in the United States because of import restrictions. It is a moist yet sliceable cheese, aged at least six months.

American Cheddar—Wisconsin Sharp, Vermont Cabot, Canadian Black Diamond

Emmenthaler (EM-en-tah-ler) is a cow's-milk cheese from Switzerland containing approximately 45% fat. Emmenthaler is the original Swiss cheese; it accounts for more than half of Switzerland's cheese production. It is mellow, rich and nutty with a natural rind and a light yellow interior full of large holes. It is ripened in three stages with the aid of fermenting bacteria. The holes or "eyes" are caused by gases expanding inside the cheese during fermentation. Authentic Emmenthaler is sold in 200-pound (90 kilograms) wheels with the word *Switzerland* stamped on the rind like the spokes of a wheel. Emmenthaler, one of the basic fondue cheeses, is also popular for sandwiches, snacks and after dinner with fruit and nuts.

Emmenthaler (Swiss)

Gruyère (groo-YAIR) is a cow's-milk cheese made near Fribourg in the Swiss Alps and containing approximately 45 to 50% fat. Gruyère is often imitated, as the name is not legally protected. True Gruyère is moist and highly flavorful, with a sweet nuttiness similar to Emmenthaler. Gruyère is aged for up to 12 months and then sold in huge wheels. It should have small, well-spaced holes and a brown, wrinkled rind. Gruyère melts easily and is often used with meats and in sauces, but it is also appropriate before or after dinner.

Gruyère

Jarlsberg (YAHRLZ-behrg) is a Swiss-type cow's-milk cheese from Norway containing approximately 45% fat. Jarlsberg closely resembles Emmenthaler in both flavor and appearance. It is mild with a delicate, sweet flavor and large holes. Jarlsberg has a pale yellow interior; it is coated with yellow wax and sold in huge wheels. It has a long shelf life and is popular for sandwiches and snacks and in cooking.

Manchego (mahn-CHAY-goh) is the best-known and most widely available Spanish sheep's-milk cheese. Its ivory to pale yellow interior is firm and compact with a few small air pockets. It has a buttery and slightly piquant flavor with an aftertaste of sheep's milk. The inedible rind is black, gray or beige with a very distinctive zigzag pattern imprinted by the traditional esparto grass molds.

There are two types of Manchego: farmhouse style, made with unpasteurized sheep's milk, and industrial, made with pasteurized milk. For both, only milk from Manchega sheep raised in the La Mancha region is used. Manchego is aged from two months (*fresco*) to one year (*curado*) to two years (*añejo* or *viejo*) and contains 45 to 57% fat. Its intense flavor and crumbly texture make it excellent for eating as is, with bread or fruit, or as the focal point of antipasto with a robust red wine or a dry sherry.

Manchego

Monterey Jack is a cheddarlike cow's-milk cheese from California containing 50% fat. It is very mild and rich, with a pale ivory interior. It is sold in wheels or loaves coated with dark wax. "Jack" is often flavored with peppers or herbs and is good for snacking and sandwiches and in Mexican dishes. Dry-aged Jack develops a tough, wrinkled brown rind and a rich, firm yellow interior. It has a nutty, sharp flavor and is dry enough for grating.

Monterey Jack

Provolone (pro-voh-LOH-neh) is a cow's-milk cheese from southern Italy containing approximately 45% fat. Provolone *dolce,* aged only two months, is mild, with a smooth texture. Provolone *piccante,* aged up to six months, is stronger and somewhat flaky or stringy. Smoked provolone is also popular, especially for snacking. Provolone is shaped in

Provolone

various ways, from huge salamis to plump spheres to tiny piglets shaped by hand. It is excellent in sandwiches and for cooking, and is often used for melting and in pizza and pasta dishes.

HARD CHESSES

Hard cheeses are not simply cheeses that have been allowed to dry out. Rather, they are carefully aged for extended periods and have a moisture content of about 30%. Hard cheeses are most often used for grating; the best flavor will come from cheeses grated as needed. Even the finest hard cheeses begin to lose their flavor within hours of grating. The most famous and popular of the hard cheeses are those from Italy, where they are known as *grana*. Hard cheeses can also be served as a table cheese or with a salad.

Asiago

Asiago (ah-zee-AH-go) is a cow's-milk cheese from Italy containing approximately 30% fat. After only one year of aging, Asiago is sharp and nutty with a cheddarlike texture. If aged for two years or more, Asiago becomes dry, brittle and suitable for grating. Either version should be an even white to pale yellow in color with no dark spots, cracks or strong aromas. Asiago melts easily and is often used in cooking.

Parmigiano-Reggiano (Parmesan) (pahr-me-ZHAN-no reg-gee-AH-no) is a cow's-milk cheese made exclusively in the region near Parma, Italy, containing from 32 to 35% fat. Parmigiano-Reggiano is one of the world's oldest and most widely copied cheeses. Used primarily for grating and cooking, it is rich, spicy and sharp with a golden interior and a hard oily rind. It should not be overly salty or bitter. Reggiano, as it is known, is produced only from mid-April to mid-November. It is shaped into huge wheels of about 80 pounds (36 kilograms) each, with the name stenciled repeatedly around the rind. Imitation Parmesan is produced in the United States, Argentina and elsewhere, but none can match the distinctive flavor of freshly grated Reggiano.

Parmigiano-Reggiano (Parmesan)

Pecorino Romano (peh-coh-REE-no roh-MAH-no) is a sheep's-milk cheese from central and southern Italy containing approximately 35% fat. Romano is very brittle and sharper than other grating cheeses, with a "sheepy" tang. Its light, grainy interior is whiter than Parmesan or Asiago. It is packed in large cylinders with a yellow rind. Romano is often substituted for, or combined with, Parmesan in cooking, but it is also good eaten with olives, sausages and red wine.

GOAT'S-MILK CHEESES

Because of their increasing popularity, cheeses made from goat's milk deserve a few words of their own. Although goats give less milk than cows, their milk is higher in fat and protein and richer and more concentrated in flavor. Cheeses made with goat's milk have a sharp, tangy flavor. They may range in texture from very soft and fresh to very hard, depending on age.

Chèvre (shehv; French for "goat") refers to small, soft, creamy cheeses produced in a variety of shapes: cones, disks, pyramids or logs. Chèvres are often coated with ash, herbs or seasonings. They are excellent for cooking and complement a wide variety of flavors. Unfortunately, they have a short shelf life, perhaps only two weeks. Cheese labeled *pur chèvre* must be made with 100% goat's milk, while others may be a mixture of cow's and goat's milk.

The finest goat's-milk cheeses usually come from France. Preferred brands include Bûcheron, exported from France in 5-pound (2-kilogram) logs; Chevrotin, one of the mildest; and Montrachet, a tangy soft cheese from the Burgundy wine region. Spurred on by the increased popularity of chèvre, several American producers have developed excellent goat's-milk cheeses in a wide variety of shapes and styles.

Assorted Soft and Goat's-Milk Cheeses (clockwise starting from the top right): log of herb-coated French goat's cheese, French Banon wrapped in leaves, cinder-coated French Sainte Maure, French Chabichon goat's cheese, French Cabichou marinated in olive oil, herbs and peppercorns and, in the center, French Camembert

► PROCESSED CHEESES

Pasteurized processed cheese is made from a combination of aged and green cheeses mixed with emulsifiers and flavorings, pasteurized and poured into molds to solidify. Manufacturers can thus produce cheeses with consistent textures and flavors. Processed cheeses are commonly used in food service operations because they are less expensive than natural cheeses. And, because they will not age or ripen, their shelf life is greatly extended. Nutritionally, processed cheeses generally contain less protein, calcium and vitamin A and more sodium than natural cheeses.

Processed cheese food contains less natural cheese (but at least 51 percent by weight) and more moisture than regular processed cheese. Often vegetable oils and milk solids are added, making cheese food soft and spreadable.

Imitation cheese is usually manufactured with dairy by-products and soy products mixed with emulsifiers, colorings and flavoring agents and enzymes. Although considerably less expensive than natural cheese, imitation cheese tends to be dense and rubbery, with little flavor other than that of salt.

► SERVING CHEESES

Cheeses may be served at any time of day. In Northern Europe, they are common for breakfast; in Great Britain, they are a staple at lunch. Cheeses are widely used for sandwiches, snacks and cooking in America, and they are often served following the entrée or instead of dessert at formal dinners.

The flavor and texture of natural cheeses are best at room temperature. So, except for fresh cheeses, all cheeses should be removed from the refrigerator 30 minutes to an hour before service to allow them to come to room temperature. Fresh cheeses, such as cottage and cream, should be eaten chilled.

Any selection of fine cheeses should include a variety of flavors and textures: from mild to sharp, from soft to creamy to firm. Use a variety of shapes and colors for visual appeal. Do not precut the cheeses, as this only causes them to become dry. Provide an adequate supply of serving knives so that stronger-flavored cheeses will not combine with and overpower milder ones. Fine cheeses are best appreciated with plain bread and crackers, as salted or seasoned crackers can mask the cheese's flavor. Noncitrus fruits are also a nice accompaniment.

AMERICAN CHEESE PRODUCTION

The first cheese factory in the United States was built in 1851 in Oneida County, New York. Herkimer County, which adjoins Oneida County, soon became the center of the American cheese industry and remained so for the next 50 years. During this time, the largest cheese market in the world was at Little Falls, New York, where farm-produced cheeses and cheeses from more than 200 factories were sold. At the turn of the century, as New York's population increased, there was a corresponding increase in demand for fluid milk. Because dairies could receive more money for fluid milk than for cheese, cheese production declined.

Although New York still produces some outstanding cheddars, the bulk of the American cheese industry gradually moved westward, eventually settling in Wisconsin's rich farmlands. The United States is now the world's largest manufacturer of cheeses, producing nearly twice as many pounds per year as its nearest competitor, France.

Over the last fifteen years there has been a resurgence of interest in traditional cheesemaking in the United States. According to the American Cheese Society there are now approximately 350 artisan producers scattered throughout the United States. These artisan cheeses are mostly handmade in small batches using all types of milk. They include farmstead cheeses, which by definition must be made on the producer's property with milk from the producer's own herd or flock. Artisan cheeses are often sold at local farmer's markets.

CHEESE TERMINOLOGY

The following terms often appear on cheese labels and may help identify or appreciate new or unfamiliar cheeses:

Affiné—French term for a cured or properly ripened cheese

Bleu—French for "blue"

Brique or *briquette*—refers to a group of French brick-shaped cheeses

Brosse—French term for cheeses that are brushed with liquid or oil during ripening

Capra—Italian for goat's-milk cheese

Carré—French term for square, flat cheeses

Cendré—French term for cheeses ripened in ashes

Coulant—French for "flowing," used to describe ripe Brie, Camembert and other cheeses when their interiors ooze or flow

Ferme or *fermier*—French adjective used to indicate farm-produced cheeses

Kaas—Dutch for "cheese"

Käse—German for "cheese"

Lait cru—French term for raw milk

Laiterie or *laitier*—French for "dairy"; appears on factory-made cheeses

Matières grasses—French term for dry matter

Mi chèvre—a French product so labeled must contain at least 25 percent goat's milk

Ost—Scandinavian for "cheese"

Pecorino—Italian term for all sheep's-milk cheeses

Queso—Spanish for "cheese"

Râpé—French term applied to cheeses that are suitable for grating

Tome or *tomme*—term used by the French, Italians and Swiss to refer to mountain cheeses, particularly from the Pyrénées or Savoie regions

Tyrophile—one who loves cheese

Vaccino—Italian term for cow's-milk cheese

Vache—French term for cow's-milk cheese

STORAGE

Most cheeses are best kept refrigerated, well wrapped to keep odors out and moisture in. Firm and hard cheeses can be kept for several weeks; fresh cheeses will spoil in 7 to 10 days because of their high moisture content. Some cheeses that have become hard or dry may still be grated for cooking or baking. Freezing is possible but not recommended because it changes the cheese's texture, making it mealy or tough.

Cheeseboard Ready for Service (starting from the top right): Shropshire Blue from Great Britain, Layered Huntsman Cheese from Great Britain, Italian Pecorino Pepato and in the center a wedge of ripe Brie cheese

WINE AND CHEESE: CLASSIC COMBINATIONS

Some cheeses are delicious with beers or ales. Others are best with strong coffee or apple cider, and nothing accompanies a Cheddar cheese sandwich as well as ice-cold milk. For most cheeses, however, the ultimate partner is wine. Wine and cheese bring out the best in each other. The proteins and fats in cheeses take the edge off harsh or acidic wines, while the tannins and acids in wines bring out the creamy richness of cheeses.

Because of their natural affinity, certain pairings are universal favorites: Stilton with port, Camembert with Bordeaux, Roquefort with Sauternes and English Cheddar with Burgundy. Although taste preferences are an individual matter, cheese-wine marriages follow two schools of thought: either pair likes or pair opposites.

Pairing like with like is simple: Cheeses are often best served with wines produced in the same region. For example, a white Burgundy such as Montrachet would be an excellent choice for cheeses from Burgundy; goat cheeses from the Rhone Valley go well with wines of that region. Hearty Italian wines such as Chianti, Barolo and Valpolicella are delicious with Italian cheese—Gorgonzola, Provolone, Taleggio. And a dry, aged Monterey Jack is perhaps the perfect mate for California Zinfandel.

Opposites do attract, however. Sweet wines such as Sauternes and Gewürztraminer go well with sharp, tangy blues, especially Roquefort. And light, sparkling wines such as Champagne or Spanish Cava are a nice complement to rich, creamy cheeses such as Brie and Camembert.

CONCLUSION

Dairy products are versatile foods used throughout the kitchen. They may be served as is or incorporated into many dishes, including soups, sauces, entrées, breads and desserts. Fine natural cheeses are useful in prepared dishes but are most important for buffets, as the cheese course during a meal or whenever cheese is the primary ingredient or dominant flavor. Dairy products spoil easily and must be handled and stored properly.

QUESTIONS FOR DISCUSSION

1 What is milkfat, and how is it used in classifying milk-based products?
2 If a recipe calls for whole milk and you have only dried milk, what do you do? Explain your answer.
3 The texture and shelf life of cheese depend on what two factors?
4 Cheeses are categorized as fresh, soft, semisoft, firm and hard. Give two examples of each, and explain how they are generally used.
5 The FDA has proposed extending the mandatory aging period for cheeses made from raw (unpasteurized) milk beyond the 60 days currently required. The FDA has also proposed banning importation of raw-milk cheeses altogether on food safety grounds. Several groups, including the American Cheese Society and Oldways Preservation & Exchange Trust, are fighting these proposals. What is the current status of the FDA proposals? What arguments are used in support of and in opposition to these proposals?

6 Use the Internet to locate a U.S. producer of European-style goat cheeses. What varieties of goat cheeses do they market?

CHAPTER**SEVEN**

MISE EN PLACE

WHEN YOU BECOME A GOOD COOK, YOU BECOME A GOOD CRAFTSMAN, FIRST. YOU REPEAT AND REPEAT AND REPEAT UNTIL YOUR HANDS KNOW HOW TO MOVE WITHOUT THINKING ABOUT IT.

—Jacques Pépin, French chef and teacher (1935–)

AFTER STUDYING THIS CHAPTER, YOU WILL BE ABLE TO:

- organize and plan your work more efficiently
- understand basic flavoring techniques
- prepare items needed prior to actual cooking
- set up and use the standard breading procedure

The French term *mise en place* (meez ahn plahs) literally means "to put in place" or "everything in its place." But in the culinary context, it means much more. Escoffier defined the phrase as "those elementary preparations that are constantly resorted to during the various steps of most culinary preparations." He meant, essentially, gathering and prepping the ingredients to be cooked as well as assembling the tools and equipment necessary to cook them.

In this chapter, we discuss many of the basics that must be in place before cooking begins: for example, creating bouquets garnis, clarifying butter, making bread crumbs, toasting nuts and battering foods. Chopping, dicing, cutting and slicing—important techniques used to prepare foods as well—are discussed in Chapter 4, Knife Skills, while specific preparations, such as roasting peppers and trimming pineapples, are discussed elsewhere.

The concept of mise en place is simple: A chef should have at hand everything he or she needs to prepare and serve food in an organized and efficient manner.

Proper mise en place can consist of just a few items—for example, those needed to prepare a small quantity of chicken soup. Or it can be quite extensive—for example, when setting up the hot line for a busy restaurant with a large menu. A proper mise en place requires the chef to consider work patterns, ingredient lists and tool and equipment needs.

Mise en place will differ from one restaurant to another. A banquet chef's mise en place could include organizing large quantities of meats, vegetables, salad ingredients, breads, condiments and pastries for several dinners, all with different menus. Regardless of the specific menu, banquet mise en place may also include gathering hot boxes, plates, chafing dishes, tongs, spoons and ladles, and setting up the dish-up line. The mise en place for the broiler station at a steakhouse could include properly storing raw steaks and chops that will be cooked to order, as well as gathering the salt, pepper, prepared sauces and accompaniments that are used during cooking or served with the finished items. The broiler cook could also be responsible for gathering plates, building a charcoal fire for the grill, and stocking his or her work area with hand tools, towels and sanitizing solution. In the restaurant situation, unlike in banquet work, the cook's mise en place is probably identical night after night. A waiter's mise en place could include brewing tea, cutting lemon wedges and refilling salt and pepper shakers—preparations that will make work go more smoothly during actual service. Regardless of the number of items used or the complexity of the recipes being prepared, completing a proper mise en place requires careful planning, efficient organization and attention to detail.

Coordination of multiple tasks is also important. An organized cook will think about everything that needs to be done and the most efficient way to complete those tasks before beginning the actual work. Taking the time to first plan the day's activities can eliminate unnecessary steps and conserve resources.

Proper mise en place also requires a good sense of timing. Knowing how long before service to begin a task, or how far in advance of service some preparations can be made, allows a cook to better plan for the efficient execution of his or her duties. In this type of planning, it is also important to consider food safety issues, such as those relating to time and temperature controls. See Chapter 2, Food Safety and Sanitation, for detailed information.

▶ SELECTING TOOLS AND EQUIPMENT

An important step in creating the proper mise en place is to identify and gather all of the tools and equipment that will be needed to prepare a recipe properly or to work a station efficiently. The tools and equipment used to prepare, cook and store foods are discussed in Chapter 3, Tools and Equipment. A few general rules to bear in mind:

- All tools, equipment and work surfaces must be clean and sanitized.
- Knives should be honed and sharpened.
- Measuring devices should be checked periodically for accuracy.
- Ovens and cooking surfaces should be preheated, as necessary.
- Mixing bowls, saucepans and storage containers should be the correct size for the task at hand.
- Serving plates, cookware, utensils, hand tools and other necessary smallwares should be gathered and stored nearby.
- Foods should be gathered and stored conveniently at the proper temperatures.
- Expiration dates on foods should be checked periodically for validity.
- Sanitizing solution, hand towels, disposable gloves and trash receptacles should be conveniently located.

▶ MEASURING INGREDIENTS

1 To use a balance scale to weigh an ingredient, place an empty container on the left, then set a counterbalance to that container on the right. Use weights and the sliding beam weight to add an amount equal to the amount of the ingredient needed.

2 Place the ingredient on the left side of the scale until the two platforms are balanced.

In order to reproduce foods consistently and for the same cost day after day, it is important that the ingredients be measured accurately each time. Menus and Recipes, ingredients may be measured by weight, volume or count. Weight refers to the mass or heaviness of an item and is measured using a scale. Volume refers

THE PREP LIST

Imagine trying to cross a stream by stepping on many different rocks. If you look at only one rock at a time, you will never have a clear picture of where you need to step next to safely get to the other side. You may completely miss the next step and find that now you have to backtrack and waste time or not get across at all. A prep list is the blueprint for how food production is going to be achieved during the work day. It gives the cook an overview of what needs to be done, how long it may take, the order in which assignments should be completed, and how each cook may interact with others in the kitchen. A prep list is not just rewriting recipes. It is reading through recipes and composing a written map of how to accomplish the tasks necessary to prepare the recipe.

The first step in organizing your work is to read and understand the recipes you will be using. Reading the recipe alerts you to other components such as sauces or stocks that must be prepared in advance. You may find that you need to change the proportions of the recipe to meet production needs. Next, it is important to break down each dish by the steps necessary to complete the mise en place and prep. This will assist you in gathering ingredients for all of your prep at one time instead of getting an item multiple times on each occasion that it is called for in the recipe.

Once each item is identified and quantified, the next step is to schedule your tasks through prioritization. Decide what needs to be done first and at what time or on what day the task should be started and completed. Follow the detailed task list you started with and this will assist you in determining the priority of your work. Do not leave anything to chance by trying to keep track of things in your head. The prep list is not only for your benefit. It can be used if another cook is assigned to help you or is needed to take over your work assignments. A clearly written prep list will allow the prep work to be completed efficiently and effectively.

CHEF DAVID ROSENTHAL is Department Chair of the Contra Costa College Culinary Program.

to the space occupied by a substance and is measured with graduated measuring cups and spoons. Count refers to the number of individual items. It is important to remember that foods do not weigh their volume. In other words, although 1 cup contains 8 fluid ounces, 1 cup of flour, honey, cinnamon, and so on does not *weigh* 8 ounces.

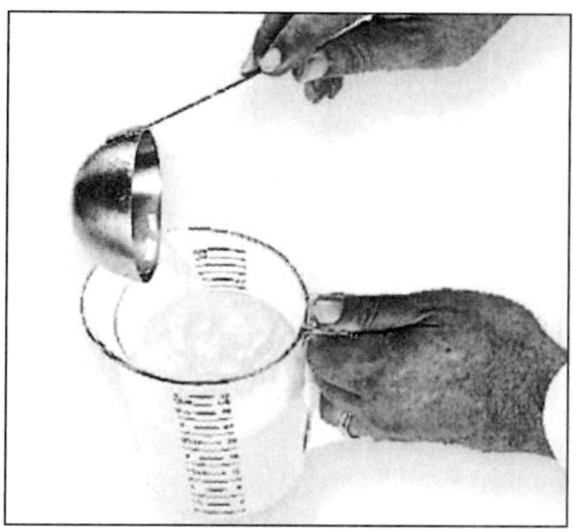

Liquids should be measured in liquid measuring cups, which may be marked in U.S. and/or metric units.

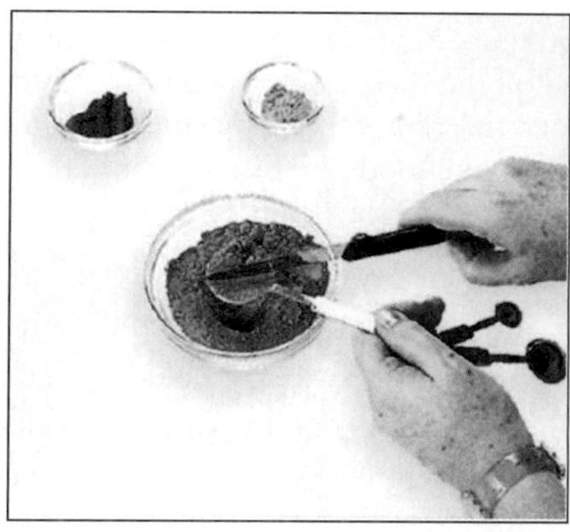

Small amounts of dry ingredients are measured by overfilling the appropriate measuring spoon, then leveling the ingredient.

▶ PREPARING INGREDIENTS

Some ingredients that are used frequently throughout the kitchen are often prepared in large quantities so that they are ready when needed for a specific recipe. For example, dry bread crumbs can be made and stored whenever a supply of bread is available. Large quantities of butter can be clarified on a back burner while other operations proceed on the line. These chores may be simple, but they are time-consuming. An entry-level cook may be assigned responsibility for this type of mise en place. Never feel that such chores are menial; consider, instead, how frustrating it would be for the chef to run out of a simple item just when it is needed during service.

▶ **ghee** a form of clarified butter in which the milk solids remain with the fat and are allowed to brown; originating in India and now used worldwide as an ingredient and cooking medium, it has a long shelf life, a high smoke point and a nutty, caramel-like flavor

CLARIFYING BUTTER

Unsalted whole butter is approximately 80% fat, 16% water and 4% milk solids. Although whole butter can be used for cooking or sauce making, sometimes a more stable and consistent product will be achieved by using butter that has had the water and milk solids removed by a process called **clarification.**

▶ PROCEDURE FOR CLARIFYING BUTTER

1. Slowly warm the butter in a saucepan over low heat without boiling or agitation. As the butter melts, the milk solids rise to the top as a foam and the water sinks to the bottom.
2. When the butter is completely melted, skim the milk solids from the top.
3. When all the milk solids have been removed, ladle the butterfat into a clean saucepan, being careful to leave the water in the bottom of the pan.
4. The clarified butter is now ready to use. One pound (454 grams) of whole butter will yield approximately 12 ounces (340 grams) of clarified butter—a yield of 75%.

Clarified butter will keep for extended periods in either the freezer or refrigerator.

Skimming milk solids from the surface of melted butter.

Ladling the butterfat into a clean pan.

TOASTING NUTS AND SPICES

Nuts are often toasted lightly before being used in baked goods, breadings, salads and sauces. Whole spices are sometimes toasted before being ground for a sauce or used as a garnish. Toasting not only browns the food, it brings out its flavor and makes it crispier and crunchier. When toasting nuts or spices in the oven or on the stove top, watch them closely as they can develop scorched flavors and burn easily.

Toasting sesame seeds in a dry sauté pan on the stove top.

MAKING BREAD CRUMBS

Almost any bread can be used to make crumbs; the choice depends on how the crumbs will be used. **Fresh bread crumbs** are made from fresh bread that is slightly dried out, approximately two to four days old. If the bread is too fresh, the crumbs will be gummy and stick together; if the bread is too stale, the crumbs will taste stale as well. **Dry bread crumbs** are made from bread that has been lightly toasted in a warm oven. Do not make crumbs from stale or molding bread, as these undesirable flavors will be apparent when the crumbs are used.

To make crumbs, the bread is cubed or torn into pieces and ground in a food processor. Dried bread can be processed to a finer consistency than fresh bread. After processing, the crumbs should be passed through a tamis and stored in a tightly closed plastic container in a cool, dry place.

For additional flavors, dried herbs and spices can be mixed into the crumbs.

1 Grind chunks of bread in a food processor.

2 Pass the crumbs through a tamis or sieve so that they will be the same size.

CONVENIENCE PRODUCTS

Convenience products have now replaced many of the chores that were typically part of a cook's routine mise en place. For example, stock and sauce bases eliminate the time and labor necessary to make these products from scratch. Fresh onions and garlic can be purchased peeled, chopped and ready to use. Bread crumbs are available in bulk, and ready-to-use clarified butter is sold in refrigerated tubs. All this convenience comes at a price, of course. A chef must carefully consider whether the savings in employee time, along with the quality and consistency of available products, justify the higher cost of some of the convenience products now on the market.

▶ Flavoring Foods

Foods are often flavored with herbs or spices, marinades or rubs before they are actually cooked. This may require the chef to prepare various flavoring or seasoning mixtures and wait for a period of time between steps in a recipe.

BOUQUET GARNI AND SACHET

A bouquet garni and sachet are used to introduce flavorings, seasonings and aromatics into stocks, sauces, soups and stews.

A **bouquet garni** is a selection of herbs (usually fresh) and vegetables tied into a bundle with twine. A standard bouquet garni consists of parsley stems, celery, thyme, leeks and carrots.

A **sachet** (also known as a *sachet d'épices*) is made by tying seasonings together in cheesecloth. A standard sachet consists of peppercorns, bay leaves, parsley stems, thyme, cloves and, optionally, garlic. The exact quantity of these ingredients is determined by the amount of liquid the sachet is meant to flavor.

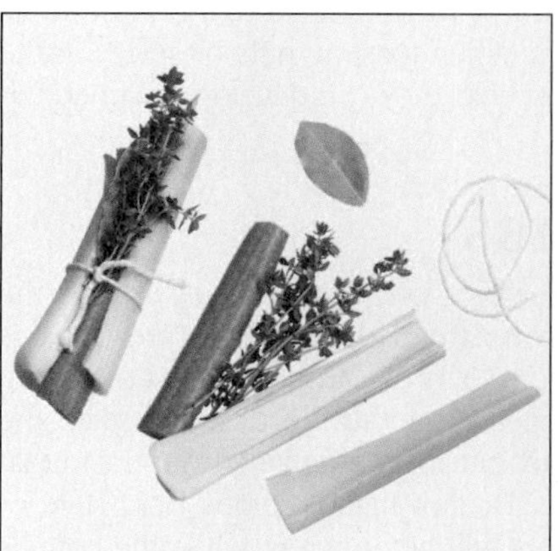

Bouquet Garni

Sachet

Bouquets garni and sachets are used to add flavors in such a way that they can be easily removed from a dish when their flavors have been extracted. A similar technique, although less commonly used, is an **oignon piqué** (also known as an *onion piquet*). To prepare an oignon piqué, peel the onion and trim off the root end. Attach one or two dried bay leaves to the onion using whole cloves as pins. The oignon piqué is then simmered in milk or stock to extract flavors.

Oignon Piqué

Oignon Brûlé

An **oignon brûlé** (also known as *onion brûlé*) French for "burnt onion," is used to flavor and color stocks, sauces and soups such as consommé. To prepare an onion brûlé, peel the onion, trim off the root end and cut it in half. Place the onion halves cut sides down in a dry skillet over medium-high heat. Cook until the onion halves char and darken. The oignon brûlé is then simmered in stocks or soups to give them a clear caramel color.

MARINADES

Marinating is the process of soaking meat or poultry in a seasoned liquid to flavor and tenderize it. Marinades can be a simple blend (herbs, seasonings and oil) or a complicated cooked recipe (red wine, fruit and other ingredients). Mild marinades should be used on more delicate meats such as veal. Game and beef require strongly flavored marinades. In wine-based marinades, white wine is usually used for white meats and poultry, and red wine is used for red meats. Not only does the wine add a distinctive flavor, but the acids in it break down connective tissues and help tenderize the meat.

Poultry, veal and pork generally require less time to marinate than game, beef and lamb. Smaller pieces of meat take less time than larger pieces. When marinating, be sure to cover the meat or poultry completely then keep it refrigerated. The quantity of marinade needed will vary depending on the size and form of the product; 2 pounds of boneless chicken breasts will require less marinade to cover than 2 pounds of whole Cornish game hens. Stir or turn foods frequently so that the marinade can penetrate evenly.

Some chefs prefer to marinate food in heavy-duty plastic food storage bags. These are useful for smaller quantities and allow for easy disposal of leftover marinades with less risk of cross-contamination. Label the bags properly and be sure to seal them tightly to prevent leaks.

Marinating chicken breasts.

RUBS AND PASTES

Additional flavors can be added to meat, fish and poultry by rubbing them with a mixture of fresh or dried herbs and spices ground together with a mortar and pestle or in a spice grinder. The flavoring blend, called a **rub,** can be used dried, or it can be mixed with a little oil, lemon juice, prepared mustard or ground fresh garlic or ginger to make a **paste** (also known as a **wet rub**). Rubs and pastes add flavor and, often, a bit of crispy crust. They do not, however, generally act as a tenderizer. They are most often used on foods that will be cooked with dry heat, especially by grilling, broiling, baking or roasting.

To apply a rub or paste, slather the mixture over the entire surface of the food to be flavored. Use enough pressure to make sure that the rub or paste adheres. (Pastes tend to adhere better than rubs.) The thicker the covering or the longer it remains on the food before cooking, the more pronounced the flavor. If the rubbed food is to be left for some time so that the flavors can be absorbed, it should be covered, refrigerated and turned from time to time.

It is best to wear disposable gloves when applying a rub or paste. Some spices can irritate or stain the skin, and cross-contamination can occur from handling raw meats.

Applying a dry rub to beef.

STEEPING

Steeping is the process of soaking dry ingredients in a liquid (usually hot) in order to either soften a food or **infuse** its flavor into the liquid. Spices, coffee beans and nuts are often steeped in hot milk to extract their flavors. The milk is then used to flavor other foods during cooking. For example, coffee beans can be steeped in hot milk and then strained out, with the coffee-flavored milk being used to make a custard sauce.

► **infuse** to flavor a liquid by steeping it with ingredients such as tea, coffee, herbs or spices

Steeping is also used for rehydrating dried fruits and vegetables such as raisins and mushrooms. Typically, the softened fruits or vegetables will be used in a recipe and the liquid discarded. Additional flavors can be achieved by using wine, spirits, stock or other flavored liquids as the rehydrating medium.

Note that in both situations, the steeping mixture is generally covered and removed from the heat to avoid evaporation or reduction of the liquid.

Steeping a vanilla bean and cinnamon sticks in warm milk to extract their flavors.

Steeping raisins in hot water to rehydrate.

▶ PREPARING TO COOK

Some techniques are done very close to or almost as a part of the final preparation of a dish.

BREADING AND BATTERING FOODS

BREADING

A breaded item is any food that is coated with bread crumbs, cracker meal, cornmeal or other dry **meal** to protect it during cooking. Breaded foods can be seasoned before the breading is applied, or seasonings may be added to the flour, bread crumbs or meal before the main item is coated. Breaded foods are generally cooked by deep-frying or pan-frying. The breading makes a solid coating that seals during cooking and prevents the fat from coming in direct contact with the food, which would make it greasy.

▶ **meal** (1) the coarsely ground seeds of any edible grain such as corn or oats; (2) any dried, ground substance (such as bonemeal)

▶ STANDARD BREADING PROCEDURE

For breading meats, poultry, fish, shellfish or vegetables, a three-step process is typically used. Called the **standard breading procedure,** it gives foods a relatively thick, crisp coating.

1. Pat the food dry and dredge it in seasoned flour. The flour adds seasoning to the food, helps seal it, and allows the egg wash to adhere.
2. Dip the floured food in an egg wash. The egg wash should contain whole eggs whisked together with approximately 1 tablespoon (15 milliliters) milk or water per egg. The egg wash will cause the crumbs or meal to completely coat the item and form a tight seal when the food is cooked.
3. Coat the food with bread crumbs, cracker crumbs or other dry meal. Shake off excess crumbs and place the breaded item in a pan. As additional breaded items are added to the pan, align them in a single layer; do not stack them or the breadings will get soggy and the foods will stick together.
4. To ensure that breading adheres after cooking, refrigerate breaded foods for at least 30 minutes before frying.

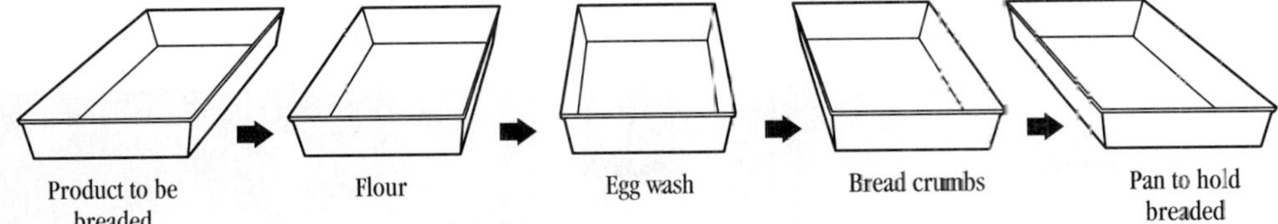

FIGURE 7.1 ▶ Setup for the standard breading procedure.

Figure 7.1 shows the proper setup for breading foods using the standard breading procedure. The following procedure helps bread foods more efficiently:

1. Assemble the mise en place as shown in Figure 7.1.
2. With your left hand, place the food to be breaded in the flour and coat it evenly. With the same hand, remove the floured item, shake off the excess flour and place it in the egg wash.
3. With your right hand, remove the item from the egg wash and place it in the bread crumbs or meal.
4. With your left hand, cover the item with crumbs or meal and press lightly to make sure the item is completely and evenly coated. Shake off the excess crumbs or meal and place the breaded food in the empty pan for finished product.

The key is to use one hand for the liquid ingredients and the other hand for the dry ingredients. This prevents your fingers from becoming coated with layer after layer of breading.

SAFETY ALERT

Batters and breading are potentially hazardous foods when eggs or milk are used in their preparation. Make small batches of batter, then discard after each use. Store fresh batter at or below 41°F (5°C). Discard crumbs, flour and eggs for breading after each use. To prevent cross-contamination when coating different foods such as vegetables and poultry, use separate batter or breading for each product.

BATTERING

Batters, like breading, coat the food being cooked, keeping it moist and preventing it from becoming excessively greasy. Batters consist of a liquid such as water, milk or beer, combined with a starch such as flour or cornstarch. Many batters also contain a leavening agent such as baking powder or whipped egg whites. Two common batters are beer batter, which uses the beer for leavening as well as for flavor and is illustrated in the recipe for Beer Battered Onion Rings and tempura batter, which is used in Tempura Vegetables with Dipping Sauce. Items coated with a batter are cooked immediately, usually by deep-frying or pan-frying. Figure 7.2 shows the proper setup for battering foods using the standard battering procedure.

▶ PROCEDURE FOR BATTERING FOODS

1. Prepare the batter.
2. Pat the food dry and dredge in flour if desired.
3. Dip the item in the batter and place it directly in the hot fat.

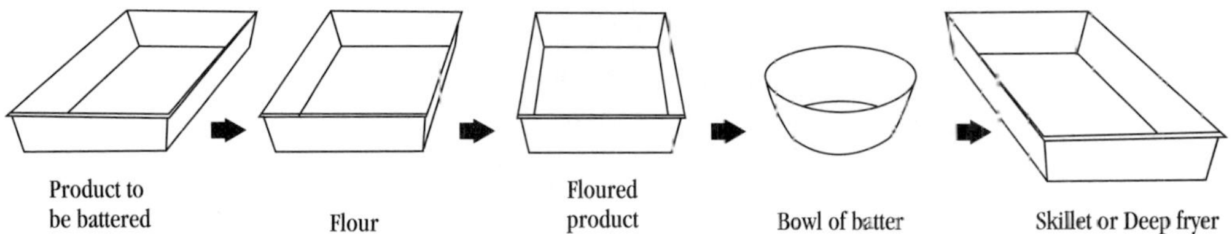

FIGURE 7.2 ▶ Setup for the standard battering procedure.

BLANCHING AND PARBOILING

1 Blanch or parboil the food as desired in boiling water.

2 Remove the food from the cooking liquid and submerge it in ice water to refresh.

▶ **blanching** very briefly and partially cooking a food in boiling water or hot fat; used to assist preparation (for example, to loosen peels from vegetables), as part of a combination cooking method or to remove undesirable flavors

▶ **parboiling** partially cooking a food in boiling or simmering liquid; similar to blanching but the cooking time is longer

▶ **parcooking** partially cooking a food by any cooking method

▶ **shocking** also called refreshing; the technique of quickly chilling blanched or parcooked foods in ice water; prevents further cooking and sets colors

Some foods, especially vegetables, are **blanched** or **parboiled** before being used in a recipe. To do so, they are immersed in a large quantity of a boiling or simmering liquid—oil or water—and partially cooked. This **parcooking** assists preparation (for example, it loosens peels from vegetables), removes undesirable flavors, softens firm foods, sets colors and shortens final cooking times. The only difference between blanching and parboiling is cooking time. Blanching is done quickly, usually only a few seconds. Parboiling lasts longer, usually several minutes. Foods that are blanched or parboiled in water (rather than fat) are often **shocked** or **refreshed** in ice water to halt the cooking process.

MAKING AN ICE BATH

Because of the risk of food-borne illness, it is important to cool hot foods quickly to a temperature below 41°F (5°C) before storing them in the refrigerator. An ice bath is an easy, efficient way to do so. An ice bath is also necessary for shocking or refreshing blanched or parcooked vegetables and for stopping the cooking of delicate mixtures such as custards.

An ice bath is simply a container of ice cubes and cold water. The combination of ice and water will chill foods more rapidly than a container of only ice. The food being chilled will also cool faster if it is in a metal container, rather than one made of plastic or glass.

Chilling Vanilla Custard Sauce in an ice bath.

CONCLUSION

As with most endeavors, consistently good cooking requires careful planning, preparation and organization. With these skills, a chef should be able to create a proper mise en place for almost any occasion.

QUESTIONS FOR DISCUSSION

1. Discuss how to create a prep list at the start of each day. Describe how the prep list can make work flow more smoothly.
2. Explain the differences between breading and battering foods.
3. Describe the correct mise en place for the standard breading procedure.
4. Choose a dessert recipe from the baking chapters of this book and describe the proper mise en place for preparing that dish.
5. How can the concepts of mise en place be applied to activities outside the kitchen?

CHAPTER EIGHT

THE QUALITIES OF AN EXCEPTIONAL COOK ARE AKIN TO THOSE OF A SUCCESSFUL TIGHTROPE WALKER: AN ABIDING PASSION FOR THE TASK, COURAGE TO GO OUT ON A LIMB AND AN IMPECCABLE SENSE OF BALANCE.

—Bryan Miller, American food writer

PRINCIPLES OF COOKING

AFTER STUDYING THIS CHAPTER, YOU WILL BE ABLE TO:

- understand how heat is transferred to foods through conduction, convection and radiation
- understand how heat affects foods
- understand the basic principles of various cooking methods

Cooking can be defined as the transfer of energy from a heat source to a food. This energy alters the food's molecular structure, changing its texture, flavor, aroma and appearance. But why is food cooked at all? The obvious answer is that cooking makes food taste better. Cooking also destroys undesirable microorganisms and makes foods easier to ingest and digest.

To cook foods successfully, you must first understand the ways in which heat is transferred: conduction, convection and radiation. You should also understand what the application of heat does to the proteins, sugars, starches, water and fats in foods.

Perhaps most important, you must understand the cooking methods used to transfer heat: broiling, grilling, roasting and baking, sautéing, pan-frying, deep-frying, poaching, simmering, boiling, steaming, braising and stewing. Each method is used for many types of food, so you will be applying one or more of them every time you cook. The cooking method you select gives the finished product a specific texture, appearance, aroma and flavor. A thorough understanding of the basic procedures involved in each cooking method helps you produce consistent, high-quality products.

This chapter describes each of the cooking methods and uses photographs to outline their general procedures. Detailed procedures and recipes applying these methods to specific foods are found in subsequent chapters.

▶ HEAT TRANSFER

Heat is a type of energy. When a substance gets hot, its molecules have absorbed energy, which causes the molecules to vibrate rapidly, expand and bounce off one another. As the molecules move, they collide with nearby molecules, causing a transfer of heat energy. The faster the molecules within a substance move, the higher its temperature. This is true whether the substance is air, water, an aluminum pot or a sirloin steak.

Heat energy may be transferred *to* foods via conduction, convection or radiation as shown in Figure 8.1. Heat then travels *through* foods by conduction. Only heat is transferred—cold is simply the absence of heat, so cold cannot be transferred from one substance to another.

CONDUCTION

Conduction is the most straightforward means of heat transfer. It is simply the movement of heat from one item to another through direct contact. For example, when the flame of a gas burner touches the bottom of a sauté pan, heat is conducted to the pan. The metal of the pan then conducts heat to the surface of the food lying in that pan.

Some materials conduct heat better than others. Water is a better conductor of heat than air. This explains why a potato cooks much faster in boiling water

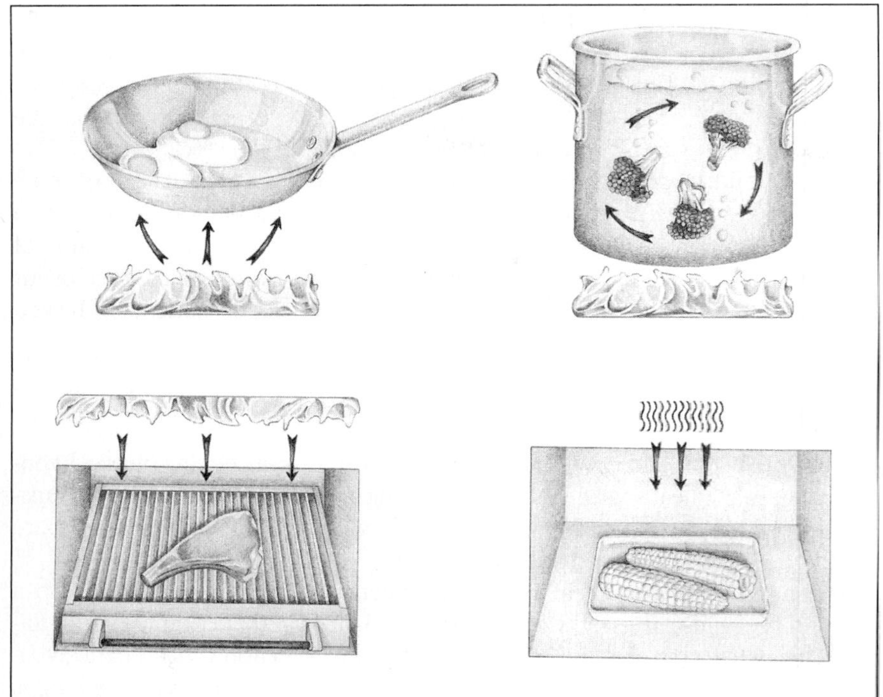

FIGURE 8.1 ▶ Arrows indicate heat patterns during conduction, convection and radiation.

than in an oven, and why you cannot place your hand in boiling water at a temperature of 212°F (100°C), but can place your hand, at least very briefly, into a 400°F (200°C) oven. Generally, metals are good conductors (as discussed in Chapter 3, Tools and Equipment, copper and aluminum are the best conductors), while liquids and gases are poor conductors.

Conduction is a relatively slow method of heat transfer because there must be physical contact to transfer energy from one molecule to adjacent molecules. Consider what happens when a metal spoon is placed in a pot of simmering soup. At first the spoon handle remains cool. Gradually, however, heat travels up the handle, making it warmer and warmer, until it becomes too hot to touch.

Conduction is important in all cooking methods because it is responsible for the movement of heat from the surface of a food to its interior. As the molecules near the food's exterior gather energy, they move more and more rapidly. As they move, they conduct heat to the molecules nearby, thus transferring heat through the food (from the exterior of the item to the interior).

In conventional heating methods (nonmicrowave), the heat source causes food molecules to react largely from the surface inward so that layers of molecules heat in succession. This produces a range of temperatures within the food, which means that the outside can brown and form a crust long before the interior is noticeably warmer. That is why a steak can be fully cooked on the outside but still rare on the inside.

CONVECTION

Convection refers to the transfer of heat through a fluid, which may be liquid or gas. Convection is actually a combination of conduction and a mixing in which molecules in a fluid (whether air, water or fat) move from a warmer area to a cooler one. There are two types of convection: natural and mechanical.

Natural convection occurs because of the tendency of warm liquids and gases to rise while cooler ones fall. This causes a constant natural circulation of heat. For example, when a pot of stock is placed over a gas burner, the molecules at the bottom of the pot are warmed. These molecules rise while cooler, heavier molecules sink. Upon reaching the pot's bottom, the cooler molecules are warmed and begin to rise. This ongoing cycle creates currents within the stock, and these currents distribute the heat throughout the stock.

Mechanical convection relies on fans or stirring to circulate heat more quickly and evenly. This explains why foods heat faster and more evenly when stirred. Convection ovens are equipped with fans to increase the circulation of air currents, thus speeding up the cooking process. But even conventional ovens (that is, not convection ovens) rely on the natural circulation patterns of heated air to transfer heat energy to items being baked or roasted.

RADIATION

Unlike conduction and convection, **radiation** does not require physical contact between the heat source and the food being cooked. Instead, energy is transferred by waves of heat or light striking the food. Two kinds of radiant heat are used in the kitchen: infrared and microwave.

Infrared cooking uses an electric or ceramic element heated to such a high temperature that it gives off waves of radiant heat that cook the food. Radiant heat waves travel at the speed of light in any direction (unlike convection heat, which only rises) until they are absorbed by a food. Infrared cooking is commonly used with toasters and broilers. The glowing coals of a fire are another example of radiant heat.

Microwave cooking relies on radiation generated by a special oven to penetrate the food, where it agitates water molecules, creating friction and heat. This energy then spreads throughout the food by conduction (and by convection in liquids). Microwave cooking is much faster than other methods because energy penetrates the food up to a depth of several centimeters, setting all water molecules in motion at the same time. Heat is generated quickly and uniformly throughout the food. Microwave cooking does not brown foods, however, and often gives meats a dry, mushy texture, making microwave ovens an unacceptable replacement for traditional ovens.

Because microwave radiation affects only water molecules, a completely waterless material (such as a plate) will not get hot. Any warmth felt in a plate used when microwaving food usually results from heat being conducted from the food to the plate.

Microwave cooking requires the use of certain types of utensils, usually heat-resistant glass or microwavable plastic. But even heat-resistant glass can shatter and is not recommended for professional use. The aluminum and stainless steel utensils most common in professional kitchens cannot be used because metal deflects microwaves, and this can damage the oven.

▶ THE EFFECTS OF HEAT

Foods are composed of proteins, carbohydrates (starches and sugars), water and fats, plus small amounts of minerals and vitamins. Changes in the shape, texture, color and flavor of foods may occur when heat is applied to each of these nutrients. By understanding these changes and learning to control them, you will be able to prepare foods with the characteristics desired. Although volumes are written on these subjects, it is sufficient for you to know the following processes as you begin your study of cooking.

PROTEINS COAGULATE

The proper term for the cooking of proteins is **coagulation.** Proteins are large, complex molecules found in every living cell, plant as well as animal. Coagulation refers to the irreversible transformation of proteins from a liquid or semiliquid state to a solid state. As proteins cook, they lose moisture, shrink and become firm. Common examples of coagulation are the firming of meat fibers during cooking, egg whites changing from a clear liquid to a white solid when heated and the setting of the structure of wheat proteins (known as gluten) in bread during baking. Most proteins complete coagulation at 160°F to 185°F (71°C to 85°C).

STARCHES GELATINIZE

Gelatinization is the proper term for the cooking of starches. Starches are complex carbohydrates present in plants and grains such as potatoes, wheat, rice and corn. When a mixture of starch and liquid is heated, remarkable changes occur. The starch granules absorb water, causing them to swell, soften and clarify slightly. The liquid visibly thickens because of the water being absorbed into the starch granules and the granules themselves swelling to occupy more space.

Gelatinization occurs gradually over a range of temperatures—150°F to 212°F (66°C to 100°C)—depending on the type of starch used. Starch gelatinization affects not only sauces or liquids to which starches are added for the express purpose of thickening, but also any mixture of starch and liquid that is heated. For example, the flour (a starch) in cake batter gelatinizes by absorbing the water from eggs, milk or other ingredients as the batter bakes. This causes part of the firming and drying associated with baked goods.

SUGARS CARAMELIZE

The process of cooking sugars is properly known as **caramelization.** Sugars are simple carbohydrates used by all plants and animals to store energy. As sugars cook, they gradually turn brown and change flavor. Caramelized sugar is used in many sauces, candies and desserts. But caramelized sugar is also partly responsible for the flavor and color of bread crusts and the browning of meats and vegetables. In fact, the process of caramelization is responsible for most flavors we associate with cooking.

Sucrose (common table sugar) begins to brown at about 338°F (170°C). The naturally occurring sugars in other foods, such as maltose, lactose and fructose, also caramelize, but at varying temperatures. Because high temperatures are required for browning (that is, caramelizing), most foods will brown only on the outside and only through the application of dry heat. Because water cannot be heated above 212°F (100°C), foods cooked with moist-heat methods do not get hot enough to caramelize. Foods cooked with dry-heat methods, including those using fats, will reach the high temperatures at which browning occurs.

WATER EVAPORATES

All foods contain some water. Some foods, especially eggs, milk and leafy vegetables, are almost entirely water. Even as much as 75 percent of raw meat is water. As the internal temperature of a food increases, water molecules move faster and faster until the water turns to a gas (steam) and vaporizes. This **evaporation** of water is responsible for the drying of foods during cooking.

FATS MELT

Fat is an energy source for the plant or animal in which it is stored. Fats are smooth, greasy substances that do not dissolve in water. Their texture varies from very firm to liquid. Oils are simply fats that remain liquid at room temperature. Fats **melt** when heated; that is, they gradually soften, then liquefy. Fats will not evaporate. Most fats can be heated to very high temperatures without burning, so they can be used as a cooking medium to brown foods.

▶ Cooking Methods

Foods can be cooked in air, fat, water or steam. These are collectively known as **cooking media.** There are two general types of cooking methods: dry heat and moist heat. (See Table 8.1.)

Dry-heat cooking methods are those using air or fat. They are broiling, grilling, roasting and baking, sautéing, pan-frying and deep-frying. Foods cooked using dry-heat cooking methods have a rich flavor caused by browning.

Moist-heat cooking methods are those using water or steam. They are poaching, simmering, boiling and steaming. Moist-heat cooking methods are used to tenderize and emphasize the natural flavors of food.

Other cooking methods employ a combination of dry- and moist-heat cooking methods. The two most significant of these **combination cooking methods** are braising and stewing.

Each of these cooking methods can be applied to a wide variety of foods—meats, fish, vegetables and even pastries. Here we describe each of the cooking methods and use photographs to outline their general procedures. Detailed procedures and recipes applying these methods to specific foods are found in subsequent chapters.

DRY-HEAT COOKING METHODS

Cooking by dry heat is the process of applying heat either directly, by subjecting the food to the heat of a flame, or indirectly, by surrounding the food with heated air or heated fat.

BROILING

Broiling uses radiant heat from an overhead source to cook foods. The temperature at the heat source can be as high as 2000°F (1093°C). The food to be broiled is placed on a preheated metal grate. Radiant heat from overhead cooks the food, while the hot grate below marks it with attractive crosshatch marks.

Table 8.1 COOKING METHODS

METHOD	MEDIUM	EQUIPMENT
Dry-Heat Cooking Methods		
Broiling	Air	Overhead broiler, salamander, rotisserie
Grilling	Air	Grill
Roasting	Air	Oven
Baking	Air	Oven
Sautéing	Fat	Stove top
Pan-frying	Fat	Stove top, tilt skillet
Deep-frying	Fat	Deep-fat fryer
Moist-Heat Cooking Methods		
Poaching	Water or other liquid	Stove top, oven, steam-jacketed kettle, tilt skillet
Simmering	Water or other liquid	Stove top, steam-jacketed kettle, tilt skillet
Boiling	Water or other liquid	Stove top, steam-jacketed kettle, tilt skillet
Steaming	Steam	Stove top, convection steamer
Combination Cooking Methods		
Braising	Fat, then liquid	Stove top, oven, tilt skillet
Stewing	Fat, then liquid	Stove top, oven, tilt skillet

Delicate foods that may be damaged by being placed directly on a metal grate or foods on which crosshatch marks are not desirable may be placed on a preheated heatproof platter and then placed under the broiler. Cooking will take place through indirect heat from the preheated platter as well as by direct heat from the broiler's overhead heat source.

▶ PROCEDURE FOR BROILING FOODS

1. Heat the broiler or salamander.
2. If necessary, use a wire brush to remove any charred or burnt particles that may be stuck to the broiler grate. The grate can be wiped with a lightly oiled towel to remove any remaining particles and to help season it.
3. Cut, trim or otherwise prepare the food to be broiled. Marinate, rub or season it, as desired. Many foods can be brushed lightly with oil to keep them from sticking to the grate.
4. Place the food in the broiler, presentation side down. If necessary, use tongs to turn or flip the item without piercing its surface.
5. Cook the food to the desired degree of doneness while developing the proper surface color. To do so, adjust the position of the item on the broiler, or adjust the distance between the grate and heat source. Doneness is often determined by touch, internal temperature or specific visual cues (for example, clear juices running from poultry).

1 Preheat the grate under the broiler, then pull it out and place the food on the hot grate, presentation side down. If the item is oblong, place it at a 45-degree angle to the bars on the cooking grate. Slide the grate back under the broiler and cook long enough for the food to develop lines where it touches the grate. Pull the sliding grate out again and turn the food over at a 90-degree angle, working from left to right.

2 Pull the sliding grate out of the broiler to turn the food as necessary in order to cook it evenly. Note the handle visible on the right, which can be used to adjust the distance between the grate and the heat source.

3 Remove the cooked item from the broiler grate.

GRILLING

Although similar to broiling, grilling uses a heat source located beneath the cooking surface. Grills may be electric or gas, or they can burn wood or charcoal, which will add a smoky flavor to the food. Specific woods such as mesquite, hickory or vine clippings can be used to create special flavors. Grilled foods are often identified by crosshatch markings.

▶ PROCEDURE FOR GRILLING FOODS

1. Heat the grill.
2. If necessary, use a wire brush to remove any charred or burnt particles that may be stuck to the grill grate. The grate can be wiped with a lightly oiled towel to remove any remaining particles and to help season it.
3. Cut, trim or otherwise prepare the food to be grilled. Marinate, rub or season it, as desired. Many foods can be brushed lightly with oil to keep them from sticking to the grate.
4. Place the food on the grill, presentation side down. If practical, rotate the food 90 degrees to produce the attractive crosshatch marks associated with grilling. Then use tongs to turn or flip the item without piercing its surface.
5. Cook the food to the desired degree of doneness while developing the proper surface color. To do so, adjust the position of the item on the grill, or adjust the distance between the grate and heat source. Doneness is often determined by touch, internal temperature or specific visual cues (for example, clear juices running from poultry).

1 Decide which side of the grilled food will be presented face up to the customer. Place the food on the hot grill with this side facing down. If the item is oblong, place it at a 45-degree angle to the bars on the cooking grate. Cook long enough for the food to develop dark charred lines where it touches the grate.

2 Rotate the food 90 degrees and allow it to cook long enough for the grates to char it to the same extent as in Step 1.

3 Turn the food over and finish cooking it. It is usually unnecessary to create the crosshatch markings on the reverse side because the customer will not see this side.

ROASTING AND BAKING

Roasting and baking are the processes of surrounding a food with dry, heated air in a closed environment. The term *roasting* is usually applied to meats and poultry, while *baking* is used when referring to fish, fruits, vegetables, starches, breads and pastry items. Heat is transferred by convection to the food's surface and then penetrates the food by conduction. The surface dehydrates and the food browns from caramelization, completing the cooking process.

Poêléing (poe-el-lay-ing) is a cooking method similar to both roasting and braising. The food is cooked in an oven, but in a covered pot with aromatic vegetables and bacon fat or butter, so that it steams in its own juices. Also known as butter roasting, the French poêlé technique is perhaps most similar to pot-roasting. Like a typical roasted dish (and unlike a typical braised dish), this method is used for tender cuts of meats and poultry that do not require long, slow cooking, and no additional liquid is added during cooking. The meat or poultry can first be browned in hot fat or it can be browned toward the end of cooking by removing the lid of the cooking vessel. Doneness is determined using the same techniques as those used for roasting. The meat or poultry is usually served with a sauce made from the pan juices mixed with a liquid and finished in the same way as a sauce for a braised dish.

► PROCEDURE FOR ROASTING OR BAKING FOODS

1. Preheat the oven.
2. Cut, trim or otherwise prepare the food to be roasted or baked. Marinate or season as desired. Brush with oil or butter, as appropriate.
3. Place the food on a rack or directly in a roasting pan or baking dish.
4. Roast the food, generally uncovered, at the desired temperature. **Baste** as necessary.
5. Cook to the desired internal temperature or doneness, remembering that many foods will undergo **carryover cooking** after they are removed from the oven.

► **baste** to moisten foods during cooking (usually grilling, broiling or roasting) with melted fat, pan drippings, a sauce or other liquids to prevent drying and to add flavor

► **carryover cooking** the cooking that occurs after a food is removed from a heat source; it is accomplished by the residual heat remaining in the food

1 Season the item to be roasted, arrange it in an uncovered pan and place it in a preheated oven.

2 Use a thermometer to check the internal temperature of the item being roasted.

SAUTÉING

Sautéing is a dry-heat cooking method that uses conduction to transfer heat from a hot sauté pan to food with the aid of a small amount of fat. Heat then penetrates the food through conduction. High temperatures are used to sauté, and the foods are usually cut into small pieces to promote even cooking.

To sauté foods properly, begin by heating a sauté pan on the stove top, then add a small amount of fat. The fat should just cover the bottom of the pan. Heat the fat to the point where it just begins to smoke. The food to be cooked should be as dry as possible when it is added to the pan to promote browning and to prevent excessive spattering. Place the food in the pan in a single layer. (The pan should be just large enough to hold the food in a single layer; a pan that is too large may cause the fat to burn.) The heat should be adjusted so that the food cooks thoroughly; it should not be so hot that the outside of the food burns before the inside is cooked. The food should be turned or tossed periodically to develop the proper color. Larger items should be turned using tongs without piercing the surface. Smaller items are often turned by using the sauteuse's sloped sides to flip them back on top of themselves. When tossing sautéed foods, keep the pan in contact with the heat source as much as possible to prevent it from cooling. Sautéing sometimes includes the preparation of a sauce directly in the pan after the main item has been removed.

Stir-frying is a variation of sautéing. A wok is used instead of a sauté pan; the curved sides and rounded bottom of the wok diffuse heat efficiently and facilitate tossing and stirring. Otherwise, stir-frying procedures are the same as those outlined for sautéing and will not be discussed separately here.

▶ PROCEDURE FOR SAUTÉING FOODS

1 Cut, pound or otherwise prepare the food to be sautéed. Season and dredge it in flour, if desired.
2 Heat a sauté pan and add enough fat (typically, oil or clarified butter) to just cover the pan's bottom.
3 Add the food to the sauté pan in a single layer, presentation side down. Do not crowd the pan.
4 Adjust the temperature so that the food's exterior browns properly without burning and the interior cooks. The heat should be high enough to complete the cooking process before the food begins to stew in its own juices.
5 Turn or toss the food as needed. Avoid burns by not splashing hot fat.
6 Cook until done. Doneness is usually determined by timing or touch.

1 Heat a small amount of oil in the sauté pan before adding the food.

2 The sloped edge of the pan can be used to toss the food. The item being sautéed should be cooked quickly.

SAFETY ALERT

Cooking with Hot Oil

When hot oil comes into contact with liquid, it can spatter, causing severe burns. Use caution when placing foods into hot fat. When pan-frying, slide food into the heated pan, letting it fall away from you so that splatters do not cause burns. Pat moist foods dry with paper towels before adding them to a deep fryer.

Oil heated to its flash point can ignite, causing burns or a serious kitchen fire. When oil is heated to its smoke point, it begins to break down creating acreolin, a harsh-smelling chemical compound. This offensive smell is a good warning that hot oil may be close to its flash point. Turn off the heat and carefully remove the pan of oil from its heat source. Allow the oil to cool completely before discarding.

PAN-FRYING

Pan-frying shares similarities with both sautéing and deep-frying. It is a dry-heat cooking method in which heat is transferred by conduction from the pan to the food, using a moderate amount of fat. Heat is also transferred to the food from the hot fat by convection. Foods to be pan-fried are usually coated in breading. This forms a seal that keeps the food moist and prevents the hot fat from penetrating the food and causing it to become greasy. (Breading procedures are explained in Chapter 7, Mise en Place.)

To pan-fry foods properly, first heat the fat in a sauté pan. Use enough fat so that when the food to be cooked is added, the fat comes one-third to halfway up the item being cooked. The fat should be at a temperature somewhat lower than that used for sautéing; it should not smoke but should be hot enough so that when the food is added it crackles and spatters from the rapid vaporization of moisture. If the temperature is too low, the food will absorb excessive amounts of fat; if it is too high, the food will burn on the outside before the interior is fully cooked. When the food is properly browned on one side, use tongs to turn it without piercing. Always turn the food away from you to prevent being burned by any fat that may splash. When the food is fully cooked, remove it from the pan, drain it on absorbent paper and serve it immediately.

▶ PROCEDURE FOR PAN-FRYING FOODS

1. Cut, pound or otherwise prepare the food to be pan-fried; then bread, batter or flour it as desired.
2. Heat a moderate amount of fat or oil in a heavy pan—usually enough to cover the item one-third to halfway up its sides.
3. Add the food to the pan, being careful not to splash the hot fat.
4. Fry the food on one side until brown. Using tongs, turn and brown the other side. Generally, pan-fried foods are fully cooked when they are well browned on both sides.
5. Remove the food from the pan and drain it on absorbent paper before serving.

1 Use tongs to carefully place the item being pan-fried into a moderate amount of hot oil.

2 Turn the item to brown the other side.

3 Drain the cooked item on absorbent paper.

DEEP-FRYING

Deep-frying is a dry-heat cooking method that uses conduction and convection to transfer heat to food submerged in hot fat. Although conceptually similar to boiling, deep-frying is not a moist-heat cooking method because the liquid fat contains no water. A key difference between boiling and deep-frying is the temperature of the cooking medium. The boiling point, 212°F (100°C), is the hottest temperature at which food can be cooked in water. At this temperature, most foods require a long cooking period and surface sugars cannot caramelize. With deep-frying, temperatures up to 400°F (200°C) are used. These high temperatures cook food more quickly and allow the food's surface to brown.

Foods to be deep-fried are usually first coated in batter or breading. This preserves moisture and prevents the food from absorbing excessive quantities of fat. Foods to be deep-fried should be of a size and shape that allows them to float freely in the fat. Foods that are to be deep-fried together should be of uniform size and shape. Delicately flavored foods should not be deep-fried in the same fat used for more strongly flavored ones, as the former could develop an odd taste from residual flavors left in the fat. Deep-fried foods should cook thoroughly while developing an attractive deep golden-brown color.

Today, most deep-frying is done in specially designed commercial fryers. These deep-fat fryers have built-in thermostats, making temperature control

▶ **recovery time** the length of time it takes a cooking medium such as fat or water to return to the desired cooking temperature after food is submerged in it

more precise. Deep-frying foods in a saucepan on the stove top is discouraged because it is both difficult and dangerous. **Recovery time** is usually very slow, and temperatures are difficult to control. Also, the fat can spill easily, leading to injuries or creating a fire hazard.

To deep-fry food, first heat the fat or oil to a temperature between 325°F and 375°F (160°C and 190°C). The cooking medium's temperature can be adjusted within this range to allow the interior of thicker foods or frozen foods to cook before their surfaces become too dark. The fat must be hot enough to quickly seal the surface of the food so that it does not become excessively greasy, yet it should not be so hot that the food's surface burns before the interior is cooked.

There are two methods of deep-frying: the basket method and the swimming method. The **basket method** uses a basket to hold foods that are breaded, are individually quick-frozen or otherwise will not tend to stick together during cooking. The basket is removed from the fryer and filled as much as two-thirds full of product. (Do not fill the basket while it is hanging over the fat, as this allows unnecessary salt and food particles to fall into the fat, shortening its life.) The filled basket is then submerged in the hot fat. When cooking is completed, the basket is used to remove the foods from the fat and hold them while excess fat drains off.

A variation on this procedure is the **double-basket method.** It is used because many foods float as they deep-fry. This may produce undesirable results because the portion of the food not submerged may not cook. To prevent this and to promote even cooking, a second basket is placed over the food held in the first basket, keeping the food submerged in the fat.

Most battered foods initially sink to the bottom when placed in hot fat, then rise to the top as they cook. Because they would stick to a basket, the **swimming method** is used for these foods. With the swimming method, battered foods are carefully dropped directly into the hot fat. (Baskets are not used.) They will rise to the top as they cook. When the surface that is in contact with the fat is properly browned, the food is turned over with a spider or a pair of tongs so that it can cook evenly on both sides. When done, the product is removed and drained, again using a spider or tongs.

▶ PROCEDURE FOR DEEP-FRYING FOODS

1. Cut, trim or otherwise prepare the food to be deep-fried. Bread or batter it, as desired.
2. Heat the oil or fat to the desired temperature.
3. Using either the basket method or the swimming method, carefully place the food in the hot fat.
4. Deep-fry the food until done. Doneness is usually determined by timing, surface color or sampling.
5. Remove the deep-fried food from the fryer and hold it over the cooking fat, allowing the excess fat to drain off.
6. Transfer the food to a hotel pan either lined with absorbent paper or fitted with a rack.
7. If the deep-fried items are to be held for later service, place them under a heat lamp; steam tables will not keep fried foods properly hot.

The basket method of deep-frying.

The double-basket method of deep-frying.

The swimming method of deep-frying.

Fats for Deep-Frying

Many types of fats can be used for deep-frying. Although animal fats, such as rendered beef fat, are sometimes used to impart their specific flavors to deep-fried foods, their low smoke points generally make them unsuitable for deep-frying unless blended with vegetable fats. By far the most common fats used for deep-frying are vegetable oils such as soybean, peanut and canola oil, all of which have high smoke points and are relatively inexpensive. See Table 8.2.

Table 8.2 REACTION TEMPERATURES OF FATS

FAT	MELT POINT	SMOKE POINT	FLASH POINT
Butter	92–98°F/33–36°C	260°F/127°C	Possible at any temperature above 300°F/150°C
Butter, clarified	92–98°F/33–36°C	335–380°F/168–193°C	Possible at any temperature above 300°F/150°C
Lard	89–98°F/32–36°C	370°F/188°C	n/a
Deep-fryer shortening, heavy-duty, premium	102°F/39°C	440°F/227°C	690°F/365°C
Canola oil	n/a	430–448°F/220–230°C	553–560°F/275–290°C
Corn oil	40–50°F/5–7°C	410°F/210°C	610°F/321°C
Cocoa butter	88–93°F/31–34°C	n/a	n/a
Cottonseed oil	55°F/13°C	450°F/232°C	650°F/343°C
Margarine	94–98°F/34–36°C	410–430°F/210–221°C	Possible at any temperature above 300°F/150°C
Olive oil, extra virgin	32°F/0°C	250°F/121°C	n/a
Olive oil, pure or pomace	32°F/0°C	410°F/210°C	437°F/225°C
Peanut oil	28°F/−2°C	450°F/232°C	540°F/283°C
Shortening, vegetable, all-purpose	120°F/49°C	410°F/210°C	625°F/329°C
Soybean oil	−5°F/−20°C	495°F/257°C	540°F/282°C
Walnut oil	n/a	450°F/232°C	620°F/326°C

n/a = not available

This data was compiled from a variety of sources and is meant as a guideline only. Because reaction temperatures depend on the exact type and ratio of fatty acids present, the actual temperatures will vary depending on the brand or manufacturer of the fat in question. Temperatures are for clean, previously unused fats. Heating a fat, even one time, can lower the smoke and flash points dramatically.

Table 8.3

FRYER FAT CAN BE DAMAGED BY:
Salt
Water
Overheating
Food particles
Oxygen

CHANGE FRYER FAT WHEN IT:
Becomes dark
Smokes
Foams
Develops off-flavors

Specially formulated deep-frying compounds are also available. These are usually composed of a vegetable oil or oils to which antifoaming agents, antioxidants and preservatives have been added. These additives increase the oil's usable life and raise its smoke point.

Deep-fryer fats may also be hydrogenated. **Hydrogenation** is a chemical process that adds hydrogen to oil, turning the liquid oil into a solid (margarine is hydrogenated vegetable oil). Hydrogenated fats are more resistant to oxidation and chemical breakdown.

To choose the right fat, consider flavor, smoke point and resistance to chemical breakdown. High-quality frying fat should have a clean or natural flavor and a high smoke point and, when properly maintained, should be resistant to chemical breakdown.

Properly maintaining deep-fryer fat will greatly extend its useful life. (See Table 8.3.) To do so:

1 Store the fat in tightly sealed containers away from strong light; cover the deep fryer when not in use. Prolonged exposure to air and light turns fat rancid.
2 Skim and remove food particles from the fat's surface during frying. Food particles cause fat to break down; if they are not removed, they will accumulate in the fryer and burn.
3 Do not salt food over the fat. Salt causes fat to break down chemically.
4 Prevent excessive water from coming into contact with the fat, pat-dry moist foods as much as possible before cooking and dry the fryer, baskets and utensils well after cleaning. Water, like salt, causes fat to break down.
5 Do not overheat the fat (turn the fryer down or off if not in use). High temperatures break down the fat.
6 Filter the fat each day or after each shift if the fryer is heavily used. Best results are obtained by using a filtering machine designed specifically for this purpose. Many large commercial fryers even have built-in filter systems. Less well-equipped operations can simply pour the hot fat through a paper filter.

MOIST-HEAT COOKING METHODS

Cooking with moist heat is the process of applying heat to food by submerging it directly into a hot liquid or by exposing it to steam.

POACHING

Poaching is a moist-heat cooking method that uses convection to transfer heat from a liquid to a food. It is most often associated with delicately flavored foods that do not require lengthy cooking times to tenderize them, such as eggs, fruit or fish.

Poaching (160°F–180°F/71°C–82°C).

Simmering (185°F–205°F/85°C–96°C).

Boiling (212°F/100°C).

For poaching, the food is placed in a liquid held at temperatures between 160°F and 180°F (71°C and 82°C). The surface of the liquid should show only slight movement, but no bubbles. It is important to maintain the desired temperature throughout the cooking process. Do not allow the liquid to reach a boil, because the agitation will cause meats to become tough and stringy and will destroy tender foods such as fresh fruit or fish.

The flavor of the poaching liquid strongly affects the ultimate flavor of the finished product, so stock, court bouillon or broth is generally used. The liquid used to poach a food is sometimes used to make an accompanying sauce.

There are two methods of poaching: submersion poaching and shallow poaching. For **submersion poaching,** the food is completely covered with the cooking liquid. There should not be too much excess liquid, however, as this could leach away much of the food's flavor. Nor should there be too little, as that could leave a portion of the food exposed, preventing it from cooking.

For **shallow poaching,** the food is placed in just enough liquid to come approximately halfway up its sides. The liquid, called a **cuisson,** is brought to a simmer on the stove top. The pan is then covered with a piece of buttered parchment paper or a lid, and cooking is completed either on the stove top or in the oven. Shallow poaching combines aspects of poaching and steaming.

▶ PROCEDURE FOR POACHING FOODS

1. Cut, trim or otherwise prepare the food to be poached.
2. Bring an adequate amount of cooking liquid to the desired starting temperature. (For some items, the cooking liquid is first brought to a boil and then reduced to the poaching temperature.) Place the food in the liquid.
3. For submersion poaching, the liquid should completely cover the food.
4. For shallow poaching, the liquid should come approximately halfway up the side of the food. If shallow poaching, cover the pan with a piece of buttered parchment paper or a lid.
5. Maintaining the proper temperature, poach the food to the desired doneness in the oven or on the stove top. Doneness is generally determined by timing, internal temperature or tenderness.
6. Remove the food and hold it for service in a portion of the cooking liquid or, using an ice bath, cool it in the cooking liquid.
7. The cooking liquid can sometimes be used to prepare an accompanying sauce or reserved for use in other dishes.

1 Season the poaching liquid as desired and bring it to the correct temperature.

2 Carefully place the food item into the poaching liquid.

3 Remove the cooked food from the poaching liquid.

SIMMERING

Simmering is another moist-heat cooking method that uses convection to transfer heat from a liquid to a food. It is often associated with foods that need to be tenderized through long, slow, moist cooking, such as less tender cuts of meat. Properly simmered foods should be moist and very tender. For simmering, the food is submerged in a liquid held at temperatures between 185°F and 205°F (85°C and 96°C). Because simmering temperatures are slightly higher than those used for poaching, there should be more action on the liquid's surface, with a few air bubbles breaking through.

As with poaching, the liquid used for simmering has a great effect on the food's flavor. Be sure to use a well-flavored stock or broth and to add mirepoix, herbs and seasonings as needed.

▶ PROCEDURE FOR SIMMERING FOODS

1 Cut, trim or otherwise prepare the food to be simmered.
2 Bring an adequate amount of the cooking liquid to the appropriate temperature (some foods, especially smoked or cured items, are started in a cold liquid). There should be enough liquid to cover the food completely.
3 Add the food to the simmering liquid.
4 Maintaining the proper cooking temperature throughout the process, simmer the food to the desired doneness. Doneness is generally determined by timing or tenderness.
5 Remove the item and hold it for service in a portion of the cooking liquid or, using an ice bath, cool the food in its cooking liquid.

1 The item being simmered should be fully submerged in the seasoned liquid.

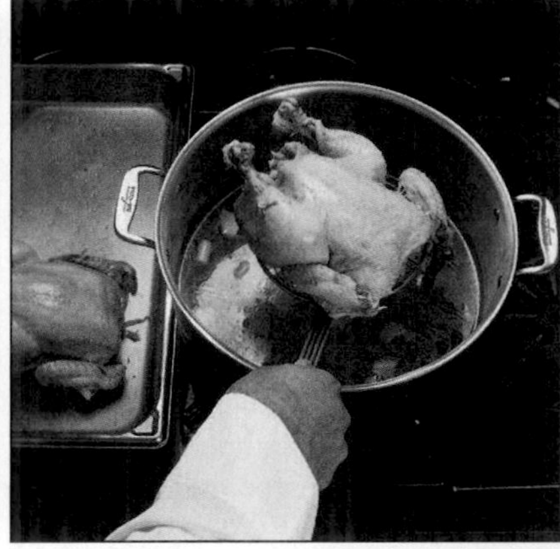

2 Remove the cooked item from the liquid.

BOILING

Boiling is another moist-heat cooking method that uses the process of convection to transfer heat from a liquid to a food. Boiling uses large amounts of rapidly bubbling liquid to cook foods. The turbulent waters and the relatively high temperatures cook foods more quickly than do poaching or simmering. Few foods, however, are cooked by true boiling. Most "boiled" meats are actually simmered. Even "hard-boiled" eggs are really only simmered. Starches such as pasta and potatoes are among the only types of food that are truly boiled.

Under normal atmospheric pressure at sea level, water boils at 212°F (100°C). The addition of other ingredients or a change in atmospheric pressure can change the boiling point, however. As altitude increases, the boiling point decreases because of the drop in atmospheric pressure. For every 1000 feet above sea level, the boiling point of water drops 2°F (1°C). In the mile-high city of Denver, for example, water boils at 203°F (95°C). Because the boiling temperature is lower, it will take longer to cook foods in Denver than in, for example, Miami.

The addition of alcohol also lowers the boiling point of water because alcohol boils at about 175°F (80°C). In contrast, the addition of salt, sugar or other substances raises the boiling point slightly. This means that foods cooked in salted water cook faster because the boiling point is one or two degrees higher than normal.

Use as much water as practical when boiling food. Whenever food is added to boiling water, it lowers the water's temperature. The greater the amount of water, however, the faster it will return to a boil.

▶ PROCEDURE FOR BOILING FOODS

1. Bring an appropriate amount of a liquid to a boil over high heat. Add oil or seasonings, if desired.
2. Add the food to be boiled to the rapidly boiling water. Bring the liquid back to a boil and adjust the temperature to maintain the boil.
3. Cook until done. Doneness is usually determined by timing or texture.
4. Remove the boiled food from the cooking liquid, draining any excess liquid.
5. Serve the boiled food immediately. Some boiled foods can be refreshed in cold water and held for later service.

1 Bring the cooking liquid to a full boil. When the item being cooked is added to the liquid, its temperature will fall.

2 After a boiled item such as pasta is cooked, it may be drained through a colander.

STEAMING

Steaming is a moist-heat cooking method that uses the process of convection to transfer heat from the steam to the food being cooked. It is most often associated with tender, delicately flavored foods, such as fish and vegetables, which do not require long cooking times. Steaming tends to enhance a food's natural flavor and helps retain its nutrients. Properly steamed foods should be moist and tender. Additional flavor can be introduced by adding wine, stock, aromatics, spices or herbs to the liquid used as the steaming medium. The steaming liquid can also often be used to make a sauce to be served with the steamed food.

The food to be steamed is usually placed in a basket or rack above a boiling liquid. The food should not touch the liquid; it should be positioned so that the steam can circulate around it. (Some foods, such as shellfish and ears of corn, however, can be placed directly in a shallow pool of boiling water.) A lid should be placed on the steaming pot to trap the steam and also create a slight pressure within the pot, which speeds the cooking process.

Another type of steaming uses a convection steamer. Convection steamers use pressurized steam to cook food very quickly in an enclosed chamber. Convection steamer cooking does not result in a flavored liquid that can be used to make a sauce.

Steamed foods should be served immediately. If held for later service, they should be refreshed and refrigerated until used.

▶ PROCEDURE FOR STEAMING FOODS

1 Cut, trim or otherwise prepare the food to be steamed.
2 If a convection steamer is not being used, prepare a steaming liquid and bring it to a boil in a covered pan or double boiler.
3 Place the food to be steamed on a rack, in a basket or on a perforated pan in a single layer. Do not crowd the items. Place the rack, basket or pan over the boiling liquid.
4 Alternatively, place the food in a shallow pool of the cooking liquid.
5 Cover the cooking assemblage and cook to the desired doneness. Doneness is usually determined by timing, color or tenderness.

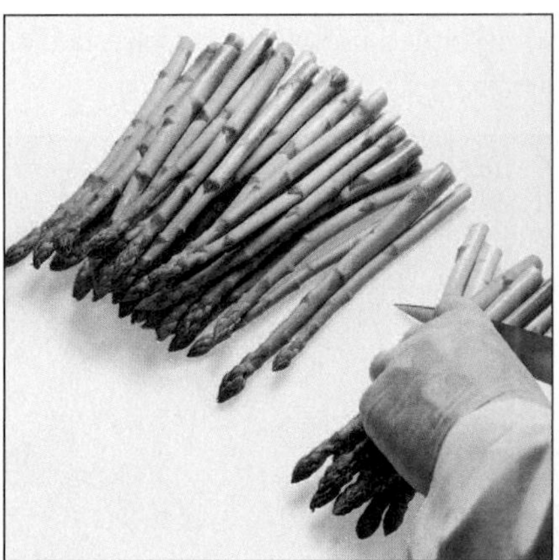

1 Trim items before steaming them so that they cook evenly.

2 A perforated hotel pan can be set over a deeper pan of water, covered and used as a steamer.

Table 8.4 MOIST-HEAT COOKING METHODS

METHOD	LIQUID'S TEMPERATURE	LIQUID'S CONDITION	USES
Poaching	160–180°F 71–82°C	Liquid moves slightly but no bubbles	Eggs, fish, fruits
Simmering	185–205°F 85–96°C	Small bubbles break through the liquid's surface	Meats, stews, chicken
Boiling	212°F 100°C	Large bubbles and rapid movement	Vegetables, pasta
Steaming	212°F or higher 100°C or higher	Food is in contact only with the steam generated by a boiling liquid	Vegetables, fish, shellfish

COMBINATION COOKING METHODS

Some cooking methods employ both dry-heat and moist-heat cooking techniques. The two principal combination methods are braising and stewing. In both methods, the first step is usually to brown the main item using dry heat. The second step is to complete cooking by simmering the food in a liquid. Combination methods are often used for less tender but flavorful cuts of meat as well as for poultry and some vegetables.

BRAISING

Braised foods benefit from the best qualities of both dry- and moist-heat cooking methods. Foods to be braised are usually large pieces that are first browned in a small amount of fat at high temperatures. As with sautéing, heat is transferred from the pan to the food mainly by the process of conduction. Vegetables and seasonings are added, and enough sauce or liquid is added to come one-third to halfway up the item being cooked. The pan is covered, and the heat is reduced. The food is then cooked at low heat, using a combination of simmering and steaming to transfer heat from the liquid (conduction) and the air (convection) to the food. This can be done on the stove top or in the oven. A long, slow cooking period helps tenderize the main item. Braised foods are usually served with a sauce made from the cooking liquid.

1 First brown the item being braised in fat.

2 Add liquid to the pan.

3 The item can be basted with the liquid during cooking.

▶ PROCEDURE FOR BRAISING FOODS

1. Cut, trim or otherwise prepare the food to be braised. Dredge it in flour, if desired.
2. Heat a small amount of fat in a heavy pan.
3. Sear the food on all sides. Some foods—notably, meats—should be removed from the pan after they are seared.
4. Add any other ingredients and sauté.
5. Add flour or roux, if used.
6. Add the cooking liquid; it should partially cover the food being braised.
7. Add aromatics and seasonings.
8. If the principal item was removed, return it to the pan.
9. Cover the pan and bring the cooking liquid to a simmer. Cook slowly, either on the stove top or in an oven at 250°F–300°F (120°C–150°C). Baste and turn the food as needed.
10. When the principal item is cooked, remove it from the pan and hold it in a warm place.
11. Prepare a sauce from the braising liquid if desired. This may be done by reducing the liquid on the stove top to intensify its flavors. If the food was braised in an unthickened stock, the stock may now be thickened using a roux, arrowroot or cornstarch. Strain the sauce or, if desired, purée the mirepoix and other ingredients and return them to the sauce. Adjust the sauce's consistency as desired.

STEWING

Stewing also uses a combination of dry- and moist-heat cooking methods. Stewing is most often associated with smaller pieces of food that are first cooked either by browning them in a small amount of fat or oil or by blanching them in a liquid. Cooking is then finished in a liquid or sauce. Stewed foods have enough liquid added to cover them completely and are simmered at a constant temperature until tender. Cooking time is generally shorter for stewing than for braising because the main items are smaller.

▶ PROCEDURE FOR STEWING FOODS

1. Trim and cut the food to be stewed into small, uniform-sized pieces. Dredge the pieces in flour, if desired.
2. Heat a small amount of fat in a heavy pan. Then sear the food on all sides, developing color as desired.
3. Add any other ingredients and sauté.
4. Add flour or roux.
5. Gradually add the cooking liquid, stirring to prevent lumps. The liquid should completely cover the principal items.
6. Bring the stew to the appropriate temperature. Cover and place in the oven at 250°F–300°F (120°C–150°C) or continue to simmer on the stove top until the principal items are tender.
7. Remove the principal items and hold them in a warm place.
8. Thicken the sauce as desired.
9. Return the principal items to the stew. If not added during the cooking process, vegetables and other garnishes may be cooked separately and added to the finished stew.

1 First brown the item being stewed in a small amount of fat.

2 Add flour to make a roux.

3 Add liquid to the pan.

4 Degrease the finished stew as necessary.

CONCLUSION

Cooking is the transfer of heat energy to foods by conduction, convection or radiation. Cooking changes the molecular structure of certain nutrients. When heat is applied, proteins coagulate, starches gelatinize, sugars caramelize, fats melt and water evaporates. Foods can be cooked using a variety of methods. Some use dry heat: broiling, grilling, roasting and baking, sautéing, pan-frying and deep-frying. Others use moist heat: poaching, simmering, boiling and steaming. Still others use a combination of the two: braising and stewing. The method used affects the texture, appearance and flavor of the cooked foods. Students must understand these principles in order to ensure that foods are cooked properly.

QUESTIONS FOR DISCUSSION

1. Describe the differences between conduction and convection. Identify four cooking methods that rely on both conduction and convection to heat foods. Explain your choices.
2. Identify two cooking methods that rely on infrared heat. What is the principal difference between these methods?
3. At the same temperature, will a food cook faster in a convection oven or a conventional oven? Explain your answer.
4. Describe the process of caramelization and its significance in food preparation. Will a braised food have a caramelized surface? Explain your answer.
5. Describe the process of coagulation and its significance in food preparation. Will a pure fat coagulate if heated? Explain your answer.
6. Describe the process of gelatinization and its significance in food preparation. Will a pure fat gelatinize? Explain your answer.
7. Name and describe two styles of deep-frying.

CHAPTER NINE

WHAT I LOVE ABOUT COOKING IS THAT AFTER A HARD DAY, THERE IS SOMETHING COMFORTING ABOUT THE FACT THAT IF YOU MELT BUTTER AND ADD FLOUR, THEN HOT STOCK, IT WILL GET THICK! IT'S A SURE THING. IT'S A SURE THING IN A WORLD WHERE NOTHING IS SURE!

—Nora Ephron, American author and filmmaker (1941–)

STOCKS AND SAUCES

PRIMITIVO WINE BAR, Colorado Springs, CO
Former Executive Chef John Broening

AFTER STUDYING THIS CHAPTER, YOU WILL BE ABLE TO:

- prepare a variety of stocks
- recognize and classify sauces
- use thickening agents properly
- prepare a variety of classic and modern sauces

▶ **fond** (1) French for "stock" or "base"; (2) the concentrated juices, drippings and bits of food left in pans after foods are roasted or sautéed; it is used to flavor sauces made directly in the pans in which foods were cooked

A **stock** is a flavored liquid. A good stock is the key to a great soup, sauce or braised dish. The French appropriately call a stock *fond* ("base"), as stocks are the basis for many classic and modern dishes.

A **sauce** is a thickened liquid used to flavor and enhance other foods. A good sauce adds flavor, moisture, richness and visual appeal. A sauce should complement food; it should never disguise it. A sauce can be hot or cold, sweet or savory, smooth or chunky.

Although the thought of preparing stocks and sauces may be intimidating, the procedures are really quite simple. Carefully follow the basic procedures outlined in this chapter, use high-quality ingredients and, with practice and experience, you will soon be producing fine stocks and sauces.

This chapter addresses classical hot sauces as well as coulis, contemporary broths, flavored oils, salsas and relishes. Cold sauces, generally based on mayonnaise and vinaigrettes, are discussed in Chapter 23, Salads and Salad Dressings

▶ STOCKS

There are several types of stocks. Although they are all made from a combination of bones, vegetables, seasonings and liquids, each type uses specific procedures to give it distinctive characteristics.

A **white stock** is made by simmering chicken, veal or beef bones in water with vegetables and seasonings. The stock remains relatively colorless during the cooking process.

A **brown stock** is made from chicken, veal, beef or game bones and vegetables, all of which are caramelized before being simmered in water with seasonings. The stock has a rich, dark color.

Both a **fish stock** and a **fumet** are made by slowly cooking fish bones or crustacean shells and vegetables without coloring them, then simmering them in water with seasonings for a short time. For a fumet, wine and lemon juice are also added. The resulting stock or fumet is a strongly flavored, relatively colorless liquid.

A **court bouillon** is made by simmering vegetables and seasonings in water and an acidic liquid such as vinegar or wine. It is used to poach fish or vegetables.

The quality of a stock is judged by four characteristics: body, flavor, clarity and color. Body develops when collagen proteins dissolve in protein-based stock. Vegetable stocks have less body than meat stocks because they lack animal protein. Flavoring vegetables such as mirepoix, herb sachets and the proper ratios of ingredients to liquid give stocks their flavor. Clarity is achieved by removing impurities during stock making. Many ingredients contribute to a stock's color. Vegetables such as leeks and carrots give white stock a light color. Browned bones and tomato paste give color to dark stocks. Improper uses of coloring ingredients can overwhelm the color and flavor of a stock.

INGREDIENTS

The basic ingredients of any stock are bones, a vegetable mixture known as a mirepoix, seasonings and water.

BONES

Bones are the most important ingredient; they add flavor, richness and color to the stock. Traditionally, the kitchen or butcher shop saved the day's bones to make stock. But because many meats and poultry items are now purchased precut or portioned, food service operations often purchase bones specifically for stock making.

Different bones release their flavor at different rates. Even though the bones are cut into 3- to 4-inch (8- to 10-centimeter) pieces, a stock made entirely of beef and/or veal bones requires six to eight hours of cooking time, while a stock made entirely from chicken bones requires only five to six hours.

Beef and Veal Bones

The best bones for beef and veal stock are from younger animals. They contain a higher percentage of **cartilage** and other **connective tissue** than do bones from more mature animals. Connective tissue has a high **collagen** content. Through the cooking process, the collagen is converted into **gelatin** and water. The gelatin adds richness and body to the finished stock.

The best beef and veal bones are back, neck and shank bones, as they have high collagen contents. Beef and veal bones should be cut with a meat saw into small pieces, approximately 3 to 4 inches (8 to 10 centimeters) long, so that they can release as much flavor as possible while the stock cooks.

▶ **cartilage** also known as gristle; a tough, elastic, whitish connective tissue that helps give structure to an animal's body

▶ **connective tissue** tissue found throughout an animal's body that binds together and supports other tissues such as muscles

▶ **collagen** a protein found in nearly all connective tissue; it dissolves when cooked with moisture

▶ **gelatin** a tasteless and odorless mixture of proteins (especially collagen) extracted from boiling bones, connective tissue and other animal parts; when dissolved in a hot liquid and then cooled, it forms a jellylike substance used as a thickener and stabilizer

Chicken Bones

The best bones for chicken stock are from the neck and back. If a whole chicken carcass is used, it can be cut up for easier handling.

Fish Bones

The best bones for fish stock are from lean fish such as sole, flounder, whiting or turbot. Bones from fatty fish (for example, salmon, tuna and swordfish) do not produce good stock because of their high fat content and distinctive flavors. The entire fish carcass can be used, but it should be cut up with a cleaver or heavy knife for easy handling and even extraction of flavors. After cutting, the pieces should be rinsed in cold water to remove blood, loose scales and other impurities.

Other Bones

Lamb, turkey, game and ham bones can also be used for white or brown stocks. Although mixing bones is generally acceptable, be careful of blending strongly flavored bones, such as those from lamb or game, with beef, veal or chicken bones. The former's strong flavors may not be appropriate or desirable in the finished product.

▶ **matignon** a standard mirepoix plus diced smoked bacon or smoked ham and, depending on the dish, mushrooms and herbs; sometimes called an edible mirepoix, it is usually cut more uniformly than a standard mirepoix and left in the finished dish as a garnish

MIREPOIX

A mirepoix is a mixture of onions, carrots and celery added to a stock to enhance its flavor and aroma. Although chefs differ on the ratio of vegetables, generally a mixture of 50 percent onions, 25 percent carrots and 25 percent celery, by weight, is used. (Unless otherwise noted, any reference to mirepoix in this book refers to this ratio.) For a brown stock, onion skins may be used to add color. It is not necessary to peel the carrots or celery because flavor, not aesthetics, is important.

The size into which the mirepoix is chopped is determined by the stock's cooking time: The shorter the cooking time, the smaller the vegetables must be chopped to ensure that all possible flavor is extracted. For white or brown stocks made from beef or veal bones, the vegetables should be coarsely

Mirepoix Ingredients

chopped into large, 1- to 2-inch (2.5- to 5-centimeter) pieces. For chicken and fish stocks, the vegetables should be more finely chopped into ½-inch (1.2-centimeter) pieces.

A white mirepoix is made by replacing the carrots in a standard mirepoix with parsnips and adding mushrooms and leeks. Some chefs prefer to use a white mirepoix when making a white stock, as it produces a lighter product. Sometimes parsnips, mushrooms and leeks are added to a standard mirepoix for additional flavors.

SEASONINGS

Principal stock seasonings are peppercorns, bay leaves, thyme, parsley stems and, optionally, garlic. These seasonings generally can be left whole. A stock is cooked long enough for all of their flavors to be extracted, so there is no reason to chop or grind them. Seasonings generally are added to the stock at the start of cooking. Some chefs do not add seasonings to beef or veal stock until midway through the cooking process, however, because of the extended cooking times. Seasonings can be added as a sachet d'épices or a bouquet garni.

Salt, an otherwise important seasoning, is not added to stock. Because a stock has a variety of uses, it is impossible for the chef to know how much salt to add when preparing it. If, for example, the stock was seasoned to taste with salt, the chef could not reduce it later; salt is not lost through reduction, and the concentrated product would taste too salty. Similarly, seasoning the stock to taste with salt could prevent the chef from adding other ingredients that are high in salt when finishing a recipe. Unlike many seasonings whose flavors must be incorporated into a product through lengthy cooking periods, salt can be added at any time during the cooking process with the same effect.

PRINCIPLES OF STOCK MAKING

Start the stock in cold water.
Simmer the stock gently.
Skim the stock frequently.
Strain the stock carefully.
Cool the stock quickly.
Store the stock properly.
Degrease the stock.

FIGURE 9.1 ▶ Principles of stock making.

The following principles, outlined in Figure 9.1, apply to all stocks. You should follow them in order to achieve the highest-quality stocks possible.

A. START THE STOCK IN COLD WATER

The ingredients should always be covered with cold water. When bones are covered with cold water, blood and other impurities dissolve. As the water heats, the impurities coagulate and rise to the surface, where they can be removed easily by skimming. If the bones were covered with hot water, the impurities would coagulate more quickly and remain dispersed in the stock without rising to the top, making the stock cloudy.

If the water level falls below the bones during cooking, add water to cover them. Flavor cannot be extracted from bones not under water, and bones exposed to the air will darken and discolor a white stock.

B. SIMMER THE STOCK GENTLY

The stock should be brought to a boil and then reduced to a simmer, a temperature of approximately 185°F (85°C). While simmering, the ingredients release their flavors into the liquid. If kept at a simmer, the liquid will remain clear as it reduces and the stock develops.

Never boil a stock for any length of time. Rapid boiling of a stock, even for a few minutes, causes impurities and fats to blend with the liquid, making it cloudy.

C. SKIM THE STOCK FREQUENTLY

A stock should be skimmed often to remove the fat and impurities that rise to the surface during cooking. If they are not removed, they may make the stock cloudy.

D. STRAIN THE STOCK CAREFULLY

Once a stock finishes cooking, the liquid must be separated from the bones, vegetables and other solid ingredients. In order to keep the liquid clear, it is important not to disturb the solid ingredients when removing the liquid. This is easily accomplished if the stock is cooked in a steam kettle or stockpot with a spigot at the bottom.

If the stock is cooked in a standard stockpot, to strain it:

1. Skim as much fat and as many impurities from the surface as possible before removing the stockpot from the heat.
2. After removing the pot from the heat, carefully ladle the stock from the pot without stirring it.
3. Strain the stock through a china cap lined with several layers of cheesecloth.

E. COOL THE STOCK QUICKLY

Most stocks are prepared in large quantities, cooled and held for later use. Great care must be taken when cooling a stock to prevent food-borne illnesses or souring. To cool a stock below the temperature danger zone quickly and safely:

1. Keep the stock in a metal container. A plastic container insulates the stock and delays cooling.
2. Vent the stockpot in an empty sink by placing it on blocks or a rack. This allows water to circulate on all sides and below the pot when the sink is filled with water. See Figure 9.2.
3. Install an overflow pipe in the drain and fill the sink with cold water or a combination of cold water and ice. Make sure that the weight of the stockpot is adequate to keep it from tipping over.
4. Let cold water run into the sink and drain out the overflow pipe. Stir the stock frequently to facilitate even, quick cooling.

In addition to this venting procedure, cooling wands can be used to speed the cooling of stocks, soups, sauces and other liquids. These wands (also known as ice paddles) are hollow plastic containers that can be filled with water or ice, sealed, frozen and then used to stir and cool liquids. Clean and sanitize the wand after each use to prevent cross-contamination.

SAFETY ALERT

Cooling and Handling Stocks

A two-stage cooling method is recommended for keeping stock out of the temperature danger zone. First cool the stock to 70°F (21°C) within 2 hours and from 70°F to below 41°F (21°F to below 5°C) in an additional 4 hours, for a total of 6 hours. To prevent bacterial growth if these temperatures have not been met, the stock must be reheated to 165°F (74°C) for 15 seconds within 2 hours.

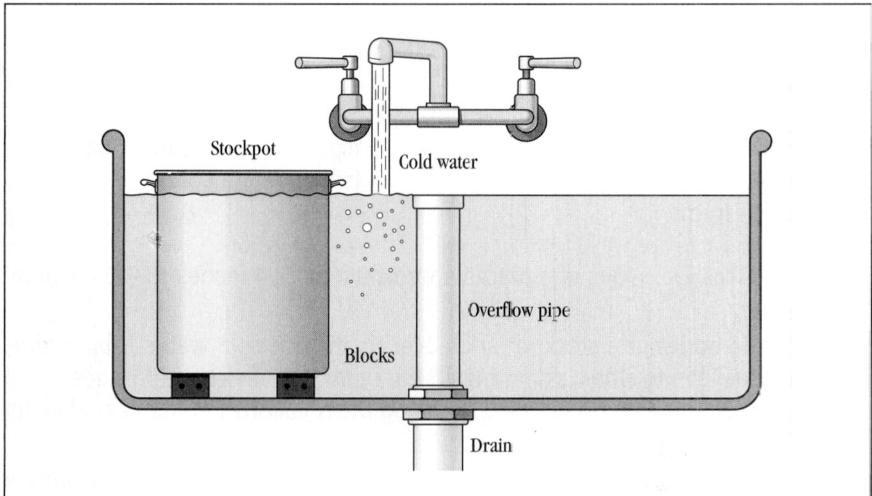

FIGURE 9.2 ▶ Venting a stockpot.

Lifting fat from the surface of a cold stock.

▶ **degrease** to remove fat from the surface of a liquid such as a stock or sauce by skimming, scraping or lifting congealed fat

F. STORE THE STOCK PROPERLY

Once the stock is cooled, transfer it to a sanitized covered container (either plastic or metal) and store it in the refrigerator. As the stock chills, fat rises to its surface and solidifies. If left intact, this layer of fat helps preserve the stock. Stocks can be stored for up to one week under refrigeration or frozen for several months.

G. DEGREASE THE STOCK

Degreasing a stock is simple: When a stock is refrigerated, fat rises to its surface, hardens and is easily lifted or scraped away before the stock is reheated.

WHITE STOCK

A white or neutral stock may be made from beef, veal or chicken bones. The finished stock should have a good flavor, good clarity, high gelatin content and little or no color. Veal bones are most often used, but any combination of beef, veal or chicken bones may be used.

BLANCHING BONES

Chefs disagree on whether the bones for a white stock should be blanched to remove impurities. Some chefs argue that blanching keeps the stock as clear and colorless as possible; others argue that blanching removes nutrients and flavor.

▶ PROCEDURE FOR BLANCHING BONES

If you choose to blanch the bones:

1. Wash the cut-up bones, place them in a stockpot and cover them with cold water.
2. Bring the water to a boil over high heat.
3. As soon as the water boils, skim the rising impurities. Drain the water from the bones and discard it.
4. Refill the pot with cold water, and proceed with the stock recipe.

RECIPE 9.1

WHITE STOCK

Mise en Place

- ▶ Cut up and wash bones.
- ▶ Peel and chop onions, carrots and celery for mirepoix.
- ▶ Prepare herb sachet.

Yield: 2 gal. (8 lt)

Bones, veal, chicken or beef	15 lb.	7 kg
Cold water	3 gal.	11 lt
Mirepoix	2 lb.	1 kg
Sachet:		
Bay leaves	2	2
Dried thyme	1/2 tsp.	2 ml
Peppercorns, crushed	1/2 tsp.	2 ml
Parsley stems	8	8

1. Cut the washed bones into pieces approximately 3–4 inches (8–10 centimeters) long.
2. Place the bones in a stockpot and cover them with cold water. If blanching, bring the water to a boil, skimming off the scum that rises to the surface. Drain off the water and the impurities. Then add the 3 gallons (11 liters) cold water and bring to a boil. Reduce to a simmer.
3. If not blanching the bones, bring the cold water to a boil. Reduce to a simmer and skim the scum that forms.
4. Add the mirepoix and sachet to the simmering stock.

5 Continue simmering and skimming the stock for 6 to 8 hours. (If only chicken bones are used, simmer for 3 to 4 hours.)
6 Strain, cool and refrigerate.

Approximate values per 1-fl.-oz. (30-ml) serving: **Calories** 4, **Total fat** 0.1 g, **Saturated fat** 0.1 g, **Cholesterol** 0 mg, **Sodium** 5 mg, **Total carbohydrates** 0 g, **Protein** 0.2 g, **Claims**—fat free; very low sodium

1 Adding water to bones for white stock.

2 Skimming the white stock.

3 Adding mirepoix to the white stock and seasonings.

BROWN STOCK

A brown stock is made from chicken, veal, beef or game bones. The finished stock should have a good flavor, rich dark brown color, good body and high gelatin content.

The primary differences between a brown stock and a white stock are that for a brown stock, the bones and mirepoix are caramelized before being simmered and a tomato product is added. These extra steps provide the finished stock with a rich dark color and a more intense flavor.

CARAMELIZING

Caramelization is the process of browning the sugars found on the surface of most foods. This gives the stock its characteristic flavor and color.

▶ **deglaze** to swirl or stir a liquid (usually wine or stock) in a sauté pan or other pan to dissolve cooked food particles remaining on the bottom; the resulting mixture often becomes the base for a sauce

▶ PROCEDURE FOR CARAMELIZING BONES

For caramelizing, do not wash or blanch the bones as this retards browning. To caramelize:

1 Place the cut-up bones in a roasting pan one layer deep. It is better to roast several pans of bones than to overfill one pan.
2 Roast the bones for approximately 1 hour in a hot oven (375°F/190°C). Stirring occasionally, brown the bones thoroughly, but do not allow them to burn.
3 Transfer the roasted bones from the pan to the stockpot.

DEGLAZING THE PAN

After the bones are caramelized, the excess fat should be removed and reserved for future use. The caramelized and coagulated proteins remaining in the roasting pan are very flavorful. To utilize them, **deglaze** the pan.

▶ **remouillage** (rhur-moo-yahj) French for "rewetting"; a stock produced by reusing the bones left from making another stock. After draining the original stock from the stockpot, add fresh mirepoix, a new sachet and enough water to cover the bones and mirepoix, and a second stock can be made. A remouillage is treated like the original stock; allow it to simmer for four to five hours before straining. A remouillage will not be as clear or as flavorful as the original stock, however. It is often used to make glazes or in place of water when making stocks.

▶ PROCEDURE FOR DEGLAZING THE PAN

1. Place the pan on the stove top over medium heat, and add enough water to cover the bottom of the pan approximately ½ inch (1.2 centimeters) deep.
2. Stir and scrape the pan bottom to dissolve and remove all the caramelized materials while the water heats.
3. Pour the deglazing liquid (also known as the deglazing liquor) over the bones in the stockpot.

▶ PROCEDURE FOR CARAMELIZING MIREPOIX

1. Add a little of the reserved fat from the roasted bones to the roasting pan after it has been deglazed. (Or use a sautoir large enough to contain all the mirepoix comfortably.)
2. Sauté the mirepoix, browning all the vegetables well and evenly without burning them.
3. Add the caramelized mirepoix to the stockpot.

Almost any tomato product can be used in a brown stock: fresh tomatoes, canned whole tomatoes, crushed tomatoes, tomato purée or paste. If using a concentrated tomato product such as paste or purée, use approximately half the amount by weight of fresh or canned tomatoes. The tomato product should be added to the stockpot when the mirepoix is added.

RECIPE 9.2

BROWN STOCK

Mise en Place

- ▶ Cut up and wash bones.
- ▶ Peel and chop onions, carrots and celery for mirepoix.
- ▶ Prepare herb sachet.

Yield: 2 gal. (8 lt)

Bones, veal or beef, cut in 3- to 4-in. (8- to 10-cm) pieces	15 lb.	7 kg
Cold water	3 gal.	11 lt
Mirepoix	2 lb.	1 kg
Tomato paste	8 oz.	250 g
Sachet:		
Bay leaves	2	2
Dried thyme	½ tsp.	2 ml
Peppercorns, crushed	½ tsp.	2 ml
Garlic cloves, crushed	3	3
Parsley stems	12	12

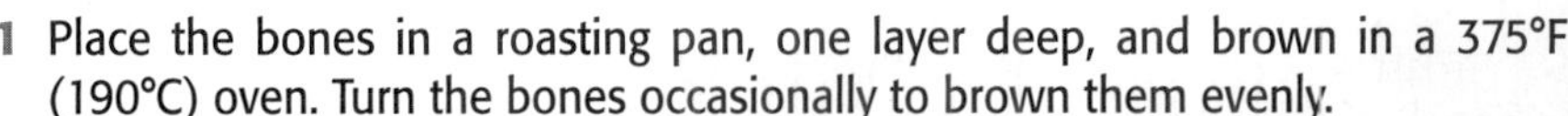

1. Place the bones in a roasting pan, one layer deep, and brown in a 375°F (190°C) oven. Turn the bones occasionally to brown them evenly.
2. Remove the bones and place them in a stockpot. Pour off the fat from the roasting pan and reserve it.
3. Deglaze the roasting pan with part of the cold water.
4. Add the deglazing liquor and the rest of the cold water to the bones, covering them completely. Bring to a boil and reduce to a simmer.
5. Add a portion of the reserved fat to the roasting pan and sauté the mirepoix until evenly browned. Then add it to the simmering stock.
6. Add the tomato paste and sachet to the stock and continue to simmer for 6 to 8 hours, skimming as necessary.
7. Strain, cool and refrigerate.

1 Caramelizing the bones.

Approximate values per 1-fl.-oz. (30-ml) serving: **Calories** 3, **Total fat** 0 g, **Saturated fat** 0 g, **Cholesterol** 0.3 mg, **Sodium** 105 mg, **Total carbohydrates** 0 g, **Protein** 0 g, **Claims**—fat free; low sodium

2 Deglazing the pan with water.

3 Caramelizing the mirepoix.

4 Adding the proper amount of water.

FISH STOCK AND FISH FUMET

A fish stock and a fish fumet (foo-may) are similar and can be used interchangeably in most recipes. Both are clear with a pronounced fish flavor and very light body. A fumet, however, is more strongly flavored and aromatic and contains an acidic ingredient such as white wine and/or lemon juice.

Only the bones and heads of lean fish and crustacean shells are used to make fish stock. Oily fish such as mackerel, salmon or tuna are not used as their pronounced flavor would overwhelm the stock. The fish bones and shells used to make a fish stock or fumet should be washed but never blanched because blanching removes too much flavor. They may be **sweated** without browning if desired, however. Because of the size and structure of fish bones and crustacean shells, stocks and fumets made from them require much less cooking time than even a chicken stock; 30 to 45 minutes is usually sufficient to extract full flavor. Mirepoix or other vegetables should be cut small so that all of their flavors can be extracted during the short cooking time.

▶ **sweat** to cook a food in a pan (usually covered), without browning, over low heat until the item softens and releases moisture; sweating allows the food to release its flavor more quickly when cooked with other foods

The procedure for making a fish stock is very similar to that for making a white stock.

COMMERCIAL BASES

Commercially produced flavor (or convenience) bases are widely used in food service operations. They are powdered or paste flavorings added to water to create stocks or, when used in smaller amounts, to enhance the flavor of sauces and soups. These products are also sold as bouillon cubes or granules. Although inferior to well-made stocks, flavor bases do reduce the labor involved in the production of stocks, sauces and soups. Used properly, they also ensure a consistent product. Because bases do not contain gelatin, stocks and sauces made from them do not benefit from reduction.

Bases vary greatly in quality and price. Sodium (salt) is the main ingredient in many bases. Better bases are made primarily of meat, poultry or fish extracts. To judge the quality of a flavor base, prepare it according to package directions and compare the flavor to that of a well-made stock. The flavor base can be improved by adding a mirepoix, standard sachet and a few appropriate bones to the mixture, then simmering for one or two hours. It can then be strained, stored and used like a regular stock. Although convenience bases are widely used in the industry, it is important to remember that even the best base is a poor substitute for a well-made stock.

RECIPE 9.3 FISH STOCK

Mise en Place

- ▶ Wash fish bones or shells.
- ▶ Peel and chop onions, carrots and celery for mirepoix.
- ▶ Prepare herb sachet.

Adding cold water to fish bones.

Yield: 1 gal. (4 lt)

Mirepoix, small dice	1 lb.	450 g
Mushroom trimmings	8 oz.	250 g
Clarified butter	2 fl. oz.	60 ml
Fish bones or crustacean shells	10 lb.	4.5 kg
Water	5 qt.	5 lt
Sachet:		
Bay leaves	2	2
Dried thyme	1/2 tsp.	2 ml
Peppercorns, crushed	1/4 tsp.	1 ml
Parsley stems	8	8

1. Sweat mirepoix and mushroom trimmings in butter until tender for 1 to 2 minutes.
2. Combine all ingredients except the sachet in a stockpot.
3. Bring to a simmer and skim impurities as necessary.
4. Add the sachet and simmer uncovered for 30 to 45 minutes.
5. Strain, cool and refrigerate.

Approximate values per 1-fl.-oz. (30-ml) serving: **Calories** 5, **Total fat** 0 g, **Saturated fat** 0 g, **Cholesterol** 0 mg, **Sodium** 100 mg, **Total carbohydrates** 0 g, **Protein** 1 g, **Claims**—fat free; low sodium

A fish stock is sometimes used to make a fish fumet; if so, the resulting product is very strongly flavored. A fish fumet is also flavored with white wine and lemon juice. When making a fumet, sweat the bones and vegetables before adding the cooking liquid and seasonings.

RECIPE 9.4 FISH FUMET

Mise en Place

- ▶ Peel onion and chop into small dice.
- ▶ Cut up and wash bones.

Yield: 2 gal. (8 lt)

Whole butter	2 oz.	60 g
Onions, small dice	1 lb.	500 g
Parsley stems	12	12
Fish bones	10 lb.	5 kg
Dry white wine	1 1/2 pt.	750 ml
Lemon juice	2 fl. oz.	60 ml
Cold water or fish stock	7 qt.	7 lt
Mushroom trimmings	2 oz.	60 g
Fresh thyme	1 sprig	1 sprig
Lemon slices	10	10

1. Melt the butter in a stockpot.
2. Add the onion, parsley stems and fish bones. Cover the pot and sweat the bones over low heat.
3. Sprinkle the bones with the wine and lemon juice.
4. Add the cold water or stock, mushroom trimmings, thyme and lemon slices. Bring to a boil, reduce to a simmer and cook approximately 30 minutes, skimming frequently.
5. Strain, cool and refrigerate.

Approximate values per 1-fl.-oz. (30-ml) serving: **Calories** 5, **Total fat** 0.7 g, **Saturated fat** 0.2 g, **Cholesterol** 0.5 mg, **Sodium** 90 g, **Total carbohydrates** 0 g, **Protein** 1 g, **Claims**—fat free; low sodium

1 Sweating the onions, parsley stems and fish bones.

2 Adding cold water and seasonings.

VEGETABLE STOCK

A good vegetable stock should be clear and light-colored. Because no animal products are used, it has no gelatin content and little body. A vegetable stock can be used instead of a meat-based stock in most recipes. This substitution is useful when preparing vegetarian dishes or as a lighter, more healthful alternative when preparing sauces and soups. Although almost any combination of vegetables can be used for stock making, more variety is not always better. Sometimes a vegetable stock made with one or two vegetables that complement the finished dish particularly well will produce better results than a stock made with many vegetables. Strongly flavored vegetables such as asparagus, broccoli and other cruciferous vegetables, spinach and bitter greens, for example, should be avoided when making an all-purpose vegetable stock. Potatoes and other starchy vegetables will cloud the stock and should not be used unless clarity is not a concern.

VEGETABLE STOCK

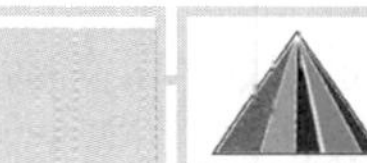

RECIPE 9.5

Yield: 1 gal. (4 lt)

Vegetable oil	2 fl. oz.	60 ml
Mirepoix, small dice	2 lb.	900 g
Leek, whites and greens, chopped	8 oz.	250 g
Garlic cloves, chopped	4	4
Fennel, small dice	4 oz.	120 g
Turnip, diced	2 oz.	60 g
Tomato, diced	2 oz.	60 g
White wine	8 fl. oz.	250 ml
Water	1 gal.	4 lt
Sachet:		
Bay leaf	1	1
Dried thyme	½ tsp.	2 ml
Peppercorns, crushed	¼ tsp.	1 ml
Parsley stems	8	8

1. Heat the oil. Add the vegetables and sweat for 10 minutes.
2. Add the wine, water and sachet.
3. Bring the mixture to a boil, reduce to a simmer and cook for 45 minutes.
4. Strain, cool and refrigerate.

Approximate values per 1-fl.-oz. (30-ml) serving: **Calories** 5, **Total fat** 0 g, **Saturated fat** 0 g, **Cholesterol** 0 mg, **Sodium** 0 mg, **Total carbohydrates** 0 g, **Protein** 0 g, **Claims**—fat free; low calorie

Mise en Place

- ▶ Peel and chop onions, carrots and celery for mirepoix.
- ▶ Clean, peel and chop leeks, garlic cloves, fennel and turnip.
- ▶ Wash and dice tomato.
- ▶ Prepare herb sachet.

Adding cold water to the sweated vegetables.

COURT BOUILLON

A court bouillon (bool-yawn), though not actually a stock, is prepared in much the same manner as stocks, so it is included here. A court bouillon (French for "short broth") is a flavored liquid, usually water and wine or vinegar, in which vegetables and seasonings have been simmered to impart their flavors and aromas.

Court bouillon is most commonly used to poach foods such as fish and shellfish. Recipes vary depending on the foods to be poached. Although a court bouillon can be made in advance and refrigerated for later use, its simplicity lends itself to fresh preparation whenever needed.

RECIPE 9.6

COURT BOUILLON

Mise en Place

- ▶ Peel and chop onions, carrots and celery for mirepoix.
- ▶ Crush peppercorns.

Yield: 1 gal. (4 lt)

Water	1 gal.	4 lt
Vinegar	6 fl. oz.	180 ml
Lemon juice	2 fl. oz.	60 ml
Mirepoix	1 lb. 8 oz.	650 g
Bay leaves	4	4
Peppercorns, crushed	1 tsp.	5 ml
Dried thyme	1 pinch	1 pinch
Parsley stems	1 bunch	1 bunch

1. Combine all ingredients and bring to a boil.
2. Reduce to a simmer and cook for 45 minutes.
3. Strain and use immediately or cool and refrigerate.

Note: This recipe can be used for poaching almost any fish, but it is particularly well suited to salmon, trout and shellfish. When poaching freshwater fish, replace the water and vinegar with equal parts white wine and water.

Approximate values per 1-fl.-oz. (30-ml) serving: **Calories** 3, **Total fat** 0 g, **Saturated fat** 0 g, **Cholesterol** 0 mg, **Sodium** 0 mg, **Total carbohydrates** 0 g, **Protein** 0 g, **Claims**—fat free; low sodium

NAGE

An aromatic court bouillon is sometimes served as a light sauce or broth with fish or shellfish. This is known as a nage (nahj), and dishes served in this manner are described as *à la nage* (French for "swimming"). After the fish or shellfish is cooked, additional herbs and aromatic vegetables are added to the cooking liquid, which is then reduced slightly and strained.

Alternatively, the used court bouillon can be strained, chilled, and clarified with egg whites and aromatic vegetables in the same manner as a consommé, discussed in Chapter 10, Soups. Finally, whole butter or cream may be added to a nage for richness.

GLAZE

A glaze is the dramatic reduction and concentration of a stock. One gallon (4 liters) of stock produces only 1 to 2 cups (2.5 to 5 deciliters) of glaze. *Glace de viande* is made from brown stock, reduced until it becomes dark and syrupy. *Glace de volaille* is made from chicken stock, and *glace de poisson* from fish stock.

Glazes are added to soups or sauces to increase and intensify flavors. They are also used as a source of intense flavoring for several of the small sauces discussed next.

▶ PROCEDURE FOR REDUCING A STOCK TO A GLAZE

1. Simmer the stock over very low heat. Be careful not to let it burn, and skim it often.
2. As it reduces and the volume decreases, transfer the liquid into progressively smaller saucepans. Strain the liquid each time it is transferred into a smaller saucepan.
3. Strain it a final time, cool and refrigerate. A properly made glaze will keep for several months under refrigeration.

1 A properly thickened glaze made from brown stock.

2 Chilled glace de viande.

Table 9.1 TROUBLESHOOTING CHART FOR STOCKS

PROBLEM	REASON	SOLUTION
Cloudy	Impurities Stock boiled during cooking	Start stock in cold water Strain through layers of cheesecloth
Lack of flavor	Not cooked long enough Inadequate seasoning Improper ratio of bones to water	Increase cooking time Add more flavoring ingredients Add more bones
Lack of color	Improperly caramelized bones and mirepoix Not cooked long enough	Caramelize bones and mirepoix until darker Cook longer
Lack of body	Wrong bones used Insufficient reduction Improper ratio of bones to water	Use bones with a higher content of connective tissue Cook longer Add more bones
Too salty	Commercial base used Salt added during cooking	Change base or make own stock; do not salt stock

▶ SAUCES

With a few exceptions, a sauce is a liquid plus thickening agent plus seasonings. Any chef can produce fine sauces by learning to do the following:

1. Make good stocks.
2. Use thickening agents properly to achieve the desired texture, flavor and appearance.
3. Use seasonings properly to achieve the desired flavors.

Classic hot sauces are divided into two groups: **mother** or **leading sauces** (Fr. *sauce mère*) and **small** or **compound sauces.** The five classic mother sauces are béchamel, velouté, espagnole (brown), tomato and hollandaise. Except for hollandaise, leading sauces are rarely served as is; more often they are used to create the many small sauces.

Not all sauces fall into the traditional classifications, however. Some sauces use purées of fruits or vegetables as their base; they are known as **coulis.** Others, such as **beurre blanc** (French for "white butter") and **beurre rouge** ("red butter"), are based on an acidic reduction in which whole butter is incorporated. **Flavored butters, flavored oils, salsas, relishes** and **pan gravy** are also used as sauces in modern food service operations.

THICKENING AGENTS

One of the most traditional and commonly used methods for thickening sauces is through the gelatinization of starches. As discussed in Chapter 8, Principles of Cooking, gelatinization is the process by which starch granules absorb moisture when placed in a liquid and heated. As the moisture is absorbed, the product thickens. Starches generally used to thicken sauces are flour, cornstarch and arrowroot. Gelatinization may sound easy, but it takes practice to produce a good sauce that:

- Is lump-free
- Has a good clean flavor that is not pasty or floury
- Has a consistency that will coat the back of a spoon (the French call this *nappe*)
- Will not separate or break when the sauce is held or reduced

ROUX

Roux (roo) is the principal means used to thicken sauces. It is a combination of equal parts, by weight, of flour and fat, cooked together to form a paste. Cooking the flour in fat coats the starch granules with the fat and prevents them from lumping together or forming lumps when introduced into a liquid. In large production kitchens, large amounts of roux are prepared and held for use as needed. Smaller operations may make roux as required for each recipe.

A SAUCY HISTORY

The word *sauce* is derived from the Latin word *salus,* meaning "salted." This derivation is entirely logical. For millennia, salt has been the basic condiment for enhancing or disguising the flavor of many foods.

Cooks of ancient Rome flavored dishes with *garum,* a golden-colored sauce made from fermented fish entrails combined with brine, condiments, water and wine or vinegar. They also used a sauce referred to as a "single" made from oil, wine and brine. When boiled with herbs and saffron, it became a "double" sauce. To this the Byzantines later added pepper, cloves, cinnamon, cardamom and coriander or spikenard (a fragrant ointment made from grains).

Medieval chefs were fond of either very spicy or sweet-and-sour sauces. A typical sauce for roasted meat consisted of powdered cinnamon, mustard, red wine and a sweetener such as honey. Bits of stale or grilled bread were used as a thickener. Other sauces were based on verjuice, an acidic stock prepared from the juice of unripe grapes. To it were added other fruit juices, honey, flower petals and herbs or spices. Perhaps this was done to hide the taste of salt-cured or less-than-fresh meats, or, more likely, to showcase the host's wealth.

Guillaume Tirel (ca. 1312–1395), who called himself **Taillevent,** was the master chef for Charles V of France. Around 1375, Taillevent wrote *Le Viandier,* the oldest known French cookbook. It includes 17 sauces. Among them is a recipe for a *cameline* sauce, made from grilled bread soaked in wine. The wine-soaked bread is then drained, squeeze-dried and ground with cinnamon, ginger, pepper, cloves and nutmeg; this mixture is diluted with vinegar. There is also a recipe for a sauce called *taillemaslée,* made of fried onions, verjuice, vinegar and mustard.

Sauces enjoyed in Renaissance Italy and France were prepared much like those of the Middle Ages, but in an important development for modern cuisine, many were based on broths thickened with cream, butter and egg yolks, and flavored with herbs and spices. Recipes for some sauces of the Renaissance, such as poivrade and Robert, are recognizable today. Many consider **François Pierre de La Varenne** (1618–1678) to be one of the founding fathers of French cuisine. His treatises, especially *Le Cuisinier français* (1651), detail the early development, methods and manners of French cuisine. His analysis and recipes mark a departure from medieval cookery and a French cuisine heavily influenced by Italian traditions. His uniquely modern writings include recipes for new foods (especially fruits and vegetables native to the Americas or the Far East) and for indigenous foods (such as saltwater fish) that were becoming more popular. La Varenne is credited with introducing roux as a thickening agent for sauces, especially velouté sauces. He emphasized the importance of *fonds* and the reduction of cooking juices to concentrate flavors. He also popularized the use of bouquets garni to flavor stocks and sauces.

Taillevent dressed as a sergeant-at-arms with three cooking pots on his shield from his grave marker.

During the early 18th century, the chef to the French Duc de Levis-Mirepoix pioneered the use of onions, celery and carrots to enhance the flavor and aroma of stocks. The mixture, named for the chef's employer, soon became the standard. An enriched stock greatly improves the quality of the sauces derived from it. Antonin Carême developed the modern system for classifying hundreds of sauces in the early 19th century. While it is unknown how many sauces Carême actually invented, he wrote treatises containing the theories and recipes for many of the sauces still used today. Carême's extravagant lists were simplified by chefs later in the 19th century, most notably by Auguste Escoffier.

There are three types of roux:

1. **White roux** is cooked only briefly and should be removed from the heat as soon as it develops a frothy, bubbly appearance. It is used in white sauces, such as béchamel, or in dishes where little or no color is desired.
2. **Blond roux** is cooked slightly longer than white roux, and should begin to take on a little color as the flour caramelizes. It is used in ivory-colored sauces, such as velouté, or where a richer flavor is desired.
3. **Brown roux** is cooked until it develops a darker color and a nutty aroma and flavor. Brown roux is used in brown sauces and dishes where a dark color is desired. It is important to remember that cooking a starch before adding a liquid breaks down the starch granules and prevents gelatinization from occurring. Therefore, because brown roux is cooked longer than white roux, more brown roux is required to thicken a given quantity of liquid.

White, Blond and Brown Roux

▶ PROCEDURE FOR PREPARING ROUX

Cooking the roux.

Whether it will be white, blond or brown, the procedure for making a roux is the same:

1. Using a heavy saucepan to prevent scorching, heat the clarified butter or other fat.
2. Add all the flour and stir to form a paste. Although all-purpose flour can be used, it is better to use cake or pastry flour because they contain a higher percentage of starch. Do not use high-gluten flour because of its greatly reduced starch content.
3. Cook the paste over medium heat until the desired color is achieved. Stir the roux often to avoid burning. Burnt roux will not thicken a liquid; it will simply add dark specks and an undesirable flavor.

The temperature and amount of roux being prepared determine the exact length of cooking time. Generally, however, a white roux needs to cook for only a few minutes, long enough to minimize the raw flour taste. Blond roux is cooked longer, until the paste begins to change to a slightly darker color. Brown roux requires a much longer cooking time to develop its characteristic color and aroma. A good roux will be stiff, not runny or pourable.

▶ INCORPORATING ROUX INTO A LIQUID

There are two ways to incorporate roux into a liquid without causing lumps:

1. Cold stock can be added to the hot roux while stirring vigorously with a whisk.
2. Room-temperature roux can be added to a hot stock while stirring vigorously with a whisk.

When the roux and the liquid are completely incorporated and the sauce begins to boil, it is necessary to cook the sauce for a time to remove any raw flour taste that may remain. Most chefs feel a minimum of 20 minutes is necessary.

When thickening stock with roux, either (a) add cold stock to hot roux, or (b) add cold roux to hot stock.

▶ GUIDELINES FOR USING ROUX

1. Avoid using aluminum pots. The scraping action of the whisk will turn light sauces gray and will impart a metallic flavor.
2. Use sufficiently heavy pots to prevent sauces from scorching or burning during extended cooking times.
3. Avoid extreme temperatures. Roux should be no colder than room temperature so that the fat is not fully solidified. Extremely hot roux is dangerous and can spatter when combined with a liquid. Stocks should not be ice cold when combined with roux; the roux will become very cold, and the solidified pieces may be very difficult to work out with a whisk.
4. Avoid overthickening. See Table 9.2. Roux does not begin to thicken a sauce until the sauce is almost at the boiling point; the thickening action continues for several minutes while the sauce simmers. If a sauce is to cook for a long time, it will also be thickened by reduction.

CORNSTARCH

Cornstarch, a very fine white powder, is a pure starch derived from corn. It is used widely as a thickening agent for hot and cold sauces and is especially pop-

Table 9.2 **PROPORTIONS OF ROUX TO LIQUID**

FLOUR	+	BUTTER	=	ROUX	+	LIQUID	=	SAUCE
6 oz./190 g	+	6 oz./190 g	=	12 oz./375 g	+	1 gal./4 lt	=	light
8 oz./250 g	+	8 oz./250 g	=	1 lb./500 g	+	1 gal./4 lt	=	medium
12 oz./375 g	+	12 oz./375 g	=	24 oz./750 g	+	1 gal./4 lt	=	heavy

Variables: The starch content of a flour determines its thickening power. Cake flour, being lowest in protein and highest in starch, has more thickening power than bread flour, which is high in protein and low in starch. In addition, a dark roux has less thickening power than a lighter one, so more will be needed to thicken an equal amount of liquid.

ular in Asian cuisines for thickening sauces and soups. Liquids thickened with cornstarch have a glossy sheen that may or may not be desirable.

One unit of cornstarch thickens about twice as much liquid as an equal unit of flour. Sauces thickened with cornstarch are less stable than those thickened with roux because cornstarch can break down and lose its thickening power after prolonged heating. Products thickened with cornstarch should not be reheated.

Incorporating Cornstarch

Cornstarch must be mixed with a cool liquid before it is introduced into a hot one. The cool liquid separates the grains of starch and allows them to begin absorbing liquid without lumping. A solution of a starch and a cool liquid is called a **slurry.**

▶ **slurry** a mixture of raw starch and cold liquid used for thickening

The starch slurry may be added to either a hot or cold liquid. If added to a hot liquid, it must be stirred continuously during incorporation. Unlike roux, cornstarch begins to thicken almost immediately if the liquid is hot. Sauces thickened with cornstarch must be cooked gently until the raw starch flavor disappears, usually about 5 minutes.

ARROWROOT

Arrowroot, derived from the roots of several tropical plants, is similar in texture, appearance and thickening power to cornstarch and is used in exactly the same manner. Arrowroot does not break down as quickly as cornstarch, and it produces a slightly clearer finished product although it is much more expensive.

BEURRE MANIÉ

Beurre manié (burr mahn-yay) is a combination of equal amounts, by weight, of flour and soft whole butter. Beurre manié is used for quick thickening at the end of the cooking process. The butter also adds shine and flavor to the sauce as it melts.

▶ PROCEDURE FOR USING BEURRE MANIÉ

1 Knead flour and butter together until smooth.

2 Form the mixture into pea-sized balls, then whisk the beurre manié gradually into a simmering sauce.

LIAISON

Unlike the thickeners already described, a liaison (lee-yeh-zon) does not thicken a sauce through gelatinization. A liaison is a mixture of egg yolks and heavy cream; it adds richness and smoothness with minimal thickening. Special care must be taken to prevent the yolks from coagulating when they are added to a hot liquid because this could curdle the sauce.

▶ PROCEDURE FOR USING A LIAISON

1. Whisk together one part egg yolk and three parts whipping cream. Combining the yolk with cream raises the temperature at which the yolk's proteins coagulate, making it easier to incorporate them into a sauce without lumping or curdling.
2. **Temper** the egg yolk and cream mixture by slowly adding a small amount of the hot liquid while stirring continuously.
3. When enough of the hot liquid has been added to the liaison to warm it thoroughly, begin adding the warmed liaison to the remaining hot liquid. Be sure to stir the mixture carefully to prevent the yolk from overcooking or lumping. Plain egg yolks coagulate at temperatures between 149°F and 158°F (65°C and 70°C). Mixing them with cream raises the temperatures at which they coagulate to approximately 180°F–185°F (82°C–85°C). Temperatures over 185°F (85°C) will cause the yolks to curdle. Great care must be taken to hold the sauce above 135°F (57°C) for food safety and sanitation reasons, yet below 185°F (85°C) to prevent curdling.

▶ **tempering** gradually raising the temperature of a cold liquid such as eggs by slowly stirring in a hot liquid

1 Adding hot liquid to the egg yolk and cream mixture.

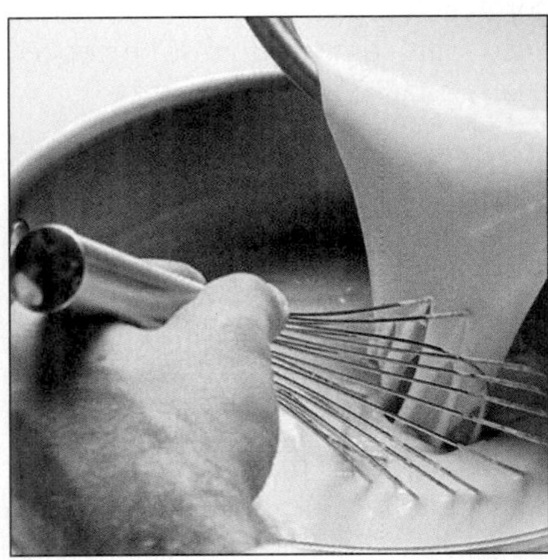

2 Adding the tempered egg yolk and cream liaison to the hot liquid.

EMULSIFICATION

Sauces can also be thickened by the process of **emulsification,** whereby unmixable liquids such as oil and water are forced into a uniform, creamy state. Usually an emulsifying agent such as the lecithin found in egg yolks must be present to aid in the process. The action of stirring or whisking a sauce to incorporate the ingredients will produce an emulsion that is **permanent, semipermanent** or **temporary.** A permanent emulsion, such as that formed when making mayonnaise, will last for several days. A semipermanent emulsion will last for a few hours. Hollandaise sauce is one example of a semipermanent emulsion. A temporary emulsion will last very briefly and usually does not contain an emulsifying agent. Rather, vigorous whisking aerates the mixture, causing the temporary suspension of liquids. Such is the case when oil and vinegar are whisked together to make a simple salad dressing. Emulsified sauces are discussed in detail in Chapter 23, Salads and Salad Dressings.

▶ **emulsification** the process by which generally unmixable liquids, such as oil and water, are forced into a uniform distribution

FINISHING TECHNIQUES

REDUCTION

As sauces cook, moisture is released in the form of steam. As steam escapes, the remaining ingredients concentrate, thickening the sauce and strengthening the flavors. This process, known as **reduction,** is commonly used to thicken sauces because no starches or other flavor-altering ingredients are needed. Sauces are often finished by allowing them to reduce until the desired consistency is reached.

▶ **reduction** cooking a liquid such as a sauce until its quantity decreases through evaporation. To reduce by one-half means that one-half of the original amount remains. To reduce by three-fourths means that only one-fourth of the original amount remains. To reduce *au sec* means that the liquid is cooked until nearly dry.

STRAINING

Smoothness is important to the success of most sauces. They can be strained through either a china cap lined with several layers of cheesecloth or a fine mesh chinois. As discussed later, often vegetables, herbs, spices and other seasonings are added to a sauce for flavor. Straining removes these ingredients as well as any lumps of roux or thickener remaining in the sauce after the desired flavor and consistency have been reached.

MONTER AU BEURRE

Monter au beurre (mohn-tay ah burr) is the process of swirling or whisking whole butter into a sauce to give it shine, flavor and richness. Compound or flavored butters, discussed later, can be used in place of whole butter to add specific flavors. Monter au beurre is widely used to enrich and finish small sauces.

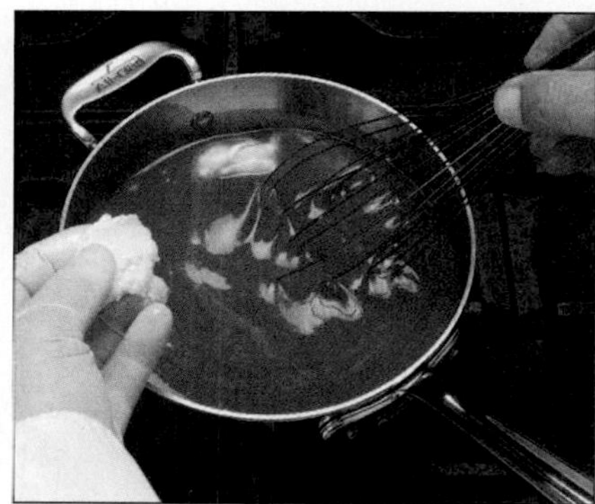

Using a wire whisk to finish a sauce with whole butter.

SAUCE FAMILIES

Leading or **mother sauces** are the foundation for the entire classic repertoire of hot sauces. The five leading sauces—béchamel, velouté, espagnole (also known as brown), tomato and hollandaise—can be seasoned and garnished to create a wide variety of small or compound sauces. These five leading sauces are distinguished principally by the liquids and thickeners used to create them. See Table 9.3.

Small or **compound sauces** are grouped into families based on their leading sauce. Some small sauces have a variety of uses; others are traditional accompaniments for specific foods. A small sauce may be named for its ingredients, place of origin or creator. Although there are numerous classic small sauces, we have included only a few of the more popular ones following each of the leading sauce recipes.

THE BÉCHAMEL FAMILY

Named for its creator, Louis de Béchameil (1630–1703), steward to Louis XIV of France, béchamel (bay-shah-mell) sauce is the easiest mother sauce to prepare. Traditionally, it is made by adding heavy cream to a thick veal velouté. Although some chefs still believe a béchamel should contain veal stock, today the sauce is almost always made by thickening scalded milk with a white roux and adding seasonings. Often used for vegetable, egg and gratin dishes, béchamel has fallen into relative disfavor recently because of its rich, heavy nature. It is nevertheless important to understand its production and its place in traditional sauce making.

A properly made béchamel is rich, creamy and absolutely smooth with no hint of graininess. The flavors of the onion and clove used to season it should be apparent but not overwhelm the sauce's clean, milky taste. The sauce should be the color of heavy cream and have a deep luster. It should be thick enough to coat foods lightly but should not taste like the roux used to thicken it.

Table 9.3 **SAUCE FAMILIES**

MOTHER SAUCE	LIQUID	THICKENER
Béchamel	Milk	Roux
Velouté	White stock	Roux
Veal velouté	Veal stock	
Chicken velouté	Chicken stock	
Fish velouté	Fish stock	
Espagnole (brown sauce)	Brown stock	Roux
Tomato sauce	Tomato	Roux (optional)
Hollandaise	Butter	Egg yolks

BÉCHAMEL

RECIPE 9.7

Yield: 1 gal. (4 lt)

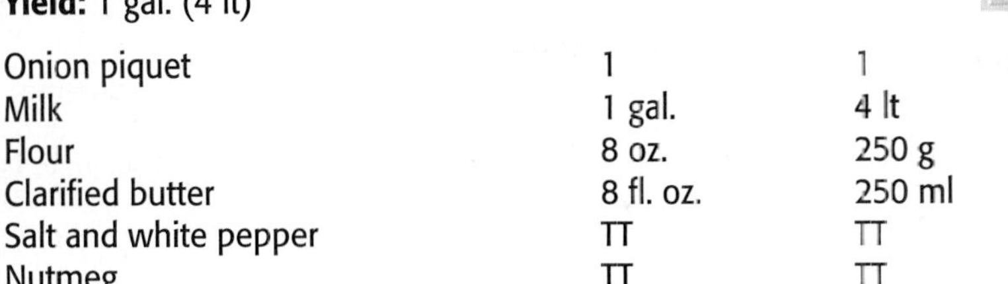

Onion piquet	1	1
Milk	1 gal.	4 lt
Flour	8 oz.	250 g
Clarified butter	8 fl. oz.	250 ml
Salt and white pepper	TT	TT
Nutmeg	TT	TT

1. Add the onion piquet to the milk in a heavy saucepan and simmer for 20 minutes.
2. In a separate pot, make a white roux with the flour and butter.
3. Remove the onion piquet from the milk. Gradually add the hot milk to the roux while stirring constantly with a whisk to prevent lumps. Bring to a boil.
4. Reduce the sauce to a simmer, add the seasonings and continue cooking for 30 minutes.
5. Strain the sauce through a china cap lined with cheesecloth. Melted butter can be carefully ladled over the surface of the sauce to prevent a skin from forming. Hold for service or cool in a water bath.

Approximate values per 6-fl.-oz. (180-ml) serving: **Calories** 240, **Total fat** 15 g, **Saturated fat** 9 g, **Cholesterol** 50 mg, **Sodium** 180 mg, **Total carbohydrates** 18 g, **Protein** 7 g, **Vitamin A** 15%, **Calcium** 25%

Mise en Place

▶ Tack a bay leaf onto a small peeled onion using a clove to make onion piquet.

Small Béchamel Sauces

With a good béchamel, producing the small sauces in its family is quite simple. The quantities given are for 1 quart (1 liter) of béchamel. The final step for each recipe is to season to taste with salt and pepper.

CREAM SAUCE Add to béchamel 8–12 fluid ounces (250–360 milliliters) scalded cream and a few drops of lemon juice.

CHEESE Add to béchamel 8 ounces (250 grams) grated Cheddar or American cheese, a dash of Worcestershire sauce and 1 tablespoon (15 milliliters) dry mustard.

MORNAY Add to béchamel 4 ounces (120 grams) grated Gruyère and 1 ounce (30 grams) grated Parmesan. Thin as desired with scalded cream. Remove the sauce from the heat and swirl in 2 ounces (60 grams) whole butter.

NANTUA Add to béchamel 4 fluid ounces (120 milliliters) heavy cream and 6 ounces (180 grams) crayfish butter. Add paprika to achieve the desired color. Garnish the finished sauce with diced crayfish meat.

SOUBISE (MODERN) Sweat 1 pound (500 grams) diced onions in 1 ounce (30 grams) whole butter without browning. Add béchamel and simmer until the onions are fully cooked. Strain through a fine chinois.

Table 9.4 **VELOUTÉ SAUCES**

Fish stock	+	Roux	=	Velouté				
Chicken stock	+	Roux	=	Velouté	+	Cream	=	Suprême
Chicken stock	+	Roux	=	Velouté	+	Liaison and lemon	=	Allemande
Veal stock	+	Roux	=	Velouté	+	Liaison and lemon	=	Allemande

THE VELOUTÉ FAMILY

Velouté (veh-loo-TAY) sauces are made by thickening a white stock or fish stock with roux. The white stock can be made from veal or chicken bones. A velouté sauce made from veal or chicken stock is usually used to make one of two intermediary sauces—allemande and suprême—from which many small sauces are derived. **Allemande** sauce is made by adding lemon juice and a liaison to either a veal or chicken velouté. (The stock used depends on the dish with which the sauce will be served.) **Suprême** sauce is made by adding cream to a chicken velouté. See Table 9.4.

▶ **allemande** (ah-leh-MAHND) an intermediary sauce made by adding lemon juice and a liaison to chicken or veal velouté

▶ **suprême** (soc-prem) an intermediary sauce made by adding cream to chicken velouté

A properly made velouté should be rich, smooth and lump-free. If made from chicken or fish stock, it should taste of chicken or fish. A velouté made from veal stock should have a more neutral flavor. The sauce should be ivory-colored, with a deep luster. It should be thick enough to cling to foods without tasting like the roux used to thicken it.

RECIPE 9.8

VELOUTÉ

Yield: 1 gal. (4 lt)

Clarified butter	8 fl. oz.	250 ml
Flour	8 oz.	250 g
Chicken, veal or fish stock	5 qt.	5 lt
Salt and white pepper	TT	TT

1. Heat the butter in a heavy saucepan. Add the flour and cook to make a blond roux.
2. Gradually add the stock to the roux, stirring constantly with a whisk to prevent lumps. Bring to a boil and reduce to a simmer. (Seasonings are optional; their use depends on the seasonings in the stock and the sauce's intended use.)
3. Simmer and reduce to 1 gallon (4 liters), approximately 30 minutes.
4. Strain through a china cap lined with cheesecloth.
5. Melted butter may be carefully ladled over the surface of the sauce to prevent a skin from forming. Hold for service or cool in a water bath.

Approximate values per 1-fl.-oz. (30-ml) serving: **Calories** 25, **Total fat** 1.5 g, **Saturated fat** 1 g, **Cholesterol** 5 mg, **Sodium** 140 mg, **Total carbohydrates** 2 g, **Protein** 1 g

Small Fish Velouté Sauces

A few small sauces can be made from fish velouté. The quantities given are for 1 quart (1 liter) fish velouté sauce. The final step for each recipe is to season to taste with salt and pepper.

BERCY Sauté 2 ounces (60 grams) finely diced shallots in butter. Then add 8 fluid ounces (250 milliliters) dry white wine and 8 fluid ounces (250 milliliters) fish stock. Reduce this mixture by one-third and add the fish velouté. Finish with butter and garnish with chopped parsley.

CARDINAL Add 8 fluid ounces (250 milliliters) fish stock to 1 quart (1 liter) fish velouté. Reduce this mixture by half and add 1 pint (500 milliliters) heavy cream and a dash of cayenne pepper. Bring to a boil and swirl in 1½ ounces (45 grams) lobster butter. Garnish with chopped lobster coral at service time.

NORMANDY Add 4 ounces (120 grams) mushroom trimmings and 4 fluid ounces (120 milliliters) fish stock to 1 quart (1 liter) fish velouté. Reduce by one-third and finish with an egg yolk and cream liaison. Strain through a fine chinois.

ALLEMANDE SAUCE

RECIPE 9.9

Yield: 1 gal. (4 lt)

Veal or chicken velouté sauce	1 gal.	4 lt
Egg yolks	8	8
Heavy cream	24 fl. oz.	675 ml
Lemon juice	1 fl. oz.	30 ml
Salt and white pepper	TT	TT

1. Bring the velouté to a simmer.
2. In a stainless steel bowl, whip the egg yolks with the cream to create a liaison. Ladle approximately one-third of the hot velouté sauce into this mixture, while whisking, to temper the yolk-and-cream mixture.
3. When one-third of the velouté has been incorporated into the now-warmed yolk-and-cream mixture, gradually add the liaison to the remaining velouté sauce while whisking continuously.
4. Reheat the sauce. Do not let it boil.
5. Add the lemon juice; season with salt and white pepper to taste.
6. Strain through a china cap lined with cheesecloth.

Approximate values per 1-fl.-oz. (30-ml) serving: **Calories** 40, **Total fat** 3.5 g, **Saturated fat** 2 g, **Cholesterol** 25 mg, **Sodium** 95 mg, **Total carbohydrates** 1 g, **Protein** 1 g, **Vitamin A** 4%

Small Allemande Sauces

Several small sauces are easily produced from an allemande sauce made with either a chicken or veal velouté. The quantities given are for 1 quart (1 liter) allemande. The final step for each recipe is to season to taste with salt and pepper.

AURORA Add to allemande 2 ounces (60 grams) tomato paste and finish with 1 ounce (30 grams) butter.

HORSERADISH Add to allemande 4 fluid ounces (120 milliliters) heavy cream and 1 teaspoon (5 milliliters) dry mustard. Just before service add 2 ounces (60 grams) freshly grated horseradish. The horseradish should not be cooked with the sauce.

MUSHROOM Sauté 4 ounces (120 grams) sliced mushrooms in ½ ounce (15 grams) whole butter; add 2 teaspoons (10 milliliters) lemon juice. Then add the allemande to the mushrooms. Do not strain.

POULETTE Sauté 8 ounces (250 grams) sliced mushrooms and ½ ounce (15 grams) diced shallot in 1 ounce (30 grams) whole butter. Add to the allemande; then add 2 fluid ounces (60 milliliters) heavy cream. Finish with lemon juice to taste and 1 tablespoon (15 milliliters) chopped parsley.

RECIPE 9.10

SUPRÊME SAUCE

Yield: 1 gal. (4 lt)

Chicken velouté sauce	1 gal.	4 lt
Mushroom trimmings	8 oz.	225 g
Heavy cream	1 qt.	1 lt
Salt and white pepper	TT	TT

1. Simmer the velouté sauce with the mushroom trimmings until reduced by one-fourth.
2. Gradually whisk in the cream and return to a simmer.
3. Adjust the seasonings.
4. Strain through a china cap lined with cheesecloth.

Approximate values per 1-fl.-oz. (30-ml) serving: **Calories** 45, **Total fat** 4 g, **Saturated fat** 2.5 g, **Cholesterol** 15 mg, **Sodium** 95 mg, **Total carbohydrates** 1 g, **Protein** 1 g, **Vitamin A** 4%

Small Suprême Sauces

The following small sauces are easily made from a suprême sauce. The quantities given are for 1 quart (1 liter) suprême sauce. The final step for each recipe is to season to taste with salt and pepper.

ALBUFERA Add to suprême sauce 3 fluid ounces (90 milliliters) glace de volaille and 2 ounces (60 grams) red pepper butter.

HUNGARIAN Sweat 2 ounces (60 grams) diced onion in 1 tablespoon (15 milliliters) whole butter. Add 1 tablespoon (15 milliliters) paprika. Stir in suprême sauce. Cook for 2 to 3 minutes, strain and finish with whole butter.

IVORY Add to suprême sauce 3 fluid ounces (90 milliliters) glace de volaille.

THE ESPAGNOLE FAMILY

The mother sauce of the espagnole (ess-spah-nyol) or brown sauce family is full-bodied and rich. It is made from a brown stock to which brown roux, mirepoix and tomato purée have been added. Most often this sauce is used to produce demi-glace. Brown stock is also used to make jus lié. Demi-glace and jus lié are intermediary sauces used to create the small sauces of the espagnole family.

RECIPE 9.11

ESPAGNOLE (BROWN SAUCE)

Mise en Place

- ▶ Peel and chop onions, carrots and celery for mirepoix.
- ▶ Prepare herb sachet.

Yield: 1 gal. (4 lt)

Mirepoix, medium dice	2 lb.	1 kg
Clarified butter	8 fl. oz.	250 ml
Flour	8 oz.	250 g
Brown stock	5 qt.	5 lt
Tomato purée	8 oz.	250 g
Sachet:		
Bay leaf	1	1
Dried thyme	1/2 tsp.	2 ml
Peppercorns, crushed	1/4 tsp.	1 ml
Parsley stems	8	8
Salt and pepper	TT	TT

1. Sauté the mirepoix in butter until well caramelized.
2. Add the flour and cook to make a brown roux.
3. Add the stock and tomato purée. Stir to break up any lumps of roux. Bring to a boil; reduce to a simmer.

4 Add the sachet.
5 Simmer for approximately 1½ hours, allowing the sauce to reduce. Skim the surface as needed to remove impurities.
6 Strain the sauce through a china cap lined with several layers of cheesecloth. Adjust seasonings and cool in a water bath or hold for service.

Approximate values per 1-fl.-oz. (30-ml) serving: **Calories** 35, **Total fat** 2 g, **Saturated fat** 1 g, **Cholesterol** 5 mg, **Sodium** 150 mg, **Total carbohydrates** 4 g, **Protein** 1 g, **Vitamin A** 6%, **Claims**—low fat; low calorie

Demi-Glace

Brown stock is used to make the espagnole or brown sauce described earlier. Espagnole sauce can then be made into demi-glace, which in turn is used to make the small sauces of the espagnole family. Demi-glace is half brown sauce, half brown stock, reduced by half. It is usually finished with a small amount of Madeira or sherry wine. Because demi-glace creates a richer, more flavorful base, it produces finer small sauces than those made directly from a brown sauce.

A properly made demi-glace is rich, smooth and lump-free. Its prominent roasted flavor comes from the bones used for the brown stock. There should be no taste of roux. The caramelized bones and mirepoix as well as the tomato product contribute to its glossy dark brown, almost chocolate, color. It should be thick enough to cling to food without being pasty or heavy.

DEMI-GLACE

RECIPE 9.12

Yield: 1 qt. (1 lt)

Brown stock	1 qt.	1 lt
Brown sauce	1 qt.	1 lt

1 Combine the stock and sauce in a saucepan over medium heat.
2 Simmer until the mixture is reduced by half (a yield of 1 quart or 1 liter).
3 Strain and cool in a water bath.

Approximate values per 1-fl.-oz. (30-ml) serving: **Calories** 30, **Total fat** 1.5 g, **Saturated fat** 0.5 g, **Cholesterol** 5 mg, **Sodium** 200 mg, **Total carbohydrates** 4 g, **Protein** 1 g, **Vitamin A** 6%, **Claims**—low fat; low calorie

Jus Lié

Jus lié (zhoo lee-ay), also known as fond lié, is used like a demi-glace, especially to produce small sauces. Jus lié is lighter and easier to make than a demi-glace, however. It is made in one of two ways:

1 A rich brown stock is thickened with cornstarch or arrowroot and seasoned.
2 A rich brown stock is simmered and reduced so that it thickens naturally because of the concentrated amounts of gelatin and other proteins.

The starch-thickened method is a quick alternative to the long-simmering demi-glace. But because it is simply a brown stock thickened with cornstarch or arrowroot, it will be only as good as the stock with which it was begun. Sauces made from reduced stock usually have a better flavor but can be expensive to produce because of high food costs and lengthy reduction time.

A properly made jus lié is very rich and smooth. It shares many flavor characteristics with demi-glace. Its color should be dark brown and glossy from the concentrated gelatin content. Its consistency is somewhat lighter than demi-glace, but it should still cling lightly to foods.

Small Brown Sauces

Demi-glace and jus lié are used to produce many small sauces. The quantities given are for 1 quart (1 liter) demi-glace or jus lié. The final step for each recipe is to season to taste with salt and pepper.

BORDELAISE Combine 16 fluid ounces (500 milliliters) dry red wine, 2 ounces (60 grams) chopped shallots, 1 bay leaf, 1 sprig thyme and 1 pinch black pepper in a saucepan. Reduce by three-fourths, then add demi-glace and simmer for 15 minutes. Strain through a fine chinois. Finish with 2 ounces (60 grams) whole butter and garnish with sliced, poached beef marrow.

CHASSEUR (HUNTER'S SAUCE) Sauté 4 ounces (120 grams) sliced mushrooms and ½ ounce (15 grams) diced shallots in whole butter. Add 8 fluid ounces (250 milliliters) white wine and reduce by three-fourths. Then add demi-glace and 6 ounces (170 grams) diced tomatoes; simmer for 5 minutes. Do not strain. Garnish with chopped parsley.

CHÂTEAUBRIAND Combine 16 fluid ounces (500 milliliters) dry white wine and 2 ounces (60 grams) diced shallots. Reduce the mixture by two-thirds. Add demi-glace and reduce by half. Season to taste with lemon juice and cayenne pepper. Do not strain. Swirl in 4 ounces (120 grams) whole butter to finish and garnish with chopped fresh tarragon.

CHEVREUIL Prepare a poivrade sauce but add 6 ounces (170 grams) bacon or game trimmings to the mirepoix. Finish with 4 fluid ounces (120 milliliters) red wine and a dash of cayenne pepper.

MADEIRA OR PORT Bring demi-glace to a boil and reduce slightly. Then add 4 fluid ounces (120 milliliters) Madeira wine or ruby port.

MARCHAND DE VIN Reduce 8 fluid ounces (250 milliliters) dry red wine and 2 ounces (60 grams) diced shallots by two-thirds. Then add demi-glace, simmer and strain.

MUSHROOM Blanch 8 ounces (250 grams) mushroom caps in 8 fluid ounces (250 milliliters) boiling water seasoned with salt and lemon juice. Drain the mushrooms, saving the liquid. Reduce this liquid to 2 tablespoons (30 milliliters) and add it to the demi-glace. Just before service stir in 2 ounces (60 grams) whole butter and the mushroom caps.

PÉRIGUEUX Add finely diced truffles to Madeira sauce. **Périgourdine** sauce is the same, except that the truffles are cut into relatively thick slices.

PIQUANT Combine 1 ounce (30 grams) shallots, 4 fluid ounces (120 milliliters) white wine and 4 fluid ounces (120 milliliters) white wine vinegar. Reduce the mixture by two-thirds. Then add demi-glace and simmer for 10 minutes. Add 2 ounces (60 grams) diced cornichons, 1 tablespoon (15 milliliters) fresh tarragon, 1 tablespoon (15 milliliters) fresh parsley and 1 tablespoon (15 milliliters) fresh chervil. Do not strain.

POIVRADE Sweat 12 ounces (340 grams) mirepoix in 2 tablespoons (30 milliliters) oil. Add 1 bay leaf, 1 sprig thyme and 4 parsley stems. Then add 16 fluid ounces (500 milliliters) vinegar and 4 fluid ounces (120 milliliters) white wine. Reduce by half, add demi-glace and simmer for 40 minutes. Then add 20 crushed peppercorns and simmer for 5 more minutes. Strain through a fine chinois and finish with up to 2 ounces (60 grams) whole butter.

ROBERT Sauté 8 ounces (250 grams) chopped onion in 1 ounce (30 grams) whole butter. Add 8 fluid ounces (250 milliliters) dry white wine and reduce by two-thirds. Add demi-glace and simmer for 10 minutes. Strain and then add 2 teaspoons (10 milliliters) prepared Dijon mustard and 1 tablespoon (15 milliliters) granulated sugar. If the finished Robert sauce is garnished with sliced sour pickles, preferably cornichons, it is known as **Charcutière.**

POIVRADE POUR GIBIER

Poivrade is also the name given a flavorful sauce traditionally made with game stock and seasoned with peppercorns. It is used for the wonderful Sauce Grand Veneur, one of the most complex small sauces in the classic repertoire. For Grand Veneur, game stock is flavored with demi-glace and finished with cream and currant jelly. The sweetness balances the strong flavor of the game meats.

THE TOMATO SAUCE FAMILY

Classic tomato sauce is made from tomatoes, vegetables, seasonings and white stock and thickened with a blond or brown roux. In today's kitchens, however, most tomato sauces are not thickened with roux. Rather, they are created from tomatoes, herbs, spices, vegetables and other flavoring ingredients simmered together and puréed.

A **gastrique** is sometimes added to reduce the acidity of a tomato sauce. To prepare a gastrique, caramelize a small amount of sugar, then thin or deglaze with vinegar. This mixture is then used to finish the tomato sauce.

A properly made tomato sauce is thick, rich and full-flavored. Its texture should be grainier than most other classic sauces, but it should still be smooth. The vegetables and other seasonings should add flavor, but none should be pronounced. Tomato sauce should not be bitter, acidic or overly sweet. It should be deep red and thick enough to cling to foods.

▶ **gastrique** (gas-streek) caramelized sugar deglazed with vinegar; used to flavor tomato or savory fruit sauces

▶ **render** (1) to melt and clarify fat; (2) to cook meat in order to remove the fat

TOMATO SAUCE

RECIPE 9.13

Yield: 1 gal. (4 lt)

Salt pork, small dice	4 oz.	120 g
Mirepoix	1 lb. 8 oz.	750 g
Tomatoes, fresh or canned	3 qt.	3 lt
Tomato purée	2 qt.	2 lt
Sachet:		
Dried thyme	1 tsp.	5 ml
Bay leaves	3	3
Garlic cloves	3	3
Parsley stems	10	10
Peppercorns, crushed	1/2 tsp.	3 ml
Salt	1 1/2 oz.	45 g
Granulated sugar	3/4 oz.	20 g
White stock	3 qt.	3 lt
Pork bones	2 lb.	1 kg

1. **Render** the salt pork over medium heat.
2. Add the mirepoix and sauté, but do not brown.
3. Add the tomatoes, tomato purée, sachet, salt and sugar.
4. Add the stock and bones.
5. Simmer slowly for 1 to 2 hours or until the desired consistency has been reached.
6. Remove the bones and sachet and pass the sauce through a food mill. Cool in a water bath and refrigerate.

Approximate values per 1-fl.-oz. (30-ml) serving: **Calories** 30, **Total fat** 0.5 g, **Saturated fat** 0.2 g, **Cholesterol** 0.7 mg, **Sodium** 240 mg, **Total carbohydrates** 4 g, **Protein** 2 g, **Vitamin A** 6%, **Claims**—low fat; low calorie

Mise en Place

- ▶ Rinse and dry salt pork and chop into fine dice.
- ▶ Peel and chop onions, carrots and celery for mirepoix.
- ▶ Prepare herb sachet.
- ▶ Wash pork bones.

1 Passing the sauce through a food mill.

2 The finished sauce.

Small Tomato Sauces

The following small sauces are made by adding the listed ingredients to 1 quart (1 liter) tomato sauce. The final step for each recipe is to season to taste with salt and pepper.

CREOLE Sauté 6 ounces (170 grams) finely diced onion, 4 ounces (120 grams) thinly sliced celery and 1 teaspoon (5 milliliters) garlic in 1 fluid ounce (30 milliliters) oil. Add tomato sauce, a bay leaf and 1 pinch thyme; simmer for 15 minutes. Then add 4 ounces (120 grams) finely diced green pepper and a dash of hot pepper sauce; simmer for 15 minutes longer. Remove the bay leaf.

SPANISH Prepare creole sauce as directed, adding 4 ounces (120 grams) sliced mushrooms to the sautéed onions. Garnish with sliced black or green olives.

MILANAISE Sauté 5 ounces (140 grams) sliced mushrooms in ½ ounce (15 grams) whole butter. Add tomato sauce and then stir in 5 ounces (140 grams) cooked ham (julienne) and 5 ounces (140 grams) cooked tongue (julienne). Bring to a simmer.

THE HOLLANDAISE FAMILY

Hollandaise and the small sauces derived from it are emulsified sauces. Egg yolks, which contain large amounts of lecithin, a natural emulsifier, are used to emulsify warm butter and a small amount of water, lemon juice or vinegar. When the egg yolks are vigorously whipped with the liquid while the warm butter is slowly added, the lecithin coats the individual fat droplets and holds them in suspension in the liquid.

A properly made hollandaise is smooth, buttery, pale lemon-yellow-colored and very rich. It is lump-free and should not exhibit any signs of separation. The buttery flavor should dominate but not mask the flavors of the egg, lemon and vinegar. The sauce should be frothy and light, not heavy like a mayonnaise.

Temperatures and Sanitation Concerns

Temperatures play an important role in the proper production of a hollandaise sauce. As the egg yolks and liquid are whisked together, they are cooked over a bain marie until they thicken to the consistency of slightly whipped cream. Do not overheat this mixture, because even slightly cooked eggs lose their ability to emulsify. The clarified butter used to make the sauce should be warm but not so hot as to further cook the egg yolks. Although hollandaise sauce can be made from whole butter, a more stable and consistent product will be achieved by using clarified butter. (Clarification is described in Chapter 7, Mise en Place.)

SAFETY ALERT

Handling Emulsified Butter Sauces

Emulsified butter sauces must be held at the specific temperatures most conducive to bacterial growth: 41°F–135°F (5°C–57°C). If the sauce is heated above 150°F (65°C), the eggs will cook and the sauce will break and become grainy. If the sauce temperature falls below 45°F (7°C), the butter will solidify, making the sauce unusable. In order to minimize the risk of food-borne illnesses:

- Always use clean, sanitized utensils.
- Schedule sauce production as close to the time of service as possible. Never hold hollandaise-based sauces more than 1½ hours.
- Make small batches of sauce.
- Never mix an old batch of sauce with a new one.

Rescuing a Broken Hollandaise

Occasionally, a hollandaise will break or separate and appear thin, grainy or even lumpy. A sauce breaks when the emulsion has not formed or the emulsified butter, eggs and liquid have separated. This may happen for several reasons: The temperature of the eggs or butter may have been too high or too low; the butter may have been added too quickly; the egg yolks may have been overcooked; too much butter may have been added or the sauce may not have been whipped vigorously enough.

To rescue and re-emulsify broken hollandaise you must first determine whether it is too hot or too cold. If it is too hot, allow the sauce to cool. If it is too cold, reheat the sauce over a double boiler before attempting to rescue it.

For 1 quart (1 liter) of broken sauce, place 1 tablespoon (15 milliliters) water in a clean stainless steel bowl and slowly beat in the broken sauce. If the problem seems to be that the eggs were overcooked or too much butter was added, add a yolk to the water before incorporating the broken sauce.

HOLLANDAISE

RECIPE 9.14

Yield: 24 fl.oz. (750 ml)

White peppercorns, crushed	½ tsp.	2 ml
White wine vinegar	3 fl. oz.	90 ml
Water	2 fl. oz.	60 ml
Egg yolks, pasteurized	6	6
Lemon juice	1½ fl. oz.	45 ml
Clarified butter, warm	1 pt.	450 ml
Salt and white pepper	TT	TT
Cayenne pepper	TT	TT

1 Combine the peppercorns, vinegar and water in a small saucepan and reduce by one-half.

2 Place the egg yolks in a stainless steel bowl. Strain the vinegar-and-pepper reduction through a chinois into the yolks. There should be ½ fluid ounce (15 milliliters) acidic reduction for each egg yolk used.

3 Place the bowl over a double boiler, whipping the mixture continuously with a wire whip. As the yolks cook, the mixture will thicken. When the mixture is thick enough to leave a trail across the surface when the whip is drawn away, remove the bowl from the double boiler. Do not overcook the egg yolks.

4 Whip in 1 fluid ounce (30 milliliters) lemon juice to stop the yolks from cooking.

5 Begin to add the warm clarified butter to the egg yolk mixture a few drops at a time, while constantly whipping the mixture to form an emulsion. Once the emulsion is started, the butter may be added more quickly. Continue until all the butter is incorporated.

6 Whip in the remaining lemon juice. Adjust the seasonings.

7 Strain the sauce through cheesecloth if necessary and hold for service in a warm (not simmering) bain marie. This sauce may be held for approximately 1 to 1½ hours.

Approximate values per 1-fl.-oz. (30-ml) serving: **Calories** 170, **Total fat** 18 g, **Saturated fat** 11 g, **Cholesterol** 90 mg, **Sodium** 180 mg, **Total carbohydrates** 0 g, **Protein** 1 g **Vitamin A** 20%

Mise en Place

- ▶ Crush white peppercorns.
- ▶ Warm clarified butter.

1 Combining the egg yolks with the vinegar and pepper reduction in a stainless steel bowl.

2 Whipping the mixture over a double boiler until it is thick enough to leave a trail when the whip is removed.

3 Using a kitchen towel and saucepot to firmly hold the bowl containing the yolks, add the butter slowly while whipping continuously.

4 Hollandaise at the proper consistency.

RECIPE 9.15

HOLLANDAISE, BLENDER METHOD

Yield: 1 qt. (1 lt.)

Egg yolks, pasteurized	9	9
Water, warm	3 fl. oz.	90 ml
Lemon juice	1 fl. oz.	30 ml
Cayenne pepper	TT	TT
Salt	1 tsp.	5 ml
White pepper	1/4 tsp.	1 ml
Tabasco sauce	TT	TT
Whole butter	24 oz.	750 g

1 Place the egg yolks, water, lemon juice, cayenne pepper, salt, white pepper and Tabasco sauce in the bowl of the blender. Cover and blend on high speed for approximately 5 seconds.

2 Heat the butter to approximately 175°F (80°C). This allows the butter to cook the yolks as it is added to them.

3 Turn the blender on and immediately begin to add the butter in a steady stream. Incorporate all the butter in 20 to 30 seconds. Adjust the seasonings.

4 If any lumps are present, strain the sauce through a mesh strainer. Transfer the sauce to a stainless steel container and adjust the seasonings. Hold for service in a bain marie, remembering the sanitation precautions discussed earlier.

Approximate values per 1-fl.-oz. (30-ml) serving: **Calories** 120, **Total fat** 12 g, **Saturated fat** 7 g, **Cholesterol** 70 mg, **Sodium** 170 mg, **Total carbohydrates** 0 g, **Protein** 1 g, **Vitamin A** 15%

Small Hollandaise Sauces

The following small sauces are easily made by adding the listed ingredients to 1 quart (1 liter) hollandaise. The final step for each recipe is to season to taste with salt and pepper. Béarnaise is presented here as a small sauce although some chefs consider it a leading sauce.

BÉARNAISE (bair-NAYZ) Combine 2 ounces (60 grams) chopped shallots, 5 tablespoons (75 milliliters) chopped fresh tarragon, 3 tablespoons (45 milliliters) chopped fresh chervil and 1 teaspoon (5 milliliters) crushed peppercorns with 8 fluid ounces (250 milliliters) white wine vinegar. Reduce to 2 fluid ounces (60 milliliters). Add this reduction to the egg yolks and proceed with the hollandaise recipe. Strain the finished sauce and season to taste with salt and cayenne pepper. Garnish with additional chopped fresh tarragon.

CHORON Combine 2 ounces (60 grams) tomato paste and 2 fluid ounces (60 milliliters) heavy cream; add the mixture to a béarnaise.

FOYOT Add to béarnaise 3 fluid ounces (90 milliliters) melted glace de viande.

GRIMROD Infuse a hollandaise sauce with saffron.

MALTAISE Add to hollandaise 2 fluid ounces (60 milliliters) orange juice and 2 teaspoons (10 milliliters) finely grated orange zest. Blood oranges are traditionally used for this sauce.

MOUSSELINE (CHANTILLY SAUCE) Whip 8 fluid ounces (250 milliliters) heavy cream until stiff. Fold it into the hollandaise just before service. Mousseline sauce is also used as a **glaçage** coating.

▶ **glaçage** (glah-sahge) browning or glazing a food, usually under a salamander or broiler

BEURRE BLANC AND BEURRE ROUGE

Beurre blanc (burr blahnk) and beurre rouge (burr rooge) are emulsified butter sauces made without egg yolks. The small amounts of lecithin and other emulsifiers naturally found in butter are used to form an oil-in-water emulsion. Although similar to hollandaise in concept, they are not considered either classic leading or compound sauces. Beurre blancs are thinner and lighter than hollandaise and béarnaise. They should be smooth and slightly thicker than heavy cream.

Beurre blanc and beurre rouge are made from three main ingredients: shallots, white (Fr. *blanc*) wine or red (Fr. *rouge*) wine and whole butter (not clarified). The shallots and wine provide flavor, while the butter becomes the sauce. A good beurre blanc or beurre rouge is rich and buttery, with a neutral flavor that responds well to other seasonings and flavorings, thereby lending itself to the addition of herbs, spices and vegetable purées to complement the dish with which it is served. Its pale color changes depending on the flavorings added. It should be light and airy yet still liquid, while thick enough to cling to food.

▶ **beurre fondu** (burr fon-DOO) French for "melted butter"; it is often served over steamed vegetables such as asparagus or poached white fish

▶ **beurre noir** (burr NWAR) French for "black butter"; used to describe whole butter cooked until dark brown (not black); sometimes flavored with vinegar or lemon juice, capers and parsley and served over fish, eggs and vegetables

▶ **beurre noisette** (burr nwah-ZEHT) French for "brown butter"; used to describe butter cooked until it is a light brown color; it is flavored and used in much the same manner as beurre noir

▶ PROCEDURE FOR PREPARING BEURRE BLANC OR BEURRE ROUGE

1. Use a nonaluminum pan to prevent discoloring the sauce. Do not use a thin-walled or nonstick pan, as heat is not evenly distributed in a thin-walled pan and a nonstick pan makes it difficult for an emulsion to set.
2. Over medium heat, reduce the wine, shallots and herbs or other seasonings, if used, until au sec (that is, nearly dry). Some chefs add a small amount of heavy cream at this point and reduce the mixture. Although not necessary, the added cream helps stabilize the finished sauce.
3. Whisk in cold butter a small amount at a time. The butter should be well chilled, as this allows the butterfat, water and milk solids to be gradually incorporated into the sauce as the butter melts and the mixture is whisked.
4. When all the butter is incorporated, strain and hold the sauce in a bain marie.

TEMPERATURE

Do not let the sauce become too hot. At 136°F (58°C) some of the emulsifying proteins begin to break down and release the butterfat they hold in emulsion. Extended periods at temperatures over 136°F (58°C) will cause the sauce to separate. If the sauce separates, it can be corrected by cooling to approximately 110°F–120°F (43°C–49°C) and whisking to reincorporate the butterfat

If the sauce is allowed to cool below 85°F (30°C), the butterfat will solidify. If the sauce is reheated it will separate into butterfat and water; whisking will not re-emulsify it. Cold beurre blanc can be used as a soft, flavored butter, however, simply by whisking it at room temperature until it smooths out to the consistency of mayonnaise.

RECIPE 9.16

BEURRE BLANC

Mise en Place

▶ Peel and mince shallot.

1 Reducing the shallots and wine au sec.

2 Whisking in the cold butter a little at a time.

3 Straining the sauce.

Yield: 1 qt. (1 lt)

White wine	1 fl. oz.	30 ml
White wine vinegar	4 fl. oz.	120 ml
Salt	1 1/2 tsp.	7 ml
White pepper	1/2 tsp.	2 ml
Shallot, minced	1 oz.	30 g
Whole butter, chilled	2 lb.	1 kg

1 Combine the white wine, white wine vinegar, salt, white pepper and shallot in a small saucepan. Reduce the mixture until approximately 2 tablespoons (30 milliliters) of liquid remain. If more than 2 tablespoons of liquid are allowed to remain, the resulting sauce will be too thin. For a thicker sauce, reduce the mixture au sec.

2 Cut the butter into pieces approximately 1 ounce (30 grams) in weight. Over low heat, whisk in the butter a few pieces at a time, using the chilled butter to keep the sauce between 100°F and 120°F (38°C and 49°C).

3 Once all the butter has been incorporated, remove the saucepan from the heat. Strain through a chinois and hold the sauce at a temperature between 100°F and 130°F (38°C and 54°C) for service.

VARIATIONS:

Beurre Rouge—Substitute a dry red wine for the white wine and red wine vinegar for the white wine vinegar.

Lemon-Dill—Heat 2 tablespoons (30 milliliters) lemon juice and whisk it into the beurre blanc. Stir in 4 tablespoons (60 milliliters) chopped fresh dill.

Pink Peppercorn—Add 2 tablespoons (30 milliliters) coarsely crushed pink peppercorns to the shallot-wine reduction when making beurre rouge. Garnish the finished sauce with whole pink peppercorns.

Approximate values per 1-fl.-oz. (30-ml) serving: **Calories** 210, **Total fat** 23 g, **Saturated fat** 14 g, **Cholesterol** 60 mg, **Sodium** 340 mg, **Total carbohydrates** 0 g, **Protein** 0 g, **Vitamin A** 20%

COMPOUND BUTTERS

A compound butter is made by incorporating various seasonings into softened whole butter. These butters, also known as *beurres composés,* give flavor and color to small sauces or may be served as sauces in their own right. For example, a slice of maître d'hôtel butter (parsley butter) is often placed on a grilled steak or piece of fish at the time of service. The butter quickly melts, creating a sauce for the beef or fish.

Butter and flavoring ingredients can be combined with a blender, food processor or mixer. Using parchment paper or plastic wrap, the butter is then rolled into a cylinder, chilled and sliced as needed. Or it can be piped into rosettes and refrigerated until firm. Most compound butters will keep for two to three days in the refrigerator, or they can be frozen for longer storage.

RECIPES FOR COMPOUND BUTTERS

For each of the following butters, add the listed ingredients to 1 pound (500 grams) of softened, unsalted butter. The compound butter should then be seasoned with salt and pepper to taste.

BASIL BUTTER Mince 2 ounces (60 grams) basil and 2 ounces (60 grams) shallots; add to the butter with 2 teaspoons (10 milliliters) lemon juice.

HERB BUTTER Add to the butter up to 1 cup (250 milliliters) mixed chopped fresh herbs such as parsley, dill, chives, tarragon or chervil.

LOBSTER OR CRAYFISH BUTTER Grind 8 ounces (250 grams) cooked lobster or crayfish meat, shells and/or coral with 1 pound (500 grams) butter. Place in a saucepan and clarify. Strain the butter through a fine chinois lined with cheesecloth. Refrigerate, then remove the butterfat when firm.

MAÎTRE D'HÔTEL BUTTER Mix into the butter 4 tablespoons (60 milliliters) finely chopped parsley, 3 tablespoons (45 milliliters) lemon juice and a dash of white pepper.

MONTPELIER BUTTER Blanch 1 ounce (30 grams) parsley, 1 ounce (30 grams) chervil, 1 ounce (30 grams) watercress and 1 ounce (30 grams) tarragon in boiling water. Drain thoroughly. Mince 2 hard-boiled egg yolks, 2 garlic cloves and 2 gherkin pickles. Blend everything into the butter.

RED PEPPER BUTTER Purée 8 ounces (250 grams) roasted, peeled red bell peppers until liquid, then add to the butter.

SHALLOT BUTTER Blanch 8 ounces (250 grams) peeled shallots in boiling water. Dry and finely dice them and mix with the butter.

1 Placing the butter on the plastic wrap.

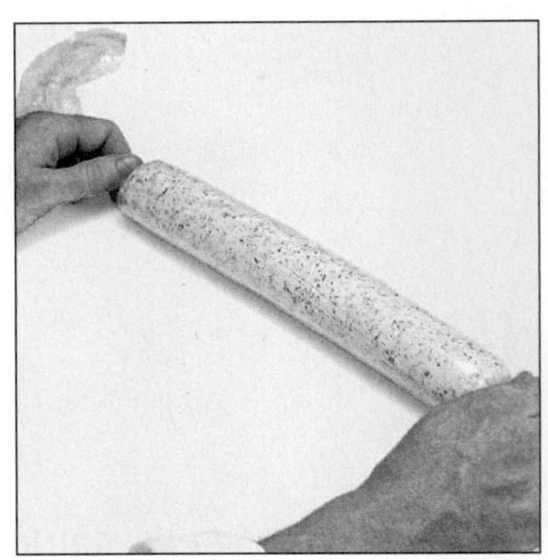

2 Rolling the butter in the plastic wrap to form a cylinder.

PAN GRAVY

Pan gravy is aptly named: It is made directly in the pan used to roast the poultry, beef, lamb or pork that the gravy will accompany. Pan gravy is actually a sauce; it is a liquid thickened with a roux. Pan gravy gains additional flavors from the drippings left in the roasting pan and by using a portion of the fat rendered during the roasting process to make the roux. This technique is used in the recipe for Roast Turkey with Chestnut Dressing and Giblet Gravy.

A properly made pan gravy should have all the characteristics of any brown sauce except that it has a meatier flavor as a result of the pan drippings.

► **gravy** a sauce made from meat or poultry juices combined with a liquid and thickening agent; usually made in the pan in which the meat or poultry was cooked

► PROCEDURE FOR PREPARING PAN GRAVY

1. Remove the cooked meat or poultry from the roasting pan.
2. If mirepoix was not added during the roasting process, add it to the pan containing the drippings and fat.
3. Place the roasting pan on the stove top and clarify the fat by cooking off any remaining moisture.
4. Pour off the fat, reserving it to make the roux.
5. Deglaze the pan using an appropriate stock. The deglazing liquid may be transferred to a saucepan for easier handling, or the gravy may be finished directly in the roasting pan.
6. Add enough stock or water to the deglazing liquid to yield the proper amount of finished gravy.
7. Determine the amount of roux needed to thicken the liquid and prepare it in a separate pan, using a portion of the reserved fat.
8. Add the roux to the liquid and bring the mixture to a simmer. Simmer until the mirepoix is well cooked, the flavor is extracted and the flour taste is cooked out.
9. Strain the gravy and adjust the seasonings.

PAN SAUCES

Sauces served with sautéed meats, poultry or fish are often made directly in the sauté pan in which the dish was cooked. Once the food is sautéed, it is removed from the pan and kept warm while the sauce is prepared. Stock, jus lié or other liquid is added to deglaze the pan. Like pan gravy, these pan sauces gain flavor from the drippings left in the pan. Unlike pan gravy, pan sauces are usually thickened by reduction, not with a starch. Pan sauces are discussed in Chapter 11, Principles of Meat Cookery.

COULIS

▶ **coulis** (koo-lee) a sauce made from a purée of vegetables and/or fruit; may be served hot or cold

The term *coulis* most often refers to a sauce made from a purée of vegetables and/or fruit that is strained before serving. A vegetable coulis can be served as either a hot or a cold accompaniment to other vegetables, starches, meat, poultry, fish or shellfish. It is often made from a single vegetable base (popular examples include broccoli, tomatoes and sweet red peppers) cooked with flavoring ingredients such as onions, garlic, shallots, herbs and spices and then puréed. An appropriate liquid (stock, water or cream) may be added to thin the purée if necessary. Vegetable coulis are often prepared with very little fat and served as a healthy alternative to a heavier, classic sauce.

A fruit coulis, often made from fresh or frozen berries, is generally used as a dessert sauce. It is usually as simple as puréed fruit thinned to the desired consistency with sugar syrup.

Typically, both vegetable and fruit coulis have a texture similar to that of a thin tomato sauce. But their textures can range from slightly grainy to almost lumpy, depending on their intended use. The flavor and color of a coulis should be that of the main ingredient. The flavors of herbs, spices and other flavoring ingredients should only complement and not dominate the coulis.

▶ PROCEDURE FOR PREPARING A COULIS

Here we include a procedure for making a vegetable coulis.

1. Cook the main ingredient and any additional flavoring ingredients with an appropriate liquid.
2. Purée the main ingredient and flavoring ingredients in a food mill, blender or food processor.
3. Combine the purée with the appropriate liquid and simmer to blend the flavors.
4. Strain, then thin and season the coulis as desired.

RED PEPPER COULIS

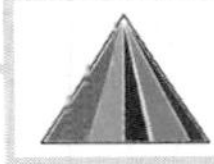

RECIPE 9.17

Yield: 1 qt. (1 lt)

Vegetable oil	1 fl. oz.	30 ml
Garlic, chopped	2 tsp.	10 ml
Onion, small dice	3 oz.	90 g
Red bell peppers, medium dice	3 lb.	1.25 kg
White wine	8 fl. oz.	250 ml
Chicken stock	1 pt.	450 ml
Salt and pepper	TT	TT

1. Heat the oil and sweat the garlic and onion until translucent, without browning.
2. Add the bell pepper and sweat until tender.
3. Deglaze the pan with the wine.
4. Add the stock, bring to a simmer and cook for 15 minutes. Season with salt and pepper.
5. Purée in a blender or food processor and strain through a china cap.
6. Adjust the consistency and seasonings and hold for service.

Approximate values per 1-fl.-oz. (30-ml) serving: **Calories** 20, **Total fat** 1 g, **Saturated fat** 0 g, **Cholesterol** 0 mg, **Sodium** 45 mg, **Total carbohydrates** 2 g, **Protein** 1 g, **Vitamin C** 50%, **Claims**—low fat; low sodium; low calorie

Mise en Place

- ▶ Peel and chop garlic.
- ▶ Peel the onion and chop into small dice.
- ▶ Wash red pepper and chop into medium dice.

1 Sweating the red peppers.

2 Puréeing the cooked peppers.

3 Straining the coulis.

CONTEMPORARY SAUCES

Modern chefs and menu writers are relying less on traditional sauces and more on salsas, relishes, juices, broths, essences and infused oils in their work. Unlike classic sauces, these modern accompaniments do not rely on meat-based stocks and starch thickeners, but rather on fresh vegetables, vegetable juices, aromatic broths and intensely flavored oils. The names for these sauces are not codified, as are those in the classic sauce repertoire. Chefs apply various terms freely, using whatever name best fits the dish and the overall menu. Most of these contemporary sauces can be prepared more quickly than their classic counterparts, and the use of fresh fruits and vegetables enhances the healthfulness of the dish. These so-called contemporary or modern sauces may have a lighter body and less fat than classic sauces, but they are still derived from classical culinary techniques and principles. The sauces should be appropriate in

▶ **chutney** a sweet-and-sour condiment made of fruits and/or vegetables cooked in vinegar with sugar and spices; some chutneys are reduced to a purée, while others retain recognizable pieces of their ingredients

flavor, texture and appearance and should complement, not overwhelm, the food they accompany.

SALSA AND RELISH

Many people think of salsa (Spanish for "sauce") as a chunky mixture of raw vegetables and chiles eaten with chips or ladled over Mexican food; they think of relish as a sweet green condiment spooned onto a hot dog. But salsas and relishes—generally, cold chunky mixtures of herbs, spices, fruits and/or vegetables—can be used as sauces for many meat, poultry, fish and shellfish items. They can include ingredients such as oranges, pineapple, papaya, black beans, jicama, tomatillos and an array of other vegetables.

Although not members of any classic sauce family, salsas and relishes are currently enjoying great popularity because of their intense fresh flavors, ease of

▶ PROCEDURE FOR PREPARING A SALSA OR RELISH

1. Cut or chop the ingredients.
2. Precook and chill items as directed in the recipe.
3. Toss all ingredients together and refrigerate, allowing the flavors to combine for at least 30 minutes before service.

RECIPE 9.18

PICO DE GALLO (TOMATO SALSA)

Mise en Place

- ▶ Wash and peel vegetables, if necessary.
- ▶ Chop tomatoes into small dice.
- ▶ Slice green onions.
- ▶ Mince garlic cloves.
- ▶ Chop cilantro leaves.
- ▶ Remove seeds from jalapeños and finely chop.

Yield: 1 qt. (1 lt)

Tomatoes, seeded, small dice	5	5
Green onions, sliced	1 bunch	1 bunch
Garlic cloves, minced	3	3
Cilantro, chopped	½ bunch	½ bunch
Jalapeños, chopped fine	3	3
Lemon juice	2 fl. oz.	60 ml
Cumin, ground	½ tsp.	2 ml
Salt and pepper	TT	TT

1. Combine all ingredients and gently toss. Adjust seasonings and refrigerate.

Approximate values per 1-fl.-oz. (30-ml) serving: **Calories** 5, **Total fat** 0 g, **Saturated fat** 0 g, **Cholesterol** 0 mg, **Sodium** 30 mg, **Total carbohydrates** 1 g, **Protein** 0 g, **Claims**—fat free; very low sodium; low calorie

VEGETABLE JUICE SAUCES

Juice extractors make it possible to prepare juice from fresh, uncooked vegetables such as carrots, beets and spinach. Thinner and smoother than a purée, vegetable juice can be heated, reduced, flavored and enriched with butter to create colorful, intensely flavored sauces. Cream or stock can be added to finish the sauce. Sauces made from vegetable juices are sometimes referred to as an **essence** or **tea** on menus.

Juice from a single type of vegetable provides the purest, most pronounced flavor, but two or more vegetables sometimes can be combined successfully. Be careful of mixing too many flavors and colors in the juice, however. Juiced vegetable sauces are particularly appropriate with pasta, fish, shellfish and poultry, and can be useful in vegetarian cuisine or as a healthier alternative to classic sauces.

▶ **essence** a sauce made from a concentrated vegetable juice

▶ PROCEDURE FOR PREPARING A VEGETABLE JUICE SAUCE

1 Wash and peel vegetables as needed.
2 Process the vegetables through a juice extractor.
3 Place the juice in a saucepan and add stock, lemon juice, herbs or other flavorings as desired.
4 Bring the sauce to a simmer and reduce as necessary.
5 Strain the sauce through a fine chinois.
6 Adjust the seasonings and whisk in whole butter to finish.

THYME-SCENTED CELERY ESSENCE

RECIPE 9.19

STOUFFER STANFORD COURT HOTEL, SAN FRANCISCO, CA
Former Executive Chef Ercolino Crugnale

Yield: 1 qt. (1 lt)

Celery juice	1 qt.	1 lt
Tomato juice	1 pt.	500 ml
Fresh thyme, chopped	½ oz.	15 g
Whole butter	6 oz.	180 g
Salt	TT	TT
Tabasco sauce	TT	TT

1 Combine the celery juice, tomato juice and thyme. Bring to a simmer and reduce to 1½ pints (750 milliliters).
2 Whisk in the butter and adjust the seasonings with salt and Tabasco sauce.
3 Strain through a chinois.

Approximate values per 1-fl.-oz. (30-ml) serving: **Calories** 50, **Total fat** 4.5 g, **Saturated fat** 2.4 g, **Cholesterol** 10 mg, **Sodium** 200 mg, **Total carbohydrates** 2 g, **Protein** 0 g

Mise en Place

- ▶ Wash celery and put through juice extractor.
- ▶ Wash tomatoes and put through juice extractor.
- ▶ Chop fresh thyme.

BROTH

Broth, which also appears on menus as a **tea, au jus, essence** or **nage,** is a thin, flavorful liquid served in a pool beneath the main food. The broth should not be so abundant as to turn an entrée into a soup, but it should provide moisture and flavor. The essence, broth or nage is often made by simply reducing and straining the liquid in which the main food was cooked. Alternatively, a specifically flavored stock—tomato, for example—can be prepared, then clarified like consommé to create a broth or essence to accompany an appetizer or entrée.

FLAVORED OIL

Small amounts of intensely flavored oils can be used to dress or garnish a variety of dishes. Salads, soups, vegetable and starch dishes and entrées can be enhanced with a drizzle of colorful, appropriately flavored oil. Because such small quantities are used, these oils provide flavor and moisture without adding too many calories or fat.

Unless the flavoring ingredient goes especially well with olive oil (for example, basil), select a high-quality but neutral oil such as peanut, safflower or canola. Although flavoring ingredients can be simply steeped in oil for a time, a

▶ **decant** to separate liquid from solids without disturbing the sediment by pouring off the liquid: vintage wines are often decanted to remove sediment

▶ **vinaigrette** a temporary emulsion of oil and vinegar seasoned with salt and pepper

better way to flavor oil is to crush, purée or cook the flavoring ingredients first. Warming the oil before infusing it with dry herbs or spices is recommended, as is **decanting** the oil to remove solids before using.

Modern chefs are also using **vinaigrettes,** a combination of oil and vinegar, citrus or other acidic liquid, as quick light sauces. Vinaigrettes give the illusion of lightness that many health-conscious customers are demanding, although the oil in such sauces can raise the fat and calorie content substantially. Vinaigrettes are discussed in Chapter 23, Salads and Salad Dressings.

▶ PROCEDURE FOR PREPARING A FLAVORED OIL

1 Purée or chop fresh herbs, fruits or vegetables. Sweat dry spices or seeds in a small amount of oil to form a paste.
2 Place the selected oil and the flavoring ingredients in a jar or other tightly lidded container.
3 Allow the mixture to stand at room temperature until sufficient flavor is extracted. This may take from 1 to 24 hours. Shake the jar periodically. Do not allow the flavoring ingredients to remain in the oil indefinitely, as the flavor may become harsh or bitter.
4 Strain the oil through a chinois lined with a coffee filter.
5 Store the flavored oil in a covered container in the refrigerator.

RECIPE 9.20

SHALLOT CURRY OIL

Mise en Place

▶ Peel and mince shallot.

Yield: 8 fl. oz. (225 ml)

Canola oil	8 fl. oz.	240 ml
Shallot, minced	1	1
Curry powder	4 Tbsp.	60 ml
Water	2 fl. oz.	60 ml

1 In a small saucepan, heat 1 tablespoon (15 milliliters) oil over medium heat. Add the shallot and sauté until softened and translucent. Do not allow the shallot to brown.
2 Add the curry powder and sauté for 1 to 2 minutes.
3 Stir in the water and bring the mixture to a boil. Reduce the heat and simmer until most of the water evaporates, leaving a paste of curry and shallots.
4 Remove from the heat and stir in the remaining oil.
5 Place the mixture in a lidded jar and set aside at room temperature for 6 to 8 hours. Shake the jar occasionally.
6 Strain the oil through a chinois lined with a coffee filter. Place the flavored oil in a covered container and refrigerate until ready to use.

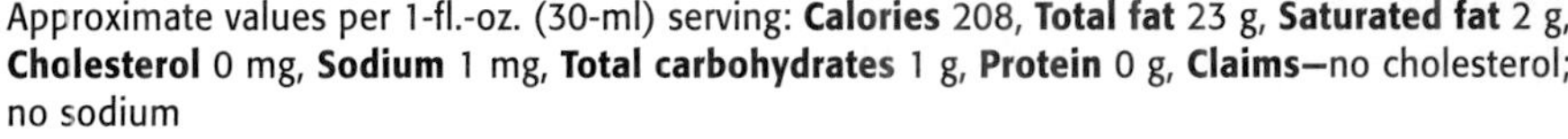

Approximate values per 1-fl.-oz. (30-ml) serving: **Calories** 208, **Total fat** 23 g, **Saturated fat** 2 g, **Cholesterol** 0 mg, **Sodium** 1 mg, **Total carbohydrates** 1 g, **Protein** 0 g, **Claims—**no cholesterol; no sodium

Sauces are used in many recipes in this book and in the professional kitchen. Table 9.5 lists some of the sauces discussed in this chapter and describes common ways to use them. Table 9.6 is a troubleshooting chart to be used when problems arise.

Table 9.5 **USING SAUCES**

SAUCE	QUALITIES	SMALL SAUCE OR FLAVORINGS	USE
Béchamel	Smooth, rich and creamy; no graininess; cream-colored with rich sheen	Cream	Vegetables, pasta, eggs, fish, shellfish
		Cheese	Vegetables, pasta
		Mornay	Fish, shellfish, poultry, vegetables
		Nantua	Fish, shellfish
		Soubise	Veal, pork, eggs
Velouté	Smooth and rich; ivory-colored; good flavor of the stock used; not pasty or heavy	Fish Velouté	
		Bercy	Poached fish
		Cardinal	Lobster, white fish, crab, eggs
		Normandy	Delicate white fish, oysters
		Allemande (veal or chicken)	
		Aurora	Eggs, chicken, sweetbreads
		Horseradish	Roast beef, corned beef, baked ham
		Mushroom	Sautéed poultry, white meats
		Poulette	Vegetables, sweetbreads
		Suprême (chicken)	
		Albufera	Braised poultry, sweetbreads
		Hungarian	Eggs, chicken, chops, sweetbreads
		Ivory	Eggs, braised poultry
Espagnole	Smooth and rich; dark brown color; good meat flavor	Bordelaise	Sautéed or grilled meats
		Chasseur	Sautéed or grilled meats and poultry
		Châteaubriand	Broiled meats
		Chevreuil	Roasted meats and game
		Madeira/Port	Grilled or roasted meats and game, ham
		Marchand de vin	Grilled or roasted meats
		Mushroom	Sautéed or grilled meats and poultry
		Périgueux/Périgourdine	Sautéed poultry, grilled meats and game, sweetbreads
		Piquant	Pork
		Poivrade	Grilled or roasted meats, game
		Robert	Pork
Tomato	Thick and rich; slightly grainy; full-flavored	Tomato	Meats, poultry, vegetables, pasta and for making small sauces
		Creole	Fish, eggs, chicken
		Spanish	Eggs, fish
		Milanaise	Pasta, grilled or sautéed poultry and white meats
Hollandaise	Smooth and rich; buttery flavor; light and slightly frothy; pale yellow color; no signs of separating	Béarnaise	Grilled or sautéed meats and fish
		Choron	Grilled meats and fish
		Foyot	Grilled meats and fish
		Grimrod	Eggs, poached fish
		Maltaise	Poached fish
		Mousseline	Poached fish, eggs, vegetables
Beurre blanc and beurre rouge	Rich and buttery; thinner than hollandaise; light and airy; pale-colored	Wide variety of seasonings and flavorings may be used	Steamed, grilled or poached fish, chicken or vegetables
Compound butter	Flavor ingredients should be evenly distributed	Wide variety of seasonings and flavorings may be used	Grilled meats, poultry and fish; finishing sauces
Pan gravy (jus lié)	Smooth; deep rich color; meaty flavor	Made from pan drippings	Roasted meats and poultry
Coulis	Rich color; moderately thin, grainy texture; strongly flavored	Made with a wide variety of vegetables or fruits	Vegetables, grilled or poached meats, poultry and fish
Salsa and relish	Chunky; bright colors; not watery	Made with a wide variety of vegetables, fruits and seasonings	Meats, fish, vegetables and poultry; used as a sauce or condiment
Flavored oil	Smooth; bright colors; intense flavors	Made with a variety of herbs, spices and seasonings	Used as a garnish

Table 9.6 **TROUBLESHOOTING CHART FOR SAUCES**

PROBLEM	REASON	SOLUTION
Lumpy	Roux undercooked	Increase cooking time of roux
	Stock cold when roux added	Heat stock before adding roux; strain through chinois to remove lumps
	Cornstarch not properly dissolved	Strain, make cornstarch slurry and cook until thickened, stirring constantly
Pasty or floury taste	Sauce undercooked after starch was added	Increase cooking time
Grainy texture	Starch or flour not properly gelatinized	Increase cooking time
	Eggs overheated in liaison	Discard sauce
Thick consistency	Too much thickener	Decrease thickener; add additional liquid
	Sauce reduced too much	Decrease cooking time; add additional liquid
Thin consistency	Not enough thickener	Add more roux or cornstarch slurry
	Starch-thickened sauce overheated	Do not reheat sauces thickened with cornstarch
	Insufficiently reduced	Continue cooking until sauce thickens
Separates, breaks	Temporary emulsion failed	Whisk sauce again (vinaigrette); cool to 110°F–120°F (43°C–49°C), then whisk again to reincorporate fat (beurre blanc); reheat sauce over double boiler, then beat into water (hollandaise)
	Eggs overcooked	Beat an egg yolk and water together, then beat into sauce (hollandaise); discard sauce if liaison was used and overheated
Gray color or metallic taste	Aluminum pan used	Discard (cream sauce); use nonreactive pan to make cream sauce

CONCLUSION

In *Le Guide culinaire,* Auguste Escoffier wrote "Indeed, stock is everything in cooking . . . without it, nothing can be done. If one's stock is good, what remains of the work is easy; if, on the other hand, it is bad or merely mediocre, it is quite hopeless to expect anything approaching a satisfactory result." Because stocks and the sauces made from them are still the basis for much of contemporary cuisine, Escoffier's words are as true today as when he wrote them.

Both the classic mother sauces and the small sauces derived from them as well as sauces such as beurre blanc and beurre rouge, coulis, flavored oils, salsas and relishes that are not based on classic recipes all share two goals: to complement the foods with which they are served and to neither mask nor disguise poorly prepared foods. With practice and care (and the right ingredients), you will be able to make great sauces.

QUESTIONS FOR DISCUSSION

1 Why are the bones of younger animals preferred for making stocks?
2 Why should a stock made from beef or veal bones cook longer than a stock made from fish bones? What is the result if a stock does not cook long enough?
3 What can cause a stock to become cloudy? How can you prevent this from happening?
4 List three differences in the production of a white stock and a brown stock.
5 List the five classic mother sauces and explain how they are used to prepare small sauces.
6 Why is demi-glace preferred when making brown sauces? Is jus lié different from classic demi-glace? Can they be used interchangeably?
7 Why are temperatures important when making hollandaise sauce? What precautions must be taken when holding hollandaise for service?
8 Compare a beurre blanc and a hollandaise sauce. How are they similar? How are they different?
9 How are compound butters used in making sauces? What are the ingredients for a traditional maître d'hôtel butter?
10 What are the differences between a salsa, a chutney and a relish? Can these items be used in place of classic sauces? Explain your answer.
11 What are the differences between a vegetable juice sauce and a broth?

CHAPTER **TEN**

A FIRST-RATE SOUP IS MORE CREATIVE THAN A SECOND-RATE PAINTING.

—Abraham Maslow, American psychologist (1908–1970)

SOUPS

HERBSAINT BAR AND RESTAURANT,
New Orleans, LA
Chef Donald Link

AFTER STUDYING THIS CHAPTER, YOU WILL BE ABLE TO:

- prepare a variety of clear and thick soups
- garnish and serve soups appropriately

The variety of ingredients, seasonings and garnishes that can be used for soups is virtually endless, provided one understands the basic procedures for making different kinds of soup. Great soups can be made from the finest and most expensive ingredients or from leftovers from the previous evening's dinner service and trimmings from the day's production. Although fresh ingredients are preferable, wise use of leftovers means that a daily soup special can be an economical, practical menu item.

This chapter extends to soups the skills and knowledge learned in Chapter 9, Stocks and Sauces. In Chapter 9, we discussed making stocks, thickening liquids, using a liaison and skimming impurities, techniques that apply to soup making as well. Here we discuss techniques such as clarifying consommés and thickening soups with vegetable purées. This chapter also covers cream soups, cold soups and guidelines for garnishing and serving a variety of soups.

Most soups can be classified by cooking technique and appearance as either clear or thick.

Clear soups include **broths** made from meat, poultry, game, fish or vegetables as well as **consommés,** which are broths clarified to remove impurities.

Thick soups include cream soups and purée soups. The most common **cream soups** are those made from vegetables cooked in a liquid that is thickened with a starch and puréed; cream is then incorporated to add richness and flavor. **Purée soups** are generally made from starchy vegetables or legumes. After the main ingredient is simmered in a liquid, the mixture—or a portion of it—is puréed.

Some soups (notably **bisques** and **chowders** as well as **cold soups** such as gazpacho and fruit soup) are neither clear nor thick soups. Rather, they use special preparation methods or a combination of the methods mentioned before.

A soup's quality is determined by its flavor, appearance and texture. A good soup should be full-flavored, with no off or sour tastes. Flavors from each of the soup's ingredients should blend and complement, with no one flavor overpowering another. Consommés should be crystal clear. The vegetables in vegetable soups should be brightly colored, not gray. Garnishes should be attractive and uniform in size and shape. The soup's texture should be very precise. If it is supposed to be smooth, then it should be very smooth and lump-free. If the soft and crisp textures of certain ingredients are supposed to contrast, the soup should not be overcooked, as this causes all the ingredients to become mushy and soft.

Garnishing is an important consideration when preparing soups. When applied to soups, the word garnish has two meanings. The first is the one more typically associated with the word. It refers to foods added to the soup as decoration—for example, a broccoli floret floated on a bowl of cream of broccoli soup. The second refers to foods that may serve not only as decorations but also as critical components of the final product—for example, noodles in a bowl of chicken noodle soup. In this context, the noodles are not ingredients because they are not used to make the chicken soup. Rather, they are added to chicken soup to create a different dish. These additional items are still referred to as garnishes, however.

ESCOFFIER'S CLASSIFICATION OF SOUPS

In his 1903 culinary treatise *Le Guide Culinaire*, Auguste Escoffier recognized many more categories of soups than we do today. They include the following:

Clear soups, which are always "clear consommés with a slight garnish in keeping with the nature of the consommé."

Purées, which are made from starchy vegetables and are thickened with rice, potato or soft bread crumbs.

Cullises, which use poultry, game or fish for a base and are thickened with rice, lentils, espagnole sauce or bread soaked in boiling salted water.

Bisques, which use shellfish cooked with a mirepoix as a base and are thickened with rice.

Veloutés, which use velouté sauce as a base and are finished with a liaison of egg yolks and cream.

Cream soups, which use béchamel sauce as a base and are finished with heavy cream.

Special soups, which are those that do not follow the procedures for veloutés or creams.

Vegetable soups, which are usually paysanne or peasant-type and "do not demand very great precision in the apportionment of the vegetables of which they are composed, but they need great care and attention, notwithstanding."

Foreign soups, "which have a foreign origin whose use, although it may not be general, is yet sufficiently common."

Because of changes in consumer health consciousness and kitchen operations, many of the distinctions between Escoffier's classic soups have now become blurred and, in some cases, eliminated. As discussed in this chapter, for example, clear consommés and vegetable soups are now made with stocks or broths; most cream soups use velouté as a base and are finished with milk or cream rather than a liaison. But not everything has changed: The procedures for making purées and bisques are essentially the same today as they were when Escoffier haunted the great kitchens of Europe.

▶ Clear Soups

All clear soups start as stock or broth. Broths may be served as finished items, used as the base for other soups or refined (clarified) into consommés.

BROTHS

The techniques for making stocks discussed in Chapter 9 are identical to those used for making broths. Like stocks, broths are prepared by simmering flavoring ingredients in a liquid for a long time. Broths and stocks differ, however, in two ways. First, broths are made with meat instead of just bones. Second, broths (often with a garnish) can be served as finished dishes, while stocks are generally used to prepare other items.

Broths are made from meat, poultry, fish or vegetables cooked in a liquid. An especially full-flavored broth results when a stock and not just water is used as the liquid. Cuts of meat from the shank, neck or shoulder result in more flavorful broths, as will the flesh of mature poultry. Proper temperature, skimming and straining help produce well-flavored, clear broths.

▶ PROCEDURE FOR PREPARING BROTHS

1. Truss or cut the main ingredient.
2. Brown the meat; brown or sweat the mirepoix or vegetables as necessary.
3. Place the main ingredient and mirepoix or vegetables in an appropriate stockpot and add enough cold water or stock to cover. Add a bouquet garni or sachet d'épices if desired.
4. Bring the liquid slowly to a boil; reduce to a simmer and cook, skimming occasionally, until the main ingredient is tender and the flavor is fully developed.
5. Carefully strain the broth through a china cap lined with damp cheesecloth; try to disturb the flavoring ingredients as little as possible in order to preserve the broth's clarity.
6. Cool and store following the procedures for cooling stocks. Or bring to a boil, garnish as desired and hold for service.

RECIPE 10.1

BEEF BROTH

Mise en Place

- ▶ Cut beef shank into pieces.
- ▶ Chop onions, carrots and celery for mirepoix.
- ▶ Wash and peel turnips and leeks and chop into medium dice.
- ▶ Prepare herb sachet.

Yield: 8 qt. (8 lt)

Beef shank, neck or shoulder cut in 2-in.- (5-cm-) thick pieces	12 lb.	5.5 kg
Vegetable oil	8 fl. oz.	250 ml
Beef stock or water, cold	2 gal.	8 lt
Mirepoix	2 lb.	900 g
Turnips, medium dice	8 oz.	250 g
Leeks, medium dice	8 oz.	250 g
Tomatoes, seeded and diced	8 oz.	250 g
Sachet:		
Bay leaf	1	1
Dried thyme	1/2 tsp.	2 ml
Peppercorns, crushed	1/2 tsp.	2 ml
Parsley stems	8	8
Garlic cloves, crushed	2	2
Salt	TT	TT

1 Brown the meat in 4 fluid ounces (120 milliliters) oil, then place it in a stockpot. Add the stock or water and bring to a simmer. Simmer gently for 2 hours, skimming the surface as necessary.

2 After the meat has simmered for 2 hours, caramelize the mirepoix in the remaining oil and add it to the liquid. Add the turnips, leeks, tomatoes and sachet.

3 Simmer until full flavor has developed, approximately 1 hour. Skim the surface as necessary.

4 Carefully strain the broth through cheesecloth and season to taste. Cool and refrigerate.

Approximate values per 6-fl.-oz. (180-ml) serving: **Calories** 70, **Total fat** 6 g, **Saturated fat** 1 g, **Cholesterol** 2 mg, **Sodium** 630 mg, **Total carbohydrates** 2 g, **Protein** 2 g

1 Browning the meat.

2 Adding mirepoix to the broth.

3 Straining the broth.

BROTH-BASED SOUPS

Broths are often used as bases for such familiar soups as vegetable, chicken noodle and beef barley.

Transforming a broth into a broth-based vegetable soup, for example, is quite simple. Although a broth may be served with a vegetable (or meat) garnish, a broth-based vegetable soup is a soup in which the vegetables (and meats) are cooked directly in the broth, adding flavor, body and texture to the finished product. Any number of vegetables can be used to make a vegetable soup; it could be a single vegetable as in onion soup or a dozen different vegetables for a hearty minestrone.

When making broth-based vegetable soups, each ingredient must be added at the proper time so that all ingredients are cooked when the soup is finished. The ingredients must cook long enough to add their flavors and soften sufficiently but not so long that they lose their identity and become too soft or mushy.

Because broth-based vegetable soups are made by simmering ingredients directly in the broth, they are generally not as clear as plain broths. But appearances are still important. So when cutting ingredients for the soup, pay particular attention so that the pieces are uniform and visually appealing. Small dice, julienne, bâtonnet or paysanne cuts are recommended.

▶ PROCEDURE FOR PREPARING BROTH-BASED VEGETABLE SOUPS

1. Sweat long-cooking vegetables in butter or fat.
2. Add the appropriate stock or broth and bring to a simmer.
3. Add seasonings such as bay leaves, dried thyme, crushed peppercorns, parsley stems and garlic, in a sachet, allowing enough time for the seasonings to fully flavor the soup.
4. Add additional ingredients according to their cooking times.
5. Simmer the soup to blend all the flavors.
6. If the soup is not going to be served immediately, cool and refrigerate it.
7. Just before service, add any garnishes that were prepared separately or do not require cooking.

RECIPE 10.2

HEARTY VEGETABLE BEEF SOUP

Mise en Place

- ▶ Peel and chop onions, carrots and celery for mirepoix.
- ▶ Wash and peel turnip and chop into fine dice.
- ▶ Peel and chop garlic.
- ▶ Cut beef into fine dice.
- ▶ Prepare herb sachet.
- ▶ While broth is simmering, peel, seed and dice tomato for concassée.

1 Sweating the vegetables.

2 The finished soup.

▶ **concassée** peeled, seeded and diced tomato

Yield: 5 qt. (5 lt)

Butter or beef fat	6 oz.	170 g
Mirepoix, small dice	3 lb.	1.5 kg
Turnip, small dice	8 oz.	250 g
Garlic cloves, chopped	2	2
Beef broth or stock	4 qt.	4 lt
Beef, small dice	1 lb.	450 g
Sachet:		
Bay leaf	1	1
Dried thyme	½ tsp.	2 ml
Peppercorns, crushed	½ tsp.	2 ml
Parsley stems	8	8
Tomato **concassée**	12 oz.	350 g
Corn kernels, fresh, frozen or canned	12 oz.	350 g
Salt and pepper	TT	TT

1 In a soup pot, sweat the mirepoix and turnip in the butter or fat until tender.

2 Add the garlic and sauté lightly.

3 Add the broth or stock and the diced beef; bring to a simmer. Add the sachet. Skim or degrease as necessary.

4 Simmer until the beef and vegetables are tender, approximately 1 hour.

5 Add the tomato concassée and corn; simmer for 10 minutes. Season to taste with salt and pepper.

6 Cool and refrigerate or hold for service.

VARIATIONS:

A wide variety of vegetables can be added or substituted in this recipe. If leeks, rutabagas, parsnips or cabbage are used, they should be sweated to bring out their flavors before the liquid is added. Potatoes, fresh beans, summer squash and other vegetables that cook more quickly should be added according to their cooking times. Rice, barley and pasta garnishes should be cooked separately and added just before service.

Approximate values per 6-fl.-oz. (180-ml) serving: **Calories** 170, **Total fat** 10 g, **Saturated fat** 5 g, **Cholesterol** 30 mg, **Sodium** 600 mg, **Total carbohydrates** 12 g, **Protein** 7 g, **Vitamin A** 20%

CONSOMMÉS

A consommé is a stock or broth that has been clarified to remove impurities so that it is crystal clear. Traditionally, all clear broths were referred to as consommés; a clear broth further refined using the process described later was referred to as a double consommé. The term *double consommé* is still used occasionally to describe any strongly flavored consommé.

Well-prepared consommés should be rich in the flavor of the main ingredient. Beef and game consommés should be dark in color; consommés made from poultry should have a golden to light amber color. They should have substantial body as a result of their high gelatin content, and all consommés should be perfectly clear with no trace of fat.

Because a consommé is a refined broth, it is absolutely essential that the broth or stock used be of the highest quality. Although the clarification process adds some flavor to the consommé, the finished consommé will be only as good as the stock or broth from which it was made.

THE CLARIFICATION PROCESS

To make a consommé, you clarify a stock or broth. The stock or broth to be clarified must be cold and grease-free. To clarify, the cold degreased stock or broth is combined with a mixture known as a **clearmeat** or **clarification.** A clearmeat is a mixture of egg whites; ground meat, poultry or fish; mirepoix, herbs and spices; and an acidic product, usually tomatoes, lemon juice or wine. (An **oignon brûlé,** also known as an onion brûlé, is also often added to help flavor and color the consommé. See Chapter 7, Mise en Place.)

▶ **oignon brûlé** French for "burnt onion"; made by charring onion halves; used to flavor and color stocks and sauces

The stock or broth and clearmeat are then slowly brought to a simmer. As the albumen in the egg whites and meat begins to coagulate, it traps impurities suspended in the liquid. As coagulation continues, the albumen-containing items combine with the other clearmeat ingredients and rise to the liquid's surface, forming a **raft.** As the mixture simmers, the raft ingredients release their flavors, further enriching the consommé.

After simmering, the consommé is carefully strained through several layers of cheesecloth to remove any trace of impurities. It is then completely degreased, either by cooling and refrigerating, then removing the solidified fat, or by carefully ladling the fat from the surface. The result is a rich, flavorful, crystal-clear consommé.

▶ PROCEDURE FOR PREPARING CONSOMMÉS

1. In a suitable stockpot (one with a spigot makes it much easier to strain the consommé when it is finished), combine the ground meat, lightly beaten egg white and other clearmeat ingredients.
2. Add the cold stock or broth and stir to combine with the clearmeat ingredients.
3. Over medium heat, slowly bring the mixture to a simmer, stirring occasionally.
4. As the raft forms, make a hole in its center so that the liquid can bubble through, cooking the raft completely and extracting as much flavor as possible from the raft ingredients.
5. Simmer the consommé until full flavor develops, approximately 1 to 1½ hours.
6. Carefully strain the consommé through several layers of cheesecloth and degrease completely.
7. If the consommé will not be used immediately, it should be cooled and refrigerated, following the procedures for cooling stocks discussed in Chapter 9. When the consommé is completely cold, remove any remaining fat that solidifies on its surface.
8. If, after reheating the consommé, small dots of fat appear on the surface, they can be removed by blotting with a small piece of paper towel.

RECIPE 10.3 BEEF CONSOMMÉ

Mise en Place

- ▶ Peel and chop onions, carrots and celery for mirepoix.
- ▶ Seed and dice tomato.
- ▶ Prepare onions brûlés and herb sachet.

Yield: 4 qt. (4 lt)

Ingredient	U.S.	Metric
Egg whites	10	10
Ground beef, lean, preferably shank, neck or shoulder	2 lb.	1 kg
Mirepoix	1 lb.	450 g
Tomatoes, seeded and diced	12 oz.	340 g
Beef broth or stock, cold	5 qt.	5 lt
Onions brûlés	2	2
Sachet:		
Bay leaves	2	2
Dried thyme	1/2 tsp.	2 ml
Peppercorns, crushed	1/2 tsp.	2 ml
Parsley stems	8	8
Cloves, whole	2	2
Salt	TT	TT

1 Whip the egg whites until slightly frothy.

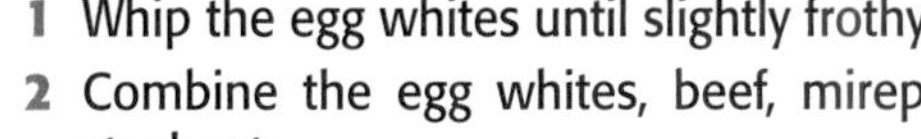

2 Combine the egg whites, beef, mirepoix and tomatoes in an appropriate stockpot.

3 Add the broth or stock; mix well and add the onions brûlés and sachet.

4 Bring the mixture to a simmer over moderate heat, stirring occasionally. Stop stirring when the raft begins to form.

5 Break a hole in the center of the raft to allow the consommé to bubble through.

6 Simmer until full flavor develops, approximately 1 1/2 hours.

7 Strain through several layers of cheesecloth, degrease and adjust the seasonings. Cool and refrigerate or hold for service.

Approximate values per 6-fl.-oz. (180-ml) serving: **Calories** 210, **Total fat** 10 g, **Saturated fat** 3.5 g, **Cholesterol** 40 mg, **Sodium** 870 mg, **Total carbohydrates** 14 g, **Protein** 15 g, **Vitamin A** 20%, **Vitamin C** 10%

1 Combining the ingredients for the clearmeat.

2 Making a hole in the raft to allow the liquid to bubble through.

3 Degreasing the consommé with a paper towel.

4 The finished consommé.

CORRECTING A POORLY CLARIFIED CONSOMMÉ

A clarification may fail for a variety of reasons. For example, if the consommé is allowed to boil or if it is stirred after the raft has formed, a cloudy consommé can result. If the consommé is insufficiently clear, a second clarification can be performed using the following procedure. This second clarification should be performed only once, however, and only if absolutely necessary, because the eggs remove not only impurities but also some of the consommé's flavor and richness.

1. Thoroughly chill and degrease the consommé.
2. Lightly beat four egg whites per gallon (4 liters) of consommé and combine with the cold consommé.
3. Slowly bring the consommé to a simmer, stirring occasionally. Stop stirring when the egg whites begin to coagulate.
4. When the egg whites are completely coagulated, carefully strain the consommé.

▶ THICK SOUPS

There are two kinds of thick soups: cream soups and purée soups. In general, cream soups are thickened with a roux or other starch, while purée soups rely on a purée of the main ingredient for thickening. But in certain ways the two soups are very similar: Some purée soups are finished with cream or partially thickened with a roux or other starch. See Tables 10.1 and 10.2.

CREAM SOUPS

Most cream soups are made by simmering the main flavoring ingredient (for example, broccoli for cream of broccoli soup) in a white stock or thin **velouté** sauce to which seasonings have been added. The mixture is then puréed and strained. After the consistency has been adjusted, the soup is finished by adding cream. In classic cuisine, thin **béchamel** sauce is often used as the base for cream soups and can be substituted for velouté in many cream soup recipes, if desired.

▶ **velouté** (veh-loo-tay) a leading sauce made by thickening a white stock (fish, veal, or chicken) with roux

▶ **béchamel** (bay-shah-mell) a leading sauce made by thickening milk with a white roux and adding seasonings

Both hard vegetables (for example, celery and squash) and soft or leafy vegetables (for example, spinach, corn, broccoli and asparagus) are used for cream soups. Hard vegetables are generally sweated in butter without browning before the liquid is added. Soft and leafy vegetables are generally added to the soup

Table 10.1 **SOUPS, THEIR THICKENING AGENTS AND FINISHES**

CATEGORY	TYPE	THICKENING AGENT OR METHOD	FINISH
Clear soups	Broths	None	Assorted garnishes
	Consommés	None	Assorted garnishes
Thick soups	Cream soups	Roux and/or puréeing	Assorted garnishes, cream or béchamel sauce
	Purée soups	Puréeing	Assorted garnishes; cream is optional
Other soups	Bisques	Roux or rice and puréeing	Garnish of main ingredient cream and/or butter
	Chowders	Roux	Cream
Cold soups	Cooked cold soups	Roux, arrowroot, cornstarch, puréeing, sour cream, yogurt	Assorted garnishes, cream, crème fraîche or sour cream
	Uncooked cold soups	Puréeing	Assorted garnishes, cream, crème fraîche or sour cream

Table 10.2 CREAM AND PURÉE SOUPS

	CREAM SOUPS	PURÉE SOUPS
Technique	Cook principal ingredient in stock or velouté sauce	Cook principal ingredient in stock or water
Thickener	Roux or roux-thickened sauce	Purée of starchy ingredients
Texture	Strained; very smooth and rich	Not strained; slightly coarse and grainy

after the liquid is brought to a boil. Because cream soups are puréed, it is important to cook the flavoring ingredients until they are soft and can be passed through a food mill easily.

All cream soups are finished with milk or cream. Using milk thins the soup while adding richness; using the same amount of cream adds much more richness without the same thinning effect. Cold milk and cream curdle easily if added directly to a hot or acidic soup.

To prevent curdling:

▶ **cream sauce** a sauce made by adding cream to a béchamel sauce

1 Never add cold milk or cream to hot soup. Bring the milk or cream to a simmer before adding it to the soup. Or, temper the milk or cream by gradually adding some hot soup to it and then incorporating the warmed mixture into the rest of the soup.
2 Add the milk or cream to the soup just before service, if possible.
3 Do not boil the soup after the milk or cream has been added.
4 Use béchamel or cream sauce instead of milk or cream to finish cream soups because the presence of roux or other starch helps prevent curdling.

▶ PROCEDURE FOR PREPARING CREAM SOUPS

1 In a soup pot, sweat hard vegetables such as squash, onions, carrots and celery in oil or butter without browning.
2 In order to thicken the soup:
   a. add flour and cook to make a blond roux, then add the cooking liquid (that is, the stock), or
   b. add the stock to the vegetables, bring the stock to a simmer and add a blond roux that was prepared separately, or
   c. add a thin velouté or béchamel sauce (which contain roux) to the vegetables.
3 Bring to a boil and reduce to a simmer.
4 Add any soft vegetables such as broccoli or asparagus, and a sachet or bouquet garni as desired.
5 Simmer the soup, skimming occasionally, until the vegetables are very tender.
6 Purée the soup by passing it through a food mill, blender, food processor or vertical cutter/mixer (VCM). Strain through a china cap if desired. If the soup is too thick, adjust the consistency by adding hot white stock.
7 Finish the soup by adding hot milk or cream or a thin béchamel or cream sauce. Adjust the seasonings and serve.

CREAM OF BROCCOLI SOUP

RECIPE 10.4

Yield: 6 qt. (6 lt)

Whole butter	3 oz.	90 g
Onions, medium dice	12 oz.	340 g
Celery, medium dice	3 oz.	90 g
Broccoli, chopped	3 lb.	1.4 kg
Chicken velouté sauce, hot	4 qt.	4 lt
Chicken stock, hot	approx. 2 qt.	approx. 2 lt
Heavy cream, hot	24 fl. oz.	700 ml
Salt and white pepper	TT	TT
Broccoli florets, blanched	8 oz.	250 g

1 Sweat the onions, celery and broccoli in the butter, without browning, until they are nearly tender.
2 Add the velouté sauce. Bring to a simmer and cook until the vegetables are tender, approximately 15 minutes. Skim the surface periodically.
3 Purée the soup, then strain it through a china cap.
4 Return the soup to the stove and thin it to the correct consistency with the stock.
5 Bring the soup to a simmer and add the cream. Season to taste.
6 Garnish with blanched broccoli florets just before service.

Mise en Place

- ▶ Clean and peel onions and celery and chop into medium dice.
- ▶ Chop broccoli.
- ▶ Prepare velouté sauce and keep warm.
- ▶ While the soup is simmering, blanch broccoli florets.

VARIATIONS:

To make cream of asparagus, cauliflower, corn, pea or spinach soup, substitute an equal amount of the chosen vegetable for the broccoli. If using fresh spinach, precook the leaves slightly before proceeding with the recipe.

Approximate values per 6-fl.-oz. (180-ml) serving: **Calories** 140, **Total fat** 12 g, **Saturated fat** 7 g, **Cholesterol** 40 mg, **Sodium** 340 mg, **Total carbohydrates** 5 g, **Protein** 4 g, **Vitamin A** 20%, **Vitamin C** 70%

1 Adding the velouté sauce.

2 Puréeing the soup through a food mill.

3 Garnishing the finished soup.

PURÉE SOUPS

Purée soups are hearty soups made by cooking starchy vegetables or legumes in a stock or broth, then puréeing all or a portion of them to thicken the soup. Purée soups are similar to cream soups in that they both consist of a main ingredient that is first cooked in a liquid, then puréed. The primary difference is that unlike cream soups, which are thickened with starch, purée soups generally do not use additional starch for thickening. Rather, purée soups depend on the starch content of the main ingredient for thickening. Also, purée soups are generally coarser than cream soups and are typically not strained after puréeing. When finishing purée soups with cream, follow the guidelines discussed previously for adding cream to cream soups.

Purée soups can be made with dried or fresh beans such as peas, lentils and navy beans, or with any number of vegetables, including cauliflower, celery root, turnips and potatoes. Diced potatoes or rice are often used to help thicken vegetable purée soups.

▶ PROCEDURE FOR PREPARING PURÉE SOUPS

1. Sweat the mirepoix in butter without browning.
2. Add the cooking liquid.
3. Add the main ingredients and a sachet or bouquet garni.
4. Bring to a boil, reduce to a simmer and cook until all the ingredients are soft enough to purée easily. Remove and discard the sachet or bouquet garni.
5. Reserve a portion of the liquid to adjust the soup's consistency. Purée the rest of the soup by passing it through a food mill, food processor, blender or VCM.
6. Add enough of the reserved liquid to bring the soup to the correct consistency. If the soup is still too thick, add hot stock as needed.
7. Return the soup to a simmer and adjust the seasonings.
8. Add hot cream to the soup if desired.

RECIPE 10.5

PURÉE OF SPLIT PEA SOUP

Mise en Place

- ▶ Dice bacon.
- ▶ Peel onions, carrots and celery and chop into medium dice for mirepoix.
- ▶ Peel and chop garlic.
- ▶ Wash and sort split peas.
- ▶ Prepare herb sachet.
- ▶ Sauté croutons in butter while the soup is simmering.

Yield: 4 qt. (4 lt)

Bacon, diced	3 oz.	90 g
Mirepoix, medium dice	1 lb.	450 g
Garlic cloves, chopped	2	2
Chicken stock	3 qt.	3 lt
Split peas, washed and sorted	1 lb.	450 g
Ham hocks or meaty ham bones	1½ lb.	650 g
Sachet:		
Bay leaves	2	2
Dried thyme	½ tsp.	2 ml
Peppercorns, crushed	½ tsp.	2 ml
Salt and pepper	TT	TT
Croutons, sautéed in butter	as needed for garnish	

▶ **render** to melt and clarify fat

1. In a stockpot, **render** the bacon by cooking it slowly and allowing it to release its fat; sweat the mirepoix and garlic in the fat without browning them.
2. Add the stock, peas, ham hocks or bones and sachet. Bring to a boil, reduce to a simmer and cook until the peas are soft, approximately 1 to 1½ hours.
3. Remove the sachet and ham hocks or bones. Pass the soup through a food mill and return it to the stockpot.
4. Remove the meat from the hocks or bones. Cut the meat into medium dice and add it to the soup.

5 Bring the soup to a simmer and, if necessary, adjust the consistency by adding hot chicken stock. Adjust the seasonings and serve, garnished with croutons.

VARIATIONS:

White beans, yellow peas and other dried beans can be soaked overnight in water and used instead of split peas.

Approximate values per 6-fl.-oz. (180-ml) serving: **Calories** 110, **Total fat** 4 g, **Saturated fat** 1.5 g, **Cholesterol** 20 mg, **Sodium** 870 mg, **Total carbohydrates** 6 g, **Protein** 11 g

1 Adding peas to the stockpot.

2 Puréeing the split pea soup.

3 Garnishing the finished soup.

ADJUSTING THE CONSISTENCY OF THICK SOUPS

Cream and purée soups tend to thicken when made in advance and refrigerated. To dilute a portion being reheated, add hot stock, broth, water or milk to the hot soup as needed.

If the soup is too thin, additional roux, beurre manié or cornstarch mixed with cool stock can be used to thicken it. If additional starch is added to thicken the soup, it should be used sparingly and the soup should be simmered a few minutes to cook out the starchy flavor. A liaison of egg yolks and heavy cream can be used to thicken cream soups when added richness is also desired. Remember, the soup must not boil after the liaison is added or it may curdle.

▶ OTHER SOUPS

Several popular types of soup do not fit the descriptions of, or follow the procedures for, either clear or thick soups. Soups such as bisques and chowders as well as many cold soups use special methods or a combination of the methods used for clear and thick soups.

BISQUES

Traditional bisques are shellfish soups thickened with cooked rice. Today, bisques are prepared using a combination of the cream and purée soup procedures. They are generally made from shrimp, lobster or crayfish and are thickened with a roux instead of rice for better stability and consistency.

Much of a bisque's flavor comes from crustacean shells, which are simmered in the cooking liquid, puréed (along with the mirepoix), returned to the cooking liquid and strained after further cooking. Puréeing the shells and returning them to the soup also adds the thickness and grainy texture associated with bisques.

Bisques are enriched with cream, following the procedures for cream soups, and can be finished with butter for additional richness. The garnish should be diced flesh from the appropriate shellfish.

▶ PROCEDURE FOR PREPARING BISQUES

1. Caramelize the mirepoix and main flavoring ingredient in fat.
2. Add a tomato product and deglaze with wine.
3. Add the cooking liquid (stock or velouté sauce).
4. Incorporate roux if needed.
5. Simmer, skimming as needed.
6. Strain the soup, reserving the solids and liquid. Purée the solids in a food mill or processor and return them to the liquid. Return to a simmer.
7. Strain the soup through a fine chinois or a china cap lined with cheesecloth.
8. Return the soup to a simmer and finish with hot cream.

To add even more richness to the bisque, monté au beurre with whole butter or a compound butter such as shrimp or lobster butter just before the soup is served. Also, if desired, add 3 ounces (90 milliliters) of sherry to each gallon (4 liters) of soup just before service.

RECIPE 10.6

SHRIMP BISQUE

Mise en Place

- ▶ Peel onions, carrots and celery and chop into small dice for mirepoix.
- ▶ Peel and chop garlic.
- ▶ Prepare fish velouté with shrimp stock.
- ▶ Prepare herb sachet.
- ▶ Peel and devein shrimp.
- ▶ Wash and chop basil in chiffonade while bisque is simmering.

Yield: 4 qt. (4 lt)

Ingredient	U.S.	Metric
Clarified butter	3 fl. oz.	90 ml
Mirepoix, small dice	1 lb.	450 g
Shrimp shells and/or lobster or crayfish shells and bodies	2 lb.	1 kg
Garlic cloves, chopped	2	2
Tomato paste	2 oz.	60 g
Brandy	4 fl. oz.	120 ml
White wine	12 fl. oz.	350 ml
Fish velouté (made with shrimp stock)	4 qt.	4 lt
Sachet:		
Bay leaf	1	1
Dried thyme	½ tsp.	2 ml
Peppercorns, crushed	½ tsp.	2 ml
Parsley stems	8	8
Heavy cream, hot	1 pt.	500 ml
Salt and white pepper	TT	TT
Cayenne pepper	TT	TT
Dry or cream sherry wine, optional	4 fl. oz.	120 ml
Shrimp, peeled and deveined	1 lb.	450 g
Fresh basil, chiffonade	as needed for garnish	

1. Caramelize the mirepoix and shrimp shells in the butter.
2. Add the garlic and tomato paste and sauté lightly.
3. Add the brandy and flambé.

4 Add the wine. Deglaze and reduce the liquid by half.
5 Add the velouté and sachet and simmer for approximately 1 hour, skimming occasionally.
6 Strain, discarding the sachet and reserving the liquid and solids. Purée the solids and return them to the liquid. Return to a simmer and cook for 10 minutes.
7 Strain the bisque through a fine chinois or china cap lined with cheesecloth.
8 Return the bisque to a simmer and add the cream.
9 Season to taste with salt, white pepper and cayenne pepper. Add sherry, if using.
10 Cook the shrimp and slice or dice them as desired. Garnish each portion of soup with cooked shrimp and the basil chiffonade.

Approximate values per 4-fl.-oz. (120-ml) serving: **Calories** 110, **Total fat** 10 g, **Saturated fat** 6 g, **Cholesterol** 60 mg, **Sodium** 160 mg, **Total carbohydrates** 2 g, **Protein** 4 g, **Vitamin A** 10%

CHOWDERS

Although chowders are usually associated with the eastern United States where fish and clams are plentiful, they are of French origin. Undoubtedly the word chowder is derived from the Breton phrase *faire chaudière*, which means to make a fish stew in a caldron. The procedure was probably brought to Nova Scotia by French settlers and later introduced to New England.

Chowders are hearty soups with chunks of the main ingredients (including, virtually always, diced potatoes) and garnishes. With some exceptions (notably, Manhattan clam chowder), chowders contain milk or cream. Although there are thin chowders, most chowders are thickened with roux. The procedures for making chowders are similar to those for making cream soups except that chowders are not puréed and strained before the cream is added.

► PROCEDURE FOR PREPARING CHOWDERS

1 Render finely diced salt pork over medium heat.
2 Sweat mirepoix in the rendered pork.
3 Add flour to make a roux.
4 Add the liquid.
5 Add the seasoning and flavoring ingredients according to their cooking times.
6 Simmer, skimming as needed.
7 Add milk or cream.

RECIPE 10.7

NEW ENGLAND–STYLE CLAM CHOWDER

Mise en Place

- ▶ Peel and dice potatoes.
- ▶ Dice the salt pork.
- ▶ Peel and dice onions and celery.
- ▶ Peel and julienne carrot garnish while chowder is simmering.

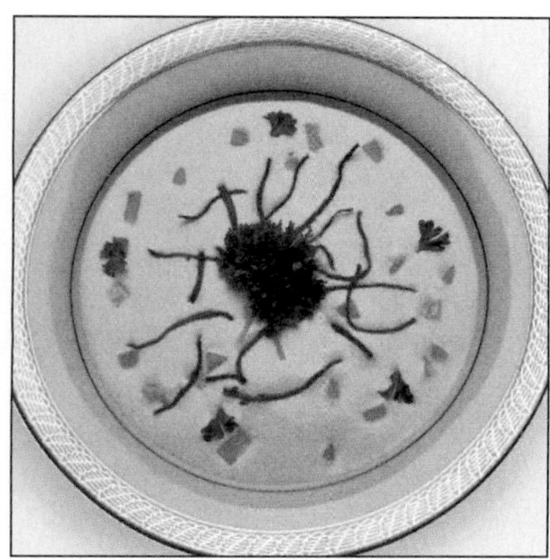

Yield: 3½ qt. (3.5 lt)

Canned clams with juice*	2 qt.	2 lt
Water or fish stock	approx. 1½ qt.	approx. 1.5 lt
Potatoes, small dice	1 lb. 4 oz.	600 g
Salt pork, small dice	8 oz.	250 g
Whole butter	2 oz.	60 g
Onions, small dice	1 lb.	500 g
Celery, small dice	8 oz.	250 g
Flour	4 oz.	120 g
Milk	1 qt.	1 lt
Heavy cream	8 fl. oz.	250 ml
Salt and pepper	TT	TT
Tabasco sauce	TT	TT
Worcestershire sauce	TT	TT
Fresh thyme	TT	TT
Fresh parsley	as needed for garnish	
Carrot, julienned	as needed for garnish	

1. Drain the clams, reserving both the clams and their liquid. Add enough water or stock so that the total liquid equals 2 quarts (2 liters).
2. Simmer the potatoes in the clam liquid until nearly cooked through. Strain and reserve the potatoes and the liquid.
3. Render the salt pork with the butter. Add the onions and celery to the rendered fat and sweat until tender but not brown.
4. Add the flour and cook to make a blond roux.
5. Add the clam liquid to the roux, whisking away any lumps.
6. Simmer for 30 minutes, skimming as necessary.
7. Bring the milk and cream to a boil and add to the soup.
8. Add the clams and potatoes, and season to taste with salt, pepper, Tabasco sauce, Worcestershire sauce and thyme.
9. Garnish each serving with fresh parsley and julienned carrot as desired.

*If using fresh clams for the chowder, wash and steam approximately ½ bushel (15 liters) chowder clams in a small amount of water to yield 1¼ quarts (1.25 liters) clam meat. Chop the clams. Strain the liquid through several layers of cheesecloth to remove any sand that may be present. Add enough water or stock so that the total liquid is 2 quarts (2 liters). Continue with the recipe, starting at step 2.

Approximate values per 6-fl.-oz. (180-ml) serving: **Calories** 250, **Total fat** 15 g, **Saturated fat** 7 g, **Cholesterol** 45 mg, **Sodium** 930 mg, **Total carbohydrates** 17 g, **Protein** 11 g, **Vitamin A** 10%, **Vitamin C** 10%, **Calcium** 15%

SAFETY ALERT

Cooked Cold Soup

Cooked cold soups, especially those made with potatoes, beans, dairy products or other high-protein foods, are potentially hazardous foods and must be chilled quickly and held at or below 41°F (5°C). Because these soups will not be reheated for service, cross-contamination is also a concern. Keep the soup covered and store above any raw meat, poultry or seafood in the cooler.

COLD SOUPS

Cold soups can be as simple as a chilled version of a cream soup or as creative as a cold fruit soup blended with yogurt. Cold fruit soups have become popular on contemporary dessert menus. Other than the fact that they are cold, cold soups are difficult to classify because many of them use unique or combination preparation methods. Regardless, they are divided here into two categories: cold soups that require cooking and those that do not.

COOKED COLD SOUPS

Many cold soups are simply a chilled version of a hot soup. For example, consommé madrilène and consommé portugaise are prepared hot and served cold.

Vichyssoise is a cold version of puréed potato-leek soup. When serving a hot soup cold, there are several considerations:

1. If the soup is to be creamed, add the cream at the last minute. Although curdling is not as much of a problem as it is with hot soups, adding the cream at the last minute helps extend the soup's shelf life.
2. Cold soups should have a thinner consistency than hot soups. To achieve the proper consistency, use less starch if starch is used as the thickener, or use a higher ratio of liquid to main ingredient if the soup is thickened by puréeing. Consistency should be checked and adjusted at service time.
3. Cold dulls the sense of taste, so cold soups require more seasoning than hot ones. Taste the soup just before service and adjust the seasonings as needed.
4. Always serve cold soups as cold as possible, using chilled bowls.

VICHYSSOISE (COLD POTATO-LEEK SOUP)

RECIPE 10.8

Yield: 4 qt. (4 lt)

Method: Purée

Leeks, white part only	2 lb.	1 kg
Whole butter	8 oz.	250 g
Russet potatoes, large dice	2 lb.	1 kg
Chicken stock	3½ qt.	3½ lt
Salt and white pepper	TT	TT
Heavy cream	24 fl. oz.	700 ml
Chives, snipped	as needed for garnish	
Fried sweet potato frizzles	as needed for garnish	

1. Split the leeks lengthwise and wash well to remove all sand and grit. Slice them thinly.
2. Sweat the leeks in the butter without browning them.
3. Add the diced potatoes and stock, season with salt and white pepper and bring to a simmer.
4. Simmer until the leeks and potatoes are very tender, approximately 45 minutes.
5. Purée the soup in a food processor, blender or food mill; strain through a fine sieve.
6. Chill the soup well.
7. At service time, incorporate the cream and adjust the seasonings. Serve in chilled bowls, garnished with snipped chives and sweet potato frizzles.

Approximate values per 6-fl.-oz. (180-ml) serving: **Calories** 300, **Total fat** 22 g, **Saturated fat** 13 g, **Cholesterol** 70 mg, **Sodium** 660 mg, **Total carbohydrates** 19 g, **Protein** 6 g, **Vitamin A** 20%, **Vitamin C** 20%

Mise en Place

- ▶ Wash and trim leeks.
- ▶ Peel and dice potatoes.
- ▶ Snip chives and prepare potato garnish while soup is chilling.

Many cooked cold soups use fruit juice (typically apple, grape or orange) as a base and are thickened with cornstarch or arrowroot as well as with puréed fruit. For additional flavor, wine is sometimes used in lieu of a portion of the fruit juice. Cinnamon, ginger and other spices that complement fruit are commonly added, as is lemon or lime juice, which adds acidity as well as flavor. Crème fraîche, yogurt or sour cream can be used as an ingredient or garnish to add richness.

RECIPE 10.9

FRESH PEACH AND YOGURT SOUP

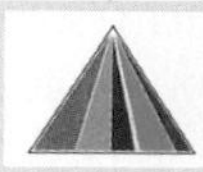

Yield: 2 qt. (2 lt) **Method:** Purée

Fresh peaches	4 lb.	1.8 kg
Dry white wine	24 fl. oz.	700 ml
Honey	4 oz.	120 g
Lemon juice	2 fl. oz.	60 ml
Cinnamon, ground	1/4 tsp.	1 ml
Plain nonfat yogurt	8 oz.	225 g
Heavy cream	TT	TT
Pistachios, chopped fine	as needed for garnish	

1 Pit and coarsely chop the peaches without peeling. Place in a nonreactive saucepan. Add the wine, honey and lemon juice. Cover and simmer for 30 minutes.
2 Purée the peach mixture in a blender. Strain and chill.
3 Stir in the cinnamon, yogurt and cream.
4 Chill thoroughly. Serve in chilled bowls, garnished with finely chopped pistachio nuts.

Approximate values per 6-fl.-oz. (180-ml) serving: **Calories** 140, **Total fat** 0 g, **Saturated fat** 0 g, **Cholesterol** 0 mg, **Sodium** 20 mg, **Total carbohydrates** 32 g, **Protein** 3 g, **Vitamin A** 10%, **Vitamin C** 25%, **Claims**—fat free; very low sodium; good source of fiber

1 Simmering the peaches.

2 Straining the peach purée.

3 The finished soup.

UNCOOKED COLD SOUPS

Some cold soups are not cooked at all. Rather, they rely only on puréed fruits or vegetables for thickness, body and flavor. Cold stock is sometimes used to adjust the soup's consistency. Dairy products such as cream, sour cream and crème fraîche are sometimes added to enrich and flavor the soup.

GAZPACHO

RECIPE 10.10

Yield: 4 qt. (4 lt) **Method:** Uncooked

Ingredient	U.S.	Metric
Tomatoes, peeled and diced	2 lb. 8 oz.	1.2 kg
Onions, medium dice	8 oz.	250 g
Green bell pepper, medium dice	1	1
Red bell pepper, medium dice	1	1
Cucumbers, peeled, seeded, medium dice	1 lb.	500 g
Garlic, minced	1 oz.	30 g
Red wine vinegar	2 fl. oz.	60 ml
Lemon juice	2 fl. oz.	60 ml
Olive oil	4 fl. oz.	120 ml
Salt and pepper	TT	TT
Cayenne pepper	TT	TT
Fresh bread crumbs (optional)	3 oz.	90 g
Tomato juice	3 qt.	3 lt
White stock	as needed	as needed
Garnish:		
Tomatoes, peeled, seeded, small dice	8 oz.	250 g
Red bell pepper, small dice	4 oz.	120 g
Green bell pepper, small dice	4 oz.	120 g
Yellow bell pepper, small dice	4 oz.	120 g
Cucumber, peeled, seeded, small dice	3 oz.	90 g
Green onion, sliced fine	2 oz.	60 g
Fresh basil	as needed for garnish	

1. Combine and purée all ingredients except the tomato juice, stock and garnish in a VCM, food processor or blender.
2. Stir in the tomato juice.
3. Adjust the consistency with the stock.
4. Stir in the vegetable garnishes and adjust the seasonings.
5. Serve in chilled cups or bowls garnished with fresh basil.

VARIATION:

Gazpacho can be made without puréeing all the ingredients. Less garnish will be required.

Approximate values per 6-fl.-oz. (180-ml) serving: **Calories** 70, **Total fat** 0.5 g, **Saturated fat** 0 g, **Cholesterol** 0 mg, **Sodium** 600 mg, **Total carbohydrates** 14 g, **Protein** 3 g, **Vitamin A** 15%, **Vitamin C** 70%, **Claims**—low fat; no cholesterol

Mise en Place

- ▶ Peel and dice the tomatoes, onions and peppers.
- ▶ Peel, seed and dice the cucumbers.
- ▶ Mince the garlic.
- ▶ Peel and finely slice the green onions.

▶ GARNISHING SOUPS

Garnishes and toppings can range from a simple sprinkle of chopped parsley on a bowl of cream soup to tiny profiteroles stuffed with foie gras adorning a crystal-clear bowl of consommé. Some soups are so full of attractive, flavorful and colorful foods that are integral parts of the soup (for example, vegetables and chicken in chicken vegetable soup) that no additional garnishes are necessary. In others, the garnish determines the type of soup. For example, a beef broth garnished with cooked barley and diced beef becomes beef barley soup.

SAFETY ALERT

Uncooked Cold Soup

Because uncooked cold soups are never heated, enzymes and bacteria are not destroyed and the soup can spoil quickly. Many cold soups also contain dairy products, which makes them a potentially hazardous food. When preparing uncooked cold soups, always prepare small batches as close to service time as possible. Keep the soup at or below 41°F (5°C) at all times. Cover and store leftovers properly.

CLASSIC CONSOMMÉS

Many classic consommés are known by their garnishes:

Consommé brunoise–blanched or sautéed brunoise of turnip, leek, celery and onion.

Consommé julienne–blanched or sautéed julienne of carrot, turnip, leek, celery, cabbage and onion.

Consommé paysanne–blanched or sautéed paysanne of leek, turnip, carrot, celery and potato.

Consommé bouquetière–assorted blanched vegetables.

Consommé madrilène–tomatoes or tomato juice; served hot or cold.

Consommé royale–cooked custard cut into tiny shapes.

Angel hair consommé–cooked angel hair (vermicelli) pasta.

Consommé with profiteroles–tiny profiteroles (pâte à choux rounds) stuffed with foie gras.

GUIDELINES FOR GARNISHING SOUPS

Although some soups (particularly consommés) have traditional garnishes, many soups depend on the chef's imagination and the kitchen's inventory for the finishing garnish. The only rules are as follows:

1. The garnish should be attractive.
2. The meats and vegetables used should be neatly cut into an appropriate and uniform shape and size. This is particularly important when garnishing a clear soup such as a consommé, as the consommé's clarity highlights the precise (or imprecise) cuts.
3. The garnish's texture and flavor should complement the soup.
4. Starches and vegetables used as garnishes should be cooked separately, reheated and placed in the soup bowl before the hot soup is added. If they are cooked in the soup, they may cloud or thicken the soup or alter its flavor, texture and seasoning.
5. Garnishes should be cooked just until done; meat and poultry should be tender but not falling apart, vegetables should be firm but not mushy, and pasta and rice should maintain their identity. These types of garnishes are usually held on the side and added to the hot soup at the last minute to prevent overcooking.

GARNISHING SUGGESTIONS

Some garnishes are used to add texture, as well as flavor and visual interest, to soups. Items such as crunchy croutons or oyster crackers, or crispy crumbled bacon on a cream soup, or diced meat in a clear broth soup add a textural variety that makes the final product more appealing.

- Clear soups—any combination of julienne cuts of the same meat, poultry, fish or vegetable that provides the dominant flavor in the stock or broth; vegetables (cut uniformly into any shape), pasta (flat, small tortellini or tiny ravioli), gnocchi, quenelles, barley, spaetzle, white or wild rice, croutons, crepes, tortillas or won tons.
- Cream soups, hot or cold—toasted slivered almonds, sour cream or crème fraîche, croutons, grated cheese or puff pastry fleurons; cream vegetable soups are usually garnished with slices or florets of the main ingredient.
- Purée soups—julienne cuts of poultry or ham, sliced sausage, croutons, grated cheese or bacon bits.
- Any soup—finely chopped fresh herbs, snipped chives, edible flowers, parsley or watercress.

▶ SOUP SERVICE

PREPARING SOUPS IN ADVANCE

Most soups can be made ahead of time and reheated as needed for service. To preserve freshness and quality, small batches of soup should be heated as needed throughout the meal service.

Clear soups are quite easy to reheat because there is little danger of scorching. If garnishes are already added to a clear soup, care should be taken not to overcook the garnishes when reheating the soup. All traces of fat should be removed from a consommé's surface before reheating.

Thick soups present more of a challenge. To increase shelf life and reduce the risk of spoilage, cool and refrigerate a thick soup when it is still a base (that is, before it is finished with milk or cream). Just before service, carefully reheat the soup base using a heavy-gauge pot over low heat. Stir often to prevent scorching. Then finish the soup (following the guidelines noted earlier) with boiling milk or cream, a light béchamel sauce or a liaison and adjust the seasonings. Always taste the soup after reheating and adjust the seasonings as needed.

TEMPERATURES

The rule is simple: Serve hot soup hot and cold soup cold. Hot clear soups should be served near boiling; 210°F (99°C) is ideal. Hot cream soups should be served at slightly lower temperatures; 190°F–200°F (88°C–93°C) is acceptable. Cold soups should be served at a temperature of 41°F (5°C) or below, and are sometimes presented in special serving pieces surrounded by ice.

CONCLUSION

Soup, often served as the first course, may determine the success or failure of an entire meal. Although a wide variety of ingredients can be used to make both clear and thick soups, including trimmings and leftovers, poor-quality ingredients make poor-quality soups. By using, adapting and combining the basic techniques described in this chapter with different ingredients, a chef can create an infinite number of new and appetizing hot or cold soups. But exercise good judgment when combining flavors and techniques, they should blend well and complement each other. Moreover, any garnishes that are added should contribute to the appearance and character of the finished soup. And remember, always serve hot soups hot and cold soups cold.

QUESTIONS FOR DISCUSSION

1. What are the differences between a stock and a broth?
2. What are the differences between a beef consommé and a beef-based broth? How are they similar?
3. What are the differences between a cream soup and a purée soup? How are they similar?
4. Create a recipe for veal consommé.
5. Discuss several techniques for serving soup. What can be done to ensure that soups are served at the correct temperature?
6. Explain how and why soups are garnished. Why is it sometimes said that the noodles in a chicken noodle soup are actually a garnish?

CHAPTER **ELEVEN**

COOKING IS AT ONCE ONE OF THE SIMPLEST AND MOST GRATIFYING OF THE ARTS, BUT TO COOK WELL ONE MUST LOVE AND RESPECT FOOD.

—Craig Claiborne, American food critic (1920–2000)

PRINCIPLES OF MEAT COOKERY

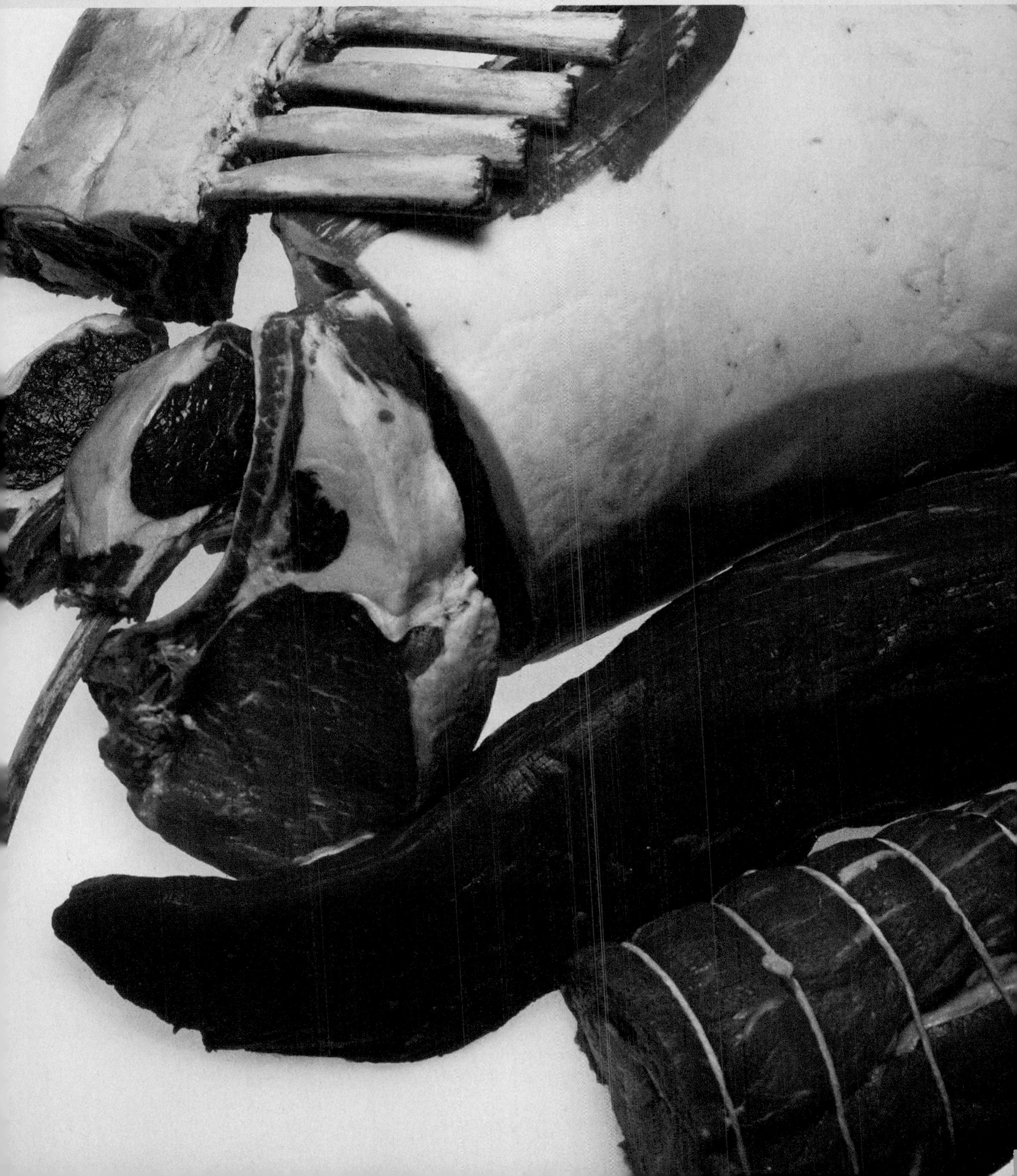

AFTER STUDYING THIS CHAPTER, YOU WILL BE ABLE TO:

- understand the structure and composition of meats
- understand meat inspection and grading practices
- purchase meats appropriate for your needs
- store meats properly
- prepare meats for cooking
- apply various cooking methods to meats

Meats—beef, veal, lamb and pork—often consume the largest portion of a food purchasing dollar. In this chapter, we discuss how to protect that investment. Students will learn how to determine the quality of meat, how to purchase meat in the form that best suits their needs and how to store it. We also discuss several of the dry-heat, moist-heat and combination cooking methods introduced in Chapter 8, Principles of Cooking, and how they can best be used so that a finished meat item is appealing to both the eye and palate. Although each of the cooking methods is illustrated with a single beef, veal, lamb or pork recipe, the analysis is intended to apply to all meats.

In Chapters 12 through 15, students will learn about the specific cuts of beef, veal, lamb and pork typically used in food service operations, as well as some basic butchering procedures. Recipes using these cuts and applying the various cooking methods are included at the end of each of those chapters.

▸ Muscle Composition

The carcasses of cattle, sheep, hogs and furred game animals consist mainly of edible lean muscular tissue, fat, connective tissue and bones. They are divided into large cuts called **primals.** Primal cuts are rarely cooked; rather, they are usually reduced to **subprimal cuts,** which in turn can be cooked as is or used to produce **fabricated cuts.** For example, the beef primal known as a short loin can be divided into subprimals, including the strip loin. The strip loin can be fabricated into other cuts, including New York steaks. The primals, subprimals and fabricated cuts of beef, veal, lamb and pork are discussed in Chapters 12 through 15, respectively; game is discussed in Chapter 17.

▸ **primal cuts** the primary divisions of muscle, bone and connective tissue produced by the initial butchering of the carcass

▸ **subprimal cuts** the basic cuts produced from each primal

▸ **fabricated cuts** individual portions cut from a subprimal

Muscle tissue gives meat its characteristic appearance; the amount of connective tissue determines the meat's tenderness. Muscle tissue is approximately 72 percent water, 20 percent protein, 7 percent fat and 1 percent minerals. (Meat shrinks during cooking as water evaporates and fats melt. Proper cooking helps prevent excessive **shrinkage,** which can cause the loss of finished weight and irregularly shaped meats after cooking.) A single muscle is composed of many bundles of muscle cells or fibers held together by connective tissue. See Figures 11.1 and 11.2. The thickness of the cells, the size of the cell bundles and the connective tissues holding them together form the grain of the meat and determine the meat's texture. When the fiber bundles are small, the meat has a fine grain and texture. Grain also refers to the direction in which the muscle fibers travel. When an animal fattens, some of the water and proteins in the lean muscle tissue are replaced with fat, which appears as **marbling.** Marbling adds tenderness and flavor to meat and is a principal factor in determining meat quality.

▸ **shrinkage** the loss of weight in a food due to evaporation of liquid or melting of fat during cooking

▸ **marbling** whitish streaks of inter- and intramuscular fat

▸ **subcutaneous fat** also known as exterior fat; the fat layer between the hide and muscles

Connective tissue forms the walls of the long muscle cells and binds them into bundles. It surrounds the muscle as a membrane and also appears as the tendons and ligaments that attach the muscles to the bone. Most connective tissue consists of either **collagen** or **elastin.** Collagen breaks down into gelatin and water when cooked using moist heat. Elastin, on the other hand, will not break down under normal cooking conditions. Because elastin remains stringy and tough, tendons and ligaments should be trimmed away before meat is cooked.

▸ **collagen** a protein found in connective tissue; it is converted into gelatin when cooked with moisture

▸ **elastin** a protein found in connective tissues, particularly ligaments and tendons; it often appears as the white or silver covering on meats known as silverskin

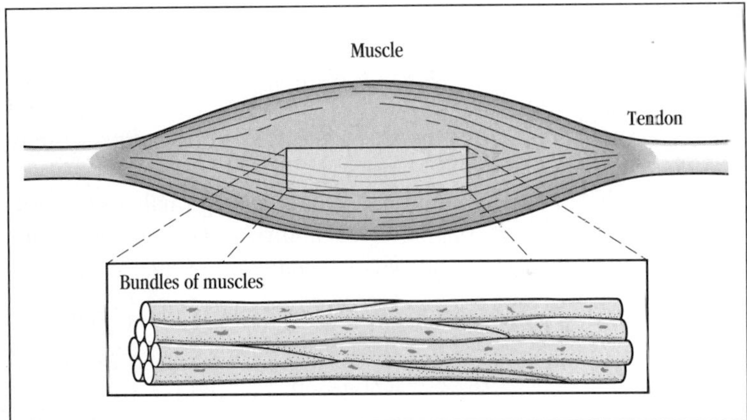

FIGURE 11.1 ▶ Muscle tissue.

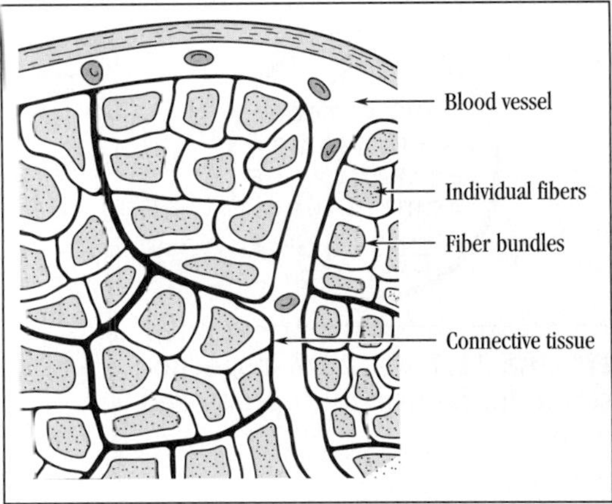

FIGURE 11.2 ▶ Crosscut of a bundle of muscle fibers.

Connective tissue develops primarily in the frequently used muscles. Therefore, cuts of meat from the shoulder (also known as the chuck), which the animal uses constantly, tend to be tougher than those from the back (also known as the loin), which are used less frequently. As an animal ages, the collagen present within the muscles becomes more resistant to breaking down through moist-heat cooking. Therefore, the meat of an older animal tends to be tougher than that of a younger one. Generally, the tougher the meat, the more flavorful it is, however.

The way that meat is fabricated also affects its tenderness. Cutting raw meat against the grain, pounding thinly sliced raw meat or grinding raw meat before cooking will tenderize tougher cuts. Butchering techniques have evolved to maximize the usability of primal cuts.

▶ **butcher** to slaughter and/or dress or fabricate animals for consumption

▶ **dress** to trim or otherwise prepare an animal carcass for consumption

▶ **fabricate** to cut a larger portion of raw meat (for example, a primal or subprimal), poultry or fish into smaller portions

▶ **carve** to cut cooked meat or poultry into portions

▶ Inspection and Grading of Meats

INSPECTION

All meat produced for public consumption in the United States is subject to USDA inspection. Inspections ensure that products are processed under strict sanitary guidelines and are wholesome and fit for human consumption. Inspections do not indicate a meat's quality or tenderness, however. Whole carcasses of beef, pork, lamb and veal are labeled with a round stamp identifying the slaughterhouse. See Figure 11.3. The stamp shown in Figure 11.4 is used for fabricated or processed meats and is found on either the product or its packaging.

FIGURE 11.3 ▶ USDA inspection stamp for whole carcasses.

DOMESTICATION OF ANIMALS

Early humans were hunter-gatherers, dependent on what their immediate environment offered for food. As "opportunistic" meat eaters, they ate meat when they could obtain it.

Anthropologists believe that the cultivation of grains and the birth of agriculture, which took place sometime around 9000 B.C.E., led directly to the domestication of animals. Sheep and goats were attracted to the fields of grain, and dogs and pigs to the garbage heaps of the new communities. Rather than allow these animals to interfere with food production, people tamed them, thus providing a steadier supply of meat. The first animals to be domesticated were most likely sheep, soon followed by goats. These animals—ruminants—can digest cellulose (humans cannot), so they could feed on stalks instead of valuable grains. Dogs and pigs, which prefer the same foods as humans, were tamed later, once there were more certain food supplies. Cattle were the most recently domesticated food animal, probably coming under control between 6100 and 5800 B.C.E.

FIGURE 11.4 ▶ USDA inspection stamp for fabricated or processed meats.

FIGURE 11.5 ▶ Quality grade stamp for USDA prime.

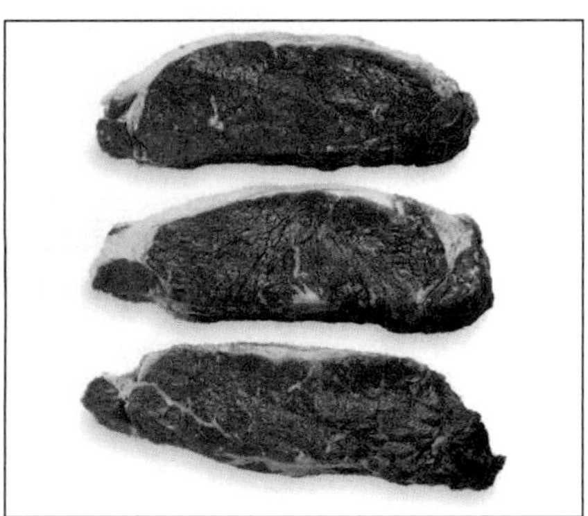

FIGURE 11.6 ▶ Quality grades of beef—no roll (top), Choice and Prime (bottom).

FIGURE 11.7 ▶ USDA yield grade stamp.

GRADING

USDA grading provides a voluntary, uniform system by which producers, distributors and consumers can measure differences in the quality of meats and make price-quality comparisons. There are two parts to this grading system: quality grades and yield grades.

Quality grades, established in 1927, are a guide to the eating qualities of meat: its tenderness, juiciness and flavor. Based on an animal's age and the meat's color, texture and degree of marbling, the USDA quality grades are:

- Beef—USDA Prime, Choice, Select, Standard, Commercial, Utility, Cutter and Canner
- Veal—USDA Prime, Choice, Good, Standard, Utility
- Lamb—USDA Prime, Choice, Good, Utility
- Pork—USDA No. 1, No. 2, No. 3, Utility

USDA Prime meats are produced in limited quantities for use in the finest restaurants, hotels and gourmet markets. They are well marbled and have thick coverings of firm fat. See Figure 11.5.

USDA Choice meat is the most commonly used grade in quality food service operations and retail markets. Choice meat is well marbled (but with less fat than Prime) and will produce a tender and juicy product.

Although lacking the flavor and tenderness of the higher grades, beef graded USDA Select or USDA Standard, and lamb and veal graded USDA Good, are also used in food service operations and retail outlets. The term "no roll" refers to beef that has not been grade-stamped (rolled) by a USDA inspector. Much of the beef sold in the United States, especially at retail, is no roll, but would have been USDA Select if graded. The lower grades of beef, lamb and veal are usually used for processed, ground or manufactured items such as meat patties or canned meat products. Figure 11.6 illustrates the three quality grades in a cut of beef.

Yield grades, established in 1965, measure the amount of usable meat (as opposed to fat and bones) on a carcass and provide a uniform method of identifying cuttability differences among carcasses. Yield grades apply only to beef and lamb and appear in a shield similar to that used for the quality grade stamp. The shields are numbered from 1 to 5, with number 1 representing the greatest yield and number 5 the smallest. See Figure 11.7. Beef and lamb can be graded for either quality or yield or both.

Grading is a voluntary program. Many processors, purveyors and retailers (especially pork and veal producers) develop and use their own labeling systems to provide quality assurance information. These private systems do not necessarily apply the USDA's standards. In fact, some pork inspection programs actually apply more stringent quality standards.

▶ AGING MEATS

When animals are slaughtered, their muscles are soft and flabby. Within 6 to 24 hours, rigor mortis sets in, causing the muscles to contract and stiffen. Rigor mortis dissipates within 48 to 72 hours under refrigerated conditions. All meats should be allowed to rest, or age, long enough for rigor mortis to dissipate completely. Meats that have not been aged long enough for rigor mortis to dissipate, or that have been frozen during this period, are known as "green meats." They will be very tough and flavorless when cooked.

Typically, initial aging takes place while the meat is being transported from the slaughterhouse to the supplier or food service operation. Beef and lamb are sometimes aged for longer periods to increase their tenderness and flavor characteristics. Pork is not aged further because its high fat content turns rancid easily, and veal does not have enough fat to protect it during an extended aging period.

WET AGING

Today, most preportioned or precut meats are packaged and shipped in vacuum-sealed plastic packages (sometimes known generically by the manufacturer's trade name, Cryovac). Wet aging is the process of storing vacuum-packaged meats under refrigeration for up to 6 weeks. This allows natural enzymes and microorganisms time to break down connective tissue, which tenderizes and flavors the meat. As this chemical process takes place, the meat develops an unpleasant odor that is released when the package is opened; the odor dissipates in a few minutes. Exercise great care when aging meats. Beef can be wet aged for the longest period; other meats must be consumed within a shorter time period. The shelf life for vacuum-sealed refrigerated pork is approximately 3 weeks.

Wet-Aged New York Strip

DRY AGING

Dry aging is the process of storing fresh meats in an environment of controlled temperature, humidity and air flow for up to six weeks. This allows enzymes and microorganisms to break down connective tissues. Dry aging is actually the beginning of the natural decomposition process. Dry-aged meats can lose from 5 to 20 percent of their weight through moisture evaporation. They can also develop mold, which adds flavor but must be trimmed off later. Moisture loss combined with additional trimming can substantially increase the cost of dry-aged meats. Dry-aged meats are generally available only through smaller distributors and specialty butchers.

Dry-Aged Beef Short Loin

▶ PURCHASING AND STORING MEATS

Several factors determine the cuts of meat your food service operation should use:

1 Menu: The menu identifies the types of cooking methods used. If meats are to be broiled, grilled, roasted, sautéed or fried, more tender cuts should be used. If they are to be stewed or braised, flavorful cuts with more connective tissue can be used.

2 Menu price: Cost constraints may prevent an operation from using the best-quality meats available. Generally, the more tender the meat, the more expensive it is. But the most expensive cuts are not always the best choice for a particular cooking method. For example, a beef tenderloin is one of the most expensive cuts of beef. Although excellent grilled, it will not necessarily produce a better braised dish than the tougher, fattier brisket.

3 Quality: Often, several cuts or grades of meat can be used for a specific dish, so each food service operation should develop its own quality specifications.

▶ **vacuum packaging** a food preservation method in which fresh or cooked food is placed in an airtight container (usually plastic). Virtually all air is removed from the container through a vacuum process, and the container is then sealed.

A TENDER HISTORY

In *Food in History,* Reay Tannahill suggests that prehistoric hunters developed weapons and stealth tactics in order to kill their quarry without alerting it to danger and provoking fright, fight or flight. She notes that muscle tissues from animals that die placidly contain glycogen. At death, glycogen breaks down into various substances, including lactic acid, a natural preservative. Animals experiencing fright, fight or flight just before death, however, use up their glycogen. Tannahill theorizes that prehistoric hunters recognized and responded to what science much later confirmed: Meat from animals that die peacefully is sweeter and more tender.

PURCHASING MEATS

Once you have identified the cuts of meat your operation needs, you must determine the forms in which they will be bought. Meats are purchased in a variety of forms: as large as an entire carcass that must be further fabricated or as small as an individual cut (known as **portion control** or **P.C.**) ready to cook and serve. You should consider the following when deciding how to purchase meats:

1 Employee skills: Do your employees have the skills necessary to reduce large pieces of meat to the desired cuts?

2 Menu: Can you use the variety of bones, meat and trimmings that result from fabricating large cuts into individual portions?

NO, IT DOESN'T GLOW

Fresh and frozen beef, lamb, pork and poultry can be irradiated in order to control the presence of microorganisms, such as *E. coli* and *Salmonella*, which can cause foodborne illnesses. Although the permitted dose of ionizing radiation kills significant numbers of insects, pathogenic bacteria and parasites on and in the meat, it does not make food radioactive or compromise the food's nutritional values. Nor does radiation noticeably alter a food's flavor, texture or appearance.

The FDA requires that any packaged food subjected to radiation for preservation be labeled "treated with radiation" or "treated by irradiation" and display the radura symbol shown here.

3. Storage: Do you have ample refrigeration and freezer space so that you can be flexible in the way you purchase your meats?
4. Cost: Considering labor costs and trim usage, is it more economical to buy larger cuts of meat or P.C. units?

IMPS/NAMP

The USDA publishes Institutional Meat Purchasing Specifications (IMPS) describing products customarily purchased in the food service industry. IMPS identifications are illustrated and described in *The Meat Buyers Guide*, published by the National Association of Meat Purveyors (NAMP). The IMPS/NAMP system is a widely accepted and useful tool in preventing miscommunications between purchasers and purveyors. Meats are indexed by a numerical system: Beef cuts are designated by the 100 series, lamb by the 200 series, veal by the 300 series, pork by the 400 series, and portion cuts by the 1000 series. Commonly used cuts of beef, veal, lamb and pork and their IMPS numbers, as well as applicable cooking methods and serving suggestions, are discussed in Chapters 12 through 15.

STORING MEATS

Meat products are highly perishable and potentially hazardous foods, so temperature control is the most important thing to remember when storing meats. Fresh meats should be stored at temperatures between 30°F and 35°F (−1°C and 2°C). Vacuum-packed meats should be left in their packaging until they are needed. Under proper refrigeration, vacuum-packed meats with unbroken seals have a shelf life of three to four weeks. If the seal is broken, shelf life is reduced to only a few days. Ground meats have a shorter shelf life than whole-muscle meats and should be consumed within one or two days. Meats that are not vacuum packed should be wrapped tightly in air-permeable paper. Do not wrap meats tightly in plastic wrap, as this creates a good breeding ground for bacteria and will significantly shorten a meat's shelf life. Store meats on trays and away from other foods to prevent cross-contamination.

When freezing meats, the faster the better. Slow freezing produces large ice crystals that tend to rupture the muscle tissues, allowing water and nutrients to drip out when the meat is thawed (Figure 11.8). Most commercially packaged meats are frozen by blast freezing, which quickly cools by blasting −40°F (−40°C) air across the meat. Most food service facilities, however, use a slower and more conventional method known as still-air freezing. Still-air freezing is the common practice of placing meat in a standard freezer at about 0°F (−18°C) until it is frozen.

FIGURE 11.8 ▶ Meat damaged by freezer burn—freezer-burned Bottom Sirloin Butt Tri Tip (left) and fresh Bottom Sirloin Butt Tri Tip (right).

The ideal temperature for maintaining frozen meat is −50°F (−45°C). Frozen meat should not be maintained at any temperature warmer than 0°F (−18°C). Moisture- and vaporproof packaging will help prevent **freezer burn.** The length of frozen storage life varies with the species and type of meat. As a general rule, properly handled meats can be frozen for 6 months. Frozen meats should be thawed at refrigerator temperatures, not at room temperature or in warm water.

▶ **freezer burn** the surface dehydration and discoloration of food that results from moisture loss at below-freezing temperatures

▶ Preparing Meats

Certain procedures are often applied to meats before cooking to add flavor and/or moisture. These include marinating and rubs, discussed in Chapter 7, Mise en Place, and trussing, barding and larding.

Loin of veal tied for roasting.

TYING AND TRUSSING

Some meats, especially roasts and whole birds, require tying or trussing before cooking. Tying larger roasts with butcher's twine holds loose pieces of meat together during cooking and ensures that the meat retains its shape. Poultry is often trussed to protect the more delicate white breast meat during cooking. Trussing techniques are discussed along with specific cuts and types of meat in Chapters 12 through 16.

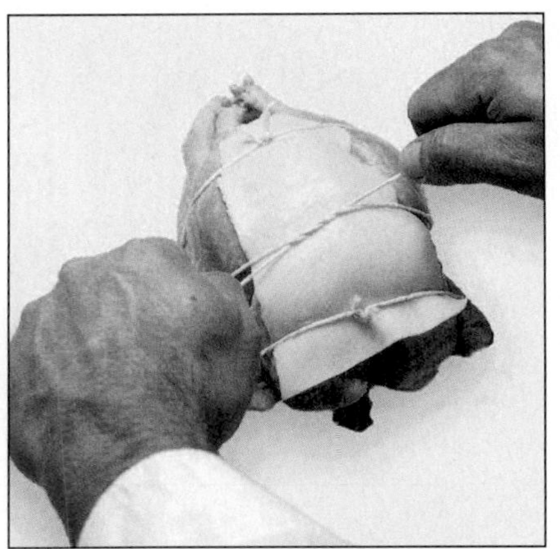

Barding a Pheasant.

BARDING

Barding is the process of covering the surface of meat or poultry with thin slices of pork fatback and tying them in place with butcher's twine. Barded meat or poultry is usually roasted. As the item cooks, the fatback continuously bastes it, adding flavor and moisture. A drawback to barding is that the fatback prevents the meat or poultry from developing the crusty exterior associated with roasting.

LARDING

Larding is the process of inserting small strips of pork fat into meat with a larding needle. Larded meat is usually cooked by braising. During cooking, the added fat contributes moisture and flavor. Although once popular, larding is rarely used today because advances in selective breeding produce consistently tender, well-marbled meat.

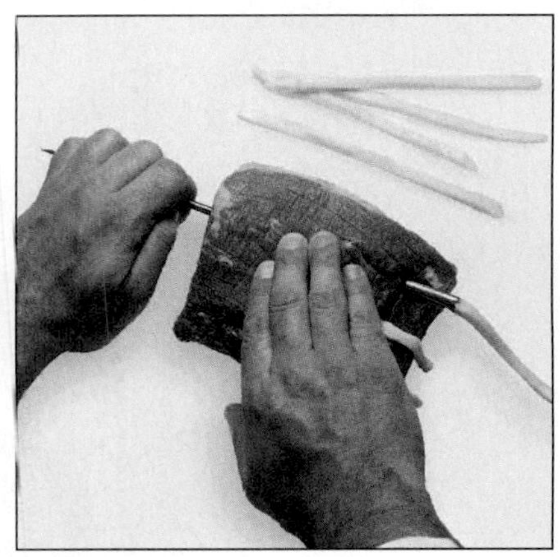

Larding Meat.

▶ Applying Various Cooking Methods

In Chapter 8, Principles of Cooking, you learned the basic techniques for broiling, grilling, roasting, sautéing, pan-frying, deep-frying, poaching, simmering, braising and stewing. In Chapters 12 through 15, you will learn more about applying these cooking methods to beef, veal, lamb and pork. Here we apply these methods to meat cookery in general.

DRY-HEAT COOKING METHODS

Dry-heat cooking methods subject food directly to the heat of a flame (broiling and grilling), hot air (roasting) or heated fat (sautéing and pan-frying). These cooking methods firm proteins without breaking down connective tissue. They are not recommended for tougher cuts or those high in connective tissue.

BROILING AND GRILLING

The broiling or grilling process adds flavor; additional flavors are derived from the seasonings. The broiler or grill should brown the meat, keeping the interior juicy. The grill should leave appetizing crosshatch marks on the meat's surface. To serve a good-quality broiled or grilled product, start with good-quality meat.

Selecting Meats to Broil or Grill

Only the most tender cuts should be broiled or grilled because direct heat does not tenderize. Fat adds flavor as the meat cooks, so the meat should be well marbled. Some external fat is also beneficial. Too much fat, however, will cause the broiler or grill to flare up, burning or discoloring the meat and adding objectionable flavors. Connective tissue toughens when meat is broiled or grilled, so trim away as much of it as possible.

Seasoning Meats to Be Broiled or Grilled

Meats that have not been marinated should be well seasoned with salt and pepper just before being placed on the broiler or grill. If they are preseasoned and allowed to rest, the salt will dissolve and draw out moisture, making it difficult to brown the meat properly. Some chefs feel so strongly about this that they season broiled or grilled meats only after they are cooked. Pork and veal, which have a tendency to dry out when cooked, should be basted with seasoned butter or oil during cooking to help keep them moist. Meats can be glazed or basted with barbecue sauce as they cook.

Cooking Temperatures

Red meats should be cooked at sufficiently high temperatures to caramelize their surface, making them more attractive and flavorful. At the same time, the broiler or grill cannot be too hot, or the meat's exterior will burn before the interior is cooked.

Because veal and pork are normally cooked to higher internal temperatures than beef and lamb, they should be cooked at slightly lower temperatures so that their exteriors are not overcooked when their interiors are cooked properly. The exterior of white meats should be a deep golden color when finished.

FIGURE 11.9 ▶ Degrees of doneness: Meat cooked rare, medium rare, medium and medium well.

Degrees of Doneness

Consumers request and expect meats to be properly cooked to specific degrees of doneness. It is your responsibility to understand and comply with these requests. Meats can be cooked very rare (or bleu), rare, medium rare, medium, medium well or well done. Figure 11.9 shows the proper color for these different degrees of doneness. Use this guide for red meats cooked by any method.

Larger cuts of meat, such as a châteaubriand or thick chops, are often started on the broiler or grill to develop color and flavor and then finished to temperature in the oven to ensure complete, even cooking.

Determining Doneness

Broiling or grilling meat to the proper degree of doneness is an art. Larger pieces of meat will take longer to cook than smaller ones, but how quickly a piece of meat cooks is determined by many other factors: the temperature of the broiler or grill, the temperature of the piece of meat when placed on the broiler or grill, the type of meat and the thick-

Table 11.1 **DETERMINING DONENESS OF BROILED AND GRILLED ITEMS**

DEGREES OF DONENESS	COLOR	DEGREE OF RESISTANCE	IDEAL TEMPERATURE
Very rare (bleu)	Very red and raw-looking center (the center is cool to the touch)	Almost no resistance	115°F–120°F 46°C–49°C
Rare	Large deep-red center	Spongy; very slight resistance	125°F–130°F 52°C–54°C
Medium rare	Bright red center	Some resistance, slightly springy	130°F–140°F 54°C–60°C
Medium	Rosy pink to red center	Slightly firm; springy	140°F–150°F 60°C–66°C
Medium well	Very little pink at the center, almost brown throughout	Firm; springy	155°F–165°F 68°C–74°C
Well done	No red	Quite firm; springs back quickly when pressed	Not recommended

ness of the cut. Because of these variables, timing alone is not a useful tool in determining doneness.

The most reliable method of determining doneness of a small piece of meat is by pressing the piece of meat with a finger and gauging the amount of resistance it yields. Very rare (bleu) meat will offer almost no resistance and feel almost the same as raw meat. Meat cooked rare will feel spongy and offer slight resistance to pressure. Meat cooked medium will feel slightly firm and springy to the touch. Meat cooked well done will feel quite firm and spring back quickly when pressed. See Table 11.1.

Accompaniments to Broiled and Grilled Meats

Because a broiler or grill cannot be deglazed to form the base for a sauce, compound butters or sauces such as béarnaise are often served with broiled or grilled meats. Brown sauces such as bordelaise, chasseur, périgueux or brown mushroom sauce also complement many broiled or grilled items. Additional sauce suggestions are found in Table 11.5.

▶ PROCEDURE FOR BROILING OR GRILLING MEATS

1. Heat the broiler or grill.
2. Use a wire brush to remove any charred or burnt particles that may be stuck to the broiler or grill grate. The grate can be wiped with a lightly oiled towel to remove any remaining particles and to help season it.
3. Prepare the item to be broiled or grilled by trimming off any excess fat and connective tissue and marinating or seasoning it as desired. The meat may be brushed lightly with oil to help protect it and keep it from sticking to the grate.
4. Place the item in the broiler or on the grill. Following the example in Chapter 8, turn the meat 90 degrees to produce the attractive crosshatch marks associated with grilling. Use tongs to turn or flip the meat without piercing the surface (this prevents valuable juices from escaping).
5. Cook the meat to the desired doneness while developing the proper surface color. To do so, adjust the position of the meat on the broiler or grill, or adjust the distance between the grate and heat source.

SAFETY ALERT

Serving Meat

The Food Safety and Inspection Service of the USDA recommends the following as safe internal temperatures for serving various meats. Note that these temperatures are approximately 10–15°F (5–8°C) higher than the temperatures generally preferred by chefs and diners. Most diners would find the USDA's recommended 160°F unacceptably overcooked for a "medium" steak. Each chef or meat cook must decide for themselves whether it is more important to their clientele to cook meat to the USDA's safety standards or to diners' requests.

Fresh Beef, Veal and Lamb	
Rare	not recommended
Medium rare	145°F (63°C)
Medium	160°F (71°C)
Well done	170°F (77°C)
Fresh Pork	
Rare	not recommended
Medium rare	not recommended
Medium	160°F(71°C)
Well done	170°F (77°C)
Ground Meat and Meat Mixtures	
Beef, veal, lamb and pork	160°F (71°C) or higher

RECIPE 11.1

GRILLED LAMB CHOPS WITH HERB BUTTER

Yield: 2 Servings **Method:** Grilling

Lamb chops, loin or rib, approx. 1 in. (2.5 cm) thick	6	6
Oil	as needed	as needed
Salt and pepper	TT	TT
Herb butter	6 thin slices or	6 small rosettes

1 Brushing the lamb chops with oil.

1. Preheat the grill for 15 minutes.
2. Brush the lamb chops with oil; season with salt and pepper.
3. Place the lamb chops on the grill, turning as necessary to produce the proper crosshatching. Cook to the desired doneness.
4. Remove the lamb chops from the grill and place a slice or rosette of herb butter on each chop.
5. Serve immediately as the herb butter melts. The plate can be placed under the broiler for a few seconds to help melt the herb butter.

Approximate values per 6.5-oz. (195-g) serving: **Calories** 623, **Total fat** 50 g, **Saturated fat** 27 g, **Cholesterol** 224 mg, **Sodium** 1186 mg, **Total carbohydrates** 0 g, **Protein** 42 g, **Vitamin A** 40%

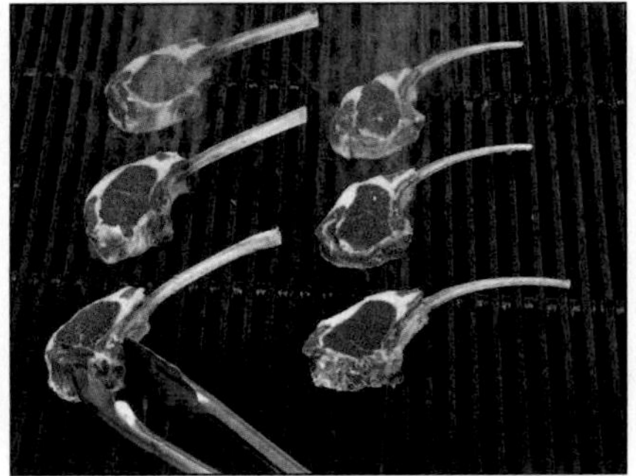

2 Placing the lamb chops on the grill.

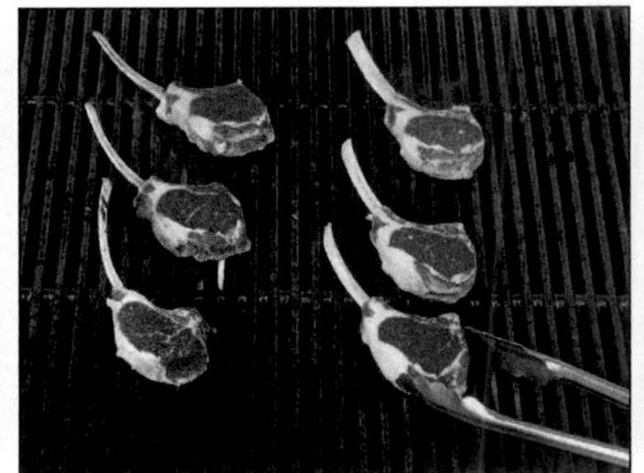

3 Rotating the lamb chops 90 degrees to create crosshatch

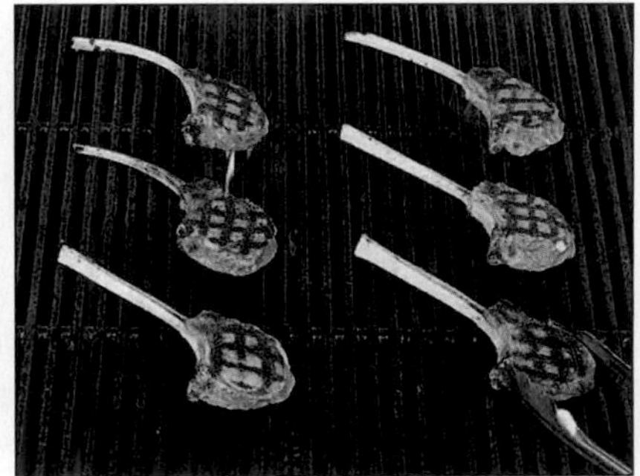

4 Turning the chops over to finish them on the other side.

ROASTING

Properly roasted meats should be tender, juicy and evenly cooked to the appropriate degree of doneness. They should have a pleasant appearance when whole as well as when sliced and plated.

Selecting Meats to Roast

Because roasting is a dry-heat cooking method and will not tenderize the finished product, meats that are to be roasted should be tender and well marbled. They are usually cut from the rib, loin or leg sections.

Seasoning Meats to Be Roasted

Seasonings are especially important with smaller roasts and roasts with little or no fat covering. With these roasts, some of the seasonings penetrate the meat while the remainder help create the highly seasoned crust associated with a good roast. A large roast with heavy fat covering (for example, a steamship round or prime rib) does not benefit from being seasoned on the surface because the seasonings will not penetrate the fat layer, which is trimmed away before service.

When practical, a roast with excess fat should be trimmed, leaving just a thin fat layer so that the roast bastes itself while cooking. A lean roast can be barded or larded before cooking to add richness and moisture. Lamb legs are sometimes studded with garlic cloves by piercing the meat with a paring knife and then pressing slivers of raw garlic into the holes.

A roast is sometimes cooked on a bed of mirepoix, or mirepoix is added to the roasting pan as the roast cooks. The mirepoix raises the roast off the bottom of the roasting pan, preventing the bottom from overcooking. This mirepoix, however, does not add any flavor to the roast. Rather, it combines with the drippings to add flavor to the jus, sauce or gravy that is made with them.

Cooking Temperatures

Small roasts such as a rack of lamb or a beef tenderloin should be cooked at high temperatures, 375°F–450°F (191°C–232°C) so that they develop good color during their short cooking times.

Traditionally, large roasts were started at high temperatures to sear the meat and seal in the juices; they were then finished at lower temperatures Studies have shown, however, that searing does not seal in juices and that roasts cooked at constant, low temperatures provide a better yield with less shrinkage than roasts that have been seared. Temperatures between 275°F and 325°F (135°C and 163°C) are ideal for large roasts. These temperatures will produce a large, evenly cooked pink center portion.

Determining Doneness

The doneness of **small roasts** such as a rack of lamb is determined in much the same way as broiled or grilled meats. With experience, the chef develops a sense of timing as well as a feel for gauging the amount of resistance by touching the meat. These techniques, however, are not infallible, especially with large roasts.

Although timing is useful as a general guide for determining doneness, there are too many variables for it to be relied on exclusively. With this caution in mind, Table 11.2 lists general cooking times for roasted meats.

The best way to determine the doneness of a **large roast** is to use an instant-read thermometer, as shown in Figure 11.10. The thermometer is inserted into the center or thickest part of the roast and away from any bones. The proper finished temperatures for roasted meats are listed in Table 11.2.

FIGURE 11.10 ▶ Proper placement of an instant-read thermometer.

Carryover Cooking and Resting

Cooking does not stop the moment a roast is removed from the oven. Through conduction, the heat applied to the outside of the roast continues to penetrate, cooking the center for several more minutes. Indeed, the internal temperature of

Table 11.2 DETERMINING DONENESS OF ROASTS

DEGREE OF DONENESS	IDEAL INTERNAL TEMPERATURE AFTER CARRYOVER	MINUTES PER POUND*
Very rare	125°F–130°F 52°C–54°C	12–15
Rare	130°F–140°F 54°C–60°C	15–18
Medium	140°F–150°F 60°C–66°C	18–20
Well done	150°F–165°F 66°C–74°C	20–25

*Assumes meat was at room temperature before roasting and cooked at a constant 325°F (163°C).

a small roast can rise by as much as 5°F–10°F (3°C–6°C) after being removed from the oven. With a larger roast, such as a 50-pound steamship round, it can rise by as much as 20°F (11°C). Therefore, remove roasted meats before they reach the desired degree of doneness, and allow carryover cooking to complete the cooking process. The temperatures listed in Table 11.2 are internal temperatures after allowing for **carryover cooking.**

▶ **carryover cooking** the cooking that occurs after a food is removed from a heat source; it is accomplished by the residual heat remaining in the food

As meat cooks, its juices flow toward the center. If the roast is carved immediately after it is removed from the oven, its juices will run from the meat, causing it to lose its color and become dry. Letting the meat rest before slicing allows the juices to redistribute themselves evenly throughout the roast so that the roast will retain more juices when carved. Small roasts, such as a rack of lamb, need to rest only 5 to 10 minutes; larger roasts such as a steamship round of beef require as much as an hour.

Accompaniments to Roasted Meats

Roasts may be served with a sauce based on their natural juices (called *au jus*), as described in the recipe for Roast Prime Rib of Beef au Jus (below) or with a pan gravy made with drippings from the roast. Additional sauce suggestions are found in Table 11.5.

▶ PROCEDURE FOR ROASTING MEATS

1 Trim excess fat, tendons and silverskin from the meat. Leave only a thin fat covering, if possible, so that the roast bastes itself as it cooks.
2 Season the roast as appropriate and place it in a roasting pan. The roast may be placed on a bed of mirepoix or on a rack.
3 Roast the meat, uncovered, at the desired temperature (the larger the roast, the lower the temperature), usually 275°F–425°F (135°C–220°C).
4 If a jus or pan gravy is desired and a mirepoix was not added at the start of cooking, it may be added 30 to 45 minutes before the roast is done, thus allowing it to caramelize while the roast finishes cooking.
5 Cook to the desired temperature.
6 Remove the roast from the oven, allowing carryover cooking to raise the internal temperature to the desired degree of doneness. Allow the roast to rest before slicing or carving it. As the roast rests, prepare the jus, sauce or pan gravy.

RECIPE 11.2

ROAST PRIME RIB OF BEEF AU JUS

Mise en Place

▶ Peel and chop garlic.
▶ Peel and chop onions, carrots and celery for mirepoix.

Yield: 18 Boneless Servings, 8 oz. (250 g) each **Method:** Roasting

Oven-ready rib roast, IMPS #109, approx. 16 lb. (7.5 kg)	1	1
Salt and pepper	TT	TT
Garlic, chopped	TT	TT
Mirepoix	1 lb.	500 g
Brown stock	2 qt.	2 lt

1 Pull back the netting, fold back the fat cap and season the roast well with the salt, pepper and garlic. Replace the fat cap and netting; place the roast in an appropriate-sized roasting pan. Roast at 300°F–325°F (150°C–160°C).
2 Add the mirepoix to the pan approximately 45 minutes before the roast is finished cooking. Continue cooking until the internal temperature reaches 125°F (52°C), approximately 3 to 4 hours. Carryover cooking will raise the internal temperature of the roast to approximately 138°F (59°C).

3 Remove the roast from the pan and allow it to rest in a warm place for 30 minutes.
4 Drain the excess fat from the roasting pan, reserving the mirepoix and any drippings in the roasting pan.
5 Caramelize the mirepoix on the stove top; allow the liquids to evaporate, leaving only brown drippings in the pan.
6 Deglaze the pan with the stock. Stir to loosen all the drippings.
7 Simmer the jus, reducing it slightly and allowing the mirepoix to release its flavor; season with salt and pepper if necessary.
8 Strain the jus through a china cap lined with cheesecloth. Skim any remaining fat from the surface with a ladle.
9 Remove the netting from the roast. Trim and slice the roast as and serve with approximately 1 to 2 ounces (30 to 60 milliliters) jus per person.

Approximate values per 9-oz. (270-g) serving: **Calories** 951, **Total fat** 79 g, **Saturated fat** 32 g, **Cholesterol** 214 mg, **Sodium** 278 mg, **Total carbohydrates** 1 g, **Protein** 56 g, **Iron** 40%

1 Draining off the excess fat.

2 Caramelizing the mirepoix.

3 Deglazing the pan with brown stock.

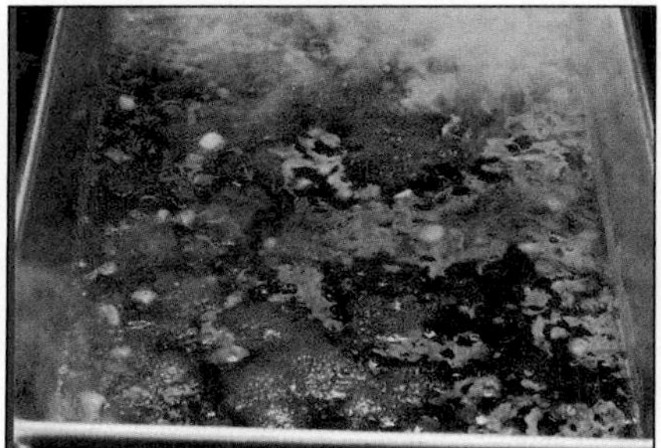

4 Simmering the jus, reducing it slightly and allowing the mirepoix to release its flavors.

5 Straining the jus through a china cap and cheesecloth.

Carving Roasts

All the efforts that went into selecting and cooking a perfect roast will be wasted if the roast is not carved properly. Roasts are always carved against the grain; carving with the grain produces long stringy, tough slices. Cutting across the muscle fibers produces a more attractive and tender portion. Portions may be cut in a single thick slice, as with Roast Prime Rib of Beef, or in many thin slices. The following photographs illustrate several different carving procedures.

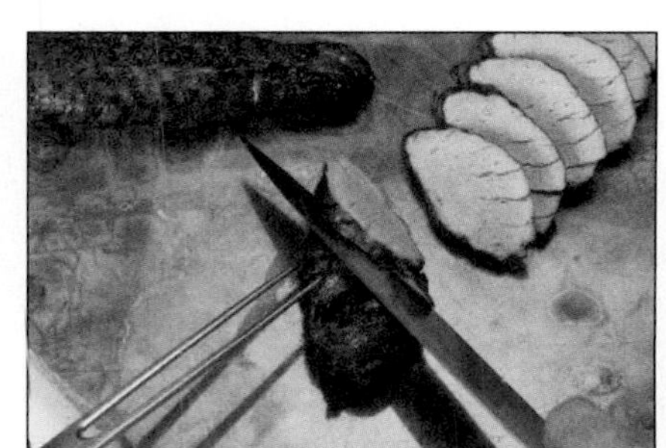

Carving pork tenderloin against the grain.

▶ PROCEDURE FOR CARVING PRIME RIB

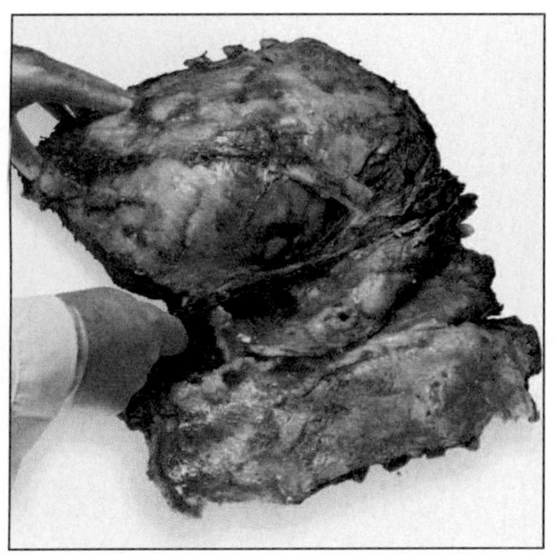

1 Removing the netting, cap fat and **chine** bones.

▶ **chine** the backbone or spine of an animal; a subprimal cut of beef, veal, lamb, pork or game carcass containing a portion of the backbone with some adjoining flesh.

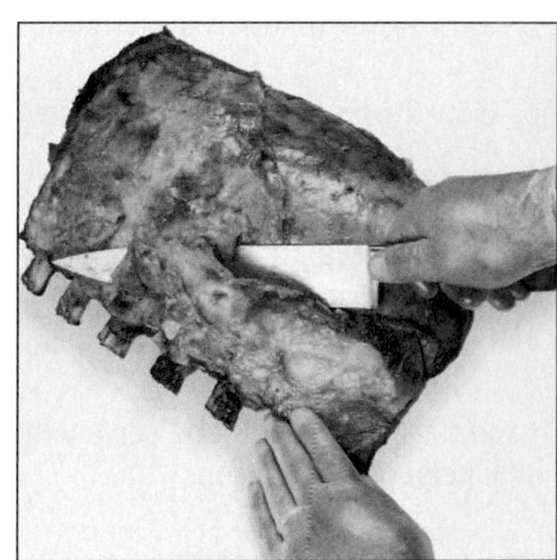

2 Trimming the excess fat from the eye muscle.

3 Slicing the rib in long, smooth strokes, the first cut (end cut) without a rib bone, the second cut with a rib bone, the third without, and so on.

▶ PROCEDURE FOR CARVING PRIME RIB ON THE SLICER

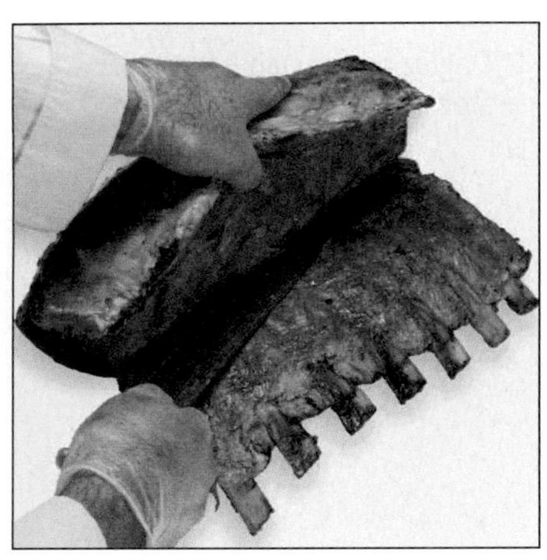

1 When producing large quantities of prime rib, it is often more practical to slice it on a slicing machine. Following the steps illustrated above, remove the netting, cap fat and chine bone; trim excess fat from the eye muscle. Then use a long slicer and completely remove the rib eye from the rib bones, being careful to stay as close as possible to the bones to avoid wasting any meat.

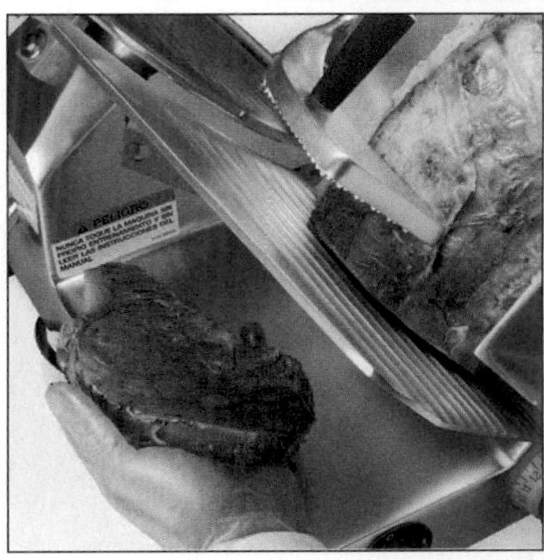

2 After placing the rib on the slicing machine, set the machine to the desired thickness. The blade will have to be adjusted often because a roast's thickness fluctuates.

▶ PROCEDURE FOR CARVING A STEAMSHIP ROUND OF BEEF

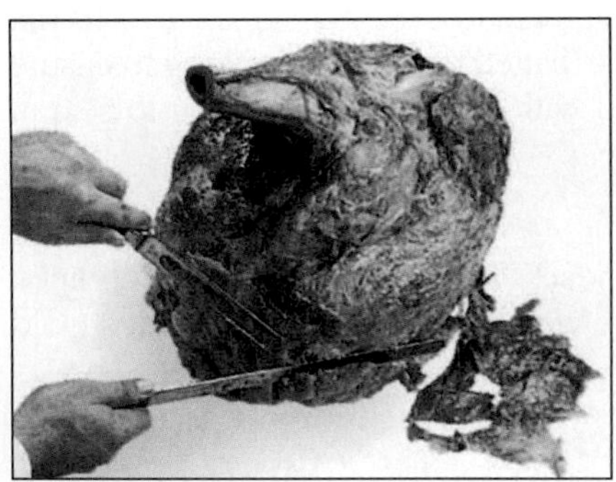

1 After setting the roast on the cutting board with the exposed femur bone (large end of the roast) down and the tibia (shank bone) or "handle" up, trim the excess exterior fat to expose the lean meat.

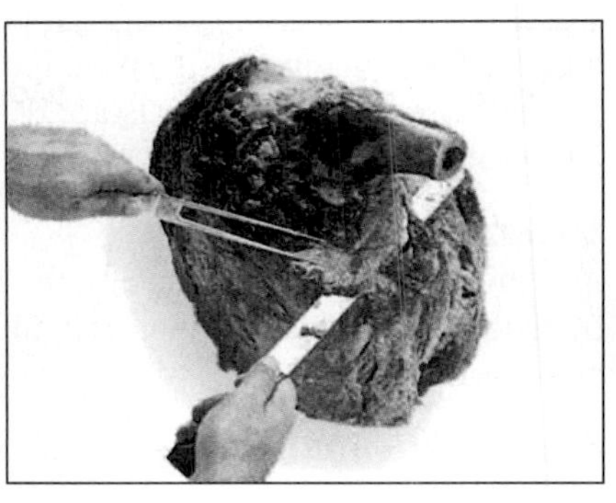

2 Begin slicing with a horizontal cut toward the shank bone, then make vertical cuts to release the slices of beef.

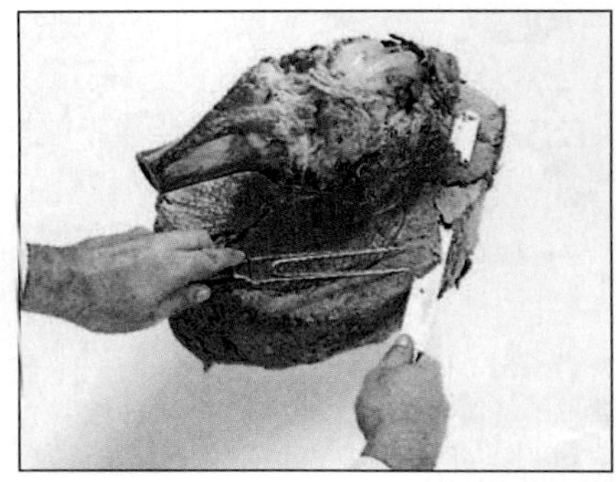

3 Keeping the exposed surface as level as possible, continue carving, turning the roast as necessary to access all sides.

▶ PROCEDURE FOR CARVING A LEG OF LAMB

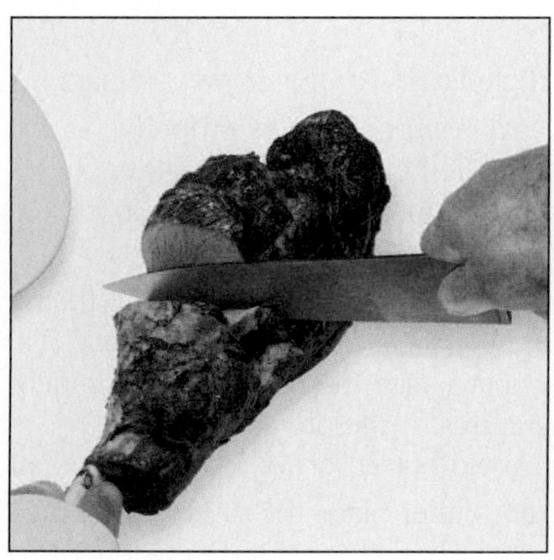

1 Holding the shank bone firmly, cut toward the bone.

2 Cutting parallel to the shank bone to remove the slices.

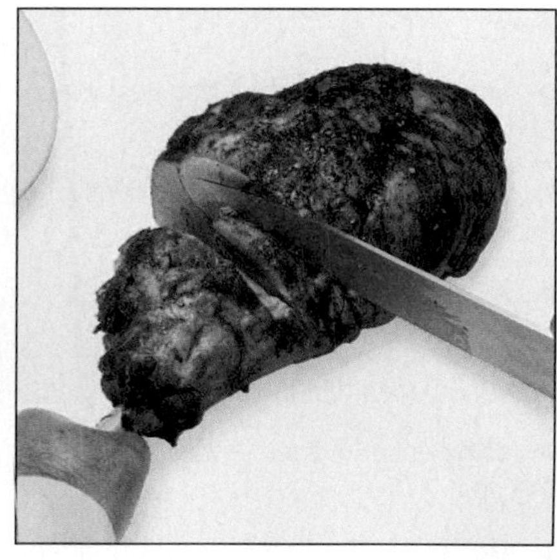

3 Rotating the leg as needed to access the meat on all sides.

SAUTÉING

Sautéing is a dry-heat cooking method in which heat is conducted by a small amount of fat. Sautéed meats should be tender (a reflection of the quality of the raw product) and of good color (determined by proper cooking temperatures) and have a good overall flavor. Any accompanying sauce should be well seasoned and complement the meat without overpowering it.

Selecting Meats to Sauté

As with broiling, grilling and roasting, you should use tender meats of the highest quality in order to produce good results when sautéing. The cuts should be uniform in size and shape in order to promote even cooking.

Seasoning Meats to Be Sautéed

The sauces that almost always accompany sautéed meats provide much of the seasoning. The meat, however, can be marinated or simply seasoned with salt and pepper. If marinated, the meat must be patted dry before cooking to ensure proper browning. Some meats are dusted with flour before cooking to seal in juices and promote even browning.

Determining Doneness

As with broiled and grilled meats, the doneness of sautéed meats is determined by touch and timing. Red meats should be well browned; veal and pork should be somewhat lighter.

▶ **fond** (1) French for "stock" or "base"; (2) the concentrated juices, drippings and bits of food left in pans after foods are roasted or sautéed; it is used to flavor sauces made directly in the pans in which the foods were cooked

Accompaniments to Sautéed Meats

Sauces served with sautéed meats are usually made directly in the sauté pan, using the **fond.** They often incorporate a previously thickened sauce. Sauce suggestions for sautéed meats are found in Table 11.5.

▶ PROCEDURE FOR SAUTÉING MEATS

▶ **cutlet** a relatively thick, boneless slice of meat

▶ **scallop** a thin, boneless slice of meat

▶ **émincé** a small, thin, boneless piece of meat

▶ **medallion** a small, round, relatively thick slice of meat

▶ **mignonette** a medallion

▶ **noisette** a small, usually round, portion of meat cut from the rib

▶ **chop** a cut of meat, including part of the rib

▶ **paillard** a scallop of meat pounded until thin, usually grilled

1. Heat a sauté pan and add enough oil or clarified butter to just cover the bottom. The pan should be large enough to hold the meat in a single layer. A pan that is too large may cause the fat or meat to burn.
2. Cut the meat into **cutlets, scallops, émincés, medallions, mignonettes, noisettes, chops** or small even-sized pieces. Season the meat and dredge in flour if desired.
3. Add the meat to the sauté pan in a single layer. Do not crowd the pan.
4. Adjust the temperature so that the meat's exterior browns properly without burning and the interior cooks. The heat should be high enough to complete the cooking process before the meat begins to stew in its own juices.
5. Small items may be tossed using the sauté pan's sloped sides to flip them back on top of themselves. Do not toss the meat more than necessary, however. The pan should remain in contact with the heat source as much as possible to maintain proper temperatures. Larger items should be turned using tongs or a kitchen fork. Avoid burns by not splashing hot fat.
6. Larger items can be finished in an oven. Either place the sauté pan in the oven or transfer the meat to another pan. The latter procedure allows a sauce to be made in the original pan as the meat continues to cook.

▶ PROCEDURE FOR PREPARING A SAUCE IN THE SAUTÉ PAN

1. If a sauce is to be made in the pan, hold the meat in a warm spot while preparing the sauce. When the meat is removed from the pan, leave a small amount of fat as well as the fond. If there is excessive fat, degrease the pan, leaving just enough to cover its bottom. Add ingredients such as garlic, shallots and mushrooms that will be used as garnishes and sauce flavorings; sauté them.
2. Deglaze the pan with wine or stock. Scrape the pan, loosening the fond and allowing it to dissolve in the liquid. Reduce the deglazing liquid by approximately three-fourths.
3. Add jus lié or stock to the pan. Cook and reduce the sauce to the desired consistency.
4. Add any ingredients that do not require cooking, such as herbs and spices. Adjust the seasonings with salt and pepper.

5 For service, the meat may be returned to the pan for a moment to reheat it and coat it with the finished sauce. The meat should remain in the sauce just long enough to reheat. Do not attempt to cook the meat in the sauce.

SAUTÉED VEAL SCALLOPS WITH WHITE WINE LEMON SAUCE

RECIPE 11.3

Yield: 6 Servings **Method:** Sautéing

Veal scallops, 3 oz. (90 g) each	12	12
Clarified butter	2 fl. oz.	60 ml
Flour	4 oz.	120 g
Salt and pepper	TT	TT
Shallots, chopped	2 Tbsp.	30 ml
White wine	6 fl. oz.	180 ml
Lemon juice	2 fl. oz.	60 ml
Brown veal stock	4 fl. oz.	120 ml
Unsalted butter	2 oz.	60 g
Lemon wedges	12	12

1 Pound the scallops to a uniform thickness, as described in Chapter 13, Veal.
2 Heat a sauté pan and add the clarified butter.
3 Dredge the scallops in flour seasoned with salt and pepper and add to the pan in a single layer. Sauté on each side for 1 to 2 minutes. As the first scallops are done, remove them to a warm platter and sauté the remaining scallops.
4 Add the chopped shallots to the pan and sauté.
5 Deglaze the pan with the wine and lemon juice.
6 Add the stock and reduce by half.
7 Swirl in the butter (monté au beurre).
8 Adjust the seasonings with salt and pepper.
9 Serve two scallops per person with approximately 1 ounce (30 milliliters) sauce. Garnish with lemon wedges.

Approximate values per 8-oz. (240-g) serving: **Calories** 537, **Total fat** 28 g, **Saturated fat** 13 g, **Cholesterol** 208 mg, **Sodium** 325 mg, **Total carbohydrates** 17 g, **Protein** 47 g, **Vitamin A** 22%

Mise en Place

▶ Peel and chop shallots.

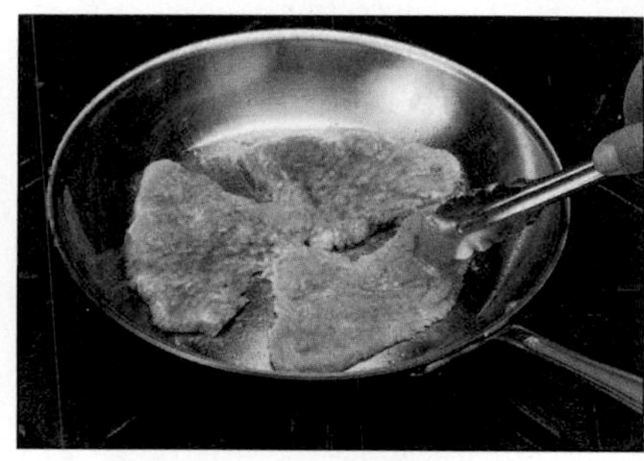

1 Adding the veal scallops to the pan. Note the relationship of scallops to pan size.

2 Adding the chopped shallots to the pan and sautéing them.

3 Deglazing the pan with white wine and lemon juice.

4 Adding the brown veal stock and reducing by half.

5 Swirling in the butter and adjusting the seasonings.

PAN-FRYING

Pan-frying uses more fat than sautéing to conduct heat. Pan-fried meats should be tender (a reflection of the quality of the raw product) and of good color (determined by proper cooking temperatures) and have a good overall flavor. Meats to be pan-fried are usually breaded. In addition to providing flavor, breading seals the meat. The breading should be free from breaks, thus preventing the fat from coming into direct contact with the meat or collecting in a pocket formed between the meat and the breading. Pan-fried items should be golden in color, and the breading should not be soggy.

Selecting Meats to Pan-Fry

As with other dry-heat cooking methods, tender meats of high quality should be used because the meat will not be tenderized by the cooking process. Meats that are pan-fried are often cut into cutlets or scallops.

Seasoning Meats to Be Pan-Fried

Pan-fried meats are usually seasoned lightly with salt and pepper either by applying them directly to the meat or by adding them to the flour and bread crumbs used in the breading procedure.

Determining Doneness

The most accurate way to determine the doneness of a pan-fried item is by timing. The touch method is difficult to use because of the large amounts of hot fat. It also may not be as accurate as with broiled or grilled meats because pan-fried meats are often quite thin. The thinness of the meat also means that thermometer readings may not be accurate.

Accompaniments to Pan-Fried Meats

Any sauce served with pan-fried meats is usually made separately because no fond is created during the pan-frying process. Sauce suggestions are listed in Table 11.5.

▶ PROCEDURE FOR PAN-FRYING MEATS

1. Slice and pound the meat into scallops, as described in Chapter 13, Veal.
2. Bread the meat using the standard breading procedure detailed in Chapter 7, Mise en Place.
3. Heat a moderate amount of fat or oil in a heavy pan. The temperature should be slightly lower than that used to sauté so that the breading will be nicely browned when the item is fully cooked.
4. Place the meat in the pan, being careful not to splash the hot fat. The fat should come one-third to halfway up the side of the meat. Fry until brown. Turn and brown the other side. Ideally, pan-fried meats should be fully cooked when they are well browned on both sides.
5. Remove the meat from the pan; drain it on absorbent paper before serving.

RECIPE 11.4 BREADED VEAL CUTLETS

Mise en Place

▶ Set up containers with flour, eggs and milk, and breadcrumbs for breading following standard breading procedure.

Yield: 10 Servings

Method: Pan-frying

Veal cutlets, 4 oz. (120 g) each	10	10
Salt and pepper	TT	TT
Flour	as needed for breading	
Eggs	as needed for breading	
Milk	as needed for breading	

Bread crumbs	as needed for breading	
Vegetable oil	as needed	as needed
Whole butter	6 oz.	180 g
Lemon wedges	20	20

1 Using a mallet, pound the cutlets to an even thickness, approximately ¼ inch (6 millimeters).
2 Season the cutlets with salt and pepper.
3 Bread the cutlets using the standard breading procedure described in Chapter 7, Mise en Place.
4 Heat a heavy pan to moderate heat; add approximately ⅛ inch (3 millimeters) oil.
5 Add the cutlets in a single layer. Do not crowd the pan. Brown on one side, then the other. Total cooking time should be approximately 4 minutes.
6 Remove the cutlets and drain on absorbent paper.
7 Melt the butter in a small pan until it foams.
8 Place one cutlet on each plate and pour approximately ½ fluid ounce (15 milliliters) butter over each portion. Garnish with lemon wedges.

1 Adding the breaded cutlets to the hot pan. Note the amount of oil in the pan.

Approximate values per 5-oz. (150-g) serving: **Calories** 501, **Total fat** 37 g, **Saturated fat** 17 g, **Cholesterol** 193 mg, **Sodium** 338 mg, **Total carbohydrates** 5 g, **Protein** 36 g, **Vitamin A** 17%

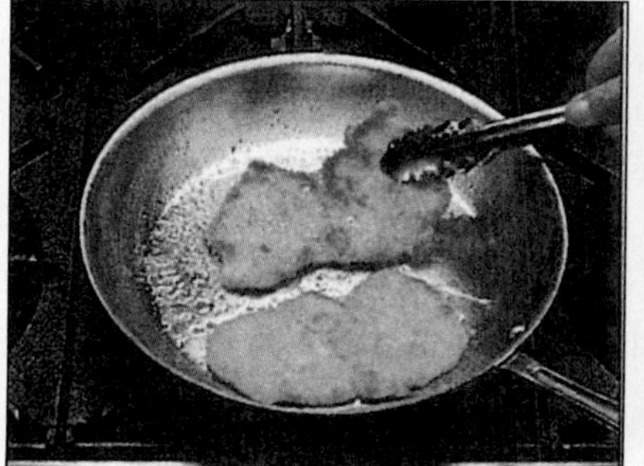

2 Turning the cutlets to brown on the second side.

3 Melting the butter in a separate pan until it foams.

4 Pouring the butter over the cutlet.

DEEP-FRYING

Deep-frying quickly cooks foods submerged in hot fat. It does not have a tenderizing effect. As even the choicest cuts of meat can always benefit from some tenderizing, deep-frying is not usually used for beef, veal, lamb or pork. There are exceptions, however. For example, commercially available frozen breaded meat cutlets are sometimes deep-fried, and some Asian dishes require deep-frying small pieces of beef or pork before finishing the meat in a sauce.

MOIST-HEAT COOKING METHODS

Moist-heat cooking methods subject food to heat and moisture. Moist heat is often, but not always, used to tenderize tougher cuts of meat through long, slow cooking. Simmering is the only moist-heat cooking method discussed here, as it is the only one frequently used with meat.

SIMMERING

Simmering is usually associated with specific tougher cuts of meat that need to be tenderized through long, slow, moist cooking. Quality simmered meats have good flavor and texture. The flavor is determined by the cooking liquid; the texture is a result of proper cooking temperatures and time.

Selecting Meats to Simmer

Meats such as fresh or corned beef brisket, fresh or cured hams and tongue are often simmered. Beef briskets and tongues, pork butts and hams are often simmered whole.

Seasoning Meats to Be Simmered

If the meat to be simmered was cured by either smoking (as with cured hams, ham hocks and smoked pork butt) or pickling (as with corned beef and pickled tongue), the cooking liquid will not be used to make a sauce and should not be seasoned. Indeed, simmering cured meats helps leach out some of the excess salt, making the finished dish more palatable.

Cooking Temperatures

Moist-heat cooking methods generally use lower temperatures than dry-heat cooking methods. Meats are normally simmered at temperatures between 180°F and 200°F (82°C and 93°C). In some food service operations, meats such as hams and corned beef are cooked at temperatures as low as 150°F (66°C) for up to 12 hours. Although lower cooking temperatures result in less shrinkage and a more tender finished product, cooking times can be increased to the point that very low cooking temperatures may not be practical.

Determining Doneness

Simmered meats are always cooked well done, which is determined by tenderness. The size and quality of the raw product determines the cooking time. Undercooked meats will be tough and chewy. Overcooked meats will be stringy and may fall apart.

To test large cuts of meat for doneness, a kitchen fork should be easily inserted into the meat and the meat should slide off the fork. Smaller pieces of meat should be tender to the bite or easily cut with a table fork.

Accompaniments to Simmered Meats

Simmered meats are often served with boiled or steamed vegetables, as in the case of corned beef and cabbage. Pickled meats are usually served with mustard or horseradish sauce on the side.

▶ PROCEDURE FOR SIMMERING MEATS

1. Cut, trim or tie the meat according to the recipe.
2. Bring an adequate amount of liquid to a boil. There should be enough liquid to cover the meat completely. Too much liquid will leach off much of the meat's flavor; too little will leave a portion of the meat exposed, preventing it from cooking. Because the dish's final flavor is determined by the flavor of the liquid, use plenty of mirepoix, flavorings and seasonings.
3. When simmering smoked or cured items, start them in cold water. This helps draw off some of the strong smoked or pickled flavors.
4. Add the meat to the liquid.
5. Reduce the heat to the desired temperature and cook until the meat is tender. Do not allow the cooking liquid to boil. Boiling results in a tough or overcooked and stringy product. If the simmered meat is to be served cold, a moister and juicier product can be achieved by removing the pot from the stove before the meat is fully cooked. The meat and the liquid can be cooled in a water bath like that for a stock, as described in Chapter 9, Stocks and Sauces. This allows the residual heat in the cooking liquid to finish cooking the meat.

NEW ENGLAND BOILED DINNER

RECIPE 11.5

Yield: 12 Servings, 6 oz. (180 g) each **Method:** Simmering

Corned beef brisket, 8 lb. (6.5 kg)	1	1
White stock	as needed	as needed
Sachet:		
Bay leaves	2	2
Dried thyme	½ tsp.	2 ml
Peppercorns, cracked	½ tsp.	2 ml
Parsley stems	10	10
Mustard seeds	1 Tbsp.	15 ml
Cinnamon sticks	2	2
Allspice berries	4	4
Baby red beets	24	24
Baby turnips	24	24
Baby carrots	24	24
Brussels sprouts	24	24
Pearl onions	24	24
Red Bliss potatoes	24	24

1 Place the beef in a pot and add enough stock to cover it. Add the sachet, bring to a boil and reduce to a simmer.
2 Simmer until the beef is tender, approximately 3 hours. Remove the beef and hold in a hotel pan in a small amount of the cooking liquid.
3 Peel or prepare the vegetables and potatoes as needed and cook separately in a portion of the cooking liquid.
4 Carve the beef and serve with two of each of the vegetables and horseradish sauce.

Approximate values per serving: **Calories** 1067, **Total fat** 58 g, **Saturated fat** 19 g, **Cholesterol** 296 mg, **Sodium** 3844 mg, **Total carbohydrates** 73 g, **Protein** 64 g, **Vitamin A** 27%, **Vitamin C** 200%, **Iron** 66%

Mise en Place

▶ Prepare herb sachet.

1 Placing the corned beef and sachet in an appropriate pot and covering with stock.

2 Presenting the carved beef with the vegetable garnish.

COMBINATION COOKING METHODS

Braising and stewing are referred to as combination cooking methods because both dry heat and moist heat are used to achieve the desired results.

BRAISING

Braised meats are first browned and then cooked in a liquid that serves as a sauce for the meat. A well-prepared braised dish has the rich flavor of the meat in the sauce and the moisture and flavor of the sauce in the meat. It should be almost fork tender but not falling apart. The meat should have an attractive color from the initial browning and final glazing.

Selecting Meats to Braise

Braising can be used for tender cuts (such as those from the loin or rib) or tougher cuts (such as those from the chuck or shank). Any meat to be braised should be well marbled with an ample fat content in order to produce a moist finished product.

If tender cuts such as veal chops or pork chops are braised, the finished dish has a uniquely different flavor and texture than if the meats were cooked by a dry-heat method. Tender cuts require shorter cooking times than tougher cuts because lengthy cooking is not needed to break down connective tissue.

More often, braising is used with tougher cuts that are tenderized by the long, moist cooking process. Cuts from the chuck and shank are popular choices, as they are very flavorful and contain relatively large amounts of collagen, which adds richness to the finished product.

Large pieces of meat can be braised, then carved like a roast. Portion control cuts and diced meats can also be braised.

Seasoning Meats to Be Braised

The seasoning and overall flavor of a braised dish is largely a function of the quality of the cooking liquid and the mirepoix, herbs, spices and other ingredients that season the meat as it cooks. However, braised meats can be marinated before they are cooked to tenderize them and add flavor. The marinade is then sometimes incorporated into the braising liquid. Salt and pepper may be added to the flour if the meat is dredged before it is browned, or the meat may be seasoned directly (although the salt may draw out moisture and inhibit browning).

A standard sachet and a tomato product are usually added at the start of cooking. The tomato product adds flavor and color to the finished sauce as well as acid to tenderize the meat during the cooking process. Final seasoning should not take place until cooking is complete and the sauce will not be reduced further.

Cooking Temperatures

Braised meats are always browned before simmering. As a general rule, smaller cuts are floured before browning; larger cuts are not. Flouring seals the meat, promotes even browning and adds body to the sauce that accompanies the meat. Whether floured or not, the meat is browned in fat. After browning, white meats should be golden to amber in color; red meats should be dark brown. Do not brown the meat too quickly at too high a temperature because it is important to develop a well-caramelized surface. The caramelized surface adds color and flavor to the final product.

The meat and the braising liquid are brought to a boil over direct heat. The temperature is then reduced below boiling and the pot is covered. Cooking can be finished in the oven or on the stove top. The oven provides gentle, even heat without the risk of scorching. If braising is finished on the stove top, proper temperatures must be maintained carefully throughout the cooking process, and great care must be taken to prevent scorching or burning. Lower temperatures and longer cooking times result in more even cooking and thorough penetration of the cooking liquid, providing a more flavorful final product.

Finishing Braised Meats

Near the end of the cooking process, the lid may be removed from oven-braised meats. Finishing braised meats without a cover serves two purposes. First, the meat can be glazed by basting it often. (As the basting liquid evaporates, the meat is browned and a strongly flavored glaze is formed.) Second, removing the lid allows the cooking liquid to reduce, thickening it and concentrating its flavors for use as a sauce.

Determining Doneness

Braised meats are done when they are tender. A fork inserted into the meat should meet little resistance. Properly braised meats should remain intact and not fall apart when handled gently.

Braised meats that fall apart or are stringy are overcooked. If the finished product is tough, it was probably undercooked or cooked at too high a temperature. If the entire dish lacks flavor, the meat may not have been properly browned or the cooking liquid may have been poorly seasoned.

Accompaniments to Braised Meats

Large braised items are often served like roasts. They are carved against the grain in thin slices and served with their sauce. Vegetables can be cooked with the braised meat, cooked separately and added when the main item has finished cooking or added at service. If the vegetables are cooked with the main item, they should be added at intervals based on their individual cooking times to prevent overcooking.

► PROCEDURE FOR BRAISING MEATS

The liquid used for braising is usually thickened in one of three ways:

- With a roux added at the start of the cooking process; the roux thickens the sauce as the meat cooks.
- Prethickened before the meat is added.
- Thickened after the meat is cooked either by puréeing the mirepoix or by using roux, arrowroot or cornstarch.

The procedure for braising meats includes variations for whichever thickening method is selected.

1. Heat a small amount of oil in a heavy pan.
2. Dredge the meat to be braised in seasoned flour, if desired, and add it to the oil.
3. Brown the meat well on all sides and remove from the pan.
4. Add a mirepoix to the pan and caramelize it well. If using roux, it should be added at this time.
5. Add the appropriate stock or sauce so that when the meat is returned to the pan the liquid comes approximately one-third of the way up the side of the meat.
6. Add aromatics and seasonings.
7. Return the meat to the sauce. Tightly cover the pot and bring it to a simmer. Cook slowly either on the stove top or by placing the covered pot directly in an oven at 250°F–300°F (120°C–150°C).
8. Cook the item, basting or turning it often so that all sides of the meat benefit from the moisture and flavor of the sauce.
9. When the meat is done, remove it from the pan and hold it in a warm place while the sauce is finished.
10. The sauce may be reduced on the stove top to intensify its flavors. If the meat was braised in a stock, the stock may be thickened using a roux, arrowroot or cornstarch. Strain the sauce or, if desired, purée the mirepoix and other ingredients and return them to the sauce. Adjust the sauce's consistency as desired.

RECIPE 11.6 AUNT RUTHIE'S POT ROAST

Mise en Place

▶ Peel onions and slice thinly.
▶ Peel and mince garlic.

1 Browning the brisket.

2 Sautéing the onions and garlic.

3 Basting the brisket. Note the proper amount of cooking liquid.

Yield: 12 Servings, 6 oz. (180 g) meat and 4 oz. (120 g.) sauce

Method: Braising

Vegetable oil	3 fl. oz.	90 ml
Beef brisket	6 lb.	2.7 kg
Onions, thinly sliced	3 lb.	1.4 kg
Garlic, minced	2 Tbsp.	30 ml
Brown veal stock	1 qt.	1 lt
Tomato sauce	1 pt.	450 ml
Brown sugar	4 oz.	120 g
Paprika	1 tsp.	5 ml
Dry mustard	2 tsp.	10 ml
Lemon juice	8 fl. oz.	250 ml
Ketchup	8 oz.	250 g
Red wine vinegar	8 fl. oz.	250 ml
Worcestershire sauce	2 fl. oz.	60 ml
Salt and pepper	TT	TT

1 Heat the oil in a large skillet. Add the beef and brown thoroughly. Remove and reserve the brisket.
2 Add the onions and garlic to the pan and sauté.
3 Add the stock and tomato sauce to the pan.
4 Return the brisket to the pan, cover tightly and bring to a boil. Braise at 325°F (160°C) for 1½ hours, basting or turning the brisket often.
5 Combine the remaining ingredients and add to the pan.
6 Continue cooking and basting the brisket until tender, approximately 1 hour. Add additional stock or water as needed during braising.
7 Remove the brisket, degrease the sauce and adjust its consistency and seasonings. Do not strain the sauce.
8 Slice the brisket against the grain and serve with the sauce.

Approximate values per serving: **Calories** 803, **Total fat** 52 g, **Saturated fat** 16 g, **Cholesterol** 224 mg, **Sodium** 3290 mg, **Total carbohydrates** 40 g, **Protein** 46 g, **Vitamin A** 25%, **Vitamin C** 100%

STEWING

Stewing, like braising, is a combination cooking method. In many ways, the procedures for stewing are identical to those for braising, although stewing is usually associated with smaller or bite-sized pieces of meat.

There are two main types of stews: brown stews and white stews.

When making **brown stews,** the meat is first browned in fat; then a cooking liquid is added. The initial browning adds flavor and color to the finished product. The same characteristics apply to a good brown stew that apply to a good braised dish: It should be fork tender and have an attractive color and a rich flavor.

There are two types of **white stews: fricassees,** in which the meat is first cooked in a small amount of fat without coloring, then combined with a cooking liquid; and **blanquettes,** in which the meat is first blanched, then rinsed and added to a cooking liquid. A white stew should have the same flavor and texture characteristics as a brown stew, but should be white or ivory in color.

Selecting Meats to Stew

Stewing uses moist heat to tenderize meat just as braising does; therefore, many of the same cuts can be used. Meats that are to be stewed should be trimmed of excess fat and connective tissue and cut into 1- to 2-inch (2.5- to 5-cm) cubes.

STEW TERMINOLOGY

Ragoût (ra-GOO)—A general term that refers to white or brown stews in which the meat is cooked by dry heat before a liquid is added. In French, *ragoût* means "to bring back the appetite."

Fricassee (FRIHK-uh-see)—A white ragoût usually made from white meat or small game, seared without browning and garnished with small onions and mushrooms.

Navarin (nah-veh-rahng)—A brown ragoût generally made with turnips, other root vegetables, onions, peas and lamb.

Blanquette (blahn-KEHT)—A white stew in which the meat is first blanched, then added to a stock or sauce to complete the cooking and tenderizing process. Blanquettes are finished with a liaison of egg yolks and heavy cream.

Chili con carne—A ragoût of ground or diced meat cooked with onions, chile peppers, cumin and other spices. Despite the objections of purists, chili sometimes contains beans.

Goulash—A Hungarian beef stew made with onions and paprika and garnished with potatoes.

Tagine—(tah-GEEN) A North African stew in which meat, poultry, fish or vegetables are flavored with onions, cilantro, spices and aromatics and then braised over a fire in a covered earthenware vessel of the same name.

Adobo—A stew of Spanish origin in which meats are simmered with onions and spices in a savory red chili sauce. In the Philippines, *adobo* refers to a stew in which ingredients meats, poultry or fish are pickled in vinegar, oil and spices before cooking.

Seasoning Meats to Be Stewed

Stews, like braised meats, get much of their flavor from their cooking liquid A stew's seasoning and overall flavor is a direct result of the quality of the cooking liquid and the vegetables, herbs, spices and other ingredients added during cooking.

Cooking Temperatures

Meats for brown stews are first cooked at high temperatures over direct heat until well browned. Meats for fricassees are first sautéed at low temperatures so that they do not develop color.

Once the cooking liquid has been added and the moist-heat cooking process has begun, do not allow the stew to boil. Stews benefit from low-temperature cooking. If practical, stews can be covered and finished in the oven.

Determining Doneness

Stewed meats are done when they are fork tender. Test them by removing a piece of meat to a plate and cutting it with a fork. Any vegetables that are cooked with the meat should be added at the proper times so that they and the meat are completely cooked at the same time.

Accompaniments to Stewed Meats

Stews are often complete meals in themselves, containing meat, vegetables and potatoes in one dish. Stews that do not contain a starch are often served with pasta or rice.

▶ PROCEDURE FOR STEWING MEATS—BROWN STEWS

Red meats, lamb and game are used in brown stews. The procedure for making a brown stew is very similar to braising.

1. Trim the meat of excess fat and silverskin and cut into 1- to 2-inch (2.5- to 5-cm) pieces.
2. Dredge the meat in flour if desired. Heat an appropriate-sized pan and add enough oil to cover the bottom. Cook the meat in the oil, browning it well on all sides. Onions and garlic can be added at this time and browned.
3. Add flour to the meat and fat and cook to make a brown roux.
4. Gradually add the liquid to the roux, stirring to prevent lumps. Bring the stew to a boil and reduce to a simmer.

5 Add a tomato product and a sachet or a bouquet garni. Cover and place in the oven or continue to simmer on the stove top until the meat is tender. Add other ingredients such as vegetables or potatoes at the proper time so that they will be done when the meat is tender.

6 When the meat is tender, remove the sachet or bouquet garni. The meat may be strained out and the sauce thickened with roux, cornstarch or arrowroot or reduced to concentrate its flavors.

7 If not added during the cooking process, vegetables and other garnishes may be cooked separately and added to the finished stew.

RECIPE 11.7

BROWN BEEF STEW

Mise en Place

- ▶ Cube trimmed beef.
- ▶ Peel onions and chop into fine dice.
- ▶ Peel and chop garlic.
- ▶ Make herb sachet.

Yield: 8 Servings, 8 oz. (240 g) each   **Method:** Stewing

Oil	2 fl. oz.	60 ml
Beef chuck or shank, trimmed and cut into 1½-in. (3.5-cm) cubes	4 lb. 8 oz.	2 kg
Salt	2 tsp.	10 ml
Black pepper	½ tsp.	2 ml
Onions, small dice	10 oz.	300 g
Garlic, chopped	1 tsp.	5 ml
Flour	1½ oz.	45 g
Red wine	8 fl. oz.	250 ml
Brown stock	1 qt.	1 lt
Tomato purée	4 oz.	120 g
Sachet:		
Bay leaves	2	2
Dried thyme	½ tsp.	2 ml
Peppercorns, crushed	½ tsp.	2 ml
Parsley stems	10	10

1 Heat a heavy pot until very hot and add the oil.

2 Season the beef with salt and pepper and add it to the pot, browning it well on all sides. Do not overcrowd the pot. If necessary, cook the beef in several batches.

3 Add the onions and garlic and sauté until the onions are slightly browned.

4 Add the flour and stir to make a roux. Brown the roux lightly.

5 Add the wine and stock slowly, stirring to prevent lumps.

6 Add the tomato purée and the sachet.

7 Bring to a simmer and cook until the beef is tender, approximately 1½ to 2 hours.

8 If desired, remove the cooked beef from the sauce and strain the sauce. Return the beef to the sauce.

9 Degrease the stew by skimming off the fat.

VARIATION:

Vegetables such as turnips, carrots, celery and pearl onions can be cooked separately and added to the stew as garnish.

Approximate values per 8-oz. (240-g) serving: **Calories** 590, **Total fat** 32 g, **Saturated fat** 11 g, **Cholesterol** 185 mg, **Sodium** 710 mg, **Total carbohydrates** 15 g, **Protein** 58 g, **Vitamin A** 45%, **Iron** 40%

1 Browning the beef.

2 Sautéing the garlic and onions until slightly browned.

3 Adding the flour and making a roux.

4 Adding the red wine and beef stock.

5 Adding the tomato purée and sachet.

6 Degreasing the stew.

▶ PROCEDURE FOR STEWING MEATS—BRAISED WHITE STEWS (FRICASSEES)

The procedure for making fricassees is similar to the procedure for brown stews. The primary difference is that the meat is sautéed but not allowed to brown. The braised white stew (fricassee) procedure outlined here is the basis for Veal Fricassee.

1. Trim the meat of excess fat and silverskin and cut into 1- to 2-inch (2.5- to 5-cm) pieces.
2. Heat an appropriate-sized pan and add enough oil to cover the bottom. Add the meat (and often an onion) to the pan and cook without browning.
3. Sprinkle the meat (and onion) with flour and cook to make a blond roux.
4. Gradually add the liquid, stirring to prevent lumps. Bring the stew to a boil and reduce to a simmer.
5. Add a bouquet garni and seasonings. Cover the stew and place in the oven or continue to simmer on the stove top, being careful not to burn or scorch the stew.
6. Continue to cook until the meat is tender. If the sauce is too thin, remove the meat from the sauce and hold the meat in a warm place. Reduce the sauce to the proper consistency on the stove top or thicken it by adding a small amount of blond roux, cornstarch or arrowroot.

▶ PROCEDURE FOR STEWING MEATS—SIMMERED WHITE STEWS (BLANQUETTES)

Unlike fricassees, blanquettes contain meat that was blanched, not sautéed. (Because the meat is cooked only by moist heat and never by dry heat, the blanquette cooking process is not a true combination cooking method; nevertheless, because of its striking similarities to stewing, it is included here.) The most common blanquette is made with veal and is known as blanquette de veau, but any white meat or lamb can be prepared in this manner using a variety of garnishes. The simmered white stew (blanquette) procedure outlined here is the basis for Banquette of Lamb.

1. Trim the meat of excess fat and silverskin and cut into 1- to 2-inch (2.5- to 5-cm) pieces.
2. Blanch the cubed meat by placing the meat in an appropriate pot, covering with cool water, adding salt, and bringing it rapidly to a boil. Drain the water. Rinse the meat to remove any impurities.
3. Return the meat to the pot and add enough stock to cover. Add a bouquet garni, salt and pepper. Simmer until the meat is tender, approximately 1 to 1½ hours.
4. Strain the meat from the stock. Discard the bouquet garni. Bring the stock to a boil, thicken it with a blond roux and simmer for 15 minutes.
5. Return the meat to the thickened stock. Add a liaison of cream and egg yolks to enrich and thicken the stew. Heat the stew to a simmer. Do not boil or the egg yolks will curdle.
6. If any vegetables are to be added, they should be cooked separately and added to the thickened stock with the meat.
7. Adjust the seasonings with a few drops of lemon juice, nutmeg or salt and pepper as needed.

CONCLUSION

Because meat may account for the largest portion of a food service operation's food-cost dollar, it should be purchased carefully, stored properly and fabricated appropriately. The various cuts and flavors of meat (beef, veal, lamb and pork) can be successfully broiled, grilled, roasted, sautéed, pan-fried, simmered, braised or stewed, provided chefs follow a few simple procedures and learn which cuts respond best to the various cooking methods.

QUESTIONS FOR DISCUSSION

1. Explain the difference between primals, subprimals and fabricated cuts of meat. Why is it important to be skilled in meat fabrication?
2. What is connective tissue composed of, and where is it found? What happens to connective tissue at normal cooking temperatures?
3. Discuss the government's role in regulating the marketing and sale of meat.
4. At what temperature should fresh meat be stored? At what temperature should frozen meat be stored?
5. Would it be better to grill or braise a piece of meat that contains a great deal of connective tissue? Explain your answer.
6. List three ways to improve the cooking qualities of lean meats. What techniques can be used to compensate for the lack of fat?
7. Describe the similarities between sautéing meats and pan-frying them. Describe the differences.
8. Describe the similarities between braising meats and stewing them. Describe the differences.

CHAPTER TWELVE

BEEF

BEEF IS THE SOUL OF COOKING.

—Marie-Antoin Carême, French chef (1784–1833)

CAFÉ ANNIE, Houston, TX
Chef-Owner Robert Del Grande
Executive Chef Ben Berryhill

AFTER STUDYING THIS CHAPTER, YOU WILL BE ABLE TO:

- identify the primal, subprimal and fabricated cuts of beef
- perform basic butchering procedures
- apply appropriate cooking methods to several common cuts of beef

Beef is the meat of domesticated cattle. Most of the beef Americans eat comes from steers, which are male cattle castrated as calves and specifically raised for beef. Although Americans are consuming less beef today than we once did, we still consume far more beef than any other meat. The beef we are eating is leaner than that of years past, thanks to advances in animal husbandry and closer trimming of exterior fat.

▶ PRIMAL AND SUBPRIMAL CUTS OF BEEF

After the steer is slaughtered, it is cut into four pieces (called quarters) for easy handling. This is done by first splitting the carcass down the backbone into two bilateral halves. Each half is divided into the forequarter (the front portion) and the hindquarter (the rear portion) by cutting along the natural curvature between the 12th and 13th ribs. The quartered carcass is then further reduced into the primal cuts and the subprimal and fabricated cuts.

The primal cuts of beef are the chuck, brisket and shank, rib, short plate, short loin, sirloin, flank and round. Figure 12.1 shows the relationship between a steer's bone structure and the primal cuts. It is important to know the location of bones when cutting or working with meats. This makes meat fabrication and carving easier and aids in identifying cuts. Figure 12.2 shows the primal cuts of beef and their location on the carcass. An entire beef carcass can range in weight from 500 to more than 800 pounds (225 to 360 kg).

▶ **boxed beef** industry terminology for primal and subprimal cuts of beef that are vacuum sealed and packed into cardboard boxes for shipping from the packing plant to retailers and food service operations

▶ **Certified Angus Beef** a brand created in 1978 to distinguish the highest-quality beef produced from descendants of the black, hornless Angus cattle of Scotland. The meat must meet American Angus Association standards for yield, marbling and age, and be graded as high choice or prime.

▶ **Kobe beef** an exclusive type of beef traditionally produced in Kobe, Japan. Wagyu cattle are fed a special diet, which includes beer to stimulate the animal's appetite during summer months. The animals are massaged with sake to relieve stress and muscle stiffness in the belief that calm, contented cattle produce better-quality meat. This special treatment produces meat that is extraordinarily tender and full-flavored, and extraordinarily expensive. Kobe Beef America introduced Wagyu cattle to the United States in 1976. KBA's cattle are raised without hormones and the meat is dry-aged for 21 days prior to sale.

FOREQUARTER

CHUCK

The primal chuck is the animal's shoulder; it accounts for approximately 28 percent of carcass weight. It contains a portion of the backbone, five rib bones and portions of the blade and arm bones.

Because an animal constantly uses its shoulder muscles, chuck contains a high percentage of connective tissue and is quite tough. This tough cut of beef, however, is one of the most flavorful.

The primal chuck is used less frequently than other primal cuts in food service operations. If cooked whole, the chuck is difficult to cut or carve because of the large number of bones and relatively small muscle groups that travel in different directions.

The primal chuck produces several fabricated cuts: cross rib pot roast, chuck short ribs, cubed or tenderized steaks, stew meat and ground chuck. Because the meat is less tender, the fabricated cuts usually benefit from moist-heat cooking or combination cooking methods such as stewing and braising. There are exceptions, however. The beef industry is developing new products from underutilized cuts of meat. Flat iron comes from the top shoulder of the chuck and is one such cut gaining in popularity as an alternative steak suitable for dry-heat cooking.

Chuck Square Cut (Two Pieces)

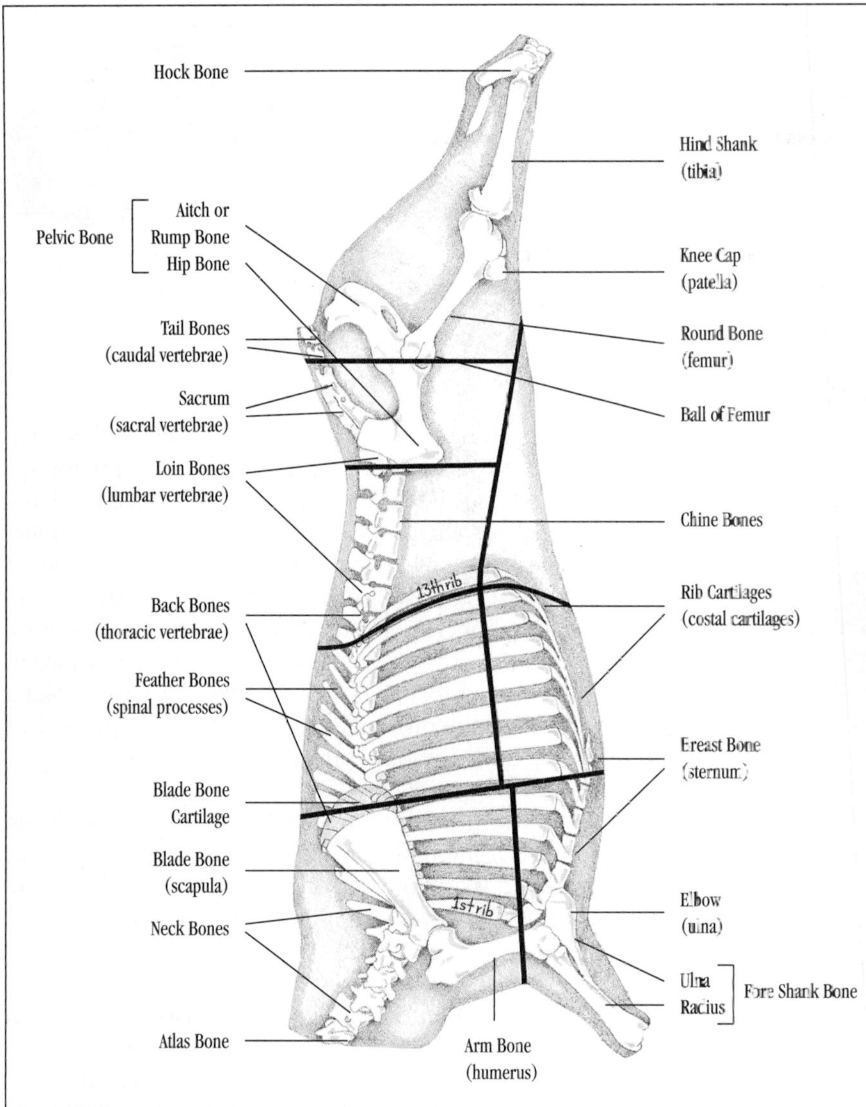

FIGURE 12.1 ▶ The skeletal structure of a steer.

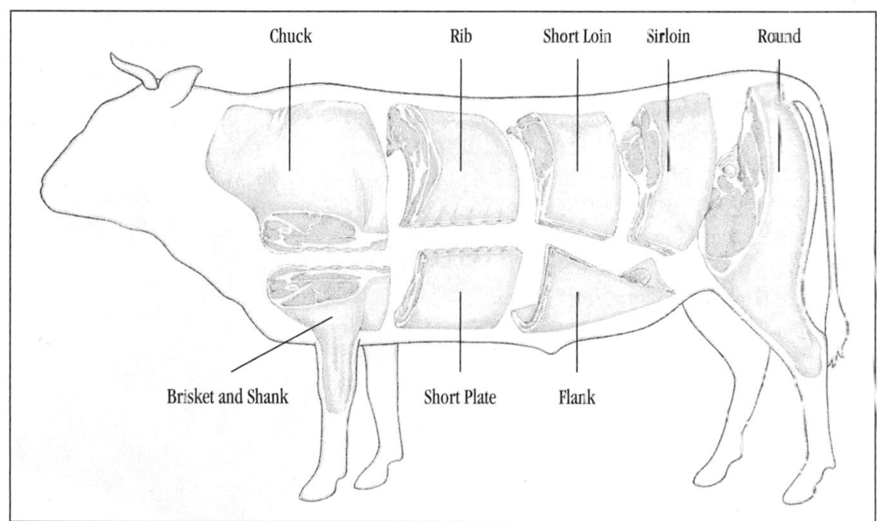

FIGURE 12.2 ▶ The primal cuts of beef.

A COW BY ANY OTHER NAME . . .

Cattle is the collective name for all domesticated oxen (genus *Bos*). Cattle are classified as follows:

Bulls—male cattle, usually not raised to be eaten.

Calves—young cows or bulls prized for their meat.

Cows—female cattle after their first calving, raised in this country principally for milk and calf production. In France, cows are used for beef when they are no longer needed for milk.

Heifers—young cows or cows before their first calving. Heifer meat and organs are becoming increasingly popular as a food source.

Stags—male cattle castrated after maturity, principally used for dog food.

Steers—male cattle castrated prior to maturity and principally raised for beef.

Shoulder Top Blade (Whole Flat Iron)

Blade Steak (Flat Iron)

BRISKET AND SHANK

The brisket and shank are located beneath the primal chuck on the front half of the carcass. Together, they form a single primal that accounts for approximately 8 percent of carcass weight. This primal consists of the steer's breast (the brisket), which contains the ribs and breast bone, and its arm (the foreshank), which contains only the shank bone.

Brisket

The ribs and breast bone are always removed from the brisket before cooking. The boneless brisket is very tough and contains a substantial percentage of fat, both intermuscular and subcutaneous. It is well suited for moist-heat and combination cooking methods such as simmering or braising. It is often pickled or corned to produce corned beef brisket, or cured and peppered to make pastrami.

Beef foreshanks are very flavorful and high in collagen. Because collagen converts to gelatin when cooked using moist heat, foreshanks are excellent for making soups and stocks. Ground shank meat is often used to help clarify and flavor consommés because of its rich flavor and high collagen content.

RIB

The primal beef rib accounts for approximately 10 percent of carcass weight. It consists of ribs 6 through 12 as well as a portion of the backbone.

Oven-Ready Rib Roast

This primal is best known for yielding roast prime rib of beef. Prime rib is not named after the quality grade USDA Prime. Rather, its name reflects the fact that it constitutes the majority of the primal cut. The eye meat of the rib (the center muscle portion) is not a well-exercised muscle and therefore is quite tender. It also contains large amounts of marbling compared to the rest of the carcass and produces rich, full-flavored roasts and steaks. Although roasting the eye muscle on the rib bones produces a moister roast, the eye meat can be removed to produce a boneless rib eye roast or cut into rib eye steaks. The rib bones that are separated from the rib eye meat are quite meaty and flavorful and can be served as barbecued beef ribs. The ends of the rib bones that are trimmed off the primal rib to produce the rib roast are known as beef short ribs. They are meaty and are often served as braised beef short ribs.

Beef Rib Eye Roll

SHORT PLATE

The short plate is located directly below the primal rib on a side of beef; it accounts for approximately 9 percent of the overall weight of the carcass. The short plate contains rib bones and cartilage and produces the short ribs and skirt steak.

Short ribs are meaty, yet high in connective tissue, and are best when braised. Skirt steak is often marinated and grilled as fajitas. Other, less meaty portions of the short plate are trimmed and ground.

Skirt Steak

HINDQUARTER

SHORT LOIN

The short loin is the anterior (front) portion of the beef loin. It is located just behind the rib and becomes the first primal cut of the hindquarter when the side of beef is divided into a forequarter and hindquarter. It accounts for approximately 8 percent of carcass weight.

Porterhouse Steak

The short loin contains a single rib, the 13th, and a portion of the backbone. With careful butchering, this small primal can yield several subprimal and fabricated cuts, all of which are among the most tender, popular and expensive cuts of beef.

The loin eye muscle, a continuation of the rib eye muscle, runs along the top of the T-shaped bones that form the backbone. Beneath the loin eye muscle on the other side of the backbone is the tenderloin, the most tender cut of all.

When the short loin is cut in cross-sections with the bone in, it produces—starting with the rib end of the short loin—club steaks (which do not contain any tenderloin), T-bone steaks (which contain only a small portion of tenderloin) and porterhouse steaks (which are cut from the sirloin end of the short loin and contain a large portion of tenderloin).

Strip Loin

The whole tenderloin can also be removed and cut into châteaubriand, filet mignon and tournedos. A portion of the tenderloin is located in the sirloin portion of the loin. When the entire beef loin is divided into the primal short loin and primal sirloin, the large end of the tenderloin (the butt tenderloin) is separated from the remainder of the tenderloin and remains in the sirloin; the smaller end of the tenderloin (the short tenderloin) remains in the short loin. If the tenderloin is to be kept whole, it must be removed before the short loin and sirloin are separated. The loin eye meat can be removed from the bones, producing a boneless strip loin, which is very tender and can be roasted or cut into boneless strip steaks.

Tenderloin

SIRLOIN

The sirloin is located in the hindquarter, between the short loin and the round. It accounts for approximately 7 percent of carcass weight and contains part of the backbone as well as a portion of the hip bone.

The sirloin produces bone-in or boneless roasts and steaks that are flavorful and tender. With the exception of the tenderloin portion, however, these subprimals and fabricated cuts are not as tender as those from the strip loin. Cuts from the sirloin are cooked using dry-heat methods such as broiling, grilling or roasting.

Top Sirloin Butt

FLANK

The flank is located directly beneath the loin, posterior to (behind) the short plate. It accounts for approximately 6 percent of carcass weight. The flank contains no bones.

Bottom Sirloin Butt Tri Tip

Flank Steak

Although quite flavorful, it is a less tender cut with a good deal of fat and connective tissue. Flank meat is usually trimmed and ground, with the exception of the flank steak or London broil. The flank also contains a small piece of meat known as the hanging tenderloin. Although not actually part of the tenderloin, it is very tender and can be cooked using any method.

ROUND

The primal round is very large, weighing as much as 200 pounds (90 kg) and accounting for approximately 24 percent of carcass weight. It is the hind leg of the animal and contains the round, aitch, shank and tail bones.

Meat from the round is flavorful and fairly tender. The round yields a wide variety of subprimal and fabricated cuts: the top round, outside round, eye round (the outside round and the eye round together are called the bottom round), knuckle and shank. See Figure 12.3. Steaks cut from the round are less tender, but because they have large muscles and limited intermuscular fat, the top round and knuckle make good roasts. The bottom round is best when braised. The hindshank is prepared in the same fashion as the foreshank.

Beef Round Rump and Shank Partially Removed (Steamship Round)

Top (or Inside) Round

BEEF: FROM COLUMBUS TO CATTLE DRIVES

Although cattle have been domesticated for several thousand years, they have been in the New World only since 1493, when Columbus brought them along on his second expedition to the West Indies. During the succeeding decades, the Spanish brought cattle to Florida and Texas, where they thrived in the dry, hot climates.

The New World's desire for beef steadily grew from the 1500s to the early 1800s. By the mid-1800s, America's demand for beef outpaced the supply available from local family farms, and so cattle ranching was born. Based principally in the Southwest and West, ranchers used the open range to support large cattle herds. Texas longhorns, descended from the original Spanish cattle stock, were the animal of choice. Prized for the quality of their meat, longhorns are hardy animals that live off the range and demand little care. They grow rapidly on forage such as mesquite beans, prickly pear, weeds, shrubs and buffalo grass. Ranchers brought the cattle from the range to slaughterhouses near consumer markets or to places such as Kansas City with rail links to the populous East Coast.

The open range, so vital to the 19th-century cattle industry, began to disappear rapidly after the signing of the Homestead Act of 1862. Squabbles with sheep ranchers further eroded the range land available for the great cattle herds to roam. And, as the railroads expanded westward, the cattle drives shortened and the economies of scale that supported cattle ranching began to dwindle. Although there are still many large cattle ranches, by the early 20th century, great cattle drives had become nothing more than fodder for Hollywood.

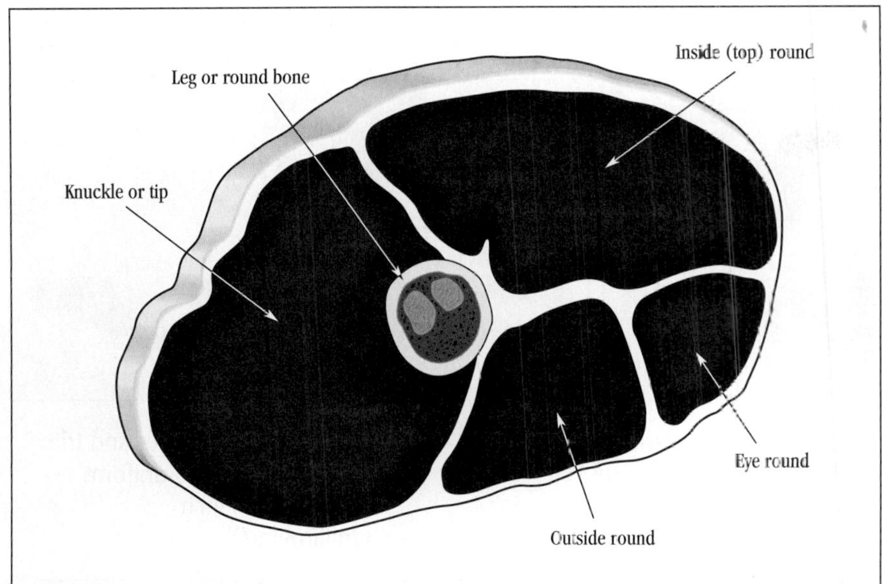

FIGURE 12.3 ▶ Cross cut of muscles in a whole round.

ORGAN MEATS

Several organ meats are used in food service operations. This group of products is known as **offal.** It includes the heart, kidney, tongue, tripe (stomach lining) and oxtail. Offal benefit from moist-heat cooking and are often used in soup, stew or braised dishes.

▶ **offal** (OFF-uhl) also called variety meats; edible entrails (for example, the heart, kidneys, liver, sweetbreads and tongue) and extremities (for example, oxtail and pig's feet) of an animal

▶ NUTRITION

Beef is a major source of protein and the primary food source of zinc as well as B vitamins, trace minerals and other nutrients. While well-marbled beef does contain a high percentage of saturated fat, lean cuts of beef such as eye round and top round roasts, top sirloin and shoulder pot roast have less fat than chicken thighs, a standard level of comparison. Excess fat should be trimmed as much as possible before cooking and serving.

▶ BUTCHERING PROCEDURES

Although many food service operations buy their beef previously cut and portioned, it is still important for a cook to be able to fabricate cuts of beef and perform basic butchering tasks.

▶ PROCEDURE FOR CUTTING A NEW YORK STEAK FROM A BONELESS STRIP LOIN

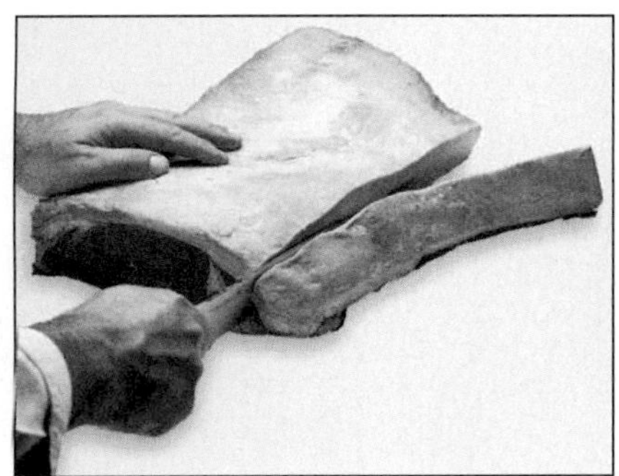

1 Square up the strip loin by trimming off the lip so it extends 1 to 2 inches (2.5 to 5 centimeters) from the eye muscle.

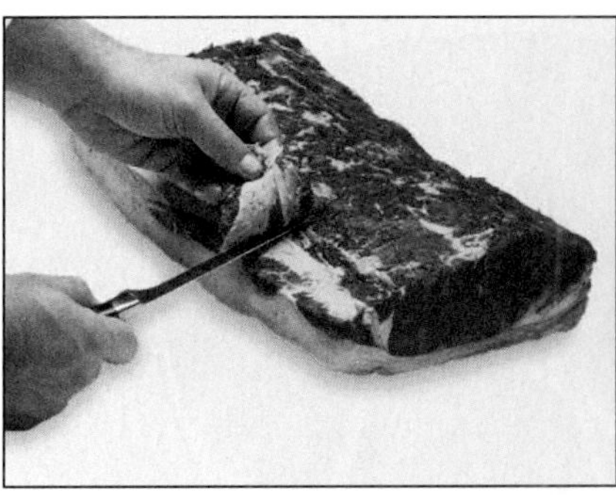

2 Turn the strip over and trim off any fat or connective tissue.

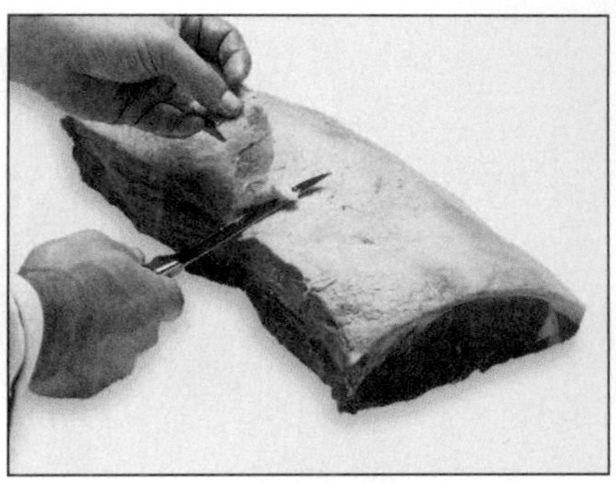

3 Turn the strip back over and trim the fat covering to a uniform thickness of 1/4 inch (6 millimeters).

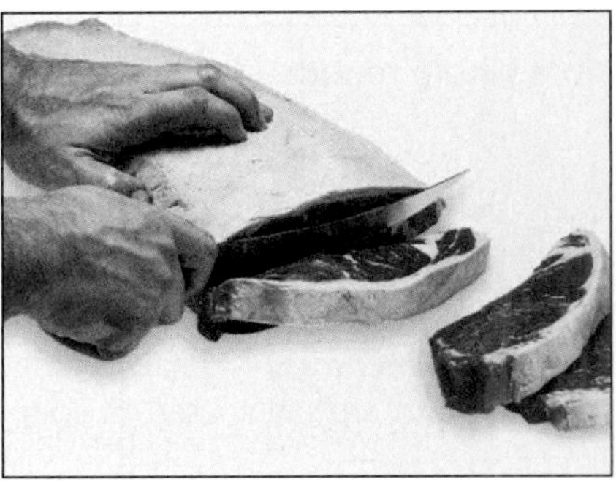

4 Cut the steaks to the thickness or weight desired.

5 The eye meat of steaks located on the sirloin end of the strip is divided by a strip of connective tissue. Steaks cut from this area are called vein steaks and are inferior to steaks cut from the rib end of the strip.

▶ PROCEDURE FOR TRIMMING A FULL BEEF TENDERLOIN AND CUTTING IT INTO CHÂTEAUBRIAND, FILET MIGNON AND TENDER TIPS

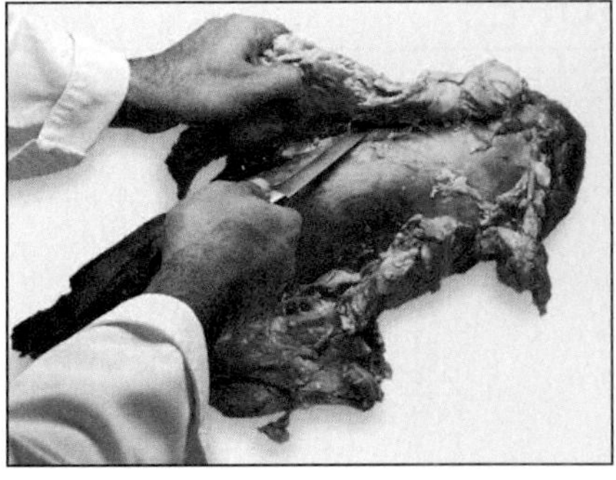

1 Cut and pull the excess fat from the entire tenderloin to expose the meat.

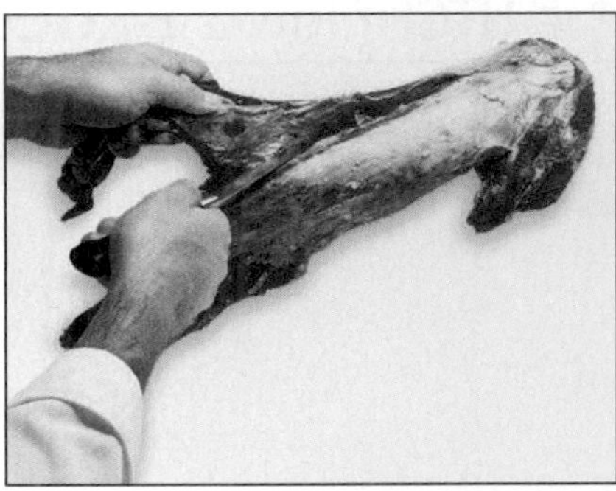

2 Remove the chain muscle from the side of the tenderloin. (Although it contains much connective tissue, the chain muscle may be trimmed and the meat used as tenderloin trimmings in various dishes.)

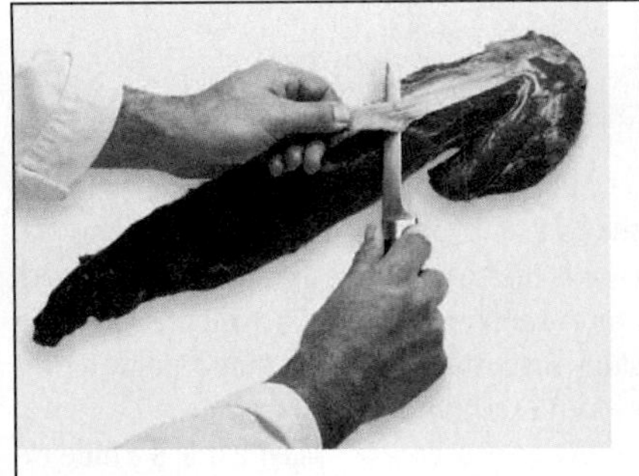

3 Trim away all of the fat and silverskin. Do so by loosening a small piece of silverskin; then, holding the loosened silverskin tightly with one hand, cut it away in long strips, angling the knife up toward the silverskin slightly so that only the silverskin is removed and no meat is wasted.

4 Cut the tenderloin as desired into (left to right) tips, châteaubriand, filet mignon, tournedos tips, and tenderloin tips.

▶ PROCEDURE FOR BUTTERFLYING MEATS

Many cuts of boneless meats such as tenderloin steaks and boneless pork chops can be butterflied to create a thinner cut that has a greater surface area and cooks more quickly.

1 Make the first cut nearly all the way through the meat, keeping it attached by leaving approximately 1/4 inch (6 millimeters) uncut.

2 Make a second cut, this time cutting all the way through, completely removing the steak from the tenderloin.

FIFTEEN SECONDS OF FLAME—A STEAK'S OWN STORY

Every cook knows that when you cook a good steak, you have to make painful compromises. You learn to blast it at high temperatures because you need more than 300°F to produce a crust with those rich, caramelized flavors that form like magic from the meat's natural sugars and amino acids. (Scientists call this process the Maillard reaction, named for the French physician who, almost a century ago, was the first to investigate similar reactions between proteins and sugars in the human body.) But you don't want the steak's interior to go much above 135°F because that's the temperature at which it stays juicy. Above that, the strands of proteins in the muscle fibers contract so much that they start to squeeze out their juices. Renowned food science author Harold McGee shocked the cooking world in 1984 when he used these principles to demonstrate that searing meat at high heat does precisely the opposite of "sealing in" those juices—it starts to dry them out.

So what usually happens when you throw your steak on the fire? You end up with a great Maillard crust, a juicy rare or rosy center—and then there's a dry, chewy "gray zone" in between.

McGee had a hunch that computers could figure out a satisfactory solution. He figured some Silicon Valley scientists could modify some mathematical simulation software to study how heat moves through meat. They could. McGee ran hundreds of simulations, in effect asking the computer: What's the best way to get the heat to diffuse through the meat so it cooks as fast and evenly as possible?

The computer told them that chefs are cooking their steaks, well, wrong. The computer simulation shows that when you throw a steak on the fire and just let it sit there, sizzling away, and then you flip the meat only once before you serve it, you're messing with the heat diffusion. There's such a huge difference between the temperatures on the side that's facing the fire and the side that's turned away that the heat inside your steak fluxes all over the place. (This applies only to beef.)

"But," McGee says, "the computer model shows that if you keep flipping the meat as you cook it, the heat diffuses through the meat much more evenly, so it cooks much more evenly. Our study suggests that the optimum flipping time is every 15 seconds."

Every 15 seconds? "Maybe that's a little extreme; it might be inconvenient," McGee says, laughing. "The computer model shows that flipping the meat every 30 seconds will work almost as well." And another recent study, at Lawrence Livermore National Laboratory, shows that frequent flipping makes steaks more healthful, too: It reduces the amount of carcinogenic compounds that can be generated when you cook over high heat by as much as 75 percent.

DANIEL ZWERDLING is a Senior Correspondent with National Public Radio. This material originally appeared in *Gourmet Magazine*

Table 12.1 USING COMMON CUTS OF BEEF

PRIMAL	SUBPRIMAL OR FABRICATED CUT	IMPS	COOKING METHODS	SERVING SUGGESTIONS
Chuck	Top blade (flat iron)	114D	Dry heat (broil or grill)	Steak; fajitas
	Chuck roll, tied	116A	Combination (braise; stew)	Pot roast; beef stew
	Stew meat	135A	Combination (stew)	Beef stew
	Ground beef	136	Dry heat (broil or grill; roast)	Hamburgers; meatloaf
			Combination (braise; stew)	Chili con carne; beef stews
Brisket and shank	Brisket	120	Moist heat (simmer)	Corned beef; New England boiled dinner
			Combination (braise)	Pot roast
	Shank	117	Combination (braise)	Shredded beef for tamales or hash
Rib	Oven-ready rib roast	109	Dry heat (roast)	Roast prime rib
	Rib eye roll	112	Dry heat (roast)	Roast prime rib
Short plate	Skirt steak	121D	Dry heat (broil or grill)	Steak; fajitas
	Short ribs	123A	Combination (braise)	Braised short ribs
Short loin	Porterhouse or T-bone steaks	173, 174	Dry heat (broil or grill)	Steaks
	Strip loin	180	Dry heat (broil or grill; roast; sauté)	New York steak; minute steak; entrecôte bordelaise
	Tenderloin	189	Dry heat (broil or grill; roast)	Tournedos Rossini; beef Wellington
Sirloin	Top sirloin butt	184	Dry heat (broil or grill; roast)	Steak; roast beef
	Tri tip	185	Dry heat (broil or grill; roast)	Steak; stir-fry; fajitas
Flank	Flank steak	193	Dry heat (broil or grill)	London broil
			Combination (braise)	Braised stuffed flank steak
Round	Steamship round	160	Dry heat (roast)	Roast beef
	Top (inside) round	168	Dry heat (roast)	Roast beef
			Combination (braise)	Braised beef roulade

CONCLUSION

Antonin Carême once said that "beef is the soul of cooking." It is also the most popular meat consumed in the United States and undoubtedly will play an important role on almost any menu. Beef's assertive flavor stands up well to most any sauce and seasonings.

Prefabricated products are readily available. But performing some basic fabrication procedures in the kitchen saves money and allows chefs to cut the meat to their exact specifications. Each primal and subprimal cut has its own distinct characteristics. The primal rib, short loin and sirloin produce the most popular and most expensive cuts of beef. Once the beef is properly fabricated, choose the appropriate dry-heat, moist-heat or combination cooking method for that cut.

QUESTIONS FOR DISCUSSION

1. List each beef primal cut and describe its location on the carcass. For each primal cut, identify two subprimal or fabricated cuts taken from it.
2. Would it be better to use the chuck for grilling or stewing? Explain your answer.
3. Which fabricated cuts contain a portion of the tenderloin? What cooking methods are best suited for these cuts? Explain your answer.
4. Most steaks are cut from the hindquarter. What popular steak is cut from the forequarter, and why is it tender when other cuts from the forequarter are relatively tough?
5. Visit the National Cattleman's Beef Association Web site to learn more. Does cooking method affect the fat and cholesterol content of a beef steak? How has consumer demand for beef products changed over the past year? 
6. Locate one or two restaurants in your area that participate in the Certified Angus Beef program. 

CHAPTER THIRTEEN

HAPPY AND SUCCESSFUL COOKING DOESN'T RELY ONLY ON KNOW-HOW; IT COMES FROM THE HEART, MAKES GREAT DEMANDS ON THE PALATE AND NEEDS ENTHUSIASM AND A DEEP LOVE OF FOOD TO BRING IT TO LIFE.

—*Georges Blanc, French chef, in* Ma Cuisine des Saisons, *1984*

BROWN PALACE, Denver, CO
Former Executive Chef Mark Black

AFTER STUDYING THIS CHAPTER, YOU WILL BE ABLE TO:

- identify the primal, subprimal and fabricated cuts of veal
- perform basic butchering procedures
- apply appropriate cooking methods to several common cuts of veal

Veal is the meat of young, usually male, calves that are by-products of the dairy industry. Dairy cows must calve before they begin to give milk. Calves that aren't used in the dairy herds are used in today's veal industry. Although veal may come from any calf under the age of nine months, most comes from calves slaughtered when they are 8 to 16 weeks old. Veal is lighter in color than beef, has a more delicate flavor and is generally more tender. Young veal has a firm texture, light pink color and very little fat. As soon as a calf starts eating solid food, the iron in the food begins to turn the young animal's meat red. Meat from calves slaughtered when they are older than five months is called calf. It tends to be a deeper red, with some marbling and external fat.

Veal's mild flavor and low fat content makes it a popular meat, especially among those looking for an alternative to beef. Its delicate flavor is complemented by both classic and modern sauces.

▸ PRIMAL AND SUBPRIMAL CUTS OF VEAL

After slaughter, the calf carcass can be split down the backbone into two bilateral halves or, more typically, cut along the natural curvature between the 11th and 12th ribs into a foresaddle (front portion) and a hindsaddle (rear portion). The veal carcass yields five primal cuts: three from the foresaddle (the shoulder, foreshank and breast, and rib), and two from the hindsaddle (the loin and leg). The veal shoulder, rib and loin primals contain both bilateral portions; that is, a veal loin contains both sides of the animal's loin.

Figure 13.1 shows the relationship between the calf's bone structure and the primal cuts. As with all meats, it is important to know the location of bones when cutting or working with veal. This makes meat fabrication and carving easier and aids in identifying cuts. Figure 13.2 shows the primal cuts of veal and their location. A veal carcass weighs in a range of 60 to 245 pounds (27 to 110 kg).

FORESADDLE

SHOULDER

Similar to the beef shoulder or chuck, the veal shoulder accounts for 21 percent of the carcass weight. It contains four rib bones (as opposed to five in the beef chuck) and portions of the backbone, blade and arm bones.

The backbone, blade and arm bones are sometimes removed and the meat roasted or stuffed and roasted. Although shoulder chops and steaks can be fabricated, they are inferior to the chops cut from more tender areas such as the loin or rib. Often the shoulder meat is ground or cubed for stew. Because of the relatively large amount of connective tissue it contains, meat from the shoulder is best braised or stewed.

FORESHANK AND BREAST

The foreshank and breast are located beneath the shoulder and rib sections on the front half of the carcass. They are considered one primal cut. Combined, they account for approximately 16 percent of the carcass weight. This primal contains rib bones and rib cartilage, breast bones and shank bones. Because

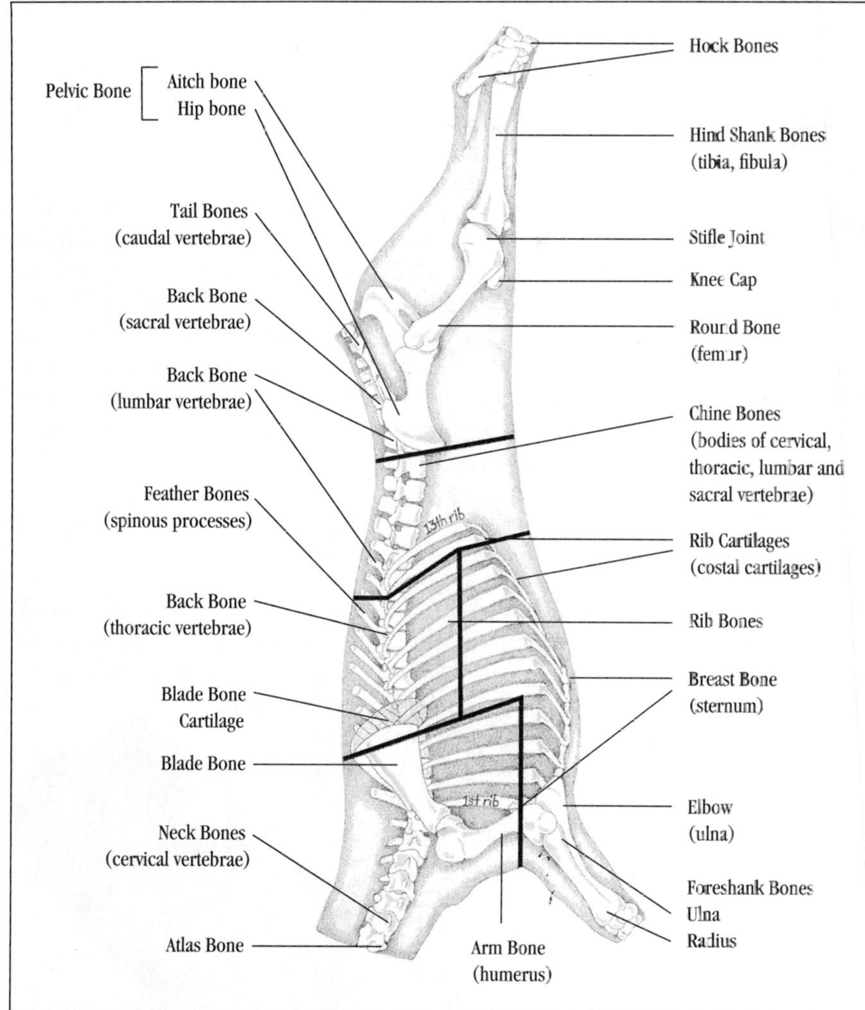

FIGURE 13.1 ▶ The skeletal structure of a calf.

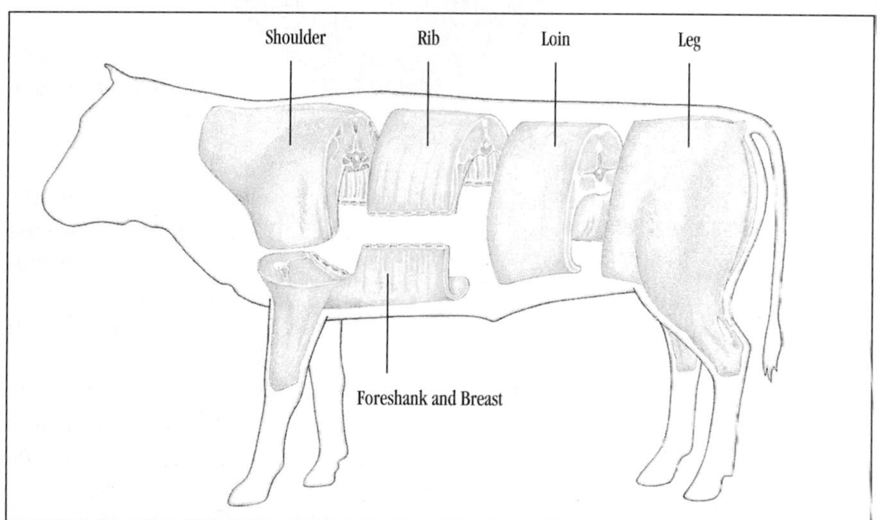

FIGURE 13.2 ▶ The primal cuts of veal.

the calf is slaughtered young, many of the breast bones are cartilaginous rather than bony.

This cartilage, as well as the ample fat and connective tissue also present in the breast, breaks down during long moist cooking, thus making the flavorful breast a good choice for braising. Veal breast can also be cubed for

FORMULA-FED VEAL VERSUS FREE-RANGE VEAL

Most veal produced today is known as formula-fed veal. Formula-fed calves are fed only nutrient-rich liquids; they are tethered in pens only slightly larger than their bodies in order to restrict their movements. Preventing the calves from eating grasses and other foods containing iron keeps their flesh white; restricting movement keeps their muscles from toughening. In recent years, controversy and allegations of cruelty have arisen concerning these methods.

An alternative to formula-fed veal is free-range veal. Free-range veal is produced from calves that are allowed to roam freely and eat grasses and other natural foods. Because they consume feed containing iron, their flesh is a reddish pink and has a substantially different flavor than meat from formula-fed calves of the same age.

Opinions differ on which has the better flavor. Some chefs prefer the consistently mild, sweet taste of formula-fed veal. Others prefer the more substantial flavor of free-range veal. The two are interchangeable in recipes. Cost, however, may be the ultimate deciding factor when determining which to use. Free-range veal is more expensive than formula-fed veal because of its limited production.

stews such as veal fricassee and veal blanquette, rolled and stuffed, or trimmed and ground.

The foreshank is also very flavorful but tough. It can be braised whole or sliced perpendicular to the shank bone and braised to produce osso buco.

RIB

The double rib, also known as a veal hotel rack, is a very tender, relatively small cut accounting for approximately 9 percent of the carcass weight. It is very popular and very expensive. The double rack consists of two racks, each with seven rib bones and a portion of the backbone.

Veal racks can be roasted either whole or split into two sides. Veal racks can be boned out; each side produces a veal rib eye and a small piece of tenderloin known as the short tenderloin, both of which make excellent roasts. More often, veal racks are trimmed and cut into chops, which can also be bone-in or boneless, to be grilled, sautéed or braised.

Veal Hotel Rack, Split

HINDSADDLE

LOIN

The veal loin is posterior to the primal rib, contains two ribs (numbers 12 and 13) and accounts for approximately 10 percent of the carcass weight. The loin consists of the loin eye muscle on top of the rib bones and the tenderloin under them.

The veal loin eye is very tender, and the tenderloin is, without a doubt, the most tender cut of veal. If the primal veal loin is separated from the primal leg before the tenderloin is removed, the tenderloin will be cut into two pieces. The small portion (short tenderloin) remains in the primal loin, and the large portion (butt tenderloin) remains in the sirloin portion of the primal leg. The tenderloin is sometimes removed and cut into medallions. The veal loin is often cut into chops, bone-in or boneless. It is usually cooked using dry-heat methods such as broiling, grilling, roasting or sautéing.

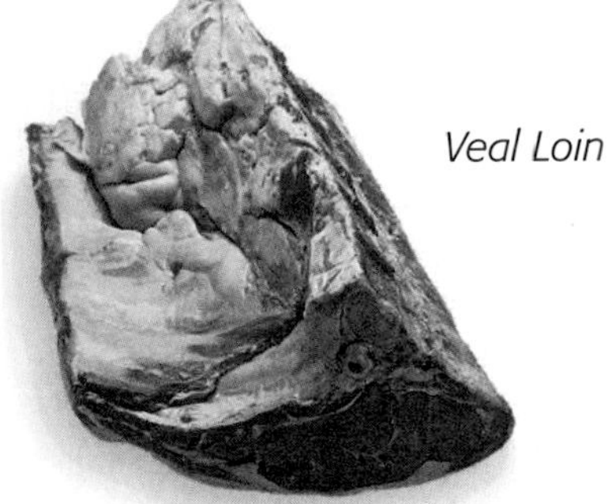

Veal Loin

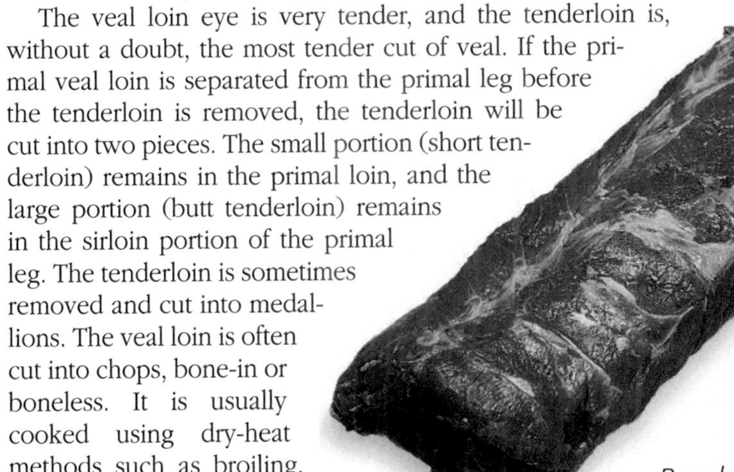

Boneless Strip Loin

Loin Chops

LEG

The primal veal leg consists of both the sirloin and the leg. Together, they account for approximately 42 percent of the carcass weight. The primal leg is separated from the loin by a cut perpendicular to the backbone immediately anterior to the hip bone, and it contains portions of the backbone, tail bone, hip bone, aitch bone, round bone and hind shank.

Although it is tender enough to be roasted whole, the veal leg is typically fabricated into cutlets and scallops. To fabricate these cuts, the leg is first broken down into its major muscles: the top round, eye round, knuckle, sirloin, bottom round (which includes the sirloin) and butt tenderloin. Each of these muscles can be reduced to scallops by trimming all fat and visible connective tissue and slicing against the grain to the desired thickness. The scallops then should be pounded carefully to tenderize them further and to prevent them from curling when cooked.

Veal Leg

The hindshank is somewhat meatier than the foreshank, but both are prepared and cooked in the same manner.

Because the veal carcass is small enough to be handled easily, it is sometimes purchased in forms larger than the primal cuts described earlier. Depending on employee skill, available equipment and storage space and an ability to utilize fully all the cuts and trimmings that fabricating meat produces, a chef may want to purchase veal in one of the following forms:

- Foresaddle: The anterior (front) portion of the carcass after it is severed from the hindsaddle by a cut following the natural curvature between the 11th and 12th ribs. It contains the primal shoulder, foreshank and breast, and rib.
- Hindsaddle: The posterior portion of the carcass after it is severed from the foresaddle. It contains the primal loin and leg.
- Back: The trimmed rib and loin sections in one piece. The back is particularly useful when producing large quantities of veal chops.
- Veal side: One bilateral half of the carcass, produced by cutting lengthwise through the backbone.

Top Round

Hindshank Cut for Osso Buco

ORGAN MEATS

Several calf organ meats are used in food service operations.

SWEETBREADS

Sweetbreads are the thymus glands of veal (Fr. *ris de veau*) and lamb (*ris d'agneau*). As an animal ages, its thymus gland shrinks; therefore, sweetbreads are not available from older cattle or sheep. Veal sweetbreads are much more popular than lamb sweetbreads in this country. Good-quality sweetbreads should be plump and firm, with the exterior membrane intact. Delicately flavored and tender, they can be prepared by almost any cooking method.

Sweetbreads

CALVES' LIVER

Calves' liver is much more popular than beef liver because of its tenderness and mild flavor. Good-quality calves' liver should be firm and moist, with a shiny appearance and without any off-odor. It is most often sliced and sautéed or broiled and served with a sauce.

Calves' Liver

KIDNEYS

Kidneys are more popular in other parts of the world than in the United States. Good-quality kidneys should be plump, firm and encased in a shiny membrane. Properly prepared kidneys have a rich flavor and firm texture; they are best prepared by moist-heat cooking methods and are sometimes used in stew or kidney pie.

Kidneys

► NUTRITION

Like beef, veal is a major source of protein as well as niacin, zinc and B vitamins. Veal has less marbling than beef. When trimmed of any visible fat, veal is lower in fat and calories than comparable beef cuts. And it is leaner than many cuts of pork and poultry.

► BUTCHERING PROCEDURES

Many food service operations purchase veal in primal or other large cuts and fabricate it in-house to their own specifications. A chef should master several important veal fabrication and butchering techniques.

▶ PROCEDURE FOR BONING A LEG OF VEAL

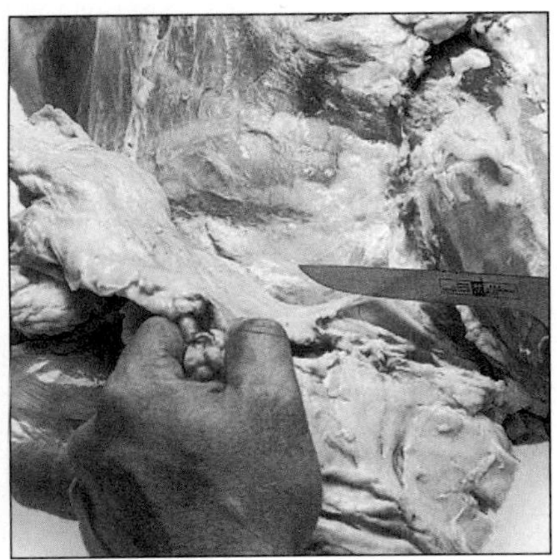

1 Remove the shank by cutting through the knee joint. Remove the excess fat and flank meat.

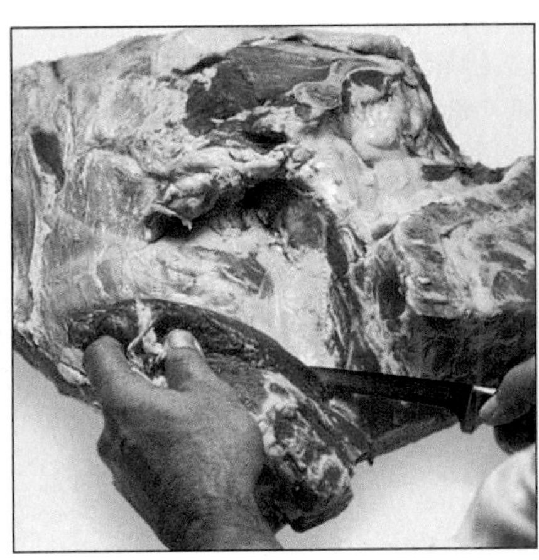

2 Remove the butt tenderloin from the inside of the pelvic bone.

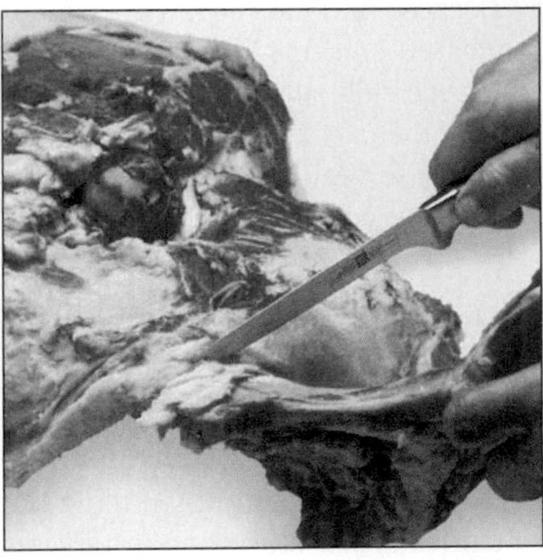

3 Remove the pelvic bone by carefully cutting around the bone, separating it from the meat. Continue until the bone is completely freed from the meat.

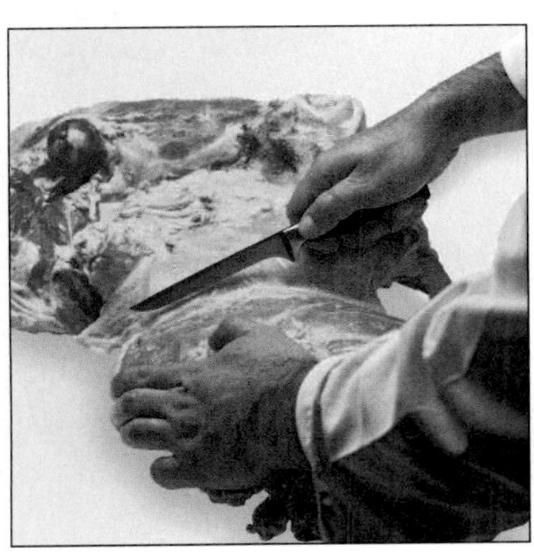

4 With the inside of the leg up, remove the top round by cutting along the natural seam.

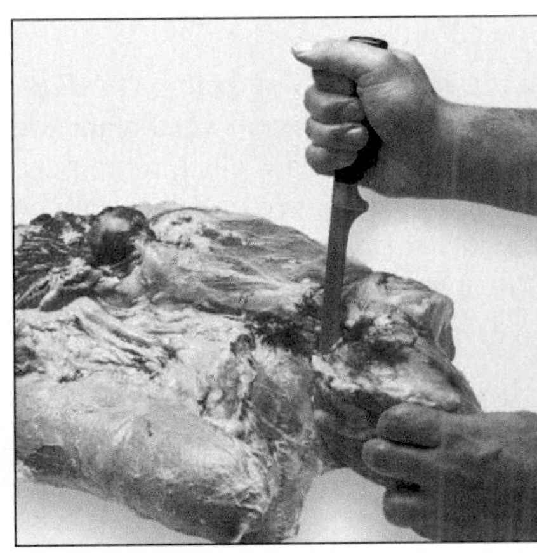

5 Remove the shank meat. (It is the round piece of meat lying between the eye round and the bone, on the shank end of the leg.)

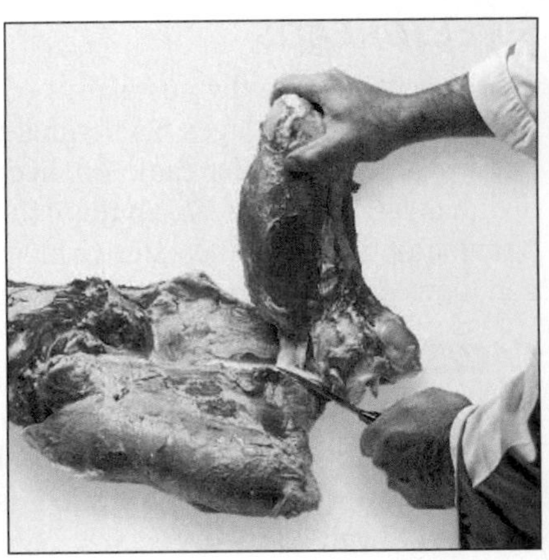

6 Remove the round bone and the knuckle together by cutting around the bone and through the natural seams separating the knuckle from the other muscles. Separate the knuckle meat from the bone.

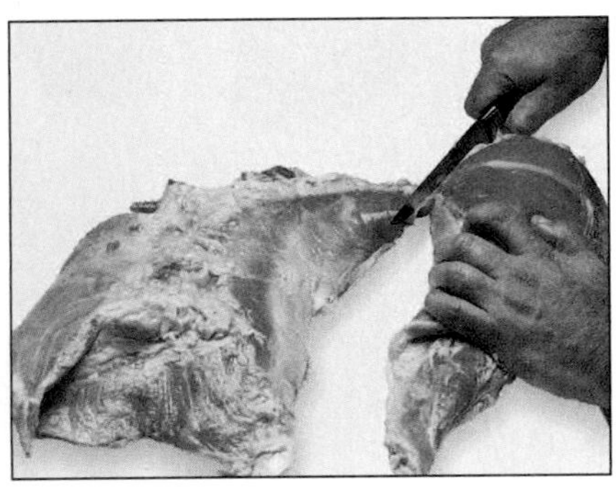

7 Remove the sirloin.

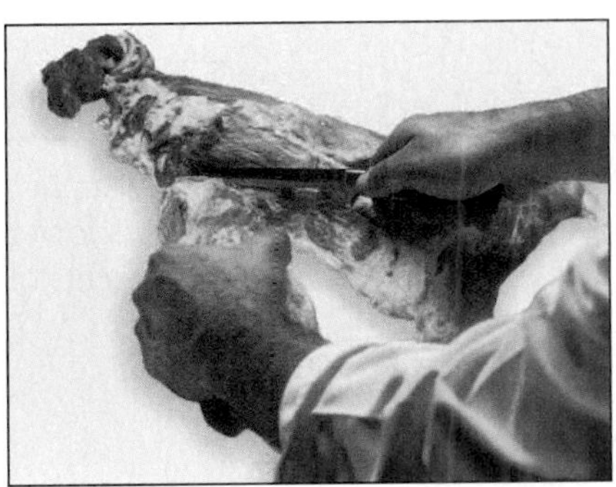

8 Remove the eye round from the bottom round.

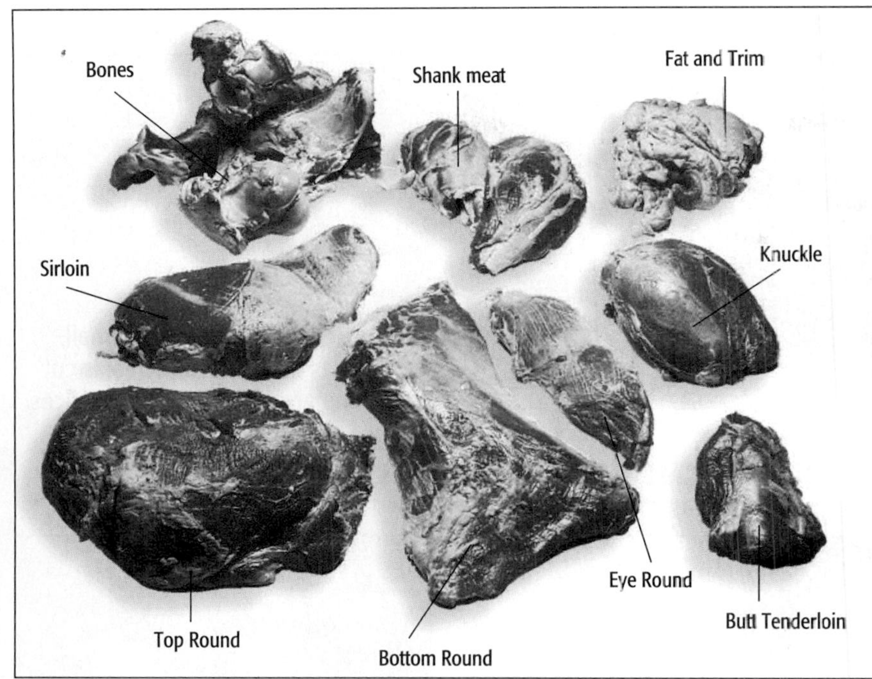

The completely boned-out veal leg, producing a top round, eye round, knuckle, shank meat, butt tenderloin, sirloin, bottom round bones and trimmings.

▶ PROCEDURE FOR CUTTING AND POUNDING SCALLOPS

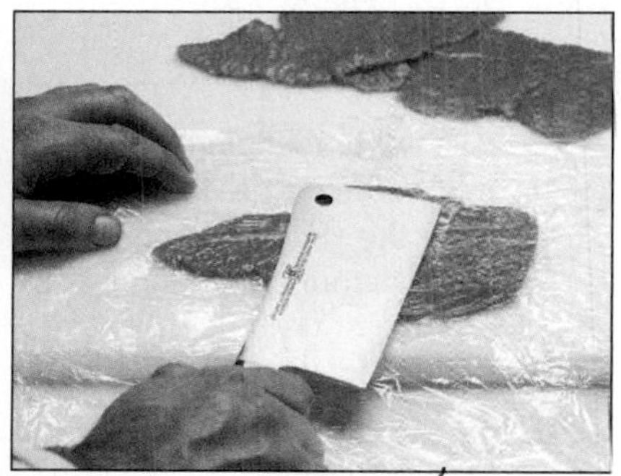

1 Veal scallops are cut from relatively large pieces of veal (here, a portion of the top round). All fat and silverskin must be trimmed. Going against the grain, cut slices approximately ¼ inch (3 millimeters) thick; cut on the bias to produce larger pieces.

2 Place the scallops between two pieces of plastic wrap and pound lightly with a spreading motion to flatten and tenderize the meat. Be careful not to tear or pound holes in the meat.

▶ PROCEDURE FOR CUTTING ÉMINCÉ

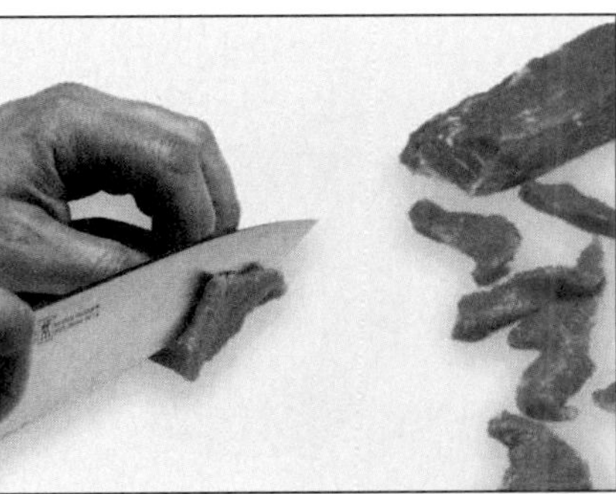

Émincé is cut from relatively small, lean pieces of meat. Here veal is cut across the grain into small, thin slices.

▶ PROCEDURE FOR BONING A VEAL LOIN AND CUTTING IT INTO BONELESS VEAL CHOPS

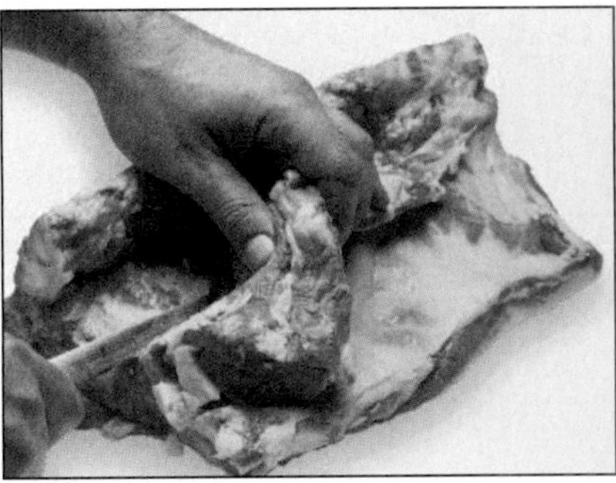

1 Remove the tenderloin in a single piece from the inside of the loin by following the vertebrae and cutting completely around the tenderloin.

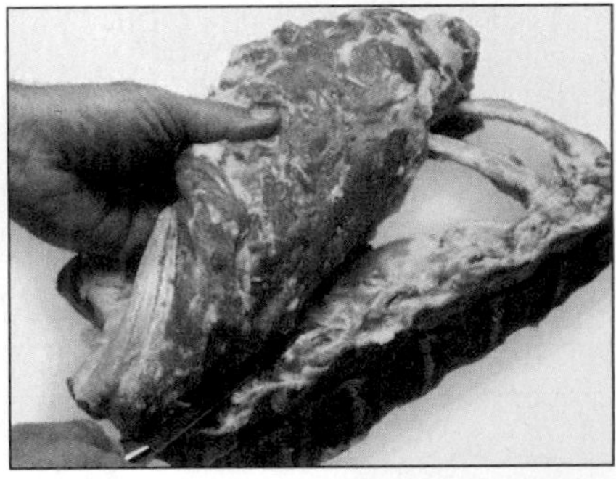

2 From the backbone side, cut along the natural curve of the backbone, separating the loin meat from the backbone.

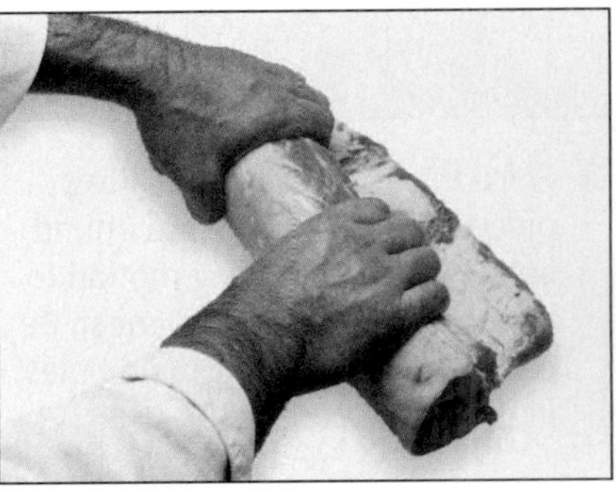

3 Trim any excess fat from the loin, and trim the flank to create a 3-inch (7.5-centimeter) lip. Tightly roll up the loin with the flank on the outside.

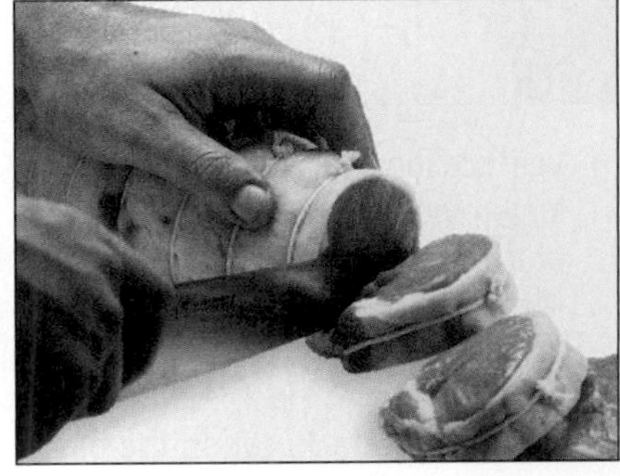

4 Tie the loin, using the procedure described next, at 1-inch (2.5-centimeter) intervals. Cut between the pieces of twine for individual boneless loin chops.

▶ PROCEDURE FOR TYING MEATS

Here we apply the tying procedure to a boneless veal loin; the same procedure can be used on any type of meat.

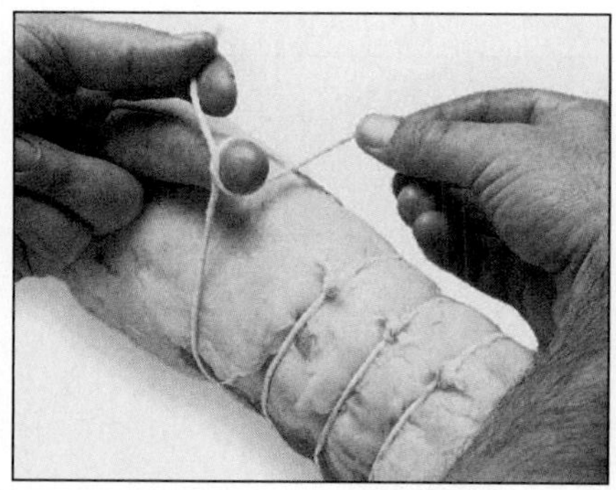

1 Cut a piece of string long enough to wrap completely around the loin. Holding one end between the thumb and forefinger, pass the other end around it and across the strings. Loop the loose end of the string around your finger.

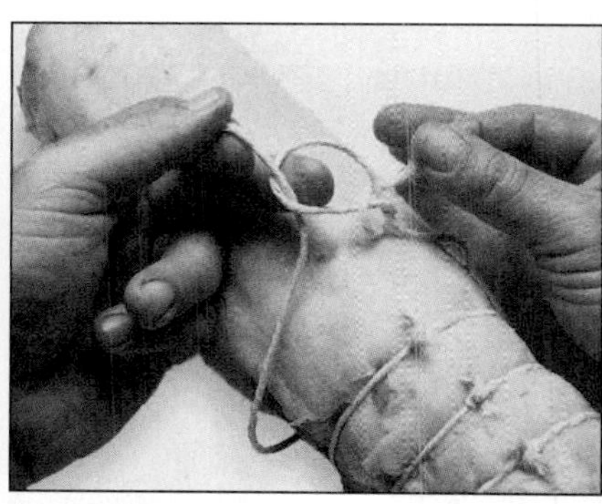

2 Wrap the string around itself and pass the loose end back through the hole.

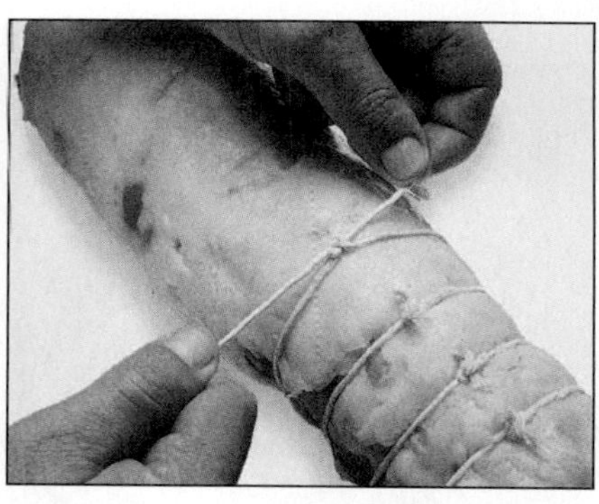

3 Pull to tighten the knot. Adjust the string so it is snug against the meat.

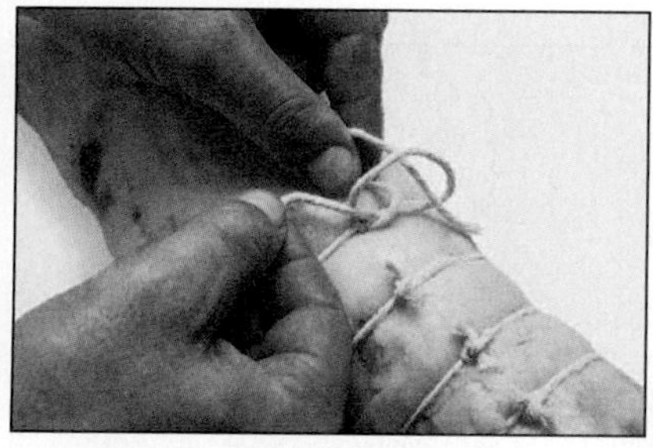

4 Loop one end of the string around your thumb and forefinger. Reach through with your thumb and forefinger and pull the other string back through the loop. Pull both strings to tighten the knot, thus preventing the first knot from loosening. Trim the ends of the strings.

5 Continue in this fashion until the entire loin is tied. The strings should be tied at even intervals, just snug enough to hold the shape of the loin; they should not dig into or cut the meat.

▶ PROCEDURE FOR CLEANING AND PRESSING SWEETBREADS

Before fabrication, submerge the sweetbreads in cold milk or water, cover and place them in the refrigerator overnight in order to soak out any blood. Then blanch them in a court bouillon for 20 minutes.

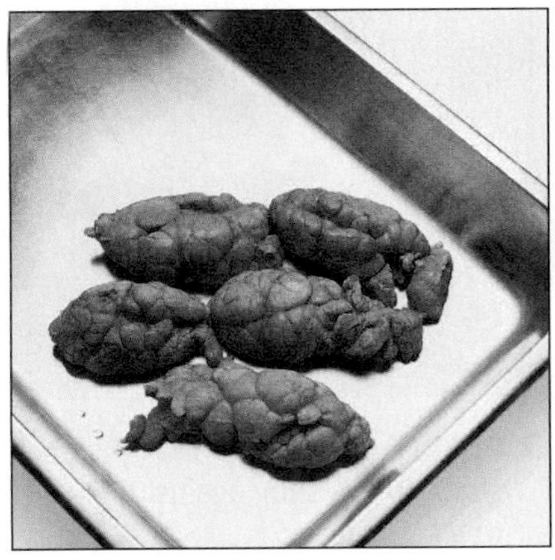

1 Remove the sweetbreads from the poaching liquid and allow them to cool.

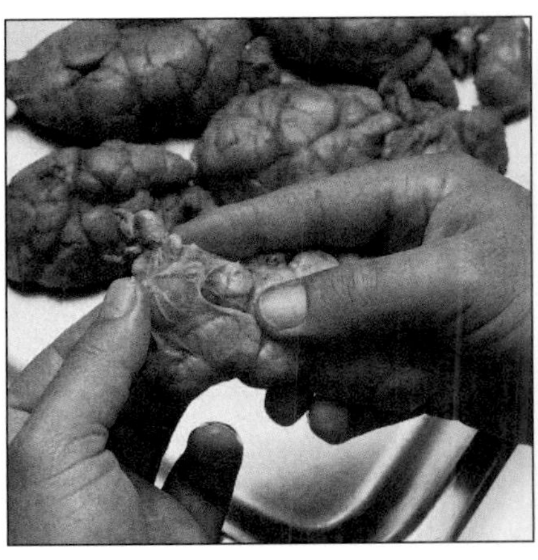

2 Using your hands, pull off any sinew or membranes that may be present on the surface of the sweetbreads.

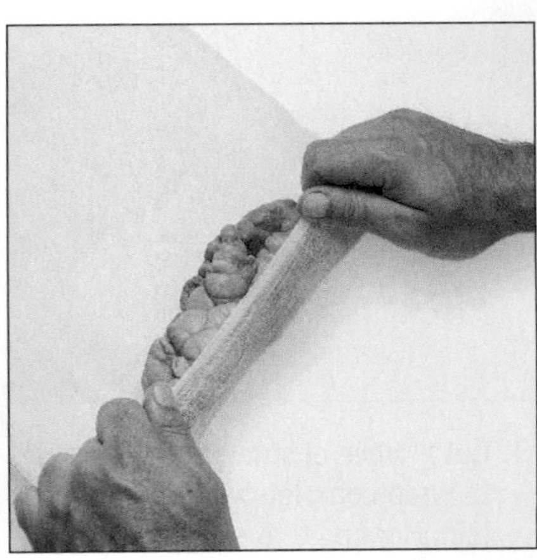

3 Wrap the sweetbreads in cheesecloth.

4 Tie the ends with butcher's twine.

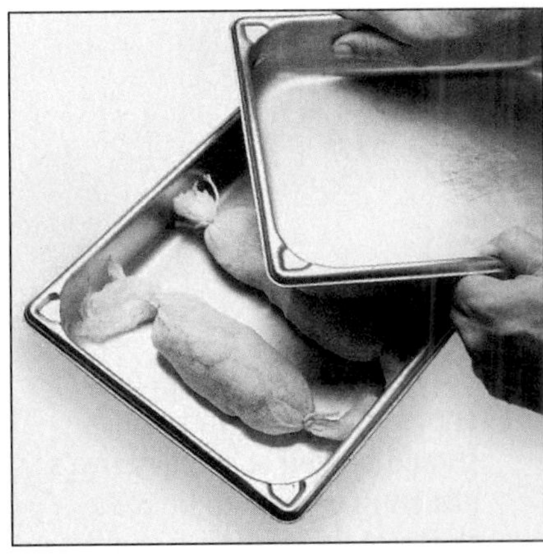

5 Place the wrapped sweetbreads in a half-size hotel pan or similar container.

6 Place another half-size hotel pan on top of the sweetbreads; place a weight in the pan to press the sweetbreads. Pressing sweetbreads in this manner improves their texture.

▶ PROCEDURE FOR CLEANING CALVES LIVER

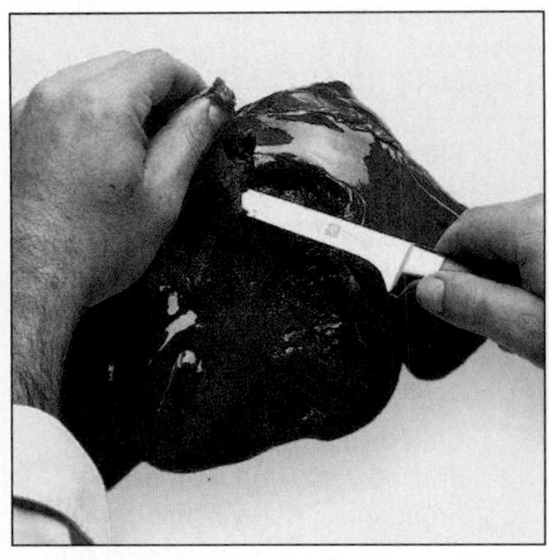

1 Trim the large sinew and outer membrane from the bottom of the liver.

2 Turn the liver over and peel the membrane off with your hands.

3 The liver can be cut into thick or thin slices as needed.

▶ PROCEDURE FOR CLEANING VEAL KIDNEYS

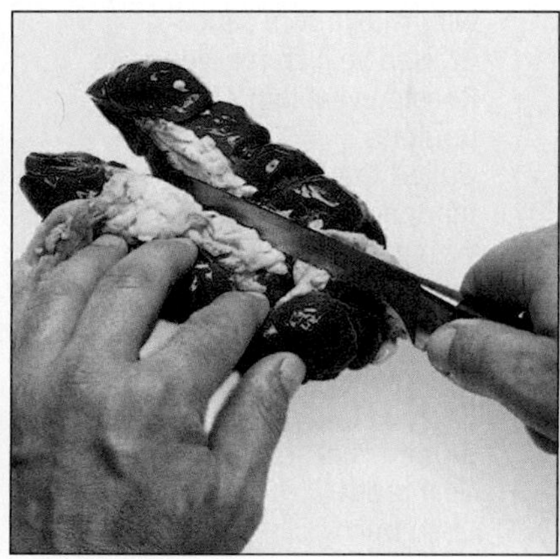

1 Split the kidneys lengthwise, exposing the fat and sinew.

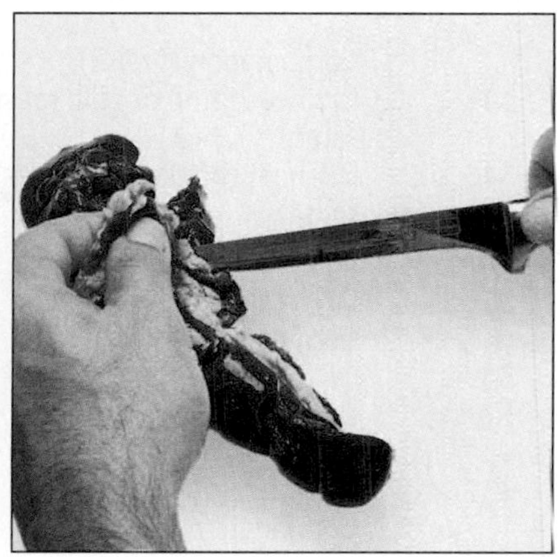

2 With a sharp knife, trim away the fat; the kidney is now ready for cooking.

Table 13.1 USING COMMON CUTS OF VEAL

PRIMAL	SUBPRIMAL OR FABRICATED CUT	IMPS	COOKING METHODS	SERVING SUGGESTIONS
Shoulder	Cubed veal	1395	Combination (stew)	Blanquette or fricassee
	Ground veal	1396	Dry heat (broil or grill)	Veal patties
			Combination (braise)	Stuffing; meatballs
Foreshank and breast	Foreshank	312	Combination (braise)	Osso buco
	Breast	313	Combination (braise)	Stuffed veal breast
Rib	Hotel rack	306	Dry heat (broil or grill; roast)	Grilled veal chop; roast veal with porcini mushrooms
	Rib chops	1306	Dry heat (broil or grill)	Grilled veal chop
			Combination (braise)	Braised veal chop with risotto
	Rib eye	307	Dry heat (broil or grill; roast)	Broiled veal rib eye with chipotle sauce; roasted veal rib eye marchand de vin
			Combination (braise)	Braised rib eye
Loin	Veal loin	331	Dry heat (broil or grill; roast; sauté)	Roasted veal loin with wild mushrooms; sautéed veal medallions with green peppercorn sauce
	Loin chops	1332	Dry heat (broil or grill; sauté)	Broiled or sautéed veal chops with mushroom sauce
			Combination (braise)	Braised veal chops lyonnaise
	Boneless strip loin	344	Dry heat (broil or grill; roast; sauté)	Roasted veal loin sauce poulette
	Veal tenderloin	346	Dry heat (broil or grill; roast; sauté)	Grilled tenderloin; roasted tenderloin; sautéed tenderloin with garlic and herbs
Leg	Leg	334	Dry heat (roast; sauté)	Veal scallopini
			Combination (stew)	Blanquette
	Top round	349A	Dry heat (roast; sauté)	Veal marsala, schnitzel
	Bottom round	NA	Dry heat (sauté)	Sautéed scallops with Calvados
			Combination (braise)	Stuffed veal scallops
	Hindshank	337	Moist heat (simmer)	Veal broth
			Combination (braise)	Osso buco
Offal	Sweetbreads	715	Dry heat (pan-fry; sauté)	Sautéed sweetbreads beurre noisette
			Combination (braise)	Braised sweetbreads Madeira
	Calves' liver	704	Dry heat (broil or grill; sauté)	Broiled or sautéed calves' liver with onion and bacon
	Kidneys	NA	Combination (braise)	Kidney pie

CONCLUSION

Although veal may not be as popular as beef or pork, it is versatile and easy to cook and adds variety to menus. Veal is much more delicately flavored than beef, with a finer texture and lighter color. Its flavor blends well with a variety of sauces and other ingredients without overpowering them. Veal can be cooked by almost any dry-heat, moist-heat or combination cooking method.

Veal quality varies greatly among purveyors. Purchase only from reputable companies to be sure of receiving a consistently high-quality product. Because veal carcasses are relatively small, they are sometimes purchased as primal cuts for further fabrication.

QUESTIONS FOR DISCUSSION

1 Compare the appearance and flavor of beef and veal.
2 What are the differences between formula-fed veal and free-range veal?
3 Describe two differences between a beef carcass and a veal carcass.
4 List each veal primal and describe its location on the carcass. For each primal, identify two subprimals or fabricated cuts taken from it
5 Would it be better to use a veal loin for grilling or braising? Explain your answer.
6 What are veal sweetbreads? Describe how sweetbreads should be prepared for cooking.
7 Certain groups oppose the use of formula-fed veal, saying that the animals are treated in an inhumane manner. What are these organizations? Are their arguments valid? What are the alternatives?

CHAPTER FOURTEEN

I LIKE A COOK WHO SMILES OUT LOUD WHEN HE TASTES HIS OWN WORK.
LET GOD WORRY ABOUT YOUR MODESTY,
I WANT TO SEE YOUR ENTHUSIASM.

—Robert Farrer Capon, American writer

LAMB

BISHOP'S RESTAURANT, Vancouver, BC
Painting by Alexandria Dikeakos, Vancouver, BC

AFTER STUDYING THIS CHAPTER, YOU WILL BE ABLE TO:

- identify the primal, subprimal and fabricated cuts of lamb
- perform basic butchering procedures
- apply appropriate cooking methods to several common cuts of lamb

Lamb is the meat of sheep slaughtered when they are less than one year old. Meat from sheep slaughtered after that age is called mutton. Spring lamb is young lamb that has not been fed grass or grains. Because lamb is slaughtered at an early age, it is quite tender and can be prepared by almost any cooking method.

Lamb has a strong and distinctive flavor. It goes well with boldly flavored sauces and accompaniments.

▶ PRIMAL AND SUBPRIMAL CUTS OF LAMB

After the young sheep is slaughtered, it is usually reduced to the primal cuts: shoulder, breast, rack, loin and leg. Like some veal primals, lamb primals are crosscut sections and contain both bilateral halves (for example, the primal leg contains both hind legs). Lamb primals are not classified into a forequarter and hindquarter like beef, or a foresaddle and hindsaddle like veal.

Figure 14.1 shows the relationship between the lamb's bone structure and the primal cuts. As with all meats, it is important to know the location of bones when cutting or working with lamb. This makes meat fabrication and carving easier and aids in identifying cuts. Figure 14.2 shows the primal cuts of lamb and their location on the carcass. A lamb carcass generally weighs between 41 and 75 pounds (20 and 35 kg).

SHOULDER

The primal lamb shoulder is a relatively large cut accounting for 36 percent of the carcass weight. The lamb shoulder contains four rib bones and the arm, blade and neck bones as well as many small, tough muscles whose grains travel in different directions.

All these bones and muscle groups make it nearly impossible to cook and carve a whole shoulder. Although the shoulder may be cut into chops, or boned and then roasted or braised, with or without stuffing, it is more commonly diced for stew or ground for patties.

BREAST

The primal lamb breast contains the breast and foreshank portions of the carcass. Together they account for approximately 17 percent of the carcass weight and contain the rib, breast and shank bones. The primal breast is located beneath the primal rack and contains the rib tips, which are cut off to produce the rack. When separated from the rest of the breast, these small ribs are called Denver ribs and can be substituted for pork ribs when desired.

Although the breast is not used extensively in food service operations, it can be stuffed and braised, either bone-in or boneless. Lamb foreshanks are quite meaty and may be braised and served as an entrée, used for broths or ground.

RACK

▶ **frenching** a method of trimming racks or individual chops of meat, especially lamb, in which the excess fat is cut away, leaving the eye muscle intact; all meat and connective tissue are removed from the rib bone

The primal lamb rack is also known as the hotel rack. It is located between the primal shoulder and loin. Containing eight ribs and portions of the backbone, it accounts for approximately 8 percent of the carcass weight.

The rack is valued for its tender rib eye muscle. The hotel rack is usually split in half and trimmed so that each set of ribs can be easily cut into chops. The split

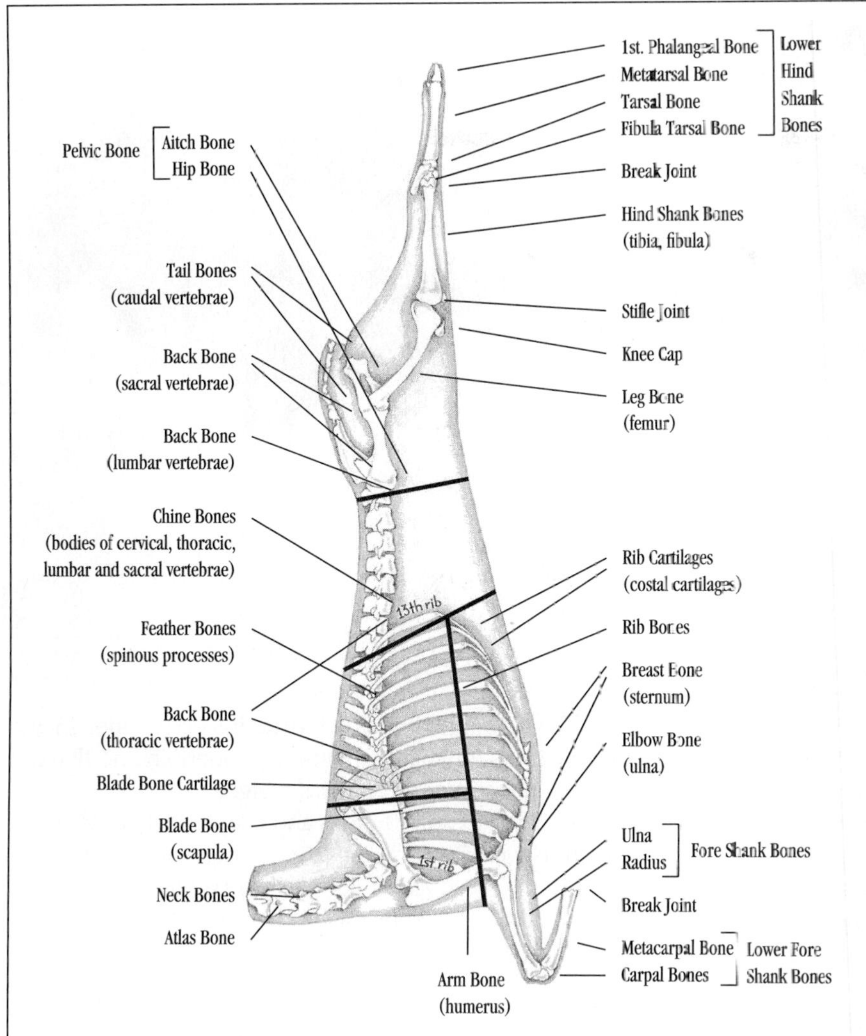

FIGURE 14.1 ▶ The skeletal structure of a lamb.

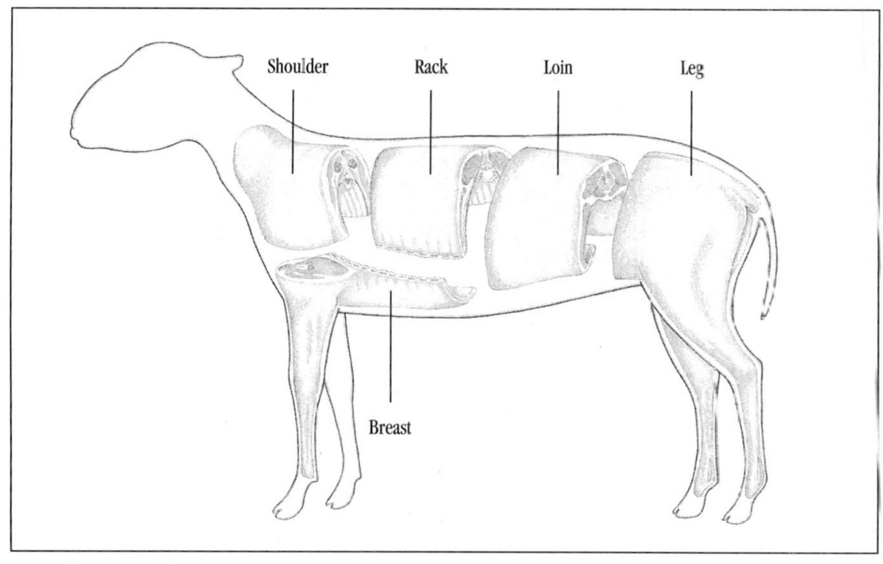

FIGURE 14.2 ▶ The primal cuts of lamb.

IMPERIALIST, COLONIALIST AND REVOLUTIONARY SHEEP

Columbus brought sheep to the New World on his second voyage in 1493. The Spanish soon established breeding centers in the Caribbean islands, then in Mexico and Panama. In 1565, people and livestock, including sheep, settled in St. Augustine, Florida.

During the 16th and 17th centuries, the Spanish established missions in Texas, New Mexico, Arizona and California in order to bridge their Florida and Mexico settlements. They brought sheep with them as an easily cared-for source of food and wool.

Sheep raising was not as easily established in the British colonies along the eastern seaboard. Many of the sheep brought with the early colonists were consumed for food during the harsh winters. More and more sheep had to be imported in order to satisfy the colonists' competing demands for food and clothing. By the mid-17th century, however, sheep were flourishing in the New England colonies and supplying an abundance of meat and wool.

In an attempt to maintain control of the wool trade, the British restricted the export of sheep to the American colonies and forbade the import of colonial wool and woolens. Retaliating against these restrictive trade practices, the colonists passed laws forbidding the use of sheep for food in order to preserve the flocks for wool. This protectionist scheme helped assure a strong supply of materials for the domestic woolen industry that flourished after the Revolutionary War.

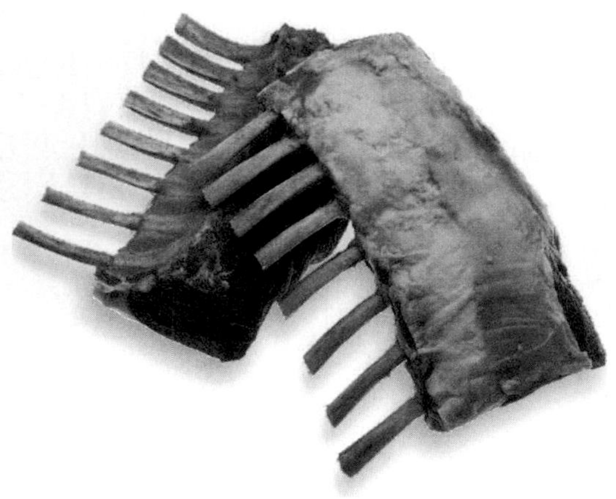

Frenched Lamb Rack

Lamb Rack

racks can then be grilled, broiled or roasted as racks or cut into single or double rib chops before cooking.

LOIN

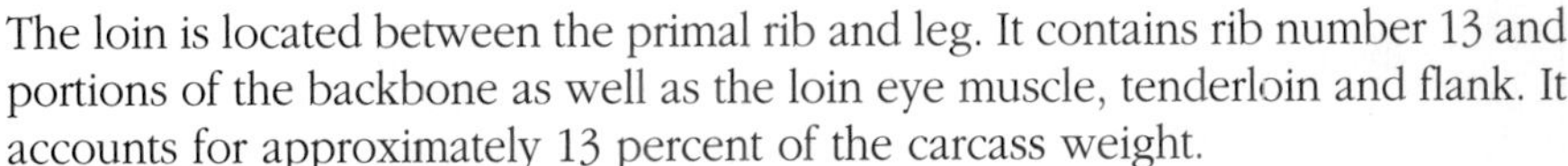

Lamb Loin Trimmed

The loin is located between the primal rib and leg. It contains rib number 13 and portions of the backbone as well as the loin eye muscle, tenderloin and flank. It accounts for approximately 13 percent of the carcass weight.

Except for the flank, the loin meat is very tender and is invariably cooked using a dry-heat method such as broiling, grilling or roasting. The loin may be boned to produce boneless roasts or chops or cut into chops with the bone in. The loin eye may be removed and cut into medallions or noisettes.

LEG

The primal leg is a large section accounting for approximately 34 percent of the carcass weight. It is the posterior portion of the carcass, separated from the loin by a straight cut anterior to the hip bone cartilage. As with veal, the cut of meat that would be the sirloin on a beef carcass is separated from the lamb loin by this cut and becomes part of the primal leg. The lamb leg contains several bones: the backbone, tail, hip, aitch, round and shank bones.

Lamb Leg

The primal leg is rarely used as is. More often, it is split into two legs and partially or fully boned. Lamb legs are quite tender—the sirloin end more so than the shank end—and are well suited to a variety of cooking methods. A bone-in leg is often roasted for buffet service or braised with vegetables or beans for a hearty dish. Steaks can also be cut from the bone-in leg, with the sirloin end producing the most tender cuts. A boneless leg can be tied and roasted, with or without stuffing, or trimmed and cut into scallops. The shank end can be diced for stew or ground for patties.

Because lamb carcasses are so easily handled, purveyors often sell them whole or cut in a variety of ways to better meet their customers' needs. As well as whole-carcass, primal and fabricated cuts, lamb can be purchased in the following forms:

Boned, Rolled and Tied Leg of Lamb

- *Foresaddle:* The anterior (front) portion of the carcass after it is severed from the hindsaddle by a cut following the natural curvature between the 12th and 13th ribs. It contains the primal shoulder, breast and foreshank and rack.

- *Hindsaddle:* The posterior portion of the carcass after it is severed from the foresaddle. It contains the primal loin and leg together with the kidneys.
- *Back:* The trimmed rack and loin sections in one piece. The back is particularly useful when producing large quantities of lamb chops.
- *Bracelet:* The primal hotel rack with the connecting breast sections.

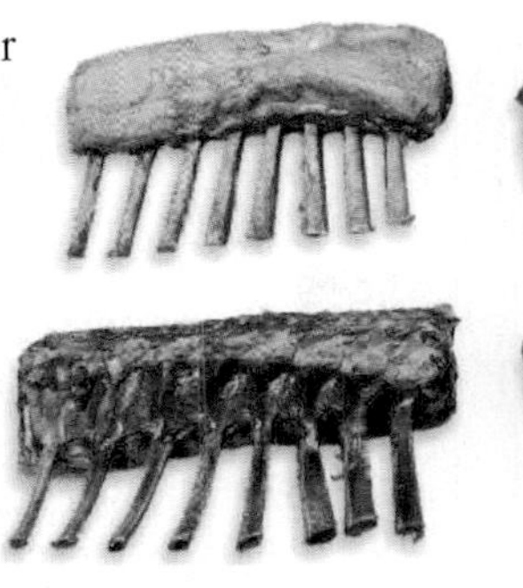

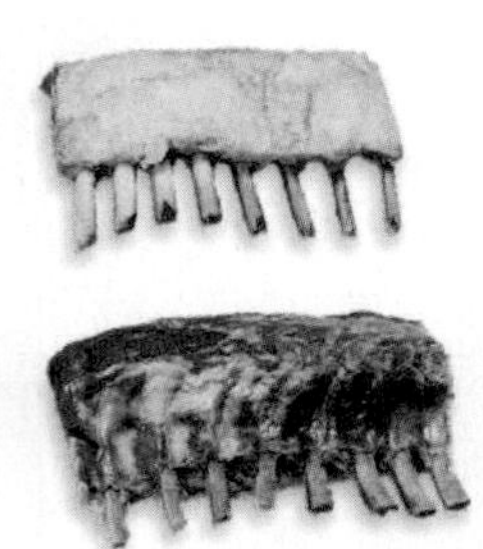

Domestic (left) and New Zealand Lamb Chops

► Nutrition

Lamb, especially when purchased in subprimal cuts to be fabricated on-site, is an economical source of high-quality protein. Lean and lower in cholesterol than other red meat proteins, lamb is a good source of iron as compared with chicken, fish or poultry. Lamb has less marbling than other red meats. Its excess fat appears on the outside of many cuts and can easily be trimmed before cooking. Grass-fed lamb, like meat from other grass-fed ruminants, is high in the powerful antioxidant conjugated linoleic acid, identified as a cancer preventative.

Domestic vs. Imported Lamb

Technologies that increase shelf life have made imported fresh lamb commonplace. Lamb imported from New Zealand and Australia accounts for nearly 50 percent of the lamb meat sold in the United States. Domestic lamb differs from imported lamb in a few ways. Domestic lamb is primarily grain fed and has a milder flavor than its grass-fed counterparts. And domestic lamb is raised to approximately 135 pounds, larger than imported lamb, resulting in larger cut sizes.

► Butchering Procedures

Lamb is unique among the common meat animals in that it is small enough to be handled easily in its carcass form. Thus, food service operations sometimes purchase lamb whole and fabricate the desired cuts themselves. This is practical if the operation has the necessary employee skills, equipment and storage space, as well as a need for all the various cuts and trimmings that butchering a whole carcass produces. A few important lamb fabrication and butchering techniques follow.

► Procedure for Frenching a Rack of Lamb

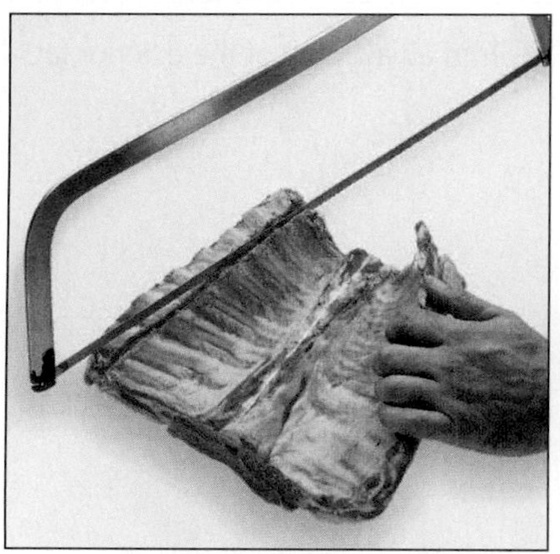

1 With a meat saw, trim the ribs to approximately 3 inches (7.5 centimeters), measuring from the rib eye on each side of the rack.

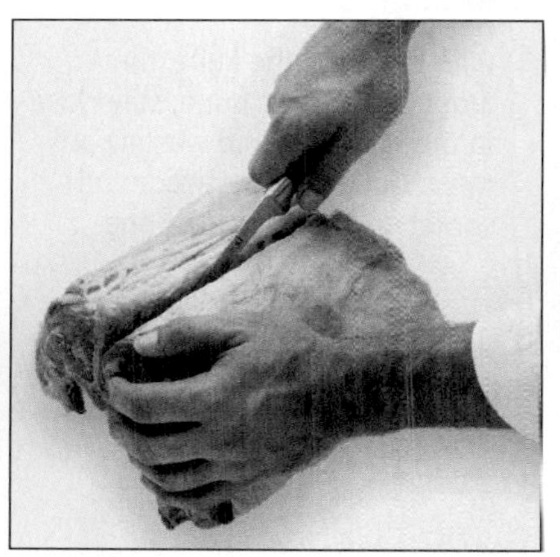

2 Turn the rack over and cut down both sides of the feather bones, completely separating the meat from the bone.

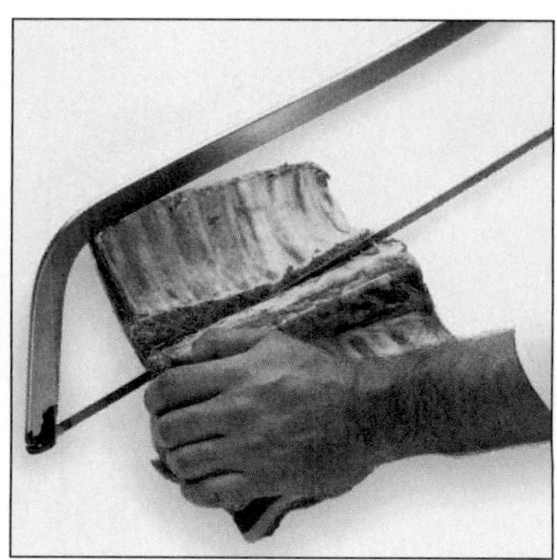

3 Turn the rack back over. Using a meat saw, cut between the ribs and the chine bone at a 45-degree angle, exposing the lean meat between the ribs and the vertebral junctures.

4 By pulling and cutting along the natural seam, remove the thick layers of fat and the meat between them from the rack's surface.

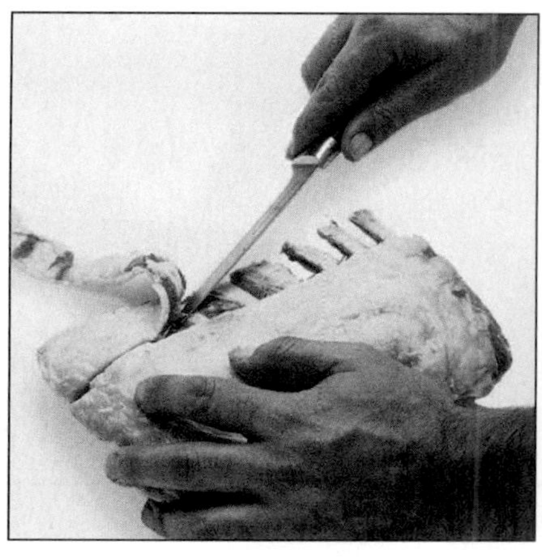

5 Make an even cut through the fat, perpendicular to the ribs, 1 inch (2.5 centimeters) from the rib eye. Trim away all meat and fat from the rib ends. The ribs should be completely clean.

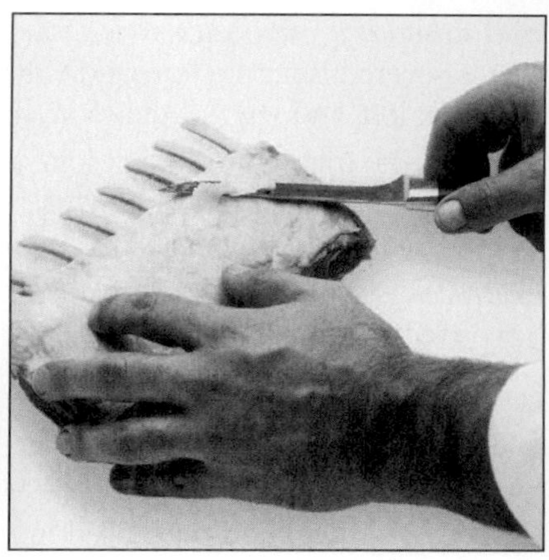

6 Trim away the fat covering. Either leave a thin layer to protect the meat during cooking or trim the fat away completely to produce a very lean rack. The rack can also be cut into chops.

▶ PROCEDURE FOR TRIMMING AND BONING A LAMB LEG FOR ROASTING OR GRILLING

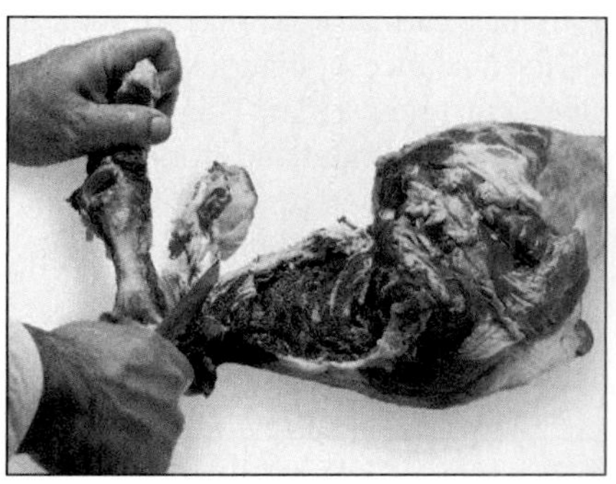

1 With the tip of the knife, trim around the pelvic bone; stay close to the bone to avoid wasting any meat. Cut the sinew inside the socket and remove the bone.

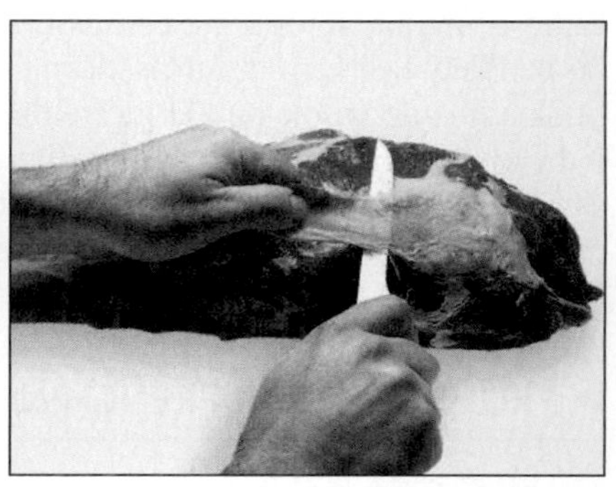

2 Trim away most of the exterior fat.

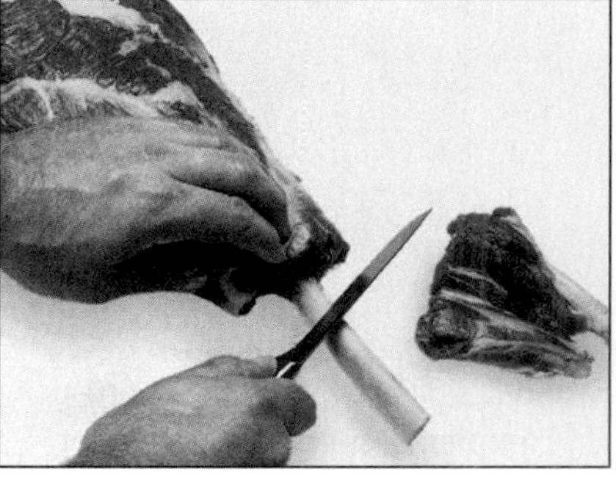

3 Cut off the shank portion completely and scrape the bone clean. This makes a handle to hold while carving the lamb.

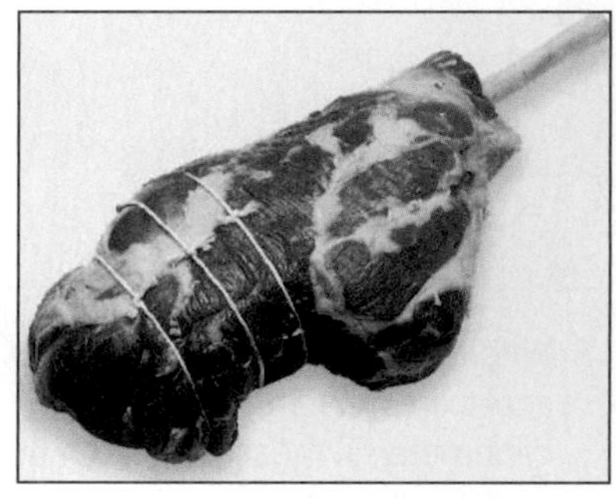

4 Fold the flap of the sirloin over on top of the ball of the leg bone and tie with butcher's twine. This helps the leg cook evenly.

▶ PROCEDURE FOR DONING A LAMB LOIN FOR ROASTING

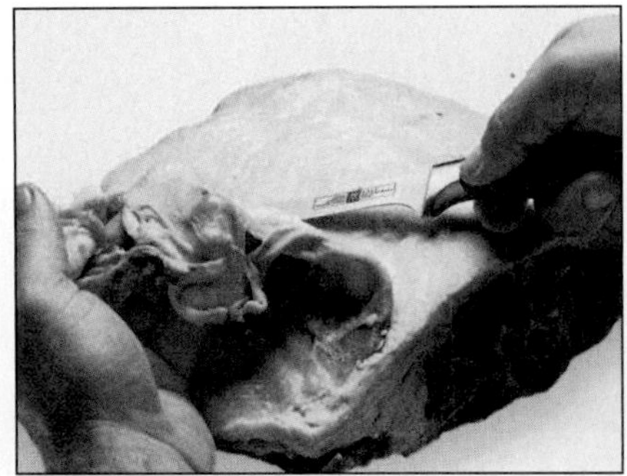

1 Start with a trimmed lamb loin (double). With the skin side up, trim the thin layer of connective tissue called the fell from the loin's surface.

2 Turn the loin over and trim the fat from around the tenderloins.

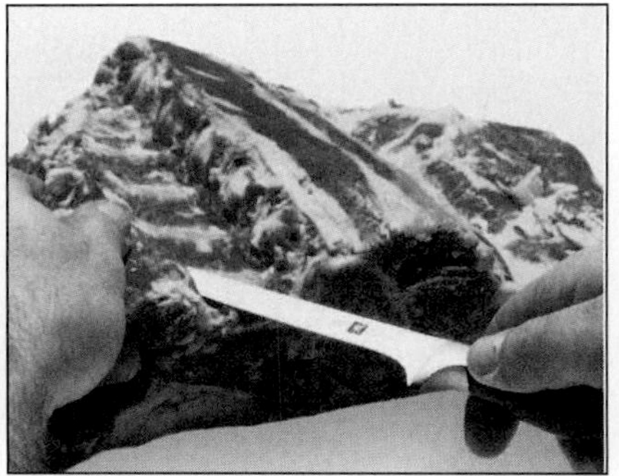

3 Starting in the middle of the backbone, cut between the tenderloin and the vertebrae, separating them but leaving the tenderloin attached to the flank. Continue until you reach the end of the vertebrae. Repeat on the other side.

4 Slide the knife under the vertebrae and the rib and cut back all the way to the backbone, separating the eye muscle from the vertebrae.

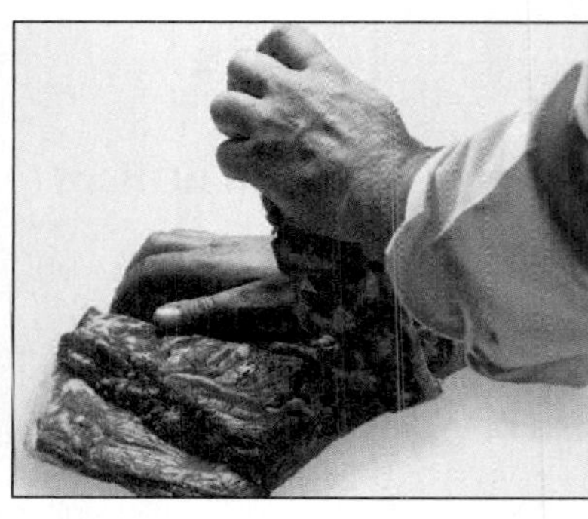

5 Pull the backbone out with your hands, keeping the loins intact.

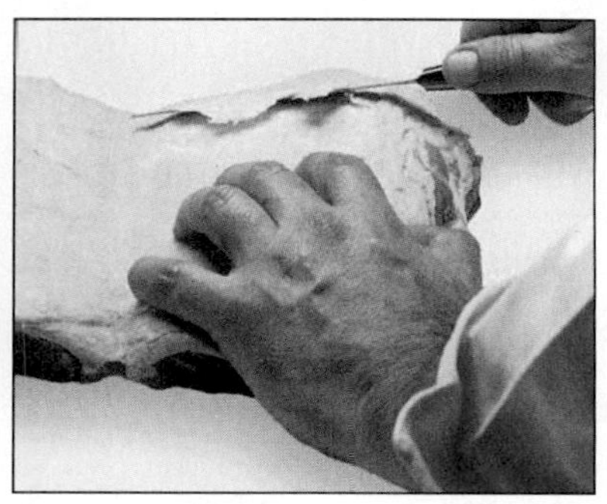

6 Turn the loins over and trim the surface fat to 1/4 inch (6 millimeters).

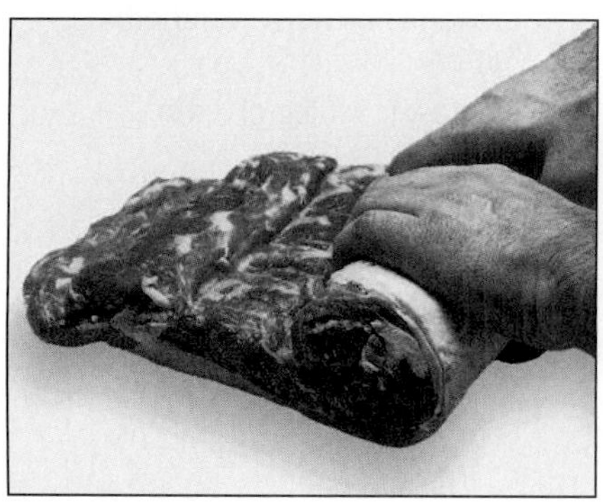

7 Roll the flank flaps under from each side.

8 Tie the roast with butcher's twine at even intervals.

▶ PROCEDURE FOR CUTTING LAMB NOISETTES FROM A LOIN

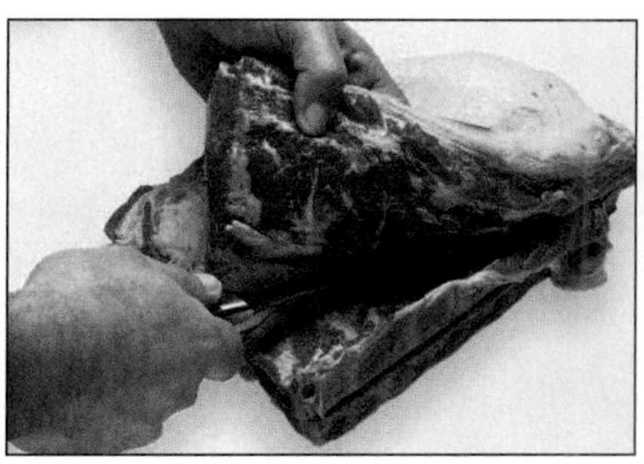

1 Remove the loin eye muscle by cutting down along the backbone and along the vertebrae. Trim the eye muscle, leaving a thin layer of fat if desired.

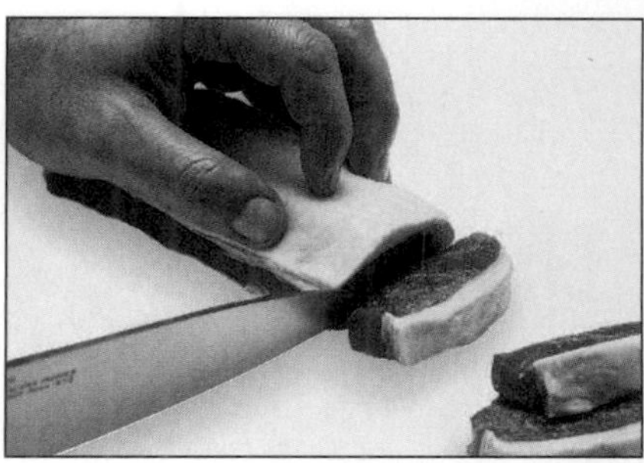

2 Cut the eye meat into noisettes of the desired thickness.

Table 14.1 USING COMMON CUTS OF LAMB

PRIMAL	SUBPRIMAL OR FABRICATED CUT	IMPS	COOKING METHODS	SERVING SUGGESTIONS
Shoulder	Shoulder lamb chop	1207	Dry heat (broil or grill)	Broiled or grilled lamb chops
	Diced lamb	1295	Combination (stew)	Lamb stew; lamb curry
	Ground lamb	1296	Dry heat (broil or grill; sauté)	Patties
Breast	Breast	209	Combination (braise)	Lamb breast stuffed with mushrooms
Hotel rack	Lamb rack	204	Dry heat (broil or grill; roast; sauté)	Roast rack of lamb with garlic and rosemary
	Frenched lamb rack	204C	Dry heat (broil or grill; roast; sauté)	Broiled lamb with mustard and hazelnut crust
Loin	Lamb loin, trimmed	232	Dry heat (broil or grill; roast; sauté)	Noisettes of lamb with roasted garlic sauce
	Loin chops	1232	Dry heat (broil or grill; sauté)	Broiled loin chops with herb butter
Leg	Lamb leg	233A	Dry heat (broil or grill; roast)	Kebabs; roast leg of lamb
	Boned, rolled, tied leg of lamb	233B	Dry heat (roast)	Roast leg of lamb

CONCLUSION

Even though lamb accounts for a small percentage of the meat consumed in this country, many people who do not prepare lamb at home will order it at a restaurant. Because lamb is slaughtered under the age of one year, its meat is tender and it can be prepared by almost any cooking method. Its strong, distinctive flavor allows chefs to offer bold, robust sauces and accompaniments that might mask the flavors of other meats.

QUESTIONS FOR DISCUSSION

1. Describe the basic differences between a lamb carcass and a beef carcass.
2. List each lamb primal and describe its location on the carcass. Identify two subprimals or fabricated cuts taken from each primal.
3. Which cooking methods are most appropriate for a breast of lamb? Explain your answer.
4. Describe the procedure for preparing a frenched rack of lamb from a primal hotel rack.
5. What is the best way to purchase lamb for a food service operation that cuts its own meat and uses large quantities of lamb chops? Explain your answer.

CHAPTER **FIFTEEN**

BUT I WILL PLACE THIS CAREFULLY FED PIG WITHIN THE CRACKLING OVEN;
AND, I PRAY, WHAT NICER DISH CAN E'ER BE GIVEN TO MAN.

—Aeschylus, ancient Greek poet (ca. 525–456 B.C.E.)

PORK

FABULOUS FOOD CATERING, Phoenix, AZ

AFTER STUDYING THIS CHAPTER, YOU WILL BE ABLE TO:

- identify the primal, subprimal and fabricated cuts of pork
- perform basic butchering procedures
- apply appropriate cooking methods to several common cuts of pork

Pork is the meat of hogs, usually butchered before they are one year old. With the exception of beef, Americans consume more pork than any other meat. The pork we eat is leaner and healthier than it once was because of advances in animal husbandry.

Because hogs are butchered at a young age, their meat is generally very tender with a delicate flavor. It is well suited to a variety of cooking methods. More than two-thirds of the pork marketed in the United States is cured to produce products such as smoked hams and smoked bacon. Cured pork products are discussed in Chapter 26, Charcuterie.

▸ PRIMAL AND SUBPRIMAL CUTS OF PORK

After a hog is slaughtered, it is generally split down the backbone, dividing the carcass into bilateral halves. Like the beef carcass, each side of the hog carcass is then further broken down into the primal cuts: shoulder, Boston butt, belly, loin and fresh ham.

Hogs are bred specifically to produce long loins; the loin contains the highest-quality meat and is the most expensive cut of pork. Pork is unique in that the ribs and loin are considered a single primal. They are not separated into two different primals, as are the ribs and loin of beef, veal and lamb.

Figure 15.1 shows the relationship between the hog's bone structure and the primal cuts. As with all meats, it is important to know the location of bones when cutting or working with pork. This makes meat fabrication and carving easier and aids in identifying cuts. Figure 15.2 shows the primal cuts of pork and their location on the carcass. A hog carcass generally weighs in a range of 120 to 210 pounds (55 to 110 kg).

SHOULDER

The primal shoulder, known as the picnic ham, is the lower portion of the hog's foreleg; it accounts for approximately 20 percent of the carcass weight. The shoulder contains the arm and shank bones and has a relatively high ratio of bone to lean meat.

Because all pork comes from hogs slaughtered at a young age, the shoulder is tender enough to be cooked by any method. It is, however, one of the least tender cuts of pork. It is available smoked or fresh. The shoulder is fairly inexpensive and, when purchased fresh, it can be cut into shoulder butt steaks or boned and cut into smaller pieces for sautéing or stewing. Whole pork shoulder is the cut preferred by many barbecue pit masters throughout the American South.

The foreshank is called the shoulder hock and is almost always smoked. Shoulder hocks are often simmered for long periods in soups, stews and braised dishes to add flavor and richness.

BOSTON BUTT

The primal Boston butt is a square cut located just above the primal pork shoulder. It accounts for approximately 7 percent of the carcass weight.

The Boston butt is very meaty and tender, with a good percentage of fat to lean meat. Containing only a small portion of the blade bone, the Boston butt is a good choice when a recipe calls for a solid piece of lean pork. The fresh

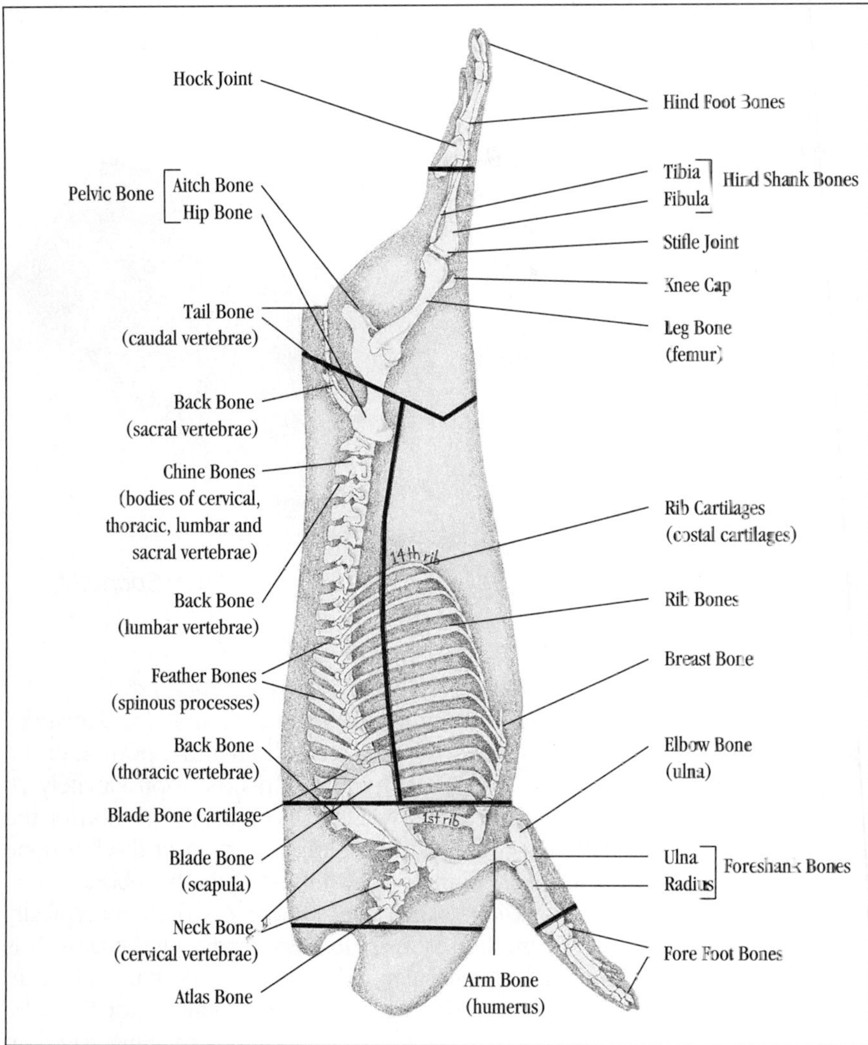

FIGURE 15.1 ▶ The skeletal structure of a hog.

HOGS: A SOURCE FOR SLOGANS

Hogs were first brought to Florida by Spanish explorers in 1539, and they thrived in this heavenly new environment. The British shipped hogs to the colonies, and as early as 1639, Virginia's colonists were supplying England with ham and bacon. During colonial days, pork was packed in barrels for shipment, giving rise to the term *meat packing.* During the War of 1812, the U.S. government shipped pork to American soldiers in barrels stamped with the letters "US" and the name of the meat packer, Sam Wilson. The soldiers referred to the meat as "Uncle Sam's meat," thus giving birth to the national government's nickname, "Uncle Sam."

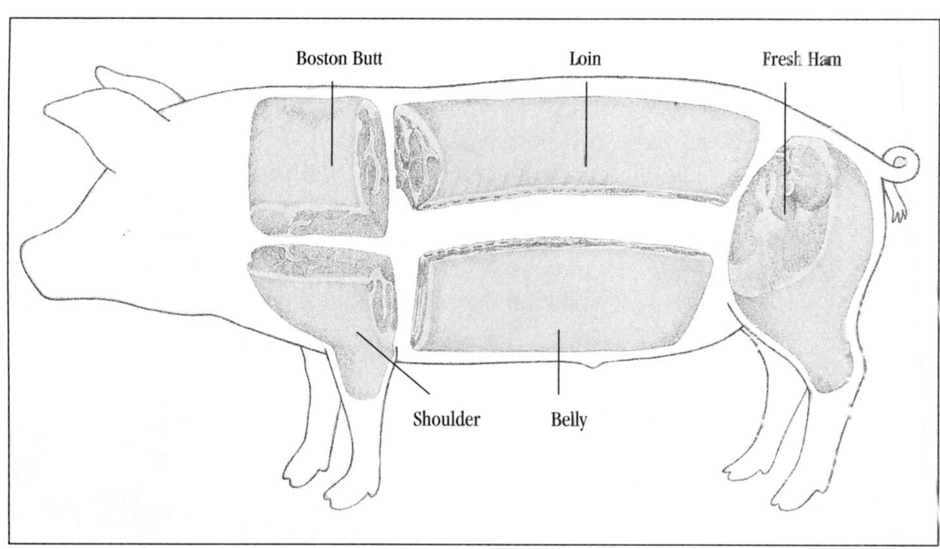

FIGURE 15.2 ▶ The primal cuts of pork.

Boston Butt

Boston butt is sometimes cut into steaks or chops to be broiled or sautéed. When the Boston butt is smoked, it is usually boneless and called a cottage ham.

BELLY

The primal pork belly is located below the loin. Accounting for approximately 16 percent of the carcass weight, it is very fatty with only streaks of lean meat. It contains the spareribs, which are always separated from the rest of the belly before cooking.

Spareribs usually are sold fresh but can also be smoked. Typically, they are simmered and then grilled or baked while being basted with a spicy barbecue sauce. The remainder of the pork belly is nearly always cured and smoked to produce bacon.

Pork Spareribs

LOIN

The loin is cut from directly behind the Boston butt and includes the entire rib section as well as the loin and a portion of the sirloin area. The primal loin accounts for approximately 20 percent of the carcass weight. It contains a portion of the blade bone on the shoulder end, a portion of the hip bone on the ham end, all the ribs and most of the backbone.

The primal pork loin is the only primal cut of pork not typically smoked or cured. Most of the loin is a single, very tender eye muscle. It is quite lean but contains enough intramuscular and subcutaneous fat to make it an excellent choice for a moist-heat cooking method such as braising, or it can be prepared with dry-heat cooking methods such as roasting or sautéing. The loin also contains the pork tenderloin, located on the inside of the rib bones on the sirloin end of the loin. The tenderloin is the most tender cut of pork; it is very versatile and can be trimmed, cut into medallions and sautéed, or the whole tenderloin can be roasted or braised. The most popular cut from the loin is the pork chop. Chops can be cut from the entire loin, the choicest being center-cut chops from the primal loin after the blade bone and sirloin portions at the front and rear of the loin are removed. The pork loin can be purchased boneless or boned and tied as a roast. A boneless pork loin is smoked to produce Canadian bacon. The rib bones, when trimmed from the loin, can be served as barbecued pork back ribs.

Although not actually part of the primal loin, fatback is the thick layer of fat—sometimes more than an inch (2.5 centimeters) thick—between the skin and the lean eye muscle. It has a variety of uses in the kitchen, especially in the preparation of charcuterie items.

Pork Loin

Pork Tenderloin

Pork Back Ribs

Pork Loin Chops

FRESH HAM

The primal fresh ham is the hog's hind leg. It is a rather large cut accounting for approximately 24 percent of the carcass weight. The ham contains the aitch, leg and hind shank bones. Fresh ham, like the legs of other meat animals, contains large muscles with relatively small amounts of connective tissue. Like many other cuts of pork, hams are often cured and smoked. But fresh hams also produce great roasts and can be prepared using almost any cooking method. When cured and smoked, hams are available in a variety of styles; they can be purchased bone-in, shankless or boneless, partially or fully cooked. Fully cooked hams are also available canned. There is a specific ham for nearly every use and desired degree of convenience. The shank portion of the ham is called the ham hock. It is used in the same manner as the shoulder hock.

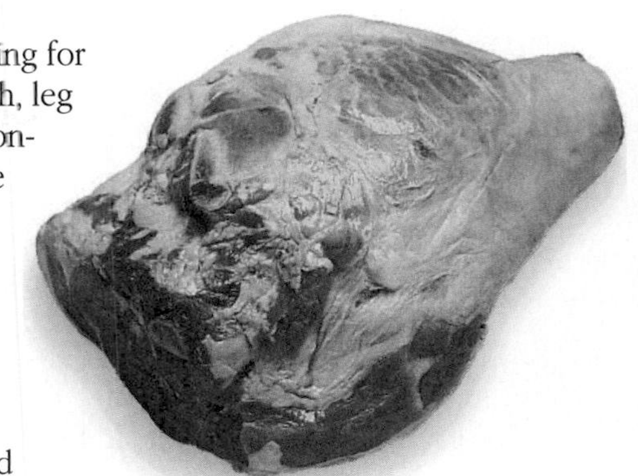

Fresh Ham

► NUTRITION

Like other meats, pork is a good source of protein, B vitamins and other essential nutrients, but it is also high in fat, especially saturated fats. Through new breeding and feeding techniques, the fat content of pork has been lowered in recent years. Cuts from the loin, such as the tenderloin and boneless loin chops, are among the leaner cuts of meat available with reduced levels of saturated fat. Sodium content of smoked and preserved pork products such as bacon, ham and sausage, which are discussed in Chapter 26, Charcuterie, is high but reduced-sodium preserved and smoked products are increasingly available.

► BUTCHERING PROCEDURES

Other than suckling pigs (which are very young, very small whole pigs used for roasting or barbecuing whole), pork products generally are not purchased in forms larger than the primal cuts described earlier. Chefs should master a few important pork fabrication and butchering techniques, however.

► PROCEDURE FOR BONING A PORK LOIN

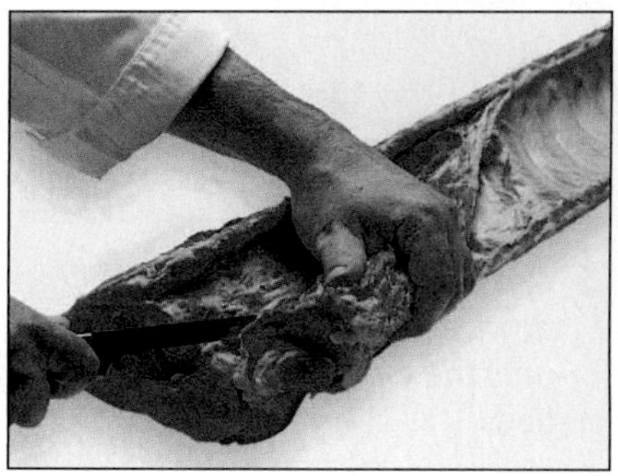

1 Starting on the sirloin end of a full pork loin, remove the tenderloin in one piece by making smooth cuts against the inside of the rib bones. Pull gently on the tenderloin as you cut.

2 Turn the loin over and cut between the ribs and the eye meat. Continue separating the meat from the bones, following the contours of the bones, until the loin is completely separated from the bones.

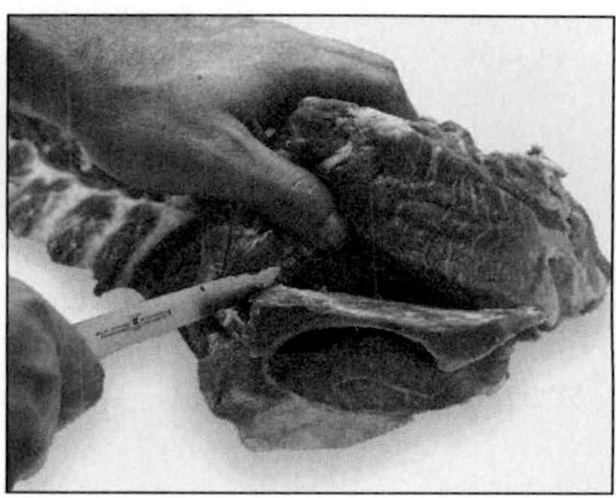

3 Trim around the blade bone on the shoulder end of the loin and remove it.

The fully boned loin consists of (from left to right) cartilage, the tenderloin, boneless loin and loin bones.

▶ PROCEDURE FOR TYING A BONELESS PORK ROAST WITH THE HALF-HITCH METHOD

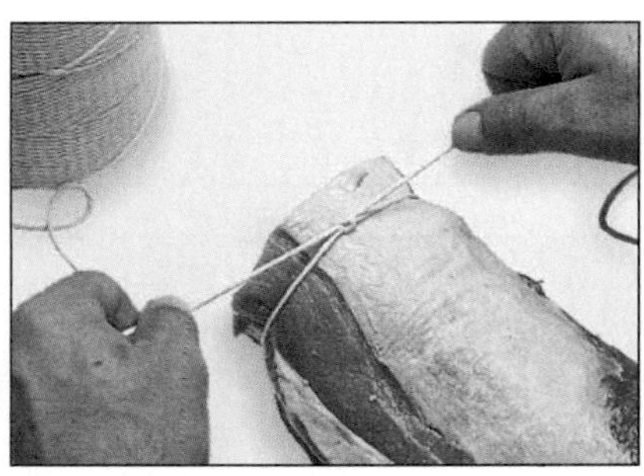

1 Wrap the loose end of the string around the pork loin and tie it with a double knot.

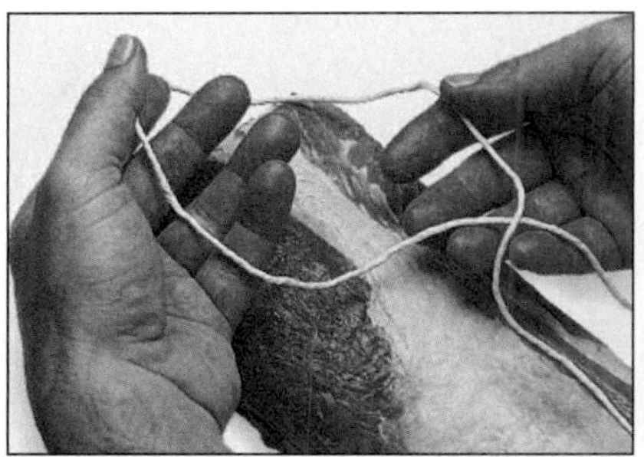

2 Make a loop and slide it down over the roast to approximately 1 inch (2.5 centimeters) from the first knot.

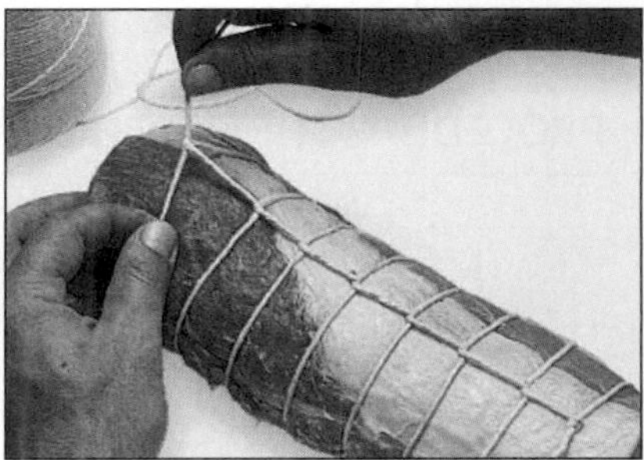

3 Make another loop and slide it down. Continue in this fashion until the whole roast has been tied.

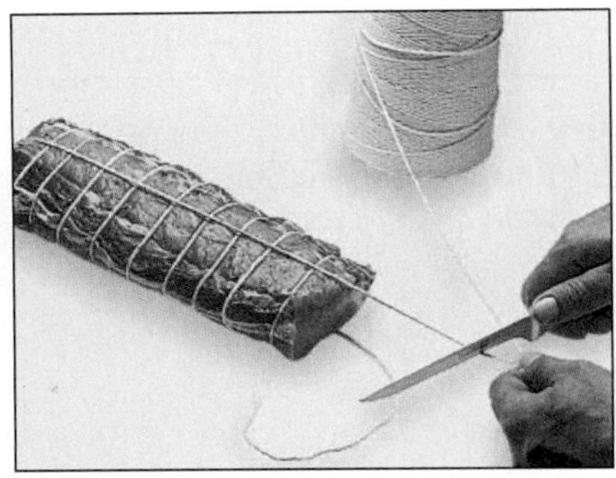

4 Turn the roast over and cut the string, leaving enough to wrap lengthwise around the roast to the original knot.

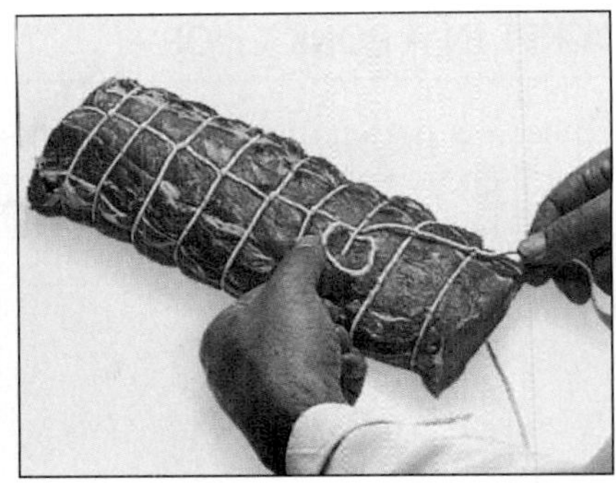

5 Wrap the string around the end of the roast, then around the string that formed the last loop. Continue in this fashion for the length of the roast, pulling the string tight after wrapping it around each loop.

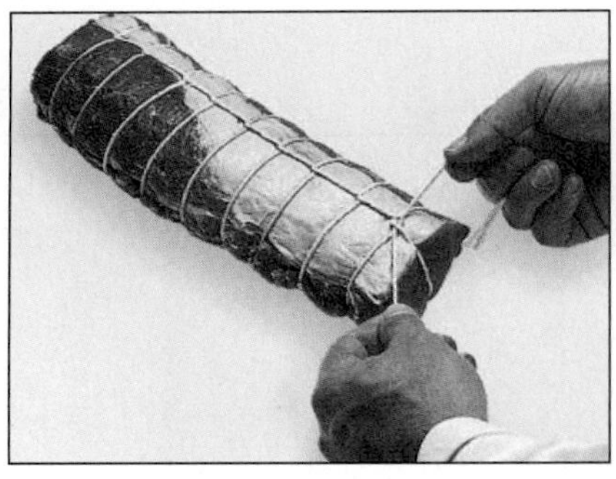

6 Turn the roast back over. Wrap the string around the front end of the roast and secure it to the first loop at the point where you tied the first knot.

7 The finished roast. Note the even intervals at which the strings are tied. They should be just snug enough to hold the shape of the roast; they should not dig in or cut the meat.

▶ PROCEDURE FOR CUTTING A CENTER-CUT PORK CHOP

A center-cut pork chop can be cut from the center portion of a bone-in pork loin without the aid of a saw by using a boning knife and a heavy cleaver. Trim the excess fat from the loin, leaving a ¼-inch (6-millimeter) layer to protect the meat during cooking.

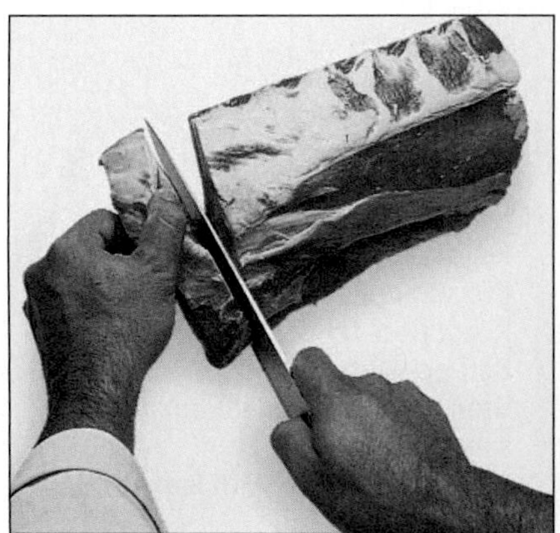

1 Cut through the meat with the knife.

2 Use the cleaver to chop through the chine bone.

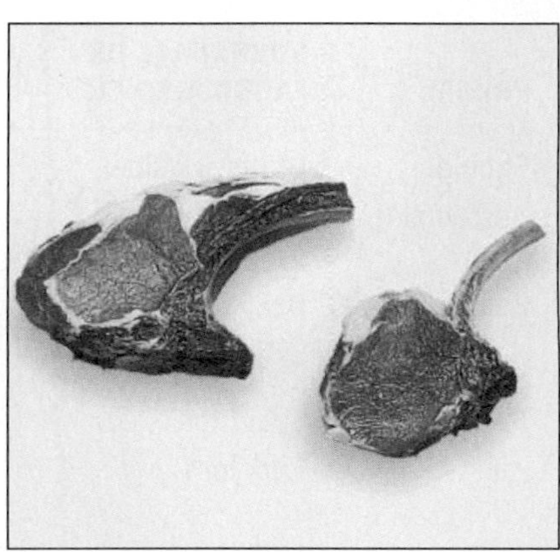

3 To produce a cleaner chop, trim the meat from the end of the rib bone. Then, with the boning knife, separate the loin meat from the chine bones and separate the chine bone from the rib with the cleaver.

▶ PROCEDURE FOR CUTTING A POCKET IN A PORK CHOP

To make a pocket in a pork chop for stuffing, start with a thick chop or a double rib chop. Cut the pocket deep enough to hold ample stuffing, but be careful not to puncture either surface of the chop.

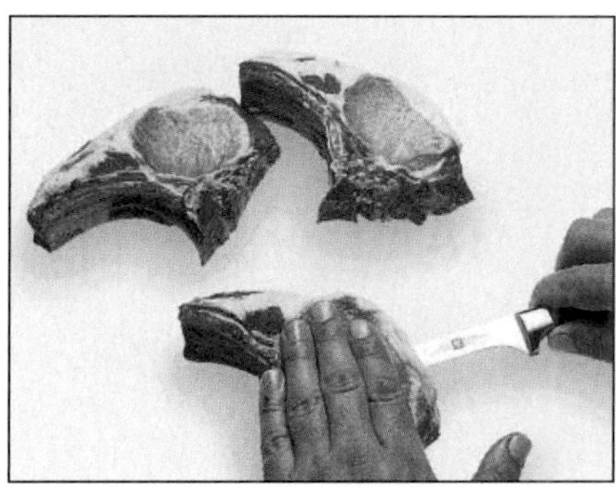

Use the tip of a boning knife to cut a pocket.

▶ PROCEDURE FOR TRIMMING A PORK TENDERLOIN

As with a beef tenderloin, the pork tenderloin must be trimmed of all fat and silverskin. Follow the procedures outlined in Chapter 12, Beef, for trimming a beef tenderloin.

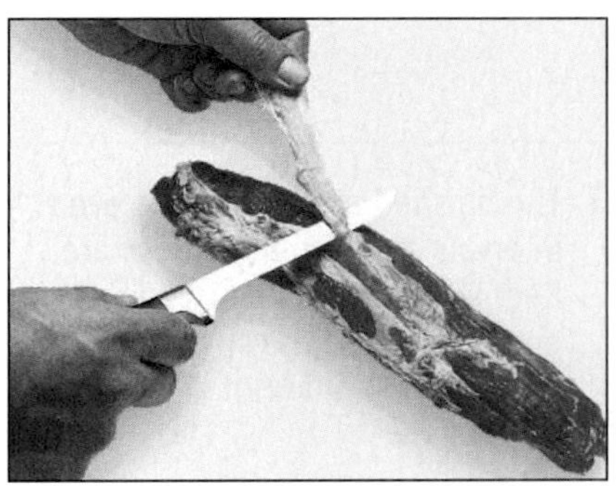

Use a boning knife to remove the silverskin from a pork tenderloin.

Table 15.1 USING COMMON CUTS OF PORK

PRIMAL	SUBPRIMAL OR FABRICATED CUT	IMPS	COOKING METHODS	SERVING SUGGESTIONS
Shoulder	Picnic shoulder	405	Dry heat (roast or bake)	Smoked picnic shoulder
Boston butt	Boston butt	406	Dry heat (broil or grill; sauté) Moist heat (simmer)	Broiled Boston butt steaks Choucroute
Belly	Bacon	539	Dry heat (sauté) Moist heat (simmer) Combination (braise)	Breakfast meat Seasoning Seasoning
	Spareribs	416A	Combination (steam, then grill)	Barbecued spareribs
Loin	Pork loin	410	Dry heat (roast) Combination (braise)	Roast pork Braised pork chops
	Pork tenderloin	415	Dry heat (broil or grill; sauté; roast)	Roast pork tenderloin
	Pork back ribs	422	Combination (steam, then grill)	Barbecued back ribs
	Pork loin chops	1410	Dry heat (broil or grill) Combination (braise)	Broiled loin chop with mushroom sauce Braised loin chop with leeks and fennel
Fresh ham	Fresh ham	401A	Dry heat (roast)	Roast pork with apricots and almonds

CONCLUSION

Pork can be enjoyed cured, processed or fresh. The mild flavor of fresh pork blends well with many different seasonings, making it a popular menu item. It is naturally tender and can be prepared by almost any dry-heat, moist-heat or combination cooking method. Properly fabricated and prepared, it can be a nutritious meat.

QUESTIONS FOR DISCUSSION

1 List each pork primal and describe its location on the carcass. Identify two subprimals or fabricated cuts taken from each primal.
2 What is unique about the primal pork loin as compared to the beef or veal loin?
3 Are fatback and bacon taken from the same primal? How are they different?
4 What is the only primal cut of pork that is not typically smoked or cured? How is it best cooked? Explain your answer.
5 What is the World Pork Expo? How is such an event useful for chefs and restauranteurs?

CHAPTER **SIXTEEN**

THE FACT IS THAT IT TAKES MORE THAN INGREDIENTS AND TECHNIQUE TO COOK A GOOD MEAL. A GOOD COOK PUTS SOMETHING OF HIMSELF INTO THE PREPARATION—HE COOKS WITH ENJOYMENT, ANTICIPATION, SPONTANEITY, AND HE IS WILLING TO EXPERIMENT.

—Pearl Bailey,
American entertainer (1918–1990)
in Pearl's Kitchen, *1973*

POULTRY

SENCHA, Colorado Springs, CO
Brent Beavers, Executive Chef

AFTER STUDYING THIS CHAPTER, YOU WILL BE ABLE TO:

- understand the structure and composition of poultry
- identify various kinds and classes of poultry
- understand poultry inspection and grading practices
- purchase poultry appropriate for your needs
- store poultry properly
- prepare poultry for cooking
- apply various cooking methods to poultry

Poultry is the collective term for domesticated birds bred for eating. They include chickens, ducks, geese, guineas, pigeons and turkeys. (Game birds such as pheasant, quail and partridge are described in Chapter 17, Game; farm-raised ratites—ostrich, emu and rhea—are discussed here.) Poultry is generally the least expensive and most versatile of all main-dish foods. It can be cooked by almost any method, and its mild flavor goes well with a wide variety of sauces and accompaniments.

In this chapter, we discuss the different kinds and classes of poultry and how to choose those that best suit your needs. You will learn how to store poultry properly to prevent food-borne illnesses and spoilage, how to butcher birds to produce the specific cuts you need and how to apply a variety of cooking methods properly.

Many of the cooking methods discussed here have been applied previously to meats. Although there are similarities with these methods, there are also many distinct differences. As you study this chapter, review the corresponding cooking methods for meats and note the similarities and differences.

► Muscle Composition

The muscle tissue of poultry is similar to that of mammals in that it contains approximately 72 percent water, 20 percent protein, 7 percent fat and 1 percent minerals; it consists of bundles of muscle cells or fibers held together by connective tissue. Unlike red meat, poultry does not contain the intramuscular fat known as marbling. Instead, a bird stores fat in its skin, its abdominal cavity and the fat pad near its tail. Poultry fat is softer and has a lower melting point than other animal fats. It is easily rendered during cooking.

As with red meats, poultry muscles that are used more often tend to be tougher than those used less frequently. Also, the muscles of an older bird tend to be tougher than those of a younger one. Because the majority of poultry is marketed at a young age, however, it is generally very tender.

The breast and wing flesh of chickens and turkeys is lighter in color than the flesh of their thighs and legs. This color difference is due to a higher concentration of the protein myoglobin in the thigh and leg muscles. Myoglobin is the protein that stores oxygen for the muscle tissues to use. More-active muscles require more myoglobin and tend to be darker than less-active ones. Because chickens and turkeys generally do not fly, their breast and wing muscles contain little myoglobin and are therefore a light color. Birds that do fly have only dark meat. Dark meat also contains more fat and connective tissue than light meat, and its cooking time is longer.

Skin color may vary from white to golden yellow, depending on what the bird was fed. Such color differences are not an indication of overall quality.

Table 16.1 **USDA CHICKEN CLASSES**

CLASS	DESCRIPTION	AGE	WEIGHT	COOKING METHOD
Game hen	Young or immature progeny of Cornish chickens or of a Cornish chicken and a White Rock chicken; very flavorful	5–6 weeks	2 lb. (1 kg) or less	Split and broil or grill; roast
Broiler/fryer	Young with soft, smooth-textured skin; relatively lean; flexible breastbone	13 weeks	3 lb. 8 oz. (1.5 kg) or less	Any cooking method; very versatile
Roaster	Young with tender meat and smooth-textured skin; breastbone is less flexible than broiler's	3–5 months	3 lb. 8 oz.–5 lb. (1.5–2 kg)	Any cooking method
Capon	Surgically castrated male; tender meat with soft, smooth-textured skin; bred for well-flavored meat; contains a high proportion of light to dark meat and a relatively high fat content	Under 8 months	6–10 lb. (2.5–4.5 kg)	Roast
Hen/stewing	Mature female; flavorful but less tender meat; nonflexible breastbone	Over 10 months	2 lb. 8 oz.–8 lb. (1–3.5 kg)	Stew or braise

▸ IDENTIFYING POULTRY

The USDA recognizes six categories or kinds of poultry: chicken, duck, goose, guinea, pigeon and turkey. Each poultry kind is divided into classes based predominantly on the bird's age and tenderness. The sex of young birds is not significant for culinary purposes. It does matter, however, with older birds; older male birds are tough and stringy and have less flavor than older female birds. Tables 16.1 through 16.6 list identifying characteristics and suggested cooking methods for each of the various kinds and classes of poultry.

Rock Cornish Game Hen

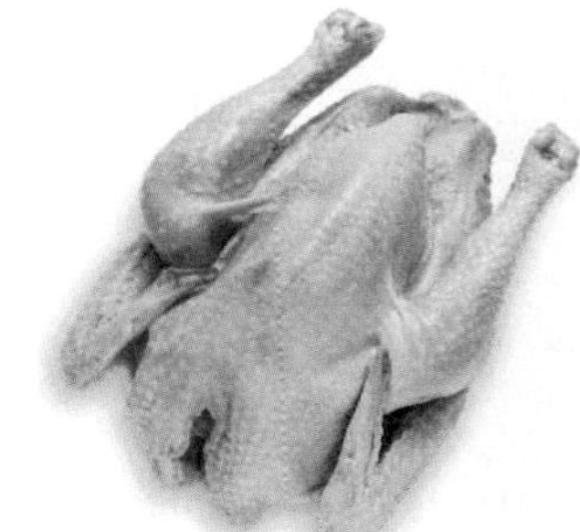

Chicken Broiler/Fryer

CHICKEN

Chicken (Fr. *poulet*) is the most popular and widely eaten poultry in the world. It contains both light and dark meat and has relatively little fat. A young, tender chicken can be cooked by almost any method; an older bird is best stewed or braised. Chicken is extremely versatile and may be seasoned, stuffed, basted or garnished with almost anything. Chicken is inexpensive and readily available, fresh or frozen, in a variety of forms.

The French *poulet de Bresse* is a special category of chicken, frequently touted as the world's finest. The only certified-origin chicken in the world, it is a blue-legged variety raised near the village of Bresse in southeastern Burgundy. These are free-range birds fed a special diet of milk products plus sweet corn and other grains. An identifying leg band is attached to each young chick, and authentic birds will be sold with the banded leg attached. They are available in the United States, at a premium price, from specialty food importers.

Capon

Table 16.2 USDA DUCK CLASSES

CLASS	DESCRIPTION	AGE	WEIGHT	COOKING METHOD
Broiler/fryer	Young bird with tender meat; a soft bill and windpipe	8 weeks or less	3 lb. 8 oz.–4 lb. (1.5–1.8 kg)	Roast at high temperature
Roaster	Young bird with tender meat; rich flavor; easily dented wind pipe	16 weeks or less	4–6 lb. (1.8–2.5 kg)	Roast
Mature	Old bird with tough flesh; hard bill and windpipe	6 months or older	4–6 lb. (1.8–2.5 kg)	Braise

▶ **duckling** a duck slaughtered before it is eight weeks old

▶ **magret** (may-gray) a duck breast, traditionally taken from the ducks that produce foie gras; it is usually served boneless but with the skin intact

DUCK

The duck (Fr. *canard*) used most often in commercial food service operations is a roaster duckling. It contains only dark meat and large amounts of fat. In order to make the fatty skin palatable, it is important to render as much fat as possible. Duck has a high percentage of bone and fat to meat; for example, a 4-pound duck will serve only two people, while a 4-pound roasting chicken will serve four people.

Roaster Duckling

GOOSE

A goose (Fr. *oie*) contains only dark meat and has very fatty skin. It is usually roasted at high temperatures to render the fat. Roasted goose is popular at holidays and is often served with an acidic fruit-based sauce to offset the fattiness.

Young Goose

Table 16.3 USDA GOOSE CLASSES

CLASS	DESCRIPTION	AGE	WEIGHT	COOKING METHOD
Young	Rich, tender dark meat with large amounts of fat; easily dented windpipe	6 months or less	6–12 lb. (2.5–5.5 kg)	Roast at high temperature, accompany with acidic sauces
Mature	Tough flesh and hard windpipe	Over 6 months	10–16 lb. (4.5–7 kg)	Braise or stew

Table 16.4 USDA GUINEA CLASSES

CLASS	DESCRIPTION	AGE	WEIGHT	COOKING METHOD
Young	Tender meat; flexible breastbone	3 months	12 oz.–1 lb. 8 oz. (0.3–0.7 kg)	Bard and roast; sauté
Mature	Tough flesh; hard breastbone	Over 3 months	1–2 lb (0.5–1 kg)	Braise or stew

Table 16.5 USDA PIGEON CLASSES

CLASS	DESCRIPTION	AGE	WEIGHT	COOKING METHOD
Squab	Immature pigeon; very tender, dark flesh and a small amount of fat	4 weeks	12 oz.–1 lb. 8 oz. (0.3–0.7 kg)	Broil, roast or sauté
Pigeon	Mature bird; coarse skin and tough flesh	Over 4 weeks	1–2 lb (0.5–1 kg)	Braise or stew

GUINEA

A guinea or guinea fowl (Fr. *pintade*) is the domesticated descendant of a game bird. It has both light and dark meat and a flavor similar to pheasant. Guinea is tender enough to sauté. Because it contains little fat, a guinea is usually barded prior to roasting. Guinea, which is relatively expensive, is not as popular here as it is in Europe.

Young Guinea

PIGEON

The young pigeon (Fr. *pigeon*) used in commercial food service operations is referred to as squab. Its meat is dark, tender and well suited for broiling, sautéing or roasting. Squab has very little fat and benefits from barding.

Squab

TURKEY

Turkey (Fr. *dinde*) is the second most popular category of poultry in the United States. It has both light and dark meat and a relatively small amount of fat. Younger turkey is economical and can be prepared in almost any manner.

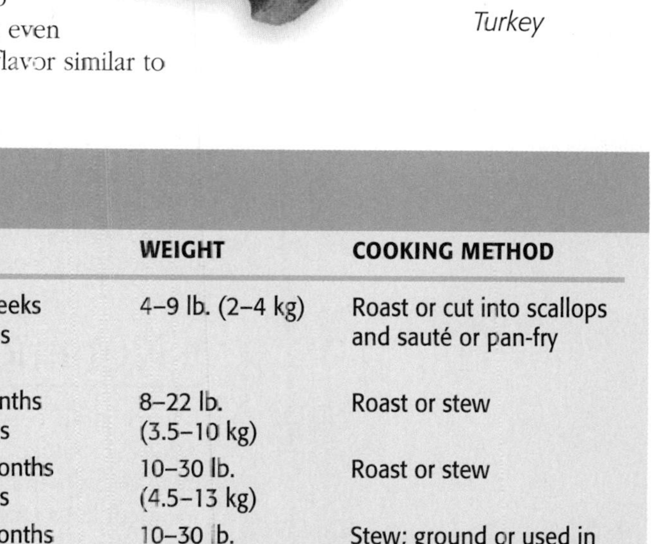

Turkey

RATITES

Ratites are a family of flightless birds with small wings and flat breastbones. They include the ostrich (which is native to Africa), the emu (native to Australia) and the rhea (native to South America). Ratite meat, which is classified as red meat even though it is poultry flesh, is a dark, cherry-red color with a flavor similar to

Table 16.6 USDA TURKEY CLASSES

CLASS	DESCRIPTION	AGE	WEIGHT	COOKING METHOD
Fryer/roaster	Immature bird of either sex (males are called toms); tender meat with smooth skin; flexible breastbone	16 weeks or less	4–9 lb. (2–4 kg)	Roast or cut into scallops and sauté or pan-fry
Young	Tender meat with smooth skin; less-flexible breastbone	8 months or less	8–22 lb. (3.5–10 kg)	Roast or stew
Yearling	Fully mature bird; reasonably tender meat and slightly coarse skin	15 months or less	10–30 lb. (4.5–13 kg)	Roast or stew
Mature	Older bird with coarse skin and tough flesh	15 months or older	10–30 lb. (4.5–13 kg)	Stew; ground or used in processed products

A TURKEY BY ANY OTHER NAME . . .

In *Food in History,* Reay Tannahill explains why we call a turkey a turkey and not a peru. Turkeys were known as *uexolotl* to 16th-century native Central Americans. They were first brought to Europe by returning Spanish explorers early in the 1500s. Turkish merchants visiting Seville, Spain, on their journeys to and from the eastern Mediterranean brought these exotic birds to England, where the English dubbed them "turkie-cocks." This was eventually shortened to "turkeys." The Turks called these birds *hindi,* suggesting that they believed the birds originated in India (as opposed to the Indies). This was a belief shared by the French, who called the bird *coq d'Inde,* which was later corrupted to *dinde* or *dindon.* The Germans followed suit, calling the bird *indianische Henn,* as did the Italians, who called it *galle d'India.* Meanwhile, in India, the bird was called a *peru*—which was a little closer to the geographical mark.

Ostrich Fan

beef, but a little sweeter, and a soft texture. It is low in fat and calories. Most ratite meat is from birds slaughtered at 10 to 13 months of age. It is generally cut from the back (which contains the very tender tenderloin), the thigh (also known as the fan) and the leg, and is available as steaks, filets, medallions, roasts, cubes or ground.

Ratite meat is often prepared like veal. The more tender cuts, such as those from the back or thigh, can be marinated and then cooked by dry-heat cooking methods, especially broiling, grilling, roasting and pan-frying. Because it has little fat, care must be taken to avoid overcooking, and these products are usually served medium rare to medium. Allowing these products to rest after cooking helps ensure tenderness. Tougher cuts, such as those from the leg, are best ground or prepared with combination cooking methods.

LIVERS, GIZZARDS, HEARTS AND NECKS

Livers, gizzards, hearts and necks are commonly referred to as giblets and can be used in a variety of ways. Gizzards (a bird's second stomach), hearts and necks are often used to make giblet gravy. Gizzards are sometimes trimmed and deep-fried; hearts are sometimes served sautéed and creamed. Necks are very flavorful and can be added to stocks for flavor and richness. Livers, hearts and gizzards are not added to stocks, however, because of their strong flavors.

Chicken livers are often used in pâtés, sautéed or broiled with onions and served as an entrée.

Chicken Giblets

FOIE GRAS

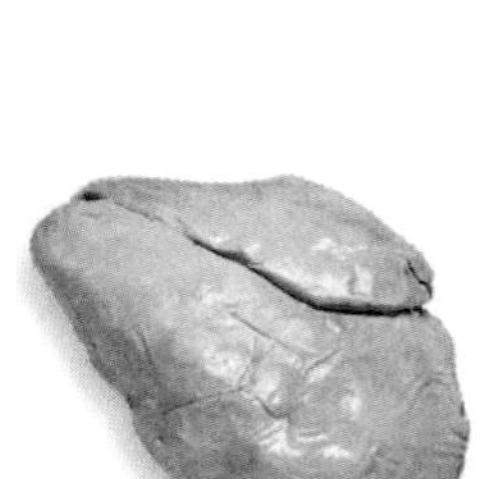

Duck Foie Gras

Foie gras is the enlarged liver of a duck or goose. Considered a delicacy since Roman times, it is now produced in many parts of the world, including the United States. Foie gras is produced by methodically fattening the birds by force-feeding them specially prepared corn while limiting their activity. Fresh foie gras consists of two lobes that must be separated, split and deveined. Good foie gras will be smooth, round and putty-colored. It should not be yellow or grainy. Goose foie gras is lighter in color and more delicate in flavor than that of duck. Duck foie gras has a deeper, winy flavor and is more frequently used than goose foie gras. Fresh foie gras can be grilled, roasted, sautéed or made into pâtés or terrines. No matter which cooking method is used, care must be taken not to overcook the liver. Foie gras is so high in fat that overcooking will result in the liver actually melting away. Most foie gras is pasteurized or canned and may consist of solid liver or small pieces of liver compacted to form a block. Canned foie gras mousse is also available, often with truffles, which are a natural accompaniment.

▶ NUTRITION

Poultry is an economical source of high-quality protein. Poultry's nutritional values are similar to those of other meats, except that chicken and turkey breast meat is lower in fat and higher in niacin than other lean meats. Generally, dark meat contains more niacin and riboflavin than white meat.

▶ INSPECTION AND GRADING OF POULTRY

INSPECTION

All poultry produced for public consumption in the United States is subject to USDA inspection. Inspections ensure that products are processed under strict sanitary guidelines and are wholesome and fit for human consumption. Inspections do not indicate a product's quality or tenderness. The round inspection stamp illustrated in Figure 16.1 can be found either on a tag attached to the wing or included in the package labeling.

FIGURE 16.1 ▶ USDA inspection stamp for poultry.

GRADING

Grading poultry is voluntary but virtually universal. Birds are graded according to their overall quality, with the grade (USDA A, B or C) shown on a shield-shaped tag affixed to the bird or on a processed product's packaging. See Figure 16.2.

According to the USDA, Grade A poultry is free from deformities, with thick flesh and a well-developed fat layer; free of pinfeathers, cuts or tears and broken bones; free from discoloration and, if it is frozen, free from defects that occur during handling or storage. Nearly all poultry used in wholesale and retail outlets is Grade A. Grade B and C birds are used primarily for processed poultry products.

Quality grades have no bearing on the product's tenderness or flavor. A bird's tenderness is usually indicated by its class (for example, a young turkey is younger and more tender than a yearling). Its grade (USDA A, B or C) within each class is determined by its overall quality.

FIGURE 16.2 ▶ Grade stamps for USDA Grade A poultry.

▶ PURCHASING AND STORING POULTRY

PURCHASING POULTRY

Poultry can be purchased in many forms: fresh or frozen, whole or cut up, bone-in or boneless, portion controlled (P.C.), individually quick-frozen (IQF) or ground. Chicken and turkey are also widely used in prepared and convenience items and are available fully cooked and vacuum-wrapped or boned and canned. Although purchasing poultry in a ready-to-use form is convenient, it is not always necessary; poultry products are easy to fabricate and portion. Whole fresh poultry is also less expensive than precut or frozen products.

As with meats, you should consider your menu, labor costs, storage facilities and employee skills when deciding whether to purchase whole fresh poultry or some other form.

STORING POULTRY

Poultry is a potentially hazardous food. It is highly perishable and particularly susceptible to contamination by salmonella bacteria. It is critical that poultry be stored at the correct temperatures.

Fresh chickens and other small birds can be stored on ice or at 32°F–34°F (0°C–2°C) for up to two days; larger birds can be stored up to four days at these temperatures. Frozen poultry should be kept at 0°F (−18°C) or below (the colder the better) and can be held for up to six months. It should be thawed gradually under refrigeration, allowing two days for chickens and as long as four days for larger birds. Never attempt to cook poultry that is still partially frozen; it will be

FREE-RANGE CHICKENS

Chicken has become increasingly popular in recent years, in part because it is inexpensive, versatile and considered healthier than meat. Indeed, more than 100 million chickens are processed weekly in this country. To meet an ever-increasing demand, chickens are raised indoors in huge chicken houses that may contain as many as 20,000 birds. They are fed a specially formulated mixture composed primarily of corn and soybean meal. Animal protein, vitamins, minerals and small amounts of antibiotics are added to produce quick-growing, healthy birds.

Many consumers feel that chickens raised this way do not have the flavor of chickens that are allowed to move freely and forage for food. Some consumers are concerned about the residual effects of the vitamins, minerals and antibiotics added to the chicken feed. To meet the demand for chickens raised the old-fashioned way, some farmers raise (and many fine establishments offer) free-range chickens.

Although the USDA has not standardized regulations for free-range chicken, generally the term *free-range* applies to birds that are allowed unlimited access to the area outside the chicken house. Often they are raised without antibiotics, fed a vegetarian diet (no animal fat or by-products), processed without the use of preservatives and raised under more humane growing methods than conventionally grown birds. Most free-range chickens are marketed at 9–10 weeks old and weigh 4½ to 5 pounds (2 to 2½ kilograms)—considerably more mature and heavier than conventional broilers. They are generally sold with heads and feet intact and are more expensive than conventionally raised chickens.

Many consumers (in both the dining room and the kitchen) feel that free-range chicken is superior in flavor and quality. Others find no perceptible differences. As a consumer, you will have to decide whether any difference is worth the added expense.

impossible to cook the product evenly, and the areas that were still frozen may not reach the temperatures necessary to destroy harmful bacteria. Never partially cook poultry one day and finish cooking it later; bacteria are more likely to grow under such conditions.

SANITATION AND CROSS-CONTAMINATION

Review the information in Chapter 2, Food Safety and Sanitation, before butchering any poultry. Be sure that all work surfaces, cutting boards, knives, hands and other equipment used to prepare poultry products are clean and sanitary. Be careful that juices and trimmings from poultry do not come in contact with other foods. Anything coming in contact with raw poultry should be cleaned and sanitized before it comes in contact with any other food. Cooked foods should never be placed in containers that were used to hold the raw product. Kitchen towels that are used to handle poultry or clean up after butchering should be sanitized before being reused to prevent cross-contamination.

Poultry should be rinsed under cold running water, then dried with clean disposable paper towels before cooking to remove any collected juices.

▶ BUTCHERING PROCEDURES

Poultry is easier to butcher than meats and is often processed on-site. You should be able to perform the following commonly encountered procedures. Because the different kinds of poultry are similar in structure, these procedures apply to a variety of birds.

▶ PROCEDURE FOR CUTTING A BIRD IN HALF

Often the first step in preparing poultry is to cut the bird in half. Broiler and fryer chickens are often split to make two portions. This procedure removes the backbone and breast bone (also known as the keel bone) for a neat finished product.

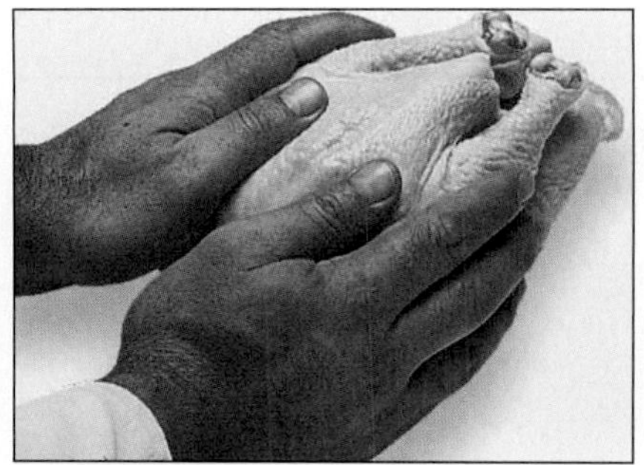

1 Square up the bird by placing it on its back and pressing on the legs and breast to create a more uniform appearance.

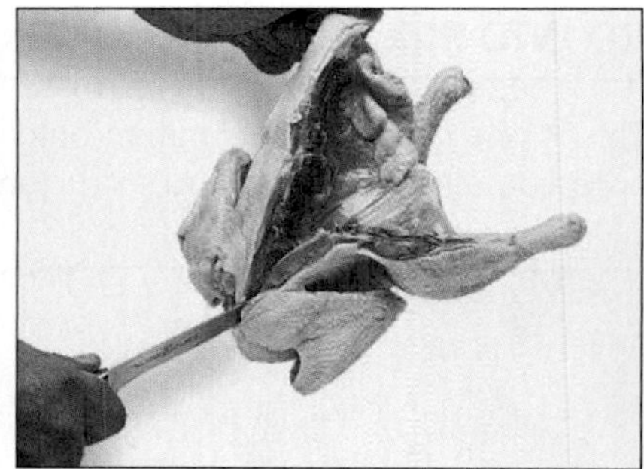

2 Place the bird on its breast and hold the tail tightly with the thumb and forefinger of one hand. Using a rigid boning knife and in a single swift movement, cut alongside the backbone from the bird's tail to the head.

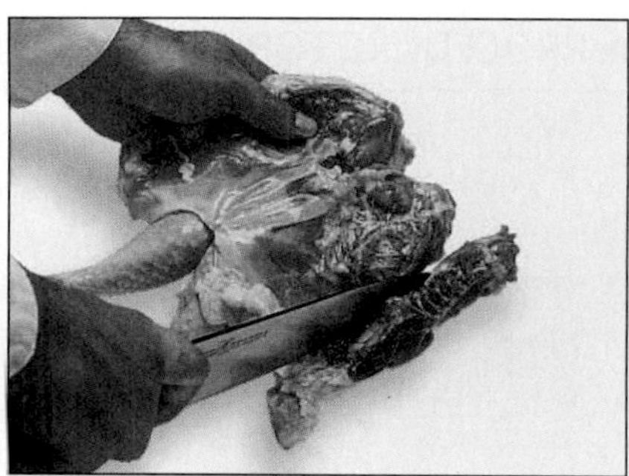

3 Lay the bird flat on the cutting board and remove the backbone by cutting through the ribs connecting it to the breast.

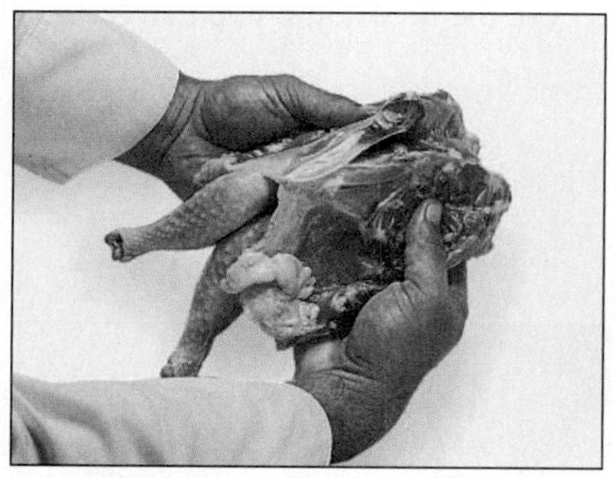

4 Bend the bird back, breaking the breast bone free.

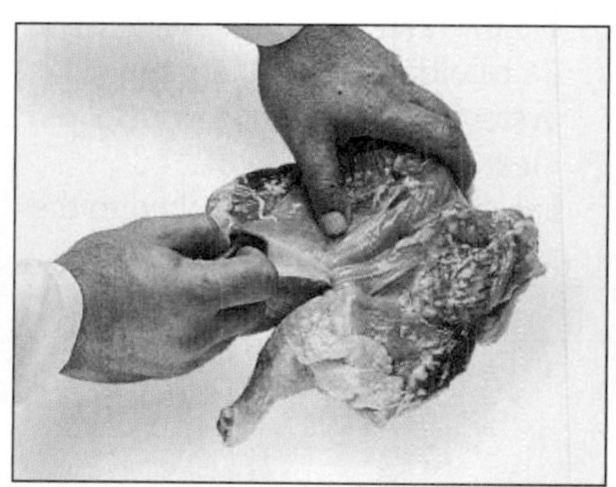

5 Run your fingers along the bone to separate the breast meat from it; pull the bone completely free. Be sure to remove the flexible cartilage completely.

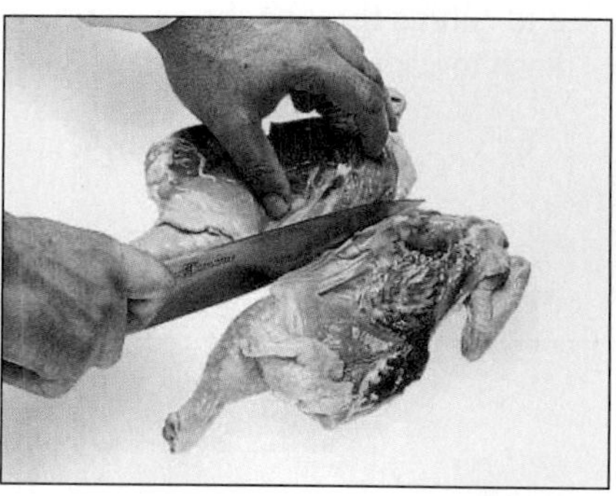

6 Cut through the skin to separate the bird into two halves. The halves are ready to be cooked; for a more attractive presentation, follow Steps 7 and 8.

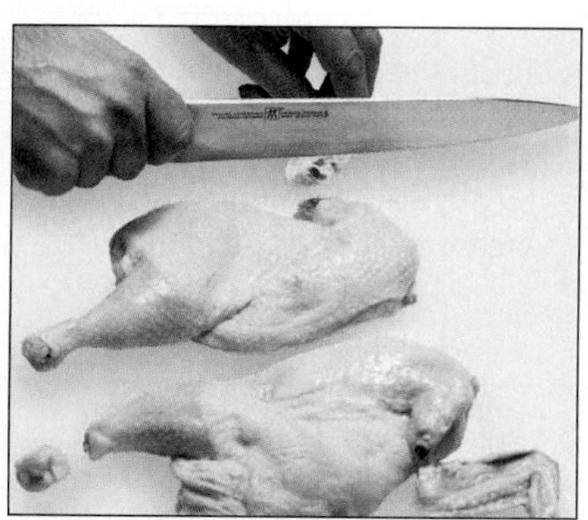

7 Trim off the wing tips and the ends of the leg bone.

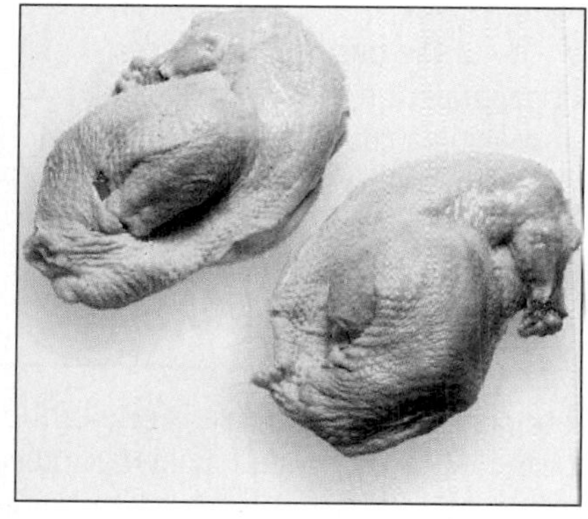

8 Make a slit in the skin below the leg and tuck the leg bone into the slit.

▶ PROCEDURE FOR CUTTING A BIRD INTO PIECES

This is one of the most common butchering procedures. It is also very simple once you understand the bird's structure and are able to find each of its joints.

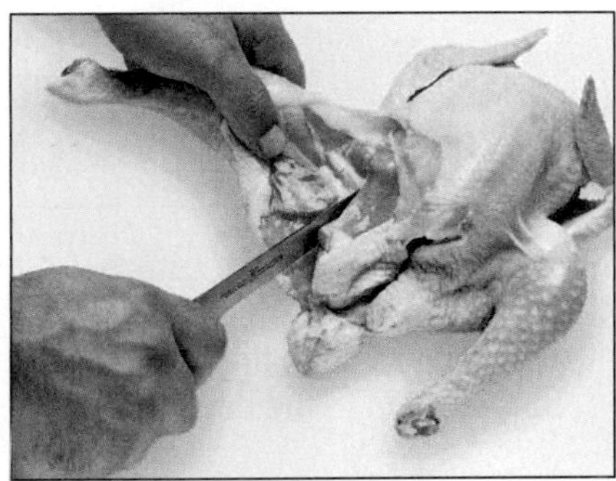

1 Remove the leg by pulling the leg and thigh away from the breast and cutting through the skin and flesh toward the thigh joint.

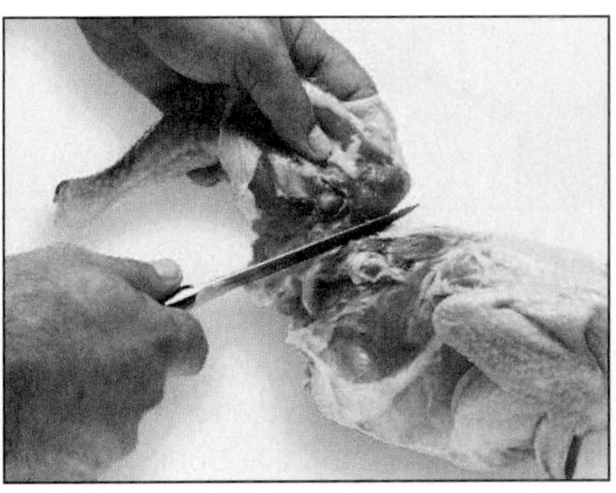

2 Cut down to the thigh joint, twist the leg to break the joint and cut the thigh and leg from the carcass. Be careful to trim around the oyster meat (the tender morsel of meat located next to the backbone); leave it attached to the thigh. Repeat with the other leg.

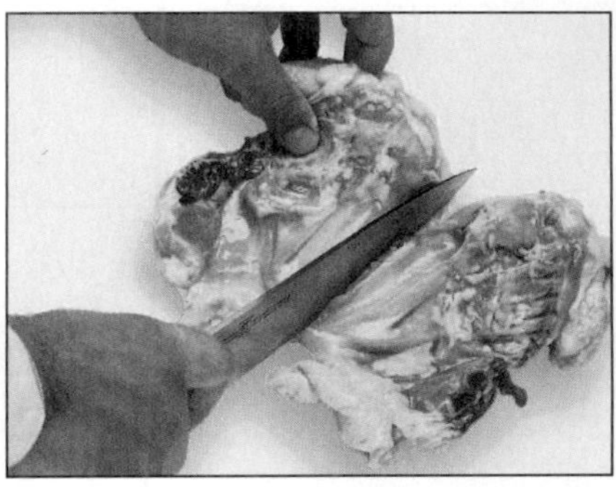

3 To split the breast, follow Steps 2 through 6 for cutting a bird in half. Cut the breast into two halves.

4 The bird is now cut into four quarters.

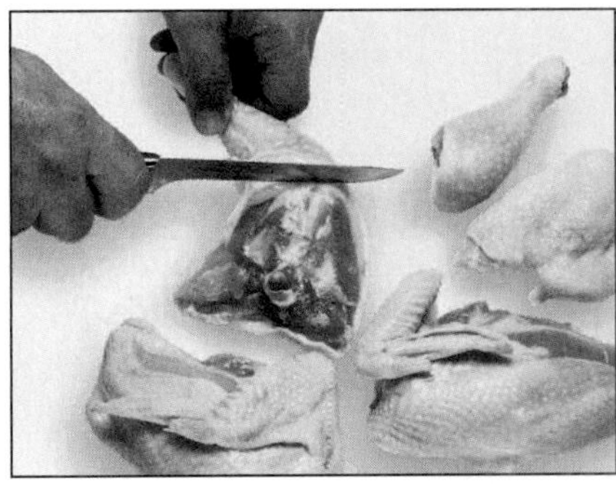

5 To cut the bird into six pieces, separate the thigh from the leg by making a cut guided by the line of fat on the inside of the thigh and leg.

6 To cut the bird into eight pieces, separate the wing from the breast by cutting the joint, or split the breast, leaving a portion of the breast meat attached to the wing.

▶ PROCEDURE FOR PREPARING A BONELESS BREAST

A boneless chicken breast is one of the most versatile and popular poultry cuts. It can be broiled, grilled, baked, sautéed, pan-fried or poached. Boneless turkey breast can be roasted or sliced and sautéed as a substitute for veal. The skin can be removed or left intact.

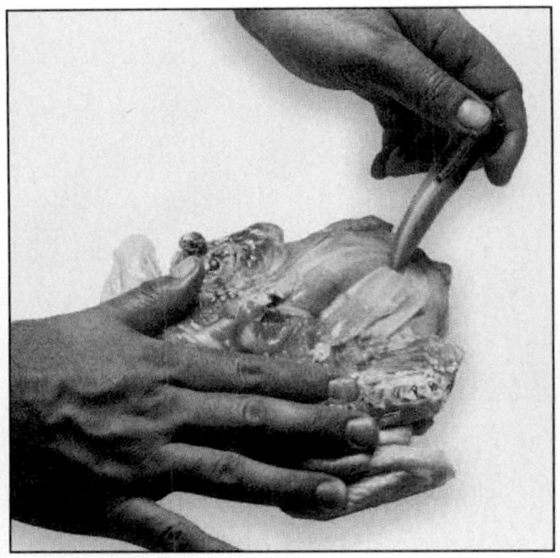

1 Remove the keel bone from the bone-in breast, following Steps 4, 5 and 6 for cutting a bird in half.

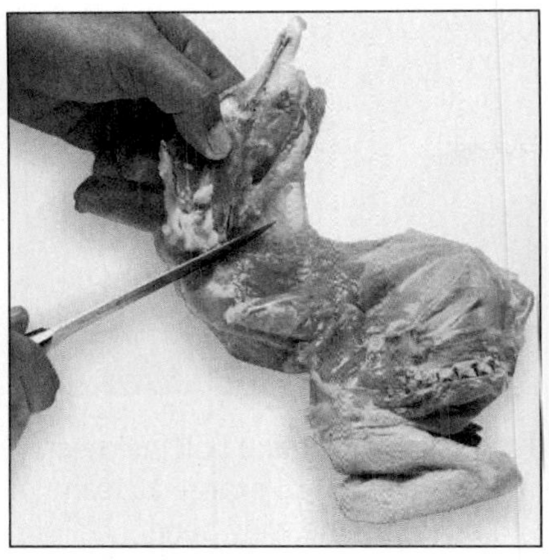

2 With the chicken breast lying skin side down, separate the rib bones, wing and wishbone from the breast. Leave the two tender pieces of meat known as the tenderloins attached to the breast. Repeat the procedure on the other side, being sure to remove the small wishbone pieces from the front of the breast.

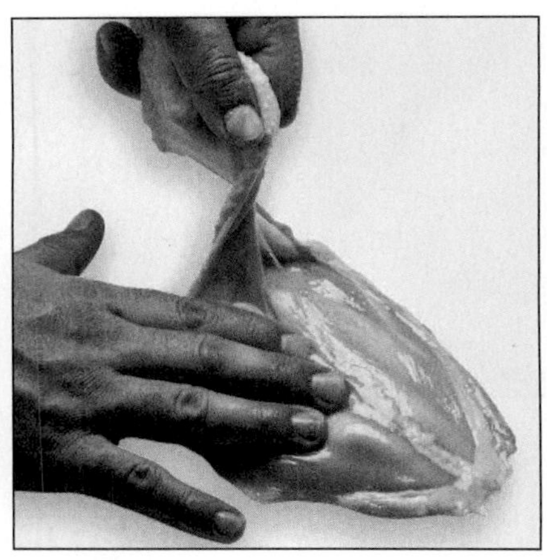

3 The skin may be left intact or removed to produce a skinless boneless breast.

▶ PROCEDURE FOR PREPARING A SUPRÊME OR AIRLINE BREAST

A chicken suprême or airline breast is half of a boneless chicken breast with the first wing bone attached. The tip of the wing bone is removed, yielding a neat and attractive portion that can be prepared by a variety of cooking methods. The skin can be left on or removed.

1 Place the chicken on its back. Remove the legs following Steps 1 and 2 for cutting a bird into pieces. Remove the backbone following Steps 2 and 3 for cutting a bird in half. Remove the keel bone from the bone-in breast, following Steps 4 and 5 for cutting a bird in half.

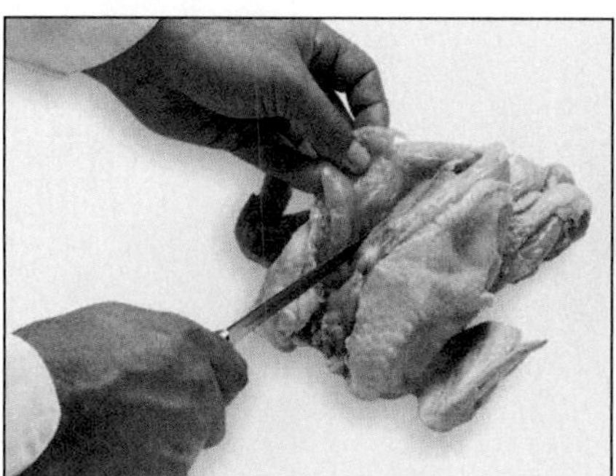

2 Cut along one side of the breast bone, separating the meat from the bone.

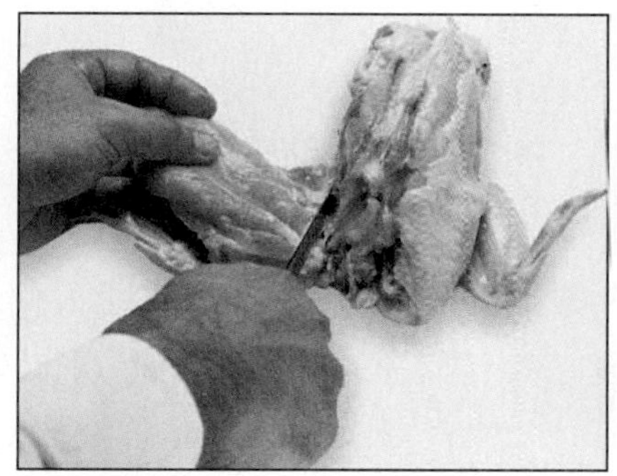

3 Following the natural curvature of the ribs, continue cutting to remove the meat from the bones.

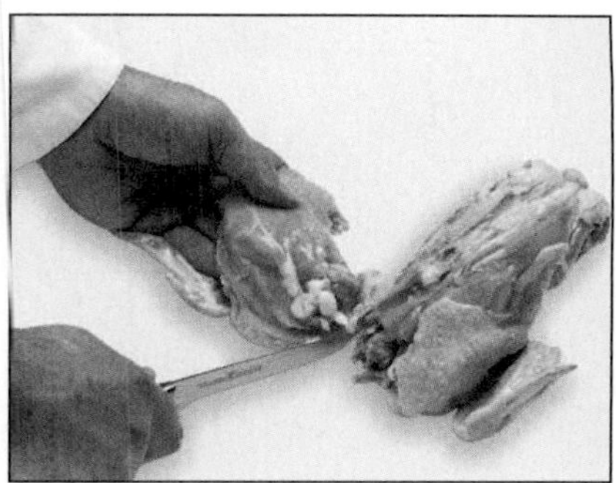

4 When you reach the wing joint, cut through the joint, keeping the wing attached to the breast portion. Cut the breast free from the carcass.

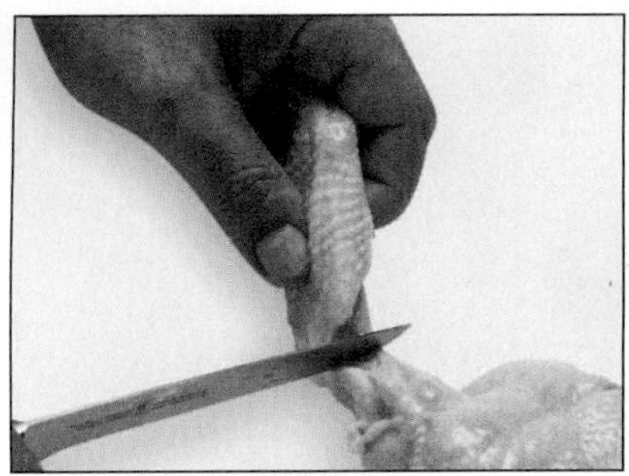

5 Make a cut on the back of the joint between the first and second wing bones.

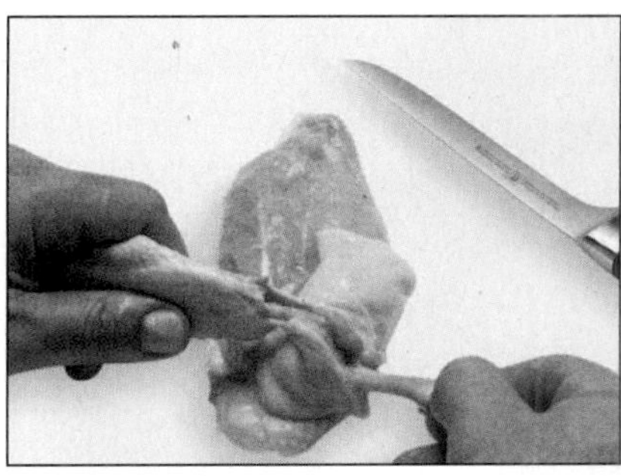

6 Break the joint and pull the meat and skin back to expose a clean bone. Trim the wing bone.

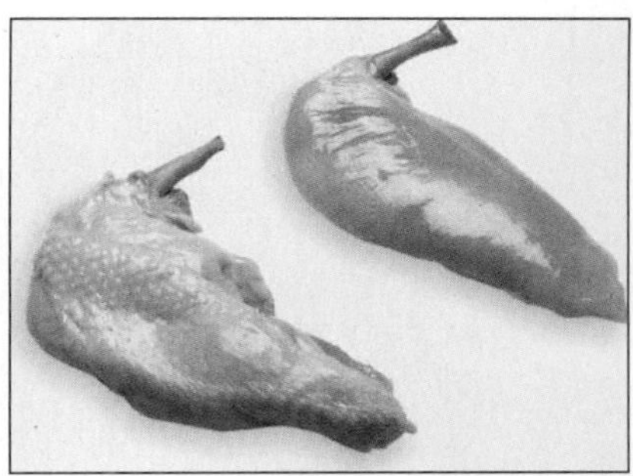

7 The suprême can be prepared skin-on or skinless.

▶ PROCEDURE FOR BONING A CHICKEN LEG AND THIGH

Chicken breasts are usually more popular than legs and thighs. There are, however, uses for boneless, skinless leg and thigh meat; they can be stuffed or used for ballotines, for example.

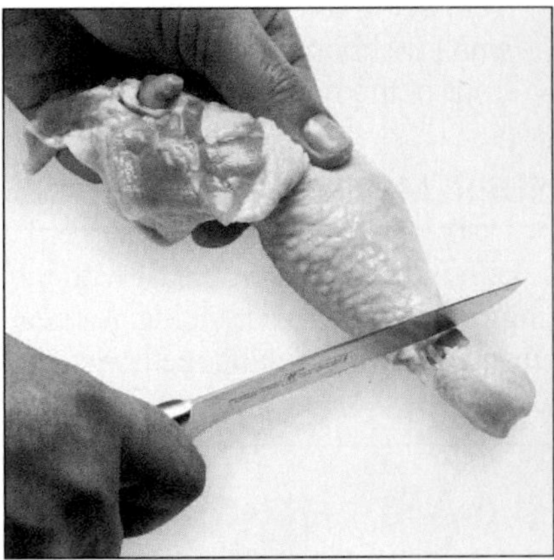

1 Carefully cut through the skin, meat and tendons at the base of the leg. Be sure to cut through completely to the bone.

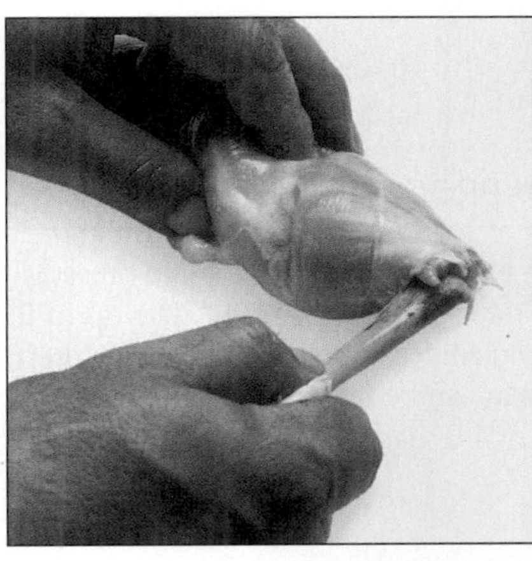

2 Pull the skin off the leg with your hands, then break the joint between the leg and thigh. Twist and pull out the leg bone.

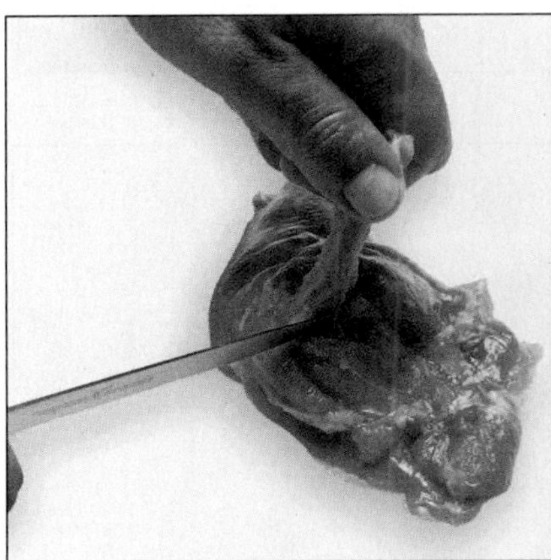

3 Working from the inside of the thigh bone, separate it from the meat.

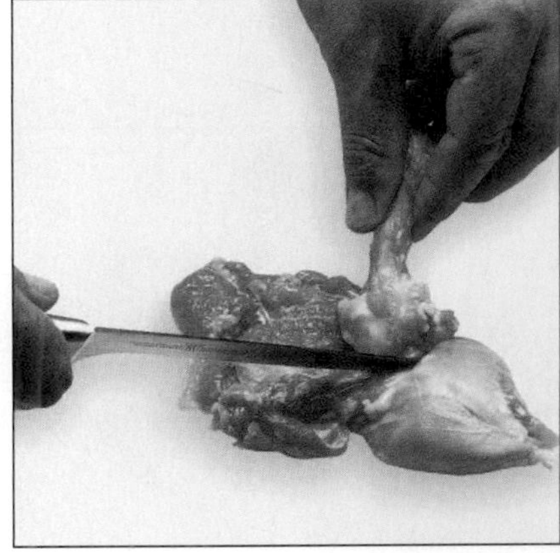

4 Cut around the cartilage at the joint between the leg and thigh and remove the thigh bone and cartilage.

▸ Marinating Poultry

Most poultry is quite mild in flavor, so a marinade is often used to add flavor and moisture, especially to poultry that will be broiled or grilled. Barbecued chicken is a simple and popular example of marinated poultry. Other poultry marinades can be a mixture of white wine or lemon juice, oil, salt, pepper, herbs and spices, such as that given in Recipe 16.1.

WHITE WINE MARINADE

RECIPE 16.1

Yield: 1 qt. (1 lt)

Garlic, minced	2 tsp.	10 ml
Onion, small dice	5 oz.	150 g
Dry white wine	24 fl. oz.	750 ml
Bay leaves	2	2
Dried thyme	2 tsp.	10 ml
White pepper	1 tsp.	5 ml
Salt	1 Tbsp.	15 ml
Lemon juice	1 fl. oz.	30 ml
Vegetable oil	4 fl. oz.	120 ml

1 Combine all ingredients. Use approximately 8 fluid ounces (240 milliliters) marinade for each double breast of chicken.

Approximate values per 1-fl.-oz. (30-ml): **Calories** 35, **Total fat** 3.5 g, **Saturated fat** 0 g, **Cholesterol** 0 mg, **Sodium** 220 mg, **Total carbohydrates** 1 g, **Protein** 0 g, **Claims—**no saturated fat; no cholesterol; no sugar; low calorie

Mise en Place

- ▶ Peel and mince garlic.
- ▶ Peel onions and chop into small dice.

Marinating chicken breasts.

Poultry absorbs flavors quickly, so if pieces are left too long in an acidic marinade, they may take on undesirable flavors. Two hours is often sufficient, with smaller pieces requiring less time in the marinade than larger ones. The texture of the protein will be affected by the acid in the marinade; marinating for more than a few hours can overly tenderize meats and poultry. Avoid using excess marinade because it will become contaminated and must be discontinued after using. To help calculate the quantity of marinade to make, figure on using approximately 8 fluid ounces (240 milliliters) of marinade for each double breast of chicken.

If the marinade contains oil, drain the poultry well to avoid flare-up when the item is placed on the broiler or grill. Use a clean kitchen towel or a paper towel to wipe excess moisture from the poultry's surface so that it browns more easily. The marinade can be used to baste the item during cooking, but leftover marinade should not be served uncooked or reused because of the danger of bacterial contamination from the raw poultry.

▶ Applying Various Cooking Methods

The principles of cooking discussed in Chapter 8 and applied to meats in earlier chapters also apply to poultry. Dry-heat methods are appropriate for young, tender birds. Moist-heat methods should be used with older, less tender products.

DRY-HEAT COOKING METHODS

Cooking poultry with dry-heat methods—broiling and grilling, roasting, sautéing, pan-frying and deep-frying—presents some unique challenges. Large birds such as turkeys benefit from low-heat cooking but are better when served with the crispy skin gained through higher temperatures. Duck and goose skins contain a great deal of fat that must be rendered during the cooking process. Small birds such as squab must be cooked at sufficiently high temperatures to crisp their skins but can be easily overcooked. Boneless chicken breasts, particularly flavorful and popular when broiled or grilled, are easily overcooked and become dry because they do not contain bones to help retain moisture during cooking. Proper application of the following dry-heat cooking methods will help meet these challenges and ensure a good-quality finished product.

BROILING AND GRILLING

Broiled and grilled poultry should have a well-browned surface and can show crosshatched grill marks. It should be moist, tender and juicy throughout. It may be seasoned to enhance its natural flavors or marinated or basted with any number of flavored butters or sauces.

Selecting Poultry to Broil or Grill

Smaller birds such as Cornish hens, chickens and squab are especially well suited for broiling or grilling. Whole birds should be split or cut into smaller pieces before cooking; their joints may be broken so that they lie flat. Quail and other small birds can be skewered before being broiled to help them cook evenly and retain their shape. Be especially careful when cooking breast portions or boneless pieces; the direct heat of the broiler or grill can overcook the item very quickly.

Seasoning Poultry to Be Broiled or Grilled

Poultry is fairly neutral in flavor and responds well to marinating. Poultry may also be basted periodically during the cooking process with flavored butter, oil or barbecue sauce. At the very least, broiled or grilled poultry should be well seasoned with salt and pepper just before cooking.

Determining Doneness

With the exception of duck breasts and squab, which are sometimes left pink, broiled or grilled poultry is always cooked well done. This makes the poultry particularly susceptible to becoming dry and tough because it contains little fat and is cooked at very high temperatures. Particular care must be taken to ensure that the item does not become overcooked.

Four methods are used to determine the doneness of broiled or grilled poultry:

1. Touch—When the item is done, it will have a firm texture, resist pressure and spring back quickly when pressed with a finger.

2 Temperature—Use an instant-read thermometer to determine the item's internal temperature. This may be difficult, however, because of the item's size and the heat from the broiler or grill. Insert the thermometer in the thickest part of the item away from any bones. It should read 165°F–170°F (74°C–77°C) at the coolest point.
3 Looseness of the joints—When bone-in poultry is done, the leg will begin to move freely in its socket.
4 Color of the juices—Poultry is done when its juices run clear or show just a trace of pink. This degree of doneness is known in French as ***à point.***

▶ **à point** (ah PWEN-tah) (1) French term for cooking to the ideal degree of doneness; (2) when applied to meat, refers to cooking it medium rare

Accompaniments to Broiled and Grilled Poultry

If the item was basted with an herb butter, it can be served with additional butter; if the item was basted with barbecue sauce, it should be served with the same sauce. Be careful, however, that any marinade or sauce that came in contact with the raw poultry is not served unless it is cooked thoroughly to destroy harmful bacteria. Additional sauce suggestions are found in Table 11.5.

Broiled or grilled poultry is very versatile and goes well with almost any side dish. Seasoned and grilled vegetables are a natural accompaniment, and deep-fried potatoes are commonly served.

▶ PROCEDURE FOR BROILING OR GRILLING POULTRY

As with meats, broiled or grilled poultry can be prepared by placing it directly on the grate. Poultry is also often broiled using a rotisserie.

1 Heat the broiler or grill.
2 Use a wire brush to remove any charred or burnt particles that may be stuck to the broiler or grill grate. The grate can be wiped with a lightly oiled towel to remove any remaining particles and help season it.
3 Prepare the item to be broiled or grilled by marinating or seasoning as desired; it may be brushed lightly with oil to keep it from sticking to the grate.
4 Place the item on the grate, presentation side (skin side) down. Following the example in Chapter 8, turn the item to produce the attractive crosshatch marks associated with grilling. Baste the item often. Use tongs to turn or flip the item without piercing the surface so that juices do not escape.
5 Develop the proper surface color while cooking the item until it is done à point. To do so, adjust the position of the item on the broiler or grill, or adjust the distance between the grate and heat source. Large pieces and bone-in pieces that are difficult to cook completely on the broiler or grill can be finished in the oven.

A commonly used procedure to cook a large volume of poultry is to place the seasoned items in a broiler pan or other shallow pan and then place the pan directly under the broiler. Baste the items periodically, turning them once when they are halfway done. Items begun this way can be easily finished by transferring the entire pan to the oven.

RECIPE 16.2

GRILLED CHICKEN BREAST WITH RED PEPPER BUTTER

Mise en Place

▶ Peel and chop garlic.

Yield: 4 Servings **Method:** Grilling

Chicken breasts, boneless, skinless	2	2
Salt and pepper	TT	TT
Garlic, chopped	1 tsp.	5 ml
Vegetable oil	1 Tbsp.	15 ml
Red pepper butter	2 oz.	60 g

1 Trim any excess fat from the breasts. Split each breast into two pieces by removing the small piece of cartilage that joins the halves.
2 Season the breasts with the salt, pepper and garlic. Coat the breasts on all sides with the vegetable oil.
3 Heat and prepare the grill.
4 Grill the chicken breasts until done, turning them 90 degrees to produce attractive crosshatch markings.
5 Remove the chicken from the grill and place on a plate for service. Place a ½-ounce (15-gram) slice of red pepper butter on top of each breast. If necessary, place the plate under a broiler or salamander for a few seconds so that the butter begins to melt.

1 Season the chicken breasts.

VARIATION:

Grilled Marinated Chicken Breasts—Omit the garlic. Marinate the chicken breasts in 8 fluid ounces (240 milliliters) White Wine Marinade for up to 1 hour. Blot excess marinade from the chicken with a paper towel before grilling.

Approximate values per serving: **Calories** 240, **Total fat** 14 g, **Saturated fat** 6 g, **Cholesterol** 95 mg, **Sodium** 60 mg, **Total carbohydrates** 1 g, **Protein** 28 g, **Vitamin A** 10%, **Vitamin C** 15%

2 Place the chicken on the grill at a 45-degree angle to the grates.

3 Using tongs, turn the chicken to cook the other side.

4 The cooked chicken is topped with red pepper butter.

ROASTING

Properly roasted (or baked) poultry is attractively browned on the surface and tender and juicy throughout. Proper cooking temperatures ensure a crisp exterior and juicy interior. Most roasted poultry is cooked until the juices run clear. Squab and duck breasts are exceptions; they are often served medium rare or pink.

Selecting Poultry to Roast

Almost every kind of poultry is suitable for roasting, but younger birds produce a more tender finished product. Because of variations in fat content, different kinds of poultry require different roasting temperatures and procedures.

Seasoning Poultry to Be Roasted

Although the mild flavor of most poultry is enhanced by a wide variety of herbs and spices, roasted poultry is often only lightly seasoned with salt and pepper. Poultry that is roasted at high temperatures should never be seasoned with herbs on its surface because the high cooking temperatures will burn them. If herbs or additional spices are used, they should be stuffed into the cavity. A mirepoix or a bouquet garni may also be added to the cavity for additional flavor. The cavities of dark-meated birds such as ducks and geese are often stuffed with fresh or dried fruits.

▶ PROCEDURE FOR TRUSSING POULTRY

Trussing is tying a bird into a more compact shape with thread or butcher's twine. Trussing allows the bird to cook more evenly, helps the bird retain moisture and improves the appearance of the finished product. There are many methods for trussing poultry, some of which require a special tool called a trussing needle. Here we show a simple method using butcher's twine.

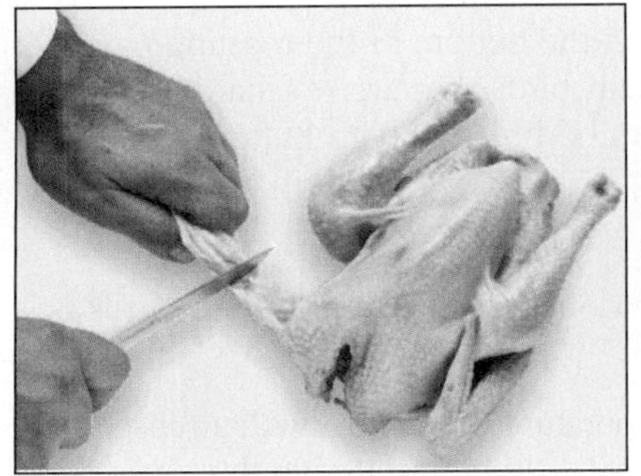

1 Square up the bird by pressing it firmly with both hands. Tuck the first joint of the wing behind the back or trim off the first and second joints as shown.

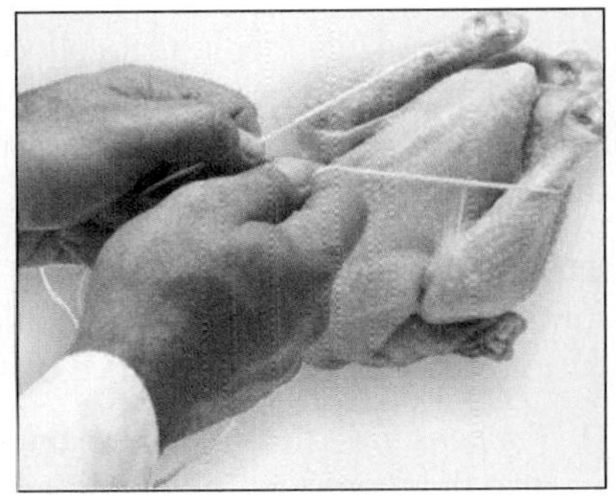

2 Cut a piece of butcher's twine approximately three times the bird's length. With the breast up and the neck toward you, pass the twine under the bird approximately 1 inch (2.5 centimeters) in front of the tail.

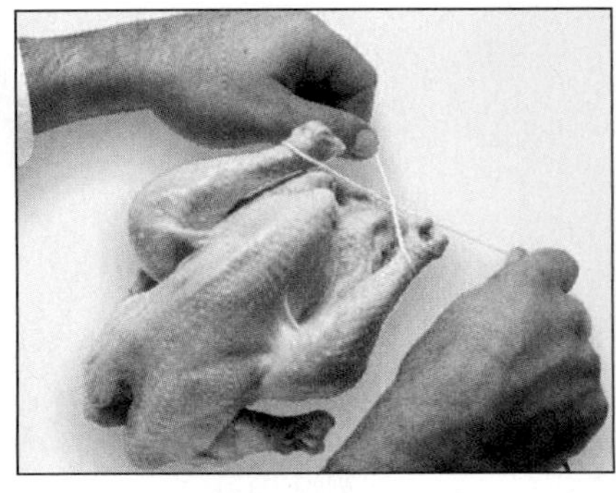

3 Bring the twine up around the legs and cross the ends, creating an X between the legs. Pass the ends of the twine below the legs.

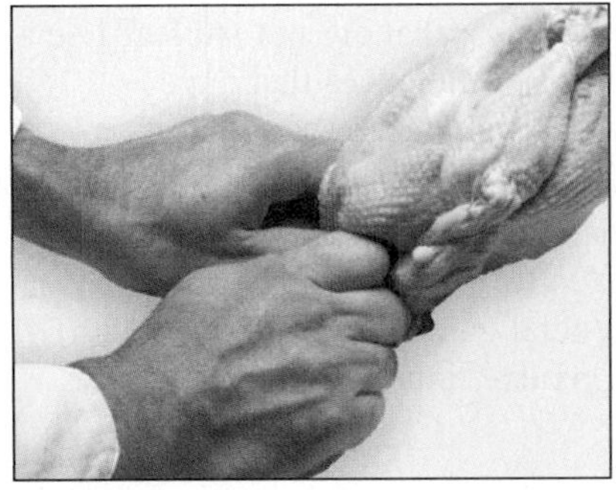

4 Pull the ends of the twine tightly across the leg and thigh joints and across the wings if the first and second joints are trimmed off, or just above the wings if they are intact.

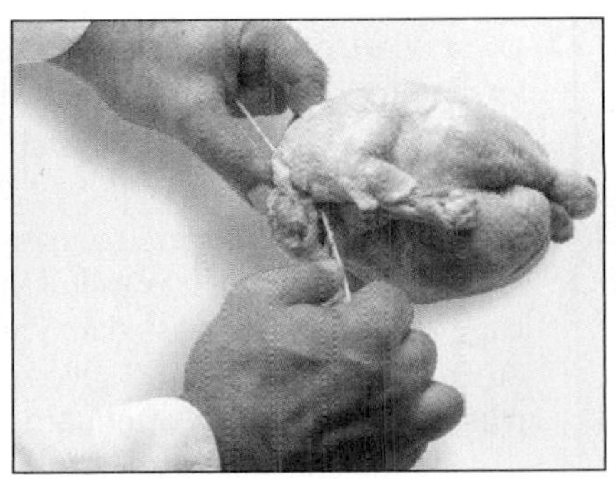

5 Pull the string tight and tie it securely just above the neck.

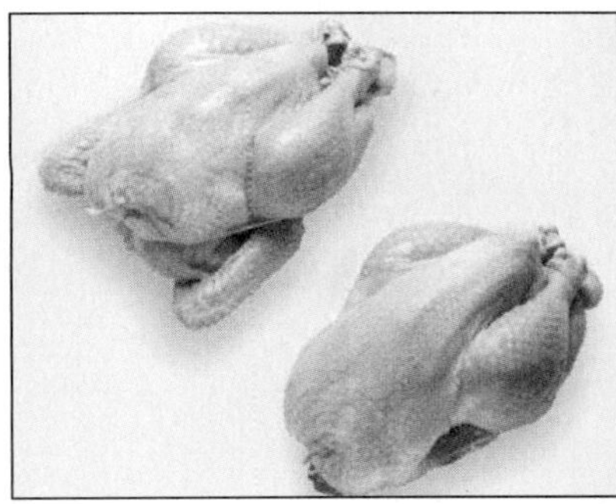

6 Two examples of properly trussed birds: one with the wings intact and one with the first and second wing joints removed.

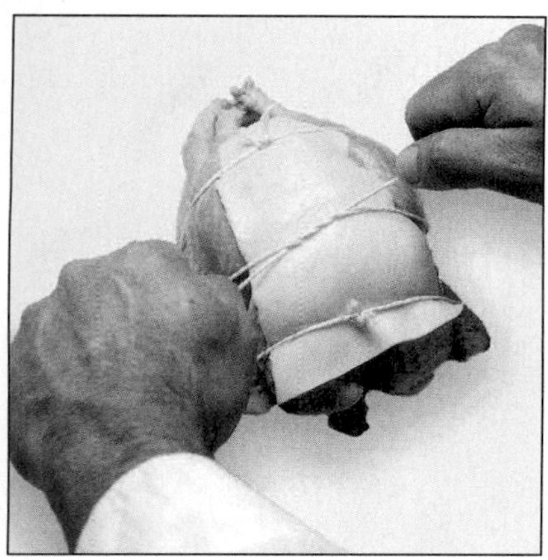

Barding a pheasant.

Barding Poultry to Be Roasted

Guineas, squabs or any skinless birds without an adequate fat covering to protect them from drying out during roasting can be barded. Bard the bird by covering its entire surface with thin slices of fatback, securing them with butcher's twine.

Cooking Temperatures

Small birds such as squab and Cornish game hens should be roasted at the relatively high temperatures of 375°F–400°F (190°C–200°C). These temperatures help produce crisp, well-colored skins without overcooking the flesh. Chickens are best roasted at temperatures between 350°F and 375°F (180°C and 190°C). This temperature range allows the skin to crisp and the flesh to cook without causing the bird to stew in its own juices. Large birds such as capons and turkeys are started at high temperatures of 400°F–425°F (200°C–220°C) to brown the skin, then finished at lower temperatures of 275°F–325°F (135°C–160°C) to promote even cooking and produce a moister product. Ducks and geese, which are very high in fat, must be roasted at the high temperatures of 375°F–425°F (190°C–220°C) to render as much fat from the skin as possible. Duck and goose skins are often pricked before roasting so that the rendered fat can escape; this helps create a crispy skin.

Basting Roasted Poultry

With the exception of fatty birds such as ducks and geese, all poultry items should be basted while they roast in order to help retain moisture. To baste a bird, spoon or ladle the fat that collects in the bottom of the roasting pan over the bird at 15-to-20-minute intervals. Lean birds that are not barded will not produce enough fat for basting and may be brushed with butter in the same manner.

Determining Doneness

Four methods are used to determine the doneness of roasted poultry. It is best to use a combination of these methods.

1. *Temperature*—Test the internal temperature of the bird with an instant-read thermometer. The thermometer should be inserted in the bird's thigh, which is the last part to become fully cooked. It should not touch the bone and should read 165°F–170°F (74°C–77°C) at the coolest point. This method works best with large birds such as capons and turkeys. Large birds are subject to some degree of carryover cooking. This is not as much of a concern with poultry as it is with meat because large birds are always cooked well done.
2. *Looseness of the joints*—The thigh and leg will begin to move freely in their sockets when the bird is done.
3. *Color of juices*—This method is used with birds that are not stuffed. Use a kitchen fork to tilt the bird, allowing some of the juices that have collected in the cavity to run out. Clear juices indicate that the bird is done. If the juices are cloudy or pink, the bird is undercooked.
4. *Time*—Because there are so many variables, timing alone is less reliable than other methods. It is useful, however, for planning production when large quantities are roasted and as a general guideline when used with other methods. Table 16.7 gives some general timing guidelines for roasting several kinds of poultry.

Table 16.7 ROASTING TEMPERATURES AND TIMES

POULTRY KIND OR CLASS	COOKING TEMPERATURES		MINUTES PER LB (500 g)
Capons	350°F–375°F	180°C–190°C	18–20 min.
Chickens	375°F–400°F	190°C–200°C	15–18 min.
Ducks and geese	375°F–425°F	190°C–220°C	12–15 min.
Game hens	375°F–400°F	190°C–200°C	45–60 min. total
Guineas	375°F–400°F	190°C–200°C	18–20 min.
Squab	400°F	200°C	30–40 min. total
Turkeys (large)	325°F	160°C	12–15 min.

Accompaniments to Roasted Poultry

The most common accompaniments to roasted poultry are bread stuffing and gravy. Large birds, such as capons and turkeys, produce adequate drippings for making sauce or pan gravy. Small birds, such as squab and Cornish game hens, are often stuffed with wild rice or other ingredients and served with a sauce that is made separately.

Ducks and geese are complemented by stuffings containing rice, fruits, berries and nuts. They are very fatty, and if stuffed, they should be roasted on a rack or mirepoix bed to ensure that the fat that collects in the pan during roasting does not penetrate the cavity, making the stuffing greasy. Ducks and geese are often served with a citrus- or fruit-based sauce. Its high acid content complements these rich, fatty birds.

▶ **dressing** another name for a bread stuffing used with poultry

▶ PROCEDURE FOR STUFFING POULTRY

Small birds such as Cornish game hens, small chickens and squab can be stuffed successfully. Stuffing larger birds, especially for volume production, is impractical and can be dangerous for the following reasons:

1. Stuffing is a good bacterial breeding ground, and because it is difficult to control temperatures inside a stuffed bird, there is a risk of food-borne illness.
2. Stuffing poultry is labor intensive.
3. Stuffed poultry must be cooked longer to cook the stuffing properly; this may cause the meat to be overcooked, becoming dry and tough.

When stuffing any bird, use the following guidelines:

1. Always be aware of temperatures when mixing the raw ingredients. All ingredients should be cold when they are mixed together, and the mixture's temperature should never be allowed to rise above 45°F (7°C).
2. Stuff the raw bird as close to roasting time as possible.
3. The neck and main body cavities should be loosely stuffed. The stuffing will expand during cooking.
4. After the cavities are filled, their openings should be secured with skewers and butcher's twine or by trussing.
5. After cooking, remove the stuffing from the bird and store separately.

SAFETY ALERT

Handling Stuffed Poultry

Stuffing is a potentially hazardous food. All ingredients used to make stuffing must be cold and stay below 45°F (7°C) when mixing and stuffing into poultry. Stuff a bird as close to cooking time as possible to keep it out of the temperature danger zone. Observe proper cooking temperatures and roast until the bird reaches an internal temperature of 165°F (74°C) as indicated by an instant-read thermometer placed deep into the stuffing. Remove all stuffing from the bird's cavity promptly. If left in the cavity, stuffing will not cool and will become a potential breeding ground for bacteria.

▶ PROCEDURE FOR ROASTING POULTRY

1. Season, bard, stuff and/or truss the bird as desired.
2. Place the bird in a roasting pan. It may be placed on a rack or a bed of mirepoix in order to prevent scorching and promote even cooking.
3. Roast uncovered, basting every 15 minutes.
4. Allow the bird to rest before carving to allow even distribution of juices. As the bird rests, prepare the pan gravy or sauce.

RECIPE 16.3

ROAST TURKEY WITH CHESTNUT DRESSING AND GIBLET GRAVY

Mise en Place

- ▶ Peel and chop onions, carrots and celery for mirepoix.
- ▶ While turkey is roasting peel and chop the onion and celery into small dice for the dressing. Beat the eggs.
- ▶ Chop parsley.
- ▶ Cook, peel and coarsely chop chestnuts for the dressing.

Yield: 16 Servings, 4 oz. (120 g) turkey, 3 oz. (90 g) dressing and 4 oz. (120 ml) gravy each

Method: Roasting

Young turkey, 12–15 lb. (5.5–6.5 kg) with giblets	1	1
Salt and pepper	TT	TT
Mirepoix	20 oz.	600 g
Onions, small dice	8 oz.	225 g
Celery, small dice	6 oz.	180 g
Whole butter	4 oz.	120 g
Dried bread cubes	2 lb.	1 kg
Eggs, beaten	2	2
Fresh parsley, chopped	1 Tbsp.	15 ml
Chicken stock	2¼ qt.	2 lt
Chestnuts, cooked and peeled, chopped coarse	8 oz.	225 g
All-purpose flour	3 oz.	90 g

1. Remove the giblets from the turkey's cavity and set aside. Season the turkey inside and out with salt and pepper. Truss the turkey.
2. Place the turkey in a roasting pan. Roast at 400°F (200°C) for 30 minutes. Reduce the temperature to 325°F (160°C) and continue cooking the turkey to an internal temperature of 165°F (74°C), approximately 2½ to 3 hours. Baste the turkey often during cooking. Approximately 45 minutes before the turkey is done, add the mirepoix to the roasting pan. If the turkey begins to overbrown, cover it loosely with aluminum foil.
3. To make the dressing, sauté the onions and celery in the butter until tender.
4. In a large bowl, toss together the bread cubes, salt, pepper, eggs, parsley, sautéed onions and celery, 4 ounces (120 milliliters) stock and the chestnuts.
5. Place the dressing in a buttered hotel pan and cover with aluminum foil or buttered parchment paper. Bake at 350°F (180°C) until done, approximately 45 minutes.
6. As the turkey roasts, simmer the giblets (neck, heart and gizzard) in 1 quart (1 liter) stock until tender, approximately 1½ hours.

7 When the turkey is done, remove it from the roasting pan and set it aside to rest. Degrease the roasting pan, reserving 3 fluid ounces (90 milliliters) of the fat to make a roux.
8 Place the roasting pan on the stove top and brown the mirepoix.
9 Deglaze the pan with a small amount of stock. Transfer the mirepoix and stock to a saucepot and add the remaining stock and the broth from the giblets. Bring to a simmer and degrease.
10 Make a blond roux with the reserved fat and the flour. Add the roux to the liquid, whisking well to prevent lumps. Simmer 15 minutes. Strain the gravy through a china cap lined with cheesecloth.
11 Remove the meat from the turkey neck. Trim the gizzard. Finely chop the neck meat, heart and gizzard and add to the gravy. Adjust the seasonings.
12 Carve the turkey and serve with a portion of chestnut dressing and giblet gravy.

Approximate values per serving: **Calories** 720, **Total fat** 23 g, **Saturated fat** 9 g, **Cholesterol** 250 mg, **Sodium** 700 mg, **Total carbohydrates** 41 g, **Protein** 87 g, **Vitamin A** 6%, **Iron** 40%

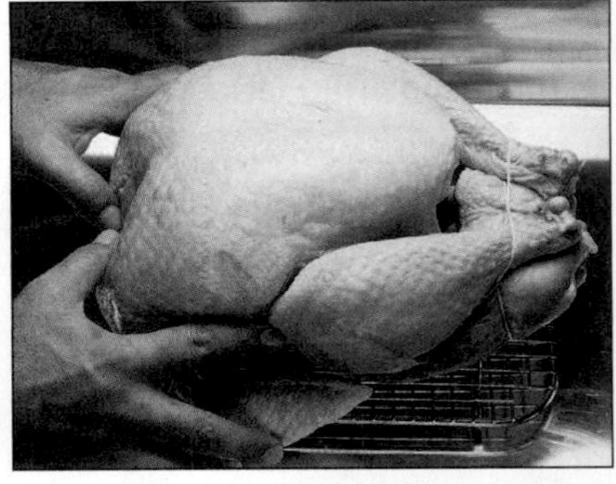

1 Placing the trussed turkey in the roasting pan.

2 Adding the mirepoix to the roasting pan.

3 Tossing the dressing ingredients together.

4 Browning the mirepoix.

5 Deglazing the roasting pan.

6 Transferring the mirepoix and stock to a saucepot.

7 Straining the gravy through a china cap and cheesecloth.

Carving Roasted Poultry

Poultry can be carved in the kitchen, at tableside or on a buffet in a variety of manners. The carving methods described next produce slices of both light and dark meat.

► PROCEDURE FOR CARVING A TURKEY, CAPON OR OTHER LARGE BIRD

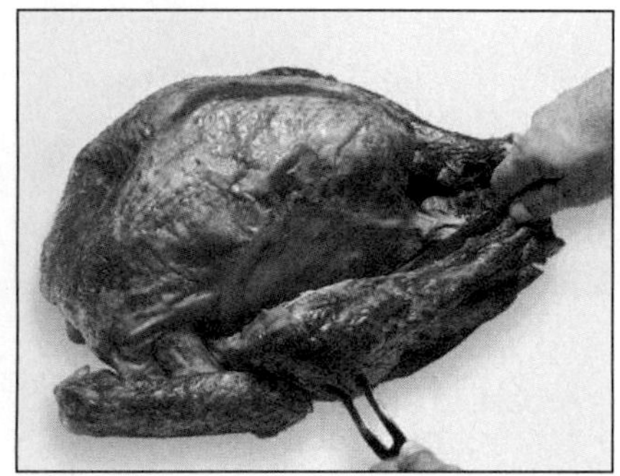

1 After roasting, allow the turkey to stand for 20 minutes so that the juices can redistribute themselves. Holding the turkey firmly with a carving fork, pry a leg outward and locate the joint. Remove the leg and thigh in one piece by cutting through the joint with the tip of a knife.

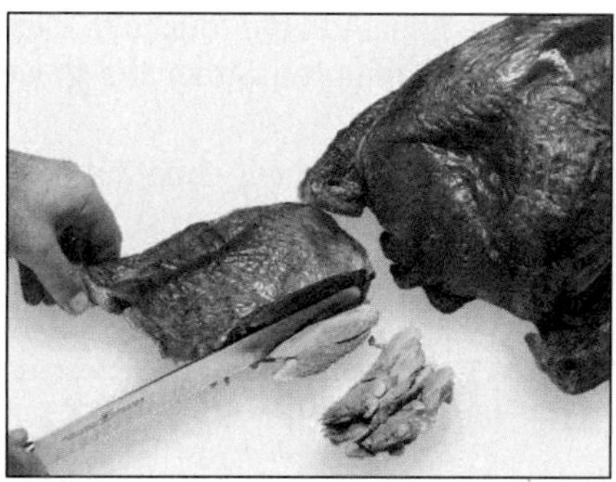

2 Repeat the procedure on the other side. Once both legs and thighs have been removed, slice the meat from the thigh by holding the leg firmly with one hand and slicing parallel to the bone.

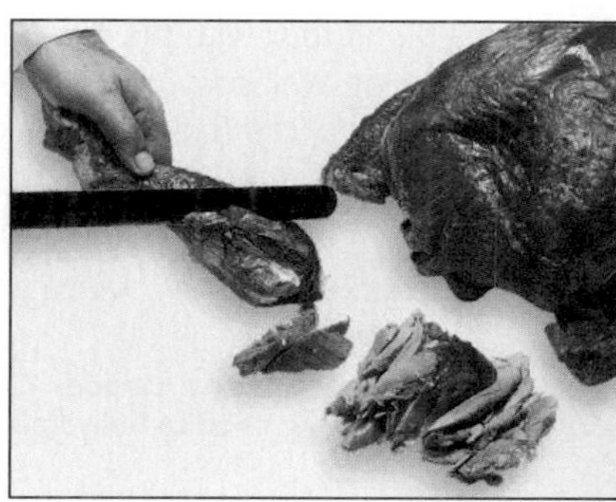

3 Separate the thigh from the leg bone by cutting through the joint. Slice the meat from the leg by cutting parallel to the bone.

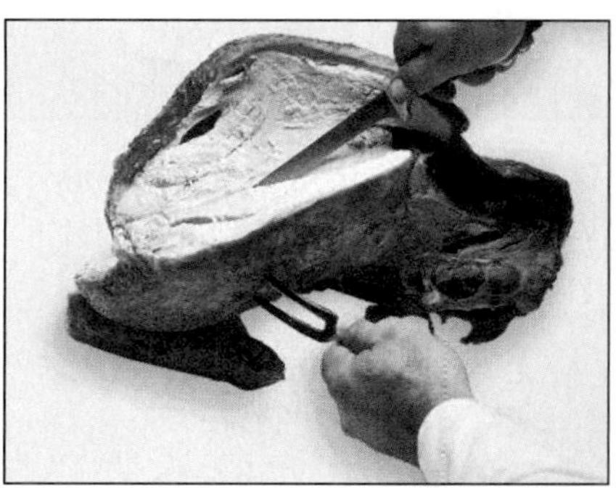

4 Cut along the backbone, following the natural curvature of the bones separating the breast meat from the ribs.

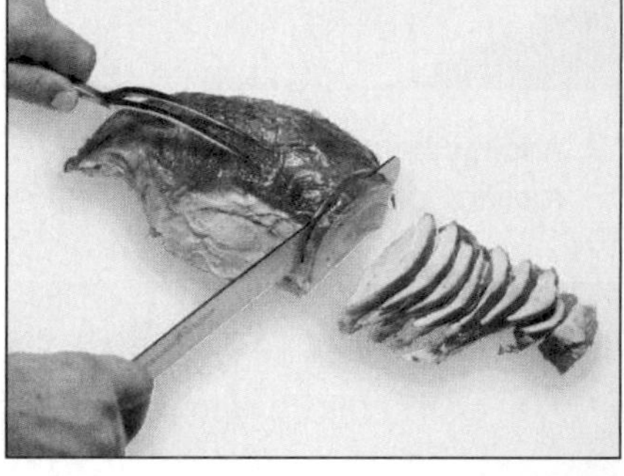

5 Remove an entire half breast and slice it on the cutting board as shown. Cut on an angle to produce larger slices.

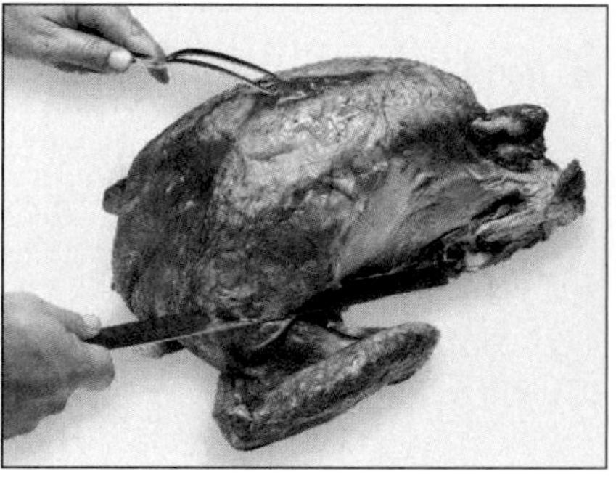

6 Alternatively, the breast can be carved on the bird. Make a horizontal cut just above the wing in toward the rib bones.

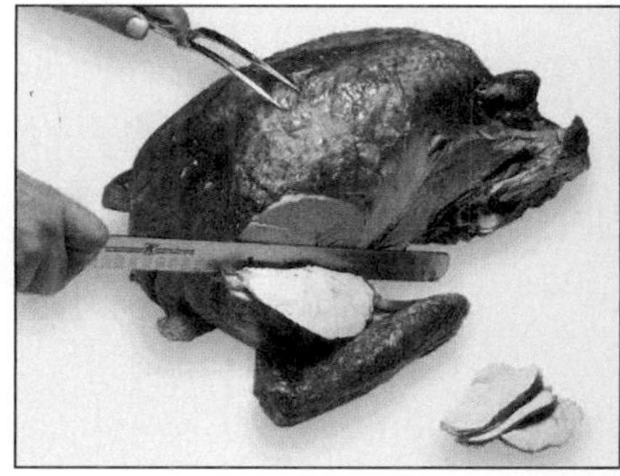

7 Slice the breast meat as shown.

▶ PROCEDURE FOR CARVING A CHICKEN OR OTHER SMALL BIRD

1 After allowing the roasted chicken to rest for 15 minutes so that the juices can redistribute themselves, cut through the skin between the leg and breast.

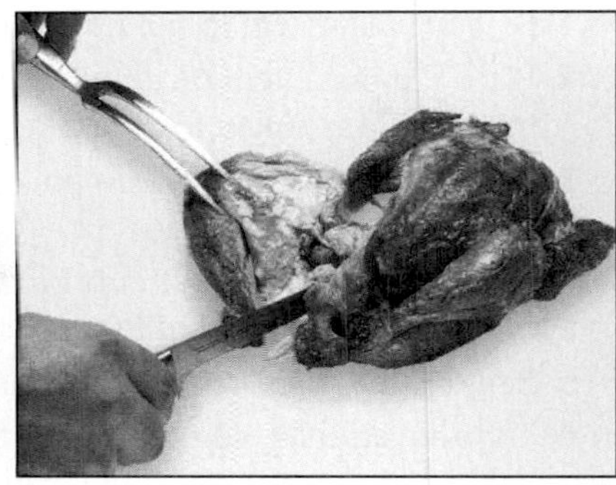

2 Use a kitchen fork to pry the leg and thigh away from the breast. Locate the thigh's ball joint and cut through it with the knife tip, separating it completely from the rest of the chicken. Be sure to cut around the delicate oyster meat, leaving it attached to the thigh.

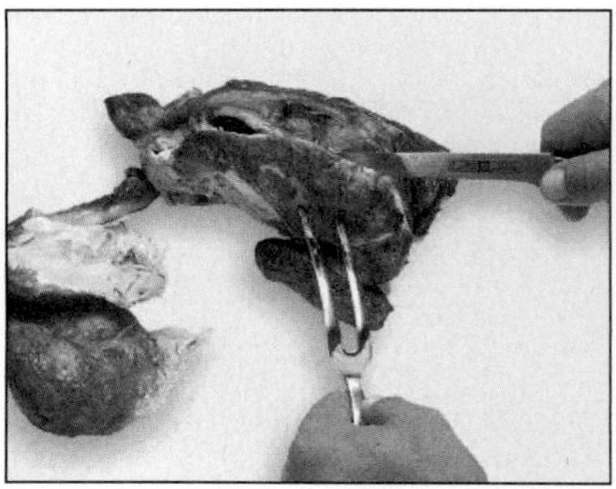

3 With the knife tip, cut through the skin and meat on one side of the breast bone. Cut and pull the meat away from the bones with the knife.

4 Cut through the wing joint, separating the breast meat and wing from the carcass. Repeat this procedure on the other side of the bird.

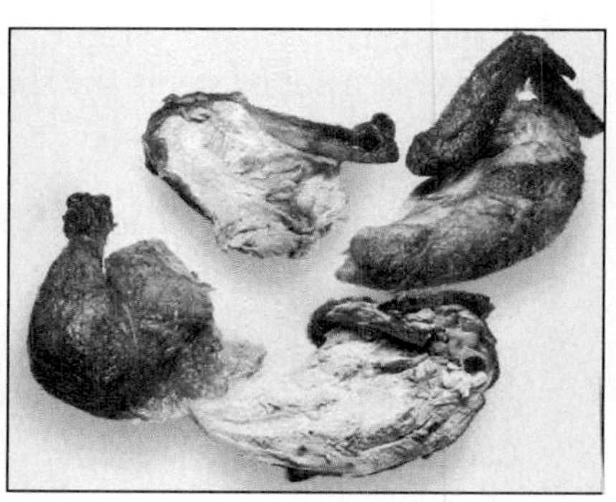

5 The chicken is now quartered.

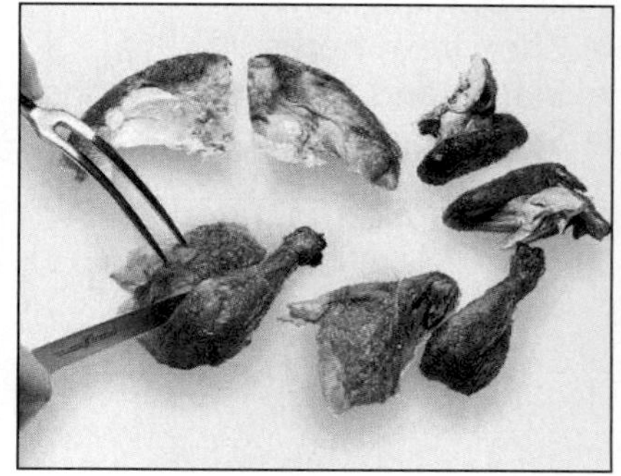

6 To cut it into eight pieces, separate the wings from the breasts and the thighs from the legs.

POÊLÉING

Poêléing (pwah-lay-ing) is a cooking method similar to both roasting and braising. The item is cooked in the oven in a covered pot so that it cooks in its own juices and steam. Although this is a moist-heat cooking technique (because the item steams in its own juices), it is used only for tender cuts, not those that need long, slow braising. The cooking time is usually shorter than that needed for dry roasting.

The item to be poêléed can first be browned in hot fat and then laid on a bed of matignon, covered and cooked in the oven. If the item was not first browned in hot fat, it can later be browned by removing the lid toward the end of cooking. Doneness is determined using the same techniques as those used for roasting.

Vegetables to be served with the dish can be added to the poêlé as it cooks or cooked separately and plated with the finished item.

The sauce for a poêlé is made from the flavorful cooking juices left in the pan. They are mixed with a liquid (stock, jus lie or demi-glace) and finished using the same techniques as those for a braised dish. The matignon can be left in the finished sauce or strained out.

▶ PROCEDURE FOR POÊLÉING POULTRY

1 Sear the main item in hot butter or oil, if desired.
2 Place the main item on a bed of matignon. Add vegetables or other ingredients as called for in the recipe.
3 Cover and cook in the oven until done. Baste periodically with pan juices or with additional butter.
4 If the main item was not first browned in hot fat, it can be browned by removing the lid toward the end of the cooking period, if desired.
5 Remove the main item when done.
6 To make a sauce, add a liquid to the matignon and cooking juices in the pan and reduce. Remove the matignon if desired and add flavorings as directed in the recipe.

RECIPE 16.4

POÊLÉ OF CHICKEN WITH PEARL ONIONS AND MUSHROOMS

Mise en Place

- ▶ Dice bacon and peel and chop onions, celery, carrots and garlic for matignon.
- ▶ Chop fresh herbs.
- ▶ Blanch and peel pearl onions.
- ▶ Stem mushrooms.

Yield: 4 Servings **Method:** Poêléing

Chickens, 2 lb. 8 oz.–3 lb. (1–1.4 kg) each	2	2
Salt and pepper	TT	TT
Fresh herbs, assorted stems and sprigs	2 oz.	60 g
Clarified butter	4 fl. oz.	120 ml
Matignon:		
Slab bacon or smoked ham, small dice	3 oz.	90 g
Onions, small dice	6 oz.	180 g
Celery, small dice	3 oz.	90 g
Carrots, small dice	3 oz.	90 g
Garlic, chopped	2 tsp.	10 ml
Pearl onions, blanched and peeled	4 oz.	120 g
Button mushrooms, stemmed	8 oz.	240 g
White wine	4 fl. oz.	120 ml
Demi-glace	2 pt.	1 qt
Tomato concassée	4 oz.	120 g
Fresh herbs, assorted, chopped	2 tsp.	10 ml

1 Season the chicken cavities with salt and pepper and stuff them with the herb stems and sprigs. Truss the birds and season the outside with salt and pepper.
2 Heat half the butter in a roasting pan that is just large enough to hold the birds without crowding. Sauté the bacon until most of the fat is rendered. Add the diced onions, celery and carrots and sauté until they begin to brown. Add the garlic and cook for 1 more minute.
3 Place the trussed chickens on top of the matignon. Baste them with the remaining butter. Cover the roasting pan with its lid and place in a 325°F (160°C) oven until done, approximately 1½ hours, basting the chickens with fat from the pan every 20 minutes. Remove the lid for the last 30 minutes of cooking to allow the chickens to brown lightly.
4 Remove the chickens from the pan and allow them to rest in a warm place. Place the roasting pan on the stove top. Remove a small amount of the accumulated fat from the roasting pan to a sauté pan and sauté the onions and mushrooms in the sauté pan until nearly tender.

5 Bring the liquid in the roasting pan to a boil; remove any excess fat or scum with a ladle. Add the wine and reduce by half. Add the demi-glace and bring to a simmer. Adjust the thickness of the sauce. If desired, strain the sauce. Add the onions, mushrooms, tomato concassée and chopped herbs to the sauce. Bring to a simmer and adjust the seasonings.
6 Carve the chickens and serve them with a portion of the sauce and vegetables.

Approximate values per serving: **Calories** 1670, **Total fat** 106 g, **Saturated fat** 39 g, **Cholesterol** 475 mg, **Sodium** 2110 mg, **Total carbohydrates** 48 g, **Protein** 129 g, **Vitamin A** 170%, **Vitamin C** 50%, **Calcium** 10%, **Iron** 45%

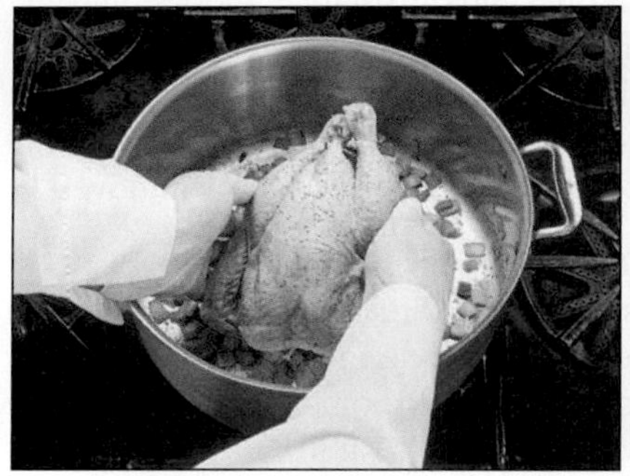

1 Place the chicken on the matignon.

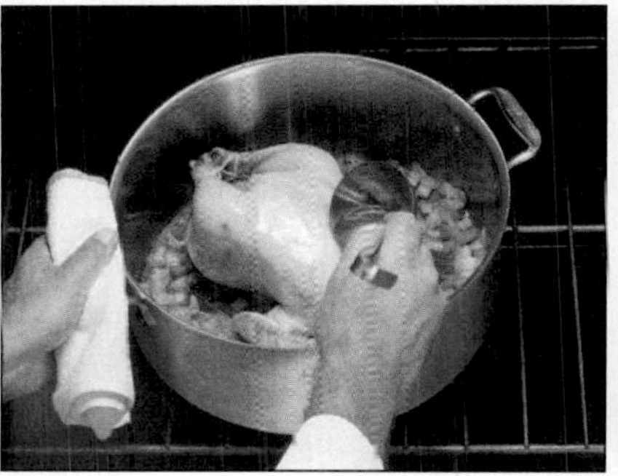

2 Baste the chicken with fat from the pan during cooking.

3 Carefully remove the cooked chicken from the pan.

SAUTÉING

Sautéed poultry should be tender and juicy, its flavor developed by proper browning. Additional flavors come from a sauce made by deglazing the pan, usually with wine, and adding garnishes, seasonings and liquids. Stir-frying is a popular method of sautéing poultry; boneless pieces are cut into strips and quickly cooked with assorted vegetables and seasonings.

Selecting Poultry to Sauté

Most poultry is quite tender and well suited for sautéing. Although small birds such as squab can be sautéed bone-in, large pieces and bone-in cuts from larger birds should not be sautéed. Boneless breasts, suprêmes, scallops and cutlets are the most common and practical cuts for sautéing. Because they are high in fat, boneless duck breasts can be sautéed without additional fat.

Seasoning Poultry to Be Sautéed

Poultry has a delicate flavor that is enhanced by a wide variety of herbs, spices, condiments and marinades. Flavor combinations are limited only by your imagination. When poultry items are dusted with flour before sautéing, the seasonings may first be added to the flour.

Cooking Temperatures

The sauté pan and the cooking fat must be hot before the poultry is added. The temperature at which the poultry is then sautéed is determined by its thickness and the desired color of the finished product. A thin, boneless slice requires relatively high temperatures so that its surface is browned before the center is overcooked. A thicker cut such as a suprême requires lower temperatures so that neither its surface nor the fond are burned before the item is fully cooked. Adjust the temperature throughout the cooking process in order to achieve the desired results, never letting the pan become too cool.

If the pan is overcrowded or otherwise allowed to cool, the poultry will cook in its own juices and absorb oil from the pan, resulting in a poor-quality product.

Determining Doneness

Thin cuts of poultry cook very quickly, so timing is a useful tool; it is less useful with thicker cuts. Experienced cooks can tell the doneness of an item by judging the temperature of the sauté pan and the color of the item being cooked.

A more practical method is to press the item with your finger and judge the resistance. Very undercooked poultry will offer little resistance and feel mushy. Slightly underdone poultry will feel spongy and will not spring back when your finger is removed. Properly cooked poultry will feel firm to the touch and will spring back when your finger is removed. Overcooked poultry will feel very firm, almost hard, and will spring back quickly when your finger is removed.

Accompaniments to Sautéed Poultry

Sautéed poultry is usually served with a sauce made directly in the pan in which the item was cooked. The sauce uses the fond for added flavor. A wide variety of ingredients, including garlic, onions, shallots, mushrooms and tomatoes, are commonly added to the pan as well as wine and stock. Table 11.5 suggests several sauces for sautéed poultry.

Sautéed items are often served with a starch such as pasta, rice or potatoes.

▶ PROCEDURE FOR SAUTÉING POULTRY

1. Heat a sauté pan and add enough fat or oil to just cover the bottom.
2. Add the poultry item, presentation side down, and cook until browned.
3. Turn the item, using tongs or by tossing the item back on itself using the pan's sloped sides.
4. Larger items can be finished in an oven. Either place the sauté pan in the oven or transfer the poultry to another pan. The latter procedure allows a sauce to be made in the original pan while the poultry cooks in the oven. Hold smaller pieces that are thoroughly cooked in a warm place so that the pan can be used for making the sauce.

▶ PROCEDURE FOR PREPARING A SAUCE IN THE SAUTÉ PAN

1. Pour off any excess fat or oil from the sauté pan, leaving enough to sauté the sauce ingredients.
2. Add ingredients such as garlic, shallots and mushrooms that will be used as garnishes and sauce flavorings; sauté them.
3. Deglaze the pan with wine, stock or other liquids. Scrape the pan, loosening the fond and allowing it to dissolve in the liquid. Reduce the liquid.
4. Add any ingredients that do not require long cooking times such as herbs and spices. Adjust the sauce's consistency and seasonings.
5. For service, the poultry can be returned to the pan for a moment to reheat it and to coat it with the sauce. The poultry should remain in the sauce just long enough to reheat. Do not attempt to cook the poultry in the sauce.
6. Serve the poultry with the accompanying sauce.

CHICKEN SAUTÉ WITH ONIONS, GARLIC AND BASIL

RECIPE 16.5

Yield: 6 Servings, 5 oz. (150 g) each **Method:** Sautéing

Chicken breasts, boneless, skinless, approx. 8 oz. (250 g) each	3	3
Salt and pepper	TT	TT
Flour	as needed for dredging	
Clarified butter	1 fl. oz.	30 ml
Onion, small dice	2 oz.	60 g
Garlic cloves, chopped	6	6
Dry white wine	4 fl. oz.	120 ml
Lemon juice	1 Tbsp.	15 ml
Tomato concassée	6 oz.	180 g
Chicken stock	4 fl. oz.	120 ml
Fresh basil leaves, chiffonade	6	6

1. Split the chicken breasts and remove the cartilage connecting the two halves.
2. Season the chicken with salt and pepper; dredge in flour.
3. Sauté the breasts in the butter, browning them and cooking à point. Hold in a warm place.
4. Add the onion and garlic to the fond and butter in the pan; sauté until the onions are translucent.
5. Deglaze the pan with the wine and lemon juice.
6. Add the tomato concassée and stock. Sauté to combine the flavors; reduce the sauce to the desired consistency.
7. Add the basil to the sauce and return the chicken breasts for reheating. Adjust the seasonings and serve one half breast per portion with a portion of the sauce.

Approximate values per 5-oz. (150-g) serving: **Calories** 230, **Total fat** 8 g, **Saturated fat** 3.5 g, **Cholesterol** 90 mg, **Sodium** 580 mg, **Total carbohydrates** 9 g, **Protein** 30 g, **Vitamin C** 10%, **Iron** 10%

Mise en Place

- ▶ Bone and skin chicken breasts.
- ▶ Peel onion and garlic and chop into fine dice.
- ▶ Slice basil in chiffonade.

1 Sautéing the breasts in butter.

2 The fond left in the pan after sautéing the chicken.

3 Sautéing the onions and garlic.

4 Deglazing the pan with white wine and lemon juice.

5 Adding tomatoes and chicken stock and sautéing to combine flavors.

6 Returning the chicken to the pan to reheat.

PAN-FRYING

Pan-fried poultry should be juicy. Its coating or batter should be crispy, golden brown, not excessively oily and free from any breaks that allow fat to penetrate. Both the poultry and the coating should be well seasoned.

Selecting Poultry to Pan-Fry

The most common pan-fried poultry is fried chicken. Young tender birds cut into small pieces produce the best results. Other cuts commonly pan-fried are boneless portions such as chicken breasts and turkey scallops.

Seasoning Poultry to Be Pan-Fried

Pan-fried poultry is usually floured, breaded or battered before cooking. (Breadings and batters are discussed in Chapter 7, Mise en Place.) Typically, the seasonings are added to the flour, breading or batter before the poultry is coated. Seasonings can be a blend of any number of dried herbs and spices. But often only salt and pepper are required because the poultry will be served with a sauce or other accompaniments for additional flavors.

Cooking Temperatures

The fat should always be hot before the poultry is added. The temperature at which it is cooked is determined by the length of time required to cook it thoroughly. Pan-frying generally requires slightly lower temperatures than those used for sautéing. Within this range, thinner items require higher temperatures to produce good color in a relatively short time. Thicker items and those containing bones require lower cooking temperatures and longer cooking times.

Determining Doneness

Even the largest pan-fried items may be too small to be accurately tested with an instant-read thermometer, and using the touch method can be difficult and dangerous because of the amount of fat used in pan-frying. So timing and experience are the best tools to determine doneness. Thin scallops cook very quickly, so it is relatively easy to judge their doneness. On the other hand, fried chicken can take as long as 30–45 minutes to cook, requiring skill and experience to determine doneness.

Accompaniments to Pan-Fried Poultry

Because pan-frying does not produce fond or drippings that can be used to make a sauce, pan-fried poultry is usually served with lemon wedges, a vegetable garnish or a separately made sauce. Fried chicken is an exception; it is sometimes served with a country gravy made by degreasing the pan, making a roux with a portion of the fat and adding milk and seasonings.

▶ PROCEDURE FOR PAN-FRYING POULTRY

1. Heat enough fat in a heavy sauté pan to cover the item to be cooked one-fourth to halfway up its side. The fat should be at approximately 325°F (160°C).
2. Add the floured, breaded or battered item to the hot fat, being careful not to splash. The fat must be hot enough to sizzle and bubble when the item is added.
3. Turn the item when the first side is the proper color; it should be half cooked at this point. Larger items may need to be turned more than once to brown them properly on all sides.
4. Remove the browned poultry from the pan and drain it on absorbent paper.

PAN-FRIED CHICKEN WITH PAN GRAVY

RECIPE 16.6

Yield: 8 Servings, 2 pieces each

Method: Pan-frying

Frying chickens, 2 lb. 8 oz.–3 lb. (1.1–1.4 kg) each, cut into 8 pieces	2	2
Salt and pepper	TT	TT
Garlic powder	2 tsp.	10 ml
Onion powder	2 tsp.	10 ml
Dried oregano	1 tsp.	5 ml
Dried basil	1 tsp.	5 ml
Flour, seasoned	9½ oz.	270 g
Buttermilk	8 fl. oz.	250 ml
Oil	as needed	as needed
Onion, small dice	4 oz.	120 g
Half-and-half or chicken stock	1½ pt.	750 ml

1. Season the chicken with salt and pepper.
2. Add the herbs and spices to 8 ounces (250 grams) of the flour.
3. Dip the chicken pieces in the buttermilk.
4. Dredge the chicken in the seasoned flour.
5. Pan-fry the chicken in oil until done, approximately 40 minutes, turning so that it cooks evenly. Reduce the heat as necessary to prevent the chicken from becoming too dark. Or remove the chicken when well browned, drain it and finish cooking it in the oven.
6. To make the pan gravy, pour off all but 3 tablespoons (45 milliliters) oil from the pan, carefully reserving the fond.
7. Add the diced onion and sauté until translucent.
8. Add 1½ ounces (45 grams) flour and cook to make a blond roux.
9. Whisk in the liquid and simmer approximately 15 minutes.
10. Strain through cheesecloth and adjust the seasonings.
11. Serve 2 pieces of chicken per person with 4 fluid ounces (120 milliliters) gravy.

Approximate values per 2-piece serving (6–7 ounces), before frying: **Calories** 650, **Total fat** 31 g, **Saturated fat** 12 g, **Cholesterol** 190 mg, **Sodium** 190 mg, **Total carbohydrates** 32 g, **Protein** 57 g, **Fiber** 1 g, **Vitamin A** 15%, **Vitamin C** 4%, **Calcium** 15%, **Iron** 20%

Mise en Place

- ▶ Cut chicken into eight pieces.
- ▶ Season flour with salt and pepper.
- ▶ Peel onion and chop into small dice.

1 Dredging the chicken in the flour mixture.

2 Adding the chicken to the oil. The bubbling fat indicates the proper cooking temperature.

3 Turning the chicken so that it cooks evenly.

4 Sautéing the diced onions until translucent.

5 Adding the liquid to the roux.

DEEP-FRYING

Young, tender poultry is an excellent and popular choice for deep-frying. The pieces should be golden brown on the outside and moist and tender on the inside. They should be neither greasy nor tough. Chopped cooked poultry can also be mixed with a heavy béchamel or velouté sauce and seasonings, breaded and deep-fried as croquettes, which are discussed in Chapter 18, Fish and Shellfish.

Selecting and Seasoning Poultry to Be Deep-Fried

Portioned chickens and whole small birds, such as Rock Cornish game hen, are best for deep-frying. Although they can be marinated or seasoned directly, it is more common to season the batter or breading that will coat them. Additional flavors come from the sauces and accompaniments served with the deep-fried poultry. Lemon wedges, sweet and sour sauce or tangy barbecue sauces are popular accompaniments to deep-fried poultry.

▶ PROCEDURE FOR DEEP-FRYING POULTRY

1. Cut, trim or otherwise prepare the poultry to be deep-fried. Season and bread or batter it, as desired.
2. Heat the fat to the desired temperature, usually around 350°F (177°C). Breaded or battered poultry cooks quickly and the fat must be hot enough to cook the food's interior without burning its surface.
3. Carefully place the poultry in the hot fat using the basket method.
4. Deep-fry the food until done. It should have a crispy, golden brown surface.
5. Remove the deep-fried poultry from the fat and hold it over the fat, allowing the excess fat to drain. Transfer the food to a hotel pan either lined with absorbent paper or fitted with a rack. Season with salt, if desired.
6. If the deep-fried poultry is to be held for later service, place it under a heat lamp.

SPICY FRIED CHICKEN TENDERS WITH CHIPOTLE DIPPING SAUCE

RECIPE 16.7

Yield: 4 Servings **Method:** Deep-frying

Chicken tenders (or tenderloins), tendons removed	24	24
Seasoned flour:		
Flour	8 oz.	450 g
Chilli powder	3 Tbsp.	45 ml
Paprika	3 Tbsp.	45 ml
Granulated garlic	2 Tbsp.	30 ml
Black pepper	2 tsp.	10 ml
Cayenne pepper	1 Tbsp.	15 ml
Dried thyme	1 Tbsp.	15 ml
Dried oregano	1 Tbsp.	15 ml
Salt	3 Tbsp.	45 ml
Egg wash:		
Eggs	4	4
Milk	4 Tbsp.	120 ml
Bread crumbs	as needed	as needed
Sauce:		
Barbecue Sauce	8 fl. oz.	240 ml
Chipotle peppers, canned, puréed	1 Tbsp.	15 ml
Honey	1 oz.	60 g

1 Lightly pound the chicken pieces to an even thickness.
2 Combine the ingredients for the seasoned flour.
3 Beat the eggs and milk.
4 Bread the chicken tenders using the standard breading procedure described in Chapter 7, Mise en Place, placing each fully breaded piece on a parchment-lined sheet pan. Refrigerate until ready to cook.
5 Place the sauce ingredients in a small saucepan and simmer until the flavors blend, approximately 5 minutes.
6 Using the basket method, deep-fry the chicken pieces at 325°F (160°C) until done, approximately 4 minutes. Drain and serve with the warm sauce.

Approximate values per serving: **Calories** 380, **Total fat** 12 g, **Saturated fat** 2.5 g, **Cholesterol** 160 mg, **Sodium** 2680 mg, **Total carbohydrates** 33 g, **Protein** 34 g, **Vitamin A** 60%, **Vitamin C** 15%, **Iron** 25%

Mise en Place

▶ Remove tendons from chicken.

MOIST-HEAT COOKING METHODS

The moist-heat cooking methods most often used with poultry are poaching and simmering. Poaching is used to cook tender birds for short periods. Simmering is used to cook older, tougher birds for longer periods in order to tenderize them. Poaching and simmering are similar procedures, the principal differences being the temperature of the cooking liquid and the length of cooking time.

POACHING AND SIMMERING

Poached or simmered poultry should be moist, tender and delicately flavored. Although the poultry is cooked in water, overcooking will cause it to become dry and tough. During cooking, some of the poultry's flavor is transferred to the cooking liquid, which can be used to make a sauce for the finished product.

Selecting Poultry to Poach or Simmer

Young birds are best suited for poaching; boneless chicken pieces are the most commonly used parts. Older, tougher birds are usually simmered. Duck and geese are rarely poached or simmered because of their high fat content.

Seasoning Poultry to Be Poached or Simmered

When poaching poultry, it is especially important to use a well-seasoned and highly flavored liquid in order to infuse as much flavor as possible into the item being cooked. Either strong stock with a sachet or a mixture of stock or water and white wine with a bouquet garni or onion piquet produces good results. The poultry should be completely covered with liquid so that it cooks evenly. However, if too much liquid is used and it is not strongly flavored, flavors may be leached out of the poultry, resulting in a bland finished product.

Poultry is often simmered in water instead of stock. A sachet and a generous mirepoix should be added to help flavor it. Typically, simmering birds results in a strong broth that may be used to complete the recipe or reserved for other uses.

Cooking Temperatures

For best results, poultry should be poached at low temperatures, between 160°F and 175°F (71°C and 79°C). Cooking poultry to the proper doneness at these temperatures produces a product that is moist and tender.

Simmering is done at slightly higher temperatures, between 185°F (85°C) and the boiling point. When simmering, do not allow the liquid to boil, as this may result in a dry, tough and stringy finished product.

Determining Doneness

Poached poultry, whether whole or boneless, is cooked just until done. An instant-read thermometer inserted in the thigh or thicker part of the bird should read 165°F (74°C). Any juices that run from the bird should be clear or show only a trace of pink.

Simmered poultry is usually cooked for longer periods to allow the moist heat to tenderize the meat. A chicken that weighs 3 pounds 8 ounces (1.5 kilograms), for example, may take 2½ hours to cook.

Accompaniments to Poached or Simmered Poultry

Poached or simmered poultry can be served hot or cold. The meat from these birds can be served cold in salads, served hot in casseroles or used in any dish that calls for cooked poultry.

Poached items are typically served with a flavored mayonnaise or a sauce made from the reduced poaching liquid, such as sauce suprême. Poultry is also often poached as a means of producing a low-calorie dish. If so, a vegetable coulis makes a good sauce, or the poultry can be served with a portion of its cooking liquid and a vegetable garnish.

Simmered poultry to be served cold will be moister and more flavorful if it is cooled in its cooking liquid. To do so, remove the pot containing the bird and the cooking liquid from the heat when the bird is still slightly undercooked. Cool the meat and broth in a water bath following the procedure in Chapter 9, Stocks and Sauces. Once cooled, remove the meat and wipe off any congealed broth before proceeding with the recipe.

▶ PROCEDURE FOR POACHING OR SIMMERING POULTRY

1. Cut or truss the item to be cooked as directed in the recipe.
2. Prepare the cooking liquid and bring it to a simmer. Submerge the poultry in the cooking liquid, or arrange the items to be poached in an appropriate pan and add the poaching liquid to the pan.
3. Poach or simmer the item to the desired doneness in the oven or on the stove top. Maintain the proper cooking temperature throughout the process.
4. Remove the poultry and hold it for service in a portion of the cooking liquid or, using an ice bath, cool the item in its cooking liquid.
5. The cooking liquid may be used to prepare an accompanying sauce or reserved for use in other dishes.

POACHED BREAST OF CHICKEN WITH TARRAGON SAUCE

RECIPE 16.8

Yield: 8 Servings, 4 oz. (120 g) each **Method:** Poaching

Chicken breasts, boneless, skinless, approx. 8 oz. (250 g) each	4	4
Whole butter	$1\frac{1}{2}$ oz.	45 g
Salt and white pepper	TT	TT
White wine	4 fl. oz.	120 ml
Chicken stock	1 pt.	450 ml
Bay leaf	1	1
Dried thyme	$\frac{1}{4}$ tsp.	1 ml
Dried tarragon	1 tsp.	5 ml
Flour	1 oz.	30 g
Heavy cream	4 fl. oz.	120 ml
Fresh tarragon sprigs	as needed for garnish	

1 Trim any rib meat and fat from the breasts. Cut the breasts into two pieces, removing the strip of cartilage that joins the halves.
2 Select a pan that will just hold the breasts when they are placed close together. Rub the pan with approximately ½ ounce (15 grams) butter.
3 Season the chicken breasts with salt and white pepper and arrange them in the buttered pan, presentation side up.
4 Add the wine, stock, bay leaf, thyme and dried tarragon.
5 Cut and butter a piece of parchment paper and cover the chicken breasts.
6 Bring the liquid to a simmer and reduce the temperature to poach the chicken.
7 Make a blond roux with 1 ounce (30 grams) butter and the flour; set aside to cool.
8 When the breasts are done, remove them from the liquid. Thicken the liquid with the roux. Add the cream. Simmer and reduce to the desired consistency.
9 Strain the sauce through cheesecloth and adjust the seasonings.
10 Serve each half breast napped with approximately 2 fluid ounces (60 milliliters) sauce; garnish each portion with a sprig of fresh tarragon.

Approximate values per 4-oz. (115-g) serving: **Calories** 250, **Total fat** 13 g, **Saturated fat** 7 g, **Cholesterol** 105 mg, **Sodium** 590 mg, **Total carbohydrates** 4 g, **Protein** 29 g, **Vitamin A** 10%

Mise en Place

▶ Bone and skin the chicken breasts.

1 Arranging the breasts in an appropriate pan.

2 Adding the white wine, chicken stock and seasonings to the pan.

3 Covering the breasts with a piece of buttered parchment paper.

4 Adding the cream to the thickened sauce.

5 Plating the poached chicken breast.

COMBINATION COOKING METHODS

Braising and stewing use both dry and moist heat to produce a moist, flavorful product. The principal difference between braising and stewing when applied to meats is the size of the cut being cooked: Large cuts of meat are braised; smaller ones are stewed. Because most poultry is relatively small, this distinction does not readily apply in poultry cookery; therefore, the two cooking methods are discussed together here.

BRAISING AND STEWING

Braised or stewed poultry should be moist and fork tender. The poultry is always served with the liquid in which it was cooked. Ducks and geese are braised or stewed in much the same way as red meats. Chicken cacciatore, coq au vin and chicken fricassee are examples of braised or stewed chicken dishes.

Selecting Poultry to Braise or Stew

Braising and stewing, being slow, moist cooking processes, are often thought of as a means to tenderize tough meats. Although they can be used to tenderize older, tougher birds, these cooking methods are more often selected as a means of adding moisture and flavor to poultry that is inherently tender, such as young ducks and chickens. Typically, the birds are disjointed and cooked bone-in, just until done, so that they retain their juiciness.

Seasoning Poultry to Be Braised or Stewed

Braised or stewed items obtain much of their flavor from the cooking liquid and other ingredients added during the cooking process. The main item and the cooking liquid should be well seasoned. If other seasonings such as an onion piquet, sachet, bouquet garni or dried herbs and spices are required, they should be added at the beginning of the cooking process rather than at the end. This allows the flavors to blend and penetrate the larger pieces of poultry. If the poultry is dredged in flour prior to browning, seasonings may be added directly to the flour. As with all dishes using combination cooking methods, the finished dish should have the flavor of the poultry in the sauce and the moisture and flavor of the sauce in the poultry.

Cooking Temperatures

Some recipes, such as chicken cacciatore and coq au vin, require the main item to be thoroughly browned during the initial stages; others, such as chicken fricassee, do not. In either case, after the liquid is added, it is important to maintain a slow simmer rather than a rapid boil. This can be done on the stove top or in the oven. Low temperatures control the cooking and produce a tender, juicy finished product.

Determining Doneness

Tenderness is the key to determining doneness. It can be determined by inserting a kitchen fork into the poultry. There should be little resistance, and the poultry should freely fall off the fork. The pieces should retain their shape, however; if they fall apart, they are overdone. Small boneless pieces can be tested by cutting into them with a fork.

Accompaniments to Braised or Stewed Poultry

All braises and stews are cooked in a liquid that results in a sauce or broth served as part of the finished dish. Rice, pasta or boiled potatoes are natural accompaniments to almost any braised or stewed dish, as are boiled vegetables.

▶ PROCEDURE FOR BRAISING OR STEWING POULTRY

1 Sear the main item in butter or oil, developing color as desired.
2 Add vegetables and other ingredients as called for in the recipe and sauté.
3 Add flour or roux if used.
4 Add the appropriate liquid.
5 Cover and simmer on the stove top or in the oven until done.
6 Add seasonings and garnishes at the appropriate times during the cooking process.
7 Finish the dish by adding cream or a liaison to the sauce or by adjusting its consistency. Adjust the seasonings.
8 Serve a portion of the poultry with the sauce and appropriate garnish.

CHICKEN FRICASSEE

RECIPE 16.9

Yield: 8 Servings, 2 pieces each

Method: Braising

Frying chickens, 2 lb. 8 oz.–3 lb. (1.1–1.4 kg) each, cut into 8 pieces	2	2
Salt and white pepper	TT	TT
Clarified butter	3 fl. oz.	90 ml
Onions, medium dice	10 oz.	300 g
Flour	3 oz.	90 g
Dry white wine	8 fl. oz.	250 ml
Chicken stock	1 qt.	1 lt
Sachet:		
Bay leaf	1	1
Dried thyme	½ tsp.	2 ml
Peppercorns, cracked	½ tsp.	2 ml
Parsley stems	8	8
Garlic clove, crushed	1	1
Heavy cream	8 fl. oz.	250 ml
Nutmeg	TT	TT

1 Season the chicken with salt and white pepper.
2 Sauté the chicken in the butter without browning. Add the onions and continue to sauté until they are translucent.
3 Sprinkle the flour over the chicken and onions and stir to make a roux. Cook the roux for 2 minutes without browning.
4 Deglaze the pan with the wine. Add the stock and sachet; season with salt. Cover and simmer until done, approximately 30 to 45 minutes.
5 Remove the chicken from the pan and hold in a warm place. Strain the sauce through cheesecloth and return it to a clean pan.
6 Add the cream and bring the sauce to a simmer. Add the nutmeg and adjust the seasonings. Return the chicken to the sauce to reheat it for service.

Approximate values per 8-oz. (240-g) serving: **Calories** 700, **Total fat** 20 g, **Saturated fat** 12 g, **Cholesterol** 60 mg, **Sodium** 795 mg, **Total carbohydrates** 113 g, **Protein** 15 g, **Vitamin A** 20%

Mise en Place

- ▶ Cut chickens into 8 pieces.
- ▶ Peel onions and chop into medium dice.
- ▶ Prepare herb sachet.

1 Sautéing the chicken and onions in butter.

2 Sprinkling the flour over the chicken.

3 Deglazing the pan with white wine.

4 Removing the chicken from the pot.

5 Straining the sauce through cheesecloth.

6 Returning the chicken to the sauce to reheat it for service.

CONCLUSION

The renowned French gastronome and author Jean-Anthelme Brillat-Savarin (1755–1826) once observed that "poultry is for the cook what canvas is for the painter." He meant, of course, that poultry, including chicken, duck, goose, guinea, pigeon and turkey, are wonderfully versatile foods that can be cooked by almost any method and with almost any seasonings, and can be served with many accompaniments and garnishes.

QUESTIONS FOR DISCUSSION

1. List the six categories or kinds of poultry recognized by the USDA. How are these categories then divided into classes?
2. How should fresh poultry be stored? Discuss several procedures that should be followed carefully when working with poultry to prevent cross-contamination.
3. What is a suprême? Describe the step-by-step procedure for preparing a chicken suprême.
4. What is trussing? Why is this technique used with poultry?
5. Which poultry items are best suited for broiling or grilling? Explain your answer.
6. Describe the characteristics of properly roasted poultry. Which classes of poultry are recommended for roasting?
7. What is foie gras? Why must you be extremely careful when cooking foie gras?

CHAPTER SEVENTEEN

GAME

ONE CAN NEVER KNOW TOO MUCH; THE MORE ONE LEARNS, THE MORE ONE SEES THE NEED TO LEARN MORE AND THAT STUDY AS WELL AS BROADENING THE MIND OF THE CRAFTSMAN PROVIDES AN EASY WAY OF PERFECTING YOURSELF IN THE PRACTICE OF YOUR ART.

—Auguste Escoffier, French chef (1846–1935)

THE SANCTUARY AT CAMELBACK, Paradise Valley, AZ
Executive Chef of Elements Charles Wiley

AFTER STUDYING THIS CHAPTER, YOU WILL BE ABLE TO:

- identify a variety of game
- understand game inspection practices
- purchase game appropriate for your needs
- store game properly
- prepare game for cooking
- apply various cooking methods to game

Game (Fr. *gibier*) are animals hunted for sport or food. Traditionally, game supplies depended on the season and the hunter's success. But game's increasing popularity in food service operations has led to farm-raising and animal husbandry techniques. As a result, pheasant, quail, deer, rabbit and other animals, although still considered game, are now farm- or ranch-raised and commercially available throughout the year.

The life of game creatures is reflected in their flesh's appearance, aroma, flavor and texture. Generally, game flesh has a dark color and a strong but not unpleasant aroma. It has a robust flavor and less fat than other meats or poultry and is more compact, becoming quite tough in older animals.

Selecting the best cooking methods for game depends on the animal's age and the particular cut of flesh. Younger animals will, of course, be more tender than older ones. Flesh from the loin or less-used muscles will also be tender and therefore can be prepared with dry-heat cooking methods. Flesh from much-used muscles, such as the leg and shoulder, will be tougher and should be prepared with combination cooking methods. Less-tender cuts can also be used in sausages, pâtés and forcemeats, as discussed in Chapter 26, Charcuterie.

▸ IDENTIFYING GAME

FURRED OR GROUND GAME

Furred game includes large animals such as deer, moose, bear, wild boar and elk as well as smaller animals such as rabbit, squirrel, raccoon and opossum. Although these animals (and many others) are hunted for sport and food, only a few species are widely available to food service operations.

Although venison, boar and elk may seem unusual to many Americans, even rarer meats are available to the daring diner. Zebra, bear, wildebeest and other "big game" animals are sometimes available through exotic game purveyors. Most often these meats are grilled, roasted or stewed.

Reptiles, particularly rattlesnake and alligator, are now also being raised on farms to meet increased demand. Reptiles are usually braised, or sliced and deep-fried. They have a mild flavor with a texture similar to lobster.

Large game animals are rarely sold whole or in primal portions. Instead, the meat is available precut into subprimals or portions. So, except for those that are used for rabbits, this chapter does not provide butchering techniques.

ANTELOPE

The blackbuck antelope, about half the size of a large deer, is ranch-raised in the United States. Although it has almost no body fat, the meat retains a high amount of moisture. The meat is fine-grained, with a flavor that is only slightly stronger than that of deer meat (venison). It should be butchered and cooked in a manner similar to venison.

BISON (AMERICAN BUFFALO)

Once found in huge herds roaming the plains states, bison or buffalo were hunted into near-extinction during the 19th century. Buffalo now live on reservations or ranches, where they are raised like beef cattle. Their meat is juicy and flavorful and may be prepared in the same manner as lean beef.

Buffalo Steak

DEER

The deer family includes elk, moose, reindeer, red-tailed deer, white-tailed deer (Fr. *chevreuil*) and mule deer. Meat from any of these animals is known as **venison** (Fr. *venaisan*). Farm-raised venison, particularly from the Scottish red deer bred in New Zealand and the United States, is commercially available all year. Axis deer, a species originally from India and Nepal, provides some of the finest-quality venison. Like cattle, axis deer graze on grass, so their meat is especially mild and tender. Venison is typically dark red with a mild aroma. It is leaner than other meats, having almost no intramuscular fat or marbling.

▶ **venison** flesh from any member of the deer family, including antelope, elk, moose, reindeer, red-tailed deer, white-tailed deer, mule deer and axis deer

The most popular commercial venison cuts are the loin, leg and rack. The loin is tender enough to roast, sauté or grill to medium rare. It can be left attached along the backbone to form a cut known as the saddle. The leg is often marinated in red wine and prepared with combination cooking methods. Other cuts can also be stewed or braised or used in sausages and pâtés. Butchering procedures for venison are similar to those for lamb discussed in Chapter 14.

Venison Saddle

RABBIT

Rabbits (Fr. *lapin*) are small burrowing animals that have long been raised for food. Rabbit has mild, lean and relatively tender flesh. Its flavor and texture are similar to chicken. Ranch-raised rabbit is available all year, either whole or cut, fresh or frozen. The average weight of a whole dressed rabbit is 2 pounds 8 ounces to 3 pounds (1.2 to 1.4 kilograms). Young rabbit can be roasted, pan-fried, stewed or braised and is popular in rustic "country-style" dishes, especially casseroles and pâtés.

MEAT OF THE FUTURE: BEEFALO

Beefalo is produced by cross-breeding a bison with a domestic beef animal. To be a registered full-blooded beefalo, the animal has to be three-eighths bison and five-eighths domestic beef. The five-eighths domestic beef portion is not restricted to any breed; it is often a combination of two or more breeds such as Hereford, Angus or Charolais. In 1985, the USDA approved a special label for beefalo; it is labeled either "Beef from Beefalo" or "Beefalo Beef."

Beefalo looks and tastes much like modern beef. The animal itself is hard to distinguish from any other beef animal. Beefalo meat is tender because the animals gain weight faster and go to market at younger ages. The meat is slightly sweeter in taste than beef.

Beefalo is lower in cholesterol than beef, fish or chicken and lower in calories and fat than beef. It offers a great alternative to beef for the diet- and health-conscious guest. The per-pound cost of beefalo may be slightly higher than beef cuts, but its low amount of interior and exterior fat gives it a higher yield with a price per usable pound comparable to beef.

Because of beefalo's finer fiber and low fat content, it cooks in one-third to one-half the time of beef and should be cooked to either rare or medium rare.

JAMES J. MUTH, MBA, CFBE, is a Chef Instructor at Grand Rapids Community College, Grand Rapids, MI.

▶ PROCEDURE FOR BUTCHERING A RABBIT

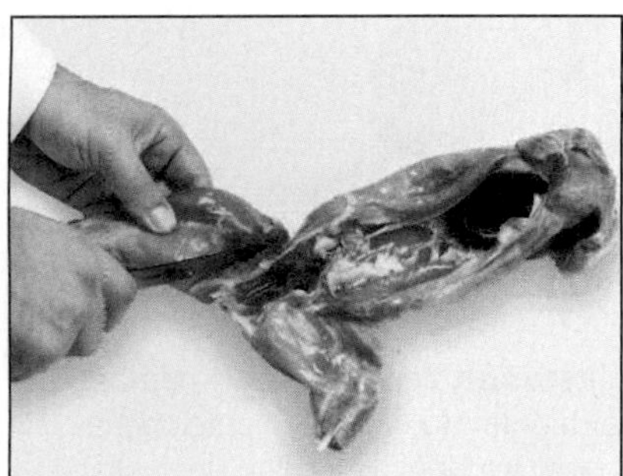

1 Place the rabbit on its back. Remove the hind legs by cutting close to the backbone and through the joint on each side. Each thigh and leg can be separated by cutting through the joint.

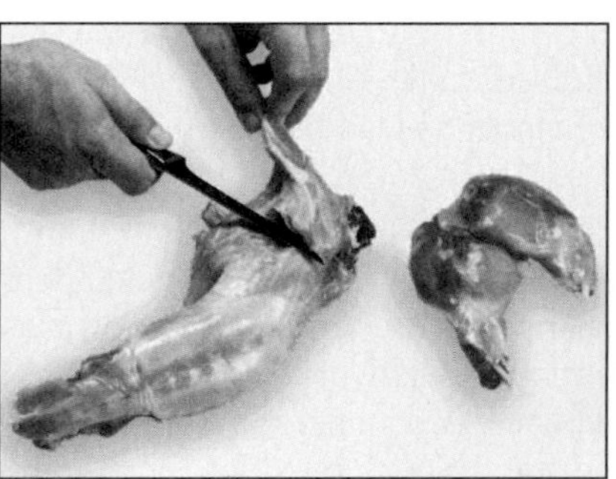

2 Remove the forelegs by cutting beneath the shoulder blades.

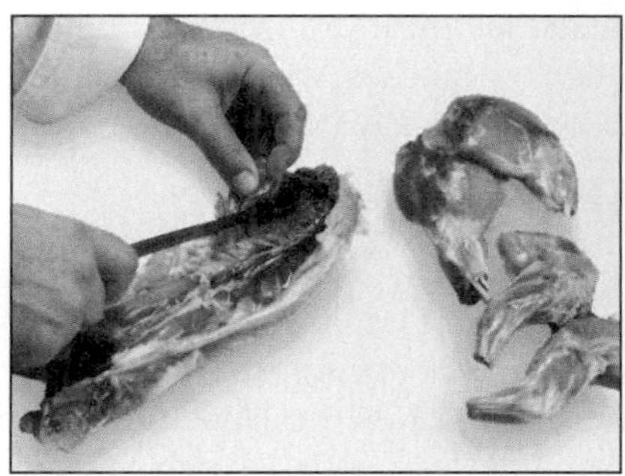

3 Cut through the breast bone and spread open the rib cage. Using a boning knife, separate the flesh from the rib bones and remove the bones.

4 Cut through the backbone to divide the loin into the desired number of pieces.

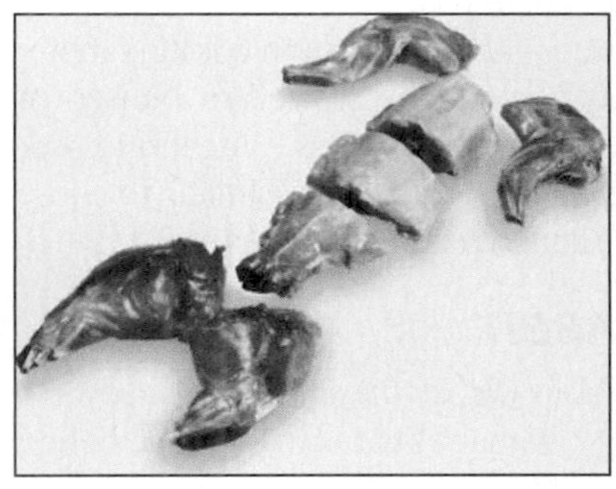

5 The cut-up rabbit: hind legs, thighs, loin in three pieces, forelegs.

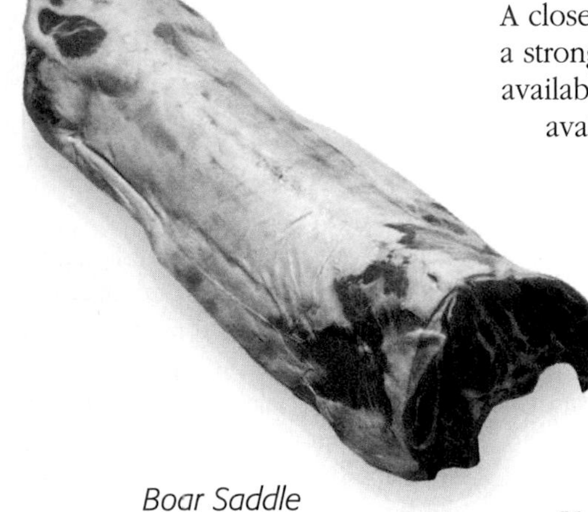

Boar Saddle

WILD BOAR

A close relative of the domesticated hog, wild boar (Fr. *sanglier*) is leaner, with a stronger flavor. Though plentiful in Europe and parts of America, wild boar is available only during autumn. A limited supply of farm- or ranch-raised boar is available all year, however.

Baby boar (under six months old) is considered a delicacy, but mature animals (one to two years old) have the best flavor. The meat is most often roasted and may be used in sausages or terrines. Boar can often be substituted in recipes for venison or pork.

FEATHERED OR WINGED GAME

Feathered game includes upland birds such as wild turkeys, pheasants, quails, doves and woodcocks; songbirds such as larks; and waterfowl such as wild geese and ducks. Wild birds cannot be sold in the United States. An ever-increasing number of these birds are being farm-raised to meet consumer demand, however.

Game birds are available whole or precut into pieces, fresh or frozen. Butchering techniques will not be shown in this chapter, as they are the same as those for domesticated poultry discussed in Chapter 16.

Table 17.1 USING FURRED GAME

ANIMAL	COMMONLY PURCHASED CUTS	COOKING METHODS	SUGGESTED USE
Antelope	Purchased and prepared in the same manner as deer		
Bison	Purchased and prepared in the same manner as lean beef		
Deer	Loin	Dry heat (roast; sauté; grill)	Sautéed medallions; whole roast loin; grilled steaks
	Leg	Combination (braise; stew)	Marinate and braise; pot roast with cranberries; chili; sausage; forcemeat
	Rack	Dry heat (roast; grill)	Grilled chops
Rabbit	Full carcass	Dry heat (sauté; pan-fry; roast; grill) Combination (braise; stew)	Pan-fried rabbit with cream gravy Braised rabbit with mushrooms
Wild boar	Loin Chops	Dry heat (roast) Combination (braise)	Roast loin with mustard crust Marinate and braise; stew with red wine and sour cream; sausage; forcemeat

Because game birds tend to have less fat than other poultry, they are often barded with fat and cooked to medium rare. If cooked well done, they become dry and stringy.

PARTRIDGE

The Hungarian and chukar partridges (Fr. *perdrix*) of Europe were introduced into the United States and Canada during the 19th century. Now found principally in the prairie and western mountain states, partridges are widely raised on game preserves and farms, producing a good commercial supply. The flavor of partridge is less delicate than that of pheasant, and the meat tends to be tougher. Partridge may be roasted or cut into pieces and sautéed or braised. Each bird weighs about 1 pound (450 grams) dressed.

Chukar Partridge

PHEASANT

The most popular of game birds, the pheasant (Fr. *faisan*) was introduced into Europe from Asia during the Middle Ages. Its mild flavor is excellent for roasting, stewing or braising. The hen is smaller and more tender than the cock. Stock made from the carcass is often used for consommé or sauce. Farm-raised birds are available fresh or frozen. A dressed bird weighs about 1 pound 8 ounces to 2 pounds 4 ounces (680 grams to 1 kilogram) and serves two people.

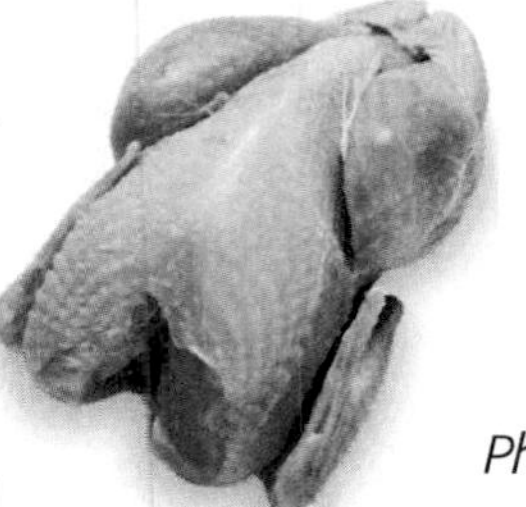

Pheasant

QUAIL

The quail (Fr. *caille*) is a migratory game bird related to the pheasant. The more popular European and Californian species are farm-raised and available all year.

Quail are very small, with only about 1 to 2 ounces (30 to 60 grams) of breast meat each. Quail may be grilled (especially on skewers), roasted, broiled or sautéed and are often boned and served whole with a stuffing of forcemeat or rice. Because they are so lean, roasted quail benefit from barding.

Quail

WILD GAME—DELICIOUS, NUTRITIOUS AND AVAILABLE

Wild game is now widely available for use in restaurants and at home. The best of wild game provides a safe, delicious and nutritious dining experience.

In almost all states, our native game animals are protected from harvesting for commercial purposes. It is a violation of state wildlife laws to kill and sell the meat from native species such as the whitetail deer, mule deer, pronghorn antelope, and so on. These laws were written when only native game was present in America. Since then, a growing number of nonnative species of deer and antelope have been introduced to ranches in America, and this has made it possible to harvest deer and antelope legally for meat production.

Oddly enough, however, meats such as antelope, venison, rabbit, and most other game meats are not subject to inspection under federal and most state meat inspection regulations. This is not because the authorities do not believe the meat should be inspected. When the meat inspection laws were written, these meats were not legally available and therefore were not included in the Federal Meat Act. County and city health codes, however, do require that any meat served to the public must be from an "approved source," which is interpreted as "inspected." Therefore, any game meat served in a restaurant should be certified as inspected by either state or federal meat inspection authorities.

Game meat is available from farmed (domesticated) deer and from free-ranging (ranched) deer and antelope. Most farmed deer are taken to a fixed conventional slaughterhouse where they are slaughtered and processed in the same way as cattle, sheep and goats. Ranched deer can be properly harvested only by an elaborate procedure that involves taking a mobile slaughter facility and meat inspector to the field, where the animals are killed by shooting them with a high-powered rifle under the supervision of the meat inspector. The carcass is then processed inside the mobile facility to avoid any contamination of the meat. This field harvesting eliminates any stress that might occur in transport of ranched deer to the slaughterhouse.

Farmed deer tend to be relatively more uniform in size and flavor. Free-ranging deer and antelope produce meat of more complex flavor due to the variety of their diet. The difference is somewhat like the difference in cultivated mushrooms and wild mushrooms, or pen-raised chickens compared with free-range chickens. Meat from free-range animals is more expensive due to higher labor and inspection costs.

Meat from both deer and antelope can be legally labeled "venison." All venison is relatively lean when compared with conventional red meats and requires special attention when cooking to avoid drying out the meat and toughening it. Tender cuts should be cooked as little as possible (rare to medium rare) to retain the maximum amount of moisture. Quick sautéing, grilling or roasting to retain a medium-rare center is most satisfactory for tender cuts such as the loin, tenderloin, and leg.

Braising is the most effective method for cooking the less tender cuts such as the shoulder, ribs and shanks. Beef broth and red wine are good liquids for braising. The toughest cut of meat will be very satisfactorily tenderized if braised for a sufficient period of time (which may be as long as two or three hours). When properly cooked, these cuts can surpass the more tender cuts in flavor.

MIKE HUGHES is the owner of the Broken Arrow Ranch in Ingram, TX.

▶ NUTRITION

Even ranch-raised game animals live in the wild and are generally more active and less well fed than domesticated animals. This lifestyle produces animals whose meat has less fat than that of domesticated animals. Most game is also lower in cholesterol and has approximately one-third fewer calories than beef. Game is also generally high in protein and minerals.

▶ INSPECTION OF GAME

The USDA and most states restrict the sale of wild game. Truly wild game can be served only by those who hunt and share their kill.

DOMESTIC GAME

Unlike meat and poultry from domesticated animals, game is not graded for quality. Farm- or ranch-raised game is subject only to voluntary inspections for wholesomeness. Generally, however, game is processed under the same federal inspection requirements as domesticated meats and poultry. State regulations vary and are constantly being expanded and improved in response to consumer demands.

IMPORTED GAME

Only USDA-approved countries are permitted to export game to the United States. On arrival in this country, game shipments are subject to USDA spot inspections.

▶ PURCHASING AND STORING GAME

PURCHASING GAME

Furred game meats are available fresh or frozen. Game birds are available cleaned and boned, fresh or frozen. Use the same criteria to determine the freshness of game as you would any other meat or poultry: The flesh should be firm, without slime or an off-odor.

Fresh game is sometimes hung before cooking to allow the meat to mature or age. During hanging, carbohydrates (glycogen) stored in muscle tissues are converted to lactic acid. This process tenderizes the flesh and strengthens its flavor. But hanging is not necessary, especially if you object to "gamy" flavors. Commercially sold game is generally fully aged and ready to use when delivered. It does not need, nor will it benefit from, hanging.

STORING GAME

As with any fresh or frozen meat, game should be well wrapped and stored under refrigeration at temperatures below 41°F (5°C). Because the flesh is generally dry and lean, frozen game should be used within four months. Thaw frozen game slowly under refrigeration to prevent moisture loss.

▶ MARINATING FURRED GAME

Tradition calls for marinating game, particularly furred game, in strong mixtures of red wine, herbs and spices. Commercially raised game does not necessarily have to be marinated. Modern animal husbandry techniques used at game ranches assure the chef of receiving meat from young, tender animals. Farm-raised game animals also have a naturally milder flavor than their truly wild cousins.

For those preferring the flavors imparted by traditional marinades, the following Red Wine Marinade, suitable for most game such as antelope, elk, rabbit, venison or wild boar, is included. After the meat is removed, the marinade may be added to the cooking liquid or reduced and used in a sauce. Do not serve uncooked marinade.

HOW TO HANG GAME

The following information may be useful if you find yourself with a need to hang freshly killed game. Most game should be eviscerated (drawn or gutted) as soon as possible, then suspended by either the hind legs or the head in a dry, well-ventilated place. Because the fur or feathers help prevent bacterial contamination, they should be left intact during hanging; game should be skinned or plucked just before butchering. The length of time necessary for hanging depends on the species and age of the animal. Two days may be sufficient for a rabbit, while up to three weeks may be necessary for a deer or boar. Hanging is generally complete when the first whiff of odor is detected (although traditionalists prefer pheasant to be hung until extremely ripe).

RECIPE 17.1

RED WINE MARINADE

Mise en Place

▶ Peel and finely chop the carrot and onions. Peel and mince the garlic.

Yield: 1½ qt. (1.5 lt)

Carrot, chopped fine	2 oz.	60 g
Onion, chopped fine	2 oz.	60 g
Garlic, minced	1 Tbsp.	15 ml
Dried thyme	1 tsp.	5 ml
Bay leaves	2	2
Juniper berries, whole	2 tsp.	10 ml
Peppercorns, whole	1 Tbsp.	15 ml
Sage, ground	½ tsp.	2 ml
Red wine	1 qt.	1 lt
Red wine vinegar	4 fl. oz.	120 ml

1 Combine all ingredients.
2 Place the meat in the marinade and marinate for the desired time. Tender, farm-raised game may need only 30 minutes; older, wild animals may need 1 to 2 days.

Approximate values per 1-fl.-oz. (30-ml): **Calories** 5, **Total fat** 0 g, **Saturated fat** 0 g, **Cholesterol** 0 mg, **Sodium** 0 mg, **Total carbohydrates** 1 g, **Protein** 0 g, **Vitamin A** 6%, **Claims—**fat free; no saturated fat; no cholesterol; no sodium; low calorie

CONCLUSION

Game is becoming increasingly popular because of consumer desires for leaner, healthier meats. Only farm-raised game can be used in food service operations. Luckily, many popular game items are now farm-raised, government-inspected and readily available. Generally, game flesh has a dark color, a strong but not unpleasant aroma and a robust flavor. You should butcher, prepare and cook game according to the comparable guidelines for other meats and poultry.

QUESTIONS FOR DISCUSSION

1 Explain the differences between truly wild game and ranch-raised game.
2 What is hanging? Is it necessary for modern food service operations to hang game?
3 Which cuts of furred game are best suited to dry-heat cooking methods? Which are best for combination cooking methods?
4 Can game birds be purchased whole? How are they fabricated?
5 What degree of doneness is best suited for game birds? Explain your answer.
6 Texas is home to several large game ranches. Explore their Internet sites to learn more about the operation of game ranches and the varieties of venison available.

CHAPTER EIGHTEEN

IN THE HANDS OF AN ABLE COOK, FISH CAN BECOME AN INEXHAUSTIBLE SOURCE OF PERPETUAL DELIGHT.

—Jean-Anthelme Brillat-Savarin (1755–1826)

FISH AND SHELLFISH

PESCE RESTAURANT, Houston, TX
Chef Mark Holley

AFTER STUDYING THIS CHAPTER, YOU WILL BE ABLE TO:

- understand the structure and composition of fish and shellfish
- identify a variety of fish and shellfish
- purchase fish and shellfish appropriate for your needs
- store fish and shellfish properly
- prepare fish and shellfish for cooking
- apply various cooking methods to fish and shellfish

Fish are aquatic vertebrates with fins for swimming and gills for breathing. Of the more than 30,000 species known, most live in the seas and oceans; freshwater species are far less numerous. Shellfish are aquatic invertebrates with shells or carapaces. They are found in both fresh and salt water.

Always an important food source, fish and shellfish have become increasingly popular in recent years, due in part to demands from health-conscious consumers. Because of increased demand and improved preservation and transportation techniques, good-quality fish and shellfish, once found only along seacoasts and lakes, are now readily available to almost every food service operation.

Many fish and shellfish species are very expensive; all are highly perishable. Because their cooking times are generally shorter and their flavors more delicate than meat or poultry, special attention must be given to fish and shellfish to prevent spoilage and to produce high-quality finished products.

In this chapter, you will learn how to identify a large assortment of fish and shellfish as well as how to properly purchase and store them, fabricate or prepare them for cooking and cook them by a variety of dry-heat and moist-heat cooking methods. This chapter presents many of the cooking methods applied to meats and poultry in the previous chapters. Review the corresponding procedures for meats and poultry, and note the similarities and differences.

STRUCTURE AND MUSCLE COMPOSITION

The fish and shellfish used in food service operations can be divided into three categories: fish, mollusks and crustaceans.

Fish (Fr. *poisson*) include both fresh- and saltwater varieties. They have fins and an internal skeleton of bone and cartilage. Based on shape and skeletal structure, fish can be divided into two groups: round fish and flatfish. **Round fish** swim in a vertical position and have eyes on both sides of their heads (Figure 18.1). Their bodies may be truly round, oval or compressed. **Flatfish** have asymmetrical, compressed bodies, swim in a horizontal position and have both eyes on top of their heads (Figure 18.2). Flatfish are bottom dwellers; most are found in deep ocean waters around the world. The skin on top of their bodies is dark, to camouflage them from predators, and can change color according to their surroundings. Their scales are small, and their dorsal and anal fins run the length of their bodies.

Mollusks (Fr. *mollusque*) are shellfish characterized by soft, unsegmented bodies with no internal skeleton. Most mollusks have hard outer shells. Single-shelled mollusks such as abalone are known as **univalves.** Those with two shells, such as clams, oysters and mussels, are known as **bivalves.** Squid and octopus, which are known as **cephalopods,** do not have a hard outer shell. Rather, they have a single thin internal shell called a *pen* or *cuttlebone.*

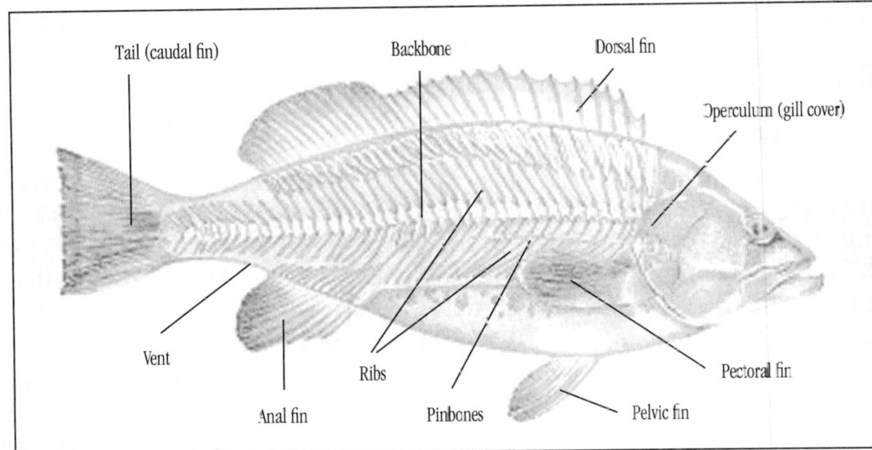

FIGURE 18.1 ▶ Bone structure of a round fish.

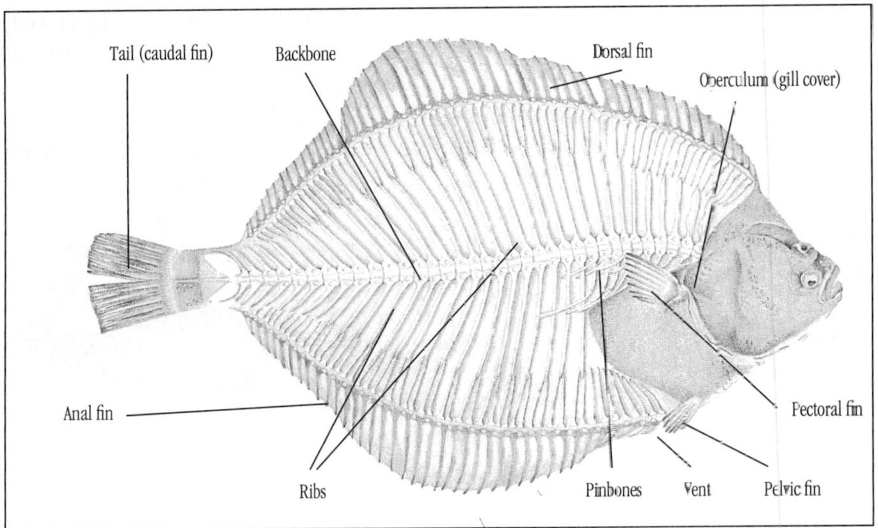

FIGURE 18.2 ▶ Bone structure of a flatfish.

SEAFOOD

Seafood means different things to different people. For some, the term applies only to shellfish or to shellfish and other small edible marine creatures. For others, it is limited to saltwater shellfish or to saltwater shellfish and fish. For yet others, it refers to all fish and shellfish, both freshwater and saltwater. Because of the term's vagueness, it is not used here.

Crustaceans (Fr. *crustacés*) are also shellfish. They have a hard outer skeleton or shell and jointed appendages. Crustaceans include lobsters, crabs and shrimp.

The flesh of fish and shellfish consists primarily of water, protein, fat and minerals. Fish flesh is composed of short muscle fibers separated by delicate sheets of connective tissue. Fish, as well as most shellfish, are naturally tender, so the purpose of cooking is to firm proteins and enhance flavor. The absence of the oxygen-carrying protein myoglobin makes fish flesh very light or white in color. (The orange color of salmon and some trout comes from pigments found in their food.) Compared to meats, fish do not contain large amounts of intermuscular fat. But the amount of fat a fish does contain affects the way it responds to cooking. Fish containing a relatively large amount of fat, such as salmon and mackerel, are known as fatty or oily fish. Fish such as cod and haddock contain very little fat and are referred to as lean fish. Shellfish are also very lean.

▶ Identifying Fish and Shellfish

Identifying fish and shellfish properly can be difficult because of the vast number of similar-appearing fish and shellfish that are separate species within each family. Adding confusion are the various colloquial names given to the same fish or the same name given to different fish in different localities. Fish with an unappealing name may also be given a catchier name or the name of a similar but more popular item for marketing purposes. Moreover, some species are referred to by a foreign name, especially on menus.

The FDA publishes a list of approved market names for food fish in *The Seafood List: FDA Guide to Acceptable Market Names for Food Fish Sold in Interstate Commerce 2002.* The list is updated regularly and available on the FDA's Web site at the Center for Food Safety and Applied Nutrition. Deviations from this list are strongly discouraged but difficult to enforce. We attempt to use the most common names for each item, whether they are zoologically accurate or not.

FISH

ROUND FISH

Bass (Fr. *bar*) commonly refers to a number of unrelated spiny-finned fish. The better-known freshwater bass varieties (largemouth, smallmouth, redeye and black) are actually members of the sunfish family. They are lean and delicate but, as game, not commercially available in the United States. The saltwater bass varieties (black sea bass and striped bass) are popular commercial items.

Black Sea Bass

Black sea bass are sometimes referred to as rock sea bass. They have a lean, firm white flesh with a mild flavor and flaky texture. They usually weigh from 1½ to 3 pounds (720 to 1360 grams) and are most prevalent in the Atlantic Ocean between New York and North Carolina. Black sea bass can be prepared by almost any cooking method and are often served whole in Chinese and Italian cuisines.

▶ **anadromous** describes a fish that migrates from a saltwater habitat to spawn in fresh water

▶ **aquafarming** also known as aquaculture; the business, science and practice of raising large quantities of fish and shellfish in tanks, ponds or ocean pens

Striped bass, often erroneously referred to as rockfish, are **anadromous.** True striped bass cannot be marketed because pollution and overfishing have damaged the supply. A hybrid of striped bass and either white bass or white perch is **aquafarmed** for commercial use, however. It is this hybrid that food service operations receive as striped bass. Whole fish weigh from 1 to 5 pounds (450 grams to 2.2 kilograms). Striped bass have a rich, sweet flavor and firm texture. They can be steamed, baked, poached or broiled.

Striped Bass

Catfish are scaleless freshwater fish common in southern lakes and rivers and now aquafarmed extensively. Aquafarm raising eliminates the "muddy" flavor once associated with catfish and ensures a year-round supply. The flesh is pure white with a moderate fat content; a mild, sweet flavor; and a firm texture. Channel catfish are the most important commercially. They usually weigh from 1½ to 5 pounds (720 grams to 2.2 kilograms). The smaller of these fish are known as **fiddlers;** they are often deep-fried and served whole. Catfish may be prepared by almost any cooking method, but are especially well suited to frying. Note that other species are often imported to the United States under the generic name *catfish*. Only products labeled "U.S. Farm-Raised Catfish" provide the consistent high quality and flavor that consumers have come to expect, however.

Catfish

The **cod** (Fr. *cabillaud*) family includes Atlantic and Pacific cod as well as pollock, haddock, whiting and hake. Cod have a mild, delicate flavor and lean, firm white flesh that flakes apart easily. Cod can be prepared by most cooking methods, although grilling is not recommended because the flesh is too flaky.

Atlantic cod are the best-selling fish in America. They are available fresh, whole or drawn, or cut into fillets or steaks. They are also available frozen and are often used for precooked or prebreaded sticks or portions. Smoked cod and dried salt cod (Sp. *bacalao*) are also available. Although cod may reach

Atlantic Cod

200 pounds (90 kilograms), most market cod weigh 10 pounds (4.4 kilograms) or less. **Scrod** is a marketing term for cod or haddock weighing less than 2½ pounds (1.1 kilograms) or less than 20 inches (50 centimeters) in length.

Haddock, the second most commercially important fish, look like thin, small Atlantic cod and weigh about 2 to 5 pounds (900 grams to 2.3 kilograms). They have a stronger flavor and more delicate texture than Atlantic cod.

Pacific cod, also known as gray cod, are found in the northern Pacific Ocean and are not as abundant as their Atlantic cousins. Pacific cod are most often available frozen; they should be labeled "true cod" to distinguish them from rock cod and black cod, which are unrelated.

Pollock, also known as Boston bluefish or blue cod, are plentiful in the northern Atlantic and Pacific Oceans. Their flesh is gray-pink when raw, turning white when cooked. Pollock are often frozen at sea, then reprocessed into surimi. They can also be salted or smoked.

Pollock

Eels (Fr. *anguilles*) are long, snakelike freshwater fish with dorsal and anal fins running the length of their bodies. (The conger eel is from a different family and has little culinary significance.) American and European eels are available live, whole, gutted or as fillets. Eels have a high fat content and firm flesh; they are sweet and mildly flavored. Their tough skin should be removed before cooking. Eels may be steamed, baked, fried or used in stews. Baby eels are a springtime delicacy, especially in Spain, where they are pan-fried in olive oil and garlic with hot red peppers. Smoked eels are also available.

Eel

The **grouper** family includes almost four hundred varieties found in temperate waters worldwide. The more common Atlantic Ocean varieties are the yellowfin grouper, black grouper, red grouper and gag; the Pacific Ocean varieties are the sea bass (also known as jewfish and different from the black sea bass) and spotted cabrilla. Although some species can reach 800 pounds or more, most commercial varieties are sold in the 5- to 20-pound (2.2- to 8.8-kilogram) range. They have lean white flesh with a mild to sweet flavor and very firm texture. Their skin, which is tough and strongly flavored, is generally removed before cooking. Grouper fillets may be baked, deep-fried, broiled or grilled.

Grouper

Herring (Fr. *hareng*) are long, silvery-blue fish found in both the northern Atlantic and Pacific Oceans. Their strongly flavored flesh has a moderate to high fat content. Whole herring weigh up to 8 ounces (225 grams). Fresh herring may be butterflied or filleted and roasted, broiled or grilled. But because herring are very soft and tend to spoil quickly, they are rarely available fresh. More often, they are smoked (and known as kippers) or cured in brine.

Very young, small herring are known as **sardines** (Fr. *sardine*). They have fatty, oily flesh with a flaky texture. Sardines are usually sold canned, whole or as skinned and boned fillets, or fried or smoked and packed in oil or sauce. Sardines are used primarily for sandwiches and salads.

Sardines

John Dory (Fr. *St. Pierre*), also known as St. Peter's fish, have a distinctive round, black spot with a yellow halo on each side of the body. Their flesh is white, firm and finely flaked. They may be filleted and prepared like flounder and are a classic bouillabaisse ingredient.

John Dory

SURIMI

Surimi is made from a highly processed fish paste colored, flavored and shaped to resemble shrimp, lobster, crab or other shellfish. Most surimi is based on Alaskan pollock, but some blends include varying amounts of real crab, shrimp or other items. Available chilled or frozen, surimi is already fully cooked and ready to add to salads, pasta, sauces or other dishes. Surimi is very low in fat and relatively high in protein. Because of processing techniques, however, it has more sodium and fewer vitamins and minerals than the real fish or shellfish it replaces. Americans now consume more than 100 million pounds of surimi each year, and its popularity continues to grow. The FDA requires that all surimi products be labeled "imitation."

Mackerel

Mackerel (Fr. *maquereau*) of culinary importance include king and Spanish mackerel as well as tuna and wahoo, which are discussed separately later. The species known as Atlantic and Pacific mackerel are not generally used for food because of their small size and high fat content. Mackerel flesh has a high fat content, gray to pink coloring, a mild flavor and flaky texture. The flesh becomes firm and off-white when cooked. Mackerel are best broiled, grilled, smoked or baked.

Mahi-mahi is the more commonly used name for dolphin or dolphinfish; this Hawaiian name is used to distinguish them from the marine mammal of the same name. (Dolphins and porpoises are marine mammals.) Also known by their Spanish name, *dorado,* mahi-mahi are brilliantly colored fish found in tropical seas. Mahi-mahi weigh about 15 pounds (6.6 kilograms) and are sold whole or as fillets. Their flesh is off-white to pink, lean and firm with a sweet flavor. Dolphinfish can be broiled, grilled or baked. The meat may become dry when cooked, however, so a sauce or marinade is recommended.

Mahi-Mahi

Monkfish are also known as angler fish, goosefish, rape and lotte. These extraordinarily ugly fish are rarely seen whole, for the large head is usually discarded before reaching market. Only the tail is edible; it is available in fillets, fresh or frozen. The scaleless skin must be removed. The flesh is lean, pearly white and very firm. Its texture and flavor have earned monkfish the nickname of "poor man's lobster." Monkfish absorb flavors easily and are baked, steamed, fried, grilled or broiled. They are also used for stews and soups.

Monkfish Tail

Orange roughy are caught in the South Pacific off the coasts of New Zealand and Australia. They have bright orange skin and firm, pearly-white flesh with a low fat content and extremely bland flavor. Orange roughy are almost always marketed as skinless, boneless frozen fillets, averaging 6 to 8 ounces (140 to 225 grams) each. Widely available year-round, they can be broiled, steamed, grilled or prepared in the same manner as cod.

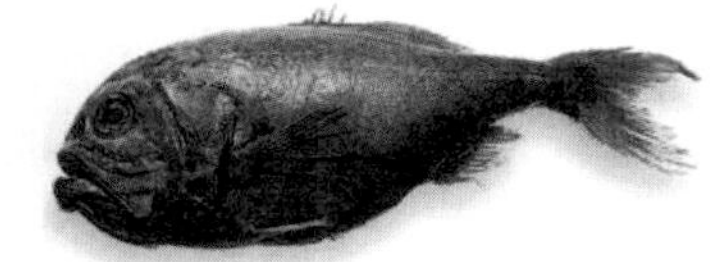
Orange Roughy

Red snapper is also known as the American or northern red snapper. Although there are many members of the snapper family, only one is the true red snapper. Red-skinned rockfish are often mislabeled as the more popular red snapper or Pacific snapper, a practice that is currently legal only in California. True red snapper have lean, pink flesh that becomes white when cooked; it is sweet-flavored and flaky. They are sold whole or as fillets with the skin left on for identification. Red snapper may reach 35 pounds, but most are marketed at only 4 to 6 pounds (1.8 to 2.7 kilograms) or as 1- to 3-pound (450-gram to 1.3-kilogram) fillets. Red snapper can be prepared using almost any cooking method. The head and bones are excellent for stock.

Red Snapper

Salmon (Fr. *saumon*) flourish in both the northern Atlantic and Pacific Oceans, returning to the freshwater rivers and streams of their birth to spawn. Salmon flesh gets its distinctive pink-red color from fat-soluble carotenoids found in the crustaceans on which they feed.

Atlantic salmon is the most important commercially, accounting for one-fourth of all salmon produced worldwide. Extensive aquafarms in Norway, Canada and Scotland produce a steady supply of Atlantic salmon. For marketing purposes, the fish's point of origin is often added to the name (for example, Norwegian, Scottish or Shetland Atlantic salmon). Atlantic salmon have a rich pink color and moist flesh. Their average weight is from 4 to 12 pounds (1.8 to 5.4 kilograms). Wild Atlantic salmon are almost never available.

Atlantic Salmon

Chinook or **king salmon** from the Pacific are also highly desirable. They average from 5 to 30 pounds (2.2 to 13.2 kilograms) and have red-orange flesh with a high fat content and rich flavor. Like other salmon, their flesh separates into large flakes when cooked. Chinooks are often marketed by the name of the river from which they are harvested (for example, Columbia, Yukon or Copper Chinook salmon). They are distinguished by the black interior of their mouth.

Chinook or King Salmon

Coho or **silver salmon** have a pinkish flesh and are available fresh or frozen, wild or from aquafarms. Wild coho average from 3 to 12 pounds (1.3 to 5.4 kilograms), while aquafarmed coho are much smaller, usually less than 1 pound (450 grams).

Other varieties, such as chum, sockeye, red, blueback and pink salmon, are usually canned but may be available fresh or frozen.

Mini Coho Salmon

Salmon can be prepared by many cooking methods: broiling, grilling, poaching, steaming or baking. Frying is not recommended, however, because of their high fat content. Salmon fillets are often cured or smoked. **Gravlax** is salmon that has been cured for one to three days with salt, sugar and dill. **Lox** is salmon that has been cured in a salted brine and then, typically, cold-smoked. **Nova** is used in the eastern United States to refer to a less-salty, cold-smoked salmon.

Sea bream is the name given to a large family of fish found in the Mediterranean (gilt-head bream), the Caribbean (porgy), the Atlantic (black sea bream) and the Indo-Pacific (emperor and snapper). Because the marketing term *bream* is applied to so many different fish, it is difficult to generalize about their characteristics. Some have very few bones, others have quite a few; some have a rich flavor, others are very mild; some weigh up to 20 pounds (9.6 kilograms), others rarely exceed 5 pounds (kilograms). Black sea bream, for example, is a good pan fish, reaching only 35 cm in length and weighing less than 6 pounds (2.9 kilograms). Their flesh is firm, mild and low in fat. Also marketed as Thai snapper, they are good for baking, grilling or frying.

Black Sea Bream

Sharks provide delicious eating, despite their less-than-appealing appearance and vicious reputation. Mako and blue sharks are the most desirable, with mako often being sold as swordfish. Sand shark, sharp-nose, blacktip, angel and thresher are also available commercially. Most sharks have lean flesh with a mild flavor and firm texture. The flesh is white with tinges of pink or red when raw, turning off-white when cooked. Makos weigh from 30 to 250 pounds (13.5 to 112.5 kilograms); other species may reach as much as 1000 pounds (450 kilograms). All sharks have cartilaginous skeletons and no bones; therefore, they are not actually fish, but rather marine invertebrates. Sharks are usually cut into loins or wheels, then into steaks or cubes. They can be broiled, grilled, baked or fried. An ammonia smell indicates that the shark was not properly treated when caught. Do not buy or eat it.

Blacktip Shark

Swordfish take their name from the long, sword-like bill extending from their upper jaw. These popular fish average about 250 pounds (112.5 kilograms). Their flesh is lean and sweet with a very firm, meatlike texture; it may be gray, pink or off-white when raw, becoming white when cooked. Swordfish are most often available cut into wheels or portioned into steaks perfect for grilling or broiling.

Swordfish Wheel

Tilapia is the name given to several species of freshwater, aquafarm-raised fish bred worldwide. They grow quickly in warm water, reaching about 3 pounds (1.3 kilograms); they are available whole or filleted, fresh or frozen. The flesh is similar to catfish—lean, white and sweet, with a firm texture. Tilapia are sometimes marketed as cherry snapper or sunshine snapper, even though they are not members of the snapper family.

Tilapia

Red Mountain Trout

Trout (Fr. *truite*) are members of the salmon family. Most of the freshwater trout commercially available are aquafarm-raised rainbow trout, although brown trout and brook trout are also being aquafarmed. Some trout species spend part of their lives at sea, returning to fresh water to spawn. On the West Coast, these are called salmon trout or steelhead. Trout have a low to moderate fat content, a flaky texture and a delicate flavor that can be easily overwhelmed by strong sauces. The flesh may be white, orange or pink. Trout are usually marketed at 8 to 10 ounces (225 to 280 grams) each, just right for an individual portion. Lake trout, sometimes known as char, are not aquafarmed and have little commercial value because of their extremely high fat content. Trout can be baked, pan-fried, smoked or steamed.

Rainbow Trout

Tuna (Fr. *thon*) varieties include the bluefin, yellowfin, bonito, bigeye and blackfin. Ahi is the popular market name for either yellowfin or bigeye tuna. All are members of the mackerel family and are found in tropical and subtropical waters around the world. Tuna are large fish, weighing up to several hundred pounds each. Bluefin, the finest and most desirable for sashimi, are becoming very scarce because of overfishing. Regular canned tuna is usually prepared from yellowfin or skipjack; canned white tuna is prepared from albacore, also known as longfin tuna. Pacific tuna that is frozen at sea to preserve its freshness is referred to as clipper fish. Any of these species may be found fresh or frozen, however. Tuna is usually cut into four boneless loins for market. The loins are then cut into steaks, cubes or chunks. The flesh has a low to moderate fat content (a higher fat content is preferred for sashimi) and a deep red color. The dark, reddish-brown muscle that runs along the lateral line is very fatty and can be removed. Tuna flesh turns light gray when cooked and is very firm, with a mild flavor. Tuna work well for grilling or broiling and may be marinated or brushed with seasoned oil during cooking. Tuna are often prepared medium rare to prevent dryness.

Yellowfin Tuna

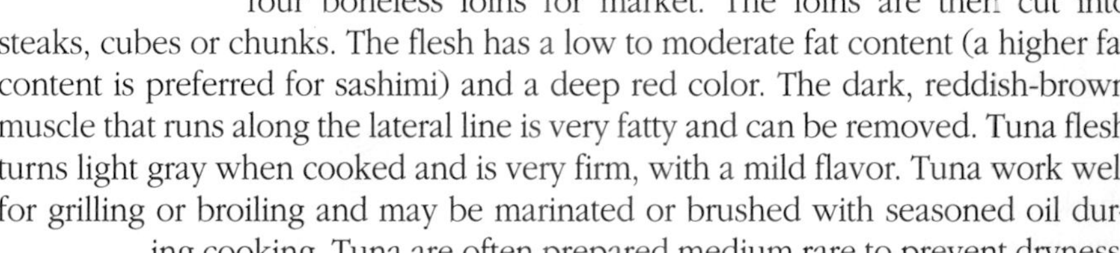

Wahoo, also known as *ono,* are found throughout tropical and subtropical waters, but are particularly associated with Hawaii (*ono* even means "good to eat" in Hawaiian). They are actually a type of mackerel and are cooked like any other mackerel.

Wahoo

Whitefish species inhabit the freshwater lakes and streams of North America. Lake whitefish, the most important commercially, are related to salmon. They are marketed at up to 7 pounds (3.2 kilograms) and are available whole or filleted. The flesh is firm and white, with a moderate amount of fat and a sweet flavor. Whitefish may be baked, broiled, grilled or smoked and are often used in processed fish products.

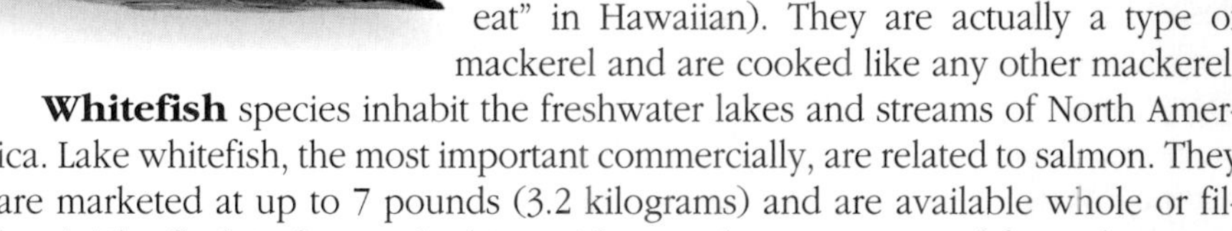

Whitefish

FLATFISH

Flounder (Fr. *flet*) have lean, firm flesh that is pearly or pinkish-white with a sweet, mild flavor. Although they are easily boned, most are deheaded and gutted at sea and sold as fresh or frozen fillets. These fillets are very thin and can dry out or spoil easily, so extra care should be taken in handling, preparing and storing them. Recipes that preserve moisture work best with flounder; poaching, steaming and frying are recommended. Many types of flounder are marketed as sole, perhaps in an attempt to cash in on the popularity of true sole. The FDA permits this practice (see Table 18.1).

English sole are actually flounder caught off the West Coast of the United States. They are usually marketed simply as "fillet of sole." They are a plentiful species of fair to average quality.

English Sole

Table 18.1 **FLOUNDER (A.K.A. SOLE)**

ATLANTIC OCEAN	PACIFIC OCEAN
Blackback/Winter flounder/Lemon sole	Arrowtooth
Fluke/Summer flounder	Petrale sole
Starry flounder	Rex sole
Yellowtail flounder	English sole
Windowpane flounder	Rock sole
Gray sole/Witch flounder	Sand sole
	Yellowfin sole
	Domestic Dover sole/Pacific flounder
	Butter sole

TRASH FISH

Ocean pout are considered a "trash fish," or fish that fishermen throw away because there is little or no consumer demand and therefore no market value.

Long ago, lobster were considered trash and good for nothing but chicken feed. More recently, monkfish was a trash fish in the U.S., and now we can't get enough. Obscure species are often trash fish until someone somewhere tastes them and realizes that they offer some incredible flavors and textures.

Searobins, dogfish, skate and whiting are still considered trash fish in America, though they are gradually becoming more popular and will someday be readily available at fish markets.

SUSAN HERRMANN LOOMIS, *The Great American Seafood Cookbook*

Petrale sole, another West Coast flounder, are generally considered the finest of the domestic "soles." They are most often available as fillets, which tend to be thicker and firmer than other sole fillets.

Petrale Sole

Domestic Dover sole are also Pacific flounder. They are not as delicate or flavorful as other species of sole or flounder. Moreover, they are often afflicted with a parasite that causes their flesh to have a slimy, gelatinous texture. Domestic Dover sole are not recommended if other sole or flounder are available.

Lemon sole are the most abundant and popular East Coast flounder. They are also known as blackback or winter flounder (during the winter, they migrate close to shore from the deeper, colder waters). They average 2 pounds (900 grams) in weight.

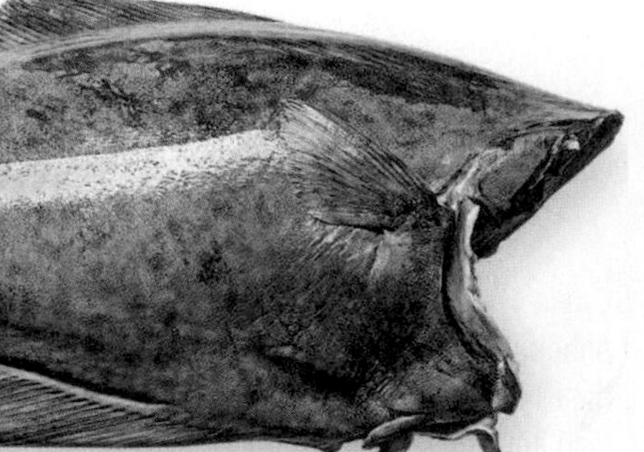
Lemon Sole

Halibut are among the largest flatfish; they often weigh up to 300 pounds (135 kilograms). The FDA recognizes only two halibut species: Atlantic (eastern) and Pacific (northern, Alaskan, western) halibut. Both have lean, firm flesh that is snow-white with a sweet, mild flavor. California halibut, which are actually flounder, are similar in taste and texture but average only 12 pounds (5.4 kilograms) each. Halibut may be cut into boneless steaks or skewered on brochettes. The flesh, which dries out easily, can be poached, baked, grilled or broiled and is good with a variety of sauces.

Alaskan Halibut

Sole (Fr. *sole*) are probably the most flavorful and finely textured flatfish. Indeed, because of the connotations of quality associated with the name, "sole" is widely used for many species that are not members of the *Soleidae* family. Even though the FDA allows many species of flatfish to be called "sole" for marketing purposes, no true sole is commercially harvested in American waters. Any flatfish harvested in American waters and marketed as sole is actually flounder.

True **Dover sole,** a staple of classic cuisine, are a lean fish with pearly-white flesh and a delicate flavor that can stand up to a variety of sauces and seasonings. They are a member of the *Soleidae* family and come only from the waters off the coasts of England, Africa and Europe. They are imported into this country as fresh whole fish or fresh or frozen fillets.

True Dover Sole

Turbot

Turbot are a Pacific flatfish of no great culinary distinction. In Europe, however, the species known as turbot (Fr. *turbot*) are large diamond-shaped fish highly prized for their delicate flavor and firm, white flesh. They are also marketed as brill.

MOLLUSKS

UNIVALVES

Univalves are mollusks with a single shell in which the soft-bodied animal resides. They are actually marine snails with a single foot, used to attach the creature to fixed objects such as rocks.

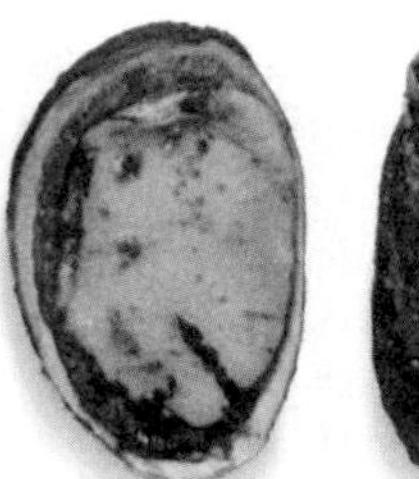

Abalone

Abalone have brownish-gray, ear-shaped shells. They are harvested in California, but California law does not permit canning abalone or shipping it out of state. Some frozen abalone is available from Mexico; canned abalone is imported from Japan. Abalone are lean with a sweet, delicate flavor similar to that of clams. They are too tough to eat unless tenderized with a mallet or rolling pin. They may then be eaten raw or prepared seviche-style. Great care must be taken when grilling or sautéing abalone, as the meat becomes very tough when overcooked.

Conch are found in warm waters off the Florida Keys and in the Caribbean. The beautiful peachy-pink shell of the queen conch is prized by beachcombers. Conch meat is lean, smooth and very firm with a sweet-smoky flavor and chewy texture. It can be sliced and pounded to tenderize it, eaten raw with lime juice or slow-cooked whole.

BIVALVES

Bivalves are mollusks with two bilateral shells attached by a central hinge.

Clams (Fr. *palourdes*) are harvested along both the East and West Coasts, with Atlantic clams being more significant commercially. Atlantic Coast clams include hard-shell, soft-shell and surf clams. Clams are available all year, either live in the shell or fresh-shucked (meat removed from the shell). Canned clams, whether minced, chopped or whole, are also available.

Littlenecks

Atlantic hard-shell clams or **quahogs** have hard, blue-gray shells. Their chewy meat is not as sweet as other clam meat. Quahogs have different names, depending upon their size. **Littlenecks** are generally under 2 inches (5 centimeters) across the shell and usually are served on the half shell or steamed. They are the most expensive clams. **Cherrystones** are generally under 3 inches (7.5 centimeters) across the shell and are sometimes eaten raw but are more often cooked. **Topnecks** are usually cooked and are often served as stuffed clams. **Chowders,** the largest quahogs, are always eaten cooked, especially minced for chowder or soup.

Cherrystones

Topnecks

Soft-shell clams, also known as Ipswich, steamer and long-necked clams, have thin, brittle shells that do not completely close because of the clam's protruding black-tipped siphon. Their meat is tender and sweet. They are sometimes fried but are more often served steamed.

Soft-Shell Clams

SNAILS

Although snails (more politely known by their French name, *escargots*) are univalve land animals, they share many characteristics with their marine cousins. They can be poached in court bouillon or removed from their shells and boiled or baked briefly with a seasoned butter or sauce. They should be firm but tender; overcooking makes snails tough and chewy. The most popular varieties are the large white Burgundy snail and the small garden variety called *petit gris.* Fresh snails are available from snail ranches through specialty suppliers. The great majority of snails, however, are purchased canned; most canned snails are produced in France or Taiwan.

Surf clams are deep-water clams that reach sizes of 8 inches (20 centimeters) across. They are most often cut into strips for frying or are minced, chopped, processed and canned.

Pacific clams are generally too tough to eat raw. The most common is the **Manila clam,** which was introduced along the Pacific coast during the 1930s. Resembling a quahog with a ridged shell, it can be served steamed or on the half shell. **Geoducks** are the largest Pacific clam, sometimes weighing up to 10 pounds (4.5 kilograms) each. They look like huge soft-shell clams with a large, protruding siphon. Their tender, rich bodies and briny flavor are popular in Asian cuisines.

Manila Clams

Cockles are small bivalves, about 1 inch (2.5 centimeters) long, with ridged shells. They are more popular in Europe than the United States and are sometimes used in dishes such as paella and fish soups or stews.

Cockles

Mussels (Fr. *moules*) are found in waters worldwide. They are excellent steamed in wine or seasoned broth and can be fried or used in soups or pasta dishes.

Blue mussels are the most common edible mussel. They are found in the wild along the Atlantic Coast and are aquafarmed on both coasts. Their meat is plump and sweet with a firm, muscular texture. The orangish-yellow meat of cultivated mussels tends to be much larger than that of wild mussels and therefore worth the added cost. Blue mussels are sold live in the shell and average from 10 to 20 per pound. Although available all year, the best-quality blue mussels are harvested during the winter months.

Blue Mussels

Greenshell (or greenlip) mussels from New Zealand and Thailand are much larger than blue mussels, averaging 8 to 12 mussels per pound. Their shells are paler gray, with a distinctive bright-green edge.

Greenshell Mussels

Oysters (Fr. *huîtres*) have a rough gray shell. Their soft, gray, briny flesh can be eaten raw directly from the shell. They can also be steamed or baked in the shell or shucked and fried, sautéed or added to stews or chowders. Most oysters available in the United States are commercially grown and sold either live in the shell or shucked. There are four main domestic species.

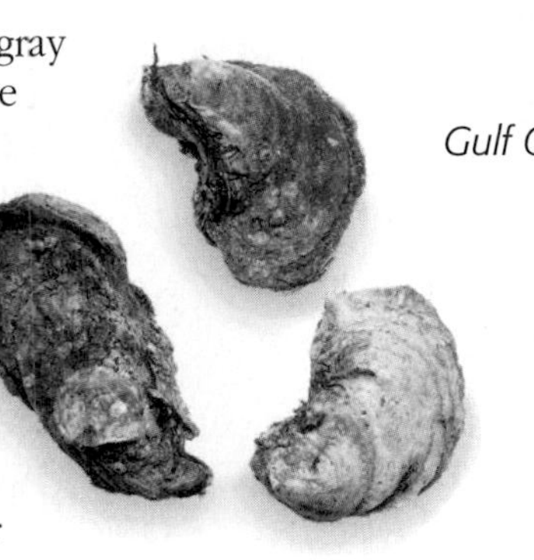

Gulf Oysters

Atlantic oysters, also called American or Eastern oysters, have darker, flatter shells than other oysters.

European flat oysters are often incorrectly called Belon (true Belon oysters live only in the Belon river of France); they are very round and flat and look like giant brownish-green Olympias.

European Flat Oysters

Olympias are the only oysters native to the Pacific Coast; they are tiny (about the size of a 50-cent coin).

Pacific oysters, also called Japanese oysters, are aquafarmed along the Pacific Coast; they have curly, thick striated shells and silvery-gray to gold to almost-white meat.

Olympia Oysters

Although it may seem as though there are hundreds of oyster species on the market, only two are commercially significant: the Atlantic oyster and the Pacific oyster. These two species yield dozens of different varieties,

Bluepoint Oysters

Hamma-Hamma Oysters

however, depending on their origin. For example, Atlantic oysters may be referred to as bluepoints, Chesapeake Bay, Florida Gulf, Long Island and so on, while Pacific oysters include Penn Cove Select, Westcott Bay, Hamma-Hamma, Kumamoto and Portuguese, among others. An oyster's flavor reflects the minerals, nutrients and salts in its water and mud bed, so a Bristol from Maine and an Apalachicola from Florida will taste very different, even though they are the same Atlantic species.

Scallops (Fr. *coquilles Saint Jacques*) contain an edible white adductor muscle that holds together the fan-shaped shells. Because they die quickly, they are almost always shucked and cleaned on board the ship. The sea scallop and the bay scallop, both cold-water varieties, and the calico scallop, a warm-water variety, are the most important commercially. Sea scallops are the largest, with an average count of 20 to 30 per pound. Larger sea scallops are also available. Bay scallops average 70 to 90 per pound; calico scallops average 70 to 110 per pound. Fresh or frozen shucked, cleaned scallops are the most common market form, but live scallops in the shell and shucked scallops with roe attached (very popular in Europe) are also available. Scallops are sweet, with a tender texture. Raw scallops should be a translucent ivory color and nonsymmetrically round and should feel springy. They can be steamed, broiled, grilled, fried, sautéed or baked. When overcooked, however, scallops quickly become chewy and dry. Only extremely fresh scallops should be eaten raw.

Sea Scallops

CEPHALOPODS

Octopus

Cephalopods are marine mollusks with distinct heads, well-developed eyes, a number of arms that attach to the head near the mouth and a saclike fin-bearing mantle. They do not have an outer shell; instead, there is a thin internal shell called a **pen** or **cuttlebone.**

Octopus is generally quite tough and requires mechanical tenderization or long, moist-heat cooking to make it palatable. Most octopus is imported from Portugal, though fresh ones are available on the East Coast during the winter. Octopus is sold by the pound, fresh or frozen, usually whole. Octopus skin is gray when raw, turning purple when cooked. The interior flesh is white, lean, firm and flavorful.

Squid, known by their Italian name, *calamari*, are becoming increasingly popular in the United States. Similar to octopuses but much smaller, they are harvested along both American coasts and elsewhere around the world (the finest are the East Coast loligo or winter squid). They range in size from an average of 8 to 10 per pound to the giant South American squid, which is sold as tenderized steaks. The squid's tentacles, mantle (body tube) and fins are edible. Squid meat is white to ivory in color, turning darker with age. It is moderately lean, slightly sweet, firm and tender, but it toughens quickly if overcooked. Squid are available either fresh or frozen and packed in blocks.

Squid

CRUSTACEANS

Crustaceans are found in both fresh and salt water. They have a hard outer shell and jointed appendages, and they breathe through gills.

Crayfish (Fr. *écrevisses*), generally called *crayfish* in the North and *crawfish* or *crawdad* in the South, are freshwater creatures that look like miniature lobsters. They are harvested from the wild or aquafarmed in Louisiana and the Pacific Northwest. They are from $3\frac{1}{2}$ to 7 inches (8 to 17.5 centimeters) in length when marketed and may be purchased live or precooked and frozen. The lean meat, found mostly in the tail, is sweet and tender. Crayfish can be boiled whole and served hot or cold. The tail meat can be deep-fried or used in soups, bisque or sauces. Crayfish are a staple of Cajun cuisine, often used in gumbo, étouffée and jambalaya. Whole crayfish become brilliant red when cooked and may be used as a garnish.

Crayfish

Crabs (Fr. *crabes*) are found along the North American coast in great numbers and are shipped throughout the world in fresh, frozen and canned forms. Crab meat varies in flavor and texture and can be used in a range of prepared dishes, from chowders to curries to casseroles. Crabs purchased live should last up to five days; dead crabs should not be used.

King crabs are very large crabs (usually around 10 pounds [4.4 kilograms] caught in the very cold waters of the northern Pacific. Their meat is very sweet and snow-white. King crabs are always sold frozen, usually in the shell. In-shell forms include sections or clusters, legs and claws or split legs. The meat is also available in "fancy" packs of whole leg and body meat, or shredded and minced pieces.

King Crab Legs

Dungeness crabs are found along the West Coast. They weigh $1\frac{1}{2}$ to 4 pounds (680 grams to 1.8 kilograms) and have delicate, sweet meat. They are sold live, precooked and frozen, or as picked meat, usually in 5-pound (2.2-kilogram) vacuum-packed cans.

Dungeness Crab

Blue crabs are found along the entire eastern seaboard and account for approximately 50 percent of the total weight of all crab species harvested in the United States. Their meat is rich and sweet. Blue crabs are available as hard-shell or soft-shell. Hard-shell crabs are sold live, precooked and frozen, or as picked meat. Soft-shell crabs are those harvested within six hours after molting and are available live (generally only from May 15 to September 15) or frozen. They are often steamed and served whole. Soft-shells can be sautéed, fried, broiled or added to soups or stews. Blue crabs are sold by size, with an average diameter of 4 to 7 inches (10 to 18 centimeters).

Blue Crab

Soft-Shell Crabs

Snow or **spider crabs** are an abundant species, most often used as a substitute for the scarcer and more expensive king crab. They are harvested from Alaskan waters and along the eastern coast of Canada. Snow crab is sold precooked, usually frozen. The meat can be used in soups, salads, omelets or other prepared dishes. Legs are often served cold as an appetizer.

Snow Crab Legs

Stone crabs are generally available only as cooked claws, either fresh or frozen (the claws cannot be frozen raw because the meat sticks to the shell). In stone crab fishery, only the claw is harvested. After the claw is removed, the crab is returned to the water, where in approximately 18 months it regenerates a new claw. Claws average $2\frac{1}{2}$ to $5\frac{1}{2}$ ounces (75 to 155 grams) each. The meat is firm, with a sweet flavor similar to lobster. Cracked claws are served hot or cold, usually with cocktail sauce, lemon butter or other accompaniments.

Lobsters have brown to blue-black outer shells and firm, white meat with a rich, sweet flavor. Lobster shells turn red when cooked. They are usually poached, steamed, simmered, baked or grilled, and can be served hot or cold. Picked meat can be used in prepared dishes, soups or sautés. Lobsters must be kept alive until just before cooking. Dead lobsters should not be eaten. The Maine, also known as American or clawed lobster, and the spiny lobster are the most commonly marketed species.

Stone Crab Claws

FIGURE 18.3 ▶ Parts of a Maine Lobster.

Maine Lobster

Maine lobsters have edible meat in both their tails and claws; they are considered superior in flavor to all other lobsters. They come from the cold waters along the northeast coast and are most often sold live. Maine lobsters may be purchased by weight (for example, 1¼ pounds [525 grams], 1½ pounds [650 grams] or 2 pounds [900 grams] each), or as chix (that is, a lobster weighing less than 1 pound [450 grams]). Maine lobsters may also be purchased as culls (lobsters with only one claw) or bullets (lobsters with no claws). They are available frozen or as cooked, picked meat.

Figure 18.3 shows a cross-section of a Maine lobster and identifies the stomach, tomalley (the olive-green liver) and coral (the roe). The stomach is not eaten; the tomalley and coral are very flavorful and are often used in the preparation of sauces and other items.

Spiny lobsters, harvested in many parts of the world, have very small claws and are valuable only for their meaty tails, which are notched with short spines. Nearly all spiny lobsters marketed in this country are sold as frozen tails, often identified as rock lobster. Those found off Florida and Brazil and in the Caribbean are marketed as warm-water tails; those found off South Africa, Australia and New Zealand are called cold-water tails. Cold-water spiny tails are considered superior to their warm-water cousins.

Slipper lobster, **lobsterette** and **squat lobster** are all clawless species found in tropical, subtropical and temperate waters worldwide. Although they are popular in some countries, their flavor is inferior to that of both Maine and spiny lobsters. **Langoustines** are small North Atlantic lobsters.

Tiger Shrimp

Shrimp (Fr. *crevettes*) are found worldwide and are widely popular. Gulf whites, pinks, browns and black tigers are just a few of the dozens of shrimp varieties used in food service operations. Although fresh, head-on shrimp are available, the most common form is raw, head-off (also called green headless) shrimp with the shell on. Most shrimp are deheaded and frozen at sea to preserve freshness. Shrimp are available in many forms: raw, peeled and deveined; cooked, peeled and deveined; and individually quick-frozen, as well as in a variety of processed, breaded or canned products. Shrimp are graded by size, which can range from 400 per pound (titi) to 8 per pound (extra-colossal), and are sold in counts per pound. For example, shrimp marketed as "21–26 count" means that there is an average of 21 to 26 shrimp per pound; shrimp marketed as "U-10" means that there are fewer than 10 shrimp per pound.

Shrimp

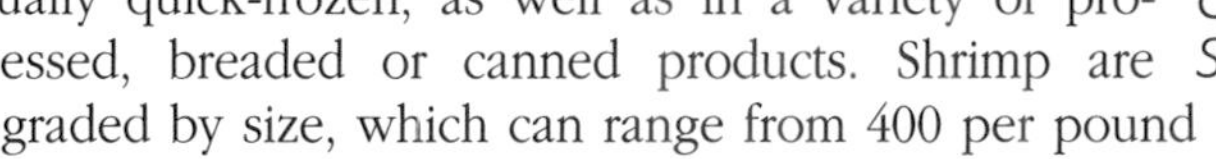

Green Headless Shrimp

Prawn is often used interchangeably with the word *shrimp* in English-speaking countries. Although it is perhaps more accurate to refer to freshwater species as prawns and saltwater species as shrimp, in commercial

Prawn

practice, prawn refers to any large shrimp. Equally confusing, *scampi* is the Italian name for the Dublin Bay prawn (which is actually a species of miniature lobster), but in the United States *scampi* refers to shrimp sautéed in garlic butter.

▶ NUTRITION

Fish and shellfish are low in calories, fat and sodium, and are high in protein and vitamins A, B and D. Fish and shellfish are also high in minerals, especially calcium (particularly in canned fish with edible bones), phosphorus, potassium and iron (especially mollusks). Fish are high in a group of polyunsaturated fatty acids called omega-3, which may help combat high blood cholesterol levels and aid in preventing some heart disease. Shellfish are not as high in cholesterol as was once thought. Crustaceans are higher in cholesterol than mollusks, but both have considerably lower levels than red meat or eggs.

The cooking methods used for fish and shellfish also contribute to their healthfulness. The most commonly used cooking methods—broiling, grilling, poaching and steaming—add little or no fat.

▶ INSPECTION AND GRADING OF FISH AND SHELLFISH

INSPECTION

Unlike mandatory meat and poultry inspections, fish and shellfish inspections are voluntary. They are performed in a fee-for-service program supervised by the United States Department of Commerce (USDC).

Type 1 inspection services cover plant, product and processing methods from the raw material to the final product. The "Packed Under Federal Inspection" (PUFI) mark or statement shown in Figure 18.4 can be used on product labels processed under Type 1 inspection services. It signifies that the product is safe and wholesome, is properly labeled, has reasonably good flavor and odor and was produced under inspection in an official establishment.

FIGURE 18.4 ▶ PUFI mark and statements.

Type 2 inspection services are usually performed in a warehouse, processing plant or cold storage facility on specific product lots. See Figure 18.5. A lot inspection determines whether the product complies with purchase agreement criteria (usually defined in a spec sheet) such as condition, weight, labeling and packaging integrity.

FIGURE 18.5 ▶ Product inspection stamp.

Type 3 inspection services are for sanitation only. Fishing vessels or plants that meet the requirements are recognized as official establishments and are included in the *USDC Approved List of Fish Establishments and Products*. The list is available to governmental and institutional purchasing agents as well as to retail and restaurant buyers. Updated copies of the list are published on the Internet.

GRADING

Only fish processed under Type 1 inspection services are eligible for grading. Each type of fish has its own grading criteria, but because of the great variety of fish and shellfish, the USDC has been able to set grading criteria for only the most common types.

The grades assigned to fish are A, B or C. Grade A products are top quality and must have good flavor and odor and be practically free of physical blemishes or defects. The great majority of fresh and frozen fish and shellfish consumed in restaurants is Grade A. See Figure 18.6. Grade B indicates good quality; Grade C indicates fairly good quality. Grade B and C products are most often canned or processed.

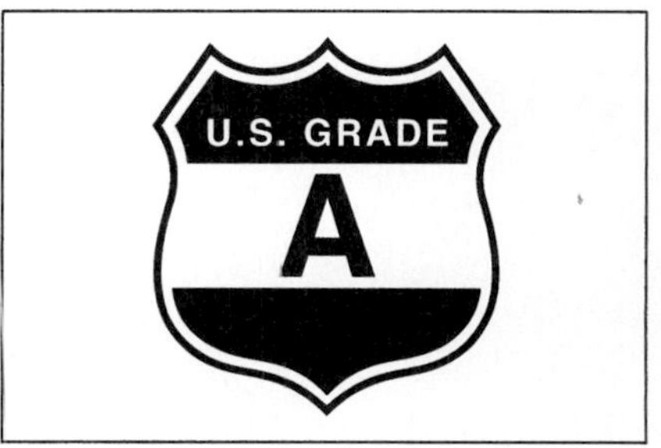

FIGURE 18.6 ▶ Grade A stamp.

HOW FRESH IS FROZEN FISH?

Fresh—The item is not and has never been frozen.

Chilled—Now used by some in the industry to replace the more ambiguous "fresh"; indicates that the item was refrigerated, that is, held at 30°F to 34°F (−1°C to 1°C).

Flash-frozen—The item was quickly frozen on board the ship or at a processing plant within hours of being caught.

Fresh-frozen—The item was quick-frozen while still fresh but not as quickly as flash-frozen.

Frozen—The item was subjected to temperatures of 0°F (−18°C) or lower to preserve its inherent quality.

Glazed—A frozen product dipped in water; the ice forms a glaze that protects the item from freezer burn.

Fancy—Code word for "previously frozen."

▶ PURCHASING AND STORING FISH AND SHELLFISH

DETERMINING FRESHNESS

Because fish and shellfish are highly perishable, an inspection stamp does not necessarily ensure top quality. A few hours at the wrong temperature or a couple of days in the refrigerator can turn high-quality fish or shellfish into garbage. It is important that chefs be able to determine for themselves the freshness and quality of the fish and shellfish they purchase or use. Freshness should be checked before purchasing and again just before cooking.

Freshness can be determined by the following criteria:

1 **Smell**—This is by far the easiest way to determine freshness. Fresh fish should have a slight sea smell or no odor at all. Any off-odors or ammonia odors are a sure sign of aged or improperly handled fish.
2 **Eyes**—The eyes should be clear and full. Sunken eyes mean that the fish is drying out and is probably not fresh.
3 **Gills**—The gills should be intact and bright red. Brown gills are a sign of age.
4 **Texture**—Generally, the flesh of fresh fish should be firm. Mushy flesh or flesh that does not spring back when pressed with a finger is a sign of poor quality or age.
5 **Fins and scales**—Fins and scales should be moist and full without excessive drying on the outer edges. Dry fins or scales are a sign of age; damaged fins or scales may be a sign of mishandling.
6 **Appearance**—Fish cuts should be moist and glistening, without bruises or dark spots. Edges should not be brown or dry.
7 **Movement**—Shellfish should be purchased live and should show movement. Lobsters and other crustaceans should be active. Clams, mussels and oysters that are partially opened should snap shut when tapped with a finger. (Exceptions are geoduck, razor and steamer clams whose siphons protrude, preventing the shell from closing completely.) Ones that do not close are dead and should not be used. Avoid mollusks with broken shells or heavy shells that might be filled with mud or sand.

PURCHASING FISH AND SHELLFISH

Fish are available from wholesalers in a variety of market forms:

▶ **Whole** or **round**—As caught, intact.

Whole or Round

▶ **Drawn**—Viscera (internal organs) are removed; most whole fish are purchased this way.

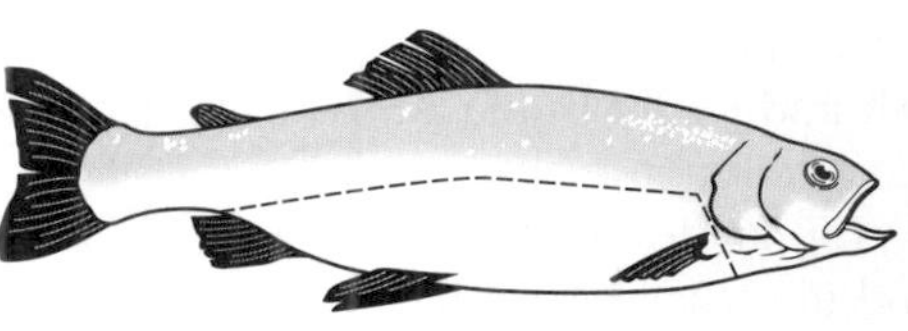
Drawn

- **Dressed**—Viscera, gills, fins and scales are removed.
- **Pan-dressed**—Viscera and gills are removed; fish is scaled and fins and tail are trimmed. The head is usually removed, although small fish, such as trout, may be pan-dressed with the head still attached. Pan-dressed fish are then pan-fried.

Dressed or Pan-Dressed

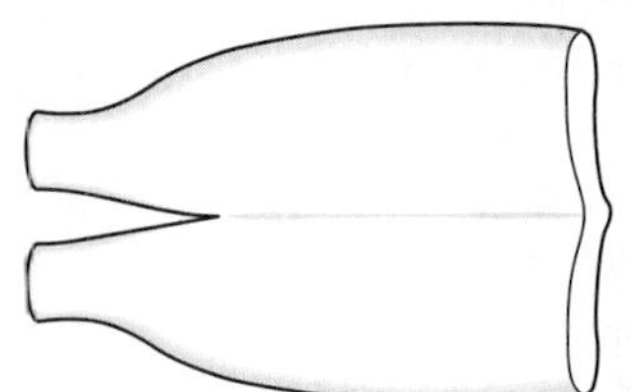

Butterflied Fillets

- **Butterflied**—A pan-dressed fish, boned and opened flat like a book. The two sides remain attached by the back or belly skin.

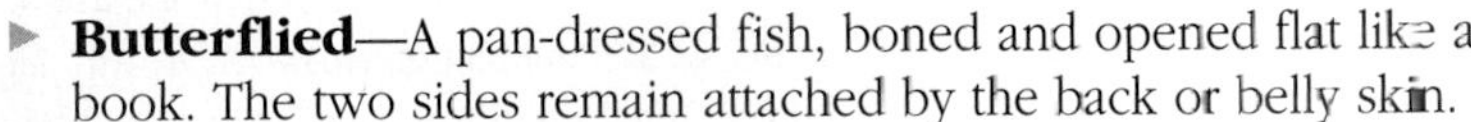

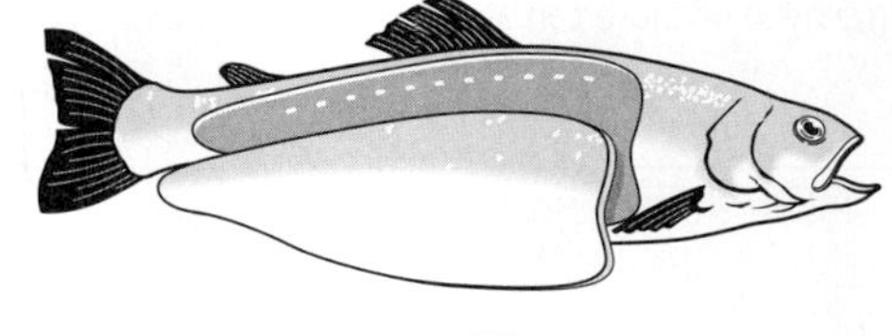

Fillets

- **Fillet**—The side of a fish removed intact, boneless or semiboneless, with or without skin.

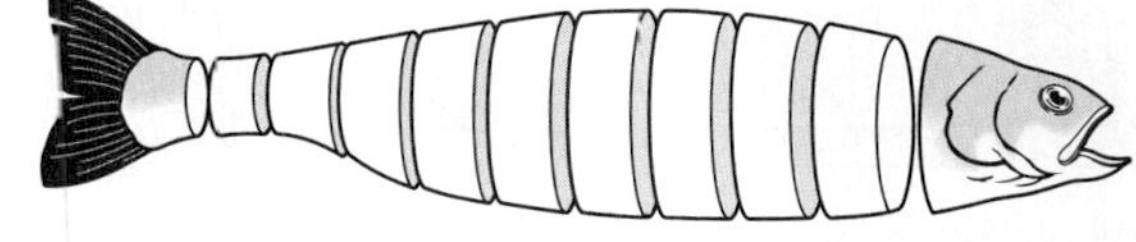

Steaks

- **Steak**—A cross-section slice, with a small section of backbone attached; usually prepared from large round fish such as salmon, swordfish or tuna.

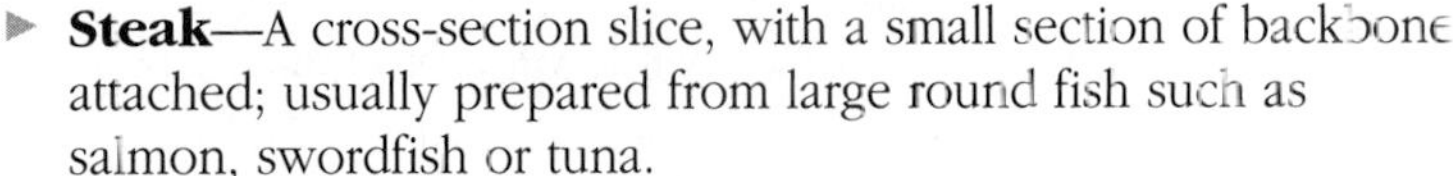

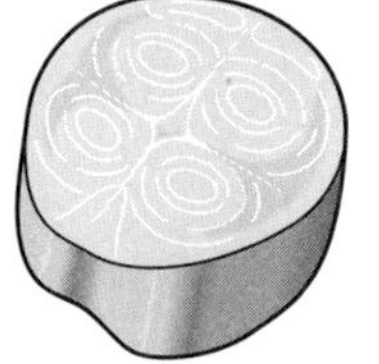

Wheel or Center-Cut

- **Wheel** or **center-cut**—Used for swordfish and sharks, which are cut into large boneless pieces from which steaks are then cut.

Chefs purchase fish in the market forms most practical for each operation. Although fish fabrication is a relatively simple chore requiring little specialized equipment, before deciding to cut fish on premises, consider the following:

1. The food service operation's ability to utilize the bones and trim that cutting whole fish produces
2. The employees' ability to fabricate fillets, steaks or portions as needed
3. The storage facilities
4. The product's intended use

Most shellfish can be purchased live in the shell, shucked (the meat removed from the shell) or processed. Both live and shucked shellfish are usually purchased by counts (that is, the number per volume). For example, standard live Eastern oysters are packed 200 to 250 (the count) per bushel (the unit of volume); standard Eastern oyster meats are packed 350 per gallon. Crustaceans are sometimes packed by size based on the number of pieces per pound; for example, crab legs or shrimp are often sold in counts per pound. Crustaceans are also sold either by grades based on size (whole crabs) or by weight (lobsters).

FARMING THE SEAS

Aquaculture or fish farming has been practiced in Asia for thousands of years. As wild fish and shellfish have been depleted by overfishing, aquaculture has grown into a major industry in the United States and many other non-Asian countries. More than 70 percent of the seafood consumed in the United States today is imported and more than 40 percent of this imported seafood is farm raised.

Aquaculture can take place in closed environments, where water is constantly circulated through tanks and ponds. Net pens or cages employed offshore can also hold vast numbers of fish. Mollusks (clams, oysters and mussels) are farmed in near-shore beds or, sometimes in the case of mussels, on long lines or even on the bases of offshore oil rigs. Catfish and trout have long been farm raised in the United States but now salmon, tilapia, hybrid striped bass, abalone, crayfish, freshwater prawns, shrimp and sturgeon are also produced. Constant experimentation is taking place with different varieties: Norwegian scientists are working with halibut, and in Ecuador sturgeon are being raised for their caviar with the help of Russian experts.

For the food service industry, aquaculture can mean that many fish are no longer seasonal; there is a constant supply, less price fluctuation and more standardized quality. Fish farming is not without its critics; environmental damage can result from poor management practices and concerns have been raised regarding the use of chemicals and antibiotics. However, as with all industry involved in food production, aquaculture is subject to federal and state regulation both for homegrown and imported products. And in response to such concerns, there is a growing organic movement within the industry.

Whole fish properly stored in a perforated pan and covered with crushed ice.

STORING FISH AND SHELLFISH

The most important concern when storing fish and shellfish is temperature. All fresh fish should be stored at temperatures between 30°F and 34°F (−1°C to 1°C). Fish stored in a refrigerator at 41°F (5°C) will have approximately half the shelf life of fish stored at 32°F (0°C).

Most fish are shipped on ice and should be stored on ice in the refrigerator as soon as possible after receipt. Whole fish should be layered directly in crushed or shaved ice in a perforated pan so that the melted ice water drains away. If crushed or shaved ice is not available, cubed ice may be used provided it is put in plastic bags and gently placed on top of the fish to prevent bruising and denting. Fabricated and portioned fish may be wrapped in moisture-proof packaging before icing to prevent the ice and water from damaging the exposed flesh. Fish stored on ice should be drained and re-iced daily.

Fresh scallops, fish fillets that are purchased in plastic trays and oyster and clam meats should be set on or packed in ice. Do not let the scallops, fillets or meats come into direct contact with the ice.

Clams, mussels and oysters should be stored at 41°F (5°C), at high humidity and left in the boxes or net bags in which they were shipped. Under ideal conditions, shellfish can be kept alive for up to one week. Never store live shellfish in plastic bags and do not ice them.

If a saltwater tank is not available, live lobsters, crabs and other crustaceans should be kept in boxes with seaweed or damp newspaper to keep them moist. Most crustaceans circulate salt water over their gills; icing them or placing them in fresh water will kill them. Lobsters and crabs will live for several days under ideal conditions.

Like most frozen foods, frozen fish should be kept at temperatures of 0°F (−18°C) or colder. Colder temperatures greatly increase shelf life. Frozen fish should be thawed in the refrigerator; once thawed, they should be treated like fresh fish.

▸ Fabricating Procedures

As discussed, fish and shellfish can be purchased in many forms. Here we demonstrate several procedures for cutting, cleaning and otherwise fabricating or preparing fish and shellfish for cooking and serving.

▶ PROCEDURE FOR SCALING FISH

This procedure is used to remove the scales from fish that will be cooked with the skin on.

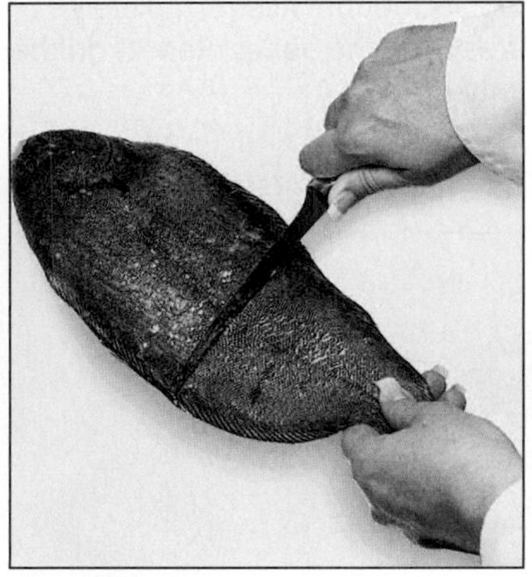

Place the fish on a work surface or in a large sink. Grip the fish by the tail and, working from the tail toward the head, scrape the scales off with a fish scaler or the back of a knife. Be careful not to damage the flesh by pushing too hard. Turn the fish over and remove the scales from the other side. Rinse the fish under cool water.

▶ PROCEDURE FOR PAN-DRESSING FLATFISH

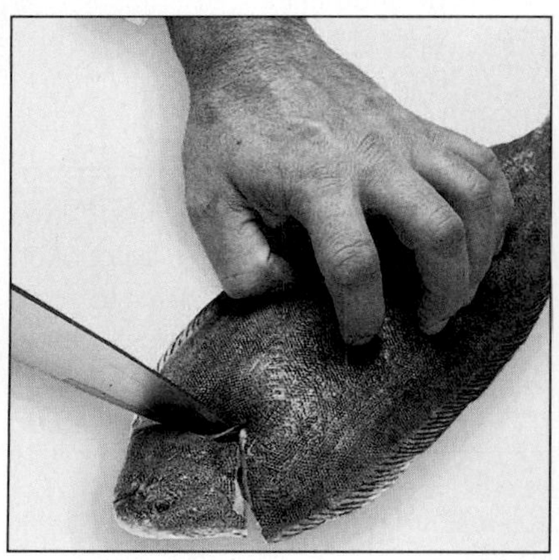

1 Place the scaled fish on a cutting board and remove the head by making a V-shaped cut around it with a chef's knife. Pull the head away and remove the viscera.

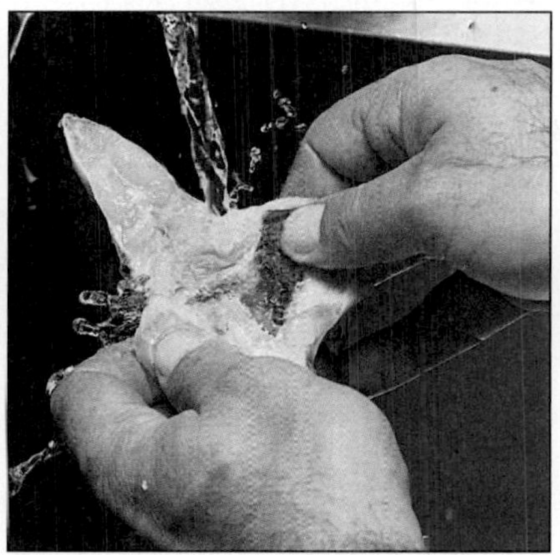

2 Rinse the fish under cold water, removing all traces of blood and viscera from the cavity.

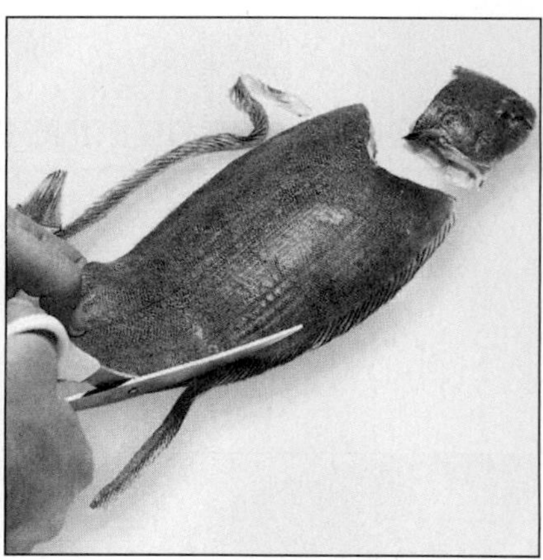

3 Using a pair of kitchen shears, trim off the tail and all of the fins.

▶ PROCEDURE FOR FILLETING ROUND FISH

Round fish produce two fillets, one from either side.

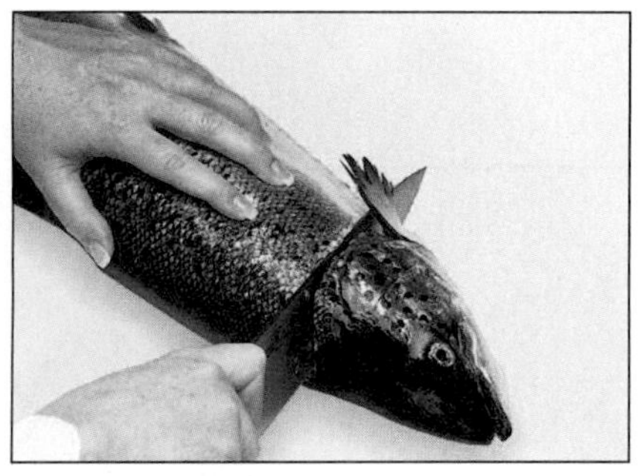

1 Using a chef's knife, cut down to the backbone just behind the gills. Do not remove the head.

2 Turn the knife toward the tail; using smooth strokes, cut from head to tail, parallel to the backbone. The knife should bump against the backbone so that no flesh is wasted; you will feel the knife cutting through the small pin bones. Cut the fillet completely free from the bones. Repeat on the other side.

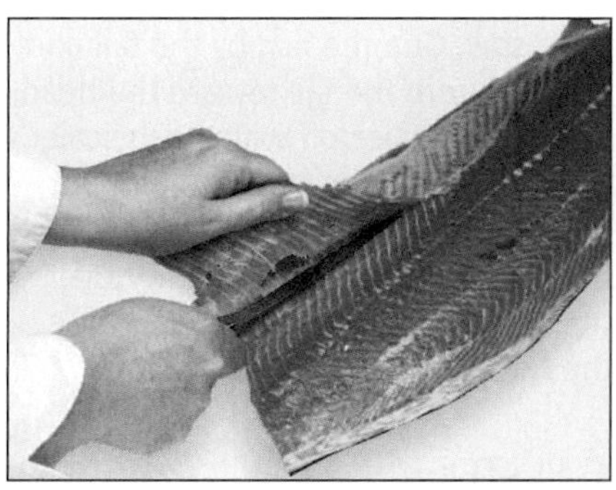

3 Trim the rib bones from the fillet with a flexible boning knife.

4 The finished fillet.

▶ PROCEDURE FOR FILLETING FLATFISH

Flatfish produce four fillets: two large bilateral fillets from the top and two smaller bilateral fillets from the bottom. If the fish fillets are going to be cooked with the skin on, the fish should be scaled before cooking (it is easier to scale the fish before it is filleted). If the skin is going to be removed before cooking, it is not necessary to scale the fish.

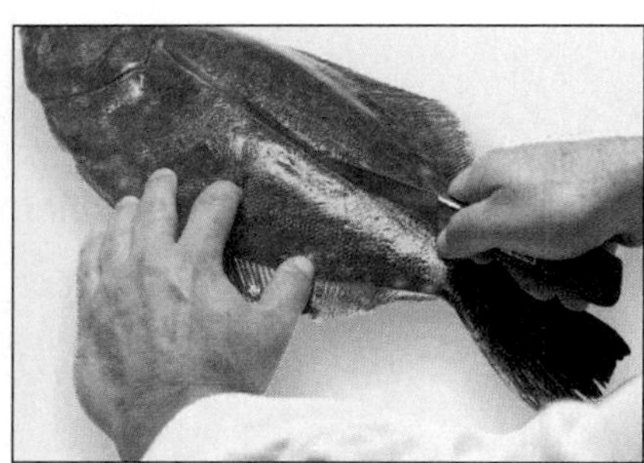

1 With the dark side of the fish facing up, cut along the backbone from head to tail with the tip of a flexible boning knife.

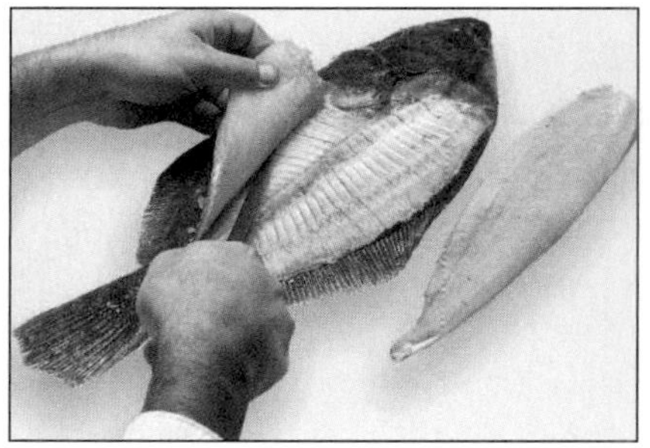

2 Turn the knife and, using smooth strokes, cut between the flesh and the rib bones, keeping the flexible blade against the bone. Cut the fillet completely free from the fish. Remove the second fillet, following the same procedure.

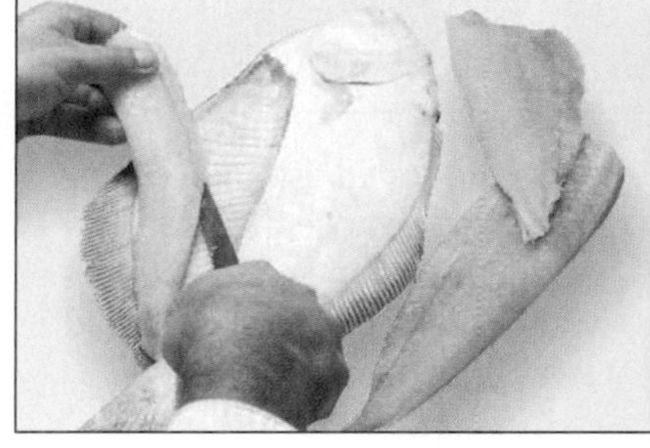

3 Turn the fish over and remove the fillets from the bottom half of the fish, following the same procedure.

▶ PROCEDURE FOR SKINNING DOVER SOLE

Dover sole is unique in that its skin can be pulled from the whole fish with a simple procedure. The flesh of other small flatfish such as flounder, petrale sole and other types of domestic sole is more delicate; pulling the skin away from the whole fish could damage the flesh. These fish should be skinned after they are filleted.

Make a shallow cut in the flesh perpendicular to the length of the fish, just in front of the tail and with the knife angled toward the head of the fish. Using a clean towel, grip the skin and pull it toward the head of the fish. The skin should come off cleanly, in one piece, leaving the flesh intact.

▶ PROCEDURE FOR SKINNING FISH FILLETS

Here we use a salmon fillet to demonstrate the procedure for skinning fish fillets. Use the same procedure to skin all types of fish fillets.

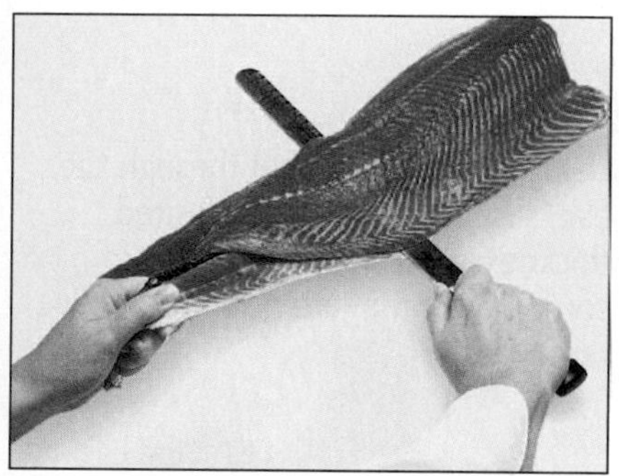

Place the fillet on a cutting board with the skin side down. Starting at the tail, use a meat slicer or a chef's knife to cut between the flesh and skin. Angle the knife down toward the skin, grip the skin tightly with one hand and use a smooth sawing motion to cut the skin cleanly away from the flesh.

▶ PROCEDURE FOR PULLING PIN BONES FROM SALMON FILLETS

Round fish fillets contain a row of intramuscular bones running the length of the fillet. Known as pin bones, they are usually cut out with a knife to produce boneless fillets. In the case of salmon, they can be removed with salmon tweezers or small needle-nose pliers.

Place the fillet (either skinless or not) on the cutting board, skin side down. Starting at the front or head end of the fillet, use your fingertips to locate the bones and use the pliers to pull them out one by one.

▶ PROCEDURE FOR CUTTING TRANCHES

A **tranche** is a slice cut from fillets of large flat or round fish. Usually cut on an angle, tranches look large and increase plate coverage.

Place the fillet on the cutting board, skin side down. Using a slicer or chef's knife, cut slices of the desired weight. The tranche can be cut to the desired size by adjusting the angle of the knife. The greater the angle, the greater the surface area of the tranche.

▶ PROCEDURE FOR CUTTING STEAKS FROM SALMON AND SIMILARLY SIZED ROUND FISH

Steaks are produced from salmon and similarly sized round fish by simply making crosscuts of the whole fish. First scale, gut and remove the fins from the fish. Then:

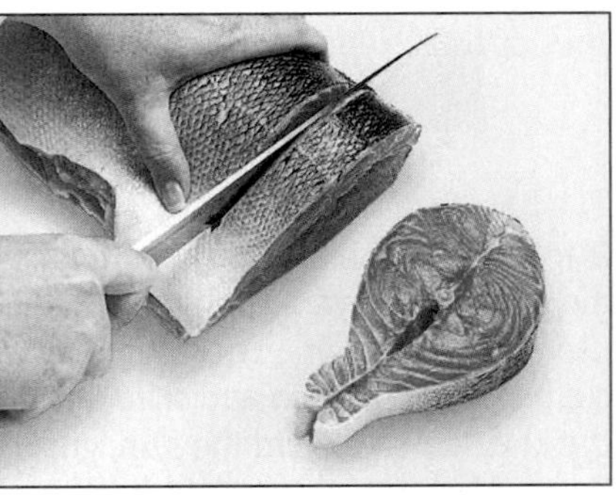

Using a chef's knife, cut through the fish, slicing steaks of the desired thickness. The steaks will contain some bones that are not necessarily removed.

▶ PROCEDURE FOR PEELING AND DEVEINING SHRIMP

Peeling and deveining shrimp is a simple procedure done in most commercial kitchens. The tail portion of the shell is often left on the peeled shrimp to give it an attractive appearance or make it easier to eat. This procedure can be used on both cooked and uncooked shrimp.

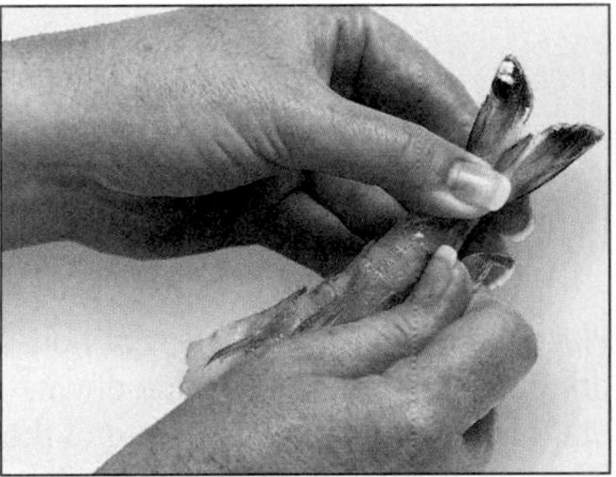

1 Grip the shrimp's tail between your thumb and forefinger. Use your other thumb and forefinger to grip the legs and the edge of the shell.

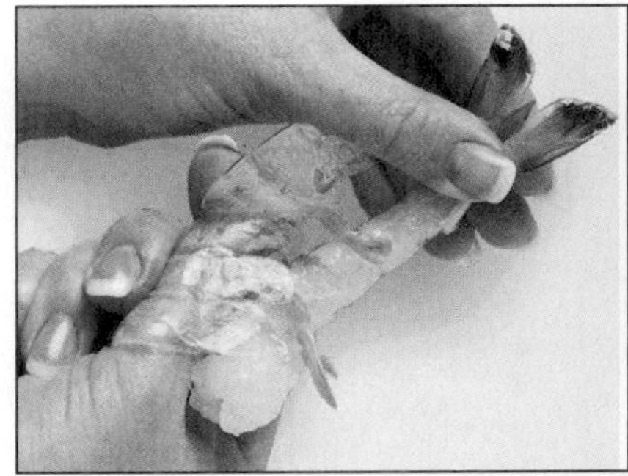

2 Pull the legs and shell away from the flesh, leaving the tail and first joint of the shell in place if desired.

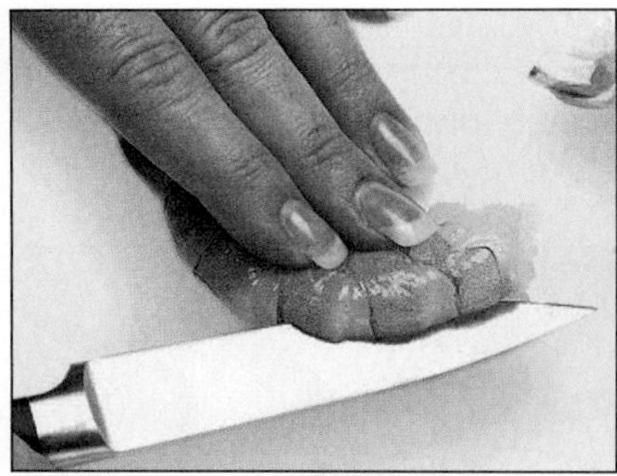

3 Place the shrimp on a cutting board and use a paring knife to make a shallow cut down the back of the shrimp, exposing the digestive tract or "vein."

4 Pull out the vein while rinsing the shrimp under cold water.

▶ PROCEDURE FOR BUTTERFLYING SHRIMP

Butterflying raw shrimp improves their appearance and increases their surface area for even cooking. To butterfly shrimp, first peel them using the procedure outlined earlier. Then:

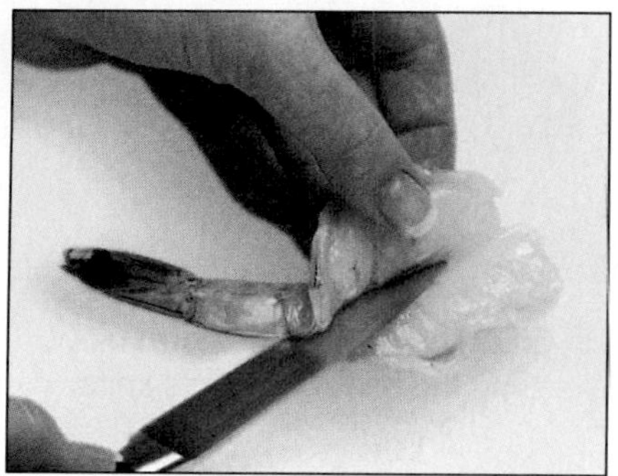

Instead of making a shallow cut to expose the vein, make a deeper cut that nearly slices the shrimp into two bilateral halves. Pull out the vein while rinsing the shrimp under cold water.

▶ PROCEDURE FOR PREPARING LIVE LOBSTERS FOR BROILING

A whole lobster can be cooked by plunging it into boiling water or court bouillon. If the lobster is to be broiled, it must be split lengthwise before cooking.

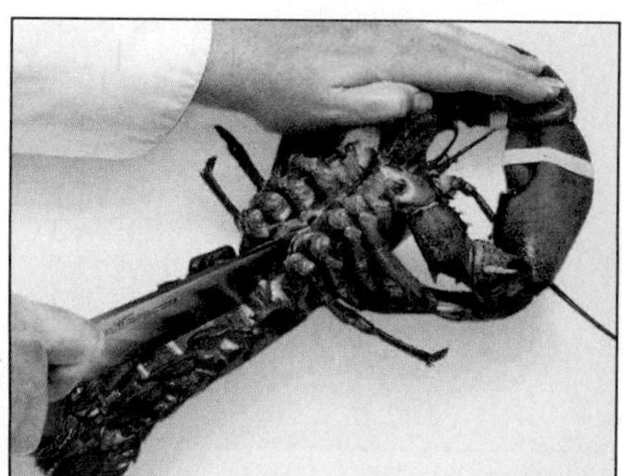

1 Place the live lobster on its back on a cutting board and pierce its head with the point of a chef's knife. Then, in one smooth stroke, bring the knife down and cut through the body and tail without splitting it completely in half.

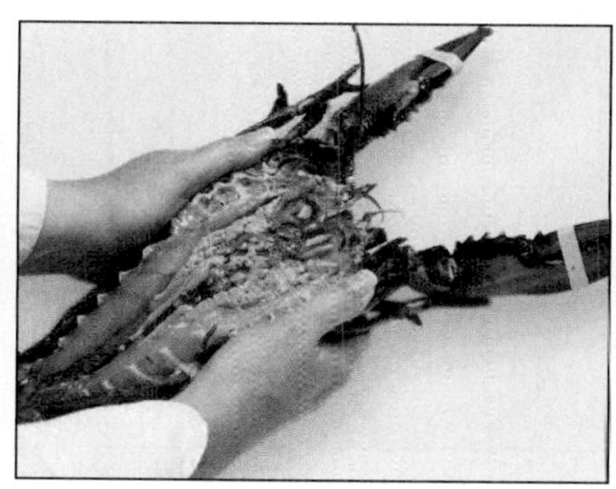

2 Use your hands to crack the lobster's back so that it lies flat. Crack the claws with the back of a chef's knife.

3 Cut through the tail and curl each half of the tail to the side. Remove and discard the stomach. The tomalley (the olive-green liver) and, if present, the coral (the roe) can be removed and saved for a sauce or other preparation.

▶ PROCEDURE FOR PREPARING LIVE LOBSTERS FOR SAUTÉING

A whole lobster may also be cut into smaller pieces for sautéing or other preparations.

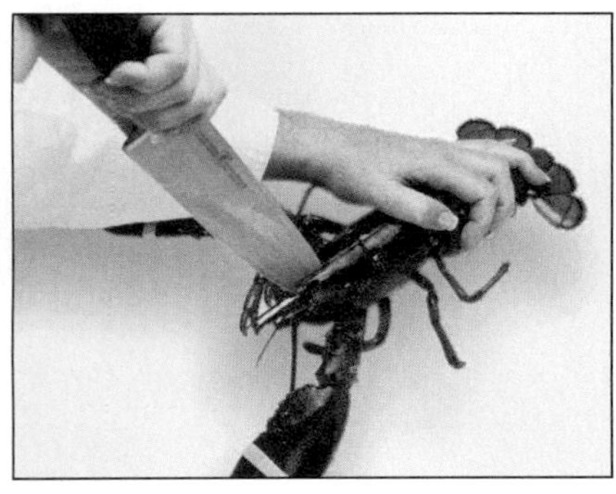

1 Using the point of a chef's knife, pierce the lobster's head.

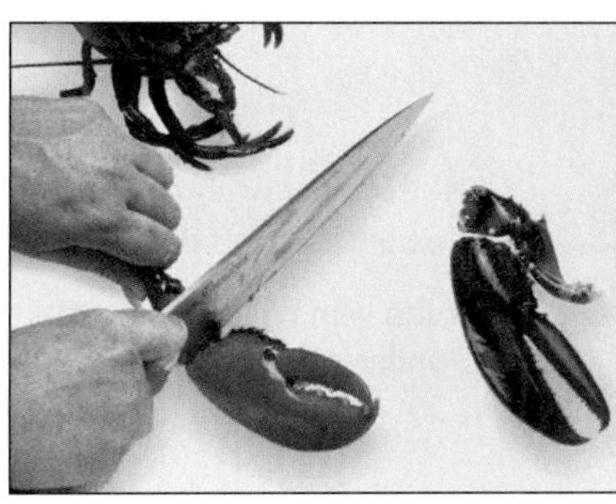

2 Cut off the claws and arms.

3 Cut the tail into cross-sections.

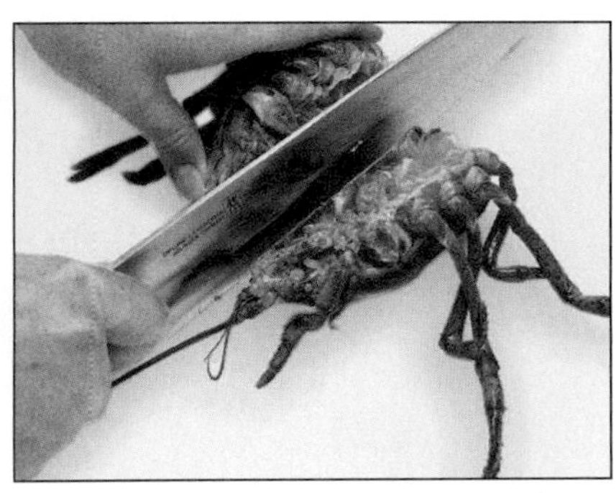

4 Split the head and thorax in half. The tomalley and coral (if present) can be removed and saved for further use. The head and legs may be added to the recipe for flavor, but there is very little meat in them and they are typically discarded.

5 Crack the claws with a firm blow, using the back of a chef's knife.

▶ PROCEDURE FOR REMOVING COOKED LOBSTER MEAT FROM THE SHELL

Many recipes call for cooked lobster meat. Cook the lobster by plunging it into a boiling court bouillon and simmering for 6 to 8 minutes per pound. Remove the lobster and allow it to cool until it can be easily handled. Then:

1 Pull the claws and large legs away from the body. Break the claw away from the leg. Split the legs with a chef's knife and remove the meat, using your fingers or a pick.

2 Carefully crack the claw with a mallet or the back of a chef's knife without damaging the meat. Pull out the claw meat in one piece.

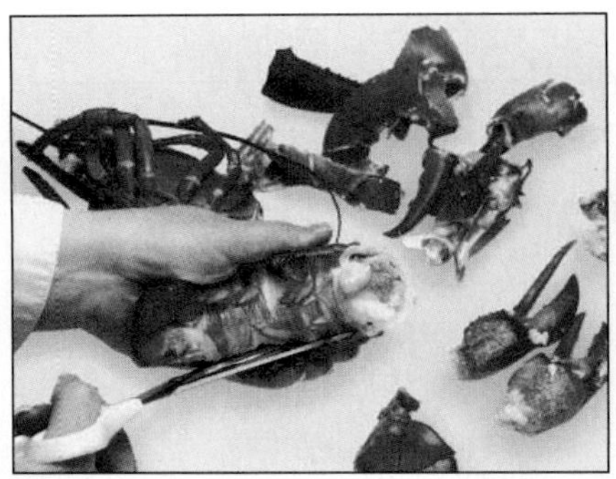

3 Pull the lobster's tail away from its body and use kitchen shears to trim away the soft membrane on the underside of the tail.

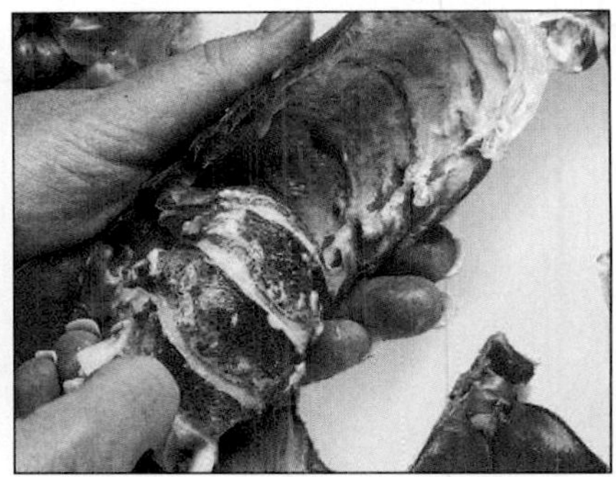

4 Pull the meat out of the shell in one piece.

▶ PROCEDURE FOR OPENING CLAMS

Opening raw clams efficiently requires practice. Like all mollusks, clams should be cleaned under cold running water with a brush to remove all mud, silt and sand that may be stuck to their shells. A knife may be more easily inserted into a clam if the clam is washed and allowed to relax in the refrigerator for at least one hour before it is opened.

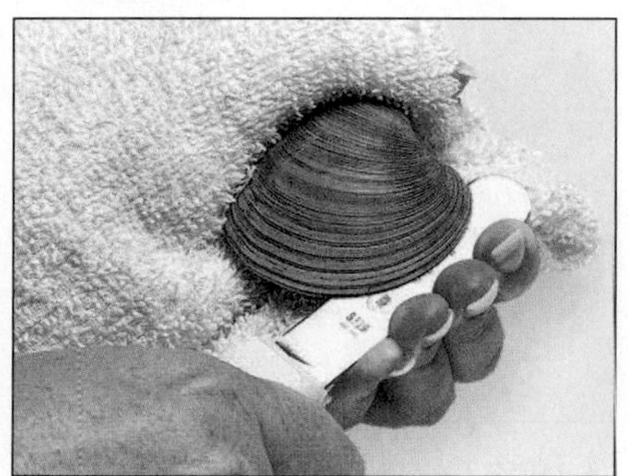

1 Hold the clam firmly in a folded towel in the palm of your hand; the notch in the edge of the shell should be toward your thumb. With the fingers of the same hand, squeeze and pull the blade of the clam knife between the clamshells. Do not push on the knife handle with your other hand; you will not be able to control the knife if it slips and you can cut yourself.

2 Pull the knife between the shells until it cuts the muscle. Twist the knife to pry the shells apart. Slide the knife tip along the top shell and cut through the muscle. Twist the top shell, breaking it free at the hinge; discard it.

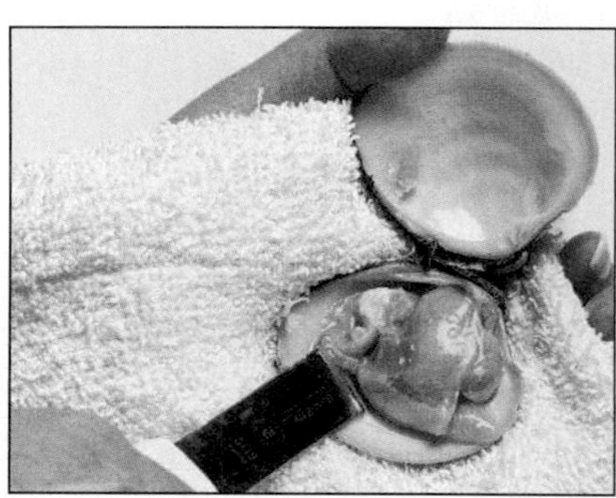

3 Use the knife tip to release the clam from the bottom shell.

▶ PROCEDURE FOR OPENING OYSTERS

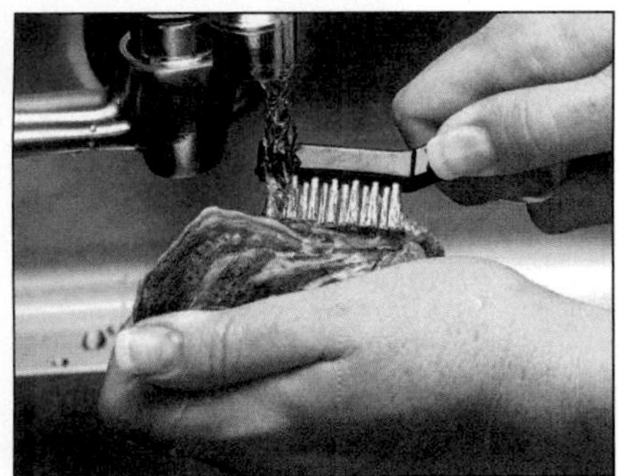

1 Clean the oyster by brushing it under running water.

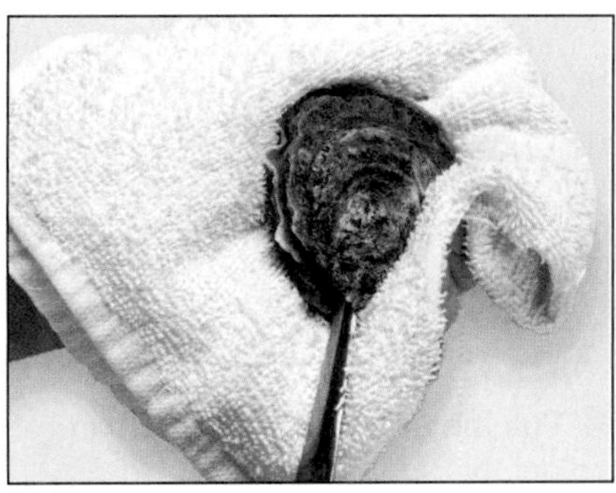

2 Hold the cleaned oyster firmly in a folded towel in the palm of your hand. Insert the tip of an oyster knife in the hinge and use a twisting motion to pop the hinge apart. Do not use too much forward pressure on the knife; it can slip and you could stab yourself.

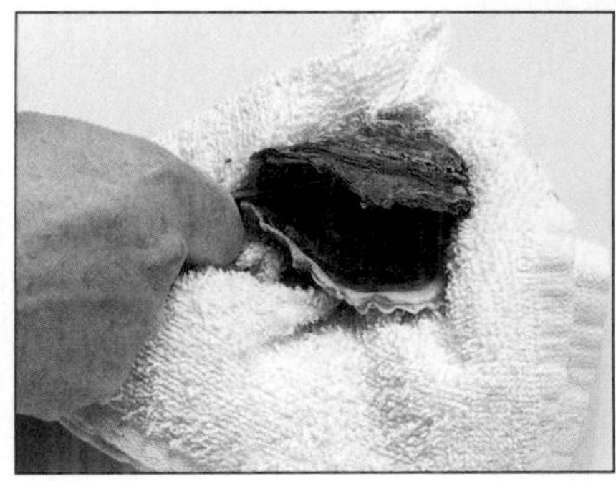

3 Slide the knife along the top of the shell to release the oyster from the shell. Discard the top shell.

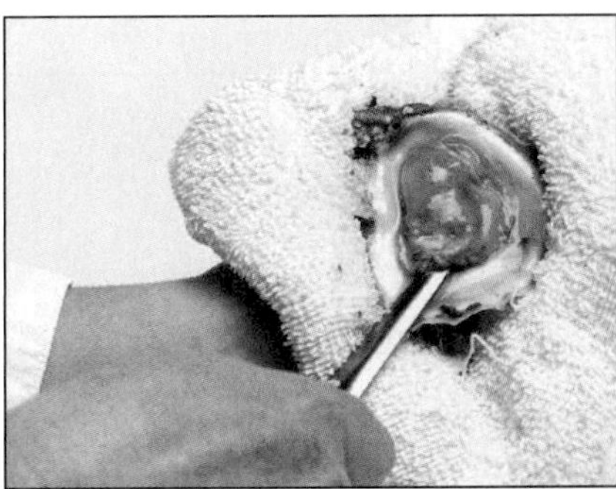

4 Use the knife tip to release the oyster from the bottom shell.

5 Fresh raw oysters on the half shell with seaweed garnish.

▶ PROCEDURE FOR CLEANING AND DEBEARDING MUSSELS

Mussels are not normally eaten raw. Before cooking, a clump of dark threads called the beard must be removed. Because this could kill the mussel, cleaning and debearding must be done as close to cooking time as possible.

1 Clean the mussel with a brush under cold running water to remove sand and grit.

2 Pull the beard away from the mussel with your fingers or a small pair of pliers.

► Applying Various Cooking Methods

Fish and shellfish can be prepared by the dry-heat cooking methods of broiling and grilling, roasting (baking), sautéing, pan-frying and deep-frying as well as the moist-heat cooking methods of steaming, poaching and simmering.

DETERMINING DONENESS

Unlike most meats and poultry, nearly all fish and shellfish are inherently tender and should be cooked just until done. Indeed, overcooking is the most common mistake made when preparing fish and shellfish. The Canadian Department of Fisheries recommends that all fish be cooked 10 minutes for every inch (2.5 centimeters) of thickness, regardless of cooking method. Although this may be a good general policy, variables such as the type and the form of fish and the exact cooking method used suggest that one or more of the following methods of determining doneness are more appropriate for professional food service operations:

1. *Translucent flesh becomes opaque*—The raw flesh of most fish and shellfish appears somewhat translucent. As the proteins coagulate during cooking, the flesh becomes opaque.
2. *Flesh becomes firm*—The flesh of most fish and shellfish firms as it cooks. Doneness can be tested by judging the resistance of the flesh when pressed with a finger. Raw or undercooked fish or shellfish will be mushy and soft. As it cooks, the flesh offers more resistance and springs back quickly.
3. *Flesh separates from the bones easily*—The flesh of raw fish remains firmly attached to the bones. As the fish cooks, the flesh and bones separate easily.
4. *Flesh begins to flake*—Fish flesh consists of short muscle fibers separated by thin connective tissue. As the fish cooks, the connective tissue breaks down and the groups of muscle fibers begin to flake, that is, separate from one another. Fish is done when the flesh begins to flake. If the flesh flakes easily, the fish will be overdone and dry.

Remember, fish and shellfish are subject to carryover cooking. Because they cook quickly and at low temperatures, it is better to undercook fish and shellfish and allow carryover cooking or residual heat to finish the cooking process.

DRY-HEAT COOKING METHODS

Dry-heat cooking methods are those that do not require additional moisture at any time during the cooking process. The dry-heat cooking methods used with fish and shellfish are broiling and grilling, roasting (usually referred to as baking when used with fish and shellfish), sautéing, pan-frying and deep-frying

BROILING AND GRILLING

After brushing with oil or butter, fish can be grilled directly on the grate or placed on a heated platter under the broiler. Broiled or grilled fish should have a lightly charred surface and a slightly smoky flavor as a result of the intense radiant heat of the broiler or grill. The interior should be moist and juicy. Broiled or grilled shellfish meat should be moist and tender with only slight coloration from the grill or broiler.

Selecting Fish and Shellfish to Broil or Grill

Nearly all types of fish and shellfish can be successfully broiled or grilled. Salmon, trout, swordfish and other oily fish are especially well suited to grilling, as are lean fish such as bass and snapper. Fillets of lean flatfish with delicate textures, such as flounder and sole, are better broiled. They should be placed on a preheated broiling (sizzler) platter before being placed under the broiler.

Oysters and clams are often broiled on the half shell with flavored butters, bread crumbs or other garnishes and served sizzling hot. Squid can be stuffed, secured with a toothpick and broiled or grilled. Brushed with butter, split lobsters, king crabs and snow crabs are often broiled or grilled. Whole lobsters can be split and broiled or grilled, or their tails can be removed, split and cooked separately. Large crab legs can also be split and broiled or grilled. Shrimp and scallops are often broiled in flavored butters or grilled on skewers for easy handling.

Seasoning Fish and Shellfish to Be Broiled or Grilled

All fish should be brushed lightly with butter or oil before being placed on the grill or under the broiler. The butter or oil prevents sticking and helps leaner fish retain moisture. For most fish, a simple seasoning of salt and pepper suffices. But most fish do respond well to marinades, especially those made with white wine and lemon juice. Because most fish are delicately flavored, they should be marinated for only a brief time. (Even marinated fish should be brushed with butter or oil before cooking.) Herbs should be avoided because they will burn from the intense heat of the broiler or grill.

Clams, oysters and other shellfish that are stuffed or cooked with butters, vegetables, bacon or other accompaniments or garnishes gain flavor from these ingredients. Be careful, however, not to overpower the delicate flavors of the shellfish by adding too many strong flavorings.

Accompaniments to Broiled and Grilled Fish and Shellfish

Lemon wedges are the traditional accompaniment to broiled or grilled fish and shellfish. But they can be served with sauces made separately. Butter sauces such as a beurre blanc are popular, as their richness complements the lean fish. Vegetable coulis are a good choice for a healthier, lower-fat accompaniment. Additional sauce suggestions are found in Table 11.5. If the item is cooked on a broiler platter with a seasoned butter, it is often served with that butter.

Almost any side dish goes well with broiled or grilled fish or shellfish. Fried or boiled potatoes, pasta and rice are all good choices. Grilled vegetables are a natural choice.

▶ PROCEDURE FOR BROILING OR GRILLING FISH AND SHELLFISH

All fish is delicate and must be carefully handled to achieve an attractive finished product. When broiling whole fish or fillets with their skin still on, score the skin by making several diagonal slashes approximately ¼ inch (6 millimeters) deep at even intervals. This prevents the fish from curling during cooking, promotes even cooking and creates a more attractive finished product. Be especially careful not to overcook the item. It should be served as hot as possible as soon as it is removed from the broiler or grill.

1. Heat the broiler or grill.
2. Use a wire brush to remove any charred or burnt particles that may be stuck to the broiler or grill grate. The grate can be wiped with a lightly oiled towel to remove any remaining particles and help season it.
3. Prepare the item to be broiled or grilled. For example, cut the fish into steaks or tranches of even thickness; split the lobster; peel and/or skewer the shrimp. Season or marinate the item as desired. Brush the item with oil or butter.
4. Place the item on a grill, presentation side down. If using a broiler, place the item directly on the grate or on a preheated broiler platter. Tender fish are usually broiled presentation side up on a broiler platter.

5 If practical, turn the item to produce the attractive crosshatch marks associated with grilling that are discussed in Chapter 8, Principles of Cooking. Items less than ½ inch (1.2 centimeters) thick cooked on a preheated broiler platter do not have to be turned over.
6 Cook the item to the desired doneness and serve immediately.

BROILED BLACK SEA BASS WITH HERB BUTTER AND SAUTÉED LEEKS

RECIPE 18.1

Yield: 1 Serving **Method:** Broiling

Black sea bass fillet, skin on, approx. 8 oz. (225 g)	1	1
Salt and pepper	TT	TT
Whole butter, melted	as needed	as needed
Leek, julienne	1	1
Lemon juice	2 tsp.	10 ml
Herb butter	2 slices	2 slices

1 Score the skin of the fillet with three diagonal cuts approximately ¼ inch (6 millimeters) deep.
2 Season the fillet with salt and pepper and brush with melted butter.
3 Place the fillet on a preheated broiler platter, skin side up, and place under the broiler.
4 Blanch the leek in boiling water until nearly tender.
5 Drain the leek and sauté in 1 tablespoon (15 milliliters) whole butter until tender. Add the lemon juice; season with salt and pepper.
6 Remove the fish from the broiler when done. Top with the herb butter and serve on a bed of sautéed leeks.

Approximate values per serving: **Calories** 260, **Total fat** 15 g, **Saturated fat** 8 g, **Cholesterol** 80 mg, **Sodium** 790 mg, **Total carbohydrates** 11 g, **Protein** 21 g, **Vitamin A** 15%, **Vitamin C** 15%

Mise en Place

- ▶ Melt whole butter and keep warm.
- ▶ Wash, clean and julienne the leek.

1 Scoring the fish skin.

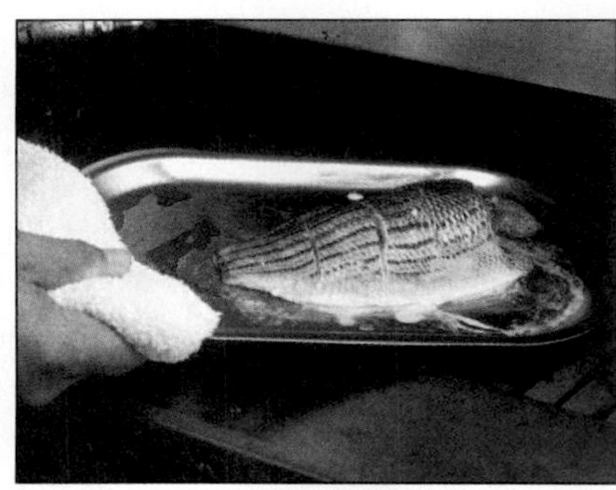

2 Placing the fish on a broiler platter, under the broiler.

3 Serving the fish on a bed of sautéed leeks.

BAKING

The terms *baking* and *roasting* are used interchangeably when applied to fish and shellfish. One disadvantage of baking fish is that the short baking time does not allow the surface of the fish to caramelize. To help correct this problem, fish can be browned in a sauté pan with a small amount of oil to achieve the added flavor and appearance of a browned surface, and then finished in an oven.

Selecting Fish and Shellfish to Bake

Fatty fish produce the best baked fish. Fish fillets and steaks are the best market forms to bake, as they cook quickly and evenly and are easily portioned. Although lean fish can be baked, it tends to become dry and must be basted often.

Seasoning Fish and Shellfish to Be Baked

The most popular seasonings for baked fish are lemon, butter, salt and pepper. Fish can also be marinated before baking for added flavor. But baked fish usually depend on the accompanying sauce for much of their flavor.

Shellfish are often stuffed or mixed with other ingredients before baking. For example, raw oysters on the half shell can be topped with spinach, watercress and Pernod (oysters Rockefeller) and baked. Shrimp are often butterflied, stuffed and baked; lobsters are split, stuffed and baked. Many food service operations remove clams from their shells; mix them with bread crumbs, seasonings or other ingredients; refill the shells and bake the mixture.

Accompaniments to Baked Fish and Shellfish

Baked fish is often served with a flavorful sauce such as a creole sauce or Beurre Blanc. Additional sauce suggestions are found in Table 11.5. Almost any type of rice, pasta or potato is a good accompaniment, as is any variety of sautéed vegetable.

▶ PROCEDURE FOR BAKING FISH AND SHELLFISH

1 Portion the fish or shellfish and arrange on a well-oiled or buttered pan, presentation side up.
2 Season as desired and brush the surface of the fish or shellfish generously with melted butter; add garnishes or flavorings as desired or directed in the recipe.
3 Place the pan in a preheated oven at approximately 400°F (200°C).
4 Baste periodically during the cooking process (more often if the fish is lean). Remove from the oven when the fish is slightly underdone.

RECIPE 18.2

BAKED RED SNAPPER

Mise en Place

- ▶ Wash and chop mint leaves.
- ▶ Peel and mince garlic.
- ▶ Melt whole butter and keep warm.

Yield: 4 Servings **Method:** Baking

Red snapper fillets, 8 oz. (250 g) each	4	4
Salt and white pepper	TT	TT
Whole butter, melted	2 oz.	60 g
Mint leaves, chopped	1 Tbsp.	15 ml
Garlic, minced	1 tsp.	5 ml
Tomato concassée	4 oz.	120 g
White wine	2 fl. oz.	60 ml
Lemon juice	2 fl. oz.	60 ml

1 Place the snapper on a buttered baking pan. Season the fillets with salt and white pepper; brush with butter.
2 Combine the mint, garlic and tomato concassée, and spoon on top of each portion of the fish.
3 Add the wine and lemon juice to the pan.
4 Bake at 400°F (200°C), basting once halfway through the cooking process, until done, approximately 15 minutes.

Approximate values per serving: **Calories** 600, **Total fat** 16 g, **Saturated fat** 8 g, **Cholesterol** 140 mg, **Sodium** 850 mg, **Total carbohydrates** 55 g, **Protein** 60 g, **Vitamin A** 25%, **Vitamin C** 35%

1 Brushing the fillets with butter.

2 Topping each portion with mint and tomato concassée.

3 The finished fish.

SAUTÉING

Sautéing is a very popular cooking method for fish and shellfish. It lightly caramelizes the food's surface, giving it additional flavor. Typically, other ingredients such as garlic, onions, vegetables, wine and lemon juice are added to the fond to make a sauce.

Selecting Fish and Shellfish to Sauté

Both fatty and lean fish may be sautéed. Flatfish are sometimes dressed and sautéed whole, as are small round fish such as trout. Larger fish such as salmon can be cut into steaks or filleted and cut into tranches. The portions should be relatively uniform in size and thickness and fairly thin to promote even cooking. Although clams, mussels and oysters are not often sautéed, scallops and crustaceans are popular sauté items.

Seasoning Fish and Shellfish to Be Sautéed

Many types of fish—especially sole, flounder and other delicate, lean fish fillets—are often dredged in plain or seasoned flour before sautéing. Seasoned butter is used to sauté some items, such as scampi-style shrimp. These items derive their flavor from the butter; additional seasonings should not be necessary.

Cooking Temperatures

The sauté pan and cooking fat must be hot before the fish or shellfish are added. Do not add too much fish or shellfish to the pan at one time, or the pan and fat will cool, letting the foods simmer in their own juices. Thin slices and small pieces of fish and shellfish require a short cooking time, so use high temperatures in order to caramelize their surfaces without overcooking. Large, thick pieces of fish or shellfish being cooked in the shell may require slightly lower cooking temperatures to ensure that they are cooked without overbrowning their surfaces.

Accompaniments to Sautéed Fish and Shellfish

Sautéed fish and shellfish are nearly always served with a sauce made directly in the sauté pan. This sauce may be as simple as browned butter (*beurre noisette*) or a complicated sauce flavored with the fond. In some cases, seasoned butter is used to sauté the fish or shellfish and the butter is then served with the main item. See Table 11.5 for additional sauce suggestions.

Mildly flavored rice and pasta are good choices to serve with sautéed fish or shellfish.

▶ PROCEDURE FOR SAUTÉING FISH AND SHELLFISH

1. Cut or portion the fish or shellfish.
2. Season the item and dredge in seasoned flour if desired.
3. Heat a suitable sauté pan over moderate heat; add enough oil or clarified butter to cover the bottom to a depth of about ⅛ inch (3 millimeters).
4. Add the fish or shellfish to the pan (fish should be placed presentation side down); cook until done, turning once halfway through the cooking process. Add other foods as called for in the recipe.
5. Remove the fish or shellfish. If a sauce is to be made in the sauté pan, follow the procedures discussed in Chapter 16, Poultry.

RECIPE 18.3

SAUTÉED HALIBUT WITH THREE-COLOR PEPPERS AND SPANISH OLIVES

Mise en Place

- ▶ Peel and slice onions.
- ▶ Peel and mince garlic.
- ▶ Wash, seed and julienne bell peppers.
- ▶ Pit and quarter olives.
- ▶ Wash and chop thyme.

Yield: 4 Servings **Method:** Sautéing

Halibut fillets, 6 oz. (170 g) each	4	4
Salt and pepper	TT	TT
Olive oil	2 fl. oz.	60 ml
Onion, sliced	3 oz.	90 g
Garlic, minced	2 tsp.	10 ml
Green bell pepper, julienne	3 oz.	90 g
Red bell pepper, julienne	3 oz.	90 g
Yellow bell pepper, julienne	3 oz.	90 g
Tomato concassée	8 oz.	250 g
Spanish olives, pitted and quartered	2 oz.	60 g
Fresh thyme, chopped	2 tsp.	10 ml
Lemon juice	2 fl. oz.	60 ml
Fish stock	2 fl. oz.	60 ml

1. Season the fillets with salt and pepper.
2. Heat a sauté pan and add the oil.
3. Sauté the halibut, turning once. Remove and reserve in a warm place.
4. Add the onion and garlic to the same pan and sauté for approximately 1 minute. Add the bell peppers and sauté for 1 to 2 minutes more.
5. Add the tomato concassée, olives and thyme; sauté briefly.
6. Add the lemon juice and deglaze the pan. Add the stock, simmer for 2 minutes to blend the flavors and adjust the seasonings.
7. Return the fish to the pan to reheat. Serve each fish fillet on a bed of vegetables with sauce and an appropriate garnish.

1 Sautéing the halibut fillets.

Approximate values per serving: **Calories** 420, **Total fat** 21 g, **Saturated fat** 3 g, **Cholesterol** 70 mg, **Sodium** 870 mg, **Total carbohydrates** 10 g, **Protein** 47 g, **Vitamin A** 15%, **Vitamin C** 110%

2 Sautéing the onions, garlic and peppers.

3 Adding the fish stock.

4 Returning the fish to the pan to reheat.

PAN-FRYING

Pan-frying is very similar to sautéing, but it uses more fat to cook the main item. Pan-fried fish is always coated with flour, batter or breading to help seal the surface and prevent the flesh from coming into direct contact with the cooking fat. Properly prepared pan-fried fish and shellfish should be moist and tender with a crisp surface. If battered or breaded, the coating should be intact with no breaks.

Selecting Fish and Shellfish to Pan-Fry

Both fatty and lean fish may be pan-fried. Trout and other small fish are ideal for pan-frying, as are portioned fillets of lean fish such as halibut. Pan-fried fish and shellfish should be uniform in size and relatively thin so that they cook quickly and evenly.

Seasoning Fish and Shellfish to Be Pan-Fried

Although fish and shellfish can be marinated or seasoned directly, it is more common to season the flour, batter or breading that will coat them. Batters, for example, can contain cheese, and breadings can contain nuts and other ingredients to add different flavors to the fish or shellfish. Review the battering and breading procedures discussed in Chapter 7, Mise en Place. Additional seasonings come from sauces and other accompaniments served with the pan-fried fish or shellfish.

Cooking Temperatures

The fat should always be hot before the fish or shellfish are added. Breaded or battered fish fillets cook very quickly, and the fat should be hot enough to brown the coating without overcooking the interior. Whole pan-fried fish take longer to cook and therefore require a slightly lower cooking temperature so that the surface does not become too dark before the interior is cooked.

Accompaniments to Pan-Fried Fish and Shellfish

Lemon wedges are the classic accompaniment to pan-fried fish and shellfish. Sauces that accompany pan-fried items are made separately. Mayonnaise-based sauces such as Tartar Sauce and Rémoulade Sauce are especially popular; rich wine-based sauces should be avoided. Vegetable coulis, such as tomato, also complement many pan-fried items. Additional sauce suggestions are found in Table 11.5.

▶ PROCEDURE FOR PAN-FRYING FISH AND SHELLFISH

1. Heat enough clarified butter or oil in a heavy sauté pan so that it will come one-third to halfway up the side of the item. The fat should be at a temperature between 325°F and 350°F (163°C and 177°C).
2. Add the floured, breaded or battered item to the pan, being careful not to splash the hot fat. Cook until done, turning once halfway through the cooking process.
3. Remove the food and drain on absorbent paper.
4. Serve it promptly with an appropriate sauce.

RECIPE 18.4

BLUE CRAB CAKES

Mise en Place

- ▶ Wash, seed and cut bell peppers into small dice.
- ▶ Wash and slice green onions.
- ▶ Crack egg into a small bowl and beat lightly with a fork.

1 Mixing all ingredients for the crab cakes.

2 Forming the crab cakes.

3 Pan-frying the crab cakes.

Yield: 15 Cakes, 2 oz. (60 g) each **Method:** Pan-frying

Blue crab meat	1 lb.	450 g
Heavy cream	6 fl. oz.	180 ml
Red bell pepper, small dice	2 oz.	60 g
Green bell pepper, small dice	2 oz.	60 g
Clarified butter	as needed	as needed
Green onions, sliced	1 bunch	1 bunch
Fresh bread crumbs	6 oz.	180 g
Salt and pepper	TT	TT
Dijon mustard	1 Tbsp.	15 ml
Worcestershire sauce	TT	TT
Tabasco sauce	TT	TT
Egg, slightly beaten	1	1

1 Carefully pick through the crab meat, removing any pieces of shell. Keep the lumps of crab meat as large as possible.
2 Place the cream in a saucepan and bring to a boil. Reduce by approximately one-half. Chill the cream well.
3 Sauté the bell peppers in a small amount of clarified butter until tender.
4 Combine the crab meat, reduced cream, bell peppers, green onions and approximately 3 ounces (90 grams) bread crumbs along with the salt, pepper, Dijon mustard, Worcestershire sauce, Tabasco sauce and egg. Mix to combine all ingredients, trying to keep the lumps of crab meat intact.
5 Using a mold, form the crab mixture into cakes of the desired size.
6 Place the remaining bread crumbs in an appropriately sized hotel pan. Place the crab cakes, a few at a time, in the hotel pan and cover with the bread crumbs. To help them adhere, press the crumbs lightly into the cakes.
7 Heat a sauté pan over moderate heat and add enough clarified butter to cover the bottom approximately 1/4 inch (6 millimeters) deep.
8 Add the crab cakes to the pan and cook until done, turning once when the first side is nicely browned. Remove and drain on absorbent paper.

Approximate values per 2-oz. (60-g) cake serving: **Calories** 130, **Total fat** 6 g, **Saturated fat** 3.5 g, **Cholesterol** 60 mg, **Sodium** 650 mg, **Total carbohydrates** 9 g, **Protein** 10 g, **Vitamin C** 15%

DEEP-FRYING

Deep-frying is the process of cooking foods by submerging them in hot fat. Typically, fish or shellfish are breaded or battered before deep-frying. Alternatively, they can be formed into croquettes or fritters. Properly deep-fried fish and shellfish should be moist and tender, not greasy or tough. Their coating should be crispy and golden brown.

Selecting Fish and Shellfish to Deep-Fry

Whole small fish and fillets of lean fish such as catfish or halibut are excellent for deep-frying. The fillets should be of uniform size and relatively thin so that they cook quickly and evenly. Fatty fish, such as salmon, are ideal for croquettes. Peeled shrimp and shucked mollusks, especially clams and oysters, can be breaded, battered or formed into fritters and deep-fried. Deep-fried breaded or battered sliced squid or octopus served with a dipping sauce makes an excellent hors d'oeuvre.

Seasoning Fish and Shellfish to Be Deep-Fried

Typically, seasonings used for deep-fried fish or shellfish are added to the breading or batter, although salt and pepper should be added after frying. Additional flavors come from sauces or accompaniments.

Accompaniments to Deep-Fried Fish and Shellfish

As with pan-fried fish and shellfish, lemon wedges and mayonnaise-based sauces such as tartar sauce and rémoulade sauce are popular accompaniments to deep-fried fish and shellfish. Spicy tomato- or soy-based dipping sauces are also excellent choices. Traditional English fish and chips is served with malt vinegar.

▶ PROCEDURE FOR DEEP-FRYING FISH AND SHELLFISH

1. Shuck, peel, cut, trim or otherwise prepare the fish or shellfish to be deep-fried. Season, bread or batter it, as desired.
2. Heat the fat to the desired temperature, usually around 350°F (177°C). Breaded or battered fish or shellfish cook quickly and the fat must be hot enough to cook the food's interior without burning its surface.
3. Carefully place the food in the hot fat using either the basket method or the swimming method.
4. Deep-fry the fish or shellfish until done. Doneness is usually determined by color, timing or sampling.
5. Remove the deep-fried food from the fat and hold it over the fryer, allowing the excess fat to drain off. Transfer the food to a hotel pan either lined with absorbent paper or fitted with a rack. Season with salt, if desired.
6. If the deep-fried fish or shellfish is to be held for later service, place it under a heat lamp.

DEEP-FRIED CATFISH FILLETS WITH TARTAR SAUCE

RECIPE 18.5

Yield: 8 Servings

Method: Deep-frying

Catfish fillets, cut into uniform-sized pieces	3 lb.	1.5 kg
Salt and pepper	TT	TT
Flour	as needed for breading	
Egg wash	as needed for breading	
Cornmeal	as needed for breading	
Tartar Sauce	12 fl. oz.	360 ml

1. Season the fillets with salt and pepper.
2. Bread the fillets using the standard breading procedure described in Chapter 7, Mise en Place.
3. Using the basket method, deep-fry the fillets until done. Drain well and serve with the Tartar Sauce.

Approximate values per 8-oz. (240-g) serving: **Calories** 600, **Total fat** 46 g, **Saturated fat** 10 g, **Cholesterol** 160 mg, **Sodium** 910 mg, **Total carbohydrates** 16 g, **Protein** 31 g, **Iron** 15%

Mise en Place

- ▶ Cut catfish into uniform-sized pieces.
- ▶ Heat deep-fat fryer.

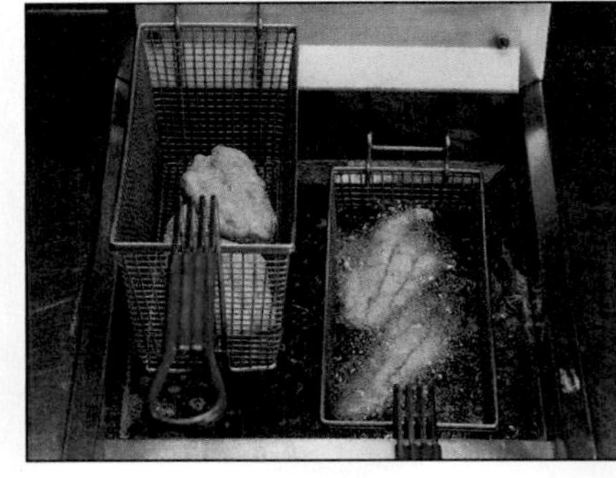

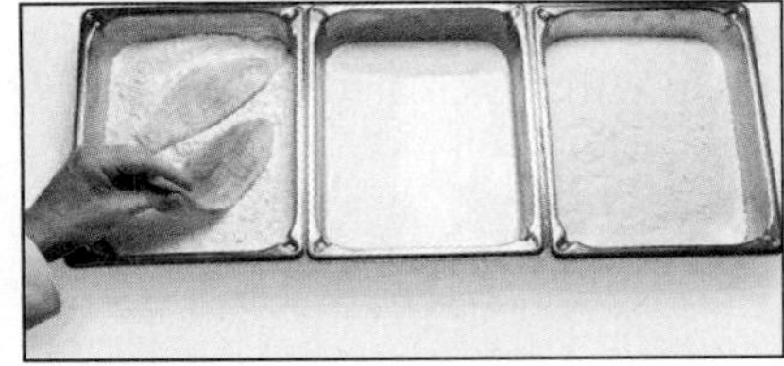

1 Flouring the seasoned fish fillets.

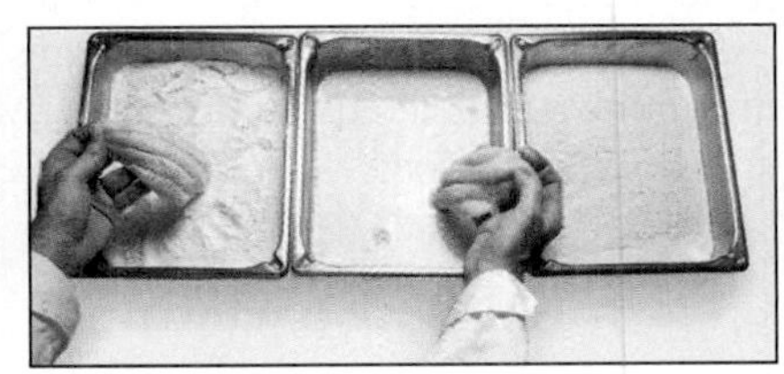

2 Passing the floured fillets through the egg wash.

3 Coating the fillets with white cornmeal.

MOIST-HEAT COOKING METHODS

Fish and shellfish lend themselves well to moist-heat cooking methods, especially steaming, poaching and simmering. Steaming best preserves the food's natural flavors and cooks without adding fat. Poaching is also popular, especially for fish. Poached fish can be served hot or cold, whole or as steaks, fillets or portions. Boiling, which is actually simmering, is most often associated with crustaceans.

STEAMING

Steaming is a very natural way to cook fish and shellfish without adding fats. Fish are steamed by suspending them over a small amount of boiling liquid in a covered pan. The steam trapped in the pan gently cooks the food while preserving its natural flavors and most nutrients. The liquid used to steam fish and shellfish can be water or a court bouillon with herbs, spices, aromatics or wine added to infuse the item with additional flavors. Mussels and clams can be steamed by placing them directly in a pan, adding a small amount of wine or other liquid and covering them. Their shells will hold them above the liquid as they cook. Fish and shellfish can also be steamed by wrapping them in parchment paper together with herbs, vegetables, butters or sauces as accompaniments and baking them in a hot oven. This method of steaming is called **en papillote.**

▶ **en papillote** (awn pa-pee-yote) a cooking method in which food is wrapped in paper or foil and then heated so that the food steams in its own moisture

Steamed fish and shellfish should be moist and tender. They should have clean and delicate flavors. Any accompaniments or sauces should complement the main item without masking its flavor. Fish and shellfish cooked en papillote should be served piping hot so that the aromatic steam trapped by the paper escapes as the paper is cut open tableside.

Selecting Fish and Shellfish to Steam

Mollusks (for example, clams and mussels), fatty fish (for example, salmon and sea bass) and lean fish (for example, sole) all produce good results when steamed. The portions should be of uniform thickness and no more than 1 inch (2.5 centimeters) thick to promote even cooking.

Seasoning Fish and Shellfish to Be Steamed

Steamed fish and shellfish rely heavily on their natural flavors and often require very little seasoning. Nevertheless, salt, pepper, herbs and spices can be applied directly to the raw food before steaming. Flavored liquids used to steam fish and shellfish will contribute additional flavors. If the liquid is served with the fish or shellfish as a broth or used to make a sauce to accompany the item, it is especially important that the liquid be well seasoned. Lemons, limes and other fruits or vegetables can also be cooked with the fish or shellfish to add flavors. Clams and mussels often do not require additional salt, as the liquor released when they open during cooking is sufficiently salty.

Accompaniments to Steamed Fish and Shellfish

Steamed fish and shellfish are popular partly because they are low in fat. In keeping with this perception, a low or nonfat sauce or a simple squeeze of lemon and steamed fresh vegetables are good accompaniments. If fat is not a concern, then an emulsified butter sauce such as Beurre Blanc or Hollandaise may be a good choice. Table 11.5 lists several sauce suggestions.

Classic New England steamed clams are served with a portion of the steaming liquid; steamed mussels are served with a sauce that is created from the wine and other ingredients used to steam them.

▶ PROCEDURE FOR STEAMING FISH AND SHELLFISH

1 Portion the fish to an appropriate size. Clean the shellfish
2 Prepare the cooking liquid. Add seasoning and flavoring ingredients as desired and bring to a boil.
3 Place the fish or shellfish in the steamer on a rack or in a perforated pan and cover tightly.
4 Steam the fish or shellfish until done.
5 Serve the fish or shellfish immediately with the steaming liquid or an appropriate sauce.

STEAMED SALMON WITH LEMON AND OLIVE OIL

RECIPE 18.6

Yield: 1 Serving **Method:** Steaming

Dressing:		
Lemon zest, blanched	1 Tbsp.	15 ml
Lemon juice	2 Tbsp.	30 ml
Salt and pepper	TT	TT
Virgin olive oil	2 Tbsp.	30 ml
White wine	8 fl. oz.	250 ml
Bay leaf	1	1
Leek, chopped	2 oz.	60 g
Fresh thyme	1 sprig	1 sprig
Peppercorns, crushed	1 tsp.	5 ml
Salmon tranche or steak, approx. 6 oz. (180 g)	1	1

1 To make the dressing, combine the lemon zest, lemon juice, salt and pepper. Whisk in the oil.
2 Combine the wine, bay leaf, leek, thyme and peppercorns in the bottom of a steamer.
3 Season the salmon with salt and pepper and place it in the steamer basket.
4 Cover the steamer and bring the liquid to a boil. Cook the fish until done, approximately 4 to 6 minutes.
5 Plate the salmon and spoon the dressing over it.

Approximate values per serving: **Calories** 620, **Total fat** 40 g, **Saturated fat** 6 g, **Cholesterol** 95 mg, **Sodium** 700 mg, **Total carbohydrates** 16 g, **Protein** 48 g, **Vitamin C** 50%

Mise en Place

▶ Blanch lemon zest.
▶ Wash, peel and chop leek.
▶ Crush peppercorns.

1 Placing the fish in the steamer.

2 Spooning the dressing over the fish.

RECIPE 18.7

RED SNAPPER EN PAPILLOTE

Mise en Place

- ▶ Wash, clean and julienne leek.
- ▶ Wash, peel if necessary, and julienne fennel bulb, carrot and celery.
- ▶ Wash, seed and julienne bell pepper.
- ▶ Cut parchment paper for papillote.

Yield: 6 Servings | **Method:** Steaming

Clarified butter	as needed	as needed
Leek, julienne	3 oz.	90 g
Fennel bulb, julienne	4 oz.	120 g
Carrot, julienne	3 oz.	90 g
Celery, julienne	3 oz.	90 g
Red bell pepper, julienne	3 oz.	90 g
Red snapper fillets, skin on, 6 oz. (180 g) each	6	6
Salt and pepper	TT	TT
Basil butter	9 oz.	270 g

1. Cut six heart-shaped pieces of parchment paper large enough to contain one portion of the fish and vegetables when folded in half.
2. Brush each piece of parchment paper with clarified butter.
3. Toss the vegetables together. Place one-sixth of the vegetables on half of each piece of the buttered parchment paper.
4. Place one portion of red snapper on each portion of vegetables, skin side up; season with salt and pepper.
5. Top each portion of fish with 1½ ounces (45 grams) basil butter.
6. Fold each piece of paper over and crimp the edges to seal it.
7. Place the envelopes (papillotes) on sheet pans and bake in a preheated oven at 450°F (230°C) for 8 to 10 minutes.
8. When baked, the parchment paper should puff up and brown. Remove from the oven and serve immediately. The envelope should be carefully cut open tableside to allow the aromatic steam to escape.

1 Cutting heart-shaped pieces of parchment paper.

Approximate values per serving: **Calories** 380, **Total fat** 19 g, **Saturated fat** 11 g, **Cholesterol** 125 mg, **Sodium** 680 mg, **Total carbohydrates** 6 g, **Protein** 46 g, **Vitamin A** 50%, **Vitamin C** 30%

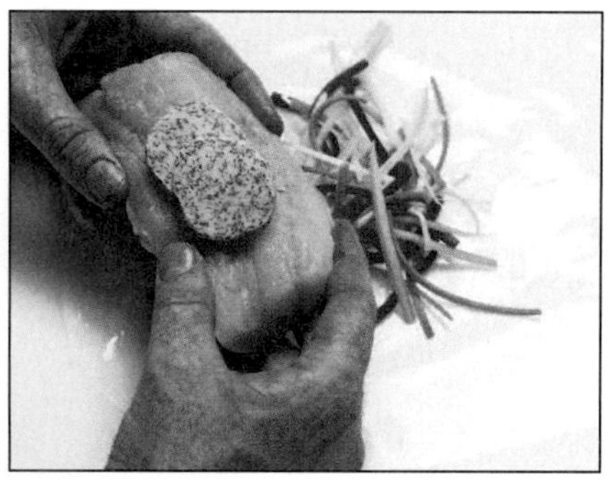

2 Placing the vegetables, red snapper and compound butter on the buttered parchment paper.

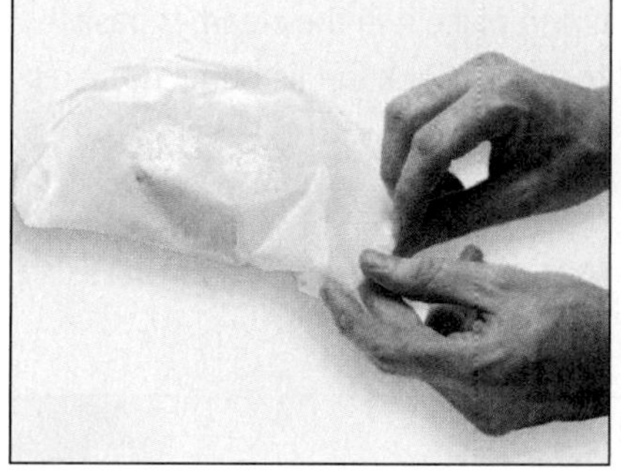

3 Crimping the edge of the parchment paper to seal it.

4 The finished papillotes.

POACHING

Poaching is a versatile and popular method for cooking fish. Shellfish are rarely poached, however. The exception is squid, which can be quickly poached and chilled for use in salads and other preparations. There are two distinct poaching methods.

The first is the **submersion method,** in which the fish is completely covered with a liquid, usually a court bouillon, fish stock or fish fumet. It is cooked until just done. The poached fish is then served (either hot or cold) with a sauce sometimes made from a portion of the cooking liquid but more often made separately. Whole fish (wrapped in cheesecloth to preserve its shape during cooking), tranches and steaks can all be cooked by submersion poaching.

The second method, called **shallow poaching,** combines poaching and steaming to achieve the desired results. The main item, usually a fillet, tranche or steak, is placed on a bed of aromatic vegetables in enough liquid to come approximately halfway up its sides. The liquid, called a **cuisson,** is brought to a simmer on the stove top. The pan is then covered with a piece of buttered parchment paper or a lid, and cooking is completed either on the stove top or in the oven. Shallow-poached fish is usually served with a sauce made with the reduced cooking liquid. (Sometimes the main item is sautéed lightly before the cooking liquid is added. If so, the cooking method is more accurately braising, as both dry- and moist-heat cooking methods are used.)

Selecting Fish to Poach

Lean white fish such as turbot, bass and sole are excellent for poaching. Some fatty fish such as salmon and trout are also excellent choices.

Seasoning Fish to Be Poached

Fish poached by either submersion or shallow poaching gain all of their seasonings from the liquid in which they are cooked and the sauce with which they are served. Therefore, it is very important to use a properly prepared court bouillon, fish fumet or a good-quality fish stock well seasoned with vegetables such as shallots, onions or carrots as well as ample herbs, spices and other seasonings. Many poached fish recipes call for wine. When using wine in either the cooking liquid or the sauce, be sure to choose a wine of good quality. Most fish are very delicately flavored, and using poor-quality wine might ruin an otherwise excellent dish. Citrus, especially lemon, is a popular seasoning; lemon juice or zest may be added to the poaching liquid, the sauce or the finished dish.

Accompaniments to Poached Fish

Poached fish cooked by submersion go well with rich sauces such as hollandaise and beurre blanc. If fat is a concern, a better choice may be a vegetable coulis (for example, broccoli or red pepper). Cold poached fish are commonly served with mayonnaise-based sauces such as sauce verte or rémoulade. Shallow-poached fish are served with sauces such as a white wine sauce or beurre blanc made from a reduction of the liquids in which the fish were poached. See Table 11.5 for additional sauce suggestions.

Poached fish are often served with rice or pasta and steamed or boiled vegetables.

▶ PROCEDURE FOR SUBMERSION POACHING

1. Prepare the cooking liquid. Whole fish should be started in a cold liquid; gradually increasing the liquid's temperature helps preserve the appearance of the fish. Portioned fish should be started in a simmering liquid to preserve their flavor and more accurately estimate cooking time.
2. Use a rack to lower the fish into the cooking liquid. Be sure the fish is completely submerged.
3. Poach the fish at 175°F–185°F (79°C–85°C) until done.
4. Remove the fish from the poaching liquid, moisten with a portion of the liquid and hold in a warm place for service. Or remove the fish from the poaching liquid, cover it to prevent drying and allow it to cool, then refrigerate.
5. Serve the poached fish with an appropriate sauce.

RECIPE 18.8

WHOLE POACHED SALMON

Mise en Place
- ▶ Scale and gut whole salmon.
- ▶ Prepare court bouillon.

Yield: 18–20 Servings   **Method:** Submersion poaching

Salmon, drawn, 4–5 lb. (1.8–2.2 kg)	1	1
Court bouillon	as needed	as needed

1 Place the fish on a lightly oiled rack or screen and secure with butcher's twine.
2 Place the rack or screen in a pot and cover with cold court bouillon.
3 Bring the court bouillon to a simmer over moderate heat. Reduce the heat and poach the fish at 175°F–180°F (79°C–85°C) until done, approximately 30 to 45 minutes.
4 If the fish is to be served hot, remove it from the court bouillon, draining well, and serve immediately with an appropriate garnish. If it is to be served cold, remove it from the court bouillon, draining well, cool and refrigerate for several hours before decorating and garnishing as desired.

Approximate values per 4-oz. (120-g) serving: **Calories** 114, **Total fat** 3 g, **Saturated fat** 1 g, **Cholesterol** 29 mg, **Sodium** 80 mg, **Total carbohydrates** 0 g, **Protein** 22 g, **Calcium** 6%

1 Arranging the whole fish on a rack.

2 Preparing the court bouillon.

3 Removing and draining the fish.

▶ PROCEDURE FOR SHALLOW POACHING

1 Butter a sauteuse and add aromatic vegetables as directed in the recipe.
2 Add the fish to the pan.
3 Add the cooking liquid to the pan.
4 Cover the pan with buttered parchment paper or a lid.
5 Bring the liquid to a simmer and cook the fish on the stove top or in the oven until done.
6 Remove the fish from the pan, moisten with a portion of the liquid and hold in a warm place for service.
7 Reduce the cuisson and finish the sauce as directed in the recipe.
8 Serve the poached fish with the sauce.

RECIPE 18.9

FILLETS OF SOLE BONNE FEMME

Mise en Place
- ▶ Peel and mince shallots.
- ▶ Wash and slice mushrooms.
- ▶ Wash, dry and chop parsley.

Yield: 2 Servings   **Method:** Shallow poaching

Sole fillets, approx. 2½ oz. (75 g) each	4	4
Salt and pepper	TT	TT
Whole butter	1 oz.	30 g
Shallots, minced	1 tsp.	5 ml
Mushrooms, sliced	4 oz.	120 g

White wine	3 fl. oz.	90 ml
Fish stock	4 fl. oz.	120 ml
Fish velouté	4 fl. oz.	120 ml
Lemon juice	TT	TT
Parsley, chopped	1 tsp.	5 ml

1 Season the sole with salt and pepper.
2 Melt the butter in a sauté pan. Add the shallots and mushrooms. To ensure even cooking, place the tail portion of each sole filet under then arrange the sole fillets over the shallots and mushrooms in the pan. Add the wine and stock.
3 Bring the liquid to a simmer. Cover the fish with buttered parchment paper and cook on the stove top or in a 350°F (180°C) oven until done, approximately 5 to 8 minutes.
4 Remove the sole and reserve in a warm place.
5 Reduce the cuisson until approximately 1 fluid ounce (30 milliliters) remains. Add the velouté. Add lemon juice to taste and adjust the seasonings. Serve the sauce with the fish, sprinkled with chopped parsley.

Approximate values per serving: **Calories** 440, **Total fat** 14 g, **Saturated fat** 5 g, **Cholesterol** 120 mg, **Sodium** 3750 mg, **Total carbohydrates** 27 g, **Protein** 42 g

1 Arranging the sole on the bed of shallots and mushrooms.

2 Covering the fish with buttered parchment paper after the liquid is added.

3 Adding the velouté to the cuisson.

SIMMERING

"Boiled" lobster, crab and shrimp are not actually boiled; rather, they are cooked whole in their shells by simmering. Although they are not as delicate as some fish, these crustaceans can become tough and are easily overcooked if the cooking liquid is allowed to boil.

Selecting Shellfish to Simmer

Lobsters, crabs and shrimp are commonly cooked by simmering. Their hard shells protect their delicate flesh during the cooking process.

Seasoning Shellfish to Be Simmered

The shellfish being simmered are not seasoned. Rather, they gain flavor by being cooked in a seasoned or flavored liquid, typically salted water or court bouillon. A sachet of pickling spice or Old Bay seasoning is sometimes used for additional flavor.

Determining Doneness

Timing is the best method for determining the doneness of simmered shellfish. This varies depending on the size of the shellfish and how quickly the liquid returns to a simmer after the shellfish is added. Shrimp cook in as little as 3 to

5 minutes; crabs cook in 5 to 10 minutes; and it can take as little as 6 to 8 minutes for a 1-pound (450-gram) lobster to cook and 15 to 20 minutes for a 2½-pound (1.1-kilogram) lobster.

Accompaniments to Simmered Shellfish

The standard accompaniments to simmered shellfish are lemon wedges and melted butter. If the shellfish is being eaten cold, the traditional sauce is a tomato-based cocktail sauce. Nearly any type of vegetable or starch goes well with simmered shellfish, the most common being fresh corn on the cob and boiled potatoes.

▶ PROCEDURE FOR SIMMERING OR BOILING SHELLFISH

1. Bring court bouillon or water to a boil.
2. Add the shellfish to the liquid. Bring the liquid back to a boil and reduce to a simmer. (Whenever an item is added to boiling water, it lowers the water's temperature. The greater the amount of water, however, the faster it will return to a boil. So to accelerate the time within which the water returns to a boil after the shellfish is added, use as much water as possible.)
3. Cook until done.
4. Remove the shellfish from the liquid and serve immediately, or cool by dropping them in ice water if they are to be eaten cold.

RECIPE 18.10

BOILED LOBSTER

Mise en Place

▶ Melt butter while the lobster is boiling.

Yield: 1 Serving **Method:** Boiling

Lobster, 1 lb. 8 oz. (675 g)	1	1
Boiling salted water	4 gal.	16 lt
Lemon wedges	4	4
Whole butter, melted	2 oz.	60 g

1. Drop the lobster into the boiling water. Bring the water back to a boil, reduce to a simmer and cook the lobster until done, approximately 12 minutes.
2. Remove the lobster from the pot, drain and serve immediately with lemon wedges and melted butter on the side.
3. If the lobster is to be eaten cold, drop it in a sink of ice water to stop the cooking process. When cool enough to handle, remove the meat from the shell following the procedures discussed earlier.

Approximate values per 1-lb. (450-g) serving: **Calories** 650, **Total fat** 26 g, **Saturated fat** 15 g, **Cholesterol** 390 mg, **Sodium** 1960 mg, **Total carbohydrates** 11 g, **Protein** 93 g, **Vitamin A** 35%, **Vitamin C** 45%

COMBINATION COOKING METHODS

Combination cooking methods are used with meats, game and poultry in part to tenderize them. Because fish and shellfish are inherently tender, they do not necessarily benefit from such procedures. As noted in the section on shallow poaching, fish can, on occasion, be lightly sautéed or browned and then poached. Although this procedure is a combination cooking method, it is used to enhance flavors and not to tenderize the product.

Some fish or shellfish recipes include the word *braised* or *stew* in the title. Note, however, that these recipes rarely follow the traditional combination cooking methods discussed in this book.

CONCLUSION

In part because of consumers' increased health awareness, more and more food service operations are expanding their selections of fish and shellfish. Their task is aided by the tremendous variety of high-quality fish and shellfish now available. A variety of dry-heat and moist-heat cooking methods can be used with these products, and a variety of sauces and accompaniments can be served with them. Regardless of how they are served, care and attention are required in order to select, store and avoid overcooking fish and shellfish.

QUESTIONS FOR DISCUSSION

1. Discuss six techniques for determining the freshness of fish and shellfish.
2. What are the physical differences between a flatfish and a round fish? How do fabrication techniques vary for these fish?
3. List four market forms for fish and discuss several factors that may determine the form most appropriate for an operation to purchase.
4. List the three categories of mollusks and give an example of a commonly used food from each category.
5. Discuss four methods for determining the doneness of fish or shellfish. Why is it important not to overcook fish and shellfish?
6. Explain the differences between shallow poaching and submersion poaching. Why is poaching a commonly used method for preparing fish and shellfish?
7. Why are combination cooking methods rarely used with fish and shellfish? Why is boiling rarely used?
8. Research international fish recipes and discuss the types of fish that can be substituted when regional varieties are not available.

CHAPTER**NINETEEN**

I HAD AN EXCELLENT REPAST—THE BEST REPAST POSSIBLE—WHICH CONSISTED SIMPLY OF BOILED EGGS AND BREAD AND BUTTER. IT WAS THE QUALITY OF THESE SIMPLE INGREDIENTS THAT MADE THE OCCASION MEMORABLE. THE EGGS WERE SO GOOD THAT I AM ASHAMED TO SAY HOW MANY OF THEM I CONSUMED. . . . IT MIGHT SEEM THAT AN EGG WHICH HAS SUCCEEDED IN BEING FRESH HAS DONE ALL THAT CAN BE REASONABLY EXPECTED OF IT.

—Henry James, American novelist (1843–1916)

EGGS AND BREAKFAST

K RESTAURANT & WINE BAR, Orlando, FL
Executive Chef Kevin Fonzo

AFTER STUDYING THIS CHAPTER, YOU WILL BE ABLE TO:

- understand the composition of eggs
- purchase and store eggs properly
- apply various cooking methods to eggs
- prepare pancakes and other griddlecakes
- understand and prepare various beverages served at breakfast and other meals
- offer customers a variety of breakfast foods

Nature designed eggs as the food source for developing chicks. Eggs, particularly chicken eggs, are also an excellent food for humans because of their high protein content, low cost and ready availability. They are extremely versatile and are used throughout the kitchen, either served alone or as ingredients in a prepared dish. Eggs are used to provide texture, flavor, structure, moisture and nutrition in everything from soups and sauces to breads and pastries.

Egg dishes are, of course, most often associated with the meals breakfast and brunch. But food service operations must offer a variety of breakfast options to appeal to a wide range of consumers.

Breakfast cookery is often one of the first line positions a new cook will be offered. This important duty requires speed, timing and precision and can help an apprentice or beginning cook develop organized, efficient work habits.

This chapter discusses cooking methods used for eggs as well as breakfast meats, griddlecakes, crêpes, cereals and the beverages coffee and tea. Other foods typically served at breakfast, such as quick breads, fruit and cheese, are discussed elsewhere in this text.

▸ EGGS

COMPOSITION

The primary parts of an egg are the shell, yolk and albumen. See Figure 19.1.

The **shell,** composed of calcium carbonate, is the outermost covering of the egg. It prevents microbes from entering and moisture from escaping, and also protects the egg during handling and transport. The breed of the hen determines shell color; for chickens, it can range from bright white to brown. Shell color has no effect on quality, flavor or nutrition.

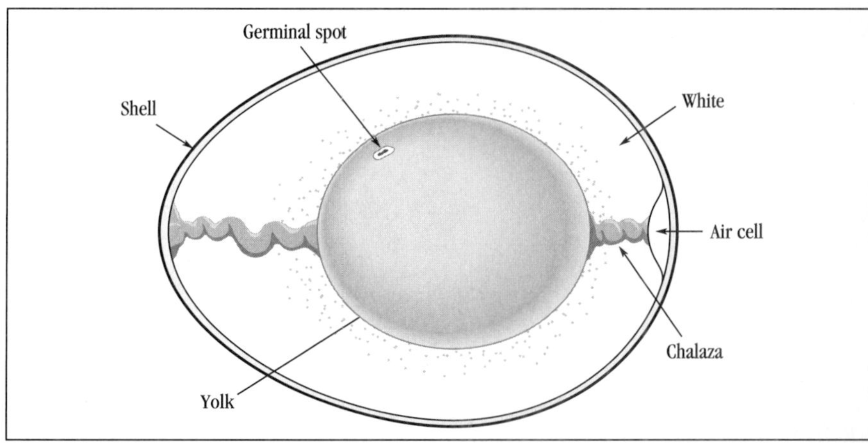

FIGURE 19.1 ▸ An egg.

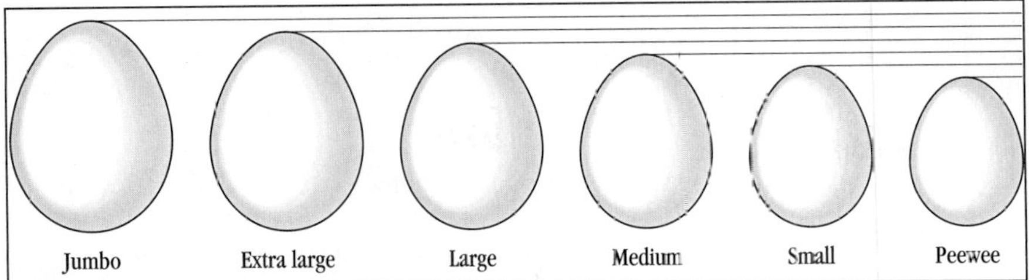

FIGURE 19.2 ▶ Egg sizes.

The **yolk** is the yellow portion of the egg. It constitutes just over one-third of the egg and contains three-fourths of the calories, most of the minerals and vitamins and all the fat. The yolk also contains lecithin, the compound responsible for emulsification in products such as hollandaise sauce and mayonnaise. Egg yolk solidifies (coagulates) at temperatures between 149°F and 158°F (65°C and 70°C). Although the color of a yolk may vary depending on the hen's feed, color does not affect quality or nutritional content.

The **albumen** is the clear portion of the egg and is often referred to as the **egg white.** It constitutes about two-thirds of the egg and contains more than half of the protein and riboflavin. Egg white coagulates, becoming firm and opaque, at temperatures between 144°F and 149°F (62°C and 65°C).

An often-misunderstood portion of the egg is the **chalazae cords.** These thick, twisted strands of egg white anchor the yolk in place. They are neither imperfections nor embryos. The more prominent the chalazae, the fresher the egg. Chalazae do not interfere with cooking or with whipping egg whites.

Eggs are sold in Jumbo, Extra Large, Large, Medium, Small and Peewee sizes, as determined by weight per dozen. See Figure 19.2. Food service operations generally use Large eggs, which weigh 24 ounces per dozen. Other sizes are based on plus or minus 3 ounces per dozen; Medium eggs weigh 21 ounces per dozen while Extra Large eggs weigh 27 ounces per dozen.

GRADING

Eggs are graded by the USDA or a state agency following USDA guidelines. The grade AA, A or B is given to an egg based on interior and exterior quality, not size. The qualities for each grade are described in Table 19.1 Grade has no effect on nutritional values.

STORAGE

Improper handling quickly diminishes egg quality. Eggs should be stored at temperatures below 45°F (7°C) and at a relative humidity of 70 to 80 percent. Eggs will age more during one day at room temperature than they will during one week under proper refrigeration. As eggs age, the white becomes thinner and the yolk becomes flatter. Although this will change the appearance of poached or fried eggs, age has little effect on nutrition or behavior during cooking procedures. Older eggs, however, should be used for hard-cooking, as the shells are easier to remove than those on fresh eggs.

Cartons of fresh, uncooked eggs will keep for at least four to five weeks beyond the pack date if properly refrigerated. Hard-cooked eggs left in their shells and refrigerated should be used within one week.

Store eggs away from strongly flavored foods to reduce odor absorption. Rotate egg stock to maintain freshness. Do not use dirty, cracked or broken eggs, as they may contain bacteria or other contaminants. Frozen eggs should be thawed in the refrigerator and used only in dishes that will be thoroughly cooked, such as baked products.

NOT JUST CHICKENS

When most people refer to an "egg," they mean a chicken's egg. But other eggs are sometimes used in the kitchen:

Bantam egg: The egg from a breed of small chicken; it is about half the size of a regular chicken egg and has the same characteristics.

Duck egg: An egg with an off-white shell and a richer flavor and higher fat content than a chicken's egg; when it is boiled, the white turns bluish and the yolk turns red-orange.

Goose egg: A white-shelled egg that is four to five times as large as a chicken egg; it also has a somewhat richer flavor.

Guinea fowl egg: An egg with an ivory shell flecked with brown; its flavor is more delicate than that of a chicken egg.

Gull egg: An egg whose shell is covered with light to dark brown blotches; it comes in various small sizes and has a slightly fishy flavor.

Ostrich egg: An egg that is 20 times as large as a chicken egg and has a thick, ivory-colored shell; its flavor is smiliar to that of a chicken egg.

Partridge egg: A small egg with a white, buff or olive shell; it has a mild flavor.

Quail egg: A small egg with a speckled brown shell; it has a rich flavor.

Turkey egg: A large egg with a brown shell; it has a delicate flavor.

Turtle egg: A reptile's egg with a soft shell that is buff or speckled; it has a mild, rich flavor.

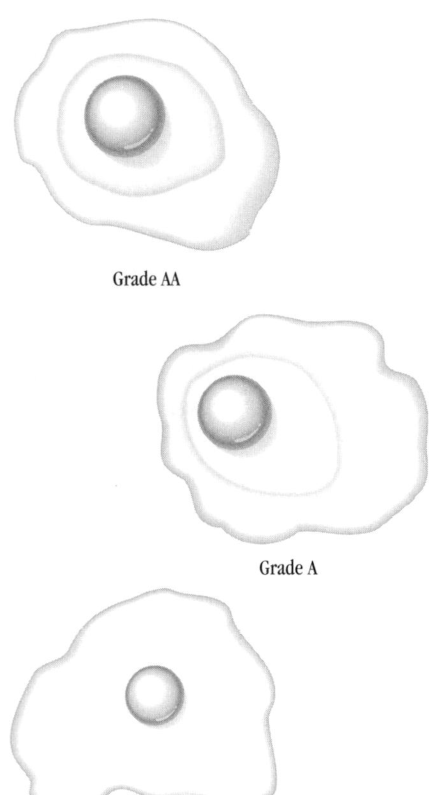
Grade AA

Grade A

Grade B

Table 19.1 **EGG GRADES**

	GRADE AA	GRADE A	GRADE B
Spread*	Remains compact	Spreads slightly	Spreads over wide area
Albumen	Clear, thick and firm; prominent chalazae	Clear and reasonably firm; prominent chalazae	Clear; weak or watery
Yolk	Firm; centered; stands round and high; free from defects	Firm; stands fairly high; practically free from defects	Enlarged and flattened; may show slight defects
Shell	Clean; of normal shape; unbroken		Slight stains permissible; abnormal shape; unbroken
Use	Any use, especially frying, poaching and cooking in shell		Baking; scrambling, used in bulk egg products

*Spread refers to the appearance of the egg when first broken onto a flat surface.

SANITATION

Eggs are a potentially hazardous food. Rich in protein, they are an excellent breeding ground for bacteria. Salmonella is of particular concern with eggs and egg products because the bacteria are commonly found in a chicken's intestinal tract. Although shells are cleaned at packinghouses, some bacteria may remain. Therefore, to prevent contamination, it is best to avoid mixing a shell with the liquid egg.

Inadequately cooking or improperly storing eggs may lead to food-borne illnesses. USDA guidelines indicate that **pasteurization** is achieved when the whole egg stays at a temperature of 140°F (60°C) for 3½ minutes. Hold egg dishes below 40°F (4°C) or above 140°F (60°C). Never leave an egg dish at room temperature for more than one hour, including preparation and service time. Never reuse a container after it has held raw eggs without thoroughly cleaning and sanitizing it.

▶ **pasteurization** the process of heating something to a certain temperature for a specific period in order to destroy pathogenic bacteria

EGG PRODUCTS

Food service operations often want the convenience of buying eggs out of the shell in the exact form needed: whole eggs, yolks only or whites only. These processed items are called egg products and are subject to strict pasteurization standards and USDA inspections. Egg products can be frozen, refrigerated or dried. Precooked, preportioned and blended egg products are also available.

EGG SUBSTITUTES

Concerns about the cholesterol content of eggs have increased the popularity of egg substitutes. There are two general types of substitutes. The first is a complete substitute made from soy or milk proteins. It should not be used in recipes in which eggs are required for thickening. The second substitute contains real albumen, but the egg yolk has been replaced with vegetable or milk products. Egg substitutes have a different flavor from real eggs, but may be useful for people on a restricted diet.

▶ NUTRITION

Eggs contain vitamins A, D, E and K and the B-complex vitamins. They are rich in minerals and contain less cholesterol now than previously. Research indicates that the cholesterol in whole eggs does not impact serum cholesterol as much as was once feared. In fact, the American Heart Association now suggests that it is acceptable to consume up to four egg yolks per week as part of a balanced diet. Egg whites do not contain cholesterol and are often added to egg dishes such as omelets to reduce total fat content.

▶ WHIPPED EGG WHITES

Egg whites are often whipped into a foam that is then incorporated into cakes, custards, soufflés, pancakes and other products. The air beaten into the egg foam gives products lightness and assists with leavening.

▶ PROCEDURE FOR WHIPPING EGG WHITES

1. Use fresh egg whites that are completely free of egg yolk and other impurities. Warm the egg whites to room temperature before whipping; this helps a better foam to form.
2. Use a clean bowl and whisk. Even a tiny amount of fat can prevent the egg whites from foaming properly.
3. Whip the whites until very foamy, then add salt or cream of tartar as directed.
4. Continue whipping until soft peaks form, then gradually add granulated sugar as directed.
5. Whip until stiff peaks form. Properly whipped egg whites should be moist and shiny; overwhipping will make the egg whites appear dry and spongy or curdled.
6. Use the whipped egg whites immediately. If liquid begins to separate from the whipped egg whites, discard them; they cannot be rewhipped successfully.

1 Egg whites whipped to soft peaks.

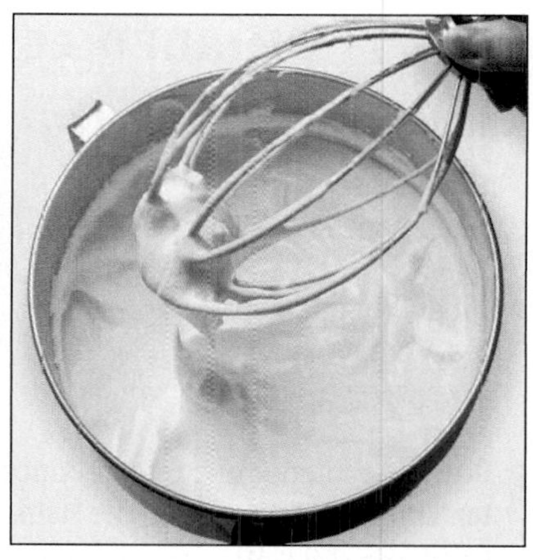

2 Egg whites whipped to stiff peaks.

3 Spongy, overwhipped egg whites.

▶ Applying Various Cooking Methods

No other food is as popular for breakfast, or as versatile, as the egg. Eggs can be cooked by almost any method and served with a wide array of seasonings, accompaniments and garnishes. Whatever cooking method is selected, be sure to prepare the eggs carefully: Overcooked eggs and those cooked at too high a temperature will be tough and rubbery. Undercooked eggs may transmit pathogenic bacteria and pose a risk of food-borne illness.

The following cooking methods are those most often used for egg-based dishes. They include dry-heat cooking methods (baking, sautéing and panfrying) and moist-heat cooking methods (in-shell cooking and poaching).

▶ Dry-Heat Cooking Methods

BAKING

SHIRRED EGGS

Baked eggs, also referred to as shirred eggs, are normally prepared in individual ramekins or baking dishes. The ramekins can be lined or partially filled with ingredients such as bread, ham, creamed spinach or artichokes. The eggs are often topped with grated cheese, fresh herbs or a sauce. When properly cooked, the egg whites should be set while the yolks are soft and creamy.

▶ PROCEDURE FOR PREPARING SHIRRED EGGS

1. Coat each ramekin with melted butter. Add flavoring ingredients as desired.
2. Break one or two eggs into each ramekin. Do not break the yolks. Season with salt and pepper.
3. Bake the eggs until the white is firm, approximately 12–15 minutes. Approximately 3–5 minutes before the eggs are done, add cream or top the eggs with grated cheese, diced ham, fresh herbs or other ingredients as desired.

RECIPE 19.1

SHIRRED EGGS WITH HAM

Mise en Place

- ▶ Melt butter.
- ▶ Slice ham.
- ▶ Heat cream.
- ▶ Grate cheese.

Yield: 1 Serving **Method:** Baking

Whole butter, melted	as needed	as needed
Baked ham, sliced thin	½ oz.	15 g
Eggs	2	2
Salt and pepper	TT	TT
Heavy cream, hot	1 Tbsp.	15 ml
Swiss cheese, grated	1 Tbsp.	15 ml

1. Brush the interior of a 6-fluid-ounce (180-milliliter) ramekin with melted butter. Line the ramekin with the ham.
2. Break the eggs into a cup and pour them carefully into the ramekin on top of the ham. Season with salt and pepper.
3. Bake at 325°F (160°C) until the eggs begin to set, approximately 8 to 10 minutes. Remove from the oven, then add the cream and cheese. Return to the oven until the eggs are cooked and the cheese is melted. Serve immediately.

Approximate values per serving: **Calories** 280, **Total fat** 22 g, **Saturated fat** 10 g, **Cholesterol** 470 mg, **Sodium** 300 mg, **Total carbohydrates** 2 g, **Protein** 17 g, **Vitamin A** 30%

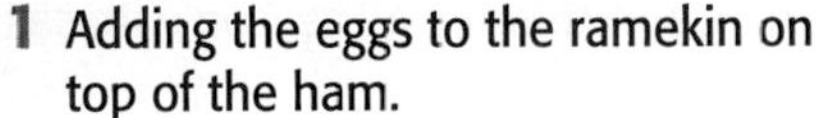

1 Adding the eggs to the ramekin on top of the ham.

2 The finished shirred eggs with ham.

QUICHE

Quiche is a classic breakfast and brunch entrée. It consists of an egg custard (eggs, cream or milk and seasonings) and fillings baked in a crust.

The filling usually includes at least one type of cheese and can also include any number of other ingredients such as cooked, diced meats (for example, sausage, crumbled bacon, ham, fish or shellfish) or blanched vegetables (for example, mushrooms, sautéed onions, asparagus or broccoli). The flavor and texture of these ingredients should complement one another without overpowering the delicate egg custard. Quiche is a good way of using leftovers, but the ingredients should still be fresh and of good quality.

The crust may be made with whole-wheat flour, cornmeal or other grains for added flavor and texture.

▶ PROCEDURE FOR PREPARING QUICHE

1. Prepare and bake a pie shell.
2. Prepare the garnishes and flavoring ingredients and add them to the pie shell.
3. Prepare a custard and add it to the pie shell. Ratios of eggs to milk or heavy cream vary depending on the specific recipe, but 6 to 8 eggs to 1 quart (1 liter) of liquid is usually sufficient to bind the custard.
4. Bake the quiche until set and it reaches 160°F (71°C) on an instant-read thermometer; allow it to cool slightly before cutting.

RECIPE 19.2

QUICHE LORRAINE

Mise en Place

- ▶ Dice, cook and drain the bacon.
- ▶ Shred cheese.
- ▶ Bake pie shell.

Yield: 1 Quiche, 10 in. (25 cm) **Method:** Baking

Bacon, diced and cooked	4 oz.	120 g
Swiss or Gruyère cheese, shredded	2 oz.	60 g
Pie shell, 10-in. (25-cm) diameter, baked	1	1
Eggs	4	4
Milk	1 pt.	450 ml
Heavy cream	4 fl. oz.	120 ml
Salt and pepper	TT	TT
Nutmeg	TT	TT

1. Place the bacon and cheese in the pie shell.
2. To make the custard, combine the eggs, milk and cream, and season with salt, pepper and nutmeg.
3. Pour the custard over the bacon and cheese and bake at 350°F (180°C) until the custard is set and it reaches an internal temperature of 160°F (71°C), approximately 1 hour.

Approximate values per ⅛-quiche serving: **Calories** 330, **Total fat** 25 g, **Saturated fat** 11 g, **Cholesterol** 105 mg, **Sodium** 420 mg, **Total carbohydrates** 14 g, **Protein** 12 g, **Vitamin A** 10%, **Calcium** 15%

SAUTÉING

SCRAMBLED EGGS

Scrambled eggs are eggs whisked with seasonings and then sautéed. They are stirred nearly constantly during cooking. The finished eggs should be light and fluffy with a tender, creamy texture. A small amount of milk or cream may be added to the eggs to provide a more delicate finished product. Overcooking or cooking at too high a temperature causes the eggs to become tough and rubbery.

Scrambled eggs are often flavored by sautéing other foods (for example, onions, mushrooms or diced ham) in the pan before adding the eggs or by adding other foods (for example, grated cheeses or herbs) to the eggs just before cooking is complete. Suggested additions include finely diced bell peppers, onions, mushrooms, zucchini or tomatoes; cottage cheese or any variety of shredded firm cheese; crumbled bacon; diced ham, turkey or beef; bits of smoked salmon, cooked shrimp or cooked sausage; and fresh herbs.

Scrambled eggs can also be prepared using only egg whites. Because all of an egg's fat is stored in the yolk, no-yolk scrambled egg dishes are lower in fat, cholesterol and calories. Water or nonfat milk can be used in place of whole milk or cream to further reduce the fat and calorie content of the finished dish. Remember that egg whites coagulate at a lower temperature than yolks, so adjust the cooking time and temperature accordingly.

▶ PROCEDURE FOR PREPARING SCRAMBLED EGGS

1. Break the eggs into a mixing bowl. Season lightly with salt and pepper. Add 1 scant tablespoon (12 milliliters) milk or cream per egg and whisk everything together.
2. Heat a sauté pan, add clarified butter or oil and heat until the fat begins to sizzle.
3. Sauté any additional ingredients in the hot fat.

4 Pour the eggs into the pan all at once. As the eggs begin to set, slowly stir the mixture with a spatula. Lift cooked portions to allow uncooked egg to flow underneath.
5 Sprinkle on additional ingredients such as cheese or herbs.
6 Cook just until the eggs are set, but still shiny and moist. Remove from the pan and serve immediately.

SCRAMBLED EGGS

RECIPE 19.3

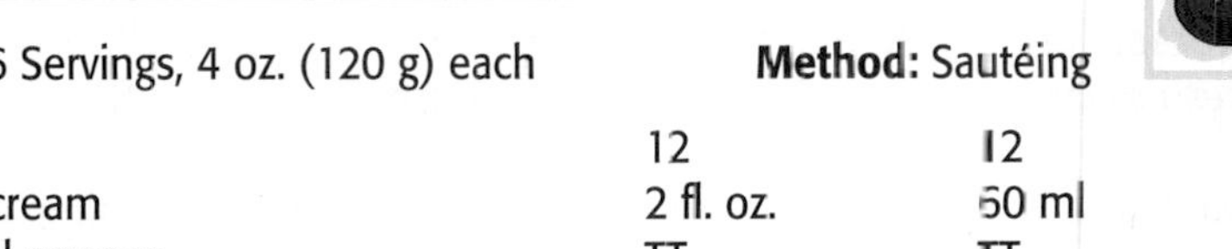

Yield: 6 Servings, 4 oz. (120 g) each **Method:** Sautéing

Eggs	12	12
Heavy cream	2 fl. oz.	60 ml
Salt and pepper	TT	TT
Clarified butter	2 fl. oz.	60 ml

1 Combine the eggs, cream, salt and pepper in a mixing bowl. Whisk until well blended.
2 Heat the butter in a sauté pan.
3 Pour the egg mixture into the hot pan and cook, stirring frequently, until set, approximately 2 minutes. The eggs should be set, but still shiny and moist.

Approximate values per 4-oz. (120-g) serving: **Calories** 250, **Total fat** 21 g, **Saturated fat** 10 g, **Cholesterol** 460 mg, **Sodium** 210 mg, **Total carbohydrates** 1 g, **Protein** 13 g, **Vitamin A** 30%

1 Stirring the scrambled eggs.

2 The properly cooked eggs.

OMELETS

Omelets are needlessly intimidating egg creations that begin as scrambled eggs. They are usually prepared as individual servings using two or three eggs. The cooked eggs are either folded around or filled with a warm savory mixture.

The filling may contain vegetables, cheeses and/or meats. Any filling ingredient that needs cooking should be cooked before being added to the omelet. Because the eggs cook relatively quickly, using raw fillings would result in overcooked eggs. A shallow, well-seasoned or nonstick pan with gently sloping sides is used for cooking omelets. Should an omelet stick to the pan, run a spatula under the omelet to loosen it.

▶ PROCEDURE FOR PREPARING FOLDED OMELETS

1 Fully cook any meats and blanch or otherwise cook any vegetables that will be incorporated into the omelet.
2 Heat an omelet pan over moderately high heat, then add clarified butter.
3 Whisk the eggs together in a small bowl. Season with salt and pepper if desired.
4 Pour the eggs into the pan and stir until they begin to set, approximately 10 seconds.
5 Pull cooked egg from the sides of the pan toward the center, allowing raw egg to run underneath. Continue doing so for 20 to 30 seconds.
6 Spoon any fillings on top of the eggs or add any other garnishes.
7 When cooked as desired, flip one side of the omelet toward the center with a spatula or a shake of the pan. Slide the omelet onto the serving plate so that it lands folded in thirds with the seam underneath.
8 Spoon any sauce or additional filling on top, garnish as desired, and serve immediately.

RECIPE 19.4 SHRIMP AND AVOCADO OMELET

Mise en Place

- Peel, devein and cut up shrimp.
- Wash, peel and slice green onions.
- Peel and dice avocado.
- Chop cilantro.

Yield: 1 Serving **Method:** Sautéing

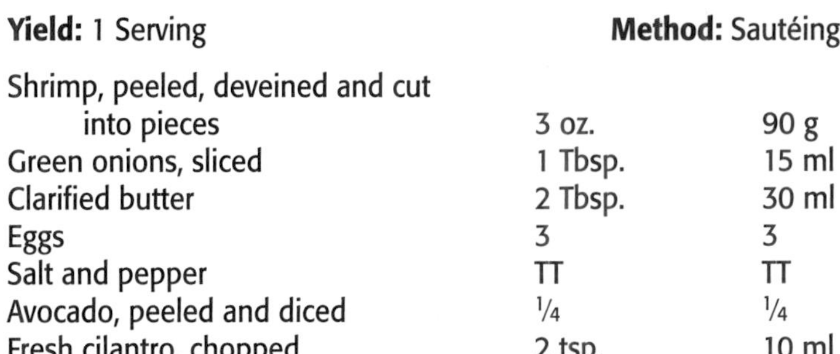

Shrimp, peeled, deveined and cut into pieces	3 oz.	90 g
Green onions, sliced	1 Tbsp.	15 ml
Clarified butter	2 Tbsp.	30 ml
Eggs	3	3
Salt and pepper	TT	TT
Avocado, peeled and diced	1/4	1/4
Fresh cilantro, chopped	2 tsp.	10 ml

1 Sauté the shrimp and onion in half of the butter until the shrimp is firm and the onions are translucent, approximately 2 minutes. Remove from the heat and set aside.

2 Heat an omelet pan and add the remaining butter.

3 Whisk the eggs together in a small bowl, season with salt and pepper and pour into the omelet pan.

4 Stir the eggs as they cook. Stop when they begin to set. Lift the edges as the omelet cooks to allow the raw eggs to run underneath.

5 When the eggs are nearly set, add the shrimp filling, avocado and cilantro. Fold the front of the eggs over and roll the omelet onto a plate.

1 Lifting the edge of the eggs to allow them to cook evenly.

Approximate values per serving: **Calories** 590, **Total fat** 47 g, **Saturated fat** 19 g, **Cholesterol** 865 mg, **Sodium** 620 mg, **Total carbohydrates** 4 g, **Protein** 39 g, **Vitamin A** 60%, **Vitamin C** 20%, **Iron** 30%

2 Adding the filling to the eggs.

3 Folding the eggs.

4 Rolling the omelet onto the plate.

French-style omelets are similar, but the eggs are cooked without a filling, then tightly rolled onto a plate for service. A cut is made into the finished omelet and the filling is spooned in.

▶ PROCEDURE FOR PREPARING FRENCH-STYLE OMELETS

1 Heat an omelet pan over moderately high heat and add clarified butter.
2 Whisk the eggs together in a small bowl. Season with salt and pepper if desired.
3 Pour the eggs into the pan and stir until they begin to set, approximately 10 seconds.
4 Pull cooked egg from the sides of the pan toward the center, allowing raw egg to run underneath. Continue doing so for 20 to 30 seconds.
5 When cooked as desired, flip one side of the omelet toward the center with a spatula or a shake of the pan. Roll the omelet onto the serving plate so that it lands with the seam underneath.

1 Rolling the omelet onto the serving plate.

2 Using a paring knife to cut into the center of the omelet.

3 Spooning in the filling.

4 The finished omelet.

FRITTATAS

Frittatas are essentially open-faced omelets of Spanish-Italian heritage. They may be cooked in small pans as individual portions or in large pans, then cut into wedges for service. A relatively large amount of hearty ingredients is mixed directly into the eggs. The eggs are first cooked on the stove top, then the pan is transferred to an oven or placed under a salamander or broiler to finish cooking.

▶ PROCEDURE FOR PREPARING FRITTATAS

1 Fully cook any meats and blanch or otherwise prepare any vegetables that will be incorporated into the frittata.
2 Heat a sauté pan and add clarified butter.
3 Whisk the eggs, flavorings and any other ingredients together; pour into the pan.
4 Stir gently until the eggs begin to set. Gently lift cooked egg at the edge of the frittata so that raw egg can run underneath. Continue cooking until the eggs are almost set.
5 Place the pan in a hot oven or underneath a salamander or broiler to finish cooking and lightly brown the top.
6 Slide the finished frittata out of the pan onto a serving platter.

RECIPE 19.5

GARDEN FRITTATA

Mise en Place

- ▶ Skin and bone chicken.
- ▶ Peel and chop garlic.
- ▶ Wash and slice mushrooms and green onions.
- ▶ Seed and mince jalapeño.
- ▶ Roast, peel, seed and julienne red peppers.
- ▶ Beat eggs.
- ▶ Shred cheese.

Yield: 1 Serving **Method:** Sautéing

Chicken breast meat, boneless, skinless	2 oz.	60 g
Garlic, chopped	1 tsp.	5 ml
Cumin, ground	TT	TT
Salt and pepper	TT	TT
Mushrooms, sliced	1 oz.	30 g
Unsalted butter	1/2 fl. oz.	15 g
Jalapeño, seeded, minced	1 tsp.	5 ml
Red bell pepper, roasted, peeled, seeded, julienned	1 oz.	30 g
Green onions, sliced	1 oz.	30 g
Fresh cilantro	2 tsp.	10 ml
Eggs, beaten	3	3
Monterey Jack or Cheddar cheese, shredded	1 oz.	30 g

1. Rub the chicken breast with the garlic, cumin, salt and pepper. Grill or broil the chicken until done. Allow it to rest briefly, then cut it into strips.
2. In a well-seasoned 9-inch (22-centimeter) sauté pan, sauté the mushrooms in the butter until tender. Add the jalapeño and sauté for 30 seconds. Add the chicken, bell pepper, green onions and cilantro and sauté until hot.
3. Add the eggs and season with salt and pepper. Cook the mixture, stirring and lifting the eggs to help them cook evenly, until they begin to set.
4. Sprinkle the cheese over the eggs and place under a salamander or broiler to melt the cheese and finish cooking the eggs. Slide the frittata onto a plate or cut into wedges for smaller portions.

Approximate values per serving: **Calories** 590, **Total fat** 39 g, **Saturated fat** 18 g, **Cholesterol** 755 mg, **Sodium** 400 mg, **Total carbohydrates** 8 g, **Protein** 51 g, **Vitamin A** 60%, **Vitamin C** 90%, **Calcium** 35%, **Iron** 20%, **Claims**—good source of fiber, vitamins A and C, calcium and iron

SAFETY ALERT

Cooking Eggs

Because of the risk of food-borne illnesses, especially salmonella, from undercooked eggs, the USDA recommends cooking all eggs until both the yolk and white are completely firm, the equivalent of over hard or well done.

PAN-FRYING

Pan-fried eggs are commonly referred to as **sunny side up** or **over easy, over medium** or **over hard.** These are visibly different products produced with proper timing and technique. Very fresh eggs are best for pan-frying, as the yolk holds its shape better and the white spreads less.

Sunny-side-up eggs are not turned during cooking; their yellow yolks remain visible. They should be cooked over medium-low heat long enough to firm the whites and partially firm the yolks: approximately 4 minutes if cooked on a 250°F (120°C) cooking surface.

For "over" eggs, the egg is partially cooked on one side, then gently flipped and cooked on the other side until done. The egg white should be firm, and its edges should not be brown. The yolk should never be broken regardless of the degree of doneness. Not only is a broken yolk unattractive, but the spilled yolk will coagulate on contact with the hot pan, making it difficult to serve.

For over-easy eggs, the yolk should remain very runny; on a 250°F (120°C) cooking surface, the egg should cook for about 3 minutes on the first side and 2 minutes on the other. Over-medium eggs should be cooked slightly longer, until the yolk is partially set. For over-hard eggs, the yolk should be completely cooked.

▶ PROCEDURE FOR PAN-FRYING EGGS

1. Select a sauté pan just large enough to accommodate the number of eggs being cooked. (An 8-inch- [20-centimeter-] diameter pan is appropriate for up to three eggs.)
2. Add a small amount of clarified butter and heat until the fat just begins to sizzle.
3. Carefully break the eggs into the pan.
4. Continue cooking over medium-low heat until the eggs reach the appropriate degree of firmness. Sunny-side-up eggs are not flipped during cooking; "over" eggs are flipped once during cooking.
5. When done, gently flip the "over" eggs once again so that the first side is up, then gently slide the cooked eggs out of the pan onto the serving plate. Serve immediately.

1 Pouring the eggs into the sauté pan.

2 Flipping the eggs.

3 Sliding the eggs onto a plate for service.

Basted eggs are a variation of sunny-side-up eggs. Basted eggs are cooked over low heat with the hot butter from the pan spooned over them as they cook. Another version of basted eggs is made by adding 1 to 2 teaspoons (5 to 10 milliliters) water to the sauté pan and then covering the pan. The steam cooks the top of the eggs.

▶ MOIST-HEAT COOKING METHODS

IN-SHELL COOKING (SIMMERING)

The difference between **soft-cooked eggs** (also called **soft-boiled**) and **hard-cooked eggs** (also called **hard-boiled**) is time. Both styles refer to eggs cooked in their shell in hot water. Despite the word *boiled* in their names, eggs cooked in the shell should never be boiled. Boiling toughens eggs and causes discoloration. Instead, the eggs should be simmered. Soft-cooked eggs are usually simmered for 3 to 5 minutes; hard-cooked eggs may be simmered for as long as 12 to 15 minutes.

Sometimes it is difficult to remove the shell from very fresh eggs. Eggs that are a few days old are better for cooking in the shell.

▶ PROCEDURE FOR PREPARING SOFT-COOKED EGGS

1. Fill a saucepan or stockpot with sufficient water to cover the eggs. Bring the water to a simmer.
2. Carefully lower each egg into the simmering water. Simmer uncovered for 3 to 5 minutes, depending on the firmness desired.
3. Lift each egg out of the water with a slotted spoon or spider. Crack the large end of the shell carefully and serve immediately.

▶ PROCEDURE FOR PREPARING HARD-COOKED EGGS

1 Repeat Steps 1 and 2 for soft-cooked eggs, simmering the eggs for 12 to 15 minutes.
2 Lift each egg out of the water with a slotted spoon or spider and place in an ice bath. When the eggs are cool enough to handle, peel them and use as desired or cover and refrigerate for up to 5 days.

POACHING

Eggs that are to be poached should always be very fresh. They should also be kept very cold until used, as cold egg whites stay together better when dropped into hot water. The water for poaching eggs is held at approximately 200°F (90°C), a gentle simmer. Poached eggs should be soft and moist; the whites should be firm enough to encase the yolk completely, but the yolk should still be runny.

Some chefs add salt to the poaching water for flavor; others believe that the salt causes the egg whites to separate. To help the egg whites cling together, add 2 tablespoons (30 milliliters) white vinegar per quart (liter) of water.

▶ PROCEDURE FOR POACHING EGGS

1 Fill a saucepan or stockpot with at least 3 inches (7.5 centimeters) water. Add salt and vinegar if desired. Bring the water to a simmer and hold at a temperature of approximately 200°F (90°C).
2 One at a time, crack the eggs into a small ramekin or cup. If a piece of shell falls into the egg, it should be removed; if the yolk breaks, the egg can be set aside for some other use.
3 Gently slide each egg into the simmering water and cook for 3 to 5 minutes.
4 Lift the poached egg out of the water with a slotted spoon. Trim any ragged edges with a paring knife. Serve immediately.

For quantity service, eggs can be poached in advance and held for up to one day. To do so, cook the eggs as described. As each egg is removed from the hot water, set it in a hotel pan filled with ice water to stop the cooking process. The eggs can then be stored in the ice water until needed. For banquet-style service, all the eggs can be reheated at once by placing the entire pan on the stove top. Or the eggs can be reheated one or two at a time by placing them in a pan of barely simmering water until they are hot.

RECIPE 19.6

POACHED EGGS

Yield: 1 Serving **Method:** Poaching

Water	as needed	as needed
Salt	1 tsp.	5 ml
Vinegar	1 fl. oz.	30 ml
Eggs	2	2

1 Bring the water to a simmer; add the salt and vinegar.
2 Crack one egg into a cup and carefully add it to the water. Repeat with the other egg.
3 Cook the eggs to the desired doneness, approximately 3 to 5 minutes. Remove them from the water with a slotted spoon and serve as desired or carefully lower them into ice water and refrigerate for later use.

Approximate values per 3½-oz. (105-g) serving: **Calories** 140, **Total fat** 10 g, **Saturated fat** 3 g, **Cholesterol** 425 mg, **Sodium** 280 mg, **Total carbohydrates** 1 g, **Protein** 12 g, **Vitamin A** 20%

1 Adding an egg to a pot of simmering water.

2 Lowering the eggs into ice water to cool them for future use.

BREAKFAST AROUND THE WORLD

In the 21st century North Americans traveling abroad will more than likely be able to order a breakfast similar to that which they would eat at home. However, in many countries residents still consume their traditional breakfast foods.

- Japan: tea; *asa-gohan*, morning rice, with side dishes of pickles, dried seaweed, tofu, fish; miso soup
- China: tea; *congee,* rice porridge, topped with meat, seafood and/or vegetables; *you tiao*, a type of fried cruller that is dipped in soy milk
- France: *café au lait*; baguette, butter and jam
- Southern Italy/Sicily: coffee *granita* served in brioche bread
- Australia: tea; steak and eggs; toast
- Egypt: *ful medames*, slow cooked beans seasoned with olive oil, lemon and garlic
- India: tea; *khichiri*, a Hindi dish of rice, lentils and spices; *appam*, a thin rice pancake with spiced meat and vegetables; *vada pavs*, deep-fried mashed potatoes wrapped in flatbread and seasoned with chutney or chilli powder
- Costa Rica: Coffee or *aqua dulce*, warm water flavored with concentrated sugar cane juice; *gallo pinto*, rice and beans with cilantro and onions
- Spain: milk, coffee, rolls and jam; *chocolate y churros*, hot chocolate with a cinnamon-sugar coated donut
- Greece: Greek coffee or instant coffee with milk; sesame bread; yogurt with honey and/or fruit
- Eastern Europe/Germany/Holland: coffee or tea; cold cuts; a variety of cheeses and breads
- Argentina: coffee or hot chocolate; *facturas*, sweet pastries with *dulce de leche*, a paste made with milk and sugar

▶ BREAKFAST & BRUNCH

Breakfast is often an on-the-go, rushed experience; hence the popularity of breakfast sandwiches, jumbo muffins and disposable coffee cups. Brunch, on the other hand, is a leisurely experience, combining breakfast and lunch into a social occasion. Brunch menus include traditional breakfast foods along with almost anything else. Unlike breakfast, brunch is often accompanied by champagne or other alcoholic beverages and concludes with a pastry or dessert.

Food service operations must offer a variety of breakfast options to appeal to a wide range of consumers. Hotels and resorts may offer a complimentary continental-style breakfast of coffee, juice and sweet rolls; a full-service à la carte dining room; a room service menu and a casual snack bar. The grand hotel Sunday and holiday brunch buffet is an American institution for celebrations and special occasions.

Office, retail and commercial complexes are peppered with small shops selling coffee, muffins, bagels and sweet rolls. Coffeehouses offering a variety of coffee blends and drinks, pastries, breads and quiche are also popular. Even fast-food facilities have expanded their menus and hours of operation to meet the needs of early-morning diners.

The foods served at breakfast include most of the foods served at other times during the day. A diner's perceptions of a proper breakfast depends on his or her cultural, ethnic, economic and geographic background as well as sleep patterns and work schedule.

Breakfast menus typically include the following items:

- ▶ Coffee, tea or other hot beverages
- ▶ Fruits or fruit juices
- ▶ Eggs
- ▶ Breads, including sweet breads
- ▶ Cereals and grains
- ▶ Potatoes
- ▶ Pancakes, waffles and French toast
- ▶ Meats or fish
- ▶ Dairy products, including milk, cheese and yogurt

Although few people could sit down to a breakfast including all of these components even occasionally, most food service operations find it necessary to offer some items from each category in order to meet their customers' expectations.

BREAKFAST MEATS

At other meals, meat is typically the principal food, but at breakfast it is usually an accompaniment. Breakfast meats tend to be spicy or highly flavored. A hearty breakfast menu may include a small beef steak (usually sirloin and often pan-fried) or pork chop. Corned beef, roast beef or roast turkey can be diced or shredded, then sautéed with potatoes and other ingredients for a breakfast hash. Fish, particularly smoked products, are also served at breakfast.

But the most popular breakfast meats are bacon (including Canadian-style bacon), ham and sausages. They are all discussed in Chapter 26, Charcuterie. **Bacon** can be cooked on a flat griddle or in a heavy skillet or baked on a sheet pan. Regardless of the method used, the cooked bacon should be drained on absorbent paper towels to remove excess fat. **Canadian-style bacon** is very lean and requires little cooking, although slices are usually sautéed briefly before serving. The round slices may be served like ham and are essential for eggs Benedict. A **ham steak** is simply a thick slice ideal for breakfast. Fully cooked ham needs to be heated only briefly on a griddle or in a sauté pan before service. The most popular **breakfast sausages** are made from uncured, uncooked meats. They can be mild to spicy, slightly sweet or strongly seasoned with sage. Recipes for country-style and other sausages are at the end of Chapter 26. Breakfast sausage is available in bulk, links or preformed patties. Link sausage is often partially cooked by steam, then browned by sautéing at service time. It should be drained on absorbent paper towels to remove excess fat before service.

GRIDDLECAKES

Pancakes and waffles are types of griddlecakes or griddle breads. They are usually leavened with baking soda or baking powder and are quickly cooked on a very hot griddle or waffle iron with very little fat. Griddlecakes should be more than just an excuse for eating butter and maple syrup, however. They should have a rich flavor and a light, tender, moist interior.

Pancake and waffle batters may be flavored with tangy buckwheat flour, fruits, whole grains or nuts. Both pancakes and waffles are usually served with plain or flavored butter and fruit compote or syrup. Waffles must be cooked in a special waffle iron, which gives the cakes a distinctive gridlike pattern and a crisp texture. Electric waffle irons are available with square, round and even heart-shaped grids. The grids should be seasoned well, then never washed. (Follow the manufacturer's directions for seasoning.) Belgian waffles are especially light and crisp because of the incorporation of whipped egg whites and/or yeast. They are often made in a waffle iron with extra deep grids and are served for breakfast or as a dessert, topped with fresh fruit, whipped cream or ice cream.

▶ PROCEDURE FOR MAKING PANCAKES

1. Prepare the batter.
2. Heat a flat griddle or large sauté pan over moderately high heat. Add clarified butter.
3. Portion the pancake batter onto the hot griddle using a portion scoop, ladle or adjustable batter dispenser. Pour the portioned batter in one spot; it should spread into an even circle. Drop the batter so that no two pancakes will touch after the batter spreads.
4. Cook until bubbles appear on the surface, and the bottom of the cake is set and golden brown. Flip the pancake using an offset spatula.
5. Cook the pancake until the second side is golden brown. Avoid flipping the pancake more than once as this causes it to deflate.

BUTTERMILK PANCAKES

RECIPE 19.7

Yield: 24 Pancakes

Flour	1 lb.	450 g
Granulated sugar	2 Tbsp.	30 ml
Baking powder	1 Tbsp.	15 ml
Salt	1½ tsp.	7 ml
Buttermilk	1½ pt.	750 ml
Unsalted butter, melted	2 oz.	60 g
Eggs, beaten	3	3
Clarified butter	as needed	as needed

1 Sift the flour, sugar, baking powder and salt together.
2 Combine the buttermilk, melted butter and eggs and add them to the dry ingredients. Mix just until the ingredients are combined.
3 If the griddle is not well seasoned, coat it lightly with clarified butter. Once its temperature reaches 375°F (190°C), drop the batter onto it in 2-fluid-ounce (60-milliliter) portions using a ladle, portion scoop or batter portioner.
4 When bubbles appear on the pancake's surface and the bottom is browned, flip the pancake to finish cooking.

Mise en Place

▶ Melt butter.
▶ Beat eggs.

VARIATIONS:

Blueberry Pancakes—Gently stir 1 pint (450 milliliters) fresh or frozen blueberries into the batter. If using frozen berries, drain them thoroughly, then pat dry with paper towels before adding them to the batter. Serve with blueberry syrup or compote.

Apple-Pecan Pancakes—Gently fold 4 ounces (120 grams) chopped cooked apples, ¼ teaspoon (2 milliliters) cinnamon and 1 ounce (30 grams) finely chopped pecans into the batter.

Approximate values per pancake: **Calories** 120, **Total fat** 4 g, **Saturated fat** 2.5 g, **Cholesterol** 35 mg, **Sodium** 250 mg, **Total carbohydrates** 17 g, **Protein** 4 g

CRÊPES

Crêpes are thin, delicate, unleavened pancakes. They are made with a very liquid egg batter cooked in a small, very hot sauté pan or crêpe pan. Crêpe batter can be flavored with buckwheat flour, cornmeal or other grains. Crêpes are not eaten plain, but are usually filled and garnished with sautéed fruits, scrambled eggs, cheese or vegetables. Crêpes can be prepared in advance, then filled and reheated in the oven.

Blintzes are crêpes that are cooked on only one side, then filled with cheese, browned in butter and served with sour cream, fruit compote or preserves. A recipe for cheese blintzes is provided at the end of this chapter.

▶ PROCEDURE FOR PREPARING CRÊPES

1 Prepare the batter at least one hour before using and keep refrigerated.
2 Heat a well-seasoned crêpe pan or small sauté pan over moderately high heat. Add a small amount of clarified butter.
3 Ladle a small amount of batter into the pan. Tilt the pan so that the batter spreads and coats the bottom evenly.

4 Cook until the crêpe is set and the bottom begins to brown, approximately 1 minute. Flip the crêpe over with a quick flick of the wrist or by lifting it carefully with a spatula.

5 Cook the crêpe for an additional 30 seconds. Slide the finished crêpe from the pan. Crêpes can be stacked between layers of parchment paper for storage.

RECIPE 19.8

CRÊPES

Mise en Place

- ▶ Prepare batter at least 1 hour before needed.
- ▶ Melt butter.

1 Coating the bottom of the pan evenly with the batter.

2 Flipping the crêpe. Notice the proper light brown color.

Yield: 30 Crêpes, 6 in. (15 cm) each

Whole eggs	6	6
Egg yolks	6	6
Water	12 fl. oz.	360 ml
Milk	18 fl. oz.	540 ml
Granulated sugar	6 oz.	180 g
Salt	1 tsp.	5 ml
Flour	14 oz.	420 g
Unsalted butter, melted	5 oz.	150 g
Clarified butter	as needed	as needed

1. Whisk together the eggs, egg yolks, water and milk. Add the sugar, salt and flour; whisk together. Stir in the melted butter. Cover and set aside to rest for at least 1 hour before cooking.
2. Heat a small sauté or crêpe pan; brush lightly with clarified butter. Pour in 1–1½ fluid ounces (30–45 milliliters) of batter; swirl to coat the bottom of the pan evenly.
3. Cook the crêpe until set and light brown, approximately 30 seconds. Flip it over and cook a few seconds longer. Remove from the pan. Repeat this process until all the batter is used.
4. Cooked crêpes may be used immediately or covered and held briefly in a warm oven. Crêpes can also be wrapped well in plastic wrap and refrigerated for 2 to 3 days or frozen for several weeks.

VARIATIONS:

Savory Crêpes—Reduce the sugar to 1 tablespoon (15 milliliters). Substitute up to 5 ounces (150 grams) buckwheat flour or whole-wheat flour for an equal amount of the all-purpose flour if desired.

Savory Crêpes Florentine—Fill Savory Crêpes with creamed spinach topped with Mornay sauce.

Approximate values per 2-oz. (60-g) crêpe: **Calories** 140, **Total fat** 7 g, **Saturated fat** 3.5 g, **Cholesterol** 95 mg, **Sodium** 100 mg, **Total carbohydrates** 17 g, **Protein** 4 g

CEREALS AND GRAINS

Oats, rice, corn and wheat are perhaps the most widely eaten breakfast foods. Processed breakfast cereals are ready-to-eat products made from these grains. Most consumers now think of breakfast cereal as a cold food, but not so long ago only hot grains were breakfast staples. Oatmeal served as a hot porridge is still popular, especially with toppings such as cream, brown sugar, fresh or dried fruit or fruit preserves. Grits, made from ground corn, are another grain product served hot at breakfast. Grits may be topped with butter and presented as a starch side dish or served in a bowl as a porridge with cream and brown sugar. Oats and oatmeal, grits and other grains are discussed in Chapter 21, Potatoes, Grains and Pasta.

Ready-to-eat (cold) cereal is usually topped with milk or light cream and sugar. Fresh or dried fruits may be added. Many products are enriched or fortified with vitamins and minerals to compensate for the nutrients lost during processing. Creative cooks can avoid overly sweet, artificially flavored commercial products by making their own ready-to-eat breakfast cereals such as **muesli** or granola, a toasted blend of whole grains, nuts and dried fruits. The results are less expensive, more nutritious and far more interesting.

▶ **muesli** (MYOOS-lee) a breakfast cereal made from raw or toasted cereal grains, dried fruits, nuts and dried milk solids and usually eaten with milk or yogurt; sometimes known as granola

CRUNCHY GRANOLA

RECIPE 19.9

Yield: 3 qt. (3 lt)

Brown sugar	8 oz.	250 g
Water, hot	4 fl. oz.	120 ml
Canola oil	6 fl. oz.	180 ml
Old-fashioned oats	18 oz.	500 g
Wheat germ	4 oz.	125 g
Coconut, shredded	2½ oz.	75 g
Salt (optional)	1 Tbsp.	15 ml
Whole-wheat flour	2 oz.	60 g
Amaranth flour	2 oz.	60 g
Unbleached all-purpose flour	2 oz.	60 g
Yellow cornmeal	2 oz.	60 g
Pecans, chopped	4 oz.	125 g

1. Dissolve the brown sugar in the hot water. Add the oil.
2. Combine the dry ingredients in a large bowl. Mix thoroughly by hand.
3. Add the brown-sugar-and-oil mixture to the dry ingredients; toss to combine.
4. Spread out the granola in a thin layer on a sheet pan. Bake at 200°F (90°C) until crisp, approximately 1½ to 2 hours. Toss lightly with a metal spatula every 30 minutes.
5. Let the baked granola cool completely at room temperature, then store in an airtight container. Chopped dried fruits, additional nuts or fresh fruits can be added at service time.

Approximate values per ¼-c. (30-g) serving: **Calories** 140, **Total fat** 7 g, **Saturated fat** 1 g, **Cholesterol** 0 mg, **Sodium** 5 mg, **Total carbohydrates** 17 g, **Protein** 3 g

FROM HEALTH FOOD TO SUGAR SNACK

The century-old, multibillion-dollar-a-year American breakfast cereal industry, unlike any other in the world, is rooted in health foods. During the 1890s, Dr. John Harvey Kellogg directed a sanitarium in Battle Creek, Michigan. Among the healthful foods prescribed for his patients was his special mixture of whole grains called "granula." John, along with his brother Will, next created and began marketing wheat flakes as a nutritious breakfast food. They were not an immediate success, however; people found a cold breakfast unappealing. Undeterred, Will continued toying with cold cereals, eventually creating flakes made from toasted corn and malt. Thanks to a massive advertising campaign, the American public finally embraced corn flakes and a financial empire was born.

Charles W. Post was a patient of Dr. Kellogg's Battle Creek Sanitarium in 1891. He adopted the principles of healthful eating espoused by the Kellogg brothers and soon opened his own spa, complete with a factory producing his "Post Toasties" and "Grape-Nuts." He promoted them as a cure for appendicitis, consumption and malaria.

Soon Battle Creek became a boomtown, home to more than 40 breakfast cereal companies. Unfortunately for the consumer, not all manufacturers—then and now—were as concerned about health as John, Will and C. W. The addition of sugar, sometimes totaling more than half the cereal's weight, makes some of today's breakfast products more sugary than candy bars. Even some of the granola cereals touted as healthier alternatives to other breakfast cereals and snacks contain 20 percent sugar or more. But at least they no longer claim to cure malaria.

▸ BEVERAGES

Water, coffee and tea are the staples of most beverage menus. Despite their relatively low price, bottled water or a good cup of coffee or tea can be extremely important to a customer's impression of a food service operation. A cup of coffee is often either the very first or the very last item consumed by a customer. Tea, whether iced or hot, is often consumed throughout the meal. Consequently, it is important to learn to prepare and serve these beverages properly. Many varieties of water are now available and some customers prefer these specialty waters to that from the tap.

Not only do these beverages complement a meal, they are important profit centers for restaurant owners. Appreciation of the proper preparation and service of these beverages is an important part of a culinary student's training.

TAKING THE CURE

In ancient times the health benefits of mineral springs were certainly appreciated and it is likely that if the water was palatable, it was not only bathed in, but also consumed. *Spas* were highly regarded for the curative power of their waters; the name comes from a town in Belgium with a famous healing spring. (It has also been written that *spa* owes its derivation to the Latin phrase *salus per aquam*, "health through water.") In the late 17th century, European entrepreneurs began to try to duplicate the naturally effervescent water of famous spas. Jacob Schweppe, a Swiss, began carbonating water around 1794 and soon moved his business to London. Dr. Louis Perrier began operating the spring in Vergeze, France, in 1863 and offered its waters bottled. Even in far-off New Zealand in 1875, Waiwera spa water was sold to health-seeking visitors, while in America Saratoga Spring Water began to be bottled in 1872. Seltzer water was originally obtained from springs at Niederselters in Germany and was popular in the 19th century. It is now produced synthetically and, like soda water, is often lightly flavored.

WATER

At one time in the United States a glass of iced water was more than likely the first thing placed in front of the customer as the menu was presented. The origin of this practice is lost to time; perhaps it was thought that sipping water would ease the waiting time until the food was served. There were also those who believed that water aided digestion. Whatever the reasons, water service has evolved as the preference for bottled water has grown. In other countries, because of suspect local water supplies, if water is ordered by a customer it is usually bottled.

Bottled water is the fastest-growing segment of the beverage industry, in part because of increased health consciousness, in part because of a perception that bottled water is safer. Waters are available from all over the globe, from Australia, France, Fiji, Germany, Italy, Wales and many points between. The list is endless and always growing. All waters imported into the United States are subject to federal regulation.

TYPES OF WATER

Bottled water is by definition potable water sold for human consumption and it is subject to FDA regulations. Bottled water comes from a variety of sources such as a municipal water supply, natural spring or well. **Spring water** is obtained from an underground source that flows naturally to the earth's surface. **Mineral water** can come from a spring, a well, or an artesian bore but by definition must contain not less than 250 parts per million total dissolved solids. This level of trace minerals distinguishes such water and frequently contributes to its unique taste.

Bottled water is sold as either **still** or **sparkling,** but within these two broad definitions are a variety of subgroups. Many brands offer either a still or sparkling version of their water. The "sparkle" is often achieved by the addition of carbon dioxide, which not only gives the beverage its spritzy taste but also prevents spoilage. The more carbonation, the more acidic the taste. Bottled waters are best served lightly chilled and without ice, unless it is requested.

▸ **artesian-well water** water obtained from an underground source; the water rises to the surface under pressure

▸ **bottled water** any water, either still or sparkling, that is bottled and sold

▸ **deionized water** water that has had the cations and anions removed by passing it over a bed of ion-exchange resins

▸ **demineralized water** water that has had all the minerals and impurities removed by passing it over a bed of ion-exchange resins

▸ **distilled water** water that has had all the minerals and impurities removed through distillation; it is generally used for pharmaceutical purposes

▸ **drinking water** water that comes from a government-approved source and has undergone some treatment and filtration; it can be bottled or available on tap and is used for drinking and general culinary purposes

COFFEE

Coffee (Fr. *café*) begins as the fruit of a small tree grown in tropical and subtropical regions throughout the world. The fruit, referred to as a cherry, is bright red with translucent flesh surrounding two flat-sided seeds. These seeds are the coffee beans. When ripe, the cherries are harvested by hand, then cleaned, fermented and hulled, leaving the green coffee beans. The beans are then roasted, blended, ground and brewed. Note that any coffee bean can be roasted to any degree of darkness, ground to any degree of fineness and brewed by any number of methods.

Only two species of coffee bean are routinely used: **arabica** and **robusta.** Arabica beans are the most important commercially and the ones from which the finest coffees are produced. Robusta beans do not produce as flavorful a drink as arabica. Nevertheless, robusta beans are becoming increasingly significant commercially, in part because robusta trees are heartier and more fertile than arabica trees. The conditions in which the beans are grown have almost as much effect on the final product as subsequent roasting, grinding and brewing. Because coffee takes much of its flavor and character from the soil, sunlight and air, the beans' origin is critical to the product's final quality. Each valley and mountain produces coffee distinct from all others, so geographic names are used to identify the beans whether they are from arabica or robusta trees. Thus, purveyors may offer beans known as Colombian, Chanchamayo (from Peru), Kilimanjaro (from Tanzania), Blue Mountain (from Jamaica), Java and Sumatra (from Indonesia) or Kona (from Hawaii), to name a few.

Although many so-called gourmet coffees are made from a single type of bean, nearly all coffee sold in the United States is a blend of various qualities and types of bean.

ROASTING COFFEE

Roasting releases and enhances the flavors in coffee. It also darkens the beans and brings natural oils to the surface. Traditionally, almost everyone roasted their own coffee beans because all coffee beans were sold green. Today, however, roasting is left to experts who possess the necessary equipment. It is important to recognize and understand some of the standard descriptions used for various types of roasting. No single international organization controls the naming of roasted coffee, however, so a coffee roaster may refer to products by any name. In general, roasts fall into four categories based on their color—light, medium, medium-dark or dark. The following descriptions are based on the most common terminology:

- **City roast:** Also called American or brown roast, city roast is the most widely used coffee style in this country. City roast, which is medium brown in color, produces a beverage that may lack brilliance or be a bit flat, yet it is the roast most Americans assume they prefer because it is the roast most often used in grocery store blends.
- **Brazilian:** Somewhat darker than a city roast, Brazilian roast should begin to show a hint of dark-roast flavor. The beans should show a trace of oil. In this context, the word *Brazilian* has no relationship to coffee grown in Brazil.
- **Viennese:** Also called medium-dark roast, Viennese roast generally falls somewhere between a standard city roast and French roast.
- **French roast:** French roast, also called New Orleans or dark roast, approaches espresso in flavor without sacrificing smoothness. The beans should be the color of semisweet chocolate, with apparent oiliness on the surface.
- **Espresso roast:** Espresso roast, also called Italian roast, is the darkest of all. The beans are roasted until they are virtually burnt. The beans should be black with a shiny, oily surface.

Green Coffee Beans

City-Roast Beans

French-Roast Beans

- **fluoridated water** water, either naturally fluoridated or treated with a fluorine-containing compound, intended to promote healthy teeth by preventing tooth decay
- **hard water** water with relatively high calcium and magnesium concentrations
- **mineral water** drinking water that comes from a protected underground water source and contains at least 250 parts per million of total dissolved solids such as calcium
- **natural water** bottled drinking water not derived from a municipal water supply; it can be mineral, spring, well or artesian-well water
- **purified water** bottled water produced by distillation, reverse osmosis, deionization or suitable processes that meet governmental standards
- **seltzer water** a flavorless natural mineral water with carbonation, originally from the German town of Niederselters
- **soda water** a flavorless water with induced carbonation, consumed plain or used as a mixer for alcoholic drinks or soda fountain confections; also known as club soda and seltzer
- **soft water** water with a relatively high sodium concentration
- **spring water** water obtained from an underground source that flows naturally to the earth's surface

GRINDING COFFEE

Unlike roasting, which is best left to the experts, the grinding of coffee beans is best left to the consumer or food service operation. Whole coffee beans stay fresh longer than ground coffee. Ground coffee kept in an airtight container away from heat and light will stay fresh for three or four days. Whole beans will stay fresh for a few weeks and may be kept frozen for several months, as long as they are dry and protected from other flavors. Frozen coffee beans do not need to be thawed before grinding and brewing. Do not refrigerate coffee.

The fineness of the grind depends entirely on the type of coffee maker being used. The grind determines the length of time it takes to achieve the optimum (19%) extraction from the beans. The proper grind is simply whatever grind allows this to happen in the time it takes a specific coffee maker to complete its brewing cycle. As a general rule, the finer the grind, the more quickly the coffee should be prepared. Follow the directions for your coffee maker or ask your specialty coffee purveyor for guidance.

BREWING COFFEE

Coffee is brewed by one of two methods: decoction or infusion. **Decoction** means boiling a substance until its flavor is removed. Boiling is the oldest method of making coffee, but is no longer used except in preparing extremely strong Turkish coffee. **Infusion** refers to the extraction of flavors at temperatures below boiling. Infusion techniques include steeping (mixing hot water with ground coffee), filtering (slowly pouring hot water over ground coffee held in a disposable cloth or paper filter) and dripping (pouring hot water over ground coffee and allowing the liquid to run through a strainer). Percolating is undesirable, as the continuous boiling ruins the coffee's flavor.

The secrets to brewing a good cup of coffee are knowing the exact proportion of coffee to water as well as the length of time to maintain contact between the two. This varies depending on the type of coffee brewing equipment being used.

Drip Coffee Maker

Drip Brewing

Drip coffee is most commonly made from a machine that operates on the principle of gravity and a filter. Water is placed in a reservoir, heated by an element and released slowly over the coffee grounds.

For drip coffee, the best results are nearly always achieved by using 2 level tablespoons of ground coffee per ¾ cup (6 fluid ounces) water. (A standard cup of coffee is three-fourths the size of a standard measuring cup; one pound of coffee yields approximately 80 level tablespoons or enough for 40 "cups" of coffee.) An Approved Coffee Measure (ACM) was developed by the Coffee Brewing Institute to measure 2 level tablespoons accurately. ACM scoops are readily available and are often included with retail coffee packages.

Premeasured packages of ground coffee are generally used with commercial brewing equipment. These packages are available in a range of sizes for making single pots or large urns of coffee. If stronger coffee is desired, use more coffee per cup of water, not a longer brewing time. For weaker coffee, prepare regular-strength coffee and dilute it with hot water. Never reuse coffee grounds.

Espresso Brewing

Espresso (from the Latin *exprimo*, "to press out") is made with a pump-driven machine that forces hot water through compressed, finely ground coffee. An espresso machine also has a steaming rod to froth the milk for espresso-based beverages, as illustrated in Figure 19.3.

Finely ground coffee to be used in espresso coffee machines is sold in bulk or in premeasured packets, or pods, that enable a consistent level of quality. Espresso measures usually come with a 1-ounce scoop on one side and a 2-ounce scoop on the other. A single serving of espresso uses about ¼ ounce

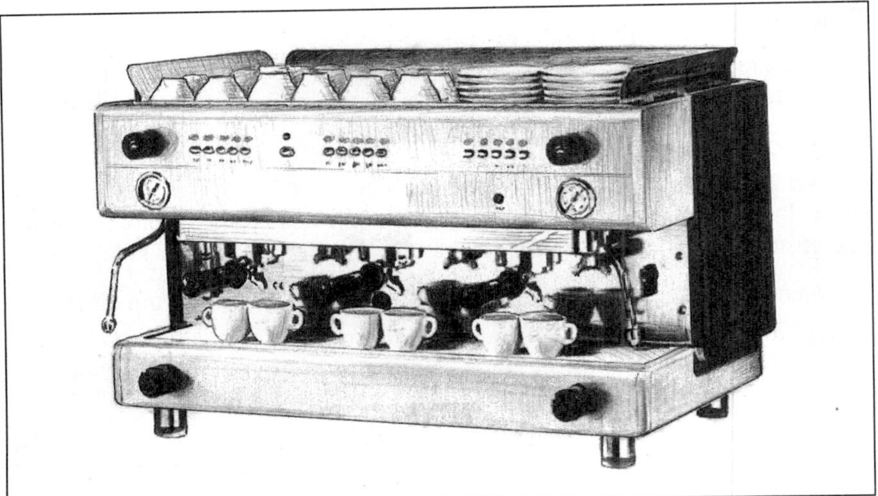

FIGURE 19.3 ▶ Espresso coffee machine with steaming rods.

(7 grams) coffee to 1½ fluid ounces (45 milliliters) water. Americans tend to prefer a larger portion, known as *espresso lungo*, made with 2 to 3 fluid ounces (60 to 90 milliliters) water. It is important that the espresso be made quickly: If the machine pumps water through the coffee for too long, too much water will be added to the cup and the intense espresso flavor will be ruined. Because the single or double "shot" of espresso forms the foundation of so many beverages, this is an important consideration.

Conditions That Affect the Quality of Brewed Coffee

Most coffees are affected by the quality of the water used to brew them. Many commercial establishments have their machines tied into their water supply, so water quality may be beyond the maker's control. Unless equipment is properly cleaned, oils from coffee form an invisible film on the inside of the maker and pots, imparting a rancid or stale flavor to each subsequent batch. Coffeepots and carafes should be cleaned well with hot water between each use; coffee makers should be disassembled and cleaned according to the manufacturer's directions. Calcification on heating elements can also reduce their effectiveness.

Finally, all coffee should be served as soon as it is brewed. Oxidation takes a toll on the aroma and flavor, which soon becomes flat and eventually bitter. Drip coffee may be held for a short time on the coffee maker's hot plate at temperatures of 185°F to 190°F (85°C to 88°C). A better holding method, however, is to immediately pour freshly brewed coffee into a thermal carafe. Never attempt to reheat cold coffee, as drastic temperature shifts destroy flavor.

TASTING COFFEE

Coffee can be judged on four characteristics: aroma, acidity, body and flavor. As a general rule, coffee will taste the way it smells. Some coffees, particularly Colombian, are more fragrant than others, however.

Acidity, also called wininess, refers to the tartness of the coffee. Acidity is a desirable characteristic that indicates snap, life or thinness. Kenyan and Guatemalan are examples of particularly acidic coffees.

Body refers to the feeling of heaviness or thickness that coffee provides on the palate. Sumatran is generally the heaviest, with Mexican and Venezuelan being the lightest.

Flavor, of course, is the most ambiguous as well as the most important characteristic. Terms such as *mellow, harsh, grassy* and *earthy* are used to describe the rather subjective characteristics of flavor.

▶ **cupping** testing coffee or tea for taste and quality, often performed by a professional taster trained to identify key coffee or tea characteristics

SERVING COFFEE

Coffee beverages can be made with specific additions and provide value-added menu alternatives. The most common ways of serving coffee are described here.

Drip Coffee or Filtered Coffee

Drip or filter coffee is the most common style of coffee served in the United States. It is served unadorned, unsweetened and black (without milk or cream). The customer then adds the desired amount of sweetener and/or milk.

- *Black:* A plain cup of unsweetened coffee with no milk or cream added.
- *Café au lait:* The French version of the Italian *caffè latte, café au lait* (or *café crème*) is made with strong coffee instead of espresso and hot, not steamed, milk. It is traditionally served in a handleless bowl.
- *Demitasse:* A small cup of strong black coffee or espresso; also refers to the small cup in which it is served.
- *Iced coffee:* Strong coffee served over ice. If desired, it is best to add sweetener before the coffee is poured over ice or shaken. Iced coffee can also be served with milk or cream. In Australia, a dollop of vanilla ice cream is often added. In Vietnam it is made with a small Vietnamese filter pot using condensed milk as a sweetener. Under no circumstances should leftover coffee be used to make iced coffee.
- *After-Dinner Coffee:* Strong coffee with the addition of liquor, liqueurs, or spices, and often sweetened and garnished with whipped cream; examples include Irish coffee, made with Irish whisky, or café brûlot, made with orange, cloves and brandy.

Espresso

Espresso

Espresso refers to a unique brewing method in which hot water is forced through finely ground and packed coffee under high pressure. Properly made espresso is strong, rich and smooth, not bitter or acidic. As the coffee drains into the cup it will be golden brown, forming a *crema* or foam that lies on top of the black coffee underneath. It is important that the small espresso cups be prewarmed. In Europe an espresso is often served with a twist of lemon on the saucer and a small glass of water on the side.

Types of Espresso Coffee

- *Espresso:* A single (shot) or double serving, black served in a demitasse.
- *Espresso machiatto:* Espresso "marked" with a tiny portion of **steamed milk.**
- *Cappuccino:* One-third espresso, one-third steamed milk and one-third **foamed milk;** the total serving is still rather small, about 4 to 6 ounces (120 to 180 milliliters).
- *Caffè latte:* One-third espresso and two-thirds steamed milk without foam; usually served in a tall glass.
- *Caffè mocha:* One-third espresso and two-thirds steamed milk, flavored with chocolate syrup; usually topped with whipped cream and chocolate shavings or cocoa.
- *Caffè freddo:* A double serving of sweetened espresso served chilled with ice or shaken with crushed ice. Can be served with milk or whipped cream, usually in a tall glass.
- *Espresso con panna:* Espresso with a dollop of whipped cream.

Cappuccino

Caffè Latte

▶ **barista** Italian for "bartender"; now used to describe someone who has been professionally trained in the art of preparing espresso and espresso-based beverages

▶ **steamed milk** milk that is heated with steam generated by an espresso machine; it should be approximately 150°F to 170°F (66°C to 77°C)

▶ **foamed milk** milk that is heated and frothed with air and steam generated by an espresso machine; it will be slightly cooler than steamed milk

- *Espresso corretto:* A shot of espresso "corrected" with the addition of liquor such as brandy or liqueur.
- *Espresso ristretto:* Espresso made with half the water normally used for a regular espresso.

Any type of milk can be used to make cappuccino, latte and other espresso beverages. Milk with higher fat content will produce a creamier tasting beverage. To froth the milk for these beverages, pour the milk into a jug, then position it under the steam spout of the espresso machine. Activate the steam control only when the head of the spout is under the surface of the milk. Moving the jug around while keeping the spout under the surface of the milk helps the steam aerate the milk, giving it a consistency resembling frothed cream.

FLAVORED COFFEES

Dried, ground chicory root has long been added to coffee, particularly by the French, who enjoy its bitter flavor. Toasted barley, dried figs and spices have also been used by various cultures for years. Coffees flavored with vanilla, chocolate, liquors, spices and nuts have recently become popular in the United States. These flavors are added to roasted coffee beans by tumbling the beans with special flavoring oils. The results are strongly aromatic flavors such as vanilla hazelnut, chocolate raspberry or maple walnut.

DECAFFEINATED COFFEE

Caffeine is an alkaloid found in coffee beans (as well as in tea leaves and cocoa beans). It is a stimulant that can improve alertness or reduce fatigue. In excess, however, caffeine can cause some people to suffer palpitations or insomnia. Regular filtered coffee contains 85 to 100 milligrams of caffeine per cup. Robusta beans contain more caffeine than the better-quality arabica beans. Decaffeinated coffee (with 97 percent or more of the caffeine removed) is designed to meet consumer desires for a caffeine-free product.

OTHER USES FOR COFFEE

In addition to its use as a beverage, coffee is also used in stews, sauces and pan gravy. It may be added to breads (such as rye and pumpernickel), cakes,

A CUP OF COFFEE HISTORY

Some anthropologists suggest that coffee was initially consumed by central African warriors in the form of a paste made from mashed coffee beans and animal fat rolled into balls. Eaten before battle, the animal fat and bean protein provided nourishment; the caffeine provided a stimulant.

A hot coffee drink may first have been consumed sometime during the ninth century A.D. in Persia. Made by a decoction of ripe beans, the drink was probably very thick and acrid. Nevertheless, by the year 1000, the elite of the Arab world were regularly drinking a decoction of dried coffee beans. The beans were harvested in Abyssinia (Ethiopia) and brought to market by Egyptian merchants. Within a century or so, *kahwa* became immensely popular with members of all strata of Arab society. Coffeehouses opened throughout the Levant, catering to customers who sipped the thick, brown brew while discussing affairs of heart and state.

Although European travelers to the Ottoman Empire had tasted coffee, and a few Arab or Turkish merchants living in Marseilles offered their guests a chance to sample the rare drink, coffee did not become popular in Europe until the 17th century. Its popularity is due in great part to Suleiman Aga, the Grand Panjandrum of the Ottoman Empire. In 1669, he arrived at the court of King Louis XIV of France as ambassador, bringing with him many exotic treasures, including coffee. Offered at his opulent parties, coffee soon became the drink of choice for the French aristocracy.

Coffee became popular in Vienna as a fortune of war. By 1683, the Turks were at the gates of Vienna. A decisive battle was fought, and the Turks fled, leaving behind stores of gold, equipment, supplies and a barely known provision—green coffee beans. One of the victorious leaders, Franz George Kolschitzky, recognized the treasure, took it as his own and soon opened the first coffeehouse in Vienna, The Blue Bottle.

Despite its growing popularity, coffee was exorbitantly expensive, in part the result of the sultan's monopoly on coffee beans. His agents, principally in Marseilles, controlled the sale of beans. But the monopoly was not to survive. By the end of the 17th century, the Dutch had stolen coffee plants from Arabia and began cultivating them in Java. By the early 18th century, the French had transported seedlings to the West Indies; from there coffee plantations spread throughout the New World.

custards, ice creams, dessert sauces and frostings. The flavor of coffee has a strong affinity for chocolate, nuts and rum.

TEA, TISANES AND RELATED BEVERAGES

Tea and tisanes are made from dried leaves, herbs, spices, flowers or fruits that are prepared by infusion, that is, steeping in fresh boiling water. **Tea** is the beverage of choice for more than half the world's population and may be served hot or cold. Eighty-five percent of the tea consumed in the United States is iced, a uniquely American preference. **Tisanes,** or herbal infusions, have long been popular for their perceived health benefits and healing properties in Europe and Asia. As customers in the United States have become familiar with herbal teas, demand for them is growing.

TEA

Tea (Fr. *thé*) is the name given to the leaves of *Camellia sinensis,* a tree or shrub that grows at high altitudes in damp tropical regions. Although tea comes from only one species of plant, there are three general types of tea—black, green and oolong. The differences among the three are the result of the manner in which the leaves are treated after picking.

Fruit Tea

Gunpowder

Darjeeling

Tea Varieties

Black tea is amber-brown and strongly flavored. Its color and flavor result from fermenting the leaves. Black tea leaves are named or graded by leaf size. Because larger leaves brew more slowly than smaller ones, teas are sorted by leaf size for efficient brewing. *Souchong* denotes large leaves, *pekoe* denotes medium-sized leaves and *orange pekoe* denotes the smallest whole leaves. (Note that orange pekoe does not refer to any type of orange flavor.) Broken tea, graded as either broken orange pekoe or broken pekoe, is smaller, resulting in a darker, stronger brew. Broken tea is most often used in tea bags. These grades apply to both Chinese and Indian black teas.

Green tea is yellowish-green in color with a bitter flavor. Leaves used for green tea are not fermented. Chinese green tea leaves are also graded according to leaf size and age. The finest green tea is Gunpowder, followed by Imperial and Hyson.

Oolong tea is partially fermented to combine the characteristics of black and green teas. Oolong is popular in China and Japan, often flavored with jasmine flowers. Oolong tea leaves are also graded by size and age.

As with coffee, tea takes much of its flavor from the geographic conditions in which it is grown. Teas are named for their place of origin—for example, Darjeeling, Ceylon (now Sri Lanka) or Assam.

Many popular and commercially available teas are actually blends of leaves from various sources. Blended and unblended teas may also be flavored with oils, dried fruit, spices, flowers or herbs; they are then referred to as **flavored teas.** Spices such as allspice, cinnamon, nutmeg and black pepper are often used to create teas flavored for cold-weather drinking. Bright herbs such as mint and citrus rind or oil, especially bergamot, which gives Earl Grey tea its flavor, add complexity to brewed teas and are also popular additions.

▶ **flavored tea** tea to which flavorings such as oils, dried fruit, spices, flowers and herbs have been added

Tea Flavors

Tea can be described according to three key characteristics: astringency or briskness, body and aroma. *Astringency* is not bitterness, which is undesirable, but a sharp, dry feeling on the tongue that contributes to the refreshing taste of a tea. *Body* refers to the feeling of thickness on the tongue. Teas range from light to full bodied. *Aroma* is the smell and flavors of the tea when brewed.

The following descriptions apply to some of the teas frequently available through wholesalers or gourmet suppliers. Taste several different ones to determine the best choice. Remember that the same tea from different blenders or distributors may taste different, and that different flavors will be more or less appropriate for different times of the day. A selection of flavors may be offered.

Variety of cups of brewed tea (from left): Chinese tea, Japanese tea, Moroccan mint tea and black tea with milk

BLACK TEAS

- *Assam*—A rich black tea from northeastern India with a reddish color. It is valued by connoisseurs, especially for breakfast.
- *Ceylon*—A full-flavored black tea with a golden color and delicate fragrance. Ideal for serving iced, it does not become cloudy when cold.
- *Darjeeling*—The champagne of teas, grown in the foothills of the Himalayas in northeastern India. It is a full-bodied, black tea with a muscat flavor.
- *Earl Grey*—A blend of black teas, usually including Darjeeling, flavored with oil of bergamot. A popular choice for afternoon tea.
- *English Breakfast*—An English blend of Indian and Sri Lankan black teas; it is full-bodied and robust, with a rich color.
- *Keemum*—A mellow black Chinese tea with a strong aroma. It is less astringent than other teas and is delicious iced.
- *Lapsang Souchong*—A large-leafed (souchong) tea from the Lapsang district of China. It has a distinctive tarry, smoky flavor and aroma, appropriate for afternoon tea or dinner.

GREEN TEAS

- *Gunpowder*—A green Chinese tea with a tightly curled leaf and gray-green color. It has a pungent flavor and a light straw color. It is often served after the evening meal.
- *Sencha* (common)—A delicate Japanese green tea that has a light color with a pronounced aroma and a bright, grassy taste.
- *White tea*—A delicate green tea made from new buds picked before they open. Allowed to wither so that natural moisture evaporates, these leaves are lightly dried to a pale silvery color. White tea has a subtle flavor.

OOLONG TEAS

- *Formosa Oolong*—A unique and expensive large-leafed oolong tea with the flavor of ripe peaches. It is appropriate for breakfast or afternoon tea.

TISANES (HERB TEAS)

Tisanes are herbal infusions that do not contain any "real" tea. They are commonly made from fresh or dried flowers, herbs, seeds or roots; chamomile, ginseng, linden flowers (Fr. *tilleul*) and lemon balm are among the more popular tisanes. In most countries there is a tradition of indigenous herbal medicine often administered in an infused form, as a tea. In Europe, a tisane may be served after a meal to aid digestion or taken before bed as an aid to sleep. (Herbal teas usually contain no caffeine, so they do not act as stimulants.) In the United States, herbal teas are gaining in popularity, but not for the first time: During the American Revolution herbal teas became known as "Liberty teas." In a professional food service establishment herbal teas are prepackaged blends and require no mixing.

TEA BAGS

The invention of the tea bag was apparently inadvertent. According to the Tea Association of America, in 1904, Thomas Sullivan, a New York tea merchant, sent potential customers samples of tea in small muslin or silk bags. Finding that they could make tea by simply pouring boiling water over the bags, Sullivan's new customers clamored for more.

Throughout the 20th century tea companies experimented and claimed supremacy for their bags, but the quality of the tea within is more important than the shape of the bag.

BREWING TEA

Tea may be brewed by the cup or the pot. In either case, it is important to use the following procedure:

1. Always begin with clean equipment and freshly drawn cold water. Water that has been sitting in a kettle or hot water tank contains less air and will taste flat or stale. Tea should never be brewed using a drip coffee system because the water is not hot enough. The resulting product will be refused by any discerning tea drinker.
2. Warm the teapot by rinsing its interior with hot water. This will help relax the tea leaves and ensure that the water will stay hot when it comes in contact with the tea.
3. Place 1 teaspoon (5 milliliters) loose tea or one tea bag per ¾ cup (6 fluid ounces/180 milliliters) of water capacity in the warmed teapot.
4. As soon as the water comes to a boil, pour the appropriate amount over the tea. Do not allow the water to continue boiling as this removes the oxygen, leaving a flat taste. The water should be at a full boil when it comes in contact with the tea so that the tea leaves will uncurl and release their flavor.
5. Replace the lid of the teapot and allow the tea to infuse for 3 to 5 minutes. Time the brew. Color is not a reliable indication of brewing time; tea leaves release color before flavor, and different types of tea will be different colors when properly brewed.
6. Remove the tea bags or loose tea from the water when brewing is complete. This can be accomplished easily if the teapot is fitted with a removable leaf basket or if a tea bag or a perforated tea ball is used. Otherwise, decant the tea through a strainer into a second warmed teapot.
7. Serve immediately, accompanied with sugar, lemon, milk (not cream) and honey as desired. Dilute the tea with hot water if necessary.
8. Do not reuse tea leaves. One pound of tea yields 200 cups, making it the most inexpensive beverage after tap water.

For iced tea, prepare regular brewed tea using 50 percent more tea. Then pour the tea into a pitcher or glass filled with ice. The stronger brew will hold its flavor better as the ice melts. If iced tea is not to be used immediately, it should be brewed at room or refrigerator temperature for some hours to prevent clouding.

SERVING TEA

Black and oolong tea may be served hot or cold, but green tea is best served hot. Black tea is served with milk or lemon and sugar; green and oolong tea are most often served plain. Adding milk to hot tea is a British preference (not normally followed in Europe or Asia) that reduces the astringency of the tea. Iced tea, an American invention, may be served plain or sweetened, and is often garnished with lemon, orange or fresh mint.

TEA BEVERAGES

The popular tea beverage—iced tea—claims its invention in the United States. Brewed-tea-and-milk beverages called *chai*, from the Chinese word for "tea," are also gaining in popularity, as are iced herbal teas. Moroccan tea is highly sweetened green tea brewed with fresh mint and served hot.

A CUP OF TEA HISTORY

Some believe that the Chinese emperor Shen Nung discovered tea drinking in 2737 B.C.E. Legend holds that the emperor was boiling his drinking water beneath a tree when some leaves fell into the pot. Enchanted with the drink, he began to cultivate the plant. Whether this is myth or truth, it is known that a hot drink made from powdered dried tea leaves whipped into hot water was regularly consumed in China sometime after the fourth century. Later, decoctions of tea leaves (as well as rice, spices and nuts) became popular. But it was not until the Ming dynasty (1368–1644) that infusions of tea leaves became commonplace.

By the ninth century, tea drinking had spread to Japan. In both Chinese and Japanese cultures, tea drinking developed into a ritual. For the Chinese, a cup of tea became the mirror of the soul. For the Japanese, it was the drink of immortality.

Tea was first transported from China to Europe by Dutch merchants during the early 1600s. By midcentury, it was introduced into England. In 1669, the British East India Company was granted a charter by Queen Elizabeth I to import tea, a monopoly it held until 1833. To ensure a steady supply, the English surreptitiously procured plants from China and started plantations throughout the Indian subcontinent, as did the Dutch.

Tea drinking became fashionable in England, at least in court circles, through Charles II (raised in exile at The Hague in Holland, he reigned from 1660 to 1685) and his Portuguese wife, Catherine of Braganza. Queen Anne of England (who reigned from 1702 to 1714) introduced several concepts that eventually became part of the English tea custom. For example, she substituted tea for ale at breakfast and began using large silver pots instead of tiny china pots.

The social custom of afternoon tea began in the late 1700s, thanks to Anna, Duchess of Bedford. Historians attribute to her the late-afternoon ritual of snacking on sandwiches and pastries accompanied by tea. She began the practice in order to quell her hunger pangs between breakfast and dinner (which was typically served at 9:30 or 10:00 P.M.).

Eventually, two distinct types of teatime evolved. Low tea was aristocratic in origin and consisted of a snack of pastries and sandwiches, with tea, served in the late afternoon as a prelude to the evening meal. High tea was bourgeois in origin, consisting of leftovers from the typically large middle-class lunch, such as cold meats, bread and cheeses. High tea became a substitute for the evening meal.

CONCLUSION

Eggs are found in practically every kitchen and served as the principal ingredient or incorporated into various dishes. How to select, handle and cook them well are basic skills all student chefs must master. They must also master the skills needed to prepare breakfast items. Breakfast is an important meal for consumers and food service operations alike. Breakfast menus may offer a variety of items, including fruits, cereals, eggs, pancakes and cured meats, or they can be devoted to one or two specialty items such as coffee and cinnamon rolls. Understanding how to prepare and serve coffee and tea is an essential skill required for breakfast and all beverage service. Whatever is served should be prepared and served with care.

QUESTIONS FOR DISCUSSION

1. Explain the difference between an omelet and a frittata.
2. Describe four different types of pan-fried eggs, and explain how each is prepared.
3. What is the difference between a soft-cooked egg and a hard-cooked egg? Why are these eggs simmered instead of boiled?
4. Explain the differences between a typical breakfast and a typical brunch. Create a sample menu for each of these meals.
5. List three types of griddlecakes and explain how they are prepared.
6. Describe the difference between drip coffee and espresso coffee.
7. Name the three principal varieties of tea.

CHAPTER TWENTY

CUISINE IS WHEN THINGS TASTE LIKE THEMSELVES.

—Julia Child, American cooking teacher and writer (1912–2004)

VEGETABLES

GREENS, San Francisco, CA
Chef Annie Somerville

AFTER STUDYING THIS CHAPTER, YOU WILL BE ABLE TO:

- identify a variety of vegetables
- purchase vegetables appropriate for your needs
- store vegetables properly
- understand how vegetables are preserved
- prepare vegetables for cooking or service
- apply various cooking methods to vegetables

Long overcooked and underrated, vegetables are enjoying a welcome surge in popularity. Gone are the days when a chef included vegetables as an afterthought to the "meat and potatoes" of the meal. Now properly prepared fresh vegetables are used to add flavor, color and variety to almost any meal. Many restaurants are featuring vegetarian entrées, an extensive selection of vegetable side dishes or an entire vegetarian menu. This trend reflects the demands of more knowledgeable and health-conscious consumers as well as the increased availability of high-quality fresh produce. (Cooking for those on a meatless diet using vegetables as well as other ingredients is discussed in Chapter 22, Vegetarian Cooking.)

In this chapter, we identify many of the vegetables typically used by food service operations. (Potatoes, although they are vegetables, are discussed in Chapter 21, Potatoes, Grains and Pasta, while salad greens are discussed in Chapter 23, Salads and Salad Dressings.) Here we also discuss how fresh and preserved vegetables are purchased, stored and prepared for service or cooking. Many of the cooking methods analyzed in Chapter 8, Principles of Cooking, are then applied to vegetables.

The term **vegetable** refers to any herbaceous plant that can be partially or wholly eaten. A herbaceous plant has little or no woody tissue. The portions we consume include the leaves, stems, roots, tubers, seeds and flowers. Vegetables contain more starch and less sugar than fruits. Therefore vegetables tend to be savory, not sweet. Also unlike fruits, vegetables are most often eaten cooked, not raw.

▸ IDENTIFYING VEGETABLES

This book presents fruits and vegetables according to the ways most people view them and use them, rather than by rigid botanical classifications. Although produce such as tomatoes, peppers and eggplants are botanically fruits, they are prepared and served like vegetables and are included here under the category we call "fruit-vegetables." Potatoes, although botanically vegetables, are discussed with other starches in Chapter 21, Potatoes, Grains and Pasta.

We divide vegetables into nine categories based on either botanical relationship or edible part: cabbages, fruit-vegetables, gourds and squashes, greens, mushrooms and truffles, onions, pods and seeds, roots and tubers, and stalks. A vegetable may have several names, varying from region to region or on a purveyor's whim. The names given here follow generally accepted custom and usage.

CABBAGES

The *Brassica* or cabbage family includes a wide range of vegetables used for their heads, flowers or leaves. They are generally quick-growing, cool-weather crops. Many are ancient plants with unknown origins. They are inexpensive, readily available and easy to prepare.

BOK CHOY

Bok choy, also known as pok choy, is a white-stemmed variety of southern Chinese cabbage. The relatively tightly packed leaves are dark green, with long white ribs attached at a bulbous stem. The stalks are crisp and mild with a flavor similar to romaine lettuce. Although bok choy may be eaten raw, it is most often stir-fried or used in soups.

Choose heads with bright white stalks and dark green leaves; avoid those with brown, moist spots. Fresh bok choy is available all year. Jars of pickled and fermented bok choy (known as Korean kim chee) are also available.

Bok Choy

BROCCOLI

Broccoli, a type of flower, has a thick central stalk with grayish-green leaves topped with one or more heads of green florets. Broccoli may be eaten raw or steamed, microwaved or sautéed and served warm or cold. Broccoli stalks are extremely firm and benefit from blanching. Stems are often slow-cooked for soups. Generally, broccoli leaves are not eaten.

Choose firm stalks with compact clusters of tightly closed dark green florets. Avoid stalks with yellow flowers. Broccoli is available all year.

Broccoli

▶ PROCEDURE FOR CUTTING BROCCOLI SPEARS

Cut off the thick, woody portion of the stalk, then cut the florets and stems into spears.

BRUSSELS SPROUTS

Brussels Sprouts

Brussels sprouts (Fr. *choux de Bruxelles*) were first cultivated around 1700. The plant produces numerous small heads arranged in neat rows along a thick stalk. The tender young sprouts are similar to baby cabbages and are usually steamed or roasted. Brussels sprouts have a strong, nutty flavor that blends well with game, ham, duck or rich meats.

Choose small, firm sprouts that are compact and heavy. The best size is ¾ to 1½ inches (2 to 4 centimeters) in diameter. They should be bright green and free of blemishes. Their peak season is from September through February.

Cauliflower

CAULIFLOWER

Cauliflower (Fr. *chou-fleur*) is the king of the cabbage family. Each stalk produces one flower or head surrounded by large green leaves. The head, composed of creamy white florets, can be cooked whole or cut into separate florets for steaming, blanching or stir-frying.

Choose firm, compact heads. Any attached leaves should be bright green and crisp. A yellow color or spreading florets indicate that the vegetable is overly mature. Cauliflower is available all year, especially from the late fall through the spring.

▶ PROCEDURE FOR CUTTING CAULIFLOWER FLORETS

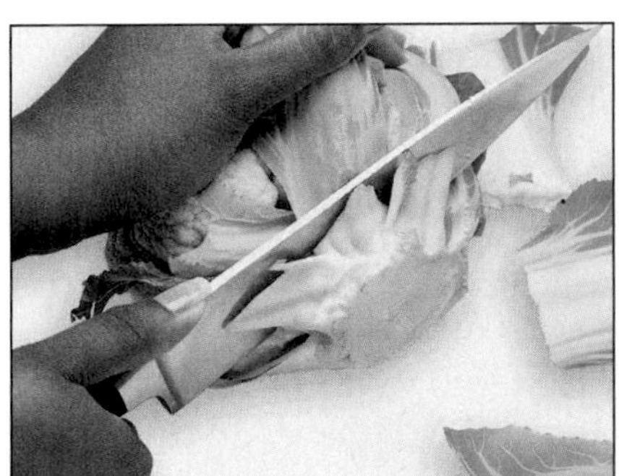

1 Cut off the stem and leaves.

2 Cut the florets off of the core.

Green and Red Cabbages

HEAD CABBAGES (GREEN AND RED)

Cabbage (Fr. *chou*) has been a staple of northern European cuisine for centuries. The familiar green cabbage has a large, firm, round head with tightly packed pale green leaves. Flat and cone-shaped heads are also available. Red (or purple) cabbage is a different strain and may be tougher than green cabbage. Cabbage can be eaten raw (as in coleslaw) or used in soups or stews; it can be braised, steamed or stir-fried. The large, waxy leaves can also be steamed until soft, then wrapped around a filling of seasoned meat.

Choose firm heads without dried cores. Cabbages are available all year.

KALE

Kale

Kale has large ruffled, curly or bumpy leaves. Its rather bitter flavor goes well with rich meats such as game, pork or ham. Kale is typically boiled, stuffed or used in soups.

Choose leaves that are crisp, with a grayish-green color. Kale is available all year; its peak season is during the winter months.

Ornamental or flowering kale, sometimes marketed as "savoy," is edible, but its pink, pur-

Ornamental Kale

ple, yellow or white-and-green variegated leaves are best used for decoration and garnish.

Kohlrabi

KOHLRABI

Although it looks rather like a round root, kohlrabi is actually a bulbous stem vegetable created by crossbreeding cabbages and turnips. Both the leaves (which are attached directly to the bulbous stem) and the roots are generally removed before sale. Depending on the variety, the skin may be light green, purple or green with a hint of red. The interior flesh is white, with a sweet flavor similar to that of turnips. (Kohlrabi can be substituted for turnip in many recipes.) Younger plants are milder and more tender than large, mature ones. The outer skin must be removed from mature stems; young stems need only to be well scrubbed before cooking. Kohlrabi can be eaten raw, or it can be cooked (whole, sliced or diced) with moist-heat cooking methods such as boiling and steaming. Kohlrabi may also be hollowed out and stuffed with meat or vegetable mixtures.

Choose small, tender stems with fresh, green leaves. Peak season for kohlrabi is from June through September.

Napa Cabbage

NAPA CABBAGE

Napa cabbage, also known as Chinese cabbage, is widely used in Asian cuisines. It has a stout, elongated head with relatively tightly packed, firm, pale green leaves. It is more moist and more tender than common green and red cabbages, with a milder, more delicate flavor. Napa cabbage may be eaten raw but is particularly well suited for stir-frying or steaming.

Choose heads with crisp leaves that are free of blemishes. Napa cabbage is available fresh all year.

Savoy

SAVOY

Savoy cabbage has curly or ruffled leaves, often in variegated shades of green and purple. (The term *savoyed* is used to refer to any vegetable with bumpy, wavy or wrinkled leaves.) Savoy cabbage tends to be milder and more tender than regular cabbages and can be substituted for them, cooked or uncooked. Savoy leaves also make an attractive garnish.

Choose heads that are loose or tight, depending on the variety, with tender, unblemished leaves. Peak season is from August through the spring.

FRUIT-VEGETABLES

Botanists classify avocados, eggplants, peppers and tomatoes as fruits because they develop from the ovary of flowering plants and contain one or more seeds. Chefs, however, prepare and serve them like vegetables; therefore they are discussed here.

AVOCADOS

Avocados include several varieties of pear-shaped fruits with rich, high-fat flesh. This light golden-green flesh surrounds a large, inedible, oval-shaped seed (pit). Some varieties have smooth, green skin; others have pebbly, almost black skin. Avocados should be used at their peak of ripeness, a condition that lasts only briefly. Firm avocados lack the desired flavor and creamy texture. Ripe avocados should be soft to the touch but not mushy. Ripe Haas avocados have almost-black skins; the skins of the other varieties remain green when ripe. Firm avocados can be left at room temperature to ripen, then refrigerated for one or two days. Avocados are most often used raw to garnish salads, mashed or puréed for sauces, sliced for sandwiches or diced for omelets. Avocado halves are

Avocados

popular containers for chilled meat, fish, shellfish or poultry salads. Because avocado flesh turns brown very quickly once cut, dip avocado halves or slices in lemon juice and keep unused portions tightly covered with plastic wrap.

Choose avocados that are free of blemishes or moist spots. The flesh should be free of dark spots or streaks. Available all year, the peak season for Haas avocados is April through October; for Fuertes avocados, it is November through April.

▶ PROCEDURE FOR CUTTING AND PITTING AVOCADOS

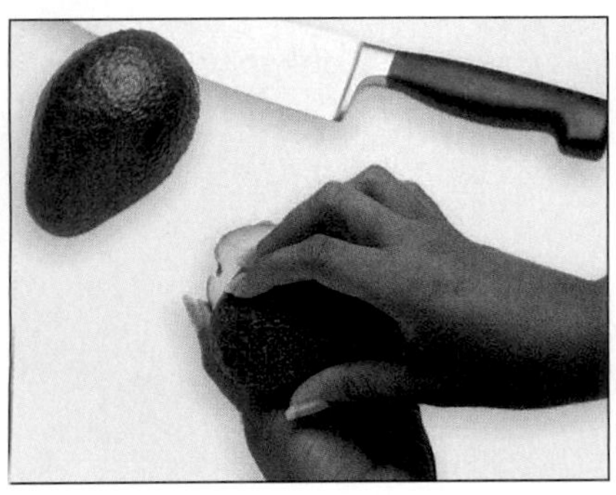

1 Cut the avocado in half lengthwise. Separate the two halves with a twisting motion.

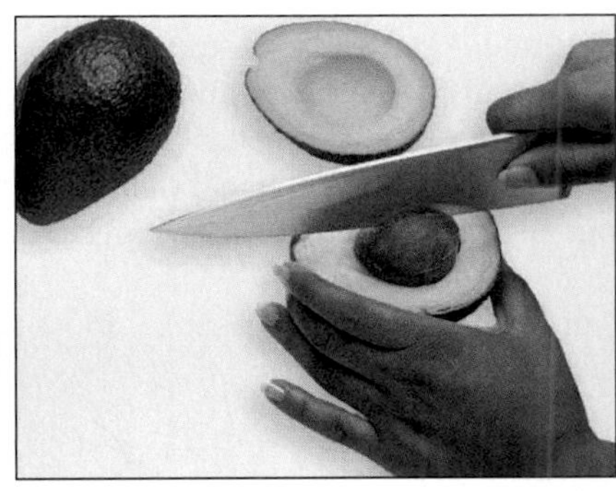

2 Insert a chef's knife into the pit and twist to remove.

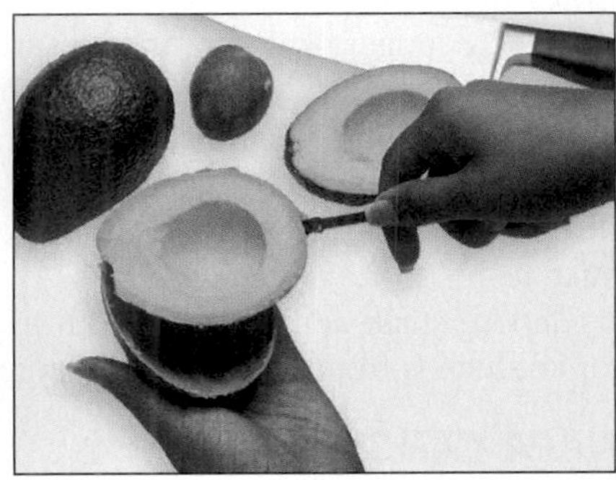

3 Scoop the flesh out of the skin with a large spoon.

EGGPLANT: TO SALT OR NOT TO SALT?

Eggplants are filled with cells that contain water and are surrounded by tiny air pockets. The presence of heat will squeeze the air out of the pockets. If the eggplant has not been salted, oil is then free to seep into these pockets and the eggplant becomes soggy when fried.

But when salt is sprinkled on an eggplant, it draws the water out of the cells. The cells then collapse, which in turn makes the air pockets collapse. As a result, no oil can seep into the tiny pockets during the frying process.

DANIEL ZWERDLING is a senior correspondent with National Public Radio. This sidebar originally appeared in *Gourmet*.

EGGPLANTS

Two types of eggplants (Fr. *aubergine*) are commonly available: Asian and western. Asian varieties are either round or long and thin, with skin colors ranging from creamy white to deep purple. Western eggplants, which are more common in the United States, tend to be shaped like a plump pear with a shiny lavender to purple-black skin. Both types have a dense, khaki-colored flesh with a rather bland flavor that absorbs other flavors well during cooking. Eggplants can be grilled, baked, steamed, fried or sautéed. They are commonly used in Mediterranean and Indian cuisines (especially in vegetarian dishes), but also appear in European and North American dishes. The skin may be left intact or removed before or after cooking, as desired. Sliced eggplants may be salted and left to drain for 30 minutes to remove moisture and bitterness before cooking.

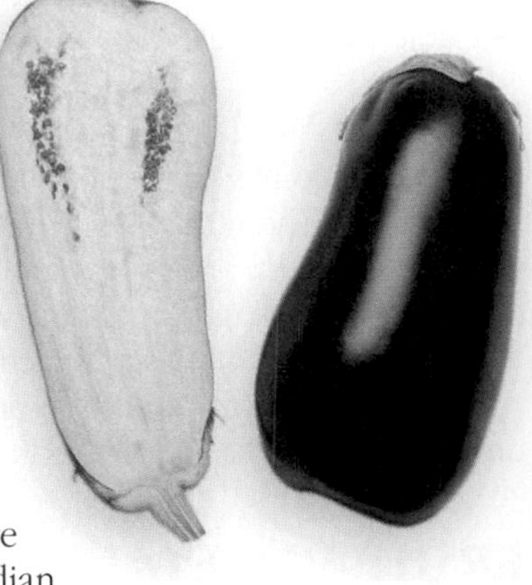

Western Eggplant

Choose plump, heavy eggplants with a smooth, shiny skin that is not blemished or wrinkled. Asian varieties tend to be softer than western. Eggplants are available all year; their peak season is during the late summer.

Asian Eggplants

Japanese Eggplant

PEPPERS

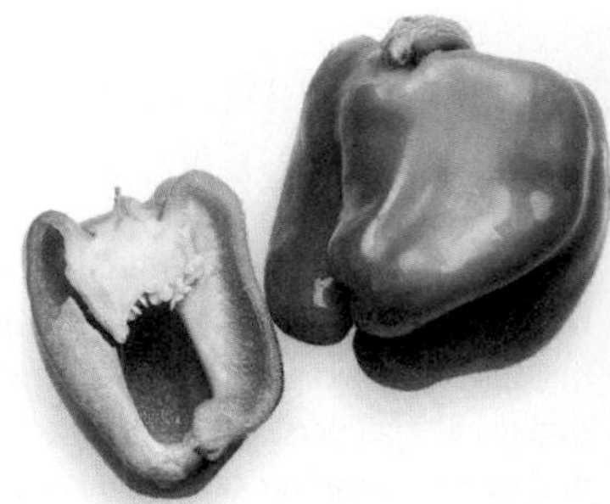

Green Bell Peppers

Members of the *Capsicum* family are native to the New World. When "discovered" by Christopher Columbus, he called them "peppers" because of their sometimes fiery flavor. These peppers, which include sweet peppers and hot peppers (chiles), are unrelated to peppercorns, the Asian spice for which Columbus was actually searching. Interestingly, New World peppers were readily accepted in Indian and Asian cuisines, in which they are now considered staples.

Fresh peppers are found in a wide range of colors—green, red, yellow, orange, purple and white—as well as shapes, from tiny teardrops to cones to spheres. They have dense flesh and a hollow central cavity. The flesh is lined with placental ribs (the white internal veins), to which tiny yellowish-white seeds are attached. A core of seeds is also attached to the stem end of each pepper.

Chile peppers get their heat from capsaicin, which is found not in the flesh or seeds, but in the placental ribs. Thus a pepper's heat can be greatly reduced by carefully removing the ribs and attached seeds. Generally, the smaller the chile, the hotter it is. The amount of heat varies from variety to variety, however, and even from one pepper to another depending on growing conditions. Hot, dry conditions result in hotter peppers than do cool, moist conditions.

When selecting peppers, choose those that are plump and brilliantly colored with smooth, unblemished skins. Avoid wrinkled, pitted or blistered peppers. A bright green stem indicates freshness. The searing heat of a Scotch bonnet or habanero can burn. Wearing gloves is recommended when working with these chile peppers.

Red and Yellow Bell Peppers

Sweet Peppers

Common sweet peppers, known as bell peppers, are thick-walled fruits available in green, red, yellow, purple, orange and other colors. They are heart-shaped or boxy, with a short stem and crisp flesh. Their flavor is warm, sweet (red peppers tend to be the sweetest) and relatively mild. Raw bell peppers may be sliced or diced and used in salads or sandwiches. Bell peppers can also be stuffed and baked, grilled, fried, sautéed or puréed for soups, sauces or condiments. Green bell peppers are available all year; other colors are more readily available during the summer and fall.

▶ PROCEDURE FOR CUTTING PEPPERS JULIENNE

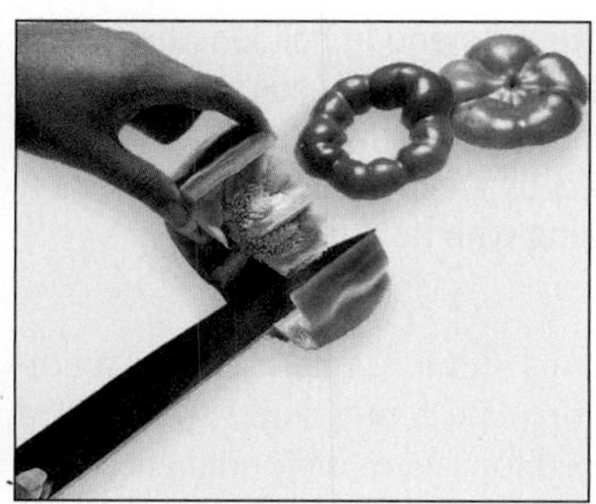

1 Trim off the ends of the pepper; cut away the seeds and core.

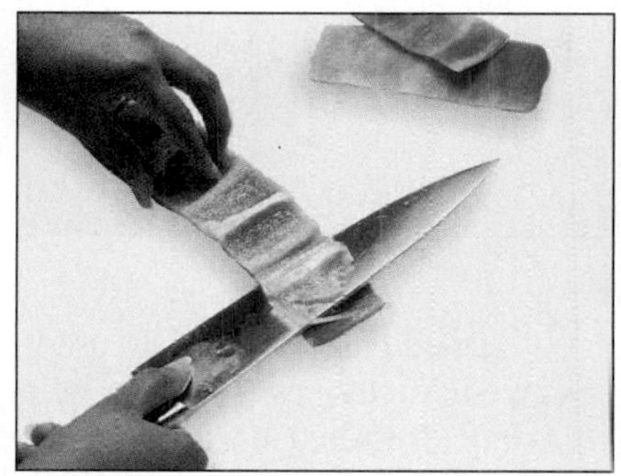

2 Cut away the pale ribs, trimming the flesh to the desired thickness.

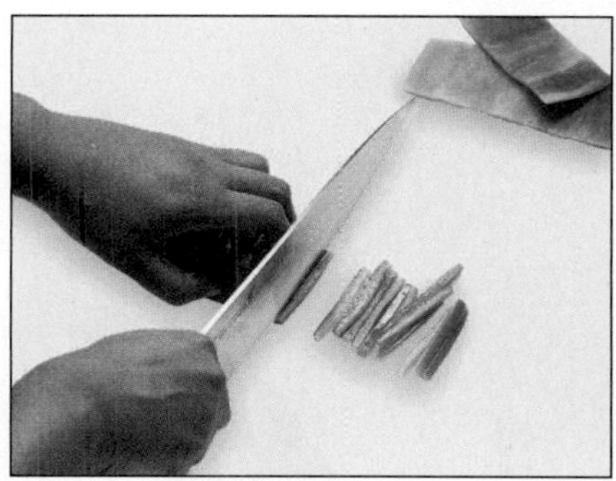

3 Slice the flesh in julienne.

CHILE PEPPER PUNGENCY

A pepper's heat can be measured by Scoville Heat Units, a subjective rating created to measure the perception of capsaicin when tasting chile peppers. The higher the rating, the larger the concentration of capsaicin and the hotter the pepper will taste. An example of some of the ranges of heat of common chile peppers as measured in this system is listed here.

Pepper	Pungency (Scoville)
Bell, sweet Italian	0
New Mexico, pimento	500–1000
Anaheim, ancho, pasilla, poblano	1000–1500
Chipotle, jalapeño	2500–10,000
Serrano	5000–23,000
De árbol	15,000–30,000
Aji, cayenne, piquin, tabasco	30,000–50,000
Habanero, Scotch bonnet	80,000–300,000
Pure capsaicin	16,000,000

Hot Peppers

Hot peppers, also known as chiles, are also members of the *Capsicum* family. Although a chile's most characteristic attribute is its pungency, each chile actually has a distinctive flavor, from mild and rich to spicy and sweet to fiery hot.

Chiles are commonly used in Asian, Indian, Mexican and Latin American cuisines. The larger (and milder) of the hot peppers, such as Anaheim and poblano, can be stuffed and baked or sautéed as a side dish. Most chiles, however, are used to add flavor and seasoning to sauces and other dishes. Fresh chiles are available all year and are also available canned in a variety of processed forms such as whole or diced, roasted, pickled or marinated.

(clockwise from bottom left) Red and Green Serrano, Green and Red Jalapeño, Yellow Hot, Poblano and Anaheim Chiles

Habanero

▶ PROCEDURE FOR CORING JALAPEÑOS

Cut the jalapeño in half lengthwise. Push the core and seeds out with your thumb. You can avoid burning your fingers by wearing rubber gloves when working with hot chiles.

Dried chiles are widely used in Mexican, Central American and southwestern cuisines. They can be ground to create a powdered spice called *chilli,* or soaked in a liquid and then puréed for sauces or condiments. Drying radically alters the flavor of chiles, making them stronger and more pungent. Just as one type of fresh chile cannot be substituted for another without altering a dish's flavor, so too dried chiles cannot be substituted without flavor changes.

Choose dried chiles that are clean and unbroken, with some flexibility. Avoid any with white spots or a stale aroma.

Dried Chiles (top to bottom): California, Ancho, De Árbol

▶ PROCEDURE FOR ROASTING PEPPERS

1 Roast the pepper over an open flame until completely charred.

2 Place the pepper in a plastic bag to sweat for a few minutes, then remove the burnt skin and rinse under running water.

A PEPPER BY ANY OTHER NAME

The popularity of southwestern cuisine, hot condiments and salsas has brought with it a new appreciation and respect for chiles. Diners and chefs may find the names given to the various chiles confusing, however. Most chiles can be used either fresh or dried; drying changes not only the pepper's flavor, but also its name. Regional variations in chile names also add to the confusion. Several of the more frequently encountered chiles are listed here according to the names most commonly used for both their fresh and dried forms:

Fresh (*Fresco*)	**Dried (*Seco*)**
Anaheim	Mild red or California
Ancho	Ancho or pastilla
Chilaca	Pastilla or negro
Jalapeño	Chipotle (smoked)
Mirasol	Guajillo
New Mexico green	New Mexico red
New Mexico red	Chile Colorado
Pimento	Paprika
Poblano	Mulato

TOMATILLOS

Tomatillos, also known as Mexican or husk tomatoes, grow on small, weedy bushes. They are bright green, about the size of a small tomato, and are covered with a thin, papery husk. They have a tart, lemony flavor and crisp, moist flesh. Although they are an important ingredient in southwestern and northern Mexican cuisines, tomatillos may not be readily available in other areas. Tomatillos can be used raw in salads, puréed for salsa or cooked in soups, stews or vegetable dishes.

Tomatillos

Choose tomatillos whose husks are split but still look fresh. The skin should be plump, shiny and slightly sticky. They are available all year; their peak season is during the summer and fall.

TOMATOES

Tomatoes (Fr. *tomate* or *pomme d'amour;* It. *pomodoro*) are available in a wide variety of colors and shapes. They vary from green (unripe) to golden yellow to ruby red; from tiny spheres (currant tomatoes) to huge, squat ovals (beefsteak). Some, such as the plum tomato, have lots of meaty flesh with only a few seeds; others, such as the slicing tomato, have lots of seeds and juice, but only a few meaty membranes. All tomatoes have a similar flavor, but the levels of sweetness and acidity vary depending on the species, growing conditions and ripeness at harvest.

(clockwise from lower right) Pear, Cherry, Plum and Beefsteak Tomatoes

Because tomatoes are highly perishable, they are usually harvested when mature but still green (unripe), then shipped to wholesalers who ripen them in temperature- and humidity-controlled rooms. The effect on flavor and texture is unfortunate.

Tomatoes are used widely in salads, soups, sauces and baked dishes. They are most often eaten raw, but can be grilled, pickled, pan-fried, roasted or sautéed as a side dish.

THREE TREASURES OF THE NEW WORLD

In lieu of many spices, golden treasures and precious gems, early Spanish explorers returned to Spain with items of much greater significance: tomatoes, potatoes and corn. Unfortunately for those who financed the voyagers, the value of this produce was not immediately appreciated.

The Spanish and the Italians hailed the tomato (whose name comes from the Aztec name *tomatl*) as an aphrodisiac—perhaps because of its resemblance to the human heart—when it arrived from the New World during the 16th century. But even though tomatoes soon became part of Spanish and Italian cuisines, most other Europeans, New World colonists and, later, Americans considered tomatoes poisonous. (There is some truth to this notion: tomato vines and leaves contain tomatine, an alkaloid that can cause health problems.) Thus for many years and in many societies, only the adventurous ate tomatoes.

The potato, first delivered to Europe from its native Peru by Francisco Pizarro in the 16th century, did not win wide acceptance in haute cuisine until Antoine-Augustin Parmentier (1737–1813), a French army pharmacist, induced King Louis XVI of France (who reigned from 1775 to 1793) to try one. The king and his courtiers liked them so much they even began wearing potato blossom boutonnières. Parmentier was ultimately honored for his starchy contribution to French cuisine by having several potato dishes named for him, such as *potage Parmentier* (potato soup). Not only did Parmentier lobby for the acceptance of the potato as a food fit for a king, he also prophesied that the potato would make starvation impossible. Potatoes ultimately did become a staple of many diets. But, sadly, the converse of Parmentier's prophecy came true during the Irish potato famine of 1846–1848, when a terrible blight destroyed the potato crop. Nearly 1.5 million people died, and an equal number emigrated to the United States. They brought with them a cuisine that incorporated potatoes; thus an appreciation of the common potato was reintroduced to its native land.

When returning from his second voyage to the New World, Columbus took corn with him. Called *mahiz* or *maize* by West Indian natives, corn had been a staple of Central American diets for at least 5000 years. Although Europeans did not actively shun corn as they did tomatoes and potatoes, corn never really caught on in most of Europe. (As with another famous New World import, corn's origin was mistakenly attributed by the British, Dutch, Germans and Russians to Turkey. They called corn "Turkish wheat"; the Turks simply called it "foreign grain.") Grown for human consumption mostly in Italy, Spain and southwestern France, corn was and still is usually eaten ground and boiled as polenta. But despite an unenthusiastic European reception, corn's popularity quickly spread well beyond Europe: Within 50 years of Columbus's journey, corn was being cultivated in lands as distant from the New World as China, India and sub-Saharan Africa.

Sun-Dried Tomatoes

Choose fresh tomatoes that are plump with a smooth, shiny skin. The color should be uniform and true for the variety. Tomatoes are available all year; most varieties have a summer peak season. Many canned tomato products are also available (for example, purée, paste, sauce or stewed whole). Sun-dried and air-dried tomatoes are available in crumbs, pieces, slivers or halves, dry or packed in oil. The dry-pack version can be soaked in oil or steeped in hot water to soften before use.

▶ PROCEDURE FOR PREPARING TOMATO CONCASSÉE

1 With a paring knife, mark an X on the bottom of the tomato just deep enough to penetrate the skin.

2 Blanch the tomato in boiling water for 20 seconds; refresh in ice water.

3 Using a paring knife, cut out the core and peel the tomato.

4 Cut the tomato in half horizontally and squeeze out the seeds and juice.

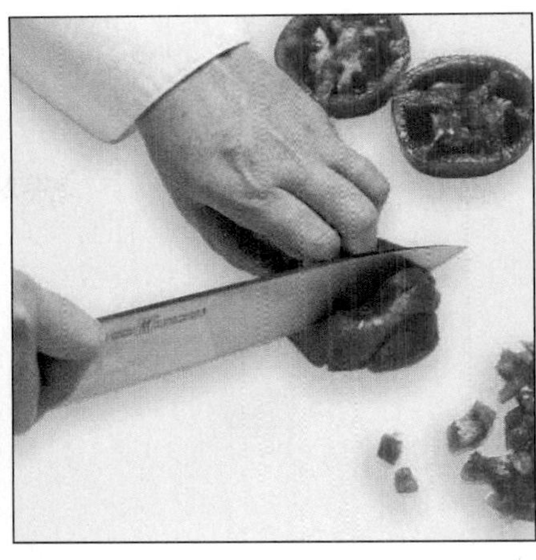

5 Chop or dice the tomato as desired for the recipe.

GOURDS AND SQUASHES

The *Cucurbitaceae* or gourd family includes almost 750 species; its members are found in warm regions worldwide. Gourds are characterized by large, complex root systems with quick-growing, trailing vines and large leaves. Their flowers are often attractive and edible. Although some members of the gourd family originated in Africa, chayotes and most squashes are native to the Americas.

CHAYOTES

The chayote, also known as the merliton or vegetable pear, is a food staple throughout Central America. The vine bears slightly lumpy, pear-shaped fruits with a smooth, light green skin and a paler green flesh. There is a single white, edible seed in the center. Chayotes are starchy and very bland and are usually combined with more flavorful ingredients. They may be eaten raw, but their flavor and texture benefit from roasting, steaming, sautéing or grilling.

Choose chayotes that have well-colored skin with few ridges. Avoid those with very soft spots or bruises. Their peak season is the late fall and winter.

Chayotes

CUCUMBERS

Cucumbers can be divided into two categories: pickling and slicing. The two types are not interchangeable. Pickling cucumbers include the cornichon, dill and gherkin. They are recognizable by their sharp black or white spines and are quite bitter when raw. Slicing cucumbers include the burpless, the seedless English (or hothouse), the lemon (which is round and yellow) and the common green market cucumber. Most have relatively thin skins and may be marketed with a wax coating to prevent moisture loss and improve appearance. Waxed skins should be peeled. All cucumbers are valued for their refreshing cool taste and astringency. Slicing cucumbers are usually served raw, in salads or mixed with yogurt and dill or mint as a side dish, especially for spicy dishes. Pickling cucumbers are generally served pickled, with no further processing.

Choose cucumbers that are firm but not hard. Avoid those that are limp or yellowed or have soft spots. The common varieties are available all year, although peak season is from April through October.

(from left to right) Pickling, Green and Hothouse Cucumbers

Acorn

Spaghetti

Banana

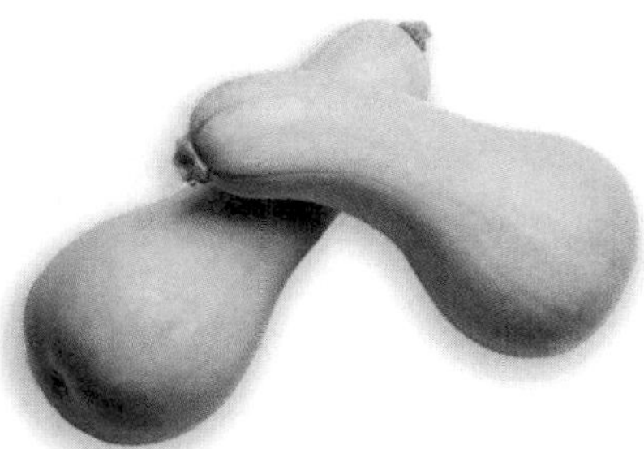

Butternut

SQUASHES

Squashes are the fleshy fruits of a large number of plants in the gourd family. Many varieties are available in a range of colors, shapes and sizes. Squashes can be classified as winter or summer based on their peak season and skin type.

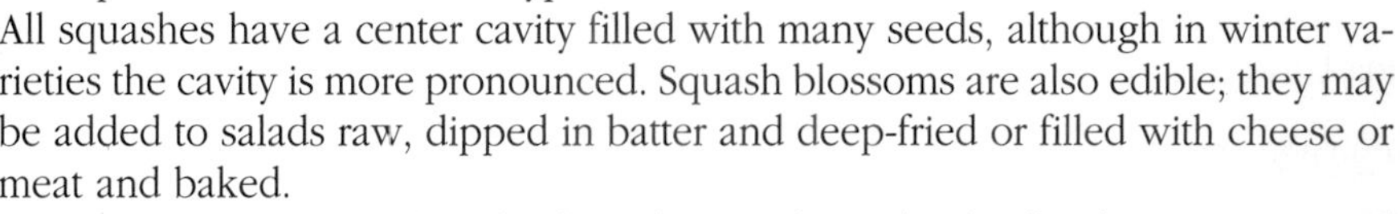

All squashes have a center cavity filled with many seeds, although in winter varieties the cavity is more pronounced. Squash blossoms are also edible; they may be added to salads raw, dipped in batter and deep-fried or filled with cheese or meat and baked.

Choose squashes with unbroken skins and good color for the variety. Avoid any squash with soft, moist spots.

Winter Squashes

Winter squashes include the acorn, banana, butternut, Hubbard, pumpkin and spaghetti varieties. They have hard skins (shells) and seeds, neither of which is generally eaten. The flesh, which may be removed from the shell before or after cooking, tends to be sweeter and more strongly flavored than that of summer squash. Winter squashes are rarely used raw; they can be baked, steamed or sautéed. Most winter squashes can also be puréed for soups or pie fillings. Their peak season is October through March.

Pumpkin

Summer Squashes

Summer squashes include the pattypan, yellow crookneck and zucchini varieties. They have soft edible skins and seeds that are generally not removed before cooking. Most summer squashes may be eaten raw, but are also suitable for grilling, sautéing, steaming or baking. Although summer squashes are now available all year, their peak season is April through September.

Yellow Crookneck

Zucchini

GREENS

The term *greens* refers to a variety of leafy green vegetables that may be served raw, but are usually cooked. Greens have long been used in the cuisines of India, Asia and the Mediterranean and are an important part of regional cuisine in the southern United States. Most have strong, spicy flavors. The milder varieties of greens that are almost always eaten raw include the lettuces discussed in Chapter 23, Salads and Salad Dressings.

Greens have an extremely high water content, which means that cooking causes drastic shrinkage. As a general rule, allow 8 ounces (250 grams) per portion before cooking.

Choose young, tender greens with good color and no limpness. Avoid greens with dry-looking stems or yellow leaves. Most greens are available fresh all year, especially from November through June. The more popular greens are also available canned or frozen.

Collard Greens

COLLARDS

Collard greens, often simply referred to as collards, are a type of cabbage with loose, leafy heads of bright green leaves. Collards have a sharp, tangy flavor and look like a cross between mustard greens and kale. Considered a staple ingredient in poverty cooking of the American South, collards are typically slow-simmered with ham hocks or bacon until very tender, then served with their cooking liquid. Collards are high in iron and vitamins A and C and are best if picked young or after the first frost of autumn.

MUSTARD

Mustard, a member of the cabbage family, was brought to America by early European immigrants. Mustard has large, dark green leaves with frilly edges. It is known for its assertive, bitter flavor. Mustard greens can be served raw in salads or used as garnish. They can also be cooked, often with white wine, vinegar and herbs.

Choose crisp, bright green leaves without discoloration.

Mustard

SORREL

Sorrel is an abundant and rather ordinary wild member of the buckwheat family. Its tartness and sour flavor are used in soups and sauces and to accent other vegetables. It is particularly good with fatty fish or rich meats. Sorrel leaves naturally become the texture of a purée after only a few minutes of moist-heat cooking.

Choose leaves that are fully formed, with no yellow blemishes.

Sorrel

SPINACH

Spinach (Fr. *épinard*) is a versatile green that grows rapidly in cool climates. It has smooth, bright green leaves attached to thin stems. Spinach may be eaten raw in salads, cooked by almost any moist-heat method, microwaved or sautéed. It can be used in stuffings, baked or creamed dishes, soups or stews. Spinach grows in sandy soil and must be rinsed repeatedly in cold water to remove all traces of grit from the leaves. It bruises easily and should be handled gently during washing. Stems and large midribs should be removed.

Spinach

Choose bunches with crisp, tender, deep green leaves; avoid yellow leaves or those with blemishes.

SWISS CHARD

Chard—the reference to "Swiss" is inexplicable—is a type of beet that does not produce a tuberous root. It is used for its wide, flat, dark green leaves. Chard can be steamed, sautéed or used in soups. Its tart, spinachlike flavor blends well with sweet ingredients such as fruit.

Choose leaves that are crisp, with some curliness or savoying. Ribs should be an unblemished white or red.

Swiss Chard

TURNIP GREENS

The leaves of the turnip root have a pleasantly bitter flavor, similar to peppery mustard greens. The dark green leaves are long, slender and deeply indented. Turnip greens are best eaten steamed, sautéed, baked or microwaved.

Turnip Greens

Portabella

Black Trumpet

Clam Shell

Pom Pom Blanc

Hen of the Woods

Morel

Porcini (cèpe or cep)

Shiitake

White

Enokidake

Oyster

MUSHROOMS AND TRUFFLES

MUSHROOMS

Mushrooms (Fr. *champignon;* It. *funghi*) are members of a broad category of plants known as fungi. (Fungi have no seeds, stems or flowers; they reproduce through spores.) Mushrooms have a stalk with an umbrellalike top. Although not actually a vegetable, mushrooms are used and served in much the same manner as vegetables.

Several types of cultivated mushroom are available. They include the common (or white), shiitake, crimini (also known as the Italian brown), straw, enokidake (also called enoki) and cloud ear (also known as wood ear or Chinese black). Button mushrooms are the smallest, most immature form of the common mushroom. The largest cultivated mushroom is the portabella, which is actually an overgrown crimini; it can grow up to 6 inches (15 centimeters) in diameter.

Many wild mushrooms are gathered and sold by specialty purveyors. Because wild mushroom spores are spread around the world by air currents, the same item may be found in several areas, each with a different common name. Wild mushrooms have a stronger earthy or nutty flavor than cultivated mushrooms, and should generally be cooked before eating.

Mushrooms, whether cultivated or gathered from the wild, are available fresh, canned or dried. Because mushrooms are composed of up to 80 percent water, dried products are often the most economical, even though they may cost hundreds of dollars per pound. Dried mushrooms can be stored in a cool, dry place for months. When needed, they are rehydrated by soaking in warm water until soft, approximately 10 to 20 minutes.

Choose fresh mushrooms that are clean, without soft or moist spots or blemishes. Fresh cultivated mushrooms are generally available all year; fresh wild mushrooms are available seasonally, usually during the summer and fall. Cultivated mushrooms with exposed gills (the

SAFETY ALERT

Mushroom Safety

Some mushrooms are deadly; others can cause severe illness. Picking edible mushrooms in the wild is not simply a process of comparing specimens with photographs or illustrations in a guidebook. So do not gather mushrooms from the wild unless you are accompanied by a well-trained, experienced mycologist or guide. Always purchase wild mushrooms from reputable purveyors.

ridges on the underside of the umbrellalike top) are old and should be avoided. Fresh mushrooms can be refrigerated in an open container for up to 5 days. Normally, it is not necessary to peel mushrooms; if they are dirty, they should be quickly rinsed (not soaked) in cool water just before use.

▶ PROCEDURE FOR FLUTING MUSHROOMS

Use the sharp edge of a straight paring knife to cut thin curves into the mushroom cap. Fluted mushrooms may be baked or poached, then used as garnish.

TRUFFLES

Truffles are actually tubers that grow near the roots of oak or beech trees. They can be cultivated only to the extent that oak groves are planted to encourage truffle growth. The two principal varieties are the Périgord (black) and the Piedmontese (white). Fresh truffles are gathered in the fall and are rarely marketed outside their locale. Truffles, especially white ones, have a strong aroma and flavor, requiring only a small amount to add their special flavor to soups, sauces, pasta and other items. Black truffles are often used as a garnish or to flavor pâtés, terrines or egg dishes. Because fresh imported truffles can cost several hundred dollars per pound, most kitchens purchase truffles canned, dried or processed.

Black Truffles

THE OLIVE

Olives (*Olea europaea*) are the fruit of a tree native to the Mediterranean area. Green olives are those harvested unripened; black olives are fully ripened. The raw fruit is inedibly bitter and must be washed, soaked and cured or pickled before eating. Green olives should have a smooth, tight skin. Ripe olives will be glossy but softer, with a slightly wrinkled skin. Many varieties and flavors are available, from the tiny black French niçoise to the large purplish Greek Kalamata. Ripe black olives are packaged in a range of seven sizes, from small to supercolossal. Unripe green olives are available in eleven sizes, from subpetite to supercolossal. Both black and green olives are available whole (with the pit), pitted, sliced, halved or in pieces. Pitted green olives are often stuffed with strips of pimento, jalapeño pepper, almonds or other foods for flavor and appearance.

Olives are used as a finger food for snacks or hors d'oeuvre, or added to salads or pasta. They may even be cooked in breads, soups, sauces, stews and casseroles. A paste made of minced ripe olives, known as tapenade, is used as a dip or condiment.

Jumbo Spanish Olives

Ripe California Olives

Kalamata Olives

Niçoise Olives

ONIONS

Onions are strongly flavored, aromatic members of the lily family. Most have edible grasslike or tubular leaves. Almost every culture incorporates them into its cuisine as a vegetable and for flavoring.

Red Onion

Yellow Onion

Shallots

Pearl Onion

Walla-Walla Sweet Onions

White Onions

BULB ONIONS

Common or bulb onions (Fr. *oignons*) may be white, yellow (Bermuda or Spanish) or red (purple). Medium-sized yellow and white onions are the most strongly flavored. Larger onions tend to be sweeter and milder. Widely used as a flavoring ingredient, onions are indispensable in mirepoix. Onions are also prepared as a side dish by deep-frying, roasting, grilling, steaming or boiling.

Pearl onions are small, about ½ inch (1.25 centimeters) in diameter, with yellow or white skins. They have a mild flavor and can be grilled, boiled, roasted or sautéed whole as a side dish, or used in soups or stews.

Sweet onion varieties include the Vidalia, Maui, Walla-Walla, Texas 1015 SuperSweet and OSO Sweet. These bulb onions have a higher water content, more sugar and less sulfuric compounds than other onions. They are best for eating raw, making them good choices for sandwiches, salads, hamburgers and the like. Cooking destroys much of their perceived sweetness and special flavor. Each sweet onion variety is available for a brief period from January through August. All have a very short shelf life and should not be stored more than a few weeks.

Choose onions that are firm and dry and feel heavy. The outer skins should be dry and brittle. Avoid onions that have begun to sprout. Store onions in a cool, dry, well-ventilated area. Do not refrigerate onions until they are cut. With the exception of sweet onions, most varieties are available all year.

GARLIC

Garlic

Garlic (Fr. *ail;* It. *aglio;* Sp. *ajo*) is also used in almost all the world's cuisines. A head of garlic is composed of many small cloves. Each clove is wrapped in a thin husk or peel; the entire head is encased in several thin layers of papery husk. Of the three hundred or so types of garlic known, only three are commercially significant. The most common is pure white, with a sharp flavor. A Mexican variety is pale pink and more strongly flavored. Elephant garlic is apple-sized and particularly mild. Although whole bulbs can be baked or roasted, garlic is most often separated into cloves, peeled, sliced, minced or crushed and used to flavor a wide variety of dishes. When using garlic, remember that the more finely the cloves are crushed, the stronger the flavor will be. Cooking reduces garlic's pungency; the longer it is cooked, the milder it becomes.

Choose firm, dry bulbs with tightly closed cloves and smooth skins. Avoid bulbs with green sprouts. Store fresh garlic in a cool, well-ventilated place; do not refrigerate. Fresh garlic is available all year. Jars of processed and pickled garlic products are also available.

LEEKS

Leeks

Leeks (Fr. *poireaux*) look like large, overgrown scallions with a fat white tip and wide green leaves. Their flavor is sweeter and stronger than scallions, but milder than common bulb onions. Leeks must be carefully washed to remove the sandy soil that gets between the leaves. Leeks can be baked, braised or grilled as a side dish, or used to season stocks, soups or sauces.

Choose leeks that are firm, with stiff roots and stems. Avoid those with dry leaves, soft spots or browning. Leeks are available all year.

▶ PROCEDURE FOR CLEANING LEEKS

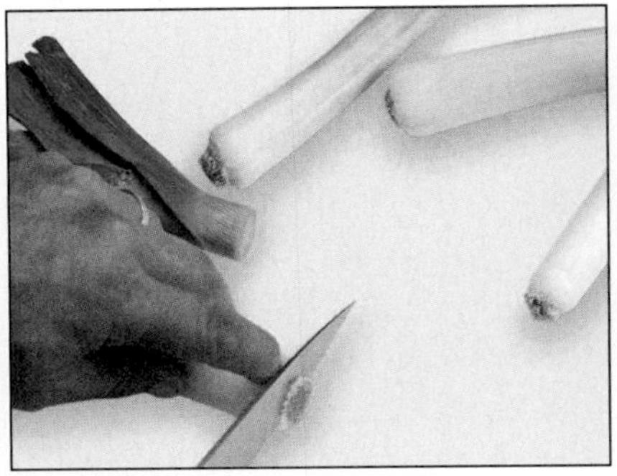

1 Trim the root end from the leek.

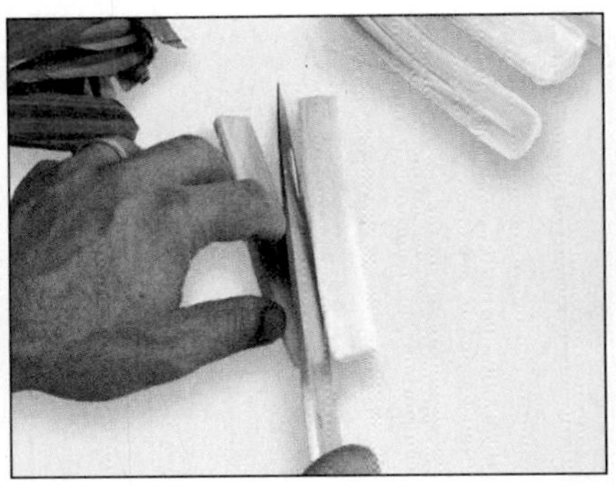

2 Cut away the dark green top and slice the white portion in half lengthwise.

3 Rinse the leek thoroughly under running water to remove soil.

SCALLIONS

Scallions

Scallions, also known as green onions or bunch onions, are the immature green stalks of bulb onions. The leaves are bright green with either a long and slender or slightly bulbous white base. Green onions are used in stir-fries and as a flavoring in other dishes. The green tops can also be sliced in small rings and used as a garnish.

Choose scallions with bright green tops and clean white bulbs. Avoid those with limp or slimy leaves. Scallions are available all year; their peak season is the summer.

SHALLOTS

Shallots

Shallots (Fr. *échalotes*) are shaped like small bulb onions with one flat side. When peeled, a shallot separates into multiple cloves, similar to garlic. They have a mild, yet rich and complex flavor. Shallots are the basis of many classic sauces and meat preparations; they can also be sautéed or baked as a side dish.

Choose shallots that are plump and well shaped. Avoid those that appear dry or have sprouted. Store shallots in a cool, dry, unrefrigerated place. Shallots are available all year.

PODS AND SEEDS

Pod and seed vegetables include corn, legumes and okra. They are grouped together here because the parts consumed are all the seeds of their respective plants. In some cases, only the seeds are eaten; in others, the pod containing the seeds is eaten as well. Seeds are generally higher in protein and carbohydrates (starch and fiber) than other vegetables.

CORN

Yellow and White Corn

Sweet corn (Fr. *maïs;* Sp. *maíz*) is actually a grain, a type of grass. Corn kernels, like peas, are plant seeds. (Dried corn products are discussed in Chapter 21, Potatoes, Grains and Pasta.) The kernels, which may be white or yellow, are attached to a woody, inedible cob. The cob is encased by strands of hairlike fibers called silks and covered in layers of thin leaves called husks. Shuck the ears (remove the silks and husks) prior to cooking; the husks may be left on for roasting or grilling. Shucked ears can be grilled, boiled, microwaved or steamed. The kernels can be cut off of the cob before or after cooking. Corn on the cob is available fresh or frozen; corn kernels are available canned or frozen.

Choose freshly picked ears with firm, small kernels. Avoid those with mold or decay at the tip of the cob or brownish silks. Summer is the peak season for fresh corn.

▶ PROCEDURE FOR CUTTING KERNELS OFF EARS OF CORN

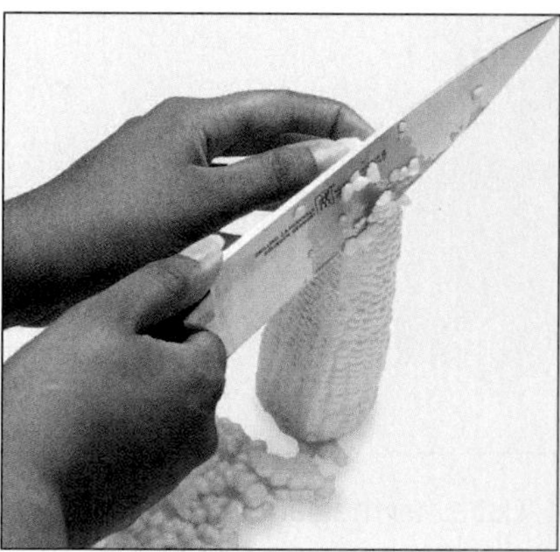

Hold the cob upright and use a chef's knife to slice off the kernels.

LEGUMES

Beans (Fr. *haricots;* It. *fagioli*) and peas (Fr. *pois*) are members of the legume family, a large group of vegetables with double-seamed pods containing a single row of seeds. Of the hundreds of known varieties of beans, some are used for their edible pods, others for shelling fresh and some only for their dried seeds. Dried beans are actually several varieties of seeds or peas left in the pod until mature, then shelled and dried.

Fresh Beans

Green Beans

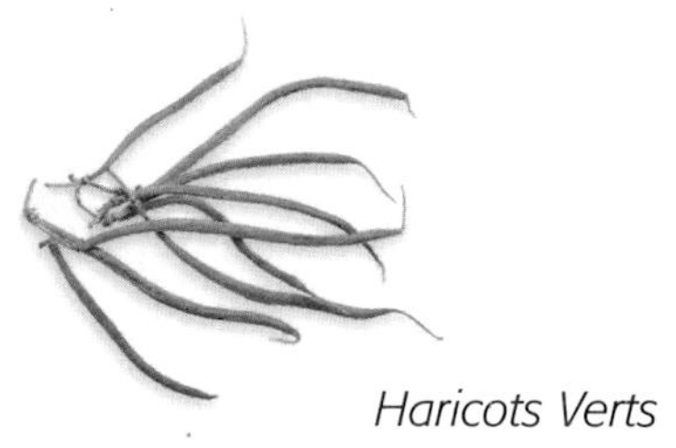

Haricots Verts

Beans used for their edible pods, commonly referred to as green beans, string beans, runner beans or snap beans, are picked when immature. Except for the stem, the entire pod can be eaten. This category includes the American green bean, the yellow wax bean and the French haricot vert, a long, slender pod with an intense flavor and tender texture. Any strings along the pod's seams should be pulled off before cooking. Beans may be left whole, cut lengthwise into thin slivers (referred to as French cut) or cut crosswise on the diagonal.

Shelling beans are those grown primarily for the edible seeds inside the pod. Common examples are flageolets, lima beans and fava (broad) beans. Their tough pods are not usually eaten.

All beans can be prepared by steaming, microwaving or sautéing. They can be added to soups or stews, and they blend well with a variety of flavors, from coconut milk to garlic and olive oil. Cooked beans can be chilled and served as a salad or crudité.

Choose beans that have a bright color without brown or soft spots. Large pods may be tough or bitter. The peak season for fresh beans is from April through December. Most bean varieties are available frozen or canned, including pickled and seasoned products.

Dried Beans

Black-Eyed Peas

Black Beans

Anthropologists report that for thousands of years, cultures worldwide have preserved some members of the legume family by drying. Common dried beans include kidney beans, pinto beans, chickpeas, lentils, black beans, black-eyed peas and split green peas. Shape is the clearest distinction among these products: Beans are oval or kidney-shaped; lentils are small, flat disks; peas are round.

Beans and peas destined for drying are left on the vine until they are fully matured and just beginning to dry. They are then harvested, shelled and quickly dried with warm air currents. Some dried legumes are sold split, which means the skin is removed, causing the seed's two halves to separate.

Lentils

Most dried beans need to be soaked in water before cooking. Soaking softens and rehydrates the beans, thus reducing cooking time. Lentils and split peas generally do not require soaking, however, and will cook faster than beans. After soaking, beans are most often simmered or baked in a liquid until soft and tender. One type may be substituted for another in most recipes, although variations in color, starch content and flavor should be considered.

Red Kidney Beans

Dried beans and peas are available in bulk or in 1-pound (450-gram) poly-bags. They should be stored in a cool, dry place, but not refrigerated. Many of these beans are also available fully cooked, then canned or frozen. Some dried beans may be fermented or processed into flour, oil or bean curd.

Great Northern Beans

Pinto Beans

▶ PROCEDURE FOR SOAKING DRIED BEANS

1 Pick through the dried beans and remove any grit, pebbles or debris.
2 Place the beans in a bowl and cover with cold water; remove any skins or other items that float to the surface.
3 Drain the beans in a colander, then rinse under cold running water.
4 Return the beans to a bowl and cover with fresh cold water. Allow approximately 3 cups (750 milliliters) water for each cup of beans.
5 Soak the beans in the cold water for the time specified in the recipe, usually several hours or overnight. Drain through a colander, discarding the water.

▶ PROCEDURE FOR QUICK-SOAKING DRIED BEANS

The soaking procedure can be accelerated by the following technique:

1 Rinse and pick through the beans.
2 Place the beans in a saucepan and add enough cool water to cover them by 2 inches (5 centimeters).
3 Bring to a boil and simmer for 2 minutes.
4 Remove from the heat, cover and soak for 1 hour.
5 Drain and discard the soaking liquid. Proceed with the recipe.

Fresh Shelling Peas

Of the shelling peas that are prepared fresh, the most common are green garden peas (English peas) and the French petit pois. Because they lose flavor rapidly after harvest, most shelling peas are sold frozen or canned. Shelling peas have a delicate, sweet flavor best presented by simply steaming until tender but still al dente. Peas may also be braised with rich meats such as ham or used in soups. Cooked peas are attractive in salads or as garnish.

Fresh Shelling Peas

Choose small fresh pea pods that are plump and moist. Peak season is April and May.

Fresh green **soy beans (soya)** (Japanese: *edamame*) are becoming a popular shelling pea in the United States. When picked before maturity, soybeans have a light green, fuzzy pod and a tender, sweet pea. Fresh green soybeans are delicious steamed in the pod, then chilled, popped open and eaten out of hand as a snack. Often served in sushi restaurants or with other Asian cuisines, they are extremely high in protein, fiber and phytochemicals. When allowed to

Soy Beans

mature and then prepared like other dried beans, however, soybeans become extremely tough, hard to digest and bitter. Mature soybeans are best used for processing into oil, tofu, sauce and other foodstuffs.

Snow Peas

Edible Pea Pods

Snow peas, also known as Chinese pea pods, are a common variety of edible pea pod. They are flat and have only a few very small green peas. Snow peas have a string along their seams that can be removed by holding the leafy stem and pulling from end to end. The pods can be eaten raw, lightly blanched or steamed, or stir-fried.

Another variety of edible pea pod is the sugar snap pea, a cross between the garden pea and snow pea, which was developed during the late 1970s. They are plump, juicy pods filled with small, tender peas. The entire pod is eaten; do not shell the peas before cooking.

Choose pea pods that are firm, bright green and crisp. Avoid those with brown spots or a shriveled appearance. Pea pods are available all year; their peak season is in March and April.

Okra

OKRA

Okra, a common ingredient in African and Arab cuisines, was brought to the United States by slaves and French settlers. It is now integral to Creole, Cajun, southern and southwestern cuisines. Its mild flavor is similar to that of asparagus. Okra is not eaten raw; it is best pickled, boiled, steamed or deep-fried. Okra develops a gelatinous texture when cooked for long periods, so it is used to thicken gumbos and stews. To avoid the slimy texture some find objectionable, do not wash okra until ready to cook, then trim the stem end only. Cook okra in stainless steel because other metals cause discoloration.

Choose small to medium pods (1½ to 2 inches [3.75 to 5 centimeters]) that are deep green, without soft spots. Pale spears with stiff tips tend to be tough. Okra's peak season is from June through September. Frozen okra is widely available.

ROOTS AND TUBERS

Taproots (more commonly referred to as roots) are single roots that extend deep into the soil to supply the above-ground plant with nutrients. Tubers are fat underground stems. Most roots and tubers can be used interchangeably. All store well at cool temperatures, without refrigeration. Potatoes, the most popular tuber, are discussed in Chapter 21, Potatoes, Grains and Pasta.

BEETS

Although records suggest that they were first eaten in ancient Greece, beets are most often associated with the colder northern climates, where they grow for most of the year. Beets can be boiled, then peeled and used in salads, soups or baked dishes.

Choose small to medium-sized beets that are firm, with smooth skins. Avoid those with hairy root tips, as they may be tough. Beets are available all year; their peak season is March to October.

Beets

CARROTS

Carrots (Fr. *carotte*), among the most versatile of vegetables, are large taproots. Although several kinds exist, the Imperator is the most common. It is long and pointed, with a medium to dark orange color and a mild, sweet flavor. Carrots

Carrots

can be cut into a variety of shapes and eaten raw, used for a mirepoix or prepared by moist-heat cooking methods, grilling, microwaving or roasting. They are also grated and used in baked goods, particularly cakes and muffins.

Choose firm carrots that are smooth and well shaped, with a bright orange color. If the tops are still attached, they should be fresh-looking and bright green. Carrots are available all year.

CELERY ROOT

Celery root, also known as celeriac, is a large, round root, long popular in northern European cuisines. It is a different plant from stalk celery, and its stalks and leaves are not eaten. Celery root has a knobby brown exterior; a creamy white, crunchy flesh; and a mild, celerylike flavor. Its thick outer skin must be peeled away; the flesh is then cut as desired. Often eaten raw, celery root can be baked, steamed or boiled. It is used in soups, stews or salads and goes well with game and rich meats. Raw celery root may be placed in acidulated water to prevent browning.

Celery Root

Choose small to medium-sized roots that are firm and relatively clean, with a pungent smell. Their peak season is October through April.

JERUSALEM ARTICHOKE

Despite their name, Jerusalem artichokes are actually tubers from a variety of sunflower unrelated to artichokes. Consequently, growers are now marketing these vegetables as *sunchokes*. Their lumpy brown skin is usually peeled away (even though it is edible) to reveal a crisp, white interior with a slightly nutty flavor. While they may be eaten raw, it is preferable to cook them before serving to make them easier to digest. Jerusalem artichokes are eaten chopped or grated into salads, or boiled or steamed for a side dish or soup.

Sunchokes

JICAMA

Jicama is actually a legume that grows underground as a tuber. It is becoming increasingly popular because of its sweet, moist flavor; crisp texture; low calorie content; and long shelf life. After its thick brown skin is cut away, the crisp, moist white flesh can be cut as desired. Jicama is often eaten raw in salads, with salsa or as a crudité. It is also used in stir-fried dishes.

Choose firm, well-shaped jicamas that are free of blemishes. Size is not an indication of quality or maturity. They are available all year; their peak season is January through May.

Jicama

PARSNIPS

Parsnips (Fr. *panais*) are taproots that look and taste like white carrots and have the texture of sweet potatoes. Parsnips should be 5 to 10 inches (12.5 to 25 centimeters) in length, with smooth skins and tapering tips. Parsnips, peeled like carrots, can be eaten raw or cooked by almost any method. When steamed until very soft, they can be mashed like potatoes.

Choose small to medium-sized parsnips that are firm, smooth and well shaped; avoid large, woody ones. Parsnips are available all year; their peak season is December through April.

Parsnips

RADISHES

Radishes (Fr. *radis*) are used for their peppery flavor and crisp texture. Radishes are available in many colors, including white, black and all shades of red; most have a creamy to pure white interior. Asian radishes, known as daikons, produce roots 2 to 4 inches (5 to 10 centimeters) in diameter and 6 to 20 inches (15 to 20 centimeters) long. Radishes can be steamed or stir-fried, but most often are

Red Radishes

eaten raw or in salads or used as garnish. Radish leaves can be used in salads or cooked as greens.

Choose radishes that are firm, not limp. Their interior should be neither dry nor hollow. Radishes are available all year.

Daikon

RUTABAGAS

Rutabagas are a root vegetable and a member of the cabbage family. Their skin is purple to yellow, and they have yellow flesh with a distinctive starchy, cabbagelike flavor. Rutabagas and turnips are similar in flavor and texture when cooked and may be used interchangeably. Rutabaga leaves are not eaten. Rutabagas should be peeled with a vegetable peeler or chef's knife, then cut into quarters, slices or cubes. They are often baked, boiled and then puréed, or sliced and sautéed. They are especially flavorful when seasoned with caraway seeds, dill or lemon juice.

Choose small to medium-sized rutabagas that are smooth and firm and feel heavy. Their peak season is January through March.

Rutabagas

TURNIPS

Also a root vegetable from the cabbage family, turnips have white skin with a rosy-red or purple blush and a white interior. Their flavor, similar to that of a radish, can be rather hot. Turnips should be peeled, then diced, sliced or julienned for cooking. They may be baked or cooked with moist-heat cooking methods, and are often puréed like potatoes.

Turnips

Choose small to medium-sized turnips that have smooth skin and feel heavy. They should be firm, not rubbery or limp. Any attached leaves should be bright green and tender. Spring is their peak season.

WATER CHESTNUTS

Water chestnuts are the tuber of an Asian plant that thrives in water. The brownish-black skin is peeled away to reveal a moist, crisp, white interior, which can be eaten raw or cooked. When cooked, water chestnuts retain their crunchy texture, making them a popular addition to stir-fried dishes. They are also used in salads and casseroles or wrapped in bacon for rumaki hors d'oeuvre.

Fresh Water Chestnuts

STALKS

▶ **cellulose** a complex carbohydrate found in the cell wall of plants; it is edible but indigestible by humans

Stalk vegetables are plant stems with a high percentage of **cellulose** fiber. These vegetables should be picked while still young and tender. Tough fibers should be trimmed before cooking.

ARTICHOKES

Artichokes (Fr. *artichaut*) are the immature flowers of a thistle plant introduced to America by Italian and Spanish settlers. Young, tender globe artichokes can be cooked whole, but more mature plants need to have the fuzzy center (known as the choke) removed first. Whole artichokes can be simmered, steamed or microwaved; they are often served with lemon juice, garlic butter or hollandaise sauce. The heart may be cooked separately, then served in salads, puréed as a filling or served as a side dish. Artichoke hearts and leafless artichoke bottoms are both available canned.

Artichokes

Choose fresh artichokes with tight, compact heads that feel heavy. Their color should be solid green to gray-green. Brown spots on the surface caused by frost are harmless. Artichokes' peak season is March through May.

▶ PROCEDURE FOR PREPARING FRESH ARTICHOKES

1 Using kitchen shears or scissors, trim the barbs from the large outer leaves of the artichoke.

2 With a chef's knife, cut away the stem and the top of the artichoke. Steam or boil the artichoke as desired.

ASPARAGUS

Asparagus (Fr. *aspèrges*), a member of the lily family, has bright green spears with a ruffle of tiny leaves at the tip. Larger spears tend to be tough and woody, but can be used in soups or for purée. Asparagus is eaten raw or steamed briefly, stir-fried, microwaved or grilled. Fresh spring asparagus is excellent with nothing more than lemon juice or clarified butter; asparagus with hollandaise sauce is a classic preparation.

Asparagus

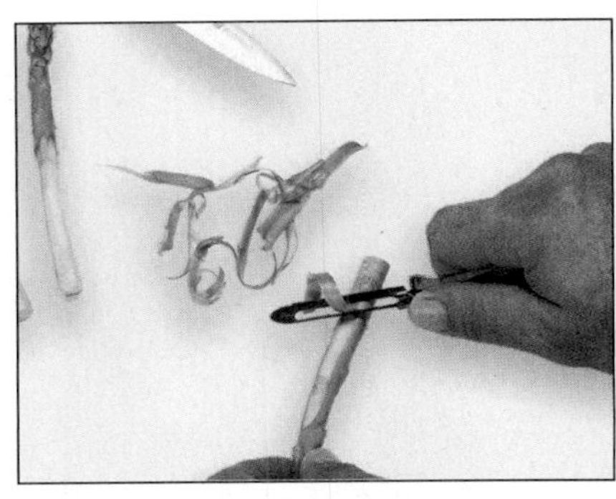

Use a sharp knife to peel away the tough outer skin from large asparagus spears.

Choose firm, plump spears with tightly closed tips and a bright green color running the full length of the spear. Asparagus should be stored refrigerated at 40°F (4°C), upright in ½ inch (1.25 centimeters) of water or with the ends wrapped in moist paper toweling. The stalks should not be washed until just before use. Canned and frozen asparagus are also available. Peak season is March through June.

A European variety of white asparagus is sometimes available fresh, or readily available canned. It has a milder flavor and soft, tender texture. It is produced by covering the stalks with soil as they grow; this prevents sunlight from reaching the plant and retards the development of chlorophyll.

BAMBOO SHOOTS

Stripped of their tough brown outer skins, the tender young shoots of certain varieties of bamboo are edible. They make excellent additions to stir-fried dishes or can be served like asparagus. Although fresh shoots are available in Asia, canned peeled shoots packed in brine or water are more common in the United States. Canned shoots should be rinsed well before use.

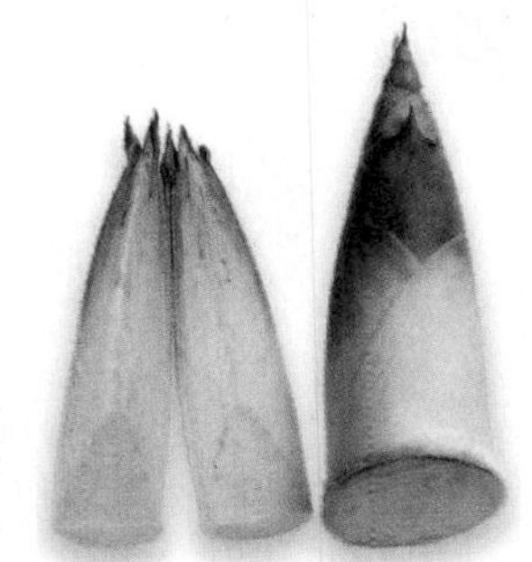

Fresh Bamboo Shoots

Celery

CELERY

Once a medicinal herb, stalk celery (Fr. *céleri*) is now a common sight in kitchens worldwide. Stalk celery is pale green with stringy curved stalks. Often eaten raw in salads or as a snack, it can be braised or steamed as a side dish. Celery is also a mirepoix component.

Choose stalks that are crisp, without any sign of dryness. Celery is available all year.

FENNEL

Fennel (Fr. *fenouil,* It. *finocchio*) is a Mediterranean favorite used for thousands of years as a vegetable (the bulb), an herb (the leaves) and a spice (the seeds). The bulb (often incorrectly referred to as sweet anise) has short, tight, overlapping celerylike stalks with feathery leaves. The flavor is similar to that of anise or licorice, becoming milder when cooked. Fennel bulbs may be eaten raw or grilled, steamed, sautéed, baked or microwaved.

Choose a fairly large, bright white bulb on which the cut edges appear fresh, without dryness or browning. The bulb should be compact, not spreading. Fresh fennel's peak season is September through May.

Fennel

Hearts of Palm

HEARTS OF PALM

Hearts of palm are the tender interiors of stems from cabbage palm trees. They are ivory-colored and slender, with a delicate flavor similar to that of asparagus. Fresh hearts of palm are sometimes available in Florida (where they are grown); canned ones are widely available everywhere. Hearts of palm are generally used uncooked in salads or marinated in herb vinaigrette.

Nopales

NOPALES

The pads of a prickly pear cactus can be prepared as a vegetable known as nopales. Cactus pads have a flavor similar to that of green bell peppers. Their texture tends to be rather gelatinous or mucilaginous, making them good for stews or sauces. To prepare fresh nopales, hold the pad with tongs and cut off the thorns and "eyes" with a sharp knife or vegetable peeler. Trim off the edge all the way around. Slice the pad into julienne strips or cubes. The pieces can be boiled or steamed and served hot, or chilled and added to salads. Nopales can also be sautéed with onions, peppers and seasonings for a side dish or added to southwestern-style casseroles.

Some cultivated varieties have thin, thornless pads. Choose pads that are stiff and heavy without blemishes. They should not be dry or soggy. Fresh cactus pads are available all year, with peak season in the late spring. Canned and pickled nopales are also available.

Baby Zucchini with Blossoms

BABY VEGETABLES

Many fine restaurants serve baby vegetables: tiny turnips, finger-length squash, miniature carrots and petite heads of cauliflower. First cultivated in Europe but

ANCIENT PLANTS AND ANCIENT WAYS VANISH

Since the days of Columbus, half of all native American crop varieties have become extinct. If this trend continues, several hundred more will become extinct in our lifetimes. Similarly, ancient farming practices have all but been abandoned. As late as the 1920s, the Tohono O'odham Indians of Arizona still used traditional methods to cultivate more than 10,000 acres without pumping groundwater. Today, only a few scattered floodwater fields remain.

When species disappear we lose an irreplaceable source of genetic diversity—a source of extraordinary genes that could someday improve modern hybrid crops. When native desert crops vanish, so does the ancient tradition of native agriculture, which has selected these crops over millennia to thrive in extreme temperatures, in alkaline soils without millions of gallons of precious water and without expensive, ecologically destructive chemicals.

Today, six highly bred species—wheat, rice, corn, sorghum, potatoes and cassava—supply most of the world's nutrition. As food crops become more and more homogeneous, they often lose their natural ability to tolerate pests, disease and drought. In the past, farmers grew thousands of food crop varieties. These traditional crop varieties contain a storehouse of genetic diversity that enables them to flourish in the most difficult environments. This broad spectrum of genetic variability is a cushion against natural predators and diseases. Wild chiles from the Sierra Madre, for example, are highly disease resistant. Their virus-tolerant genes have been bred into commercial varieties of bell pepper and jalapeños.

Native Seeds/SEARCH, one of the country's first regional seed banks, was founded to keep ancient desert plants and traditional farming methods from disappearing forever. Since 1983 we've ridden mules into remote areas and made more than 1200 collections of desert-adapted crops and wild relatives. We've gathered the seeds of chapalote (a brown popcorn), blue indigo (used for dyes), tepary (a heat- and drought-tolerant bean), teosinte (a wild relative of corn), wild chiles and other plants. These seeds are available to researchers, gardeners, farmers and seed banks. Seeds are offered free to Native Americans.

Each loss of biological and cultural diversity alters and damages the balance of life on earth, often in ways we do not understand. Each loss of leaf, stem and flower diminishes our earth's richness and beauty in ways we often don't appreciate until they're gone.

DR. GARY PAUL NABHAN, Native Seeds/SEARCH, Tucson, AZ

Chiogghi Beets

Baby Yellow Squash with Blossoms

Baby Globe Carrots

now widely available throughout the United States, baby vegetables include both hybrids bred to be true miniatures as well as regular varieties that are picked before maturity. Baby vegetables are often marketed with blossoms or greens still attached. They tend to be easily bruised and are highly perishable. Many baby vegetables can be eaten raw, but they are usually left whole, then steamed or lightly sautéed and attractively presented as an accompaniment to meat, fish or poultry entrées.

▶ Nutrition

Most vegetables are more than 80 percent water; the remaining portions consist of carbohydrates (primarily starches) and small amounts of protein and fat. The relative lack of protein and fat makes most vegetables especially low in calories.

Much of a vegetable's physical structure is provided by generally indigestible substances such as cellulose and lignin, also known as fiber. This fiber produces the characteristic stringy, crisp or fibrous textures associated with vegetables.

Vegetables are also a good source of vitamins and minerals. Care must be taken during preparation to preserve their nutritional content, however. Once

BACK TO BASICS

Great strides in agriculture have been made during the past two centuries. Pesticides, fungicides and herbicides now eliminate or control pests that once would have devoured, ruined or choked crops. Chemical fertilizers increase yields of many of the world's staples. But not everyone has greeted these developments with open arms.

During the past few decades, scientific and medical investigators have documented, or at least suggested, health risks associated with certain synthetic pesticides, fertilizers and other products. These findings have led to a renewed interest in a now multibillion-dollar-a-year back-to-the-basics approach to farming: organic farming. Specialty farms, orchards and even wineries now offer organically grown products (or, in the case of wineries, wines made from organically grown grapes). These products come with few, if any, intentional additives and should be free of any incidental additives. Proponents argue that these products are better for you and better for the health of the farm workers.

The U.S. Department of Agriculture regulates the production and labeling of organically grown foods. It requires that any natural food labeled "100 percent organic" must contain only organic ingredients–that is, those grown and manufactured without the use of added hormones, pesticides, synthetic fertilizers, and so on; soil cannot have been treated with unapproved synthetics for three years for a crop to be called organic. To be labeled organic or to display the USDA organic seal, processed foods must contain at least 95 percent organic ingredients by weight. Processed foods with 70 to 95 percent organic ingredients may be labeled "made with organic ingredients"; processed foods with less than 70 percent organic ingredients may list those ingredients on the information panel but may not use the term *organic* anywhere on the front of the package.

peeled or cut, vegetables lose nutrients to the air or to any liquid in which they are allowed to soak. Vitamins are concentrated just under the skin, so peel vegetables thinly, if at all.

▶ PURCHASING AND STORING FRESH VEGETABLES

Fresh vegetables should be selected according to seasonal availability. Using a vegetable at the peak of its season has several advantages: Price is at its lowest, selection is at its greatest and the vegetable's color, flavor and texture are at their best.

GRADING

The USDA has a voluntary grading system for fresh vegetables traded on wholesale markets. The system is based on appearance, condition and other factors affecting waste or eating quality. Grades for all vegetables include, in descending order of quality, U.S. Extra Fancy, U.S. Fancy, U.S. Extra No. 1 and U.S. No. 1. There are also grades that apply only to specific vegetables, for example, U.S. No. 1 Boilers for onions.

Consumer or retail grading is currently required only for potatoes, carrots and onions. It uses alphabetical listings, with Grade A being the finest.

PURCHASING

Fresh vegetables are sold by weight or count. They are packed in cartons referred to as cases, lugs, bushels, flats or crates. The weight or count packed in each of these containers varies depending on the size and type of vegetable as well as the packer. For example, celery is packed in 55-pound cartons containing 18 to 48 heads, depending on the size of each head.

Some of the more common fresh vegetables (for example, onions, carrots, celery and lettuces) can be purchased from wholesalers trimmed, cleaned and cut according to your specifications. Although the unit price will be higher for diced onions than for whole onions, for example, the savings in time, labor, yield loss and storage space can be substantial. Processed vegetables may suffer a loss of nutrients, moisture and flavor, however.

RIPENING

Although vegetables do not ripen in the same manner as fruits, they do continue to breathe (respire) after harvesting. The faster the respiration rate, the faster the produce ages or decays. This decay results in wilted leaves and dry, tough or woody stems and stalks. Respiration rates vary according to the vegetable variety, its maturity at harvest and its storage conditions after harvest.

Ripening proceeds more rapidly in the presence of ethylene gas. Ethylene gas is emitted naturally by fruits and vegetables and can be used to encourage further ripening in some produce, especially fruit-vegetables such as tomatoes. Items harvested and shipped when mature but green (unripe) can be exposed to ethylene gas to induce color development (ripening) just before sale.

STORING

Some fresh vegetables are best stored at cool temperatures, between 40°F and 60°F (4°C and 16°C), ideally in a separate produce refrigerator. These include winter squash, potatoes, onions, shallots and garlic. If a produce refrigerator is not available, store these vegetables at room temperature in a dry area with good ventilation. Do not store them in a refrigerator set at conventional temperatures. Colder temperatures convert the starches in these vegetables to sugars, changing their texture and flavor.

Most other vegetables benefit from cold storage at temperatures between 34°F and 40°F (2°C and 4°C) with relatively high levels of humidity. Greens and other delicate vegetables should be stored away from apples, tomatoes, bananas and melons, as the latter give off a great deal of ethylene gas.

▶ PURCHASING AND STORING PRESERVED VEGETABLES

Preservation techniques are designed to extend the shelf life of vegetables. These methods include irradiation, canning, freezing and drying. Except for drying, these techniques do not substantially change the vegetable's texture or flavor. Canning and freezing can also be used to preserve cooked vegetables.

IRRADIATED VEGETABLES

The irradiation process uses ionizing radiation (usually gamma rays of cobalt 60 or cesium 137) to sterilize foods. When foods are subjected to radiation, parasites, insects and bacteria are destroyed, ripening is slowed and sprouting is prevented. Irradiation works without a noticeable increase in temperature; consequently, the flavor and texture of fresh foods are not affected. Some nutrients, however, may be destroyed. Irradiated vegetables do not need to be sprayed with post-harvest pesticides, and they have an extended shelf life.

The FDA classifies irradiation as a food additive. Although irradiation is not yet approved for all foods, grains, fruits and vegetables may be treated with low-dose radiation. Irradiated foods must be labeled "Treated with radiation" or "Treated by irradiation." The symbol shown in Figure 20.1 may also be used.

Irradiated produce is purchased, stored and used like fresh produce.

FIGURE 20.1 ▶ Irradiation symbol.

CANNED VEGETABLES

Canned vegetables are the backbone of menu planning for many food service operations. In commercial canning, raw vegetables are cleaned and placed in a

HYDROPONICS: WORKING WATER

Hydroponics is the science of growing plants without soil in water. Plants are grown in an inert medium such as gravel, peat, sand or other sterile material. Nutrients are distributed in water that is circulated over the plant's roots. In a hydroponic farm, the temperatures and light are controlled to maximize production. Because hydroponic farms are indoors, plants can be grown in any climate; both Canada and Holland are major producers of vegetables grown under such conditions.

sealed container, then subjected to high temperatures for a specific period. Heating destroys the microorganisms that cause spoilage, and the sealed environment created by the can eliminates oxidation and retards decomposition. But the heat required by the canning process also softens the texture of most vegetables and alters their nutritional content; many vitamins and minerals may be lost through the canning process. Green vegetables may also suffer color loss, becoming a drab olive hue.

Canned vegetables are graded by the USDA as U.S. Grade A or Fancy, U.S. Grade B or Extra-Select, and U.S. Grade C or Standard. U.S. Grade A vegetables must be top quality, tender and free of blemishes. U.S. Grade C vegetables may lack uniformity or flavor, but can be used in casseroles or soups if cost is a concern.

Combinations of vegetables as well as vegetables with seasonings and sauces are available canned. For example, corn kernels are available canned in water, in seasonings and sauces, combined with other vegetables or creamed. Canned vegetables are easy to serve because they are essentially fully cooked during the canning process.

Canned vegetables are purchased in cases of standard-sized cans (see Appendix II). Canned vegetables can be stored almost indefinitely at room temperature. Once a can is opened, any unused contents should be transferred to an appropriate storage container and refrigerated. Cans with bulges should be discarded immediately, without opening.

FROZEN VEGETABLES

Frozen vegetables are almost as convenient to use as canned. However, they often require some cooking, and expensive freezer space is necessary if an inventory is to be maintained. Regardless, freezing is a highly effective method for preserving vegetables. It severely inhibits the growth of microorganisms that cause spoilage without destroying many nutrients. Generally, green vegetables retain their color, although the appearance and texture of most vegetables may be somewhat altered because of their high water content: Ice crystals form from the water in the cells and burst the cells' walls.

Some vegetables are available individually quick-frozen (IQF). This method employs blasts of cold air, refrigerated plates, liquid nitrogen, liquid air or other techniques to chill the vegetables quickly. Speeding the freezing process can greatly reduce the formation of ice crystals.

Combinations of vegetables as well as vegetables with seasonings and sauces are available frozen. Some frozen vegetables are raw when frozen; others are blanched before freezing so that final cooking time is reduced. Many others are fully cooked before freezing and need only to be thawed or heated for service. Frozen vegetables generally do not need to be thawed before being heated. Once thawed or cooked, they should be stored in the refrigerator and reheated in the same manner as fresh vegetables. Do not refreeze previously frozen vegetables.

Frozen vegetables are graded in the same manner as canned vegetables. They are usually packed in cases containing 1- to 2-pound (450- to 900-gram) boxes or bags. All frozen vegetables should be sealed in moisture-proof wrapping and kept at a constant temperature of 0°F (−18°C) or below. Temperature fluctuations can draw moisture from the vegetables, causing poor texture and flavor loss. Adequate packaging also prevents freezer burn, an irreversible change in the color, texture and flavor of frozen foods.

DRIED VEGETABLES

Except for beans, peas, peppers, mushrooms and tomatoes, few vegetables are commonly preserved by drying. Unlike other preservation methods, drying dramatically alters flavor, texture and appearance. The loss of moisture concentrates flavors and sugars and greatly extends shelf life.

► Applying Various Cooking Methods

Vegetables are cooked in order to break down their cellulose and gelatinize their starches. Cooking gives vegetables a pleasant flavor; creates a softer, more tender texture; and makes them more digestible. Ideally, most vegetables should be cooked as briefly as possible in order to preserve their flavor, nutrients and texture. Unfortunately, sometimes one must choose between emphasizing appearance and maintaining nutrition because cooking methods that preserve color and texture often remove nutrients.

ACID/ALKALI REACTIONS

The acid or alkali content of the cooking liquid affects the texture and color of many vegetables. This is of greater concern with moist-heat cooking methods, but it is also a consideration with dry-heat cooking methods, as they often call for blanched or parboiled vegetables.

TEXTURE

The acidity or alkalinity of the vegetable's cooking liquid influences the finished product's texture. If an acid such as lemon juice, vinegar or wine is added to the liquid for flavoring, the vegetable will resist softening and will require a longer cooking time. On the other hand, an alkaline cooking medium will quickly soften the vegetable's texture and may cause it to become mushy. Alkalinity also causes nutrient loss (especially thiamin) and may impart a bitter flavor. Alkalinity can be caused by tap water, detergent residue on utensils or the addition of baking soda (a base) to the cooking liquid. (You could add, for example, ⅛ teaspoon [0.6 milliliter] baking soda per cup [225 milliliters] of beans to speed the softening of dried beans.)

COLOR

The acidity or alkalinity of the liquid also affects the plant's pigments, causing both desirable and undesirable color changes. There are three principal pigment categories: chlorophyll, carotenoid and flavonoid. A plant's unique color is the result of a combination of these pigments. Chlorophyll pigments predominate in green vegetables such as spinach, green beans and broccoli. Carotenoid pigments predominate in orange and yellow vegetables such as carrots, tomatoes, red peppers and winter squashes. Flavonoid pigments predominate in red, purple and white vegetables such as red cabbage, beets and cauliflower.

Initially, as vegetables are cooked, their original colors intensify. Exposure to heat makes pigments, especially chlorophyll, appear brighter. Exposure to acids and bases affects both chlorophyll and flavonoid pigments. Acids will gradually turn green vegetables an olive-drab color, while a slight alkalinity promotes chlorophyll retention. The opposite occurs with vegetables containing flavonoids: They retain desirable colors in a slightly acidic environment while losing colors in an alkaline one. (Carotenoids are not affected by either acidity or alkalinity.) Color changes alone do not affect flavor, but the altered appearance can make the product so visually unappealing as to become inedible (Table 20.1).

Colors also change as the naturally occurring acids in vegetables are released during cooking. If the cooking pan is kept covered, the acids can concentrate, creating richer flavonoid pigments but destroying chlorophyll pigments.

Thus, if color is the one and only concern, vegetables with a high amount of chlorophyll should be cooked in an alkaline liquid, and vegetables with a high amount of flavonoids should be cooked in an acidic liquid. But remember, the improvement in color usually comes at the expense of texture and nutrients.

Table 20.1 **ACID/ALKALI REACTIONS**

		EFFECT OF ACID ON:		EFFECT OF ALKALI ON:*		
VEGETABLE	**PIGMENT FAMILY**	**COLOR**	**TEXTURE**	**COLOR**	**TEXTURE**	**COOK COVERED?**
Spinach, broccoli	chlorophyll	drab olive green	firm	bright green	mushy	no
Carrots, rutabagas	carotenoid	no change	firm	no change	mushy	no difference
Cauliflower	flavonoid	white	firm	yellow	mushy	yes
Red cabbage	flavonoid	red	firm	blue	mushy	yes

*Alkalinity always causes a loss of thiamin and other nutrients.

1 Spinach cooked with an alkali (left) and an acid.

2 Cauliflower cooked with an alkali (left) and an acid.

3 Red cabbage cooked with an alkali (left) and an acid.

GUIDELINES FOR VEGETABLE COOKERY

The following general guidelines for vegetable cookery should be considered regardless of the cooking method used:

1. Vegetables should be carefully cut into uniform shapes and sizes to promote even cooking and provide an attractive finished product.
2. Cook vegetables for as short a time as possible to preserve texture, color and nutrients.
3. Cook vegetables as close to service time as possible. Holding vegetables in a steam table continues to cook them.
4. When necessary, vegetables may be blanched in advance, refreshed in ice water and refrigerated. They can then be reheated as needed.
5. White and red vegetables (those with flavonoid pigments) may be cooked with a small amount of acid such as lemon juice, vinegar or white wine to help retain their color.
6. When preparing an assortment of vegetables, cook each type separately, then combine them. Otherwise, some items would become overcooked in the time required to properly cook others.

DETERMINING DONENESS

There are so many types of vegetables, with such varied responses to cooking, that no one standard for doneness is appropriate. Each item should be evaluated on a recipe-by-recipe basis. Generally, however, most cooked vegetables are done when they are just tender when pierced with a fork or the tip of a paring knife. Leafy vegetables should be wilted but still have a bright color.

Avoid overcooking vegetables by remembering that some carryover cooking will occur through the residual heat contained in the foods. Always rely on subjective tests—sight, feel, taste and aroma—rather than the clock.

> **VEGETABLE SAUNA**
>
> "Sweating vegetables" in a little oil over low heat in a covered pot is, in effect, a vegetable sauna. All of the flavors of the vegetables emerge slowly in a juicy tangle, in a much more intense manner than if you simply added them just-cut to a stock. Like roasting garlic, it is a way to enlarge the natural flavors very dramatically.
>
> *China Moon Cookbook* by BARBARA TROPP

DRY-HEAT COOKING METHODS

BROILING AND GRILLING

Broiling and grilling use high heat to cook vegetables quickly. This preserves their nutritional content and natural flavors. The radiant heat of the broiler or grill caramelizes the vegetables, creating a pleasant flavor that is not generally achieved when vegetables are cooked by other methods.

Selecting and Preparing Vegetables to Broil or Grill

Broiling is often used to cook soft vegetables such as tomatoes or items that might not rest easily on a grill rack. Broiling is also used to warm and brown items just before service. If necessary, the vegetables can be basted to prevent them from drying out under the broiler's direct heat. Sometimes a cooked vegetable is napped with sauce or clarified butter and placed briefly under the broiler as a finishing touch at service time.

A large range of vegetables can be grilled. Carrots, peppers, squashes, eggplants and similar vegetables should be cut into broad, thin slices. They can then be placed on the grill in the same manner as a portion of meat or fish to create attractive crosshatchings. (See Chapter 8, Principles of Cooking.) Smaller vegetables such as mushrooms, cherry tomatoes and pearl onions can be threaded onto skewers for easy handling. (Bamboo or wooden skewers should be soaked in cold water for 15 minutes before using to help prevent them from burning on the grill.)

Seasoning Vegetables to Be Broiled or Grilled

Vegetables contain little fat and therefore benefit greatly from added fat when being broiled or grilled. The added fat can be a brushing of clarified butter or a marinade such as one made from olive oil and herbs. Some vegetables may be brushed with butter and coated with bread crumbs or Parmesan before broiling.

► PROCEDURE FOR BROILING OR GRILLING VEGETABLES

1. Heat the grill or broiler.
2. Use a wire brush to remove any charred or burnt particles that may be stuck to the broiler or grill grate. The grate may be wiped with a lightly oiled towel to remove any remaining particles and help season it.
3. Prepare the vegetables to be broiled or grilled by cutting them into appropriate shapes and sizes, then seasoning, marinating or otherwise preparing them as desired or directed in the recipe.
4. Place the vegetables on the broiler grate, broiler platter or grill grate and cook to the desired doneness while developing the proper surface color.

RECIPE 20.1

GRILLED VEGETABLE SKEWERS

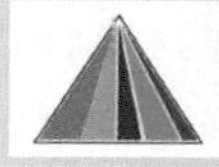

Mise en Place

- ▶ Peel and chop garlic.
- ▶ Wash broccoli and cauliflower and cut into large florets.
- ▶ Peel and dice onion.
- ▶ Wash and seed bell pepper and cut into large dice.
- ▶ Wash mushroom caps.

Grilling skewers of marinated vegetables.

Grilled sliced vegetables as an accompaniment to an entrée plate.

Yield: 12 Skewers **Method:** Grilling

Marinade:		
Rice wine vinegar	4 fl. oz.	120 ml
Vegetable oil	8 fl. oz.	250 ml
Garlic, chopped	1 oz.	30 g
Dried thyme	2 tsp.	10 ml
Salt	1 Tbsp.	15 ml
Black pepper	½ tsp.	2 ml
Zucchini	6 oz.	180 g
Yellow squash	6 oz.	180 g
Broccoli florets, large	12	12
Cauliflower florets, large	12	12
Onion, large dice	24 pieces	24 pieces
Red bell pepper, large dice	12 pieces	12 pieces
Mushroom caps, medium	12	12

1. Combine all the marinade ingredients and set aside.
2. Cut the zucchini and yellow squash into ½-inch- (1.2-centimeter-) thick semicircles.
3. Blanch and refresh the zucchini, yellow squash, broccoli florets, cauliflower florets, onion and bell pepper as discussed later under Moist-Heat Cooking Methods.
4. Drain the vegetables well and combine them with the marinade. Add the mushroom caps to the marinade. Marinate the vegetables for 30 to 45 minutes, remove and drain well.
5. Skewer the vegetables by alternating them on 6-inch (10-centimeter) bamboo skewers.
6. Place the vegetable skewers on a hot grill and cook until done, turning as needed. The vegetables should brown and char lightly during cooking. Serve hot.

VARIATION:

Grilled Sliced Vegetables—Slice the zucchini, yellow squash, onion and bell pepper into large pieces. Marinate and then grill these vegetables along with the broccoli, cauliflower and mushroom caps without skewering.

Approximate values per serving: **Calories** 60, **Total fat** 2.5 g, **Saturated fat** 0 g, **Cholesterol** 0 mg, **Sodium** 610 mg, **Total carbohydrates** 8 g, **Protein** 2 g, **Vitamin C** 90%, **Claims**—low fat; no cholesterol; good source of fiber

ROASTING AND BAKING

The terms *roasting* and *baking* are used interchangeably when referring to vegetables. Roasting or baking is used to bring out the natural sweetness of many vegetables while preserving their nutritional values. The procedures are basically the same as those for roasting meats.

Selecting and Preparing Vegetables to Roast or Bake

Hearty vegetables such as winter squash and eggplant are especially well suited for roasting or baking. Vegetables such as onions, carrots and turnips are sometimes cooked alongside roasting meats or poultry. The vegetables add flavor to the finished roast and accompanying sauce, and the fats and juices released from the cooking roast add flavor to the vegetables.

Vegetables can be baked whole or cut into uniform-sized pieces. Squash, for example, is usually cut into large pieces. Vegetables may be peeled or left unpeeled, depending on the desired finished product.

Seasoning Vegetables to Be Roasted or Baked

Vegetables may be seasoned with salt and pepper and rubbed with butter or oil before baking, or they may be seasoned afterward with a wide variety of herbs and spices. Some vegetables, such as winter squashes and sweet potatoes, may be seasoned with brown sugar or honey as well.

▶ PROCEDURE FOR ROASTING OR BAKING VEGETABLES

1. Wash the vegetables. Peel, cut and prepare them as desired or directed in the recipe.
2. Season the vegetables and rub with oil or butter if desired.
3. Place the vegetables in a baking dish and bake in a preheated oven until done.

BAKED BUTTERNUT SQUASH

RECIPE 20.2

Yield: 4 Servings, 4 oz. (120 g) each **Method:** Baking

Butternut squash, medium dice	1 lb.	450 g
Clarified butter	as needed	as needed
Salt and pepper	TT	TT
Cinnamon	1/4 tsp.	1 ml
Cardamom, ground	1/8 tsp.	0.5 ml
Brown sugar	2 Tbsp.	30 ml
Lemon juice	2 Tbsp.	30 ml
Whole butter, melted	2 oz.	60 g

1. Place the squash in a buttered pan. Season with salt, pepper, cinnamon, cardamom and sugar.
2. Drizzle the lemon juice and melted butter over the top of the squash.
3. Bake, uncovered, in a 350°F (180°C) oven until tender, approximately 50 minutes.

Approximate values per 4-oz. (120-g) serving: **Calories** 190, **Total fat** 12 g, **Saturated fat** 7 g, **Cholesterol** 30 mg, **Sodium** 700 mg, **Total carbohydrates** 20 g, **Protein** 1 g, **Vitamin A** 90%, **Vitamin C** 35%

Mise en Place

- ▶ Wash and peel butternut squash and cut into medium dice.
- ▶ Melt whole butter and keep warm.

SAUTÉING

Sautéed vegetables should be brightly colored and slightly crisp when done and show little moisture loss. When sautéing vegetables, all preparation must be complete before cooking begins because timing is important and cooking progresses rapidly. Have all vegetables, herbs, spices, seasonings and sauces ready before beginning.

Selecting and Preparing Vegetables to Sauté

A wide variety of vegetables can be sautéed. Whatever vegetables are used, they should be cut into uniform-sized pieces to ensure even cooking.

Quick-cooking vegetables such as summer squashes, onions, greens, stalks, fruit-vegetables and mushrooms can be sautéed without any preparation except washing and cutting. Other vegetables such as Brussels sprouts, green beans, winter squashes, broccoli, cauliflower and most root vegetables are usually first blanched or otherwise partially cooked by baking, steaming or simmering. They are then sautéed to reheat and finish. Carrots, squash and other vegetables are sometimes finished by sautéing in butter and then adding a small amount of honey or maple syrup to glaze them. Some cooked vegetables are reheated by simply sautéing them in a small amount of stock or sauce.

Seasoning Vegetables to Be Sautéed

Sautéed vegetables can be seasoned with a great variety of herbs and spices. Seasonings should be added toward the end of the cooking process after all other ingredients have been incorporated in order to accurately evaluate the flavor of the finished dish.

Because sautéing vegetables uses slightly lower temperatures than sautéing meats and poultry, usually whole butter can be used instead of clarified butter. For additional flavors, fats such as bacon fat, olive oil, nut oils or sesame oil can be used in place of butter.

▶ PROCEDURE FOR SAUTÉING VEGETABLES

1. Wash the vegetables and cut into uniform shapes and sizes.
2. Heat a sauté pan and add enough fat to just cover the bottom. The pan should be large enough to hold the vegetables without overcrowding.
3. When preparing an assortment of vegetables, add the ingredients according to their cooking times (first add the vegetables that take the longest to cook). Plan carefully so that all vegetables will be done at the same time. Do not overcrowd the pan; maintain high enough heat so that the vegetables do not cook in their own juices.
4. Toss the vegetables using the sloped sides of the sauté pan or wok to flip them back on top of themselves. Do not toss more than necessary. The pan should remain in contact with the heat source as much as possible to maintain proper temperatures.
5. Add any sauces or vegetables with high water content, such as tomatoes, last.
6. Season the vegetables as desired with herbs or spices, or add ingredients for a glaze.

RECIPE 20.3

STIR-FRIED ASPARAGUS WITH SHIITAKE MUSHROOMS

Mise en Place

▶ Peel and chop garlic.

Yield: 4 Servings, 4 oz. (120 g) each **Method:** Sautéing

Asparagus	1 lb.	450 g
Shiitake mushrooms, fresh	6 oz.	180 g
Vegetable oil	1 Tbsp.	15 ml
Sesame oil	1 Tbsp.	15 ml
Garlic, chopped	2 tsp.	10 ml
Oyster sauce	4 fl. oz.	120 ml
Crushed red chiles, optional	TT	TT

1. Wash the asparagus, trim the ends and slice on the bias into 1- to 2-inch (2.5- to 5-centimeter) pieces.
2. Wash the mushrooms, trim off the stems and slice the caps into ½-inch- (1.2-centimeter-) thick slices.
3. Heat the oils in a wok or sauté pan.
4. Add the garlic and stir-fry for a few seconds.

5 Add the asparagus and mushrooms and stir-fry for 1 minute.
6 Add the oyster sauce and crushed red chiles (if used) and continue to stir-fry until the asparagus is nearly tender, approximately 3 minutes.

Approximate values per 4-oz. (120-g) serving: **Calories** 140, **Total fat** 8 g, **Saturated fat** 1 g, **Cholesterol** 10 mg, **Sodium** 1130 mg, **Total carbohydrates** 13 g, **Protein** 5 g, **Vitamin C** 50%

PAN-FRYING

Pan-frying is not as popular as other techniques for cooking vegetables. Green tomatoes, however, are sometimes seasoned, floured and pan-fried; eggplant slices are seasoned, floured, pan-fried and used for eggplant Parmesan. When pan-frying vegetables, follow the procedures outlined in Chapter 8, Principles of Cooking.

DEEP-FRYING

Deep-frying is a popular method of preparing vegetables such as potatoes, squashes and mushrooms. They can be served as hors d'oeuvre, appetizers or accompaniments to a main dish. Vegetables can also be grated or chopped and incorporated into fritters or croquettes. Any deep-fried item should have a crisp, golden exterior with a tender, nongreasy center.

Selecting and Seasoning Vegetables to Be Deep-Fried

Except for potatoes (which are discussed in Chapter 21, Potatoes, Grains and Pasta), most vegetables are breaded or battered before deep-frying. Slow-cooking vegetables such as broccoli and cauliflower should be blanched in boiling water before breading or battering. Blanching speeds cooking and allows the interior to cook completely before the surface burns.

Although vegetables that will be deep-fried can be marinated or seasoned directly, it is more common to season the batter or breading that will coat them. Additional flavors come from the sauces and accompaniments served with the deep-fried vegetables. Creamy herb dressings or spicy tomato or soy-based dipping sauces are popular accompaniments.

▶ PROCEDURE FOR DEEP-FRYING VEGETABLES

1 Slice, trim or otherwise prepare the vegetables to be deep-fried. Blanch them if necessary. Season and bread or batter them, as desired.
2 Heat the fat to the desired temperature, usually between 325°F and 350°F (160°C and 180°C). Breaded or battered vegetables cook quickly and the fat must be hot enough to cook the food's interior without burning its surface.
3 Carefully place the vegetables in the hot fat using either the basket method or swimming method as appropriate.
4 Deep-fry the vegetables until done. They should have a crispy, golden brown surface.
5 Remove the deep-fried vegetables from the fat and hold them over the fryer, allowing the excess fat to drain off. Transfer the food to a hotel pan either lined with absorbent paper or fitted with a rack. Season with salt, if desired.
6 If the deep-fried vegetables are to be held for later service, place them under a heat lamp.

RECIPE 20.4

BEER-BATTERED ONION RINGS

Yield: 1 qt. (1 lt) batter, enough for approx. 4 lb. (1.8 kg) rings

Method: Deep-frying

Flour	10 oz.	300 g
Baking powder	2 tsp.	10 ml
Salt	2 tsp.	10 ml
White pepper	1/4 tsp.	1 ml
Egg	1	1
Beer	1 pt.	450 ml
Onions, whole	4 lb.	1.8 kg
Flour	as needed for dredging	

1 Sift the dry ingredients together.
2 Beat the egg in a separate bowl. Add the beer to the beaten egg.
3 Add the egg-and-beer mixture to the dry ingredients; mix until smooth.
4 Peel the onions and cut in 1/2-inch- (1.2-centimeter-) thick slices.
5 Break the slices into rings and dredge in flour.
6 Dip the rings in the batter a few at a time. Using the swimming method, deep-fry at 375°F (191°C) until done. Drain on absorbent paper, season with additional salt and white pepper and serve hot.

Approximate values per 1-oz. (30-g) serving: **Calories** 230, **Total fat** 10 g, **Saturated fat** 2.5 g, **Cholesterol** 5 mg, **Sodium** 460 mg, **Total carbohydrates** 31 g, **Protein** 4 g

1 Dredging the onion rings in flour.

2 Dipping the floured rings in batter.

3 Frying the onion rings using the swimming method.

MOIST-HEAT COOKING METHODS

BLANCHING AND PARBOILING

Blanching and parboiling are variations on boiling; the difference between them is the length of cooking time. Blanched and parboiled vegetables are often finished by other cooking methods such as sautéing.

Blanching is the partial cooking of foods in a large amount of boiling water for a very short time, usually only a few seconds. Besides preparing vegetables for further cooking, blanching is used to remove strong or bitter flavors, soften firm foods, set colors or loosen skins for peeling. Kale, chard, snow peas and tomatoes are examples of vegetables that are sometimes blanched for purposes other than preparation for further cooking.

Parboiling is the same as blanching, but the cooking time is longer, usually several minutes. Parboiling is used to soften vegetables and shorten final cooking times. Parboiling is commonly used for preparing root vegetables, cauliflower, broccoli and winter squashes.

BOILING

Vegetables are often boiled. Boiled vegetables can be served as they are, or they can be further prepared by quickly sautéing with other ingredients, puréeing or mashing. Boiled vegetables are also chilled, then used in salads.

Starchy root vegetables are generally not boiled but rather simmered slowly so that the heat penetrates to their interiors and cooks them evenly. Green vegetables should be boiled quickly in a large amount of water in order to retain their color and flavor.

REFRESHING

Unless the boiled, blanched or parboiled vegetables will be eaten immediately, they must be quickly chilled in ice water after they are removed from the cooking liquid. This prevents further cooking and preserves (sets) their colors. This process is known as **refreshing** or **shocking** the vegetables. The vegetables are removed from the ice water as soon as they are cold. Never soak or hold the vegetables in the water longer than necessary, or valuable nutrients and flavor will be leached away.

▶ **refreshing** submerging a food in cold water to quickly cool it and prevent further cooking, also known as shocking; usually used for vegetables

▶ PROCEDURE FOR REFRESHING VEGETABLES

1 Blanch, parboil or boil the vegetables to the desired doneness.

2 Remove the vegetables from the cooking liquid and submerge them in ice water just until they are cold.

Selecting and Preparing Vegetables to Boil

Nearly any type of vegetable can be boiled. Carrots, cabbages, green beans, turnips and red beets are just a few of the most common ones. Vegetables can be large or small, but they should be uniform in size to ensure even cooking. Some vegetables are cooked whole and require only washing before boiling. Others must be washed, peeled and trimmed or cut into smaller or more manageable sizes.

Seasoning Vegetables to Be Boiled

Often vegetables are boiled in nothing more than salted water. Lemon juice, citrus zest, wine and other acidic ingredients are sometimes added to white and red vegetables; if so, they should be added to the liquid before the vegetables. Herbs and spices in a sachet or a bouquet garni are often used to add flavor to boiled vegetables and should be added according to the recipe.

After boiling, vegetables are sometimes finished with herbs, spices, butter, cream or sauces.

▶ PROCEDURE FOR BOILING VEGETABLES

1. Wash, peel and trim the vegetables and cut into uniform shapes and sizes.
2. Bring an adequate amount of water, stock, court bouillon or other liquid to a boil. The liquid should cover the vegetables, and they should be able to move around freely without overcrowding.
3. Add seasonings if desired or directed in the recipe.
4. Add the vegetables to the boiling liquid. If more than one vegetable is to be cooked and they have different cooking times, they should be cooked separately to ensure that all are cooked to the proper doneness. The pot may be covered if cooking white, red or yellow vegetables. Do not cover the pot when boiling green vegetables.
5. Cook the vegetables to the desired doneness.
6. Remove the vegetables from the water with a slotted spoon or a spider or drain through a colander.
7. Refresh the vegetables in ice water, drain and refrigerate until needed, or finish the hot boiled vegetables as desired and serve immediately.

RECIPE 20.5

BRUSSELS SPROUTS IN PECAN BUTTER

Mise en Place

▶ Chop pecans.

Yield: 6 Servings, 3 oz. (90 g) **Method:** Boiling

Brussels sprouts	1 lb.	450 g
Whole butter	2 oz.	60 g
Pecans, chopped	4 oz.	120 g
Salt and pepper	TT	TT

1. Trim the Brussels sprouts and mark an X in the bottom of each with a paring knife to promote even cooking.
2. Boil the sprouts in salted water until tender, approximately 10 minutes.
3. Drain and hold the sprouts in a warm place.
4. Heat the butter in a sauté pan until noisette. Add the pecans and toss to brown them.
5. Add the Brussels sprouts and toss to reheat and blend flavors. Adjust the seasonings and serve.

VARIATION:

Substitute asparagus, green beans or fingerling potatoes for the Brussels sprouts in this recipe.

Approximate values per 3-oz. (90-g) serving: **Calories** 240, **Total fat** 21 g, **Saturated fat** 6 g, **Cholesterol** 20 mg, **Sodium** 480 mg, **Total carbohydrates** 10 g, **Protein** 4 g, **Vitamin A** 15%, **Vitamin C** 80%

1 Marking an X in the bottom of each Brussels sprout.

2 Boiling the Brussels sprouts in the appropriate amount of water.

3 Tossing the Brussels sprouts with the butter and pecans.

▶ PROCEDURE FOR COOKING DRIED BEANS

Dried beans are best rehydrated by soaking as discussed earlier and then cooking in a boiling (actually simmering) liquid. After rehydration and cooking, the beans can be served or further cooked in baked, sautéed or puréed dishes.

1. After soaking, place the drained beans in a heavy saucepan and cover with cold water or stock. Allow approximately three times as much liquid as there are beans. Add flavoring ingredients as directed in the recipe, but do not add acids or salt until the beans have reached the desired tenderness. Acids and salt cause the exterior of beans to toughen and resist any further efforts at tenderizing.
2. Slowly bring the liquid to a boil. Boil uncovered for 10 minutes or as directed in the recipe. Use a ladle to remove any scum that rises to the surface.
3. Cover and reduce the heat. Allow the mixture to simmer until the beans are tender. Whole beans generally require 1 to 2½ hours, lentils 20 to 35 minutes and split peas 30 to 60 minutes. Add additional hot liquid if necessary. Do not stir the beans during cooking.
4. Drain the cooked beans through a colander.

RECIPE 20.6

WHITE BEAN SALAD

Mise en Place

- ▶ Wash and peel carrot and celery and cut into small dice.
- ▶ Wash, peel and slice leek.
- ▶ Wash, peel and slice shallots.
- ▶ Wash and mince green onions.
- ▶ Wash and chop parsley and thyme.

Yield: 3 pt. (1.5 lt)

White beans	12 oz.	360 g
Water	as needed	as needed
Carrot, small dice	4 oz.	120 g
Celery, small dice	2 oz.	60 g
Leek, sliced	2 oz.	60 g
Dressing:		
Red wine vinegar	3 Tbsp.	45 ml
Fresh lemon juice	2 tsp.	10 ml
Dijon mustard	1 Tbsp.	15 ml
Shallot, minced	1 Tbsp.	15 ml
Olive oil	6 fl. oz.	180 ml
Salt and pepper	TT	TT
Green onions, minced	2	2
Parsley, chopped	1 Tbsp.	15 ml
Fresh thyme, chopped	1 Tbsp.	15 ml

1 Pick through the beans to remove any grit, pebbles or debris. Place the beans in a bowl of water and remove any skins or other items that float to the top. Drain and rinse the beans. Place the beans in a clean bowl and soak them for at least 1 hour or overnight.

2 Drain the beans and place them in a saucepot with 6 cups (1.5 liters) water. Bring to a boil, reduce to a simmer and cook until the beans are tender, approximately 1 hour. Drain the beans, spread on a sheet pan, cool and refrigerate.

3 Blanch and refresh the carrot, celery and leek. Drain and chill.

4 To make the dressing, combine the vinegar, lemon juice and mustard. Add the shallot and whisk in the oil a little bit at a time. Season with salt and pepper.

5 Toss the beans with the blanched vegetables, green onions, parsley and thyme. Add the dressing and toss together. Adjust the seasonings and serve chilled.

Approximate values per ½-c. (120-ml) serving: **Calories** 250, **Total fat** 15 g, **Saturated fat** 2 g, **Cholesterol** 0 mg, **Sodium** 40 mg, **Total carbohydrates** 23 g, **Protein** 8 g, **Vitamin A** 50%, **Calcium** 10%, **Iron** 20%

1 Draining the beans.

2 Blanching the vegetables.

3 Tossing the salad ingredients together.

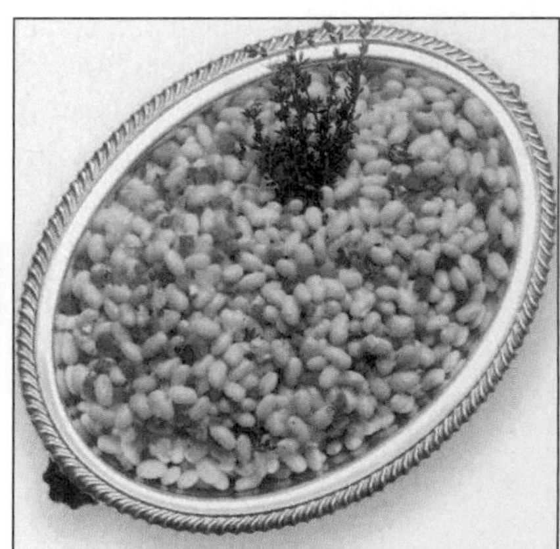

4 The finished salad ready for buffet service.

STEAMING

Vegetables can be steamed in a convection steamer or by placing them in a basket or on a rack and suspending them over boiling liquid in a wok, saucepan or hotel pan. Vegetables can also be pan-steamed by cooking them in a covered pan with a small amount of liquid; most of the cooking is done by steam because only a small portion of the food is submerged in the liquid. Steamed vegetables can be eaten plain, partially cooked and sautéed lightly to finish, incorporated into casseroles or puréed. If they are not served immediately, they must be refreshed and refrigerated until used.

Properly steamed vegetables should be moist and tender. They generally retain their shape better than boiled vegetables. Vegetables cook very rapidly in steam, and overcooking is a common mistake.

Selecting and Preparing Vegetables to Steam

Nearly any vegetable that can be boiled can also be steamed successfully. All vegetables should be washed, peeled and trimmed if appropriate and cut into uniform-sized pieces. Pan-steaming is appropriate for vegetables that are small or cut into fairly small pieces such as peas and beans or broccoli and cauliflower florets.

Seasoning Vegetables to Be Steamed

Steaming produces vegetables with clean, natural flavors. Foods cooked in convection steamers can be seasoned with herbs and spices; convection steamers use plain water to produce steam, so the foods being cooked do not gain flavor from the cooking liquid. Vegetables steamed over liquids or pan-steamed in small amounts of liquids can be flavored by using stocks or court bouillon as the cooking liquid. Herbs, spices and aromatic vegetables can be added to any liquid for additional flavor.

▶ PROCEDURE FOR STEAMING VEGETABLES

1 Wash, peel and trim the vegetables and cut into uniform shapes and sizes.

2 If a convection steamer is not being used, prepare a steaming liquid and bring it to a boil in a covered pan or double boiler.

3 Place the vegetables in a perforated pan in a single layer; do not crowd the pan. Place the pan over the boiling liquid or add the vegetables to the liquid.

4 Cover the pan and cook to the desired doneness.

5 Remove the vegetables from the steamer and serve, or refresh and refrigerate until needed.

RECIPE 20.7

BROCCOLI ALMONDINE

Mise en Place

▶ Peel and mince garlic.

1 Placing the broccoli spears in a perforated pan.

2 Drizzling the browned almonds and butter over the broccoli.

Yield: 6 Servings, 6 oz. (180 g) each **Method:** Steaming

Broccoli, fresh	2 lb.	1 kg
Salt and pepper	TT	TT
Whole butter	2 oz.	60 g
Almonds, sliced	1 oz.	30 g
Garlic clove, minced	1	1
Lemon juice	2 fl. oz.	60 ml

1 Cut the broccoli into uniform spears. Rinse and sprinkle lightly with salt and pepper.

2 Place the broccoli in a single layer in a perforated hotel pan and cook in a convection steamer until tender but slightly crisp, approximately 3 minutes.

3 Melt the butter in a sauté pan. Add the almonds and garlic and cook just until the nuts are lightly browned.

4 Arrange the broccoli on plates for service and sprinkle with the lemon juice. Drizzle the almonds and butter over the broccoli and serve immediately.

Approximate values per 6-oz. (180-g) serving: **Calories** 160, **Total fat** 10 g, **Saturated fat** 5 g, **Cholesterol** 20 mg, **Sodium** 500 g, **Total carbohydrates** 10 g, **Protein** 6 g, **Vitamin A** 35%, **Vitamin C** 110%

COMBINATION COOKING METHODS

BRAISING AND STEWING

Braised and stewed vegetables are cooked slowly in a small amount of liquid. The liquid, including any given off by the vegetables, is reduced to a light sauce, becoming part of the finished product. Generally, a braised dish is prepared with only one vegetable; a stew is a mixture of several vegetables. The main ingredients are sometimes browned in fat before the liquid is added in order to enhance flavor and color.

Both braises and stews can be exceptionally flavorful because they are served with all of their cooking liquid. (Boiled vegetables lose some of their flavor to the cooking liquid.) Braised and stewed vegetables generally can be held hot for service longer than vegetables prepared by other cooking methods.

Selecting and Preparing Vegetables to Braise or Stew

Various lettuces, especially romaine and Boston, are often braised. Cabbages, Belgium endive, leeks and many other vegetables are also commonly braised. Stews may contain a wide variety of vegetables such as summer squashes, eggplant, onions, peppers, tomatoes, carrots, celery and garlic. Leafy green vegetables and winter squashes are less commonly braised or stewed.

The vegetables should be washed and peeled or trimmed if appropriate. Vegetables to be braised may be left whole, cut into uniform pieces or shredded, as desired. Lettuces are usually cut into halves or quarters; cabbage is usually shredded.

Seasoning Vegetables to Be Braised or Stewed

Both braises and stews usually include flavoring ingredients such as garlic, herbs, bacon or mirepoix. The liquid may consist of water, wine, stock or tomato juice. Vegetables can even be braised in butter and sugar or honey to create a glazed dish.

Both braises and stews can be seasoned with a variety of herbs and spices. Add the seasonings before covering the pot to finish the cooking process. Strongly flavored vegetables such as celery root and turnips are usually parboiled first in order to reduce their strong presence.

▶ PROCEDURE FOR BRAISING AND STEWING VEGETABLES

1. Wash, peel, trim and cut the vegetables.
2. Sauté or sweat the flavoring ingredients in fat to release their flavors. Or sauté or sweat the main ingredients in fat.
3. For a braise, add the main ingredient in a single layer. For a stew, add the ingredients according to their cooking times or as directed in the recipe.
4. Add the cooking liquid; it should partially cover the vegetables Bring the liquid to a boil, reduce to a simmer, cover and cook in the oven or on the stove top until done.
5. If desired, remove the main ingredients from the pan and reduce the sauce or thicken it with beurre manié, cornstarch or arrowroot. Then return the main ingredients to the sauce.

BRAISED CELERY WITH BASIL

RECIPE 20.8

Yield: 12 Servings, 3 oz. (90 g) each **Method:** Braising

Celery heads	3	3
Onions, small dice	8 oz.	250 g
Garlic, minced	2 tsp.	10 ml
Whole butter	2 oz.	60 g
Olive oil	2 Tbsp.	30 ml
Fresh thyme	1 tsp.	5 ml
Fresh basil leaves, chiffonade	20	20
Dry white wine	8 fl. oz.	250 ml
Chicken stock	1 pt.	500 ml
Salt and pepper	TT	TT

1. Trim the outer ribs from the celery heads, leaving only the tender hearts. Trim the heads to 6-inch (15-centimeter) lengths. Trim the root slightly, leaving each head together. Cut each head lengthwise into quarters.
2. Sauté the onions and garlic in the butter and oil, without coloring, until tender. Add the celery quarters to the pan and sauté, turning occasionally.
3. Add the thyme, basil, wine and stock. Bring to a boil, reduce to a simmer, cover and braise in the oven at 350°F (180°C) until tender, approximately 1 hour.
4. Remove the celery and reserve. Reduce the cooking liquid on the stove top until it thickens. Adjust the liquid's seasonings and return the celery to the pan to reheat. Serve the celery with a portion of the sauce.

Approximate values per 3-oz. (90-g) serving: **Calories** 60, **Total fat** 4.5 g, **Saturated fat** 1.5 g, **Cholesterol** 5 mg, **Sodium** 170 mg, **Total carbohydrates** 2 g, **Protein** 1 g

Mise en Place

- ▶ Wash and peel onions and cut into small dice.
- ▶ Wash, peel and mince garlic.
- ▶ Slice basil in chiffonade.

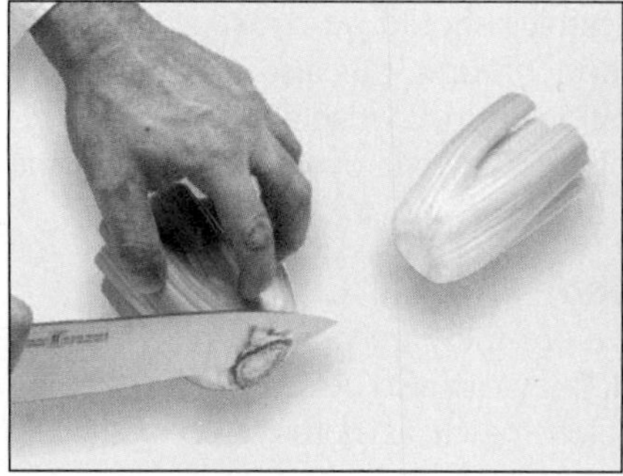

1 Trimming the celery.

2 Adding the liquid to the celery.

3 Reducing the sauce.

MICROWAVING

Fresh vegetables are among the few foods that can be consistently well prepared in a microwave oven. Often microwave cooking can be accomplished without any additional liquid, thus preserving nutrients. With microwaving, colors and flavors stay true, and textures remain crisp.

Microwave cooking is actually a form of steaming. As explained in Chapter 8, Principles of Cooking, microwaves agitate water molecules, thus creating steam. The water may be the moisture found naturally in the food or may be added specifically to create the steam.

Cooking time depends on the type of microwave oven as well as on the freshness, moisture content, maturity and quantity of vegetables being prepared.

Selecting and Preparing Vegetables to Microwave

Any vegetable that can be steamed successfully can be microwaved with good results. Because typical microwave ovens are relatively small, they are impractical for producing large quantities of food. They are most useful for reheating small portions of vegetables that have been blanched or partially cooked using another cooking method.

Seasoning Vegetables to Be Microwaved

Microwaving, like steaming, brings out the natural flavors of food. Herbs and spices can be added to the vegetables before they are microwaved. Or, after microwaving, the vegetables can be tossed with butter, herbs and spices or combined with a sauce.

▶ PROCEDURE FOR MICROWAVING VEGETABLES

1. Wash, peel and trim the vegetables and cut into uniform shapes and sizes.
2. Place the vegetables in a steamer designed for microwave use or arrange the vegetables in a microwavable dish. Cover the vegetables with the lid or plastic wrap. If using plastic wrap, it should be punctured to allow some steam to escape during cooking.
3. Cook the vegetables to the desired doneness, allowing for some carryover cooking, or reheat the previously cooked vegetables until hot. Stir or turn the vegetables as necessary to promote even cooking.
4. Serve the vegetables or refresh and refrigerate until needed.

PURÉEING

Puréeing is a technique often used with vegetables. Cooked vegetable purées can be served as is, or they can be used as an ingredient in other preparations such as pumpkin pie, mashed potatoes or vegetable soufflés. Purées can also be bound with eggs, seasoned and used to make vegetable timbales and terrines.

Puréed vegetables are generally first cooked by baking, boiling, steaming or microwaving. White, red and yellow vegetables should be cooked until quite soft. They are more easily puréed when hot or warm; this also helps ensure a smooth finished purée. For most preparations, green vegetables must be refreshed after cooking and puréed while cold, or they will overcook and become discolored.

Seasoning Vegetables to Be Puréed

Vegetables for purées can be seasoned before they are puréed following the guidelines for the cooking procedure used. They can also be seasoned after they are puréed with a wide variety of ingredients such as herbs, spices, cheese, honey or brown sugar.

Finishing Puréed Vegetables

Purées can be finished with stocks, sauces, butter or cream to add richness and flavor. First purée the main ingredient, then add additional liquids to obtain the desired consistency.

▶ PROCEDURE FOR PURÉEING VEGETABLES

1. Cook the vegetables. White, red and yellow vegetables should be cooked until very soft. Green vegetables should be cooked until tender but not overcooked to the point of being discolored.
2. Purée the vegetables in a VCM, food processor or blender or by passing them through a food mill.
3. Season or finish the puréed vegetables as desired or directed in the recipe, or use them in another recipe.

PARSNIP PURÉE

RECIPE 20.9

Yield: 2 qt. (2 lt) **Method:** Boiling/Puréeing

Parsnips	4 lb.	1.8 kg
Russet potatoes	1 lb. 8 oz.	750 g
Heavy cream, hot	8 fl. oz.	250 ml
Whole butter, melted	4 oz.	120 g
Salt and white pepper	TT	TT

1. Peel the parsnips and potatoes and cut into large pieces of approximately the same size.
2. Boil the vegetables separately in salted water until tender.
3. Drain the vegetables well. Purée them together through a food mill.
4. Add the cream and butter and mix to combine. Adjust the consistency by adding cream as desired. Season the mixture with salt and white pepper and serve hot.

VARIATIONS:

Turnip Purée—Substitute turnips for the parsnips.

Winter Squash Purée—Select approximately 6½ pounds (3 kilograms) winter squash (such as acorn, butternut, pumpkin) and cut them in halves or quarters. Scoop out the seeds and then roast the squash, cut side down, in a 375°F (190°C) oven until tender. Scoop the flesh from the shells and substitute it for the parsnips.

Approximate values per ½-c. (120-ml) serving: **Calories** 240, **Total fat** 12 g, **Saturated fat** 7 g, **Cholesterol** 35 mg, **Sodium** 220 mg, **Total carbohydrates** 31 g, **Protein** 3 g, **Vitamin A** 10%, **Vitamin C** 35%

Mise en Place

▶ Heat the cream and melt the butter while the parsnips and potatoes are cooking.

1 Passing the parsnips and potatoes through a food mill.

2 The finished Parsnip Purée.

CONCLUSION

Vegetables are an essential part of the human diet. They provide the body with vitamins, minerals and fiber and appeal to the appetite with flavor, color and texture. Increasing market availability of fresh, high-quality vegetables as well as new hybrids offers an ever-increasing variety of vegetables from which to choose. Vegetables are a relatively inexpensive food that can be prepared in limitless ways. They can be served as an entire meal or as an accompaniment to or part of a wide variety of other dishes. And when cooking vegetables, remember what James Beard (1903–1985), the great American food consultant, culinary educator and writer, once said: "No vegetable exists which is not better slightly undercooked."

QUESTIONS FOR DISCUSSION

1 Explain how the season affects the price, quality and availability of vegetables.

2 List and describe three processing techniques commonly used to extend the shelf life of vegetables.

3 What special concerns exist regarding the storage of fresh vegetables? Explain why some vegetables should not be refrigerated.

4 Why is it important to cut vegetables into a uniform size before cooking?

5 Discuss several techniques used for determining the doneness of vegetables. Is carryover cooking a concern when preparing vegetables? Explain your answer.

6 Discuss the role of acid in a cooking liquid used for preparing vegetables. Which vegetables, if any, benefit from an acidic cooking environment?

7 Describe the necessary mise en place and procedure for refreshing vegetables.

8 Locate information on farmer's markets in your area. What are the advantages and disadvantages of purchasing vegetables from a local grower?

9 Many people are very concerned about the use of genetically modified organisms (GMOs) and bioengineered products in the foods they eat. What is the federal government's position on these foodstuffs? What organizations are working to prohibit the use of GMOs? Why? Do you agree or disagree with their arguments?

CHAPTER TWENTY-ONE

POTATOES, GRAINS AND PASTA

COOKING SHOULD BE A CAREFULLY BALANCED REFLECTION OF ALL THE GOOD THINGS OF THE EARTH.

—Jean (1926–1983) and Pierre (1928–) Troisgros, French chefs

AFTER STUDYING THIS CHAPTER, YOU WILL BE ABLE TO:

- identify a variety of potatoes
- apply various cooking methods to potatoes
- identify a variety of grains
- apply various cooking methods to grains
- identify pasta products
- make fresh pasta
- cook pasta

Potatoes, grains (corn, rice, wheat and others) and pastas are collectively known as starches. Some of these foods are vegetables; others are grasses. Pastas, of course, are prepared products made from grains. Starches are, for the most part, staple foods: foods that define a cuisine and give it substance. All are high in starchy carbohydrates, low in fat and commonly used as part of a well-balanced meal.

Today's chefs are rediscovering traditional and ethnic dishes that rely on grains seldom used in typical American food service operations. Pasta, made from a variety of grains in numerous shapes and flavors and accompanied by countless sauces and garnishes, now regularly appears on many menus alongside the ubiquitous potato prepared for many classic and modern dishes.

▶ POTATOES

Potatoes (Fr. *pommes de terre*) are one of the few vegetables native to the New World, probably originating in the South American Andes. Botanically, potatoes are succulent, nonwoody annual plants. The portion consumed is the tuber, the swollen fleshy part of the underground stem. Potatoes are hardy and easy to grow, making them inexpensive and widely available. Americans eat nearly 50 pounds of potatoes annually, making potatoes one of the top 20 vegetables in the United States.

IDENTIFYING POTATOES

Discussed here are some of the more commonly used types of potatoes. Other varieties are regularly being developed or rediscovered and tested in the market place.

Choose potatoes that are heavy and very firm with clean skin and few eyes. Avoid those with many eyes, sprouts, green streaks, soft spots, cracks or cut edges. Most varieties are available all year. When ordering potatoes, note that size A is larger than size B, which must be between 1½ and 2¼ inches (3.75 and 5.5 centimeters) in diameter.

New potatoes are small, immature potatoes (of any variety) that are harvested before their starches develop. Although red potatoes can be "new," not all new potatoes are necessarily red-skinned. Conversely, not all red-skinned potatoes are new. True new potatoes are waxy with a high moisture content and a thin, delicate skin.

FINGERLINGS

Fingerlings

Fingerling potatoes are typically heirloom varieties, related to the original potato varieties from the Andes. They are generally small, long and finger-shaped or oblong with good flavor. The Russian Banana looks like a small banana and has a firm texture and rich, buttery flavor. The red-streaked French Fingerling has a nutty flavor while the red Ruby Crescent has a strong, earthy flavor. All fingerling varieties tend to be low in starch and are good for roasting and in potato salads.

PURPLE POTATOES

Purple (or blue) potatoes have a deep purple skin. The flesh is bright purple, becoming lighter when cooked. They are mealy, with a flavor and texture similar to russets. The most common varieties are All Blue and Caribe, which were also quite popular in the mid-19th century.

Purple Potatoes

RED POTATOES

Red potatoes have a thin red skin and crisp, white, waxy flesh, best suited to boiling or steaming. They do not have the dry, mealy texture that successful baking requires. Red potatoes are round, instead of long or oblong; popular varieties are Red Pontiac and Norland.

Red Potatoes

RUSSET (BURBANK) POTATOES

Russet potatoes, commonly referred to as Idaho potatoes, are the standard baking potato. They are long with rough, reddish-brown skin and mealy flesh. Russets are excellent baked and are the best potatoes for frying. They tend to fall apart when boiled. They are marketed in several size categories and should be purchased in the size most appropriate for their intended use.

Russet Potatoes

WHITE POTATOES

White potatoes are available in round or long varieties. They have a thin, tender skin with a tender, waxy yellow or white flesh. Round white potatoes are also referred to as chef or all-purpose potatoes. White potatoes are usually cooked with moist heat or used for sautéing. White Rose and Finnish Yellow (or Yellow Finn) are popular varieties.

Another variety of white potato known as the **Yukon Gold** is a medium-sized, slightly flattened, oval potato. They have a delicate pale yellow skin with shallow pink eyes. Their pale yellow flesh has a creamy texture and rich, buttery, nutty flavor. Yukon Gold potatoes are suitable for most cooking methods and will retain their yellow color when baked, boiled or fried. First bred by botanists in Canada, Yukon Golds are now grown throughout the United States. Other lesser-known gold-fleshed varieties include Michigold, Donna, Delta Gold, Banana and Saginaw Gold.

White Potatoes

Yukon Gold Potatoes

SWEET POTATOES

Sweet potatoes are from a different botanical family than ordinary potatoes, although they are also tubers that originated in the New World. Two types are commonly available. One has yellow flesh and a dry, mealy texture; it is known as a boniato, white or Cuban sweet potato. The other has a darker orange, moister flesh and is high in sugar; it is known as a red sweet potato. Both types have thick skins ranging in color from light tan to brownish red. (Sometimes dark-skinned sweet potatoes are erroneously labeled yams.) Sweet potatoes should be chosen according to the desired degree of sweetness. They are best suited for boiling, baking and puréeing, although the less sweet varieties can be deep-fried. The cooked flesh can also be used in breads, pies and puddings. Sweet potatoes are available canned, often in a spiced or sugary sauce.

Sweet Potatoes

YAMS

Yams are a third type of tuber, botanically different from both sweet and common potatoes. Yams are less sweet than sweet potatoes, but they can be used interchangeably. The flesh of yams ranges from creamy white to deep red. Yams are Asian in origin and are now found in Africa, South America and the southern United States.

Red Yams

NUTRITION

Potatoes contain a high percentage of easily digested complex carbohydrates and little or no fat. They are also a good source for minerals and vitamins, especially vitamin B_6, vitamin C and potassium, although much of the vitamin C can be destroyed when potatoes are cooked in liquid such as for boiled or mashed potatoes.

PURCHASING AND STORING POTATOES

MEALY VERSUS WAXY

One of the most important considerations in selecting potatoes is choosing between the mealy and waxy varieties. It is important to understand the differences and purchase the type of potatoes best suited to the type of dish being prepared. A comparison of mealy and waxy potatoes and their uses is presented in Table 21.1.

Mealy potatoes (also known as starchy potatoes) have a high starch content and thick skin. They are best for baking and are often ordered from suppliers simply as "bakers." Their low sugar content also allows them to be deep-fried long enough to fully cook the interior without burning the exterior. Mealy potatoes tend to fall apart when boiled, making them a good choice for whipped or puréed potatoes.

Waxy potatoes have a low starch content and thin skin. They are best for boiling. They will not develop the desired fluffy texture when baked. They tend to become limp and soggy when deep-fried because of their high moisture content.

GRADING

Like other vegetables, potatoes are subject to the voluntary USDA grading system. Although U.S. Fancy is the highest grade, most potatoes sold on the wholesale market are U.S. No. 1. Potatoes sold on the retail market can also be graded as either U.S. Grade A or U.S. Grade B.

PURCHASING

Potatoes are usually packed in 50-pound cartons. Counts vary depending on average potato size. For example, in a 100-count carton, each potato would weigh an average of 8 ounces. Eighty-, 90- and 100-count cartons are the most common. Generally, larger-sized potatoes (that is, smaller counts) are more expensive. Size does not affect quality, however, so the size selected should be determined by intended use.

Table 21.1 COMPARISON OF MEALY AND WAXY POTATOES

	CONTENT OF:			BEST TO:			
	STARCH	MOISTURE	SUGAR	BAKE	BOIL	SAUTÉ	DEEP-FRY
Mealy: russet, white rose, purple	high	low	low	✓			✓
Waxy: red, new (red), Finnish yellow	low	high	high		✓	✓	

STORING

Temperatures between 50°F and 65°F (10°C and 18°C) are best for storing potatoes. Do not store potatoes in the refrigerator. At temperatures below 40°F (4°C), potato starch turns to sugar, making the cooked product too sweet and increasing the risk that the potato will turn gray or streaky when cooked. Potatoes with a high sugar content also burn more easily when fried.

Potatoes should be stored in a dark room, as light promotes chlorophyll production, turning them green and bitter. A green patch indicates the possible presence of solanine, a toxin harmful if eaten in large amounts, and should be peeled away. Solanine is also present in the eyes and sprouts, and they, too, should be removed and discarded before cooking.

Under proper conditions, fresh baking or general-purpose potatoes should last for two months; new potatoes will keep for several weeks. Do not wash potatoes until ready to use, as washing promotes spoilage.

Once peeled, potatoes should be stored covered in water and refrigerated to prevent enzymatic browning.

APPLYING VARIOUS COOKING METHODS

Potatoes have a relatively neutral flavor, making them a perfect accompaniment to many savory dishes. They can be prepared with almost any dry- or moist-heat cooking method: baking, sautéing, pan-frying, deep-frying, boiling or steaming. They can be combined with other ingredients in braises and stews. Potatoes are used in soups (vichyssoise), dumplings (gnocchi), breads, pancakes (latkes), puddings, salads and even vodka.

Many potato dishes, both classic and modern, employ more than one cooking method. For example, lorette potatoes require boiling and deep-frying; hash browns require parboiling, then sautéing. Even French fries are best when first blanched in hot oil before final deep frying.

DETERMINING DONENESS

Most potatoes are considered done when they are soft and tender or offer little resistance when pierced with a knife tip. Fried potatoes should have a crisp, golden-brown surface; the interior should be moist and tender.

ROASTING AND BAKING

Potatoes are often roasted with meat or poultry, becoming coated with the fat and drippings released from the main item as it cooks. Either mealy or waxy potatoes, peeled or unpeeled, can be roasted successfully.

Mealy potatoes such as russets are ideal for baking. The skin is left intact, although it may be pierced with a fork to allow steam to escape. A true baked potato should not be wrapped in foil or cooked in a microwave; this changes the cooking method to steaming and prevents a crisp skin from forming. A properly baked potato should be white and fluffy, not yellowish or soggy. Once baked, potatoes can be eaten plain (or with butter, sour cream and other garnishes) or used in other recipes.

SAFETY ALERT

Cooked potato dishes, especially those with cream, butter or custard, are potentially hazardous foods. They must be held for service at 135°F (57°C) or higher. Be sure to reheat potato dishes to 165°F (74°C) or higher.

▶ PROCEDURE FOR BAKING POTATOES

1. Scrub the potatoes well.
2. Using a fork, pierce the potato skins.
3. Rub the potatoes with oil and salt if desired. Do not wrap them in foil.
4. Bake the potatoes until done. A paring knife should penetrate them easily.

RECIPE 21.1

BAKED POTATOES

1 Piercing the potatoes.

2 Seasoning the potatoes with salt.

Yield: 8 Servings **Method:** Baking

Russet potatoes	8	8
Vegetable oil	3 Tbsp.	45 ml
Kosher salt	3 Tbsp.	45 ml

1 Scrub the potatoes well, but do not peel them. Pierce the skin of each potato to allow steam to escape.

2 Rub the potatoes with oil, then sprinkle with salt.

3 Place the potatoes on a rack over a sheet pan. Bake in a 400°F (200°C) oven until done, approximately 1 hour. The potatoes should yield to gentle pressure, and a paring knife inserted in the thickest part should meet little resistance.

4 Hold uncovered in a warm spot and serve within 1 hour.

VARIATION:

Twice-Baked Potatoes (Yield: 16 Servings)—Cut baked potatoes in half lengthwise. Carefully scoop out the flesh, leaving the skins intact. Whip the potato flesh with 8 ounces (240 grams) sour cream, 2 ounces (60 grams) butter and 2 ounces (60 grams) cooked, crumbled bacon and then add salt and pepper to taste. Thin with hot milk if necessary. The mixture should be light and fluffy, not lumpy. Pile the filling back into the skins, mounding the tops. Brush the mounded potatoes with clarified butter and sprinkle with Parmesan. Arrange on a sheet pan and bake at 425°F (220°C) until thoroughly reheated and lightly browned.

Approximate values per 7.5-oz. (225-g) potato: **Calories** 270, **Total fat** 5 g, **Saturated fat** 0.5 g, **Cholesterol** 0 mg, **Sodium** 2630 mg, **Total carbohydrates** 51 g, **Protein** 5 g, **Vitamin C** 45%, **Claims**—low saturated fat; no cholesterol; good source of fiber

Baking en Casserole

Many classic potato dishes require baking either raw or parboiled potatoes with sauce, cheese, meat or other seasonings in a baking dish or casserole. Well-known examples include scalloped potatoes, which are baked in béchamel sauce, and potatoes au gratin, which are topped with cheese and baked. These dishes usually develop a crisp, brown crust, which is part of their appeal.

The casserole should hold its shape when cut; the potatoes should be tender, and the sauce should be smooth, not grainy.

Potato casseroles can be fully baked, then held loosely covered in a steam table for service. Portions can be reheated or browned briefly under a broiler or salamander at service time.

▶ PROCEDURE FOR BAKING POTATOES EN CASSEROLE

1 Prepare the potatoes by washing, peeling, slicing or partially cooking as desired or as directed in the recipe.

2 Add the potatoes to the baking pan in layers, alternating with the sauce, cream, cheese or other ingredients. Or combine the potatoes with the other ingredients and place in a buttered baking pan.

3 Bake the potatoes until done.

GRATIN DAUPHINOISE

RECIPE 21.2

Yield: 4–5 lb. (1.8–2.2 kg) **Method:** Baking en casserole

Russet potatoes	3 lb.	1.3 kg
Whole butter	as needed	as needed
Salt and white pepper	TT	TT
Nutmeg	1/4 tsp.	2 ml
Gruyère, grated	8 oz.	240 g
Half-and-half	24 fl. oz.	720 ml
Egg yolks	3	3

1 Peel the potatoes and cut into very thin slices.
2 Place a single layer of potatoes in a well-buttered, full-size hotel pan.
3 Season with salt, white pepper and a small amount of nutmeg. Sprinkle on a thin layer of cheese.
4 Add another layer of potatoes, seasonings and cheese and repeat until all the potatoes and about three-fourths of the cheese are used.
5 Heat the half-and-half to a simmer. Whisk the egg yolks together in a bowl, then gradually add the hot half-and-half.
6 Pour the cream-and-egg mixture over the potatoes. Top with the remaining cheese.
7 Bake uncovered at 350°F (180°C) until the potatoes are tender and golden brown, approximately 50 to 60 minutes.

Approximate values per 4-oz. (120-g) serving: **Calories** 160, **Total fat** 8 g, **Saturated fat** 5 g, **Cholesterol** 55 mg, **Sodium** 160 mg, **Total carbohydrates** 15 g, **Protein** 6 g, **Vitamin C** 15%, **Calcium** 15%

Mise en Place

▶ Grate Gruyère cheese.

1 Layering gratin potatoes.

2 The finished gratin potatoes.

SAUTÉING AND PAN-FRYING

Waxy potatoes, such as red- and white-skinned varieties, are best for sautéing or pan-frying. Often they are first parboiled or even fully cooked—a convenient way to use leftover boiled potatoes. They are then cooked in fat following the general procedures for sautéing and pan-frying discussed in Chapter 8, Principles of Cooking.

The fat can be clarified butter, oil, bacon fat or lard, depending on the desired flavor of the finished dish. The fat must be hot before the potatoes are added so that they will develop a crust without absorbing too much fat. Sautéed potatoes should have a crisp, well-browned crust and tender interior. They should be neither soggy nor greasy.

Potatoes can be sautéed or pan-fried by two methods: tossing and still-frying. The **tossing method** is used to cook relatively small pieces of potatoes in a small amount of fat. The potatoes are tossed using the pan's sloped sides so that they brown evenly on all sides. The **still-frying method** is used to create a disc-shaped potato product. The shredded or sliced potatoes are added to the pan, usually covering its bottom, and allowed to cook without stirring or flipping until they are well browned on the first side. The entire mass is then turned and cooked on the second side. When the potatoes are done, they can be cut into wedges for service.

▶ PROCEDURE FOR SAUTÉING AND PAN-FRYING POTATOES

1 Wash, trim, peel, cut and/or cook the potatoes as desired or as directed in the recipe.
2 Heat the pan, add the fat and heat the fat. Add the potatoes to the hot fat. Do not overcrowd the pan. Use enough fat to prevent the potatoes from sticking to the pan. Depending on the recipe, use either the tossing method or the still-frying method.
3 Add garnishes, seasonings and other ingredients as desired or as directed in the recipe.
4 Cook the potatoes until done.

RECIPE 21.3

LYONNAISE POTATOES

Mise en Place

▶ Peel and julienne onions.

Yield: 8 Servings, 4 oz. (120 g) each **Method:** Sautéing

Potatoes, waxy	2 lb.	1 kg
Onions, sliced thinly	8 oz.	240 g
Clarified butter	4 fl. oz.	120 ml
Salt and pepper	TT	TT

1 Partially cook the potatoes by baking, boiling or steaming. Allow them to cool.
2 Peel the potatoes and cut into 1/4-inch- (1/2-centimeter-) thick slices.
3 Sauté the onions in half of the butter until tender but not brown. Remove the onions from the pan with a slotted spoon and set aside.
4 Add the remaining butter to the pan. Add the potatoes and sauté, tossing as needed, until well browned on all sides.
5 Return the onions to the pan and sauté to combine the flavors. Season to taste with salt and pepper.

Approximate values per 4-oz. (120-g) serving: **Calories** 170, **Total fat** 12 g, **Saturated fat** 7 g, **Cholesterol** 30 mg, **Sodium** 650 mg, **Total carbohydrates** 16 g, **Protein** 1 g, **Vitamin A** 10%

DEEP-FRYING

Potato chips and French fries (Fr. *pomme frites*) are extremely popular in a variety of shapes, sizes and seasonings. Although a wide range of shapes, sizes and preseasoned frozen products are available, fresh fried potatoes can be a delicious, economical menu item.

Top-quality russet potatoes are recommended for deep-frying. The peel may be removed or left attached. If peeled, the potatoes should be soaked in clear, cold water until ready to cut and cook. This keeps them crisp and white by leaching some of the starch that might otherwise make the potatoes gummy or cause smaller cuts to stick together when cooked.

Deep-fried potatoes are usually blanched in oil ranging in temperature from 250°F to 300°F (120°C to 150°C) until tender and translucent. They are then drained and held for service, at which time they are finished in hotter oil, usually at a temperature between 350°F and 375°F (180°C and 190°C).

Deep-frying is also used to finish cooking several classic potato dishes such as croquettes and dauphine, in which fully cooked potatoes are puréed, seasoned, shaped and fried.

Deep-fried potatoes should be drained on absorbent paper briefly and served immediately.

▶ PROCEDURE FOR DEEP-FRYING POTATOES

1. Wash, peel or trim the potatoes as desired.
2. Cut the potatoes into uniform-sized pieces.
3. Using the basket method, blanch the potatoes in deep fat at 250°F (121°C) for 2 to 3 minutes, depending on the size of the pieces.
4. Drain the potatoes and spread them out in a single layer on a baking sheet or in a hotel pan.
5. Just before service, submerge the potatoes in deep fat at 350°F–375°F (177°C–191°C), using the basket method.
6. Cook until golden brown. Remove from the fat, drain, salt to taste and serve immediately.

DEEP-FRIED POTATOES

RECIPE 21.4

RUTH'S CHRIS STEAK HOUSE, PHOENIX, AZ

Yield: Varies **Method:** Deep-frying

Mealy potatoes, such as Idaho 70 count	as needed	as needed
Hot fat	as needed	as needed
Salt and pepper	TT	TT
Parsley, chopped	as needed for garnish	

1. Peel if necessary, then cut each potato into the desired shape; for example:
   Cottage fries—circles 1/4 inch (6 millimeters) thick
   Shoestring potatoes—long juliennes (allumettes)
   French fries—sticks 3/8 inch × 3/8 inch × 3 inches (1 centimeter × 1 centimeter × 7 centimeters)
   Steak fries—four large wedges
2. Using the basket method, deep-fry the potatoes in 250°F (120°C) fat until lightly browned, approximately 2 to 3 minutes. Remove and drain. Hold the partially cooked potatoes in a single layer on a baking sheet or in a hotel pan.
3. For service, deep-fry the partially cooked potatoes in 350°F (180°C) fat until golden in color and done. Season to taste with salt and pepper.
4. Garnish with parsley if desired.

Approximate values per 1-oz. (30-g) serving: **Calories** 90, **Total fat** 4.5 g, **Saturated fat** 1.5 g, **Cholesterol** 0 mg, **Sodium** 60 mg, **Total carbohydrates** 11 g, **Protein** 1 g

Mise en Place

▶ Wash and chop parsley.

Cottage Fries

Shoestring Potatoes

French Fries

Steak Fries

MORE THAN A FRENCH FRY

Thanks to the genius of Carême, Escoffier and others, few vegetables have as extensive a classic repertoire as potatoes. Some of these dishes begin with the duchesse (duh-SHEES) potatoes mixture; in this regard, duchesse potatoes can be considered the mother of many classic potato preparations. For example,

Duchesse + Tomato concassée = *Marquis*

Duchesse + Chopped truffles + Almond coating + Deep-frying = *Berny*

Duchesse + Shaping + Breading + Deep-frying = *Croquettes*

Duchesse + Pâte à choux = *Dauphine*

Dauphine + Grated Parmesan + Piped shape + Deep-frying = *Lorette*

Other classic potato preparations not based on duchesse potatoes include the following:

Anna—Thin potato slices are arranged in several circular layers in a round pan coated with clarified butter; additional butter is brushed on, and the potatoes are baked until crisp, then cut into wedges for service.

Boulangère—Onions and potatoes are sautéed in butter, then transferred to a baking pan or added to a partially cooked roast in a roasting pan; stock is added, and the potatoes are cooked uncovered until done.

Château—Tournéed potatoes are sautéed in clarified butter until golden and tender.

Parisienne—Small spheres are cut from raw, peeled potatoes with a Parisienne scoop; they are seasoned and sautéed in clarified butter, then tossed with a meat glaze and garnished with chopped parsley.

Rösti—Potatoes are shredded, seasoned and pan-fried in the shape of a pie, then cut into wedges for service.

BOILING

Waxy potatoes are best for all moist-heat cooking methods. Boiled potatoes (which are actually simmered) may be served as is or used in multistep preparations such as purées, salads, soups and baked casseroles. Potatoes are usually boiled in water, although stock may be used or milk added for flavor. Always begin cooking potatoes in cold liquid to ensure even cooking. Unlike other vegetables, potatoes should not be refreshed in cold water; it makes them soggy.

▶ PROCEDURE FOR BOILING POTATOES

1. Wash, peel or trim the potatoes as desired.
2. Cut the potatoes into uniform-sized pieces to promote even cooking. The pieces should not be too small, or they will absorb a large amount of water as they cook, making the final product soggy.
3. Add the potatoes to enough cool liquid to cover them by several inches. Bring to a boil, reduce to a simmer and cook until done. If a slightly firm finished product is desired, remove and drain the potatoes when they are slightly underdone and allow carryover cooking to finish cooking them.
4. Drain the potatoes in a colander and serve or use for further preparation.

RECIPE 21.5

MASHED POTATOES

Mise en Place

▶ Melt butter and heat milk while potatoes are cooking.

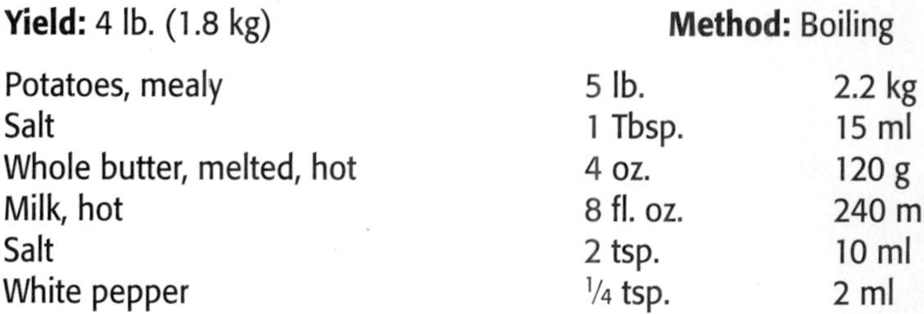

Yield: 4 lb. (1.8 kg) **Method:** Boiling

Potatoes, mealy	5 lb.	2.2 kg
Salt	1 Tbsp.	15 ml
Whole butter, melted, hot	4 oz.	120 g
Milk, hot	8 fl. oz.	240 ml
Salt	2 tsp.	10 ml
White pepper	1/4 tsp.	2 ml

1 Wash and peel the potatoes. Cut each potato into four to six uniform-sized pieces.

2 Place the potatoes in a pot, cover them with water and add 1 tablespoon (15 milliliters) salt to the water. Bring the water to a boil, reduce to a simmer and cook until the potatoes are tender. Do not overcook the potatoes.

3 When the potatoes are cooked, drain them well in a colander. The potatoes must be very dry. Transfer them to the bowl of an electric mixer. Using the whip attachment, whip the potatoes for 30 to 45 seconds. Scrape the sides and bottom of the bowl and whip for another 15 seconds or until the potatoes are smooth and free of lumps. The potatoes must be smooth before adding any liquids or they will remain lumpy.

4 Add the butter, milk and seasonings. Whip on low speed to incorporate all of the ingredients. Scrape the sides and bottom of the bowl and whip again for several seconds. Adjust consistency and seasoning.

VARIATIONS:

Garlic Mashed Potatoes—Sweat 1 ounce (30 grams) chopped garlic in the melted butter for 5 to 10 minutes without browning. Strain the butter if desired. Add the hot garlic butter in place of the melted butter in the recipe.

Horseradish Mashed Potatoes—Add 1 ounce (30 grams) freshly grated horseradish to the potatoes with the seasonings.

Approximate values per 4-oz. (120-g) serving: **Calories** 190, **Total fat** 7 g, **Saturated fat** 4.5 g, **Cholesterol** 20 mg, **Sodium** 350 mg, **Total carbohydrates** 29 g, **Protein** 3 g, **Vitamin C** 20%

1 Adding water to the uniformly cut potatoes.

2 Checking the consistency of the mashed potatoes.

▶ GRAINS

Botanically, grains are grasses that bear edible seeds. Corn, rice and wheat are the most significant. Both the fruit (that is, the seed or kernel) and the plant are called a grain.

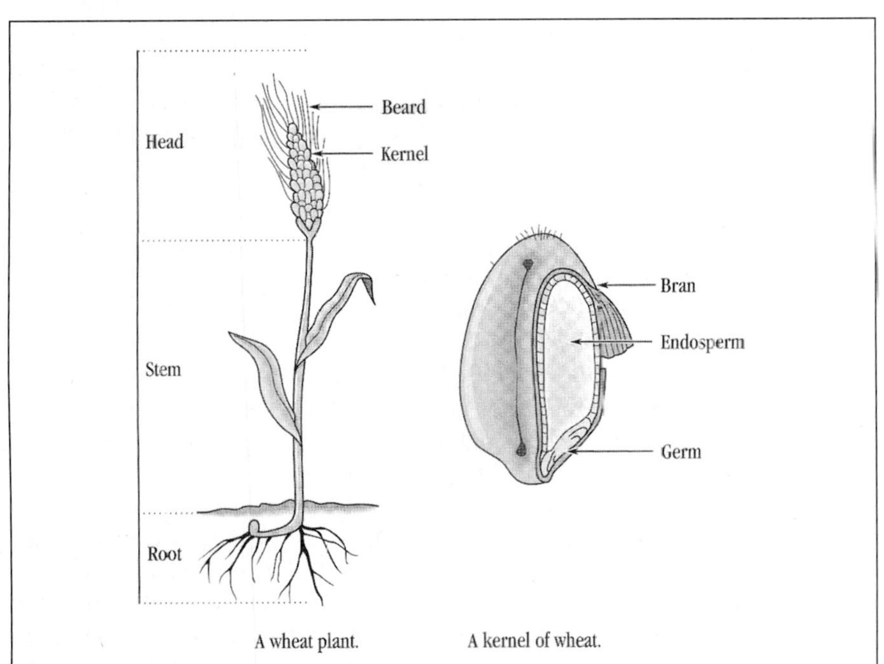

FIGURE 21.1 ▶ Wheat

Most grain kernels are protected by a **hull** or husk. All kernels are composed of three distinct parts: the **bran, endosperm** and **germ.** (See Figure 21.1.) The bran is the tough outer layer covering the endosperm. Bran is a good source of fiber and B-complex vitamins. The endosperm is the largest part of the kernel and is a source of protein and carbohydrates (starch). It is the part used primarily in milled products such as flour. The germ is the smallest portion of the grain and is the only part that contains fat. It is also rich in thiamin. The bran, endosperm and germ can be separated by milling.

▶ **cracking** a milling process in which grains are broken open

▶ **grinding** a milling process in which grains are reduced to a powder; the powder can be of differing degrees of fineness or coarseness

▶ **hulling** a milling process in which the hull or husk is removed from grains

▶ **pearling** a milling process in which all or part of the hull, bran and germ are removed from grains

IDENTIFYING GRAINS

This section presents information on corn, rice and wheat as well as several minor grains that are nutritionally significant and gaining popularity.

Some products are available in a stone-ground form. This means that the grains were ground with a stone mill rather than by the steel blades typically used for **cracking, grinding, hulling** and **pearling.** Stone grinders are gentler and more precise, so they are less likely to overgrind the grain. Stone-ground products will always be labeled as such and are usually more expensive than steel-ground ones.

CORN

Corn (Sp. *maíz;* It. *granturco*) is the only grain that is also eaten fresh as a vegetable. (Fresh corn is discussed in Chapter 20, Vegetables.) Its use as a dried grain dates back several thousand years in Central America and long preceded its use as a vegetable.

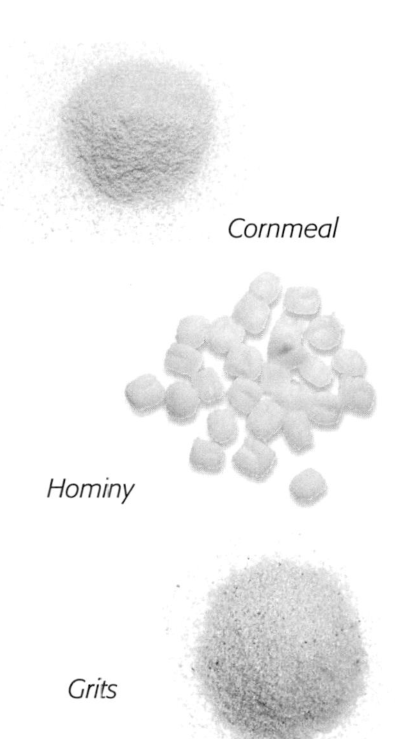
Cornmeal
Hominy
Grits

Cornmeal

Cornmeal is made by drying and grinding a special type of corn known as dent, which may be yellow, white or blue. Cornmeal is most often used in breads, as a coating for fried foods or cooked as polenta or mush. Products made with cornmeal have a gritty texture and a sweet but starchy flavor.

Hominy

Hominy, also known as posole or samp, is dried corn that has been soaked in hydrated lime or lye. This causes the kernels to swell, loosening the hulls. The hulls and germs are removed and the kernels dried. These white or yellow kernels resemble popcorn, but with a soft, chewy texture and smoky-sour flavor. Hominy is available dried or cooked and canned. It may be served as a side dish or used in stews or soups. **Masa harina,** a finely ground flour made from dried hominy, is used for making breads, tortillas, tamales and other Mexican and southwestern dishes.

Grits

Grits are traditionally made by grinding dried hominy. These tiny white granules may be used in baked dishes but are most often served as a hot breakfast cereal, usually topped with butter or cheese. Quick-cooking and instant grits are available.

RICE

Rice (Fr. *riz;* It. *riso;* Sp. *arroz*) is the starchy seed of a semiaquatic grass. Probably originating on the Indian subcontinent or in Southeast Asia, rice is used as a staple by more than half the world's population.

Rice can be incorporated into almost any cuisine, from Asian to Spanish to classic French. Its flavor adapts to the foods and seasonings with which the rice is cooked or served. Its texture adds an appealing chewiness to meat and poultry dishes, salads, breads and puddings. Rice is not limited to a side dish, but may be used in stews or curries; for stuffing vegetables or game birds; and in puddings, salads, beverages (such as Mexican horchata) and breads.

Rice is divided into three types based on seed size: **long-grain, medium-grain** and **short-grain.** Long-grain rice is the most versatile and popular worldwide. The grains remain firm, fluffy and separate when cooked. (Long-grain rice can, however, become sticky if overcooked or stirred frequently during cooking.) Short-grain rice has more starch and becomes quite tender and sticky when cooked. Italian risotto, Japanese sushi and Spanish paella are all traditionally made with short-grain rice. The appearance and starch content of medium-grain rice falls somewhere in between. Medium-grain rice becomes sticky when cool, so it is best eaten freshly made and piping hot.

Converted Rice

Long-grain, medium-grain and short-grain rice are available in different processed forms. All rice is originally brown. The grains can be left whole, with the bran attached, for **brown rice.** Or they can be pearled for the more familiar polished **white rice.** Both brown rice and white rice can be processed into converted rice and instant rice.

Converted rice is parboiled to remove the surface starch. This procedure also forces nutrients from the bran into the grain's endosperm. Therefore, converted rice retains more nutrients than regular milled white rice, although the flavor is the same. Converted rice is neither precooked nor instant; in fact, it cooks more slowly than regular milled white rice.

Instant or **quick-cooking rice** is widely available and useful if time is a concern. Instant rice is created by fully cooking and then flash-freezing milled rice. Unfortunately, this processing removes some of the nutrients and flavor.

Arborio Rice

Arborio Rice

Arborio is a round, short-grain rice used primarily in Italian dishes such as risotto. It is very sticky, with a white color and mild flavor.

Basmati Rice

Basmati is one of the finest long-grain rices in the world. It grows in the Himalayan foothills and is preferred in Indian cuisine. It is highly aromatic, with a sweet, delicate flavor and a creamy yellow color. Basmati rice is usually aged to improve its aromatic qualities and should be washed well before cooking. **Jasmine rice** is another aromatic long-grain rice. Similar to basmati, it is grown in Thailand and used throughout Southeast Asia.

Basmati Rice

Brown Rice

Brown Rice

Brown rice is the whole natural grain of rice. Only the husk has been removed. Brown rice has a nutty flavor; its chewy texture is caused by the high-fiber bran. Brown rice absorbs more water and takes longer to cook than white rice.

Sticky Rice

Sticky rice is a short-grain rice used in many Asian cuisines. The short grains are fat and round with a high starch content and a pearly white color. When cooked, the grains tend to clump together, forming a sticky mass. Sticky rice must be soaked for several hours before being cooked. Also known as glutinous rice or sweet rice, it can be ground into flour and used for dumplings and pastries. Japanese sake and mirin and Chinese shaoxing are made from fermented sticky rice, as is rice vinegar.

Wild Rice

Wild Rice

Wild rice is prepared in the same manner as traditional rice, although it is actually the seed of an unrelated reedlike aquatic plant. Wild rice has long, slender grains with a dark brown to black color. It has a nuttier flavor and chewier texture than traditional rice. Three grades are available: giant (the best quality, with very long grains); fancy (a medium-sized grain, suitable for most purposes); and select (a short grain, suitable for soups, pancakes or baked goods). Cultivated in California, Idaho and Washington, it is generally served with game, used as a

Table 21.2 **GUIDELINES FOR COOKING RICE**

TYPE OF RICE	RATIO RICE: WATER (BY VOLUME)	PREPARATION	COOKING TIME (SIMMERING)	YIELD FROM 1 CUP RAW RICE
Arborio	1:2.5–3	Do not rinse or soak	15–20 min.	2½–3 c. (560–675 ml)
Basmati	1:1.75	Rinse well; soak	15 min.	3 c. (675 ml)
Brown, long-grain	1:2.5	Do not rinse; may soak	45–50 min.	3–4 c. (675–900 ml)
Converted	1:2.5	Do not rinse	20–25 min.	3–4 c. (675–900 ml)
White, long-grain (regular milled)	1:2	Do not rinse	15 min.	3 c. (675 ml)
Wild	1:3	Rinse	35–60 min., depending on grade	3–4 c. (675–900 ml)

Wild Pecan Rice

stuffing for poultry or combined with regular rice for a side dish. Wild rice is expensive, but small quantities are usually sufficient.

Wild Pecan Rice

Wild pecan rice is neither wild nor made with pecans. It is a unique long-grain rice grown only in the bayou country of southern Louisiana. Wild pecan rice has a nutty flavor and exceptionally rich aroma.

Guidelines for Cooking Rice

Rice may be rinsed before cooking to remove dirt and debris, but doing so also removes some of its nutrients. It is not necessary to rinse most American-grown rice, which is generally clean and free of insects. Rice may also be soaked before cooking. Soaking softens the grains, removes some starch and speeds cooking.

The standard ratio for cooking rice is two parts liquid to one part rice. The actual ratio varies, however, depending on the type of rice. Guidelines for cooking rice are found in Table 21.2.

SAFETY ALERT

Once cooked, rice is highly perishable. Because of its neutral pH and high protein content, cooked rice is a potentially hazardous food. To avoid the risk of food-borne illnesses, be sure to hold hot rice at 135°F (57°C) or higher. Leftover rice must be quickly cooled and stored at 41°F (5°C) or below. Leftover rice must be reheated to 165°F (74°C) or higher.

WHEAT

Wheat (Fr. *blé*) is most often milled into the wide range of flours. But wheat and products derived from it are also used as starchy side dishes or ingredients in soups, salads, ground meat dishes and breads. These products include cracked wheat, bulgur and couscous. When cooked, they are slightly chewy with a mild flavor. All should be fluffy; none should be soggy or sticky.

Wheat germ and **wheat bran** are widely available and highly touted for their nutritional values. Bran and germ are not generally used plain, but may be added to bread or other cooked dishes.

Cracked Wheat

Cracked wheat is the whole wheat kernel (known as a **berry**) broken into varying degrees of coarseness. It is not precooked, and the kernel's white interior should be visible. The bran and germ are still intact, so cracked wheat has a great deal of fiber but a short shelf life. Whole wheat berries must be soaked for several hours before cooking. Cracked wheat can be fully cooked by long, gentle simmering.

Bulgur

Bulgur

Bulgur is a wheat berry that has had the bran removed; it is then steam-cooked, dried and ground into varying degrees of coarseness. Bulgur has a nutlike flavor and texture; it is a uniform golden-brown color (uncooked cracked wheat is not) and requires less cooking time than cracked wheat.

Generally, cracked wheat and bulgur cannot be substituted for one another in recipes.

Bulgur needs only to be soaked in water, then drained, for use in salads, or briefly cooked when used in stews or pilafs. Bulgur is good with grilled meats and as an alternative to rice in stuffings and other dishes. The fine grind is most often used in packaged mixes such as tabouli; the medium grind is most often available in bulk.

Couscous

Couscous is made by removing the bran and germ from **durum wheat** berries. The endosperm is then steamed, pressed to form tiny pellets and dried. Couscous is available in varying degrees of coarseness; medium-fine is the most popular. Couscous is prepared by steaming over water or stock in a pot called a couscousière. Couscous, traditionally served with North African stews, can be used or served like rice.

Couscous

▶ **durum wheat** a species of very hard wheat with a particularly high amount of protein; it is used to make couscous or milled into semolina, which is used for making pasta

OTHER GRAINS

Barley

Barley is one of the oldest culinary grains, used by humans since prehistoric times. Barley is extremely hardy, growing in climates from the tropics to the near-Arctic. Although much of the barley crop is used to make beer or feed animals, some does find its way into soups, stews and stuffings. The most common type is pearled to produce a small, round white nugget of endosperm. It has a sweet, earthy flavor similar to oats, and goes well with onions, garlic and strong herbs. Barley's texture ranges from chewy to soft, depending on the amount of water in which it is cooked. Its starchiness can be used to thicken soups or stews.

Barley

Buckwheat/Kasha

Buckwheat is not a type of wheat; it is not even a grain. Rather, it is the fruit of a plant distantly related to rhubarb. Buckwheat is included here, however, because it is prepared and served in the same manner as grains.

The whole buckwheat kernel is known as a **groat.** The product most often sold as buckwheat is actually kasha, which is a hulled, roasted buckwheat groat. Kasha is reddish brown with a strong, nutty, almost scorched flavor. It is available whole or ground to varying degrees of coarseness. Whole kasha remains in separate grains after cooking; the finer grinds become rather sticky. Kasha can be served as a side dish, usually combined with pasta or vegetables, or it can be chilled and used in salads.

Buckwheat/Kasha

Raw buckwheat groats are ground into flour typically used in pasta, blini and other pancakes. Buckwheat flour contains no gluten-forming proteins, and it tends to remain grainy, with a sandy texture. Therefore, it should not be substituted for all the wheat flour in breads or baked goods.

Millet

Millet is a high-protein cereal grain with a bland, slightly nutty flavor and a white color. Used principally as animal fodder in the United States, millet can be cooked and eaten like rice or toasted like buckwheat and cooked like kasha. It can also be ground for flour (when used for baking, it is best combined with wheat flour). Millet is usually sold hulled, as the husk is extremely hard.

Millet

ANCIENT GRAINS FOR MODERN TIMES

As an awareness of the nutritional benefits of eating whole grains grows, long-neglected grains are regaining popularity with chefs and consumers. Farro (*Triticum dicoccum*) is one of the oldest forms of wheat; it was a staple in the diet of ancient Roman armies. Farro is still eaten cooked as a whole grain in Tuscany, where it is prized for its chewy, nutty flavor. Spelt (*Triticum aestivum* var. *spelta*), a related subspecies of common wheat, is also prized for its taste and consistency. Farro must be soaked like beans before cooking, whereas spelt may be cooked without soaking. Treat these grains like barley. Use them to add texture to soups or cook them to add to salads and vegetable dishes.

Oats

Oats

After rice, oats are probably the most widely accepted whole-grain product in the American diet. Oats are consumed daily as a hot breakfast cereal (oatmeal) and are used in breads, muffins, cookies and other baked goods.

An oat groat is the whole oat kernel with only the husk removed. It contains both the bran and germ. *Steel-cut oats,* sometimes known as Irish oats, are groats that are toasted and then cut into small pieces with steel blades. *Rolled oats,* marketed as "old-fashioned oats," are groats that have been steamed, then rolled into flat flakes. *Quick-cooking oats* are simply rolled oats cut into smaller pieces to reduce cooking time. *Instant oats* are partially cooked and dried before rolling so that they need only to be rehydrated in boiling water. Rolled oats and quick-cooking oats can be used interchangeably, but instant oats should not be substituted in most recipes.

Oat bran is the outer covering of a hulled oat. It is available as a separate product, although rolled and cut oats do contain some oat bran.

The term *oatmeal* is commonly used to refer to both processed groats and the cooked porridge made from them. The processed groats known as oatmeal are a gray-white color with a starchy texture and sweet flavor. They cook into the soft, thick porridge with a robust flavor called oatmeal.

Quinoa

Quinoa

Quinoa (keen-wa) is native to the South American Andes and was a common food of the Incas, who referred to it as the "mother grain." Although not botanically a true grain, quinoa's tiny seeds are treated as such. The grains (seeds) are small, flattened spheres, approximately 1⁄16 inch (1.5 millimeters) in diameter, ringed with the germ. They become translucent when cooked and have a slightly smoky or sesamelike flavor. Several varieties of quinoa are available, ranging in color from dark brown to almost white. The larger whiter varieties are most common and are considered superior.

Quinoa seeds have a natural, bitter-tasting coating, which protects them from birds and insects. Consequently, they should be placed in a fine-meshed colander and rinsed well with cool water for several minutes before use. Quinoa can then be cooked like rice, and will absorb about twice its volume of water. For a nuttier taste, toast the grain in a hot dry pan for about 5 minutes before adding the liquid. Quinoa can also be eaten as a hot breakfast cereal served in lieu of rice or used as a thickener for soups or stews and in salads, casseroles, breads and desserts. Quinoa flour, ground from whole seeds, has a delicate nutty flavor. A gluten-free product, it is suitable for anyone bothered by wheat allergies. Quinoa is marketed as the world's "supergrain" because the seeds form a complete protein (with all of the essential amino acids) and contain important vitamins and minerals as well as carbohydrates and fat. Quinoa should be kept in the refrigerator or freezer for long-term storage. The leaves of the quinoa plant are similar to spinach and can be eaten as a vegetable.

NUTRITION

Grains are an excellent source of vitamins, minerals, proteins and fiber. The amount of milling or refining and the method of preparation affect their nutritional values, however. Unrefined and less-refined grains are excellent sources of dietary fiber. Rice is also quite nutritious: It is low in sodium and calories and contains all the essential amino acids. Some grains, especially white rice and oats, are usually enriched with calcium, iron and B-complex vitamins.

PURCHASING AND STORING GRAINS

PURCHASING

When buying grains, look for fresh, plump ones with a bright, even color. Fresh grains should not be shriveled or crumbly; there should be no sour or musty odors.

Grains are sold by weight. They come in bags or boxes ranging from 1 to 100 pounds. Ten-, 25- and 50-pound units are usually available.

STORING

All grains should be stored in airtight containers placed in a dark, cool, dry place. Airtight containers prevent dust and insects from entering. Airtight containers and darkness also reduce nutrient loss caused by oxidation or light. Coolness inhibits insect infestation; dryness prevents mold.

Vacuum-sealed packages will last for extended periods. Whole grains, which contain the oily germ, can be refrigerated to prevent rancidity.

APPLYING VARIOUS COOKING METHODS

Three basic cooking methods are used to prepare grains: simmering, risotto and pilaf. Unlike simmered grains, those cooked by either the risotto or pilaf method are first coated with hot fat. The primary distinction between the pilaf and risotto methods is the manner in which the liquid is then added to the grains. See Figure 21.2. When grains are used in puddings, breads, stuffings and baked casseroles, they are almost always first fully cooked by one of these methods.

DETERMINING DONENESS

Most grains should be cooked until tender, although some recipes do require a chewier (al dente) product. Doneness can usually be determined by cooking time and the amount of liquid remaining in the pan. Some grains, such as wild rice, are fully cooked when they puff open.

In general, grains will be fully cooked when almost all the cooking liquid has been absorbed. This is indicated by the appearance of tunnel-like holes between the grains. Grains can be cooked until almost all of the liquid is absorbed, then removed from the heat and left to stand, covered, for 5 to 10 minutes. This allows the cooked grains to absorb the remaining moisture without burning.

SIMMERING

The most commonly used method for preparing grains is simmering. To do so, simply stir the grains into a measured amount of boiling salted water in a saucepan on the stove top. When the liquid returns to a boil, lower the heat, cover and simmer until the liquid is absorbed and the grains are tender. The grains are not stirred during cooking.

The grains can be flavored by using stock as the cooking liquid. Herbs and spices can also be added.

▶ PROCEDURE FOR SIMMERING GRAINS

1. Bring the cooking liquid to a boil.
2. Stir in the grains. Add herbs or spices as desired or as directed in the recipe.
3. Return the mixture to a boil, cover and reduce to a simmer.
4. Simmer the grains until tender and most of the liquid is absorbed.
5. Remove the grains from the heat.
6. Drain if appropriate or keep covered and allow the excess moisture to evaporate, approximately 5 minutes. Fluff the grains with a fork before service.

SIMMERING	=	Grain	→	Boiling liquid	→	Cover and simmer
RISOTTO	=	Sauté grain	→	Hot liquid added gradually	→	Stir constantly
PILAF	=	Sauté grain	→	All liquid added at once	→	Cover and simmer

FIGURE 21.2 ▶ Cooking Methods for Grains

RECIPE 21.6

SIMMERED RICE

Yield: 1 ½ pt. (750 ml) **Method:** Simmering

Water	1 pt.	500 ml
Salt	8 oz.	2 ml
White rice	8 oz.	250 ml

1 Bring the water and salt to a boil in a heavy saucepan. Slowly add the rice.
2 Cover the pan and reduce the heat so that the liquid simmers gently. Cook until the rice is tender and the water is absorbed, approximately 15 to 20 minutes.
3 Remove from the heat and transfer to a hotel pan. Do not cover. Allow any excess moisture to evaporate for approximately 5 minutes.
4 Fluff the rice and serve, or refrigerate for use in another recipe.

Approximate values per ½-c. (120-ml) serving: **Calories** 150, **Total fat** 0 g, **Saturated fat** 0 g, **Cholesterol** 0 mg, **Sodium** 192 mg, **Total carbohydrates** 34 g, **Protein** 3 g, **Iron** 8%, **Claims**—fat free; no sugar

RISOTTO METHOD

Risotto is a classic northern Italian rice dish in which the grains remain firm but merge with the cooking liquid to become a creamy, almost puddinglike dish. True risotto is made with a short-grain starchy rice such as Arborio, but the risotto method can also be used to cook other grains such as barley and oats.

The grains are not rinsed before cooking, as this removes the starches needed to achieve the desired consistency. The grains are coated, but not cooked, in a hot fat such as butter or oil. A hot liquid is then gradually added to the grains so that the mixture is kept at a constant simmer. The cooking liquid should be a rich, flavorful stock. Unlike simmering and the pilaf method, the risotto method requires frequent, sometimes constant, stirring.

When finished, the grains should be creamy and tender, but still al dente in the center. Grated cheese, heavy cream, cooked meat, poultry, fish, shellfish, herbs and vegetables can be added to create a flavorful side dish or a complete meal.

▶ PROCEDURE FOR PREPARING GRAINS BY THE RISOTTO METHOD

1 Bring the cooking liquid (usually a stock) to a simmer.
2 Heat the fat in a heavy saucepan over moderate heat. Add any onions, garlic or other flavoring ingredients and sauté for 1 to 2 minutes without browning.
3 Add the grains to the saucepan. Stir well to make sure the grains are well coated with fat. Do not allow the grains to brown.
4 Add any wine and cook until it is fully absorbed.
5 Begin to add the simmering stock, 4 fluid ounces (120 milliliters) at a time, stirring frequently. Wait until each portion of cooking liquid is almost fully absorbed before adding the next.
6 Test for doneness after the grains have cooked for approximately 18 to 20 minutes.
7 Remove from heat and stir in butter, grated cheese, herbs or other flavoring ingredients as directed. Garnish and serve immediately.

RISOTTO MILANESE

RECIPE 21.7

Yield: 24 Servings, 4 oz. (120 g) each **Method:** Risotto

Chicken stock	2½ qt.	2.5 lt
Saffron threads, crushed	½ tsp.	2 ml
Water, hot	2 fl. oz.	60 ml
Whole butter	4 oz.	120 g
Onions, minced	5 oz.	150 g
Arborio rice	1 lb. 8 oz.	720 g
Dry white wine	8 fl. oz.	250 ml
Parmesan, grated	4 oz.	120 g

1 Bring the stock to a simmer. Soak the saffron threads in 2 fluid ounces (60 milliliters) hot water.

2 Heat 3 ounces (90 grams) of the butter in a large, heavy saucepan. Add the onion and sauté until translucent.

3 Add the rice to the onion and butter. Stir well to coat the grains with butter, but do not allow the rice to brown. Add the wine and stir until it is completely absorbed.

4 Add the saffron and soaking liquid. Add the simmering stock, 4 fluid ounces (120 milliliters) at a time, stirring frequently. Wait until the stock is absorbed before adding the next 4-fluid-ounce (120-milliliter) portion.

5 After approximately 18 to 20 minutes, all the stock should be incorporated and the rice should be tender. Remove from the heat and stir in the remaining 1 ounce (30 grams) of butter and the grated cheese. Serve immediately.

VARIATIONS:

Risotto with Radicchio (al Radicchio)—Omit the saffron and Parmesan. Just before the risotto is fully cooked, stir in 4 fluid ounces (120 milliliters) heavy cream and 3 ounces (90 grams) finely chopped radicchio leaves.

Risotto with Four Cheeses (al Quattro Formaggi)—Omit the saffron. When the risotto is fully cooked, remove from the heat and stir in 2 ounces (60 grams) each of grated Parmesan, Gorgonzola, Fontina and mozzarella. Garnish with toasted pine nuts and chopped parsley.

Risotto with Smoked Salmon (al Salmone Affumicato)—Omit the butter, saffron and Parmesan. Sauté the onion in 3 fluid ounces (90 milliliters) corn or safflower oil instead of butter. When the risotto is fully cooked, remove from the heat and stir in 8 fluid ounces (240 milliliters) half-and-half, 3 fluid ounces (90 milliliters) fresh lemon juice and 8–10 ounces (240–300 grams) good-quality smoked salmon. Garnish with chopped fresh parsley and dill. Serve with lemon wedges.

Approximate values per 4-oz. (120-g) serving: **Calories** 110, **Total fat** 6 g, **Saturated fat** 3.5 g, **Cholesterol** 15 mg, **Sodium** 470 mg, **Total carbohydrates** 9 g, **Protein** 5 g

Mise en Place

- ▶ Heat water.
- ▶ Peel and mince onions.
- ▶ Grate cheese.

1 Sautéing the rice and onions in butter.

2 Adding the stock gradually while stirring frequently.

3 Stirring in the butter and grated cheese.

PILAF METHOD

For the pilaf method, the raw grains are lightly sautéed in oil or butter, usually with onions or seasonings for additional flavor. Hot liquid, often a stock, is then added. The pan is covered and the mixture is left to simmer until the liquid is absorbed.

▶ PROCEDURE FOR PREPARING GRAINS BY THE PILAF METHOD

1. Bring the cooking liquid (either water or stock) to a boil.
2. Heat the fat in a heavy saucepan over moderate heat. Add any onions, garlic or other flavorings and sauté for 1 to 2 minutes without browning.
3. Add the grains to the saucepan. Stir well to make sure the grains are well coated with fat. Do not allow the grains to brown.
4. All at once, add the hot cooking liquid to the sautéed grains.
5. Return the liquid to a boil, reduce to a simmer and cover.
6. Allow the mixture to simmer, either in the oven or on the stove top, until the liquid is absorbed.

RECIPE 21.8

CLASSIC RICE PILAF

Mise en Place

- ▶ Peel onion and chop into fine dice.
- ▶ Heat chicken stock.

Yield: 3 lb. (1.4 kg) **Method:** Pilaf

Clarified butter	1 fl. oz.	30 ml
Olive oil	1 fl. oz.	30 ml
Onion, fine dice	3 oz.	90 g
Bay leaf	1	1
Long-grain rice	1 lb.	450 g
Chicken stock, boiling	1 qt.	1 lt
Salt	TT	TT

1. Heat the butter and oil in a heavy sautoir or saucepot.
2. Add the onion and bay leaf and sauté until the onion is tender, but not brown.
3. Add the rice and stir to coat it completely with the hot fat. Do not allow the rice to brown.
4. Pour in the boiling stock and season with salt.
5. Cover the pot tightly and place it in a 350°F (180°C) oven. Bake until the liquid is absorbed and the rice is fluffy and tender, approximately 18 to 20 minutes.
6. Transfer the cooked rice to a hotel pan and fluff the rice with a fork. Remove the bay leaf and keep the rice hot for service.

VARIATION:

Spanish Rice—Substitute 2 ounces (60 grams) bacon fat for the butter. Add three chopped garlic cloves and 1 tablespoon (15 milliliters) pure ground chilli powder with the diced onion. In Step 3, sauté the rice until it browns slightly. In place of the chicken stock, use half chicken stock and half chopped canned tomatoes with juice. Add 1 tablespoon (15 milliliters) chopped cilantro when adding the liquids.

Approximate values per 6-oz. (180-g) serving: **Calories** 130, **Total fat** 7 g, **Saturated fat** 3 g, **Cholesterol** 7.5 mg, **Sodium** 440 g, **Total carbohydrates** 12 g, **Protein** 4 g

1 Sautéing the rice in butter.

2 Adding the hot stock to the rice.

3 Fluffing the finished rice.

▸ PASTA

Pasta is made from an unleavened dough of wheat flour mixed with a liquid. The liquid is usually egg and/or water. The flour can be from almost any grain: wheat, buckwheat, rice or a combination of grains. The dough can be colored and flavored with puréed vegetables, herbs or other ingredients, and it can be cut or **extruded** into a wide variety of shapes and sizes.

▸ **extrusion** the process of forcing pasta dough through perforated plates to create various shapes; pasta dough that is not extruded must be rolled and cut

Pasta can be cooked fresh while the dough is still moist and pliable, or the dough can be allowed to dry completely before cooking. Pasta can be filled or sauced in an endless variety of ways. It can stand alone or be used in salads, desserts, soups or casseroles.

Pasta is widely used in the cuisines of Asia, North America and Europe. In Italy, pasta dishes are usually served as a separate course, often referred to as the *minestre;* in other European countries, Asia and the United States, pasta dishes may be served as an appetizer, entrée or side dish.

IDENTIFYING PASTAS

The better-known pastas are based on the Italian tradition of kneading wheat flour with water and eggs to form a smooth, resilient dough. This dough is then rolled very thin and cut into various shapes before being boiled in water or dried for longer storage.

Commercially prepared dried pasta products are usually made with semolina flour. Semolina flour, ground from hard durum wheat and available from specialty purveyors, has a rich cream color and produces a very smooth, durable dough. Semolina dough requires a great deal of kneading, however, and bread flour is an acceptable substitute when preparing fresh pasta by hand.

Semolina

Asian pasta, generally known as noodles, is made from wheat, rice, bean or buckwheat flour. It is available fresh or dried from commercial purveyors and at specialty markets.

ITALIAN-STYLE PASTA

Although all Italian-style pasta is made from the same type of dough, the finest commercial pastas are those made with pure semolina flour, which gives the dough a rich, yellow color. Gray or streaked dough probably contains softer flours. Dried pasta should be very hard and break with a clean snap. The surface should be lightly pitted or dull. (A smooth or glossy surface will not hold or absorb sauces as well.)

THE MACARONI MYTH

The popular myth holds that noodles were first invented in China and discovered there by the Venetian explorer Marco Polo during the 13th century. He introduced the food to Italy and from there the rest of Europe. Although there is little doubt that the Chinese were making noodles by the first century A.D., it is now equally clear that they were not alone.

Middle Eastern and Italian cooks were preparing macaroni long before Marco Polo's adventures. A clear reference to boiled noodles appears in the *Jerusalem Talmud* of the fifth century A.D. There, rabbis debate whether noodles violate Jewish dietary laws (they do, but only during Passover). Tenth-century Arabic writings refer to dried noodles purchased from vendors. Literary references establish that dishes called *lasagna, macaroni* and *ravioli* were all well known (and costly) in Italy by the mid-13th century.

Pasta's current popularity dates from the 18th century, when mass production by machine began in Naples, Italy. English gentlemen on their "grand tours" of the European continent developed a fondness for pasta; the word *macaroni* became a synonym for a dandy or a vain young man. Macaroni arrived in America with English colonists, who preferred it with cream sauce and cheese or in a sweet custard. Domestic factories soon opened, and by the Civil War (1861–1865), macaroni was available to the working class. Pasta became a staple of the American middle-class diet following the wave of Italian immigrants in the late 19th century.

During the 1980s pasta became ubiquitous. Restaurants began serving it in ways previously unimagined. Corner grocery stores and local supermarkets began offering at least a dozen different shapes, often fresh and sometimes flavored. Dedicated cooks began to make pasta from scratch, though they sometimes tossed it with bottled sauce. Many also became interested in Asian noodles. Chinese, Japanese, Korean and Thai restaurants expanded their menu offerings to include traditional noodle dishes that were eagerly ordered by curious consumers. Pasta's popularity continues to grow as chefs discover the versatility of this inexpensive, nutritious food.

▶ **macaroni** any dried pasta made with wheat flour and water; only in the United States does the term refer to elbow-shaped tubes

Dried pasta, both domestic and imported, is available in a wide range of flavors and shapes. In addition to the traditional white (plain), green (spinach) and red (tomato) pastas, manufacturers are now offering flavor combinations such as lemon-peppercorn, whole wheat–basil and carrot-ginger. Small pieces of herbs or other flavorings are often visible in these products.

There are hundreds of recognized shapes of pasta, but only two or three dozen are generally available in the United States. When experimenting with unusual flavors and shapes, be sure to consider the taste and appearance of the final dish after the sauce and any garnishes are added.

Italian-style pasta can be divided into three groups based on the shape of the final product: ribbons, tubes and shapes. There is no consistent English nomenclature for these pastas; the Italian names are recognized and applied virtually worldwide. (A specific shape or size may be given different names in different regions of Italy, however. These distinctions are beyond the scope of this text.)

Ribbons

Pasta dough can be rolled very thin and cut into strips or ribbons of various widths. All ribbon shapes work well with tomato, fish and shellfish sauces. Thicker ribbons, such as spaghetti and fettuccine, are preferred with cream or cheese sauces. Sheets of fresh pasta dough can be filled and shaped to create ravioli, cappelletti and tortellini. Filled pasta is usually served with a light cream- or tomato-based sauce that complements the filling's flavors.

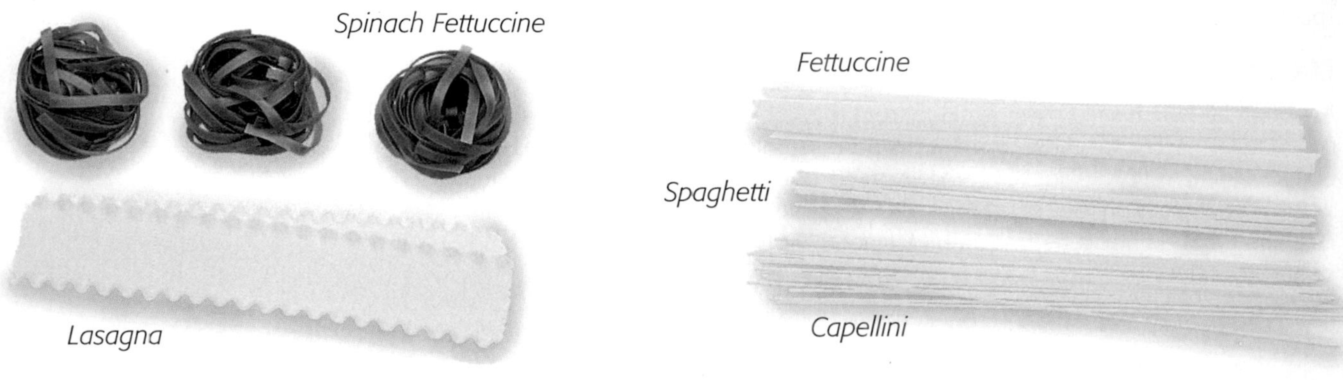

Tubes

Cylindrical forms or tubes are made by extrusion. The hollow tubes can be curved or straight, fluted or smooth. Tubes are preferred for meat and vegetable sauces and are often used in baked casseroles.

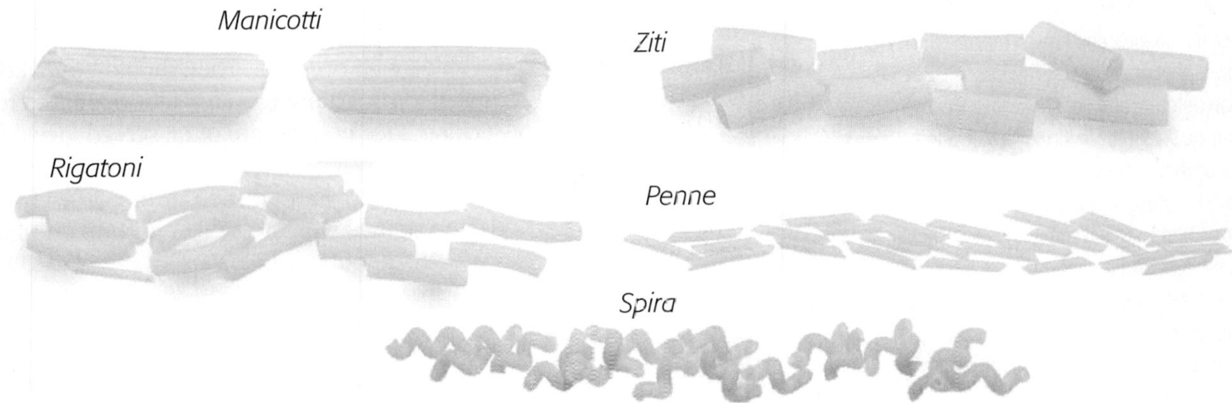

Shapes

The extrusion process can also be used to shape pasta dough into forms. The curves and textures produced provide nooks and crevices that hold sauces well. Shaped pastas, such as conchiglie, farfalle and fusilli, are preferred with meat sauces and oil-based sauces such as pesto. Larger shaped pastas can be cooked, then stuffed with meat or cheese fillings and baked or served as a casserole.

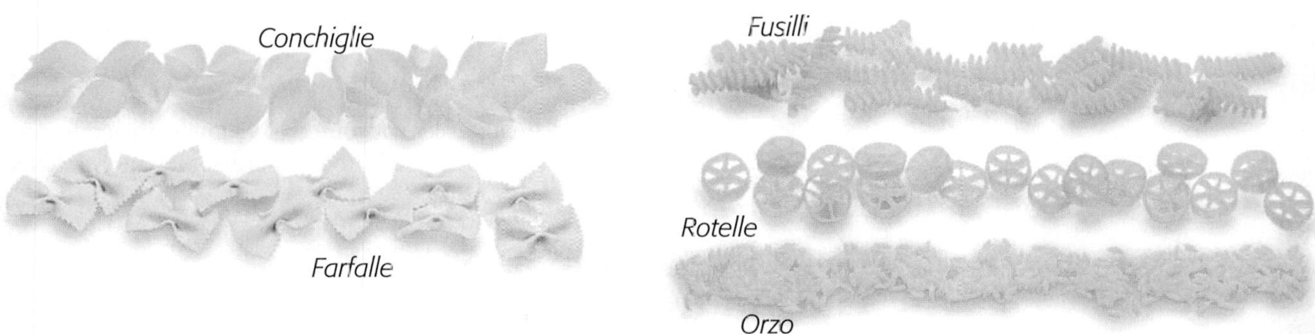

ASIAN NOODLES

Asian noodles are not cut into the same wealth of shapes and sizes as Italian-style pasta, nor are they flavored or colored with vegetable purées, herbs or other ingredients.

Virtually all Asian noodles are ribbons—some thin, some thick—folded into bundles and packaged. Differences arise because of the flours used for the dough.

Most dried Asian noodles benefit by soaking in hot water for several minutes before further preparation. The water softens the noodle strands; the bundles separate and the noodles cook more evenly.

Wheat Noodles

Wheat noodles, also known as egg noodles, are the most popular and most widely available of the Asian noodles. They are thin, flat

DUMPLINGS

A **dumpling** is a small mound of dough cooked by steaming or simmering in a flavorful liquid. Dumplings are found in many cuisines: Italian gnocchi, Jewish matzo balls, German spaetzle, Chinese wontons, Belorussian pelmeni and Polish pierogi. Dumplings can be sweet or savory, plain or filled.

Plain or **drop dumplings** are made with a breadlike dough, often leavened with yeast or chemical leavening agents. They should be light and tender, but firm enough to hold their shape when cooked. Drop dumplings may be served with stews or broths, or coated with butter or sauce as an appetizer or side dish.

Filled dumplings are made by wrapping noodle dough around seasoned meat, vegetables, cheese or fruit. These parcels are then steamed, fried or baked and served as a snack food, appetizer or side dish. A recipe for deep-fried wontons is included in Chapter 27, Hors d'Oeuvre and Canapés.

noodles with a springy texture; they are available fresh or dried. Dried egg noodles can be deep-fried after boiling to create crisp golden noodles (chow mein) used primarily as a garnish.

Japanese wheat noodles, known as *somen* (if thin) and *udon* (if thick), may be round, square or flat. They are eaten in broth or with a dipping sauce.

Rice Noodles

Rice noodles are thin dried noodles made with rice flour. They should be soaked in hot water before cooking and rinsed in cool running water after boiling to remove excess starch and prevent sticking. Rice noodles are often served in soups or sautéed.

Rice vermicelli, which has very fine strands, can be fried in hot oil without presoaking. In only a few seconds, the strands will turn white, puff up and become crunchy. Mounds of crunchy rice noodles can be used as a base for sautéed dishes or for presenting hors d'oeuvre.

Bean Starch Noodles

Bean starch noodles are also known as spring rain noodles, bean threads, bean noodles or cellophane noodles. They are thin, transparent noodles made from mung beans. Dried bean noodles can be fried in the same manner as rice vermicelli. Otherwise, they must be soaked in hot water before using in soups, stir-fries or braised dishes.

Buckwheat Noodles

Buckwheat flour is used in the noodles of northern Japan and the Tokyo region, known as soba noodles. Soba noodles are available fresh or dried and do not need soaking before cooking. They are traditionally served in broth or with a dipping sauce, but may be substituted for Italian-style pasta if desired.

NUTRITION

Pastas are very low in fat and are an excellent source of vitamins, minerals, proteins and carbohydrates. Also, the processed products are sometimes enriched with additional nutrients.

PURCHASING AND STORING PASTA PRODUCTS

Pasta products are purchased by weight, either fresh or dried. Tubes and shapes are not generally available fresh. Dried products, by far the most common, are available in boxes or bags, usually in 1-, 10- and 20-pound units. They can be stored in a cool, dry place for several months. Fresh pasta can be stored in an airtight wrapping in the refrigerator for a few days or in the freezer for a few weeks.

PREPARING FRESH PASTA

MAKING FRESH PASTA

Fresh pasta is easy to make, requiring almost no special equipment and only a few staples. The basic form is the **sfoglia,** a thin, flat sheet of dough that is cut into ribbons, circles or squares.

Although pasta dough can be kneaded by hand, stretched and rolled with a rolling pin and cut with a chef's knife, pasta machines make these tasks easier. Pasta machines are either electric or manual. Some electric models mix and knead the dough, then extrude it through a cutting disk. An extrusion machine is most practical in a food service operation that regularly serves large quantities of pasta. The pasta machine more often encountered is operated manually with a hand crank. It has two rollers that knead, press and push the dough into a thin, uniform sheet. Adjacent cutting rollers slice the thin dough into various widths for fettuccine, spaghetti, capellini and the like.

BASIC PASTA DOUGH

RECIPE 21.9

Yield: 4 lb. (1.8 kg)

Eggs	15	15
Olive oil	1 fl. oz.	30 ml
Salt	1 Tbsp.	15 ml
Bread flour*	2 lb. 8 oz.	1.1 kg

1 Place the eggs, oil and salt in a large mixer bowl. Use the paddle attachment to combine.

2 Add one-third of the flour and stir until the mixture begins to form a soft dough. Remove the paddle attachment and attach the dough hook.

3 Gradually add more flour until the dough is dry and cannot absorb any more flour.

4 Remove the dough from the mixer, wrap it well with plastic wrap and set it aside at room temperature for 20 to 30 minutes.

5 After the dough has rested, roll it into flat sheets by hand or with a pasta machine. Work with only a small portion at a time, keeping the remainder well covered to prevent it from drying out.

6 While the sheets of dough are pliable, cut them into the desired width with a chef's knife or pasta machine. Sheets can also be used for making ravioli, as illustrated next.

*Semolina flour can be substituted for all or part of the bread flour in this recipe, although it makes a stronger dough that is more difficult to work with by hand.

VARIATIONS:

Garlic-Herb—Roast one head of garlic. Peel and purée the cloves and add to the eggs. Add up to 2 ounces (60 grams) finely chopped assorted fresh herbs just before mixing is complete.

Spinach—Add 8 ounces (250 grams) cooked, puréed and well-drained spinach to the eggs. Increase the amount of flour slightly if necessary.

Tomato—Add 4 ounces (120 grams) tomato paste to the eggs; omit the salt. Increase the amount of flour slightly if necessary.

Chipotle—Purée 6 ounces (180 grams) canned chipotle chiles in adobo sauce in a blender or food processor. Add the purée to the egg-and-oil mixture. Use additional flour, if necessary.

Approximate values per 1-oz. (30-g) serving: **Calories** 80, **Total fat** 2 g, **Saturated fat** 0.5 g, **Cholesterol** 50 mg, **Sodium** 125 mg, **Total carbohydrates** 13 g, **Protein** 3 g

1 Adding the flour to the mixing bowl and using the paddle until the mixture forms a soft dough.

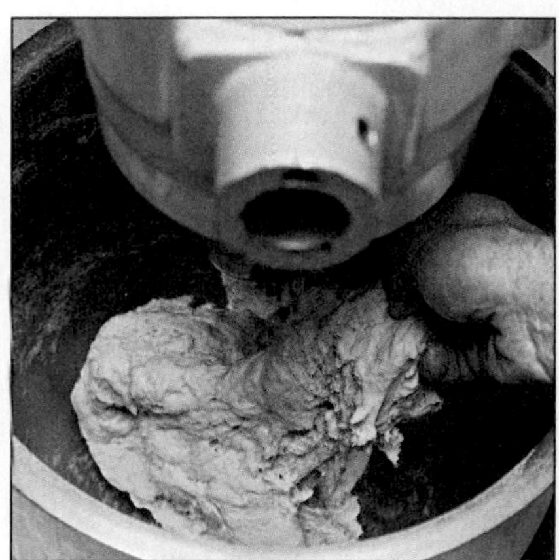

2 The finished dough.

▶ PROCEDURE FOR ROLLING AND CUTTING PASTA DOUGH

1. Work with a small portion of the dough. Leave the rest covered with plastic wrap to prevent it from drying out.
2. Flatten the dough with the heel of your hand.
3. Set the pasta machine rollers to their widest setting. Insert the dough and turn the handle with one hand while supporting the dough with the other hand. Pass the entire piece of dough through the rollers.
4. Dust the dough with flour, fold it in thirds and pass it through the pasta machine again.
5. Repeat the folding and rolling procedure until the dough is smooth. This may require four to six passes.
6. Tighten the rollers one or two marks, then pass the dough through the machine. Without folding it in thirds, pass the dough through the machine repeatedly, tightening the rollers one or two marks each time.
7. When the dough is thin enough to see your hand through it, but not so thin that it begins to tear, it is ready to use or cut into ribbons. This sheet is the *sfoglia*.
8. To cut the sfoglia into ribbons, gently feed a manageable length of dough through the desired cutting blades.
9. Lay out the pasta in a single layer on a sheet pan dusted with flour to dry. Layers of pasta ribbons can be separated with parchment paper.

1 Passing the entire piece of dough through the pasta machine.

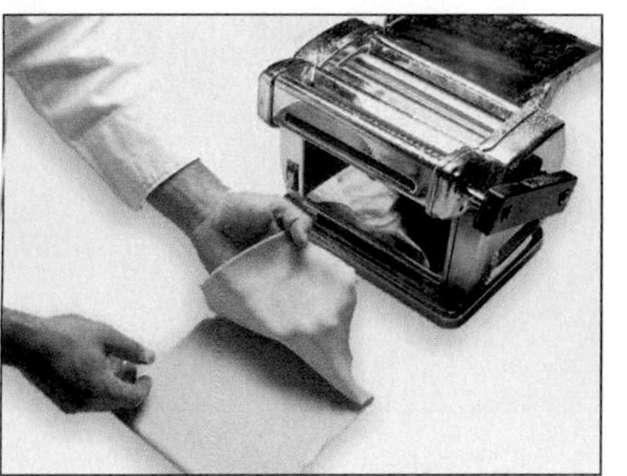

2 Folding the dough in thirds.

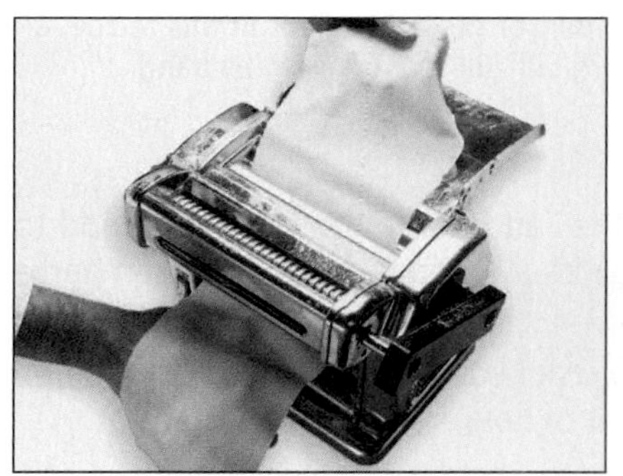

3 Passing the dough through the pasta machine to achieve the desired thickness.

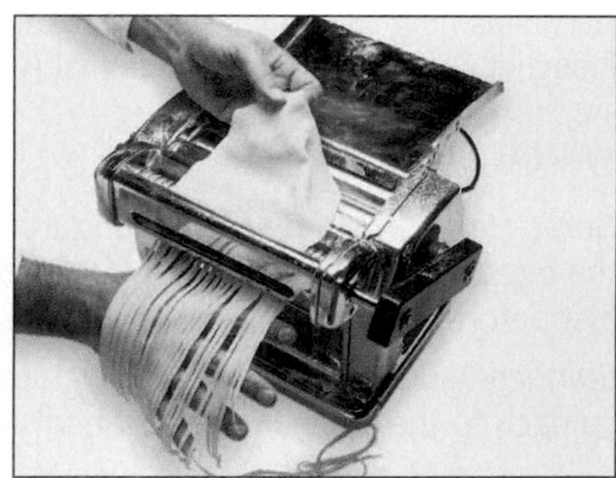

4 Using the pasta machine to cut the dough to the desired width.

FILLING PASTA

Sheets of raw pasta dough can be filled or folded to create ravioli (squares), tortellini (round "hats" with a brim of dough), lunettes (circles of dough folded into half-moons), agnolotti (squares of dough folded into rectangles), cappelletti (squares of dough folded and shaped into rings) and other shapes. The filled pieces of dough are then cooked in boiling water using the procedure for cooking pasta ribbons discussed later. The filling can include almost anything—cheese, herbs, vegetables, fish, shellfish, meat or poultry. It can be uncooked or precooked. But any meat filling should be fully cooked before the pasta is assembled, as the time it takes for the dough to cook may not be sufficient to cook the filling.

Cannelloni is a different type of filled pasta: A large square of cooked dough is wrapped around a meat or cheese filling and baked. Popular lasagna dishes are similar. Lasagna are wide, flat sheets of pasta that are cooked and then layered with cheese, tomato sauce and meat or vegetables as desired. The finished casserole is baked and cut into portions.

Some of the larger, commercially prepared pasta shapes such as large shells (conchigloni or rigate) or large tubes (manicotti) can be partially cooked in boiling water, then filled, sauced and baked as a casserole.

Asian noodle dough is also made into filled items such as dumplings, wontons, egg rolls (made with egg noodle dough) and spring rolls (made with rice paper). These items are usually steamed, pan-fried or deep-fried. When making filled pasta, consider the flavors and textures of the filling, dough and sauce. Each should complement the others.

▶ PROCEDURE FOR PREPARING RAVIOLI

1. Prepare a basic pasta dough of the desired flavor.
2. Prepare and chill the desired filling.
3. Roll out two thin sheets of dough between the rollers of a pasta machine. Gently lay the dough flat on the work surface.
4. Using a piping bag or a small portion scoop, place small mounds of filling on one of the dough pieces. Space the filling evenly, allowing approximately 2 inches (5 centimeters) between each mound.
5. Brush the exposed areas of dough with water.
6. Gently place the second sheet of dough over the mounds and press firmly around each mound to remove air pockets and seal the dough.
7. Cut between the mounds with a chef's knife, pastry wheel or circular cutter.

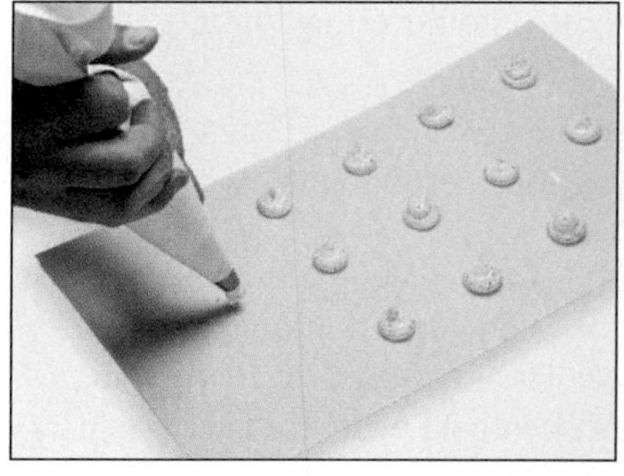

1 Piping the filling onto the dough.

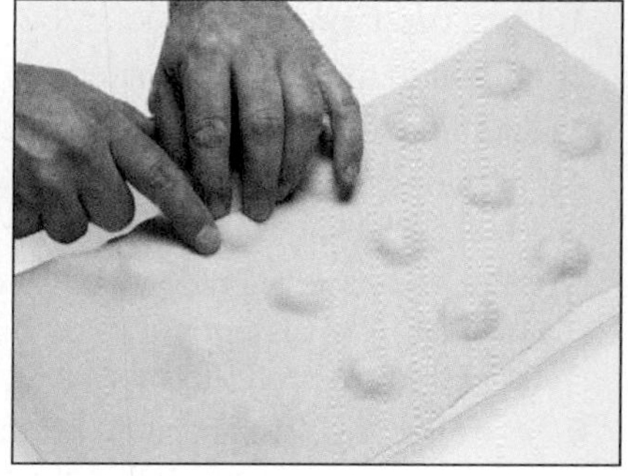

2 Pressing around the mounds of filling to seal the dough and remove any air pockets.

3 Cutting around the mounds with a circular cutter.

COOKING METHOD

DETERMINING DONENESS

Italian-style pastas are properly cooked when they are **al dente,** firm but tender. Cooking times vary depending on the shape and quantity of pasta, the amount of water used, the hardness of the water and even the altitude. Fresh

▶ **al dente** (al DEN-tay) Italian for "to the tooth"; used to describe a food, usually pasta, that is cooked only until it gives a slight resistance when one bites into it

pasta cooks rapidly, sometimes in seconds. Noodles and dried pasta may require several minutes.

Although package or recipe directions offer some guidance, the only way to accurately test doneness is to bite into a piece. When the pasta is slightly firmer than desired, remove it from the stove and drain. It will continue to cook through residual heat.

Unlike Italian pasta, Asian noodles are not served al dente. Rather, they are either boiled until very soft or stir-fried until very crisp.

BOILING

All Italian-style pasta and most Asian noodles are cooked by just one method: boiling. The secret to boiling pasta successfully is to use ample water. Allow 1 gallon (4 liters) of water for each pound (450 grams) of pasta.

Use a saucepan or stockpot large enough to allow the pasta to move freely in the boiling water; otherwise, the starch released by the dough will make the pasta gummy and sticky. The water should be brought to a rapid boil, then all the pasta should be added at once.

Salt should be added to the water. Pasta absorbs water and salt during cooking. Adding salt to the pasta after it is cooked will not provide the same seasoning effect.

Chefs disagree on whether to add oil to the cooking water. Purists argue against adding oil, on the theory that it makes the dough absorb water unevenly. Others think oil should be added to reduce surface foam. Another theory is that oil keeps the pasta from sticking, although this works only when added to cooked, drained pasta.

Asian noodles may be prepared by boiling until fully cooked, or they may be parboiled and then stir-fried with other ingredients to finish cooking.

▶ PROCEDURE FOR COOKING PASTA TO ORDER

1. Bring the appropriate amount of water to a boil over high heat.
2. Add oil to the water if desired.
3. Add the pasta and salt to the rapidly boiling water.
4. Stir the pasta to prevent it from sticking together. Bring the water back to a boil and cook until the pasta is done.
5. When the pasta is properly cooked, immediately drain it through a colander. A small amount of oil may be gently tossed into the pasta if desired to prevent it from sticking together.
6. Serve hot pasta immediately, or refresh it in cold water for later use in salads or other dishes. (Do not rinse pasta that is to be served hot.)

▶ PROCEDURE FOR COOKING DRIED PASTA IN ADVANCE

Fresh pasta is so delicate and cooks so rapidly (sometimes in as little as 15 seconds) that it should be cooked to order. Dried pasta, however, can be cooked in advance for quantity service.

1. Follow the preceding directions for cooking pasta, but stop the cooking process when the pasta is about two-thirds done.
2. Drain the pasta, rinse it lightly and toss it in a small amount of oil.
3. Divide the pasta into appropriate-sized portions. Individual portions can be wrapped in plastic or laid on a sheet pan and covered. Refrigerate until needed.
4. When needed, place a portion in a china cap and immerse in boiling water to reheat. Drain, add sauce and serve immediately.

ACCOMPANIMENTS TO PASTA

Pasta is widely accepted by consumers and easily incorporated in a variety of cuisines—from Italian and Chinese to Eastern European and spa. It is used in broths; as a bed for stews, fish, shellfish, poultry or meat; or tossed with sauce. Today's creative chefs are constantly developing nontraditional but delicious ways of serving pasta.

Pasta and Broths

Small shapes can be cooked in the broth with which they are served, or cooked separately, then added to the hot liquid at service time. Soups such as *cappelletti in brodo* and chicken noodle are examples of these techniques.

Pasta Sauces

There are hundreds of Italian pasta sauces as well as sauces for Italian-style pasta, but most can be divided into six categories: ragus, seafood sauces, vegetable sauces, cream sauces, garlic-oil sauces and uncooked sauces. Recipes for a selection of pasta sauces are included in Chapter 9, Stocks and Sauces.

Although there are no firm rules governing the combinations of sauces and pasta, Table 21.3 offers some of the more common combinations.

Table 21.3 COMBINING SAUCES, PASTA AND GARNISHES

SAUCE	DESCRIPTION	PASTA SHAPE	GARNISH
Ragù	Braised dishes used as sauce; flavorings, meat or poultry are browned, then a tomato product and stock, wine, water, milk or cream are added	Ribbons, tubes, shapes, filled	Grated cheese
Seafood	White seafood sauces are flavored with herbs and made with white wine or stock; red seafood sauces are tomato-based	Ribbons (fettuccine and capellini)	Fish or shellfish
Vegetable	Includes both traditional sauces made with tomatoes and stock, flavored with garlic and red pepper, and modern sauces such as primavera	Ribbons, tubes, filled	Meatballs, sausage, grated cheese
Cream	Uses milk or cream and sometimes roux; usually cheese is added	Thick ribbons (spaghetti and fettuccine), filled	Ham, peas, sausage, mushrooms, smoked salmon, nuts, grated cheese
Garlic-oil	(It. *aglio-olio*) Olive oil flavored with garlic and herbs; can be hot or cold, cooked or uncooked (pesto is an uncooked, cold sauce)	Ribbons, shapes, filled	Grated cheese (if uncooked or cold), herbs
Uncooked	A variety of dressings and garnishes such as fresh tomatoes, basil and olive oil; or olive oil, lemon juice, parsley, basil and hot red pepper flakes; capers, anchovies, olives, fresh herbs, fresh vegetables, flavored oils and cubed cheeses can also be used	Ribbons, shapes	Cubed or grated cheese, fresh vegetables, herbs

CONCLUSION

Most meals would seem incomplete without a starch. The most popular starches are potatoes, grains (especially rice) and pasta. All are low in fat and a good source of energy. Most can be prepared with several dry- and moist-heat cooking methods, and all can be sauced, seasoned or flavored in limitless ways.

QUESTIONS FOR DISCUSSION

1 Explain the differences between mealy and waxy potatoes. Give two examples of each.
2 Describe the two methods of sautéing or pan-frying potatoes.
3 Explain why duchesse potatoes are regarded as the "mother" of many classic potato dishes. Name and describe two such dishes.
4 All grains are composed of three parts. Name and describe each of these parts.
5 Describe and compare the three general cooking methods used to prepare grains.
6 Name the three categories of Italian-style pasta shapes and give an example of each.
7 Why is it necessary to use ample water when cooking pasta? Should pasta be cooked in salted water? Should oil be added to the cooking water? Explain your answers.
8 Discuss the differences between cooking fresh pasta and cooking dried, factory-produced pasta.

9 Different names are given to Italian pasta shapes from one region of Italy to another. Research the various regional Italian cuisines to determine other names for different types of pastas.

10 Each of the types of sauce listed in Table 21.3 comes from a specific region of Italy. Which region is most closely associated with each type of sauce? Why?

CHAPTER **TWENTY-TWO**

VEGETARIAN COOKING

VEGETARIAN FOOD LEAVES A DEEP IMPRESSION ON OUR NATURE. IF THE WHOLE WORLD ADOPTS VEGETARIANISM, IT CAN CHANGE THE DESTINY OF HUMANKIND.

—Albert Einstein, mathematician and physicist (1879–1955)

AFTER STUDYING THIS CHAPTER, YOU WILL BE ABLE TO:

- understand the range of vegetarian diets and motivations supporting vegetarianism
- use a variety of protein products as alternatives to meat, poultry, fish or dairy
- create interesting, varied and balanced vegetarian dishes, meals and menus

A growing number of people—approximately six million in the United States today—are choosing to forgo some or all animal products in their diets. Given this growing trend, a chef needs to know how to cater to a vegetarian diner. A chef needs to understand that it is not necessarily enough to simply remove the meat from the center of the plate and replace it with pasta. Nor is it always sufficient to offer a plate composed of several starch and vegetable side dishes as if it were a balanced and inviting meal.

In this chapter we discuss what it is to be a vegetarian and the motivations supporting this diet. We also explore ways in which a chef can offer a variety of flavorful and appealing vegetarian dishes that will satisfy even the most discriminating of vegetarian diners—and maybe a few meat eaters as well.

▸ VARIATIONS ON VEGETARIANISM

▸ **vegetarian** a person who does not eat any meat, poultry, game, fish, shellfish or animal by-products such as gelatin or animal fats; may also exclude dairy products or eggs from the diet

Although the term *vegetarian* was not widely used until 1847, when England's Vegetarian Society first adopted it to describe people who excluded all animal products from their diets, millions of people have, for thousands of years, eaten little to no meat. Some have done so for religious or philosophical beliefs, others for environmental or health concerns. Still others have done so simply because they did not have regular access to meat.

One of the earliest known proponents of a vegetarian diet was the Greek mathematician and philosopher Pythagoras (c. 569–475 B.C.E.). He believed that there was a kinship among all living creatures and therefore chose not to eat the flesh of slaughtered animals. Over the next two centuries or so, his beliefs were refined and his followers eventually adopted an ethical code that included vows not to kill living creatures (including animals traditionally sacrificed to the gods) and to never eat meat. His teachings and those of his followers became sufficiently widespread that for centuries—indeed, until the 19th century A.D.—the term **Pythagoreans** was used to describe people who chose to eat only plant products by choice.

Other than for small groups of Pythagoreans and some devout, ascetic religious (especially monastic) communities and sects, vegetarianism as a diet of choice never really caught hold in Europe or North America until the 19th and 20th centuries. And even then, until the 1970s, vegetarianism was more often than not chosen as part of a puritanical or spiritual lifestyle devoted to moderation and abstinence from liquor, caffeine and other stimulants.

Today there are many variations on the vegetarian diet. Some vegetarian diets (and lifestyles) exclude the consumption and use of all animal products (and even some plant products), while others allow the adherent to consume some animal or animal-based products. A person who follows a vegetarian diet can be any of the following:

- **Vegan** (VEE-gun)—A person who eats no meat, fish or poultry or any products derived from animals such as milk, cheese, eggs, honey or gelatin; also referred to as a **strict** or **pure vegetarian.**
- **Raw foodist**—Typically, a vegan who eats only raw or slightly warmed plant products (adherents believe that cooking foods to a temperature of 116°F [47°C] or above destroys enzymes and nutrients). A person on a raw

foods diet, also referred to as a **living foodist,** may soak certain foods such as nuts and sprouts to soften them and increase nutrient absorption.

- **Fructarian** or **fruitarian**—A person who eats only fruits, nuts, seeds and other plant products that can be gathered without harming the plant (some eat only plant matter that has already fallen off the plant).
- **Ovo-vegetarian**—A vegetarian who eats eggs but not dairy products.
- **Ovo-lacto-vegetarian** or **lacto-ovo-vegetarian**—A person who eats plant products as well as dairy products and eggs (although some may not eat cheeses made with animal-based enzymes such as rennet, or eggs produced by factory farms). This diet is one of the most typical of vegetarian diets and these terms are often used interchangeably with the term **vegetarian.**
- **Lacto-vegetarian**—A vegetarian who eats dairy products but not eggs.
- **Demi-vegetarian**—A vegetarian or ovo-lacto-vegetarian who eats fish.
- **Macrobioticist**—A person who follows a diet devised in the 1920s by a Japanese teacher who adhered to a simple meal plan of brown rice, miso soup and sea vegetables (seaweed). Derived from an ancient style of eating common in Asia, this dietary philosophy is based on Chinese concepts of balancing the opposite forces called *yin* and *yang*. Brown rice, whole grains, and vegetables form the basis of the diet. Fruits, nuts, refined sugars and refined foods are avoided, although fish is occassionally eaten on such diets.

► MOTIVATIONS FOR VEGETARIANISM

For millennia, people have followed vegetarian diets for a variety of reasons, including religious and ethical beliefs. More recently, environmental and health concerns have become the major motivations for adopting some sort of vegetarian diet.

RELIGION

Religion has longed played a leading role in defining how and what people eat. Although few religions actually mandate a complete vegetarian diet for their followers, many of the world's major religions promote meatless diets, in part as a spiritual ideal and in part in recognition of man's kinship with animals.

Hinduism. This vast and complex civilization and religion is based, in part, on the Vedas, sacred texts written approximately 4000 years ago. Based on these and later teachings, the priestly caste developed a religious and ethical standard of conduct called *ahimsa*. Ahimsa is the desire not to cause harm or injury; that is, a person should strive to act in a nonviolent fashion. Many observant Hindus (especially members of the priestly caste known as the Brahmins) believe that ahimsa applies to man's relationship with animals. Because they consider the slaughtering of animals for consumption a violent act, they believe that they must follow a vegetarian diet. This diet will, however, often include milk and other dairy products, as animals give these foods willingly and are not injured in the process. Other observant Hindus believe that ahimsa extends only to interactions with other people and therefore will eat meat, although most will abstain from eating beef as the cow is considered sacred. Hinduism is the predominant religion of India, but is practiced in cities worldwide by Indian immigrants and their families, as many as 800 million people worldwide.

Buddhism. As with Hindus, not all Buddhists are vegetarians. There are essentially two major schools of Buddhist thought and these schools differ on several important teachings, including vegetarianism. One school of Buddhism follows certain ancient texts that suggest that the Buddha ate meat, but did so as not to offend those who provided him and his fellow monks and nuns with these charitable offerings. These texts also record the Buddha as stating that a person can eat meat provided the person does not hear, see or suspect that the animal was specifically killed for him or her to consume. Thus, this school of Buddhism does not actually prohibit its followers from eating animal products. The second school of Buddhism does not follow these particular texts and practitioners of this school generally adhere to a vegetarian diet. They do so because the Buddha taught that nonviolence, love and compassion are all extremely important virtues that must be extended to all living creatures.

In the modern Buddhist world, attitudes toward vegetarianism also vary by location. In China and Vietnam, monks and other strictly observant Buddhists typically do not eat meat, while in Japan and Korea some will (especially fish), although most do not. In Sri Lanka and Southeast Asia, Buddhists generally do not practice vegetarianism. The Dalai Lama, the spiritual leader of Buddhists worldwide, regularly preaches nonviolence and encourages all Buddhists to maintain vegetarian diets.

Jainism. Based on their blend of Hindu and Buddhist beliefs, observant Jains are vegans. They try to practice as pure a form of ahimsa as possible. Indeed, some Jains continually sweep the path before them and wear gauze masks over their mouths so as not to harm insects by inadvertently treading on them or breathing them in. Similarly, they will not eat root vegetables and bulbs such as garlic and onions as harvesting them may kill worms and other small animals living in the soil. A majority of the world's Jains live in India.

Judaism and Christianity. The book of Genesis suggests that the original diet in the Garden of Eden was vegan. It is only later, after the Deluge, that the descendants of Noah were given permission to eat meat. Based on these scriptures, some Jews and Christians believe that God originally intended humans to be vegetarians, even though the consumption of meat is allowed. Moreover, some observant Jews and Christians are preparing for the coming of the Messiah by practicing vegetarianism. They interpret the Bible to suggest that when the Messiah arrives there will be a return to an Eden-like society, including vegetarianism. Ellen White, one of the founders of the Seventh-Day Adventist Church, was a vegetarian activist; today approximately half of the practicing Adventists in the United States follow a vegetarian diet.

ETHICS AND ANIMAL RIGHTS

Irrespective of religious teachings concerning cruelty to animals, some vegetarians refuse to eat meat because of an emotional aversion to inflicting pain and harm on other living creatures or an objection to the manner in which animals are raised and slaughtered. Early in the 20th century Americans were made aware of cruel and unsanitary practices in slaughterhouses by Upton Sinclair, whose 1906 novel *The Jungle* led to federal regulation of the meat industry. More recently, those beliefs gained much credence with the 1975 publication of *Animal Liberation* by an Australian ethics professor, Peter Singer. Along with lurid descriptions of factory farms, slaughterhouses and scientific laboratories, he presents several ethical arguments on why we should neither eat nor experiment on animals. His book helped spark the animal rights movement in the United States, including the founding of PETA (People for the Ethical Treatment of Animals), a strong proponent of vegetarianism.

ENVIRONMENTAL CONCERNS

Many vegetarians cite environmental concerns as one of the principal reasons they chose to forgo animal products in their diet and to advocate that others do so as well. They often rely on arguments first raised in a scholarly fashion by

Frances Moore Lappé in *Diet for a Small Planet*. Published in 1971, *Diet for a Small Planet* explores the problems of world hunger and concludes that world hunger is caused, in great part, by the wasteful use of agricultural resources on supporting animals raised for meat. She notes, for example, that at the time she was writing the book, more than 80 percent of the grain grown in the United States was fed to livestock. She then argues that if Americans cut their meat consumption by just 10 percent, there would be enough grain left over to feed much of the world's hungry people. Although she did not necessarily advocate a complete vegetarian diet for all, she did urge people to reduce their consumption of animal products.

Lappé's best-selling book was quickly adopted by the small but growing vegetarian community in the United States. They saw it as a manifesto that vegetarianism was good for the body and for the planet. A small number of health food stores and vegetarian restaurants began to open across the United States; generally, first in college towns along the West and East Coasts and then in other cities. For some, vegetarianism as a lifestyle meshed well with the growing hippie lifestyle of the 1960s and 1970s.

An equally influential text is John Robbins' 1987 book *Diet for a New America*. Robbins explores the prolific use of natural resources and the environmental damage caused by agricultural systems dedicated to raising animals for consumption. He also exposes the perceived horrors of factory farming and related practices such as restricting calves to pens in order to create a whiter, more tender and delicate veal and warehousing thousands of chickens in cramped cages and coops to facilitate egg production. In addition, Robbins documents the unhealthfulness of a meat-based diet and the healthfulness of a vegetarian diet. Robbins' book is sometimes credited with launching the vegan movement in the United States.

Today some people strongly believe that the production of meat and animal products at current and likely future levels is environmentally unsustainable. They argue that modern industrial agriculture is changing ecosystems faster than they can adapt. They maintain that while vegetarian agriculture produces some of the same problems as animal production, the environmental impact of animal production is significantly greater. For example, they note that free-range animal production requires land for grazing, which encourages ranchers to encroach on undeveloped lands and clear-cut woodlands. They also point out that overgrazed lands lose their ability to support animal production, which makes further agricultural expansion necessary. While they acknowledge that factory-farm animal production uses less land, they argue that it requires enormous quantities of animal feed that must be grown over large areas of land, requires considerable resources such as water and energy and creates large quantities of polluting wastes. For them, vegetarianism is an environmental imperative. A large and growing body of literature studies the effects of all types of agriculture on the environment.

▶ THE VEGETARIAN DIET

Vegetarianism has become more mainstream over the last century, evolving from a diet followed mainly due to religious or philosophical beliefs to people who now choose a plant-based diet for health reasons. The Dietary Guidelines for Americans 2005, as well as recommendations from the major health groups (American Cancer Society, American Heart Association, American Dietetic Association), stress the importance of fruits, vegetables, legumes and whole grains—the foundation of a plant-based diet. Studies have shown that the incidence of chronic diseases such as obesity, cardiovascular disease, cancer and Type 2 diabetes are lower for vegetarians than for nonvegetarians. It is important to note that other healthy lifestyle factors (not smoking, moderate use or abstinence from alcohol, and exercise) that vegetarians typically follow might also be responsible for the lower disease rates. All of these factors together probably account for the decreased incidence of disease among vegetarians.

Many people who believe that a plant-based diet is associated with a reduced incidence of disease find it difficult to give up all animal foods. They adapt the principles of vegetarianism to their lifestyles by choosing a diet plan loosely based on vegetarianism—the "flextarian" plan. Although it is not recognized as a conventional vegetarian diet, people who follow this eating pattern choose a plant-based diet augmented with lean fish and occasional servings of poultry.

Although plant-based diets offer many healthful qualities, careful planning is vital to ensure that the vegetarian is consuming adequate protein, minerals, vitamins and calories. The American Dietetic Association has determined that eating an assortment of plant foods over the course of a day can provide all the essential amino acids required for good nutrition. But the quality of plant protein and the ability of the body to absorb it may vary. Vegetarian protein needs can be met by consuming soy foods whose protein has been determined to be as effective a source as animal protein.

A vegetarian diet can meet calcium requirements when plant foods that are good sources of calcium such as greens and cruciferous vegetables are eaten. Vegetarians who elect to consume dairy and eggs do not need to be concerned with meeting adequate calcium intake requirements. Soy products that are fortified with calcium and other vitamins are also readily available. The type of iron found in plant foods may not be as readily absorbed as iron from animal sources; therefore, supplements are recommended.

There are no natural plant sources of Vitamin B_{12}, which is crucial for good nutrition, especially for pregnant women and infants. Consumption of dietary supplements, fortified foods or dairy foods is necessary to provide an adequate amount of Vitamin B_{12} for vegetarians.

Vegans have to be particularly mindful of their food choices, because they avoid all animal-based foods. Vegans usually supplement their diet with multivitamin mineral supplements and include fortified and enriched foods. An-

TO BE OR NOT TO BE: VEGETARIAN

In the not-too-distant past, vegetarianism was linked with aging hippies, musty health food stores and the religiously observant. Not any more. Now most supermarkets stock vegetarian burgers, soy cheeses, tofu and rice milk, while national chains of modern, upscale grocers cater specifically to vegetarian and health-conscious shoppers. Even fast-food restaurants now offer foods such as vegetarian submarine sandwiches and soy-filled tacos.

So just how many vegetarians are there in the United States? The Vegetarian Resource Group has tried to answer this question. In a 2003 poll, it asked adult respondents, "Which of the following foods, if any, [do] you never eat? Meat, Poultry, Fish/Seafood, Dairy Products, Eggs, Honey." Approximately 2.8 percent of the sample population responded that they did not eat meat, poultry or fish, while 6.5 percent indicated they did not eat red meat. When the same question was asked in 1994 and again in 1997, only about 1 percent indicated that they were vegetarian (defined as those who never eat meat, poultry or fish).

Adults aren't the only vegetarians. According to another Vegetarian Resource Group poll in 2000, 2 percent of children ages 6 to 17 responded that they never eat meat, fish or poultry, while 6 percent don't eat red meat.

Significantly, nonvegetarians also enjoy meatless dishes from time to time. According to a 1999 poll, approximately 57 percent of U.S. adults say they "sometimes, often or always" order a vegetarian entrée when dining out.

This growing demand for vegetarian food clearly has an impact on restaurants and institutional food service operations. When more than half of the population sometimes orders vegetarian cuisine, it is no longer sufficient to offer a one-dish-fits-all vegetarian entrée. As with nonvegetarian dishes, flavor, freshness, quality and variety will keep customers satisfied and eager to return.

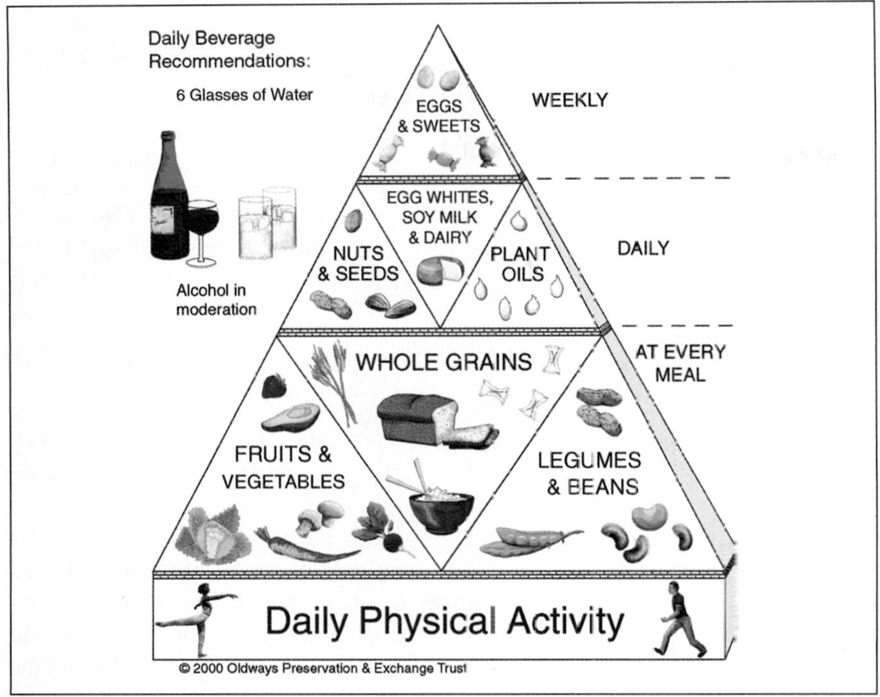

FIGURE 22.1 ▶ Traditional Healthy Vegetarian Diet Pyramid

other area in which a vegetarian diet may be lacking are the fatty acids naturally occurring in fish such as salmon and mackerel. To compensate, dietitians advise that vegetarians consume a good quantity of linolenic acid in their diet. A diet rich in nuts, canola oil, flax and other seeds and soy products is recommended.

Vegetarians who consume dairy and/or eggs generally have an easier time meeting their nutrient needs. All vegetarians must choose carefully to be certain to meet their calorie needs, however, if they are also attempting to eat a low-fat diet. High-fiber foods such as vegetables, whole grains, legumes, and fruits can reduce calorie intake because these foods tend to make people feel full sooner. Protein intake is not usually a concern for vegetarians who eat a variety of foods. Overall, a carefully planned plant-based diet is a healthy, satisfying way to eat. Those who want to maintain good health while on a vegetarian diet can be helped in making proper food choices by following eating plans such as that shown in Figure 22.1.

▶ Ingredients for Vegetarian Cooking

A diet rich in a variety of fruits, vegetables, starches and grains, well prepared and properly seasoned, will satisfy even those adhering to the more strict vegetarian diets. Chefs can prepare flavorful, visually stimulating dishes with a traditional range of ingredients available in most restaurant kitchens. Potatoes, grains, starches, vegetables and fruits—discussed in Chapter 20, Vegetables; Chapter 21, Potatoes, Grains, and Pasta; Chapter 23, Salads and Salad Dressings; and Chapter 24, Fruits—form the backbone of vegetarian cooking. To help chefs in planning vegetarian dishes, Table 22.1 lists foods that are eaten by the most common types of vegetarians.

Table 22.1 **DIET PATTERNS OF MAJOR FORMS OF VEGETARIAN DIETS**

FOOD GROUPS CONSUMED	TYPE OF VEGETARIAN				
	OVO-LACTO	OVO-	LACTO-	VEGAN	FRUITARIAN
Grains	Yes	Yes	Yes	Yes	No
Legumes	Yes	Yes	Yes	Yes	No
Nuts, seeds	Yes	Yes	Yes	Yes	Yes
Vegetables	Yes	Yes	Yes	Yes	No
Fruits	Yes	Yes	Yes	Yes	Yes
Dairy	Yes	No	Yes	No	No
Eggs	Yes	Yes	No	No	No

While the professional kitchen offers hundreds of foods appropriate for all vegetarian diets, chefs can use a number of ingredients to enhance the complexity of their vegetarian cooking. Some foods that replace the protein found in animal products are featured here, as well as other ingredients that may mimic more traditional animal-based foods.

SOYBEAN-BASED INGREDIENTS

The versatile and protein-rich soybean forms the basis for a wide range of products used in vegetarian and traditional ethnic cuisines worldwide. Soy-based foods have been favorites in Asian cooking for centuries. While there are brown, black and green varieties, most soybeans are yellow. Fresh green soybeans, called edamame, are steamed and eaten as a snack. According to the United Soybean Board, soy protein is the only plant protein that is equivalent to animal protein; it is a rich source of phytochemicals, making soy an ideal ingredient for vegetarian cooking. Soy can be made into a diverse range of foods including flour, "milk," cheese and oil.

Soy milk is made from dried soybeans that are soaked and then finely ground and pressed to extract a milky liquid. (Soy milk can be made in any kitchen by soaking, then cooking dried soybeans in hot water before grinding, straining and simmering the liquid.) Soy milk is believed to have originated in China, where it is traditionally served as a sweet or savory breakfast beverage or soup base with a distinct beany flavor. Soy milk comes in liquid or powdered form. Liquid soy milk resembles skim milk and has a slight nutty flavor. Most liquid soy milk is sold in aseptic packaging, giving it a one-year shelf life if unopened. Like other dairy products, once opened, liquid soy milk requires refrigeration and lasts from 5 to 7 days or according to recommendations of the manufacturer. Powdered soy milk is shelf-stable and lasts for a year at room temperature. Many dairy substitutes are made from soy milk, such as soy cheese, soy yogurt and flavored soy beverages.

Soy milk can be used measure-for-measure in all recipes that call for dairy milk. Manufacturing technologies have evolved to produce soy milk products with a richer texture and flavor, more suitable for enriching sauces. When cooking with soy milk, be aware that it can separate at high temperatures. Simmer foods with soy milk gently and add the soy milk near the end of the cooking time to prevent it from separating.

Tofu or bean curd (Fr. *fromage de soja*) is a staple of Japanese and Chinese cuisines and is gaining acceptance in American kitchens because of its high nutritional value, low cost and flavor adaptability. Tofu is made by processing soybeans into soy milk, which is then coagulated or cultured and formed into a cake. The result is a soft, creamy-white substance similar to cheese. Tofu is easy to digest and is a good source of protein, low in fat and sodium with no cholesterol.

Tofu is an ancient foodstuff, probably created in China during the second century A.D. It was introduced to Japan by Buddhist priests during the eighth century and was "discovered" by Western travelers during the 17th century. Today, Japanese tofu is said to be the finest, perhaps because of the superiority of the soybeans grown in the Yamato region, near the city of Kyoto. Japanese cuisine values the natural flavor and texture of tofu and uses it in a tremendous variety of ways. Chinese cuisine uses it as an additive, not as a principal ingredient.

Tofu may be eaten fresh; added to soup, broth or noodle dishes; tossed in cold salads; grilled, deep-fried or sautéed; or puréed to make a creamy spread. Its flavor is bland, but it readily absorbs flavors from other ingredients.

Two types of tofu are widely available: cotton (or traditional) and silken. **Cotton tofu** is the most common. The soy milk is coagulated (nowadays with calcium sulfate). The curds are then placed in a perforated mold lined with cloth and pressed with a weight to remove the liquid. Cotton tofu is solid, with an irregular surface caused by the weave of the cotton fabric in which it is wrapped for pressing. This traditional tofu comes in three styles: soft, firm and extra firm, each style being progressively drier and firmer. Select the style of tofu suited to the preparation. Firmer tofu is solid enough to be grilled or sautéed. It absorbs the favors of rubs and marinades. Softer tofu may be scrambled like eggs or processed to form a smooth spread.

Silken tofu (Japanese: *kinugoshi*) has a silky-smooth appearance and texture and a somewhat more delicate flavor than cotton tofu. Silken tofu is made in a process similar to the way yogurt is cultured. No curds are formed, nor is whey produced. This makes a tofu with a custardlike texture suitable for processing into a creamy substance, good to use as a base for dips or in spreads or smoothies. Because the water has not been pressed out of silken tofu, it should not be cooked at high temperatures or for a long time, as it falls apart easily. Silken tofu can also be drained to make a thicker spread with a consistency similar to mascarpone or cream cheese.

Silken Tofu

Fresh tofu is usually packaged in water. It should be refrigerated and kept in water until used. If the water is drained and changed daily, the tofu should last for 1 week. Tofu can be frozen for several months, though its texture may be slightly altered after thawing. Weight down the firm tofu while it is thawing to create a denser, firmer product, suitable for grilling. Place a sheet pan on top of the tofu, then place a heavy object such as a #10 can on top of the sheet pan. Drain the liquid from the tofu before using.

White Miso

Miso (MEE-so) is a thick paste made by salting and fermenting soybeans and rice or barley. After soaking, the soybeans are steamed, then crushed. The mixture is blended with water. Rice or barley is added along with salt before the mixture is inoculated with a living culture, *koji* or aspergillis mold. After fermenting and aging, often in large wooden barrels for as long as a year, the paste is ready to use. In Japan, where the manufacture of miso is a fine art akin to cheese making in France, there are countless styles of miso ranging in color from pale to rust and in taste from sweet to salty. In the United States, two types of miso are commonly available: sweet **white miso** (*shiro miso*) and dark or **red miso.** Creamy-colored white miso contains a high percentage of rice and has a mild, somewhat sweet flavor. Dark or red miso, which contains a higher percentage of soybeans, is aged longer and has a stronger, saltier flavor.

Red Miso

Miso can be used in cold and warm preparations but should never be boiled; it contains beneficial enzymes and bacteria that can be killed at high temperatures. A pungent seasoning, miso should be used judiciously so as not to overpower a dish. As little as 1 teaspoon (5 milliliters) per portion can be adequate

Tempeh

Texturized Soy Protein

Seitan

to flavor a simple broth. With its high salt content, miso will keep indefinitely under refrigeration.

Tempeh (TEHM-pay) is a type of bean cake made from fermented whole soybeans mixed with a grain such as rice or millet. The mixture is inoculated with rhizopus mold, which binds the grains into a firm cake. The traditional food of Indonesia, tempeh has a chewy consistency and a yeasty, nutty flavor.

With its chunky texture, tempeh makes a pleasant meat substitute. It lends itself to being marinated for grilling or sautéing. When crumbled, tempeh can be added to soups or stews to replace ground beef, poultry or pork. A firm cake, tempeh is easily sliced or cut into cubes. Because of the type of live culture used to make it, tempeh should be cooked prior to eating. Proper cooking also tempers its pronounced flavor. Tempeh is sold both fresh and frozen. It lasts for approximately 1 week in the refrigerator or several months when frozen.

Textured soy protein, also known as textured soy flour or TSP, a proprietary name, is a defatted soy protein that is dried and then compressed into granules or chunks or extruded into shapes. Food manufacturers use it as a meat extender and in commercially produced meat replacements. Granulated texturized soy protein must be rehydrated before cooking which causes it to take on a texture similar to that of meat. Larger forms of texturized soy protein benefit from simmering after rehydration. Adding some vinegar or lemon juice to the simmering liquid helps speed rehydration. A shelf-stable dry product, texturized soy protein can be stored for up to a year when tightly sealed at room temperature. Once it has been rehydrated, texturized soy protein must be refrigerated and should be used within a few days.

OTHER POPULAR INGREDIENTS IN VEGETARIAN COOKING

Seitan (SAY-tan), often referred to as "wheat meat", is a form of wheat gluten, the insoluble protein in wheat. A staple in the diets of Buddhist monks for centuries, seitan has a firm, chewy texture and a bland flavor. Seitan is made by preparing a dough from wheat gluten or wheat flour and water. The dough is repeatedly rinsed to remove any remaining starch or bran. The spongy pieces of seitan are then simmered in a broth of soy sauce or tamari with ginger, garlic and kombu (seaweed). Cooking tenderizes seitan and imbues it with the flavors of the cooking liquid. As it absorbs flavors, seitan can be flavored to mimic many foods. Using seasonings associated with poultry such as thyme and sage brings out a more chickenlike flavor in the seitan, whereas using dark soy sauce and meaty mushrooms can give it a meatlike flavor. Seitan should be added to a dish near the end of cooking, as it is already fully cooked. Fully cooked fresh seitan is sold refrigerated in irregularly sized chunks. Once opened it should be consumed within a few days. Powdered seitan mix is also available.

GRAIN BEVERAGES

Many grains and nuts can be used to produce beverages that can be used in place of stock or dairy products when making soups, sauces and custards. Almond, hazelnut, oat and rice milks are commercially available. These ingredients tend to be lower in fat but higher in carbohydrates than their dairy counterparts—and they are cholesterol-free.

ANALOGOUS FOODS

Numerous products made from soy, wheat, grains, or other plant materials are designed to mimic the appearance and texture of popular animal-based products. These commercially prepared products offer a texture and appearance similar to that of their animal-protein-based counterparts. While their flavors are less successful in imitating the actual flavor of their fish, meat or poultry counterparts, many offer consumers the pleasure of eating familiar foods in traditional dishes.

Plant-based products are available in the form of "nuggets," "burgers," "sausage," "hot dogs," "ground meat," "bacon," "cold cuts" and even "pastrami." Soy protein extract and judicious use of appropriate seasonings, such as sage in a turkey stuffing analogue, help mimic the flavor of their meat counterparts.

In most cases, these analogous food products may be prepared in the same way as their meat, poultry or fish counterparts. Steaming, sautéing, simmering, grilling and baking work well. Follow the manufacturer's directions, keeping in mind that these products are usually fully cooked, requiring only crisping and heating, and could suffer in overcooking.

▶ Vegetarian Cuisine: Rebalancing the Center of the Plate

The principles of vegetarian cuisine are no different from those of the classic kitchen. When creating an appetizing and satisfying vegetarian dish, chefs use the same professional judgment as when preparing a roast or steak. Flavors must be in balance. Ingredients must be thoughtfully selected and skillfully prepared. Only the ingredients themselves vary. Chefs need to understand the basic principles of cooking and work with the textures and flavors offered by plant-based ingredients.

Chefs also need to understand the unique role played by animal products in specific recipes they are considering adapting for a vegetarian diner. As discussed in Chapter 11, Principles of Meat Cookery, the muscle fibers in different cuts of meat, poultry and game yield foods with a chewy texture not easily mimicked by vegetable or soy analogues.

Well-marbled meat has fat throughout. When cooked, this fat melts, adding tenderness and flavor to the finished dish. It may be necessary to add fat to enhance flavor and add moisture to dishes cooked without meats. Replacing animal protein in a main dish with an equal amount of tofu, texturized soy protein, grain, bean purée or plant food may not result in a dish with the same appearance and depth of flavor as the original made with meat. Chefs must carefully choose the ingredients they use. Vegetables should be chosen for their flavor and texture. The mouthfeel each ingredient contributes to a finished dish should also be considered. Ripe avocados, for example, have a rich, creamy texture that can mimic the mouthfeel of a soft cream cheese.

Baking without eggs poses a number of challenges because of the function eggs perform in many baked goods. Quick-bread formulas using chemical leavening may be better suited to adapting to vegetarian preparation than creaming-style cakes.

With these considerations in mind, here are some suggestions on how to plan and prepare to add vegetarian dishes to a restaurant menu.

- *Use or adapt items from the regular menu.* Many items on existing menus may be vegetarian or can easily be adapted for a vegetarian diner. Soups, salads, stir-fried vegetables and pasta dishes lend themselves to vegetarian ingredients.
- *Grains and beans add texture and satiation.* Think about these versatile starches as the center-of-the-plate offerings when planning a vegetarian menu. Chewy grains such as cooked bulgur, barley and millet offer a good textural appeal that can be lacking in plant-based cuisine. Ensuring that a customer feels sufficiently fed is another consideration, something that a plate of steamed vegetables might not offer.
- *Take advantage of meaty vegetables and soy products as main attractions in a vegetarian dish.* Eggplant, mushrooms (especially portabellas), okra, sweet potatoes and parsnips have flavor and body that mimics that of meat. Pan-fried breaded eggplant slices or grilled whole portabella mushroom caps offer hearty vegetable alternatives to a slice of chicken or beef.

HAUTE VEGETABLES

Today, America's most respected chefs are elevating plant-based cuisine to the highest culinary art. Internationally acclaimed chefs Thomas Keller of the French Laundry in Yountville, California, and Per Se in New York City and Charlie Trotter of the eponymous restaurant in Chicago both offer a vegetable tasting menu each evening in their respective restaurants. While not strictly vegetarian—dairy products are used in abundance—Chef Keller explores the flavors and versatility of vegetables in his multicourse menu. Chef Trotter regularly offers a strictly raw food menu demonstrating that vegetarian dining can have a place in the finest restaurant.

Some dishes from one of Chef Keller's vegetable tasting menus:

Creamed Ramp Top "Pierogis," French Laundry Garden Shallots, Cipollini Onion "Rissolée," Glazed Ramp Bulbs with "Sauce Soubise" and Chive-Infused Extra Virgin Olive Oil

"Fricassée" of Roasted Marble Potatoes, California Grey Morel Mushrooms, Split English Peas and English Pea "Purée"

Some dishes from one of Chef Trotter's raw vegetable tasting menus:

Root Vegetable Salad with Eggplant and Purple Tomatillo Vinaigrette

Green and White Cauliflower with Shaved Asparagus Salad, Date Purée and Garlic Blossoms

- *Compose dishes with an eye to balancing color.* We eat with our eyes as well as our taste buds. When combining grains and beans on a plate, consider using different colors, such as black beans and red rice or yellow lentils and black-eyed peas.
- *Balance textures on the same plate.* Look for complementary and contrasting textures in a vegetarian plate. When serving a creamy purée, such as mashed sweet potatoes, for example, balance the texture with something crunchy or crisp such as fried zucchini or a risotto cake.
- *Layer flavors for complexity of taste.* A dish prepared with few ingredients need not be bland or boring. Combine cooking methods in one dish to bring out a complex taste. Sun-dried tomatoes added to a fresh tomato sauce add a rich dimension of taste that might otherwise be lacking.
- *Create a vegetarian pantry stocked with ingredients that help enhance plant-based cooking.* Without base flavor notes created from rich meat stocks, vegetarian dishes can lack depth of flavor. Varieties of fresh and dried mushrooms help enrich flavorful stocks, soups and stews. Dried seaweed such as kombu (sea kelp) adds a briny flavor mimicking seafood stock. Soy sauce and miso can give a vegetable broth a savory taste and appealing dark color, as can wine reductions. Richly flavored nut oils such as sesame oil, hazelnut oil and walnut oil can add complex tastes to dishes prepared without rich meat stocks or butter. Olives and dried fruit have intense flavors and pleasing textures that can add variety to a vegetarian dish. Toasted sesame and other seeds and nuts add bursts of flavor and a textural contrast to a dish.
- *Seek inspiration from ethnic cuisines in which vegetarian food is traditional.* Asian, Indian, Mexican, Middle Eastern and South American cuisines offer many exciting vegetarian options. Recipes in this book for Cambodian-Style Red Pork, Indonesian Fried Noodles with Pork, Thai Green Curry with Chicken and Eggplant and Samosas are just as frequently prepared without meat or poultry in their native countries as we have done in our recipe variations.

VEGETARIAN RECIPE OPTIONS

On Cooking contains a wealth of recipes suitable for a vegetarian eating plan. Recipes suitable for vegetarians who consume dairy and eggs are marked in this book with a  . Many other recipes can easily be adapted by substituting vegetable stock for meat stock, for example, or by using oil for sautéing in place of butter. To help adapt recipes for vegetarian cooking, some common alternatives to animal-based foods appear in Table 22.2.

Table 22.2 **VEGETARIAN INGREDIENT SUBSTITUTES**

INSTEAD OF	IN THIS APPLICATION	USE	COMMENTS
Butter	Sautéing	Vegetable oil or vegetable oil spray	
	Flavoring	Nut oil: hazelnut, pecan or walnut; nut butter: almond, cashew, peanut or sesame butter	Additional oil or liquid may be needed; thin nut butters with oil, fruit juices or nut, rice or soy milks
	Spreading	Ground nut spread: almond, cashew, peanut or sesame butter; vegetable purées: bean, roasted eggplant, red pepper	
	Baking	Dried fruit or cooked vegetable purées	Quick breads, cookies and general baking; may affect color, taste and texture
Cream	Hot soups, sauces	Soy or rice milk; puréed silken tofu	Add at last moment, heating gently to prevent separation
	Cold creams or spreads	Enriched soy milk	Oil may be needed to improve mouthfeel
Sour cream, yogurt	Beverage or custard	Soy coffee creamer	
	Cold creams or spreads	Puréed silken tofu	
Eggs	Leavening	Chemical leavening	Consider loss of color from lack of egg yolk; texture will be denser than product containing eggs
	Emulsifier in sauces such as mayonnaise	Form a temporary emulsion; form emulsion using ground nuts or soaked bread	
Beef, fish or poultry stock	Sauces, soups, stews	Vegetable stock; broth made from miso or seaweed	
Demi-glace	Sauces, stews	Rich vegetable stock made with a larger proportion of vegetables, reduced and thickened with starch	
Gelatin	Thickening, gelling	Agar	Gels more firmly than gelatin
Prepared sauces made with fish such as nuoc mam, oyster or Worcestershire	Flavoring	Soy sauce, balsamic or red wine vinegar	

CONCLUSION

A request for restaurant meals made exclusively with plant foods is no longer exceptional. Consumers choose to forgo eating meat, poultry or fish for a variety of personal and religious reasons. In fact, nutritional science increasingly recommends that all consumers eat a diet high in fiber and the vitamins found in vegetables, grains, fruits and legumes. Today's consumers, accustomed to making their own food choices, are frequently turning to a plant-based diet, and professional chefs need to understand how to create flavorful vegetarian options. While many delicious meals can be prepared using the vegetables, grains and starches studied throughout this book, a number of special ingredients made from soy and other products help vary the flavors and textures of vegetarian dishes.

QUESTIONS FOR DISCUSSION

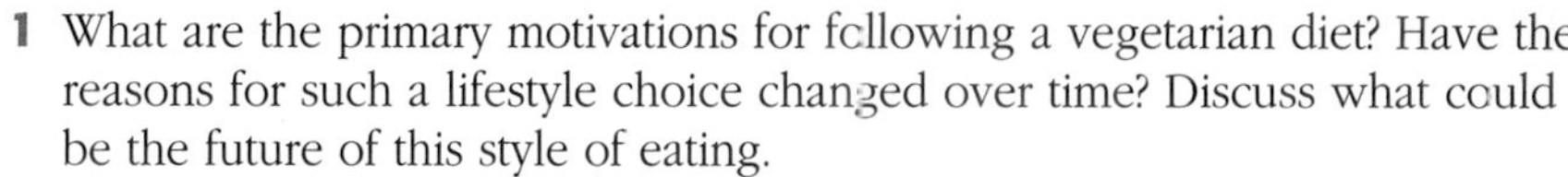

1. What are the primary motivations for following a vegetarian diet? Have the reasons for such a lifestyle choice changed over time? Discuss what could be the future of this style of eating.
2. What are three important ingredients that can be used to replace meat in a vegetarian dish? Discuss the ingredients used to prepare each product and ways in which it can be used in vegetarian cooking.
3. What are the five most common forms of vegetarianism and what are the types of foods each group permits itself to eat?
4. Identify three popular recipes that use meat, fish or poultry. Discuss how you would adapt such recipes for the vegetarian customer.

5. Vegetarian restaurants and restaurants that offer vegetarian menu options exist in every state. Schools, corporations, airlines and hospitals even offer vegetarian menu options. Use the Internet to research vegetarian menus. Analyze two or three such menus and discuss how they address the concerns of their customers.

CHAPTER TWENTY-THREE

SALADS AND SALAD DRESSINGS

ACCORDING TO THE SPANISH PROVERB,
FOUR PERSONS ARE WANTED FOR TO MAKE A GOOD SALAD:
A SPENDTHRIFT FOR OIL, A MISER FOR VINEGAR,
A COUNSELOR FOR SALT, AND A MADMAN TO STIR IT ALL UP.

—Abraham Hayward, English writer (1801–1884)

AFTER STUDYING THIS CHAPTER, YOU WILL BE ABLE TO:

- identify a variety of salad greens
- prepare a variety of salad dressings
- prepare a variety of salads
- present salads attractively

This chapter discusses all types of salads: the small plate of crisp iceberg lettuce with tomato wedges, cucumber slices and ranch dressing; the dinner plate of sautéed duck breast fanned across bright red grilled radicchio and toothy green arugula, sprayed with a vinaigrette dressing; the scoop of shredded chicken, mango chutney and seasonings, bound with mayonnaise; and the bowl of artichokes and mushrooms marinated in olive oil and lemon juice.

Each of these dishes fits the definition of a salad: a single food or a mix of different foods accompanied or bound by a dressing. A salad can contain meat, grains, fruits, nuts or cheese and absolutely no lettuce. It can be an appetizer, a second course served after the appetizer, an entrée (especially at lunch), a course following the entrée in the European manner or even dessert.

The color, texture and flavor of each salad ingredient should complement those of the others, and the dressing should complement all the ingredients. Harmony is critical to a salad's success—no matter what type of salad is being prepared.

This chapter opens with a section identifying greens commonly used in salads. A discussion of salad dressings follows. Finally, techniques for preparing green salads (both tossed and composed), bound salads, vegetable salads and fruit salads are discussed.

▸ SALAD GREENS

IDENTIFYING SALAD GREENS

Salad greens are not necessarily green: Some are red, yellow, white or brown. They are all, however, leafy vegetables. Many are members of the lettuce or chicory family.

LETTUCE

Lettuce (Fr. *laitue;* It. *lattuga*) has been consumed for nearly as long as people have kept records of what they and others ate. Archaeologists found that Persian royalty were served lettuce at their banquets more than 2500 years ago. Now grown and served worldwide, lettuces are members of the genus *Lactuca*. The most common types of lettuce are butterhead, crisp head, leaf and romaine.

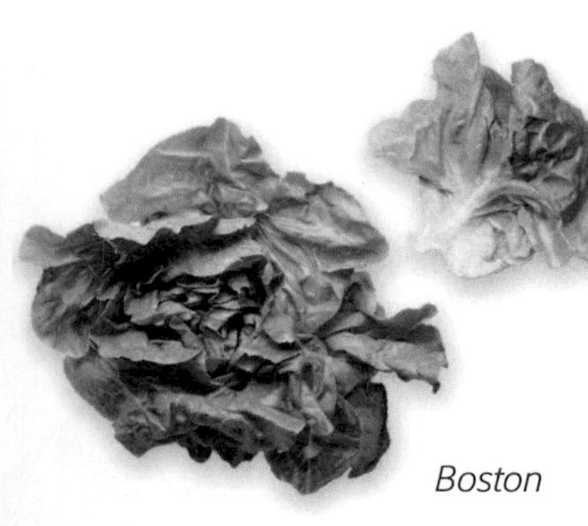
Boston

Boston

Boston and bibb are two of the most popular butterhead lettuces. Their soft, pliable, pale green leaves have a buttery texture and flavor. Boston is larger and paler than bibb. Both Boston and bibb lettuce leaves form cups when separated from the heads; these cups make convenient bases for holding other foods on cold plates.

Iceberg

Iceberg lettuce is the most common of all lettuce varieties in the United States; it outsells all other varieties combined. Its tightly packed spherical head is composed of crisp, pale green leaves with a very mild flavor. Iceberg lettuce remains crisp for a relatively long time after being cut or prepared. Select heads that are firm but not hard and leaves that are free of burnt or rusty tips.

Leaf

Leaf lettuce grows in bunches. It has separate, ruffle-edged leaves branching from a stalk. Because it does not grow into a firm head, it is easily damaged during harvest and transport. Both red and green leaf lettuce have bright colors, mild flavors and tender leaves. Good-quality leaf lettuce should have nicely shaped leaves free of bruises, breaks or brown spots.

Iceberg

Romaine

Romaine lettuce, also known as **cos,** is a loosely packed head lettuce with elongated leaves and thick midribs. Its outer leaves are dark green and although they look coarse, they are crisp, tender and tasty without being bitter. The core leaves are paler and more tender but still crisp. Romaine has enough flavor to stand up to strongly flavored dressings such as the garlic and Parmesan cheese used in a Caesar salad. A good-quality head of romaine has dark green outer leaves that are free of blemishes or yellowing.

Baby Lettuces

Innovative chefs are always looking for new and different foods to add a twist or flair to their dishes. This has led to the popularity of baby lettuces and other specialty greens. Baby greens have similar but more subtle flavors than their mature versions. They are often less bitter and are always more tender and delicate. Because of their size and variety, they are perfect for composed salads. **Mesclun** is a mixture of several kinds of baby lettuces.

Red and Green Leaf Lettuces

Brune d'Hiver

Lola Rosa

Red Sails

Romaine

Baby Red Oak Leaf

Baby Green Bibb

Baby Red Bibb

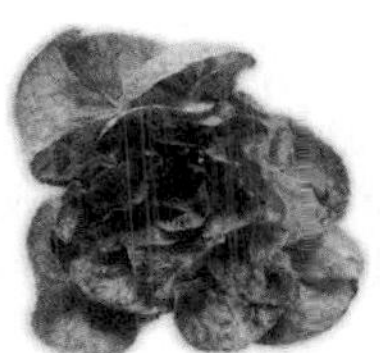

Pirate

Baby Red Romaine

Micro Greens

Micro greens are even smaller than baby lettuces. They are the first true leaves of virtually any edible greens, such as lettuce, spinach, kale and so on. Micro greens are very fragile and must be handpicked and carefully packaged for delivery. Chefs enjoy using them as garnish, especially on entrée and appetizer plates.

CHICORY

Chicories come in a variety of colors, shapes and sizes; most are slightly bitter. Chicories are quite hearty and can also be cooked, usually grilled or braised.

Belgian Endive

Belgian Endive

Belgian endive grows in small, tight heads with pointed leaves. It is actually the shoot of a chicory root. The small sturdy leaves are white at the base with yellow fringes and tips. (A purple-tipped variety is sometimes available.) Whole leaves can be separated, trimmed and filled with soft butters, cheeses or spreads and served as an hors d'oeuvre, or they can be used for composed salads. The leaves, cut or whole, can also be added to cold salads. Heads of Belgian endive are often braised or grilled and served with meat or poultry. As the name suggests, Belgian endive is imported from Belgium but a commercial crop is now produced in California as well.

Curly Endive

Curly Endive

In the United States, curly endive is often called by its family name, chicory, or its French name, frisée (free-ZAY). The dark green outer leaves are pointed, sturdy and slightly bitter. The yellow inner leaves are more tender and less bitter. Curly endive has a strong flavor that goes well with strong cheeses, game and citrus. It is often mixed with other greens to add texture and flavor.

Escarole

Radicchio

Escarole

Escarole (es-kah-ROLE), sometimes called broadleaf endive, has thick leaves and a slightly bitter flavor. It has green outer leaves and pale green or yellow center leaves. Escarole is very sturdy and is often mixed with other greens for added texture. Its strong flavor stands up to full-flavored dressings and is a good accompaniment to grilled meats and poultry.

Radicchio

Radicchio (rah-DEE-kee-oh) resembles a small red cabbage. It retains its bright reddish color when cooked and is popular braised or grilled and served as a vegetable side dish. Because of its attractive color, radicchio is popular in cold salads, but it has a very bitter flavor and should be used sparingly and mixed with other greens in a tossed salad. The leaves form cups when separated and can be used to hold other ingredients when preparing composed salads. Radicchio is quite expensive and availability is sometimes limited.

Arugula

Dandelion

OTHER SALAD GREENS AND INGREDIENTS

Leafy vegetables besides lettuce and chicory, as well as other ingredients, are used to add texture, flavor and color to salads. A partial listing follows.

Arugula

Arugula (ah-ROO-guh-lah), also known as rocket, is a member of the cabbage family. Arugula leaves are somewhat similar to broad dandelion leaves in size and shape. The best are 2 to 4 inches (5 to 10 centimeters) long. Arugula has a very strong, spicy, peppery flavor—so strong, in fact, that it is rarely served by itself. It is best when used to add zip to salads by combining it with other greens.

Dandelion

Dandelion grows as a weed throughout most of the United States. It has long, thin, toothed leaves with a prominent midrib. When purchasing dandelion for salads, look for small leaves; they are more tender and less bitter. Older, tougher leaves can be cooked and served as a vegetable.

Mâche

Mâche

Mâche (mahsh) or lamb's lettuce is very tender and very delicately flavored. Its small, curved, pale to dark green leaves have a slightly nutty flavor. Because its flavor is so delicate, mâche should be combined only with other delicately flavored greens such as Boston or bibb lettuce and dressed sparingly with a light vinaigrette dressing.

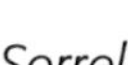

Sorrel

Sorrel

Sorrel, sometimes called sourgrass, has leaves similar to spinach in color and shape. Sorrel has a very tart, lemony flavor that goes well with fish and shellfish. It should be used sparingly and combined with other greens in a salad. Sorrel can also be made into soups, sauces and purées.

Spinach

Spinach

Like sorrel, spinach can be cooked or used as a salad green. As a salad green, it is popularly served tossed with hot bacon dressing. Spinach is deep green with a rich flavor and tender texture. Good-quality spinach should be fairly crisp. Avoid wilted or yellowed bunches.

Sprouts

Sprouts

Sprouts are not salad greens but are often used as such in salads and sandwiches. Sprouts are very young alfalfa, daikon or mustard plants. Alfalfa sprouts are very mild and sweet. Daikon and mustard sprouts are quite peppery.

Watercress

Watercress

Watercress has tiny, dime-sized leaves and substantial stems. It has a peppery flavor and adds spice to a salad. Good-quality fresh watercress is dark green with no yellowing. To preserve its freshness, watercress must be kept very cold and moist. It is normally packed topped with ice. Individual leaves are plucked from the stems and rinsed just before service.

Nasturtiums

Edible Flowers

Many specialty produce growers offer edible, pesticide-free blossoms. They are used for salads and as garnishes wherever a splash of color would be appreciated. Some flowers such as nasturtiums, calendulas and pansies are grown and picked specifically for eating. Others, such as yellow cucumber flowers and squash blossoms, are by-products of the vegetable industry.

Squash blossoms and other very large flowers should be cut in julienne strips before being added to salads. Pick petals from large and medium-sized flowers. Smaller whole flowers can be tossed in a salad or used as a garnish when composing a salad. Very small flowers or petals should be sprinkled on top of a salad so that they are not hidden by the greens.

Calendulas

Pansies

Fresh Herbs

Basil, thyme, tarragon, oregano, dill, cilantro, marjoram, mint, sage, savory and even rosemary are used to add interesting flavors to otherwise ordinary salads. Because many herbs have strong flavors, use them sparingly so that the delicate flavors of the greens are not overpowered. Leafy herbs such as basil and sage can be cut chiffonade. Other herbs can be picked from their stems or chopped before being tossed with the salad greens. Flowering herbs such as chive blossoms are used like

SAFETY ALERT

Flowers

Many flowers and blossoms are toxic, especially those grown from bulbs. Even flowers that would otherwise be edible may contain pesticides that can be harmful if ingested. Use only flowers grown specifically for use as food; purchase edible flowers only from reputable purveyors.

other edible flowers to add color, flavor and aroma. Refer to Chapter 5, Flavors and Flavorings, for more information on herbs.

NUTRITION

Salad greens are an especially healthful food. Greens contain virtually no fat and few calories and are high in vitamins A and C, iron and fiber. But when greens are garnished with meat and cheese and tossed with a dressing (many of which are oil based), fat and calories are added. In an attempt to maintain the healthful nature of greens, low-fat or fat-free dressings should be available to customers.

PURCHASING AND STORING SALAD GREENS

PURCHASING

Lettuces are grown in nearly every part of the United States; nearly all types are available year-round. Other important salad greens such as spinach are available all year; many of the specialty greens are seasonal.

Lettuce is generally packed in cases of 24 heads with varying weights. Other salad greens are packed in trays or boxes of various sizes and weights.

Because salad greens are simply washed and eaten, it is extremely important that they be as fresh and blemish-free as possible. Try to purchase salad greens daily. All greens should be fresh looking, with no yellowing. Heads should be heavy, with little or no damage to the outer leaves.

Many types of salad greens are available precut and prewashed. These greens are often vacuum packed to increase shelf life, although delicate greens are sometimes loosely packaged in 5- to 10-pound (2- to 5-kilogram) boxes. Precut and prewashed greens are relatively expensive, but can reduce labor costs dramatically.

STORING

Although some types of salad greens are hearty enough to keep for a week or more under proper conditions, all salad greens are highly perishable. Generally, softer-leaved varieties such as Boston and bibb tend to perish more quickly than the crisper-leaved varieties such as iceberg and romaine. Frequently, greens that have wilted slightly can be revived by soaking them in chilled water for up to an hour. The greens should then be drained and refrigerated until crisp.

Greens should be stored in their original protective cartons in a specifically designated refrigerator. Ideally, greens should be stored at temperatures between 34°F and 38°F (1°C and 3°C). (Most other vegetables should be stored at warmer temperatures of 40°F to 50°F [4°C to 10°C].) Greens should not be stored with tomatoes, apples or other fruits that emit ethylene gas, which causes greens to wilt and accelerates spoilage.

Do not wash greens until needed as excess water causes them to deteriorate quickly.

PREPARING SALAD GREENS

Unless salad greens are purchased precut and prewashed, they will need to undergo some preparation before service, principally tearing, cutting, washing and drying.

TEARING AND CUTTING

Some chefs want all salad greens torn by hand. Delicate greens such as butterhead and baby lettuces look nicer, and it is less likely they will be bruised if hand-torn. But often it is not practical to hand-tear all greens. It is perfectly acceptable to cut hardy greens with a knife. And it can be more practical to snip small lettuce leaves and fresh herbs with kitchen scissors.

▶ PROCEDURE FOR CUTTING ROMAINE LETTUCE

1 To cut romaine lettuce, trim the outer leaves and damaged tips with a chef's knife and split the head lengthwise.

2 Make one or two cuts along the length of the head, leaving the root intact, then cut across the width of the head.

3 Alternative method: Trim the outer leaves and damaged tips with a chef's knife. Pull the leaves from the core and cut the rib out of each leaf. The leaf can then be cut to the desired size.

▶ PROCEDURE FOR CORING ICEBERG LETTUCE

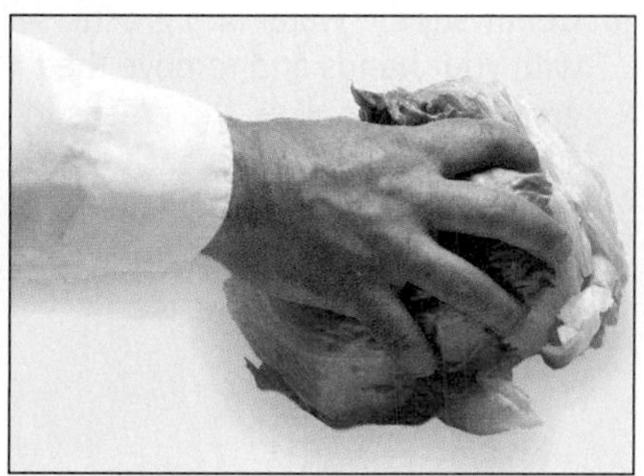

1 Loosen the core by gripping the head and smacking the core on the cutting board. (Do not use too much force or you may bruise the lettuce).

2 Remove the core and cut the lettuce as desired.

▶ PROCEDURE FOR REMOVING THE MIDRIB FROM SPINACH

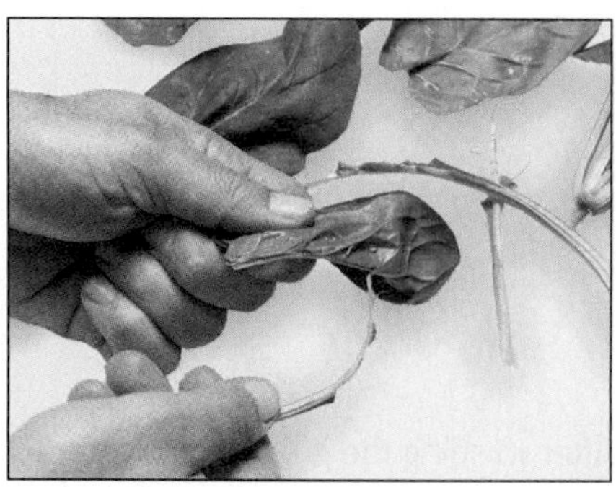

Fold the leaf in half and pull off the stem and midrib. Only the tender leaf should remain.

SAFETY ALERT

Hand Washing

Because salads are not cooked, it is especially important to be extra careful about proper hand washing when preparing them. Remember that many health departments require single-use gloves to be worn—and changed frequently—whenever working with products that will not be cooked before service.

WASHING

All lettuces and other salad greens should be washed before use. Even though they may look clean, greens may harbor hidden insects, sand, soil and pesticides. All greens should be washed after they are torn or cut. Whole heads can be washed by repeatedly dipping them in cold water and allowing them to drain. But washing whole heads is not recommended: It will not remove anything trapped near the head's center, and water trapped in the leaves can accelerate spoilage.

▶ PROCEDURE FOR WASHING SALAD GREENS

1 Fill a sink with very cold water. Place the cut or torn greens in the water.

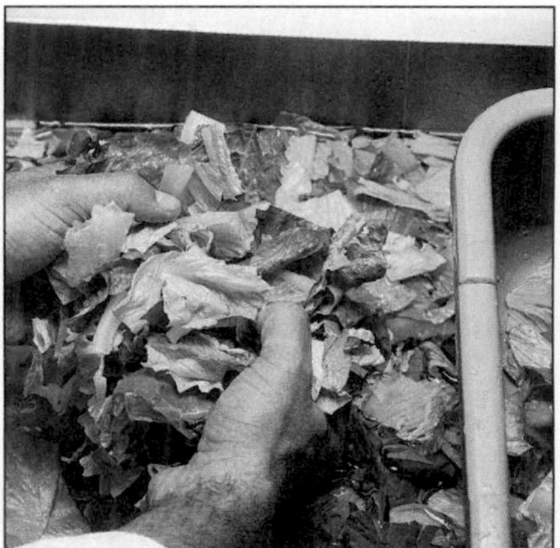

2 Gently stir the water and greens with your hands and remove the greens. Do not allow the greens to soak. Using fresh water each time, repeat the procedure until no grit can be detected on the bottom of the sink after the greens are removed.

DRYING

Salad greens should be dried after washing. Wet greens do not stay as crisp as thoroughly dried ones. Also, wet greens tend to repel oil-based dressings and dilute their flavors. Greens may be dried by draining them well in a colander and blotting them with absorbent cloth or paper towels, or, preferably, they can be dried in a salad spinner, which uses centrifugal force to remove the water.

▶ PROCEDURE FOR DRYING GREENS

After washing the greens, place them in the basket of a salad spinner and spin for approximately 30 seconds.

▶ SALAD DRESSINGS

A dressing is a sauce for a salad. Just as sauces for hot foods should complement rather than mask the flavor of the principal food, the sauce (dressing) for a salad should complement rather than mask the flavors of the other ingredients. Although a great many ingredients can be used to make salad dressings, most are based on either a mixture of oil and vinegar, called a vinaigrette, or a mayonnaise or other emulsified product.

Vinaigrette-style dressings can be made without oil; creamy dressings similar to mayonnaise-based dressings can be made with sour cream, yogurt or buttermilk instead of mayonnaise. Nevertheless, for all practical purposes these dressings are still prepared like vinaigrettes and mayonnaise-based dressings and they are treated that way here.

VINAIGRETTE DRESSINGS

The simple vinaigrette also known as basic **French dressing** is a temporary emulsion of oil and vinegar seasoned with salt and pepper. The standard ratio is three parts oil to one part vinegar. The ratio can vary, however. When using strongly flavored oils, less than three parts oil to one part vinegar generally suffices. In some recipes, all or part of the vinegar is replaced with citrus juice, in which case it may take more than one part vinegar and citrus juice to three parts oil to achieve the proper acidity level. Mild or sweet vinegars such as balsamic may require less oil to balance the flavors in the dressing. The best way to determine the correct ratio of oil to vinegar is to taste the dressing, preferably on the food it will dress.

▶ **French dressing** classically, a vinaigrette dressing made from oil, vinegar, salt and pepper; in the United States, the term also refers to a commercially prepared dressing that is creamy, tartly sweet and red-orange in color

Oils and vinegars have unique flavors that can be mixed and matched to achieve the correct balance for a particular salad. Olive oil goes well with red wine vinegar; nut oils go well with white wine or sherry vinegars. Neutral-flavored oils such as canola, corn or safflower can be mixed with a flavored vinegar.

Oil and vinegar repel each other and will separate almost immediately when mixed. They should be whisked together immediately before use.

OILS

Many types of oil can be used to make salad dressings. Light, neutral-flavored oils such as canola, corn, cottonseed, soybean and safflower are relatively low priced and used extensively for this purpose. Other oils can be used to add flavor. Olive oil is very popular; both mild-flavored pure olive oil and full-flavored extra virgin olive oil are used. Nut oils such as hazelnut and walnut are expensive, but they add unique and interesting flavors. Infused oils are also popular.

VINEGARS

Many different vinegars can be used to make salad dressings. Red wine vinegar is the most common because it is inexpensive and its flavor blends well with many foods. But other vinegars such as cider, balsamic and white wine are also used. Fruit-flavored vinegars (particularly raspberry) are extremely popular and widely available, as are herb- and garlic-flavored ones.

Flavored vinegars are easy to make. Fruit, herbs or garlic are added to a wine vinegar (either red or white) and left for several days for the flavors to blend. The vinegar is then strained and used as desired.

Acidic juices such as lemon, orange and lime are sometimes substituted for all or part of the vinegar in a salad dressing.

NOT JUST FOR SALADS

With its light taste and texture, vinaigrette dressing makes an appealing sauce where a light touch is desired. It is quick to make and versatile; changing the taste of a vinaigrette is only a matter of switching the type of oil and vinegar used. Its balanced acidity makes vinaigrette a good foil for fish dishes, as shown in Pan-Seared Sea Bass with Beet Vinaigrette and Stuffed Striped Bass Cartoccio, served with a truffle and sherry vinegar dressing.

OTHER FLAVORING INGREDIENTS

Herbs, spices, shallots, garlic, mustard and sugar are only a few of the many flavoring ingredients used to enhance a vinaigrette dressing. Items such as herbs, shallots and garlic should be minced or chopped before being added to the dressing. If dried herbs are used, the dressing should rest for at least 1 hour to allow the flavors to develop. Other ingredients may be added at any time.

▶ PROCEDURE FOR PREPARING A VINAIGRETTE

1. Choose an oil and vinegar that complement each other as well as the foods they will dress.
2. Combine the vinegar, seasonings and any other flavorings in a bowl.
3. Whisk in the oil gradually.
4. Allow the finished dressing to rest a few hours at room temperature before using so that the flavors can blend.
5. Rewhisk immediately before use.

RECIPE 23.1

BASIC VINAIGRETTE DRESSING

Whisking together the vinaigrette dressing.

Yield: 1 qt. (1 lt)

Wine vinegar	8 fl. oz.	250 ml
Salt	2 tsp.	10 ml
Pepper	TT	TT
Salad oil	24 fl. oz.	750 ml

1. Combine the vinegar, salt and pepper and mix well. Whisk in the oil gradually. Store at room temperature.

VARIATIONS:

Dijon Vinaigrette—Add 4 ounces (120 grams) Dijon-style mustard to the vinegar and proceed with the recipe.

Herb Vinaigrette—Add 2 tablespoons (30 milliliters) fresh herbs or 1 tablespoon (15 milliliters) dried herbs such as basil, tarragon, thyme, marjoram and chives to the vinaigrette.

Approximate values per 1-fl.-oz. (30-ml) serving: **Calories** 190, **Total fat** 22 g, **Saturated fat** 3 g, **Cholesterol** 0 mg, **Sodium** 75 mg, **Total carbohydrates** 0 g, **Protein** 0 g, **Claims**—no cholesterol; low sodium; no sugar

▶ **emulsion** a uniform mixture of two unmixable liquids; it is often temporary (for example, oil in water)

MAYONNAISE VS. SALAD DRESSING

Commercially prepared salad dressing is often used as a substitute for "real" mayonnaise. Although it may look, smell and spread like the real thing, salad dressing tends to be sweeter than mayonnaise. Salad dressing costs less than real mayonnaise because it is made without egg yolks, relying instead on chemical thickening agents. The cost is reduced further because the FDA requires salad dressing to contain only 30 percent oil, while mayonnaise must contain at least 65 percent oil.

MAYONNAISE

Although most food service operations buy commercially made mayonnaise, every chef should know how it is made to more fully understand how to use it and why it reacts the way it does when used. Knowing how to make mayonnaise also allows the chef to create a mayonnaise with the exact flavorings desired.

Mayonnaise is an **emulsion.** An emulsion, or emulsified sauce, is formed when two liquids that would not ordinarily form a stable mixture are forced together and held in suspension. To make mayonnaise, oil is whisked together with a very small amount of vinegar. (It is the water in the vinegar that does not normally mix with oil.) As the oil and vinegar are whisked together, the oil breaks into microscopic droplets that are separated from each other by a thin barrier of vinegar. If left alone, the droplets would quickly regroup, forming a large puddle of oil and a small puddle of vinegar. To prevent the oil droplets from regrouping, an emulsifier is added. For mayonnaise, the emulsifier is lecithin, a protein found in egg yolks. (The acid in the vinegar also helps form the emulsion.) Lecithin has the unique ability to combine with both oil and water. It surrounds the oil droplets, preventing them from coming in contact with each other and regrouping.

The balance of vinegar, oil, lecithin and agitation (whipping) is crucial to achieve a proper emulsion. The higher the proportion of oil to vinegar, the thicker the sauce will be. The higher the proportion of vinegar to oil, the thinner the sauce will be. (For example, the Emulsified Vinaigrette Dressing is a thin emulsion.) Some chefs add ½ fluid ounce (15 milliliters) boiling water to each 7 ounces (200 milliliter) finished mayonnaise to help maintain the emulsion.

There is a limit to how much oil each egg yolk can emulsify, however. One yolk contains enough lecithin to emulsify approximately 7 ounces (200 milliliters) of oil. If more than that amount of oil per egg yolk is added, the sauce will break; that is, the oil and vinegar will separate, and the mayonnaise will become very thin. Often mayonnaise that has broken can be repaired by beating the broken mayonnaise into additional egg yolks or prepared mayonnaise until the emulsion reforms. To repair a broken mayonnaise, slowly beat 7 fluid ounces (210 milliliters) broken mayonnaise into one egg yolk or 4 fluid ounces (120 milliliters) prepared mayonnaise. Adjust the amount of egg yolk or prepared mayonnaise to be used according to the batch that has broken.

SAFETY ALERT

Mayonnaise

The raw eggs in freshly prepared mayonnaise make it a potentially hazardous food. Use pasteurized eggs if possible, chill the ingredients before mixing and keep the finished mayonnaise at 41°F (5°C) or below. Although there is sufficient acid in commercially prepared mayonnaise to serve as a deterrent to bacterial growth, homemade mayonnaise should not be handled in the same manner as it does not necessarily have the same protection.

INGREDIENTS

A neutral-flavored vegetable oil is most often used for a standard mayonnaise. Other oils are used to contribute their special flavors. For example, olive oil is used to make a strong garlic mayonnaise called aïoli.

Wine vinegar is used for a standard mayonnaise. Flavored vinegars such as tarragon vinegar are often used to create unique flavors.

Seasonings vary according to the intended use but typically include dry mustard, salt, pepper and lemon juice.

▶ PROCEDURE FOR PREPARING MAYONNAISE

1. Gather all ingredients and hold at room temperature. Room-temperature ingredients emulsify more easily than cold ones.
2. By hand or in an electric mixer or food processor, whip the egg yolks on high speed until frothy.
3. Add the seasonings to the yolks and whip to combine. Salt and other seasonings will dissolve or blend more easily when added at this point rather than to the finished mayonnaise.
4. Add a small amount of the liquid (for example, vinegar) from the recipe and whip to combine.
5. With the mixer on high or whisking vigorously by hand, begin to add the oil very slowly until an emulsion forms.
6. After the emulsion forms, the oil can be added a little more quickly but still in a slow, steady stream. The mayonnaise can now be whipped at a slightly slower speed.
7. The mayonnaise will become very thick as more oil is added. A small amount of liquid can be added if it becomes too thick. Alternate between oil and liquid two or three times until all the oil is added and the correct consistency is reached. Important: A large egg yolk can emulsify up to 7 fluid ounces (200 milliliters) of oil; adding more oil may cause the mayonnaise to break.
8. Adjust the seasonings and refrigerate immediately.

CONVENIENCE PRODUCTS

A great many prepared and dry-mix salad dressings are available. Although they vary greatly in quality, they can be very economical; they offer consistency, reduced labor costs and, sometimes, reduced food costs. Some of these products use stabilizers, artificial flavorings and colors; nearly all contain preservatives. When considering the advantages of prepared or dry-mix salad dressings, always keep quality in mind.

RECIPE 23.2

MAYONNAISE

Yield: 1 qt. (1 lt)

Egg yolks, pasteurized	4	4
Salt	1 tsp.	5 ml
White pepper	TT	TT
Dry mustard	1 tsp.	5 ml
Wine vinegar	3 Tbsp.	45 ml
Salad oil	28 fl. oz.	840 ml
Lemon juice	TT	TT

1. Place the egg yolks in the bowl of a mixer and whip on high speed until thick and lemon-colored.
2. Add the dry ingredients and half the vinegar to the yolks; whisk to combine.
3. Begin to add the oil a drop at a time until the mixture begins to thicken and an emulsion begins to form.
4. Add the remaining oil in a slow steady stream, thinning the mayonnaise occasionally by adding a little vinegar. Continue until all the oil and vinegar have been incorporated.
5. Adjust the seasonings and add lemon juice to taste.
6. Refrigerate until needed.

Approximate values per 1-fl.-oz. (30-ml) serving: **Calories** 230, **Total fat** 26 g, **Saturated fat** 3.5 g, **Cholesterol** 25 mg, **Sodium** 75 mg, **Total carbohydrates** 0 g, **Protein** 0

1 Whipping the egg yolks until frothy.

2 Adding the oil very slowly, allowing the emulsion to form.

3 The finished mayonnaise.

MAYONNAISE-BASED DRESSINGS

Mayonnaise-based salad dressings are salad dressings that use mayonnaise as a base, with other ingredients added for flavor, color and texture. These ingredients include dairy products (especially buttermilk and sour cream), vinegar, fruit juice, vegetables (either puréed or minced), tomato paste, garlic, onions, herbs, spices, condiments, capers, anchovies and boiled eggs. Recipes for several mayonnaise-based salad dressings appear at the end of this chapter.

Table 23.1 **TROUBLESHOOTING MAYONNAISE**

PROBLEM	CAUSE	SOLUTION
Too thin	Not enough oil added	Continue adding oil until mixture thickens
	Too much lemon juice or vinegar added	Adjust formula
Too thick	Too much oil added for the amount of yolks	Adjust formula
	Insufficient vinegar used	Add more vinegar
Sauce breaks or curdles	Inadequate emulsification when mixing	Wisk vigorously adding oil slowly; use electric mixer to make a more stable emulsion; attempt repairing the mayonnaise
	Oil too cold when added	Use room-temperature oil; attempt repairing the mayonnaise
	Oil added too quickly	Attempt repairing the mayonnaise
	Too much oil added	Adjust formula using additional egg yolks or less oil; attempt repairing the mayonnaise

EMULSIFIED VINAIGRETTE DRESSINGS

An emulsified vinaigrette is a standard vinaigrette dressing emulsified with whole eggs. An emulsified vinaigrette dressing is thinner and lighter than a mayonnaise-based dressing and heavier than a basic vinaigrette. Its flavor is similar to a basic vinaigrette, but it will not separate and it clings to greens quite easily.

▶ PROCEDURE FOR PREPARING AN EMULSIFIED VINAIGRETTE DRESSING

1. Gather all ingredients and hold at room temperature. Room-temperature ingredients emulsify more easily than cold ones.
2. Whip the eggs until frothy.
3. Add the dry ingredients and any flavorings such as garlic, shallots and herbs.
4. Add a small amount of the liquid from the recipe and whip to incorporate the ingredients.
5. With the mixer on high or whisking vigorously by hand, begin adding the oil very slowly until the emulsion forms.
6. After the emulsion is formed, add the oil a little more quickly, but still in a slow, steady stream.
7. Alternate between oil and liquid two or three times until all the oil is added. The dressing should be much thinner than mayonnaise. If it is too thick, it can be thinned with a little water, vinegar or lemon juice. Determine which to use by first tasting the dressing.

RECIPE 23.3 EMULSIFIED VINAIGRETTE DRESSING

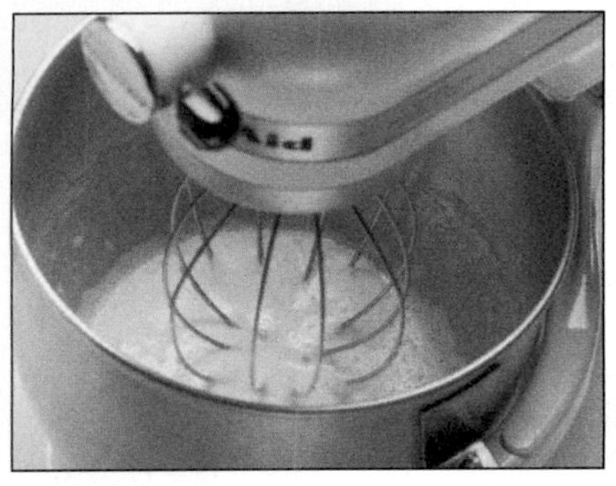

1 Whipping the whole eggs.

2 Adding the oil drop by drop to establish the emulsion.

3 The finished emulsified vinaigrette dressing.

Yield: 1 qt. (1 lt)

Eggs, pasteurized	2	2
Salt	1 Tbsp.	15 ml
White pepper	1/2 tsp.	2 ml
Paprika	1 Tbsp.	15 ml
Dry mustard	1 Tbsp.	15 ml
Granulated sugar	1 Tbsp.	15 ml
Herbes de Provence	1 Tbsp.	15 ml
Cayenne pepper	TT	TT
Wine vinegar or cider vinegar	4 fl. oz.	120 ml
Salad oil	24 fl. oz.	720 ml
Lemon juice	3 fl. oz.	90 ml

1 Place the eggs in the bowl of a mixer and whip at high speed until frothy.
2 Add the dry ingredients and approximately 1 fluid ounce (30 milliliters) vinegar to the eggs; whip to combine.
3 While whipping at high speed, begin adding the oil very slowly until an emulsion forms.
4 Add the remaining oil in a slow, steady stream. Occasionally thin the dressing by adding a little vinegar and lemon juice. Continue until all the oil, vinegar and lemon juice have been incorporated.
5 Adjust the flavor and consistency.
6 Refrigerate until needed.

Approximate values per 1-fl.-oz. (30-ml) serving: **Calories** 200, **Total fat** 22 g, **Saturated fat** 3 g, **Cholesterol** 15 mg, **Sodium** 220 mg, **Total carbohydrates** 1 g, **Protein** 1 g

▶ PREPARATION METHODS

There are two types of **green salads:** tossed and composed. The more informal **tossed salad** is prepared by placing the greens, garnishes and dressing in a large bowl and tossing to combine. A **composed salad** usually has a more elegant look. It is prepared by arranging each of the ingredients on plates in an artistic fashion.

Other types of salads include **bound salads,** which are cooked meats, poultry, fish, shellfish, pasta or potatoes bound with a dressing; **vegetable salads;** and **fruit salads.**

GREEN SALADS

TOSSED SALADS

Tossed salads are made from leafy vegetables such as lettuce, spinach, watercress, arugula or dandelion greens. They may consist only of greens and dressing, or they can be garnished with fruits, vegetables, nuts or cheese. They can be dressed with many different types of dressings, from a light oil and vinegar to a hearty hot bacon. It is important that salad dressings be added at the last possible moment before service. Acidic dressings cause most greens to wilt and become soggy.

Matching Dressings and Salad Greens

There is a simple rule to follow when choosing dressings for salads: The more delicate the texture and flavor of the greens or other ingredients, the lighter and more subtle the dressing should be. Vinaigrette-based dressings are much lighter

Table 23.2 **MATCHING DRESSINGS AND SALAD GREENS**

DRESSING	GREENS
Vinaigrette dressing made with vegetable oil and red wine vinegar	Any greens: iceberg, romaine, leaf lettuce, butterhead lettuce, escarole, curly endive, Belgian endive, radicchio, baby lettuces, sorrel, arugula, dandelion, micro greens
Vinaigrette dressing made with a nut oil and white wine or sherry vinegar	Delicate greens; butterhead lettuce, bibb lettuce, Belgian endive, baby lettuces, mâche, watercress, micro greens
Vinaigrette dressing made with vegetable oil and balsamic vinegar.	Any greens; romaine, leaf lettuce, radicchio, arugula
Emulsified vinaigrette dressing	Any greens; romaine, leaf lettuce, butterhead lettuce, escarole, curly endive, Belgian endive, radicchio, baby lettuces, sorrel, arugula, watercress
Mayonnaise-based dressing such as blue cheese or green goddess	Hardy greens; iceberg, romaine, leaf lettuce, escarole, curly endive, sorrel, dandelion

than mayonnaise-based or similar dressings and should be used with butterhead lettuces, mâche or other delicate greens. Crisp head lettuce such as iceberg and hardy lettuce such as romaine can stand up to heavier, mayonnaise-based or similar dressings. Table 23.2 lists some popular greens and dressing combinations.

Salad Garnishes

It is impossible to make a complete list of the garnishes that can be combined with salad greens for a tossed salad. The following is a partial list:

- Vegetables—nearly any vegetable (raw, blanched or fully cooked) cut into appropriate sizes and uniform shapes
- Fruits—citrus segments, apples or pears; dried fruits such as raisins, currants or apricots
- Meats, poultry, fish and shellfish—cooked meats and poultry sliced or diced neatly and uniformly; poached, grilled or cured fish, diced or flaked; small, whole cooked shellfish such as shrimp and scallops; lobster or crab sliced, diced or chopped
- Cheeses—grated hard cheeses such as Parmesan, Romano or Asiago; semihard cheeses such as Cheddar or Swiss, cut julienne or shredded
- Nuts—nearly any are appropriate, roasted, candied or smoked
- Croutons—assorted breads, seasoned in various ways and toasted

▶ PROCEDURE FOR MAKING TOSSED SALADS

1. Select greens with various colors, textures and flavors.
2. Carefully cut or tear, wash and dry the greens.
3. Prepare the garnishes as directed or desired.
4. Prepare the dressing.
5. Combine the greens, garnishes and dressing by tossing them together, or toss the greens and garnishes and, using a spray bottle, spray the greens with the dressing.

RECIPE 23.4

MESCLUN SALAD WITH RASPBERRY VINAIGRETTE

Yield: 6 Servings **Method:** Tossed

Baby lettuces, assorted	approx. 8 heads	approx. 8 heads
Mâche	4 oz.	120 g
Fresh herbs	2 Tbsp.	30 ml
Edible flowers	approx. 12	approx. 12
Raspberry Vinaigrette	4 fl. oz.	120 ml

1. Trim, wash and dry the baby lettuces and mâche.
2. Pick the fresh herbs from their stems. Leafy herbs such as basil may be cut chiffonade or left as whole leaves.
3. If desired, pick the petals from the edible flowers. Small flowers may be left whole.
4. Place the lettuces and mâche in a bowl and add the herbs. Ladle the Raspberry Vinaigrette over them and toss gently, using two spoons.
5. Transfer the salad to six cold plates. Some of the larger leaves may be used as liners if desired.
6. Garnish each salad with flowers or flower petals.

Approximate values per serving: **Calories** 150, **Total fat** 9 g, **Saturated fat** 1 g, **Cholesterol** 0 mg, **Sodium** 180 mg, **Total carbohydrates** 14 g, **Protein** 4 g, **Vitamin A** 35%, **Vitamin C** 120%

COMPOSED SALADS

Transferring composed salads to chilled plates for service.

Composed green salads usually use a green as a base and are built by artistically arranging other ingredients on the plate. There are usually four components: the base, body, garnish and dressing.

The **base** is usually a layer of salad greens that line the plate on which the salad will be served. Depending on the desired effect, the leaves can be cup-shaped or flat.

The **body** is the main ingredient. It can be lettuce or other greens, or another salad made from cooked or blended ingredients, such as chicken salad or fruit.

The **garnish** is added to the salad for color, texture and flavor. It can be as substantial as a grilled, sliced duck breast or as simple as a sprinkling of chopped herbs; it can be warm or cold. The choice is unlimited, but whatever is used should always complement and balance the flavor of the body.

The **dressing** should complement rather than mask the other flavors in the salad. If the body already contains a dressing, such as a bound salad, additional dressing may not be necessary.

Composed green salads are usually dressed by ladling the dressing over the salad after it is plated. Alternatively, the individual ingredients can be dressed before they are arranged on the plate. A third method that may be limited by the intricacy of the salad but will save precious time during a busy period is to prepare individual salads on a sheet pan. Then, just before service, mist them with dressing using a spray bottle designated for this purpose; then transfer them to chilled plates using a spatula.

▶ PROCEDURE FOR MAKING COMPOSED SALADS

1. Gather all ingredients for the salad and wash, trim, cut, cook, chill or otherwise prepare them as necessary or as called for in the recipe.
2. Arrange all ingredients artistically on the plates, dressing each ingredient as desired or as directed in the recipe.
3. At service time, heat or cook any items that are being served hot and add them to the salad.

SALAD NIÇOISE

RECIPE 23.5

Yield: 6 Servings

Method: Composed

Red wine vinegar	4 fl. oz.	120 ml
Salt and pepper	TT	TT
Virgin olive oil	12 fl. oz.	360 ml
Fresh basil leaves, chiffonade	12	12
Chicory	1 head	1 head
Tomatoes	6	6
Cucumbers	1 lb. 8 oz	720 g
Green beans	12 oz.	360 g
Eggs, hard-boiled, chilled	6	6
Artichokes	6	6
Romaine lettuce, large leaves, washed	12	12
New potatoes, size B, boiled, quartered, chilled	12 oz.	360 g
Green bell peppers, bâtonnet	2	2
Tuna, fresh, grilled and chilled	1 lb. 8 oz.	720 g
Niçoise olives	4 oz.	120 g

1. Make a vinaigrette dressing using the red wine vinegar, salt, pepper, olive oil and basil.
2. Wash and dry the chicory.
3. Core each tomato and cut into eight wedges.
4. Peel and slice the cucumbers.
5. Trim the green beans and cook al dente.
6. Peel the eggs and cut into wedges.
7. Cook the artichokes. Trim the outer leaves from each artichoke, leaving only the heart. Remove the choke from the heart and cut each heart into quarters.
8. Line each cold plate with two romaine lettuce leaves, then arrange the remaining ingredients artistically. Use the contrasting shapes, colors and textures to create an attractive presentation.
9. At service time, whisk the dressing to combine the ingredients and pour approximately 2½ fluid ounces (75 milliliters) over each salad.

Approximate values per serving: **Calories** 890, **Total fat** 70 g, **Saturated fat** 11 g, **Cholesterol** 200 mg, **Sodium** 760 mg, **Total carbohydrates** 21 g, **Protein** 44 g, **Vitamin A** 130%, **Vitamin C** 60%, **Iron** 30%

Mise en Place

- ▶ Wash and chop basil in chiffonade.
- ▶ Hard-boil eggs and chill.
- ▶ Wash lettuce.
- ▶ Boil and quarter potatoes and chill.
- ▶ Wash bell peppers and cut in bâtonnet.
- ▶ Grill tuna and chill.

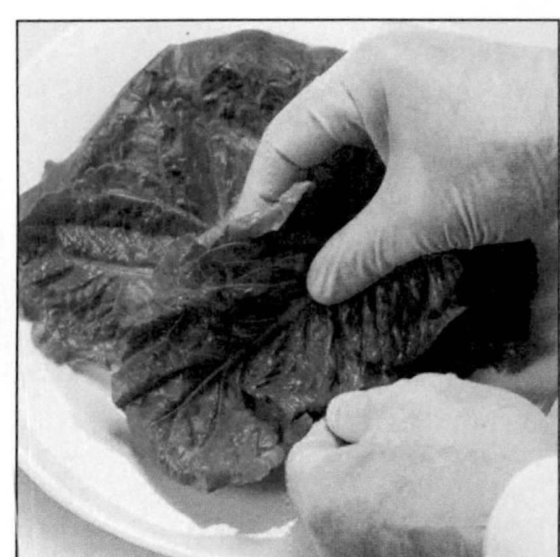

1 Lining a cold salad plate with a base of lettuce leaves.

2 The composed Salad Nicoise.

BOUND SALADS

The creative chef can prepare a wide variety of salads by combining cooked meats, poultry, fish, shellfish, potatoes, pasta, grains and/or legumes with a dressing and garnishes. Although the combinations vary greatly, these salads are grouped here because their ingredients are all bound. That is, each salad consists of one or more ingredients held together in a cohesive mass. The binding agent can be either a vinaigrette or a mayonnaise-based or similar dressing. The ingredients should be evenly distributed throughout, and the degree of cohesiveness can range from tightly packed to flaky and easily separated.

The foods that can be used to produce bound salads are so varied that it is impossible to list them all. Generalizing preparation techniques is also very difficult. There are as many ways to prepare a bound salad as there are ingredients, dressings and garnishes.

Bound salads can be used as the body of a composed salad (for instance, a serving of egg salad on a bed of greens). Some are used in sandwiches but not ordinarily as side dishes—for example, tuna or chicken salad. Some are served as side dishes but not in sandwiches—for example, potato or pasta salad. Follow specific recipes and traditional uses for each salad to build confidence. Then use these skills and imagination to create enticing new salad combinations.

▶ GUIDELINES FOR MAKING BOUND SALADS

1. Preparing a salad from cooked foods is a good opportunity to use leftovers, but be sure they are fresh and of good quality. The finished salad can be only as good as each of its ingredients.
2. When making a bound salad, choose ingredients whose flavors blend well and complement each other.
3. Choose ingredients for color; a few colorful ingredients will turn a plain salad into a spectacular one.
4. To improve appearance, cut all ingredients the same size.
5. All ingredients should be cut into pieces that are small enough to be eaten easily with a fork.
6. Be sure all meats, poultry, fish and shellfish are properly cooked before using them. Improperly cooked foods can cause food-borne illness and spoilage.
7. Always chill cooked ingredients well before using them. Warm ingredients promote bacterial growth, especially in mayonnaise-based salads.
8. Always use dressings sparingly. They should enhance the flavors of the other salad ingredients, not mask them.

RECIPE 23.6

CHUTNEY CHICKEN SALAD

Mise en Place

- ▶ Cook chicken and chill.
- ▶ Wash and peel celery and chop into small dice.
- ▶ Wash and slice green onions.

Adding grapes to the chicken salad.

Yield: 8 lb. (3.6 kg) **Method:** Bound

Chicken meat, cooked	5 lb.	2.2 kg
Celery, small dice	8 oz.	250 g
Green onions, sliced	3 oz.	90 g
Mango chutney	12 oz.	360 g
Mayonnaise	1 lb.	500 g
Seedless grapes	12 oz.	360 g

1. Remove any bones, skin and fat from the chicken and cut the meat into large dice.
2. Combine the chicken meat, celery, green onions, mango chutney and mayonnaise in a bowl; mix well.
3. Cut the grapes in half. Add them to the chicken mixture and toss gently to combine.

Approximate values per 4-oz. (120-g) serving: **Calories** 230, **Total fat** 14 g, **Saturated fat** 3 g, **Cholesterol** 70 mg, **Sodium** 135 mg, **Total carbohydrates** 4 g, **Protein** 22 g

VEGETABLE SALADS

Vegetable salads are made from cooked or raw vegetables or a combination of both. They can be served on buffets, as an appetizer or as a salad course. As with other salads, vegetable salads must successfully combine color, texture and flavor. Some vegetable salads such as coleslaw and carrot-raisin salad are made with mayonnaise. Most, however, are made by either marinating the vegetables or combining them in a vinaigrette dressing.

Almost any vegetable can be successfully marinated. The amount of time depends on the vegetables and the marinade, but several hours to overnight is usually sufficient for flavors to blend. Soft vegetables such as mushrooms, zucchini and cucumbers can be added directly to a cold marinade. Hard vegetables such as carrots and cauliflower should be blanched in salted water, refreshed, drained and then added to a cold marinade. Carrots, artichokes, mushrooms, cauliflower, zucchini, pearl onions and the like are sometimes simmered quickly in a marinade flavored with lemon juice and olive oil, and then served cold. This style is called **à la grecque.**

▶ **à la grecque** (ah lah grehk) a preparation style in which vegetables are marinated in olive oil, lemon juice and herbs, then served cold

Many marinated salads will last several days under proper refrigeration. As the salads age in the marinade, they will change in appearance and texture. This may or may not be desirable. For example, mushrooms and artichokes become more flavorful, while green vegetables are discolored by the acids in the marinade. If marinated salads are prepared in advance, check their appearance as well as their seasonings carefully at service time.

▶ PROCEDURE FOR PREPARING VEGETABLE SALADS

1 Gather and wash all vegetables.
2 Trim, cut, shred or otherwise prepare the vegetables as desired or as directed in the recipe.
3 Blanch or cook the vegetables if necessary.
4 Combine the vegetables with the marinade or dressing. Adjust the seasonings.

TOMATO AND ASPARAGUS SALAD WITH FRESH MOZZARELLA

RECIPE 23.7

Yield: 6 Servings

Asparagus	2 lb.	1 kg
Basic Vinaigrette Dressing	12 fl. oz.	360 ml
Tomatoes	6	6
Leaf lettuce	1 head	1 head
Fresh mozzarella	12 oz.	360 g
Fresh basil leaves, chiffonade	12	12

1 Trim the asparagus and blanch in salted water. Refresh, drain and marinate in 6 fluid ounces (180 milliliters) Basic Vinaigrette Dressing for approximately 15 minutes.
2 Core each tomato and cut into six wedges.
3 Clean the lettuce and separate the leaves.
4 Slice the mozzarella into 18 slices.
5 Arrange the tomatoes, cheese and asparagus on six plates using the lettuce as a base. Pour on the remaining dressing and garnish with the basil.

Approximate values per serving: **Calories** 410, **Total fat** 32 g, **Saturated fat** 9 g, **Cholesterol** 35 mg, **Sodium** 370 mg, **Total carbohydrates** 11 g, **Protein** 19 g, **Vitamin A** 20%, **Vitamin C** 110%, **Calcium** 40%

Mise en Place

▶ Wash basil and cut in chiffonade.

FRUIT SALADS

There are so many different fruits with beautiful bright colors and sweet delicious flavors that preparing fruit salads is easy work. Fruit salads are a refreshing addition to buffets and can be served as the first course of a lunch or dinner. A more elaborate fruit salad can be served as a light lunch.

Always prepare fruit salads as close to service time as possible. The flesh of many types of fruit becomes soft and translucent if cut long before service. Other fruits such as apples, bananas and peaches turn brown in a matter of minutes after cutting. Refer to Chapter 24, Fruits, for more information on this browning reaction and for information on specific fruits. Many fruit salad recipes are found at the end of that chapter.

If a fruit salad is dressed at all, the dressing is usually sweet and made with honey or yogurt mixed with fruit juices or purées. Alternatively, Grand Marnier, crème de menthe or other liqueurs sprinkled over the salad can serve as a dressing. Fruit salads can be tossed or composed. Either should offer the diner a pleasing blend of colors, shapes, sizes, flavors and textures.

CONCLUSION

A salad can be a small part of a meal or the entire meal. There are many styles of salads, and a seemingly endless variety of foods can be used to prepare them. Salads are extremely popular, especially with those interested in lighter dining alternatives. Chefs can tempt these diners by determining the appropriate style of the salads and skillfully combining the main ingredients and dressing to achieve a delicious and appealing balance of colors, textures and flavors.

QUESTIONS FOR DISCUSSION

1. Name several factors that will cause salad greens to wilt or deteriorate.
2. Describe the proper procedure for washing and drying lettuce.
3. Explain the difference between a vinaigrette and an emulsified vinaigrette dressing.
4. Describe the procedure for making mayonnaise. How can the flavor of a mayonnaise be altered?
5. Describe a typical bound salad. How does a bound salad differ from a dressed salad?
6. List five ways salads can be presented or offered on a menu.

CHAPTER TWENTY-FOUR

FRUITS

TALKING OF PLEASURE, THIS MOMENT I WAS WRITING WITH ONE HAND, AND WITH THE OTHER HOLDING TO MY MOUTH A NECTARINE—HOW GOOD HOW FINE. IT WENT DOWN ALL PULPY, SLUSHY, OOZY, ALL ITS DELICIOUS EMBONPOINT MELTED DOWN MY THROAT LIKE A LARGE, BEATIFIED STRAWBERRY.

—John Keats, English poet (1795–1821)

BRENNAN'S RESTAURANT,
New Orleans, LA
Chef Michael Roussel
(1938–2005)

AFTER STUDYING THIS CHAPTER, YOU WILL BE ABLE TO:

- identify a variety of fruits
- purchase fruits appropriate for various needs
- store fruits properly
- understand how fruits are preserved
- prepare fruits for cooking or service
- apply various cooking methods to fruits

Botanically, a fruit is an organ that develops from the ovary of a flowering plant and contains one or more seeds. Culinarily, a fruit is the perfect snack food; the basis of a dessert, colorful sauce or soup or an accompaniment to meat, fish, shellfish or poultry. No food group offers a greater variety of colors, flavors and textures than fruit.

This chapter identifies many of the fruits typically used by food service operations. It then addresses general considerations in purchasing fresh and preserved fruits. A discussion follows about some of the cooking methods presented in Chapter 8, Principles of Cooking, as they apply to fruits. Recipes in which a fruit is the primary ingredient are presented at the chapter's end.

▸ IDENTIFYING FRUITS

This book presents fruits according to the ways most people view them and use them, rather than by rigid botanical classifications. Fruits are divided here into eight categories: berries, citrus, exotics, grapes, melons, pomes, stone fruits and tropicals, according to either their shape, seed structure or natural habitat. Botanically, tomatoes, beans, eggplant, capsicum peppers and other produce are fruits. But in ordinary thinking, they are not; they are vegetables and are discussed in Chapter 20, Vegetables.

A fruit may have several names, varying from region to region or on a purveyor's whim. Botanists are also constantly reclassifying items to fit new findings. The names given here follow generally accepted custom and usage.

BERRIES

Berries are small, juicy fruits that grow on vines and bushes worldwide. Berries are characterized by thin skins and many tiny seeds that are often so small they go unnoticed. Some of the fruits classified here as berries do not fit the botanical definition (for example, raspberries and strawberries), while fruits that are berries botanically (for example, bananas and grapes) are classified elsewhere.

Berries may be eaten plain or used in everything from beer to bread, soup to sorbet. They make especially fine jams and compotes.

Berries must be fully **ripened** on the vine, as they will not ripen further after harvesting. Select berries that are plump and fully colored. Avoid juice-stained containers and berries with whitish-gray or black spots of mold. All berries should be refrigerated and used promptly. Do not wash berries until just before they are needed, as washing removes some of their aroma and softens them.

▸ **ripe** fully grown and developed; a ripe fruit's flavor, texture and appearance are at their peak, and the fruit is ready to use as food

BLACKBERRIES

Blackberries are similar to raspberries, but are larger and shinier, with a deep purple to black color. Thorny blackberry vines are readily found in the wild; commercial production is limited. Their peak season is mid-June through August. Loganberries, Marionberries, olallie berries and boysenberries are blackberry hybrids.

Blackberries

BLUEBERRIES

Blueberries (Fr. *myrtilles*) are small and firm, with a true blue to almost black skin and a juicy, light gray-blue interior. Cultivated berries (high-bush varieties)

tend to be larger than wild (low-bush) ones. Blueberries are native to North America and are grown commercially from Maine to Oregon and along the Atlantic seaboard. Their peak season is short, from mid-June to mid-August.

Blueberries

CRANBERRIES

Cranberries, another native North American food, are tart, firm fruit with a mottled red skin. They grow on low vines in cultivated bogs (swamps) throughout Massachusetts, Wisconsin and New Jersey. Rarely eaten raw, they are made into sauce or relish or are used in breads, pies or pastries. Cranberries are readily available frozen or made into a jelly-type sauce and canned. Although color does not indicate ripeness, cranberries should be picked over before cooking to remove those that are soft or bruised. Their peak harvesting season is from Labor Day through October, leading to the association of cranberries with Thanksgiving dinner.

Cranberries

CURRANTS

Currants are tiny, tart fruits that grow on shrubs in grape-like clusters. The most common are a beautiful, almost translucent red, but black and golden (or white) varieties also exist. All varieties are used for jams, jellies and sauces, and black currants are made into a liqueur, crème de cassis. Although rarely grown in the United States, currants are very popular and widely available in Europe, with a peak season during the late summer. (The dried fruits called currants are not produced from these berries; they are a special variety of dried grapes.)

White Currants

Red Currants

RASPBERRIES

Raspberries (Fr. *framboises*) are perhaps the most delicate of all fruits. They have a tart flavor and velvety texture. Red raspberries are the most common, with black, purple and golden berries available in some markets. When ripe, the berry pulls away easily from its white core, leaving the characteristic hollow center. Because they can be easily crushed and are susceptible to mold, most of the raspberries grown are marketed frozen. They grow on thorny vines in cool climates from Washington State to western New York and are imported from New Zealand and South America. The peak domestic season is from late May through November.

Raspberries

STRAWBERRIES

Strawberries (Fr. *fraises*) are brilliant red, heart-shaped fruits that grow on vines. The strawberry plant is actually a perennial herb; the berry's flesh is covered by tiny black seeds called achenes, which are the plant's true fruits. Select berries with a good red color and intact green leafy hull. (The hulls can be easily removed with a paring knife.) Avoid berries with soft or brown spots. Huge berries may be lovely to look at, but they often have hollow centers and little flavor or juice. Although strawberries are available to some extent all year, fresh California strawberries are at their peak from April through June.

Strawberries

The tiny wild or Alpine berries, known by their French name, *fraises des bois*, have a particularly intense flavor and aroma. They are not widely available in the United States.

▶ PROCEDURE FOR FANNING STRAWBERRIES

Cut thin parallel slices into the base of the strawberry without cutting through the stem. Press lightly to fan out the strawberry, exposing the cut slices.

CITRUS

Citrus fruits include lemons, limes, grapefruits, tangerines, kumquats, oranges and several hybrids. They are characterized by a thick rind, most of which is a bitter white pith (albedo) with a thin exterior layer of colored skin known as the **zest.** Their flesh is segmented and juicy. Citrus fruits are acidic, with a strong aroma; their flavors vary from bitter to tart to sweet.

▶ **zest** the colored outer portion of the rind of citrus fruit; contains the oil that provides flavor and aroma

Citrus fruits grow on trees and shrubs in tropical and subtropical climates worldwide. All citrus fruits are fully ripened on the tree and will not ripen further after harvesting. They should be refrigerated for longest storage.

Select fruits that feel heavy and have thin, smooth skins. Avoid those with large blemishes or moist spots.

GRAPEFRUITS

Grapefruits (Fr. *pamplemousses*) are large and round with a yellow skin, thick rind and tart flesh. They are an 18th-century hybrid of the orange and pummelo (a large, coarse fruit used mostly in Middle and Far Eastern cuisines). Two varieties of grapefruit are widely available all year: white-fleshed and pink- or ruby-fleshed. White grapefruits produce the finest juice, although pink grapefruits are sweeter. Fresh grapefruits are best eaten raw or topped with brown sugar and lightly broiled.

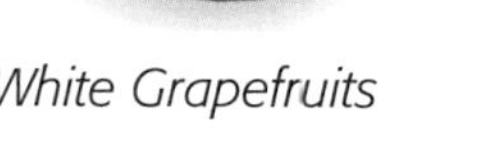

White Grapefruits

Red Grapefruits

KUMQUATS

Kumquats are very small, oval-shaped, orange-colored fruits with a soft, sweet skin and slightly bitter flesh. They can be eaten whole, either raw or preserved in syrup, and may be used in jams and preserves.

Kumquats

LEMONS

The most commonly used citrus fruits, lemons (Fr. *citrons*), are oval-shaped, bright yellow fruits available all year. Their strongly acidic flavor makes them unpleasant to eat raw but perfect for flavoring desserts and confections. Lemon juice is also

Lemons

widely used in sauces, especially for fish, shellfish and poultry. Lemon zest is candied or used as garnish. Rubbing the skin of a lemon or other citrus fruit with a sugar cube extracts much of the aromatic oil. The cube can then be crushed or dissolved to use in formulas calling for citrus flavor.

LIMES

Limes (Fr. *limons*) are small fruits with thin skins ranging from yellow-green to dark green. Limes are too tart to eat raw and are often substituted for lemons in prepared dishes. They are also juiced or used in cocktails, curries or desserts. Lime zest can be grated and used to give color and flavor to a variety of dishes. Limes are available all year; their peak season is during the summer. The key lime is a small tart lime variety native to South Florida and used to make key lime pie.

Limes

Key Limes

ORANGES

Oranges (Sp. *naranja*) are round fruits with a juicy, orange-colored flesh and a thin, orange skin. They can be either sweet or bitter.

Valencia oranges and navel oranges (a seedless variety) are the most popular sweet oranges. They can be juiced for beverages or sauces, and the flesh may be eaten raw, added to salads, cooked in desserts or used as a garnish. The zest may be grated or julienned for sauces or garnish. Sweet oranges are available all year; their peak season is from December to April.

Navel Oranges

Blood oranges are also sweet but are small, with a rough, reddish skin. Their flesh is streaked with a blood-red color. Blood oranges are available primarily during the winter months and are eaten raw, juiced or used in salads or sauces. When selecting sweet oranges, look for fruits that feel plump and heavy, with unblemished skin. The color of the skin depends on weather conditions; a green rind does not affect the flavor of the flesh.

Valencia Oranges

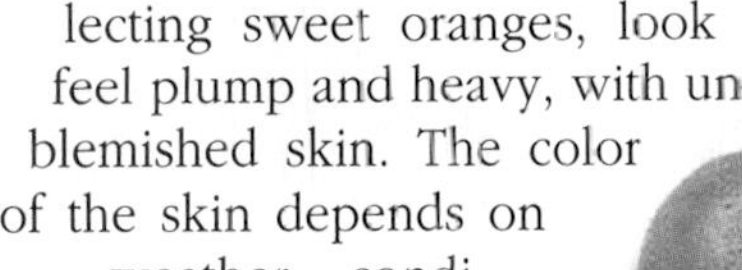

Blood Oranges

Bitter oranges include the Seville and bergamot. They are used primarily for the essential oils found in their zest. Oil of bergamot gives Earl Grey tea its distinctive flavor; oil of Seville is essential to curaçao, Grand Marnier and orange flower water. Seville oranges are also used in marmalades and sauces for meats and poultry.

TANGERINES

Tangerines, sometimes referred to as mandarins, are small and dark orange. Their rind is loose and easily removed to reveal sweet, juicy, aromatic segments. Tangerines are most often eaten fresh and uncooked, but are available canned as mandarin oranges.

Tangelos are a hybrid of tangerines and grapefruits. They are the size of a medium orange; they have a bulbous stem end and few to no seeds.

Tangerines

▶ PROCEDURE FOR SEGMENTING CITRUS FRUITS

1 Citrus segments, known as supremes, are made by first carefully cutting off the entire peel (including the bitter white pith) in even slices.

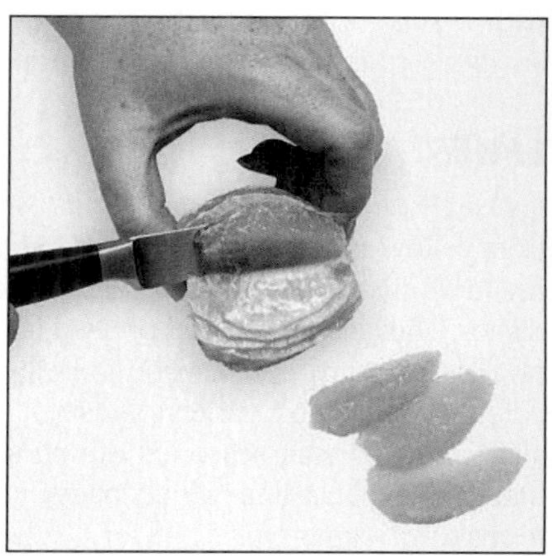

2 Individual segments are then removed by gently cutting alongside each membrane.

▶ PROCEDURE FOR ZESTING CITRUS FRUITS

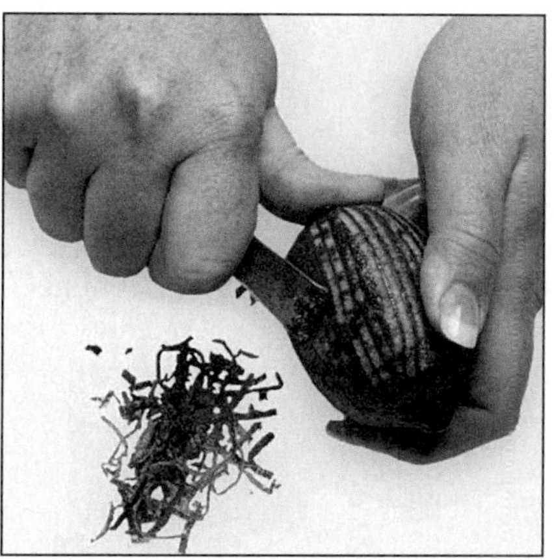

A five-hole zester is used to remove paper-thin strips of the colored rind.

▶ PROCEDURE FOR CUTTING CITRUS PEELS

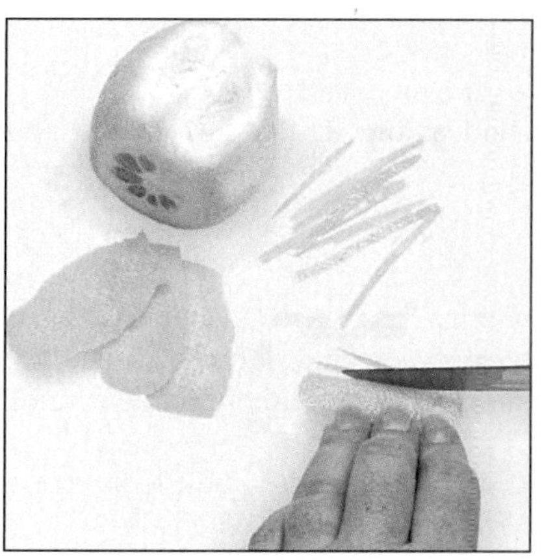

Large strips of citrus zest may be used as a garnish or to flavor soups or sauces.

EXOTICS

Improved transportation has led to the increasing availability (although sporadic in some areas) of exotic or unusual fresh fruits such as figs, persimmons, pomegranates, prickly pears, rhubarb and star fruits. Other exotic fruits, such as breadfruit, durian, feijoa and loquat, are still available only on a limited basis from specialty purveyors and are not discussed here.

HYBRIDS AND VARIETIES

Several fruits are extremely responsive to selective breeding and crossbreeding and have been toyed with by botanists and growers since at least the time of ancient Rome. Two distinct products are recognized: hybrids and varieties. **Hybrids** result from crossbreeding fruits from different species that are genetically unalike. The result is a unique product. Citrus is particularly responsive to hybridization. **Varieties** result from breeding fruits of the same species that have different qualities or characteristics. Breeding two varieties of apples, for example, produces a third variety with the best qualities of both parents.

FIGS

Figs (Fr. *figues*) are the fruit of ficus trees. They are small, soft, pear-shaped fruits with an intensely sweet flavor and rich, moist texture made crunchy by a multitude of tiny seeds. Fresh figs can be sliced and served in salads or with cured meats such as prosciutto. They can also be baked, poached or used in jams, preserves or compotes.

Dark-skinned figs, known as Mission figs, are a variety planted at Pacific Coast missions during the 18th century. They have a thin skin and small seeds and are available fresh, canned or dried. The white-skinned figs grown commercially include the White Adriatic, used principally for drying and baking, and the all-purpose Kadota. The most important domestic variety, however, is the Calimyrna. These large figs have a rich yellow color and large nutty seeds. Fresh Calimyrna figs are the finest for eating out of hand; they are also available dried.

Calimyrna Figs

For the best flavor, figs should be fully ripened on the tree. Unfortunately, fully ripened figs are very delicate and difficult to transport. Most figs are in season from June through October; fresh Calimyrna figs are available only during June.

GOOSEBERRIES

Several varieties of gooseberry (Fr. *groseille maquereau*) are cultivated for culinary purposes. One well-known variety is the European gooseberry, a member of the currant family that grows on spiny bushes in cool, moist regions of the Northern Hemisphere. Its berries can be relatively large, like a small plum, but are usually less than 1 inch (2.5 centimeters) in diameter. The skin, which is firm and smooth or only slightly hairy, can be green, white (actually gray-green), yellow or red. The tart berries contain many tiny seeds. They are eaten fresh or used for jellies, preserves, tarts and other desserts or as a traditional accompaniment to rich or fatty dishes, such as goose and mackerel. North American gooseberry varieties are smaller, perfectly round, and pink to deep red at maturity. Although more prolific, these varietals lack flavor and are generally considered inferior to European gooseberries.

Cape Gooseberries

Cape gooseberries, also known as physalis, ground cherries and poha, are unrelated to European and American gooseberries. Native to Peru, they became popular during the 19th century along the African Cape of Good Hope, for which they are named. Australia and New Zealand are currently the largest producers. Cape gooseberries are covered with a paper-thin husk or calyx. About the size of a cherry, they have a waxy, bright orange skin and many tiny seeds. Their flavor is similar to coconut and oranges, but tarter. Cape gooseberries may be eaten raw, made into jam or used in desserts. Fresh, they make an especially striking garnish.

GUAVA

Guava (GWAH-vah) are a small, oval or pear-shaped fruit with a strong fragrance and a mild, slightly grainy flesh. They are excellent in jams and preserves, and

Guava

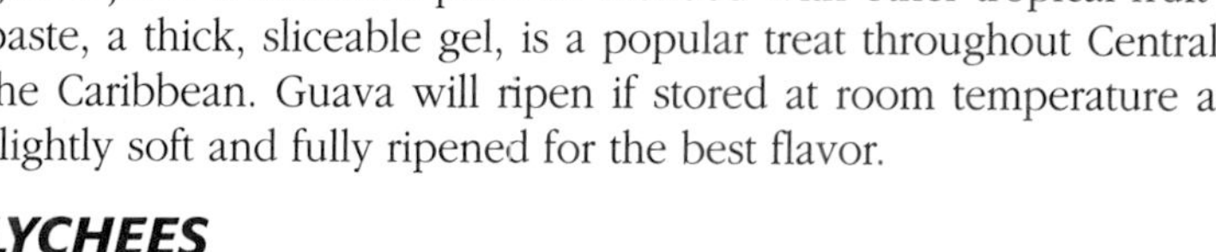

guava juice is available plain or blended with other tropical fruit juices. Guava paste, a thick, sliceable gel, is a popular treat throughout Central America and the Caribbean. Guava will ripen if stored at room temperature and should be slightly soft and fully ripened for the best flavor.

LYCHEES

Lychees

The lychee (LEE-chee), also spelled *litchi* or *leechee,* is the fruit of a large tree native to southern China and Southeast Asia. The fruits, which grow in clusters, are oval to round, red and about 1 inch (2.5 centimeters) in diameter. The tough outer skin encloses juicy, white, almost translucent flesh and one large seed. Neither the skin nor the seed are edible. The fruit travels well and is now cultivated in Florida and Hawaii, so supplies are relatively stable. Lychees are eaten fresh out of hand or juiced, and are widely available canned or dried. Fresh lychees are mild but sweet with a pleasant perfume.

MANGOSTEENS

Mangosteens

The mangosteen, another native of Southeast Asia, is cultivated in Java, Sumatra and the Philippines. Mangosteens (no relation to mangos) are the size of a small orange, with flattened ends. They have a thick, hard, deep reddish-purple rind with hard white petal-shaped protrusions at the stem end. The interior flesh is snow-white and segmented, looking something like a mandarin orange. The texture is juicy and delicate with a slightly astringent flavor. Because the fruit must ripen on the tree and keeps only a short time, it is rarely found fresh except in outdoor local markets. Mangosteens are usually eaten fresh, although canned fruit and mangosteen juice is available.

PERSIMMONS

Persimmons

Persimmons, sometimes referred to as kaki or Sharon fruits, are a bright orange, acorn-shaped fruit with a glossy skin and a large papery blossom. The flesh is bright orange and jellylike, with a mild but rich flavor similar to honey and plums. Persimmons should be peeled before use; any seeds should be discarded. Select bright orange fruits and refrigerate only after they are completely ripe. When ripe, persimmons will be very soft and the skin will have an almost translucent appearance.

Ripe persimmons are delicious eaten raw; halved and topped with cream or soft cheese; or peeled, sliced and added to fruit salads. Persimmon bread, muffins, cakes and pies are also popular. Underripe persimmons are almost inedible, however. They are strongly tannic with a chalky or cottony texture.

Persimmons are tree fruits grown in subtropical areas worldwide, although the Asian varieties—now grown in California—are the most common. Fresh persimmons are available from October through January.

POMEGRANATES

Pomegranates

An ancient fruit native to Persia (now Iran), pomegranates (POM-uh-gran-uhtz) have long been a subject of poetry and a symbol of fertility. Pomegranates are round, about the size of a large orange, with a pronounced calyx. The skin forms a hard shell with a pinkish-red color. The interior is filled with hundreds of small, red seeds (which are, botanically, the actual fruits) surrounded by juicy red pulp. An inedible yellow membrane separates the seeds into compartments. Pomegranates are sweet-sour, and the seeds are pleasantly crunchy. The bright red seeds make an attractive garnish. Pomegranate juice is a popular beverage in Mediterranean cuisines, and grenadine syrup is made from concentrated pomegranate juice.

Select heavy fruits that are not rock-hard, cracked or heavily bruised. Whole pomegranates can be refrigerated for several weeks. Pomegranates are available from September through December; their peak season is in October.

PRICKLY PEARS

Prickly pear fruits, also known as cactus pears and Barbary figs, are actually the berries of several varieties of cactus. They are barrel- or pear-shaped, about the size of a large egg. Their thick, firm skin is green or purple with small sharp pins and nearly invisible stinging fibers. Their flesh is spongy, sweet and a brilliant pink-red, dotted with small black seeds. Prickly pears have the aroma of watermelon and the flavor of sugar water.

Prickly Pears

Once peeled, prickly pears can be diced and eaten raw, or they can be puréed for making jams, sauces, custards or sorbets, to which they give a vivid pink color. Prickly pears are especially common in Mexican and southwestern cuisines.

Select fruits that are full-colored, heavy and tender, but not too soft. Avoid those with mushy or bruised spots. Ripe prickly pears can be refrigerated for a week or more. Prickly pears are grown in Mexico and several southwestern states and are available from September through December.

▶ PROCEDURE FOR PEELING PRICKLY PEARS

1 To avoid being stung by a prickly pear, hold it steady with a fork, then use a knife to cut off both ends.

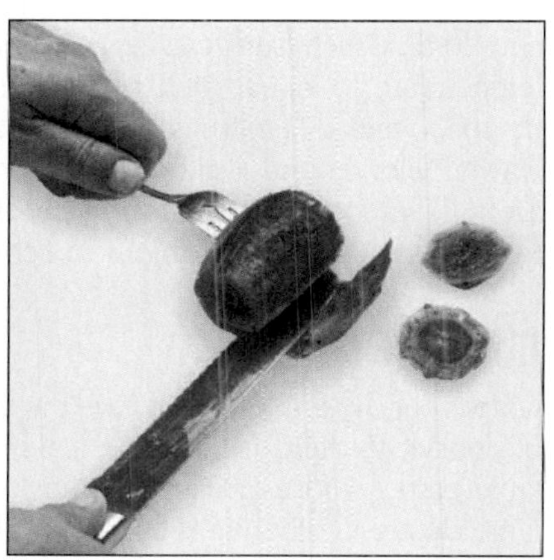

2 Cut a lengthwise slit through the skin. Slip the tip of the knife into the cut and peel away the skin by holding it down while rolling the fruit away.

RAMBUTANS

Rambutans (ram-BOOT-enz), the fruit of a tree in the soapberry family, are closely related to lychees. Native to Malaysia, they are now cultivated throughout Southeast Asia. The bright-red, oval fruit is about the size of a small hen's egg, and is covered with long, soft spines, hence the name "hairy" lychees. The interior has a white, lightly acidic pulp. Rambutans darken with age, so select brightly colored fruit with soft, fleshy spines. Rambutans are eaten fresh and used in preserves and ice cream; they are also available canned.

Rambutans

RHUBARB

Although botanically a vegetable, rhubarb (ROO-barb) is most often prepared as a fruit. It is a perennial plant that grows well in temperate and cold climates.

Rhubarb

Only the pinkish-red stems are edible; the leaves contain high amounts of oxalic acid, which is toxic.

Rhubarb stems are extremely acidic, requiring large amounts of sugar to create the desired sweet-sour taste. Cinnamon, ginger, orange and strawberry are particularly compatible with rhubarb. It is excellent for pies, cobblers, preserves or stewing. Young, tender stalks of rhubarb do not need to be peeled. When cooked, rhubarb becomes very soft and turns a beautiful light pink color.

Fresh rhubarb is sold as whole stalks, with the leaves removed. Select crisp, unblemished stalks. Rhubarb's peak season is during the early spring, from February through May. Frozen rhubarb pieces are readily available and are excellent for pies, tarts or jams.

STAR FRUITS

Star fruits, also known as carambola, are oval, up to 5 inches (12.5 centimeters) long, with five prominent ribs or wings running their length. A cross-section cut is shaped like a star. The edible skin is a waxy orange-yellow; it covers a dry, paler yellow flesh. Its flavor is similar to that of plums, sweet but bland. Star fruits do not need to be peeled or seeded. They are most often sliced and added to fruit salad or used as a garnish. Unripe fruits can be cooked in stews or chutneys.

Color and aroma are the best indicators of ripeness. The fruits should be a deep golden-yellow and there should be brown along the edge of the ribs. The aroma should be full and floral. Green fruits can be kept at room temperature to ripen, then refrigerated for up to 2 weeks. Star fruits are cultivated in Hawaii, Florida and California, though some are still imported from the Caribbean. Fresh fruits are available from August to February.

Star Fruits

GRAPES

Grapes (Fr. *raisins;* Sp. *uvas*) are the single largest fruit crop in the world, due, of course, to their use in wine making. This section, however, discusses only table grapes, those grown for eating. Grapes are berries that grow on vines in large clusters. California is the world's largest producer, with more than a dozen varieties grown for table use. Grapes are classified by color as white (which are actually green) or black (which are actually red). White grapes are generally blander than black ones, with a thinner skin and firmer flesh.

The grape's color and most of its flavor are found in the skin. Grapes are usually eaten raw, either alone or in fruit salads. They are also used as a garnish or accompaniment to desserts and cheeses. Dried grapes are known as raisins (Fr. *raisins sec;* usually made from Thompson Seedless or muscat grapes), currants (made from Black Corinth grapes and labeled Zante currants) or sultanas (made from sultana grapes).

Grapes are available all year because the many varieties have different harvesting schedules. Look for firm, unblemished fruits that are firmly attached to the stem. A surface bloom or dusty appearance is caused by yeasts and indicates recent harvesting. Wrinkled grapes or those with brown spots around the stem are past their prime. All grapes should be rinsed and drained prior to use.

Red Flame Grapes

RED FLAME GRAPES

Red Flame grapes are a seedless California hybrid, second only in importance to the Thompson Seedless. Red Flame grapes are large and round with a slightly tart flavor and variegated red color.

THOMPSON SEEDLESS GRAPES

Thompson Seedless Grapes

The most commercially important table grapes are a variety known as Thompson Seedless, which are pale green with a crisp texture and sweet flavor. Their peak season is from June to November. Many are dried in the hot desert sun of California's San Joaquin Valley to produce dark raisins. For golden raisins, Thompson Seedless grapes are treated with sulfur dioxide to prevent browning, then dried mechanically.

OTHER TABLE GRAPES

Of the table grapes containing seeds, the most important varieties are the Concord, Ribier and Emperor. They range from light red to deep black, and all three are in season during the autumn. Concord grapes, one of the few grape varieties native to the New World, are especially important for making juices and jellies.

Virtually all the fine wine made in the world comes from varieties of a single grape species, *Vitis vinifera*. It is grown in the United States, Europe, South Africa, South America, the Middle East, Australia and wherever fine wine is made. The variety of grapes used in any given wine determines the wine's character, which is discussed in Chapter 5, Flavor and Flavorings.

Concord Grapes

MELONS

Like pumpkins and cucumbers, melons are members of the gourd family (*Cucurbitaceae*). The dozens of melon varieties can be divided into two general types: sweet (or dessert) melons and watermelons. Sweet melons have a tan, green or yellow netted or furrowed rind and dense, fragrant flesh. Watermelon has a thick, dark green rind surrounding crisp, watery flesh.

Melons are almost 90 percent water, so cooking destroys their texture, quickly turning the flesh to mush. Most are served simply sliced, perhaps with a bit of lemon or lime juice. Melons also blend well in fruit salads or with rich, cured meats such as prosciutto. Melons may be puréed and made into sorbet or chilled, uncooked soup.

Melons should be vine-ripened. A ripe melon should yield slightly and spring back when pressed at the blossom end (opposite the stem). It should also give off a strong aroma. Avoid melons that are very soft or feel damp at the stem end. Ripe melons may be stored in the refrigerator, although the flavor will be better at room temperature. Slightly underripe melons can be stored at room temperature to allow flavor and aroma to develop.

CANTALOUPES

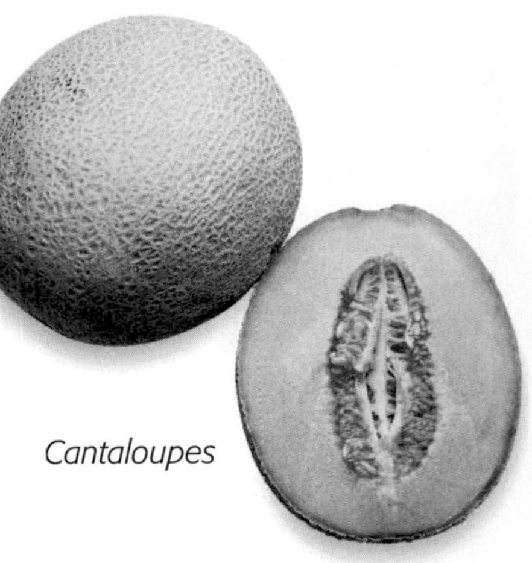

Cantaloupes

American cantaloupes, which are actually muskmelons, are sweet melons with a thick, yellow-green netted rind, a sweet, moist, orange flesh and a strong aroma. (European cantaloupes, which are not generally available in this country, are more craggy and furrowed in appearance.) As with all sweet melons, the many small seeds are found in a central cavity. Cantaloupes are excellent for eating alone and are especially good with ham or rich meats.

Avoid cantaloupes with the pronounced yellow color or moldy aroma that indicates overripeness. Mexican imports ensure a year-round supply, although their peak season is summer.

CASABA MELONS

The casaba melon is a teardrop-shaped sweet melon. It has a coarse, yellow skin and a thick, ridged rind; its flesh is creamy white to yellow. Casaba melons are used like cantaloupes. Casaba melons do not have an aroma, so selection must be based on a deep

Casaba Melons

Crenshaw Melons

skin color and the absence of dark or moist patches. Their peak season is during September and October.

CRENSHAW MELONS

Crenshaw (or cranshaw) melons have a mottled, green-yellow ridged rind and orange-pink flesh. They are large pear-shaped sweet melons with a strong aroma. The flesh has a rich, spicy flavor and may be used like cantaloupe. Crenshaws are available from July through October; their peak season is during August and September.

HONEYDEW MELONS

Honeydew melons are large oval sweet melons with a smooth rind that ranges from white to pale green. Although the flesh is generally pale green, with a mild, sweet flavor, pink- or gold-fleshed honeydews are also available. Like casaba melons, honeydew melons have little to no aroma. They are available almost all year; their peak season is from June through October.

Gold Honeydews

Green Honeydews

SANTA CLAUS MELONS

Santa Claus Melons

Santa Claus or Christmas melons are large, elongated sweet melons with a green-and-yellow-striped, smooth rind. The flesh is creamy white or yellow and tastes like casaba. They are a winter variety, with peak availability during December, which explains the name.

WATERMELONS

Watermelons are large (up to 30 pounds or 13.5 kilograms) round or oval-shaped melons with a thick rind. The skin may be solid green, green-striped or mottled with white. The flesh is crisp and extremely juicy with small, hard, black seeds throughout. Seedless hybrids are available. Most watermelons have pink to red flesh, although golden-fleshed varieties are becoming more common. Watermelons are of a different genus from the sweet melons described earlier. They are native to tropical Africa and are now grown commercially in Texas and several southern states.

Watermelons

Gold Watermelons

POMES

Pomes are tree fruits with thin skin and firm flesh surrounding a central core containing many small seeds called pips or carpels. Pomes include apples, pears and quince.

APPLES

Apples (Fr. *pommes*), perhaps the most common and commonly appreciated of all fruits, grow on trees in temperate zones worldwide. They are popular because of their convenience, flavor, variety and availability.

Apples can be eaten raw out of hand, or they can be used in a wide variety of cooked or baked dishes. They are equally useful in breads, desserts or vegetable dishes and go well with game, pork and poultry. Classic dishes prepared with apples are often referred to as *à la Normande*. Apple juice (cider) produces alcoholic and nonalcoholic beverages and cider vinegar.

Of the hundreds of known apple varieties, only 20 or so are commercially significant in the United States. Several varieties and their characteristics are noted in Table 24.1. Most have a moist, creamy white flesh with a thin skin of yellow, green or red. They range in flavor from very sweet to very tart, with an equally broad range of textures, from firm and crisp to soft and mealy.

In Europe, apples are divided into distinct cooking and eating varieties. Cooking varieties are those that disintegrate to a purée when cooked. American varieties are less rigidly classified. Nevertheless, not all apples are appropriate for all types of cooking. Those that retain their shape better during cooking are the best choices when slices or appearance are important. Varieties with a higher malic acid content break down easily, making them more appropriate for applesauce or juicing. Either type may be eaten out of hand, depending on personal preference.

Although not native to North America, apples are now grown commercially in 35 states, with Washington and New York leading in production. Apples are harvested when still slightly underripe, then stored in a controlled atmosphere (temperature and oxygen are greatly reduced) for extended periods until ready for sale. Modern storage techniques make fresh apples available all year, although their peak season is during the autumn.

Rome
Red Delicious
Granny Smith
Golden Delicious

McIntosh
Gala

Table 24.1 **APPLE VARIETIES**

VARIETY	SKIN COLOR	FLAVOR	TEXTURE	PEAK SEASON	USE
Fiji	Yellow-green with red highlights	Sweet-spicy	Crisp	All year	Eating, in salads
Gala	Yellow-orange with red stripes	Sweet	Crisp	Aug.–March	Eating, in salads, sauce
Golden Delicious	Glossy, greenish-gold	Sweet	Semifirm	Sept.–Oct.	In tarts, with cheese, in salads
Granny Smith	Bright green	Tart	Firm and crisp	Oct.–Nov.	Eating, in tarts
Jonathan	Brilliant red	Tart to acidic	Tender	Sept.–Oct.	Eating, all-purpose
McIntosh	Red with green background	Tart to acidic	Soft	Fall	Applesauce, in closed pies
Pippin (Newton)	Greenish-yellow	Tart	Semifirm	Fall	In pies, eating, baking
Red Delicious	Deep red	Sweet but bland	Soft to mealy	Sept.–Oct.	Eating
Rome	Red	Sweet-tart	Firm	Oct.–Nov.	Baking, pies, sauces
Winesap	Dark red with streaks	Tangy	Crisp	Oct.–Nov.	Cider, all-purpose

When selecting apples, look for smooth, unbroken skins and firm fruits, without soft spots or bruises. Badly bruised or rotting apples should be discarded immediately. They emit quantities of ethylene gas that speed spoilage of nearby fruits. (Remember the saying that "one bad apple spoils the barrel.") Store apples chilled for up to 6 weeks. Apple peels (the skin) may be eaten or removed as desired, but in either case, apples should be washed just prior to use to remove pesticides and any wax that was applied to improve appearance. Apple slices can be frozen (often with sugar or citric acid added to slow spoilage) or dried.

▶ PROCEDURE FOR CORING APPLES

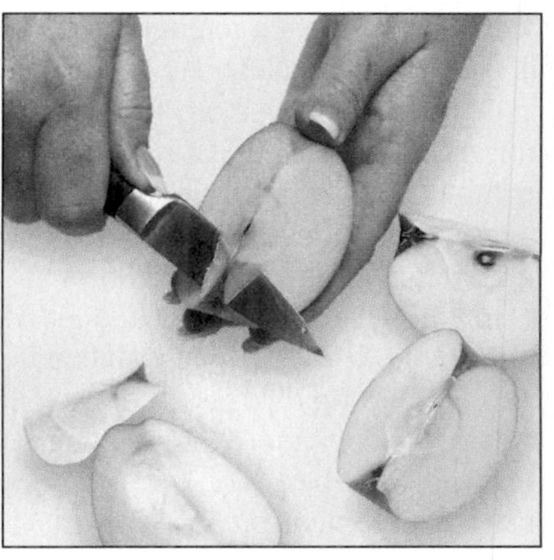

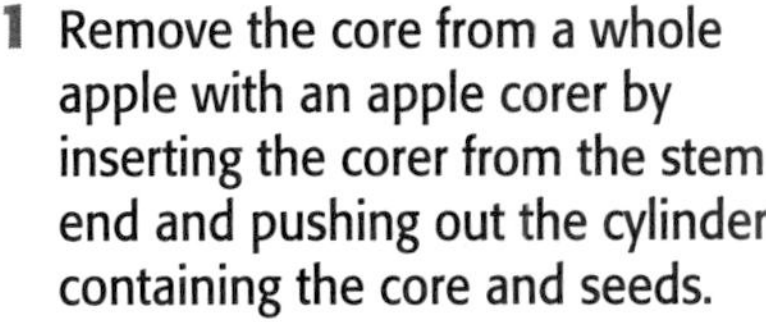

1 Remove the core from a whole apple with an apple corer by inserting the corer from the stem end and pushing out the cylinder containing the core and seeds.

2 Alternatively, first cut an apple into quarters, then use a paring knife to cut away the core and seeds.

PEARS

Pears (Fr. *poires*) are an ancient tree fruit grown in temperate areas throughout the world. Most of the pears marketed in the United States are grown in California, Washington and Oregon.

Although thousands of pear varieties have been identified, only a dozen or so are commercially significant. Several varieties and their characteristics are noted in Table 24.2. Pear varieties vary widely in size, color and flavor. They are most often eaten out of hand, but can be baked or poached. Pears are delicious with cheese, especially blue cheeses, and can be used in fruit salads, compotes or preserves.

Asian pears, also known as Chinese pears or apple-pears, are of a different species than common pears. They have the moist, sweet flavor of a pear and the round shape and crisp texture of an apple. They are becoming increasingly popular in the United States, particularly those known as Twentieth Century or Nijisseiki.

When selecting pears, look for fruits with smooth, unbroken skin and an intact stem.

Anjou

Asian Pears

Bartlett

Red d'Anjou

Bosc

Table 24.2 **PEAR VARIETIES**

VARIETY	APPEARANCE	FLAVOR	TEXTURE	PEAK SEASON	USE
Anjou (Beurre d'Anjou)	Greenish-yellow skin; egg-shaped with short neck; red variety also available	Sweet and juicy	Firm, keeps well	Oct.–May	Eating, poaching
Bartlett (Williams)	Thin yellow skin; bell-shaped; red variety also available	Very sweet, buttery, juicy	Tender	Aug.–Dec.	Eating, canning, in salads
Bosc	Golden-brown skin; long tapered neck	Buttery	Dry, holds its shape well	Sept.–May	Poaching, baking
Comice	Yellow-green skin; large and chubby	Sweet, juicy	Smooth	Oct.–Feb.	Eating
Sekel	Tiny; brown to yellow skin	Spicy	Very firm, grainy	Aug.–Dec.	Poaching, pickling

Pears will not ripen properly on the tree, so they are picked while still firm and should be allowed to soften before use. Underripe pears may be left at room temperature to ripen. A properly ripened pear should have a good fragrance and yield to gentle pressure at the stem end. Pears can be prepared or stored in the same ways as apples.

QUINCE

Common quince (kwince; Fr. *coing*) resemble large, lumpy yellow pears. Their flesh is hard, with many pips or seeds, and they have a wonderful fragrance. Too astringent to eat raw, quince develop a sweet flavor and pink color when cooked with sugar. Quince are used in meat stews, jellies, marmalades and pies. They have a high **pectin** content and may be added to other fruit jams or preserves to encourage gelling.

Fresh quince, usually imported from South America or southeast Europe, are available from October through January. Select firm fruits with a good yellow color. Small blemishes may be cut away before cooking. Quince will keep for up to a month under refrigeration.

Quince

HEIRLOOM VARIETIES

Older fruit and vegetable varieties are often less suited to the demands of commercial agriculture. They may bruise easily and be irregular in size and appearance. Many chefs and home gardeners are finding that these heirloom varieties are more flavorful than their photogenic descendants. Seeds and rootstocks from these older varieties are being cultivated in an attempt to preserve the flavors from the past.

▶ **pectin** a gelatin-like carbohydrate obtained from certain fruits; used to thicken jams and jellies

STONE FRUITS

Stone fruits, also known as drupes, include apricots, cherries, nectarines, peaches and plums. They are characterized by a thin skin, soft flesh and one woody stone or pit. Although most originated in China, the shrubs and trees producing stone fruits are now grown in temperate climates worldwide.

The domestic varieties of stone fruits are in season from late spring through summer. They tend to be fragile fruits, easily bruised and difficult to transport, and have a short shelf life. Do not wash them until ready to use, as moisture can cause deterioration. Stone fruits are excellent dried and are often used to make liqueurs and brandies. (The kernel inside the pits of many stone fruits contains amygdalin, a compound that has a bitter almond flavor. Eating the raw kernel can cause digestive discomfort or more serious side effects and should be avoided. When cooked it is harmless and can add flavor to jams and creams.)

APRICOTS

Apricots (Fr. *abricots*) are small, round stone fruits with a velvety skin that varies from deep yellow to vivid orange. Their juicy orange flesh surrounds a dark, almond-shaped pit. Apricots can be eaten out of hand, poached, stewed, baked

Apricots

or candied. They are often used in fruit compotes or savory sauces for meat or poultry, and are also popular in quick breads and fruit tarts or puréed for dessert sauces, jams, custards or mousses.

Apricots have a short season, peaking during June and July, and do not travel well. Select apricots that are well shaped, plump and fairly firm. Avoid ones that are greenish-yellow or mushy. Fresh apricots will last for several days under refrigeration, but the flavor is best at room temperature. If fresh fruits are unavailable, canned apricots are usually an acceptable substitute. Dried apricots and apricot juice (known as nectar) are readily available.

CHERRIES

Rainier Cherries

Bing Cherries

From the northern states, particularly Washington, Oregon, Michigan and New York, come the two most important types of cherry: the sweet cherry and the sour (or tart) cherry.

Sweet cherries (Fr. *cerises*) are round to heart-shaped, about 1 inch (2.5 centimeters) in diameter, with skin that ranges from yellow to deep red to nearly black. The flesh, which is sweet and juicy, may vary from yellow to dark red. The most common and popular sweet cherries are the dark red Bings. Yellow-red Royal Ann and Rainier cherries are also available in some areas.

Sweet cherries are often marketed fresh, made into maraschino cherries or candied for use in baked goods. Fresh sweet cherries have a very short season, peaking during June and July. Cherries will not ripen further after harvesting. Select fruits that are firm and plump with a green stem still attached. There should not be any brown spots around the stem. A dry or brown stem indicates that the cherry is less than fresh. Once the stem is removed, the cherry will deteriorate rapidly. Store fresh cherries in the refrigerator and do not wash them until ready to use.

Sour cherries are light to dark red and are so acidic they are rarely eaten uncooked. The most common sour cherries are the Montmorency and Morello. Most sour cherries are canned or frozen, or cooked with sugar and starch (usually cornstarch or tapioca) and sold as prepared pastry and pie fillings.

Both sweet and sour varieties are available dried.

▶ PROCEDURE FOR PITTING CHERRIES

Remove the stem and place the cherry in the pitter with the indentation facing up. Squeeze the handles together to force out the pit.

PEACHES AND NECTARINES

Peaches

Peaches (Fr. *pêches*) are moderate-sized, round fruits with a juicy, sweet flesh. Nectarines are a variety of peach, the main difference between the two being their skin. Peaches have a thin skin covered with fuzz, while nectarines have a thin, smooth skin. The flesh of either fruit ranges from white to pale orange. Although their flavors are somewhat different, they may be substituted for each other in most recipes.

Peaches and nectarines are excellent for eating out of hand or in dessert tarts or pastries. They are also used in jams, chutneys, preserves and savory relishes, having a particular affinity for Asian and Indian dishes. Although the skin is edible, peaches are generally peeled before being used. (Peaches are easily peeled if blanched first.)

Nectarines

Peaches and nectarines are either freestones or clingstones. With freestones, the flesh separates easily from the stone; freestone fruits are commonly eaten out of hand. The flesh of clingstones adheres firmly to the stone; they hold their shape better when cooked and are the type most often canned.

Select fruits with a good aroma; an overall creamy, yellow or yellow-orange color; and an unwrinkled skin free of blemishes. Red patches are not an indication of ripeness; a green skin indicates that the fruit was picked too early and it will not ripen further. Peaches and nectarines will soften but do not become sweeter after harvesting.

The United States, especially California, is the world's largest producer of peaches and nectarines. Their peak season is through the summer months, with July and August producing the best crop. South American peaches are sometimes available from January to May. Canned and frozen peaches are readily available.

PLUMS

Plums (Fr. *prunes*) are round to oval-shaped fruits that grow on trees or bushes. Dozens of plum varieties are known, although only a few are commercially significant. Plums vary in size from very small to 3 inches (7.5 centimeters) in diameter. Their thin skin can be green, red, yellow or various shades of blue-purple.

Santa Rosa Plums

Plums are excellent for eating out of hand. Plums can also be baked, poached or used in pies, cobblers or tarts; they are often used in jams or preserves, and fresh slices can be used in salads or compotes.

Fresh plums are widely available from June through October; their peak season is in August and September. When selecting plums, look for plump, smooth fruits with unblemished skin. Generally, they should yield to gentle pressure, although the green and yellow varieties remain quite firm. Avoid plums with moist, brown spots near the stem. Plums may be left at room temperature to ripen, then stored in the refrigerator. Prunes, discussed later, are produced by drying special plum varieties, usually the French Agen.

Damson Plums

TROPICALS

Tropical fruits are native to the world's hot, tropical or subtropical regions. Most are now readily available throughout the United States thanks to rapid transportation and distribution methods. All can be eaten fresh, without cooking. Their flavors complement each other and go well with rich or spicy meat, fish and poultry dishes.

BANANAS

Common yellow bananas (Fr. *bananes*) are actually the berries of a large tropical herb. Grown in bunches called hands, they are about 7 to 9 inches (17.5 to 22.5 centimeters) long, with a sticky, soft, sweet flesh. Their inedible yellow skin is easily removed. Baby bananas (Nino, Ladyfinger or Finger Bananas) measure 4 to 5 inches long (10 to 12.5 centimeters) with yellow or red skin. Their flesh is more dense and sweeter than most larger banana varieties and their diminutive size makes them ideal for many dessert applications.

Properly ripened bananas are excellent eaten out of hand or used in salads. Lightly bruised or overripe fruits are best used for breads or muffins. Bananas blend well with other tropical fruits and citrus. Their unique flavor is also complemented by curry, cinnamon, ginger, honey and chocolate.

Fresh bananas are available all year. Bananas are always harvested when still green, because the texture and flavor will be adversely affected if the fruits are

Common Yellow Bananas

Plantains

allowed to turn yellow on the tree. Unripe bananas are hard, dry and starchy. Because bananas ripen after harvesting, it is acceptable to purchase green bananas if there is sufficient time for final ripening before use. Bananas should be left at room temperature to ripen. A properly ripened banana has a yellow peel with brown flecks. The tip should not have any remaining green coloring. As bananas continue to age, the peel darkens and the starches turn to sugar, giving the fruits a sweeter flavor. Avoid bananas that have large brown bruises or a gray cast (a sign of cold damage).

Plantains, also referred to as cooking bananas, are larger than but not as sweet as common bananas. They are frequently cooked as a starchy vegetable in tropical cuisines.

DATES

Dates (Fr. *dattes*) are the fruit of the date palm tree, which has been cultivated since ancient times. Dates are about 1 to 2 inches (2.5 to 5 centimeters) long, with a paper-thin skin and a single grooved seed in the center. Most are golden to dark brown when ripe.

Medjool Dates

Although dates appear to be dried, they are actually fresh fruits. They have a sticky-sweet, almost candied texture and rich flavor. Dates provide flavor and moisture for breads, muffins, cookies and tarts. They can also be served with fresh or dried fruits, or stuffed with meat or cheese as an appetizer.

Pitted dates are readily available in several packaged forms: whole, chopped or extruded (for use in baking). Whole unpitted dates are available in bulk. Date juice is also available for use as a natural sweetener, especially in baked goods. Although packaged or processed dates are available all year, peak season for fresh domestic dates is from October through December. When selecting dates, look for those that are plump, glossy and moist.

KIWIS

Kiwis

Kiwis, sometimes known as kiwifruits or Chinese gooseberries, are small oval fruits, about the size of a large egg, with a thin, fuzzy brown skin. The flesh is bright green with a white core surrounded by hundreds of tiny black seeds.

Kiwis are sweet, but somewhat bland. They are best used raw, peeled and eaten out of hand or sliced for fruit salads or garnish. Although kiwis are not recommended for cooking because heat causes them to fall apart, they are a perfect addition to glazed fruit tarts and can be puréed for sorbets, sauces or mousses. Kiwis contain an enzyme similar to that in fresh pineapple and papaya, which has a tenderizing effect on meat and prevents gelling.

MANGOES

Mangoes

Mangoes (Fr. *mangues*) are oval or kidney-shaped fruits that normally weigh between 6 ounces and 1 pound (180 and 500 grams). Their skin is smooth and thin but tough, varying from yellow to orange-red, with patches of green, red or purple. As mangoes ripen, the green disappears. The juicy, bright orange flesh clings to a large, flat pit.

A mango's unique flavor is spicy-sweet, with an acidic tang. Mangoes can be puréed for use in drinks or sauces, or the flesh can be sliced or cubed for use in salads, pickles, chutneys or desserts. Mangoes go well with spicy foods such as curry and with barbecued meats.

Although Florida produces some mangoes, most of those available in the United States are from Mexico. Their peak season is from May through August. Select fruits with good color that are firm and free of blemishes. Ripe mangoes should have a good aroma, and should not be too soft or shriveled. Allow mangoes to ripen completely at room temperature, then refrigerate for up to 1 week.

FRIEDA AND THE KIWIFRUIT

How did a fuzzy brown unknown become a media darling and a hugely viable crop? The answer is, thanks to Frieda Caplan. In 1962 Frieda, founder of Frieda's, Inc., launched her historical worldwide promotion of kiwifruit. Acting on a suggestion that Chinese gooseberries, then grown only in New Zealand, might sell better under the name *kiwifruit* (the kiwi is the national bird of New Zealand), Frieda unleashed a produce giant. This story of the kiwifruit is studied throughout the world as one of the great successes in food marketing.

In 1980, after 18 years of Frieda's continual, creative, aggressive and expensive marketing, the kiwifruit became a North American star when *nouvelle cuisine* chefs prominently featured it in their mixes of strawberry, banana, melon and pineapples. Since that time, the question asked most commonly of Frieda's, Inc., is "What will be the next kiwifruit?"

The answer is that there will never be another kiwifruit. When the kiwifruit was accepted into the world's fruit vernacular, there was an unconditional paradigm shift. Today, new specialty produce does not have to go through the rigorous acceptance process inflicted on the kiwifruit. There can never be another kiwifruit because the marketing climate and consumer palate have shifted in a wonderful, irreversible way. Now when a new fruit such as red bananas or yellow seedless watermelon comes onto the market, the consuming public does not react with fear and say, "Bananas are supposed to be yellow," or, "It really isn't watermelon if there aren't any seeds and it's not red." They respond with positive open minds (much the same as Frieda did when she purchased her first flat of kiwifruit in 1962) and a newfound knowledge that new foods will bring quality and variety, not discord, to their diets.

KAREN CAPLAN is Frieda's eldest daughter and president of Frieda's, Inc.

▶ PROCEDURE FOR PITTING AND CUTTING MANGOES

1 Cut along each side of the pit to remove two sections.

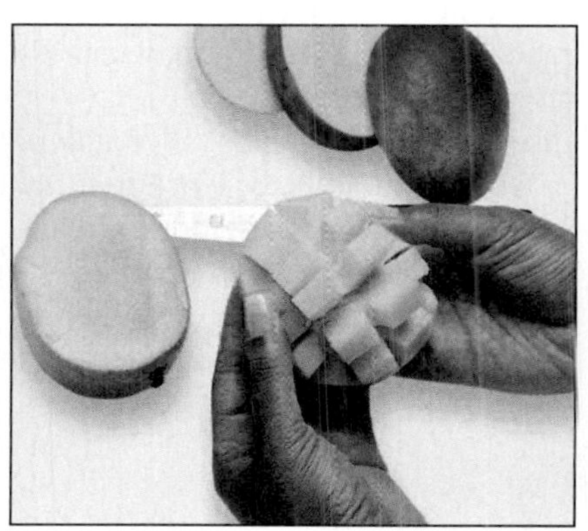

2 Each section can then be cubed using the "hedgehog" technique: Make crosswise cuts through the flesh, just to the skin; press up on the skin side of the section, exposing the cubes.

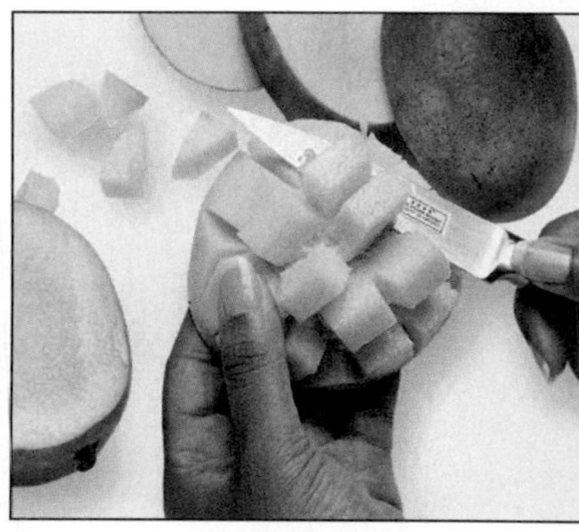

3 The mango may be served like this or the cubes can be cut off to use in salads or other dishes.

PAPAYAS

The papaya (puh-PIE-yuh) is a greenish-yellow fruit shaped rather like a large pear and weighing 1 to 2 pounds (500 to 1000 grams). When halved, it resembles a melon. The flesh is golden to reddish-pink; its center cavity is filled with round, silver-black seeds resembling caviar. Ripe papayas can be eaten raw, with only a squirt of lemon or lime juice. They can also be puréed for sweet or spicy sauces, chilled soups or sorbets.

Papayas contain **papain,** which breaks down proteins, and therefore papayas are an excellent meat tenderizer. Meats can be marinated with papaya juice or slices before cooking. Papain, however, makes fresh papayas unsuitable for use in gelatins because it inhibits gelling. Unripe (green) papayas are often used in pickles or chutneys, and can be baked or stewed with meat or poultry.

Papayas

▶ **papain** an enzyme found in papayas that breaks down proteins; used as the primary ingredient in many commercial meat tenderizers

Red Papayas

Papaya seeds are edible, with a peppery flavor and slight crunch. They are occasionally used to garnish fruit salads or add flavor to fruit salsas and compotes.

Papayas are grown in tropical and subtropical areas worldwide. Although they are available year-round, their peak season is from April through June. Select papayas that are plump, with a smooth, unblemished skin. Color is a better determinant of ripeness than is softness: The greater the proportion of yellow to green skin color, the riper the fruit. Papayas may be held at room temperature until completely ripe, then refrigerated for up to 1 week.

Passion Fruit

PASSION FRUITS

Passion fruits (Fr. *fruits de la passion*) have a firm, almost shell-like purple skin with orange-yellow pulp surrounding large, black, edible seeds. They are about the size and shape of large hen eggs, with a sweet, rich and unmistakable citrusy flavor. The pulp is used in custards, sauces and ice creams.

Select heavy fruits with dark, shriveled skin and a strong aroma. Allow them to ripen at room temperature, if necessary, then refrigerate. Passion fruits are now grown in New Zealand, Hawaii and California and should be available all year, although their peak season is in February and March. Bottles or frozen packs of purée are readily available and provide a strong, true flavor.

PINEAPPLES

Pineapples (Fr. *ananas*) are the fruit of a shrub with sharp spear-shaped leaves. Each fruit is covered with rough, brown eyes, giving it the appearance of a pine cone. The pale yellow flesh, which is sweet and very juicy, surrounds a cylindrical woody core that is edible but too tough for most uses. Most pineapples weigh approximately 2 pounds (1 kilogram), but dwarf varieties are also available.

Pineapples are excellent eaten raw, alone or in salads. Slices can be baked or grilled to accompany pork or ham. The cuisines of Southeast Asia incorporate pineapple into various curries, soups and stews. Pineapple juice is a popular beverage, often used in punch or cocktails. Canned or cooked pineapple can be added to gelatin mixtures, but avoid using fresh pineapple; an enzyme (bromelin) found in fresh pineapple breaks down gelatin.

Pineapples do not ripen after harvesting. They must be left on the stem until completely ripe, at which time they are extremely perishable. The vast majority of pineapples come from Hawaii. Fresh pineapples are available all year, with peak supplies in March through June. Select heavy fruits with a strong, sweet aroma and rich color. Avoid those with dried leaves or soft spots. Pineapples should be used as soon as possible after purchase. Pineapples are also available canned in slices, cubes or crushed, dried or candied.

Pineapples

▶ PROCEDURE FOR TRIMMING AND SLICING PINEAPPLES

1 Slice off the leaves and stem end. Stand the fruit upright and cut the peel off in vertical strips.

2 Cut the peeled fruit in quarters, then cut away the woody core.

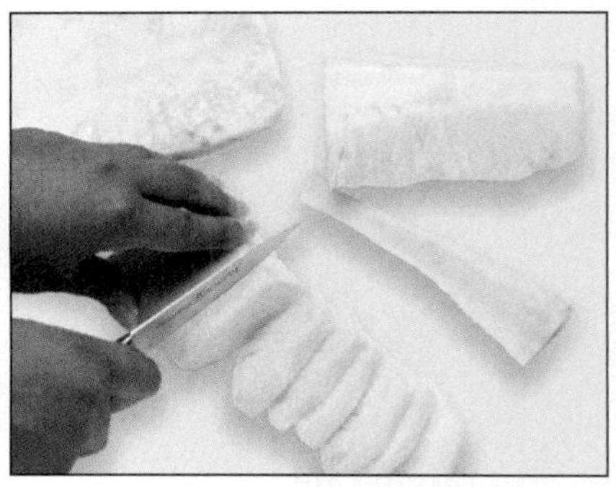

3 The flesh can then be cut as desired.

▶ NUTRITION

Most fruits are quite nutritious. They have a high water content (usually 75 to 95 percent) and low protein and fat contents, all of which makes them low in calories. They are also an excellent source of fiber, and the sugar content of ripe fruits is a good source of energy. Some fruits, such as citrus, melons and strawberries, contain large amounts of vitamin C (which may be destroyed, however, by cooking or processing). Deep yellow and green fruits, such as apricots, mangoes and kiwis, are high in vitamin A; bananas, raisins and figs are a good source of potassium.

▶ PURCHASING FRESH FRUITS

Fresh fruits have not been subjected to any processing (such as canning, freezing or drying). Fresh fruits may be ripe or unripe, depending on their condition when harvested or the conditions under which they have been stored. In order to use fresh fruits to their best advantage, it is important to make careful purchasing decisions. It is important to pay attention to the size of each piece of fruit, its grade or quality, its ripeness on delivery and its nutritional content in order to serve fruit in an appropriate and cost-effective manner.

GRADING

Fresh fruits traded on the wholesale market may be graded under the USDA's voluntary program. The grades, based on size and uniformity of shape, color and texture as well as the absence of defects, are U.S. Fancy, U.S. No. 1, U.S. No. 2 and U.S. No. 3. Most fruits purchased for food service operations are U.S. Fancy. Fruits with lower grades are suitable for processing into sauces, jams, jellies or preserves.

RIPENING

Several important changes take place in a fruit as it ripens. The fruit reaches its full size; its pulp or flesh becomes soft and tender; its color changes. In addition, the fruit's acid content declines, making it less tart, and its starch content converts into the sugars fructose and glucose, which provide the fruit's sweetness, flavor and aroma.

Unfortunately, these changes do not stop when the fruit reaches its peak of ripeness. Rather, they continue, deteriorating the fruit's texture and flavor and eventually causing spoilage.

Depending on the species, fresh fruits can be purchased either fully ripened or unripened. Figs and pineapples, for example, ripen only on the plant and are harvested at or just before their peak of ripeness, then rushed to market. They should not be purchased unripened as they will never attain full flavor or texture after harvesting. On the other hand, some fruits, including bananas and pears, continue to ripen after harvesting and can be purchased unripened.

With most harvested fruits, the ripening time as well as the time during which the fruits remain at their peak of ripeness can be manipulated. For instance, ripening can be delayed by chilling. Chilling slows the fruit's **respiration rate** (fruits, like animals, consume oxygen and expel carbon dioxide). The slower the respiration rate, the slower the conversion of starch to sugar. For quicker ripening, fruit can be stored at room temperature.

▶ **respiration rate** the speed with which the cells of a fruit use oxygen and produce carbon dioxide during ripening

Ripening is also affected by ethylene gas, a colorless, odorless hydrocarbon gas. Ethylene gas is naturally emitted by ripening fruits and can be used to encourage further ripening in most fruits. Apples, tomatoes, melons and bananas give off the most ethylene and should be stored away from delicate fruits and vegetables, especially greens. Fruits that are picked and shipped unripened can be exposed to ethylene gas to induce ripening just before sale. Conversely, to extend the life of ripe fruits a day or two, isolate them from other fruits and keep them well chilled.

Fresh fruits will not ripen further once they are cooked or processed. The cooking or processing method applied, however, may soften the fruits or add flavor.

PURCHASING

Fresh fruits are sold by weight or by count. They are packed in containers referred to as crates, bushels, cartons, cases, lugs or flats. The weight or count packed in each of these containers varies depending on the type of fruit, the purveyor and the state in which the fruits were packed. For example, Texas citrus is packed in cartons equal to 7⁄10 of a bushel; Florida citrus is packed in cartons equal to 4⁄5 of a bushel. Sometimes fruit size must be specified when ordering. A 30-pound case of lemons, for example, may contain 96, 112 or 144 individual lemons, depending on their size.

Some fresh fruits, especially melons, pineapples, peaches and berries, are available trimmed, cleaned, peeled or cut. Sugar and preservatives are sometimes added. They are sold in bulk containers, sometimes packed in water. These items offer a consistent product with a significant reduction in labor costs. The purchase price may be greater than that for fresh fruits, and flavor, freshness and nutritional qualities may suffer somewhat from the processing.

▶ Purchasing and Storing Preserved Fruits

Preservation techniques are designed to extend the shelf life of fruits in essentially fresh form. These methods include irradiation, acidulation, canning, freezing and drying. Except for drying, these techniques do not substantially change the fruits' texture or flavor. Canning and freezing can also be used to preserve cooked fruits.

Preserves such as jellies and jams are cooked products and are discussed later in this chapter.

IRRADIATED FRUITS

As described in Chapter 20, Vegetables, some fruits can be subjected to ionizing radiation to destroy parasites, insects and bacteria. The treatment also slows ripening without a noticeable effect on the fruits' flavor and texture. Irradiated fruits must be labeled "treated with radiation," "treated by irradiation" or with the symbol shown in Figure 22.1.

ACIDULATION

Apples, pears, bananas, peaches and other fruits turn brown when cut. Although this browning is commonly attributed to exposure to oxygen, it is actually caused by the reaction of enzymes.

Enzymatic browning can be retarded by immersing cut fruits in an acidic solution such as lemon or orange juice. This simple technique is sometimes referred to as **acidulation.** Soaking fruits in water or lemon juice and water (called acidulated water) is not recommended. Unless a sufficient amount of salt or sugar is added to the water, the fruits will just become mushy. But if enough salt or sugar is added to retain texture, the flavor will be affected.

CANNED FRUITS

Almost any type of fruit can be canned successfully; pineapple and peaches are the largest sellers. In commercial canning, raw fruits are cleaned and placed in a sealed container, then subjected to high temperatures for a specific amount of time. Heating destroys the microorganisms that cause spoilage, and the sealed environment created by the can eliminates oxidation and retards decomposition. But the heat required by the canning process also softens the texture of most fruits. Canning has little or no effect on vitamins A, B, C and D because oxygen is not present during the heating process. Canning also has no practical effect on proteins, fats or carbohydrates.

In solid-pack cans, little or no water is added. The only liquid is from the fruits' natural moisture. Water-pack cans have water or fruit juice added, which must be taken into account when determining costs. Syrup-pack cans have a sugar syrup—light, medium or heavy—added. The syrup should also be taken into account when determining food costs, and the additional sweetness should be considered when using syrup-packed fruits. Cooked fruit products such as pie fillings are also available canned.

Canned fruits are purchased in cases of standard-sized cans (see Appendix II). Once a can is opened, any unused contents should be transferred to an appropriate storage container and refrigerated. Cans with bulges should be discarded immediately, without opening.

FROZEN FRUITS

Freezing is a highly effective method for preserving fruits. It severely inhibits the growth of microorganisms that cause fruits to spoil. Freezing does not destroy nutrients, although the appearance or texture of most fruits can be affected because of their high water content. This occurs when ice crystals formed from the water in the cells burst the cells' walls.

Many fruits, especially berries and apple and pear slices, are now individually quick-frozen (IQF). This method employs blasts of cold air, refrigerated plates, liquid nitrogen, liquid air or other techniques to chill the produce quickly. Speeding the freezing process can greatly reduce the formation of ice crystals.

Fruits can be trimmed and sliced before freezing and are also available frozen in sugar syrup, which adds flavor and prevents browning. Berries are frozen whole, while stone fruits are usually peeled, pitted and sliced. Fruit purées are also available frozen.

Golden Raisins

Currants

Frozen fruits are graded as U.S. Grade A (Fancy), U.S. Grade B (Choice or Extra Standard), or U.S. Grade C (Standard). The "U.S." indicates that a government inspector has graded the product, but packers may use grade names without an actual inspection if the contents meet the standards of the grade indicated.

IQF fruits can be purchased in bulk by the case. All frozen fruits should be sealed in moisture-proof wrapping and kept at a constant temperature of 0°F (−18°C) or below. Temperature fluctuations can cause freezer burn. Frozen berries such as blueberries and blackberries should not be thawed before adding to batters because their juice can easily discolor the batter.

DRIED FRUITS

Drying is the oldest known technique for preserving fruits, having been used for more than 5000 years. When ripe fruits are dried, they lose most of their moisture. This concentrates their flavors and sugars and dramatically extends shelf life. Although most fruits can be dried, plums (prunes), grapes (raisins, sultanas and currants), apricots and figs are the fruits most commonly dried. The drying method can be as simple as leaving ripe fruits in the sun to dry naturally or the more cost-efficient technique of passing fruits through a compartment of hot, dry air to quickly extract moisture.

Kiwis

Persimmons

Apricots

Dried fruits actually retain from 16 to 26 percent residual moisture, which leaves them moist and soft. They are often treated with sulfur dioxide to prevent browning (oxidation) and to extend shelf life. Dried fruits may be eaten out of hand; added to cereals or salads; baked in muffins, breads, pies or tarts; stewed for chutneys or compotes; or used as a stuffing for roasted meats or poultry. Before use, dried fruits may be softened by steeping them for a short time in a hot liquid such as water, wine, rum, brandy or other liquor. Some dried fruits should be simmered in a small amount of water before use.

Store dried fruits in airtight containers to prevent further moisture loss; keep in a dry, cool area away from sunlight. Dried fruits may mold if exposed to both air and high humidity.

Apples

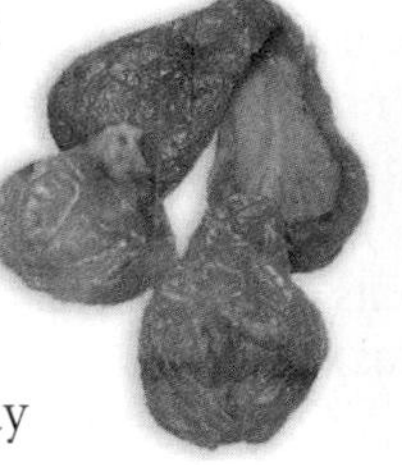

Pears

▶ JUICING

▶ **juice** the liquid extracted from any fruit or vegetable

▶ **nectar** the diluted, sweetened juice of peaches, apricots, guavas, black currants or other fruits, the juice of which would be too thick or too tart to drink straight

▶ **cider** mildly fermented apple juice; nonalcoholic apple juice may also be labeled cider

Fruit juice is used as a beverage, alone or mixed with other ingredients, and as the liquid ingredient in other preparations. Juice can be extracted from fruits (and some vegetables) in two ways: pressure and blending.

Pressure is used to extract juice from fruits such as citrus that have a high water content. Pressure is applied by hand-squeezing or with a manual or electric reamer. All reamers work on the same principle: A ribbed cone is pressed against the fruit to break down its flesh and release the juice. Always strain juices to remove seeds, pulp or fibrous pieces.

A blender or an electric juice extractor can be used to liquefy less-juicy fruits and vegetables such as apples, carrots, tomatoes, beets and cabbage. The extractor pulverizes the fruit or vegetable, then separates and strains the liquid from the pulp with centrifugal force.

Interesting and delicious beverages can be made by combining the juice of one or more fruits or vegetables pineapple with orange, apple with cranberry, strawberry with tangerine and papaya with orange. Color should be considered when creating mixed-juice beverages, however. Some combinations can cause rather odd color changes. Although yellow and orange juices are not a problem, those containing red and blue flavonoid pigments (such as Concord grapes, cherries, strawberries, raspberries and blueberries) can create some unappetizing colors. Adding an acid such as lemon juice helps retain the correct red and blue hues.

▶ Applying Various Cooking Methods

Although most fruits are edible raw and typically served that way, some fruits can also be cooked. Commonly used cooking methods are broiling and grilling, baking, sautéing, deep-frying, poaching, simmering and preserving.

When cooking fruits, proper care and attention are critical. Even minimal cooking can render fruits overly soft or mushy. To combat this irreversible process, sugar can be added. When fruits are cooked with sugar, the sugar will be absorbed slowly into the cells, firming the fruits. Acids (notably lemon juice) also help fruits retain their structure. (Alkalis, such as baking soda, cause the cells to break down more quickly, reducing the fruits to mush.)

DETERMINING DONENESS

There are so many different fruits with such varied responses to cooking that no one standard for doneness is appropriate. Each item should be evaluated on a recipe-by-recipe basis. Generally, however, most cooked fruits are done when they are just tender when pierced with a fork or the tip of a paring knife. Simmered fruits, such as compotes, should be softer, cooked just to the point of disintegration. Avoid overcooking fruits by remembering that some carryover cooking will occur through the residual heat contained in the foods. Always rely on subjective tests—sight, feel, taste and aroma—rather than the clock.

DRY-HEAT COOKING METHODS

BROILING AND GRILLING

Fruits are usually broiled or grilled just long enough to caramelize sugars; cooking must be done quickly in order to avoid breaking down the fruits' structure. Good fruits to broil or grill are pineapples, apples, grapefruits, bananas, persimmons and peaches. The fruits may be cut into slices, chunks or halves as appropriate. A coating of sugar, honey or liqueur adds flavor, as do lemon juice, cinnamon and ginger.

When broiling fruits, use an oiled sheet pan or broiling platter. When grilling fruits, use a clean grill grate or thread the pieces onto skewers. Only thick fruit slices will need to be turned or rotated to heat fully. Broiled or grilled fruits can be served alone, as an accompaniment to meat, fish or poultry or as topping for ice creams or custards.

▶ PROCEDURE FOR BROILING OR GRILLING FRUITS

1. Select ripe fruits and peel, core or slice as necessary.
2. Top with sugar or honey to add flavor and aid caramelization.
3. Place the fruits on the broiler platter, sheet pan or grill grate.
4. Broil or grill at high temperatures, turning as necessary to heat the fruits thoroughly but quickly.

RECIPE 24.1

BROILED GRAPEFRUIT

Yield: 8 Servings **Method:** Broiling

Ruby grapefruits	4	4
Sweet sherry	2 Tbsp.	30 ml
Brown sugar	4 Tbsp.	60 ml

1. Cut each grapefruit in half (perpendicular to the segments), then section with a sharp knife, carefully removing any visible seeds.
2. Sprinkle the grapefruit halves with the sherry and sugar.
3. Arrange on a baking sheet and place under a preheated broiler. Cook briefly, only until well heated and the sugar caramelizes. Serve immediately.

Approximate values per serving: **Calories** 70, **Total fat** 0 g, **Saturated fat** 0 g, **Cholesterol** 0 mg, **Sodium** 0 mg, **Total carbohydrates** 16 g, **Protein** 1 g, **Vitamin C** 80%, **Claims**—fat free; no sodium

BAKING

After washing, peeling, coring or pitting, most pomes, stone fruits and tropicals can be baked to create hot, flavorful desserts. Fruits with sturdy skins, particularly apples and pears, are excellent for baking alone, as their skin (peel) holds in moisture and flavor. They can also be used as edible containers by filling the cavity left by coring with a variety of sweet or savory mixtures.

Combinations of fruits can also be baked successfully; try mixing fruits for a balance of sweetness and tartness (for example, strawberries with rhubarb or apples with plums).

Several baked desserts are simply fruits (fresh, frozen or canned) topped with a crust (called a cobbler), strudel (called a crumple or crisp) or batter (called a buckle). Fruits, sometimes poached first, can also be baked in a wrapper of puff pastry, flaky dough or phyllo dough to produce an elegant dessert.

▶ PROCEDURE FOR BAKING FRUITS

1. Select ripe but firm fruits and peel, core, pit or slice as necessary.
2. Add sugar or any flavorings.
3. Wrap the fruits in pastry dough if desired or directed in the recipe.
4. Place the fruits in a baking dish and bake uncovered in a moderate oven until tender or properly browned.

RECIPE 24.2

BAKED APPLES

Yield: 8 Servings **Method:** Baking

Apples, Red or Golden Delicious	8	8
Raisins	6 oz.	180 g
Orange zest	1½ Tbsp.	23 ml
Brown sugar	4 oz.	120 g

1. Rinse and core each apple. The peels should be scored or partially removed to allow the pulp to expand without bursting the skin during baking.
2. Plump the raisins by soaking them in boiling water for 10 minutes. Drain the raisins thoroughly.
3. Combine the raisins, zest and sugar. Fill the cavity of each apple with this mixture.

4 Stand the apples in a shallow baking dish. Add enough water to measure about ½ inch (1.2 centimeters) deep.
5 Bake the apples at 375°F (190°C) for 15 minutes. Reduce the temperature to 300°F (150°C) and continue baking until the apples are tender but still hold their shape, approximately 1 hour. Occasionally, baste the apples with liquid from the baking dish.

Approximate values per apple: **Calories** 220, **Total fat** 0.5 g, **Saturated fat** 0 g, **Cholesterol** 0 mg, **Sodium** 10 mg, **Total carbohydrates** 52 g, **Protein** 1 g, **Vitamin C** 15%, **Claims**—low fat; no cholesterol; very low sodium; good source of fiber

SAUTÉING

Fruits develop a rich, syrupy flavor when sautéed briefly in butter, sugar and, if desired, spices or liqueur. Cherries, bananas, apples, pears and pineapples are good choices. They should be peeled, cored and seeded as necessary and cut into uniform-size pieces before sautéing.

For dessert, fruits are sautéed with sugar to create a caramelized glaze or syrup. The fruits and syrup can be used to fill crêpes or to top spongecakes or ice creams. Liquor may be added and the mixture flamed (flambéed) in front of diners, as with Bananas Foster.

For savory mixtures, onions, shallots or garlic are often added.

In both sweet and savory fruit sautés, the fat used should be the most appropriate for the finished product. Butter and bacon fat are typical choices.

▶ PROCEDURE FOR SAUTÉING FRUITS

1 Peel, pit and core the fruits as necessary and cut into uniform-size pieces.
2 Melt the fat in a hot sauté pan.
3 Add the fruit pieces and any flavoring ingredients. Do not crowd the pan, as this will cause the fruit to stew in its own juices.
4 Cook quickly over high heat.

SAVORY FRUIT COMPOTE

RECIPE 24.3

Yield: 2 lb. (1 kg) **Method:** Sautéing

Onions, fine dice	6 oz.	180 g
Whole butter or bacon fat	1 oz.	30 g
Apples (tart) or peaches, peeled	3	3
Apricots	3	3
Granulated sugar	4 oz.	120 g
Hot paprika	TT	TT
Salt and white pepper	TT	TT

1 Sweat the onions in the butter or bacon fat without browning.
2 Slice the apples or peaches and apricots into thin, even pieces. Add the apples to the onions and sauté for 1 to 2 minutes. Add the apricots.
3 Sprinkle the sugar over the fruits and cook, uncovered, over medium heat until tender. Season with paprika, salt and white pepper.
4 Serve warm as an accompaniment to roast pork, game or other meat.

Approximate values per 1-oz. (30-g) serving: **Calories** 60, **Total fat** 1.5 g, **Saturated fat** 1 g, **Cholesterol** 5 mg, **Sodium** 50 mg, **Total carbohydrates** 12 g, **Protein** 0 g, **Vitamin A** 4%, **Claims**—low fat; low cholesterol; low sodium

Mise en Place

▶ Wash and peel onions and cut into fine dice.
▶ Peel apples or peaches.

DEEP-FRYING

Few fruits are suitable for deep-frying. Apples, bananas, pears, pineapples and firm peaches mixed in or coated with batter, however, produce fine results. These fruits should be peeled, cored, seeded and cut into evenly sized slices or chunks. They may also need to be dried with paper towels so that the batter or coating can adhere.

Fruit fritters are also a popular snack or dessert item. Fritters contain diced or chopped fish, shellfish, vegetables or fruits bound together with a thick batter and deep-fried. Because frying time is very short, the main ingredient is usually precooked. Fritters are spooned or dropped directly into the hot fat; they form a crust as they cook. Popular examples are clam fritters, corn fritters, artichoke fritters and apple fritters.

▶ PROCEDURE FOR DEEP-FRYING FRUIT—FRITTERS

1. Cut, chop and otherwise prepare the food to be made into fritters.
2. Precook any ingredients if necessary.
3. Prepare the batter as directed.
4. Scoop the fritters into deep fat at 350°F (180°C), using the swimming method.
5. Cook until done. The fritters should be golden brown on the outside and moist but set on the inside.
6. Remove the fritters from the fat and hold them over the fryer, allowing the excess fat to drain off. Transfer the food to a hotel pan either lined with absorbent paper or fitted with a rack. Serve hot.
7. If the fritters are to be held for later service, place them under a heat lamp.

RECIPE 24.4

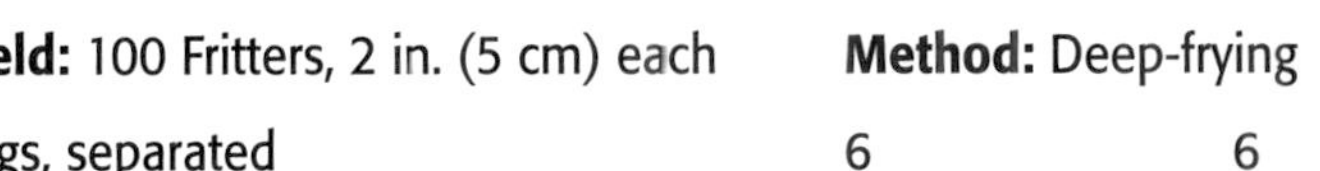

APPLE FRITTERS

Mise en Place

- ▶ Separate eggs.
- ▶ Peel and core apples and cut into medium dice.

1 Adding the dry ingredients to the liquids.

Yield: 100 Fritters, 2 in. (5 cm) each

Method: Deep-frying

Eggs, separated	6	6
Milk	1 pt.	500 ml
Flour	1 lb.	450 g
Baking powder	1 Tbsp.	15 ml
Salt	1 tsp.	5 ml
Granulated sugar	2 oz.	60 g
Cinnamon, ground	½ tsp.	2 ml
Apples, peeled, cored, medium dice	1 lb. 8 oz.	700 g
Powdered sugar	as needed	as needed

1. Combine the egg yolks and milk.
2. Sift together the flour, baking powder, salt, sugar and cinnamon. Add the dry ingredients to the milk-and-egg mixture; whisk until smooth.
3. Allow the batter to rest 1 hour.
4. Stir the apples into the batter.
5. Just before the fritters are to be cooked, whip the egg whites to soft peaks and fold into the batter.
6. Scoop the fritters into deep fat at 350°F (180°C), using the swimming method. Cook until uniformly browned approximately 5 minutes.
7. Dust with powdered sugar and serve hot.

2 Folding the egg whites into the batter.

3 Dropping the fritters into the deep fat.

4 Dusting the fritters with powdered sugar.

VARIATION:

Banana Fritters—Omit the cinnamon and apples. Add 3 tablespoons (45 milliliters) finely grated orange zest, 4 fluid ounces (120 milliliters) orange juice and 2 large bananas, peeled and diced (not puréed).

Approximate values per fritter: **Calories** 60, **Total fat** 4 g, **Saturated fat** 1 g, **Cholesterol** 15 mg, **Sodium** 5 mg, **Total carbohydrates** 6 g, **Protein** 1 g

MOIST-HEAT COOKING METHODS

POACHING

One of the more popular cooking methods for fruits is poaching. Poaching softens and tenderizes fruits and infuses them with additional flavors such as spices or wine. Poached fruits can be served hot or cold and used in tarts or pastries or as an accompaniment to meat or poultry dishes.

The poaching liquid can be water, wine, liquor or sugar syrup. (As noted earlier, sugar helps fruits keep their shape, although it takes longer to tenderize fruits poached in sugar syrup.) The low poaching temperature (185°F/85°C) allows fruits to soften gradually. The agitation created at higher temperatures would damage them.

Cooked fruits should be allowed to cool in the flavored poaching liquid or syrup. Most poaching liquids can be used repeatedly. If they contain sufficient sugar, they can be reduced to a sauce or glaze to accompany the poached fruits.

▶ PROCEDURE FOR POACHING FRUITS

1 Peel, core and slice the fruits as necessary.
2 In a sufficiently deep, nonreactive saucepan, combine the poaching liquid (usually water or wine) with sugar, spices, citrus zest and other ingredients as desired or as directed in the recipe.
3 Submerge the fruits in the liquid. Place a circle of parchment paper over the fruits to help them stay submerged.
4 Place the saucepan on the stove top over a medium-high flame; bring to a boil.
5 As soon as the liquid boils, reduce the temperature. Simmer gently.
6 Poach until the fruits are tender enough for the tip of a small knife to be easily inserted. Cooking time depends on the type of fruit used, its ripeness and the cooking liquid.

7 Remove the saucepan from the stove top and allow the liquid and fruits to cool.

8 Remove the fruits from the liquid and then refrigerate. The liquid can be returned to the stove top and reduced until thick enough to use as a sauce or glaze or refrigerated for further use.

RECIPE 24.5

PEARS POACHED IN RED WINE

Mise en Place

▶ Chop the fresh basil.

Yield: 8 Servings **Method:** Poaching

Ripe pears, Anjou or Bartlett	8	8
Zinfandel wine	52 fl. oz.	1500 ml
Whole peppercorns	8–10	8–10
Vanilla bean	1	1
Granulated sugar	12 oz.	360 g
Fresh basil, chopped	1 oz.	30 g
Orange zest	from 1 orange	from 1 orange

1 Peel and core the pears, leaving the stems intact.

2 Combine the remaining ingredients in a large nonreactive saucepan. Arrange the pears in the liquid in a single layer.

3 Place the pears on the stove top over a medium-high flame. Bring to just below a boil, then immediately reduce the heat and allow the liquid to simmer gently. Cover with a round of parchment paper if necessary to keep the pears submerged.

4 Continue poaching the pears until tender, approximately 1 to 1½ hours. Remove the saucepan from the stove and allow the pears to cool in the liquid.

5 Remove the pears from the poaching liquid and return the liquid to the stove top. Reduce until the liquid is thick enough to coat the back of a spoon, then strain.

6 Serve the pears chilled or at room temperature in a pool of the reduced wine syrup.

Approximate values per 7-oz. (210-g) serving: **Calories** 410, **Total fat** 1.5 g, **Saturated fat** 0 g, **Cholesterol** 0 mg, **Sodium** 35 mg, **Total carbohydrates** 91 g, **Protein** 6 g, **Vitamin A** 40%, **Calcium** 90%, **Iron** 110%, **Claims**—low fat; no cholesterol; low sodium; high fiber

SIMMERING

Simmering techniques are used to make stewed fruits and compotes. Fresh, frozen, canned and dried fruits can be simmered or stewed. As with any moist-heat cooking method, simmering softens and tenderizes fruits. The liquid used can be water, wine or the juices naturally found in the fruits. Sugar, honey and spices may be added as desired. Stewed or simmered fruits can be served hot or cold, as a first course, a dessert or an accompaniment to meat or poultry dishes.

▶ PROCEDURE FOR SIMMERING FRUITS

1 Peel, core, pit and slice the fruits as necessary.

2 Bring the fruits and cooking liquid, if used, to a simmer. Cook until the fruit is tender.

3 Add sugar or other sweeteners as desired or as directed in the recipe.

DRIED FRUIT COMPOTE

RECIPE 24.6

Yield: 3 lb. (1.5 kg) **Method:** Simmering

Dried apricots	5 oz.	150 g
Prunes, pitted	5 oz.	150 g
Dried pears or apples	5 oz.	150 g
Dried peaches	5 oz.	150 g
Water, hot	24 fl. oz.	720 ml
Cinnamon stick	1	1
Light corn syrup	12 fl. oz.	360 ml
Cointreau	2 fl. oz.	60 ml

Mise en Place

► Pit the prunes.

1. Coarsely chop the fruits. Place the pieces in a nonreactive saucepan and add the water and cinnamon stick.
2. Bring the mixture to a simmer, cover and cook until tender, approximately 12–15 minutes.
3. Add the corn syrup and Cointreau. Simmer uncovered until thoroughly heated. Remove the cinnamon stick. Serve warm or refrigerate for longer storage.

Approximate values per 1-oz. (30-g) serving: **Calories** 60, **Total fat** 0 g, **Saturated fat** 0 g, **Cholesterol** 0 mg, **Sodium** 15 mg, **Total carbohydrates** 15 g, **Protein** 0 g, **Claims**—fat free, very low sodium

PRESERVING

Fresh fruits can be preserved with sugar if the fruit-and-sugar mixture is concentrated by evaporation to the point that microbial spoilage cannot occur. The added sugar also retards the growth of, but does not destroy, microorganisms.

Pectin, a substance present in varying amounts in all fruits, can cause cooked fruits to form a semisolid mass known as a gel. Fruits that are visually unattractive but otherwise of high quality can be made into gels, which are more commonly known as **jams, jellies, marmalades** and **preserves.**

The essential ingredients of a fruit gel are fruit, pectin, acid (usually lemon juice) and sugar. They must be carefully combined in the correct ratio for the gel to form. For fruits with a low pectin content (such as strawberries) to form a gel, pectin must be added, either by adding a fruit with a high pectin content (for example, apples or quinces) or by adding packaged pectin.

► **concentrate** also known as a fruit paste or compound; a reduced fruit purée, without a gel structure, used as a flavoring

► **jam** a fruit gel made from fruit pulp and sugar

► **jelly** a fruit gel made from fruit juice and sugar

► **marmalade** a citrus jelly that also contains unpeeled slices of citrus fruit

► **preserve** a fruit gel that contains large pieces or whole fruits

Apple Jelly

Apricot Jam

Orange Marmalade

CONCLUSION

Fruits, whether fresh, frozen, canned or dried, are one of the most versatile and popular of foods. Fruits can be used uncooked or incorporated into a soup, salad, bread, meat dish or dessert. When selecting fresh fruits, it is important to consider seasonal availability, storage conditions and ripeness. When using them, it is important that they be at their peak of ripeness for the best flavor, texture, aroma and appearance.

QUESTIONS FOR DISCUSSION

1. Define ripeness and explain why ripe fruits are most desirable. How does the ripening process affect the availability of some fruits?
2. Describe the proper storage conditions for most fruits. Which fruits emit ethylene gas, and why is this a consideration when storing fruits?
3. Explain why some apple varieties are preferred for cooking, while other varieties are preferred for eating. Which variety is generally preferred for making applesauce?
4. Which types of fruits are best for dry-heat cooking methods? Explain your answer. Why is sugar usually added when cooking any type of fruit?
5. List and describe three ways to prepare fruits for extended storage.

6. Research a tropical or exotic fruit that is not available in your local area. Where is this fruit originally from? How is it eaten or used in cooking? What challenges face producers and importers in bringing this fruit to market in the United States?

CHAPTER TWENTY-FIVE

THE GENTLE ART OF GASTRONOMY IS A FRIENDLY ONE. IT HURDLES THE LANGUAGE BARRIER, MAKES FRIENDS AMONG CIVILIZED PEOPLE, AND WARMS THE HEART.

—Samuel Chamberlain, American author (1895–1975)

SANDWICHES

WILDFLOWER BREAD COMPANY, Scottsdale, AZ

AFTER STUDYING THIS CHAPTER, YOU WILL BE ABLE TO:

- select high-quality sandwich ingredients
- identify different types and styles of sandwiches
- prepare sandwiches to order

A sandwich is often the first meal a person learns to prepare. Even those who claim that they cannot cook often make delicious hot and cold sandwiches without considering it cooking. Mastering a grilled cheese sandwich or assembling the quintessential BLT may not require a degree in the culinary arts, but it does require the ability to select and use ingredients wisely.

Sandwiches, which are usually quick and easy to assemble, lend themselves well to a chef's creativity. Fancy sandwiches can become sensational menu additions in even the most formal restaurants, and amazing sandwiches can keep lunch customers visiting regularly. Sandwiches offer food service operations economical opportunities for using leftovers, and they offer customers, especially those with smaller budgets or appetites, meals to eat out of hand. Thus, the ability to correctly prepare hot and cold sandwiches to order is a fundamental skill in many food service operations.

► Ingredients for Sandwiches

Sandwiches are constructed from bread, a spread and one or more fillings. These components should be selected and combined carefully so that the finished sandwich is flavorful and visually appealing.

BREAD

Bread provides more than a convenient means for handling a sandwich. It holds or contains the spread and fillings and gives the sandwich its shape. Bread also adds flavor, texture, nutrition and color, and often determines the overall look of the finished product.

Health consciousness and consumer willingness to try new and unusual foods gives today's chefs the freedom to create sandwiches without relying on two slices of white bread. Virtually any bread can be used in sandwich making: rolls, biscuits, bagels, croissants, fruit and nut breads, whole-grain breads and savory breads as well as flatbreads such as naan, lavosh and tortillas; pocket breads such as pitas; and flavorful breads such as focaccia and Swedish limpa.

Whatever bread is used and whether its flavor is mild or intense, the bread should complement the fillings and not overpower them. The bread should be fresh (although day-old bread is easier to slice and is excellent toasted) and its texture should be able to withstand moisture from the spread and fillings without becoming soggy or pasty. An overly hard or crusty bread, however, may make the sandwich difficult to eat.

SPREAD

A spread is used to add flavor, moisture and richness to the sandwich, and sometimes helps to hold or bind it together. Some spreads, especially plain or flavored butters, also act as a barrier to prevent the moisture in the filling from soaking into the bread.

There are three principal spreads: butter, mayonnaise and vegetable purées.

BUTTER

One of the most common spreads, plain butter adds flavor and richness; it is also an excellent moisture barrier. Flavored or compound butters, discussed in Chapter 9, Stocks and Sauces, make excellent sandwich spreads, adding flavor dimensions to the finished product. For example, try caper butter on a Cajun-style blackened beef sandwich or a red chile honey butter on a smoked turkey sandwich. Any butter spread should be softened or whipped so that it will spread easily without tearing the bread.

MAYONNAISE

Perhaps the most popular sandwich spread, mayonnaise adds moisture, richness and flavor and complements most meat, poultry, fish, shellfish, vegetable, egg and cheese fillings. Like butter, mayonnaise can be made more exciting by adding flavoring ingredients. Condiments (for example, coarse-grained mustard or grated horseradish), herbs, spices and spice blends (for example, curry or chilli powder) and other ingredients such as sun-dried tomatoes and pesto sauce can be stirred into fresh or commercially prepared mayonnaise. Fresh mayonnaise can also be prepared with flavored oils, such as olive oil, walnut oil or chile oil. See Chapter 23, Salads and Salad Dressings, for recipes and additional information on mayonnaise.

VEGETABLE PURÉES

Puréed vegetables are often used as sandwich spreads; after all, lunch boxes everywhere would be incomplete without a purée of roasted peanuts (more commonly known as peanut butter) and fruit jelly. More sophisticated examples include black olive tapenade for a sandwich of Italian meats and cheeses, or a well-seasoned chickpea purée with lemon and tahini paste for a vegetarian sandwich. Unlike butter, vegetable purées usually will not provide a moisture barrier between the bread and the fillings.

FILLING

The filling is the body of the sandwich, providing most of its flavor. A sandwich often contains more than one filling. For example, the filling in a Reuben sandwich is corned beef, cheese and sauerkraut, while in a BLT it is bacon, lettuce and tomato. Fillings for cold sandwiches must be precooked and properly chilled, although some hot sandwich fillings may be cooked to order.

When choosing fillings, be sure that the flavors complement each other. Their textures may be similar or contrasting. If an ingredient, such as lettuce, is supposed to be crisp, it should be very crisp, not limp. If an ingredient is supposed to be tender and moist, make sure it is so. Improperly prepared, poor-quality or mishandled filling ingredients can ruin an otherwise wonderful sandwich.

Popular fillings include the following:

BEEF

Although the classic hot beef sandwich is the hamburger, other hot or cold beef products are commonly used. For example, hot or cold small steaks, slices of larger cuts such as the tenderloin, thin slices of roast beef and so on make excellent fillings. Also popular are hot or cold slices of cured beef products, including corned beef, pastrami and tongue as well as beef sausages such as salami, bologna and hot dogs.

PORK

Various ham and bacon products, served either hot or cold, are extremely popular. In addition, pork loin and tenderloin are light, white meats that adapt well to various flavor combinations and cooking methods. Barbecued pork, pork sausages and pork hot dogs are also popular.

HERO WORSHIP

Americans love sandwiches—not only the everyday classics, but larger-than-life regional masterpieces that go by colorful, often-interchangeable names: hoagies, submarines, heroes and so on. I've even heard them called "Dagwoods," after the Bumstead of comics fame who makes his monumental sandwiches in the middle of the night, invariably with a piece of Swiss cheese hanging over the side and an olive on a toothpick spear. They're "hoagies" in my native Philadelphia, supposedly after the Hog Island shipyard, where Italian workers ate big stuffed sandwiches during World War I. "Submarine" was coined in the next war, it is said, at a Connecticut submarine base. A sandwich is a "hero" when it's so huge it takes a hero to eat it—this from food journalist Clementine Paddleford, writing in the 1930s about New York's Manganaro's deli.

Call it what you like, and make what you like of it. Dagwood puts everything but the kitchen sink in his sandwich. Manganaro's still fills its version to the brim with Italian antipasti—meats, cheeses, peppers, lettuce and tomatoes. In my hometown, everything's optional but the Italian bread, lettuce, tomato, onion and salad oil. New Englanders eat something called a "grinder," a hero stuffed with hot meatballs, sausage and peppers, veal parmigiana or the like. These are aptly named and a real workout for the jaw! New Orleans has two big sandwiches: the round muffuletta, dressed in garlicky green-olive salad, and the warming po' boy, which is often soaked in gravy. Cuban immigrants press ham, roast pork, cheese and sweet pickles between slabs of French bread in a plancha, a kind of sandwich iron. But perhaps you have a better idea. Try it! Give it a jaunty title and who knows—perhaps both the recipe and its name will live on.

from *SHEILA LUKINS USA COOKBOOK*, by Sheila Lukins, Workman Publishing, 1997

SAFETY ALERT

Sandwich Sanitation

Sandwiches, whether hot or cold, present a particularly dangerous environment for the spread of food-borne illnesses. The use of uncooked lettuce and other vegetables, the use of high-protein foods such as meat and poultry, the combination of hot and cold ingredients and the presence of uncooked eggs in spreads such as homemade mayonnaise offer bacteria attractive homes. Cross-contamination can be an especially common problem because of the repeated use of spatulas, spreaders, scales, knives, cutting boards and, deadliest of all, human hands. Take extra care to wash hands frequently and to use disposable gloves properly; clean work surfaces and tools with a sanitizer often during service. The cardinal rule for proper food handling applies as well: Keep hot foods hot; keep cold foods cold. Review Chapter 2, Food Safety and Sanitation, for further information.

POULTRY

Sliced turkey breast, either roasted or smoked, and processed turkey are often used in hot and cold sandwiches. Moreover, food substitutes such as turkey bologna, turkey pastrami, turkey hot dogs and turkey ham are becoming increasingly popular because they generally have a lower fat content than the beef or pork original. Boneless chicken breast, either sliced or whole, is also quite popular because it can be prepared by a variety of methods and complements a broad range of flavors.

FISH AND SHELLFISH

Although fried fish fillets are an old standard, grilled fish sandwiches are gaining in popularity. Canned fish products, particularly tuna and salmon, are also widely used. Often fish and shellfish, especially tuna, shrimp and crab, are used for mayonnaise-based bound salads. Sardines and anchovies are less popular than other fish, but are sometimes mixed into bound salads or arranged artistically on open-faced sandwiches.

VEGETABLES

Vegetables add texture, moisture, flavor and nutrition to most any sandwich. Fresh vegetables such as lettuce, onions and tomatoes are commonly used in combination with meat, cheese and other fillings. Celery or bell peppers add a nice crunchy texture to cheese or mayonnaise-based bound salad fillings. Vegetables, however, can stand on their own as sandwich fillings. Marinated, grilled vegetables can be used in hot or cold sandwiches, and a combination of sliced, fresh vegetables and a flavorful dressing wrapped in soft lavosh or a tortilla becomes a portable salad.

EGGS

Hard-cooked eggs are most often used as an ingredient in a mayonnaise-based salad, where they are chopped and combined with pickle relish and seasonings. Hard-cooked eggs can also be sliced thin and used as an attractive garnish on open-faced sandwiches. Fried or scrambled eggs can be layered between pieces of bread or rolled in a tortilla for a breakfast sandwich.

CHEESE

Cheese is available in such a variety of textures, flavors, colors and styles that it is a welcome addition to nearly any sandwich. Sliced cheese can be used as a filling in hot or cold sandwiches, and melted cheese or a cheese sauce makes an excellent topping for hot open-faced sandwiches. Flavored cream cheese is also used as a spread or filling, particularly with bagels and fruit or nut breads.

BOUND SALADS

Protein salads bound with mayonnaise or salad dressing are popular sandwich fillings. Examples include chicken, tuna, egg and ham salads. Bound salads are discussed in Chapter 23, Salads and Salad Dressings.

▶ TYPES OF SANDWICHES

Sandwiches can be hot or cold, closed or open-faced, depending on the way in which the ingredients are assembled and presented.

HOT SANDWICHES

Hot closed sandwiches include those in which the filling ingredients are served hot, such as a hamburger or hot dog, and those where the entire sandwich is heated for service, such as a grilled cheese or Monte Cristo. Hot closed sandwiches can be categorized as basic, grilled or deep-fried.

Basic hot closed sandwiches are generally those in which the principal filling is served hot between two pieces of bread. These sandwiches may also include fillings that are not hot, such as tomato slices and lettuce leaves. Variations of the basic hot closed sandwich include tacos, quesadillas, burros (or burritos) and wraps, in which the hot and/or cold fillings are folded or wrapped in a tortilla or other supple flatbread.

▶ PROCEDURE FOR PREPARING WRAP SANDWICHES

1 The tortilla is topped with a spread or dressing.

2 Vegetables and meat, fish or poultry items are mounded across the tortilla.

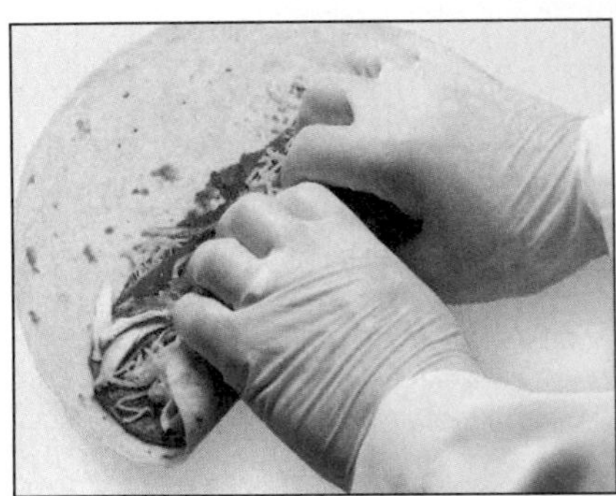

3 The tortilla is rolled tightly around the filling.

Grilled sandwiches are those in which the filling is placed between two pieces of bread, which are buttered on the outside and then browned on a griddle or in a sauté pan. (A sandwich grill also known as a panini grill, with a heated hinged lid, makes easy work of grilling sandwiches as it allows them to be toasted on each side without flipping.) In grilled sandwiches, the filling will be warmed during this procedure but will not cook. Therefore, fillings such as bacon or sliced meat should be fully cooked before the sandwich is assembled and grilled.

Cooking grilled cheese sandwiches.

Deep-fried sandwiches are made by dipping a closed sandwich in egg batter or bread crumbs and then deep-frying it. The most common example is the Monte Cristo: white bread filled with sliced ham, Swiss cheese and Dijon mustard.

The hot open-faced turkey or steak sandwich proved long ago that sandwiches do not need to be eaten by hand. In the typical **hot open-faced sandwich,** bread (grilled, toasted or fresh) is placed on a serving plate, covered with hot meat or other filling and topped with an appropriate gravy, sauce or cheese. The completed dish is often browned under a broiler immediately before service. Condiments and garnishes are usually served on the side. Figure 25.1 illustrates various methods used to prepare the bread and assemble hot open-faced sandwiches.

Perhaps the ultimate hot open-faced sandwich is the **pizza.** Bread dough is topped with sauce, cheese, meat and vegetables, then baked. Small personal-sized pizzas are a popular menu item in even upscale restaurants

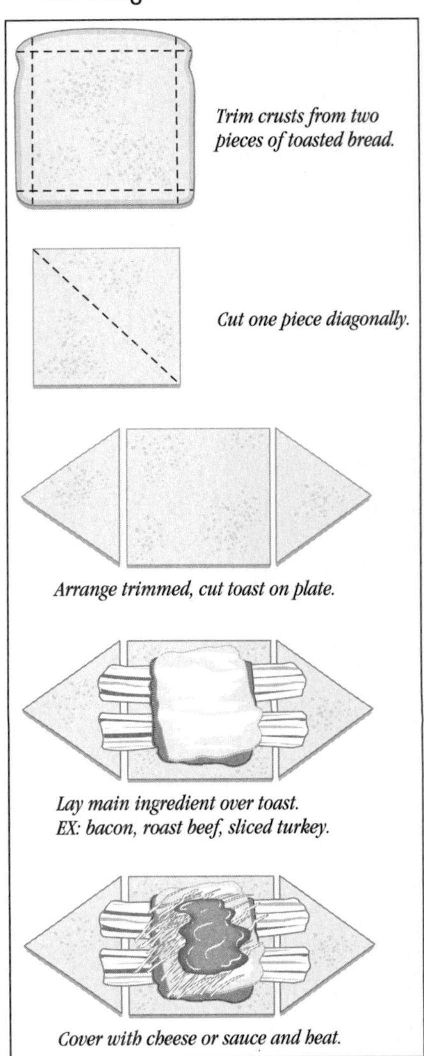

FIGURE 25.1 ▶ Arranging hot open-faced sandwiches.

COLD SANDWICHES

Cold sandwiches are simply sandwiches that are eaten cold. They are made with raw ingredients that are not intended to be cooked, such as vegetables and cheese, or with meat, poultry, fish or shellfish that is precooked and then chilled before use as a filling. Cold sandwiches may be closed or open-faced.

Cold closed sandwiches contain two or more pieces of bread with one or more fillings and one or more spreads. Cold closed sandwiches are usually eaten with the hands and come in three basic styles: basic, multidecker and tea.

Basic cold sandwiches are made with two pieces of bread or one split roll, one spread and one or more fillings. A tuna salad sandwich and an Italian-style submarine are both examples of basic cold closed sandwiches. A variation of the basic cold sandwich is a wrap with cold fillings—for example, an herb-flavored tortilla spread with peanut sauce and wrapped around spinach leaves, diced grilled chicken and cold cooked rice.

Multidecker cold sandwiches are made with three or more pieces of bread, one or more spreads and two or more fillings. The club sandwich, in which sliced turkey, bacon, lettuce and tomato are layered with three slices of toasted bread, is a classic example of a multidecker sandwich.

▶ PROCEDURE FOR PREPARING COLD MULTIDECKER SANDWICHES

1 The first slice of toasted bread is spread with butter or mayonnaise, then topped with meat and vegetables.

2 The second slice of bread is added, then spread with mayonnaise.

3 A second layer of vegetables and meat is added.

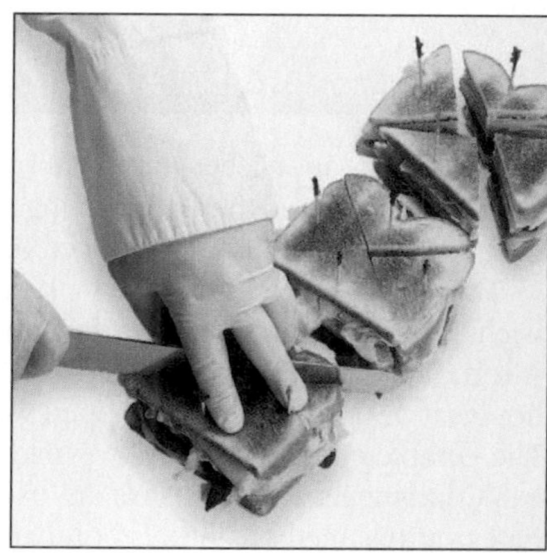

4 The finished sandwich is cut into quarters for service.

Open-faced sandwiches featuring smoked salmon (top), roast beef and shrimp (bottom) are attractively garnished with items that complement the principal ingredient.

Tea sandwiches are small, fancy constructions made with light, soft, trimmed breads and delicate fillings and spreads. They are usually cut or rolled into shapes such as diamonds, circles or pinwheels and served as a finger food at parties and receptions. The name derives from their service at afternoon tea.

Cold open-faced sandwiches are simply larger versions of canapés, which are discussed in Chapter 27, Hors d'Oeuvre and Canapés. The most popular style is the open-faced Norwegian sandwich known as **smørbrød.** As with canapés, much emphasis is placed on visual appeal. A single slice of bread is coated with a spread, then covered with thin slices of meat, poultry or fish, or a thin layer of a bound salad. Carefully cut and arranged garnishes such as hard-cooked eggs, fresh herbs, pickles, onions and radishes are used to complete the presentation. A simple version of an open-faced cold sandwich is a delicatessen classic—a bagel with lox and cream cheese.

HISTORY OF SANDWICHES

One of the earliest recorded references to foods eaten between two pieces of bread tells of Rabbi Hillel, a great Jewish teacher who lived sometime between 70 B.C.E. and 70 A.D. He created the Passover custom of eating *haroseth* (chopped nuts and apples) and *mohror* (bitter herbs) between two pieces of matzo (unleavened bread). This "sandwich" was intended to represent the mortar used by the Jews to build the Egyptians' pyramids and the bitter sadness of their internment away from the land of Israel.

The term *sandwich* came into use approximately 200 years ago. The Fourth Earl of Sandwich, Sir John Montague (1718–1792), is credited with popularizing the concept of eating meats and cheeses between two slices of bread. Apparently the earl, not wanting to leave the gaming tables that he loved so much, would demand that his servants bring him meat and bread. He combined the two and ate them with one hand, allowing him a free hand to continue playing at the tables. Some historians argue that a more likely scenario is that, as the head of defense, the earl was kept busy planning British strategy for the Revolutionary War underway in the American colonies. Whichever the case, the name stuck.

Sandwiches became more popular in the United States when soft white bread became common in the early 20th century. Today, sandwiches are found on breakfast, lunch and dinner menus and are served by every type of food service operation, from the most casual diner to the fanciest four-star dining room.

▶ **smørbrød** (SMURR-brur) Norwegian cold open-faced sandwiches; similarly, the Swedish term *smörgåsbord* (SMORE-guhs-bohrd) refers to a buffet table of bread and butter, salads, open-faced sandwiches, pickled or marinated fish, sliced meats and cheeses

▶ SANDWICH MISE EN PLACE

Sandwiches are generally prepared to order, and their preparation usually requires a great deal of handwork. Therefore, the goal is to assemble all ingredients and equipment within easy reach to minimize movement and ensure efficiency at the time of final assembly. Because each menu and food service operation has its own requirements, there is no one correct station setup, but there are a few basic guidelines.

1 *Prepare ingredients.* All sandwich ingredients should be cooked, mixed, sliced and prepared ahead of service to facilitate quick, efficient assembly at service time. So, before service, slice the meats, cheeses and vegetables; clean and dry lettuce and other fresh vegetable ingredients; blend the flavored spreads; mix the bound salads; and so on.
2 *Arrange and store ingredients.* Arrange all sandwich ingredients within easy reach of the work area. Cold items must be properly refrigerated at all times. A sandwich bar, similar to a steam table but with refrigerated compartments, is frequently used for this purpose. Under-counter refrigeration can be used for backup supplies and less frequently used ingredients. Sliced meats, cheeses and vegetables must be well covered to prevent dehydration or contamination. Many ingredients can be preportioned, either by weight or count, then wrapped in individual portions for storage.
3 *Select and arrange equipment.* The heavy equipment needed for making sandwiches can include preparation equipment such as meat slicers, griddles, grills, fryers and broilers as well as storage equipment such as refrigerated sandwich bars for cold ingredients and steam tables for hot ingredients. Even the simplest sandwich menu will require the use of basic hand tools such as spatulas, spreaders, portion scoops, knives and cutting boards. Be sure that the supply of such items is adequate to permit quick handwork and to avoid delays or cross-contamination.

FIGURE 25.2 ▶ A typical sandwich bar.

GREATEST HITS FROM THE SANDWICH COUNTER

Writing in his monumental *Le Guide culinaire* of 1903, Auguste Escoffier describes just two types of sandwiches: those "with two slices of buttered bread . . . covering a slice of ham or tongue, etc." and "the kind served at elaborate functions," which are much smaller, and in which the "sandwiched product (whatever this be)" is diced. Among his list of common sandwich ingredients are ham, beef, chicken, foie gras, caviar and watercress.

Today's cook must recognize a somewhat wider variety of sandwiches, however. And, as the following list shows, often a sandwich's popular name bears no connection to its ingredients.

BLT—Bacon, lettuce and tomato between two slices of toasted bread.

Club—Three slices of toasted bread usually layered with bacon, lettuce and tomato plus turkey or chicken. The sandwich, and its name, most likely originated at the Saratoga Club during the 1890s.

Croque Monsieur—Ham and cheese sandwich dipped in beaten egg and grilled; made popular by bars and bistros throughout Paris.

Deli—Contains any of various meats commonly sold in a delicatessen, such as pastrami, corned beef, turkey, ham, roast beef and so on. Usually the meat is sliced very thin and piled very high between two slices of white or rye bread.

Fluffernutter—Peanut butter and marshmallow fluff spread on—what else?—white bread; popular during the 1960s.

French Dip—Thin slices of roast beef in a crusty French-bread roll served au jus.

Gyro—Well-seasoned rotisserie-roasted lamb, thinly sliced and served wrapped in pita bread with onions and cucumber-yogurt dressing. A Greek-American creation, the gyro (YEAR-o) became popular at Greek lunch counters in New York City during the 1970s.

Patty Melt—Ground beef patty with grilled onions and cheese, grilled between two slices of buttered rye bread.

Po' Boy—French bread loaf split and filled with various ingredients, especially fried oysters or shrimp and rémoulade sauce. Created during the 1920s, it is New Orleans' version of a submarine sandwich.

Reuben—Corned beef, Swiss (Emmenthaler) cheese, sauerkraut and mustard or Thousand Island dressing grilled between two slices of rye bread. The Reuben was probably created during the early 1900s by Arnold Reuben, owner of New York City's Reuben's Restaurant.

▶ PRESENTING AND GARNISHING SANDWICHES

Sandwiches, especially cold closed sandwiches, are usually cut into halves, thirds or quarters for service. Cutting makes a sandwich easier for the customer to handle and allows for a more attractive presentation; the sandwich wedges can be arranged to add height to the plate and to expose the fillings' colors and textures. For sit-down service, hot closed sandwiches such as hamburgers are often presented open-faced. Condiments, such as mustard and mayonnaise, and garnishes, such as sliced tomatoes, onions, pickles and lettuce leaves, are served on the side or on one of the open bun halves. This tends to be a more attractive presentation, and it allows the customer to assemble and add ingredients to the sandwich as desired.

Although a sandwich can be a meal unto itself, it may be served with a salad or starch accompaniment. Potato chips or french-fried potatoes are, of course, standard fare, perhaps because they are also finger foods and they provide a crunchy texture. Bound salads, such as potato and macaroni, are also common starch accompaniments. Plated sandwiches have long been served with coleslaw, fruit salad or a small mixed green salad as side dishes. Even the standard soup-and-sandwich combo—half a sandwich with a cup of soup—remains a popular lunch selection.

CONCLUSION

High-quality sandwiches are made from fresh, carefully prepared ingredients, presented in an appetizing and appealing manner. Flavors, colors and textures of the bread, spread and filling should be appropriate and complementary. Breads should be fresh, never stale, and appropriate for the finished sandwich. Spreads should be carefully chosen to add additional flavors and moisture to the sandwich but should not be used to cover or mask dry or poor-quality fillings or breads. Fillings provide the dominant flavor and are usually the source of the sandwich's name; they should be flavorful and properly prepared. The appearance of even the most basic sandwich can be improved by careful assembly and precise trimming and cutting.

QUESTIONS FOR DISCUSSION

1. List examples for each of the three primary sandwich components.
2. Explain the differences between a hot open-faced and a hot closed sandwich.
3. List several hand tools used in sandwich production, and explain the need for an ample supply of these tools.
4. Why is cross-contamination a concern when preparing sandwiches? What simple steps can be taken to avoid the spread of pathogenic microorganisms?

CHAPTER TWENTY-SIX

THERE ARE ONLY
TWO QUESTIONS TO ASK
ABOUT FOOD.
IS IT GOOD?
AND IS IT AUTHENTIC?
WE ARE OPEN
[TO] NEW IDEAS,
BUT NOT IF IT MEANS
DESTROYING OUR HISTORY.
AND FOOD IS HISTORY.

—Giuliano Bugialli, quoted in The New York Times, *May 9, 1984*

CHARCUTERIE

CHEF LELAND ATKINSON,
Washington, DC

AFTER STUDYING THIS CHAPTER, YOU WILL BE ABLE TO:

- prepare a variety of forcemeats
- assemble and cook a variety of pâtés, terrines and sausages
- understand the proper methods for brining, curing and smoking meats and fish
- identify several cured pork products

Traditionally, charcuterie (shar-COO-tuhr-ree) was limited to the production of pork-based pâtés, terrines and galantines. Over the years, however, the term has come to include similar products made with game, poultry, fish, shellfish and even vegetables. Many of these are discussed here.

Charcuterie is an art and science in itself. This chapter is not intended to be a complete guide to the charcutier's art. Instead, this chapter focuses on procedures for making common charcuterie items that can be prepared easily in most kitchens. The preparation of sausages as well as curing methods, including salt curing, brining and both cold and hot smoking is discussed. The chapter ends with information about several cured pork products.

▸ Forcemeats and Their Uses

A **forcemeat** is a preparation made from uncooked ground meats, poultry, fish or shellfish that is seasoned and then emulsified with fat. Forcemeats are the primary ingredient used to make pâtés, terrines, galantines and sausages.

The word *forcemeat* is derived from the French word *farce,* meaning "stuffing." Depending on the preparation method, a forcemeat can be very smooth and velvety, well-textured and coarse, or anything in between. Regardless of its intended use, it has a glossy appearance when raw and will slice cleanly when cooked. A properly emulsified forcemeat provides a rich flavor and a comforting texture on the palate.

Forcemeats are emulsified products. Emulsification is the process of binding two ingredients that ordinarily would not combine. (Emulsified sauces are discussed in Chapter 9, Stocks and Sauces; emulsified salad dressings are discussed in Chapter 23, Salads and Salad Dressings.) The proteins present in the meat, poultry, fish and shellfish combine easily with both fat and liquids. In forcemeats, these proteins act as a stabilizer that allows the fat and liquids, which ordinarily would not combine, to bind. When improperly emulsified forcemeats are cooked, they lose their fat, shrink and become dry and grainy. To ensure proper emulsification of a forcemeat:

1. The ratio of fat to other ingredients must be precise.
2. Temperatures must be maintained below 41°F (5°C).
3. The ingredients must be mixed properly.

FORCEMEAT INGREDIENTS

Forcemeats are usually meat, poultry, fish or shellfish combined with binders, seasonings and sometimes garnishes. Selections from each of these basic categories are used to make an array of forcemeats. All ingredients must be of the finest quality and added in just the right proportions.

MEATS

The **dominant meat** is the meat, poultry, fish or shellfish that gives the forcemeat its name and essential flavor. When preparing meats, poultry or fish for forcemeat, it is important to trim all silverskin, gristle and small bones so that the meat will be more easily ground and will produce a smoother finished product.

Many forcemeats contain some pork. Pork adds moisture and smoothness to the forcemeat. Without it, poultry-based forcemeats tend to be rubbery, while venison and other game-based forcemeats tend to be dry. The traditional ratio is one part pork to two parts dominant meat.

Many forcemeats also contain some liver. Pork liver is commonly used, as is chicken liver. Liver contributes flavor as well as binding to the forcemeat. For a finer texture, grind the livers and then force them through a drum sieve before incorporating them into the forcemeat.

FATS

Here, fat refers to a separate ingredient, not the fat in the dominant meat or pork, both of which should be quite lean in order to ensure the correct ratio of fat to meat. Usually pork fatback or heavy cream is used to add moisture and richness to the forcemeat. Because fat carries flavor, it also promotes the proper infusion of flavors and smoke.

BINDERS

There are two principal types of binders: panadas and eggs.

A **panada** (pah-nahd) is something other than fat that is added to a forcemeat to enhance smoothness (especially in fish mousselines, which tend to be slightly grainy in texture), to aid emulsification (especially in vegetable terrines, in which the protein levels are insufficient to bind on their own) or both (for example, in liver mousses). It should not make up more than 20 percent of the forcemeat's total weight. Usually a panada is nothing more than crustless white bread soaked in milk or, more traditionally, a heavy béchamel or rice.

Eggs or egg whites are used as a primary binding agent in some styles of forcemeat. If used in forcemeats that have a large ratio of liver or liquids, they also add texture.

SEASONINGS

Forcemeats are seasoned with salt, curing salt, marinades and various herbs and spices.

Salt not only adds flavor to a forcemeat but also aids in the emulsification of the meat and fat. As with other foods, a forcemeat that lacks salt will taste flat.

Curing salt is a mixture of salt and sodium nitrite. Sodium nitrite controls spoilage by inhibiting bacterial growth. Equally important, curing salt preserves the rosy pink colors of some forcemeats that might otherwise oxidize to an unappetizing gray. Although currently regarded as substantially safer than the previously used potassium nitrate (saltpeter), some studies suggest that sodium nitrite is a carcinogen. For a typical consumer, however, the amount of sodium nitrite consumed from cured meats should not pose a substantial health threat.

Traditionally, ingredients for forcemeats were marinated for long periods, sometimes days, before grinding. The trend today is for a shorter marinating time so that the true flavors of the main ingredients shine through. Both classic and contemporary marinades include herbs, citrus zest, spices and liquors, all of which lend flavor, character and nuance to the forcemeat.

Pâté spice is a mixture of spices and dried herbs that can be premixed and used as needed.

RECIPE 26.1

PÂTÉ SPICE

Yield: 7⅔ oz. (220 g)

Cloves	1 oz.	30 g
Dried ginger	1 oz.	30 g
Nutmeg	1 oz.	30 g
Paprika	1 oz.	30 g
Dried basil	⅔ oz.	20 g
Black pepper	⅔ oz.	20 g
White pepper	⅔ oz.	20 g
Bay leaf	⅓ oz.	10 g
Dried thyme	1 oz.	30 g
Dried marjoram	⅓ oz.	10 g

1 Grind all the ingredients in a spice grinder. Pass through a sieve to remove any large pieces.

VARIATION:

This mixture can be used as is, or mix 1 ounce (30 grams) (or any amount desired) with 1 pound (450 grams) salt. The salt-and-spice mixture can then be used to season forcemeats; ⅓ ounce (10 grams) per pound of forcemeat usually suffices for most pâtés.

Approximate values per 1-oz. (30-g) serving: **Calories** 20, **Total fat** 1 g, **Saturated fat** 0 g, **Cholesterol** 0 mg, **Sodium** 0 mg, **Total carbohydrates** 3 g, **Protein** 1 g, **Vitamin A** 6%

A forcemeat's seasoning and texture can be tested by cooking a small portion before the entire forcemeat is cooked. (Unlike sauces, stews and other dishes, a forcemeat cannot be tasted during the cooking process to adjust the seasonings.) A small portion of a hearty forcemeat can be sautéed; a small portion of a more delicate forcemeat should be poached for 3 to 5 minutes. When cooked, the forcemeat should hold its shape and be slightly firm but not rubbery. If it is too firm, add a little cream.

GARNISHES

Forcemeat garnishes are meats, fat, vegetables or other foods added in limited quantities to provide contrasting flavors and textures and to improve appearance. The garnishes are usually diced, chopped or more coarsely ground than the dominant meat. Common garnishes include pistachio nuts, diced fatback, truffles or truffle peelings and diced ham or tongue.

An X-Blade and Assorted Dies for a Standard Grinder

EQUIPMENT FOR PREPARING FORCEMEATS

To properly prepare forcemeats, certain equipment is required. A food chopper or food processor and a heavy-duty drum sieve with a metal band are essential tools used to make forcemeat. A standard meat grinder or meat-grinding attachment with various-sized grinding dies is also useful especially when preparing meats for coarse pâtés and sausage.

PREPARING FORCEMEATS

The three common forcemeat preparations are **country-style, basic** and **mousseline.** Each can be produced easily in a typical food service operation. Other types of forcemeat preparations such as the emulsified mixture used to make hot dogs and bratwurst are not commonly encountered in food service operations and are not discussed here.

When preparing any forcemeat, certain guidelines must be followed:

1. Forcemeat preparations include raw meats, liver, eggs and dairy products. If improperly handled, these potentially hazardous foods create a good environment for the growth of microorganisms. To avoid the risk of food-borne illness, temperatures must be carefully controlled, and all cutting boards and food contact surfaces must be as sanitary as possible at all times.
2. To ensure a proper emulsification, the forcemeat must be kept cold—below 41°F (5°C)—at all times. Refrigerate all moist ingredients, and keep forcemeats in progress in an ice bath. Chilling or freezing metal grinder and food processor parts helps keep the ingredients as cold as possible.
3. Cut all foods into convenient sizes that fit easily into grinder openings. Do not overstuff grinders or overfill food processors. When grinding items twice, always begin with a larger die, followed by a medium or small die. For exceptional smoothness, press the forcemeat through a sieve after grinding to remove any lumps or pieces of membrane.

SAFETY ALERT

Forcemeats

Forcemeats are potentially hazardous foods and must be kept cold—41°F (5°C) or below—both before and after cooking. Because of the way meat and other ingredients are ground together, any surface bacteria will become distributed throughout the forcemeat. Chill metal grinders, food processor parts and other equipment prior to use and keep all cutting boards, knives and food contact surfaces clean and sanitary. Check the internal temperature carefully when cooking to ensure that it reaches at least 165°F (74°C) for poultry-based forcemeats, 155°F (68°C) for fish- or vegetable-based forcemeats or 145°F (63°C) for meat-based forcemeats.

COUNTRY-STYLE FORCEMEATS

A traditional country-style forcemeat is heavily seasoned with onions, garlic, pepper, juniper berries and bay leaves. It is the simplest of the forcemeats to prepare and yields the heartiest and most distinctive pâtés and sausages.

The dominant meat for a country-style forcemeat is usually ground once through the grinder's large die, then ground again through the medium die. This produces the characteristic coarse, country-style texture. As with most forcemeats, the dominant meat for a country-style forcemeat is usually marinated and seasoned prior to grinding and then mixed with some liver.

▶ PROCEDURE FOR PREPARING A COUNTRY-STYLE FORCEMEAT

1. Chill all ingredients and equipment thoroughly. Throughout preparation, they should remain at temperatures below 41°F (5°C).
2. Cut all meats into an appropriate size for grinding.
3. Marinate, under refrigeration, the dominant meat and pork with the desired herbs, spices and liquors.
4. If using liver, grind it and force it through a sieve.
5. Cut the fatback into an appropriate size and freeze.
6. Prepare an ice bath for the forcemeat. Then grind the dominant meat, pork and fat as directed in the recipe, usually once through the grinder's largest die and a second time through the medium die.
7. If using liver, eggs, panada or garnishes, fold them in by hand, remembering to keep the forcemeat over an ice bath at all times.
8. Cook a small portion of the forcemeat; adjust the seasonings and texture as appropriate.
9. Refrigerate the forcemeat until needed.

RECIPE 26.2 COUNTRY-STYLE FORCEMEAT

Mise en Place

- ▶ Chill the equipment.
- ▶ Dice pork and fatback.
- ▶ Clean and dice pork liver.
- ▶ Peel onion and cut into small dice.
- ▶ Peel and mince garlic.
- ▶ Wash and chop fresh parsley.

Yield: 5 lb. (2.2 kg)

Lean pork, diced	2 lb.	900 g
Pâté Spice	2 Tbsp.	30 ml
Salt	1 Tbsp.	15 ml
Black pepper	TT	TT
Brandy	2 fl. oz.	60 ml
Pork liver, cleaned and diced	1 lb.	450 g
Fatback, diced	1 lb.	450 g
Onion, small dice	3 oz.	90 g
Garlic, minced	1 Tbsp.	15 ml
Fresh parsley, chopped	3 Tbsp.	45 ml
Eggs	6	6

1. Combine the diced pork with the Pâté Spice, salt, pepper and brandy; marinate under refrigeration for several hours.
2. Grind the liver and force it through a drum sieve. Reserve.
3. Grind the marinated pork and fatback through the grinder's large die.
4. Grind half of the pork and fatback a second time through the medium die along with the onion, garlic and parsley.
5. Working over an ice bath, combine the coarse and medium ground pork with the liver and eggs.
6. Cook and taste a small portion of the forcemeat and adjust the seasonings as necessary.

The forcemeat is now ready to use as desired in the preparation of pâtés, terrines, galantines and sausages.

Approximate values per 1-oz. (30-g) serving: **Calories** 90, **Total fat** 8 g, **Saturated fat** 3 g, **Cholesterol** 50 mg, **Sodium** 105 mg, **Total carbohydrates** 1 g, **Protein** 5 g, **Vitamin A** 30%

1 Marinating the meat and fatback with herbs and spices.

2 Forcing the ground liver through a sieve.

3 Grinding half of the meat a second time.

4 Incorporating the liver and eggs into the ground meat mixture over an ice bath to keep the forcemeat cold.

BASIC FORCEMEATS

Smoother and more refined than a country-style forcemeat, a basic forcemeat is probably the most versatile of all. It should be well seasoned, but the seasonings should not mask the dominant meat's flavor. Examples of basic forcemeats are those used in most game pâtés and terrines as well as traditional pâtés en croûte.

A basic forcemeat is made by grinding the meat and fat separately—the meat twice and the fat once. The fat is then worked into the meat, either by hand or in a food processor or chopper. A quicker method involves grinding the fat and meat together and then blending them in a food processor. Whichever method is used, some recipes call for the incorporation of crushed ice to minimize friction, reduce temperature and add moisture.

▶ PROCEDURE FOR PREPARING A BASIC FORCEMEAT

1 Chill all ingredients and equipment thoroughly. Throughout preparation, they should remain at temperatures below 41°F (5°C).

2 Cut all meats into an appropriate size for grinding.

3 Marinate, under refrigeration, the dominant meat and pork with the desired herbs, spices and liquors.

4 If using liver, grind it and force it through a sieve.

5 Cut the fatback into an appropriate size and freeze.

6 Grind the meats twice, once through the grinder's large die and then through the medium die; hold on an ice bath.

7 Grind the chilled or frozen fat once through the medium die and add it to the meat mixture.

8 Work the fat into the meat over an ice bath or in a well-chilled food processor or chopping machine.

9 Over an ice bath, add any required eggs, panada and/or garnishes and work them into the mixture.

10 Cook a small portion of the forcemeat in stock or water; adjust the seasonings and texture as appropriate.

11 Refrigerate the forcemeat until needed.

An alternative method for preparing a basic forcemeat replaces Steps 6 to 9 with the following procedures:

6a Grind the meats and fats together twice.

7a Place them in a food processor or chopper and blend until smooth.

8a Add any required eggs or panada while the machine is running and blend them in with the meat and fat.

9a Remove the forcemeat from the machine and, working over an ice bath, fold in any garnishes by hand.

Whichever method is used, a particularly warm kitchen or a lengthy running time in the food processor or chopping machine may necessitate the addition of small quantities of crushed ice to properly emulsify the forcemeat. Add the ice bit by bit while the machine is running.

RECIPE 26.3 BASIC FORCEMEAT

Mise en Place

- ▶ Chill the equipment.
- ▶ Dice veal, lean pork and fatback.
- ▶ Cut ham into medium dice.
- ▶ Chop black olives coarsely.

Yield: 4 lb. 8 oz. (2 kg)

Veal, diced	1 lb. 8 oz.	650 g
Lean pork, diced	1 lb. 8 oz.	650 g
Brandy	2 fl. oz.	60 ml
Pâté Spice	2 tsp.	10 ml
Salt	1½ tsp.	7 ml
White pepper	TT	TT
Fatback, diced	1 lb. 8 oz.	650 g
Eggs	4	4
Ham, medium dice	4 oz.	120 g
Pistachio nuts	2 oz.	60 g
Black olives, chopped coarse	2 oz.	60 g

1. Combine the veal and pork with the brandy, Pâté Spice, salt and white pepper; marinate under refrigeration for several hours.
2. Grind the meats through the grinder's large die and again through the small die.
3. Grind the fatback through the grinder's small die.
4. Combine the meat and fat in the bowl of a food processor and blend until they are emulsified.
5. Work in the eggs until the forcemeat is smooth and well emulsified. Do not overprocess the forcemeat.
6. Fold in the ham, pistachio nuts and olives.
7. Cook a small portion of the forcemeat by poaching or sautéing it. Taste and adjust the seasonings as necessary.

The forcemeat is now ready to use as desired in the preparation of pâtés, terrines, galantines and sausages.

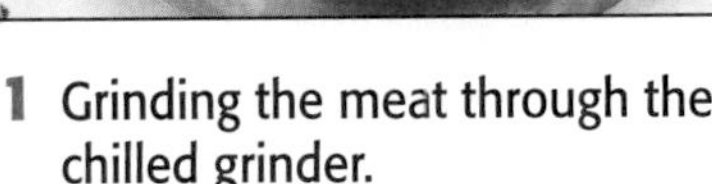

1 Grinding the meat through the chilled grinder.

Approximate values per 1-oz. (30-g) serving: **Calories** 140, **Total fat** 12 g, **Saturated fat** 4.5 g, **Cholesterol** 45 mg, **Sodium** 80 mg, **Total carbohydrates** 1 g, **Protein** 7 g

2 Combining the fat with the meat in the food processor.

3 Adding the eggs to the meat.

4 Folding the garnishes into the forcemeat.

MOUSSELINE FORCEMEATS

A properly made mousseline (moos-uh-LEEN) forcemeat is light, airy and delicately flavored. It is most often made with fish or shellfish but sometimes with veal, pork, feathered game or poultry. (A mousseline forcemeat is not the same as a mousse, which usually contains gelatin and is discussed later.)

A mousseline forcemeat is prepared by processing ground meats and cream in a food processor; often egg whites are added to lighten and enrich the mixture. The proportion of fish or dominant meat to eggs to cream is very important: too many egg whites, and the mousseline will be rubbery; too few, and it may not bind together. If too much cream is added, the mousseline will be too soft or will fall apart during cooking.

A mousseline forcemeat can be served hot or cold. It can be used to make fish sausages and a variety of timbales and terrines, or it can be used to make quenelles, which are discussed later. A shrimp mousseline is used with Paupiettes of Sole.

▶ PROCEDURE FOR PREPARING A MOUSSELINE FORCEMEAT

1. Chill all ingredients and equipment thoroughly. Throughout preparation, they should remain at temperatures below 41°F (5°C).
2. Cut all meats into an appropriate size for processing.
3. Grind the meat in a cold food processor until smooth. Do not overprocess.
4. Add eggs and pulse until just blended.
5. Add cream and seasonings in a steady stream while the machine is running. Stop the machine and scrape down the sides of the bowl once or twice during the processing. Do not run the machine any longer than necessary to achieve a smooth forcemeat.
6. If desired, pass the forcemeat through a drum sieve to remove any sinew or bits of bone.
7. Over an ice bath, fold in any garnishes by hand.
8. Poach a small amount of the mousseline in stock or water. Taste and adjust the seasonings and texture as necessary.
9. Refrigerate until ready for use.

RECIPE 26.4

MOUSSELINE FORCEMEAT

Mise en Place

▶ Chill the equipment.

Yield: 4 lb. (1.8 kg)

Fish, scallops, skinless chicken breast or lean veal	2 lb.	900 g
Egg whites	4	4
Salt	1 Tbsp.	15 ml
White pepper	TT	TT
Nutmeg, ground	TT	TT
Cayenne pepper	TT	TT
Heavy cream	up to 1 qt.	up to 900 ml

1 Grind the dominant meat through a large die.
2 Process the meat in a food processor until smooth.
3 Add the egg whites one at a time and pulse the processor until they are incorporated.
4 Scrape down the sides of the processor's bowl and add the spices.
5 With the machine running, add the cream in a slow, steady stream. Check the consistency, adding only enough cream to make a firm but smooth forcemeat.
6 Scrape down the bowl again and process the mousseline until it is smooth and well mixed. Do not overprocess.
7 Remove the mousseline from the machine and hold in an ice bath. If additional smoothness is desired, force the mousseline through a drum sieve in small batches using a plastic scraper or rubber spatula.
8 Cook a small portion of the forcemeat by poaching it. Taste and adjust the seasonings and texture as necessary.

The forcemeat is now ready to cook as quenelles or use as desired in the preparation of pâtés, terrines, galantines and sausages.

Note: Forcemeat made only from fish will use the least amount of cream. Frozen meat will absorb less cream than meat that is merely chilled.

Approximate values per 1-oz. (30-g) serving: **Calories** 80, **Total fat** 7 g, **Saturated fat** 4 g, **Cholesterol** 30 mg, **Sodium** 25 mg, **Total carbohydrates** 1 g, **Protein** 4 g, **Vitamin A** 8%

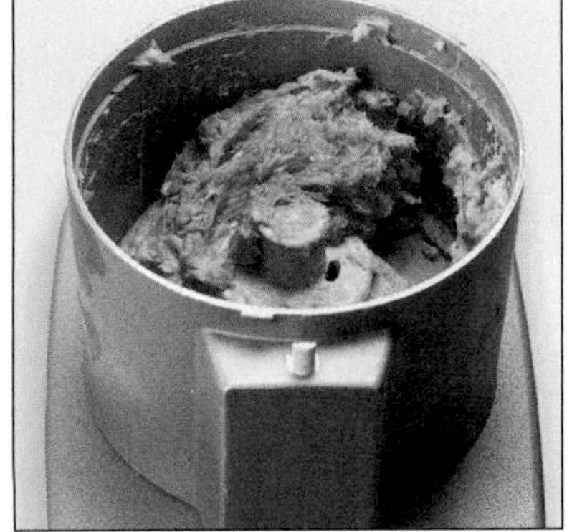

1 Processing the ground meat in a cold food processor just until smooth.

2 Adding the egg whites and pulsing until blended.

3 Adding the cream in a steady stream while the machine runs.

4 Passing the forcemeat through a drum sieve to ensure a smooth finished product.

QUENELLES

Quenelles (kuh-NEHL) are small dumpling-shaped portions of a mousseline forcemeat poached in an appropriately flavored stock. Quenelles are a traditional garnish for many soups and a popular appetizer usually accompanied by a tomato coulis or a sauce based on a fish velouté. The technique used for making and poaching quenelles is also used for testing the seasoning and consistency of a mousseline forcemeat.

▶ PROCEDURE FOR PREPARING QUENELLES

1. Prepare a mousseline forcemeat.
2. Bring an appropriately flavored poaching liquid to a simmer.
3. Use two spoons to form the forcemeat into oblong-shaped dumplings. For small quenelles, use small spoons; for larger quenelles, use larger spoons.
4. Poach the quenelles until done. Test by breaking one in half to check the center's doneness.
5. Small soup-garnish-sized quenelles can be chilled in ice water, drained and held for service. Reheat them in a small amount of stock before garnishing the soup.

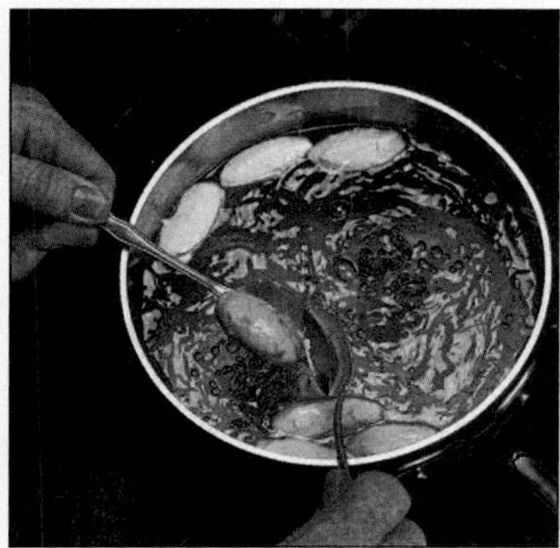

Forming the quenelles using two spoons and poaching until done.

▶ USING FORCEMEATS

Forcemeats are used as basic components in the preparation of other foods, including terrines, pâtés, galantines and sausages. Aspic jelly is also an important component of these products.

TERRINES, PÂTÉS AND GALANTINES

Traditionally, a **pâté** (pah-tay) was a fine savory meat filling wrapped in pastry, baked and served hot or cold. A **terrine** was considered more basic, consisting of coarsely ground and highly seasoned meats baked in an earthenware mold and always served cold. (The mold is also called a terrine, derived from the French word *terre,* meaning "earth.") Today, many types of pâtés are baked in loaf-type pans without a crust, which according to tradition would make them terrines, while pâtés baked in pastry are called **pâtés en croûte** (pah-TAY awn croot). Thus, the terms *pâté* and *terrine* are now used almost interchangeably. **Galantines** (GAL-uhn-teen) are made from forcemeats of poultry, game or suckling pig wrapped in the skin of the bird or animal and poached in an appropriate stock. They are usually served cold. **Ballotines** (bahl-lo-teen) are similar, but generally use only deboned poultry legs and are served hot.

Terrines, pâtés and galantines are often made with forcemeats layered with garnishes to produce a decorative or mosaic effect when sliced. A wide variety of foods can be used as garnishes, including strips of ham, fatback or tongue; mushrooms or other vegetables; truffles and pistachio nuts. Garnishes should always be cooked before they are added to the pâté, terrine or galantine, or they will shrink during cooking, creating air pockets.

PÂTÉ PANS, MOLDS AND TERRINES

Pâté pans, molds and terrines come in a variety of shapes and sizes. Pâtés that are not baked in a crust can be prepared in standard metal loaf pans of any shape, although rectangular ones make portioning the cooked pâté much easier. For pâtés en croûte, the best pans are collapsible or hinged, thin-metaled ones. They make it easier to remove the pâté after baking. Collapsible and hinged pans come in various shapes and sizes, from small plain rectangles to large intricately fluted ovals. Traditional earthenware molds and terrines as well as ones made from enameled cast iron, metal, glass or even plastic are available. Most terrines are rectangular or oval in shape. Several of these pans are illustrated in Chapter 3, Tools and Equipment.

TERRINES

Terrines are forcemeats baked in a mold without a crust. The mold can be the traditional earthenware dish or some other appropriate metal, enameled cast iron or glass mold. Any type of forcemeat can be used to make a terrine. The terrine can be as simple as a baking dish filled with a forcemeat and baked until done. A more attractive terrine can be constructed by layering the forcemeat with garnishes to create a mosaic effect when sliced. A terrine can even be layered with different forcemeats—for example, a pink salmon mousseline layered with a white pike mousseline.

▶ PROCEDURE FOR PREPARING TERRINES

1. Prepare the desired forcemeat and garnishes and keep refrigerated until needed.
2. Line a mold with thin slices of fatback, blanched leafy vegetables or other appropriate liner. (Some chefs claim that the fatback keeps the terrine moist during cooking; most modern chefs do not agree but nevertheless use it for aesthetic purposes.) The lining should overlap slightly, completely covering the inside of the mold and extending over the edge of the mold by approximately 1 inch (2.5 centimeters). Alternatively, line the mold with plastic wrap.
3. Fill the terrine with the forcemeat and garnishes, being careful not to leave air pockets. Tap the mold several times on a solid work surface to remove any air pockets.
4. Fold the liner or plastic wrap over the forcemeat and, if necessary, use additional pieces to completely cover its surface.
5. If desired, garnish the top of the terrine with herbs that were used in the preparation of the forcemeat.
6. Cover the terrine with its lid or aluminum foil and bake in a water bath in a 350°F (180°C) oven. Regulate the oven temperature so that the water stays between 170°F and 180°F (77°C and 82°C).
7. Cook the terrine to an internal temperature of 165°F (74°C) for poultry-based forcemeats, 155°F (68°C) for fish-based forcemeats or 145°F (63°C) for meat-based forcemeats.
8. Remove the terrine from the oven and allow it to cool slightly. If desired, pour off any fat and liquid from around the terrine and cover it with cool liquid aspic jelly.

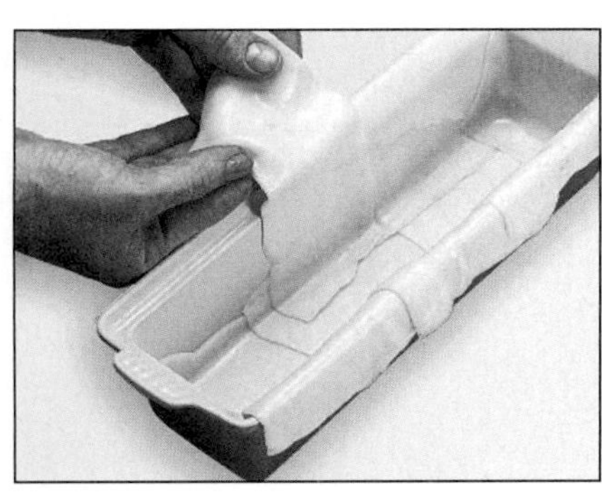

1 Lining a mold with thin slices of fatback.

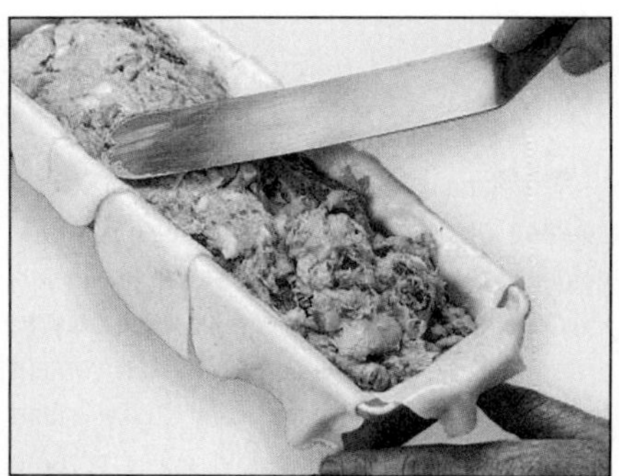

2 Filling the terrine with the forcemeat and garnish.

3 Placing the herb-decorated terrine in a water bath.

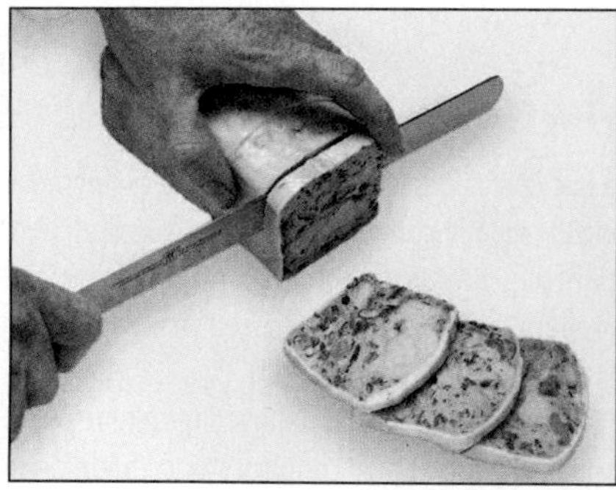

4 Slicing the finished terrine.

Types of Terrines

Several types of terrines are not made from traditional forcemeats, many others are not made from forcemeats at all. But all are nonetheless called terrines because they are molded or cooked in the earthenware mold called a terrine. These include liver (and foie gras) terrines, vegetable terrines, brawns or aspic terrines, mousses, rillettes and confits.

Liver terrines are popular and easy to make. Puréed poultry, pork or veal livers are mixed with eggs and a panada of cream and flour, then baked in a fatback-lined terrine. Although most livers purée easily in a food processor, a smoother finished product is achieved if the livers are forced through a drum sieve after or in lieu of puréeing them in the processor.

Foie gras terrines are made with the fattened geese or duck livers called foie gras. Foie gras is unique, even among other poultry livers, in that it consists almost entirely of fat. (See Chapter 16, Poultry.) It requires special attention during cooking; if it is cooked improperly or too long, it turns into a puddle of very expensive fat.

Vegetable terrines, which have a relatively low fat content, are becoming increasingly popular. Beautiful vegetable terrines are made by lining a terrine with a blanched leafy vegetable such as spinach, then alternating layers of two or three separately prepared vegetable fillings to create contrasting colors and flavors. A different style of vegetable terrine is made by suspending brightly colored vegetables in a mousseline forcemeat to create a mosaic pattern when sliced.

Brawns or **aspic terrines** are made by simmering gelatinous cuts of meat (most notably, pigs' feet and head, including the tongue) in a rich stock with wine and flavorings. The stock is enriched with the gelatin and flavor from the meat, creating an unclarified aspic jelly. The meat is then pulled from the bone, diced and packed into the terrine mold. The stock is reduced to concentrate its gelatin content, strained through cheesecloth and poured over the meat in the terrine. After the terrine has set, it is removed from the mold and sliced for service. The finished product is a rustic and flavorful dish.

A more elegant-appearing brawn is made by lining a terrine mold with aspic jelly, arranging a layer of garnish (for example, sliced meats, vegetables or low-acid fruits) along the mold's bottom, adding aspic jelly to cover the garnish and repeating the procedure until the mold is full.

A **mousse** can be sweet or savory. A savory mousse—which is not a mousseline forcemeat—is made from fully cooked meats, poultry, game, fish, shellfish or vegetables that are puréed and combined with a béchamel or other appropriate sauce, bound with gelatin and lightened with whipped cream. A mousse can be molded in a decorated, aspic-jelly-coated mold such as that described next, or it can be formed in molds lined with plastic wrap, which is peeled off after the mousse is unmolded. A small mousse can be served as an individual portion; a larger molded mousse can be displayed on a buffet.

GARNISHING SLICED TERRINES AND PÂTÉS

Cornichons sliced into decorative fans are an attractive garnish for sliced country terrines and Pâtés en croûte.

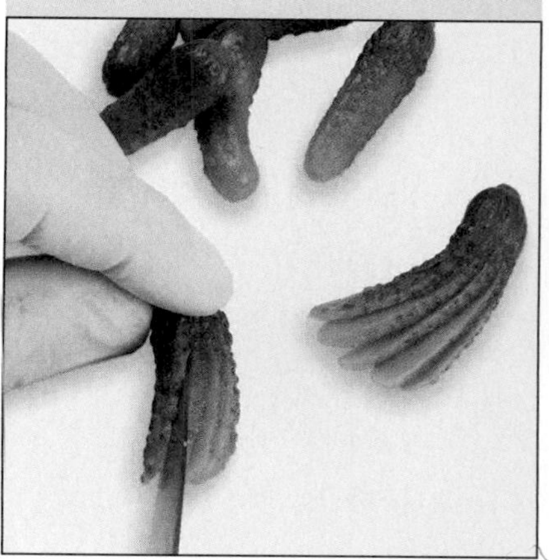

ASPIC JELLY

Aspic jelly is a savory jelly produced by increasing the gelatin content of a strong stock and then clarifying the stock following the process for preparing consommé discussed in Chapter 10, Soups.

Although gelatin is a natural ingredient present in all good meat or poultry stocks, additional gelatin is usually added to the stock in order to assist gelling (setting). One way is to produce a stock with an extremely high gelatin content by using gelatinous meats and bones such as calves' feet, pigs' ears and pork skin; another is to add plain gelatin to a finished stock. An easier method of preparing aspic jelly is to add gelatin directly to a flavorful finished consommé.

In addition to adding flavor and shine, a coating of aspic jelly prevents displayed foods from drying out and inhibits the oxidation of sliced red meats. Aspic jelly is often lightly flavored with liquors such as Madeira and cut into decorative garnishes for both plated presentations and buffet displays. Decorative platters on which pâtés are displayed may be coated with aspic jelly, as shown in the chapter opening photograph. It is also used to bind savory mousses, glaze slices of pâté and coat molded mousses. Aspic jelly is funneled into cooked pâtés en croûte to fill the gaps created when the forcemeat shrinks during the cooking process. Aspic jelly is also the basis of aspic molds or terrines (often simply called aspics), in which layers of cooked meats or vegetables are bound together and held in place by the aspic jelly. Many of these uses are discussed later.

The gelatin content of aspic jelly varies depending on its intended use. Table 26.1 lists guidelines for quantities of gelatin to use in various applications. Aspic jelly to be used only on a display can have a very high gelatin content for easier handling. Aspic jelly to be eaten should be fairly firm when cold, gelled at room temperature but tender enough to melt quickly in the mouth when eaten. To test the gelatin content of a liquid, pour a teaspoon (5 milliliters) onto a plate and refrigerate the plate for a few minutes. If the liquid does not gel firmly, additional gelatin can be softened in a small amount of cool liquid, then added to the hot liquid.

Rillettes and **confits** are actually preserved meats. Rillettes (ree-YEHT) are prepared by seasoning and slow-cooking pork or fatty poultry such as duck or goose in generous amounts of their own fat until the meat falls off the bone. The warm meat is mashed and combined with a portion of the cooking fat. The mixture is then packed into a crock or terrine, and rendered fat is strained over the top to seal it. Rillettes are eaten cold as a spread accompanied by bread or toast.

Confit (kohn-FEE) is prepared in a similar manner except that before cooking, the meat or poultry is often lightly salt-cured to draw out some moisture. The confit is then cooked until very tender but not falling apart. Confits are generally served hot. Like rillettes, confits can be preserved by sealing them with a layer of strained rendered fat. Properly prepared and sealed rillettes and confits will keep for several weeks under refrigeration.

Although it is sometimes incorrectly called chicken liver pâté, **chopped chicken liver** is prepared in a similar fashion to a rillette. Chopped chicken liver, however, will not have the keeping qualities of traditional rillettes or confits because it is not normally sealed in a crock or terrine with rendered fat. It should be eaten within a day or two of its preparation.

Table 26.1 GELATIN CONCENTRATIONS

TYPE OF GEL	AMOUNT OF GELATIN PER GALLON (4 LITERS) WATER	TYPICAL USE
Soft	2 oz. (60 g)	Cubed aspic jelly for edible garnishes
Firm	4 oz. (120 g)	Brushing slices of pâté or galantine; glazing edible centerpieces; molding terrines, aspics and brawns that will be sliced
Very firm	8 oz. or more (225 g or more)	Nonedible purposes such as coating nonedible centerpieces or trays for presentations

Preparing Molds When Making Terrines

A mold can be lined with aspic jelly, then decorated and filled with cold mousse. The aspic-jelly-coated mousse is then unmolded for an attractive presentation.

▶ PROCEDURE FOR PREPARING ASPIC-JELLY-COATED CHILLED MOUSSES

1 Set a metal mold in ice water and add 8 fluid ounces (250 milliliters) cool liquid aspic jelly. Swirl the mold so the aspic jelly adheres to all sides. Pour out the excess aspic jelly. Repeat as needed to achieve the desired thickness; ¼ inch (6 millimeters) or less is usually sufficient.

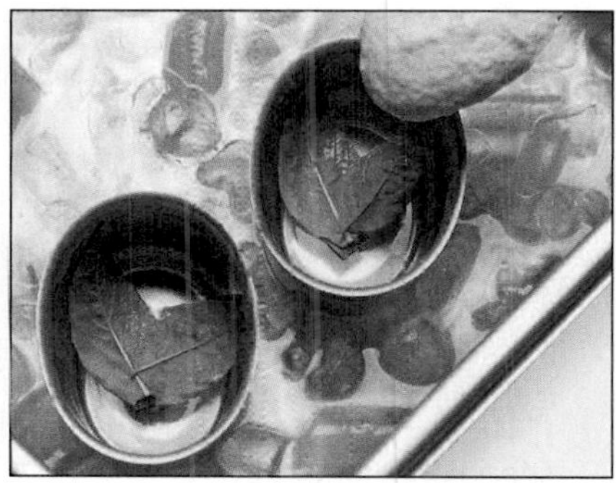

2 Garnish the mold by dipping pieces of vegetable or other foods in the liquid aspic jelly and placing them carefully inside the aspic-jelly-coated mold. The mold can now be filled with a cold filling such as a mousse.

3 Refrigerate the mold until it is well chilled. Unmold the aspic by dipping the mold in warm water, then inverting and tapping the mold on a plate.

▶ PROCEDURE FOR GLAZING PÂTÉ SLICES WITH ASPIC JELLY

Slices of chilled terrines, pâtés en croûte or gallantines (discussed next) may be garnished and coated with aspic to preserve their color, prevent drying and create a more attractive presentation.

1 Cool the clarified aspic jelly by slowly stirring it over an ice bath.

2 Brush or spoon the aspic jelly over slices of chilled pâté arranged on a cooling rack. Repeat the process until the coating reaches the desired thickness.

PÂTÉS EN CROÛTE

Considered by some to be the pinnacle of the charcutier's art, pâtés en croûte are forcemeats baked in a crust. The forcemeat can be country-style, basic or mousseline, but a basic forcemeat is most commonly used. Although pâtés en croûte can be baked without using a mold, a mold helps produce a more attractive finished product.

Making Pâté Dough (Pâte au Pâté)

The crust surrounding a baking forcemeat must be durable enough to withstand the long baking process and hold in the juices produced as the pâté bakes. Unfortunately, some of the more durable crusts are tough and unpleasant to eat.

The goal is to achieve a balance so that the crust will hold the juices of the baking pâté and still be relatively pleasant to the palate. Some pâtés, especially more delicate ones such as fish mousselines, can be wrapped in brioche dough.

RECIPE 26.5

DOUGH FOR PÂTÉ

Yield: 1 lb. 8 oz. (680 g)

All-purpose flour	1 lb.	450 g
Shortening	7 oz.	200 g
Salt	1½ tsp.	7 ml
Water	5 fl. oz.	150 ml
Egg	1	1

1. Place the flour in the bowl of a mixer. Add the shortening and mix on low speed until smooth.
2. Combine the salt, water and egg; add them to the flour and shortening mixture.
3. Knead until smooth and refrigerate. The dough will be easier to work with if allowed to rest for at least 1 hour.

Approximate values per 1-oz. (30-g) serving: **Calories** 150, **Total fat** 9 g, **Saturated fat** 2 g, **Cholesterol** 10 mg, **Sodium** 100 mg, **Total carbohydrates** 15 g, **Protein** 2 g

Assembling, Baking and Glazing Pâté

After preparing a forcemeat and pastry dough, all that remains is to assemble and bake the pâté en croûte. The amount of pastry dough and forcemeat needed is determined by the size of the mold or pan chosen. Once the pâté is baked and cooled, aspic jelly is poured into holes in the dough to fill the space created when the pâté shrank during cooking. Slices of pâté can also be glazed with aspic for a more formal presentation.

▶ PROCEDURE FOR ASSEMBLING AND BAKING PÂTÉS EN CROÛTE

1. Prepare the pâté dough and the forcemeat, keeping the forcemeat refrigerated until needed.
2. Roll out the dough into a rectangular shape ⅛ inch (3 millimeters) thick.
3. Using the pâté mold as a pattern, determine how much dough is needed to line its inside; allow enough dough along each side of the mold's length to cover the top when folded over. Mark the dough. Cut the dough slightly larger than the marked lines. Cut a second rectangular piece of dough that is slightly larger than the top of the mold; it will be used as a lid.
4. Lightly butter the inside of the mold.
5. Lightly dust the large rectangle of dough with flour, fold it over and transfer it to the mold.
6. Use your thumbs and a dough ball made from dough trimmings to form the dough neatly into the corners of the mold. Continue until the dough is of even thickness on all sides and in the corners.
7. Trim the dough, leaving ¾ inch (2 centimeters) on the ends and enough dough to cover the top along the sides.
8. Line the dough-covered mold with thin slices of fatback or ham, allowing ¾ inch (2 centimeters) extra around the top of the mold, or as directed in the recipe. This layer helps protect the pastry crust from coming in contact with the moist forcemeat, which would make it soggy.

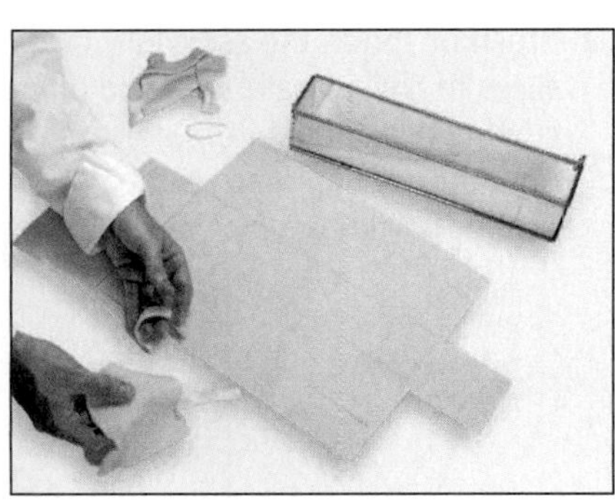

1 Cutting the dough into a large rectangle.

9 Fill the lined mold with the forcemeat to ½ inch (1.2 centimeters) below the top of the mold, pressing it well into the corners to avoid air pockets. Layer and garnish as appropriate.

10 Fold the fatback or ham over the top of the forcemeat, using additional pieces if necessary to cover its entire surface. Fold the pastry over the forcemeat.

11 Brush the exposed surface of the pastry with egg wash; carefully cap with the top piece of dough. Press any overlapping dough down inside the sides of the mold with a small spatula.

12 Using round cutters, cut one or two holes in the top to allow steam to escape during cooking. Egg-wash the surface. Place a doughnut-shaped piece of dough around each of the holes. Egg-wash any decorations.

13 Bake the pâté in a preheated 450°F (230°C) oven for 15 minutes. Then cover the surface of the pâté with aluminum foil. Reduce the heat to 350°F (180°C) and continue baking until the internal temperature reaches 165°F (74°C) for poultry-based forcemeats, 155°F (68°C) for fish-based forcemeats or 145°F (63°C) for meat-based forcemeats.

14 Allow the pâté to cool for at least 1 hour or overnight. Using a funnel, pour cool liquid aspic jelly through the holes to fill the space created when the pâté shrank during cooking. Allow the pâté en croûte to cool overnight before slicing.

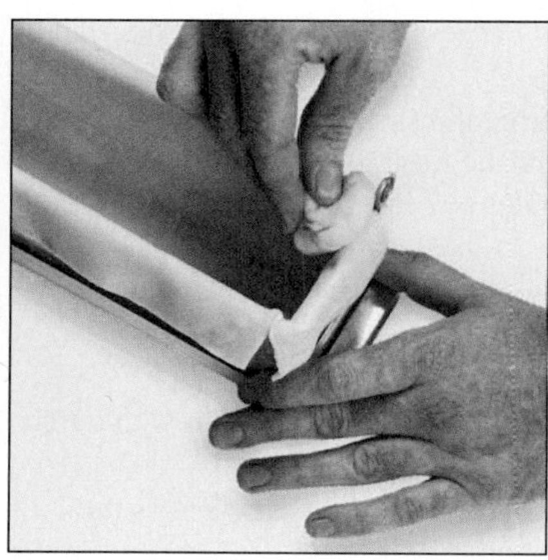

2 Pressing the dough into the mold with a floured dough ball.

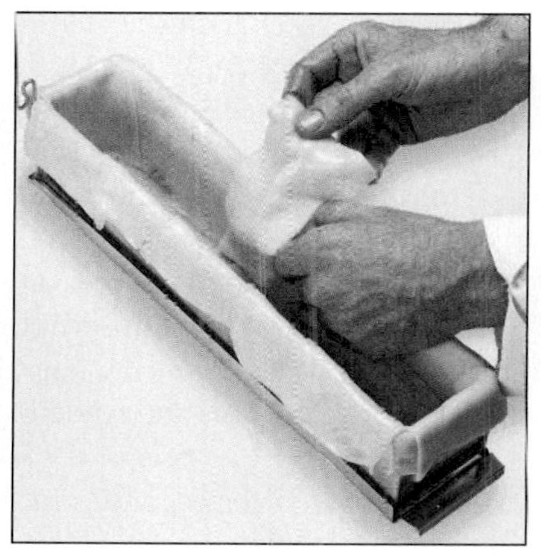

3 Lining the dough-covered mold with thin slices of fatback.

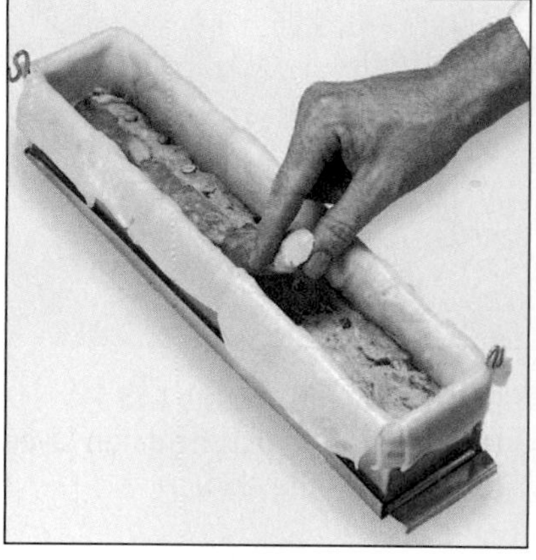

4 Filling the lined mold with the forcemeat and garnish.

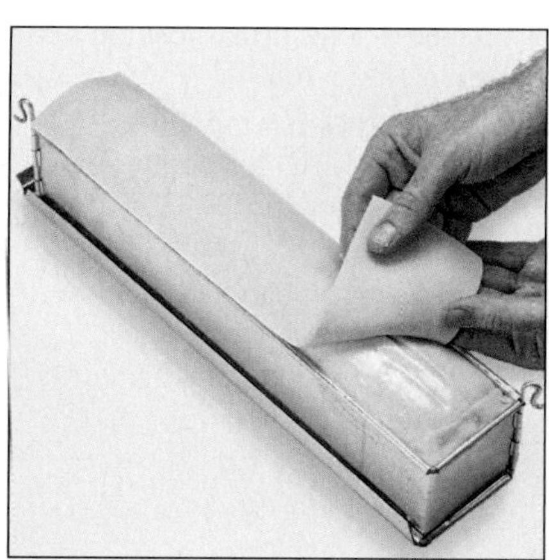

5 Placing the top on the pâté.

6 Pouring aspic jelly into the steam hole of the baked pâté through an aluminum foil chimney.

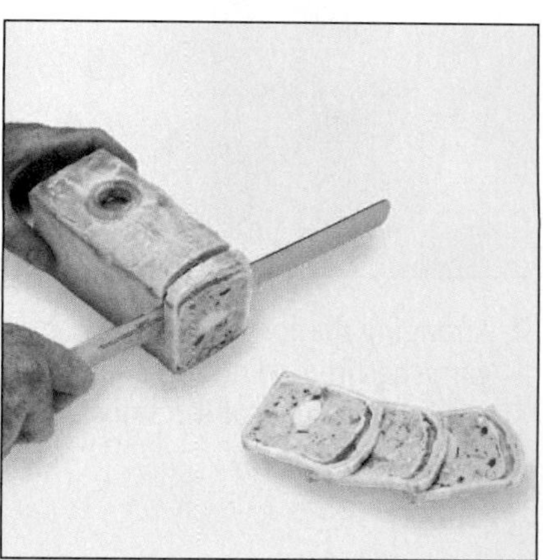

7 Slicing the pâté with a thin-bladed knife.

GALANTINES

A classic galantine is a boned chicken stuffed with a chicken-based forcemeat to resemble its original shape and then poached. Today, galantines are still most often prepared from whole ducks or chickens, but they can also be made from game, veal, fish or shellfish. When appropriate, the forcemeat is stuffed in the skin, which has been removed in one piece, sometimes with flesh still attached. When the skin is not available, or in the case of fish and shellfish where there is no skin, the galantine is made by forming the forcemeat into a cylindrical shape and wrapping it in cheesecloth, or plastic wrap and foil, before poaching. Galantines are always served cold and are often displayed on buffets, sliced and glazed with aspic jelly.

A ballotine is similar to a galantine. It is made by removing the bones from a poultry leg, filling the cavity with an appropriate forcemeat and poaching or braising the leg with vegetables. Ballotines are often served hot with a sauce made from the cooking liquid.

▶ PROCEDURE FOR PREPARING A POULTRY GALANTINE

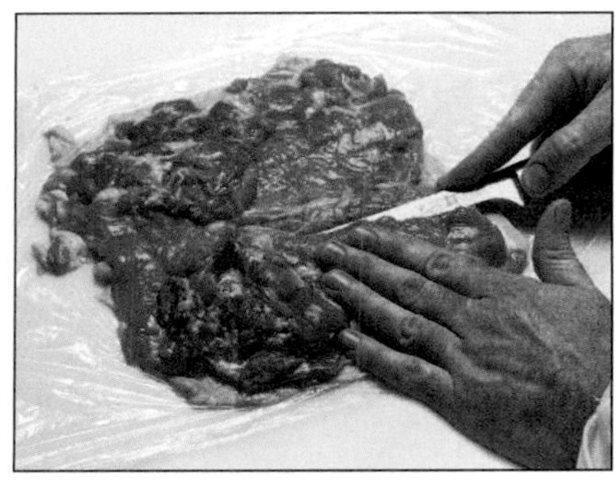

1 Butterflying the breasts and tenderloins and placing a thin layer of meat over the skin.

2 Arranging the forcemeat and garnishes in a cylindrical shape across the center of the skin.

1. Bone the chicken by cutting through the skin along the length of the backbone and then following the natural curvature of the carcass. Keep all the meat attached to the skin. Remove the legs and wings by cutting through the joints when you reach them; leave the legs and wings attached to the skin. Then cut off the wings. Bone the thighs and legs, leaving the skin and meat attached to the rest of the bird. Trim the skin to form a large rectangle.
2. Prepare a forcemeat using the meat from the skinned bird or any other appropriate meat. Reserve a portion of the meat as garnish if desired. Prepare any other garnishes. Refrigerate the forcemeat and garnishes until needed.
3. Spread out the skin and meat on plastic wrap or several layers of cheesecloth with the skin side down and the flesh up.
4. Remove the chicken tenderloins and pull the tendon out of each. Butterfly the breasts and tenderloins and cover the entire skin with a thin layer of meat.
5. Arrange the forcemeat and garnishes in a cylindrical shape across the center of the skin.
6. Using the plastic or cheesecloth to assist the process, tightly roll the skin around the forcemeat and garnishes to form a tight cylinder.
7. Tie the ends of the cheesecloth with butcher's twine and secure the galantine at even intervals using strips of cheesecloth. If plastic wrap was used, wrap the galantine with heavy-duty aluminum foil.
8. Poach the galantine in water (or a full-flavored stock if wrapped in cheesecloth) to an internal temperature of 165°F (74°C) for poultry-based forcemeats, 155°F (68°C) for fish-based forcemeats or 145°F (63°C) for meat-based forcemeats.
9. Cool the galantine in its cooking liquid until it can be handled. Remove the cheesecloth or plastic wrap and aluminum foil and rewrap the galantine in clean cheesecloth or plastic wrap. Refrigerate overnight before decorating or slicing.

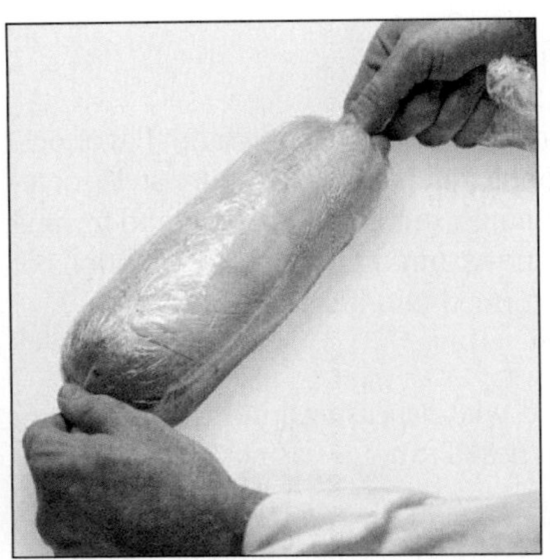

3 Using plastic wrap to roll the galantine into a tight cylinder.

4 Securing the galantine with heavy-duty aluminum foil.

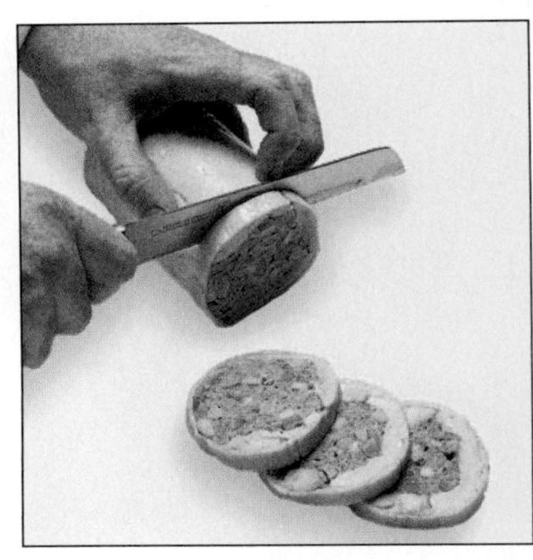

5 Slicing the finished product.

SAUSAGES

Sausages are forcemeats stuffed into casings. For centuries, sausages consisted of ground meat, usually pork, and seasonings. Today, sausages are made not only from pork, but also from game, beef, veal, poultry, fish, shellfish and even vegetables.

There are three main types of sausages:

1. **Fresh sausages** include breakfast sausage links and Italian sausages. They are made with fresh ingredients that have not been cured or smoked.
2. **Smoked** and **cooked sausages** are made with raw meat products treated with chemicals, usually the preservative sodium nitrite. Examples are kielbasa, bologna and hot dogs.
3. **Dried** or **hard sausages** are made with cured meats, then air-dried under controlled conditions. Dried sausages may or may not be smoked or cooked. Dried or hard sausages include salami, pepperoni and soppressata.

Smoked and cooked sausages and dried or hard sausages are rarely prepared in typical food service operations. Rather, they are produced by specialty shops and will not be discussed here. We do, however, discuss the ingredients and procedures for a variety of fresh sausages that can be prepared in almost any kitchen.

SAUSAGE COMPONENTS

Sausage Meats

Sausage meats are forcemeats with particular characteristics and flavorings. Coarse Italian and lamb sausages, for example, are simply a country-style forcemeat without liver and with different seasonings, stuffed into casings and formed into links. Hot dogs, bratwurst and other fine-textured sausages are variations of basic forcemeats stuffed into casings and formed into links.

Sausage Casings

Although sausage mixtures can be cooked without casings, most sausages are stuffed into casings before cooking. Two types of sausage casings are commonly used in food service operations:

1. **Natural casings** are portions of hog, sheep or cattle intestines. Their diameters are measured in millimeters, and they come in several sizes depending upon the animal or portion of the intestine used. Sheep casings are considered the finest-quality small casings. Both hog and sheep casings are used to make hot dogs and many types of pork sausage. Beef casings are quite large and are used to make sausages such as ring bologna and Polish sausage. Most natural casings are purchased in salt packs. In order to rid them of salt and impurities, the casings must be carefully rinsed in warm water and allowed to soak in cool water for at least 1 hour or overnight before use.
2. **Collagen casings** are manufactured from collagen extracted from cattle hides. They are generally inferior to natural casings in taste and texture, but they do have advantages: Collagen casings do not require any washing or soaking prior to use, and they are uniform in size.

PREPARING SAUSAGES

Equipment for Making Sausages

Sausage-stuffing machines are best for those who engage in large-scale sausage production. Otherwise, all that is needed is a grinder with a sausage nozzle. Nozzles are available in several sizes to accommodate the various casing sizes.

Sausage Nozzles

▶ PROCEDURE FOR PREPARING SAUSAGES

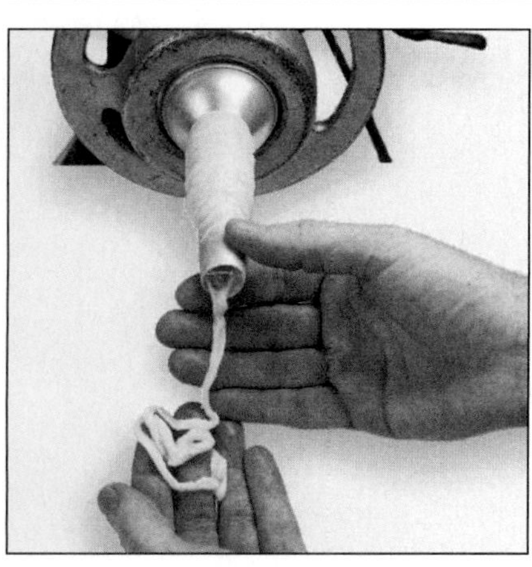

1 Sliding the casing over the nozzle of the sausage stuffer.

1. Prepare a forcemeat.
2. Thoroughly chill all parts of the sausage stuffer that will come in contact with the forcemeat.
3. Rinse and soak the casings if using natural ones. Cut the casings into 4- to 6-foot (1.2- to 1.8-meter) lengths.
4. Put the sausage in the sausage stuffer.
5. Slide the entire casing over the nozzle of the sausage stuffer. Tie the end in a knot and pierce with a skewer to prevent an air pocket.
6. Support and guide the casing off the end of the nozzle as the sausage is extruded from the nozzle into the casing.
7. After all the sausage has been stuffed into the casing, twist or tie the sausage into uniform links of the desired size.

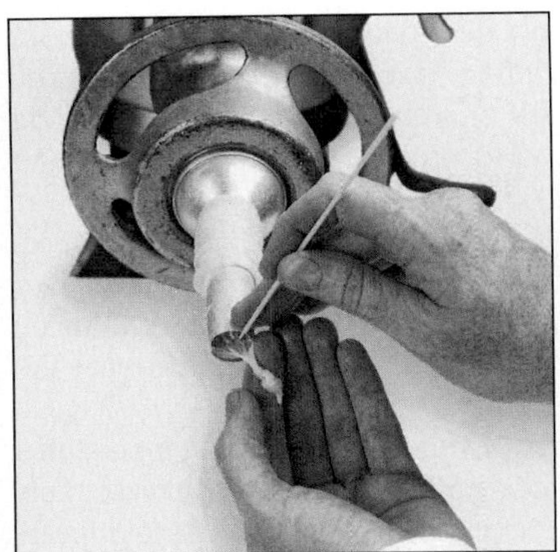

2 Knotting and piercing the casing with a skewer.

3 Supporting and guiding the casing off the end of the nozzle as the sausage is extruded from the machine into the casing.

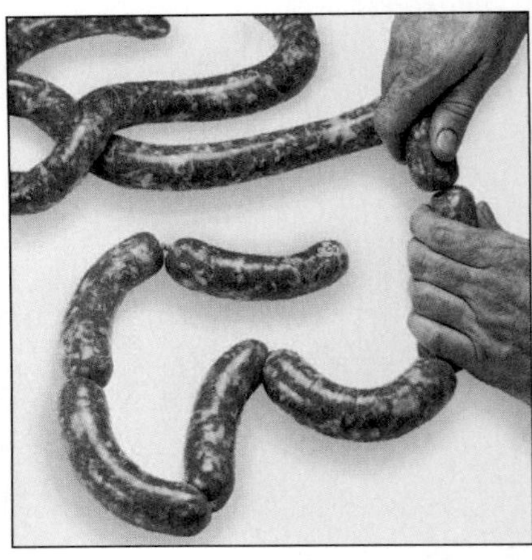

4 Twisting the sausage into uniform links.

▶ Salt Curing, Brining and Smoking

Curing, brining and smoking are ancient techniques for preserving food. Today, foods such as hams, corned beef and smoked salmon are salt-cured, brined or smoked primarily for flavor. Cured meats have a characteristic pink color caused by the reaction of sodium nitrite, which is added during processing, with the naturally occurring myoglobin protein in the meat.

SALT CURING

Salt curing is the process of surrounding a food with salt or a mixture of salt, sugar, nitrite-based curing salt, herbs and spices. Salt curing dehydrates the food, inhibits bacterial growth and adds flavor. It is most often used with pork products and fish. Salt curing is not a quick procedure—and the time involved adds money to production costs. For example, country-style hams are salt-cured. Proper curing requires approximately one and a half days per pound of ham, which means three weeks for the average ham.

Some salt-cured hams such as Smithfield and prosciutto are not actually cooked. The curing process preserves the meat and makes it safe to consume raw. Gravlax is a well-known salmon dish prepared by salt-curing salmon fillets with a mixture of salt, sugar, pepper and dill.

BRINING

A brine is actually a very salty marinade. Most brines have approximately 20 percent salinity, which is equivalent to 1 pound (450 grams) of salt per gallon (4 liters) of water. As with dry-salt cures, brines can also contain sugar, nitrites, herbs and spices. Brining is sometimes called pickling.

Today, most cured meats are prepared in large production facilities where the brine is injected into the meat for rapid and uniform distribution. Commercially brined corned beef is cured by this process, as are most common hams. After brining, hams are further processed by smoking.

SMOKING

There are two basic methods of smoking foods: cold smoking and hot smoking. The principal difference is that hot smoking actually cooks the food, while cold smoking does not.

▶ **andouille** (an-DOO-ee) a very spicy smoked pork sausage, popular in Cajun cuisine

▶ **chorizo** (chor-EE-zoh) a coarse, spicy pork sausage flavored with ground chiles and removed from its casing before cooking; used in Mexican and Spanish cuisines

▶ **mortadella** (mohr-tah-DEH-lah) an Italian smoked sausage made with ground beef, pork and pork fat, flavored with coriander and white wine; it is air-dried and has a delicate flavor; also a large American bologna-type pork sausage studded with pork fat and garlic

▶ **pepperoni** (peh-peh-ROH-nee) a hard, thin, air-dried Italian sausage seasoned with red and black pepper

▶ **soppressata** (soh-preh-SAH-tah) a hard, aged Italian salami, sometimes coated with cracked peppercorns or herbs

Both are done in a **smoker** specifically designed for this purpose. Smokers can be gas or electric; they vary greatly in size and operation. But they have several things in common. All consist of a chamber that holds the food being smoked, a means of burning wood to produce smoke and a heating element.

Different types of wood can be used to smoke food. Specific woods are selected to impart specific flavors. Hickory is often used for pork products; alder is excellent for smoked salmon. Maple, chestnut, juniper, mesquite and many other woods are also used. Resinous woods such as pine give food a bitter flavor and should be avoided.

Cold smoking is the process of exposing foods to smoke at temperatures of 50°F to 85°F (10°C to 29°C). Meat, poultry, game, fish, shellfish, cheese, nuts and even vegetables can be cold-smoked successfully. Most cold-smoked meats are generally salt cured or brined first. Salt curing or brining adds flavor, allows the nitrites (which give the ham, bacon and other smoked meats their distinctive pink color) to penetrate the flesh and, most important, extracts moisture from the food, allowing the smoke to penetrate more easily. Cold-smoked foods are actually still raw. Some, such as smoked salmon (lox), are eaten without further cooking. Most, such as bacon and hams, must be cooked before eating.

Hot smoking is the process of exposing foods to smoke at temperatures of 200°F to 250°F (93°C to 121°C). As with cold smoking, a great variety of foods can be prepared by hot smoking. Meats, poultry, game, fish and shellfish that are hot-smoked also benefit from salt curing or brining. Although most hot-smoked foods are fully cooked when removed from the smoker, many are used in other recipes that call for further cooking.

While most smoking requires specialized equipment, two affordable options exist for imparting a smoked flavor to foods. A stove top smoker, which resembles a hotel pan with a tight-fitting lid, can be used to hot-smoke small cuts of meat, fish, poultry or vegetables. Wood chips are scattered inside the bottom of the pan. Foods to be smoked sit on top of a mesh rack placed inside the box. The heat of the stove top ignites the woodchips, permeating the food with a smoky flavor. Foods smoked in this manner must reach proper internal cooking temperatures to be served without additional cooking. The recipe for Smoked Tomato Coulis is prepared using this type of smoker. Liquid smoke is a flavoring made from smoke, which has been condensed from the burning of wood chips. When used judiciously it can impart a pleasant smoky taste to barbecue sauces and marinades.

Sliced Bacon

Canadian Bacon

Pancetta

PORK PRODUCTS

Preparing hams and curing and smoking pork products are a traditional part of charcuterie. Although most bacon and ham are now produced in large commercial facilities, the chef still works with these products and must be able to identify them properly.

Most bacon comes from a hog's fatty belly.

Common bacon is produced by brining and cold-smoking trimmed pork belly. It is available in slab or sliced form. Sliced bacon is purchased by count (number of slices) per pound; thick-sliced bacon runs 10–14 slices per pound, while thin-sliced bacon may contain as many as 28–32 slices per pound.

Canadian bacon is produced from a boneless pork loin, trimmed so that only a thin layer of fat remains on its surface. It is then brined and smoked.

Pancetta (pan-CHEH-tuh) is an Italian pork-belly bacon that is not smoked. It is salt-cured, peppered and often rolled into a cylinder shape. It can be sliced into rounds and fried; it is diced, rendered and combined with sauce to make fettuccine carbonara.

IMPS No. 501, Ham Short Shank, Cured and Smoked

A **fresh ham** is a hog's hind leg; it is a primal cut. Many processed products produced from the primal fresh ham are also called ham.

Ham, in the United States, describes a variety of processed pork products, most of which come from the primal fresh ham. **Boneless** or **formed hams** are produced by separating a primal ham into its basic muscles, defatting the meat, curing it, stuffing the meat into casings of various sizes and shapes and cooking it. Boneless or formed hams either are smoked or have chemical smoke flavoring added during the curing process. The quality of boneless or formed hams varies greatly. The best hams are formed from only one or two large muscles and have low fat content and no added water other than that used during the curing process. Hams of lesser quality are formed from many small pieces of muscle and have a higher fat and water content. Many boneless or formed hams are listed in *The Meat Buyers Guide* and are indexed by the NAMP/IMPS system.

IMPS No. 510, Ham, Boneless, Skinless, Cured and Smoked, Fully Cooked

Country ham is a specialty of the southeastern United States. Country hams are dry-cured, smoked and hung to air-dry for a period ranging from several weeks to more than a year. During drying, a mold develops on the ham rind that must be scrubbed off before the ham is cooked. It is best cooked by first soaking, then slow simmering. The most famous country hams are Virginia hams; those from Smithfield, Virginia, are considered the finest. Only hams produced in rural areas can be called country hams; others must be labeled country-style ham.

Prosciutto (proh-SHOO-toe) is the Italian word for ham. What we call prosciutto in this country is called **Parma** in Italy. Parma ham, produced near that Italian city, is made from hogs fed on the whey of cheese processed nearby. It is salt-cured and air-dried but not smoked. The curing process makes it safe and wholesome to consume raw. Several domestic varieties of prosciutto are produced, varying widely in quality. Imported prosciuttos are much larger than the domestic varieties because Italian hogs are larger when butchered.

Prosciutto

Westphalian ham is dry-cured, brined and then smoked with beechwood. Authentic Westphalian hams are produced in the Westphalia region of Germany and are quite similar to prosciutto. They are sold bone-in or boneless. Their characteristic flavor is derived from the juniper berries used in the curing process and the beechwood used for smoking.

▸ SAUCE CHAUD-FROID

Sauce chaud-froid (shoh-FRAWH) (French for "hot-cold") is prepared hot but served cold. Traditionally used to coat meats, poultry or fish that were eaten cold, sauce chaud-froid is now more typically used to coat a whole poached salmon or whole roasted poultry item, which is then further decorated and used as a centerpiece. As with aspic jelly, chaud-froid that is to be eaten should be fairly firm when cold, gelled at room temperature but tender enough to melt quickly in the mouth when eaten. Chaud-froid used for decorative purposes only should have a heavier gelatin content and be quite firm, which makes it easier to work with.

A classic sauce chaud-froid is a mixture of one part cream and two parts stock (veal, chicken and/or fish) strengthened with gelatin. Depending on the stock used, this coating ranges in color from cream to beige. A more modern sauce chaud-froid (also known as a mayonnaise chaud-froid or mayonnaise collée) is based on mayonnaise; it is easier to make than the classic sauce and provides a whiter product, which is more desirable when used for centerpieces.

RECIPE 26.6

MAYONNAISE CHAUD-FROID

Yield: 2 qt. (2 lt)

Aspic jelly (firm to very firm)	1 qt.	1 lt
Mayonnaise (commercially made)	1 lb.	450 g
Sour cream	1 lb.	450 g

1 Melt the aspic jelly.
2 In a stainless steel bowl, combine the mayonnaise with the sour cream and mix until smooth.
3 Stir the aspic jelly into the mayonnaise and sour cream mixture until smooth.
4 Warm the sauce over a double boiler, stirring gently with a spoon until smooth and all the air bubbles disappear.

▶ PROCEDURE FOR COATING FOODS WITH SAUCE CHAUD-FROID

1 Cook (usually by poaching or roasting), trim and otherwise prepare the item to be decorated.
2 Place the item on a cooling rack over a clean sheet pan and refrigerate until ready to decorate. (Sauce that drips into the clean pan can be reused.)
3 Warm an ample amount of sauce chaud-froid in a stainless steel bowl over a double boiler until it is completely melted. Stir the sauce gently with a spoon rather than a whisk in order to prevent air bubbles from forming.
4 When the sauce is warm and smooth, remove the bowl from the double boiler and place it in an ice bath.
5 Using the back of a large ladle, stir the sauce by spinning the bowl and holding the ladle stationary. This should be done almost continuously while the sauce cools. Do not scrape the solidified chaud-froid from the sides of the bowl, as lumps will form.
6 When the sauce has cooled to room temperature, remove the item to be decorated from the refrigerator and place it on the worktable.
7 Coat the item with the sauce in a single, smooth motion. Use a ladle if the item is small; if it is large, pour the sauce directly from the bowl. The sauce should adhere to the cold food, and the coating should be free of bubbles or runs.
8 Repeat as necessary, reusing the sauce that drips onto the sheet pan, until the desired thickness is achieved.
9 Using a paring knife, carefully cut away any sauce from areas that are to be left uncoated.
10 Decorate the item as desired with vegetable flowers or other garnishes. If desired, finish the item by coating the vegetable garnishes with a layer of clear aspic jelly, using the same procedure.

1 Scoring the skin of the fish.

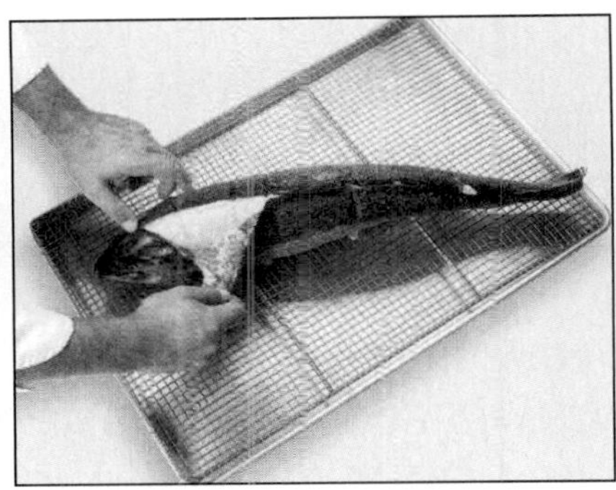

2 Removing the skin.

3 Removing the dark flesh and preparing the fish for the first coating of sauce chaud-froid.

4 Glazing the fish with the sauce chaud-froid.

5 Decorating the fish with vegetable flowers.

CONCLUSION

The classic art of charcuterie is as popular today as ever. Consumers regularly enjoy high-quality pâtés, sausages, hams and other charcuterie products.

Although production procedures have changed as new technologies and equipment have developed, the basic principles remain the same: Terrines, pâtés and sausages can be produced only from high-quality forcemeats, and temperature control is fundamental to the proper production of forcemeats and other charcuterie products.

Armed with a basic knowledge of the procedures used for charcuterie, experienced chefs can use imagination and creativity to produce a variety of enticing charcuterie products.

QUESTIONS FOR DISCUSSION

1. Explain why the art of charcuterie is relevant to the training of modern chefs.
2. Compare the three styles of forcemeat.
3. In what way is a terrine different from a pâté? How does a pâté differ from a pâté en croûte?
4. Describe the differences and the similarities between a ballotine and a galantine.
5. Describe the typical procedure for making sausages. Why is the selection of casings important?
6. Explain the difference between hot smoking and cold smoking. Describe a food typically prepared by each of these methods.
7. Describe the differences and the similarities between aspic jelly and sauce choud-froid. In what ways are aspic jelly and sauce choud-froid used?

CHAPTER TWENTY-SEVEN

EATING IS NOT MERELY A MATERIAL PLEASURE. EATING WELL GIVES A SPECTACULAR JOY TO LIFE AND CONTRIBUTES IMMENSELY TO GOODWILL AND HAPPY COMPANIONSHIP. IT IS OF GREAT IMPORTANCE TO THE MORALE.

—Elsa Schiaparelli,
Italian fashion designer
(1890–1973)

HORS D'OEUVRE AND CANAPÉS

PREP CHEF, INC.,
Phoenix, AZ
Chef Sidney Brodsky

AFTER STUDYING THIS CHAPTER, YOU WILL BE ABLE TO:

- prepare and serve a variety of cold and hot hors d'oeuvre, including canapés
- choose hors d'oeuvre, including canapés, that are appropriate for the meal or event

Hors d'oeuvre, whether hot or cold, are very small portions of foods served before the meal to whet the appetite. Hors d'oeuvre and canapés can be passed elegantly by waiters or displayed on buffets. Appetizers, or starters, whether hot or cold, are generally the first course or introduction to a meal; they are more typically served with dinner than with lunch. Sometimes there is very little difference between an hors d'oeuvre and an appetizer.

Preparing hors d'oeuvre, including canapés, uses skills from almost every work station. Because they can consist of meat, poultry, fish, shellfish, vegetables, potatoes, grains, pasta, fruits, baked goods and sauces, they require a detailed knowledge of these foods and how they are prepared.

The French term *hors d'oeuvre* translates as "outside the work." Its usage was correct under the classic kitchen brigade system, for it was the service staff's responsibility to prepare small tidbits for guests to enjoy while the kitchen prepared the meal. Today, however, the kitchen staff prepares the hors d'oeuvre as well as the meals. Cold hors d'oeuvre (a final *s* is added as an Americanized plural) are usually prepared by the garde-manger; hot ones are prepared in the main kitchen.

There are really only two limitations on the type of food and manner of preparation that can be used for hors d'oeuvre: the chef's imagination and the foods at his or her disposal. There are, however, a few guidelines.

GUIDELINES FOR PREPARING HORS D'OEUVRE

1. They should be small, one to two bites.
2. They should be flavorful and well seasoned without being overpowering.
3. They should be visually attractive.
4. They should complement whatever foods may follow without duplicating their flavors.

▸ COLD HORS D'OEUVRE

Cold hors d'oeuvre are divided here into five broad categories based on preparation method, principal ingredient or presentation style: canapés, caviar, crudités, dips and sushi. These categories may vary somewhat from classical teachings, but they are completely appropriate for modern menus and food service operations.

UN ARTISTE DE L'HORS D'OEUVRE

Well may it be said that a good hors d'oeuvre artist is a man to be prized in any kitchen, for, although his duties do not by any means rank first in importance, they nevertheless demand of the chef the possession of such qualities as are rarely found united in one person: reliable and experienced taste, originality, keen artistic sense, and professional knowledge.

Auguste Escoffier, *Le Guide culinaire*

CANAPÉS

Canapés are tiny open-faced sandwiches. They are constructed from a base, a spread and one or more garnishes.

The most common **canapé base** is a thin slice of bread cut into an interesting shape and toasted. Although almost any variety of bread can be used, spiced, herbed or otherwise flavored breads may be inappropriate for some spreads or garnishes. Melba toasts, crackers and slices of firm vegetables such as cucumbers or zucchini are also popular canapé bases. Whatever item is used, the base must

Table 27.1 A SELECTION OF CANAPÉ SPREADS AND SUGGESTED GARNISHES

SPREAD	SUGGESTED GARNISHES
Anchovy butter	Hard-cooked eggs, capers, green or black olive slices
Blue cheese	Grape half, walnuts, roast beef roulade, pear slice, currants, watercress
Caviar butter	Caviar, lemon, egg slice, chives
Deviled ham	Cornichons, mustard butter, sliced radish
Horseradish butter	Smoked salmon, roast beef, smoked trout, marinated herring, capers, parsley
Lemon butter	Shrimp, crab, caviar, salmon, chives, parsley, black olive slices
Liver pâté	Truffle slice, cornichon
Mustard butter	Smoked meats, pâté, dry salami coronet, cornichon
Pimento cream cheese	Smoked oyster, sardine, pimento, parsley
Shrimp butter	Poached bay scallops, shrimp, caviar, parsley
Tuna salad	Capers, cornichons, sliced radish
Wasabi mayonnaise	Grilled tuna, smoked fish, sliced daikon, sprouts

be strong enough to support the weight of the spread and garnish without falling apart when handled.

The **canapé spread** provides much of the canapé's flavor. Spreads are usually flavored butters, cream cheese or a combination of the two. Several examples of spreads are listed in Table 27.1. Each spread is made by adding the desired amount of the main ingredient (chopped or puréed as appropriate) and seasonings to softened butter or cream cheese and mixing until combined. Quantities and proportions vary according to individual tastes. Other canapé spreads include bound salads (for example, tuna or egg), finely chopped shrimp or liver mousse. Any of a number of ingredients can be combined for spreads, using the following guidelines:

Salmon Rosette Canapés

Shrimp and Caviar Canapés

Salami Cornet Canapés

GUIDELINES FOR PREPARING CANAPÉ SPREADS

1. The spread's texture should be smooth enough to produce attractive designs if piped through a pastry bag fitted with a decorative tip.
2. The spread's consistency should be firm enough to hold its shape when piped onto the base, yet soft enough to stick to the base and hold the garnishes in place.
3. The spread's flavor should complement the garnishes and be flavorful enough to stimulate the appetite without being overpowering.

A spread may be a substantial portion of the canapé as well as its distinguishing characteristic. Or it can be applied sparingly and used more as a means of gluing the garnish to the base than as a principal ingredient.

Canapés with bread bases tend to become soggy quickly from both the moisture in the spread and the moisture in the refrigerator where they are stored. Using a spread made with butter will help keep the bread bases crisper, as will buttering the base with a thin coat of softened plain butter before piping on the spread. The best way to ensure a crisp base is to make the canapés as close to service time as possible.

The variety of canapé garnishes is vast. The garnish can dominate or complement the spread, or it can be a simple sprig of parsley intended to provide visual appeal but little flavor. Although several ingredients can be used to garnish the same canapé, remember the limitations imposed by the canapé's size and purpose. Traditional garnishes can be made by shaping thinly sliced smoked salmon into rosettes, or thin slices of salami into cornets, into which additional spread can be piped. The natural shape of a boiled, peeled shrimp also makes an attractive canapé garnish.

▶ PROCEDURE FOR PREPARING CANAPÉS

This procedure can be adapted and used with a variety of ingredients to produce a variety of canapés. If the canapé base is a bread crouton, begin with Step 1. If some other product is used as the base, prepare that base and begin with Step 4.

1. Trim the crust from an unsliced loaf of bread. Slice the bread lengthwise approximately ⅓ inch (8 millimeters) thick.
2. Cut the bread slices into the desired shapes using a serrated bread knife or canapé cutter. See Figure 27.1.
3. Brush the bread shapes with melted butter and bake in a 350°F (180°C) oven until they are toasted and dry. Remove and cool. Alternatively, the entire bread slice can be buttered and toasted, then cut into shapes.
4. If desired, spread each base with a thin layer of softened plain butter.
5. Apply the spread to the base. If a thin layer is desired, use a palette knife. If a thicker or more decorative layer is desired, pipe the spread onto the base using a pastry bag and decorative tip. Alternatively, the entire bread slice can be buttered, toasted, cooled, covered with a spread and then cut into the desired shapes.
6. Garnish the canapé as desired.
7. If desired, glaze each canapé with a thin coating of aspic jelly. The aspic jelly can be applied with a small spoon or a spray bottle designated for that purpose.

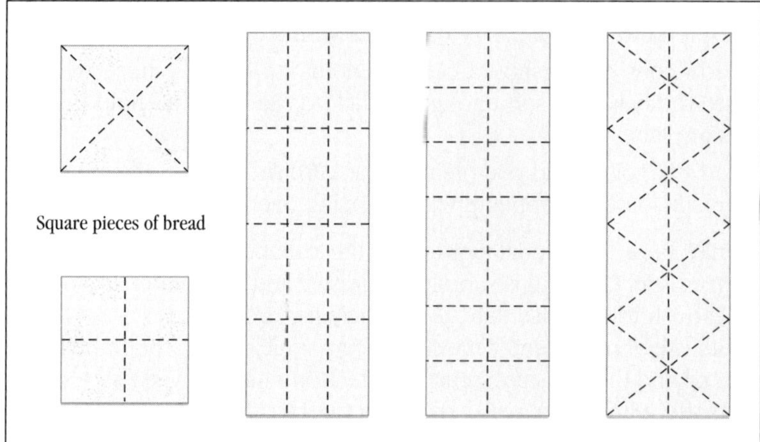

FIGURE 27.1 ▶ Bread can be sliced into several basic shapes to avoid waste.

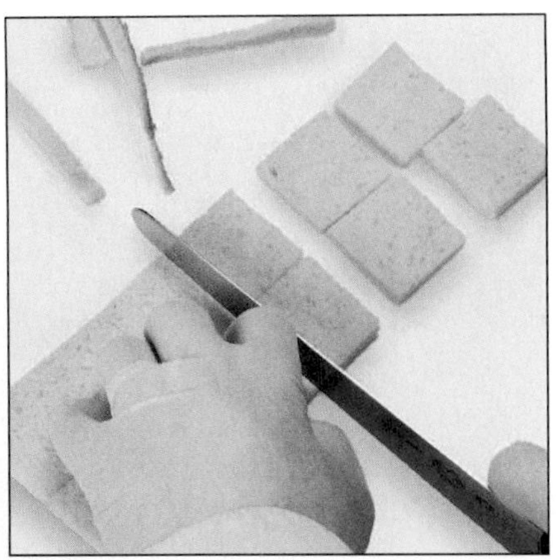

1 Slicing bread into the desired shapes.

2 Applying the spread to the base with a palette knife.

3 Piping the spread onto the base.

4 Coating the entire slice of toasted bread with a spread before cutting it into canapés.

5 Garnishing the canapés.

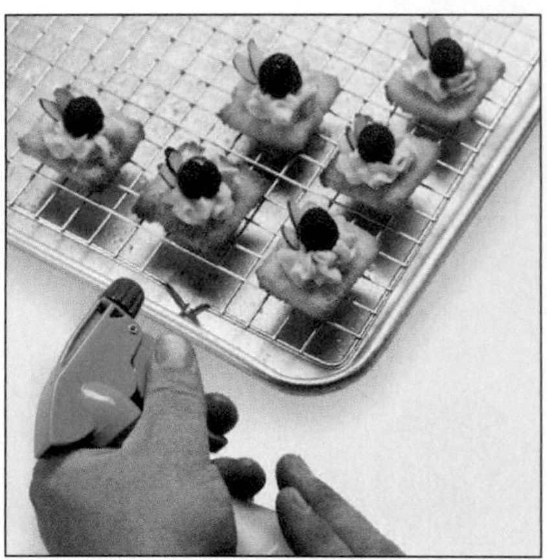

6 Spraying the finished canapés with aspic.

BARQUETTES, TARTLETS AND PROFITEROLES

Barquettes, tartlets and profiteroles are all adaptations of the basic canapé. A barquette is a tiny boat-shaped shell made from a savory dough such as pâte brisée. A **tartlet** is simply a round version of a barquette. A **profiterole** is a small puff made from pâte à choux. These three items can be prepared like canapés by filling them with flavored spreads and garnishing as desired.

▶ PROCEDURE FOR PREPARING BARQUETTES

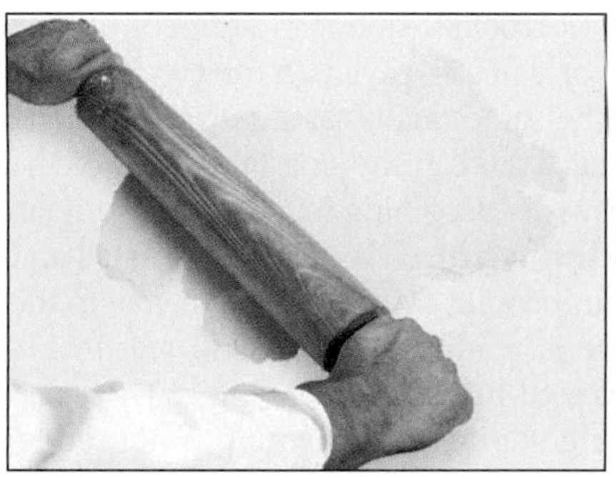

1 Rolling out the pastry dough.

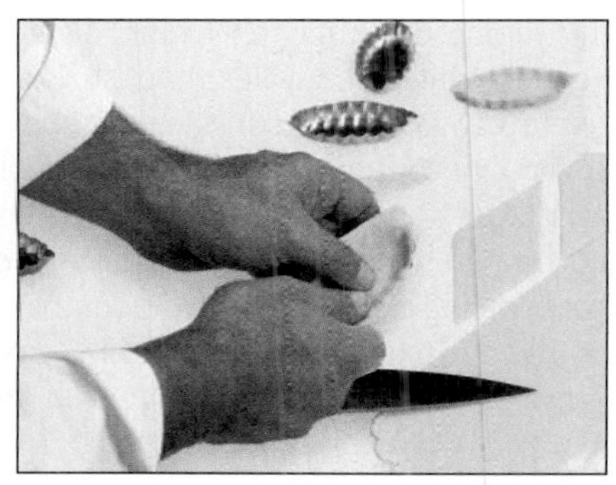

2 Pressing the dough into the barquette shells.

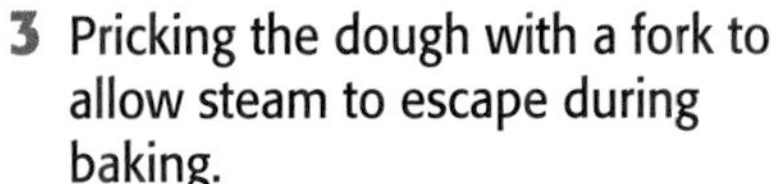

3 Pricking the dough with a fork to allow steam to escape during baking.

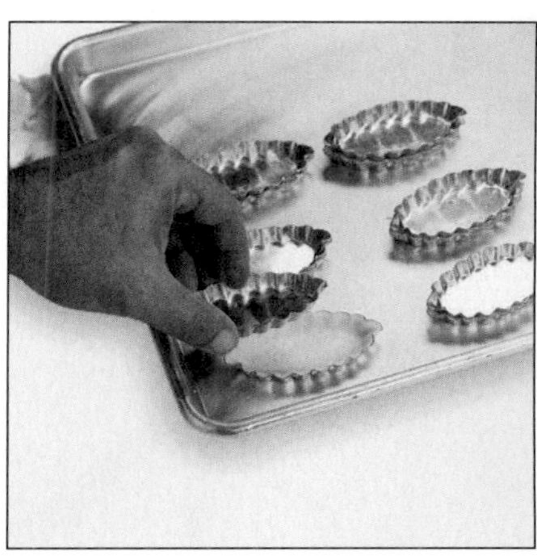

4 Placing a second barquette shell on top of the dough to prevent it from rising as it bakes.

OTHER TYPES OF CANAPÉS

Vegetables such as cherry tomatoes, blanched snow peas, mushroom caps and Belgian endive leaves are sometimes used as canapé bases. They are filled and garnished in the same manner as barquettes, tartlets and profiteroles.

Beluga Caviar

Sevruga Caviar

Osetra Caviar

American Salmon Roe

CAVIAR

Caviar, considered by many to be the ultimate hors d'oeuvre, is the salted roe (eggs) of the sturgeon fish. In the United States, only sturgeon roe can be labeled simply "caviar." Roe from other fish must be qualified as such on the label (for example, salmon caviar or lumpfish caviar).

Most of the world's caviar comes from sturgeon harvested in the Caspian Sea and imported from Russia and Iran. Imported sturgeon caviar, classified according to the sturgeon species and the roe's size and color, includes beluga, osetra and sevruga as well as pressed caviar. **Beluga** is the most expensive caviar, and comes from the largest species (the sturgeon can weigh up to 1750 pounds [800 kilograms]); the dark gray and well-separated eggs are the largest and most fragile kind. **Osetra** is considered by some connoisseurs to be the best caviar; the eggs are medium-sized, golden yellow to brown and quite oily. **Sevruga** is harvested from small sturgeon; the eggs are quite small and light to dark gray. **Pressed caviar** is a processed caviar made from osetra and sevruga roes. The eggs are cleaned, packed in linen bags and hung to drain; as salt and moisture drain away, the natural shape of the eggs is destroyed and the eggs are pressed together. Approximately 3 pounds (1.3 kilograms) of roe produce only 1 pound (450 grams) of pressed caviar; pressed caviar has a spreadable, jamlike consistency.

Most of the caviar consumed in the United States, however, comes from either domestic sturgeon or other fish and is labeled American sturgeon caviar, golden whitefish caviar, lumpfish caviar or salmon caviar. **American sturgeon caviar** is not considered to be of the same quality as Russian or Iranian caviars; nevertheless, roe from sturgeon harvested in the coastal waters of the American Northwest and the Tennessee River is becoming increasingly popular, due in part to its relatively low price. **Golden whitefish caviar** is a small and very crisp roe; it is a natural golden color and comes from whitefish native to the northern Great Lakes. **Lumpfish caviar** is readily available and reasonably priced; it is produced from lumpfish harvested in the North Atlantic. The small and very crisp eggs are dyed black, red or gold; the food coloring is not stable, however, and when used to garnish foods, colored lumpfish caviar tends to bleed. **Salmon caviar,** the eggs of the chum and silver salmon, is a very popular garnish. The eggs are large with a good flavor and natural orange color.

PURCHASING AND STORING CAVIARS

Although all caviar is processed with salt, some caviar is labeled **malassol,** which means "little salt." Caviar should smell fresh, with no off-odors. The eggs should be whole, not broken, and they should be crisp and pop when pressed with the tongue. Excessive oiliness may be caused by a large number of broken eggs. The best way to test caviar's quality is to taste it. Remember, price alone does not necessarily indicate quality.

Most caviar can be purchased fresh or pasteurized in tins or jars ranging from 1 ounce (28 grams) to more than 4 pounds (2 kilograms). Some caviars are also available frozen. (Frozen caviar should be used only as a garnish and should not be served by itself.) In order to ensure the freshest possible product, always purchase caviar in small quantities as often as possible based on the needs of the restaurant.

Fresh caviar should be stored at 32°F (0°C). Because most refrigerators are considerably warmer than that, store the caviar on ice in the coldest part of the refrigerator and change the ice often. If properly handled, fresh caviar will last one to two weeks before opening and several days after opening. Pasteurized caviar does not require refrigeration until it is opened and will last several days in the refrigerator after opening.

SERVING CAVIARS

Fine caviar should be served in its original container or a nonmetal bowl on a bed of crushed ice, accompanied only by lightly buttered toasts or blinis and sour cream. Connoisseurs prefer china, bone or other nonmetal utensils for serving caviar because metal reacts with the caviar, producing off-flavors.

Lesser-quality caviars are often served on ice, accompanied by minced onion, chopped hard-cooked egg whites and yolks (separately), lemon, sour cream and buttered toasts.

Lumpfish and other nonsturgeon caviars are usually not served by themselves. Rather, they are used as ingredients in or garnishes for other dishes.

CRUDITÉS

Crudité, a French word meaning "raw thing," generally refers to raw or slightly blanched vegetables served as an hors d'oeuvre. Although almost any vegetable will do, the most commonly used are broccoli, cauliflower, carrots, celery, asparagus and green beans, all of which are often blanched, and cucumbers, zucchini, yellow squash, radishes, green onions, cherry tomatoes, Belgian endive leaves, mushrooms, peppers and jicama, which are served raw.

When preparing crudités, use only the freshest and best-looking produce available. Because they are displayed and eaten raw, blemishes and imperfections cannot be disguised. Vegetables, both blanched and raw, should be cut into attractive shapes. Crudités are usually served with one or more dips.

DIPS

Dips can be served hot or cold and as an accompaniment to crudités, crackers, chips, toasts, breads or other foods.

Cold dips often use mayonnaise, sour cream or cream cheese as a base. The methods for preparing mayonnaise-based and sour cream-based dips are identical to those for making mayonnaise-based salad dressings discussed in Chapter 23, Salads and Salad Dressings. The principal difference is that dips are normally thicker than dressings.

To use cream cheese as a base, first soften it by mixing it in an electric mixer fitted with a paddle. Then add the flavoring ingredients such as chopped cooked vegetables, chopped

Artful Array of Crudités and Dip

cooked fish or shellfish, herbs, spices, garlic or onions. Adjust the consistency of the dip by adding milk, buttermilk, cream, sour cream or other appropriate liquid.

Some cold dips such as guacamole and hummus use purées of fruits, vegetables or beans as the base.

Hot dips often use a béchamel, cream sauce or cheese sauce as a base and usually contain a dominant flavoring ingredient such as chopped spinach or shellfish.

Dips can be served in small bowls or hollowed-out cabbages, squash, pumpkins or other vegetables. Hot dips are often served in chafing dishes.

The combinations of ingredients and seasonings that can be used to make dips as well as the foods that are dipped in them are limited only by the chef's imagination.

RECIPE 27.1

CLAM DIP

Mise en Place

- ▶ Drain clams.
- ▶ Wash and slice green onions.

Yield: 3 pt. (1.5 lt)

Cream cheese, softened	1 lb.	450 g
Worcestershire sauce	2 Tbsp.	30 ml
Dijon mustard	1 Tbsp.	15 ml
Sour cream	1 lb.	450 g
Canned clams, drained	1 lb.	450 g
Lemon juice	2 Tbsp.	30 ml
Salt and pepper	TT	TT
Tabasco sauce	TT	TT
Green onions, sliced	2 oz.	60 g

1 Blend the cream cheese in the bowl of an electric mixer fitted with a paddle.
2 Add the Worcestershire sauce, mustard and sour cream; mix until smooth.
3 Add the clams and lemon juice and season with salt, pepper and Tabasco.
4 Add the green onions and mix well.

Approximate values per 2-Tbsp. (30-ml) serving: **Calories** 70, **Total fat** 5 g, **Saturated fat** 3.5 g, **Cholesterol** 20 mg, **Sodium** 55 mg, **Total carbohydrates** 1 g, **Protein** 4 g, **Iron** 15%, **Claims**—low sodium; low sugar

SAFETY ALERT

The raw fish and cooked rice in sushi and sashimi are potentially hazardous foods. Many species of fin fish carry parasites that are harmless to the fish but can cause illness in humans. To destroy these parasites, such fish should be frozen prior to service according to procedures outlined in the *Model Food Code.* Cooked sushi rice should be kept chilled at 41°F (5°C) or lower. Observe the strictest sanitation standards when preparing these dishes to prevent cross-contamination. Many health departments enforce strict regulations to ensure that sushi and sashimi are properly prepared and served. Check local regulations for the most accurate information for your area.

SUSHI

Generally, **sushi** refers to cooked or raw fish and shellfish rolled in or served on seasoned rice. **Sashimi** is raw fish eaten without rice. In Japan, the word sushi (or **zushi**) refers only to the flavored rice. Each combination of rice and another ingredient or ingredients has a specific name. These include *nigiri zushi* (rice with raw fish), *norimaki zushi* (rice rolled in seaweed), *fukusa zushi* (rice wrapped in omelet), *inari zushi* (rice in fried bean curd) and *chirashi zushi* (rice with fish, shellfish and vegetables). Although a Japanese sushi master spends years perfecting style and technique, many types of sushi can be produced in any professional kitchen with very little specialized equipment.

INGREDIENTS

Fish

The key to good sushi and sashimi is the freshness of the fish. All fish must be of the highest quality and absolutely fresh, preferably no more than one day out of the water. Ahi and yellowfin tuna, salmon, flounder and sea bass are typically used for sushi. Cooked shrimp and eel are also popular.

Rice

Sushi rice is prepared by adding seasonings such as vinegar, sugar, salt and rice wine (sake or mirin) to steamed short-grain rice. The consistency of the rice is very important. It must be sticky enough to stay together when formed into finger-shaped oblongs, but not too soft.

Seasonings

Seasonings include the following:

- Shoyu—Japanese soy sauce, which is lighter and more delicate than the Chinese variety.
- Wasabi—A strong aromatic root, purchased as a green powder. It is sometimes called green horseradish, although it is not actually related to the common horseradish.
- Pickled ginger—Fresh ginger pickled in vinegar, which gives it a pink color.
- Nori—A dried seaweed purchased in sheets; it adds flavor and is sometimes used to contain the rolled rice and other ingredients.

ZUSHI (SUSHI RICE)

RECIPE 27.2

Yield: 2 lb. (1 kg)

Short-grain rice	1 lb.	450 g
Water	20 fl. oz.	600 ml
Rice vinegar	2 fl. oz.	60 ml
Granulated sugar	3 Tbsp.	45 ml
Salt	2½ tsp.	12 ml
Mirin	1 fl. oz.	30 ml

1. Wash the rice and allow it to drain for 30 minutes.
2. Combine the rice and water in a saucepan. Bring to a boil, lower to a simmer, cover and steam for 20 minutes.
3. Combine the rice vinegar, sugar, salt and mirin and add to the rice. Mix well and cool to room temperature.

Approximate values per 1-oz. (30-g) serving: **Calories** 60, **Total fat** 0 g, **Saturated fat** 0 g, **Cholesterol** 0 mg, **Sodium** 140 mg, **Total carbohydrates** 13 g, **Protein** 1 g, **Claims**—fat free

Adding the seasonings to the cooked rice.

NIGIRI SUSHI

RECIPE 27.3

Yield: 24 Pieces

Sushi-quality fish fillets such as ahi, salmon, flounder or sea bass	1 lb.	450 g
Wasabi powder	1 oz.	30 g
Water	1 fl. oz.	30 ml
Sushi rice	2 lb.	900 g
Pickled ginger, sliced	2 oz.	60 g
Shoyu	3 fl. oz.	90 ml

1. Trim the fish fillets of any skin, bone, imperfections or blemishes. Cut the fillets into 24 thin slices, approximately 2 inches by 1 inch (5 centimeters by 2.5 centimeters).
2. Mix the wasabi powder and water to form a paste.
3. With your hands, form a 1½-ounce (50-gram) portion of rice into a finger-shaped mound.
4. Rub a small amount of wasabi on one side of a slice of fish.
5. Holding the rice mound in one hand, press the fish, wasabi side down, onto the rice with the fingers of the other hand.
6. Serve with additional wasabi, pickled ginger and shoyu.

Approximate values per piece: **Calories** 80, **Total fat** 2 g, **Saturated fat** 0 g, **Cholesterol** 10 mg, **Sodium** 310 mg, **Total carbohydrates** 11 g, **Protein** 5 g, **Claims**—low fat; low cholesterol; no sugar

Mise en Place

- Prepare and chill sushi rice.

▶ PROCEDURE FOR FORMING NIGIRI SUSHI

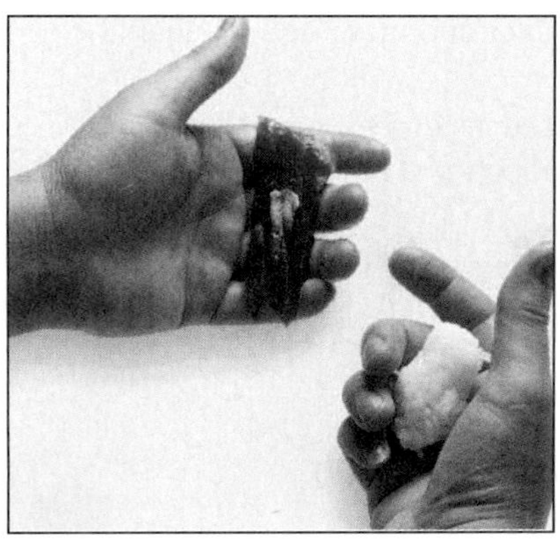

1 Forming a finger-shaped rice mound.

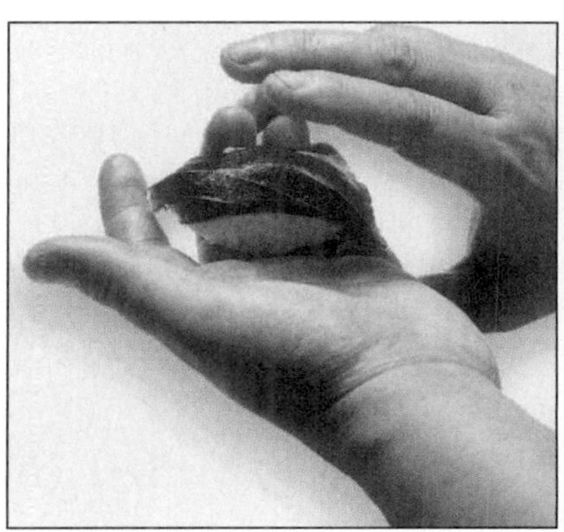

2 Pressing the fish onto the rice.

RECIPE 27.4

NORIMAKI ZUSHI

Mise en Place

▶ Prepare and chill sushi rice.

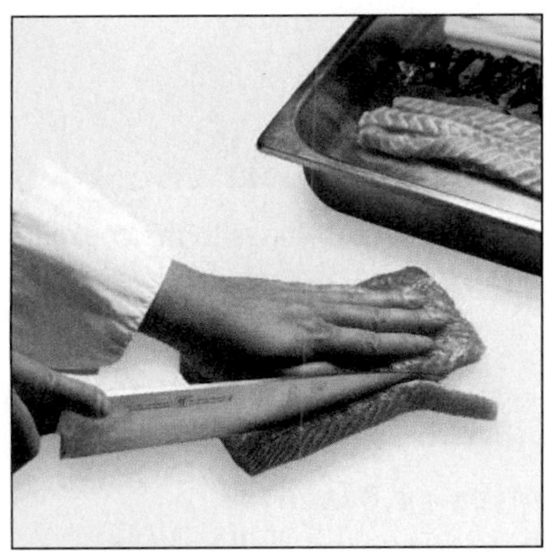

1 Preparing the garnishes for the sushi roll.

2 Spreading the rice over the nori.

Yield: 36 Pieces

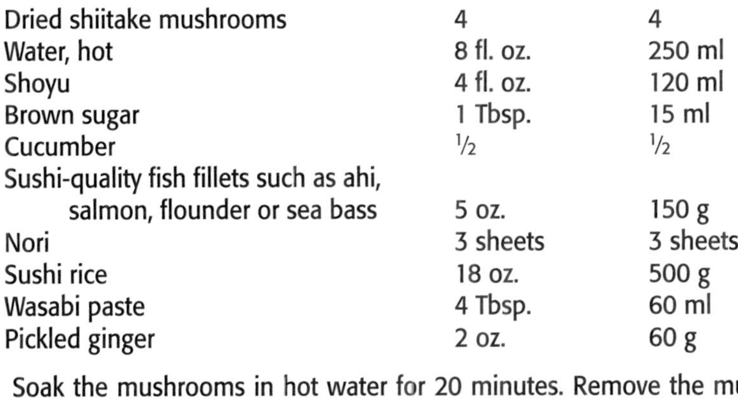

Ingredient	U.S.	Metric
Dried shiitake mushrooms	4	4
Water, hot	8 fl. oz.	250 ml
Shoyu	4 fl. oz.	120 ml
Brown sugar	1 Tbsp.	15 ml
Cucumber	½	½
Sushi-quality fish fillets such as ahi, salmon, flounder or sea bass	5 oz.	150 g
Nori	3 sheets	3 sheets
Sushi rice	18 oz.	500 g
Wasabi paste	4 Tbsp.	60 ml
Pickled ginger	2 oz.	60 g

1. Soak the mushrooms in hot water for 20 minutes. Remove the mushrooms and reserve 4 ounces (120 grams) of the liquid. Trim off the mushroom stems.
2. Julienne the mushroom caps. Combine the reserved soaking liquid with 2 tablespoons (30 milliliters) of the shoyu and the sugar. Simmer the caps in this liquid and reduce au sec. Remove from the heat and refrigerate.
3. Peel and seed the cucumber; cut it into strips the size of pencils, approximately 6 inches (15 centimeters) long.
4. Trim the fish fillets of any skin, bone, imperfections or blemishes. Cut the fillets into strips the same size as the cucumbers.
5. Cut the sheets of nori in half and place one half sheet on a napkin or bamboo rolling mat. Divide the rice into six equal portions; spread one portion over each half sheet of nori, leaving a ½-inch (1.2-centimeter) border of nori exposed.
6. Spread 1 teaspoon (5 milliliters) of wasabi paste evenly on the rice.
7. Lay one-sixth of the mushrooms, cucumber and fish strips in a row down the middle of the rice.
8. Use the napkin or bamboo mat to roll the nori tightly around the rice and garnishes.
9. Slice each roll into six pieces and serve with the remaining shoyu, pickled ginger and wasabi.

Approximate values per piece: **Calories** 40, **Total fat** 0 g, **Saturated fat** 0 g, **Cholesterol** 5 mg, **Sodium** 220 mg, **Total carbohydrates** 6 g, **Protein** 2 g, **Vitamin C** 15%, **Claims**—fat free; low cholesterol; low calorie

3 Adding the garnishes in a row down the middle of the rice.

4 Rolling the nori around the rice and garnishes.

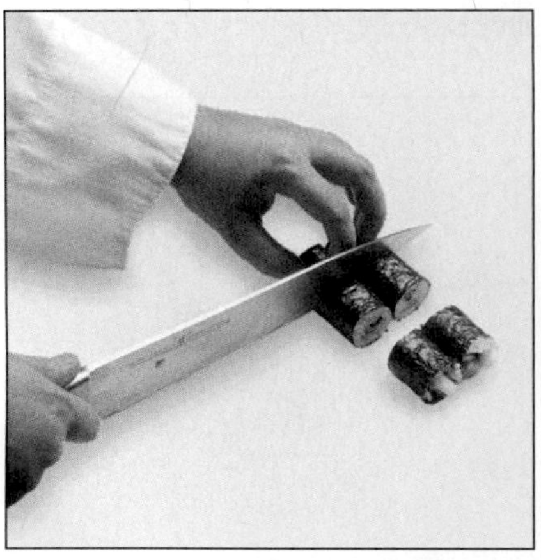

5 Slicing the roll into six pieces.

► Hot Hors d'Oeuvre

To provide a comprehensive list of hot hors d'oeuvre would be virtually impossible; therefore, just a few of the more commonly encountered ones that can be easily made in almost any kitchen are discussed here.

FILLED PASTRY SHELLS

Because savory (unsweetened) barquettes and tartlets, éclair puffs and bouchées can hold a small amount of liquid, they are often baked and then filled with warm meat, poultry or fish purées or ragoûts, garnished and served hot. They become soggy quickly, however, and must be prepared at the last possible minute before service.

BROCHETTES

Hors d'oeuvre brochettes are small skewers holding a combination of meat, poultry, game, fish, shellfish or vegetables. The foods are typically marinated, then baked, grilled or broiled, and are usually served with a dipping sauce. Brochettes can be small pieces of boneless chicken breast marinated in white wine and grilled; beef cubes glazed with teriyaki sauce; lamb or chicken satay (saté) with peanut sauce or rabbit and shiitake mushrooms skewered on a sprig of fresh rosemary.

In order to increase visual appeal, the main ingredients should be carefully cut and consistent in size and shape. The ingredients are normally diced, but strips of meat and poultry can also be threaded onto the skewers.

As hors d'oeuvre, the skewers should be very small, slightly larger than a toothpick. When assembling brochettes, leave enough exposed skewer so that diners can pick them up easily. Wooden skewers have a tendency to burn during cooking. Soaking them in water before assembling helps reduce the risk of burning.

RECIPE 27.5

RABBIT AND SHIITAKE SKEWERS

Yield: 12 Skewers

Rabbit	1	1
Shiitake mushrooms	2 lb.	1 kg
Fresh rosemary	12 sprigs	12 sprigs
Salt and pepper	TT	TT
Olive oil	2 fl. oz.	60 ml

1 Bone the rabbit and cut the pieces into ½-inch (1.2-centimeter) cubes. One rabbit should produce 36 cubes.
2 Wash the mushrooms. Trim and discard the stems.
3 Cut enough of the mushrooms into ½-inch (1.2-centimeter) dice to produce 24 pieces.
4 Skewer three pieces of rabbit and two pieces of mushroom alternately onto each rosemary sprig.
5 Season the skewers and the remaining mushrooms with salt and pepper and brush with oil. Grill the skewers and the mushroom caps over medium heat, being careful not to burn the rosemary sprigs.
6 Slice the mushroom caps and arrange a portion of sliced mushrooms and two rabbit skewers on each plate.

Approximate values per skewer: **Calories** 160, **Total fat** 8 g, **Saturated fat** 1.5 g, **Cholesterol** 30 mg, **Sodium** 20 mg, **Total carbohydrates** 11 g, **Protein** 12 g

MEATBALLS

Meatballs made from ground beef, veal, pork or poultry and served in a sauce buffet style are a popular hot hors d'oeuvre. One of the best known is the Swedish meatball. It is made from ground beef, veal and pork bound with eggs and bread crumbs and served in a velouté or cream sauce seasoned with dill. Other sauces that can be used in the same manner are mushroom sauce, red wine sauce or any style of tomato sauce.

RECIPE 27.6

SWEDISH MEATBALLS

Mise en Place

- ▶ Peel onion and chop into fine dice.
- ▶ Grind fresh bread for bread crumbs.
- ▶ Heat demi-glace and cream and chop dill while the meatballs are baking.

Yield: 4 lb. 8 oz. (2 kg)

Onions, small dice	8 oz.	250 g
Whole butter	2 oz.	60 g
Ground beef	2 lb.	1 kg
Ground pork	2 lb.	1 kg
Bread crumbs, fresh	4 oz.	120 g
Eggs	3	3
Salt	1 Tbsp.	15 ml
Black pepper	TT	TT
Nutmeg, ground	TT	TT
Allspice, ground	TT	TT
Lemon zest, grated	1 tsp.	5 ml
Demi-glace, hot	1 qt.	1 lt
Heavy cream, hot	8 fl. oz.	250 ml
Fresh dill, chopped	2 Tbsp.	30 ml

1 Sauté the onions in the butter without coloring. Remove and cool.
2 Combine the onions with all of the ingredients except the demi-glace, cream and dill. Mix well.

3 Portion the meat with a #20 scoop; form into balls with your hands and place on a sheet pan.
4 Bake the meatballs at 400°F (200°C) until firm, approximately 15 minutes. Remove the meatballs from the pan with a slotted spoon, draining well, and place in a hotel pan.
5 Combine the demi-glace, cream and dill; pour over the meatballs.
6 Cover the meatballs and bake at 350°F (180°C) until done, approximately 20 minutes. Skim the grease from the surface and serve.

Approximate values per 5-oz. (150-g) serving: **Calories** 250, **Total fat** 15 g, **Saturated fat** 7 g, **Cholesterol** 105 mg, **Sodium** 420 mg, **Total carbohydrates** 7 g, **Protein** 20 g, **Calcium** 30%

RUMAKI

Traditionally, rumaki were made by wrapping chicken livers in bacon and broiling or baking them. Today, however, many other foods prepared in the same fashion are called rumaki. For example, blanched bacon can be wrapped around olives, pickled watermelon rind, water chestnuts, pineapple, dates or scallops. These morsels are then broiled, baked or fried and served piping hot.

RUMAKI

RECIPE 27.7

Yield: 60 Pieces

Chicken livers	1 lb.	450 g
Marinade:		
Brown sugar	1 Tbsp.	15 ml
Water, hot	1 Tbsp.	15 ml
Dark soy sauce	1 Tbsp.	15 ml
Garlic, minced	1 Tbsp.	15 ml
Bacon, sliced thin	30 slices	30 slices
Water chestnuts, sliced	60 slices	60 slices

1 Trim the livers and cut into 60 equal-sized pieces. Place the livers in a stainless steel bowl.
2 Combine the marinade ingredients. Pour the marinade over the livers and refrigerate for 1 hour.
3 Cut the bacon slices in half, spread them on a sheet pan and parcook at 375°F (190°C) for approximately 5 minutes. Pour off and discard the excess fat.
4 Drain the livers. Roll one piece of liver and one water chestnut slice in one piece of bacon and secure with a toothpick. Repeat with the remaining ingredients. Place on a baking rack over a sheet pan with the seam side down.
5 Bake the rumaki in a 400°F (200°C) convection oven until the bacon is crisp and the liver is cooked, approximately 10 minutes. Do not overcook or the rumaki will be dry. Serve hot.

Mise en Place

▶ Slice water chestnuts while liver is marinating in Step 2.

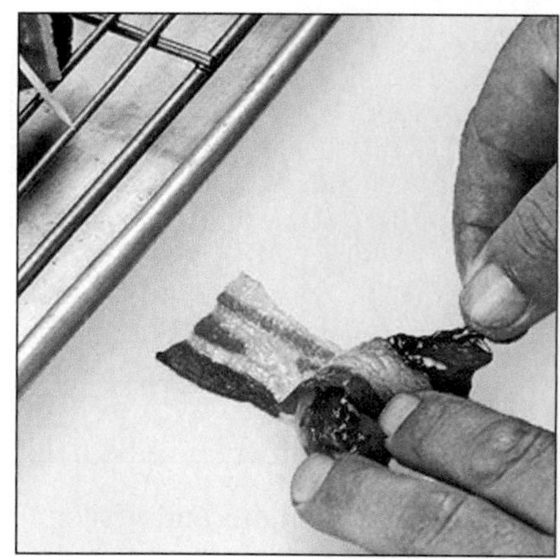

1 Rolling rumaki.

2 The finished rumaki.

Approximate values per piece: **Calories** 60, **Total fat** 5 g, **Saturated fat** 1.5 g, **Cholesterol** 30 mg, **Sodium** 170 mg, **Total carbohydrates** 1 g, **Protein** 4 g, **Vitamin A** 10%

STUFFED WONTON SKINS

Wonton skins are an Asian noodle dough used to produce a wide variety of hors d'oeuvre such as a miniature version of the traditional egg roll or a puff filled with a mixture of seasoned cream cheese and crab. Or they can be stuffed with a wide variety of pork, chicken, shellfish and vegetables before cooking. As hors d'oeuvre, stuffed wonton skins can be steamed, but they are more often pan-fried or deep-fried. (Wonton skins can also be baked and used as a canapé base.)

RECIPE 27.8

STUFFED WONTONS WITH APRICOT SAUCE

Mise en place

- ▶ Peel and chop garlic.
- ▶ Wash and slice green onions.

1 Brushing the wonton edges with water.

2 Folding the wontons and sealing the edges.

3 The finished wontons.

Yield: 24 Pieces

Cream cheese	8 oz.	250 g
Crab meat	8 oz.	250 g
Garlic, chopped	1 tsp.	5 ml
Green onions, sliced	1 oz.	30 g
Salt and pepper	TT	TT
Worcestershire sauce	TT	TT
Sesame oil	TT	TT
Wonton skins	24	24
Apricot Sauce (recipe follows)	as needed	as needed

1. Place the cream cheese in the bowl of a mixer and mix until soft.
2. Add the crab meat, garlic and green onions. Season with salt and pepper, Worcestershire sauce and a drop or two of sesame oil.
3. Place several wonton skins on a work surface. Brush the edges with water. Place 1 tablespoon (15 milliliters) of the cream cheese mixture in the center of each skin. Fold the wonton skin in half to form a triangle; seal the edges.
4. Using the swimming method, deep-fry the wontons at 350°F (180°C) for 10 seconds. Remove the wontons, drain well and refrigerate.
5. At service time, deep-fry the wontons at 350°F (180°C) until crisp, approximately 1 minute. Serve with Apricot Sauce.

Approximate values per piece, with sauce: **Calories** 130, **Total fat** 8 g, **Saturated fat** 2.5 g, **Cholesterol** 20 mg, **Sodium** 105 mg, **Total carbohydrates** 11 g, **Protein** 4 g

APRICOT SAUCE

Yield: 8 oz. (250 g)

Apricot preserves	8 oz.	250 g
Fresh ginger, grated	1 Tbsp.	15 ml
Dry mustard	1 tsp.	5 ml
Red wine vinegar	½ fl. oz.	15 ml

1. Combine all ingredients and heat until the preserves melt and the flavors blend.

Approximate values per 1-oz. (30-g) serving: **Calories** 70, **Total fat** 0 g, **Saturated fat** 0 g, **Cholesterol** 0 mg, **Sodium** 10 mg, **Total carbohydrates** 19 g, **Protein** 0 g, **Claims**—fat free

OTHER HOT HORS D'OEUVRE

Other types of hot hors d'oeuvre include layers of phyllo dough wrapped around various fillings; vegetables such as mushrooms that are stuffed and baked; tiny red potatoes filled with sour cream and caviar or Roquefort cheese and walnuts; tiny artichoke or clam fritters or any of the hundreds of varieties of chicken wings that are seasoned or marinated, baked, fried, broiled or grilled and served with a cool and soothing or outrageously spicy sauce.

The secret is to use creativity, to keep the ingredients harmonious and, if the hors d'oeuvre are to precede dinner, not to allow them to duplicate the foods to be served or overpower them with excessively spicy flavors.

▶ SERVING HORS D'OEUVRE

Hors d'oeuvre are not served only as a precursor to dinner. At many events, the only foods served may be butlered hors d'oeuvre, an hors d'oeuvre buffet or a combination of the two. Whether the hors d'oeuvre are being served before dinner or as dinner, butler style or buffet style, they must always be attractively prepared and displayed.

All events have themes and varying degrees of formality. Long buffets with overflowing baskets of crudités and sweet potato chips with dips presented in hollowed squashes and cabbages may be appropriate for one event, while elegant silver trays of carefully prepared canapés passed among guests by white-gloved, tuxedoed service staff may be appropriate for another. When preparing and serving hors d'oeuvre, always keep the event's theme in mind and plan accordingly.

When choosing hors d'oeuvre, select an assortment that contrasts flavors, textures and styles. There are no limits to the variety of hors d'oeuvre that can be served, but three to four cold and three to four hot selections are sufficient for most occasions. The following is a sample selection of hot and cold hors d'oeuvre that contrast flavors, textures and styles as well as types of food.

COLD

- Canapés of smoked salmon on brioche
- Barquettes filled with Roquefort cheese and garnished with grapes
- Tiny tortilla cups filled with grilled chicken and spicy tomato salsa

HOT

- Tiny pouches of shrimp wrapped in phyllo dough
- Date and chorizo rumaki
- Rabbit and shiitake skewers
- Small chèvre tarts

BUTLER SERVICE

Butler service hors d'oeuvre, or "passed" hors d'oeuvre, are presented to guests on trays by the service staff. The hors d'oeuvre can be hot or cold and should be very small to make it easier for the guests to eat them without the aid of a knife or fork. Hot and cold hors d'oeuvre should be passed separately so that they can be kept at the correct temperatures. For a one-hour cocktail reception before a dinner, three to five hors d'oeuvre per person is usually sufficient. If hors d'oeuvre are the only food being served, however, four to five pieces per person per hour may be more appropriate.

BUFFET SERVICE

An hors d'oeuvre buffet should be beautiful and appetizing. It may consist of a single table to serve a small group of people or several huge multilevel displays designed to feed thousands. Colors, flavors and textures must all be taken into account when planning the menu.

Both hot and cold hors d'oeuvre may be served on buffets. Hot hors d'oeuvre are often kept hot by holding them in chafing dishes. Alternatively, hot hors d'oeuvre can be displayed on trays or platters; the trays and platters, however, must be replaced frequently to ensure that the food stays hot. Cold hors d'oeuvre can be displayed on trays, mirrors, platters, baskets, leaves, papers or other serving pieces to create the desired look.

ARRANGING BUFFET PLATTERS

When displaying hors d'oeuvre and other foods on mirrors, trays or platters, the foods should be displayed in a pattern that is pleasing to the eye and flows toward the guest or from one side to the other. An easy and attractive method for accomplishing this is to arrange the items on a mirror or tray with an attractive centerpiece. The food can be placed in parallel diagonal lines, alternating the various styles and shapes. Three alternative arrangements are shown in the following photographs. Be careful not to make the tray or mirror too fussy or cluttered, however; often the best approach is to keep it simple.

Creating interesting levels and height will also add to the visual excitement when displaying hors d'oeuvre platters.

CONCLUSION

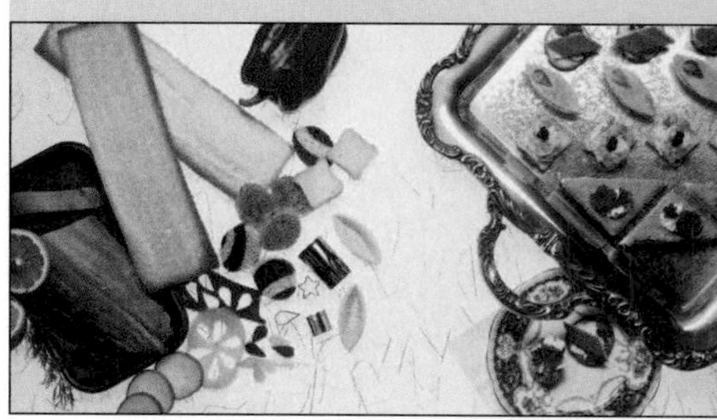

The preparation of hors d'oeuvre provides an opportunity for the chef to demonstrate his or her creativity, knowledge of food and skills in presentation and garnishing. Because hors d'oeuvre often serve as the guests' introduction to the meal to come, it is especially important that these foods be properly prepared and of the highest quality.

QUESTIONS FOR DISCUSSION

1. Discuss four guidelines that should be followed when preparing hors d'oeuvre.
2. Identify and describe the three parts of a canapé.
3. Describe the differences between beluga, osetra and sevruga caviars, and explain how these differ from domestic caviars.
4. Create an hors d'oeuvre menu for a small cocktail party. Include three hot and three cold items and explain the reasons for your selections.

CHAPTER TWENTY-EIGHT

NO ONE WHO COOKS, COOKS ALONE. EVEN AT HER MOST SOLITARY, A COOK IN THE KITCHEN IS SURROUNDED BY GENERATIONS OF COOKS PAST, THE ADVICE AND MENUS OF COOKS PRESENT, THE WISDOM OF COOKBOOK WRITERS.

—Laurie Colwin, cookbook author and American writer (1944–1992)

PRINCIPLES OF THE BAKESHOP

AFTER STUDYING THIS CHAPTER, YOU WILL BE ABLE TO:

- recognize many of the specialized tools and equipment used in the bakeshop
- recognize and select ingredients used in the bakeshop
- control the development of gluten
- cook sugar correctly
- understand the baking process

▶ **formula** the standard term used throughout the industry for a bakeshop recipe; formulas rely on weighing to ensure accurate measuring of ingredients

Flour, sugar, eggs, milk, butter, flavorings—with this simple list of ingredients a seemingly endless variety of sweet goods, from breads to sauces to pastries, can be made. But to produce consistently good brioche, Bavarians, biscuits or the like, careful attention must be paid to the character and quantity of each ingredient, the way the ingredients are combined and how heat is applied to them. Unlike, for example, a cut of meat that can be grilled, roasted, sautéed or braised and still be the same cut of meat, bakeshop products depend on careful, precise preparation for their very identity.

Accurate measurements are critical in the bakeshop. It is equally important to follow bakeshop **formulas** carefully and completely. Unlike other types of cooking, baking mistakes often cannot be discovered until the product is finished, by which time it is too late to correct them. For example, if salt is left out when preparing a stew, the mistake can be corrected by adding salt at service time. If salt is left out of a batch of bread dough, the mistake cannot be corrected after the bread has baked, and its texture and flavor may be ruined. It is probably more important to follow a written formula, measure ingredients precisely and combine them accurately in the bakeshop than anywhere else in the kitchen.

In order to provide a thorough introduction to the skills needed in a bakeshop, this book focuses on preparing the types of breads and desserts usually found in a small retail shop or restaurant. Because this book is not designed for large wholesale or commercial bakeries, mixes, stabilizers and mechanical preparation and shaping skills are not included.

▶ Bakeshop Tools and Equipment

Beginning cooks may find the tools of the bakeshop a bit complex. Indeed, the tools required for a professional pâtisserie are quite specialized. A well-rounded chef need not be concerned with possessing every gadget available, but should recognize and be familiar with most of the items shown in Figure 28.1. Although many of these hand tools will make a task easier, most can be improvised by a creative chef. Several of the items shown, such as the springform pans, tartlet pans and petit four molds, are used for shaping or holding batters and doughs. The various spatulas are used for spreading icings or fillings. The piping tools and cake comb are used for decorating and finishing baked goods. When purchasing tools and equipment for the bakeshop, look for quality and durability.

Bakeshop ovens may be conventional, convection or steam injection models. Convection ovens can reduce cooking time, but the air currents may damage delicate products such as spongecake or puff pastry. Steam injection ovens use conventional heat flow but allow the baker to automatically add steam to the cooking chamber as needed to produce crisp-crusted breads. Although expensive, steam injection ovens are a necessity for commercial bakeries and most larger restau-

FIGURE 28.1 ▶ Bakeshop Tools (clockwise from center back): cake turntable, cake pans, flan ring, tartlet pans, cannoli form, offset spatulas, flat cake spatula, blade for scoring breads, flower nail, rectangular tartlet pans, piping bag and tips, metal spatula, dough cutter, rolling pin, springform pan, copper sugar pot (on cooling rack), nest of round cutters

rant and hotel bakeshops. Baking instructions in the following chapters are based on the use of a conventional oven. If a convection oven is used instead, remember that the temperature and baking time may need to be reduced.

▶ INGREDIENTS

Although substituting ingredients may have little or no effect on some dishes (carrots can be substituted for turnips in a stew, for instance), this is not the case with baked goods. Different flours, fats, liquids and sweeteners function differently. Bread flour and cake flour are not the same, nor are shortening and butter. If one ingredient is substituted for another, the results will be different.

Understanding ingredients, why they function the way they do and how to adjust for their differences will make the baking experience more successful and consistent. This chapter discusses flours, sugar and other sweeteners, fats, thickeners and flavorings such as chocolate, vanilla and nuts. Flavorings such as herbs, spices and liquors are discussed in Chapter 5, Flavors and Flavorings. Dairy products, also common in baked goods, are discussed in Chapter 6, Dairy Products, and eggs, coffee and tea are discussed in Chapter 19, Eggs and Breakfast.

FLOURS

Flour provides bulk and structure to baked goods. Some flours are used to thicken liquids in items such as puddings and pie fillings, or to prevent foods from sticking during preparation and baking. Flour is produced when grain kernels are milled or ground into a powder. Grains are grasses that bear edible seeds. Corn, rice and wheat are the most significant grains for human consumption, but the most frequently used—and therefore the most important—ingredient in the bakeshop is wheat flour.

WHEAT FLOUR

Wheat flour (Fr. *farine*) is produced by milling wheat kernels (berries). As discussed in Chapter 21, Potatoes, Grains and Pasta, a wheat kernel has an outer covering called bran. It is composed of several layers that protect the endosperm, which contains starches and proteins. The innermost part is the germ, which contains fat and serves as the wheat seed (see Figure 23.1). During milling, the kernels first pass through metal rollers to crack them, then the bran and germ are removed through repeated stages of sifting and separation. The remaining endosperm is then ground into flour. Flour made from the portion of the endosperm closest to the germ (also known as patent flour) is finer; flour made from the portion of the endosperm nearer the bran (clear flour) is coarser and darker.

Composition of Flour

Flour consists primarily of five nutrients: fat, minerals, moisture, starches and proteins. Fat and minerals each generally account for less than 1 percent of flour's content. The moisture content of flour is also relatively low—when packaged, it cannot exceed 15 percent under government standards. But its actual moisture content varies depending on climatic conditions and storage. In damp areas, flour absorbs moisture from the atmosphere.

Starches constitute 63 to 77 percent of flour and are necessary for the absorption of moisture during baking. This process, known as gelatinization, occurs primarily at temperatures above 140°F (60°C). Starches also provide food for yeast during fermentation.

▶ **gluten** an elastic network of proteins created when wheat flour is moistened and manipulated

Flour proteins are of crucial importance because of their gluten-forming potential. **Gluten** is the tough, rubbery substance created when wheat flour is mixed with water. Gluten strands are both plastic (that is, they change shape under pressure) and elastic (they resume their original shape when that pressure is removed). Gluten is responsible for the volume, texture and appearance of baked goods. It provides structure and enables dough to retain the gases given off by leavening agents. Without gluten, there could be no raised breads: The gases created by yeast fermentation or chemical leaveners would simply escape if there were no network of gluten strands to trap them in the dough.

In general, the higher a flour's protein content, the greater that flour's gluten-forming potential. In some cases, however, flour with, for example, 13% protein may perform better than one with 14% protein because the proteins in the flour are of superior quality. The proteins responsible for gluten formation are *glutenin* and *gliadin*. Flour does not contain gluten; only a dough or batter can contain gluten. Gluten is produced when glutenin and gliadin are moistened and manipulated, as when they are stirred or kneaded. In order to make a chewy product such as a crusty French loaf, a flour with a high protein content must be used. Lower-protein flours are used for tender soft products such as cakes or muffins. Table 28.1 lists the protein content and uses for several common flours. Substituting one type of flour for another may be acceptable in some formulas as long as the ratio of fats, moisteners and other ingredients is adjusted accordingly. In most cases, however, substituting one type of flour for another will result in a changed and probably less desirable product.

Gluten development is affected by a number of factors, including mixing time and the presence of fat. Generally, the longer a substance is mixed, the more gluten will develop. Extreme overmixing in industrial equipment can break down the gluten structure, however. The type and balance of ingredients in a formula will also affect gluten development. Fats coat the protein in the flour, in-

Table 28.1 PROTEIN CONTENT OF FLOURS

TYPE OF FLOUR	PERCENT PROTEIN	USES
Cake	7–9.5	Tender cakes
Pastry	7.5–12	Biscuits, pie crusts
All-purpose	10–13	General baking
Bread	12–15	Yeast breads
Whole-wheat	13–14	Breads
High-gluten	14–15	Bagels; used to increase protein content of weaker flour such as rye, whole-grain or specialty flours

hibiting the formation of the gluten bond. Flour needs to absorb liquid in order for the proteins to bond into gluten. Firm bread dough that can be kneaded and shaped before baking requires a high-protein flour. When this dough is made with water it will bake into a product with a solid structure. When whole milk is used in the same formula, the product will be more tender because the milkfat weakens the gluten bond.

The character of the wheat determines the character of the flour. Wheat is classified as soft or hard depending on the kernel's hardness. The harder the wheat kernel, the higher its protein content. Soft wheat yields a soft flour with a low protein content. **Soft flour,** also called **weak flour,** is best for tender products such as cakes. Hard wheat yields a **hard flour** with a high protein content. Hard flour, also known as **strong flour,** is used for yeast breads.

Various types of flour are created by mixing or blending flours from different varieties of wheat. All-purpose flour, a blend of hard and soft flours, is designed for use in a wide range of foods. It is also referred to throughout this book because it is readily available in quantities appropriate for small food service operations. Large bakeshops rarely use all-purpose flour; instead, they choose flours specifically milled and blended for specific characteristics.

Aging and Bleaching

Any flour develops better baking qualities if allowed to rest for several weeks after milling. Freshly milled flour produces sticky doughs and products with less volume than those made with aged flour. During aging, flour turns white through a natural oxidation process referred to as bleaching.

Natural aging and bleaching are somewhat unpredictable, time-consuming processes, however, so chemicals are often used to do both. Potassium bromate and chlorine dioxide gas rapidly age flour. Chlorine dioxide and other chemicals bleach flour by removing yellow pigments in order to obtain a uniform white color. Bleaching destroys small amounts of the flour's naturally occurring vitamin E. Many artisan bakers use unbleached and unbromated flours exclusively. (It should be noted, however that potassium bromate has been identified as a possible carcinogen and may not be added to flour milled and sold in Canada or Europe.)

SPECIALTY FLOURS

Whole-wheat flour is made by milling the entire wheat kernel, including the bran and nutritious germ. Whole-wheat flour has a nutty, sweet flavor and brown, flecked color. Products made with whole-wheat flour will be denser, with less volume than those made with white flour; bran particles cut through the gluten strands in the dough, resulting in a heavier crumb. Whole-wheat flour has a reduced shelf life because fats in the germ can become rancid during storage. Whole-wheat pastry and high-gluten flours are available. Though not a flour, **wheat**

Whole-Wheat Flour

germ is often used in place of some flour in recipes for flavor and fiber. Wheat germ, preferably toasted, can be used in place of up to one-third of the wheat flour in a dough formula. The finished product will have a denser texture, however.

Vital wheat gluten (gluten flour) is the pure protein extracted from wheat flour. With an average protein content of 75%, it is used to boost the protein content of weaker flours such as rye and whole-wheat flour. It must be blended with other ingredients to form a dough or batter.

Self-rising flour is an all-purpose flour to which salt and a chemical leavener, usually baking powder, have been added. It is not recommended for professional use. Chemicals lose their leavening ability over time and may cause inconsistent results. Furthermore, different formulas call for different ratios of salt and leaveners; no commercial blend is appropriate for all purposes.

Nonwheat flours, also referred to as **composite flours,** are made from grains, seeds or beans. Corn, soybeans, rice, oats, buckwheat, potatoes and other items provide flours, but none of them contain the gluten-forming proteins of wheat flour. Composite flours are generally blended with a high-protein wheat flour for baking. Substituting composite flour for wheat flour changes the flavor and texture of the product.

Rye Flour

Rye flour is commonly used in bread baking. It is milled from the rye berry much as wheat flour is milled from the wheat berry. Rye flour comes in four grades or colors: white, medium, dark and rye meal. White rye flour is made from only the center of the rye berry. Medium and dark rye flours are made from the whole rye berry after the bran is removed and have the most intense rye flavor. Rye meal is the entire rye berry milled into a flour of different granulations, most often a coarse-textured flour. Some mills refer to their rye meal as pumpernickel flour. Others use pumpernickel to describe dark rye flour. All rye flours have a warm, pungent flavor similar to caraway and a gray-brown color. Although rye flour contains proteins, they will not form gluten, so bread made with 100% rye flour will be dense and flat. Therefore, rye flour is usually blended with a high-protein wheat flour to produce a more acceptable product.

NUTRITION

Flours are generally high in carbohydrates and low in fat. The grains from which they are milled are often rich in vitamins and minerals. Some of these nutrients, however, are lost during milling. In enriched flours, thiamin, riboflavin, niacin and iron are added at levels set by the government.

PURCHASING AND STORING

Most flours are purchased in 50- and 100-pound bags. They should be stored in a lit, ventilated room at temperatures no higher than 80°F (27°C). Flour can be stored in a refrigerator or freezer if necessary to prevent the onset of rancidity. Refrigeration may cause the flour to absorb moisture, however, which will limit the flour's ability to absorb additional moisture during actual use. An open bag of flour should be transferred to a closed container to prevent contamination. Even unopened bags of flour should not be stored near items with strong odors, as flour readily absorbs odors. Whole grains should be stored in airtight containers in cool, dry, dark conditions. Coolness inhibits insect infestations; dryness prevents mold. Using airtight containers stored in darkness helps prevent nutrient loss.

SUGAR AND SWEETENERS

Sugar (Fr. *sucre*) and other sweeteners serve several purposes in the bakeshop: They provide flavor and color, tenderize products by weakening gluten strands, provide food for yeasts, serve as a preservative and act as a creaming or foaming agent to assist with leavening.

SUGAR

Sugars are carbohydrates. They are classified as either (1) single or simple sugars (monosaccharides), such as glucose and fructose, which occur naturally in honey and fruits, or (2) double or complex sugars (disaccharides), which may occur naturally, such as lactose in milk, or in refined sugars.

The sugar most often used in the kitchen is **sucrose,** a refined sugar obtained from both the large tropical grass called sugar cane (*Saccharum officinarum*) and the root of the sugar beet (*Beta vulgaris*). Sucrose is a disaccharide, composed of one molecule each of glucose and fructose. The chemical composition of beet and cane sugars is identical. The two products taste, look, smell and react the same. Sucrose is available in many forms: white granulated, light or dark brown granulated, molasses and powdered.

▶ **sucrose** the chemical name for common refined sugar; it is a disaccharide, composed of one molecule each of glucose and fructose

Sugar Manufacturing

Common refined or table sugar is produced from sugar cane or sugar beets. The first step in sugar production is to crush the cane or beet to extract the juice. This juice contains tannins, pigments, proteins and other undesirable components that must be removed through refinement. Refinement begins by dissolving the juice in water, then boiling it in large steam evaporators. The solution is then crystallized in heated vacuum pans. The uncrystallized liquid by-product, known as molasses, is separated out in a centrifuge. The remaining crystallized product, known as raw sugar, contains many impurities; the USDA considers it unfit for direct use in food.

Raw sugar is washed with steam to remove some of the impurities. This yields a product known as turbinado sugar. Refining continues as the turbinado is heated, liquefied, centrifuged and filtered. Chemicals may be used to bleach and purify the liquid sugar. Finally, the clear liquid sugar is recrystallized in vacuum pans as granulated white sugar.

Pure sucrose is sold in granulated and powdered forms and is available in several grades. Because there are no government standards regulating grade labels, various manufacturers' products may differ slightly.

Types of Sugar

Turbinado sugar, sometimes called Demerara sugar, is the closest consumable product to raw sugar. It is partially refined and light brown in color, with coarse crystals and a caramel flavor. It is sometimes used in beverages and certain baked goods. Because of its high and variable moisture content, turbinado sugar is not recommended as a substitute for granulated or brown sugar.

Sanding sugar has a large, coarse crystal structure that prevents it from dissolving easily. It is used almost exclusively for decorating cookies and pastries.

Granulated sugar is the all-purpose sugar used throughout the kitchen. The crystals are a fine, uniform size suitable for a variety of purposes. **Sugar cubes** are formed by pressing moistened granulated sugar into molds and allowing it to dry. Most cubes are used for beverage service.

Brown sugar is simply regular refined cane sugar with some of the molasses returned to it. Light brown sugar contains approximately 3.5 percent molasses; dark brown sugar contains about 6.5 percent. **Molasses** adds moisture and a distinctive flavor. Brown sugar can be substituted for refined sugar, measure for measure, in any formula where its flavor is desired. Because of the added moisture, brown sugar tends to lump, trapping air into pockets. Always store brown sugar in an airtight container to prevent it from drying and hardening.

Superfine or castor sugar is granulated sugar with a smaller-sized crystal. It can be produced by processing regular granulated sugar in a food processor for a few moments. Superfine sugar dissolves quickly in liquids and produces light and tender cakes.

Powdered sugar (Fr. *sucre en poudre*) or confectioner's sugar is made by grinding granulated sugar crystals through varying degrees of fine screens.

Clockwise from top left: Demerara sugar cubes; light brown sugar, powdered sugar, sugar cubes, brown sugar crystals, granulated sugar

Powdered sugar cannot be made in a food processor. It is widely available in various degrees of fineness: 10X is the finest and most common; 6X and 4X are progressively coarser. Because of powdered sugar's tendency to lump, 3% cornstarch is added to absorb moisture. Powdered sugar is most often used in icings and glazes and for decorating baked products.

LIQUID SWEETENERS

Except for leavening, liquid sweeteners can be used to achieve the same benefits as sugar in baked goods. Most of these liquids have a distinctive flavor as well as sweetness. Some liquid sweeteners are made from sugar cane; others are derived from other plants, grains or bees.

Corn syrup is produced by extracting starch from corn kernels and treating it with acid or an enzyme to develop a sweet syrup. This syrup is extremely thick or viscous and less sweet tasting than honey or refined sugar. Its viscosity gives foods a thick, chewy texture. It stabilizes products made with sugar preventing them from recrystalization. Corn syrup is available in light and dark forms; the dark syrup has caramel color and flavor added. Corn syrup is a **hygroscopic** (water-attracting) sweetener, which means it will attract water from the air on humid days and lose water through evaporation more slowly than granulated sugar. Thus, it keeps products moister and fresher longer.

Honey

Honey (Fr. *miel*) is a strong sweetener consisting of fructose and glucose. It is created by honeybees from nectar collected from flowers. Its flavor and color vary depending on the season, the type of flower the nectar came from and its age. Commercial honey is often a blend, prepared to be relatively neutral and consistent. Like corn syrup, honey is highly hygroscopic. Its distinctive flavor is found in several ethnic foods such as baklava and halvah, and beverages such as Drambuie and Benedictine.

Maple syrup is made from the sap of sugar maple trees. Sap is collected during the spring, then boiled to evaporate its water content, yielding a sweet brown syrup. One sugar maple tree produces about 12 gallons of sap each season; 30–40 gallons of sap will produce 1 gallon of syrup. Pure maple syrup must weigh not less than 11 pounds per gallon; it is graded according to color, flavor and sugar content. The more desirable products, Grades AA and A, have a light amber color and delicate flavor. Pure maple syrup is expensive, but it does add a distinct flavor to baked goods, frostings and, of course, pancakes and waffles. Maple-flavored syrups, often served with pancakes, are usually corn syrups with artificial colorings and flavorings added.

Molasses

As mentioned earlier, **molasses** (Fr. *mélasse*) is the liquid by-product of sugar refining. Edible molasses is derived only from cane sugar, as beet molasses has an unpleasant odor and bitter flavor. Unsulfured molasses is not a true by-product of sugar making. It is intentionally produced from pure cane syrup and is preferred because of its lighter color and milder flavor. Sulfured molasses is a by-product and contains some of the sulfur dioxide used in secondary sugar processing. It is darker and has a strong, bitter flavor.

The final stage of sucrose refinement yields blackstrap molasses, which is somewhat popular in the American South. Blackstrap molasses is very dark and thick, with a strong, unique flavor.

Sorghum molasses is produced by cooking down the sweet sap of a brown corn plant known as sorghum, which is grown for animal feed. The flavor and appearance of sorghum molasses are almost identical to that of unsulfured sugar cane molasses.

NUTRITION

Sweeteners are carbohydrates. They are high in calories and contain no fiber, protein, fat, vitamin A or vitamin C. They contain only trace amounts of thiamin, riboflavin and niacin.

COOKING SUGAR

Sugar can be incorporated into a prepared item in its dry form or first liquefied into a syrup. **Sugar syrups** (not to be confused with liquid sweeteners such as molasses) take two forms: **simple syrups,** which are mixtures of sugar and water, and **cooked syrups,** which are made of melted sugar cooked until it reaches a specific temperature.

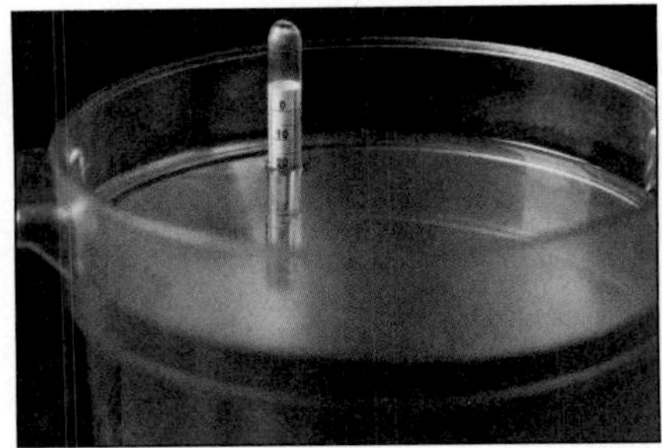

Using a Baumé hydrometer or saccharometer.

Simple Sugar Syrups

Simple or stock syrups are solutions of sugar and water. They are used to moisten cakes and to make sauces, sorbets, and beverages.

The syrup's **density** or concentration is dictated by its intended purpose. Cold water will dissolve up to double its weight in sugar; heating the solution forms denser, more concentrated syrups. A hydrometer, which measures specific gravity and shows degrees of concentration on the Baumé scale, is the most accurate guide to density. The higher the number, the greater the density of the solution.

▶ **density** the relationship between the mass and volume of a substance ($D = m/v$). For example, as more and more sugar is dissolved in a liquid, the heavier or denser the liquid will become. Sugar density is measured on the Baumé scale using a hydrometer or saccharometer.

Simple syrups can be prepared without the aid of a hydrometer, however. To make a simple sugar syrup, specific amounts of water and sugar are combined in a saucepan and brought to a boil. Once the solution boils, it is important not to stir, as this may cause recrystallization or lumping. For successful simple sugar syrups, the following formulas must be followed precisely.

- Light syrup—Boil 2 parts water with 1 part sugar for 1 minute. This concentration would measure 17°–20° on the Baumé scale. A light syrup can be used for making sorbet or moistening spongecake.
- Medium syrup—Boil 1½ parts water with 1 part sugar for 1 minute. This concentration would measure 21°–24° on the Baumé scale. A medium syrup can be used for candying citrus peel.
- Heavy syrup—Boil equal parts water and sugar for 1 minute. This concentration would measure 28°–30° on the Baumé scale, and the solution should be at 220°F (104°C). Heavy syrup is a basic, all-purpose syrup kept on hand in many bakeshops.

Cooked Sugars

Caramel sauce, meringue, buttercream, candy and other confections often need liquid sugar that will be firm when cool or have a cooked caramel flavor. For these purposes, sugar needs to be cooked to temperatures far higher than for simple syrups. A small amount of water is generally added at the beginning to help the sugar dissolve evenly. As the mixture boils, the water evaporates, the solution's temperature rises and its density increases. The syrup's concentration depends on the amount of water remaining in the final solution: The less water, the harder the syrup will become when cool.

The sugar's temperature indicates its concentration. If a great deal of water is present, the temperature will not rise much above 212°F (100°C). As water evaporates, however, the temperature will rise until it reaches 320°F (160°C), the point at which all water is evaporated. At temperatures above 320°F (160°C), the pure sugar begins to brown or caramelize. As sugar caramelizes, its sweetening power decreases dramatically. At approximately 375°F (191°C), sugar will burn, developing a bitter flavor. If allowed to continue cooking, sugar will ignite.

Preparing cooked sugar syrups and caramel.

Sugar solutions are unstable because of their molecular structure. They can recrystallize because of agitation or uneven heat distribution. To prevent recrystallization:

1. Always use a heavy, clean saucepan, preferably copper.
2. Stir the solution to make sure all sugar crystals dissolve before it reaches a boil. Do not stir the solution after it begins boiling, however.

Brushing sugar crystals from the side of the pan.

3 An **interferent** may be added when the solution begins to boil. Cream of tartar, vinegar, glucose (a monosaccharide) and lemon juice are known as interferents because they interfere with the formation of sugar crystals. Some formulas specify which interferent to use, although most are used in such small quantities that their flavor cannot be detected.

4 Brush down the sides of the pan with cold water to wash off crystals that may be deposited there. These sugar crystals may seed the solution, causing more crystals (lumps) to form if not removed. Instead of using a brush to wash away crystals, the pan can be covered for a few moments as soon as the solution comes to a boil. Steam will condense on the cover and run down the sides of the pan, washing away the crystals.

The concentration of sugar syrup should be determined with a candy thermometer that measures very high temperatures. If a thermometer is not available, use the traditional but less accurate ice-water test: Spoon a few drops of the hot sugar into a bowl of very cold water. Check the hardness of the cooled sugar with your fingertips. Each stage of cooked sugar is named according to its firmness when cool—for example, soft ball or hard crack. Table 28.2 lists the various stages of cooked sugar and the temperature for each. Each stage is also identified by the ice-water test result. Note that even a few degrees makes a difference in the syrup's concentration.

Soft ball stage.

Hard ball stage.

Hard crack stage.

SAFETY ALERT

Be extremely careful when working with hot sugar syrups. Because sugar can be heated to very high temperatures, these syrups can cause severe burns. Do not touch liquefied or caramelized sugar with your bare hand until it has cooled completely.

FATS

Fat is the general term for butter, margarine, lard, shortening and oil. Fats provide flavor and color, add moisture and richness, assist with leavening, help extend a product's shelf life and shorten gluten strands, producing tender baked goods.

The flavor and texture of a baked good depends on the type of fat used and the manner in which it is incorporated with other ingredients. In pastry doughs,

Table 28.2 STAGES OF COOKED SUGAR

STAGE	TEMPERATURE	ICE-WATER TEST—ONE DROP:
Thread	236°F (113°C)	Spins a 2-in. (5-cm) thread when dropped
Soft Ball	240°F (116°C)	Forms a soft ball
Firm Ball	246°F (119°C)	Forms a firm ball
Hard Ball	260°F (127°C)	Forms a hard, compact ball
Soft Crack	270°F (132°C)	Separates into a hard, but not brittle, thread
Hard Crack	300°F (149°C)	Separates into a hard, brittle sheet
Caramel	338°F (170°C)	Liquid turns dark brown in the pan

solid fat shortens or tenderizes the gluten strands; in bread doughs, fat increases loaf volume and lightness; in cake batters, fat incorporates air bubbles and helps leaven the mixture. Fats should be selected based on their flavor, melting point and ability to form emulsions. See Table 28.3.

Most bakeshop ingredients combine completely with liquids; fats do not. Fats will not dissolve but will break down into smaller and smaller particles through mixing. With proper mixing, these fat particles are distributed, more or less evenly, throughout the other ingredients, causing fat and liquid to blend or emulsify.

Butter and Margarine

Butter is prized in the bakeshop for its flavor; however, it melts at a relatively low temperature of approximately 93°F (33°C) and burns easily. Unsalted butter is preferred for baking because it tends to be fresher, and additional salt might interfere with product formulas. Margarine melts at a slightly higher temperature than butter, making it useful for some rolled-in doughs such as puff pastry or Danish. Because they require higher temperatures to melt, margarine and other vegetable-based shortenings can leave a greasy taste on the tongue. For detailed information on butter and margarine, see Chapter 6, Dairy Products.

Lard

Lard (Fr. *saindoux*) is rendered pork fat. It is a solid white product of almost 100 percent pure fat; it contains only a small amount of water. Lard yields flaky, flavorful pastries, such as pie crusts, but is rarely used commercially because it turns rancid quickly.

Lard

Shortenings

Any fat is a **shortening** in baking because it shortens gluten strands and tenderizes the product. What is generally referred to as shortening, however, is a type of solid, white, generally flavorless fat, specially formulated for baking. Shortenings are made from animal fats and/or vegetable oils that are solidified through hydrogenation. These products are 100% fat with a relatively high melting point. Solid all-purpose shortening is ideal for greasing baking pans because it is flavorless and odorless. When substituting shortening in a formula calling for butter, additional liquid must be added to compensate for the lack of moisture in the shortening.

Emulsifiers may be added to regular shortening to assist with moisture absorption and retention as well as leavening. **Emulsified shortenings,** also known as high-ratio shortenings, are used in the commercial production of cakes and frostings when the formula contains a large amount of sugar. If a formula calls for an emulsified shortening, use it. If you substitute any other fat, the product's texture suffers.

Table 28.3 MELTING POINT OF FATS*

Fat	Melting point
Butter, whole	92°F–98°F (33°C–36°C)
Butter, clarified	92°F–98°F (33°C–36°C)
Cocoa butter	88°F–93°F (31°C–34°C)
Lard	89°F–98°F (32°C–36°C)
Margarine, solid	94°F–98°F (34°C–36°C)
Shortening, all-purpose vegetable	120°F (49°C)
Shortening, emulsified vegetable	115°F (46°C)
Shortening, heavy-duty fryer	97°F–107°F (36°F–42°C)

*The melting point of any fat depends on its specific ratio of fatty acids, its intended use and its manufacturer. Natural products such as butter and lard will vary more from one lot to the next than will manufactured products such as margarine or shortening. (This information was obtained from a variety of manufacturers and assumes that the fat is pure and previously unused.)

Oil

Unlike butter and other fats, **oil** blends thoroughly throughout a mixture. It therefore coats more of the proteins, and the gluten strands produced are much shorter, a desirable result in fine-textured products such as muffins or chiffon cakes. For baking, select a neutral-flavored oil unless the distinctive taste of olive oil is desired, as in some breads. Never substitute oil in a formula requiring a solid shortening. For detailed information on oil, see Chapter 5, Flavors and Flavorings.

THICKENERS

STARCHES

Starches are often used as thickening agents in bakeshop products. Cornstarch, arrowroot and flour can be used as thickeners for pastry creams, sauces, custards and fruit fillings. **Cornstarch** is a grain-based starch. It must be dissolved in cold water, then added to the mixture to be thickened and then heated. Once it reaches just below the boiling point it must be cooked until it thickens into an opaque gel. Products thickened with cornstarch should not be vigorously stirred once cooled or they can break down and soften. Products thickened with cornstarch tend to separate when thawed after freezing.

Pearl Tapioca

Arrowroot is dissolved in cold water and added to a liquid to thicken it. Used primarily to thicken hot sauces, arrowroot can break down if overcooked, making it most appropriate for thickening sauces that will be served immediately.

Although less commonly encountered in professional bakeshops, tapioca can be used to thicken a variety of pastry products. **Tapioca** is a starch produced from the root of the tropical cassava (manioc) plant. It is available as a flour or as balls, referred to as pearls. Tapioca flour can be used in the same manner as cornstarch to thicken sauces and fruit mixtures. Pearl tapioca is used to thicken milk for tapioca pudding or to thicken fruit pie fillings. Most pearl tapioca must be soaked in a cold liquid for several hours before cooking. Instant tapioca, which is smaller, needs to soak for only 20 to 30 minutes before cooking.

GELATIN

One of the most commonly used thickeners in the bakeshop is **gelatin,** a natural product derived from collagen, an animal protein. It is available in two forms: granulated gelatin and sheet (also called leaf) gelatin. A two-step process is necessary to use either form: The gelatin must first be softened in a cold liquid, **bloomed,** then dissolved in a hot liquid.

▶ **bloom** to soften granulated gelatin in a cold liquid before dissolving and using

Granulated gelatin is available in bulk or in ¼-ounce (7-gram) envelopes (slightly less than 1 tablespoon). One envelope is enough to set 1 pint (500 milliliters) of liquid into a firm gel for aspic or decorating, or 3 cups (720 milliliters) of liquid into a softer mousse consistency. Granulated gelatin should be softened in four times its weight of cold liquid for at least five minutes, then heated gently to dissolve. The initial softening in a cold liquid is necessary to separate the gelatin molecules so that they will not lump together when the hot liquid is added. Melting over a double boiler prevents scorching.

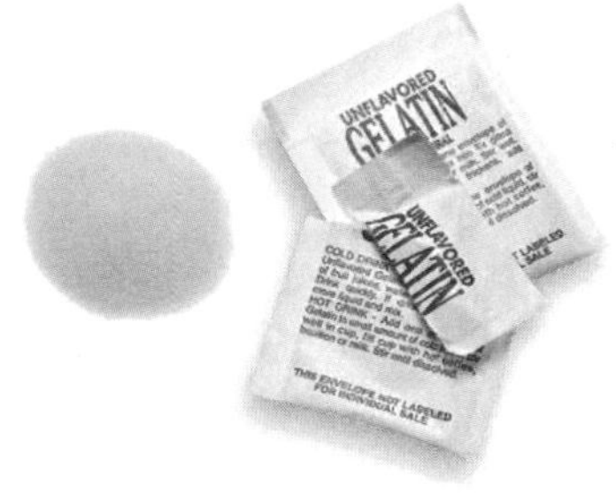

Granulated Gelatin

Sheet or **leaf gelatin** is available in 1-kilogram boxes, sometimes further packaged in envelopes containing five or six sheets. The sheets are produced in varying thicknesses and weights; the average weighs about ⅒ ounce (3 grams) per sheet. They must be separated and soaked in ice water until very soft, at least 15 minutes. They are then removed from the water, squeezed to remove excess moisture and stirred into a hot liquid until completely dissolved. When sheet gelatin is added to a hot liquid it is not necessary to melt it first.

▶ PROCEDURE FOR USING SHEET GELATIN

1 Gelatin sheets are submerged in ice water for several minutes to soften.

2 Softened gelatin sheets are then removed from the ice water and incorporated into a hot liquid.

Granulated and sheet gelatin can be substituted weight for weight in any formula. Sheet gelatin, though more expensive, is preferred for its lack of flavor and color. It also tends to dissolve more readily and evenly and has a longer shelf life than the granulated form. Once incorporated into a product such as a Bavarian, gelatin can be frozen, or melted and reset once or twice, without a loss of thickening ability. Because it scorches easily, gelatin and mixtures containing gelatin should not be allowed to boil. Products thickened with gelatin, such as mousse or custard, can become rubbery after a few days in the refrigerator.

FLAVORINGS

Many flavoring ingredients are used in the bakeshop. Practically any herb, spice, beverage or extract can be used to give baked goods, creams and confections their characteristic flavors. As with all baking ingredients, select flavoring components for overall quality and freshness, and combine flavorings carefully to achieve a balanced, good-tasting finished product. Recommendations for bakeshop uses for herbs and spices can be found in Chapter 5, Flavors and Flavorings.

EMULSIONS AND EXTRACTS

Emulsions and extracts are liquid flavoring agents derived from various flavoring oils (**essential oils**) taken from fruits, beans, spices or seeds.

▶ **essential oils** pure oils extracted from the skins, peels and other parts of plants used to give their aroma and taste to flavoring agents in foods, cosmetics and other products

Emulsions are flavoring oils mixed into water with the aid of emulsifiers. Lemon and orange are the most common emulsions. Emulsions are much stronger than extracts and should be used carefully and sparingly. **Extracts** are mixtures of flavoring oils or essential oils and ethyl alcohol. Vanilla, almond and lemon are frequently used extracts. An extract may be made with pure flavoring oils or with artificial flavors and colors. Contents are regulated by the FDA, and package labels must indicate any artificial ingredients. Emulsions and extracts are highly volatile. They should be stored in sealed containers in a cool area away from direct light.

VANILLA

Vanilla (Fr. *vanille*) is the most frequently used flavoring in the bakeshop. It comes from the pod fruit, called a bean, of a vine in the orchid family. Vanilla beans are purchased whole, individually or by the pound. They should be soft and pliable, with a rich brown color and good aroma. The finest vanilla comes from Tahiti and Madagascar.

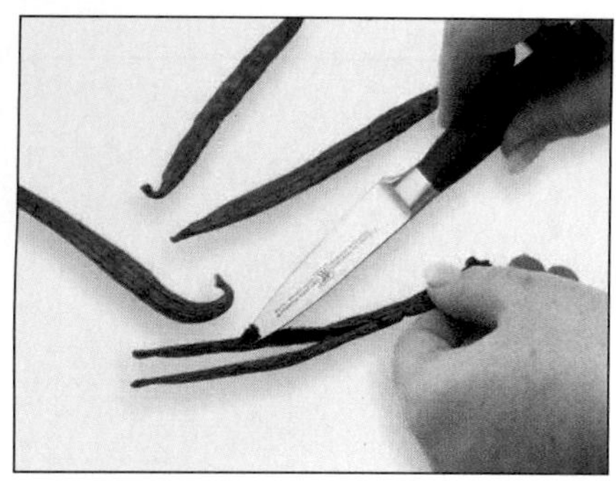

Scraping seeds from the interior of a vanilla bean.

To use a vanilla bean, cut it open lengthwise with a paring knife. Scrape out the moist seeds with the knife's tip and stir them into the mixture being flavored. The seeds do not dissolve and will remain visible as small black or brown flecks. After all the seeds have been removed, the bean can be stored in a covered container with sugar to create vanilla sugar. Because the intensity of vanilla extract varies, it is difficult to recommend an equivalent in vanilla beans. Generally, ½ fluid ounce (15 milligrams) vanilla extract can be substituted for 1 vanilla bean; however, taste should be the ultimate guide.

Vanilla beans should be stored in an airtight container in a cool, dark place. During storage, the beans may develop a white coating. This is not mold, but rather crystals of vanilla flavor known as vanillin. It should not be removed.

Pure vanilla extract is an easy and less expensive way to give bakeshop products a true vanilla flavor. It is dark brown and aromatic, and comes in several strengths referred to as folds. The higher the number of folds, the stronger the flavor of the extract. Any product labeled "vanilla extract" must not contain artificial flavorings and must be at least 35 percent alcohol by volume. Vanilla extract should be stored at room temperature in a closed, opaque container. It should not be frozen.

Artificial or imitation vanilla flavoring is made with synthetic **vanillin.** Artificial flavoring is available in a clear form, which is useful for white buttercreams in which the dark brown color of pure vanilla extract would be undesirable. Although inexpensive, artificial vanilla is, at best, weaker and less aromatic than pure extract. It can also impart a chemical or bitter taste to foods.

CHOCOLATE

Chocolate is one of the most popular flavorings—perhaps the most popular—for candies, cookies, cakes and pastries. Chocolate is also served as a beverage and is an ingredient in the traditional spicy Mexican mole sauce. Chocolate is available in a variety of forms and degrees of sweetness.

CHOCOLATE PRODUCTION

Chocolate (Fr. *chocolat*) begins as yellow fruit pods dangling from the trunk and main branches of the tropical cacao tree. A native species of the Amazon rainforest, the cacao tree is found in the Caribbean, parts of Africa, Asia and Latin America. Each pod contains about 40 almond-sized cocoa beans. After the pods ripen, the beans are placed in the sun for several days to dry and ferment. While time-consuming, this process helps develop the aroma and essential oils in the beans. They are then cleaned, dried, cured and roasted to develop flavor and reduce bitterness. Next, the beans are crushed to remove their shells, yielding the prized chocolate **nib.**

Cocoa Beans

Like coffee beans, chocolate beans are blended to the specifications of the chocolate manufacturer to obtain the desired flavor and aroma of their end product, a trade secret closely guarded unless the finest beans are used. Nibs are shipped to manufacturers worldwide where they can be further roasted. They are crushed into a thick (nonalcoholic) paste known as **chocolate liquor** or **chocolate mass.** Chocolate mass contains about 53 percent fat, known as **cocoa butter.** The chocolate mass is further refined depending on the desired product. If **cocoa powder** is to be produced, virtually all the cocoa butter is removed. Adding more cocoa butter, sugar, milk solids and flavorings to the chocolate mass creates a variety of other products. Most manufacturers of fine chocolates use the Swiss technique of **conching** to increase smoothness. Conching involves stirring large vats of blended chocolate with a heavy granite roller or paddle to smooth out sugar crystals and mellow the flavor, a process that may last from 12 hours to 3 days.

▶ **conching** stirring melted chocolate with large stone or metal rollers to create a smooth texture in the finished chocolate

TASTING CHOCOLATES

There are three types of cocoa beans: a very hardy, abundant African variety used as a base bean, and two flavorful, aromatic varieties used for flavor. Unlike wine or coffee, it is difficult to taste processed chocolate and tell which beans were used. Most chocolates are blends, created by their manufacturer to be unique yet consistent. Varietal chocolates, those made from one type of bean grown in one specific area, have become trendy, though expensive, for both chocolate bars and baking chocolates.

Roasting greatly affects the final flavor of chocolate. Generally, German and Spanish manufacturers use a high (or strong) roast; Swiss and American makers use a low (or mild) roast.

Refining is also a matter of national taste. Swiss and German chocolate are the smoothest, followed by English chocolates. American chocolate is noticeably grainier.

FROM CACAO TO CHOCOLATE CHIPS

To understand the history of chocolate, a chef or chocoholic must first understand the fundamental difference between its original use as a beverage and its later transformation into a candy.

The cacao tree (called *Theobroma cacao,* meaning "food of the gods") originated in the river valleys of South America and was carried into what is now Mexico by the Mayans before the seventh century A.D. It was cultivated by Mayans, Aztecs and Toltecs not only as a source of food but also as currency. Chocolate was consumed only as a treasured drink. Cacao beans were roasted, crushed to a paste and steeped in water, then thickened with corn flour to create a cold, bitter beverage. Sometimes honey, vanilla or spices, including chiles, were added. The Aztec emperor Montezuma was so enamored with the beverage that he reportedly consumed 50 cups at each meal.

Columbus brought cacao beans to Spain from his fourth voyage to the New World in 1504. (The common term *cocoa* is actually a western European mispronunciation of the proper term *cacao,* caused by confusion with another New World delicacy, the coconut.) But almost 20 years passed before Spanish conquistadors, led by Cortez, understood the beans' value. With Montezuma's encouragement, Cortez and his soldiers slowly acquired a taste for the bitter beverage, spurred on by the intoxicating effects of caffeine.

Cortez's most important contribution to the history of chocolate was to take beans with him when he left Mexico. He planted them on the islands he passed on his return to Spain: Trinidad, Haiti and Fernando Po, from which the giant African cocoa industry grew. Through Cortez's far-sighted efforts, Spain controlled all aspects of the cocoa trade until well into the 18th century.

The Spanish began drinking chocolate at home during the 16th century. It was usually mixed with two other expensive imports, sugar and vanilla, and frothed with a carved wooden swizzle stick known as a *molinet.* This thick, cold drink was made from tablets of crushed cocoa beans produced and sold by monks. The Spanish believed that cocoa cured all ills and supplied limitless stamina. In the early 17th century, cocoa beverages, now served hot, crept into France via royal marriages.

Cocoa spread through the rest of Europe by different routes. The Dutch, who had poached on Spanish trade routes for many years, eventually realized the value of the unusual beans they found on Spanish ships. Holland soon became the most important cocoa port outside Spain. From there, a love of cocoa spread to Germany, Scandinavia and Italy. In 1655, England acquired Jamaica and its own cocoa plantations.

Chocolate Chef, sculpted by Pastry Chef Rubin Foster

Until the Industrial Revolution, cocoa was made by hand using mortar and pestle or stone-grinding disks to crush the cocoa nibs. By the 1700s, cocoa factories had opened throughout Europe. James Baker opened the first cocoa factory in the United States in 1765.

Conrad van Houten, a Dutch chemist, patented "chocolate powder" in 1825. His work marked the beginning of a shift from drinking to eating chocolate. It also paved the way for everything we know as chocolate today. Van Houten developed a screw press that removed most of the cocoa butter from the bean, leaving a brown, flaky powder, essentially the same substance as modern cocoa powder.

Eventually, it was discovered that the extra cocoa butter resulting from the production of cocoa powder could be added to ground beans to make the paste more malleable, smoother and more tolerant of added sugar. The English firm of Fry and Sons introduced the first eating chocolate in 1847. Their recipe was the same then as today: crushed cocoa beans, cocoa butter and sugar.

In 1876, Swiss chocolatier Daniel Peter invented solid milk chocolate using the new condensed milk created by baby food manufacturer Henri Nestlé. Pennsylvania cocoa manufacturer Milton Hershey introduced his milk chocolate bars in 1894, followed by Hershey's Kisses in 1907. Nestlé Foods introduced the chocolate chip, perfect for cookies, in 1939.

Chocolate quality is actually the product of several factors besides flavor. All of the following factors should be evaluated when selecting chocolates:

1. Appearance—color should be even and glossy, without any discoloration
2. Smell—should be chocolaty with no off-odors or staleness
3. Break—should snap cleanly without crumbling
4. Texture—should melt quickly and evenly on the tongue

TYPES OF CHOCOLATE

Unsweetened chocolate is pure hardened chocolate liquor without any added sugar or milk solids. It is frequently used in baking and is sometimes referred to as "baking chocolate." Unsweetened chocolate is approximately 53 percent cocoa butter and 47 percent cocoa solids. Its flavor is pure and chocolatey, but the absence of sugar makes it virtually inedible as is.

Clockwise from lower left: semisweet chips, disks of chocolate liquor, block of bittersweet chocolate, block of milk chocolate, disks of white chocolate, alkalized cocoa powder

Both **bittersweet** and **semisweet chocolates** contain at least 35 percent chocolate liquor plus additional cocoa butter, sugar, flavorings and sometimes emulsifiers. Generally, semisweet chocolate will be sweeter than bittersweet chocolate, but there are no precise definitions, so flavor and sweetness will vary from brand to brand. Both are excellent eating chocolates and can usually be substituted measure for measure in any formula.

Couverture (koo-vehr-TYOOR) refers to high-quality chocolate containing at least 32 percent cocoa butter. Professional chocolatiers generally prefer couverture chocolate, which has a higher fluidity than other chocolates when melted. It is available in a range of flavors, such as bittersweet, semisweet and milk chocolate. Couverture has a glossy appearance and can be used to create a thin, smooth coating on confections and pastries.

MELTING CHOCOLATE

Two important rules for melting chocolate:

1. Chocolate must never exceed 120°F or there will be a loss of flavor.
2. Water—even a drop in the form of steam—must never touch the chocolate.

When a droplet of water enters melted chocolate, the chocolate becomes lumpy (a process called *seizing*). There must be a minimum of 1 tablespoon water per ounce of chocolate to keep this from happening.

If seizing does occur, the addition of fat such as vegetable shortening, clarified butter, or cocoa butter will somewhat restore the chocolate to a workable condition.

For melting chocolate, unlined copper is the traditional "chocolate pot" because it is so responsive to changes in temperature. Aluminum or heatproof glass also works well. Ideally, chocolate should be heated to 120°F, the point at which all the different fat fractions in the cocoa butter are melted.

When melting chocolate or cocoa butter, temperatures exceeding 120°F adversely affect the flavor. There are many acceptable methods for melting dark chocolate. If the heat source does not exceed 120°F it is fine to add the dark chocolate in large pieces and leave it to melt unmonitored. When the heat source is capable of bringing the chocolate over 120°F, however, the chocolate should be finely chopped or grated to ensure uniformity of melting. The chocolate must be carefully watched and stirred to avoid overheating. If using a double boiler, water in the lower container should not exceed 140°F and the upper container should not touch the water. The chocolate should be stirred constantly.

Milk and white chocolate must always be stirred frequently while melting because they contain milk solids which seed (lump) if left undisturbed.

Remove chocolate from the heat source when it reaches 115°F as the temperature may continue to rise, and stir vigorously to prevent overheating and to distribute the cocoa butter evenly.

Always melt chocolate uncovered as moisture could condense on the lid, drop back in the chocolate, and cause seizing.

—ROSE LEVY BERANBAUM, *The Cake Bible*

Government standards require that **sweet chocolate** contain not less than 15 percent chocolate liquor and varying amounts of sugar, milk solids, flavorings and emulsifiers. As the name implies, sweet chocolate is sweeter, and thus less chocolatey, than semisweet chocolate.

Milk chocolate is the favorite eating chocolate in the United States. It contains sugar, vanilla, perhaps other flavorings and, of course, milk solids. The milk solids that make the chocolate milder and sweeter than other chocolates also make it less suitable for baking purposes. Do not substitute milk chocolate for dark chocolate in any product that must be baked, as the milk solids tend to burn. If melted slowly and carefully, milk chocolate can be used in glazes, mousses or candies.

Dutch-Processed Cocoa Powder (left) and American-Style Non-Alkalized Cocoa Powder

Chocolate chips are drops of chocolate available in count sizes from 14 to 160 per ounce, (the average chips are 800 to 1000 per pound). They are easy additions to cookies, muffins and cakes. Like the larger **chocolate chunks,** chips are available in many flavors including white chocolate, butterscotch, peanut butter and fruit flavors. **Pistoles** or **calets** are small round pieces of chocolate, often the finest couverture, designed to eliminate the need for chopping chocolate in the bakeshop—especially useful when tempering.

Cocoa powder is the brown powder left after the fat (cocoa butter) is removed from cocoa beans. It does not contain any sweeteners or flavorings and is used primarily in baked goods. Alkalized or Dutch-processed cocoa powder has been treated with an alkaline solution, such as potassium carbonate, to raise the powder's pH from 5.5 to 7 or 8. Alkalized powder is darker and milder than nonalkalized powder and has a reduced tendency to lump. Either can be used in baked goods, however.

Chocolate Pistoles

Cocoa Butter

Chocolate liquor is approximately 53 percent fat, known as **cocoa butter.** Cocoa butter has long been prized for its resistance to rancidity and its use as a cosmetic. Cocoa butter has a very precise melting point, just below body temperature. Fine chocolatiers use high percentages of cocoa butter to give their chocolates melt-in-the-mouth quality.

White Chocolate

This ivory-colored substance is not the product of an albino cocoa bean. It is actually a confectionery product that does not contain any chocolate solids or liquor. (Thus it is usually labeled *white confectionery* or *coating* in the United States.) The finest white chocolate couverture contains a minimum of 31% cocoa butter, a maximum of 55% sugar, 20% milk solids, vanilla or other flavors. Other products replace all or part of the cocoa butter with vegetable oils. These confectionery products will be less expensive than those containing pure cocoa butter, but their flavor and texture will be noticeably inferior. White chocolate melts at a lower temperature than dark chocolate and burns easily. It is excellent for mousses, sauces, and candy making but is less often used in baked products.

Imitation Chocolate or Chocolate-Flavored Coating

A less-expensive product substituted in many prepared foods, imitation chocolate is made with hydrogenated vegetable oils instead of cocoa butter, as little as 8% defatted cocoa powder and as much as 55% sugar, plus emulsifiers, flavorings and perhaps milk solids. The resulting product melts at a higher temperature and requires no tempering. Imitation chocolates have an inferior taste and leave a waxy feel in the mouth, though when quality is no concern, they may be used in most cases when chocolate is required. Products containing imitation chocolate should be labeled "chocolate flavored."

NUTRITION

Chocolate is high in calories and fat. It contains minimal amounts of vitamin A and trace amounts of other vitamins as well as some sodium, phosphorus, potassium and other minerals.

TO TEMPER OR NOT TO TEMPER

The number-one mystique that surrounds chocolate has to do with tempering. From the dessert maker and pastry chef's point of view, I take a radical position: I do not think it is necessary or practical to temper. But what are we talking about anyway?

Briefly, tempering is a process of slowly raising and lowering the temperature of melted chocolate, stirring constantly, until the complex fat crystals in the cocoa butter stabilize and "behave" in concert with each other. At a cool room temperature, chocolate that has been tempered will dry rapidly to a hard and shiny piece that breaks with a snap. It shrinks slightly as it dries, enabling it to release easily from a mold. A tempered chocolate piece keeps at room temperature for months without losing its luster or snap. Any bar of chocolate that you purchase to eat or to melt has been tempered. Once melted or exposed to heat, however, it loses its temper, though it can be retempered.

Chocolate that is melted but not tempered will dry slowly, at room temperature, to a soft, almost cakey texture. It will stick inside a mold. Untempered chocolate "blooms"—that is, it becomes dull and streaky, or it takes on a mottled appearance—unless it is refrigerated immediately.

Candy makers almost always temper the chocolate they use. But dessert chefs have little need to temper. There is no reason to temper the chocolate used in cake and torte batters, buttercreams, and most ganaches. The same is true for mousses, custards, and creams. Chocolate that will be stored in the refrigerator or consumed quickly need not be tempered. Chocolate glazes, properly handled, do not require tempering to remain shiny for the short life of the dessert.

—ALICE MEDRICH, *Cocolat: Extraordinary Chocolate Desserts*

STORING CHOCOLATE

All chocolates should be stored at a cool, consistent temperature, away from strong odors and moisture. Chocolate should never be stored under refrigeration. Dark chocolate, white chocolate and cocoa powder can be kept for up to one year without loss of flavor. Milk chocolate will not keep as well because it contains milk solids.

Chocolate may develop grayish-white spots during storage referred to as **bloom.** Two types of bloom can develop on chocolate. **Fat bloom** occurs when cocoa butter crystals rise and crystallize on the chocolate's surface. Chocolate stored above 70°F (21°C) will develop fat bloom over time. Because fat bloom has no effect on taste, tempering the product will remedy the problem. **Sugar bloom** occurs when moisture collects on the surface of the chocolate and blends with the sugar in the chocolate, leaving a white sugar film. The result is a gritty chocolate that cannot be improved by tempering.

NUTS

Nuts (Fr. *noix*) provide texture and flavor to baked goods and are often substituted for all or part of the wheat flour in a pastry such as Linzer Tart or a dacquoise. A nut is the edible single-seed kernel of a fruit surrounded by a hard shell. A hazelnut is an example of a true nut. The term is used more generally, however, to refer to any seed or fruit with an edible kernel in a hard shell. Walnuts and peanuts are examples of non-nut "nuts" (peanuts are legumes that grow underground; walnuts have two kernels). Nuts are high in fat, making them especially susceptible to rancidity and odor absorption. Nuts should be stored in nonmetal, airtight containers in a cool, dark place. Most nuts may be kept frozen for up to one year.

Nuts are often roasted in a low (275°F/135°C) oven or in a sauté pan over low heat before being used in order to heighten their flavor. Allowing roasted nuts to cool to room temperature before grinding prevents them from releasing too much oil. Some nuts such as hazelnuts, pistachios, almonds, peanuts and cashews are ground into nut butters used to flavor pastries. When sweetened, nut butter is referred to as a paste, and is used to flavor chocolates, ice creams and other baked items.

Almonds

Almonds (Fr. *amande*) are the seeds of a plumlike fruit native to western India that was first cultivated by the ancient Greeks. It is now a major commercial crop in California. Almonds are available whole, sliced, slivered or ground. Blanched almonds have had their brown, textured skins removed; natural almonds retain their skins. Unless the brown color of natural almond skin is undesirable, the two types can be used interchangeably in recipes. Almonds are frequently used in pastries and candies and are the main ingredient in almond paste and marzipan.

Almond Paste

Brazil nuts (Fr. *noix du Brésil*), sometimes referred to as cream nuts, are the large, oval-shaped seeds of huge trees that grow wild in the rain forests of Central and South America. Their high oil content gives them a rich, buttery flavor and a tender texture. Brazil nuts are available both in the shell and shelled, and are eaten raw, roasted, salted and in ice creams and bakery and confectionery products.

Brazil Nuts

Cashews

Cashews (Fr. *noix de caju*), native to the Amazon, are actually the seeds of a plant related to poison ivy. Because of toxins in the shell, cashews are always sold shelled. They are expensive and have a pronounced flavor. Cashews make a wonderful addition to cookies and candies.

Chestnuts

Chestnuts (Fr. *marrons*) are true nuts that must be cooked before using. Available steamed, dried, boiled or roasted, they are often sold as a canned purée, with or without added sugar. Candied or glazed chestnuts are also available. Most chestnuts are grown in Europe, primarily Italy, but new varieties are beginning to flourish in North America. Their distinctive flavor is found in many sweet dishes and pastries.

Coconuts (Fr. *noix de coco*) are the seeds from one of the largest of all fruits. They grow on the tropical coconut palm tree. The nut is a dark brown oval, covered with coarse fibers. The shell is thick and hard; inside is a layer of white, moist flesh. The interior also contains a clear liquid known as **coconut water.** (This is not the same as **coconut milk** or **coconut cream,** both of which are prepared from the flesh.) Coconut has a mild aroma, a sweet, nutty flavor and a crunchy, chewy texture. Fresh coconuts are readily available but require some effort to use. Coconut flesh is available shredded or flaked, with or without added sugar. Coconut purée is sold as a pastry ingredient and in ethnic markets. Coconut is most often used in pastries and candies and is also an important ingredient in Indian and Caribbean cuisines. A good fresh coconut should feel heavy; you should be able to hear the coconut water sloshing around inside. Avoid cracked, moist or moldy coconuts.

Coconuts

▶ **coconut water** the thin, slightly opaque liquid contained within a fresh coconut

▶ **coconut milk** a coconut-flavored liquid made by pouring boiling water over shredded coconut; may be sweetened or unsweetened; do not substitute cream of coconut for coconut milk

▶ **coconut cream** (1) a coconut-flavored liquid made like coconut milk but with less water; it is creamier and thicker than coconut milk; (2) the thick fatty portion that separates and rises to the top of canned or frozen coconut milk; do not substitute cream of coconut for true coconut cream

▶ **cream of coconut** a canned commercial product consisting of thick, sweetened coconut-flavored liquid; used for baking and in beverages

Hazelnuts

Hazelnuts (Fr. *noisette*) are true nuts that grow wild in the northwestern and upper midwestern states. The cultivated form, known as a filbert, is native to temperate regions throughout the Northern Hemisphere. A bit larger than the hazelnut, the filbert has a weaker flavor than its wild cousin. Both nuts look like smooth brown marbles. Filberts are more abundant, so are generally less expensive. Their distinctive flavor goes well with chocolate and coffee.

Hazelnut Paste

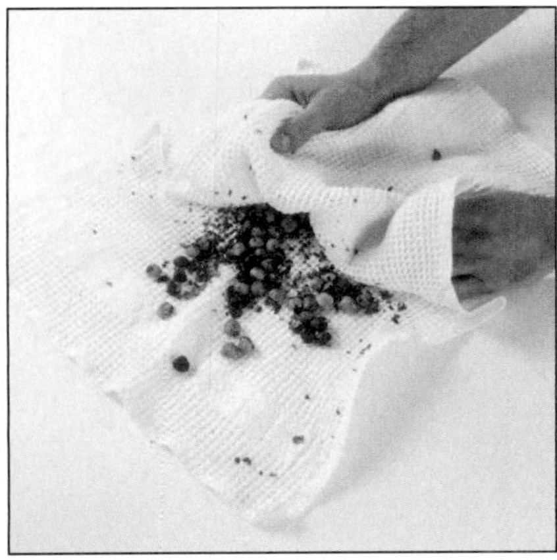

Rubbing toasted hazelnuts with a towel to remove the skin.

To remove the hazelnut's skin, roast whole nuts in a 275°F (135°C) oven for 12 to 15 minutes. They should give off a good aroma and just begin to darken. While they are still hot, rub the nuts in a dry towel or against a mesh sifter to remove the skin.

Hazelnut paste (Fr. *praline*) is a smooth composition made from finely ground roasted hazelnuts and sugar. It is used to flavor creams, chocolates and icings. Gianduja (zhahn-DOO-yah) refers to chocolate blended with hazelnut paste. It is used as a filling or in candies.

Macadamias

Macadamia nuts are small, round, creamy white nuts with a sweet, rich flavor and high fat content, native to Australia. The shell is extremely hard and must be removed by machine, so the macadamia is always sold out of the shell. Its flavor blends well with fruit, coconut and white and dark chocolate.

Peanuts (Fr. *arachide*), also known as groundnuts, are actually legumes that grow underground. The peanut is native to South America; it made its way into North America via Africa and the slave trade. Peanuts may be eaten raw or roasted and are available shelled or unshelled, with or without their thin red skins. Peanuts are ubiquitous ground with a bit of oil into peanut butter.

Peanuts

Pecans (Fr. *noix de pacane*), native to the Mississippi River Valley, are perhaps the most popular nuts in America. Their flavor is rich and mapley and appears most often in breads, sweets and pastries. They are available whole in the shell or in various standard sizes and grades of pieces.

Pine nuts (Fr. *pignon*), also known as piñon nuts and pignole, are the seeds of several species of pine tree. The small, creamy white, teardrop-shaped nuts are commonly used in pastries from Spain, Italy and the American Southwest. They are rarely chopped or ground because of their small size, and will need roasting only if being used in a dish that will not receive further cooking.

Pecans

Pine Nuts

Pistachios (Fr. *pistaches*) are native to central Asia, where they have been cultivated for more than 3000 years. California now produces most of the pistachios marketed in this country. Pistachios are unique for the green color of their meat. When ripe, the shell opens naturally at one end, aptly

Pistachios

referred to as "smiling," which makes shelling the nuts quite easy. Red pistachios are dyed, not natural. Pistachios are sold whole, shelled or unshelled, and are used in pastries and confections.

Walnuts (Fr. *noix*), relatives of the pecan, are native to Asia, Europe and North America. The black walnut, native to Appalachia, has a dark brown meat and a strong flavor. The English walnut, now grown primarily in California, has a milder flavor, is easier to shell and is less expensive. Walnuts are more popular than pecans outside the United States. They are used in baked goods and are pressed for oil.

English Walnuts

► Measuring Ingredients

The precise, accurate measurement of ingredients is extremely important for bakeshop products. As a result, baking formulas often use weight, even for liquid ingredients. Measuring ingredients by weight is more accurate and, once the basic procedures are mastered, it will be faster than measuring by volume. It is also important to remember that most foods do not weigh their volume. In other words, 1 cup of flour equals 8 fluid ounces of flour (a measure of volume) but it does not contain 8 ounces of flour by weight. For best results, use the measurement specified in each recipe. Because accurate weights are so important, balance scales are commonly employed in the bakeshop. Procedures for using these scales are shown in Chapter 7, Mise en Place.

► Mixing Methods

A critical step in the production of all baked goods is the mixing of ingredients. The techniques used to mix or combine ingredients affect the baked good's final volume, appearance and texture. Mixing distributes ingredients evenly. Mixing activates the proteins in wheat flour, causing the formation of the elastic structure called gluten. Mixing incorporates air (**aerates**) into a mixture to help it rise and develop a light texture when baked. Different mixing methods ensure that ingredients are combined in the proper order to achieve the desired results.

► **aerate** to incorporate air into a mixture through sifting and mixing

There are several mixing methods—**beating, blending, creaming, cutting, folding, kneading, sifting, stirring** and **whipping.** (See Table 28.4.) Learn the differences among these mixing methods, then use the designated method with the appropriate equipment or tool to ensure a good-quality finished product.

Baked goods are made from doughs and batters. A **dough** has a low water content. The water-protein complex known as gluten forms the continuous medium into which other ingredients are embedded. A dough is usually prepared by beating, blending, cutting or kneading and is often stiff enough to cut into various shapes.

A **batter** generally contains more liquids, fat, and sugar than a dough. Gluten development is minimized and liquid forms the continuous medium in which other ingredients are dispersed. A batter bakes into softer, moister products. A batter is usually prepared by blending, creaming, stirring or whipping and is generally thin enough to pour.

Table 28.4 **MIXING METHODS**

METHOD	PURPOSE	EQUIPMENT
Beating	Vigorously agitating foods to incorporate air or develop gluten	Spoon or electric mixer fitted with a paddle
Blending	Mixing two or more ingredients until evenly distributed	Spoon, rubber spatula, whisk or electric mixer fitted with a paddle
Creaming	Vigorously combining fat and sugar while incorporating air	Electric mixer fitted with a paddle on medium speed
Cutting	Incorporating solid fat into dry ingredients only until lumps of the desired size remain	Pastry cutters, fingers or electric mixer fitted with a paddle
Folding	Very gently incorporating ingredients such as whipped cream or whipped eggs with dry ingredients, a batter or cream	Rubber spatula or balloon whisk
Kneading	Working a dough to develop gluten	Hands or electric mixer fitted with a dough hook; if done by hand, the dough must be vigorously and repeatedly folded and turned in a rhythmic pattern
Sifting	Passing one or more dry ingredients through a wire mesh to remove lumps and combine and aerate	Rotary or drum sifter or mesh strainer
Stirring	Gently mixing ingredients by hand until evenly distributed and blended	Spoon, whisk or rubber spatula
Whipping	Beating vigorously to incorporate air	Whisk or electric mixer fitted with a whip

▶ THE BAKING PROCESS

Many changes occur in a dough or batter as it bakes. A pourable liquid solidifies into a tender, light cake; a sticky mass becomes chewy cookies; a soft, elastic dough becomes firm, crusty French bread. These physical changes are the result of the ingredients used, the mixing methods employed and the effect of heat applied during the baking process. Namely, gases form and are trapped within the dough or batter; starches, proteins and sugars cook; fats melt; moisture evaporates and staling begins.

By learning to control these changes, the student baker also learns to control the final product. Control can be exerted in the selection of ingredients and the methods by which those ingredients are combined, as well as the baking temperature and duration. Batters and dough pass through nine stages during and after the baking process.

GASES FORM

A baked good's final texture is determined by the amount of leavening or rise that occurs both before and during baking. This rise is caused by the gases present in the dough or batter. These gases are carbon dioxide, air and steam. See Table 28.5. Air and carbon dioxide are present in doughs and batters before they are heated. (Air may be incorporated during the mixing process. Carbon dioxide is released as a by-product of leaveners used in the mixture.) Other gases are formed when heat is applied. For example, steam is created as the moisture in a dough is heated; yeast and baking powder rapidly release additional carbon dioxide when placed in a hot oven. These gases then expand and leaven the product.

Table 28.5 **LEAVENING AGENTS IN BAKED GOODS**

LEAVENING AGENT	PRESENT IN:
Air	All products, especially those containing whipped eggs or creamed fat
Steam	All products when liquids evaporate or fats melt
Carbon dioxide	Products containing baking soda, baking powder, baking ammonia or yeast

GASES ARE TRAPPED

The stretchable network of proteins created in a batter or dough, either egg proteins or gluten, traps gases in the product. Without an appropriate network of proteins, the gases would just escape without causing the mixture to rise.

STARCHES GELATINIZE

Starches are complex carbohydrates present in plants and grains such as potatoes, wheat, rice and corn. Flour made from these and other grains is the primary ingredient in most baked goods. When starch granules in a batter or dough reach a temperature of approximately 140°F (60°C), they absorb additional moisture—up to 10 times their own weight—and expand. This contributes to the baked good's structure.

PROTEINS COAGULATE

Gluten and dairy and egg proteins begin to coagulate (solidify) when the dough or batter reaches a temperature of 160°F (71°C). This process provides most of the baked good's structure.

Proper baking temperatures are important for controlling the point at which proteins coagulate. If the temperature is too high, proteins will solidify before the gases in the product have expanded fully, resulting in a product with poor texture and volume. If the temperature is too low, gases will escape before the proteins coagulate, resulting in a product that may collapse.

FATS MELT

As fats melt, steam is released and fat droplets are dispersed throughout the product. These fat droplets coat the starch (flour) granules, thus moistening and tenderizing the product by keeping the gluten strands short. Shortenings melt at different temperatures. It is important to select a fat with the proper melting point for the product being prepared.

WATER EVAPORATES

Throughout the baking process, the water contained in the liquid ingredients will turn to steam and evaporate. This steam is a useful leavener. As steam is released, the dough or batter dries out starting from the outside and the result is the formation of a crust.

SUGARS CARAMELIZE

As sugars are heated above 320°F (160°C), they caramelize, adding flavor and causing the product to darken. Caramelization of sugars is responsible for most of the flavors associated with baked goods. Because high temperatures are required for caramelization, most foods will brown only on the outside and only through the application of dry heat.

CARRYOVER BAKING

The physical changes in a baked good do not stop when it is removed from the oven. The residual heat contained in the hot baking pan and within the product itself continues the baking process as the product cools. This is why a crisp-style cookie or biscuit may be soft and seem a bit underbaked when removed from the oven; it will finish baking as it cools.

STALING

Staling is a change in a baked good's texture and aroma caused by both moisture loss and changes in the structure of the starch granules. Stale products have lost their fresh aroma and are firmer, drier and more crumbly than fresh goods.

Staling is not just a general loss of moisture into the atmosphere; it is also a change in the location and distribution of water molecules within the product. This process, known as **starch retrogradation,** occurs as starch molecules cool, becoming more dense and expelling moisture.

▶ **starch retrogradation** the process whereby starch molecules in a batter or dough lose moisture after baking; the result is baked goods that are dry or stale

In breads, this moisture migrates from the interior to the drier crust, causing the crust to become tough and leathery. If the product is not well wrapped, moisture will escape completely into the surrounding air. In humid conditions, unwrapped bread crusts absorb moisture from the atmosphere, resulting in the same loss of crispness. The flavor and texture of breads can be revived by reheating them to approximately 140°F (60°C), the temperature at which starch gelatinization occurs. Usually, products can be reheated only once without causing additional quality loss.

The retrogradation process is temperature dependent. It occurs most rapidly at temperatures of approximately 40°F (4°C). Therefore, baked products should not be refrigerated unless they contain perishable components such as cream fillings. It is better to store products frozen or at room temperature, as long as food safety is not of concern.

Products containing fats and sugars, which retain moisture, tend to stay fresh longer. Commercial bakeries usually add chemical emulsifiers, modified shortening or special sweeteners to retard staling, but these additives are not as practical for small-scale production.

CONCLUSION

Of the many stations of the kitchen, the bakeshop often requires the most conscientious attention to detail. The correct use of flour, thickeners, sugar, fat, chocolate and other flavorings is essential. During preparation and baking, doughs and batters go through many physical changes. One of the most important is the development of gluten, the elastic network of wheat proteins created when doughs and batters are prepared, which gives baked goods body and structure. Student chefs should understand the changes baked goods undergo and learn to control or adjust them as needed.

QUESTIONS FOR DISCUSSION

1. What is the importance of protein in flour for bread making? Name the general types of flours available and their different uses in the bakeshop.
2. Discuss the four functions of sugar and sweeteners in baked goods.
3. Many varieties of fat and shortening are available to today's baker and pastry chef. Discuss which fats are preferred for various bakeshop applications.
4. Use the Internet to locate a U.S. producer of European-style pastry ingredients. What type of flavorings and nut products do they produce and market?
5. Discuss the various mixing methods and the tools used.
6. What elements in baked goods make them rise?
7. List and describe the nine steps in the baking process.
8. Explain what process causes staling. List the ways to minimize staling of breads and cakes.

CHAPTER TWENTY-NINE

I WANT ORDER AND TASTE.
A WELL DISPLAYED MEAL
IS ENHANCED ONE HUNDRED PER CENT
IN MY EYES.

—Marie-Antoine Carême,
French chef (1783–1833)

PLATE PRESENTATION

AFTER STUDYING THIS CHAPTER, YOU WILL BE ABLE TO:

- understand the basic principles of plate presentation
- use a variety of techniques to add visual appeal to plated foods

Finally, the real test has come. It is time to put down the spatula and set the whisk aside. The food must be served. But it is important that the creativity and skill that went into cooking, baking or otherwise preparing the foods are not wasted because of a sloppy presentation or an unattractive setting.

While food preparation is very much a science, food presentation is an art. Good plate presentation results from careful attention to the colors, shapes, textures and arrangements of the foods. Great plate presentation requires experience and style.

This chapter describes several methods of presenting foods. For every guideline suggested, there are exceptions. Nor are these examples meant to take the place of more traditional techniques. They are intended only to spark the imagination. With experience, a chef's personal style will evolve. The final step in food preparation is to justify the hours of hard work spent cooking the food by serving and presenting it properly.

Service is the process of delivering the selected foods to diners in the proper fashion. Hot foods should be served very hot and on heated plates; cold foods should be served very cold and on chilled plates. Foods should be cooked to the proper degree of doneness: A roast rack of lamb ordered medium rare should be medium rare—not medium, not rare. Pasta should be served al dente—slightly chewy, not mushy. Bread should be fresh, not stale. Portion sizes should be appropriate. First courses and appetizers should be small enough so that the diner can still appreciate the courses that follow.

Presentation is the process of offering the selected foods to diners in a fashion that is visually pleasing. When presenting foods, always bear in mind that diners consume first with their eyes and then with their mouths. The foods must be pleasantly and appropriately colored, cut or molded. The colors, textures, shapes and arrangements of all foods must work together to form a pleasing composition on the plate. Any decorative touches such as the manipulation of sauces or the addition of garnishes should be done thoughtfully and well. Most important, plates should be neat and clean. Inspect all plates before they leave the kitchen; wipe fingerprints, drops of sauce or specks of food from their rims with a clean towel.

Presentation techniques are divided here into two broad categories: those applied to specific foods and those applied to the plate as a whole. Most of the techniques and concepts described here are illustrated with foods or recipes that appear elsewhere in the text.

▶ THE FOOD

The most attractive foods will always be the ones that are properly prepared, but they can be made even more attractive by cutting or molding them into various shapes. Both of these techniques preserve the integrity of the food; that is, neither changes the food itself, but only changes the way the food is presented.

PREPARING FOODS PROPERLY

Foods look best when prepared properly. A sirloin steak grilled medium rare should be pink inside; its surface should glisten and be branded with well-defined and neatly executed crosshatch marks. When serving asparagus with hollandaise, the stalks should be bright green and crisp looking; the hollandaise sauce should be smooth and shiny, not grainy and dingy. A lemon meringue pie should be attractively browned on top; the filling should be a true lemony yellow and the crust golden brown and without cracks.

Whether a recipe calls for browning foods under a salamander before service, poaching a galantine of chicken wrapped in cheesecloth to maintain its shape or adding vinegar when braising red cabbage, proper cooking procedures can enhance the texture, shape and color of many cooked foods. Throughout this text, we have discussed the proper cooking procedures for many, many foods. Use them.

CUTTING FOODS

The careful cutting of foods often increases their visual appeal and reflects the chef's attention to detail. Here we distinguish between cutting foods to decorate the plate and cutting the foods to be consumed. Decorative garnishes such as tomato and radish roses, scallion brushes, watermelon boats and the like fall within the former category. Cutting foods into beautiful garnishes is an art unto itself, requiring skill and practice. Although beyond the scope of this text, books on creating food garnishes are listed in the Bibliography.

Fried Julienned Red Beets

The latter category includes the meats, poultry, fish, shellfish, vegetables and starches that are the meal. Each should be carefully cut. Vegetables can be cut into uniform shapes and sizes such as julienne, bâtonnet or tournée. Firm vegetables such as beets, carrots, leeks, lotus root, parsnips, potatoes, scallions and turnips can be sliced or julienned and deep-fried to add color, flavor and texture to a plated dish.

If serving sliced meats or poultry, the slices should be of an even thickness; fish can be cut into tranches. Individual stew ingredients and soup or salad garnishes should be of uniform sizes. All these techniques are simple, fundamental and effective.

Fried Julienned Carrots

Some foods take the shape of the pan in which they are cooked. Polenta and gratin or escalloped potatoes, for example, can be presented attractively when baked in and removed from individual casseroles, or they can be baked in a hotel pan and then cut into various shapes.

Fried Julienned Leeks

GARNISHES (AN ADMITTEDLY CRANKY ADMONITION)

I am a strong believer in the simple, edible garnish that has a close flavor kinship to the dish. In my world, dyed daikon flamingos, writhing carrot dragons, and blinking Christmas lights in the empty eye sockets of a stir-fried lobster—all garnishes of the Hong Kong sort—are out. So, too, are radish flowers, tomato rosettes, and vegetable pellets sculpted to look like suppositories. I find all of this loathsome.

In my own rather minimalist style, the fanciest I get is an occasional scallion brush. Otherwise, a leggy piece of coriander or a flourish of scallion rings are all that our already colorful dishes require. Or, if the dish is green, a confetti of finely diced red bell pepper will do the job.

The issue is a visible one, but it needs to make sense on your tongue. A garnish is primarily designed to tickle the eye, but it also should meld seamlessly with the other flavors on the plate or contrast with them in a meaningful way.

Garnishing the rims of plates—a current feature of trendy restaurants in the 90s—is something I find very peculiar. I spill and splatter my own food quite nicely, thank you, and don't want the kitchen to do it for me.

Ditto the rage for a whole chive aloft each appetizer or a cage of spun sugar looming above a dessert. It is admittedly wonderful to give a little height to a dish: One can arrange cold shrimp, for example, in a lively tumble with just a touch or two. But the unrelated vertical garnish is often absurd, a bit of Dr. Seuss on the plate.

I sound cranky, and perhaps I am! Restaurant cooks frequently spend too much time decorating their food, and too little time paying attention to its taste. This, I think, is sad.

—Barbara Tropp, *China Moon Cookbook*

Fried Sliced Lotus Root

Fried Julienned Sweet Potato

Fried Julienned Potatoes

▶ PROCEDURE FOR CUTTING POLENTA

Cutting polenta into various shapes.

1. Cook the polenta according to the recipe. When it is done, pour it onto a well-oiled half-sheet pan. Then chill it until firm.
2. Once the polenta is firm, flip the pan over onto a worktable. Lift off the pan; the polenta will come out easily. Using a chef's knife or circular cutters, cut the polenta into the desired shape. The polenta can be sautéed or grilled for service.

▶ PROCEDURE FOR CUTTING GRATIN OR ESCALLOPED POTATOES

Cutting potatoes with a circular cutter.

1. Select a recipe that produces a firm finished product so that the finished dish will hold its shape after cutting.
2. Bake the potatoes in a well-greased pan and refrigerate until cold and firm. Then cut the potatoes into various shapes with a chef's knife or circular cutters and remove them to a clean pan with a spatula.
3. For service, reheat the potatoes in a 325°F (160°C) oven until hot.

MOLDING FOODS

Some foods, particularly grains or vegetables bound by sauces, can be molded into attractive shapes by using metal rings, circular cutters or other forms. These molded forms create height and keep the plate neat and clean.

▶ PROCEDURE FOR MOLDING GRAINS

1. Fill a timbale, soup cup or other mold of the appropriate size and shape with the hot grains, firmly pressing them together.
2. For à la carte service, immediately unmold the grains onto the serving plate by placing the mold upside down on the plate and tapping its rim.
3. For banquet service, place the filled molds in a hotel pan and refrigerate until needed. Shortly before service, fill the hotel pan with hot water to a point about two-thirds up the side of the molds. Be careful not to splash any water onto the grains. Cover the pan with foil and place in the oven. Heat until the grains are hot, then plate as desired.

Unmolding a timbale of rice.

▶ PROCEDURE FOR MOLDING VEGETABLES

1 Position a ring mold on the plate and fill it with the vegetables. Press the foods into the ring to help them hold the shape. Level the top.

2 Carefully lift off the ring.

Many soft and creamy savory or sweet foods can be molded into small ovals such as for the dumpling-shaped quenelle discussed in Chapter 26, Charcuterie. Purées and mousses such as mashed potatoes, risotto and salmon mousseline as well as ice creams, custards and sorbets can be attractively shaped using two large spoons.

Forming grapefruit sorbet into a quenelle shape using two spoons.

▶ The Plate

▶ **composition** a completed plate's structure of colors, shapes and arrangements

Properly cooked, carefully cut and appropriately molded foods should not be haphazardly slapped onto a plate. Rather, choose and position the foods carefully to achieve a plate presentation with a balanced, harmonious **composition.**

The composition can be further enhanced by decorating the plate with garnishes, crumbs or sauces. Some of these techniques (for example, decorating the plate with powdered sugar) do not substantially affect the flavors of the foods; they only make the completed presentation more attractive. Other techniques (for example, garnishing a dessert with finely chopped nuts or painting a plate with two sauces) add flavor and texture to the finished dish.

CHOOSING PLATES

Restaurant china designed to withstand the rigors of repeated use is available in many different shapes, sizes, colors and styles. It is often the chef's responsibility to choose the china appropriate for the food being served. Frequently, specific plates will be used for specific dishes, such as a tulip sundae glass for an ice cream dish.

SIZES AND SHAPES

Most plates are round, but oval plates (also referred to as platters) and rectangular, square and triangular plates are becoming more common. Plates are available in a variety of sizes from a small 4-inch (10-centimeter) bread plate to a huge 14-inch (35-centimeter) charger or base plate. Plates are typically concave; their depths vary within a limited range of about 1 inch (2.5 centimeters). Most plates have rims; rim widths also vary. Soup bowls can be rimmed or rimless. Soup plates are usually larger and shallower than soup bowls and have wide rims. Soup cups are also available. There are also dozens of plate designs intended for a specific purpose, such as plates with small indentations for holding escargots, or long, rectangular plates with grooves for holding asparagus.

Chewy Date Bars with Caramel Ice Cream

Choose plates large enough to hold the food comfortably without overcrowding or spilling. Oversized, rimmed soup plates are popular for serving any food with a sauce. Be careful when using oversized plates, however, as the food may look sparse, creating poor value perception.

Whether a round, oval or less conventionally shaped plate is used, be sure to choose one with a size and shape that best highlights the food and supports the composition. For example, in the photograph to the left, the rectangular dish with round corners and raised rim accentuates the geometrically simple yet effective composition of the square date bar and spherical scoop of ice cream.

COLORS AND PATTERNS

White and cream are by far the most common colors for restaurant china. Almost any food looks good on these neutral colors.

Colored and patterned plates can be used quite effectively to accent food, however. The obvious choice is to contrast dark plates with bright- or light-colored foods and light plates with dark-colored foods. The food should always be the focal point of any plate. The colors and shapes in the pattern should blend well and harmonize with the foods served. The crisp pattern of blue dots along the plate rim shown to the left, for example, harmonizes well with the beige sauce and symmetrically placed shrimp skewers.

Grilled Prawn Brochette with Butternut Squash Risotto

ARRANGING FOODS ON PLATES

Plates should be composed to make the food appetizing to the customer. Strive for a well-balanced plate composition that can be achieved with careful consideration of the shapes, colors, textures and arrangement of foods on the plate.

SHAPES

For visual interest and pure drama, combine a variety of shapes on the plate. The plate shown to the right is an excellent example of simple shapes artfully combined: ovals of evenly sliced lamb loin with cleanly cut triangles of crisp potatoes and long, thin spears of asparagus. The three very different shapes lend contrast and character to the dish.

Lamb Loin with Rösti Potatoes

COLORS

Foods come in a rainbow of colors and to the extent appropriate, foods of different colors should be presented together. Generally, the colors should provide balance and contrast. But no matter how well prepared or planned, some dishes simply have dull, boring or similar colors. If so, try adding another ingredient or garnish for a splash of color. The vivid red lobster claws and the shiny black mussel shells shown here add striking color notes to a paella dish that would otherwise be dominated by yellow rice, tan chicken, brown sausages and gray clam shells.

Paella

TEXTURES

Texture refers to the sensation perceived when eating a food as well as the appearance of the surface of the food. It may be crisp, crumbly, grainy, flaky smooth or creamy. Mashed potatoes and carrot purée both look smooth and soft Salmon mousseline and spinach soufflé both have slightly grainy surfaces. Rösti potatoes and meatloaf both appear coarse. The flavors of each food in these pairs differ; their visual textures do not.

Typically, foods with similar textures look boring together; foods with different textures look more exciting. Serve carrots cut into julienne with the mashed potatoes to achieve a balance of hard and soft textures; steamed leaf spinach with the salmon mousseline for a combination of smooth and grainy textures; and a baked potato with the meatloaf for pairing fluffy and coarse textures. These pairs generally maintain the same range of flavors as the first set of pairs while providing different visual textures.

Achieving a balance of texture on a plate can be as simple as adding a crisp garnish such as the fried julienned vegetables shown here served with a rack of lamb.

Rack of Lamb Garnished with Fried Julienned Vegetables

The cassoulet shown to the right harmoniously combines several textures in one dish: the pebbly beans, the slices of smooth slab bacon and coarse sausage and the bumpy skin of the duck leg. Indeed, the variation in textures is so dramatic and appealing that many diners may not even notice that all the principal ingredients are essentially the same color.

Cassoulet

ARRANGEMENTS

Having decided on the colors, textures and shapes of the foods that will go on the plate, the next choice is where to place each individual item to achieve a balanced and unified composition. Mostly this takes judgment and style, but there are a few general guidelines.

▶ GUIDELINES FOR ARRANGING FOODS ON A PLATE

1. Strike a balance between overcrowding the plate and leaving large gaps of space. Foods should not touch the plate rim nor necessarily be confined to the very center.
2. Choose a focal point for the plate—that is, the point to which the eye is drawn. This is usually the highest point on the plate. Design the plate with the highest point to the rear or center. Avoid placing foods of equal heights around the edge of the plate, leaving a hole in the center—the eye will naturally be drawn to that gap.

Grilled Duck with Roasted Vegetables

3 The plate's composition should flow naturally. For example, make the highest point the back of the plate and have the rest of the food become gradually shorter toward the front of the plate. Slicing and fanning foods can attract the eye and help establish flow.

The grilled duck with roasted vegetables shown here elegantly illustrates these principles. Height is established by a structure composed of the duck leg and thigh, sliced turnips and baby carrots. The structure sits toward the back of the plate. Its height, placement and striking appearance make it the focal point. The neatly sliced duck breast is then fanned across the plate in front of this focal point, drawing the viewer into the plate.

DECORATING PLATES

Using herbs to garnish a plate.

The colors, textures, shapes and arrangements of foods on a plate can be improved or highlighted by decorating a plate with herbs, greens, spices and other garnishes, baked hippen masse dough and sauces. If any of these are to be applied after the principal food is placed on the plate, be prepared to do so quickly so that the food is served at its proper temperature.

PLATE DUSTING

An attractive method for decorating dessert plates is to cover the entire plate with a dusting of powdered sugar, cocoa powder or both before placing the dessert on the plate. Use sugar on dark-colored plates and cocoa on light-colored plates. These items can be dusted onto the plate with a shaker can or sifter in a free-form fashion or into any desired pattern by using a template. The template can be a doily or a stencil placed over the plate before it is dusted.

Provided they complement the food, very finely chopped nuts can also be used to decorate plates for sweet or savory foods. Plates for savory foods can also be decorated by sprinkling them with finely chopped herbs such as thyme or minced vegetables such as a combination of brightly colored peppers.

Slicing strawberry fans to use as plate garnish.

GARNISHING PLATES WITH HERBS AND GREENS

Using fresh herbs and greens is one of the easiest ways to add color, texture and flow to a plate. Whether the herbs or greens are an ingredient in the dish or merely a decoration, they should always complement the foods and be consistent with their seasonings. A sprig of fresh rosemary garnishing a beautifully roasted rack of lamb or tiny leaves of chervil garnishing delicately poached fillets of sole are natural combinations. Sprigs of fresh green mint (often with a fresh berry or two or a strawberry cut in a fan) can be the perfect decoration for a dessert plate. Microgreens add a delicate-tasting, light and lacy garnish to many dishes.

A dessert garnished with fresh mint and berries.

Garnishing a plate with chopped fresh rosemary.

Garnishing an appetizer with microgreens.

GARNISHING PLATES WITH HIPPEN MASSE

A popular presentation technique is to pipe batters into intricate designs and then bake them to form crisp, rigid, cookielike garnishes. These garnishes are then used to create height and add texture.

SAVORY HIPPEN MASSE

RECIPE 29.1

ARIZONA BILTMORE, PHOENIX, AZ

Yield: 1 lb. (450 g)

Egg whites, room temperature	8 oz.	250 g
Wondra flour	4 oz.	120 g
Heavy cream	3 fl. oz.	90 ml
Granulated sugar	1 oz.	30 g
Salt and white pepper	TT	TT
Dried thyme, crushed	1 tsp.	5 ml

1 Lightly beat the egg whites together to blend. Stir in all the flour at once.
2 Blend in the cream, then add the remaining ingredients.
3 Strain the batter through a china cap and allow to rest for 30 minutes.
4 Lightly oil the back of a very flat sheet pan. Pipe the hippen masse onto the pan using a plastic squeeze bottle. Pipe the batter into decorative patterns appropriate for the desired plate presentation.
5 Bake at 375°F (190°C) until set and lightly browned, approximately 3 to 4 minutes. Remove from the oven, then remove the decorations from the sheet pan while still slightly warm.

Miss en place

- Bring eggs to room temperature.
- Crush thyme.
- Preheat oven to 375°F (190°C).

1 Piping the batter onto an oiled sheet pan.

2 Using the baked batter as a component when composing a plate.

DECORATING PLATES WITH SAUCES

The sauce is an integral part of most any dish: It adds flavor and moisture; it also adds color, texture and flow to the plate. A rich, glossy bordelaise or Madeira sauce pooled beneath sautéed tournedos of beef is a classic example. A chunky salsa of tomatoes, papaya and pineapple beneath a juicy piece of grilled swordfish is a more contemporary approach.

Sauces are also used in other, less traditional ways to add visual appeal. For example, if using a vinaigrette dressing for grilled foods, let the oil and vinegar separate and pool on the plate, creating the interesting effect shown here.

One or more colored sauces can also be used to paint plates. One technique is simply to drizzle or splatter the sauce onto the plate. In the photograph shown here, the sauce boldly splattered across the plate is the same rich magenta beet vinaigrette as that pooled beneath the sea bass; the plate's drama is heightened by the contrasting tomato ovals and potato spikes.

Alternatively, one or more colored sauces can be applied to a plate using squirt bottles to create abstract patterns or representational designs. Salad dressings or reduced balsamic vinegar can be artfully squirted over the entire plate to create interest and eye appeal as shown here.

Painting plates with different-colored sauces also facilitates flow and adds color. Although this technique can be used with hot sauces, it is more often used with cold sauces (such as vanilla, caramel, chocolate and fruit-flavored ones) for dessert presentations. The sauces must be thick enough to hold the pattern once it is created, and they should all be the same viscosity.

Grilled Quail with Balsamic Raspberries

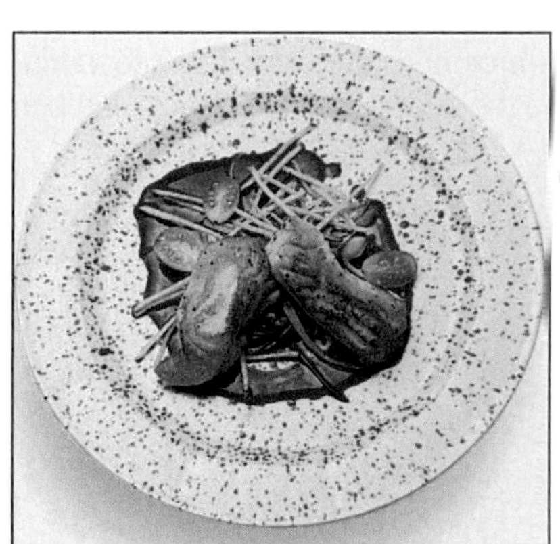

Pan-Seared Sea Bass with Beet Vinaigrette

Squirting a salad plate with a balsamic vinegar reduction.

▶ PROCEDURE FOR PAINTING A DESIGN WITH SAUCES

1 Apply the sauces to the plate in parallel lines of alternating colors.

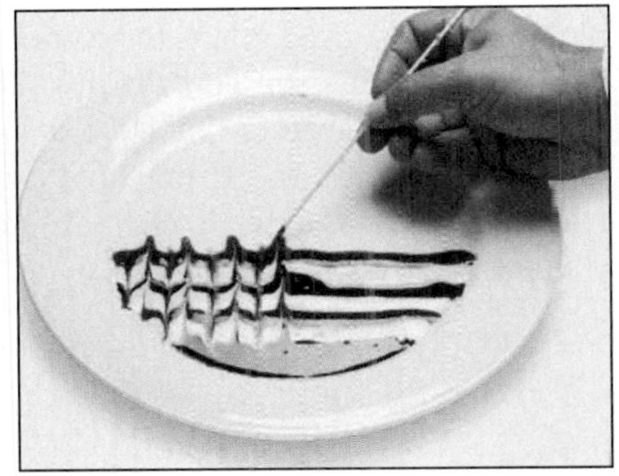

2 Carefully pull a toothpick through the sauces, perpendicular to the parallel lines in the sauces.

▶ PROCEDURE FOR PAINTING A SPIDER WEB DESIGN

1 Pool one sauce evenly across the entire base of the plate, then apply a contrasting sauce onto the base sauce in a spiral.

2 Draw a thin-bladed knife or a toothpick through the sauces from the center point toward the edge. Then, leaving a ½-inch (1.2-centimeter) space along the edge, draw a knife blade or toothpick from the edge to the center.

Other patterns can be produced by squirting the sauces onto the plate in different patterns or by pulling the knife or toothpick through the sauces in different directions. As shown below, a circle of chocolate-sauce dots in a pool of vanilla sauce is pulled to create a border of hearts.

CONCLUSION

Although the techniques described in this chapter—as well as many other techniques—can be used to create a variety of effects, often the most elegant plates are those with the simplest designs. Thoughtful presentation improves the appeal and appearance of any food as well as the completed plate, but it cannot mask poor-quality, poorly prepared or bland-tasting foods. Employing the technical skills learned in the kitchen classroom and the techniques discussed in this chapter, the student chef can create a variety of masterful plate presentations.

QUESTIONS FOR DISCUSSION

1. Explain why proper service and presentation are important in food service operations.
2. Distinguish between cutting and molding foods for visual appeal and creating garnishes out of foods.
3. How can the selection of serviceware such as bowls and platters affect the visual appeal of the foods served?
4. List and describe four techniques for garnishing plates.
5. Describe how color, texture, shape and arrangement can be used to create a well-balanced plate composition.

CHAPTER **THIRTY**

STRANGE TO SEE HOW A GOOD DINNER AND FEASTING RECONCILES EVERYBODY.

—Samuel Pepys, English artist (1633–1703), in his Diary

BUFFET PRESENTATION

THE PHOENICIAN, Scottsdale, AZ

AFTER STUDYING THIS CHAPTER, YOU WILL BE ABLE TO:

- understand the basic principles of buffet presentation
- use a variety of techniques to create and maintain appealing buffets

A buffet offers diners all the dishes from a selected menu, usually at one time, in a single, attractive setting. A buffet offers food service professionals the opportunity to exercise their creativity by identifying themes and then creating menus, displays and decorations with these themes in mind.

In this chapter, we use the word *buffet* to describe both the event at which all the dishes from a menu are served at once as well as the table on which these foods are displayed and from which diners serve themselves or are served by wait staff. Buffet foods can be virtually any of those found in this book.

PLANNING THE BUFFET

Buffets must be carefully designed to provide foods from a planned menu in an attractive fashion to a given number of people within a specified time. Doing this well requires a collaborative effort among the chef, the catering sales staff and the dining room manager, banquet manager or other senior front-of-the-house staff. Together, they identify the theme for the event and choose the menu. If the event is designed for a specific client, then the client should be invited to join in the planning.

The **theme** sets the tone of the event. It defines a motif: an elegant Sunday brunch, a black-and-white formal, a Mexican fiesta, a New England clambake. Regardless of the purpose for the event—a wedding, bar mitzvah, business luncheon, charity ball or the like—the theme defines the menu, decorations, props, linens and dinnerware; it can even define the music, lighting and wait staff uniforms. In Figures 30.1 through 30.4, we present examples of menus, decorations and buffet plans for various themed events.

Once the theme is identified, a **menu** is designed. Essentially, a lunch or dinner buffet offers an à la carte menu; the only differences are that at a buffet, the foods are presented all at once and the diners generally serve themselves or are served by wait staff stationed at the buffet table. Like an à la carte menu, the buffet menu should contain selections of first courses (soups and/or salads), entrées (hot and/or cold meat, poultry, fish and/or shellfish dishes), accompaniments (vegetables, starches and breads), desserts and beverages. Depending on the event, the menu may need to reflect particular dietary or religious concerns, such as the need for vegetarian entrées or kosher-style selections. Although costs are a consideration, the principal factors limiting a menu are the client's desires and the chef's imagination.

When planning the menu, it is important to offer dishes consistent with the theme. If the theme is a Greek wedding feast, do not offer tortilla chips and salsa. It may be necessary, however, to occasionally bend this rule in order to include one of the client's favorite foods or to offer an item not traditionally associated with the theme, such as beef at a Hawaiian luau.

It is also important to consider visual appeal and avoid repetition. Therefore:

- *Offer dishes featuring different principal ingredients.* This avoids repetition and offers diners a wider array of choices. Even fussy diners should be able to find something they want to eat. Therefore, if the buffet features two entrées, make one beef and the other poultry; if there is a third, use fish or shellfish. If there are two starch dishes, make one a pasta and the other a potato dish. Also, avoid repeating ingredients in different dishes; for example, if the entrée is a stir fry of beef and broccoli, do not offer steamed broccoli as a vegetable side dish.

KEEPING KOSHER

To one degree or another, many observant Jews keep kosher; that is, they adhere to dietary laws rooted in the Torah (the first five books of the Old Testament) and developed over the centuries by Jewish scholars. These laws (1) categorize foods and (2) define basic dietary principles.

Kosher foods—Only meat from animals that chew their cud and have split hooves can be eaten. These include cattle, goats, deer and other game; swine are not a kosher species. Poultry can be kosher, provided it is not from a bird of prey; thus, chicken, duck, goose and turkey are allowed, but hawk and eagle are not. Even if the species is kosher, the animal must still be slaughtered and butchered according to religious rules. For fish to be kosher, it must have both scales and gills; this eliminates catfish and eel, and no shellfish can be kosher. Dairy products are kosher if the species from which they come is kosher; for cheese to be kosher, it must be made without rennet. Fresh fruits and vegetables are always kosher, as are baked goods, provided they are not made with animal fats. Commercially prepared foods marked with U, K or a similar symbol (often in a circle) indicates that the food product is kosher, the producer having used appropriate ingredients and met certain standards and its facilities having been inspected and approved by a rabbi.

Kosher dietary principles—All foods are either (1) meat, (2) dairy, or (3) pareve (parve). The principal dietary rule for keeping kosher is that meat and dairy foods cannot be cooked or eaten together. Over the centuries, this rule has been refined to the point that people keeping kosher will have two sets of cooking utensils, dishes and even dishcloths, one devoted to meat, the other to dairy, so that there is no accidental mixing. Particularly observant Jews will even wait for one to six hours after eating a meat dish before consuming a dairy dish. Pareve refers to neutral (neuter) foods such as fruits, vegetables, breads, fish, eggs and certain commercially prepared foods that can be eaten with either meat or dairy items.

Not all Jews keep strictly kosher. Those who do will dine out only in a restaurant that regularly observes the same religious laws that they do at home, or in one that has been specially inspected and approved by a rabbi for the particular occasion (an option often used by catering facilities to accommodate kosher weddings, bar mitzvahs, bat mitzvahs and other Jewish celebrations). Other Jews will keep kosher by not eating any shellfish, meat, poultry or fish from nonkosher species or mixing dairy and meat, but they will not insist that separate meat and dairy cooking and eating utensils be used. They will generally dine in nonkosher restaurants, provided that the menu (sometimes referred to as "kosher-style") offers appropriate selections from kosher species.

- *Offer foods cooked by different methods.* For example, serve beef bourguignonne (a hot braised meat dish), roast turkey (a hot or cold roasted poultry dish) and salmon with dill sauce (a cold poached fish dish). Again, this avoids repetition.
- *Offer foods with different colors.* Fettuccine Alfredo and poached fish in a béarnaise sauce may both taste good, but they look boring next to each other. Offer a salsa verde or pesto instead of the béarnaise sauce, or a penne with asparagus and tomatoes in place of the Alfredo This will increase the buffet's visual appeal.

KEEPING HALAL

Similarly, many Muslims follow dietary laws based on the Qur'an (the revealed book), the Hadith (the sayings or traditions of the prophet Muhammad) and the collective wisdom of Muslim scholars. *Halal,* which means "allowed" or "lawful," refers to foods and beverages that can be consumed by observant Muslims. Foods and beverages that are *haram* are not allowed, and those that are of a questionable or suspect nature are referred to as *mushbooh.*

As all fruits and vegetables are halal, the majority of Muslim dietary laws address permitted and prohibited meats. Cooked (not raw) beef, lamb and chicken are halal, provided the animals are slaughtered and butchered according to certain rituals and methods. Fish and shellfish are also halal. Pork, game, carnivorous animals, birds of prey, carrion (the meat of animals that died of natural causes), and blood are haram, as are products derived from them. Eggs and dairy products from permitted animals are halal. as are baked goods made with ingredients from permitted animals. Any halal food contaminated with blood, pork or other haram product is deemed haram and cannot be eaten. Alcohol, whether consumed as a beverage, used as a flavoring or even present in a cleaning solution for dishes, is haram. Gelatin, emulsifiers, animal-based fats and certain dairy products are considered mushbooh unless certified as halal. Halal certification is often denoted as a capital H inside a triangle.

In food service operations, it is best if equipment dedicated solely to halal cooking is used. If this is impractical and the same equipment is used to cook halal and haram foods, the equipment must be thoroughly sanitized before it can be used for halal products. Normally, a careful visual inspection of the equipment suffices.

- *Offer foods with different textures.* If two or more soups are served, make one a clear soup and the other a cream or purée soup; use a variety of tossed and bound salads, each with different principal ingredients.
- *Offer seasonally appropriate foods.* A rich lamb stew may be easy to prepare and may hold well in a chafing dish but it is not appropriate to offer at a summer luncheon. Offer sliced grilled leg of lamb instead. This will be a lighter option.
- *Offer foods appropriate to the time of year.* Buffet menus may be planned months in advance. Consider the availability of the produce needed in the menu being offered. A fresh tomato, basil and mozzarella salad is ideal for a summer buffet but a poor choice in the winter months when hothouse tomatoes may be all that is available.

When defining the theme and creating the menu, costs must be considered. Often a client will place a limit on what he or she wants to spend for the buffet. It is then the responsibility of the chef, sales staff and/or dining room manager to create an attractive and satisfying buffet that meets this budget, while providing a reasonable profit to the food service operation. One typical method of meeting these sometimes-conflicting needs is to plan a menu that balances both high-end and less expensive items.

▶ Designing the Buffet

After the theme is set, members of the planning group should study the room, garden, patio or other space where the event will be held. They need to allocate space for the buffet table(s), the dining tables and, depending on the function, one or more bars, a dance floor, a stage for musicians, a podium for speakers, audiovisual equipment for presentations and so on. When doing so, common sense should be used: The buffet should be in an area with easy access to both the kitchen and the dining tables—neither the wait staff nor the diners should have to cross a dance floor or walk in front of a podium to get to the food. Similarly, a stage or podium should be within good sightlines of the dining tables.

Table 30.1 **STANDARD BUFFET TABLES**

SHAPE	SIZES	SIZES FOR TABLECLOTHS OR SKIRTING
Rectangle	6 feet × 30 inches	90 × 128 inches (floor length)
	8 feet × 30 inches	60 × 125 inches (lap length) or 90 × 153 inches (floor length)
Round	24-inch diameter	80-inch diameter (floor length)
	36-inch diameter	96-inch diameter (floor length)
	48-inch diameter	80-inch diameter (lap) or 108-inch diameter (floor)
	60-inch diameter	96-inch diameter (lap) or 120-inch diameter (floor)
	72-inch diameter	108-inch diameter (lap) or 132-inch diameter (floor)
Half-round	30-inch radius at 180° angle (i.e., half of a 60-inch diameter round)	160 inches of skirting
Quarter-round (wedge)	30-inch radius at 90° angle (i.e., one-quarter of a 60-inch-diameter round)	110 inches of skirting
Serpentine	Outside curve measures 8 feet, inside curve measures 4 feet, ends measure 30 inches (i.e., one-quarter of a circle's circumference)	Specialty cloths needed

DÉCOR

Linens: buffet and dining tables draped with floor-length colored linens, buffet table with a contrasting overlay; linen napkins in the same colors as the tablecloths and overlay.

Centerpieces: fresh flowers (tulips, mums, lilies and greenery).

Serviceware: polished stainless steel or brass trays and chafing dishes; ceramic bowls.

Dinnerware: white or ivory china, stainless flatware and plain stemware.

Music: none

Wait staff uniforms: bistro attire (white button-down shirts, long tie, black pants and long aprons).

KEY FOR THE BUFFET TABLE

a. Rectangular table, 8 feet x 30 inches
1. Basket of flatware rolled in linen napkins
2. Dinner plates
3. Sunset Salad
4. Raspberry Vinaigrette
5. Caesar Salad
6. Chafing dish of Vegetable Medley
7. Centerpiece
8. Chafing dish of Dauphine Potatoes
9. Sweet and Flavored Butters
10. Baskets of Rolls
11. Chafing dish of Chicken with Wild Mushroom Sauce
12. Chafing dish of Salmon Fillets
13. Dessert plates
14. Cheesecake
15. Fruit Platter
16. Sacher Torte
17. Caramel Sauce for the Cheesecake
18. Raspberry Sauce for the Sacher Torte

Note: Beverages will be in pitchers on the table and replenished by the wait staff; coffee will be offered by circulating wait staff.

SUNSET SALAD OF MIXED GREENS, CITRUS WEDGES AND CRISPY BEET FRIZZLES WITH A RASPBERRY VINAIGRETTE

CAESAR SALAD WITH HERBED CROUTONS AND SHREDDED PARMESAN

OVEN-ROASTED BREAST OF CHICKEN WITH WILD MUSHROOM SAUCE

GRILLED SALMON FILLET ON A BED OF SAUTÉED LEEKS AND GREENS

DAUPHINE POTATOES

MEDLEY OF ZUCCHINI, YELLOW SQUASH AND CARROTS

ASSORTED ROLLS WITH SWEET AND FLAVORED BUTTERS

PISTACHIO CITRUS CHEESECAKE WITH CARAMEL SAUCE

FRESH FRUIT PLATTER

SACHER TORTE WITH RASPBERRY SAUCE

ICED TEA, LEMONADE AND SPARKLING WATER
FRENCH ROAST COFFEE

A SINGLE-SIDED BUFFET TO FEED 50 PEOPLE

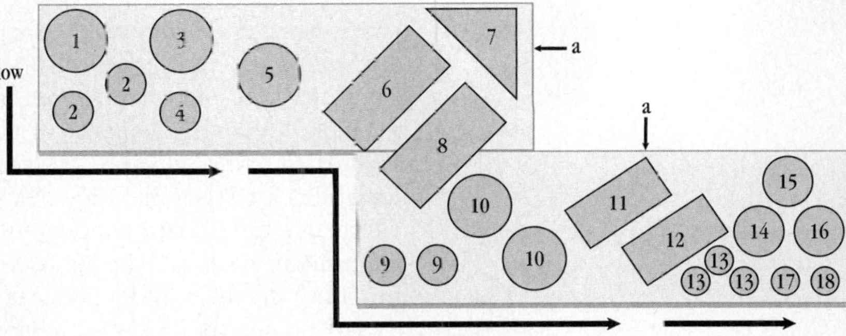

FIGURE 30.1 ▶ Business Luncheon Buffet

DÉCOR

Linens: buffet and dining tables draped in bright colors (yellow, orange, red, fuschia and/or turquoise) with overlays of brightly colored Mexican serapes; brightly-colored linen napkins tied with raffia.

Centerpieces: Large cacti in pots with raffia ties, surrounded with river rocks and sand.

Decorations: piñatas, sombreros, fresh chiles, brightly colored paper flowers, brightly colored papier maché vegetables, raffia, small potted cacti in turquoise-painted terra-cotta pots.

Serviceware: copper or beaten tin trays, copper chafing dishes, wooden or earthenware bowls and platters.

Dinnerware: brightly colored china (red, yellow and/or turquoise), hammered stainless steel flatware and Mexican green or blue glass stemware.

Music: strolling mariachi band.

Wait staff uniforms: jeans and white shirts with a colored serape over the shoulders.

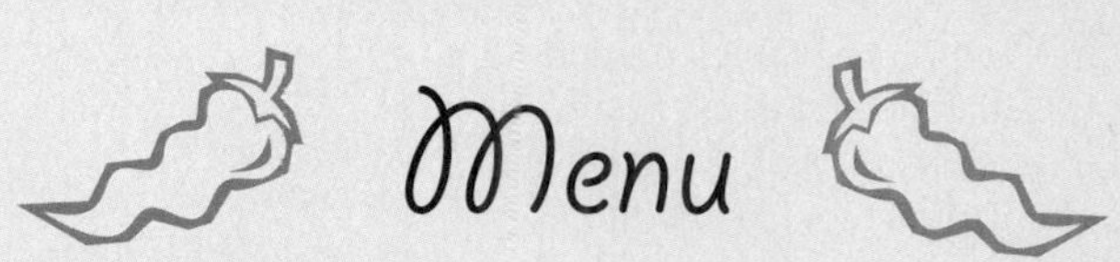

Crudités of Red and Green Bell Peppers, Carrots, Cauliflower, Broccoli, Jicama and Snap Peas with Sun-Dried Tomato Dip

Tri-colored Tortilla Chips with Fresh Tomato-Cilantro Salsa, Zesty Guacamole and Sour Cream

Warm Chorizo Chili Con Queso

Petit Blue Corn and Shrimp Tamales with Cilantro Cream

Soft Tacos of Grilled Pork Loir and Marinated Boneless Chicken Breast, Served with Ancho-Chile Honey Sauce, Tomato Cilantro Salsa, Avocado, Grated Queso Blanco and Diced Tomatoes

Goat Cheese and Green Chile Chimichangas with Roasted Habañero Sauce

Fresh Fruit Salad of Watermelon, Honeydew, Cantaloupe, Pineapple, Papaya, Berries and Grapes with Tequila Lime Splash

Mexican Celebration Cookies

Piñon Nut Tarts

Lemon Curd Tarts

Mocha Mousse Cups with Cinnamon

Fresh Roasted Mexican Coffee

Fresh Mint Lemonade, Peach Iced Tea with Lemon and Sparkling Water

Assorted Wines and Mexican Beers

FIGURE 30.2 ▶ Mexican Fiesta

Once the room's layout is determined, the chef and/or banquet or dining room manager decides on the shape of the buffet table. A buffet table is usually composed of one or more standard-sized tables grouped together in a functional and attractive shape. Standard table shapes and sizes are found in Table 30.1; arrangements of the various sizes and shapes are shown in Figures 30.1 through 30.4. The buffet table can then be draped with a floor-length linen tablecloth, or a tablecloth with a detachable skirt can be used. An alternative to standard-sized tables shrouded in linen is to use unique pieces of furniture such as cabinets, sideboards, consoles, armoires, desks or other furniture, draped with linens or not.

The number of diners is a critical consideration when determining the size, arrangement and placement of the buffet table. As a general rule, a single-sided buffet can comfortably serve 50–75 people. See Figure 30.1. If more than 100 guests are expected, the buffet should be designed with at least two service lines. See Figure 30.2. Even so, many guests will still have to wait in line, although their wait should not be excessive.

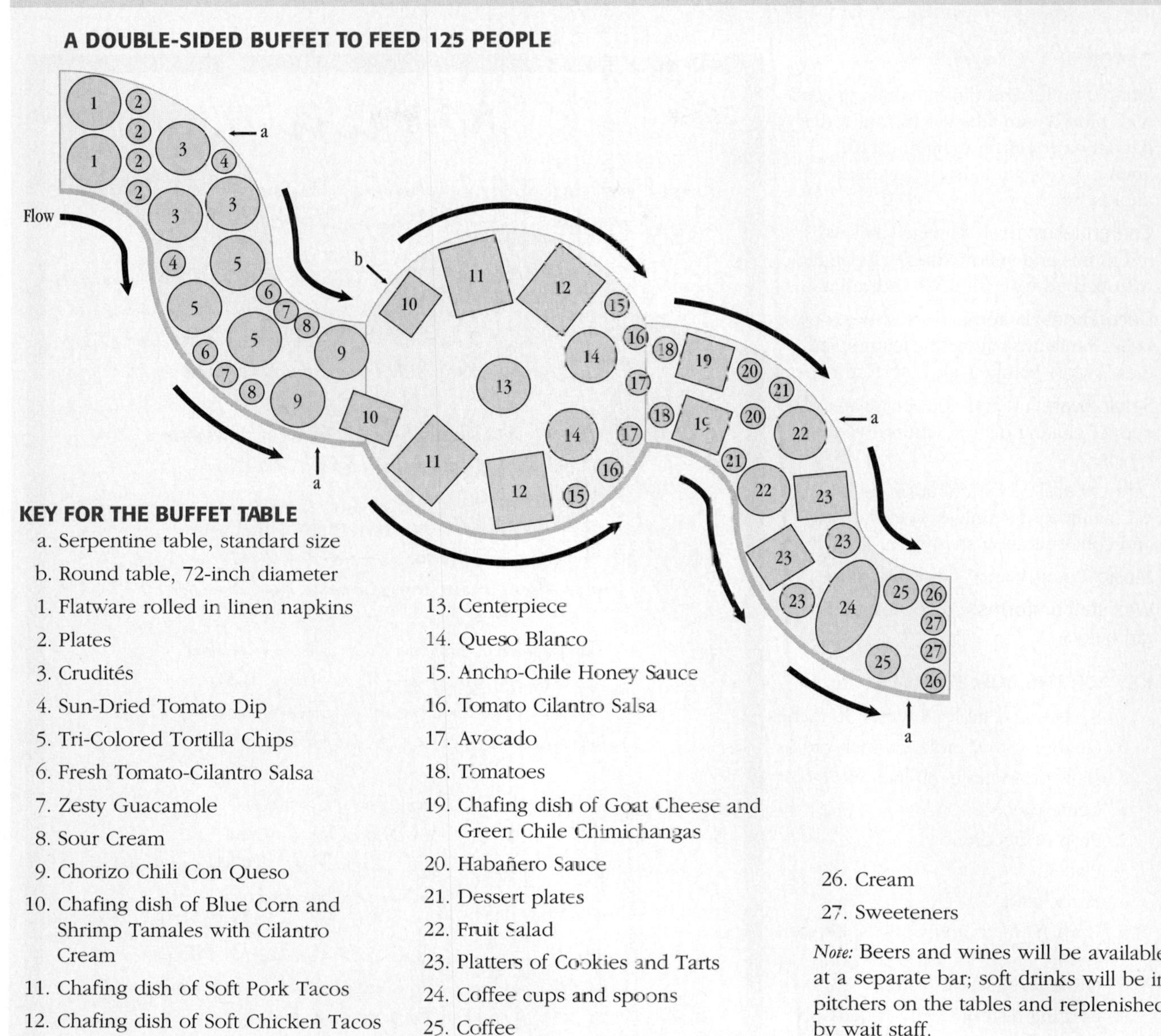

Several techniques can be used to serve large groups efficiently. One option is to use a double-sided buffet line. On a double-sided buffet, the same foods are served on both sides of the table. See Figure 30.2. All diners approach the table from the same direction and at the start of the buffet, the line is split, with half of the diners diverted to either side. Or a single-sided buffet can be divided into two, three or more zones, each of which offers the identical foods. See Figure 30.3. Either option requires that the buffet provide the diners with appropriate visual cues to recognize that the two sides of the table or two ends of the table are offering identical fare.

Another option for serving larger crowds is to divide the menu among various stations that are scattered throughout the room or series of rooms. See Figure 30.4. One station can be devoted to cold salads or to an elaborate display of cold fish and shellfish surrounding an ice sculpture. Another can be devoted to pasta prepared to order by a line cook assigned to the station; equipped with a portable gas or electric burner, the chef can finish precooked

DÉCOR

Linens: buffet and dining tables draped with blue denim tablecloths and red bandanna overlays; cobalt and red linen napkins with silver cow head napkin rings.

Centerpieces: fresh flowers (daisies, red mums and yellow lilies), decorated with barbed wire (dulled) and raffia.

Decorations: lanterns, horseshoes, cowbells, miniature hay bales, leather saddles, saddle blankets and western rope.

Serviceware: tin and copper trays and copper chafing dishes, earthenware bowls.

Dinnerware: cobalt china on tin chargers, hammered stainless steel flatware and cobalt-rimmed stemware.

Music: Country and Western band.

Wait staff uniforms: cowboy and cowgirl outfits.

Menu

Fresh Fruit Salad of Watermelon, Honeydew, Cantaloupe, Pineapple, Papaya, Mango, Berries and Grapes

Platter of Chilled Carrots, Cauliflower, Broccoli, Asparagus, Snap Peas, Bell Peppers, Eggplant, Bermuda Onions, Summer Squash and Zucchini Marinated in Flavored Oils, Seasoned with Fresh Herbs and Grilled

Chilled Corn, Tomato and Confetti Pepper Salad with Creamy Basil Dressing

Corn on the Cob Grilled in the Husk
Grilled Yukon Gold Potatoes
with Red Chile Sour Cream and Butter

Barbecued Chicken and Chile-Rubbed
Black Angus New York Strip Steak
Served with Chipotle Lime Sauce,
Southwestern Béarnaise and Flour Tortillas

Warm Blackberry Cobbler
with Vanilla Bean Ice Cream
Strawberry Rhubarb Tarts with Fresh Whipped Cream
Fudgy Homemade Brownies

Fresh Mint Lemonade and Sparkling Water
Kettle Coffee with Cream and Sweeteners
Assorted Wines and Beers

KEY FOR THE BUFFET TABLE

a. Rectangular table, 8 feet × 30 inches
b. Quarter-round table, 30-inch radius
c. Half-round table, 30-inch radius

1. Centerpiece
2. Prop or decoration
3. Plates
4. Fruit Salad
5. Corn, Tomato and Confetti Pepper Salad
6. Grilled Vegetable Platter
7. Chafing dish of Corn on the Cob
8. Chafing dish of Grilled Potatoes
9. Red Chile Sour Cream
10. Butter
11. Prop or decoration
12. Chafing dish of Barbecued Chicken
13. Flour Tortillas
14. Chafing dish of New York Strip Steak
15. Chipotle Lime Sauce
16. Southwestern Béarnaise
17. Prop or decoration
18. Dessert plates
19. Strawberry Rhubarb Tarts
20. Brownies
21. Blackberry Cobbler
22. Vanilla Bean Ice Cream

Note: Beers and wines will be available at a separate bar; soft drinks will be in pitchers on the table and replenished by the wait staff; coffee will be offered by circulating wait staff.

BUFFET DIVIDED INTO TWO ZONES TO FEED 150 PEOPLE

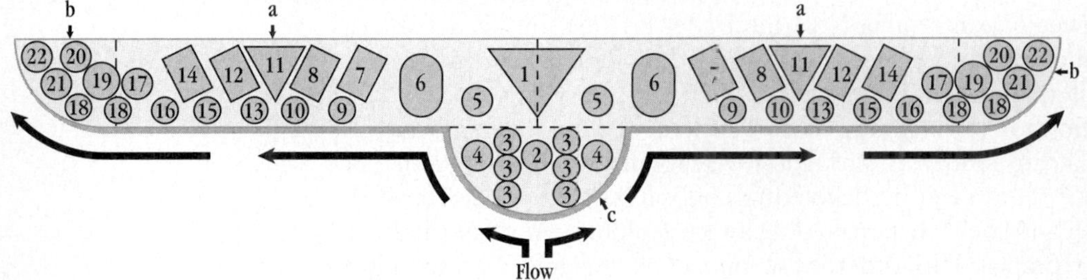

FIGURE 30.3 ▶ Western Barbecue Buffet

A small kitchen becomes the setting for an elegant and unusual brunch buffet
The Hyatt Regency Scottsdale at Gainey Ranch, Scottsdale, AZ

pasta in the diner's choice of sauce. Other stations can offer roasted meats and poultry kept warm by an infrared heat lamp and carved to order by the station chef. See Figure 30.4.

The excitement and beauty of a well-designed buffet table depends principally on two factors: (1) the arrangement of the foods on their individual serving pieces, and (2) the arrangement of the foods and decorations on the buffet table.

ARRANGING FOODS ON SERVING PIECES

The chef is responsible for determining how the foods will be arranged on their serving pieces. Most hot foods will be presented in chafing dishes, while cold or room-temperature foods are usually served on trays, platters, bowls or mirrors.

Chafing Dish

Chafing dishes are metal dishes, usually rectangular or round, with a heat source (flame or electric) located beneath, which is used to keep the foods warm; the foods are usually placed in a hotel pan or other receptacle that sits inside the chafing dish above a pan of hot water. Chafing dishes are usually covered in copper, silver or stainless steel.

Trays, platters and mirrors for presenting foods are available in four basic shapes: square, rectangle, round and oval. They come in a wide variety of materials, including metal (silver, copper, tin and steel), ceramics (china and earthenware), glass, mirrors (glass and acrylic), plastic, wood and stone (especially marble). The choice depends on the theme. Silver and mirror trays create a more formal feel at an event; ceramic and wood lend a more casual look.

Once the tray, platter, bowl or mirror is chosen, the chef must artfully arrange the food on it. When designing the presentation, the chef should consider:

1. *Height*—The eye is naturally drawn toward the highest point on a tray; typically, this will be the centerpiece. It can be a garnish or a **grosse piece.** Although it is sometimes in the center of the tray, it is more often located toward the rear, either in the middle or off to one side. Foods placed at a level higher than the centerpiece usually distract from the overall appearance.
2. *Pattern*—Whenever possible, foods should be arranged in an interesting pattern. Three different types of canapés, each chosen for contrasting

► **grosse piece** a centerpiece consisting of a large piece of the principal food offered; for example, a large wheel of cheese with slices of the cheese cascading around it

Butlered Hors d'Oeuvre

Red Potatoes with Gorgonzola, Bacon and Walnuts
Mushroom Phyllo Triangles
Popovers with Shrimp and Chive Filling
Asparagus Spears Tied with Red Pepper

Buffet

Station One

Tropical Fruit Display
Caesar Salad with Herbed Croutons and Shredded Parmesan
Salad of Bibb Lettuce and Blue Cheese with Citrus Vinaigrette
Platter of Assorted Pâtés, Galantines and Ballotines
Assorted Rolls with Sweet and Flavored Butters
Tiered Display of Imported Cheeses, including Stilton, Saint André, Port Salut, Gouda, Black Diamond Cheddar and Brie Baked in Phyllo with Apricots and Fresh Basil, Garnished with Apple Slices and Grape Clusters
Lavosh and Cracker Bread

Station Two

Antipasto of Assorted Salami, Prosciutto, Sliced Cheeses, Marinated Mushrooms and Artichokes, Olives, Roasted Peppers and Wedges of Melon Wrapped with Prosciutto
Penne with Fresh Tomatoes and Basil Tossed with Extra Virgin Olive Oil
Cheese-Filled Tortellini with Wild Mushroom Alfredo Sauce
Pastas Prepared to Order by the Chef
Wheel of Parmesan
Focaccia, Garlic Twists, Breadsticks and Assorted Rolls
Sweet and Flavored Butters

Station Three

Herb-Rubbed, Grilled Tenderloin of Beef Carved by the Chef with Béarnaise Sauce and Sage-Merlot Sauce
Assorted Rolls with Sweet and Flavored Butters
Chicken Satay with Chile Peanut Sauce
Grilled Swordfish with Tomatillo Sauce

Station Four

Three-Tiered Wedding Cake
bottom layer — Black Forest
middle layer — White Cake with White Chocolate Mousse, Strawberries and Chocolate Ganache
top layer — Carrot Cake
Petits Fours
Fruit Tartlets
Chocolate-Dipped Strawberries
French Roast Coffee and Hot Tea with Deluxe Condiments

Assorted Beers, Alcoholic Beverages, Still and Sparkling Wines, Sparkling Water and Soft Drinks

DÉCOR

Linens: buffet and dining tables draped with floor-length ivory linens with overlays of tulle and lace, accented with gold ribbons and tassels, linen napkins tied with ribbons and tassels and decorated with flowers.

Centerpieces: fresh flowers (calla lilies, white orchids, roses, tulips, ivy and greenery) and candles (votives, pillars or hurricanes) wrapped in ivy.

Serviceware: fancy silver and mirror trays, silver chafing dishes, china or glass bowls.

Dinnerware: ivory gold-rimmed china on gold chargers, silver flatware and gold-rimmed stemware.

Music: harpist, violinist or quartet.

Wait staff uniforms: tuxedos.

FIGURE 30.4 ▶ Formal Wedding Buffet

A FOUR-STATION BUFFET (INCLUDING TWO STAFFED BY CHEFS) TO FEED 200 PEOPLE

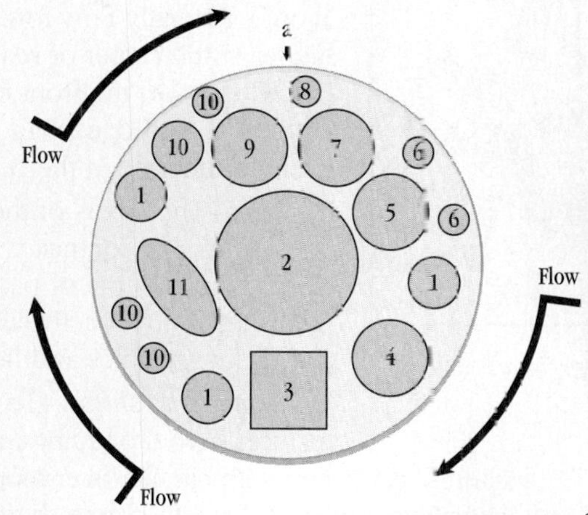

KEY FOR STATION ONE:

a. Round table, 72-inch diameter
1. Salad plates
2. Centerpiece
3. Tropical Fruit Display
4. Caesar Salad
5. Basket of Rolls overflowing onto the table
6. Sweet and Flavored Butters
7. Bibb Lettuce Salad
8. Citrus Vinaigrette
9. Platter of Pâtés, Galantines and Ballotines
10. Baskets of Lavosh and Cracker Breads
11. Tiered Cheese Display

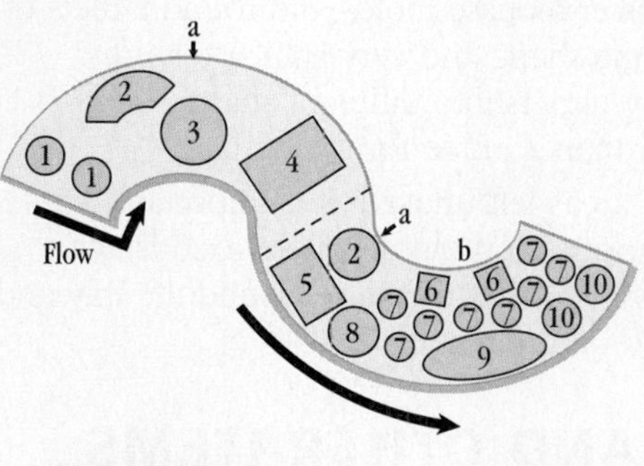

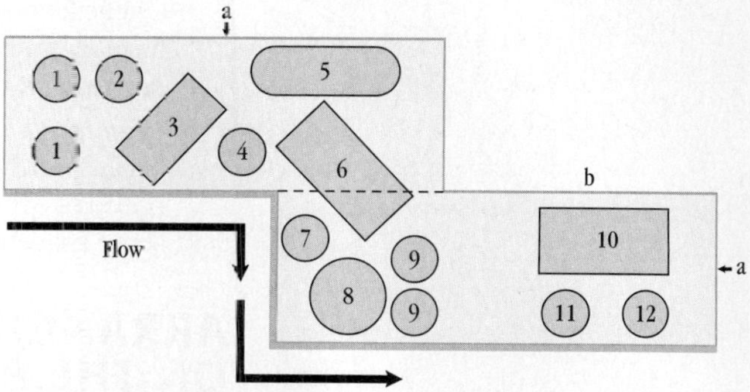

KEY FOR STATION TWO:

a. Serpentine table, standard size
b. Chef's station
1. Plates
2. Centerpiece
3. Antipasto
4. Chafing dish of Penne Pasta
5. Chafing dish of Cheese Tortellini
6. Induction burners for chef
7. Garnishes for the pastas made to order, including mushrooms, grilled chicken, walnuts, peas, roasted bell peppers and shrimp, and sauces for the pasta, including Alfredo and tomato basil
8. Large hollowed wheel of Parmesan
9. Basket of Focaccia, Garlic Twists, Breadsticks and Assorted Rolls
10. Sweet and Flavored Butters

KEY FOR STATION THREE:

a. Rectangular table, 6 feet x 30 inches
b. Chef's station
1. Plates
2. Decoration or prop
3. Chafing dish of Swordfish
4. Tomatillo Sauce
5. Centerpiece
6. Chafing dish of Chicken Satay
7. Chile Peanut Sauce
8. Basket of Assorted Rolls
9. Sweet and Flavored Butters
10. Carving station with heat lamp for the Tenderloin of Beef
11. Sage-Merlot Sauce
12. Béarnaise Sauce

KEY FOR STATION FOUR:

a. Round table, 48-inch diameter
b. Serpentine table, standard size
1. Three-Tiered Wedding Cake
2. Cake and dessert plates
3. Petits Fours
4. Fruit Tartlets
5. Chocolate-Dipped Strawberries
6. Tray of coffee mugs
7. Carafe of hot water with assorted tea bags
8. Urn of regular coffee
9. Garnishes for coffee including raw sugar cubes, artificial sweeteners, cream, whipped cream, candied citrus peel, mint swizzle sticks, cinnamon sticks, rock-sugar sticks and chocolate shavings
10. Urn of decaffeinated coffee

Note: Soft drinks as well as assorted wines, beers and other alcoholic beverages will be available at a separate bar; sparkling water, assorted wines and champagne will be served by the wait staff.

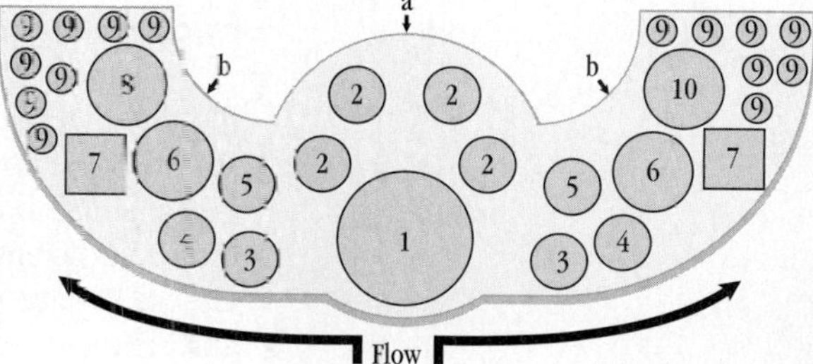

A Variety of Canapés Displayed on a Silver Tray

shapes, colors and textures, can march across a mirrored surface in alternating lines. Crudités can flow from baskets, hollowed squashes or bell peppers. Spirals of different pâtés can swirl around one another. Foods should generally flow toward the diner. Stack foods higher in the center or rear of the tray so that they cascade toward the front or edges. (Trays that are higher around all the edges than in the center tend to draw the eye into the hole in the center.)

3 *Color*—The colors of the principal foods should complement or contrast with each other. If they cannot (for example, a tray of pâtés or cheeses), they should be garnished with attractively contrasting colored foods such as fruits, vegetables and herbs.

4 *Texture and shape*—Try to use a variety of shapes and textures. Avoid building trays with circular slices of galantine garnished with circular liver mousse molds and round tartlets of a vegetable purée; all have the same shape and very similar textures. Instead, try molding the mousse or tartlets into different shapes or preparing a vegetable salad rather than a purée for the tartlets.

5 *Negative space*—This refers to the areas left unused. It is important because the space enhances the appeal of the object it surrounds and prevents overcrowding. Try leaving a border of space around the tray and some space within clusters of food on the platter.

ARRANGING FOODS AND OTHER ITEMS ON THE BUFFET TABLE

When designing the shape of the buffet table, the chef and/or banquet or dining room manager must also consider how the various foods, centerpieces and props will be laid out on the table. Besides color, height, shape and texture, they should consider the following:

1 *Flow*—Regardless of whether a single buffet table, a main buffet table with one or more stations or only stations are used, the foods should be placed in a logical order that affords the diner the chance to construct a meal in the same order as one that would be served to him or her. The start of the buffet line should be obvious and accessible; usually, it is near the entrance to the room.

Typically, on a single- or double-sided buffet table, the first items offered the diner are plates. (Flatware and napkins can be located at the start or the end of the buffet or on the dining tables.) The first foods to be offered should be soups and salads. These should be followed by appetizers such as cold sliced meats, pâtés, shellfish and the like. Entrées should be next, along with their vegetable and starch accompaniments. Desserts should be the last items on the buffet. (Beverages can be available on the buffet table at a bar, or on the dining tables or offered by circulating wait staff.)

Stations offer the designer greater flexibility. They also help minimize the line that usually forms at a single buffet table, allowing diners to go in various directions, although this can sometimes cause traffic problems. Like a single buffet table, each station can be designed so that it offers diners sufficient selections to create a complete meal. The stations can also be arranged around a room in a sequence mirroring a meal: soups and salads on the first station diners would approach, appetizers on the next, and so on. A third option is to arrange the stations so that the one

Pasta Station
The Phoenician, Scottsdale, AZ

with the most spectacular display of centerpiece, foods and decorations or the one featuring a chef making foods to order will be the center of attention, with the other stations scattered around the room. Regardless of how they are arranged, each should be self-contained with plates and accompaniments for the main items.

2 *Spacing*—Allow approximately 1 linear foot for each item on the buffet. Thus, if 16 items are to be placed on the table, including plates, a centerpiece and large props, then the buffet table must be approximately 16 feet long. If extremely large centerpieces are used or if food is presented on oversized platters, this will, of course, affect the total table space needed.

3 *Reach*—Try to place all foods within easy reach of the diners. Try to avoid stacking one item behind another. But if items must be placed farther back on the table, try setting them on **risers** or on pedestals in order to add height to the platter. This extra height not only adds visual interest, it allows the diner to reach over the dish in front without disturbing its arrangement. Also, if possible, place foods that will not drip or splatter behind ones that will; that way, sauce from the back dish will not drip into the front dish on its way to the diner's plate. Trays with foods that will not shift can be propped at a slight angle to make the contents more accessible and attractive.

▶ **risers** boxes (including the plastic crates used to store glassware) covered with linens, paper or other decorative items and used on a buffet table as a base for platters, trays or displays

4 *Accompaniments*—Place the appropriate garnishes, sauces or other accompaniments near their principal foods. Also, place a small plate or napkin near a platter for any serving utensils.

5 *Centerpieces*—A centerpiece brings focus to the buffet, and its height or dominance increases the visual appeal of the overall table design. A centerpiece can be a floral arrangement or a sculpture made of ice, tallow, pastillage, chocolate, blown or pulled sugar or other material. The centerpiece can also be a grosse piece such as a whole roast turkey or whole poached salmon decorated with sauce chaud-froid. See Chapter 26, Charcuterie.

Display of Fresh Fruit and Bread for Sunday Brunch Buffet
The Phoenician, Scottsdale, AZ

6 *Decorations*—In addition to the centerpiece, other nonedible objects or props may grace the buffet table. Sometimes these are nothing more than smaller or modified versions of the centerpiece, such as flowers or leaves from a floral centerpiece. Of course, anything from a saddle to a silver candelabra can be used, depending on the buffet's theme. Whatever items are chosen, they should be well cleaned and arranged artfully but not in a manner that interferes with a diner's ability to see and reach the food. Props can also be used to mark divisions in the meal; for example, grouping all salads between one set of props divides them from the entrées. Sometimes, unusable or dead space will result because of constrictions of room or food. If it cannot be avoided, try filling the space with props or other decorations.

7 *Labels*—Unlike a restaurant with a printed menu and an attentive wait staff, an unattended buffet may not give the diner an opportunity to inquire about particular dishes. This can be remedied by placing attractively printed cards bearing the name of the dish in front of any items that the chef feels need identification.

▶ Presenting and Maintaining the Buffet

PORTIONING FOODS

A common problem when planning a buffet is overproduction. Many novice chefs want to make enough of each menu item to serve the entire group. But this is unnecessary. Most people tend to sample a little from many dishes and try not to gorge themselves. Some chefs use a simple, although far from foolproof, formula of 1 pound (450 grams) of food per person as a starting point and then adjust this number depending on factors such as the general composition of the group (a luncheon for female executives may require less food than one for male football players), the number of items offered (the more dishes to choose from, the smaller the portions most people will take), the structure of the event (that is, whether it will be convenient for people to return to the buffet for second helpings) and whether diners serve themselves or are served by wait staff or chefs at the buffet.

Generally, portions should be small, especially if more than one item is served in each food category. For example, if a grilled salmon fillet with Lyonnaise potatoes and a medley of sautéed vegetables is served as an entrée from an à la carte menu, a typical serving would be 6 ounces (180 grams) of fish, 4 ounces (120 grams) of potato and 4 ounces (120 grams) of vegetables. If the same salmon fillet with its accompaniments is served as one of three entrées on a dinner buffet for 100 people, the total of available fish should be 2 to 3 ounces (60 to 90 grams) of fish per portion multiplied by 100 portions, 1 to 1.5 ounces (30 to 45 grams) of potatoes per portion multiplied by 100 portions and 1 ounce (30 grams) of vegetables per portion (diners tend to take smaller portions of vegetables than of starches) multiplied by 100 portions. Similarly, if a dessert tart from an à la carte menu has a 4-inch (10-centimeter) diameter, the version offered on a dessert buffet should have a 2-inch (5-centimeter) diameter.

Experience suggests that most diners tend to serve themselves larger portions of foods found at the start of the buffet than at its middle. Thus, if caviar is being served, it may make economic sense to place it somewhere farther down the line than at the start of the buffet.

PRESENTING HOT FOODS

Keeping hot foods hot on a buffet is a particular challenge, and an important one, for both food safety and presentation concerns. If possible, hot foods should be served in relatively small quantities on warm platters that are exchanged frequently. This is not always possible, however. More often, hot foods are maintained in chafing dishes or under heat lamps.

To maintain the quality of foods kept in a chafing dish, use the following guidelines:

- Choose foods that hold well. Rare meats and delicate pastas do not hold well in a chafing dish; they become overcooked and unattractive quickly. Instead, try braised meats (which may actually benefit from the extended cooking) or hearty pastas such as tortellini or penne. This guideline also applies to garnishes: Bunches of delicate herbs such as basil do not do well in a chafing dish; instead, try sprigs of rosemary or thyme.
- Cook small amounts of delicate foods at a time and change the insert pan in a chafing dish often. This prevents foods from sitting too long.
- Ladle a small amount of sauce in the bottom of the pan before placing sliced meats in the pan, or serve sliced meats, poultry or fish on a bed of vegetables. The sauce or the vegetable bed helps to absorb the heat from the chafing dish, insulating the more delicate items and providing a bit of steam to help keep the foods moist.
- Keep the chafing dish closed whenever possible. This holds in the steam, which helps keep the food moist. But a closed chafing dish distracts from a buffet's appeal and slows down the flow of diners through the buffet line.

Heat lamps are generally used for keeping large cuts of meats or poultry warm during carving. These foods, however, become dry rapidly and should be replaced periodically. Of course, time and temperature principles of food safety must also be followed.

SAFETY ALERT

Buffets

A properly maintained buffet is important for visual and culinary reasons. It is also important for food safety reasons. Because the public has access to the food, cross-contamination is a potential problem. In addition to keeping foods at the proper temperatures, the following steps should be followed:

- Do not add new food to old food in a serving dish or chafing dish.
- Do not use a chafing dish to heat food; make sure food is at the proper internal temperature before transferring it to a chafing dish or putting it under a heat lamp.
- Check food temperatures with food thermometers at established time intervals to ensure that food is being held at safe serving temperatures.
- Be careful of steam when changing pans in a chafing dish; do not leave the pan of hot water uncovered.
- Provide clean utensils for each dish and replace them often.
- Provide an ample supply of clean plates, so that diners do not reuse plates from which they have eaten.

A BLOCK OF ICE, A CHAIN SAW, A CHISEL AND A LITTLE CAUTION AND CREATIVITY

Ice carvings have long been popular buffet centerpieces; they add elegance and sophistication to the setting and occasion. As with other arts, it may take years to master ice carving. Nevertheless, with some practice and care, chefs can usually create acceptable ice sculptures after only a few tries.

Blocks of carving ice are specially prepared to remove air bubbles. These large blocks (20 × 10 × 46 inches [50 × 25 × 115 centimeters]) weigh approximately 300 pounds (135 kilograms), and special ice tongs and caution are required when handling them.

At 0°F (−18°C), ice is very brittle and difficult to carve without breaking. Therefore, carving ice must be tempered before carving. To temper the ice, remove it from the freezer and allow it to rest at room temperature for approximately 1 hour. When the surface is clear of frost, carving can begin.

A single carving can take from one to several hours to complete. Although chisels and specially designed saws for ice carving work quite well, chain saws are commonly used to speed up the process. Because most carving is done indoors, electric saws are used; unlike gas saws, they do not leave a greasy residue on the ice's surface. Be very careful when using any chain saw, particularly an electric one around melting ice and pools of water.

To begin, trace the outline of the figure you want to carve on the surface of all four sides of the block of ice. There are several excellent ice carving books, some of which provide stencils for this purpose. Then start removing the ice using a large saw or a chainsaw. As the figure begins to take shape, use smaller chisels and specialized tools to create the desired effect. Some carvers use chain saws for the entire process, however. After some practice, you will develop your own style and preferences.

When the carving is complete, carefully return the ice to the freezer until needed. When setting it on a buffet, use a pan designed to hold an ice carving and provide drainage. Avoid placing ice sculptures under hot air vents. At room temperature and average humidity, ice melts at the rate of approximately ½ inch (1.2 centimeters) per hour from all sides. Keep this in mind when carving thin pieces or small details into the surface.

THE PHOENICIAN RESORT

The Phoenician Resort in Scottsdale, Arizona, is one of America's premier resorts. It offers several dining options, including the award-winning fine-dining room Mary Elaine's. Sunday brunch is a popular event at The Phoenician, especially in the Terrace Dining Room, where chefs create a lavish multistationed buffet utilizing interior spaces and exterior patios. The Terrace's Sunday brunch buffet, which is pictured in the preceding pages, typically serves 450 guests and is prepared and maintained by 20 cooks. It takes the staff 12 hours to set up some 13 stations for each week's 4-hour-long brunch. In addition to a wide selection of hot and cold entrées, meat and poultry carving stations, fresh fruits and vegetables, pasta, salads, pâtés, freshly baked breads and pastries, guests enjoy four varieties of imported caviar and consume an average of 120 pounds of boiled shrimp.

Display of Fish and Shellfish for Sunday Brunch Buffet
The Phoenician, Scottsdale, AZ

PRESENTING COLD FOODS

Keeping cold foods cold on a buffet table is a little less of a challenge. As with hot foods, it is best if cold foods are served in relatively small quantities on cold platters that are exchanged frequently. Alternatively, the items can be set on a bed of ice—usually a large bowl filled with ice into which a smaller bowl containing the food is placed.

REPLENISHING FOODS

Dishes from the buffet table should be removed when they are approximately two-thirds empty or have deteriorated in some fashion (for example, when the aspic on pâtés has softened, cut fruits have browned or a hot food has crusted over). Once the old dish has been removed, its fresh replacement should be placed on the buffet immediately, and it should be as carefully arranged and garnished as the original. If items from the old dish are to be combined with a replacement dish, this should be done in the kitchen and not at the buffet table. Batches of temperature-sensitive or potentially hazardous foods should not be combined, however.

SERVING FOODS

Once the banquet or restaurant manager has completed the planning for a buffet, it usually falls to a captain to supervise the actual event. The captain directs the crew setting up the room as well as the stewards who bring the food, flatware, china and glassware from the kitchen to the buffet.

The captain also supervises the wait staff. One of the front waiters' principal responsibilities is to maintain the appearance of the buffet and to replenish items as needed. Depending on the function, front waiters can be stationed behind the buffet table to serve diners, circulate in the crowd with trays of hors d'oeuvre or drinks (passing foods in this fashion is called **butler service**) or serve beverages to diners seated at the dining tables. Back waiters generally police the room and clear tables. They should be particularly vigilant in removing used plates from a dining table after a diner has gone to the buffet for more food and before he or she returns to the dining table with a new plate.

Typically, servers or chefs are placed only at stations where foods are prepared or carved to order. This helps control portioning. It also provides a greater opportunity for staff to police the buffet and therefore ensure that the table and the individual items remain neat, attractive and fresh. Finally, placing wait staff or kitchen staff at the buffet allows diners to ask questions about the foods presented.

THE BUFFET: AN ANCIENT EXTRAVAGANZA

The origin of the buffet is obscure, but it is possible that the idea evolved from Italian banquets of the early Renaissance. Gathering together to eat and drink on festive occasions was not new; one only has to think of banqueting scenes on ancient Egyptian or Roman frescoes. But the word, *banchetto,* was new, and referred not only to the event but the long table or bench at which the many guests were seated.

As the influence of Italian art and manners spread throughout Europe, the French adopted the "banquet." Not only was it an occasion for eating and drinking prodigious amounts, but the resplendent display of food was often accompanied by an equally resplendent display of silver on dining room buffets or sideboards. And it was the chefs who were responsible for these imaginative displays. Paintings from the period of Louis XIV depict the unbridled creativity that went into these tableaux.

From France to England to America, the idea of the buffet migrated across time. There is *rijstaffel* in the Netherlands and *smorgasbord* in Scandinavia. In America, the Chinese restaurant buffet began around the time of the 1849 gold rush, perhaps the first instance of the "all you can eat" experience. It cost $1.00. The "midnight chuck wagon" buffet at the El Rancho in 1940s Las Vegas popularized the "all you can eat" buffet. It cost $1.50.

Whatever the case, the buffet has come a long way from the 16th-century Medici banquet that featured a ram poached in water, reinserted into its skin (horns and all) and set lifelike into a gold basin.

CONCLUSION

A buffet is more than a salad bar at a restaurant—that is, merely food laid out for the diner to grab. A buffet is an opportunity for a chef to use his or her creativity to plan and present an entire menu in an attractive fashion. But a successful buffet requires careful planning, attention to detail and the help of many professionals in the food service facility.

QUESTIONS FOR DISCUSSION

1 What is a grosse piece? How is it different from a centerpiece?
2 What food safety and sanitation factors must be considered when planning a buffet? Explain your answer.
3 Describe three things that can be done to keep hot foods attractive and fresh when using a chafing dish.
4 Describe two things that can be done to keep cold foods cold on a buffet.
5 List five different stations serving hot foods at a buffet and the equipment necessary for each.
6 Redesign the Western-themed buffet in Figure 30.3 to include three stations.

7 Where can you go for current information on new trends and styles of buffet arrangements? What resources are available to assist caterers in business management?

APPENDIX I

▸ Professional Organizations

American Cheese Society
304 West Liberty Street, Suite 201
Louisville, KY 40202
(502) 583-3783
http://www.cheesesociety.org

American Culinary Federation (ACF)
180 Center Place Way
St. Augustine, FL 32095
(800) 624-9458
http://www.acfchefs.org

American Dietetic Association (ADA)
120 South Riverside Plaza, Suite 2000
Chicago, Illinois 60606-6995
(800) 877-1600
http://www.eatright.org

American Institute of Baking (AIB)
P.O. Box 3999
Manhattan, KS 66505-3999
(785) 537-4750
http://www.aibonline.org

American Institute of Wine & Food (AIWF)
1303 Jefferson Street, Suite 100B
Napa, CA 94559
(800) 274-2493
http://www.aiwf.org

Chefs Collaborative
262 Beacon Street
Boston, MA 02116
(617) 236-5200
http://www.chefscollaborative.org

Club Managers Association of America (CMAA)
1733 King Street
Alexandria, VA 22314
(703) 739-9500
http://www.cmaa.org

International Association of Culinary Professionals (IACP)
304 West Liberty Street, Suite 201
Louisville, KY 40202
(502) 581-9786
http://www.iacp.com

International Food Service Executives Association
836 San Bruno Avenue
Henderson, NV 89015
(888) 234-3732
http://www.ifsea.org

The James Beard Foundation
167 West 12th Street
New York, NY 10011
(800) 36-BEARD
http://www.jamesbeard.org

Les Dames d'Escoffier International
P.O. Box 4961
Louisville, KY 40204
(502) 456-1851
http://www.ldei.org

National Ice Carving Association
P.O. Box 3593
Oak Brook, IL 60522-3593
(630) 871-8431
http://www.nica.org

National Restaurant Association

1200 17th Street, NW
Washington, DC 20036
(202) 331-5900
http://www.restaurant.org

Oldways Preservation Trust

266 Beacon Street
Boston, MA 02116
(617) 421-5500
http://www.oldwayspt.org

Personal Chefs Network

(877) 905-CHEF
http://www.personalchefsnetwork.com

Research Chefs Association

5775 Peachtree-Dunwoody Road, Building G, Suite 500
Atlanta, GA 30342
(404) 252-3663
http://www.culinology.com

Share Our Strength (SOS)

1730 M Street NW, Suite 700
Washington, DC 20036
(800) 969-4767
http://www.strength.org

Slow Food USA

20 Jay Street, Suite 313
Brooklyn, NY 11201
(718) 260-8000
http://www.slowfoodusa.org

Southern Foodways Alliance

Center for the Study of Southern Culture
Barnard Observatory
University, MS 38677
(662) 915-5993
http://www.southernfoodways.com

U.S. Personal Chef Association

481 Rio Rancho Blvd. NE
Rio Rancho, NM 87124
(800) 995-2138
http://www.uspca.com

Women Chefs and Restaurateurs (WCR)

304 West Liberty Street, Suite 201
Louisville, KY 40202
(502) 581-0300
http://www.womenchefs.org

APPENDIX II

▸ MEASUREMENT AND CONVERSION CHARTS

MEASUREMENT CONVERSION CHARTS

FORMULAS FOR EXACT MEASURES

	WHEN YOU KNOW:	**MULTIPLY BY:**	**TO FIND:**
Mass (weight)	ounces	28.35	grams
	pounds	0.45	kilograms
	grams	0.035	ounces
	kilograms	2.2	pounds
Volume (capacity)	teaspoons	5.0	milliliters
	tablespoons	15.0	milliliters
	fluid ounces	29.57	milliliters
	cups	0.24	liters
	pints	0.47	liters
	quarts	0.95	liters
	gallons	3.785	liters
	milliliters	0.034	fluid ounces
Temperature	Fahrenheit	5/9 (after subtracting 32)	Celsius
	Celsius	9/5 (then add 32)	Fahrenheit

ROUNDED MEASURES FOR QUICK REFERENCE

1 oz.		= 30 g
4 oz.		= 120 g
8 oz.		= 240 g
16 oz.	= 1 lb.	= 480 g
32 oz.	= 2 lb.	= 960 g
36 oz.	= 2¼ lb.	= 1000 g (1 kg)
¼ tsp.	= 1/24 fl. oz.	= 1 ml
½ tsp.	= 1/12 fl. oz.	= 2 ml
1 tsp.	= 1/6 fl. oz.	= 5 ml
1 Tbsp.	= ½ fl. oz.	= 15 ml
1 c.	= 8 fl. oz.	= 240 ml
2 c. (1 pt.)	= 16 fl. oz.	= 480 ml
4 c. (1 qt.)	= 32 fl. oz.	= 960 ml
4 qt. (1 gal.)	= 128 fl. oz.	= 3.75 lt
32°F		= 0°C
122°F		= 50°C
212°F		= 100°C

CONVERSION GUIDELINES

1 gallon	=	4 quarts 8 pints 16 cups (8 fluid ounces) 128 fluid ounces
1 fifth bottle	=	approximately 1½ pints or exactly 26.5 fluid ounces
1 measuring cup	=	8 fluid ounces (a coffee cup generally holds 6 fluid ounces)
1 large egg white	=	1 ounce (average)
1 lemon	=	1 to 1¼ fluid ounces of juice
1 orange	=	3 to 3½ fluid ounces of juice

SCOOP SIZES

SCOOP NUMBER	LEVEL MEASURE
6	⅔ cup
8	½ cup
10	⅖ cup
12	⅓ cup
16	¼ cup
20	3 ⅕ tablespoons
24	2 ⅔ tablespoons
30	2 ⅕ tablespoons
40	1 ⅗ tablespoons

The number of the scoop determines the number of servings in each quart of a mixture: for example, with a No. 16 scoop, one quart of mixture will yield 16 servings.

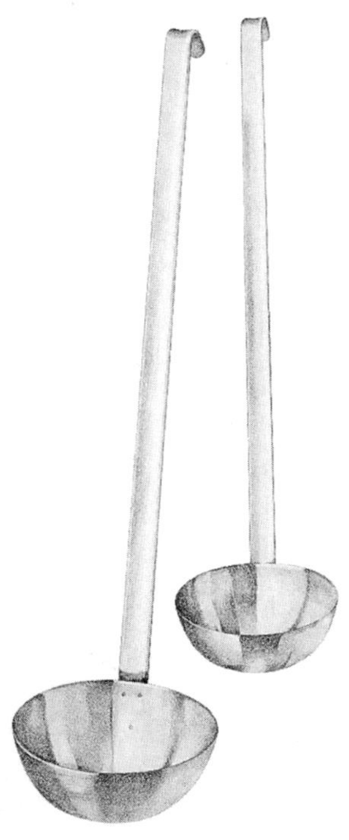

LADLE SIZES

SIZE	PORTION OF A CUP	NUMBER PER QUART	NUMBER PER LITER
1 fl. oz.	⅛	32	34
2 fl. oz.	¼	16	17
2⅔ fl. oz.	⅓	12	13
4 fl. oz.	½	8	8.6
6 fl. oz.	¾	5⅓	5.7

CANNED GOOD SIZES

SIZE	NO. OF CANS PER CASE	AVERAGE WEIGHT	AVERAGE NO. CUPS PER CAN
No. 1/4	1 & 2 doz.	4 oz.	1/2
No. 1/2	8	8 oz.	1
No. 300	1 & 2 doz.	14 oz.	1 3/4
No. 1 tall (also known as 303)	2 & 4 doz.	16 oz.	2
No. 2	2 doz.	20 oz.	2 1/2
No. 2 1/2	2 doz.	28 oz.	3 1/2
No. 3	2 doz.	33 oz.	4
No. 3 cylinder	1 doz.	46 oz.	5 2/3
No. 5	1 doz.	3 lb. 8 oz.	5 1/2
No. 10	6	6 lb. 10 oz.	13

Various standard cans—(left to right, front row) No. 1/2 flat, No. 1/4; (middle row) No. 300, No. 1 tall, No. 1/2; (back row) No. 10, No. 3 cylinder, No. 5

APPENDIX III

▶ Fresh Produce Availability Chart

The availability of fresh, locally grown produce depends on local climate and growing conditions. Gardeners in central Arizona may be enjoying vine-ripened tomatoes in March, while gardeners in Michigan or New England may still be buried under snow. Just by looking at what's available in the produce department of your local supermarket, you may not be able to tell whether it is July or January. That's because consumers have become accustomed to having the same foods available all year. Modern transportation and storage methods allow us to have out-of-season foods anytime, anywhere. But though we depend on and enjoy this convenience, it contributes to hidden costs that are not usually considered. These include loss of farmlands and natural resources involved in the marketing and movement of these foods.

Chefs across the country are now shopping for fruits and vegetables at local farmer's markets and working with local farmers who grow products especially for their kitchens. While any good produce wholesalers or even supermarkets will carry out-of-season, imported produce, the taste will be inferior and the cost will be much higher.

Locally grown, in-season products appeal to restaurant patrons and demonstrate your concern for both food quality and the viability of local farmers and foragers. Chefs can also work with local farmers before planting begins to determine what specialty items grow well in the area and to encourage farmers to grow products that the restaurant agrees to purchase at harvest. Many states now have programs to assist and encourage chefs and farmers to work together. It's a shift from demand-driven (chef) to supply-driven (farm) choices.

With only 2 percent of the U.S. population farming the land, few Americans give a second thought to the sources of their food. Many of us may have lost our connection to agriculture, but none of us has lost our dependence on that connection. By creating markets for local agriculture, we can ensure that farmland remains active and viable. What happens to farmers remains crucial to our nation's well-being. Even if we never set foot on a farm, our connection to the farmer and the land is there every time we buy a loaf of bread, munch an apple, plan a daily special or design a restaurant's menu.

The following chart is intended as only a general guide to the best availability of freshly harvested produce items grown in the continental United States. State departments of agriculture can provide charts of local produce availability and information on local farmer's markets and sustainable agriculture programs.

PRODUCT	JAN	FEB	MAR	APR	MAY	JUN	JUL	AUG	SEP	OCT	NOV	DEC
	WINTER DEC 21–MAR 19		SPRING MAR 20–JUN 20			SUMMER JUN 21–SEP 21			AUTUMN SEP 22–DEC 20			
Apples								X	X	X	X	
Apricots						X	X					
Artichokes			X	X	X							
Asparagus				X	X	X						
Avocados, Hass				X	X	X	X	X	X	X		

PRODUCT	JAN	FEB	MAR	APR	MAY	JUN	JUL	AUG	SEP	OCT	NOV	DEC
Beans, green					X	X	X	X	X			
Beets								X	X	X		
Blueberries					X	X	X	X				
Broccoli	X	X	X						X	X	X	X
Brussels sprouts	X	X							X	X	X	X
Cabbage	X	X	X	X	X				X	X	X	X
Cantaloupe						X	X	X	X			
Cauliflower	X	X	X	X	X				X	X	X	X
Celery root	X	X	X	X						X	X	X
Cherries					X	X	X	X				
Chestnuts									X	X	X	X
Citrus	X	X	X	X	X	X			X	X	X	X
Collards	X										X	X
Corn						X	X	X				
Cranberries									X	X	X	X
Cucumbers					X	X	X	X				
Dates										X	X	X
Eggplants						X	X	X	X			
Figs						X	X	X	X	X		
Grapes						X	X	X	X	X	X	
Greens			X	X	X	X						
Kohlrabi						X	X					
Leeks	X	X	X							X	X	X
Lettuce			X	X	X	X	X	X	X			
Lychees						X	X					
Mangos					X	X	X	X				
Mushrooms, morels			X	X	X							
Mushrooms, truffles	X	X									X	X
Okra					X	X	X	X	X			
Onions						X	X	X	X			
Onions, sweet				X	X	X						
Papayas			X	X	X	X						
Peaches					X	X	X	X				
Pears	X	X	X	X						X	X	X
Peas, English				X	X							
Peas, field							X	X				
Pecans											X	X
Peppers, bell						X	X	X	X			
Peppers, chile									X	X	X	X
Persimmons										X	X	X
Pineapples			X	X	X	X	X	X				
Plums						X	X	X	X			
Pome-granates									X	X	X	X
Potatoes								X	X	X		
Prickly pears									X	X	X	X
Pumpkins									X	X	X	
Raspberries						X	X	X	X			
Rhubarb		X	X	X	X							
Spinach	X	X	X	X	X					X	X	X

PRODUCT	JAN	FEB	MAR	APR	MAY	JUN	JUL	AUG	SEP	OCT	NOV	DEC
Squash, summer				X	X	X	X	X	X			
Squash, winter	X	X	X							X	X	X
Strawberries		X	X	X	X	X						
Tomatoes						X	X	X	X			
Turnips				X	X					X	X	
Water-melons						X	X	X				

APPENDIX IV

▸ IF YOU WANT TO LEARN MORE ABOUT FOOD SAFETY

So many people who read this book in advance of publication have suggested that more information about foodborne diseases be discussed. The following facts were obtained from the Centers for Disease Control and Prevention.

WHAT CAUSES FOODBORNE ILLNESS?

Consuming contaminated foods or beverages causes foodborne illness. These different diseases have many different symptoms, so there is no one "syndrome." However, the microbe or toxin enters the body through the gastrointestinal tract, and often causes the first symptoms there, so nausea, vomiting, abdominal cramps, and diarrhea are common symptoms in many foodborne diseases

WHAT ARE THE MOST COMMON FOODBORNE DISEASES?

The most commonly recognized foodborne infections are those caused by the bacteria *campylobacter*, *salmonella*, *E. coli 0157:H7*, and a group of viruses called calicivirus, also known as Norwalk and Norwalk-like viruses.

- *Campylobacter* is a bacterial pathogen that causes fever, diarrhea, and abdominal cramps. It is the most commonly identified bacterial cause of diarrheal illness in the world. These bacteria live in the intestines of healthy birds, and most raw poultry meat has campylobacter on it. Eating undercooked chicken, or other food that has been contaminated with juices dripping from raw chicken, is the most frequent source of this infection.
- *Salmonella* is also a bacterium that is widespread in the intestines of birds, reptiles, and mammals. It can spread to humans via a variety of different foods of animal origin. The illness it causes, *salmonellosis*, typically includes fever, diarrhea, and abdominal cramps. In persons with poor underlying health or weakened immune systems, it can invade the bloodstream and cause life-threatening infections.
- *E. coli* 0157:H7 is a bacterial pathogen that has a reservoir in cattle and other similar animals. Human illness typically follows consumption of food or water that has been contaminated with microscopic amounts of cow feces. The illness it causes is often a severe and bloody diarrhea and painful abdominal cramps, without much fever. In 3% to 5% of cases, a serious complication called hemolytic uremic syndrome (HUS) can occur several weeks after the initial symptoms, and includes temporary anemia, profuse bleeding, and kidney failure.
- *Calicivirus*, or Norwalk-like virus is an extremely common cause of foodborne illness, though it is rarely diagnosed because the laboratory test is not widely available. It causes an acute gastrointestinal illness, usually with more vomiting than diarrhea that resolves within two days.
- Unlike many foodborne pathogens that have animal reservoirs, it is believed that Norwalk-like viruses spread primarily from one infected person to another. Infected cooks can contaminate a salad or sandwich as they prepare it, if they have the virus on their hands. Infected fishermen have contaminated oysters as they have harvested them.

In addition to disease caused by direct infection, some foodborne diseases are caused by the presence of a toxin in the food that was produced by a microbe in the food.

- For example, the bacterium *Staphylococcus aureus* can grow in some foods and produce a toxin that causes intense vomiting. The rare but deadly disease botulism occurs when the bacterium *Clostridium botulinum* grows and produces a powerful paralytic toxin in foods. These toxins can produce illness even if the microbes that produced them are no longer there.
- Other toxins and poisonous chemicals can cause foodborne illness. People can become ill if a pesticide is inadvertently added to a food or if naturally poisonous substances are used to prepare a meal.
- Every year people become ill after mistaking poisonous mushrooms for safe species, or after eating poisonous reef fishes.

The spectrum of foodborne diseases is constantly changing. A century ago, typhoid fever, tuberculosis, and cholera were common foodborne diseases.

Improvements in food safety, such as pasteurization of milk, safe canning, and the disinfection of water supplies have conquered those diseases.

Today other foodborne infections have taken their places—including some that have only recently been discovered.

- In the last 15 years, several important diseases of unknown cause have turned out to be complications of foodborne infections. For example, we now know that the Guillain-Barre syndrome can be caused by campylobacter infections, and that the most common cause of acute kidney failure in children, hemolytic uremic syndrome, is caused by infection with E. coli 0157:H7 and related bacteria. In the future, other diseases whose origins are currently unknown may turn out to be related to foodborne infections.

WHEN TO CONSULT YOUR DOCTOR ABOUT A DIARRHEAL ILLNESS

A heathcare provider should be consulted for a diarrheal illness that lasts for more than 3 days and is accompanied by high fever (temperature over 101.5 degrees F, measured orally), blood in the stools, prolonged vomiting that prevents keeping liquids down which can lead to dehydration, signs of dehydration, including a decrease in urination, dry mouth and throat, and feeling dizzy when standing up.

HOW MANY CASES OF FOODBORNE DISEASE ARE THERE IN THE UNITED STATES?

An estimated 76 million cases of foodborne disease occur each year in the United States. The great majority of these cases is mild and cause symptoms for only a day or two. Some cases are more serious, and CDC estimates that there are 325,000 hopitalizations and 5,200 deaths related to foodborne diseases each year. The most severe cases tend to occur in the very old, the very young, those who already have an illness that reduces their immune system function, and in healthy people exposed to a very high dose or organism.

HOW DO PUBLIC HEALTH DEPARTMENTS TRACK FOODBORNE DISEASES?

Routine monitoring of important diseases by public health departments is called disease surveillance. Each state decides which diseases are to be under surveillance in that state.

In most states, diagnosed cases of *salmonella*, *E. coli 0157:H7* and other serious infections are routinely reported to the health department. The county reports them to the state health department that reports them to the CDC.

Tens of thousands of cases of these "notifiable conditions" are reported every year. For example, nearly 35,000 cases of *salmonella* infection were reported to CDC in 1998.

However, most foodborne infections go undiagnosed and unreported, either because the ill person does not see a doctor, or the doctor does not make a specific diagnosis. Also, infections with some microbes are not reportable in the first place.

To get more information about infections that might be diagnosed but not reported, CDC developed a special surveillance system called FoodNet. FoodNet provides the best available information about specific foodborne infections in the United States, and summarizes them in an annual report. In addition to tracking the number of reported cases of individual infections, states also collect information about foodborne outbreaks, and report a summary of that information to CDC.

About 400 to 500 foodborne outbreaks investigated by local and state health departments are reported each year. This includes information about many diseases that are not notifiable and thus are not under individual surveillance, so it provides some useful general information about foodborne illnesses.

WHAT ARE FOODBORNE DISEASE OUTBREAKS AND WHY DO THEY OCCUR?

An outbreak of foodborne illness occurs when a group of people consume the same contaminated food and two or more of them come down with the same illness. It may be a group that ate a meal together somewhere, or it may be a group of people who do not know each other at all, but who all happened to buy and eat the same contaminated item from a grocery store or restaurant.

For an outbreak to occur, something must have happened to contaminate a batch of food that was eaten by a group of people. Often, a combination of events contributed to the outbreak. A contaminated food may be left out at room temperature for many hours, allowing the bacteria to multiply to high numbers, and then be insufficiently cooked to kill the bacteria.

Many outbreaks are local in nature. They are recognized when a group of people realize that they all became ill after a common meal, and someone calls the local health department. This classic local outbreak might follow a catered meal at a reception, a pot-luck supper, or eating a meal at an understaffed restaurant on a particularly busy day. However, outbreaks are increasingly being recognized that are more widespread, that affect persons in many different places, and that are spread out over several weeks.

The vast majority of reported cases of foodborne illness is not part of recognized outbreaks, but occurs as individual or "sporadic" cases. It may be that many of these cases are actually part of unrecognized widespread or diffuse outbreaks. Detecting and investigating such widespread outbreaks is a major challenge to our public health system. This is the reason that new and more sophisticated laboratory methods are being used at CDC and in state public health department laboratories.

HOW DOES FOOD BECOME CONTAMINATED?

We live in a microbial world, and there are many opportunities for food to become contaminated as it is produced and prepared. Many foodborne microbes are present in healthy animals (usually in their intestines) raised for food. Meat and poultry carcasses can become contaminated during slaughter by contact with small amounts of intestinal contents. Similarly, fresh fruits and vegetables can be contaminated if they are washed or irrigated with water that is contaminated with animal manure or human sewage.

- Some types of *salmonella* can infect a hen's ovary so that the internal contents of a normal looking egg can be contaminated with *salmonella* even before the shell is formed.
- Oysters and other filter-feeding shellfish can concentrate *vibrio* bacteria that are naturally present in seawater, or other microbes that are present in human sewage dumped into the sea.

Later in food processing, other foodborne microbes can be introduced from infected humans who handle the food or by cross-contamination from some other raw agricultural product.

- For example, *Shigella* bacteria, hepatitis A virus, and Norwalk virus can be introduced by unwashed hands of people handling food who are themselves infected.
- In the kitchen, microbes can be transferred from one food to another food by using the same knife, cutting board, or other utensil to prepare both without washing the surface or utensil in between.
- A food that is fully cooked can become recontaminated if it touches other raw foods or drippings from raw foods that contain pathogens.
- The way that food is handled after it is contaminated can also make a difference in whether or not an outbreak occurs. Many bacterial microbes need to multiply to a larger number before enough are present in food to cause disease. Given warm moist conditions and an ample supply of nutrients, one bacterium that reproduces by dividing itself every half-hour can produce 16 billion progeny in 12 hours.

As a result, lightly contaminated food left out overnight can be highly infectious by the next day. If the food were refrigerated promptly, the bacteria would not multiply at all. However, in general, refrigeration or freezing prevents virtually all bacteria from growing but generally preserves them in a state of suspended animation. This general rule has a few surprising exceptions:

- Two foodborne bacteria, *Listeria monocytogenes* and *Yersinia enterocolitica*, can actually grow at refrigerated temperatures. High-salt, high-sugar, or high-acid levels keep bacteria from growing, which is why salted meats, jam, and pickled vegetables are traditionally preserved foods.

Microbes are killed by heat. If food is heated to an internal temperature about 160 degrees F. for even a few seconds, this is sufficient to kill parasites, viruses, or bacteria.

- The exception is the *clostridium bacteria*, which produce a heat-resistant form called a spore. *Clostridium* spores are killed only at temperatures above boiling. This is why canned foods must be cooked to a high temperature under pressure as part of the canning process. The toxins produced by bacteria vary in their sensitivity to heat.
- The *staphylococcal toxin*, which causes vomiting, is not killed even if it is boiled.
- Fortunately, the potent toxin that causes botulism is completely inactivated by boiling.

WHAT FOODS ARE MOST ASSOCIATED WITH FOODBORNE ILLNESS?

Raw foods of animal origin are the most likely to be contaminated—that is, raw meat and poultry, raw eggs, unpasteurized milk, and raw shellfish. Because filter-feeding shellfish strain microbes from the sea over many months, they are particularly likely to be contaminated if there are any pathogens in the seawater. Foods that mingle the products of many individual animals, such as bulk raw milk, pooled raw eggs, or ground beef, are particularly hazardous because a pathogen present in any one of the animals may contaminate the whole batch. A single hamburger may contain meat from hundreds of animals.

A single restaurant omelet may contain eggs from hundreds of chickens. A glass of raw milk may contain milk from hundreds of cows. A broiler chicken carcass can be exposed to drippings and juices of many thousands of other birds that went through the same cold water tank after slaughter.

When consumed raw, fruits and vegetables are a particular concern. Washing can decrease but not eliminate contamination, so the home cooks can do little to protect themselves.

Recently a number of outbreaks have been traced to fresh fruits and vegetables that were processed under less than sanitary conditions. These outbreaks show that the quality of the water used for washing and chilling the produce after it is harvested is critical. Using water that is not clean can contaminate many boxes of produce.

- Fresh manure used to fertilize vegetables can also contaminate them. Alfalfa sprouts and other raw sprouts pose a particular challenge, as the conditions under which they are sprouted are ideal for growing microbes as well as sprouts, and because they are eaten without further cooking. That means that a few bacteria present on the seeds can grow to high numbers of pathogens on the sprouts.
- Unpasteurized fruit juice can also be contaminated if there are pathogens in or on the fruit that is used to make it.

WHAT CAN HOME COOKS DO TO PROTECT THEIR FAMILIES AND THEMSELVES FROM FOODBORNE ILLNESS?

A few simple precautions can reduce the risk of foodborne dieases:

COOK Meat, poultry, and eggs thoroughly. Using a thermometer to measure the internal temperature of meat is a good way to be sure that it is cooked sufficiently to kill bacteria. For example, ground beef should be cooked to an internal temperature of 160 degrees F. Eggs should be cooked until the yolk is firm.

SEPARATE Don't cross-contaminate one food with another. Avoid cross-contaminating foods by washing hands, utensils, and cutting boards after they have been in contact with raw meat or poultry and before they touch another food. Put cooked meat on a clean platter, rather than back on one that held the raw meat.

CHILL Refrigerate leftovers promptly. Bacteria can grow quickly at room temperature, so refrigerate leftover foods if they are not going to be eaten within 4 hours. Large volumes of food will cool more quickly if they are divided into several shallow containers for refrigeration.

CLEAN Wash produce. Rinse fresh fruits and vegetables in running tap water to remove visible dirt and grime. Remove and discard the outermost leaves of a head of lettuce or cabbage. Because bacteria can grow well on the cut surface of fruit or vegetable, be careful not to contaminate these foods while slicing them on the cutting board, and avoid leaving cut produce at room temperature for many hours. As a home cook, don't be a source of foodborne illness yourself. Wash your hands with soap and water before preparing food. Avoid preparing food for others if you yourself have a diarrheal illness. Changing a baby's diaper while preparing food is a bad idea that can easily spread disease.

Report suspected foodborne illnesses to your local health department. The local public health department is an important part of the food safety system. Often calls from concerned citizens are how outbreaks are first detected. If a public health official contacts you to find out more about an illness you had, your cooperation is important. In public health investigations, it can be as important to talk to healthy people as to ill people. Your cooperation may be needed even if you are not ill.

ARE SOME PEOPLE MORE LIKELY TO CONTRACT A FOODBORNE ILLNESS? IF SO, ARE THERE SPECIAL PRECAUTIONS THEY SHOULD TAKE?

Some persons at particularly high risk should take more precautions:

- Pregnant women, the elderly, and those with weakened immune systems are at higher risk for severe infections such as *Listeria* and should be particularly careful not to consume undercooked animal products.
- They should avoid soft French-style cheeses, pates, uncooked hot dogs, and sliced deli meats, which have been sources of *Listeria* infections. Persons at high risk should also avoid alfalfa sprouts and unpasteurized juices.

- A bottle-fed infant is at most risk for severe infections with *salmonella* or other bacteria that can grow in a bottle of warm formula if it is left at room temperature for many hours. Particular care is needed to be sure the baby's bottle is cleaned and disinfected and that leftover milk formula or juice is not held in the bottle for many hours.
- Persons with liver disease are susceptible to infections with a rare but dangerous microbe called *Vibrio vulnificus*, found in oysters. They should avoid eating raw oysters.

WHAT CAN CONSUMERS DO WHEN THEY EAT IN RESTAURANTS?

You can protect yourself first by choosing which restaurant to patronize. Restaurants are inspected by the local health department to make sure they are clean and have adequate kitchen facilities. Find out how restaurants did on their most recent inspections and use that score to help guide your choice. While this is not true in many jurisdictions, the latest Inspector's Report may be posted in the restaurant. Some restaurants have specifically trained their staff in principles of food safety. This is also good to know in deciding which restaurant to patronize.

You can also protect yourself from foodborne illness when ordering specific foods, just as you would at home. When ordering a hamburger, ask for it to be cooked to a temperature of 160 degrees F., and send it back if it is still pink in the middle. Before you order something that is made with many eggs pooled together, such as scrambled eggs, omelets, or French toast, ask the waiter whether it was made with pasteurized egg, and choose something else if it was not.

HOW CAN FOOD BE MADE SAFER IN THE FIRST PLACE?

There is only so much the consumer can do. Making food safe in the first place is a major effort, involving the farm and fishery, the production plant or factory, and many other points from the farm to the table. Many different groups in public health, industry, regulatory agencies, and academia have roles to play in making the food supply less contaminated.

Consumers can promote general food safety with their dollars, by purchasing foods that have been processed for safety. For example, milk pasteurization was a major advance in food safety that was developed 100 years ago. Buying pasteurized milk rather than raw unpasteurized milk still prevents an enormous number of foodborne diseases every day. Now juice pasteurization is a recent important step forward that prevents *E. coli 0157:H7* infections, *salmonella*, and many other diseases. Consumers can look for and buy pasteurized fruit juices and ciders.

In the future, meat and other foods will be available that has been treated for safety with irradiation. These technologies are likely to be as important a step forward as the pasteurization of milk.

Foodborne diseases are largely preventable, though there is no simple one-step prevention measure like a vaccine. Instead, measures are needed to prevent or limit contamination all the way from farm to table.

A variety of good agricultural and manufacturing practices can reduce the spread of microbes among animals and prevent contamination of foods. Careful review of the whole food production process can identify the principal hazards, and the control points where contamination can be prevented, limited, or eliminated. A formal method for evaluating the control of risk in foods exists and is called a Hazard Analysis Critical Control Point (HACCP) system.

Early in the century, large botulism outbreaks occurred when canned foods were cooked insufficiently to kill botulism spores. After research was done to find out exactly how much heat was needed to kill the spores, the canning industry and the government regulators went to great lengths to be sure every can was sufficiently cooked. As a result, botulism related to commercial canned foods has disappeared in this country.

Similarly, the introduction of careful pasteurization of milk eliminated a large number of milk-borne diseases. This occurred after sanitation in dairies had already reached a high level.

In the future, other foods can be made much safer by new pasteurizing technologies, such as in-shell pasteurization of eggs, and irradiation of ground beef. Just as with milk, these new technologies should be implemented in addition to good sanitation, not as a replacement for it.

So, in the end, it is up to the consumer to demand a safe food supply; up to industry to produce it; up to researchers to develop better ways of doing so; and up to government to see that it happens, to make sure it works and to identify problems still in need of solutions.

WHAT IS CDC DOING TO CONTROL AND PREVENT FOODBORNE DISEASE?

- The Centers for Disease Control and Prevention (CDC) is part of the U.S. Public Health Service, with a mission to use the best scientific information to monitor, investigate, control, and prevent public health problems. Using the tools of epidemiology and laboratory science, CDC provides scientific assessment of public health threats. CDC works closely with state health departments to monitor the frequency of specific diseases and conducts national surveillance for them.

- CDC provides expert epidemiologic and microbiologic consultation to health departments and other federal agencies on a variety of public health issues, including foodborne disease, and it stations epidemiologists in state health departments to help with the surveillance and investigation of many problems.
- CDC can also send a team into the field to conduct emergency field investigations for large or unusual outbreaks, in collaboration with state public health officials. CDC researchers develop new methods for identifying, characterizing, and fingerprinting the microbes that cause disease. We translate laboratory research into practical field methods that can be used by public health authorities in states and counties.
- CDC is not a regulatory agency. Government regulation of food safety is carried out by the Food and Drug Administration (FDA), the U.S. Department of Agriculture (USDA), and National Marine Fisheries Service, and other regulatory agencies.
- CDC maintains regular contact with regulatory agencies. When new public health threats appear, CDC learns what they are and how they can be controlled through rapid scientific field and laboratory investigation. CDC shares the results of these investigations with the states, with the regulatory federal agencies and with the industries themselves. Although CDC does not regulate the safety of food, CDC assesses the effectiveness of current prevention efforts and provides independent scientific assessment of what the problems are, how they can be controlled, and of where there are gaps in the knowledge of the CDC staff.

WHAT ARE SOME UNSOLVED PROBLEMS IN FOODBORNE DISEASE?

As new foodborne problems emerge, several questions need to be answered before the problem can be successfully controlled. It takes careful scientific observation and research to answer these questions. Some pressing unanswered questions include the following:

- How do the foodborne pathogens spread among the animals themselves, and how can this be prevented?
- This includes *E. coli* 0157:H7 among cattle, *Salmonella enteritis* among egg-laying hens, and *campylobacter* in broiler chickens.
- If it were possible to prevent the animals from becoming infected in the first place, there would not be as much illness in the humans who eat them.

WHAT IS THE MICROBIAL CAUSE OF OUTBREAKS IN WHICH NO PATHOGEN CAN BE IDENTIFIED BY CURRENT METHODS?

This is true for over half of the reported foodborne outbreaks. Will wider application of existing experimental diagnostic methods help, or are there outbreaks caused by pathogens we simply do not yet know how to identify?

- What would be the impact of basic food safety education of restaurant workers on the risk of foodborne disease among restaurant patrons?
- How can the food and water that animals consume be made safer?
- How can we dispose of animal manure usefully, without threatening the food supply and the environment?
- How can basic food safety principles be most effectively taught to school children?
- How can we be sure food safety standards in other countries are as good as those in the United States? As we import more of our fresh foods from other countries, we need to be confident that they are produced with the same level of safety as food in the United States.
- What control strategies in the slaughter plant will reduce the contamination of poultry meat with *campylobacter*?
- How can irradiation pasteurization of certain high risk foods, such as ground beef, be used most effectively?
- How do raspberries in Central America get contaminated with *cyclospora* in the first place? Does this parasite have an animal reservoir?
- How can alfalfa sprouts and other raw sprouts be produced safely? Sprouts are unique among foods in that the conditions for sprouting are also perfect for bacterial growth, and they are not cooked after that.

Table A.1 **SUMMARY OF AGENTS THAT CAUSE FOOD-BORNE ILLNESS**

CAUSATIVE AGENT (*SPOREFORMING BACTERIA)	TYPE OF ILLNESS	SYMPTOMS ONSET	COMMON FOODS	PREVENTION
Anisakis spp.	Parasitic infection	Coughing, vomiting 1 hr to 2 wks	Raw or undercooked seafood, especially bottom-feeding fish	Cook fish to proper temperature throughout; freeze to meet *2001 FDA Food Code* specification
**Bacillus cereus*	Bacterial intoxication or toxin-mediated infection	1) Diarrhea, abdominal cramps (8 to 16 hrs) 2) Vomiting type, vomiting, diarrhea, abdominal crams (30 minutes to 6 hrs)	1) Diarrheal type: meats, milk, vegetables 2) Vomiting type: rice, starchy foods; grains and cerals	Properly heat, cool, and reheat foods
Campylobacter jejuni	Bacterial infections	Watery, bloody diarrhea (2 to 5 days)	Raw chicken, raw milk, raw meat	Properly handle and cook foods; avoid cross-contamination
Ciguatoxin	Fish toxin, originating from toxic algae of tropical waters	Vertigo, hot/cold flashes, diarrhea, vomiting (15 minutes to 24 hrs)	Marine finfish, including grouper, barracuda, snappers, jacks, mackerel, triggerfish, reef fish	Purchase fish from a reputable supplier; cooking WILL NOT inactivate the toxin
**Clostridium botulinum*	Bacterial intoxication	Dizziness, double vision, difficulty in breathing and swallowing, headache (12 to 36 hours)	Improperly canned foods, vacuum packed refrigerated foods, cooked foods in anaerobic mass	Properly heat process anaerobically packed foods; DO NOT use home canned foods
**Clostridium perfringens*	Bacterial toxin-mediated infections	Intense abdominal pains and severe diarrhea (8 to 22 hrs)	Spices, gravy, improperly cooled foods (especially meats and gravy dishes)	Properly cook, cool, and reheat foods
Cryptosporidium parvum	Parasitic infection	Severe watery diarrhea within 1 week of ingestion	Contaminated water, food contaminated by infected food workers	Use potable water supply; practice good personal hygiene and hand washing
Cyclospora cayetanensis	Parasitic infection	Watery and explosive diarrhea, loss of appetite, bloating (1 week)	Water, strawberries, raspberries, and raw vegetables	Good sanitation; reputable supplier
Food Allergens	An allergic reaction usually involving the skin, mouth, digestive tract, or airways	Skin: hives, rashes, and itching Mouth: swelling and itching of lips and tongue Digestive tract: vomiting and diarrhea Airways: difficulty breathing, wheezing	Foods that contain milk, egg, wheat, nuts and peanuts, fish and shellfish	Packaged and prepared foods must be properly labeled if they contain common food allergens so sensitive people can avoid them

Table A.1 **SUMMARY OF AGENTS THAT CAUSE FOOD-BORNE ILLNESS (CONTINUED)**

CAUSATIVE AGENT (*SPOREFORMING BACTERIA)	TYPE OF ILLNESS	SYMPTOMS ONSET	COMMON FOODS	PREVENTION
Giardia lamblia	Parasitic infection	Diarrhea within 1 week of contact	Contaminated water	Potable water supply; good personal hygiene and hand washing
Hepatitis A virus	Viral infection	Fever, nausea, vomiting, abdominal pain, fatigue, swelling of the liver, jaundice (15 to 50 days)	Foods that are prepared with human contact, contaminated water	Wash hands and practice good personal hygiene; avoid raw seafood
Listeria monocytogenes	Bacterial infection	1) Healthy adult: flu-like symptoms 2) Highly susceptible population: septicemia, meningitis, encephalitis, birth defects (1 day to 3 weeks)	Raw milk, dairy items, raw meats, refrigerated ready-to-eat foods, processed ready-to-eat meats such as hot dogs, raw vegetables, and seafood	Properly store and cook foods; avoid cross contamination; rotate processed refrigerated foods using "first-in, first-out" to ensure timely use
Mycotoxins	Intoxication	1) Acute onset: hemorrhage, fluid buildup, possible death 2) Chronic: cancer from small doses over time	Moldy grains: corn, corn products, peanuts, pecans, walnuts and milk	Purchase food from a reputable supplier; keep grains and nuts dry; protect products from humidity
Norwalk virus	Viral infections	Vomiting, diarrhea, abdominal pain, headache, and low grade fever; onset 24 to 48 hrs	Sewage, contaminated water, contaminated salad ingredients, raw clams, oysters	Use potable water; cook all shellfish; handle food properly; meet time temperature guidelines for PHF
Rotavirus	Viral infection	Diarrhea (especially in children and infants), vomiting, low grade fever, 1 to 3 days onset; lasts 4 to 8 days	Sewage, contaminated water, contaminated salad ingredients, raw seafood	Good personal hygiene and hand washing; proper food-handling practices
Salmonella spp.	Bacterial infection	Nausea, fever, vomiting, abdominal cramps, diarrhea (6 to 48 hrs)	Raw meats, raw poultry, eggs, milk, dairy products	Properly cook foods; avoid cross-contamination
Scombrotoxin	Seafood toxin originating from histamine-producing bacteria	Dizziness, burning feeling in the mouth, facial rash or hives, peppery taste in mouth, headache, itching, teary eyes, runny nose (1 to 30 minutes)	Tuna, mahi-mahi, bluefish, sardines, mackerel, anchovies, amberjack, abalone	Purchase fish from a reputable supplier; store fish at low temperatures to prevent growth
Shellfish toxins: PSP, DSP, DAP, NSP	Intoxication	Numbness of lips, tongue, arms, legs, neck; lack of muscle coordination (10 to 30 minutes)	Contaminated mussels, clams, oysters, scallops	Purchase from a reputable supplier Shiga toxin-producing

Table A.1 SUMMARY OF AGENTS THAT CAUSE FOOD-BORNE ILLNESS (CONTINUED)

CAUSATIVE AGENT (*SPOREFORMING BACTERIA)	TYPE OF ILLNESS	SYMPTOMS ONSET	COMMON FOODS	PREVENTION
Escherichia coli	Bacterial infection or toxin-mediated infection	Bloody diarrhea followed by kidney failure and hemolytic uremic syndrome (HUS) in severe cases (12 to 72 hours)	Undercooked hamburger, raw milk, unpasteurized apple cider, and lettuce	Practice good food sanitation; hand washing; properly handle and cook foods
Shigella spp.	Bacterial infection	Bacillary dysentery, diarrhea, fever, abdominal cramps, dehydration (1 to 7 days)	Foods that are prepared with human contact: salads, raw vegetables, milk, dairy products, raw poultry, non-potable water, ready-to-eat meat	Wash hands and practice good personal hygiene; properly cook foods
Staphylococcus aureus	Bacterial intoxication	Nausea, vomiting, abdominal cramps, headaches (2 to 6 hours)	Foods that are prepared with human contact cooked or processed foods	Wash hands and practice good personal hygiene; cooking WILL NOT inactivate the toxin
Toxoplasma gondii	Parasitic infection	Mild cases of the disease involve swollen lymph glands, fever, headache, and muscle aches. Severe cases may result in damage to the eye or brain (10 to 13 days)	Raw meats, raw vegetables, and fruits	Good sanitation; reputable supplier; proper cooking
Trichinella spiralis	Parasitic infection from a nematode worm	Nausea, vomiting, diarrhea, sweating, muscle soreness (2 to 28 days)	Primarily undercooked pork products and wild game meats (bear, walrus)	Cook foods to the proper temperature throughout
Vibrio spp.	Bacterial infection	Headache, fever, chills, diarrhea, vomiting, severe electrolyte loss, gastroenteritis (2 to 48 hrs)	Raw or improperly cooked fish and shellfish	Practice good sanitation, properly cook foods, avoid serving raw seafood

RESOURCES

GOVERNMENT AGENCIES PROVIDING FOOD SAFETY PROGRAMS

Centers for Disease Control and Prevention (CDC) — www.cdc.org

EPA Office of Prevention, Pesticides and Toxic Substances — www.epa.gov./internet/oppts

Gateway to Government Food Safety Information — www.foodsafety.gov

National Marine Fisheries Services — www.seafood.nmfs.noaa.gov

USDA/FDA Food and Nutrition Information Center — www.nal.usda.gov/fnic/

USDA Food Safety and Inspection Service (FSIS) — www.fsis.usda.gov

United States Department of Agriculture (SDA) — www.usda gov

United States Food and Drug Administration (FDA) — www.fda.gov

United States Environmental Protection Agency (EPA) — www.epa.gov

Canadian Food Safety Sites Involving HACCP — foodnet.fic.ca/safety/safety.html

INDEPENDENT FOOD SAFETY ORGANIZATIONS

Conference for Food Protection — www.foodprotect.org

Food and Agriculture Organization — www.fao.org

International Food Information Council – ificinfo.health.org/

Partnerships for Food Safety Education — www.fightbac.org

The Food Allergy Network — www.foodalergy.com

World Health Organization — www.who.int

INDUSTRY FOOD SAFETY ORGANIZATIONS

American Meat Institute — www.meatami.org

The American Egg Board — www.aeb.org

The Food Marketing Institute — www.fmi.org

The Food Marketing Institute-Retail Food Establishment Industry Facts — www.fmi.org/facts_figs/superfact

The National Chicken Council — www.eatchicken.com

U.S. Poultry and Egg Association — www.poultryegg.org

Pest Control

Supply Companies

Actron, Inc. — www.actroninc.com

Do-It-Yourself Pest Control — www.doyourowonpestcontrol.com

Insect-O-Cutor — www.insect-o-cutor.com

Killgerm/PestWest, USA — www.Pestwest.com

PCO — www.pco.ca

The Orkin Company — www.orkin.com

PEST MANAGEMENT ORGANIZATIONS

Association of Applied Insect Ecologists — www.aaie.com

National Pest Management Association — www.pestworld.org

Pest Control Industry — www.pestweb.com

Pest Control Technology magazine — www.pctonline.com

Virginia Polytechnic Institute and University Pesticide Programs — www.vtpp.ext.vt.eduvm.cfsan.fda.gov/~mow/intro.html

SUPPLIERS OF EQUIPMENT AND PRODUCTS USED FOR CLEANING AND SANITIZING

All QA Products — www.allqa.com

Bowerman Associates — www.ebowerman.com

Champion Industries — www.championindustries.com

DiverseyLever, Inc. — www.diverseylever.com

Ecolab — www.ecolab.com

Paper Thermometer Company — www.mv.com/ipusers/paperthermometer/

Steritech— www.stertech.com

The Soap and Detergent Association — www.sdahq.org

SOURCES OF FOOD SAFETY EDUCATION INFORMATION

Food Safety Day — www.foodsci.purdue.edu/publications/foodsafetyday

Prentice Hall — www.prenhall.com

The Food Marketing Institute — www.fmi.org

Partnerships for Food Safety Education — www.fightbac.org

SOURCES FOR CAREERS AVAILABLE IN FOOD SAFETY

According to The Food Safety Information Handbook by Cynthia A. Roberts, Oryx Press, many trade associations and professional societies offer scholarship, internship, or fellowship opportunities. If this book has made you more aware of this important subject, and has given you a passion to seek a career in the culinary field, here, from Roberts' valuable book is a list for more information:

American Culinary Federation, Inc.
St. Augustine, FL
800-624-9458
www.acschefs.org
offers scholarships

American Dietetic Association (ADA)
Chicago, IL
800-877-1600
www.eatright.org
offers scholarships

American Institute of Baking (AIB)
Manhattan, KS
785-537-4750 ext 179
www.aibonline.org
offers scholarships

American School Food Service Association (ASFSA)
Alexandria, VA
703-739-3900
www.asfsa.org
offers scholarships and interships

American Society for Healthcare Food Service Administrators (ASFSA)
Chicago, IL
312 422-3870
www.asfsa.org

Centers for Disease Control and Prevention (CDC)
Atlanta, GA
770-488-3257
www.cdc.gov

Institute of Food Technologists (IFT)
Chicago, IL
312-782-8424
www.ift.org

International Association of Culinary Professionals (IACP)
Louisville, KY
502-581-9786
www.iacpfoundation.org

National Association of College and University Food Services (NACUFS)
East Lansing, MI
517-332-2494
www.nacufs.org

National Environmental Health Association
Denver, CO
303-756-9090
ask for Megan Thompson
Write for a scholarship application and information.

The Asparagus Club Scholarship
Send request to Scholarship Program Administrators, Inc.
Post Office Box 23737
Nashville, TN 27202-3737

National Meat Association (NMA)
Oakland, CA
510-763-1533

National Restaurant Association Educational Foundation
Chicago, IL
800-765-2122 ext. 733
www.nra.org

BIBLIOGRAPHY
and Recommended Reading

General Interest

Bennion, Marion, and Barbara Scheule. *Introductory Foods*. 12th ed. Upper Saddle River, N.J.: Prentice Hall, 2003.

Bickel, Walter, ed. and trans. *Hering's Dictionary of Classical and Modern Cookery*. 13th English ed. London: Virtue, 1994.

Davidson, Alan. *The Oxford Companion to Food*. Oxford, England: Oxford University Press, 1999.

Dornenburg, Andrew, and Karen Page. *Becoming a Chef*. New York: Wiley, 2003.

———. *Culinary Artistry*. New York: Wiley, 1996.

Escoffier, Auguste. *The Escoffier Cook Book and Guide to the Fine Art of Cookery for Connoisseurs, Chefs, Epicures*. (Trans. of *Le Guide culinaire*.) New York: Crown, 1969.

Herbst, Sharon Tyler. *The New Food Lover's Companion*. 3rd ed. Hauppauge, New York: Barron's Educational Series, 2001.

Kamman, Madeleine. *The New Making of a Cook*. New York: Morrow, 1997.

Labensky, Steven, Gaye G. Ingram, and Sarah R. Labensky. *Webster's New World Dictionary of Culinary Arts*. 2nd ed. Upper Saddle River, N.J.: Prentice Hall, 2000.

Larousse Gastronomique. English ed. New York: Potter, 2001.

Marranca, Bonnie, ed. *A Slice of Life: Contemporary Food Writers on Food*. New York: Overlook Press, 2003.

Molt, Mary. *Food for Fifty*. 12th ed. Upper Saddle River, N.J.: Prentice Hall, 2005.

Pépin, Jacques. *The Art of Cooking*. New York: Knopf, 1987.

———. *La Technique*. New York: Pocket Books, 1987.

Peterson, James. *Essentials of Cooking*. New York: Artisan, 2000.

Point, Fernand. *Fernand Point: Ma Gastronomie*. English ed. Wilton, Conn.: Lyceum Books, 1974.

Saulnier, Louis. *Le Répertoire de la Cuisine*. Revised ed. New York: Barron's Educational Series, 1976.

Willan, Anne. *La Varenne Pratique*. New York: Crown, 1989.

Food History

Anderson, Jean. *The American Century Cookbook: The Most Popular Recipes of the 20th Century*. New York: Potter, 1997.

Coe, Sophie D., and Michael D. Coe. *The True History of Chocolate*. New York: Thames & Hudson, 1996.

Cooper, Ann. *A Woman's Place Is in the Kitchen: The Evolution of Women Chefs*. Stamford, Conn.: Thomson, 1997.

Fussell, Betty. *The Story of Corn*. New York: Knopf, 1992.

Kurlansky, Mark. *Cod: A Biography of the Fish That Changed the World*. New York: Walker, 1997.

Lovegren, Sylvia. *Fashionable Food: Seven Decades of Food Fads*. New York: Macmillan General Reference, 1995.

Mintz, Sidney W. *Sweetness and Power: The Place of Sugar in Modern History*. New York: Viking Press, 1995.

Norman, Barbara. *Tales of the Table: A History of Western Cuisine*. Upper Saddle River, N.J.: Prentice Hall, 1972.

Revel, Jean-François. *Culture and Cuisine*. (Trans. of *Un Festin en paroles*.) New York: Da Capo Press, 1982.

Rupp, Rebecca. *Blue Corn and Square Tomatoes*. Pownal, Vt.: Garden Way, 1987.

Schlossberg, Eli W. *The World of Orthodox Judaism*. Northvale, N.J.: Aronson, 1996.

Shapiro, Laura. *Perfection Salad: Women and Cooking at the Turn of the Century*. New York: Farrar, Straus & Giroux, 1986.

Tannahill, Reay. *Food in History*. Revised ed. New York: Crown, 1995.

Toussaint-Samat, Maguelonne. *A History of Food,* trans. Anthea Bell. Cambridge, Mass.: Blackwell, 1992.

Wheaton, Barbara Ketcham. *Savoring the Past: The French Kitchen and Table from 1300 to 1789.* Reprint ed. New York: Touchstone Books, 1996.

Willan, Anne. *Great Cooks and Their Recipes: From Taillevent to Escoffier.* Boston: Little, Brown, 1992.

Sanitation and Safety

International Life Sciences Institute. *A Simple Guide to Understanding and Applying the Hazard Analysis Critical Control Point Concept.* Washington, D.C.: ILSI Press, 1993.

Loken, Joan K. *The HACCP Food Safety Manual.* New York: Wiley, 1995.

McSwane, David, Nancy Rue and Richard Linton. *Essentials of Food Safety and Sanitation.* 2nd ed. Upper Saddle River, N.J.: Prentice Hall, 2005.

National Assessment Institute. *Handbook for Safe Food Service Management.* 2nd ed. Upper Saddle River, N.J.: Prentice Hall, 1998.

National Restaurant Association Educational Foundation. *ServSafe Essentials.* New York: Wiley, 2004.

Nutrition

Baskette, Michael, and Eleanor Mainella. *The Art of Nutritional Cooking.* 2nd ed. Upper Saddle River, N.J.: Prentice Hall, 1999.

Drummond, Nina, and Lisa M. Brefore. *Nutrition for Foodservice and Culinary Professionals.* New York: Wiley, 2003.

Freyberg, Nicholas, and Willis A. Gortner. *The Food Additives Book.* New York: Bantam Books, 1982.

Food Costing and Business Skills

Cullen, Noel. *Life Beyond the Line: A Front-of-the-House Companion for Culinarians.* Upper Saddle River, N.J.: Prentice Hall, 2001.

Drysdale, John, and Jennifer Adams Aldrich. *Profitable Menu Planning.* 3rd ed. Upper Saddle River, N.J.: Prentice Hall, 2002.

Labensky, Sarah R. *Applied Math for Food Service.* Upper Saddle River, N.J.: Prentice Hall, 1998.

Miller, Jack E. *Menu Pricing and Strategy.* 4th ed. New York: Van Nostrand Reinhold, 1996.

Schmidt, Arno. *Chef's Book of Formulas, Yields, and Sizes.* 2nd ed. New York: Van Nostrand Reinhold, 1996.

Tools

Bridge, Fred, and Jean F. Tibbetts. *The Well-Tooled Kitchen.* New York: Morrow, 1991.

Williams, Chuck, ed. *Williams-Sonoma Kitchen Companion.* New York: Time-Life Books, 2000.

Wolf, Burton, ed. *The New Cooks' Catalogue.* New York: Knopf, 2000.

General Ingredients

Anderson, Burton. *Treasures of the Italian Table: Italy's Celebrated Foods and the Artisans Who Make Them.* New York: Morrow, 1994.

Cost, Bruce. *Asian Ingredients: A Guide to Foodstuffs of China, Japan, Korea, Thailand and Vietnam.* New York: Quill Harper Collins, 2000.

DeMers, John. *The Community Kitchen's Complete Guide to Gourmet Coffee.* New York: Simon & Schuster, 1986.

Dowell, Philip, and Adrian Bailey. *Cook's Ingredients.* New York: Morrow, 1980.

Jordan, Michele Anna. *The Good Cook's Book of Oil & Vinegar.* Reading, Mass.: Addison-Wesley, 1992.

Morris, Sallie, and Lesley Mackley. *The Spice Ingredients Cookbook.* New York: Lorenz Books, 1997.

Norman, Jill. *The Complete Book of Spices.* American ed. New York: Viking Studio Books, 1991.

Ortiz, Elisabeth Lambert. *The Encyclopedia of Herbs, Spices and Flavorings.* 1st American ed. New York: Dorling Kindersley, 1992.

Schapira, Joel, and Karl Schapira. *The Book of Coffee and Tea.* New York: St. Martin's Press, 1975.

Ward, Susie, et al. *The Gourmet Atlas.* New York: Macmillan, 1997.

Dairy and Cheese

Fletcher, Janet. *The Cheese Course.* San Francisco: Chronicle Books, 2002.

Jenkins, Steven. *Steven Jenkins' Cheese Primer.* New York: Workman, 1996.

Lambert, Paula. *The Cheese Lover's Cookbook & Guide.* New York: Simon & Schuster, 2000.

Marquis, Vivienne, and Patricia Haskell. *The Cheese Book.* New York: Simon & Schuster, 1985.

Masui, Kazuko, and Tomoko Yamada. *French Cheeses.* New York: Dorling Kindersley, 1996.

Werlin, Laura. *The All-American Cheese and Wine Book.* New York: Stewart, Tabori & Chang, 2003.

Flavors and Food Science

Coates, Clive. *An Encyclopedia of the Wines and Domaines of France.* Davis, Calif.: University of California Press, 2001.

Corriher, Shirley O. *Cookwise.* New York: Morrow, 1997.

Delwiche, Jeannine. "Are there 'basic' tastes?" *Trends in Food Science & Technology,* 7, Special Issue on Flavor Perception (December 1996): 411–415.

Heath, Henry B. *Source Book of Flavors.* Norwalk, Conn.: AVI, 1981.

MacNeil, Karen. *The Wine Bible.* New York: Workman, 2001.

McGee, Harold. *On Food and Cooking.* Revised ed. New York: Scribner, 2004.

McWilliams, Margaret. *Foods: Experimental Perspectives.* 4th ed. Upper Saddle River, N.J.: Prentice Hall, 2001.

Parsons, Russ. *How to Read a French Fry*. Boston: Houghton Mifflin, 2001.

Robinson, Jancis. *The Oxford Companion to Wine*. 2nd ed. Oxford, England: Oxford University Press, 1999.

Schmid, Albert. *Hospitality Managers Guide to Wines, Beers and Spirits*. Upper Saddle River, NJ: Prentice Hall, 2004.

Stocks, Sauces and Soups

Clayton, Bernard. *The Complete Book of Soups and Stews*. New York: Simon & Schuster, 1987.

Davis, Deidre. *A Fresh Look at Saucing Foods*. Reading, Mass.: Addison-Wesley, 1993.

Editors of *Cook's Illustrated* Magazine. *The Best Recipe: Soup and Stew*. Boston: Boston Common Press, 2001.

Kafka, Barbara. *Soup: A Way of Life*. New York: Artisan, 1998.

Larousse, David Paul. *The Sauce Bible: Guide to the Saucier's Craft*. New York: Wiley, 1993.

Peterson, James. *Sauces: Classical and Contemporary Sauce Making*. 2nd ed. New York: Van Nostrand Reinhold, 1998.

Sokolov, Raymond A. *The Saucier's Apprentice*. New York: Knopf, 1976.

Meat

Aidells, Bruce, and Denis Kelly. *The Complete Meat Cookbook*. New York: Houghton Mifflin, 1998.

Ellis, Merle. *The Great American Meat Cookbook*. New York: Knopf, 1996.

Knox, Luc, and Keith Richmond. *The World Encyclopedia of Meat, Game and Poultry*. New York: Lorenz Books, 2000.

The Meat Buyers Guide. Reston, Va.: National Association of Meat Purveyors, 1990.

Game

Cameron, Angus, and Judith Jones. *The L. L. Bean Game and Fish Cookbook*. New York: Random House, 1983.

Hibler, Jane. *Wild about Game: 150 Recipes for Cooking Farm-Raised and Wild Game from Alligator and Antelope to Venison and Wild Turkey*. New York: Broadway Books, 1998.

Little, Carolyn. *The Game Cookbook*. Wiltshire, England: Crowood Press, 1988.

Marrone, Teresa. *Dressing and Cooking Wild Game*. New York: Prentice Hall, 1987.

Webster, Harold W., Jr. *The Complete Venison Cookbook*. Brandon, Miss.: Quail Ridge Press, 1996.

Fish and Shellfish

Cronin, Isaac, Jay Harlow, and Paul Johnson. *The California Seafood Cookbook*. Berkeley, Calif.: Aris Books, 1983.

Howarth, A. Jan. *The Complete Fish Cookbook*. New York: St. Martin's Press, 1983.

King, Shirley. *Fish, The Basics*. Revised and updated ed. New York: Chapters, 1996.

———. *Saucing the Fish*. New York: Simon & Schuster, 1986.

Loomis, Susan Herrmann. *The Great American Seafood Cookbook*. New York: Workman, 1988.

McClane, A. J. *The Encyclopedia of Fish Cookery*. New York: Holt, Rinehart & Winston, 1989.

Peterson, James. *Fish and Shellfish*. New York: Morrow, 1998.

The Seafood Handbook: Seafood Standards. Rockland, Maine: Seafood Business Magazine, 1991.

The Seafood List: FDA Guide to Acceptable Market Names for Food Fish Sold in Interstate Commerce. Washington, D.C.: Center for Food Safety and Applied Nutrition, 2001.

Eggs and Breakfast Cookery

Bristow, Linda Kay. *Bread and Breakfast*. San Ramon, Calif.: 101 Productions, 1985.

Davids, Kenneth. *Coffee: A Guide to Buying, Brewing, and Enjoying*. 5th ed. New York: St. Martin's Griffin, 2001.

Eggcyclopedia. 2nd ed. Park Ridge, Ill.: American Egg Board, 1989.

Fox, Margaret S., and John Bear. *Morning Food from Café Beaujolais*. Berkeley, Calif.: Ten Speed Press, 1994.

Jamison, Cheryl A., and Bill Jamison. *A Real American Breakfast: The Best Meal of the Day, Any Time of the Day*. New York: Morrow, 2002.

Pettigrew, Jane. *The Tea Companion*. Jackson, Tenn.: Running Press Book Publishers, 2004.

Vegetables and Fruits

Andrews, Jean. *Peppers: The Domesticated Capsicums*. Austin: University of Texas Press, 1984.

Brown, Marlene. *International Produce Cookbook and Guide*. Los Angeles: HP Books, 1989.

Davidson, Alan. *Fruit: A Connoisseur's Guide and Cookbook*. New York: Simon & Schuster, 1991.

DeWitt, Dave, and Nancy Gerlach. *The Whole Chile Pepper Book*. Boston: Little, Brown, 1990.

Goldstein, Joyce. *Italian Slow and Savory*. San Francisco: Chronicle Books, 2004.

Greenburg, Patricia. *The Whole Soy Cookbook*. New York: Random House, 1998.

Ingram, Christine. *The New Guide to Vegetables*. New York: Hermes House, 1997.

Madison, Deborah, *Local Flavors: Cooking and Eating from America's Farmer's Markets*. New York: Broadway, 2002.

Miller, Mark, with John Harrisson. *The Great Chile Book*. Berkeley, Calif.: Ten Speed Press, 1991.

Murdich, Jack. *Buying Produce*. New York: Morrow, 1986.

Nathan, Amy. *Salad*. San Francisco: Chronicle Books, 1985.

Payne, Rolce Redard, and Dorrit Speyer Senior. *Cooking with Fruit.* New York: Crescent Books, 1995.

Peterson, James, and Justin Schwartz. *Vegetables.* New York: Morrow, 1998.

Routhier, Nicole. *Nicole Routhier's Fruit Cookbook.* New York: Workman, 1996.

Schmidt, Jimmy. *Cooking for All Seasons.* New York: Macmillan, 1991.

Schneider, Elizabeth. *Vegetables from Amaranth to Zucchini: The Essential Reference.* New York: Morrow, 2001.

Grains and Pasta

Bugialli, Giuliano. *On Pasta.* New York: Simon & Schuster, 1988.

Della Croce, Julia. *Pasta Classica.* Reprint ed. San Francisco: Chronicle Books, 1996.

Greene, Bert. *The Grains Cookbook.* New York: Workman, 1988.

Kummer, Corby. "Pasta." *The Atlantic,* 258, no. 1 (July 1986): 35–47.

Leblang, Bonnie Tandy, and Joanne Lamb Hayes. *Rice.* New York: Harmony Books, 1991.

Spier, Carol. *Food Essentials: Grains and Pasta.* New York: Crescent Books, 1993.

Vegetarian Cooking

Bergeron, Ken. *Professional Vegetarian Cooking.* New York: Wiley, 1999.

Harris, William. *The Scientific Basis of Vegetarianism.* Honolulu, Hawaii: Health Publishers, 1995.

Holthaus, Fusako. *Tofu Cookery.* Tokyo: Kodansha International, 1992.

Madison, Deborah. *Vegetarian Cooking for Everyone.* New York: Broadway Books, 1997.

Melino, Vesanto, and Brenda Davis. *The New Becoming Vegetarian: The Essential Guide to a Healthy Vegetarian Diet.* Summertown, Tenn.: Healthy Living Publications, 2003.

Messina, Mark, and Virginia Messina. *The Vegetarian Way.* New York: Three Rivers Press, 1996.

Charcuterie

Editors of Time-Life Books. *The Good Cook: Terrines, Pâtés and Galantines.* London: Time-Life International, 1981.

Ehlert, Friedrich W., et al. *Pâtés and Terrines.* Reprint ed. London: Hearst Books, 1990.

Grigson, Jane. *The Art of Charcuterie.* Reprint ed. New York: Echo Press, 1991.

Breads

Albright, Barbara, and Leslie Weiner. *Mostly Muffins.* New York: St. Martin's Press, 1984.

Alston, Elizabeth. *Biscuits and Scones.* New York: Potter, 1988.

Clayton, Bernard. *Bernard Clayton's New Complete Book of Breads.* Revised ed. New York: Fireside Books, 1995.

David, Elizabeth. *English Bread and Yeast Cookery.* Notes by Karen Hess. American ed. New York: Viking Press, 1980.

Glezer, Maggie. *Artisan Baking Across America.* New York: Artisan, 2000.

Hensperger, Beth. *The Bread Bible: Beth Hensperger's 300 Favorite Recipes.* San Francisco: Chronicle Books, 1999.

Ortiz, Joe. *The Village Baker: Classic Regional Breads from Europe and America.* Berkeley, Calif.: Ten Speed Press, 1993.

Reinhart, Peter. *The Bread Baker's Apprentice.* Berkeley, Calif.: Ten Speed Press, 2001.

Pastries and Desserts

Braker, Flo. *The Simple Art of Perfect Baking.* Shelburne, Vt.: Chapters, 1992.

Daley, Regan. *In the Sweet Kitchen: The Definitive Baker's Companion.* New York: Artisan, 2001.

Fletcher, Helen S. *The New Pastry Cook.* New York: Morrow, 1986.

Friberg, Bo. *The Professional Pastry Chef.* 4th ed. New York: Wiley, 2002.

Healy, Bruce, and Paul Bugat. *Mastering the Art of French Pastry.* Woodbury, N.Y.: Barron's, 1984.

Heatter, Maida. *Maida Heatter's Book of Great Desserts.* Kansas City, Mo.: Andrews McMeel, 1999.

Hyman, Philip, and Mary Hyman, trans. *The Best of Gaston Lenotre's Desserts.* Woodbury, N.Y.: Barron's, 1983.

Labensky, Sarah, and Eddy Van Damme. *On Baking: A Textbook of Baking and Pastry Fundamentals.* Upper Saddle River, N.J.: Prentice Hall, 2005.

London, Sheryl, and Mel London. *Fresh Fruit Desserts: Classic and Contemporary.* New York: Prentice Hall, 1990.

Luchetti, Emily. *A Passion for Desserts.* San Francisco: Chronicle Books, 2003.

Purdy, Susan G. *A Piece of Cake.* Reprint ed. New York: Macmillan, 1993.

Silverton, Nancy. *Desserts by Nancy Silverton.* New York: Harper & Row, 1986.

Teubner, Christian, ed. *The Chocolate Bible.* New York: Penguin Studio, 1997.

Hors D'Oeuvre and Buffets

Aloni, Nicole. *Secrets from a Caterer's Kitchen.* Tucson, Ariz.: HP Books, 2001.

Duffy, Gillian. *Hors d'Oeuvres.* New York: Morrow, 1998.

Janericco, Terence. *The Book of Great Hors d'Oeuvre.* New York: Wiley, 1990.

Larousse, David Paul. *The Professional Garde Manger.* New York: Wiley, 1996.

Sanders, Ed, et al. *Catering Solutions*. Upper Saddle River, N.J.: Prentice Hall, 2000.

Schmidt, Arno, and Inja Nam. *The Book of Hors d'Oeuvres and Canapes*. New York: Van Nostrand Reinhold, 1996.

Simmons, Bob, and Coleen Simmons. *Tapas Fantasticas: Appetizers with a Spanish Flair*. San Leandro, Calif.: Bristol, 1999.

International Cuisines

Alford, Jeffrey. *Hot Sour Salty Sweet: A Culinary Journey Through Southeast Asia*. New York: Artisan, 2000.

Bayless, Rick, with Deann Groen Bayless. *Authentic Mexican: Regional Cooking from the Heart of Mexico*. New York: Morrow, 1987.

Bugialli, Giuliano. *The Fine Art of Italian Cooking*. New York: Random House, 1990.

Casas, Penelope. *The Foods and Wines of Spain*. New York: Knopf, 1991.

Downer, Lesley. *At the Japanese Table*. San Francisco: Chronicle Books, 1993.

Field, Carol. *Celebrating Italy*. New York: Morrow, 1990.

Gin, Maggie. *Regional Cooking of China*. San Francisco: 101 Productions, 1984.

Harris, Jessica. *The Africa Cookbook: Tastes of a Continent*. New York: Simon & Schuster, 1998.

Hazan, Marcella. *Essentials of Classic Italian Cooking*. New York: Knopf, 1993.

Jaffrey, Madhur. *An Invitation to Indian Cooking*. New York: Ecco Press, 1999.

Kasper, Lynn Rossetto. *The Splendid Table: Recipes from Emilia-Romagna, the Heartland of Northern Italian Food*. New York: Morrow, 1992.

Kennedy, Diana. *The Cuisines of Mexico*. Revised ed. New York: Harper & Row, 1986.

Lo, Kenneth. *The Encyclopedia of Chinese Cooking*. New York: Bristol Books, 1997.

McDermott, Nancie. *Real Thai: The Best of Thailand's Regional Cooking*. San Francisco: Chronicle Books, 1992.

Pham, Mai. *Pleasures of the Vietnamese Table*. New York: HarperCollins, 2001.

Roden, Claudia. *The New Book of Middle Eastern Food*. New York: Knopf, 2000.

Rojas-Lombardi, Felipe. *The Art of South American Cooking*. New York: HarperCollins, 1991.

Rose, Evelyn. *The New Complete International Jewish Cookbook*. New York: Carroll & Graf, 1992.

Routhier, Nicole. *Foods of Vietnam*. New York: Stewart, Tabori & Chang, 1989.

Rozin, Elisabeth. *Ethnic Cuisine: How to Create the Authentic Flavors of 30 International Cuisines*. Reprint ed. New York: Penguin Books USA, 1992.

Solomon, Charmaine. *The Complete Asian Cookbook*. Revised ed. Boston: Tuttle, 2002.

———. *Encyclopedia of Asian Food*. Boston: Periplus Editions, 1998.

Toomre, Joyce. *Classic Russian Cooking: Elena Molokhovets' A Gift to Young Housewives*, trans., introduced and annotated by Joyce Toomre. Bloomington: Indiana University Press, 1992.

Von Bremzen, Anya, and John Welchman. *Please to the Table: The Russian Cookbook*. New York: Workman, 1990.

Garnishing

Budgen, June. *The Book of Garnishes*. Los Angeles: HP Books, 1986.

Haydock, Robert, and Yukiko Haydock. *Japanese Garnishes*. New York: Holt, Rinehart & Winston, 1980.

Huang, Su-Huei. *Great Garnishes*. Monterey Park, Calif.: Wei-Chuan, 1990.

Lynch, Francis Talyn. *Garnishing: A Feast for Your Eyes*. Los Angeles: HP Books, 1987.

Rosen, Harvey. *How to Garnish*. Lakewood, N.J.: International Culinary Consultants, 1998.

Texido, Amy. *Glorious Garnishes: Crafting Easy & Spectacular Food Decorations*. Asheville, N.C.: Lark Books, 1996.

Books by Contributing Chefs

Ash, John, and Sid Goldstein. *American Game Cooking*. Reading, Mass.: Addison-Wesley, 1991.

Atkinson, Leland. *Cocina! A Hands-On Guide to the Techniques of Southwestern Cooking*. Berkeley, Calif.: Ten Speed Press, 1996.

Beranbaum, Rose Levy. *The Cake Bible*. New York: Morrow, 1988.

Bishop, John. *Bishop's: The Cookbook*. Vancouver, Canada: Douglas & McIntyre, 1997.

Brennan, Pip, Jimmy Brennan, and Ted Brennan. *Breakfast at Brennan's and Dinner, Too*. New Orleans, La.: Brennan's Inc., 1994.

Carpenter, Hugh, and Teri Sandison. *Chopstix: Quick Cooking with Pacific Flavors*. New York: Stewart, Tabori & Chang, 1990.

Golden, Harris. *Golden's Kitchen: The Artistry of Cooking and Dining on the Light Side*. Revised 2nd ed. Phoenix, Ariz.: Quail Run Books, 1989.

Goldstein, Joyce. *Back to Square One: Old-World Food in a New-World Kitchen*. New York: Morrow, 1992.

———. *Kitchen Conversations: 160 Mediterranean-Style Recipes from One of America's Most Innovative Chefs*. New York: Morrow, 1996.

———. *Sephardic Flavors: Jewish Cooking of the Mediterranean*. San Francisco: Chronicle Books, 2000.

Guerithault, Vincent. *Vincent's Cookbook*. Berkeley, Calif.: Ten Speed Press, 1994.

Harris, Jessica. *Beyond Gumbo: Creole Fusion Food from the Atlantic Rim*. New York: Simon & Schuster, 2003.

———. *Iron Pots and Wooden Spoons: Africa's Gifts to New World Cooking*. New York: Simon & Schuster, 1999.

———. *Tasting Brazil: Brazilian Recipes and Reminiscences*. New York: Macmillan, 1992.
Lukins, Sheila. *Sheila Lukins USA Cookbook*. New York: Workman, 1997.
Medrich, Alice. *Cocolat*. New York: Warner Books, 1990.
Miller, Mark. *Coyote Cafe*. Berkeley, Calif.: Ten Speed Press, 1989.
Milliken, Mary Sue, and Susan Feniger. *City Cuisine*. New York: Morrow, 1989.
Pépin, Jacques. *The Apprentice: My Life in the Kitchen*. Boston: Houghton Mifflin, 2003.
———. *Jacques Pépin Celebrates*. New York: Knopf, 2001.
Portale, Alfred. *Alfred Portale's Gotham Bar and Grill Cookbook*. New York: Doubleday, 1997.
Puck, Wolfgang. *The Wolfgang Puck Cookbook: Recipes from Spago, Chinois and Points East and West*. New York: Random House, 1996.
———. *Wolfgang Puck Adventures in the Kitchen*. New York: Gramercy, 2004.
Richard, Michel. *Michel Richard's Home Cooking with a French Accent*. New York: Morrow, 1993.
Roberts, Michael. *Secret Ingredients*. New York: Bantam Books, 1988.
Smith, Andrew F. *The Tomato in America: Early History, Culture and Cookery*. Reprint ed. Champaign: University of Illinois Press, 2001.
———. *The Oxford Encyclopedia of Food and Drink in America*. Oxford, England: Oxford University Press, 2004
Somerville, Annie. *Fields of Greens: New Vegetarian Recipes from the Celebrated Greens Restaurant*. New York: Bantam Books, 1993.
Susser, Allen. *Allen Susser's New World Cuisine and Cookery*. New York: Doubleday, 1995.
Tausend, Marilyn. *Cocina de la Familia: More Than 200 Authentic Recipes from Mexican-American Home Kitchens*. New York: Fireside, 1999.
———. *Williams-Sonoma Collection: Mexican*. New York: Simon & Schuster, 2004.
Tropp, Barbara. *China Moon Cookbook*. New York: Workman, 1992.

GLOSSARY

à la—(ah lah) French for "in the manner or style of"; used in relation to a food, it designates a style of preparation or presentation

à la carte—(ah lah kart) (1) a menu on which each food and beverage is listed and priced separately; (2) foods cooked to order as opposed to foods cooked in advance and held for later service

à la grecque—(ah lah grehk) a preparation style in which vegetables are marinated in olive oil, lemon juice and herbs, then served cold

à point—(ah PWEN-tah) (1) French term for cooking to the ideal degree of doneness; (2) when applied to meat, refers to cooking it medium rare

absorption—the ability of flour to absorb moisture when mixed into dough, which varies according to protein content, growing, and storage conditions

acid—a substance that neutralizes a base (alkaline) in a liquid solution; foods such as citrus juice, vinegar and wine that have a sour or sharp flavor (most foods are slightly acidic); acids have a pH of less than 7

acidulation—the browning of cut fruit caused by the reaction of an enzyme (polyphenoloxidase) with the phenolic compounds present in these fruits; this browning is often mistakenly attributed to exposure to oxygen

acini di pepe—from the Italian word for "peppercorn"; a tiny pasta shaped like peppercorns primarily used for soups; orzo can be substituted

additives—substances added to many foods to prevent spoilage or improve appearance, texture, flavor or nutritional value; they may be synthetic materials copied from nature (for example, sugar substitutes) or naturally occurring substances (for example, lecithin). Some food additives may cause allergic reactions in sensitive people.

adobo seasoning—a commercial spice blend; although several brands are available, most include dried chiles, Mexican oregano, cumin, black pepper, garlic powder and onion powder

aerate—to incorporate air into a mixture through sifting and mixing

aerobic bacteria—those that thrive on oxygen

aging—(1) the period during which freshly killed meat is allowed to rest so that the effects of rigor mortis dissipate; (2) the period during which freshly milled flour is allowed to rest so that it will whiten and produce less sticky doughs; the aging of flour can be chemically accelerated

airline breast—a boneless chicken breast with the first wing bone attached

albumen—the principal protein found in egg whites

al dente—(al DEN-tay) Italian for "to the tooth"; used to describe a food, usually pasta, that is cooked only until it gives a slight resistance when one bites into it

alkali—also known as a base, any substance with a pH higher than 7; baking soda is one of the few alkaline foods

alkaloid—a number of bitter organic substances with alkaline properties; found most often in plants and sometimes used in drugs

allemande—(ah-leh-MAHND) an intermediary sauce made by adding lemon juice and a liaison to chicken or veal velouté

allumette—(al-yoo-MEHT) (1) a matchstick cut of ⅛ inch × ⅛ inch × 2 inches (3 millimeters × 3 millimeters × 5 centimeters) usually used for potatoes; (2) a strip of puff pastry with a sweet or savory filling

American service—restaurant service in which the waiter takes the orders and brings the food to the table; the food is placed on dishes (plated) in the kitchen, making it a relatively fast method for seated service

amino acid—the basic molecular component of proteins; each of the approximately two dozen amino acids contains oxygen, hydrogen, carbon and nitrogen atoms

anadromous—describes a fish that migrates from a saltwater habitat to spawn in fresh water

anaerobic bacteria—those that are able to live and grow without the presence of oxygen

andouille—(an-DOO-ee) a very spicy smoked pork sausage, popular in Cajun cuisine

angus beef, Certified—a brand created in 1978 to distinguish the highest-quality beef produced from descendants of the black, hornless Angus cattle of Scotland

animal husbandry—the business, science and practice of raising domesticated animals

anterior—at or toward the front of an object or place; opposite of posterior

appetizers—also known as first courses, usually small portions of hot or cold foods intended to whet the appetite in anticipation of the more substantial courses to follow

aquafarming—also known as aquaculture, the business, science and practice of raising large quantities of fish and shellfish in tanks, ponds or ocean pens

aroma—the sensations, as interpreted by the brain, of what we detect when a substance comes in contact with sense receptors in the nose

aromatic—a food added to enhance the natural aromas of another food; aromatics include most flavorings, such as herbs and spices, as well as some vegetables

artesian-well water—water obtained from an underground source; the water rises to the surface under pressure

aspic; aspic jelly—a clear jelly usually made from a clarified stock thickened with gelatin; used to coat foods, especially charcuterie items, and for garnish

as purchased (A.P.)—the condition or cost of an item as it is purchased or received from the supplier

au gratin—(oh GRAH-tan) foods with a browned or crusted top; often made by browning a food with a bread-crumb, cheese and/or sauce topping under a broiler or salamander

au jus—(oh zhew) roasted meats, poultry or game served with their natural, unthickened juices

au sec—(oh sek) cooked until nearly dry

bacteria—single-celled microorganisms, some of which can cause diseases, including food-borne diseases

bagel—a dense, donut-shaped yeast roll; it is cooked in boiling water, then baked, which gives it a shiny glaze and chewy texture

bain marie—(bane mah-ree) (1) a hot-water bath used to gently cook food or keep cooked food hot; (2) a container for holding food in a hot-water bath

baked Alaska—ice cream set on a layer of spongecake and encased in meringue, then baked until the meringue is warm and golden

baked blind—describes a pie shell or tart shell that is baked unfilled, using baking weights or beans to support the crust as it bakes

baking—a dry-heat cooking method in which foods are surrounded by hot, dry air in a closed environment; similar to roasting, the term baking is usually applied to breads, pastries, vegetables and fish

baking powder—a mixture of sodium bicarbonate and one or more acids, generally cream of tartar and/or sodium aluminum sulfate, used to leaven baked goods; it releases carbon dioxide gas if moisture is present in a formula. Single-acting baking powder releases carbon dioxide gas in the presence of moisture only; double-acting baking powder releases some carbon dioxide gas upon contact with moisture, and more gas is released when heat is applied.

baking soda—sodium bicarbonate, an alkaline compound that releases carbon dioxide gas when combined with an acid and moisture; used to leaven baked goods

ballotine—(bahl-lo-teen) similar to a galantine; usually made by stuffing a deboned poultry leg with forcemeat; it is then poached or braised and normally served hot

banneton—(BAN-tahn) a traditional woven basket, often lined with canvas, in which yeast bread is placed to rise before baking

barbecue—(1) to cook foods over dry heat created by the burning of hardwood or hardwood charcoals; (2) a tangy tomato- or vinegar-based sauce used for grilled foods; (3) foods cooked by this method and/or with this sauce

barding—tying thin slices of fat, such as bacon or pork fatback, over meats or poultry that have little to no natural fat covering in order to protect and moisten them during roasting

barista—Italian for "bartender"; now used to describe someone who has been professionally trained in the art of preparing espresso and espresso-based beverages

base—a substance that neutralizes an acid in a liquid solution; ingredients such as sodium bicarbonate (baking soda) that have an alkaline or bitter flavor; bases have a pH of more than 7

baste—to moisten foods during cooking (usually grilling, broiling or roasting) with melted fat, pan drippings, a sauce or other liquids to prevent drying and to add flavor

bâtonnet—(bah-toh-nah) foods cut into matchstick shapes of ¼ inch × ¼ inch × 2 inches (6 millimeters × 6 millimeters × 5 centimeters)

batter—(1) a semiliquid mixture containing flour or other starch used to make cakes and breads. The gluten development is minimized and the liquid forms the continuous medium in which other ingredients are disbursed; generally contains more fat, sugar and liquids than a dough; (2) a semiliquid mixture of liquid and starch used to coat foods for deep-frying.

Baumé scale—(boh-may) *see* hydrometer

bavarian cream—a sweet dessert mixture made by thickening custard sauce with gelatin and then folding in whipped cream; the final product is poured into a mold and chilled until firm

beard—a clump of dark threads found on a mussel

béarnaise—(bare-NAYZ) a sauce made of butter and egg yolks and flavored with a reduction of vinegar, shallots, tarragon and peppercorns

beating—a mixing method in which foods are vigorously agitated to incorporate air or develop gluten; a spoon or electric mixer with its paddle attachment is used

béchamel—(bay-shah-mell) a leading sauce made by thickening milk with a white roux and adding seasonings

beefalo—the product of crossbreeding a bison (American buffalo) and a domestic beef animal.

beer—an alcoholic beverage made from water, hops and malted barley, fermented by yeast

beignets—squares or strips of éclair paste deep-fried and dusted with powdered sugar

berry—(1) the kernel of certain grains such as wheat; (2) small, juicy fruits that grow on vines and bushes

beurre blanc—(burr BLANHK) French for "white butter"; an emulsified butter sauce made from shallots, white wine and butter

beurre composé—(burr kom-poh-ZAY) *see* compound butter

beurre fondu—(burr fon-DOO) French for "melted butter"; it is often served over steamed vegetables such as asparagus or poached white fish

beurre manié—(burr man-YAY) a combination of equal amounts by weight of flour and soft, whole butter; it is whisked into a simmering sauce at the end of the cooking process for quick thickening and added sheen and flavor

beurre noir—(burr NWAR) French for "black butter"; used to describe whole butter cooked until dark brown (not black); sometimes flavored with vinegar or lemon juice, capers and parsley and served over fish, eggs and vegetables

beurre noisette—(burr nwah-ZEHT) French for "brown butter"; used to describe butter cooked until it is a light brown color; it is flavored and used in much the same manner as beurre noir

beurre rouge—(burr ROOGE) French for "red butter"; an emulsified butter sauce made from shallots, red wine and butter

biological hazard—a danger to the safety of food caused by disease-causing microorganisms such as bacteria, molds, yeasts, viruses or fungi

biscuit method—a mixing method used to make biscuits, scones and flaky doughs; it involves cutting cold fat into the flour and other dry ingredients before any liquid is added

bisque—(bisk) a soup made from shellfish; classic versions are thickened with rice

bivalves—mollusks such as clams, oysters and mussels that have two bilateral shells attached at a central hinge

blanching—very briefly and partially cooking a food in boiling water or hot fat; used to assist preparation (for example, to loosen peels from vegetables), as part of a combination cooking method or to remove undesirable flavors

blanquette—(blahn-KEHT) a white stew made of a white sauce and meat or poultry that is simmered without first browning

blending—a mixing method in which two or more ingredients are combined just until they are evenly distributed

bloom—(1) a white, powdery layer that sometimes appears on chocolate if the cocoa butter separates; (2) a measure of gelatin's strength; (3) to soften granulated gelatin in a cold liquid before dissolving and using

blue cheese—(1) a generic term for any cheese containing visible blue-green molds that contribute a characteristic tart, sharp flavor and aroma; also known as a blue-veined cheese or bleu; (2) a group of Roquefort-style cheeses made in the United States and Canada from cow's or goat's milk rather than ewe's milk and injected with molds that form blue-green veins; also known as blue mold cheese or blue-veined cheese

boiling—a moist-heat cooking method that uses convection to transfer heat from a hot (approximately 212°F/100°C) liquid to the food submerged in it; the turbulent waters and higher temperatures cook foods more quickly than do poaching or simmering

bombe—two or more flavors of ice cream, or ice cream and sherbet, shaped in a spherical mold; each flavor is a separate layer that forms the shell for the next flavor

bordelaise—(bor-dil-AYZ) a brown sauce flavored with a reduction of red wine, shallots, pepper and herbs and garnished with marrow

bottled water—any water, either still or sparkling, that is bottled and sold

bouchées—(boo-SHAY) small puff pastry shells that can be filled and served as bite-size hors d'oeuvre or petit fours

bound salad—a salad composed of cooked meats, poultry, fish, shellfish, pasta or potatoes combined with a dressing

bouquet garni—(boo-KAY gar-NEE) fresh herbs and vegetables tied into a bundle with twine and used to flavor stocks, sauces, soups and stews

bouquetière—(boo-kuh-TYEHR) a garnish (bouquet) of carefully cut and arranged fresh vegetables

boxed beef—industry terminology for primal and subprimal cuts of beef that are vacuum sealed and packed into cardboard boxes for shipping from the packing plant to retailers and food service operations

braising—a combination cooking method in which foods are first browned in hot fat, then covered and slowly cooked in a small amount of liquid over low heat; braising uses a combination of simmering and steaming to transfer heat from the liquid (conduction) and the air (convection) to the foods

bran—the tough outer layer of a cereal grain and the part highest in fiber

brandy—an alcoholic beverage made by distilling wine or the fermented mash of grapes or other fruits.

brawn—also called an aspic terrine, made from simmered meats packed into a terrine and covered with aspic

brazier; brasier—a pan designed for braising; usually round with two handles and a tight-fitting lid

breading—(1) a coating of bread or cracker crumbs, cornmeal or other dry meal applied to foods that will typically be deep-fried or pan-fried; (2) the process of applying this coating

brigade—a system of staffing a kitchen so that each worker is assigned a set of specific tasks; these tasks are often related by cooking method, equipment or the types of foods being produced

brine—a mixture of salt, water and seasonings used to preserve foods

brioche—(bree-OHSH) a rich yeast bread containing large amounts of eggs and butter

brochettes—(bro-SHETTS) skewers, either small hors d'oeuvre or large entrée size, threaded with meat, poultry, fish, shellfish and/or vegetables and grilled, broiled or baked; sometimes served with a dipping sauce

broiling—a dry-heat cooking method in which foods are cooked by heat radiating from an overhead source

broth—a flavorful liquid obtained from the long simmering of meats and/or vegetables

brown sauce—*see* espagnole

brown stew—a stew in which the meat is first browned in hot fat

brown stock—a richly colored stock made of chicken, veal, beef or game bones and vegetables, all of which are caramelized before they are simmered in water with seasonings

brunch—a late-morning to early-afternoon meal that takes the place of both breakfast and lunch; a brunch menu often offers breakfast foods as well as almost anything else

brunoise—(BROO-nwaz) (1) foods cut into cubes of ⅛ inch × ⅛ inch × ⅛ inch (3 millimeters × 3 millimeters × 3 millimeters); a 1⁄16-inch (1.5-millimeter) cube is referred to as a fine brunoise; (2) foods garnished with vegetables cut in this manner

buffet service—restaurant service in which diners generally serve themselves foods arranged on a counter or table or are served by workers assigned to specific areas of the buffet. Usually buffet-service-style restaurants charge by the meal; restaurants offering buffet service that charge by the dish are known as cafeterias.

bun—any of a variety of small, round yeast rolls; can be sweet or savory

butcher—to slaughter and/or dress or fabricate animals for consumption

butler service—restaurant service in which servers pass foods (typically hors d'oeuvre) or drinks arranged on trays

buttercream—a light, smooth, fluffy frosting of sugar, fat and flavorings; egg yolks or whipped egg whites are sometimes added. There are three principal kinds: simple, Italian and French.

butterfly—to slice boneless meat, poultry or fish nearly in half lengthwise so that it spreads open like a book

cafeteria—see Buffet service

caffeine—an alkaloid found in coffee beans, tea leaves and cocoa beans that acts as a stimulant

cake—in American usage, refers to a broad range of pastries, including layer cakes, coffeecakes and gâteaux; can refer to almost anything that is baked, tender, sweet and sometimes frosted

calf—(1) a young cow or bull; (2) the meat of calves slaughtered when they are older than five months

calorie—the unit of energy measured by the amount of heat required to raise 1000 grams of water one degree Celsius; it is also written as kilocalorie or kcal

canapé—(KAN-ah-pay) a tiny open-faced sandwich served as an hors d'oeuvre; usually composed of a small piece of bread or toast topped with a savory spread and garnish

capon—(kay-pahn) the class of surgically castrated male chickens; they have well-flavored meat and soft, smooth skin

capsaicin—(kap-SAY-ee-zin) an alkaloid found in a chile pepper's placental ribs that provides the pepper's heat

caramelization—the process of cooking sugars; the browning of sugar enhances the flavor and appearance of foods

carbohydrates—a group of compounds composed of oxygen, hydrogen and carbon that supply the body with energy (4 calories per gram); carbohydrates are classified as simple (including certain sugars) and complex (including starches and fiber)

carotenoid—a naturally occurring pigment that predominates in red and yellow vegetables such as carrots and red peppers

carryover cooking—the cooking that occurs after a food is removed from a heat source; it is accomplished by the residual heat remaining in the food

cartilage—also known as gristle; a tough, elastic, whitish connective tissue that helps give structure to an animal's body

carve—to cut cooked meat or poultry into portions

casings—membranes used to hold forcemeat for sausages; they can be natural animal intestines or manufactured from collagen extracted from cattle hides

casserole—(1) a heavy dish, usually ceramic, for baking foods; (2) foods baked in a casserole dish

caul fat—a fatty membrane from pig or sheep intestines; it resembles fine netting and is used to bard roasts and pâtés and to encase forcemeat for sausages

cellulose—a complex carbohydrate found in the cell wall of plants; it is edible but indigestible by humans

cephalopods—mollusks with a single, thin internal shell called a pen or cuttlebone, well-developed eyes, a number of arms that attach to the head and a saclike fin-bearing mantle; include squid and octopus

Certified Angus Beef—a brand created in 1978 to distinguish the highest-quality beef produced from descendants of the black, hornless Angus cattle of Scotland. The meat must meet American Angus Association standards for yield, marbling and age, and be graded as high choice or prime.

chafing dish—a metal dish with a heating unit (flame or electric) used to keep foods warm at tableside or during buffet service

chalazae cords—thick, twisted strands of egg white that anchor the yolk in place

charcuterie—(shahr-COO-tuhr-ree) the production of pâtés, terrines, galantines, sausages and similar foods

cheesecloth—a light, fine mesh gauze used to strain liquids and make sachets

chef de cuisine—(chef duh qui-zine) also known simply as chef; the person responsible for all kitchen operations, developing menu items and setting the kitchen's tone and tempo

chef de partie—(chef duh par-tee) also known as station chef; produces the menu items under the direct supervision of the chef or sous-chef

chef's knife—an all-purpose knife used for chopping, slicing and mincing; its tapering blade is 8–14 inches (20–35 centimeters) long

chemical hazard—a danger to the safety of food caused by chemical substances, especially cleaning agents, pesticides and toxic metals

chèvre—(SHEHV-ruh) French for "goat"; generally refers to a cheese made from goat's milk

chiffonade (chef-fon-nahd)—to finely slice or shred leafy vegetables or herbs

chile—a member of the capsicum plant family; may be used fresh or dried or dried and ground into a powder

chili—a stewlike dish containing chiles

chilli—a commercial spice powder containing a blend of seasonings

china cap—a cone-shaped strainer made of perforated metal

chine—the backbone or spine of an animal; a subprimal cut of beef, veal, lamb, pork or game carcass containing a portion of the backbone with some adjoining flesh.

chinois—(sheen-WAH) a conical strainer made of fine mesh, used for straining and puréeing foods

chlorophyll—a naturally occurring pigment that predominates in green vegetables such as cabbage

cholesterol—a fatty substance found in foods derived from animal products and in the human body; it has been linked to heart disease

chop—(1) a cut of meat, including part of the rib; (2) to cut into pieces when uniformity of size and shape is not important

chorizo—(chor-EE-zoh) a coarse, spicy pork sausage flavored with ground chiles and removed from its casing before cooking; used in Mexican and Spanish cuisines

choux pastry—(shoo paste-re) see Éclair paste

chowder—a hearty soup made from fish, shellfish and/or vegetables, usually containing milk and potatoes and often thickened with roux

churros—a Spanish and Mexican pastry in which sticks of éclair paste flavored with cinnamon are deep-fried and rolled in sugar while still hot

chutney—a sweet-and-sour condiment made of fruits and/or vegetables cooked in vinegar with sugar and spices; some chutneys are reduced to a purée, while others retain recognizable pieces of their ingredients

cider—mildly fermented apple juice; nonalcoholic apple juice may also be labeled cider

citrus—fruits characterized by a thick rind, most of which is a bitter white pith (albedo) with a thin exterior layer of colored skin (zest); their flesh is segmented and juicy and varies from bitter to tart to sweet

clarification—(1) the process of transforming a broth into a clear consommé by trapping impurities with a clearmeat consisting of the egg white protein albumen, ground meat, an acidic product, mirepoix and other ingredients; (2) the clearmeat used to clarify a broth

clarified butter—purified butterfat; the butter is melted and the water and milk solids are removed

classic cuisine—a late 19th- and early 20th-century refinement and simplification of French grande cuisine. Classic (or classical) cuisine relies on the thorough exploration of culinary principles and techniques, and emphasizes the refined preparation and presentation of superb ingredients.

clean—to remove visible dirt and soil

clear soups—unthickened soups, including broths, consommés and broth-based soups

clearmeat—*see* clarification

club roll—a small oval-shaped roll made of crusty French bread

coagulation—the irreversible transformation of proteins from a liquid or semiliquid state to a drier, solid state; usually accomplished through the application of heat

cocoa butter—the fat found in cocoa beans and used in fine chocolates

coconut cream—(1) a coconut-flavored liquid made like coconut milk but with less water; it is creamier and thicker than coconut milk; (2) the thick fatty portion that separates and rises to the top of canned or frozen coconut milk; do not substitute cream of coconut for true coconut cream

coconut milk—a coconut-flavored liquid made by pouring boiling water over shredded coconut; may be sweetened or unsweetened; do not substitute cream of coconut for coconut milk

coconut water—the thin, slightly opaque liquid contained within a fresh coconut

cojita—(ko-HEE-ta) an aged, hard, salty Mexican cow's-milk cheese; similar to feta, although not soaked in brine

colander—a perforated bowl, with or without a base or legs, used to strain foods

collagen—a protein found in connective tissue; it is converted into gelatin when cooked with moisture

combination cooking methods—cooking methods, principally braising and stewing, that employ both dry-heat and moist-heat procedures

composed salad—a salad prepared by arranging each of the ingredients (the base, body, garnish and dressing) on individual plates in an artistic fashion

composition—a completed plate's structure of colors, shapes and arrangements

compound butter—also known as a beurre composé, a mixture of softened whole butter and flavorings used as a sauce or to flavor and color other sauces

compound sauces—see Small sauces

concassée—peeled, seeded and diced tomato

concasser—(kon-kaas) to pound or chop coarsely; usually used for tomatoes or parsley

concentrate—also known as a fruit paste or compound; a reduced fruit purée, without a gel structure, used as a flavoring

conching—stirring melted chocolate with large stone or metal rollers to create a smooth texture in the finished chocolate

condiment—traditionally, any item added to a dish for flavor, including herbs, spices and vinegars; now also refers to cooked or prepared flavorings such as prepared mustards, relishes, bottled sauces and pickles

conduction—the transfer of heat from one item to another through direct contact

confit—(kohn-FEE) meat or poultry (often lightly salt-cured) slowly cooked and preserved in its own fat and served hot

connective tissue—tissue found throughout an animal's body that binds together and supports other tissues such as muscles

consommé—(kwang-soh-MAY) a rich stock or broth that has been clarified with clearmeat to remove impurities

contaminants—biological, chemical or physical substances that can be harmful when consumed in sufficient quantities

contamination—the presence, generally unintentional, of harmful organisms or substances

convection—the transfer of heat caused by the natural movement of molecules in a fluid (whether air, water or fat) from a warmer area to a cooler one; mechanical convection is the movement of molecules caused by stirring

conversion factor (C.F.)—the number used to increase or decrease ingredient quantities and recipe yields

cookery—the art, practice or work of cooking

cookie press—also known as a cookie gun, a hollow tube fitted with a plunger and an interchangeable decorative tip or plate; soft cookie dough is pressed through the tip to create shapes or patterns

cookies—small, sweet, flat pastries; usually classified by preparation or makeup techniques as drop, icebox, bar, cutout, pressed and wafer

cooking—(1) the transfer of energy from a heat source to a food; this energy alters the food's molecular structure, changing its texture, flavor, aroma and appearance; (2) the preparation of food for consumption

cooking medium—the air, fat, water or steam in which a food is cooked

coring—the process of removing the seeds or pit from a fruit or fruit-vegetable

cost of goods sold—the total cost of food items sold during a given period; calculated as beginning inventory plus purchases minus ending inventory

cost per portion—the amount of the total recipe cost divided by the number of portions produced from that recipe; the cost of one serving

coulibiac—a creamy mixture of salmon fillet, rice, hard-cooked eggs, mushrooms, shallots and dill enclosed in a pastry envelope usually made of brioche dough

coulis—(koo-lee) a sauce made from a purée of vegetables and/or fruit; may be served hot or cold

count—the number of individual items in a given measure of weight or volume

coupe—another name for an ice cream sundae, especially one served with a fruit topping

court bouillon—(kort boo-yon) water simmered with vegetables, seasonings and an acidic product such as vinegar or wine; used for simmering or poaching fish, shellfish or vegetables

cows—female cattle after their first calving, principally raised for milk and calf production

cracking—a milling process in which grains are broken open

cream filling—a pie filling made of flavored pastry cream thickened with cornstarch

creaming—a mixing method in which softened fat and sugar are vigorously combined to incorporate air

cream of coconut—a canned commercial product consisting of thick, sweetened coconut-flavored liquid; used for baking and in beverages

cream puffs—baked rounds of éclair paste cut in half and filled with pastry cream, whipped cream, fruit or other filling

creams—also known as crèmes; include light, fluffy or creamy-textured dessert foods made with whipped cream or whipped egg whites, such as Bavarian creams, chiffons, mousses and crème Chantilly

cream sauce—a sauce made by adding cream to a béchamel sauce

cream soup—a soup made from vegetables cooked in a liquid that is thickened with a starch and puréed; cream is then incorporated to add richness and flavor

crème anglaise—(khrem ahn-GLEHZ) also known as crème à l'anglaise; *see* vanilla custard sauce

crème brûlée—(krehm broo-lay) French for "burnt cream"; used to describe a rich dessert custard topped with a crust of caramelized sugar

crème caramel—(khrem kair-ah-MEHL) like crème renversée (rehn-vehr-SAY) and flan, a custard baked over a layer of caramelized sugar and inverted for service

crème Chantilly—(khrem shan-TEE) heavy cream whipped to soft peaks and flavored with sugar and vanilla; used to garnish pastries or desserts or folded into cooled custard or pastry cream for fillings

crème Chiboust—(krehm chee-boos) a vanilla pastry cream lightened by folding in Italian meringue; traditionally used in a gâteau St. Honoré

crème pâtissière—(khrem pah-tees-SYEHR) *see* pastry cream

crêpe—(krayp) a thin, delicate unleavened griddlecake made with a very thin egg batter cooked in a very hot sauté pan; used in sweet and savory preparations

critical control point—a step during the processing of food when a mistake can result in the transmission, growth or survival of pathogenic bacteria

croissant—(krwah-SAHN) a crescent-shaped roll made from a rich, rolled-in yeast dough

croquembouche—a pyramid of small puffs, each filled with pastry cream; a French tradition for Christmas and weddings, it is held together with caramelized sugar and decorated with spun sugar or marzipan flowers

croquette—(crow-keht) a food that has been puréed or bound with a thick sauce (usually béchamel or velouté), made into small shapes and then breaded and deep-fried

cross-contamination—the transfer of bacteria or other contaminants from one food, work surface or piece of equipment to another

croûte, en—(awn KROOT) describes a food encased in a bread or pastry crust

crouton—(KROO-tawn) a bread or pastry garnish, usually toasted or sautéed until crisp

crudités—(croo-dee-TAYS) generally refers to raw or blanched vegetables served as an hors d'oeuvre and often accompanied by a dip

crullers—a Dutch pastry in which a loop or strip of twisted éclair paste is deep-fried

crumb—the interior of bread or cake; may be elastic, aerated, fine grained or coarse grained

crustaceans—shellfish characterized by a hard outer skeleton or shell and jointed appendages; include lobsters, crabs and shrimp

cuisine—the ingredients, seasonings, cooking procedures and styles attributable to a particular group of people; the group can be defined by geography, history, ethnicity, politics, culture or religion

cuisson—(kwee-sohn) the liquid used for shallow poaching

cupping—testing coffee or tea for taste and quality, often performed by a professional taster trained to identify key coffee or tea characteristics

curdling—the separation of milk or egg mixtures into solid and liquid components; caused by overcooking, high heat or the presence of acids

curing salt—a mixture of salt and sodium nitrite that inhibits bacterial growth; used as a preservative, often for charcuterie items

custard—any liquid thickened by the coagulation of egg proteins; its consistency depends on the ratio of eggs to liquid and the type of liquid used; custards can be baked in the oven or cooked in a bain marie or on the stove top

cutlet—a relatively thick, boneless slice of meat

cutting—(1) reducing a food to smaller pieces; (2) a mixing method in which solid fat is incorporated into dry ingredients until only lumps of the desired size remain

cutting loss—the unavoidable and unrecoverable loss of food during fabrication; the loss is usually the result of food particles sticking to the cutting board or the evaporation of liquids

cuttlebone—also known as the pen, the single, thin internal shell of cephalopods

cycle menu—a menu that changes every day for a certain period and then repeats the same daily items in the same order (for example, on a seven-day cycle, the same menu is used every Monday)

dairy products—include cow's milk and foods produced from cow's milk such as butter, yogurt, sour cream and cheese; sometimes other milks and products made from them are included (e.g., goat's milk cheese)

decant—to separate liquid from solids without disturbing the sediment by pouring off the liquid; vintage wines are often decanted to remove sediment

decline phase—a period during which bacteria die at an accelerated rate, also known as the negative growth phase

decoction—(1) boiling a food until its flavor is removed; (2) a procedure used for brewing coffee

decorator's icing—*see* royal icing

deep-frying—a dry-heat cooking method that uses convection to transfer heat to a food submerged in hot fat; foods to be deep-fried are usually first coated in batter or breading

deglaze—to swirl or stir a liquid (usually wine or stock) in a pan to dissolve cooked food particles remaining on the bottom; the resulting mixture often becomes the base for a sauce

degrease—to remove fat from the surface of a liquid such as a stock or sauce by skimming, scraping or lifting congealed fat

deionized water—water that has had the cations and anions removed by passing it over a bed of ion-exchange resins

demi-glace—(deh-me glass) French for "half-glaze"; a mixture of half brown stock and half brown sauce reduced by half

demineralized water—water that has had all the minerals and impurities removed by passing it over a bed of ion-exchange resins

density—the relationship between the mass and volume of a substance ($D = m/v$). For example, as more and more sugar is dissolved in a liquid, the heavier or denser the liquid will become. Sugar density is measured on the Baumé scale using a hydrometer or saccharometer.

dessert wines—sweet wines made from grapes left on the vine until they are overly ripe, such as Sauternes or wines labeled "Late Harvest"; during fermentation, some of the sugar is not converted to alcohol, but remains in the wine, giving it its characteristic intense sweet taste

détrempe—a paste made with flour and water during the first stage of preparing a pastry dough, especially rolled-in doughs

deveining—the process of removing a shrimp's digestive tract

deviled—describes meat, poultry or other food seasoned with mustard, vinegar and other spicy seasonings

diagonals—oval-shaped slices

dice—to cut into cubes with six equal-sized sides

dip—a thick, creamy sauce, served hot or cold, to accompany crudités, crackers, chips or other foods, especially as an hors d'oeuvre; dips are often based on sour cream, mayonnaise or cream cheese

direct contamination—the contamination of raw foods in their natural setting or habitat

distillation—the separation of alcohol from a liquid (or, during the production of alcoholic beverages, from a fermented mash); it is accomplished by heating the liquid or mash to a gas that contains alcohol vapors; this steam is then condensed into the desired alcoholic liquid (beverage)

distilled water—water that has had all the minerals and impurities removed through distillation; it is generally used for pharmaceutical purposes

diver scallops—scallops that are harvested from the ocean by divers who hand-pick each one; diver scallops tend to be less gritty than those harvested by dragging, and hand-harvesting is more ecologically friendly

docking—pricking small holes in an unbaked dough or crust to allow steam to escape and to prevent the dough from rising when baked

dough—a mixture of flour and other ingredients used in baking; has a low moisture content, and gluten forms the continuous medium into which other ingredients are embedded; it is often stiff enough to cut into shapes

drawn—a market form for fish in which the viscera is removed

dredging—coating a food with flour or finely ground crumbs; usually done prior to sautéing or frying or as the first step of the standard breading procedure

dress—to trim or otherwise prepare an animal carcass for consumption

dressed—a market form for fish in which the viscera, gills, fins and scales are removed

dressing—another name for a bread stuffing used with poultry

drinking water—water that comes from a government-approved source and has undergone some treatment and filtration; it can be bottled or available on tap and is used for drinking and general culinary purposes

drupes—*see* stone fruits

dry-heat cooking methods—cooking methods, principally broiling, grilling, roasting and baking, sautéing, pan-frying and deep-frying, that use air or fat to transfer heat through conduction and convection; dry-heat cooking methods allow surface sugars to caramelize

drying—a preservation method in which the food's moisture content is dramatically reduced; drying changes the food's texture, flavor and appearance

duchesse potatoes—(duh-shees) a purée of cooked potatoes, butter and egg yolks, seasoned with salt, pepper and nutmeg; can be eaten as is or used to prepare several classic potato dishes

duckling—a duck slaughtered before it is eight weeks old

dumpling—any of a variety of small starchy products made from doughs or batters that are simmered or steamed; can be plain or filled

durum wheat—a species of very hard wheat with a particularly high amount of protein; it is used to make couscous or milled into semolina, which is used for making pasta

duxelles—a coarse paste made of finely chopped mushrooms sautéed with shallots in butter used in sauces and stuffing

éclair paste—(ay-clahr) also known as pâte à choux; a soft dough that produces hollow baked products with crisp exteriors; used for making éclairs, cream puffs and savory products

éclairs—baked fingers of éclair paste filled with pastry cream; the top is then coated with chocolate glaze or fondant

edible portion (E.P.)—the amount of a food item available for consumption or use after trimming or fabrication; a smaller, more convenient portion of a larger or bulk unit

egg wash—a mixture of beaten eggs (whole eggs, yolks or whites) and a liquid, usually milk or water, used to coat doughs before baking to add sheen

elastin—a protein found in connective tissues, particularly ligaments and tendons; it often appears as the white or silver covering on meats known as silverskin

émincé—a small, thin, boneless piece of meat

emulsification—the process by which generally unmixable liquids, such as oil and water, are forced into a uniform distribution

emulsion—a uniform mixture of two unmixable liquids; it is often temporary (for example, oil in water)

endosperm—the largest part of a cereal grain and a source of protein and carbohydrates (starch); the part used primarily in milled products

en papillote—(awn pa-pee-yote) a cooking method in which food is wrapped in paper or foil and then heated so that the food steams in its own moisture

entrée—the main dish of an American meal, usually meat, poultry, fish or shellfish accompanied by a vegetable and starch; in France, the first course, served before the fish and meat courses

enzymes—proteins that aid specific chemical reactions in plants and animals

escalope—(eh-SKAL-ohp) *see* scallop

escargot—(ays-skahr-go) French for "snail"; those used for culinary purposes are land snails (genus Helix); the most popular are the large Burgundy snails and the smaller but more flavorful common or garden snail known as petit gris

espagnole—(ess-spah-nyol) also known as brown sauce, a leading sauce made of brown stock, mirepoix and tomatoes thickened with brown roux; often used to produce demi-glace

essence—a sauce made from a concentrated vegetable juice

essential nutrients—nutrients that must be provided by food because the body cannot or does not produce them in sufficient quantities

essential oils—pure oils extracted from the skins, peels and other parts of plants used to give their aroma and taste to flavoring agents in foods, cosmetics and other products

ethnic cuisine—the cuisine of a group of people having a common cultural heritage, as opposed to the cuisine of a group of people bound together by geography or political factors

ethylene gas—a colorless, odorless hydrocarbon gas naturally emitted from fruits and fruit-vegetables that encourages ripening

evaporation—the process by which heated water molecules move faster and faster until the water turns to a gas (steam) and vaporizes; evaporation is responsible for the drying of foods during cooking

ewe's milk—milk produced by a female sheep; it has approximately 7.9% milkfat, 11.4% milk solids and 80.7% water

extracts—concentrated mixtures of ethyl alcohol and flavoring oils such as vanilla, almond and lemon

extrusion—the process of forcing pasta dough through perforated plates to create various shapes; pasta dough that is not extruded must be rolled and cut

fabricate—to cut a larger portion of raw meat (for example, a primal or subprimal), poultry or fish into smaller portions

fabricated cuts—individual portions cut from a subprimal

facultative bacteria—those that can adapt and will survive with or without oxygen

fancy—(1) fish that has been previously frozen; (2) a quality grade for fruits, especially canned or frozen

fatback—fresh pork fat from the back of the pig, used primarily for barding

fats—(1) a group of compounds composed of oxygen, hydrogen and carbon atoms that supply the body with energy (9 calories per gram); fats are classified as saturated, monounsaturated or polyunsaturated; (2) the general term for butter, lard, shortening, oil and margarine used as cooking media or ingredients

fermentation—the process by which yeast converts sugar into alcohol and carbon dioxide; it also refers to the time that yeast dough is left to rise—that is, the time it takes for carbon dioxide gas cells to form and become trapped in the gluten network

feuilletées—(fuh-YETS) square, rectangular or diamond-shaped puff pastry boxes; may be filled with a sweet or savory mixture

fiber—also known as dietary fiber; indigestible carbohydrates found in grains, fruits and vegetables; fiber aids digestion

FIFO (first in, first out)—a system of rotating inventory, particularly perishable and semiperishable goods, in which items are used in the order in which they are received

filé—(fee-lay) a seasoning and thickening agent made from dried, ground sassafras leaves

filet, fillet—(fee-lay) (1) filet: a boneless tenderloin of meat; (2) fillet: the side of a fish removed intact, boneless or semiboneless, with or without skin; (3) to cut such a piece

fish velouté—a velouté sauce made from fish stock

flambé—(flahm-BAY) food served flaming; produced by igniting brandy, rum or other liquor

flan—a firm savory or sweet egg custard; dessert variety is baked over a layer of caramelized sugar and inverted for service

flash-frozen—describes food that has been frozen very rapidly using metal plates, extremely low temperatures or chemical solutions

flash point—the temperature at which a fat ignites and small flames appear on the surface of the fat

flatfish—fish with asymmetrical, compressed bodies that swim in a horizontal position and have both eyes on the top of the head; include sole, flounder and halibut

flavonoids—plant pigments that dissolve readily in water, found in red, purple and white vegetables such as blueberries, red cabbage, onions and tea

flavor—an identifiable or distinctive quality of a food, drink or other substance perceived with the combined senses of taste, touch and smell

flavored tea—tea to which flavorings such as oils, dried fruit, spices, flowers and herbs have been added

flavoring—an item that adds a new taste to a food and alters its natural flavors; flavorings include herbs, spices, vinegars and condiments; the terms *seasoning* and *flavoring* are often used interchangeably.

fleuron—(fluh-rawng) a crescent-shaped piece of puff pastry used as a garnish

flour—a powdery substance of varying degrees of fineness made by milling grains such as wheat, corn or rye

fluoridated water—water, either naturally fluoridated or treated with a fluorine-containing compound, intended to promote healthy teeth by preventing tooth decay

foamed milk—milk that is heated and frothed with air and steam generated by an espresso machine; it will be slightly cooler than steamed milk

foie gras—(fwah grah) liver of specially fattened geese

fold—a measurement of the strength of vanilla extract

folding—incorporating light, airy ingredients into heavier ingredients by gently moving them from the bottom of the bowl up over the top in a circular motion, usually with a rubber spatula

fond—(1) French for "stock" or "base"; (2) the concentrated juices, drippings and bits of food left in pans after foods are roasted or sautéed; it is used to flavor sauces made directly in the pans in which foods were cooked

fondant—(FAHN-dant) a sweet, thick opaque sugar paste commonly used for glazing pastries such as napoleons or making candies

fond lié—(fahn lee-ay) *see* jus lié

fondue—a Swiss specialty made with melted cheese, wine and flavorings; eaten by dipping pieces of bread into the hot mixture with long forks

food cost—the cost of the materials that go directly into the production of menu items

food cost percentage—the ratio of the cost of foods used to the total food sales during a set period, calculated by dividing the cost of food used by the total sales in a restaurant

Food Guide Pyramid—a dietary guide that prioritizes and proportions food choices among six general food groups

forcemeat—a preparation made from uncooked ground meats, poultry, fish or shellfish, seasoned, and emulsified with fat; commonly prepared as country-style, basic and mousseline and used for charcuterie items

formula—the standard term used throughout the industry for a bakeshop recipe; formulas rely on weighing to ensure accurate measuring of ingredients

frangipane—(fran-juh-pahn) a sweet almond and egg filling cooked inside pastry

free-range chickens—chickens allowed to move freely and forage for food; as opposed to chickens raised in coops

free-range veal—the meat of calves that are allowed to roam freely and eat grasses and other natural foods; this meat is pinker and more strongly flavored than that of milk-fed calves

freezer burn—the surface dehydration and discoloration of food that results from moisture loss at below-freezing temperatures

French dressing—classically, a vinaigrette dressing made from oil, vinegar, salt and pepper; in the United States, the term also refers to a commercially prepared dressing that is creamy, tartly sweet and red-orange in color

French service—restaurant service in which one waiter (a captain) takes the order, does the tableside cooking and brings the drinks and food; the secondary or back waiter serves bread and water, clears each course, crumbs the table and serves the coffee

frenching—a method of trimming racks or individual chops of meat, especially lamb, in which the excess fat is cut away, leaving the eye muscle intact; all meat and connective tissue are removed from the rib bone

fresh-frozen—describes a food that has been frozen while still fresh

fricassee—(FRIHK-uh-see) a white stew in which the meat is cooked in fat without browning before the liquid is added

frittata—(free-tah-ta) an open-faced omelet of Spanish-Italian heritage

frosting—also known as icing, a sweet decorative coating used as a filling between the layers or as a coating over the top and sides of a cake

fruit—the edible organ that develops from the ovary of a flowering plant and contains one or more seeds (pips or pits)

frying—a dry-heat cooking method in which foods are cooked in hot fat; includes sautéing and stir-frying, pan-frying and deep-frying

fumet—(foo-may) a stock made from fish bones or shellfish shells and vegetables simmered in a liquid with flavorings

fungi—a large group of plants ranging from single-celled organisms to giant mushrooms; the most common are molds and yeasts

fusion cuisine—the blending or use of ingredients and/or preparation methods from various ethnic, regional or national cuisines in the same dish; also known as transnational cuisine

galantine—(GAL-uhn-teen) similar to a ballotine; a charcuterie item made from a forcemeat of poultry, game or suckling pig usually wrapped in the skin of the bird or animal and poached in an appropriate stock; often served cold, usually in aspic

game—birds and animals hunted for sport or food; many game birds and animals are now ranch-raised and commercially available

game hen—the class of young or immature progeny of Cornish chickens or of a Cornish chicken and White Rock chicken; they are small and very flavorful

ganache—(ga-nosh) a rich blend of chocolate and heavy cream and, optionally, flavorings, used as a pastry or candy filling or frosting

garde-manger—(gar mawn-zhay) (1) also known as the pantry chef, the cook in charge of cold food production, including salads and salad dressings, charcuterie items, cold appetizers and buffet items; (2) the work area where these foods are prepared

garnish—(1) food used as an attractive decoration; (2) a subsidiary food used to add flavor or character to the main ingredient in a dish (for example, noodles in chicken noodle soup)

gastrique—(gas-streek) caramelized sugar deglazed with vinegar; used to flavor tomato or savory fruit sauces

gastronomy—the art and science of eating well

gâteau—(gah-toe) (1) in American usage, refers to any cake-type dessert; (2) in French usage, refers to various pastry items made with puff pastry, éclair paste, short dough or sweet dough

gaufrette—(goh-FREHT) a thin lattice or waffle-textured slice of vegetable cut on a mandoline

gaufrette potatoes—(goh-FREHT) thin, fried, lattice-cut slices of potato

gelatin—a tasteless and odorless mixture of proteins (especially collagen) extracted from boiling bones, connective tissue and other animal parts; when dissolved in a hot liquid and then cooled, it forms a jellylike substance used as a thickener and stabilizer

gelatinization—the process by which starch granules are cooked; they absorb moisture when placed in a liquid and heated; as the moisture is absorbed, the product swells, softens and clarifies slightly

gelato—(jah-lah-to) an Italian-style ice cream that is denser than American-style ice cream

genoise—(zhen-waahz) (1) a form of whipped-egg cake that uses whole eggs whipped with sugar; (2) a French spongecake

germ—the smallest portion of a cereal grain and the only part that contains fat

ghee—a form of clarified butter in which the milk solids remain with the fat and are allowed to brown; originating in India and now used worldwide as an ingredient and cooking medium, it has a long shelf life, a high smoke point and a nutty, caramel-like flavor

giblets—the collective term for edible poultry viscera, including gizzards, hearts, livers and necks

gizzard—a bird's second stomach

glaçage—(glah-sahge) browning or glazing a food, usually under a salamander or broiler

glace de poisson—(glahss duh pwah-sawng) a syrupy glaze made by reducing a fish stock

glace de viande—(glahss duh vee-awnd) a dark, syrupy meat glaze made by reducing a brown stock

glace de volaille—(glahss duh vo-lahy) a light brown, syrupy glaze made by reducing a chicken stock

glaze—(1) any shiny coating applied to food or created by browning; (2) the dramatic reduction and concentration of a stock; (3) a thin, flavored coating poured or dripped onto a cake or pastry

global cuisine—foods (often commercially produced items) or preparation methods that have become ubiquitous throughout the world; for example, curries and French-fried potatoes

glucose—a thick, sweet syrup made from cornstarch, composed primarily of dextrose; light corn syrup can usually be substituted for it in baked goods or candy making

gluten—an elastic network of proteins created when wheat flour is moistened and manipulated

goat's milk—milk produced by a female goat; it has approximately 4.1% milkfat, 8.9% milk solids and 87% water

gougère éclair—pastry flavored with cheese baked and served as a savory hors d'oeuvre

gourmand—a connoisseur of fine food and drink, often to excess

gourmet—a connoisseur of fine food and drink

gourmet foods—foods of the highest quality, perfectly prepared and beautifully presented

grading—a series of voluntary programs offered by the U.S. Department of Agriculture to designate a food's overall quality

grains—(1) grasses that bear edible seeds, including corn, rice and wheat; (2) the fruit (that is, the seed or kernel) of such grasses

gram—the basic unit of weight in the metric system; equal to approximately 1/30 of an ounce

grande cuisine—the rich, intricate and elaborate cuisine of the 18th- and 19th-century French aristocracy and upper classes. It is based on the rational identification, development and adoption of strict culinary principles. By emphasizing the how and why of cooking, grande cuisine was the first to distinguish itself from regional cuisines, which tend to emphasize the tradition of cooking.

grate—to cut a food into small, thin shreds by rubbing it against a serrated metal plate known as a grater

gravy—a sauce made from meat or poultry juices combined with a liquid and thickening agent; usually made in the pan in which the meat or poultry was cooked

green meats—freshly slaughtered meats that have not had sufficient time to age and develop tenderness and flavor

gremolata—(greh-moa-LAH-tah) an aromatic garnish of chopped parsley, garlic and lemon zest used for osso buco

grilling—a dry-heat cooking method in which foods are cooked by heat radiating from a source located below the cooking surface; the heat can be generated by electricity or by burning gas, hardwood or hardwood charcoals

grind—to pulverize or reduce food to small particles using a mechanical grinder or food processor

grinding—a milling process in which grains are reduced to a powder; the powder can be of differing degrees of fineness or coarseness

gristle—*see* cartilage

grosse piece—a centerpiece consisting of a large piece of the principal food offered; for example, a large wheel of cheese with slices of the cheese cascading around it

gum paste—a smooth dough of sugar and gelatin that can be colored and used to make decorations, especially for pastries

HACCP—*see* Hazard Analysis Critical Control Points

halal—describes food prepared in accordance with Muslim dietary laws

hanging—the practice of allowing eviscerated (drawn or gutted) game to age in a dry, well-ventilated place; hanging helps tenderize the flesh and strengthen its flavor

hard water—water with relatively high calcium and magnesium concentrations

haricot vert—a French variety of green bean characterized by its long, slender pod with an intense flavor and tender texture

Hazard Analysis Critical Control Points (HACCP)—a rigorous system of self-inspection used to manage and maintain sanitary conditions in all types of food service operations; it focuses on the flow of food through the food service facility to identify any point or step in preparation (known as a critical control point) where some action must be taken to prevent or minimize a risk or hazard

Heimlich maneuver—the first-aid procedure for choking victims in which sudden upward pressure is applied to the upper abdomen in order to force any foreign object from the windpipe

herb—any of a large group of aromatic plants whose leaves, stems or flowers are used as a flavoring; used either dried or fresh

high-ratio cake—a form of creamed-fat cake that uses emulsified shortening and a two-stage mixing method

hollandaise—(ohll-uhn-daze) an emulsified sauce made of butter, egg yolks and flavorings (especially lemon juice)

homogenization—the process by which milk fat is prevented from separating out of milk products

hors d'oeuvre—(ohr durv) very small portions of hot or cold foods served before the meal to stimulate the appetite

hotel pan—a rectangular, stainless steel pan with a lip allowing it to rest in a storage shelf or steam table; available in several standard sizes

hull—also known as the husk, the outer covering of a fruit, seed or grain

hulling—a milling process in which the hull or husk is removed from grains

hybrid—the result of crossbreeding different species that are genetically unalike; often a unique product

hybrid menu—a menu combining features of a static menu with a cycle menu or a market menu of specials

hydrogenation—the process used to harden oils; hydrogen atoms are added to unsaturated fat molecules, making them partially or completely saturated and thus solid at room temperature

hydrometer—a device used to measure specific gravity; it shows degrees of concentration on the Baumé scale

hygroscopic—describes a food that readily absorbs moisture from the air

icing—*see* frosting

IMPS/NAMP—see NAMP/IMPS

incidental food additives—those inadvertently or unintentionally added to foods during processing, such as pesticide residues on fruits

induction cooking—a cooking method that uses a special coil placed below the stove top's surface in combination with specially designed cookware to generate heat rapidly with an alternating magnetic field

infection—in the food safety context, a disease caused by the ingestion of live pathogenic bacteria that continue their life processes in the consumer's intestinal tract

infrared cooking—a heating method that uses an electric or ceramic element heated to such a high temperature that it gives off waves of radiant heat that cook the food

infuse—to flavor a liquid by steeping it with ingredients such as tea, coffee, herbs or spices

infusion—(1) the extraction of flavors from a food at a temperature below boiling; (2) a group of coffee brewing techniques, including steeping, filtering and dripping; (3) the liquid resulting from this process

instant-read thermometer—a thermometer used to measure the internal temperature of foods; the stem is inserted in the food, producing an instant temperature readout

intentional food additives—those added to foods on purpose, such as the chemicals used to ensure longer shelf life or food colorings

intoxication—in the food safety context, a disease caused by the toxins that bacteria produce during their life processes

inventory—the listing and counting of all foods in the kitchen, storerooms and refrigerators

IQF (individually quick-frozen)—describes the technique of rapidly freezing each individual item of food such as slices of fruit, berries or pieces of fish before packaging; IQF foods are not packaged with syrup or sauce

irradiation—a preservation method used for certain fruits, vegetables, grains, spices, meat and poultry in which ionizing radiation sterilizes the food, slows ripening and prevents sprouting

jam—a fruit gel made from fruit pulp and sugar

jelly—a fruit gel made from fruit juice and sugar

juice—the liquid extracted from any fruit or vegetable

julienne—(ju-lee-en) (1) to cut foods into stick-shaped pieces, approximately ⅛ inch × ⅛ inch × 2 inches (3 millimeters × 3 millimeters × 5 centimeters); a fine julienne has dimensions of 1⁄16 inch × 1⁄16 inch × 2 inches (1.5 millimeters × 1.5 millimeters × 5 centimeters); (2) the stick-shaped pieces of cut food

jus lié—(zhoo lee-ay) also known as fond lié; a sauce made by thickening brown stock with cornstarch or similar starch; often used like a demi-glace, especially to produce small sauces

Kaiser roll—a large round yeast roll with a crisp crust and a curved pattern stamped on the top; used primarily for sandwiches

kneading—working a dough to develop gluten

Kobe beef—an exclusive type of beef traditionally produced in Kobe, Japan. Wagyu cattle are fed a special diet, which includes beer to stimulate the animal's appetite during summer months. The animals are massaged with sake to relieve stress and muscle stiffness in the belief that calm, contented cattle produce better-quality meat. This special treatment produces meat that is extraordinarily tender and full-flavored, and extraordinarily expensive. Kobe Beef America introduced Wagyu cattle to the United States in 1976. KBA's cattle are raised without hormones and the meat is dry-aged for 21 days prior to sale.

kosher—describes food prepared in accordance with Jewish dietary laws

lactose—a disaccharide that occurs naturally in mammalian milk; milk sugar

lag phase—a period, usually following transfer from one place to another, during which bacteria do not experience much growth

lamb—the meat of sheep slaughtered under the age of one year

lard—the rendered fat of hogs

larding—inserting thin slices of fat, such as pork fatback, into low-fat meats in order to add moisture

lardons—diced, blanched, fried bacon

leading sauces—also known as mother sauces, the foundation for the entire classic repertoire of hot sauces; the five leading sauces (béchamel, velouté, espagnole [also known as brown], tomato and hollandaise) are distinguished by the liquids and thickeners used to make them; they can be seasoned and garnished to create a wide variety of small or compound sauces

leavener—an ingredient or process that produces or incorporates gases in a baked product in order to increase volume, provide structure and give texture

lecithin—a natural emulsifier found in egg yolks

legumes—(lay-gyooms) (1) French for "vegetables"; (2) a large group of vegetables with double-seamed seed pods; depending upon the variety, the seeds, pod and seeds together, or the dried seeds are eaten

liaison—(lee-yeh-zon) a mixture of egg yolks and heavy cream used to thicken and enrich sauces

liqueur—a strong, sweet, syrupy alcoholic beverage made by mixing or redistilling neutral spirits with fruits, flowers, herbs, spices or other flavorings; also known as a cordial

liquor—an alcoholic beverage made by distilling grains, fruits, vegetables or other foods; includes rum, whiskey and vodka

liter—the basic unit of volume in the metric system, equal to slightly more than a quart

log phase—a period of accelerated growth for bacteria

lozenges—diamond-shaped pieces, usually of firm vegetables

macaroni—any dried pasta made with wheat flour and water; only in the United States does the term refer to elbow-shaped tubes

macerate—to soak foods in a liquid, usually alcoholic, to soften them

macronutrients—the nutrients needed in large quantities: carbohydrates, proteins, fats and water

madeira—(muh-DEH-rah) a Portuguese fortified wine heated during aging to give it a distinctive flavor and brown color

magret—(may-gray) a duck breast, traditionally taken from the ducks that produce foie gras; it is usually served boneless but with the skin intact

maître d'hotel (maître d')—(may-tr doh-tel) (1) the leader of the dining room brigade, also known as the dining room manager; oversees the dining room or "front of the house" staff; (2) a compound butter flavored with chopped parsley and lemon juice

makeup—the cutting, shaping and forming of dough products before baking

mandoline—a stainless steel, hand-operated slicing device with adjustable blades

marbling—whitish streaks of inter- and intramuscular fat

marinade—the liquid used to marinate foods; it generally contains herbs, spices and other flavoring ingredients as well as an acidic product such as wine, vinegar or lemon juice

marinate—to soak a food in a seasoned liquid in order to tenderize the food and add flavor to it

market menu—a menu based upon product availability during a specific period; it is written to use foods when they are in peak season or readily available

marmalade—a citrus jelly that also contains unpeeled slices of citrus fruit

marquise—a frozen mousselike dessert, usually chocolate

marsala—(mar-SAH-lah) a flavorful fortified sweet-to-semidry Sicilian wine

marzipan—(MAHR-sih-pan) a paste of ground almonds, sugar and egg whites used to fill and decorate pastries

matignon—a standard mirepoix plus diced smoked bacon or smoked ham and, depending on the dish, mushrooms and herbs

matzo—thin, crisp unleavened bread made only with flour and water; can be ground into meal that is used for matzo balls and pancakes

mayonnaise—a thick, creamy sauce consisting of oil and vinegar emulsified with egg yolks, usually used as a salad dressing

meal—(1) the coarsely ground seeds of any edible grain such as corn or oats; (2) any dried, ground substance (such as bonemeal)

mealy potatoes—also known as starchy potatoes; those with a high starch content and thick skin; they are best for baking

medallion—a small, round, relatively thick slice of meat

melting—the process by which certain foods, especially those high in fat, gradually soften and then liquefy when heated

menu—a list of foods and beverages available for purchase

meringue—(muh-reng) a foam made of beaten egg whites and sugar

metabolism—all the chemical reactions and physical processes that occur continuously in living cells and organisms

meter—the basic unit of length in the metric system, equal to slightly more than 1 yard

mezzaluna—a two-handled knife with one or more thick, crescent-shaped blades used to chop and mince herbs and vegetables

micronutrients—the nutrients needed only in small amounts; vitamins and minerals

microorganisms—single-celled organisms as well as tiny plants and animals that can be seen only through a microscope

microwave cooking—a heating method that uses radiation generated by a special oven to penetrate the food; it agitates water molecules, creating friction and heat; this energy then spreads throughout the food by conduction (and by convection in liquids)

mignonette—(1) a medallion; (2) a vinegar sauce with shallots

milk-fed veal—also known as formula-fed veal; the meat of calves fed only a nutrient-rich liquid and kept tethered in pens; this meat is whiter and more mildly flavored than that of free-range calves

milling—the process by which grain is ground into flour or meal

mince—to cut into very small pieces when uniformity of shape is not important

minerals—inorganic micronutrients necessary for regulating body functions and proper bone and tooth structures

mineral water—drinking water that comes from a protected underground water source and contains at least 250 parts per million of total dissolved solids such as calcium

mirepoix—(meer-pwa) a mixture of coarsely chopped onions, carrots and celery used to flavor stocks, stews and other foods; generally, a mixture of 50 percent onions, 25 percent carrots and 25 percent celery, by weight, is used

mirin—a sweet, viscous Japanese wine made from glutinous rice, generally used to flavor and sweeten glazes and sauces

mise en place—(meez on plahs) French for "putting in place"; refers to the preparation and assembly of all necessary ingredients and equipment

miso—(ME-so) a thick paste made by salting and fermenting soybeans and rice or barley; generally used as a flavoring

mix—to combine ingredients in such a way that they are evenly dispersed throughout the mixture

moist-heat cooking methods—cooking methods, principally

simmering, poaching, boiling and steaming, that use water or steam to transfer heat through convection; moist-heat cooking methods are used to emphasize the natural flavors of foods

mojo criollo—a citrus and herb marinade used in Latino cuisines; bottled brands are available in Hispanic markets

molding—the process of shaping foods, particularly grains and vegetables bound by sauces, into attractive, hard-edged shapes by using metal rings, circular cutters or other forms

molds—(1) algaelike fungi that form long filaments or strands; for the most part, molds affect only food appearance and flavor; (2) containers used for shaping foods

mollusks—shellfish characterized by a soft, unsegmented body, no internal skeleton and a hard outer shell

monounsaturated fats—see Unsaturated fats

monter au beurre—(mohn-tay ah burr) to finish a sauce by swirling or whisking in butter (raw or compound) until it is melted; used to give sauces shine, flavor and richness

mortadella—(mohr-tah-DEH-lah) an Italian smoked sausage made with ground beef, pork and pork fat, flavored with coriander and white wine; it is air-dried and has a delicate flavor; also a large American bologna-type pork sausage studded with pork fat and garlic

mortar and pestle—a hard bowl (the mortar) in which foods such as spices are ground or pounded into a powder with a club-shaped tool (the pestle)

mother sauces—(French sauce mère), *see* leading sauces

mousse—(moose) a soft, creamy food, either sweet or savory, lightened by adding whipped cream, beaten egg whites or both

mousseline—(moos-uh-leen) a cream or sauce lightened by folding in whipped cream

mouthfeel—the sensation created in the mouth by a combination of a food's taste, smell, texture and temperature

muesli—(MYOOS-lee) a breakfast cereal made from raw or toasted cereal grains, dried fruits, nuts and dried milk solids and usually eaten with milk or yogurt; sometimes known as granola

muffin method—a mixing method used to make quick-bread batters; it involves combining liquid fat with other liquid ingredients before adding them to the dry ingredients

muscles—animal tissues consisting of bundles of cells or fibers that can contract and expand; they are the portions of a carcass usually consumed

mushrooms—members of a broad category of plants known as fungi; they are often used and served like vegetables

mutton—the meat of sheep slaughtered after they reach the age of one year

NAMP/IMPS—the Institutional Meat Purchasing Specifications (IMPS) published by the U.S. Department of Agriculture; the IMPS are illustrated and described in The Meat Buyer's Guide published by the National Association of Meat Purveyors (NAMP)

nappe—(nap) (1) the consistency of a liquid, usually a sauce, that will coat the back of a spoon; (2) to coat a food with sauce

national cuisine—the characteristic cuisine of a nation

natural water—bottled drinking water not derived from a municipal water supply; it can be mineral, spring, well or artesian-well water

navarin—(nah-veh-rahng) a brown ragoût generally made with turnips, other root vegetables, onions, peas and lamb

neapolitan—a three-layered loaf or cake of ice cream; each layer is a different flavor and a different color, a typical combination being chocolate, vanilla and strawberry

nectar—the diluted, sweetened juice of peaches, apricots, guavas, black currants or other fruits, the juice of which would be too thick or too tart to drink straight

neutral spirits or grain spirits—pure alcohol (ethanol or ethyl alcohol); they are odorless, tasteless and a very potent 190 proof (95% alcohol)

New American cuisine—a late-20th-century movement that began in California but has spread across the United States; it stresses the use of fresh, locally grown, seasonal produce and high-quality ingredients simply prepared in a fashion that preserves and emphasizes natural flavors

noisette—a small, usually round, portion of meat cut from the rib

noodles—flat strips of pasta-type dough made with eggs; may be fresh or dried

nouvelle cuisine—French for "new cooking"; a mid-20th-century movement away from many classic cuisine principles and toward a lighter cuisine based on natural flavors, shortened cooking times and innovative combinations

nut—(1) the edible single-seed kernel of a fruit surrounded by a hard shell; (2) generally, any seed or fruit with an edible kernel in a hard shell

nutrients—the chemical substances found in food that nourish the body by promoting growth, facilitating body functions and providing energy; there are six categories of nutrients: proteins, carbohydrates, fats, water, minerals and vitamins

nutrition—the science that studies nutrients

oblique cuts—(oh-BLEEK) small pieces with two angle-cut sides

offal—(OFF-uhl) also called variety meats; edible entrails (for example, the heart, kidneys, liver, sweetbreads and tongue) and extremities (for example, oxtail and pig's feet) of an animal

oignon brûlé—French for "burnt onion"; made by charring onion halves; used to flavor and color stocks and sauces

oignon piqué—(ohn-nawng pee-KAY) French for "pricked onion"; a bay leaf tacked with a clove to a peeled onion; used to flavor sauces and soups

oil—a type of fat that remains liquid at room temperature

organic farming—a method of farming that does not rely on synthetic pesticides, fungicides, herbicides or fertilizers

orzo—a rice-shaped pasta

oven spring—the rapid rise of yeast goods in a hot oven, resulting from the production and expansion of trapped gases

overhead costs—expenses related to operating a business, including but not limited to costs for advertising, equipment leasing, insurance, property rent, supplies and utilities

overrun—the amount of air churned into an ice cream during freezing

paillard—a scallop of meat pounded until thin, usually grilled

palate—(1) the complex of smell, taste and touch receptors that contribute to a person's ability to recognize and appreciate flavors; (2) the range of an individual's recognition and appreciation of flavors

panada; panade—(pah-nahd) (1) something other than fat added to a forcemeat to enhance smoothness, aid emulsification or both; it is often béchamel, rice or crustless white bread soaked in milk; (2) a mixture for binding stuffings and dumplings, notably quenelles, often choux pastry, bread crumbs, frangipane, puréed potatoes or rice

pan-broiling—a dry-heat cooking method that uses conduction to transfer heat to a food resting directly on a cooking surface; no fat is used and the food remains uncovered

pan-dressed—a market form for fish in which the viscera, gills and scales are removed and the fins and tail are trimmed

panettone—(pan-eh-TONE-nay) sweet Italian yeast bread filled with raisins, candied fruits, anise seeds and nuts; traditionally baked in a rounded cylindrical mold and served as a breakfast bread or dessert during the Christmas holidays

pan-frying—a dry-heat cooking method in which food is placed in a moderate amount of hot fat

pan gravy—a sauce made by deglazing pan drippings from roast meat or poultry and combining them with a roux or other starch and stock

papain—an enzyme found in papayas that breaks down proteins; used as the primary ingredient in many commercial meat tenderizers

papillote, en—(awn pa-pee-yote) a cooking method in which food is wrapped in paper or foil and then heated so that the food steams in its own moisture

parboiling—partially cooking a food in boiling or simmering liquid; similar to blanching but the cooking time is longer

parchment (paper)—heat-resistant paper used throughout the kitchen for tasks such as lining baking pans, wrapping foods to be cooked en papillote and covering foods during shallow poaching

parcooking—partially cooking a food by any cooking method

parfait—ice cream served in a long, slender glass with alternating layers of topping or sauce; also the name of the mousselike preparation that forms the basis for some still-frozen desserts

paring knife—a short knife used for detail work, especially cutting fruits and vegetables; it has a rigid blade approximately 2–4 inches (5–10 centimeters) long

Paris-Brest—rings of baked éclair paste cut in half horizontally and filled with light pastry cream and/or whipped cream; the top is dusted with powdered sugar or drizzled with chocolate glaze

parisienne—(pah-ree-zee-en) spheres of fruits or vegetables cut with a small melon ball cutter

parstock (par)—the amount of stock necessary to cover operating needs between deliveries

pasta—(1) an unleavened paste or dough made from wheat flour (often semolina), water and eggs; the dough can be colored and flavored with a wide variety of herbs, spices or other ingredients and cut or extruded into a wide variety of shapes and sizes; it can be fresh or dried and is boiled for service; (2) general term for any macaroni product or egg noodle

pasteurization—the process of heating something to a certain temperature for a specific period in order to destroy pathogenic bacteria

pastillage—(pahst-tee-azh) a paste made of sugar, cornstarch and gelatin; it may be cut or molded into decorative shapes

pastry cream—also known as crème pâtissière, a stirred custard made with egg yolks, sugar and milk and thickened with starch; used for pastry and pie fillings

pâte—French for *dough*

pâté—(pah-TAY) traditionally, a fine savory meat filling wrapped in pastry, baked and served hot or cold; as opposed to a terrine, which was a coarsely ground and highly seasoned meat mixture baked in an earthenware mold and served cold; today, the words pâté and terrine are generally used interchangeably

pâte à choux—(paht ah shoo) *see* éclair paste

pâte à glacer—a specially formulated chocolate coating compound with vegetable oils designed to retain its shine without tempering; it is used as a coating or frosting chocolate

pâte au pâté—(paht ah pah-TAY) a specially formulated pastry dough used for wrapping pâté when making pâté en croûte

pâte brisée—(paht bree-zay) a dough that produces a very flaky baked product containing little or no sugar; flaky dough is used for prebaked pie shells or crusts; mealy dough is a less flaky product used for custard, cream or fruit pie crusts

pâté en croûte—(pah-tay awn croot) a pâté baked in pastry dough such as pâte au pâté

pâte feuilletée—(paht fuh-yuh-tay) also known as puff pastry; a rolled-in dough used for pastries, cookies and savory products; it produces a rich and buttery but not sweet baked product with hundreds of light, flaky layers

pâte sucrée—(paht soo-kray) a dough containing sugar that produces a very rich, crisp (not flaky) baked product; also known as sweet dough, it is used for tart shells

pathogen—any organism that causes disease; usually refers to bacteria; undetectable by smell, sight or taste

pâtissier—(pah-tees-sir-yair) a pastry chef; the person responsible for all baked items, including breads, pastries and desserts

paupiette—a thin slice of meat or fish that is rolled around a filling of finely ground meat or vegetables, then fried, baked or braised in wine or stock

paysanne—(pahy-sahn) foods cut into flat square, round or triangular items with dimensions of ½ inch × ½ inch × ⅛ inch (1.2 centimeters × 1.2 centimeters × 3 millimeters)

pearling—a milling process in which all or part of the hull, bran and germ are removed from grains

pectin—a gelatin-like carbohydrate obtained from certain fruits; used to thicken jams and jellies

pepperoni—(peh-peh-ROH-nee) a hard, thin, air-dried Italian sausage seasoned with red and black pepper

persillade—(payr-se-yad) (1) a food served with or containing parsley; (2) a mixture of bread crumbs, parsley and garlic used to coat meats, especially lamb

pH—a measurement of the acid or alkali content of a solution, expressed on a scale of 0 to 14.0. A pH of 7.0 is considered neutral or balanced. The lower the pH value, the more acidic the substance. The higher the pH value, the more alkaline the substance.

physical hazard—a danger to the safety of food caused by particles such as glass chips, metal shavings, bits of wood or other foreign matter

pickle—(1) to preserve food in a brine or vinegar solution; (2) food that has been preserved in a seasoned brine or vinegar, especially cucumbers. Pickled cucumbers are available whole, sliced, in wedges, or chopped as a relish, and may be sweet, sour dill-flavored or hot and spicy.

pigment—any substance that gives color to an item

pilaf—a cooking method for grains in which the grains are lightly sautéed in hot fat and then a hot liquid is added; the mixture is simmered without stirring until the liquid is absorbed

poaching—a moist-heat cooking method that uses convection to transfer heat from a hot (approximately 160°F–180°F [71°C–82°C]) liquid to the food submerged in it

polyunsaturated fats—*see* unsaturated fats

pomes—members of the Rosaceae family; tree fruits with a thin skin and firm flesh surrounding a central core containing many small seeds (called pips or carpels); include apples, pears and quince

ponzu—(pon zoo) Japanese dipping sauce traditionally made with lemon juice or rice wine vinegar, soy sauce, mirin or sake, seaweed and dried bonito flakes

pork—the meat of hogs, usually slaughtered under the age of one year

posole—also known as hominy or samp; dried corn that has been soaked in hydrated lime or lye; posole (Sp. pozole) also refers to a stewlike soup made with pork and hominy served in Mexico and Central America

posterior—at or toward the rear of an object or place; opposite of anterior

potentially hazardous foods—foods on which bacteria can thrive

poultry—the collective term for domesticated birds bred for eating; they include chickens, ducks, geese, guineas, pigeons and turkeys

preserve—a fruit gel that contains large pieces or whole fruits

primal cuts—the primary divisions of muscle, bone and connective tissue produced by the initial butchering of the carcass

prix fixe—(pree feks) French for "fixed price"; refers to a menu offering a complete meal for a set price; also known as table d'hôte

professional cooking—a system of cooking based on a knowledge of and appreciation for ingredients and procedures

profiteroles—small baked rounds of éclair paste filled with ice cream and topped with chocolate sauce

proofing—the rise given shaped yeast products just prior to baking

proteins—a group of compounds composed of oxygen, hydrogen, carbon and nitrogen atoms necessary for manufacturing, maintaining and repairing body tissues and as an alternative source of energy (4 calories per gram); protein chains are constructed of various combinations of amino acids

pudding—a thick, spoonable dessert custard, usually made with eggs, milk, sugar and flavorings and thickened with flour or another starch

puff pastry—*see* pâte feuilletée

pulled sugar—a doughlike mixture of sucrose, glucose and tartaric acid that can be colored and shaped by hand into decorative items

pulses—dried seeds from a variety of legumes

pumpernickel—(1) coarsely ground rye flour; (2) bread made with this flour

purée—(pur-ray) (1) to process food to achieve a smooth pulp; (2) food that is processed by mashing, straining or fine chopping to achieve a smooth pulp

purée soup—a soup usually made from starchy vegetables or legumes; after the main ingredient is simmered in a liquid, the mixture, or a portion of it, is puréed

purified water—bottled water produced by distillation, reverse osmosis, deionization or suitable processes that meet governmental standards

putrefactives—bacteria that spoil food without rendering it unfit for human consumption

quality grades—a guide to the eating qualities of meat—its tenderness, juiciness and flavor—based on an animal's age and the meat's color, texture and degree of marbling

quenelle—(kuh-nehl) a small, dumpling-shaped portion of a mousseline forcemeat poached in an appropriately flavored stock; it is shaped by using two spoons

quiche—a savory tart or pie consisting of a custard baked in a pastry shell with a variety of flavorings and garnishes

quick bread—a bread, including loaves and muffins, leavened by chemical leaveners or steam rather than yeast

radiation cooking—a heating process that does not require physical contact between the heat source and the food being cooked; instead, energy is transferred by waves of heat or light striking the food. Two kinds of radiant heat used in the kitchen are infrared and microwave.

raft—a crust formed during the process of clarifing consommé; it is composed of the clearmeat and impurities from the stock, which rise to the top of the simmering stock and release additional flavors

ragoût—(rah-goo) (1) traditionally, a well-seasoned, rich stew containing meat, vegetables and wine; (2) any stewed mixture

ramekin—a small, ovenproof dish, usually ceramic

rancidity—the decomposition of fats by exposure to oxygen, resulting in off-flavors and destruction of nutritive components

ratites—a family of flightless birds with small wings and flat breastbones; they include the ostrich, emu and rhea

recipe—a set of written instructions for producing a specific food or beverage; also known as a formula

recovery time—the length of time it takes a cooking medium such as fat or water to return to the desired cooking temperature after food is submerged in it

red fish—a name applied to various species of fish around the world. In the United States, it generally refers to a member of the drum family found in the southern Atlantic and the Gulf of Mexico. It has a reddish-bronze skin and firm, ivory flesh with a mild flavor and a typical market weight of 2 to 8 pounds (0.9 to 3.6 kilograms); it is also known as channel bass, red drum and red bass.

red rice—an unmilled short- or long-grain rice from the Himalayas; it has a russet-colored bran and an earthy, nutty flavor

reduction—cooking a liquid such as a sauce until its quantity decreases through evaporation. To reduce by one-half means that one-half of the original amount remains. To reduce by three-fourths means that only one-fourth of the original amount remains. To reduce au sec means that the liquid is cooked until nearly dry.

refreshing—submerging a food in cold water to quickly cool it and prevent further cooking, also known as shocking; usually used for vegetables

regional cuisine—a set of recipes based on local ingredients, traditions and practices; within a larger geographical, political, cultural or social unit, regional cuisines are often variations of one another that blend together to create a national cuisine

relish—a cooked or pickled sauce usually made with vegetables or fruits and often used as a condiment; can be smooth or chunky, sweet or savory and hot or mild

remouillage—(rhur-moo-yahj) French for "rewetting"; a stock produced by reusing the bones left from making another stock. After draining the original stock from the stockpot, add fresh mirepoix, a new sachet and enough water to cover the bones and mirepoix, and a second stock can be made. A remouillage is treated like the original stock; allow it to simmer for four to five hours before straining. A remouillage will not be as clear or as flavorful as the original stock, however. It is often used to make glazes or in place of water when making stocks.

render—(1) to melt and clarify fat; (2) to cook meat in order to remove the fat

respiration rate—the speed with which the cells of a fruit use oxygen and produce carbon dioxide during ripening

restaurateur—a person who owns or operates an establishment serving food, such as a restaurant

ribbon—a term used to describe the consistency of a batter or mixture, especially a mixture of beaten egg and sugar; when the beater or whisk is lifted, the mixture will fall back slowly onto its surface in a ribbonlike pattern

ricer—a sievelike utensil with small holes through which soft food is forced; it produces particles about the size of a grain of rice

rillette—(ree-yeh) meat or poultry slowly cooked, mashed and preserved in its own fat; served cold and usually spread on toast

ripe—fully grown and developed; a ripe fruit's flavor, texture and appearance are at their peak, and the fruit is ready to use as food

risers—boxes (including the plastic crates used to store glassware) covered with linens, paper or other decorative items and used on a buffet table as a base for platters, trays or displays

risotto—(re-zot-toe) (1) a cooking method for grains in which the grains are lightly sautéed in butter and then a liquid is gradually added; the mixture is simmered with near-constant stirring until the still-firm grains merge with the cooking liquid; (2) a Northern Italian rice dish prepared this way

roasting—a dry-heat cooking method that heats food by surrounding it with hot, dry air in a closed environment or on a spit over an open fire; similar to baking, the term roasting is usually applied to meats, poultry, game and vegetables

roe—(roh) fish eggs

roll cuts—*see* oblique cuts

rolled fondant—a cooked mixture of sugar, glucose and water formulated to drape over cakes

rolled-in dough—a dough in which a fat is incorporated in many layers by using a rolling and folding procedure; it is used for flaky baked goods such as croissants, puff pastry and Danish pastry

rondeau—(ron-doe) a shallow, wide, straight-sided pot with two loop handles

rondelles—(ron-dellz) disk-shaped slices

rotate stock—to use products in the order in which they were received; all perishable and semiperishable goods, whether fresh, frozen, canned or dry, should be used according to the first in, first out (FIFO) principle

rotisserie—cooking equipment that slowly rotates meat or other foods in front of a heating element

roulade—(roo-lahd) (1) a slice of meat, poultry or fish rolled around a stuffing; (2) a filled and rolled spongecake

round fish—fish with round, oval or compressed bodies that swim in a vertical position and have eyes on both sides of their heads; include salmon, swordfish and cod

rounding—the process of shaping dough into smooth, round balls; used to stretch the outside layer of gluten into a smooth coating

roux—(roo) a cooked mixture of equal parts flour and fat, by weight, used as a thickener for sauces and other dishes; cooking the flour in fat coats the starch granules with the fat and prevents them from lumping together or forming lumps when introduced into a liquid

royal icing—also known as decorator's icing, an uncooked mixture of confectioner's sugar and egg whites that becomes hard and brittle when dry; used for making intricate cake decorations

rub—a mixture of fresh or dried herbs and spices ground together; it can be used dried, or it can be mixed with a little oil, lemon juice, prepared mustard or ground fresh garlic or ginger to make a wet rub

Russian service—restaurant service in which the entrée, vegetables and starches are served from a platter onto the diner's plate by a waiter

sabayon—(sa-by-on) also known as zabaglione; a foamy, stirred custard sauce made by whisking eggs, sugar and wine over low heat

sachet d'épices; sachet—(sah-shay day-pea-say) French for "bag of spices"; aromatic ingredients tied in a cheesecloth bag and used to flavor stocks and other foods; a standard sachet contains parsley stems, cracked peppercorns, dried thyme, bay leaf, cloves and, optionally, garlic

salad—a single food or a mix of different foods accompanied or bound by a dressing

salad dressing—a sauce for a salad; most are based on a vinaigrette, mayonnaise or other emulsified product

salad greens—a variety of leafy vegetables that are usually eaten raw

salamander—a small broiler used primarily for browning or glazing the tops of foods

salsa—(sahl-sah) Spanish for "sauce"; (1) generally, a cold chunky mixture of fresh herbs, spices, fruits and/or vegetables used as a sauce for meat, poultry, fish or shellfish; (2) in Italian usage, a general term for pasta sauces

salt-curing—the process of surrounding a food with salt or a mixture of salt, sugar, nitrite-based curing salt, herbs and spices; salt-curing dehydrates the food, inhibits bacterial growth and adds flavor

sanding sugar—granulated sugar with a large, coarse crystal structure that prevents it from dissolving easily; used for decorating cookies and pastries

sanitation—the creation and maintenance of conditions that will prevent food contamination or food-borne illness

sanitize—to reduce pathogenic organisms to safe levels

sansho—dried berries of the prickly ash tree, ground into a powder that is also known as Szechuan pepper, fagara and Chinese pepper; generally used in Japanese cooking to season fatty foods

sashimi—(sah-shee-mee) raw fish eaten without rice; usually served as the first course of a Japanese meal

saturated fats—fats found mainly in animal products and tropical oils; usually solid at room temperature; the body has more difficulty breaking down saturated fats than either monounsaturated or polyunsaturated fats

sauce—generally, a thickened liquid used to flavor and enhance other foods

sausage—a seasoned forcemeat usually stuffed into a casing; a sausage can be fresh, smoked and cooked, dried or hard

sautéing—(saw-tay-ing) a dry-heat cooking method that uses conduction to transfer heat from a hot pan to food with the aid of a small amount of hot fat; cooking is usually done quickly over high temperatures

sauteuse—(saw-toose) the basic sauté pan with sloping sides and a single long handle

sautoir—(saw-twahr) a sauté pan with straight sides and a single long handle

savory—a food that is not sweet

scald—to heat a liquid, usually milk, to just below the boiling point

scallop—a thin, boneless slice of meat

score—to cut shallow gashes across the surface of a food before cooking

Scoville Heat Units—a subjective rating for measuring a chile's heat; the sweet bell pepper usually rates 0 units, the tabasco pepper rates from 30,000 to 50,000 units and the habanero pepper rates from 100,000 to 300,000 units

seafood—an inconsistently used term encompassing some or all of the following: saltwater fish, freshwater fish, saltwater shellfish, freshwater shellfish and other edible marine life

sear—to brown food quickly over high heat; usually done as a preparatory step for combination cooking methods

season—(1) traditionally, to enhance flavor by adding salt; (2) more commonly, to enhance flavor by adding salt and/or pepper as well as herbs and spices; (3) to mature and bring a food (usually beef or game) to a proper condition by aging or special preparation; (4) to prepare a pot, pan or other cooking surface to prevent sticking

seasoning—an item added to enhance the natural flavors of a food without dramatically changing its taste; salt is the most common seasoning

seitan—(SAY-tan) a form of wheat gluten; it has a firm, chewy texture and a bland flavor; traditionally simmered in a broth of soy sauce or tamari with ginger, garlic and kombu (seaweed)

seltzer water—a flavorless natural mineral water with carbonation, originally from the German town of Niederselters

semi à la carte—describes a menu on which some foods (usually appetizers and desserts) and beverages are priced and ordered separately, while the entrée is accompanied by and priced to include other dishes such as a salad, starch or vegetable

semifreddi—(seh-mee-frayd-dee) also known as still-frozen desserts; items made with frozen mousse, custard or cream into which large amounts of whipped cream or meringue are folded in order to incorporate air; layers of spongecake and/or fruits may be added for flavor and texture; include frozen soufflés, marquise, mousses and neapolitans

semolina—*see* durum wheat

sfoglia—(sfo-glee-ah) a thin, flat sheet of pasta dough that can be cut into ribbons, circles, squares or other shapes

shallow poaching—a moist-heat cooking method that combines poaching and steaming; the food (usually fish) is placed on a vegetable bed and partially covered with a liquid (cuisson) and simmered

shellfish—aquatic invertebrates with shells or carapaces

sherbet—a frozen mixture of fruit juice or fruit purée that contains milk and/or eggs for creaminess

shocking—also called refreshing; the technique of quickly chilling blanched or parcooked foods in ice water; prevents further cooking and sets colors

shortening—(1) a white, flavorless, solid fat formulated for baking or deep-frying; (2) any fat used in baking to tenderize the product by shortening gluten strands

shred—to cut into thin but irregular strips

shrinkage—the loss of weight in a food due to evaporation of liquid or melting of fat during cooking

shuck—(1) a shell, pod or husk; (2) to remove the edible portion of a food (for example, clam meat, peas or an ear of corn) from its shell, pod or husk

side masking—the technique of coating only the sides of a cake with a garnish such as chopped nuts

sifting—shaking one or more dry substances through a sieve or sifter to remove lumps, incorporate air and mix

silverskin—the tough connective tissue that surrounds certain muscles; see Elastin

simmering—(1) a moist-heat cooking method that uses convection to transfer heat from a hot (approximately 185°F–205°F [85°C–96°C]) liquid to the food submerged in it; (2) maintaining the temperature of a liquid just below the boiling point

skim—to remove fat and impurities from the surface of a liquid during cooking

slice—to cut an item into relatively broad, thin pieces

slurry—a mixture of raw starch and cold liquid used for thickening

small sauces— also known as compound sauces; made by adding one or more ingredients to a leading sauce; they are grouped together into families based on their leading sauce; some small sauces have a variety of uses, while others are traditional accompaniments for specific foods

smoke point—the temperature at which a fat begins to break down and smoke

smoking—any of several methods for preserving and flavoring foods by exposing them to smoke; includes cold smoking (in which the foods are not fully cooked) and hot smoking (in which the foods are cooked)

smørbrød—(SMURR-brur) Norwegian cold open-faced sandwiches; similarly, the Swedish term smörgåsbord (SMORE-guhs-bohrd) refers to a buffet table of bread and butter, salads, open-faced sandwiches, pickled or marinated fish, sliced meats and cheeses

soda water—a flavorless water with induced carbonation, consumed plain or used as a mixer for alcoholic drinks or soda fountain confections; also known as club soda and seltzer

soft water—water with a relatively high sodium concentration

solid pack—canned fruits or vegetables with little or no water added

soppressata—(soh-preh-SAH-tah) a hard, aged Italian salami, sometimes coated with cracked peppercorns or herbs

sorbet—(sore-bay) a frozen mixture of fruit juice or fruit purée; similar to sherbet but without milk products

soufflé—(soo-flay) either a sweet or savory fluffy dish made with a custard base lightened with whipped egg whites and then baked; the whipped egg whites cause the dish to puff when baked

sous-chef—(soo-shef) a cook who supervises food production and who reports to the executive chef; he or she is second in command of a kitchen

specifications; specs—standard requirements to be followed in procuring items from suppliers

spice—any of a large group of aromatic plants whose bark, roots, seeds, buds or berries are used as a flavoring; usually used in dried form, either whole or ground

springform pan—a circular baking pan with a separate bottom and a side wall held together with a clamp that is released to free the baked product

spring lamb—the meat of sheep slaughtered before they have fed on grass or grains

spring water—water obtained from an underground source that flows naturally to the earth's surface

spun sugar—a decoration made by flicking dark caramelized sugar rapidly over a dowel to create long, fine, hairlike threads

squab—the class of young pigeon used in food service operations

staling—also known as starch retrogradation; a change in the distribution and location of water molecules within baked products; stale products are firmer, drier and more crumbly than fresh baked goods

standard breading procedure—the procedure for coating foods with crumbs or meal by passing the food through flour, then an egg wash and then the crumbs; it gives foods a relatively thick, crisp coating when deep-fried or pan-fried

standardized recipe—a recipe producing a known quality and quantity of food for a specific operation

staples—(1) certain foods regularly used throughout the kitchen; (2) certain foods, usually starches, that help form the basis for a regional or national cuisine and are principal components in the diet

starch—(1) complex carbohydrates from plants that are edible and either digestible or indigestible (fiber); (2) a rice, grain, pasta or potato accompaniment to a meal

starch retrogradation—the process whereby starch molecules in a batter or dough lose moisture after baking; the result is baked goods that are dry or stale

starchy potatoes—*see* mealy potatoes

static menu—a menu offering patrons the same foods every day

station chef—the cook in charge of a particular department in a kitchen

steak—(1) a cross-section slice of a round fish with a small section of the bone attached; (2) a cut of meat, either with or without the bone

steamed milk—milk that is heated with steam generated by an espresso machine; it should be approximately 150°F to 170°F (66°C to 77°C)

steamer—(1) a set of stacked pots with perforations in the bottom of each pot; they fit over a larger pot filled with boiling or simmering water and are used to steam foods; (2) a perforated insert made of metal or bamboo placed in a pot and used to steam foods; (3) a type of soft-shell clam from the East Coast; (4) a piece of gas or electric equipment in which foods are steamed in a sealed chamber

steaming—a moist-heat cooking method in which heat is transferred from steam to the food being cooked by direct contact; the food to be steamed is placed in a basket or rack above a boiling liquid in a covered pan

steel—a tool, usually made of steel, used to hone or straighten knife blades

steep—to soak food in a hot liquid in order to either extract its flavor or soften its texture

steers—male cattle castrated prior to maturity and principally raised for beef

sterilize—to destroy all living microorganisms

stewing—a combination cooking method similar to braising but generally involving smaller pieces of meat that are first blanched or browned, then cooked in a small amount of liquid that is served as a sauce

stir-frying—a dry-heat cooking method similar to sautéing in which foods are cooked over very high heat using little fat while stirring constantly and briskly; often done in a wok

stirring—a mixing method in which ingredients are gently mixed by hand until blended, usually with a spoon, whisk or rubber spatula

stock—(French fond) a clear, unthickened liquid flavored by soluble substances extracted from meat, poultry or fish and their bones as well as from a mirepoix, other vegetables and seasonings

stone fruits—members of the genus Prunus, also known as drupes; tree or shrub fruits with a thin skin, soft flesh and one woody stone or pit; include apricots, cherries, nectarines, peaches and plums

straight dough method—a mixing method for yeast breads in which all ingredients are simply combined and mixed

strain—to pour foods through a sieve, mesh strainer or cheesecloth to separate or remove the liquid component

streusel—a crumbly mixture of fat, flour, sugar and sometimes nuts and spices, used to top baked goods

subcutaneous fat—also known as exterior fat; the fat layer between the hide and muscles

submersion poaching—a poaching method in which the food is completely covered with the poaching liquid

subprimal cuts—the basic cuts produced from each primal

sucrose—the chemical name for common refined sugar; it is a disaccharide, composed of one molecule each of glucose and fructose

sugar—a carbohydrate that provides the body with energy and gives a sweet taste to foods

sugar syrups—either simple syrups (thin mixtures of sugar and water) or cooked syrups (melted sugar cooked until it reaches a specific temperature)

sundae—a great and gooey concoction of ice cream, sauces (hot fudge, marshmallow and caramel, for example), toppings (nuts, candies and fresh fruit to name a few) and whipped cream

suprême—(soo-prem) an intermediary sauce made by adding cream to chicken velouté

sushi—(szu-she) cooked or raw fish or shellfish rolled in or served on seasoned rice

sweat—to cook a food in a pan (usually covered), without browning, over low heat until the item softens and releases moisture; sweating allows the food to release its flavor more quickly when cooked with other foods

sweetbreads—the thymus glands of a calf or lamb

syrup—sugar that is dissolved in liquid, usually water, and often flavored with spices or citrus zest

syrup pack—canned fruits with a light, medium or heavy syrup added

table d'hôte—(tab-bluh dote) see Prix fixe

tahini—(tah-HEE-nee) a thick, oily paste made from crushed sesame seeds

tamale—a Mexican baked dish consisting of seasoned meats, poultry and or vegetables wrapped a corn husk spread with masa

tang—the portion of a knife's blade that extends inside the handle

tart—a sweet or savory filling in a baked crust made in a shallow, straight-sided pan without a top crust

tartlet—a small, single-serving tart

taste—the sensations, as interpreted by the brain, of what we detect when food, drink or other substances come in contact with our taste buds

tempeh—(TEHM-pay) fermented whole soybeans mixed with a grain such as rice or millet; it has a chewy consistency and a yeasty, nutty flavor

temper—to heat gently and gradually; refers to the process of slowly adding a hot liquid to eggs or other foods to raise their temperature without causing them to curdle

temperature danger zone—the broad range of temperatures between 41°F and 135°F (5°C and 57°C) at which bacteria multiply rapidly

tempering—a process for melting chocolate during which the temperature of the cocoa butter is carefully stabilized; this keeps the chocolate smooth and glossy

terrine—(teh-reen) (1) traditionally, a loaf of coarse forcemeat cooked in a covered earthenware mold and without a crust; today, the word is used interchangeably with pâté; (2) the mold used to cook such items, usually a rectangle or oval shape and made of ceramic

thickening agents—ingredients used to thicken sauces; include starches (flour, cornstarch and arrowroot), gelatin and liaisons

timbale—(tim-bull) (1) a small pail-shaped mold used to shape foods; (2) a preparation made in such a mold

tisanes—(teh-zahns) beverages made from herbal infusions that do not contain any tea

tofu—also known as bean curd; it is created from soymilk using a method similar to the way animal milk is separated into curds and whey in the production of cheese

togarishi—a Japanese spice and sesame seed blend available at Asian markets

tomato sauce—a leading sauce made from tomatoes, vegetables, seasonings and white stock; it may or may not be thickened with roux

toque—(toke) the tall white hat worn by chefs

torchon—(TOR-shahn) French for a cloth or towel, such as a dishcloth. The term is sometimes used to refer to dishes in which the item has been shaped into a cylinder by being wrapped in a cloth or towel.

torte—in Central and Eastern European usage, refers to a rich cake in which all or part of the flour is replaced with finely chopped nuts or bread crumbs

tossed salad—a salad prepared by placing the greens, garnishes and salad dressing in a large bowl and tossing to combine

total recipe cost—the total cost of ingredients for a particular recipe; it does not reflect overhead, labor, fixed expenses or profit

tourner—(toor-nay) to cut into football-shaped pieces with seven equal sides and blunt ends

toxins—by-products of living bacteria that can cause illness if consumed in sufficient quantities

tranche—(tranch) an angled slice cut from fish fillets

trans fats—a type of fat created when vegetable oils are solidified through hydrogenation

tripe—the edible lining of a cow's stomach

truffles—(1) flavorful tubers that grow near the roots of oak or beech trees; (2) rich chocolate candies made with ganache

truss—to tie poultry with butcher's twine into a compact shape for cooking

tube pan—a deep round baking pan with a hollow tube in the center

tuber—the fleshy root, stem or rhizome of a plant from which a new plant will grow; some, such as potatoes, are eaten as vegetables

tunneling—large tubular holes in muffins and cakes, a defect caused by improper mixing

unit cost—the price paid to acquire one of the specified units

univalves—single-shelled mollusks with a single muscular foot, such as abalone

unsaturated fats—fats that are normally liquid (oils) at room temperature; they may be monounsaturated (from plants such as olives and avocados) or polyunsaturated (from grains and seeds such as corn, soybeans and safflower as well as from fish)

vacuum packaging—a food preservation method in which fresh or cooked food is placed in an airtight container (usually plastic). Virtually all air is removed from the container through a vacuum process, and the container is then sealed.

vanilla custard sauce—also known as crème anglaise; a stirred custard made with egg yolks, sugar and milk or half-and-half and flavored with vanilla; served with or used in dessert preparations

vanillin—(1) whitish crystals of vanilla flavor that often develop on vanilla beans during storage; (2) synthetic vanilla flavoring

variety—the result of breeding plants of the same species that have different qualities or characteristics; the new plant often combines features from both parents

variety meats—*see* offal

veal—the meat of calves under the age of nine months

vegan—(VEE-gun) a vegetarian who does not eat dairy products, eggs, honey or any other animal product; vegans usually also avoid wearing and using animal products such as fur, leather or wool

vegetable—any herbaceous plant (one with little or no woody tissue) that can be partially or wholly eaten; vegetables can be classified as cabbages, fruit-vegetables, gourds and squashes, greens, mushrooms and truffles, onions, pods and seeds, roots and tubers and stalks

vegetarian—a person who does not eat any meat, poultry, game, fish, shellfish or animal by-products such as gelatin or animal fats; may also exclude dairy products or eggs from the diet

velouté—(veh-loo-tay) a leading sauce made by thickening a white stock (fish, veal, or chicken) with roux

venison—flesh from any member of the deer family, including antelope, elk, moose, reindeer, red-tailed deer, white-tailed deer, mule deer and axis deer

vent—(1) to allow the circulation or escape of a liquid or gas; (2) to cool a pot of hot liquid by setting the pot on blocks in a cold water bath and allowing cold water to circulate around it

vinaigrette—a temporary emulsion of oil and vinegar seasoned with salt and pepper

vinegar—a thin, sour liquid used as a preservative, cooking ingredient and cleaning solution

viniculture—the art and science of making wine from grapes

vintner—a winemaker

viruses—the smallest known form of life; they invade the living cells of a host and take over those cells' genetic material, causing the cells to produce more viruses; some viruses can enter a host through the ingestion of food contaminated with those viruses

viscera—internal organs

vitamins—compounds present in foods in very small quantities; they do not provide energy but are essential for regulating body functions

viticulture—the art and science of growing grapes used to make wines; factors considered include soil, topography (particularly, sunlight and drainage) and microclimate (temperature and rainfall)

vol-au-vents—deep, individual portion–sized puff pastry shells, often shaped as a heart, fish or fluted circle; they are filled with a savory mixture and served as an appetizer or main course

volume—the space occupied by a substance; volume measurements are commonly expressed as liters, teaspoons, tablespoons, cups, pints and gallons

wash—a glaze applied to dough before baking; a commonly used wash is made with whole egg and water

water bath—*see* bain marie

water buffalo's milk—milk produced by a female water buffalo; it has approximately 7.5% milkfat, 10.3% milk solids and 82.2% water

water pack—canned fruits with water or fruit juice added

waxy potatoes—those with a low starch content and thin skin; they are best for boiling

weight—the mass or heaviness of a substance; weight measurements are commonly expressed as grams, ounces and pounds

whetstone—a dense, grained stone used to sharpen or hone a knife blade

whipping—a mixing method in which foods are vigorously beaten in order to incorporate air; a whisk or an electric mixer with its whip attachment is used

white stew—*see* fricassee and blanquette

white stock—a light-colored stock made from chicken, veal, beef or fish bones simmered in water with vegetables and seasonings

whitewash—a thin mixture or slurry of flour and cold water used like cornstarch for thickening

whole butter—butter that is not clarified, whipped or reduced-fat

wine—an alcoholic beverage made from the fermented juice of grapes; may be sparkling (effervescent) or still (non-effervescent) or fortified with additional alcohol

work section—*see* work station

work station—a work area in the kitchen dedicated to a particular task, such as broiling or salad making; work stations using the same or similar equipment for related tasks are grouped together into work sections

yeasts—microscopic fungi whose metabolic processes are responsible for fermentation; they are used for leavening bread and in cheese, beer and wine making

yield—the total amount of a product made from a specific recipe; also, the amount of a food item remaining after cleaning or processing

yield grades—a grading program for meat that measures the amount of usable meat on a carcass

zabaglione—*see* sabayon

zest—the colored outer portion of the rind of citrus fruit; contains the oil that provides flavor and aroma

zushi—(zhoo-she) the seasoned rice used for sushi

INDEX

[Note: Recipes are in boldface type and are listed under main ingredients, cooking method, or category of food. Thus Grilled Potato Salad may be found under Potatoes, Grilling, and Salads. Some well-known or international dishes are also listed as unique entries.]